Eminent Contributors to Psychology

Eminent Contributors to Psychology

Volume I

A Bibliography of Primary References

ROBERT I. WATSON, SR., Editor

University of New Hampshire

SPRINGER PUBLISHING COMPANY

NEW YORK

Of making many books there is no end.

Ecclesiastes XII, 12

Library of Congress Catalog Card Number: 73–88108

International Standard Book Number: 0–8261–1450–4

Library of Congress Cataloging in Publication Data

Watson, Robert Irving, 1909–
    Eminent contributors to psychology.

    CONTENTS: v. 1. A bibliography of primary
references.

    1. Psychology—Bibliography—Collected works.
I. Title. [DNLM: 1. Psychology. 2. Bibliography.
Z7201 W341e]
Z7201.W37   016.15   73–88108
ISBN 0–8261–1450–4

Printed in U.S.A.

TABLE OF CONTENTS

ACKNOWLEDGMENTS

The reference selection process was facilitated by the generous cooperation of 239 specialists in the United States, Canada, and Europe, as well as in Australia, India, Sudan, and Colombia. In most instances I asked a specialist for help with one or two contributors. There were, however, three individuals whose counsel was so freely and enthusiastically given that I imposed on them to an even greater extent: Josef Brožek, of Lehigh; Philip H. Gray, of Montana; and Otto Marx, of Boston. To these scholars and to those who follow go my heartfelt thanks:

E. H. Ackerknecht, Zurich; D. C. Adkins, Hawaii; A. O. Aldridge, Illinois; L. B. Ames, Gesell Institute; H. L. Ansbacher, Vermont; R. Ardila, National University of Colombia; M. B. Arnold, Loyola; D. Bakan, York (Canada); K. M. Baker, Chicago; D. Bannister, Bexley Hospital (England); S. Balaraman, Madras, India; F. M. Barnard, Western Ontario; S. H. Bartley, Michigan State; F. A. Beach, California at Berkeley; J. Beck, Oregon; L. W. Beck, Rochester; S. J. Beck, Chicago; W. Bernard, Bellmore, Long Island (N.Y.); C. Bibby, Kingston-upon-Hull; J. L. Blau, Columbia; M. Blaug, London (England); M. Bleuler, Zollikon (Switzerland); A. L. Blumenthal, Harvard; D. C. Bollotte, Dijon (France); D. Bonneville, Florida; J. A. Boydston, Southern Illinois; M. A. B. Brazier, California at Los Angeles (Medical Center); W. G. Bringmann, Windsor (Canada); B. R. Bugelski, Buffalo; C. Buhler, Los Angeles, California; D. M. Bullard, Sr., Rockville, Maryland; M. E. Bunch, Washington University (St. Louis); R. W. Burkhardt, Jr., Harvard; J. C. Burnham, Ohio State; H. E. Burtt, Ohio State; R. S. Calinger, Rensselaer; D. P. Campbell, Minnesota; D. T. Campbell, Northwestern;

G. Canguilhem, Paris; M. Capek, Boston; J. Cardno, Tasmania; E. T. Carlson, Payne Whitney, Cornell Medical; L. Carmichael, National Geographic Society; D. Cartwright, Michigan; R. B. Cattell, Illinois; R. Chauvin, Laboratoire d'Ethologie Expérimentale (France); J. T. Clark, Canisius; T. N. Clark, Chicago; G. J. Clifford, California at Berkeley; J. F. Corso, Cortland; L. A. Coser, Stony Brook; M. Cowan, City College of New York; E. H. Craigie, Toronto, Canada; H. F. Crovitz, V. A. Hospital, Durham, N.C.; N. Dain, Rutgers, Newark; J. G. Darley, Minnesota; H. S. Decker, Payne Whitney, Cornell Medical; D. Denny-Brown, Harvard Medical; R. W. Dexter, Kent State; S. Diamond, Pasadena, California; E. E. Doll, Tennessee; W. Doney, Dartmouth; S. Drake, Toronto (Canada); J. Drever, Jr., Dundee (Scotland); H. Dreyfus, California at Berkeley; H. Düker, Marburg; C. P. Duncan, Northwestern; J. Dupont, Paris (France); E. Dzendolet, Massachusetts at Amherst; F. N. Egerton III, Wisconsin—Parkside; J. A. Elias, City College of New York; H. F. Ellenberger, Montreal; B. Elevitch, Boston; A. Ellis, Institute for Rational Living (New York); H. Evans, Harvard; R. B. Evans, New Hampshire; J. R. Ewalt, Massachusetts Mental Health Center (Boston); O. Ewert, Ruhr; O. Fellows, Columbia; G. A. Ferguson, McGill; M. Fisch, Illinois; G. Forlano, Bureau of Educational Research (Brooklyn); P. Fraisse, Paris; J. Fraser, Jung Foundation (New York); F. S. Freeman, Sarasota, Florida; P. L. Gardiner, Oxford; A. I. Gates, Montrose, New York; E. A. Gavin, St. Catherine's College; A. R. Gilbert, Buckhannon, Virginia; B. v. H. Gilmer, Carnegie-Mellon; R. Gotesky, Northern Illinois; S. H. Greenblatt, Dartmouth-Hitchcock

Medical Center; R. R. Greenson, Institute of Psychoanalysis, Los Angeles; R. Grimsley, Bristol; G. N. Grob, Rutgers; H. Grundfest, College of Physicians and Surgeons, Columbia; H. Guerlac, Cornell; H. Gulliksen, Princeton; R. Hahn, California at Berkeley; R. Hall, York (England); K. Hammond, Colorado; R. Handy, Buffalo; E. Hanfmann, Watertown, Massachusetts; T. L. Hankins, Washington (Seattle); H. F. Harlow, Wisconsin; H. H. Harman, Educational Testing Service (Princeton); M. Harrower, Gainesville, Florida; S. Hathaway, Minnesota; L. S. Hearnshaw, Liverpool; P. L. Heath, Edinburgh; D. O. Hebb, McGill; F. Heider, Kansas; H. Helson, California at Berkeley; M. Henle, New School for Social Research; E. R. Hilgard, Stanford; W. L. Hine, York (Canada); R. C. Hinkle, Ohio State; H. M. Hoenigwald, Pennsylvania; I. L. Horowitz, Rutgers; J. B. Hunsdahl, Royal Danish School for Educational Studies (Copenhagen); W. A. Hunt, Loyola; L. M. Hurvich, Pennsylvania; D. H. Hymes, Pennsylvania; F. W. Irwin, Pennsylvania; W. H. Ittelson, City University of New York; I. Janis, Yale; J. Jaynes, Princeton; J. R. Kantor, Chicago, Illinois; W. Kaufmann, Princeton; H. C. Kelman, New York City; J. C. Kenna, British Psychological Society (London); D. R. Kenshalo, Florida State; D. King-Hele, Surrey (England); I. Kohler, Innsbruck; D. L. Krantz, Lake Forest; D. Krech, California at Berkeley; S. B. Kutash, Maplewood, N.J.; A. A. Landauer, Western Australia; C. A. Larson, Rutgers, Jersey City; E. Laurence, Sussex (England); C. D. Leake, California Medical (San Francisco); L. LeBarre, Duke; Y. LeGrand, Musée National d'Histoire Naturelle (Paris); E. Lesky, Vienna; T. H. Levere, Toronto; A. Lewis, Institute of Psychiatry, Maudsley Hospital (London); D. P. C. Lloyd, London (England); L. E. Loemker, Emory; R. T. Louttit, Massachusetts at Amherst; J. W. Macfarlane, California at Berkeley; R. MacLeod, Cornell; P. W. McReynolds,

Nevada; G. Mandler, Toronto; M. E. Maron, California at Berkeley; M. E. Marshall, Carleton (Canada); M. A. May, Hamden, Connecticut; R. W. Mayer, San Francisco State; W. Mays, Manchester (England); M. Mead, Fordham; H. Meltzer, St. Louis, Missouri; R. K. Merton, Columbia; W. Metzger, Münster; E. S. Mills, New Hampshire; T. Mischel, Colgate; H. Misiak, New York City; F. C. T. Moore, Khartoum (Sudan); G. Mora, Poughkeepsie, New York; C. W. Morris, Florida (Gainesville); C. R. Myers, Toronto; R. Naroll, Buffalo; J. R. Nuttin, Louvain; C. O'Brien, Alberta; N. Pastore, Queens (New York); J. Perkins, Swarthmore; H. S. Perry, Cambridge, Massachusetts; J. W. Petras, Central Michigan; C. Pfaffmann, Rockefeller; R. W. Pickford, Glasgow; R. H. Pollack, Georgia; W. Pomeroy, New York City; J. A. Popplestone, Akron; L. G. Portenier, Red Cloud, Nebraska; C. C. Pratt, Pennington, New Jersey; A. C. Rancurello, Dayton; A. C. Raphelson, Michigan at Flint; N. V. Riasanovsky, California at Berkeley; J. M. Reisman, Memphis State; R. A. Rice, Vermont; R. G. Rinard, New Hampton, New York; B. K. Rome, Pacific Palisades, California; S. Rosenzweig, Washington (St. Louis); D. Ross, Washington, D.C.; W. A. Russell, Minnesota; F. Schiller, California Medical School (San Francisco); J. M. Schneck, New York City; F. Seaman, Idaho; M. H. Segall, Syracuse; L. Shaffer, Oradell, New Jersey; D. Shakow, National Institute of Mental Health; M. R. Sheehan, Hunter; R. E. Shor, New Hampshire; M. L. Simmel, Brandeis; I. K. Skrupskelis, South Carolina; D. W. Smith, Arizona; W. M. Smith, Dartmouth; G. S. Speer, Illinois Institute of Technology; J. T. Spence, Texas; H. Spiegelberg, Washington (St. Louis); S. S. Stevens, Harvard; G. W. Stocking, Jr., Chicago; O. Strunk, Jr., School of Theology, Boston; J. F. Szwed, Pennsylvania; S. Tax, Chicago; R. A. Tsanoff, Rice; J. Tuckmann, Suicide Prevention Center (Phila-

Acknowledgments   viii

delphia); C. E. Turley, Swedenborg School of
Religion (Newton, Massachusetts); L. Tyler,
Oregon; S. G. Vandenberg, Colorado; P. W.
Van der Pas, South Pasadena; W. Van Hoorn,
Leiden; P. E. Vernon, Calgary; G. von Bonin,
Mill Valley, California; A. A. Walsh, New
Hampshire; H. H. Walzer, Zurich; E. Weigl,
Deutsche Akademie der Wissenschaften (Ber-
lin, DDR); E. Weisskopf-Joelson, Georgia; A.
Wellek, Mainz; W. H. Werkmeister, Florida
State; M. Wertheimer, Colorado; R. H. Wil-
kins, Duke Medical School; L. P. Williams,
Cornell; H. A. Witkin, Brooklyn; W. Witte,
Münster; T. H. Wolf, Illinois at Chicago Circle;
K. H. Wolff, Brandeis; D. L. Wolfle, Washing-
ton (Seattle); P. T. Young, Claremont, Califor-
nia; P. Zagorin, Rochester; G. Zunini, Univer-
sità Cattolica del Sacro Cuore (Milan); A.
Zweig, Oregon.

Over the years, graduate and undergraduate
students at the University of New Hampshire
gave indispensable help. It is with pleasure and
affection that I acknowledge the cooperation
of Stephanie Ackerman, Deeda Aho, Brian
Arthur, Richard A. Bagg, Susan Bagg, James
Blight, Karla Boughton, Denise Condon, Ken-

neth R. Gibson, Deborah Goodrich, R. John
Huber, Richard Kushner, and Marilyn Merrifield.

There is also a debt to the administration
of the University of New Hampshire in general
and to the Department of Psychology in particular. Both have been understanding and
helpful and in countless ways smoothed the
path toward completion of this work. Reference
services in general and inter-library loan in
particular loomed large in this enterprise. To
Professor Hugh Pritchard, Reference Librarian
at the Dimond Library, University of New
Hampshire, go my special thanks.

This project could not have come to completion without the assistance of two secretaries,
first, Mrs. Roberta Hubbard and then Mrs.
Elfriede Archer, whose thorough knowledge of
French and German was of great value.

The understanding of the enterprise by Dr.
Ursula Springer and the meticulous copy
editing of Esther Gollobin of Springer Publishing Company made the relation of editor and
publisher an unusually pleasant and cooperative one.

As has been the case for many years and
for many books, my wife, Hazel, contributed
both psychological strength and practical help.

INTRODUCTION

Psychology has lacked a convenient, detailed, and general bibliography of its literature. Behavioral scientists in the United States have the *Psychological Index* and *Psychological Abstracts* and various specialized publications, while workers in other countries have somewhat comparable indexing and abstracting periodicals and books. However, all these sources share the common characteristics of being relatively unselective, despite a nationalistic emphasis, and of including only literature from just before the beginning of the century to the present. Many bibliographical problems can be solved through their use, but something else is also needed to bring together this literature in more selective fashion and to extend it back to the beginning of the modern period.

It was decided to divide the venture into two volumes and, at least, to consider the possibility of supplementation later. The first volume was devoted to the major primary references for more than 500 individuals living between 1600 and 1967, selected in a manner described in the next section of the introduction. About 12,000 references are cited—an average of 23 references per person, with a range from one to 80. The second volume contains more than 50,000 selected secondary references to the work of the same contributors to psychology.[1]

Both for the sake of discriminating use on the part of the reader and to call attention to the distinctive features of this work, several

[1] Naturally, this will include thousands of the references, reported as primary, which serve as secondary references to the work of other primary contributors. Moreover, there are references by many of these contributors not included in the first volume because they were not considered to be of sufficient importance. Book reviews and necrologies are illustrative. Systematic search of the name index of the second volume will yield these additional titles.

points should be stated at the outset. Examination of the names of the individuals will show that there can be little quarrel with the statement that at least a majority of them are important contributors to psychology. To have at one's fingertips a list of the major publications of James, Freud, and Hull (and 535 others) is a convenience at the very least, even if used only to verify a reference one has already decided to include in a paper or book. At a higher level of complexity, psychologist readers will find, for example, that it is a source to turn to when the name of an individual can be associated with a particular contentual theme—audition with Helmholtz, intelligence with Binet; a methodological problem—the phenomenological approach with Husserl, projective techniques with Rorschach; a school—Gestalt psychology with Köhler, behaviorism with Watson; a particular intellectual epoch—the Enlightenment with Voltaire, the dawning of modern science with Newton; the interrelation of psychological study with other fields—neurology with Head, evolution with Darwin; an issue in the philosophy of science—empiricism with Locke, rationalism with Descartes; or a country—Russia with Pavlov, Germany with Wundt. Other uses will, of course, occur to the reader.

Users from other disciplines will find the works of Kant (and 87 other philosophers), Cannon (and 93 other physiologist-biologists), and Jung (and 53 other psychoanalyst-psychiatrists).

It is hoped that individuals carrying out the inevitable literature search with problems in psychology and in related fields will find its contents a useful and convenient way of approaching their topic. My "private" reason for enduring the painstaking process of its prepara- tion was to increase the popularity of work in the history of the behavioral sciences by mak- ing it a shade more convenient to do.

Although the reader is strongly advised to examine the remainder of this introduction, it should be noted at this point that a concise practical guide to the use of the volume is given on pages xxi–xxiii ff.

METHOD OF ASCERTAINING EMINENCE

A list of 1,040 contributors to psychology, who lived between 1600 and 1967, was com- piled by Edwin G. Boring and Robert I. Wat- son. The names were submitted to a repre- sentative panel of nine leading psychologists from the United States, France, Japan, and Belgium, who were asked to rate each name according to the following scale:

one check mark if he recognized the name in the history of psychology, even if he could not specify the person's contribution;

two check marks if he could identify the person's contribution to psychology, even if not very precisely;

three check marks if he considered the per- son important enough to be included among the 500 most distinguished psychologists since 1600 and not living.

A triple check was scored as 3, a double check as 2, a single check as 1, and a blank as zero. The scores were then summed for an overall score. Prior to carrying out the study, it had been decided to report on about 500 of the top-rated individuals. A cutoff score at 11 yielded 538 eminent contributors to psy- chology. This lowest score was achieved, for example, if seven judges gave one check while two others gave two checks. At the other end of the scale, a score of 27, the highest obtain-

able, indicated that all nine judges rated this particular individual with the maximum three checks.

The manner of selection and the method by which the contributions were estimated by the international panel have been described in more detail in an article by Edith L. Annin, Edwin G. Boring, and Robert I. Watson, "Important Psychologists, 1600–1967" (*J. hist. Behav. Sci.*, 1968, *4*, 303–315). In it, the authors present the names of the 538 individuals in alpha- betical order, with dates of birth and death, as well as another list arranged by score. In this volume the birth and death dates reported parenthetically after the names are either those reported in the original study or those belatedly identified as correct or added in a follow-up study in which a check was run on the pre- viously reported dates (Marilyn R. Merrifield & Robert I. Watson, Eminent psychologists: Corrections and additions, *J. hist. Behav. Sci.*, 1970, *6*, 261–262).

A subsequent study supplied information about the person's particular field of endeavor, his nationality, and the temporal period in which the contributions were made (Robert I. Watson & Marilyn R. Merrifield,, Character- istics of individuals eminent in psychology in temporal perspective: Part I, *J. hist. Behav. Sci.*, 1973, *9*, 339–359.) Consideration of place of birth, education, and professional activity entered into the decision of nationality. The decision was clear-cut in many cases, but a variety of problems was encountered due to the crossing of national boundaries in the case of some individuals. Anything more compli- cated than dual nationality was too unwieldly to be considered. Where two nationalities are reported, they are given in chronological se- quence. For readers interested in the rationale for nationality classification, the above-men- tioned article may be helpful.

Concerning the group as a whole, it will suffice to report that 178 were "German," 163 were "American," 86 were "British," 79 were "French," and 32 fell into the catch-all category of "other." These summary figures include more than the nationals of the countries mentioned. For example, the German national-linguistic grouping includes Austrians as well as German-speaking Swiss and the Dutch, Hungarians, and Scandinavians who wrote both in their native language and in German; the French grouping includes French-speaking Swiss and Belgians.

The 538 individuals were selected because of their contributions to psychology. That is not, however, the same as saying that all were psychologists in the sense of having a primary identification with the field. In the panelists' judgment, many individuals with expertise in peripheral fields did make relevant contributions to psychology and warranted inclusion on the list. Indeed, more than half must be designated as being primarily identified with a field other than psychology in the narrower sense. As a result, the use of twenty-two categories was necessary to encompass all of them. In addition to 228 psychologists *per se,* there were 310 other contributors, including 92 philosophers; 103 biologists, physiologists, anatomists, neurologists, ophthalmologists, and geneticists; 55 psychoanalysts, psychiatrists, and hypnotists; and 20 anthropologists and sociologists. Other, less frequently used, categories included astronomer-mathematicians, mathematicians, linguists, statisticians, chemists, physicists, educators, logicians, theologians, and laymen.

We have attempted to use as few categories of specialization as possible while still giving due attention to the complexity of the task. Accordingly, the criteria applied included the field given in the authoritative sources consulted, the person's self-appraisal, and those aspects of his writing that were most relevant to psychology. Problems arose particularly when authority and self-estimate were in agreement, but relevance to psychology was dis-

crepant. There is no question that Coleridge was much more a poet and that Goethe and Schiller were much more poet-dramatists—in their own eyes and in those of the public—but because all of them were relevant to psychology as philosophers, they were so designated. Josef Breuer, a general practitioner and otologist and never, strictly speaking, a psychoanalyst, was nevertheless so designated. A philosopher all of the time and a psychologist only some of the time, William James was reluctantly surrendered to philosophy. For readers who take issue with particular categorizations used in this volume, the detailed discussion in the Watson and Merrifield papers previously referred to may offer greater justification.

It is inevitable that some individuals will wish to second-guess the panel—that is, to question the omission of some names which, in their opinion, should have been on the list. I shall take advantage of my strategic position to play the second-guessing game, primarily because of the network of relations—impressionistic citation indexes, as it were—that emerged during my examination of thousands of books and articles. Some of the individuals who were omitted—despite widely different contexts—seemed to serve as important links between those selected on the list. Their names (in alphabetical order with parenthetical statement of the panel score) are: Walter Bagehot (9), Charles Baudouin (10), Hermann Boerhaave (8), Bernard Bosanquet (9), Robert Boyle (9), George Combe (4), Moritz Drobisch (7), David Ferrier (10), Wilhelm Griesinger (5), Jean-Baptiste von Helmont (9), Robert Hooke (8), Francis Hutcheson (4), Claude H. de Saint-Simon (10), Max Scheler, Anthony Shaftesbury (8), Georg Ernst Stahl (8), Carl Wernicke, Thomas Willis (8), and Adolphe Wohlgemuth (10). Thirteen of these 19 scholars would have been included if all individuals scoring 8, 9, or 10 had been added. But so, too, would 122 others whose absence did not seem to constitute a significant omission. In retrospect, the cutoff score of 11 still seems justified. Two of the individuals, however, were not listed in the original sample of over 1,000: Max Scheler and Carl Wernicke. Consequently, they had no chance of being selected. These are especially regrettable omissions for which I, as one of the two framers of the original list, must apologize.

CRITERIA FOR SELECTION OF REFERENCES

Some effort has been made to keep the number of primary references proportionate to the importance of the person (as reflected by his panel score). A revised estimate, always in an upward direction, was made for the number of primary references "appropriate" for individuals scoring in the groupings of 11–15, 16–20, 21–24, and 25–27.

The number of references stubbornly refused to fit any neat categorization. "Equally" eminent men of the same temporal period are divergent in productivity. Some attained eminence on the basis of relatively few seminal works; others achieved it almost by the sheer weight of numerous publications whose importance differed relatively little. Another factor influencing the length of a list, despite roughly comparable eminence, was the change in publication format. At the beginning of the modern period, everyone published in book form, and it would be impossible to cite more than about a dozen distinct publications for Descartes or Geulincx. More recently, with articles becoming the preferred form of publication, accelerated rates of publication have resulted, albeit at different times in different fields. In the preparation of this work, certain deviations from planned patterns were decided upon. Deliberate adjustments, for example,

were made for psychologists close to the present day who did not summarize their research in book or monographic form. Such individuals were given more journal citations and, therefore, a longer list of references. All individuals scoring 25–27 may in one sense be equal; however, to paraphrase an Orwellian thought, some are more equal than others. A certain amount of variation arose from the differing anticipated needs of the volume.

The citing of definitive and complete collected works meets some bibliographic needs. Individual titles judged to be of greatest significance to psychology must also be cited in original book or article form. There are the important research studies that produced a considerable proportion of the secondary references cited in Volume 2. There are books and articles illustrating relatively little-known facets of the psychological works of a writer better known for work in another area. Nevertheless, cutting across these categorizations is a master theme: citations of the most important work of each person.

The task of meeting various needs is made even more complex if the work was originally published in a language other than English. In many instances, if an adequate translation of a work is available, the original work is not cited (except for the date of original publication). If the translation, for some reason, is judged less authoritative, the original foreign version must also be cited. Another exception to preference for English citation occurs with those books that have recently been reprinted in languages other than English, thereby becoming more easily accessible than the English translations; in these cases, the foreign version is also cited. Still another exception was made concerning collected works. Whenever the choice could be made, an edition accepted as standard is cited even though much of the same material may be available in the English translation, e.g., the Adam and Tannery edition of Descartes. When better ones are known to be available, poor translations are passed over in discreet silence, by simple omission. If no other translations are available, the poor ones are cited.

Within the hazy limits of psychology, another source of selection must be clarified. Psychologists are sometimes casually known only for their work in a circumscribed field. To remedy this narrowness, we deliberately sought references to lesser-known phases of their work. Alfred Binet is a case in point. "Everyone" would know and expect to find references about his work on intelligence testing. A significantly smaller number would know about his studies of thinking, imageless thought, and perception. But it would be a surprise, perhaps, to all but the specialist to know that he also worked on graphology and on the psychology of the theater.

As has been indicated, many of these scholars are eminent in philosophy, physiology, psychiatry, social science, and other fields. One should approach their works selectively in order to isolate, to some extent at least, that which is most relevant to psychology. Nevertheless, some of the primary and secondary works concerning these scholars naturally tend to be nonpsychological. It was decided to treat them as important figures in the general history of science, and some of the literature pertinent to their major area of specialization is also cited. This is all the more justified because the materials most relevant to psychology are often imbedded in broader fields of interest. A Descartes, a Goethe, or a James must be understood against the background of his total work, and selection was made with this in mind. Moreover, since a philosophical position throws light on psychological views, philosophical literature was sometimes included, especially when a person on the list of eminent contributors was discussing the work of another contributor. Within this broader context, a sub-

sidiary selection criterion was also applied. If circumstances permitted, emphasis was placed upon contributions within the framework of the biological and social sciences and the philosophy of science rather than the physical sciences. Nevertheless, while some attention had to be paid to major contributions, irrespective of field, these references do not reflect the deeper and fuller scope that would have resulted if the source book had not been edited to present historical literature from the perspective of psychological science. There is, therefore, no claim to a complete coverage of the literature from other fields, be they philosophy, physiology, statistics, sociology, genetics, mathematics, or whatever.

A few other considerations about selection must be mentioned. Research articles placed in larger context by later inclusion in a monograph or book were eliminated in favor of the book. The book references would lead back to these omitted articles; if the reverse procedure had been followed, this would not have been possible. In most cases, citations are not made of works in which the individual's major service was that of editor. Exceptions are made for those whose reputations, in part, rested upon contributions of this nature—e.g., James Mark Baldwin and Carl Murchison. Individual chapters included in personally edited volumes are cited, however, if they meet the criteria required for their other reported contributions. Dissertations eventuating in books or articles are included without any special identification. Neither unpublished dissertations nor manuscript collections are included.

COLLECTION AND VERIFICATION OF REFERENCES

It might appear that the most straightforward approach in starting to collect primary references published by psychologists after 1894 would be to turn directly to the *Psychological Index* and to its successor, *Psychological Abstracts*—bibliographic sources of which psychologists have every right to be proud. Instead, it was decided to use them as devices for checking the accuracy of some citations. The reasoning was as follows: although reference production would have proceeded rapidly, the use of these guides would be nonselective. References, important and unimportant, crucial and trivial, would have poured forth. In addition, when all relevant references had been found from these sources, there would still remain the even more important task of selection. It was therefore decided to start with the editor's personal files—then numbering a mere 2,000 primary references—and to proceed more or less cautiously by first searching the various obvious historical sources, such as the relevant publications of Boring, Titchener, Woodworth, Helmholtz, and Murchison, and then turning to other historical works, bibliographic volumes, various word-books, biographies, bibliographies in the *Journal of the History of the Behavioral Sciences,* the *Biographical Memoirs of the National Academy of Sciences,* and equivalent series for other countries, necrologies in the various journals, *Festschrift* volumes, and collections of papers. The same procedures and types of sources were used in searching for the relevant literature of biology, physiology, anthropology, sociology, philosophy, and the history of science, e.g., *Isis* bibliographies, *International Encyclopedia of Social Sciences,* the *Encyclopedia of Philosophy,* Garrison and Morton, and lists of the Syntopicon of the *Great Books of the Western World.* Also consulted were thousands of more specific sources that were pertinent to only one or a few of the individuals. In progressing from the more obvious to the less obvious bibliographic sources, the repetitions of identical references which occurred

not only provided the opportunity to check citations for discrepancies but also gave us a very rough idea of the importance attributed to these particular references. Even before turning to the process of formal checking for accuracy, which we shall describe below, over 25 percent of the references had been checked for agreement among two, three, or more secondary statements and notations of agreement or disagreement made on the reference cards.

While no exact record was kept of just how many references were actually examined directly, it is in the neighborhood of 70 percent of the total.

Consistent errors were often found. Inspection of the article or book in question often showed that "consistent" verification from various lists could be an illusion created by one source copying from the previous one.

For a reference not examined directly, the source used to check it was not the same as that used to generate it. The check sources for a considerable number were the *Psychological Index and Abstracts,* the *Library of Congress Catalogue* and *National Union Catalogue,* and related publications. After they were used, 30 or 40 percent of the references, not examined directly, were still unchecked.

The next most productive sources for books proved to be the *British Museum: General Catalogue of Printed Books,* the *Catalogue Général des Livres Imprimés de la Bibliothèque Nationale,* and the *Deutsches Bücherverzeichnis.* After these, there was a considerable mélange of sources. The literature reviews of *L'Année psychologique* and the *Zeitschrift für Psychologie* were not particularly productive, perhaps because they covered the same material as the *Index* and *Abstracts.* More fruitful were *American Bibliography, Books in Print, Catalogue Général de la Librairie Française, English Catalogue of Books, La France Littéraire* and its extension, *La Littérature Française*

Contemporaine, Index Medicus (including its earlier versions), *Index of Psychoanalytic Writings, Internationale Bibliographie der Zeitschriftenliteratur, La Librairie Française: Les Livres de l'Année, Royal Society London Catalogue of Scientific Papers, The United States Catalog,* trade catalogs, reprint catalogs, critical reviews, and major definitive texts.

Previous bibliographies varied in the extent to which they supplied what we would consider to be complete referencing. For example, the *British Museum* does a superlative job in some respects; however, they omit the publisher in most instances. In reporting later editions, almost all sources did not report the original date of publication.

When viewed from the perspective of the fields involved, certain differences in the amount of available bibliographic sources became apparent. Psychology, in the narrower sense, is relatively well supplied with sources. The long tradition of philosophy has also produced a reasonably ample supply. It is physiology that is conspicuously lacking in reference collections. This is especially the case for nineteenth-century German physiology; this country, field, and period gave more trouble in verifying citations than any other.

As already stated, it was impossible to inspect directly all references reported. Errors are inevitable. If another edition is published, corrections could be made. In the meantime, a tentative plan is under consideration to issue a list of corrections in the *Journal of the History of the Behavioral Sciences.* Suggestions, corrections, and additions, addressed to the Editor, would be appreciated.

Although used only sparingly, several stratagems were resorted to when sighting became impracticable or impossible, and yet some relevant bit of information was still missing—in particular, the names of publishers or the pages of a certain article. In the case of articles in collections, sometimes the original journal,

volume, and pages were omitted, with the title followed only by the publication date but with complete citation to the collection. Used only as a last resort, since it was a glaring and obvious failure, primary books are given with the ignominious admission: "publisher not known" (this "defeat" was experienced less than five times).

A source of considerable anxiety in the collection of references was the possibility that I would confuse the work of two different individuals. This thought, which almost gave me nightmares throughout the project, was narrowly averted relatively late in the process of reference selection. Most of the publications of Francis M. Urban were signed "F. M."; they dealt with psychophysics, and most of them appeared in American and German journals during the first two decades of this century. At practically the last moment I stumbled upon a partial bibliography of *Friedrich* M. Urban and discovered that he too signed with his initials, published on psychophysics in the same American and German journals, and covered the same time span! Editors evidently had become aware of the two Urbans, for some articles appeared with (Philadelphia) or (Brunn) after the name. To the best of my ability, I have reported only the works of Francis M. Urban. There is still a strong possibility that his panel score of 14 was inflated by Friedrich's work being credited by the panelists to Francis.

The literature search actually ended in December 1971, but about fifty early-1972 publications have been added. No titles were included on the basis of anticipated publication except for open-ended citation of some series already partly in print by that date—e.g., the *Collected Works* of Jung, of which most volumes had appeared by that date.

When the references collected seemed reasonably complete and balanced, I sought the help of specialists. Cooperation was first asked through explanatory letters addressed to individuals known to be especially knowledgeable about one or two particular contributors. The great majority agreed. They were sent xeroxed copies of the selected references, and criticisms, deletions, and additions were requested. In most instances their advice was followed, but the Editor reserved the right to disagree. Any errors of commission or omission are still his. In all, advice on 349 contributors was received from 239 individuals. Their names are listed in the section devoted to acknowledgments.

SHORT-TITLE PRIMARY READINGS AND FULL REFERENCES

In recent years, books of short excerpts not confined to the works of one man have become quite common. Below is the list of books cited. To facilitate reference from the text to this listing, the alphabetical arrangement is that of the short titles.

(Ackermann, *Theories*) Ackermann, R. J. (Ed.), *Theories of knowledge: A critical introduction.* New York: McGraw-Hill, 1965.

(Anastasi, *Individual Differences*) Anastasi, Anne (Ed.), *Individual differences.* New York: Wiley, 1965.

(Arnold, *Emotion*) Arnold, Magda B. (Ed.), *The nature of emotion: Selected readings.* Baltimore, Md.: Penguin Books, 1968.

(Beardslee, *Perception*) Beardslee, D. C., & Wertheimer, M. (Eds.), *Readings in perception.* Princeton, N.J.: Van Nostrand, 1958.

(Beck & Molish, *Reflexes*) Beck, S. I. & Molish, H. B. (Eds.), *Reflexes to intelligence: A reader in clinical psychology.* Glencoe, Ill.: Free Press, 1959.

(Bindra & Stewart, *Motivation*) Bindra, D., & Stewart, Jane (Eds.), *Motivation: Selected readings.* Baltimore, Md.: Penguin Books, 1966.

(Bodenheimer, *Biology*) Bodenheimer, F. S.

(Ed.), *The history of biology: An introduction.* London: Dawsons, 1958.

(Boe & Church, *Punishment*) Boe, E. E., & Church, R. M. (Eds.), *Punishment: Issues and experiments.* New York: Appleton-Century-Crofts, 1968.

(Borgatta, *Present-day Sociology*) Borgatta, E. F., & Meyer, H. J. (Eds.), *Sociological theory: Present-day sociology for the past.* New York: Knopf, 1956.

(Brinton, *Age Reason*) Brinton, C. (Ed.), *The portable age of reason reader.* New York: Viking Press, 1956.

(Burnham, *Science*) Burnham, J. C. (Ed.), *Science in America: Historical selections.* New York: Holt, Rinehart & Winston, 1971.

(Chisholm, *Realism*) Chisholm, R. M. (Ed.), *Realism and the background of phenomenology.* New York: Free Press, 1960.

(Clarke & O'Malley, *Brain*) Clarke, E., & O'Malley, C. D. (Eds.), *The human brain and spinal cord: A historical study illustrated by writings from antiquity to the twentieth century.* Berkeley, Calif.: University of California Press, 1968.

(Clendening, *Source Book*) Clendening, L. (Ed.), *Source book of medical history.* New York: Dover, 1960. (1942)

(Coser, *Sociological Thought*) Coser, L. A. (Ed.), *Masters of sociological thought: Ideas in historical and social context.* New York: Harcourt Brace Jovanovich, 1971.

(Coser & Rosenberg, *Sociological Theory*) Coser, L. A., & Rosenberg, B. (Eds.), *Sociological theory: A book of readings.* New York: Macmillan, 1957.

(Count, *Race*) Count, E. W. (Ed.), *This is race.* New York: Schuman, 1950.

(Cubberley, *Public Educators*) Cubberley, E. P. (Ed.), *Readings in public education in the United States: A collection of sources and readings to illustrate the history of educational practice and progress in the United States.* Boston: Houghton Mifflin, 1934.

(Curtis, *Knowledge*) Curtis, J. E., & Petras, J. W. (Eds.), *The sociology of knowledge: A reader*. London: Duckworth, 1970.

(Dampier, *Literature*) Dampier, W. C., & Dampier, Margaret (Eds.), *Readings in the literature of science: Being extracts from the writings of men of science to illustrate the development of scientific thought*. New York: Harper, 1959.

(Dember, *Perception*) Dember, W. N. (Ed.), *Visual perception: The nineteenth century*. New York: Wiley, 1964.

(Dennis, *Psychology*) Dennis, W. (Ed.), *Readings in the history of psychology*. New York: Appleton-Century-Crofts, 1948.

(Dennis, *Readings Developmental*) Dennis, W. (Ed.), *Historical readings in developmental psychology*. New York: Appleton-Century-Crofts, 1972.

(Drever, *Sourcebook*) Drever, J., Jr. (Ed.), *Sourcebook in psychology: A course of selected readings by authorities*. New York: Philosophical Library, 1960.

(Fisch, *Philosophers*) Fisch, M. H. (Ed.), *Classic American philosophers*. New York: Appleton-Century-Crofts, 1951.

(Fried, *Anthropology*) Fried, M. H. (Ed.), *Readings in anthropology*. Vol. 2: *Readings in cultural anthropology*. New York: Crowell, 1959.

(Fulton & Wilson, *Physiology*) Fulton, J. F., & Wilson, L. G. (Eds.), *Selected readings in the history of physiology*. (2nd ed.) Springfield, Ill.: Thomas, 1966. (1930)

(Gabriel & Fogel, *Biology*) Gabriel, M. L., & Fogel, S. (Eds.), *Great experiments in biology*. Englewood Cliffs, N.J.: Prentice-Hall, 1955.

(Gardiner, *Philosophy*) Gardiner, P. L. (Ed.), *Nineteenth-century philosophy*. New York: Free Press, 1969.

(Goldschmidt, *Mankind*) Goldschmidt, W. (Ed.), *Exploring the ways of mankind*. New York: Holt, Rinehart & Winston, 1960.

(Goshen, *Documentary*) Goshen, C. E. (Ed.), *Documentary history of psychiatry: A source book on historical principles*. New York: Philosophical Library, 1967.

(Grinder, *Genetic Psychology*) Grinder, R.E. (Ed.), *A history of genetic psychology: The first science of human development*. New York: Wiley, 1967.

(Grob & Beck, *American Ideas*) Grob, G. N., & Beck, R. N. (Eds.), *American ideas: Source readings in the intellectual history of the United States*. (2 vols. in 1.) New York: Free Press, 1963.

(Gruber, *Creative Thinking*) Gruber, H. E., Terrell, G., & Wertheimer, M. (Eds.), *Contemporary approaches to creative thinking*. New York: Atherton Press, 1962.

(Hall, *Nature's Laws*) Hall, Marie B. (Ed.), *Nature and laws: Documents of the scientific revolution*. New York: Harper & Row, 1970.

(Hall, *Source Book*) Hall, T. S. (Ed.), *A source book in animal biology*. New York: McGraw-Hill, 1951.

(Hameline, *Anthologie*) Hameline, D. (Ed.), *Anthologie des psycholoques français contemporains*. Paris: Presses Universitaires de France, 1969.

(Herrnstein & Boring, *Source Book*) Herrnstein, R. J., & Boring, E. G. (Eds.), *A source book in the history of psychology*. Cambridge: Harvard University Press, 1965.

(Hirst, *Perception*) Hirst, R. J. (Ed.), *Perception and the external world*. New York: Macmillan, 1965.

(Hoebel & Jennings, *Anthropology*) Hoebel, E. A., Jennings, J. E., & Smith, E. R. (Eds.), *Readings in anthropology*. New York: McGraw-Hill, 1955.

(Hunter & Macalpine, *Psychiatry*) Hunter, R., & Macalpine, Ida (Eds.), *Three hundred years of psychiatry, 1535–1860*. London: Oxford University Press, 1963.

(Hutchins, *Great Books*) Hutchins, R. M. (Ed.), *Great books of the western world*. (54 vols.) Chicago: Encyclopaedia Britannica, 1952.

(Jenkins & Paterson, *Individual Differences*) Jenkins, J. J., & Paterson, D. G. (Eds.), *Studies in individual differences: The search for intelligence.* New York: Appleton-Century-Crofts, 1961.

(Johnston, *Scottish Philosophy*) Johnston, G. A. (Ed.), *Selections from the Scottish philosophy of common sense.* Chicago: Open Court, 1915.

(Kessen, *Child*) Kessen, W. (Ed.), *The child.* New York: Wiley, 1965.

(Krich, *Sexual Revolution*) Krich, A. (Ed.), *The sexual revolution.* Vol. 1. New York: Dell, 1963.

(Kroeber, *Source Book*) Kroeber, A. L., & Waterman, T. T. (Eds.), *Source book in anthropology.* Berkeley, Calif.: University of California Press, 1920.

(Kurtz, *American Thought*) Kurtz, P. (Ed.), *American thought before 1900: A sourcebook from puritanism to Darwinism.* New York: Macmillan, 1966.

(Lawrence & O'Connor, *Phenomenology*) Lawrence, N., & O'Connor, D. *Readings in existential phenomenology.* Englewood Cliffs, N.J.: Prentice-Hall, 1967.

(Lindzey & Hall, *Personality*) Lindzey, G., & Hall, C. S. (Eds.), *Theories of personality: Primary sources and research.* New York: Wiley, 1965.

(MacAdam, *Color Science*) MacAdam, D. L. (Ed.), *Sources of color science.* Cambridge: M.I.T. Press, 1970.

(McNall, *Sociological Perspectives*) McNall, S. G. (Ed.), *Sociological perspectives: Introductory readings.* Boston: Little, Brown, 1968.

(Madden, *Scientific Thought*) Madden, E. H. (Ed.), *The structure of scientific thought: An introduction to the philosophy of science.* Boston: Houghton Mifflin, 1960.

(Mandler & Mandler, *Thinking*) Mandler, Jean M., & Mandler, G. (Eds.), *Thinking:*

From association to Gestalt. New York: Wiley, 1964.

(Mann & Kreyche, *Reflections Man*) Mann, J. A., & Kreyche, G. F. (Eds.), *Reflections on man: Readings in philosophical psychology from classical philosophy to existentialism.* New York: Harcourt, Brace & World, 1966.

(Margolis, *Introduction*) Margolis, J. (Ed.), *An introduction to philosophical inquiry: Contemporary and classical sources.* New York: Knopf, 1968.

(Matson, *Being*) Matson, F. W. (Ed.), *Being, becoming and behavior.* New York: Braziller, 1967.

(Miller, *Mathematics*) Miller, G. A. (Ed.), *Mathematics and psychology.* New York: Wiley, 1964.

(Moore & Hartmann, *Industrial Psychology*) Moore, B. V., & Hartmann, G. W. (Eds.), *Readings in industrial psychology.* New York: Appleton, 1931.

(Mueller, *American Philosophy*) Mueller, W. G., Sears, L., & Schlabach, Anne V. (Eds.), *The development of American philosophy.* (2nd ed.) Boston: Houghton Mifflin, 1960. (1940)

(Murphy, *Western*) Murphy, G., & Murphy, Lois B. (Eds.), *Western psychology: From the Greeks to William James.* New York: Basic Books, 1969.

(Nash, *Models*) Nash, P. (Ed.), *Models of man: Explorations in the western educational tradition.* New York: Wiley, 1968.

(Newman, *Mathematics*) Newman, J. R. (Ed.), *The world of mathematics.* (2 vols.) New York: Simon & Schuster, 1956.

(O'Brien & Schrag, *Sociology*) O'Brien, R. W., Schrag, C. G., & Martin, W. T. (Eds.), *Readings in general sociology.* Boston: Houghton Mifflin, 1951.

(Park & Burgess, *Sociology*) Park, R. E. & Burgess, E. W. (Eds.), *Introduction to the science of sociology.* Chicago: University of Chicago Press, 1921.

(Parsons, *Society*) Parsons, T., Shils, E., Naegels, K. D., & Pitts, J. R. (Eds.), *Theories of Society: Foundations of modern sociological theory.* (2 vols.) Glencoe, Ill.: Free Press, 1961.

(Perez, *Readings*) Perez, J. R., *et al.* (Eds.), *General psychology: Selected readings.* New York: Van Nostrand, Reinhold, 1967.

(Popkin, *Philosophy*) Popkin, R. H. (Ed.), *The philosophy of the 16th and 17th centuries.* New York: Free Press, 1966.

(Pressey, *Casebook*) Pressey, S. L., & Janney, J. E. (Eds.), *Casebook of research in educational psychology.* New York: Harper, 1937.

(Price, *Education*) Price, K. (Ed.), *Education and philosophical thought.* Boston: Allyn & Bacon, 1967.

(Rabkin & Carr, *Abnormal*) Rabkin, L. Y., & Carr, J. E. (Eds.), *Sourcebook in abnormal psychology.* Boston: Houghton Mifflin, 1967.

(Rand, *Classical Philosophers*) Rand, B. (Ed.), *Modern classical philosophers: Selections illustrating modern philosophy from Bruno to Bergson.* (2nd ed.) Boston: Houghton Mifflin, 1924. (1908)

(Rand, *Classical Psychologists*) Rand, B. (Ed.), *The classical psychologists: Selections illustrating psychology from Anaxagoras to Wundt.* Boston: Houghton Mifflin, 1912.

(Rand, *Moralists*) Rand, B. (Ed.), *The classical moralists: Selections illustrating ethics from Socrates to Martineau.* Boston: Houghton Mifflin, 1909.

(Rapaport, *Thought*) Rapaport, D. (Ed.), *Organization and pathology of thought: Selected sources.* New York: Columbia University Press, 1951.

(Reeves, *Body Mind*) Reeves, Joan W. (Ed.), *Body and mind in western thought: An introduction to some origins of modern psychology.* London: Penguin Books, 1958.

Riopelle, *Problem Solving*) Riopelle, A. J. (Ed.), *Animal problem solving: Selected readings.* Baltimore, Md.: Penguin Books, 1967.

(Robinson, *Scottish Philosophy*) Robinson, D. S. (Ed.), *The story of Scottish philosophy.* New York: Exposition Press, 1961.

(Rook, *Origins*) Rook, A. (Ed.), *The origins and growth of biology.* London: Penguin Books, 1964.

(Rorty, *Pragmatic Philosophy*) Rorty, Amelie (Ed.), *Pragmatic philosophy: An anthology.* Garden City, N.Y.: Doubleday, 1966.

(Rosenblith & Allinsmith, *Causes Behavior*) Rosenblith, Judy F., & Allinsmith, W. (Eds.), *The causes of behavior: Readings in child development and educational psychology.* Boston: Allyn & Bacon, 1962.

(Ross, *Social Order*) Ross, H. L. (Ed.), *Perspective on the social order: Readings in sociology.* (2nd ed.) New York: McGraw-Hill, 1968.

(Russell, *Motivation*) Russell, W. A. (Ed.), *Milestones in motivation: Contributions to the psychology of drive and purpose.* New York: Appleton-Century-Crofts, 1970.

(Sahakian, *Personality*) Sahakian, W. S. (Ed.), *Psychology of personality: Readings in theory.* Chicago: Rand McNally, 1965.

(Sahakian, *Psychology*) Sahakian, W. S. (Ed.), *History of psychology.* Itasca, Ill.: Peacock, 1968.

(Schneider, *Scottish Moralists*) Schneider, L. (Ed.), *The Scottish moralists on human nature and society.* Chicago: University of Chicago Press, 1967.

(Schwartz & Bishop, *Moments Discovery*) Schwartz, G., & Bishop, P. W. (Eds.), *Moments of discovery.* (2 vols.) New York: Basic Books, 1958.

(Shipley, *Classics*) Shipley, T. (Ed.), *Classics in psychology.* New York: Philosophical Library, 1961.

(Shor, *Hypnosis*) Shor, R. E., & Orne, M. T. (Eds.), *The nature of hypnosis: Selected basic writings.* New York: Holt, Rinehart & Winston, 1965.

(Slotkin, *Anthropology*) Slotkin, J. S. (Ed.),

Readings in early anthropology. Chicago: Aldine, 1965.

(Smith, *Source Book*) Smith, D. E. (Ed.), *A source book in mathematics.* New York: Mc-Graw-Hill, 1929. (Reprinted 1959)

(Strain, *Philosophies Education*) Strain, J. P. (Ed.), *Modern philosophies of education: A book of readings.* New York: Random House, 1970.

(Teevan, *Vision*) Teevan, R. C., & Birney, R. C. (Eds.), *Color vision: An enduring problem in psychology.* Princeton, N.J.: Van Nostrand, 1961.

(Thomas, *Source Book*) Thomas, W. I. (Ed.), *Source book for social origins.* (6th ed.) Boston: Badger, 1909.

(Tinterow, *Hypnosis*) Tinterow, M. M. (Ed.), *Foundations of hypnosis: From Mesmer to Freud.* Springfield, Ill.: Thomas, 1970.

(Torrey, *Les Philosophes*) Torrey, N. L. (Ed.), *Les philosophes: The philosophers of the enlightenment and modern democracy.* New York: Capricorn Books, 1960.

(Ulich, *Educational Wisdom*) Ulich, R. (Ed.), *Three thousand years of educational wisdom: Selections from great documents.* Cambridge: Harvard University Press, 1947.

(Valentine, *Experimental*) Valentine, W. L. (Ed.), *Readings in experimental psychology.* New York: Harper, 1931.

(Vetter, *Personality*) Vetter, H. J., & Smith, B. D. (Eds.), *Personality theory: A source book.* New York: Appleton-Century-Crofts, 1971.

(Wiseman, *Intelligence*) Wiseman, S. (Ed.), *Intelligence and ability: Selected readings.* Baltimore, Md.: Penguin Books, 1967.

(Wrenn, *Contributions*) Wrenn, R. L. (Ed.), *Basic contributions to psychology: Readings.* Belmont, Calif.: Wadsworth, 1966.

(Zajonc, *Animal Social*) Zajonc, R. B. (Ed.), *Animal social psychology: A reader of experimental studies.* New York: Wiley, 1969.

GUIDE TO ARRANGEMENT OF REFERENCES
AND CITATION FORMS

This section discusses the manner in which the references are arranged and presented. At first the overall arrangement is described; then the way in which books and articles are cited is indicated. Footnotes indicating the rationale of the procedures, and the qualifications and exceptions made, must be consulted when problems are encountered in interpreting a particular reference.

An alphabetical arrangement is followed for the 538 individuals whose selected works are cited in this volume. The full name [2] is first given, followed by dates of birth and death. Then the country (or countries) where his principal work was done, along with the scholar's major field of endeavor, are reported (see pages x–xi for details). Last, in parentheses, the eminence rating score is indicated (see pages x–xi for information on how these ratings were derived). References follow.

Listed first for each contributor are collections of complete, selected works and letters, arranged by date of publication. That they are

collections is indicated by an entry of "C" following the reference.

Following the collections individual books and articles are intermingled; they too are arranged chronologically by date of original publication. If a work—a book or an article—in this part of the list is included in a previously listed collection, its previously listed collection source is identified parenthetically by short title and "*op. cit.*"

Primary entries for a given individual close with an alphabetical listing of the short titles of books of primary readings in which some excerpts from the work of the individual appear. A list of short-title entries (and their abbreviations) will be found on pp. xvi–xx.

An entry of "B" or "Bl" following a reference indicates, respectively, an autobiography or letter collection, and a bibliography.[3]

Each *book entry* gives the title of the book in italics, the place of publication, the publisher's name in short title, and the copyright date. If necessary, other materials are interpolated, such as the number of volumes (if more than one), the particular edition [4] (if not

---

[2] Names of Russians are given in a form most familiar to American readers despite the fact that consistent transliteration might call for another spelling. Thus, Vygotsky is retained rather than the more accurate Vygotskii.

Despite a thorough search, some birth and death dates cannot be specified precisely. This is the case with Francis M. Urban, who last published in 1950 and was known then to be living in Brazil. This was the most frustrating failure, since he was rather prolific and taught at a university in the United States. No definite information could be obtained. For failure to obtain the death date of Alfons Pilzecker and both the birth and death dates of Adolf Jost there is perhaps more justification. The former published two papers and the latter only one. Both were students of G. E. Müller and no trace could be found of them after 1890, the apparent date of their departure from Göttingen, and possibly from university life itself.

[3] Biographies and bibliographies prepared by others will be found in Volume 2, which is devoted to the secondary literature.

[4] The effort to cite the most recent edition for each work, even though it was a sensible procedure, created some complications. Errors of omission, for example, have taken place because the release of later editions may not have been noted. Moreover, many continental publishers report each printing as a new edition, whether or not revisions have been made. There may also be some uncertainty about the exact status of a particular edition, including the fact that some popular volumes have been revised posthumously by persons other than the author. Historical study of any depth requires that this matter be worked through carefully. The present bibliographies do not pretend to solve these problems for the scholar.

the first), and the initials and name of the translator(s) and/or editor(s).

The date of original publication is always reported. If no other date is reported, it may be assumed that the copyright and original publication dates are the same. Otherwise, the original date of publication is reported in parentheses. In most instances this date is given immediately after the citation of the full reference and its copyright date. The parenthetical date of the original publication appears after the title itself when material is being cited from a collected work with its own copyright date.

Some problems are created by reference to second or subsequent editions. In most instances the last edition known is the one cited.[5] The vicissitudes of the various editions of a particular book, sometimes as many as thirty, are not indicated in the citations since the parenthetical date is that of the original publication, regardless of the edition being cited. The date given for the copyright of the particular printing is cited in the usual fashion, after the name of the publisher. This latter date may not necessarily be the original publication date of the particular edition.[6]

[5] Some exceptions to the rule of citing only the last edition occur because of the particular value of another edition. Two works of Woodworth are cases in point. The third edition of his *Schools of psychology* is a classic, but it was revised subsequently; consequently, the fourth edition, written in collaboration with Mary R. Sheehan, is also cited. Two editions of Woodworth's *Experimental psychology* are cited: the original or 1938 edition (which also has an earlier history in mimeograph form) and his second edition, written in collaboration with Harold Schlosberg. (In the reported secondary literature there is still a third edition prepared by J. W. Kling and Lorren A. Riggs.)

[6] Especially prominent in references carrying other than the original copyright date are the products of various reprint houses, such as Dawsons, Olms, Editions Culture et Civilisation, Dover, Hafner, and Scholars' Facsimiles and Reprints. Since the works are probably more generally accessible in these editions, they are often the ones indicated here. Major libraries would, of course, have the originals

of these reprints. Articles republished in book form, if the original full journal citation is not given (which would include the date), show the date of original publication in parentheses following the title.

Renewal of copyright, and reissuance in a later printing which is then copyrighted, are the two most obvious sources of this discrepancy between the date reported for the publication and the edition mentioned, because only the original first-edition date is reported in parentheses. This might be confusing in citing volumes that are reissued and bear a date later than that of the first appearance of that edition, since accessibility and availability in translation were considered in selecting the particular printing to be cited. For example, Kant's *Critique of pure reason* is cited for the second edition's date, 1787, while the date in parentheses is that of the first edition, 1781. There would have been no problem if the second edition, in its original publication in Riga by Hartknock, had been cited, for that would have carried the correct 1787 date of the second edition. To do so would have been accurate, but not as helpful to the reader, since this particular publication is quite rare and is in the original German. Instead, an English version of the second edition is cited, with a 1933 copyright date.

In translated works, a second or subsequent edition cited parenthetically after the title refers to the edition in the language from which it was translated; it does not mean that the translation in itself is a second edition.

Some books published in the same year as the original work are translations or later editions of that volume. Since translations into English were reported whenever possible, this has resulted in multiple listings of the same title. If a later foreign edition of the translated edition is known, it too is reported.

For works kept in print, the original publication date is given. Works going out of print and then reappearing, even with the same publisher, are reported as reprinted; or the reference given is of the new copyright date, but the original date of publication is still shown in parentheses. When a work has been known to appear in a paperback edition or in book-size microfilm, it is reported as "reprinted"; accordingly, the date of that reprinting is supplied. (The word "reprinted" is used loosely in connection with some two to three hundred volumes. Actually, they are facsimiles by microfilm-xerography from University Microfilms. Many were requested by the Editor for the University of New Hampshire Library shelves and became available through this service.)

An apparent violation of citation fidelity had to be instituted because of the not-uncommon publishing practice of listing an editor in such fashion that he appears to be the "author." As a hypothetical example, a title cited on the spine of the book, or even on the title page, as "T. Brown, *Kant the*

In the case of an *article*, the title is reported first, followed by the journal's name (abbreviated and in italics), the year of publication, the volume number, and the inclusive pages. If the article appeared earlier in another language, the title is followed by a parenthetical statement of the year in which it first appeared. Periodicals that start pagination for each issue within a volume list the number of that issue in parentheses following the volume number.

With a few exceptions, the abbreviations used to identify journal titles are those adopted by the American Psychological Association, as reported in the 1957 volume of the *Publication Manual*. In turn, these abbreviations, plus additions, are based on the *World List of Scientific Periodicals*.[7]

---

thinker," might turn out to be the selected works of Kant, edited by Brown, and more correctly cited as "Kant, I. *Kant the thinker*. Ed. T. Brown."

A more legitimate variant of this practice involves works, edited by others, especially posthumous ones; the title page is so arranged as to carry the editor as the source of the publication and the author is mentioned in the title—e.g., Margaret Mead, Editor of *An anthropologist at work: Writings of Ruth Benedict*. Many "Complete works," edited posthumously, follow this practice. In all citations of this nature, the editor is listed parenthetically after the title, and the book is considered as a primary publication of the person whose writings are included.

If books have been published simultaneously in the United States and England by one or more publishers, only the city and publisher in the United States are cited. It is also not uncommon for a book to be published simultaneously by different publishers in two German- or two French-speaking countries. French or German cities and publishers are cited in preference to those in Belgium, Switzerland, and Austria. Translations from the Latin, Scandinavian,

Flemish, or Spanish languages into English, French, or German are cited in preference to the original publications. Titles of untranslated works in these languages are cited in the language of origin. The titles of untranslated works published in Japanese, in Russian, and in other Slavic languages are cited only in English translation and placed in parentheses. While some readers may object to this practice, I believe that those who are unfamiliar with these languages are by far a majority of those who will use this volume.

[7] Some changes in journal title abbreviations were dictated by considerations of space. For example, "*Arch. ges. Psychol.*" was cited without a preceding "*Pflügers,*" as would be customary in Europe and called for by the *World List*—an omission which saved at least a page overall. However, the tendency to develop an esoteric code of one's own was resisted and a special list of abbreviations rendered unnecessary.

Over the years, some journals have changed their names rather drastically but maintained volume sequence number. To avoid confusion it was decided in some instances to use the abbreviation of the latest name: *Char. & Pers.* is reported as *J. Pers.*; *Psychol. Rev. Monogr. Suppl.* as *Psychol. Monogr.*; *Ped. Sem.* as *J. genet. Psychol.*; *J. Phil. Psychol. Sci. Meth.* as *J. Phil.*; and so on. Where the change was not likely to lead to confusion—e.g., *J. abnorm. Psychol.*, later *J. abnorm. soc. Psychol.*—some journals are presented under the title appropriate to the year of publication.

Publication of the same article in more than one journal—e.g., simultaneously in *Fortnightly Review*, *Macmillan's Magazine*, and *Nature*—created a problem that was not always solved consistently. In most instances, to save space, only one source is given even though others are known to exist.

When a volume includes two or more years, the inclusive years are reported even though the article in question appeared in an issue carrying a specific year. The following frequently cited journals maintained this policy of spanning more than one year with an issue over an appreciable period of their existence: *Philosophische Studien, American Journal of Psychology, Archives de Psychologie* (Geneva), and the *British Journal of Psychology*.

The following illustrations, drawn from the works of Gordon Allport, indicate graphically the organization of the bibliographic entries:

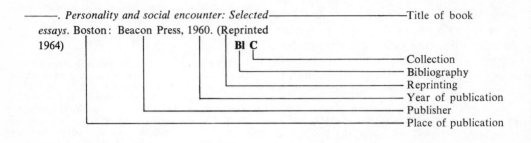

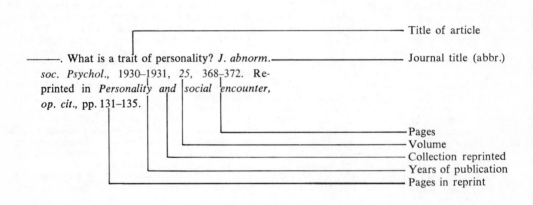

KARL ABRAHAM
1877-1925
German Psychoanalyst (20)

Abraham, K. *Selected papers*. Trans. by D. Bryant & A. Strachey. London: Hogarth Press, 1965. (1927)   **C Bl**

————. *Clinical papers and essays on psychoanalysis*. Ed. by Hilda C. Abraham & trans. by Hilda C. Abraham *et al*. London: Hogarth Press, 1955.   **C Bl**

Freud, S., & ————. *A psychoanalytic dialogue: The letters of Sigmund Freud and Karl Abraham, 1907–1926*. Ed. by Hilda C. Abraham & E. L. Freud. New York: Basic Books, 1966.   **B C**

————. The experiencing of sexual traumas as a form of sexual activity. (1907) Reprinted in *Selected papers, op cit.*, pp. 47–63.

————. On the significance of sexual trauma in childhood for the symptomatology of dementia praecox. (1907) Reprinted in *Clinical papers, op. cit.*, pp. 13–20.

————. The psychological relations between sexuality and alcoholism. (1908) Reprinted in *Selected papers, op. cit.*, pp. 80–89.

————. The psycho-sexual differences between hysteria and dementia praecox. (1908) Reprinted in *Selected papers, op. cit.*, pp. 64–79.

————. *Dreams and myths: A study in race psychology*. Trans. by W. A. White. New York: Nervous & Mental Disease Publishing, 1913. (1909) Reprinted in *Clinical papers, op. cit.*, pp. 151–209.

————. Hysterical dream states. (1910) Reprinted in *Selected papers, op. cit.*, pp. 90–124.

————. *Giovanni Segantini: Ein psychoanalytischer Versuch*. Vienna: Deuticke, 1925. (1911)

————. Notes on the psychoanalytical investigation and treatment of manic-depressive insanity and allied conditions. (1911) Reprinted in *Selected papers, op. cit.*, pp. 137–156.

————. Ansätze zur psychoanalytischen Erforschung und Behandlung des manisch-depressiven

Irreseins und verwandter Zustände. *Zbl. Psychoanal.*, 1912, *2*(6), 302–315.

————. Kritik zu C. G. Jung. Versuch einer Darstellung der psychoanalytischen Theorie. *Int. Z. Psychoanal.*, 1914, *2*, 72–82.

————. Ueber Einschränkungen und Umwandlungen der Schaulust bei den Psychoneurotikern nebst Bemerkungen über analoge Erscheinungen in der Völkerpsychologie. *Jb. Psychoanal.*, 1914, *6*, 25–88.

————. The first pregenital stage of the libido. (1916) Reprinted in *Selected papers, op. cit.*, pp. 248–279.

————. Ejaculation praecox. (1917) Reprinted in *Selected papers, op. cit.*, pp. 280–298.

————. Ueber eine besondere Form des neurotischen Widerstandes gegen die psychoanalytische Methodik. *Int. Z. Psychoanal.*, 1919, *5*, 173–180.

————. Manifestations of the female castration complex. (1920) Reprinted in *Selected papers, op. cit.*, pp. 338–369.

————. The narcissistic evaluation of excretory processes in dreams and neuroses. (1920) Reprinted in *Selected papers, op. cit.*, pp. 318–322.

————. The cultural significance of psycho-analysis. (1920) Reprinted in *Clinical papers, op. cit.*, pp. 116–136.

————. Contributions to the theory of the anal character. (1921) Reprinted in *Selected papers, op. cit.*, pp. 370–392.

————. The influence of oral erotism on character formation. (1924) Reprinted in *Selected papers, op. cit.*, pp. 393–406.

————. A short study of the development of the libido, viewed in the light of mental disorders. (1924) Reprinted in *Selected papers, op. cit.*, pp. 418–501.

————. Character-formation on the genital level of the libido-development. (1924) Reprinted in *Selected papers, op. cit.*, pp. 407–417.

————. Psycho-analytical notes on Coue's method of self-mastery. (1925) Reprinted in *Clinical papers, op. cit.*, pp. 306–327.

NARZISS KASPAR ACH
1871-1946
German Psychologist (26)

Ach, N. Ueber die geistige Leistungsfähigkeit im Zustande des eingeengten Bewusstseins. *Z. Hypno.*, 1899, *9*, 1–84.

————. Ueber die Beeinflussung der Auffassungsfähigkeit durch einige Arzneimittel. *Psychol. Arb.*, 1900, *3*, 203–288. (Also Leipzig: Engelmann, 1900)

————. Ueber die Otolithenfunction und den Labyrinthtonus. *Arch. ges. Physiol.*, 1901, *86*, 122–146.

————. *Ueber die Willenstätigkeit und das Denken: Eine experimentelle Untersuchung mit einem Anhange: Ueber das Hippsche Chronoskop.* Göttingen: Vandenhoeck & Ruprecht, 1905. **Bl**

————. *Ueber den Willensakt und das Temperament: Eine experimentelle Untersuchung.* Leipzig: Quelle & Meyer, 1910.

————. *Ueber den Willen.* Leipzig: Quelle & Meyer, 1910.

————. Willensakt und Temperament. Eine Widerlegung. *Z. Psychol.*, 1911, *58*, 263–276.

————. *Ueber den Willensakt. Eine Replik.* Leipzig: Quelle & Meyer, 1911.

————. *Eine Serienmethode für Reaktionsversuche. Bemerkung zur Untersuchung des Willens.* Leipzig: Quelle & Meyer, 1912.

————. Willensuntersuchungen in ihrer Bedeutung für die Pädagogik. *Z. pädag. Psychol.*, 1913, *14*, 1–11.

————. *Ueber die Erkenntnis a priori insbesondere in der Arithmetik.* Leipzig: Quelle & Meyer, 1913.

————. Wille. In E. Korschelt *et al.* (Eds.), *Handwörterbuch der Naturwissenschaften.* Vol. 10. Jena: Fischer, 1915, pp. 619–627.

————. Zur Psychologie der Amputierten. Ein Beitrag zur praktischen Psychologie. *Arch. ges. Psychol.*, 1920, *40*, 89–116. (Also Leipzig: Engelmann, 1920)

————. *Ueber die Begriffsbildung.* Bamberg: Buchner, 1921.

————. *Untersuchungen zur Psychologie, Philosophie und Pädagogie.* Vol. 5. Göttingen: Calvör, 1925.

————, Kühle, P. E., & Passarge, E. Beiträge zur Lehre von der Perseveration. *Z. Psychol.*, 1926, Suppl. 12. (Also Leipzig: Barth, 1926) (Reprinted 1970)

————. *Der Chronotyper (Zeitdrucker).* (VIII International Congress of Psychology.) Groningen: Noordhoff, 1927, pp. 217–218.

————. Experimentelle Untersuchungen über die freie Wahlentscheidung. *Proc. 8th Int. Cong. Psychol.*, Groningen: Noordhoff, 1927, pp. 219–222.

————. Ueber die Entstehung des Bewusstseins der Willensfreiheit. *Ber. Kongr. dtsch. Ges. Psychol.*, Bonn, 1928, 91–97.

————. Psychologie und Technik bei Bekämpfung von Auto-Unfällen. *Industr. Psychotechn.*, 1929, *6*, 87–97.

————. Zur Frage der Enge des Bewusstseins. *Arch. ges. Psychol.*, 1930, *74*, 261–274.

————, Düker, H., & Lubrich, W. Experimentellpsychologische Untersuchungen der Brauchbarkeit von Strassensperrschildern. *Psychotechn. Z.*, 1931, *6*, 97–106.

————. Zur psychologischen Grundlegung der sprachlichen Verständigung. *Ber. Kongr. dtsch. Ges. Psychol.*, Hamburg, 1932, *12*, 123–134.

————, Gerdessen, H., Kohlhagen, F., & Margaritzky, S. *Finale Qualität und Objektion.* Leipzig: Akademische Verlagsgesellschaft, 1932.

————. Das Kompensations- oder Produktionsprinzip der Identifikation. *Ber. Kongr. dtsch. Ges. Psychol.*, Hamburg, 1932, *12*, 280–288.

————. Ueber den Begriff des Unbewussten in der Psychologie der Gegenwart. *Z. Psychol.*, 1933, *129*, 223–245.

————. *Ueber die Determinationspsychologie und ihre Bedeutung für das Führerproblem.* Leipzig: Barth, 1933.

————. Ueber die Determinationspsychologie und ihre Bedeutung für das Führerproblem. *Ber. Kongr. dtsch. Ges. Psychol.*, Leipzig, 1934, *13*, 111–112.

————. Willens– und Charakterbildung. *Ber. Kongr. dtsch. Ges. Psychol.*, Tübingen, 1935, *14*, 274–281.

————. *Analyse des Willens.* Berlin: Urban & Schwarzenberg, 1935.

————. Zur neueren Willenslehre. *Ber. 15. Kongr. dtsch. Ges. Psychol.*, Jena, 1936, *15*, 125–156.

————. Ueber Suggestibilität und Hypnotisierbarkeit. *Z. ges. Neurol. Psychiat.*, 1937, *158*, 402–406.

————. *Lehrbuch der Psychologie.* Bamberg: Buchner, 1944.

Mandler & Mandler, *Thinking*; Rapaport, *Thought*

ALFRED ADLER
1870-1937
Austrian-American Psychiatrist (27)

Adler, A. *The practice and theory of individual psychology.* (2nd ed.) Trans. by P. Radin. New York: Harcourt, Brace, 1927. (1920)   **C**

————, Furtmüller, C., & Wexberg, E. (Eds.), *Heilen und Bilden: Grundlagen der Erziehungskunst für Aerzte und Pädagogen.* (2nd ed.) Munich: Bergmann, 1922. (1914, 1921)   **C**

————. *The individual psychology of Alfred Adler: A systematic presentation in selections from his writings.* Ed. by H. L. & Rowena R. Ansbacher. New York: Basic Books, 1956.   **B C**

————. *Superiority and social interest: A collection of later writings.* Ed. by H. L. & Rowena R. Ansbacher. Evanston, Ill.: Northwestern University Press, 1964.   **Bl C**

————. *Gesundheitsbuch für das Schneidergewerbe.* Berlin: Heymanns, 1898.

————. *Study of organ inferiority and its psychical compensation: A contribution to clinical medicine.* Trans. by S. E. Jeliffe. New York: Nervous & Mental Disease Publishing, 1917. (1907)

————. Die Theorie der Organminderwertigkeit und ihre Bedeutung für Philosophie und Psychologie. *Univ. Wien, Phil. Ges., Wiss. Beil.*, 1908, *21*, 11–26.

————. *The neurotic constitution: Outline of a comparative individualistic psychology and psychotherapy.* Trans. by B. Glueck & J. E. Lind. New York: Dodd, 1926. (1912)

————. *Ueber den nervösen Charakter. Grundzüge einer vergleichenden Individual-Psychologie und Psychotherapie.* (4th ed.) Munich: Bergmann, 1928. (1912)

————. Traum und Traumdeutung. *Zbl. Psychoanal.*, 1913, *3*, 574–583.

————. *Das Problem der Homosexualität: Erotisches Training und erotischer Rückzug.* (2nd ed.) Leipzig: Hirzel, 1930. (1917, 1926)

————. *Die andere Seite: Eine massenpsychologische Studie über die Schuld des Volkes.* Vienna: Heidrich, 1919.

————. *Understanding human nature.* Trans. by W. B. Wolfe. New York: Greenberg, 1946. (1927) (Reprinted 1957)

————. *Menschenkenntnis.* (5th ed.) Zurich: Rascher, 1947. (1927)

————. Individual psychology. *J. abnorm. soc. Psychol.*, 1927, *22*, 116–122.

————. Individualpsychologie und Wissenschaft. *Int. Z. indiv. Psychol.*, 1927, *5*, 401–408.

————. The psychology of power. (1928) *J. indiv. Psychol.*, 1966, *22*, 166–172.

————. *The case of Miss R.: The interpretation of a life story.* Trans. by Eleanore & F. Jensen. New York: Greenberg, 1929. (1928)

————. Feelings and emotions from the standpoint of individual psychology. In M. L. Reymert (Ed.), *Feelings and emotions: The Wittenberg symposium.* Worcester, Mass.: Clark University Press, 1928, pp. 316–321.

————. *Problems of neurosis: A book of casehistories.* Ed. by P. Mairet. London: Kegan

Paul, Trench & Truebner, 1929. (Reprinted 1964)

————. *Individualpsychologie in der Schule: Vorlesungen für Lehrer und Erzieher.* Leipzig: Hirzel, 1929.

————. *The science of living.* Ed. by H. L. Ansbacher. Garden City, N.Y.: Doubleday, 1969. (1929)

————. Individual psychology: Some of the problems fundamental to all psychology. In C. Murchison (Ed.), *Psychologies of 1930.* Worcester, Mass.: Clark University Press, 1930, pp. 395–405.

————. *The education of children.* Trans. by Eleanore & F. Jensen. New York: Greenberg, 1930. (Reprinted 1970)

————. *The pattern of life.* Ed. by W. B. Wolfe. New York: Cosmopolitan Book, 1930.

————. *The problem child: The life of the difficult child as analyzed in specific cases.* Trans. by G. Daniels. New York: Capricorn Books, 1963. (1930, 1952)

————. *The case of Mrs. A.: The diagnosis of a life style.* London: Daniel, 1933. (1931)

————. Individual psychology and experimental psychology. *J. Pers.,* 1932–1933, *1,* 265–267.

————. *Social interest: A challenge to mankind.* Trans. by J. Linton & R. Vaughan. New York: Putnam, 1939. (1933) (Reprinted 1964)

————. Mass psychology. (1934) *Int. J. indiv. Psychol.,* 1937, *3,* 111–120.

————. The structure of neuroses. *Int. J. indiv. Psychol.,* 1935, *1*(2), 3–12. Reprinted in *Superiority and social interest, op cit.,* pp. 83–95.

————. Prevention of neurosis. *Int. J. indiv. Psychol.,* 1935, *1*(4), 3–12.

————. Psychiatric aspects regarding individual and social disorganization. *Amer. J. Sociol.,* 1936–1937, *42,* 773–780.

————. The neurotic's picture of the world. *Int. J. indiv. Psychol.,* 1936, *2*(3), 3–13. Reprinted in *Superiority and social interest, op. cit.,* pp. 96–111.

————. On the interpretation of dreams. *Int. J. indiv. Psychol.,* 1936, *2*(7), 3–16.

————. Significance of early recollections. *Int. J. indiv. Psychol.,* 1937, *3,* 283–287. Reprinted in E. L. Hartley, H. G. Birch, & Ruth E. Hartley (Eds.), *Outside readings in psychology.* New York: Crowell, 1950, pp. 361–365.

————. The progress of mankind. (1937) *Int. J. indiv. Psychol.,* 1947, *13,* 9–13. Reprinted in K. A. Adler & Danica Deutsch (Eds.), *Essays in individual psychology.* New York: Grove Press, 1959, pp. 3–8, and in *Superiority and social interest, op. cit.,* pp. 23–28.

————. [Autobiographical notes.] In Phyllis Bottome, *Alfred Adler: A biography.* New York: Putnam's, 1939, pp. 9–12. Reprinted as How I chose my career. *Indiv. Psychol. Bull.,* 1947, *6,* 9–11.   **B**

Beck & Molish, *Reflexes;* Lindzey & Hall, *Personality;* Sahakian, *Personality;* Sahakian, *Psychology;* Shipley, *Classics;* Vetter, *Personality*

(JEAN) LOUIS (RODOLPHE) AGASSIZ
1807-1873
Swiss-American Biologist (13)

Agassiz, J. L. R. *Contributions to the natural history of the United States of America.* (4 vols.) Boston: Little, Brown, 1857–1862.   **C**

————. *Geological sketches.* Boston: Houghton Mifflin, 1886.   **C**

————. *The intelligence of Louis Agassiz: A specimen book of scientific writings.* Ed. by G. Davenport. Boston: Beacon Press, 1963.   **C**

————. *Correspondence between Spencer Fulberton Baird and Louis Agassiz, two pioneer American naturalists.* Ed. by E. C. Herber. Washington, D.C.: Smithsonian Institution, 1963.   **C**

————, & Gould, A. *Principles of zoology.* New York: Arno, 1970. (1848)

————. *Bibliographia zoologiae et geologiae.* (4 vols.) Ed. by H. E. Strickland. New York: Johnson Reprint, 1968. (1848–1854)   **Bl**

————. *Essay on classification.* Ed. by E. Lurie.

Cambridge: Harvard University Press, 1962. (1859)

————. On the origin of species. *Amer. J. Sci.,* 1860, *30* (2nd ser.), 142–154.

————. *Methods of study in natural history.* New York: Arno, 1970. (1863)

————. *The structure of animal life.* (3rd ed.) New York: Scribner, Armstrong, 1874. (1866)

————, & Agassiz, Elizabeth C. *A journey in Brazil.* Boston: Houghton Mifflin, 1909. (1868)
B

————. Evolution and permanence of type. *Atlantic Mon.,* 1874, *33,* 92–101.

JEAN LE ROND D'ALEMBERT
1717-1783
French Philosopher (15)

Alembert, J. L. R. d'. *Mélange de littérature, d'histoire, et de philosophie.* (5 vols.) Amsterdam: Chatelain, 1770.   **C**

————. *Select eulogies.* (2 vols.) Trans. by J. Aiken. London: Strahan, 1799.   **C**

————. *Oeuvres complètes de d'Alembert.* (5 vols.) Geneva: Slatkine, 1967. (1821–1822)
B Bl C

————. *Oeuvres et correspondances inédites de d'Alembert.* Ed. by C. Henry. Geneva: Slatkine, 1967. (1887)   **C**

————. *Traité de dynamique dans lequel les lois de l'équilibre et du mouvement des corps sont réduites au plus petit nombre possible et démontrées d'une manière nouvelle, et où l'on donne un principe général pour trouver le mouvement de plusieurs corps qui agissent les uns sur les autres, d'une manière quelconque.* Brussels: Culture et Civilisation, 1967. (1743)

————. *Traité de l'équililibre et du mouvement des fluides, pour servir de suite au traité de dynamique.* Brussels: Culture et Civilisation, 1966. (1744)

————. *Preliminary discourse to the encyclopedia of Diderot.* Trans. by R. N. Schwab. India-

napolis. Ind.: Bobbs-Merrill, 1963. (1751) Reprinted in French in *Oeuvres complètes,* Vol. 1, *op. cit.,* pp. 14–114.

Diderot, D., ————, et al. *Encyclopedia: Selections.* Trans. by Nelly S. Hoyt & T. Cassirer. Indianapolis, Ind.: Bobbs-Merrill, 1965. (1751–1772)

Diderot, D., & ————. *Encyclopédie ou dictionnaire raisonné des sciences, des arts et des métiers.* (35 vols.) Stuttgart-Bad Canstatt: Frommann, 1966. (1751–1772)

Diderot, D., & ————. *The "Encyclopédie" of Diderot and d'Alembert: Selected articles.* Ed. by J. Lough. Cambridge: Cambridge University Press, 1954. (1751–1772)

————, & Voltaire. *Correspondance avec Voltaire (1752–1778).* Reprinted in *Oeuvres complètes,* Vol. 5, *op. cit.,* pp. 46–247.   **B**

————. *Essai d'une nouvelle théorie de la résistance des fluides.* Brussels: Culture et Civilisation, 1966. (1752)

————. *Recherches sur différents points importants du système du monde.* Brussels: Culture et Civilisation, 1966. (1754–1756)

————. *Analyse de l'esprit des lois.* (1758) Reprinted in *Oeuvres complètes,* Vol. 3, *op. cit.,* pp. 466–476.

————. Eloge de M. le Président de Montesquieu. (1758) In *Eloges historiques.* Reprinted in *Oeuvres complètes,* Vol. 3, *op. cit.,* pp. 440–466.

————. *Essai sur les éléments de philosophie, ou sur les principes des connaissances humaines, avec les éclaircissements.* (1759) Reprinted in *Oeuvres complètes,* Vol. 1, *op. cit.,* pp. 115–348.

————. Essay on taste. (1759) In A. Gerard (Ed.), *An essay on taste.* (3rd ed.) Edinburgh: Bell & Creech, 1780. (Reprinted 1971)

————. *Dialogue entre Descartes et Christine, reine de Suède, aux Champs Élysées.* (1771) Reprinted in *Oeuvres complètes,* Vol. 4, *op. cit.,* pp. 468–475.

Brinton, *Age Reason ;* Torrey, *Les Philosophes*

FRANZ ALEXANDER
1891-1964
German-American Psychoanalyst (18)

Alexander, F. *The scope of psychoanalysis:1921–1961. Selected papers of Franz Alexander*. New York: Basic Books, 1961. **C**

————. The castration complex in the formation of character. (1922) *Int. J. Psycho-Anal.*, 1923, *4*, 11–42. Reprinted in *The scope of psychoanalysis, op. cit.*, pp. 3–30.

————, & Staub, H. *The criminal, the judge, and the public*. Glencoe, Ill.: Free Press, 1956. (1929)

————. *The psychoanalysis of the total personality: The application of Freud's theory of the ego to the neuroses*. New York: Nervous & Mental Disease Publishing, 1930. (1927) (Reprinted 1959)

————. *The medical value of psychoanalysis*. New York: Norton, 1936. (1932)

————. On Ferenczi's relaxation principle. *Int. J. Psycho-Anal.*, 1933, *14*, 183–192.

————, & Healy, W. *Roots of crime: Psychoanalytic studies*. New York: Knopf, 1935.

————. The logic of emotions and its dynamic background. *Int. J. Psycho-Anal.*, 1935, *16*, 399–413. Reprinted in *The scope of psychoanalysis, op. cit.*, pp. 116–128.

————. The problem of psychoanalytic technique. *Psychoanal. Quart.*, 1935, *4*, 588–611. Reprinted in *The scope of psychoanalysis, op. cit.*, pp. 225–243.

————. Psychoanalysis and social disorganization. *Amer J. Sociol.*, 1936–1937, *42*, 781–813. Reprinted in *The scope of psychoanalysis, op. cit.*, pp. 384–411.

————. Psychoanalysis revised. *Psychoanal. Quart.*, 1940, *9*, 1–36. Reprinted in *The scope of psychoanalysis, op. cit.*, pp. 137–164.

————. A jury trial of psychoanalysis. *J. abnorm. soc. Psychol.*, 1940, *35*, 305–323.

————. *Our age of unreason: A study of the irrational forces in social life*. (Rev. ed.) Philadelphia: Lippincott, 1951. (1942)

————. Fundamental concepts of psychosomatic research: Psychogenesis, conversion, specificity. *Psychosom. Med.*, 1943, *5*, 205–210. Reprinted in M. H. Marx (Ed.), *Psychological theory: Contemporary readings*. New York: Macmillan, 1959, pp. 460–471.

————, French, T. M., *et al. Psychoanalytic therapy: Principles and application*. New York: Ronald Press, 1946.

————. Educative influence of personality factors in the environment. In C. Kluckhohn & H. A. Murray (Eds.), *Personality in nature, society, and culture*. New York: Knopf, 1948, pp. 421–435.

————. *Fundamentals of psychoanalysis*. (3rd ed.) New York: Norton, 1963. (1948)

————, & French, T. M. *Studies in psychosomatic medicine: An approach to the cause and treatment of vegetative disturbances*. New York: Ronald Press, 1948.

————. *Psychosomatic medicine: Its principles and applications*. New York: Norton, 1950.

————. The evolution and present trends of psychoanalysis. *Acta Psychol.*, 1950, *7*, 126–132. Reprinted in H. Brand (Ed.), *The study of personality: A book of readings*. New York: Wiley, 1954, pp. 78–82.

————. Analysis of the therapeutic factors in psychoanalytic treatment. *Psychoanal. Quart.*, 1950, *19*, 482–500. Reprinted in *The scope of psychoanalysis, op. cit.*, pp. 261–275.

————, & Ross, Helen. *The impact of the Freudian psychiatry*. Chicago: University of Chicago Press, 1952.

————, & Ross, Helen (Eds.), *Dynamic psychiatry*. Chicago: University of Chicago Press, 1952.

————, & Ross, Helen (Eds.), *20 years of psychoanalysis: A symposium in celebration of the twentieth anniversary of the Chicago Institute for Psychoanalysis*. New York: Norton, 1953. **B**

————. *Psychoanalysis and psychotherapy*. New York: Norton, 1956.

———. Unexplored areas in psychoanalytic theory and treatment. Part I. *Behav. Sci.*, 1958, *3*, 293–316. Reprinted in *The scope of psychoanalysis, op. cit.*, pp. 183–201.

———. *The western mind in transition: An eye-witness story.* New York: Random House, 1960.
B

———. Social significance of psychoanalysis and psychotherapy. *Arch. gen. Psychiat.*, 1964, *11*, 235–244.

———. Neurosis and creativity. *Amer. J. Psychoanal.*, 1964, *24*, 116–130.

———, Eisenstein, S., & Grotjahn, M. (Eds.), *Psychoanalytic pioneers.* New York: Basic Books, 1966.
B

———, & Selesnick, S. T. *The history of psychiatry: An evaluation of psychiatric thought and practice from prehistoric times to the present.* New York: Harper & Row, 1966.

Rosenblith, *Causes Behavior*

GORDON WILLARD ALLPORT
1897-1967
American Psychologist (27)

Allport, G. W. *The nature of personality: Selected papers.* Cambridge: Addison-Wesley, 1950.
Bl C

———. *Personality and social encounter: Selected essays.* Boston: Beacon Press, 1960. (Reprinted 1964)
Bl C

———. *The person in psychology: Selected essays.* Boston: Beacon Press, 1968.
Bl C

———. The standpoint of Gestalt psychology. *Psyche*, 1924, *4*, 354–361.

———. Eidetic imagery. *Brit. J. Psychol.*, 1924–1925, *15*, 99–120.

———. The eidetic image and the after-image. *Amer. J. Psychol.*, 1928, *40*, 418–425.

———. A test for ascendance-submission. *J. abnorm. soc. Psychol.*, 1928–1929, *23*, 118–136.

———. Change and decay in the visual memory image. *Brit. J. Psychol.*, 1930–1931, *21*, 133–148.

———. What is a trait of personality? *J. abnorm. soc. Psychol.*, 1930–1931, *25*, 368–372. Reprinted in *Personality and social encounter, op. cit.*, pp. 131–135.

Vernon, P. E., & ———. A test for personal values. *J. abnorm. soc. Psychol.*, 1931–1932, *26*, 231–248.

———, & Vernon, P. E. *Studies in expressive movement.* New York: Macmillan, 1933. (Reprinted 1967)

———. Attitudes. In ·C. Murchison (Ed.), *A handbook of social psychology.* Worcester, Mass.: Clark University Press, 1935, pp. 798–844. Reprinted in *The nature of personality, op. cit.*, pp. 1–47.

———, & Cantril, H. *The psychology of radio.* New York: Harper, 1935.

———, & Odbert, H. S. Trait names: A psycho-lexical study. *Psychol. Monogr.*, 1936, *47*, No. 211.

———. *Personality: A psychological interpretation.* New York: Holt, 1937.

———. The functional autonomy of motives. *Amer. J. Psychol.*, 1937, *50*, 141–156. Reprinted in *The nature of personality, op. cit.*, pp. 76–91.

———. Personality: A problem for science or a problem for art? *Rev. Psihol.*, 1938, *1* (4), 1–15. Reprinted in *The nature of personality, op. cit.*, pp. 198–210.

———, & Bruner, J. S. Fifty years of change in American psychology. *Psychol. Bull.*, 1940, *37*, 757–776.

———. The psychologist's frame of reference. *Psychol. Bull.*, 1940, *37*, 1–28. Reprinted in *The nature of personality, op. cit.*, pp. 48–75.

———. Motivation in personality: Reply to Mr. Bertocci. *Psychol. Rev.*, 1940, *47*, 533–554. Reprinted in H. Brand (Ed.), *The study of personality: A book of readings.* New York: Wiley, 1954, pp. 83–99, & in *The nature of personality, op. cit.*, pp. 92–113.

———, Bruner, J.S., & Jandorf, E. M. Personality under social catastrophe: Ninety life-histories of the Nazi revolution. *J. Pers.*, 1941, *10*, 1–22.

Abridged in C. Kluckhohn & H. A. Murray (Eds.), *Personality in nature, society and culture.* (2nd ed.) New York: Knopf, 1953, pp. 436–455.

————. *The use of personal documents in psychological science.* (Bull. No. 49) New York: Social Science Research Council, 1942.

————. The productive paradoxes of William James. *Psychol. Rev.,* 1943, *50,* 95–120. Reprinted in *The person in psychology, op. cit.,* pp. 298–325.

————. The ego in contemporary psychology. *Psychol. Rev.,* 1943, *50,* 451–478. Reprinted in *The nature of personality, op. cit.,* pp. 114–141, & in *Personality and social encounter, op. cit.,* pp. 71–93.

————. The psychology of participation. *Psychol. Rev.,* 1945, *52,* 117–132. Reprinted in *The nature of personality, op. cit.,* pp. 142–157.

————, & Postman, L. The basic psychology of rumor. *Trans. N.Y. Acad. Sci., Sec. Psychol.,* 1945, *8,* 61–81. Reprinted in T. M. Newcomb & E. L. Hartley (Eds.), *Readings in social psychology.* (Rev. ed.) New York: Holt, 1952, pp. 160–171; in Eleanor E. Maccoby, T. M. Newcomb, & E. L. Hartley (Eds.), *Readings in social psychology.* (3rd ed.) New York: Holt, 1958, pp. 54–65; in D. Katz, D. Cartwright, S. Eldersveld, & A. McG. Lee (Eds.), *Public opinion and propaganda.* New York: Dryden Press, 1954, pp. 394–404; & in W. Schramm (Ed.), *The process and effects of mass communication.* Urbana, Ill.: University of Illinois Press, 1954, pp. 141–155.

————. Personalistic psychology as science: A reply. *Psychol. Rev.,* 1946, *53,* 132–135. Reprinted in *The nature of personality, op. cit.,* pp. 183–186.

————. Effect: A secondary principle of learning. *Psychol. Rev.,* 1946, *53,* 335–347. Reprinted in *The nature of personality, op. cit.,* pp. 170–182.

————. Geneticism versus ego-structure in theories of personality. *Brit. J. educ. Psychol.,* 1946, *16,* 57–68. Reprinted in *The nature of personality, op. cit.,* pp. 158–169, & in *Personality and social encounter, op. cit.,* pp. 137–151.

————, & Postman, L. *The psychology of rumor.* New York: Holt, 1947.

————. The genius of Kurt Lewin. *J. Pers.,* 1947, *16,* 1–10. Reprinted in *The person in psychology, op. cit.,* pp. 360–370.

————. Scientific models and human morals. *Psychol. Rev.,* 1947, *54,* 182–192. Reprinted in M. H. Marx (Ed.), *Psychological theory: Contemporary readings.* New York: Macmillan, 1959, pp. 156–170; in M. H. Marx (Ed.), *Theories in contemporary psychology.* New York: Macmillan, 1963, pp. 258–271; in *Personality and social encounter, op. cit.,* pp. 55–68; & in *The nature of personality, op. cit.,* pp. 187–197.

————. Prejudice: A problem in psychological and social causation. *J. soc. Issues,* 1950 (Supp. Series). Reprinted in T. Parsons & E. A. Shils (Eds.), *Toward a general theory of action.* Cambridge: Harvard University Press, 1951, pp. 365–387.

————. The trend in motivational theory. *Amer. J. Orthopsychiat.,* 1953, *25,* 107–119. Reprinted in *Personality and social encounter, op. cit.,* pp. 95–105.

————. The psychological nature of personality. *Personalist,* 1953, *34,* 347–357. Reprinted in *Personality and social encounter, op. cit.,* pp. 17–38.

————. *The nature of prejudice.* Reading, Mass.: Addison-Wesley, 1954. (Reprinted abridged 1958)

————. *Becoming: Basic considerations for a psychology of personality.* New Haven: Yale University Press, 1955. (Reprinted 1960)

————. European and American theories of personality. In H. P. David & H. v. Bracken (Eds.), *Perspectives in personality theory.* New York: Basic Books, 1957, pp. 3–24.

————. Personality: Normal and abnormal. *Sociol. Rev.,* 1958, *6*(N.S.), 167–180.

————. What units shall we employ? In G. Lindzey (Ed.), *Assessment of human motives.* New York: Rinehart, 1958, pp. 239–259. Reprinted in *Personality and social encounter, op. cit.,* pp. 111–129.

———. The open system in personality theory. *J. abnorm. soc. Psychol.*, 1960, *61*, 301–310. Reprinted in *Personality and social encounter, op. cit.*, pp. 39–54.

———. *Pattern and growth in personality.* New York: Holt, Rinehart & Winston, 1961.

———. The general and unique in psychological science. *J. Pers.*, 1962, *30*, 405–422. Reprinted in *The person in psychology, op. cit.*, pp. 81–102.

———. The fruits of eclecticism: Bitter or sweet? *Acta Psychol.*, 1964, *23*, 27–44. Reprinted in *The person in psychology, op. cit.*, pp. 3–27.

———. *Letters from Jenny.* New York: Harcourt, Brace & World, 1965.

———. Traits revisited. *Amer. Psychologist*, 1966, *21*, 1–10. Reprinted in *The person in psychology, op. cit.*, pp. 43–66.

———. Gordon W. Allport. In E. G. Boring & G. Lindzey (Eds.), *A history of psychology in autobiography.* Vol. 5. New York: Appleton-Century-Crofts, 1967, pp. 1–25. Reprinted in *The person in psychology, op. cit.*, pp. 376–409. **B**

———. The personalistic psychology of William Stern. In B. B. Wolman (Ed.), *Historical roots of contemporary psychology.* New York: Harper & Row, 1968, pp. 321–337. Reprinted in *The person in psychology, op. cit.*, pp. 271–297.

———. The historical background of modern social psychology. In G. Lindzey & E. Aronson (Eds.), *The handbook of social psychology.* Vol. 1. *Historical introduction: Systematic positions.* (2nd ed.) Reading, Mass.: Addison-Wesley, 1968, pp. 1–80. (1954)

Beck & Molish, *Reflexes;* Lindzey & Hall, *Personality;* Matson, *Being;* Perez, *Readings;* Russell, *Motivation;* Sahakian, *Personality;* Sahakian, *Psychology;* Vetter, *Personality;* Wrenn, *Contributions*

ADELBERT AMES, Jr.
1880-1955
American Ophthalmologist (16)

Ames, A., Jr., & Proctor, C. A. Dioptrics of the eye. *J. opt. Soc. Amer.*, 1921, *5*, 22–84.

———, Gliddon, G. H., & Ogle, K. N. Size and shape of ocular images. I. Methods of determination and physiologic significance. *Arch. Ophthalm.*, 1932, *7*, 576–597.

———, & Ogle, K. N. Size and shape of ocular images. III. Visual sensitivity to differences in the relative size of the ocular images of the two eyes. *Arch. Ophthalm.*, 1932, *7*, 904–924.

———. The space eikonometer test for aniseikonia. *Amer. J. Ophthalm.*, 1945, *28*, 248–263.

———. Binocular vision as affected by relations between uniocular stimulus-patterns in commonplace environments. *Amer. J. Psychol.*, 1946, *59*, 333–357.

———, Cantril, H., Hastorf, A. H. J., & Ittelson, W. H. Psychology and scientific research. I: The nature of scientific inquiry. II: Scientific inquiry and scientific method. III: The transactional view in psychological research. *Science*, 1949, *110*, 461–464, 491–497, 517–522.

———. Architectural form and visual sensations. In T. Creighton (Ed.), *Building for modern man.* Princeton, N.J.: Princeton University Press, 1949, pp. 82–91.

———. Sensations, their nature and origin. *Transformation*, 1950, *1*, 11–12.

Ittelson. W. H., & ———. Accommodation, convergence and their relation to apparent distance. *J. Psychol.*, 1950, *30*, 43–62.

———. Visual perception and the rotating trapezoidal window. *Psychol. Monogr.*, 1951, *65*, No. 324.

———. An interpretative manual for the demonstrations in the Psychology Research Center, Princeton University: The nature of our perceptions, prehensions and behavior. Princeton, N.J.: Princeton University Press, 1955. Reprinted in W. H. Ittelson, *The Ames demonstrations in perception, together with an interpretative manual by Adelbert Ames, Jr.* New York: Hafner, 1968.

———. The morning notes of Adelbert Ames, Jr.: Including a correspondence with John Dewey. Ed. by H. Cantril. New Brunswick, N.J.: Rutgers University Press, 1960. **B**

FRANK ANGELL
1857-1939
American Psychologist (16)

Angell, F. Untersuchungen über die Schätzung von Schallintensitäten nach der Methode der mittleren Abstufungen. *Phil. Stud.*, 1892, 7, 414–468.

———, & Harwood, H. Experiments on discrimination of clangs for different intervals of time. *Amer. J. Psychol.*, 1899, *11*, 67–79.

———. Discrimination of clangs for different intervals of time. II. *Amer. J. Psychol.*, 1900, *12*, 58–79.

———. Discrimination of shades of gray for different intervals of time. *Phil. Stud.*, 1902, *19*, 1–21.

Coover, J. E., & ———. General practice effect of special exercise. *Amer. J. Psychol.*, 1907, *18*, 328–340.

———. On judgments of "like" in discrimination experiments. *Amer. J. Psychol.*, 1907, *18*, 253–260.

———. A note on some of the physical factors affecting reaction time, together with a description of a new reaction key. *Amer. J. Psychol.*, 1911, *22*, 86–93.

———. Duration, energy and extent of reaction movements—simple and flying reactions. *Amer. J. Psychol.*, 1919, *30*, 224–236.

———. Notes on the horizon illusion. I. *Amer. J. Psychol.*, 1924, *35*, 98–102.

———. Notes on the horizon illusion. II. *J. gen. Psychol.*, 1932, *6*, 133–156.

JAMES ROWLAND ANGELL
1869-1949
American Psychologist (27)

Angell, J. R., & Pierce, A. H. Experimental research upon the phenomena of attention. *Amer. J. Psychol.*, 1892, *4*, 528–541.

———, & Moore, A. W. Reaction time: A study in attention and habit. *Psychol. Rev.*, 1896, *3*, 245–258.

———. Thought and imagery. *Phil. Rev.*, 1897, *6*, 646–651.

———, Spray, J. N., & Mahood, E. W. An investigation of certain factors affecting the relations of dermal and optical space. *Psychol. Rev.*, 1898, *5*, 579–594.

———. Habit and attention. *Psychol. Rev.*, 1898, *5*, 179–183.

———, & Thompson, H. B. The relations between certain organic processes and consciousness. *Psychol. Rev.*, 1899, *6*, 32–69.

———, & Fite, W. The monaural localization of sound. *Psychol. Rev.*, 1901, *8*, 225–246.

———, & Fite, W. Further observations on the monaural localization of sound. *Psychol. Rev.*, 1901, *8*, 449–458.

———. A preliminary study of the significance of partial tones in the localization of sound. *Psychol. Rev.*, 1903, *10*, 1–14.

———. The relations of structural and functional psychology to philosophy. *Phil. Rev.*, 1903, *12*, 243–271.

———. *Psychology: An introductory study of the structure and functions of human consciousness.* (4th ed.) New York: Holt, 1908. (1904)

———. Psychology at the St. Louis Congress. *J. Phil.*, 1905, *2*, 533–546.

———. The province of functional psychology. *Psychol. Rev.*, 1907, *14*, 61–91.

———. The doctrine of formal discipline in the light of the principles of general psychology. *Educ. Rev.*, 1908, *36*, 1–14.

———. The influence of Darwin on psychology. *Psychol. Rev.*, 1909, *16*, 152–169.

———. Methods for the determination of mental imagery. In Report of the committee of the American Psychological Association on the standardizing of procedures in experimental tests. *Psychol. Monogr.*, 1910, *13*, No. 53, pp. 61–107.

———. Imageless thought. *Psychol. Rev.*, 1911, *18*, 295–323.

———. *Chapters from modern psychology*. New York: Longmans, Green, 1912.

———. Behavior as a category of psychology. *Psychol. Rev.*, 1913, *20*, 255–270.

———. A reconsideration of James's theory of emotion in the light of recent criticisms. *Psychol. Rev.*, 1916, *23*, 251–261.

———. *An introduction to psychology*. New York: Holt, 1918.

———. *The development of research in the U.S.* Washington, D.C.: National Research Council, 1919.

———. The organization of research. *Sci. Mon.*, N.Y., 1920, *11*, 26–42.

———. James Rowland Angell. In C. Murchison (Ed.), *A history of psychology in autobiography*. Vol 3. Worcester, Mass.: Clark University Press, 1936, pp. 1–38. (Reprinted 1961)

B

———. *American education: Addresses and articles*. New Haven: Yale University Press, 1937. (Reprinted 1970)

———. *The higher patriotism*. Stanford, Calif.: Stanford University Press, 1938.

———. *War propaganda and the radio*. Philadelphia: University of Pennsylvania Press, 1940.

Dennis, *Psychology* ; Herrnstein & Boring, *Source Book* ; Sahakian, *Psychology*

ROSWELL PARKER ANGIER
1874-1946
American Psychologist (12)

Angier, R. P. The aesthetics of unequal division. *Psychol. Monogr.*, 1903, No. 17, pp. 541–561.

———. Vergleichende Messung der kompensatorischen Rollungen beider Augen. *Z. Psychol.*, 1904, *37*, 235–249.

———. Vergleichende Bestimmungen der Peripheriewerte des trichromatischen und des deuteranopischen Auges. *Z. Psychol.*, 1904, *37*, 401–413.

———. Die Schätzung von Bewegungsgrössen bei Vorderarmbewegungen. *Z. Psychol.*, 1905, *39*, 429–447.

———, & Trendelenburg, W. Bestimmungen über das Mengenverhältnis komplementärer Spektralfarben in Weissmischungen. *Z. Psychol.*, 1905, *39*, 284–293.

———. Ueber den Einfluss des Helligkeitskontrastes auf Farbenschwellen. *Z. Sinnesphysiol.*, 1906, *41*, 353–363.

———. The coördinative mechanisms of the central nervous system. *Psychol. Bull.*, 1911, *8*, 119–125.

———. The conflict theory of emotion. *Amer. J. Psychol.*, 1927, *39*, 390–401.

ANDRAS ANGYAL
1902-1960
Austrian-American Psychiatrist (13)

Angyal, A. Der Schlummerzustand. *Z. Psychol.*, 1927, *103*, 65–99.

———. Einige Beobachtungen über raumhafte Tastphänomene. *Arch. ges. Psychol.*, 1929, *71*, 351–356.

———. Warum vergisst man die Träume? *Z. Psychol.*, 1930, *118*, 191–199.

———. Ueber die Raumlage vorgestellter Örter. *Arch. ges. Psychol.*, 1930, *78*, 47–94.

———. Zur Frage der Traumsymbolik. *Zbl. Psychother.*, 1931, *4*, 107–119.

———. Die Lagebeharrung der optisch vorgestellten räumlichen Umgebung. *Neue psychol. Stud.*, 1931, *6*(3), 291–310.

———. Die Bedeutung der Lage bei räumlichen Gebilden. *Kwart. Psychol.*, 1932, *3*, 5–42.

Ponzo, M., & ———. Zur Systematik der Gewichts-Empfindungen. *Arch. ges. Psychol.*, 1933, *88*, 629–634.

———. The perceptual basis of somatic delusions in a case of schizophrenia. *Arch. Neurol. Psychiat.*, Chicago, 1935, *34*, 270–279.

——. The experience of the body self in schizophrenia. *Arch. Neurol. Psychiat.,* Chicago, 1936, *35,* 1029–1053.

——. Disturbances of activity in a case of schizophrenia. *Arch. Neurol. Psychiat.,* Chicago, 1937, *38,* 1047–1054.

——. The concept of bionegativity. *Psychiatry,* 1938, *1,* 303–307.

——. The structure of wholes. *Phil. Sci.,* 1939, *6,* 25–37.

——, *et al.* Physiologic aspects of schizophrenic withdrawal. *Arch. Neurol. Psychiat.,* Chicago, 1940, *44,* 621–626. Reprinted in S. S. Tomkins (Ed.), *Contemporary psychopathology: A source book.* Cambridge: Harvard University Press, 1947, pp. 254–258.

——. *Foundations for a science of personality.* New York: Commonwealth Fund, 1941.

——. Disgust and related aversions. *J. abnom. soc. Psychol.,* 1941, *36,* 393–412.

——. Basic sources of human motivation. *Trans. N.Y. Acad. Sci.,* 1943, *6,* 5–13.

——. Disturbances of thinking in schizophrenia. In J. S. Kasanin (Ed.), *Language and thought in schizophrenia.* Berkeley, Calif.: University of California Press, 1944, pp. 115–123. (Reprinted 1964)

——. The holistic approach in psychiatry. *Amer. J. Psychiat.,* 1948, *105,* 178–182.

——. The psychodynamic process of illness and recovery in a case of catatonic schizophrenia. *Psychiatry,* 1950, *13,* 149–165.

——. A theoretical model for personality studies. *J. Pers.,* 1951, *20,* 131–142.

——. The convergence of psychotherapy and religion. *J. pastoral Care,* 1952, *5,* 4–14.

——. *Neurosis and treatment: A holistic theory.* Ed. by Eugenia Hanfmann & R. M. Jones. New York: Wiley, 1965.   **Bl**

Lindzey & Hall, *Personality;* Sahakian, *Personality*

HERMANN AUBERT
1826-1892
German Physiologist (20)

Aubert, H. Ueber den Raumsinn der Netzhaut. *Jb. schles. ges. vaterl. Kult.,* 1856, *43,* 33–34.

——. Ueber die Gränzen der Farbenwahrnehmung auf den seitlichen Theilen der Retina. *Arch. Ophthalm.,* Berlin, 1857, *3,* 38–64.

——, & Foerster, R. Untersuchungen über den Raumsinn der Retina. *Arch. Ophthalm.,* Berlin, 1857, *3,* 1–67.

——. Beiträge zur Kenntniss des indirecten Sehens. *Arch. Ophthalm.,* Berlin, 1858, *4,* 16–35, 215–239.

——. Ueber das Verhalten der Nachbilder auf den peripherischen Teilen der Netzhaut. *Untersuch. Naturlehre Mensch. Thiere,* 1858, *4,* 215–239.

——, & Kammler, A. Untersuchungen über den Druck und Raumsinn der Haut. *Untersuch. Naturlehre Mensch. Thiere,* 1859, *5,* 145–179.

——. Ueber die durch den elektrischen Funken erzeugten Nachbilder. *Untersuch. Naturlehre Mensch. Thiere,* 1859, *5,* 279–314.

——. Beiträge zur Physiologie der Netzhaut. *Abh. schles. Ges.,* 1861, *1,* 49–103, 344.

——. *Die Caphalopoden des Aristoteles in zoologischer, anatomischer und naturgeschichtlicher Beziehung besprochen.* Leipzig: Engelmann, 1862.

——. Untersuchungen über die Sinnesthätigkeit der Netzhaut. *Ann. Phys. Chem.,* 1862, *115,* 87–116, *116,* 249–278.

——. *Physiologie der Netzhaut.* Breslau: Morgenstern, 1865. (First part, 1864)

——. Grundzüge der physiologischen Optik. In A. Graefe & T. Saemisch (Eds.), *Handbuch der gesammten Augenheilkunde.* Vol. 2, Part 2. Leipzig: Engelmann, 1876.

——. Die Innervation der Kreislaufsorgane. In L. Hermann (Ed.), *Handbuch der Physiologie.* Vol. 4. Leipzig: Vogel, 1883, pp. 344–460.

——. Die Bewegungsempfindung. *Arch. ges.*

Physiol., 1886, *39,* 347–370 ; 1887, *40, 459–480,* 623–624.

———. *Physiologische Studien über die Orientierung.* Tübingen: Laupp, 1888.

———. Die innerliche Sprache und ihr Verhalten zu den Sinneswahrnehmungen und Bewegungen. *Z. Psychol.,* 1890, *1,* 52–59.

FRANCIS AVELING
1875-1941
English Psychologist (11)

Aveling, F. The relation of thought-process and percept and perception. *Brit. J. Psychol.,* 1911, *4,* 211–227.

———. *On the consciousness of the universal and the individual ; a contribution to the phenomenology of the thought processes.* London: Macmillan, 1912.

———, & Hargreaves, H. L. Suggestibility with and without prestige in children. *Brit. J. Psychol.,* 1921, *12,* 53–75.

Field, G. C., ———, & Laird, J. Is the conception of the unconscious of value in psychology? *Mind,* 1922, *31,* 413–442.

———, & McDowall, R. J. S. The effect of the circulation on the electrical resistance of the skin. *J. Physiol.,* 1925, *60,* 316–321.

———, McDowall, R. J. S., & Wells, H. M. On the physiology of the so-called psychogalvanic reflex. *J. Physiol.,* 1925, *60,* vii–viii.

———. The psychology of conation and volition. *Brit. J. Psychol.,* 1925–1926, *16,* 339–353.

———. The standpoint of psychology. *Brit. J. Psychol.,* 1925–1926, *16,* 159–170.

———. The conative indications of the psychogalvanic phenomenon. *Proc. 8th Int. Cong. Psychol.,* Groningen, 1926, *8,* 227–234.

———. *Directing mental energy.* New York: Doran, 1927.

———. The relevance of visual imagery to the process of thinking. *Brit. J. Psychol.,* 1927, *18,* 15–22.

———. Emotion, conation, and will. In M. L. Reymert (Ed.), *Feelings and emotions: The Wittenberg symposium.* Worcester, Mass.: Clark University Press, 1928, pp. 49–57.

———. The psychogalvanic phenomenon. *Proc. & Papers 9th Int. Cong. Psychol.,* New Haven, 1929, 63–65.

———. Notes on the emotion of fear as observed in conditions of warfare. *Brit. J. Psychol.,* 1929, *20,* 137–144.

———. *Personality and will.* New York: Appleton, 1931.

———. The perception of tachistoscopically exposed symbols. *Brit. J. Psychol.,* 1932, *22,* 193–199.

———. The influence of volition upon thinking. *Brit. J. Psychol.,* 1932, *22,* 324–332.

———. The status of psychology as an empirical science. *Nature,* 1933, *132,* 841–843, 881–882.

———. *Psychology: The changing outlook.* London: Watts, 1937.

RICHARD HEINRICH LUDWIG
AVENARIUS
1843-1896
Swiss Philosopher (23)

Avenarius, R. *Ueber die beiden ersten Phasen des Spinozischen Pantheismus und das Verhältnis der zweiten und dritten Phase, nebst einem Anhang über Reihenfolge und Abfassungszeit der älteren Schriften Spinozas.* Leipzig: Author, 1868.

———. *Philosophie als Denken der Welt, gemäss dem Prinzip des kleinsten Kraftmaasses: Prolegomena zu einer Kritik der reinen Erfahrung.* Leipzig: Reisland, 1876.

———. *Ueber die Stellung der Psychologie zur Philosophie. Vtljsch. wiss. Phil.,* 1877, *1,* 471–488.

———. *Kritik der reinen Erfahrung.* (2 vols.) Leipzig: Reisland, 1888–1890. (Reprinted 1971)

———. *Der menschliche Weltbegriff.* (4th ed.) Leipzig: Reisland, 1927. (1891)

———. Bemerkungen zum Begriff des Gegenstandes der Psychologie. *Vtljsch. wiss. Phil.*, 1894, *18*, 137–161, 400–420; 1895, *19*, 1–18, 129–145.

———. *Zur Terminalfunktion.* Berlin: Tetzlaff, 1913.

JOSEPH FRANCOIS FELIX BABINSKI
1857-1932
French Neurologist (20)

Babinski, J. *Exposé des titres et travaux scientifiques.* Paris: Masson, 1913.　　　　C

———. *Oeuvres scientifiques: Recueil des principaux travaux.* Ed. by J.-A. Barré, J. Chaillous, & A. Charpentier. Paris: Masson, 1934.
　　　　　　　　　　　　　　　　　Bl C

———. *Recherches servant à établir que certaines manifestations hystériques peuvent être transférées d'un sujet à l'autre sous l'influence de l'aimant.* Paris: Delahaye & Lecrosnier, 1886.

———. *Grand et petit hypnotisme.* Paris: Lecrosnier & Basé, 1889.

———. *Hypnotisme et hystérie. Du rôle de l'hypnotisme en thérapeutique.* Paris: Librairie de l'Académie de Médecine, 1891.

———. Sur le réflexe cutané plantaire dans certaines affections organiques du système nerveux central. *C. r. soc. biol.*, 1896, 9th ser., *3*, 207–208. Reprinted in *Oeuvres scientifiques, op. cit.*, pp. 27–28.

———. On the phenomenon of the toes and its semiotic value. (1898) In R. H. Wilkins & I. A. Brody, Babinski's sign. *Arch. Neurol.*, 1967, *17*, 442–445.

———. Du phénomène des orteils dans l'épilepsie. *C. r. soc. biol.*, 1899, *51*, 343–346.

———. De l'asynergie cérébelleuse. *Rev. neurol.*, 1899, *7*, 784–785, 806–816.

———. Analyse de quelques troubles moteurs et sensitifs d'origine cérébrale. *J. Méd. int.*, 1900, *4*, 704–708.

———. Diagnostic différentiel entre l'hémiplégie organique et de l'hémiplégie hystérique. *Trib. méd.*, 1900, *23*, 551–553. Reprinted in *Oeuvres scientifiques, op. cit.*, pp. 91–111.

———. De l'influence des lésions de l'appareil auditif sur le vertige voltaique. *C. r. soc. biol.*, 1901, *53*, 77–80.

———, & Nageotte, J. Hémiasynergie, latéropulsion et myosis bulbaires avec hémianesthésie et hémiplégie croisées. *Rev. neurol.*, 1902, *10*, 358–365.

———. Définition de l'hystérie. *Rev. hypno.*, 1902, *16*, 193–201. Reprinted in *Oeuvres scientifiques, op. cit.*, pp. 457–464.

———. Sur le rôle du cervelet dans les actes volitionnels à succession rapide de mouvements. *Rev. neurol.*, 1902, *10*, 1013–1014.

———. On abduction of the toes. (1903) In R. H. Wilkins & I. A. Brody, Babinski's sign. *Arch. Neurol.*, 1967, *17*, 445–446.

———. Einführung in die Semiotik des Nervensystems. Ueber objektive Symptome, die der Wille nicht imstande ist, zu reproduzieren, ihre Wichtigkeit in der gerichtlichen Medizin. *Wien. klin.-ther. Wochenschr.*, 1905, *12*, 161–168.

———. Suggestion et hystérie. Á propos de l'article de M. Bernheim intitulé "Comment je comprends le mot hystérie." *Bull. Méd.*, 1907, *21*, 273-276.

———. My conception of hysteria and hypnotism (pithiatism). *Alienist Neurol.*, 1908, *29*, 1–29. (1906) Reprinted in *Oeuvres scientifiques, op. cit.*, pp. 465–485.

———, & Dagnan-Bouveret, J. Emotion et hystérie. *J. Psychol. norm. path.*, 1912, *9*, 97–146.

———, & Weill, G. A. Mouvements réactionnels d'origine vestibulaire et mouvements contreréactionnels. *C. r. soc. biol.*, 1913, *75*, 98–100.

———. Réflexes de défense. I. Etude clinique. *Rev. neurol.*, 1915, *22*, 145–154. Reprinted in *Oeuvres scientifiques, op. cit.*, pp. 115–126.

————, & Froment, J. *Hysteria or pithiatism, and reflex nervous disorders in the neurology of war.* Trans. & ed. by J. D. Rolleston. London: London University Press, 1918. (1917)

————. *Réflexes de défense. Brain,* 1922, *45,* 149–184.

Clarke & O'Malley, *Brain*

FRANCIS BACON
1561-1626
English Philosopher (23)

Bacon, F. *The essays or counsels, civil and moral.* Mt. Vernon, N.Y.: Pauper, (n.d.).   **C**

————. *The works.* (14 vols.) Collected & ed. by J. Spedding, R. L. Ellis, & D. D. Heath. New York: Garrett, 1968. (1858–1874)   **C**

————. *The physical and metaphysical works of Lord Bacon, including the advancement of learning and novum organum.* London: Bell, 1886.   **C**

————. *The philosophical works of Francis Bacon.* Ed. by J. M. Robertson. London: Routledge, 1905.   **C**

————. *The advancement of learning and New Atlantis.* Ed. by T. Case. London: Oxford University Press, 1906, 1951.   **C**

————. *Essays, advancement of learning, New Atlantis, and other pieces.* Ed. by R. F. Jones. Garden City, N.Y.: Odyssey Press, 1937.   **C**

————. *Francis Bacon, selected writings.* Ed. by H. G. Dick. New York: Random House, 1955.   **C**

————. *The new organon and related writings.* Ed. by F. H. Anderson. New York: Liberal Arts Press, 1960.   **C**

Bodenheimer, *Biology* ; Brinton, *Age Reason* ; Curtis, *Knowledge* ; Hall, *Nature's Laws* ; Hutchins, *Great Books* ; Park & Burgess, *Sociology* ; Popkin, *Philosophy* ; Rand, *Classical Philosophers* ; Reeves, *Body Mind* ; Schwartz & Bishop, *Moments Discovery* ; Slotkin, *Anthropology* ; Ulich, *Educational Wisdom*

ALEXANDER BAIN
1818-1903
Scottish Psychologist (26)

Bain, A. *Practical essays.* London: Longmans, Green, 1884.   **C**

————. *Dissertations on leading philosophical topics.* London: Longmans, Green, 1903.   **C**

————. *The senses and the intellect.* (4th ed.) London: Longmans, Green, 1894. (1855)

————. *The emotions and the will.* (4th ed.) New York: Longmans, Green, 1899. (1859)

————. *On the study of character, including an estimate of phrenology.* London: Parkeson & Bourn, 1861.

————. *A historical view of the theories of the soul. Fortn. Rev.,* 1866, *3,* 47–62.

————. *The feelings and the will viewed physiologically. Fortn. Rev.,* 1866, *3,* 575–588.

————. *The intellect viewed physiologically. Fortn. Rev.,* 1866, *3,* 735–748.

————. *On the correlation of force in its bearing on mind. Macmillan's Mag.,* 1867, *16,* 372–383.

————. *Mental and moral science: A compendium of psychology and ethics.* (3rd ed.) (2 vols.) London: Longmans, 1884. (1868)

————. *Logic.* (2nd ed.) London: Longmans, Green, Reader & Dyer, 1873. (1870)

————. *Mind & body: The theories of their relation.* (8th ed.) New York: Appleton, 1887. (1873)

————. *The gratification derived from the infliction of pain. Mind,* 1876, *1,* 429–431.

————. *Education as a science.* (10th ed.) New York: Appleton, 1902. (1879)

————. *Mr. Galton's statistics of mental imagery. Mind,* 1880, *5,* 564–573.

————. *Mr. Spencer's psychological congruities.* Part 1, 2. *Mind,* 1881, *6,* 266–270, 394–406.

————. *John Stuart Mill: A criticism ; with personal recollections.* London: Longmans, Green, 1882.   **B**

————. *James Mill: A biography.* New York: Kelly, 1967. (1882)   **B**

————. Mr. James Ward's "Psychology." *Mind*, 1886, *11*, 457–477.

————. On association controversies. *Mind*, 1887, *12*, 161–182. Reprinted in *Dissertations on leading philosophical topics, op. cit.*, pp. 27–57.

————. On feeling as indifference. *Mind*, 1887, *12*, 576–579 ; 1889, *14*, 97–106.

————. Definition and demarcation of the subject-sciences. *Mind*, 1888, *13*, 527–548. Reprinted in *Dissertations on leading philosophical topics, op. cit.*, pp. 105–131.

————. The empiricist position. *Mind*, 1889, *14*, 369–392. Reprinted in *Dissertations on leading philosophical topics, op. cit.*, pp. 132–161.

————. On physiological expression in psychology. *Mind*, 1891, *16*, 1–22. Reprinted in *Dissertations on leading philosophical topics, op. cit.*, pp. 162–188.

————. Notes on volition. *Mind*, 1891, *16*, 253–258.

————. Pleasure and pain. *Mind*, 1892, *1*(N.S.), 161–187. Reprinted in *Dissertations on leading philosophical topics, op. cit.*, pp. 187–222.

————. The respective spheres and mutual helps of introspection and psycho-physical experiment in psychology. *Mind*, 1893, *2*(N.S.), 42–53. Reprinted in *Dissertations on leading philosophical topics, op. cit.*, pp. 241–255.

————. Definition and problem of consciousness. *Mind*, 1894, *3*(N.S.), 348–361. Reprinted in *Dissertations on leading philosophical topics, op. cit.*, pp. 223–240.

————. *Autobiography.* Ed. by W. L. Davidson ; bibliog. by J. P. Anderson. London: Longmans, Green, 1904.   **B Bl**

Drever, *Sourcebook* ; Herrnstein & Boring, *Source Book* ; Mandler & Mandler, *Thinking ;* Rand, *Classical Psychologists ;* Sahakian, *Psychology*

JOHN WALLACE BAIRD
1869-1919
American Psychologist (17)

Baird, J. W. The influence of accommodation and convergence upon the perception of depth. *Amer. J. Psychol.*, 1903, *14*, 150–200.

————. Accommodation and convergence—a protest. *J. Phil.*, 1904, *I*, 323–324.

————. *The color sensitivity of the peripheral retina.* Washington, D.C.: Carnegie Institution, 1905.

————. The contraction of the color zones in hysteria and neurasthenia. *Psychol. Bull.*, 1906, *3*, 249–254.

————. Erwiderung zu einigen Bemerkungen von Prof. A. Kirschmann. *Arch. ges. Psychol.*, 1907, *9*, 86–90.

————. The problems of color blindness. *Psychol. Bull.*, 1908, *5*, 294–300.

————. Memory, imagination, learning and the higher mental processes (experimental). *Psychol. Bull.*, 1911, *8*, 243–253 ; 1912, *9*, 321–336 ; 1913, *10*, 333–347 ; 1914, *11*, 305–324 ; 1915, *12*, 333–354.

————. The phenomena of indirect color vision. *Psychol. Rev.*, 1914, *21*, 70–78.

————. The role of intent in mental functioning. In Various, *Philosophical essays in honor of James Edwin Creighton.* New York: Macmillan, 1917, pp. 307–317.

JAMES MARK BALDWIN
1861-1934
American Psychologist (25)

Baldwin, J. M. *Fragments in philosophy and science, being collected essays and addresses.* New York: Scribner's, 1902.   **C**

————. *Handbook of psychology.* I. *Senses & intellect.* (2nd rev. ed.) New York: Holt, 1890. (1889)

————. *Handbook of psychology.* II. *Feeling & will.* New York: Holt, 1891.

――. *Elements of psychology*. New York: Holt, 1893.

――. Psychology past and present. *Psychol. Rev.*, 1894, *1*, 363–391.

――. The origin of emotional expression. *Psychol. Rev.*, 1894, *1*, 610–623.

――. Imitation: A chapter in the natural history of consciousness. *Mind*, 1894, *3*(N.S.), 26–55.

――, & Shaw, W. J. Memory for square size. *Psychol. Rev.*, 1895, *2*, 236–239.

――. The effect of size-contrast upon judgments of position in the retinal field. *Psychol. Rev.*, 1895, *2*, 244–259.

――, & Shaw, W. J. Types of reaction. *Psychol. Rev.*, 1895, *2*, 259–273.

――. *Mental development in the child and the race: Methods and processes*. (3rd ed.) New York: Macmillan, 1911. (1895)

――. The "type-theory" of reaction. *Mind*, 1896, *5*(N.S.), 81–90.

――. *Social and ethical interpretations in mental development: A study in social psychology*. (4th ed.) New York: Macmillan, 1906. (1897)

――. The genesis of the ethical self. *Phil. Rev.*, 1897, *6*, 225–241.

――. *The story of the mind*. New York: McClure, Phillips, 1904. (1898)

―― (Ed.), *Dictionary of philosophy and psychology*. (3 vols. in 4) New York: Macmillan, 1905. (1901)

――. A scheme of classification for psychology. *Psychol. Rev.*, 1901, *8*, 60–64.

――. *Development and evolution*. New York: Macmillan, 1902.

――. Notes on social psychology and other things. *Psychol. Rev.*, 1902, *9*, 57–69, 185.

――. Sketch of the history of psychology. *Psychol. Rev.*, 1905, *12*, 144–165.

――. *Thought and things: A study of the development and meaning of thought or* genetic logic. Vol. 1: *Functional logic, or genetic theory of knowledge*. Vol. 2: *Experimental logic, or genetic theory of thought*. Vol. 3: *Interests and art, being real logic and genetic epistemology*. New York: Macmillan, 1906–1911.

――. *Darwin and the humanities*. Baltimore, Md.: Review Publishing, 1909.

――. Darwinism and logic: A reply to Professor Creighton. *Psychol. Rev.*, 1909, *16*, 431–436.

――. The influence of Darwin on theory of knowledge and philosophy. *Psychol. Rev.*, 1909, *16*, 207–218.

――. *Individual and society, or psychology and sociology*. Boston: Badger, 1911.

――. *History of psychology*. (2 vols.) New York: Putnam, 1913. (Reprinted 1970)   **Bl**

――. *Genetic theory of reality, being the outcome of genetic logic as issuing in the aesthetic theory of reality called pancalism*. New York: Putnam, 1915. (Reprinted 1970)

――. *Between two wars (1861–1921)*. (2 vols.) Boston: Stratford, 1926.   **B**

――. James Mark Baldwin. In C. Murchison (Ed.), *A history of psychology in autobiography*. Vol 1. Worcester, Mass.: Clark University Press, 1930, pp. 1–30.   **B**

Borgotta, *Present-day Sociology*; Herrnstein & Boring, *Source Book*; Kessen, *Child*; Sahakian, *Psychology*

PHILIP BOSWOOD BALLARD
1865-1950
English Psychologist (11)

Ballard, P. B. *Handwork as an educational medium*. (2nd ed.) New York: Macmillan, 1915. (1910)

――. Obliviscence and reminiscence. *Brit. J. Psychol. Monogr. Suppl.*, 1913, *1*, No. 2.

――. *Mental tests*. London: Hodder & Stoughton, 1920.

———. The limit of the growth of intelligence. *Brit. J. Psychol.*, 1921–1922, *12*, 125–141.

———. *Group tests of intelligence.* London: University of London, 1922.

———. *The new examiner.* London: Hodder & Stoughton, 1923.

———. *The changing school.* London: Hodder & Stoughton, 1925.

———. *Fundamental arithmetic.* London: University of London Press, 1926–1928.

———. *Teaching the essentials of arithmetic.* London: University of London Press, 1928.

———. *Thought and language.* London: University of London Press, 1934.

———. Geometry: Its values and methods. *Brit. J. educ. Psychol.*, 1936, *6*, 23–42.

———. *Teaching and testing English.* London: University of London Press, 1939.

HARRY BANISTER
1882-1963
English Psychologist (11)

Banister, H. The effect of binaural phase differences on the localisation of tones at various frequencies. *Brit. J. Psychol.*, 1924–1925, *15*, 280–307.

———. Three experiments on the localisation of tones. *Brit. J. Psychol.*, 1925–1926, *16*, 265–292.

———. Phase effect and the localisation of sound: An examination of the Myers-Watson hypothesis. *Phil. Mag.*, 1926, *2*, 402–431.

———. A suggestion towards a new hypothesis regarding the localisation of sound. *Brit. J. Psychol.*, 1926–1927, *17*, 142–153.

———. The transmission of sound through the head. *Phil. Mag.*, 1926, *2*, 144–161.

———. Auditory theory: A criticism of Professor Boring's hypothesis. *Amer. J. Psychol.*, 1927, *38*, 436–440.

———, & Pollock, K. G. The accommodation of the eye. *Brit. J. Psychol.*, 1928–1929, *19*, 394–396.

———. Hearing. I. In C. Murchison (Ed.), *The foundations of experimental psychology.* Worcester, Mass.: Clark University Press, 1929, pp. 273–312.

Hartridge, H., & ———. Hearing. II. In C. Murchison (Ed.), *The foundations of experimental psychology.* Worcester, Mass.: Clark University Press, 1929, pp. 313–349.

———. Audition. I. Auditory phenomena and their stimulus correlations. In C. Murchison (Ed.), *A handbook of general experimental psychology.* Worcester, Mass.: Clark University Press, 1934, pp. 880–923.

———. *Psychology and health.* New York: Macmillan, 1935.

———. Another approach to the problem of accident causation. *Brit. J. Psychol.*, 1938, *28*, 304–314.

———, & Zangwill, O. L. Experimentally induced visual paramnesias. *Brit. J. Psychol.*, 1941–1942, *32*, 30–51.

———, & Zangwill, O. L. Experimentally induced olfactory paramnesias. *Brit. J. Psychol.*, 1941–1942, *32*, 155–175.

———, & Ravden, M. The environment and the child. *Brit. J. Psychol.*, 1945, *35*, 82–87.

HENRI ETIENNE BEAUNIS
1830-1921
French Physiologist (18)

Beaunis, H., & Bouchard, A. *Nouveaux éléments d'anatomie descriptive et d'embryologie.* Paris: Baillière, 1868.

———. *Programme du cours complémentaire de physiologie fait à la faculté de médecine de Strasbourg (semestre d'été, 1869).* Paris: Baillière, 1872.

———. *Les principes de la physiologie.* Paris: Berger-Levrault, 1875.

———. *Nouveaux éléments de physiologie humaine, comprenant les principes de la physiol-*

ogie comparée et de la physiologie générale.
(3rd ed.) (2 vols.) Paris: Baillière, 1888. (1876)

————, & Bouchard, A. *Précis d'anatomie et de dissection.* Paris: Baillière, 1877.

————. Sur la comparaison du temps de réaction des différentes sensations. *Rev. phil.,* 1883, *15,* 611–620.

————. *Recherches expérimentales sur les conditions de l'activité cérébrale et sur la physiologie des nerfs.* (2 vols.) Paris: Baillière, 1884–1886. (1883)

————. L'expérimentation en psychologie par le somnambulisme provoqué. *Rev. phil.,* 1885, *20,* 1–36, 113–135.

————. Influence de la durée de l'expectation sur le temps de réaction des sensations visuelles. *Rev. phil.,* 1885, *20,* 330–332.

————. *Le somnambulisme provoqué.* Paris: Baillière, 1896. (1886)

————. Une expérience sur le sens musculaire. *Rev. phil.,* 1887, *22,* 328–330.

————. Recherches sur la mémoire des sensations musculaires. *Rev. phil.,* 1888, *25,* 569–574.

————. *Les sensations internes.* Paris: Alcan, 1889.

————. *L'évolution du système nerveux.* Paris: Baillière, 1890.

————. *Travaux du laboratoire de psychologie physiologique des hautes études ; à la Sorbonne.* Paris: Baillière, 1893.

————. Contribution à la psychologie du rêve. *Amer. J. Psychol.,* 1903, *14,* 7–23 (271–287).

————. Comment fonctionne mon cerveau ; essai de psychologie introspective. *Rev. phil.,* 1909, *67,* 29–40.

————. Le mécanisme cérébral. Observations personnelles. *Rev. phil.,* 1910, *69,* 464–482.

————. L'émotion musicale. *Rev. phil.,* 1918, *86,* 353–369.

————. Les aveugles de naissance et le monde extérieur. *Rev. phil.,* 1921, *91,* 15–74.

JOHN GILBERT BEEBE-CENTER
1897-1958
American Psychologist (19)

Beebe-Center, J. G., & Pratt, C. C. A test of Birkhoff's aesthetic measure. *J. gen. Psychol.,* 1927, *17,* 339–353.

————. The law of affective equilibrium. *Amer. J. Psychol.,* 1929, *41,* 54–69.

————. General affective value. *Psychol. Rev.,* 1929, *36,* 472–480.

————. The relation between affectivity and specific processes in sense organs. *Psychol. Rev.,* 1930, *37,* 327–333.

————. The variability of affective judgments upon odors. *J. exp. Psychol.,* 1931, *14,* 91–93.

————. *The psychology of pleasantness and unpleasantness.* New York: Van Nostrand, 1932. (Reprinted 1966)

Gardiner, H. M., Metcalf, Ruth C., & ————. *Feeling and emotion: A history of theories.* New York: American Book, 1937.

————, & Stevens, S. S. Cardiac acceleration in emotional situations. *J. exp. Psychol.,* 1937, *21,* 72–87.

————, & Stevens, S. S. The emotional responses: Changes of heart-rate in a gun-shy dog. *J. exp. Psychol.,* 1938, *23,* 239–257.

Harsh, C. M., ————, & Beebe-Center, Roxanna. Further evidence regarding preferential judgment of polygonal forms. *J. Psychol.,* 1939, *7,* 343–350.

Berg, R. L., & ————. Cardiac startle in man. *J. exp. Psychol.,* 1941, *28,* 262–279.

————, & McFarland, R. A. Psychology in South America. *Psychol. Bull.,* 1941, *38,* 627–667.

————, & Beebe-Center, Roxanna. Measurement of affective power in terms of ratios of partial E^2s. *Amer. J. Psychol.,* 1946, *59,* 290–295.

————, Black, P., Hoffman, A. C., & Wade, Marjorie. Relative per diem consumption as a measure of preference in the rat. *J. comp. physiol. Psychol.,* 1948, *41,* 239–251.

———, & Waddell, D. A general psychological scale of taste. *J. Psychol.*, 1948, *26*, 517–524.

———. Standards for use of the gust scale. *J. Psychol.*, 1949, *28*, 411–419.

———, Feeling and emotion. In H. Helson (Ed.), *Theoretical foundations of psychology.* New York: Van Nostrand, 1951, pp. 254–317.

———, Rogers, M. S., & Atkinson, W. H. Intensive equivalences for sucrose and NaCl solutions. *J. Psychol.*, 1955, *39*, 371–372.

CLIFFORD WHITTINGHAM BEERS
1876-1943
American Layman (17)

Beers, C. W. *A mind that found itself: An autobiography.* (5th ed.) Garden City, N.Y.: Doubleday, 1960. (1908) **B**

———. *The after care of the insane.* New Haven: Bradley & Scoville, 1909.

———. *The value of social service as an agency in the prevention of nervous and mental disorders.* New Haven: Connecticut Society for Mental Hygiene, 1910.

VLADIMIR MIKHAILOVICH
BEKHTEREV
1857-1927
Russian Physiologist (27)

Bekhterev, V. M. *(Principles of brain function.)* (7 vols.) St. Petersburg: Brockhaus & Efron, 1903-1907. **C**

———. *(Selected works: Articles and addresses.)* Ed. by V. N. Myasishchev. Moscow: Medgiz, 1954. **B Bl C**

———. *(On the function of the semicircular canals of the labyrinth.)* St. Petersburg: Ettinger, 1882.

———. Ueber die functionelle Beziehung der unteren Oliven zum Kleinhirn und die Bedeutung derselben für die Erhaltung des Körpergleichgewichts. *Arch. ges. Physiol.*, 1882, *29*, 257–265.

———. Ergebnisse der Durchschneidung des N. acusticus, nebst Erörterung der Bedeutung der semicirculären Canäle für das Körpergleichgewicht. *Arch. ges. Physiol.*, 1883, *30*, 312–347.

———. Zur Physiologie des Körpergleichgewichts: Die Funktion der centralen grauen Substanz des dritten Hirnventrikels. *Arch. ges. Physiol.*, 1883, *31*, 479–530.

———. Ueber die Verbindung der sogenannten peripheren Gleichgewichtsorgane mit dem Kleinhirnstiele. *Arch. ges. Physiol.*, 1884, *34*, 362–388.

———. Zur Frage über den Ursprung der Hörnerven und über die physiologische Bedeutung des N. vestibularis. *Zbl. Physiol.*, 1887, *6*, 193–198, 264.

———, & Mislavsky, N. Zur Frage der die Speichelsekretion anregenden Rindenfelder. *Neurol. Zbl.*, 1889, *9*, 190–193.

———. Ueber die Erscheinungen, welche die Durchschneidung der Hinterstränge des Rükenmarks bei Thieren herbeiführt, und die Beziehung dieser Stränge zur Gleichgewichtsfunction. *Arch. Anat. Physiol.*, 1890, *2*, 489–504.

———, & Mislavsky, N. Zur Frage über die Innervation des Magens. *Neurol. Zbl.*, 1890, *9*, 195–199.

———. *Die Leitungsbahnen im Gehirn und Rükenmark.* (2nd ed.) Leipzig: Georgi, 1898. (1893)

———. Der hintere Zweihügel als Centrum für das Gehör, die Stimme und die Reflexbewegungen. *Neurol. Zbl.*, 1895, *14*, 706–712.

———. *(Role of the organs of equilibrium in space perception.)* St. Petersburg: Rikker, 1896.

———. Ueber die Gehörcentra der Hirnrinde. *Arch. Anat. Physiol.*, 1899 (suppl. vol.), 391–402.

———. Ueber paradoxe Pupillenreaction und über pupillenverengernde Fasern im Gehirn. *Deutsch. Z. Nervenk.*, 1900, *16*, 186–208.

———. Ueber objective Symptome localer Hyperästhesie und Anästhesie bei den sogenannten traumatischen Neurosen und bei Hysteria. *Neurol. Zbl.,* 1900, *19,* 205–208, 388–389.

———. Ueber die Lokalisation der Geschmackzentren in der Gehirnrinde. *Arch. Anat. Physiol.,* 1900 (suppl. vol.), 145–151.

———. *Psyche und Leben.* Wiesbaden: Bergmann, 1908. Also *L'activité psychique et la vie.* Paris: Boulangé, 1907. (1902)

———. *La suggestion et son rôle dans la vie sociale.* Trans. by P. Keraval. Paris: Boulangé, 1910. (1903)

———. La psychologie objective. (1904) *Rev. sci.* 1906, *6,* 353–357, 390–396.

———. Der Einfluss der Gehirnrinde auf Geschlechtsorgane, die Prostata und die Milchdrüsen. *Arch. Anat. Physiol.,* 1905, 524–537.

———. Des signes objectifs de la suggestion pendant le sommeil hypnotique. *Arch. Psychol.,* Geneva, 1905, *5,* 103–107.

———. *Die Persönlichkeit und die Bedingungen ihrer Entwicklung und Gesundheit.* Wiesbaden: Bergmann, 1906.

———. *Objektive Psychologie oder Psychoreflexologie: Die Lehre von den Associations-Reflexen.* Leipzig: Teubner, 1913. Also *La psychologie objective.* Paris: Alcan, 1913. (1907–1910)

———. Ueber die reproduktive und associative Reaction beider Bewegungen. (1908) *Z. Therap.,* 1909, *1,* No. 1.

———. *Ueber die Functionen der Nervencentra.* (3 vols.) Jena: Fischer, 1908–1911.

———. Die objective Psychologie und ihre Begründung. *J. Psychol. Neurol.,* 1909, *14,* 16–37, 150–165.

———. Die objektive Untersuchung der neuropsychischen Sphäre der Geisteskranken. *Z. Psychother. med. Psychol.,* 1909, *1,* 257–289.

———. Ueber die Lokalisation der motorischen Appraxie. *Monatsch. Psychiat. Neurol.,* 1909, *25,* 42–51.

———. Objective Untersuchung der neurophysischen Sphäre im Kindesalter. *Z. Psychother. med. Psychol.,* 1910, *2,* 129–141.

———. *(Hypnosis, suggestion and psychotherapy and their therapeutic significance.)* St. Petersburg: n.p., 1911.

———. La psychologie objective appliquée à l'étude de la criminalité. *Arch. anthrop.,* 1911, *25,* 161–189.

———. La psychologie sociale considérée comme une science objective. *Rev. psychol.,* 1911, *4,* 304–313.

———. *(Objective psychological methods applied to the study of delinquency.)* St. Petersburg: Publisher unknown, 1912.

———. Ueber die Hauptäusserungen der neuropsychischen Tätigkeit beim objektiven Studium derselben. *Z. Psychol.,* 1912, *60,* 280–301.

———. Was ist Psycho-Reflexologie? *Deutsch. med. Wochensch.,* 1912, *38,* 1481–1487.

———. Sur la psycho-réflexologie ou psychologie objective. *Arch. int. Neurol.,* 1913, *1,* 273–288, 365–374.

———. Ueber die individuelle Entwicklung der neuropsychischen Sphäre nach psychoreflexologischen Befunden. *Z. Psychother. med. Psychol.,* 1913, *5,* 65–77.

———. Ueber die biologische Entwicklung der menschlichen Sprache. *Folia neuro-biol.,* 1913, *7,* 595–610.

———. La localisation des psycho-réflexes dans l'écorce cérébrale. *Scientia,* 1915, *20,* 444–457.

———. *General principles of human reflexology: An introduction to the objective study of personality.* (4th ed.) Trans. by Emma & W. Murphy. London: Jarrolds, 1932. (1918) (Reprinted 1971)

———. *Die kollektive Reflexologie.* Halle: Marhold, 1928. (1921)

———. *(Objective study of personality.)* Petrograd: Publisher unknown, 1923.

———. Studium der Funktionen der praefrontal und anderer Gebiete der Hirnrinde vermittelst der assoziativ-motorischen Reflexe. *Schweiz. Arch. Neurol. Psychiat.,* 1923, *13,* 61–76.

————, & de Lange, M. Die Ergebnisse des Experiments auf dem Gebiete der kollectiven Reflexologies. *Z. angew. Psychol.*, 1924, *24*, 305–344.

————, & Shchelovanov, N. M. Toward the establishment of a developmental reflexology. (1924) *Sov. Psychol.*, 1969, *8*(1), 7–25.

————. *(Psychology, reflexology, and Marxism.)* Leningrad: Giz, 1925.

————. *(Function of the brain viewed from reflexological viewpoint.)* Leningrad: Soikin, 1926.

————, Vasiliev, L. L., & Everbov, A. F. *(Reflexology of human work.)* Moscow: Soikin, 1926.

————. Dialectical materialism and reflexology. *Pod. Znamenem Marksizma*, 1926, 7–8, 69–94.

————. Ueber die Perversion. *Psychol. Med.*, 1927, *2*, 197–205, 233–253.

————. Wladimir Bechterew. In L. R. Grote (Ed.), *Die Medizin der Gegenwart in Selbstdarstellungen.* Vol. 6. Leipzig: Meiner, 1927, pp. 1–52. **B Bl**

————. Ueber komplizierte Reflexerscheinung bei Affektion des zentralen motorischen Neurons. *Z. ges. Neurol. Psychiat.*, 1927, *108*, 41–55.

————. *(The brain and its activity.)* Leningrad: Giz, 1928.

————. Emotions as somato-mimetic reflexes. In M. L. Reymert (Ed.), *Feelings and emotions: The Wittenberg symposium.* Worcester, Mass.: Clark University Press, 1928, pp. 270–283.

————. (Concerning emotions as mimic-somatic reflexes.) *Nov. Refl. Fiziol. Nerv. Sist.*, 1929, *3*, 17–30.

————. *La réflexologie collective.* Ed., trans., & pref. by N. Kostyleff. Neuchâtel: Delachaux & Niestlé, 1957.

————, & Shchelovanov, N. M. Toward the establishment of a developmental reflexology. *Sov. Psychol.*, 1970, *8*, 7–25.

Park & Burgess, *Sociology;* Sahakian, *Psychology*

CHARLES BELL
1774-1842
English Anatomist (24)

Bell, C. *An exposition of the natural system of the nerves of the human body with a republication of the papers delivered to the Royal Society, on the subject of nerves.* London: Spottiswoode, 1824. **C**

————. *The nervous system of the human body as explained in a series of papers read before the Royal Society of London.* Edinburgh: Black, 1836. **C**

————. *Letters of Sir Charles Bell, K.H., F.R.S.L., & E., selected from his correspondence with his brother George Joseph Bell.* London: Murray, 1870. **B C**

————, & Bell, J. *The anatomy of the human body.* (4 vols.) New York: Collins, 1812. (1797–1804) Reprinted 1829 & 1834 as *The anatomy and physiology of the human body.*

————. *A system of dissections, explaining the anatomy of the human body, the manner of displaying the parts, and their varieties in disease.* (2nd ed.) (2 vols.) Edinburgh: Mundell & Son, 1799–1803. (1798–1800) (Reprinted 1809, 1814)

————. *The anatomy of the brain explained in a series of engravings.* London: Longman & Rees, 1802.

————. *The anatomy and philosophy of expression as connected with the fine arts.* (5th ed.) London: Bohn, 1865. (1806)

————. *Expression: Its anatomy and philosophy.* (New ed.) New York: Fowler & Wells, 1883. (1806)

————. *Idea of a new anatomy of the brain: Submitted for the observations of his friends.* London: Strahan & Preston, 1811. Reprinted in *J. Anat. Physiol.*, 1869, *3*, 153–166; in English with German translation, Leipzig: Barth, 1911; in *Medical classics.* Vol. 1. Baltimore, Md.: Williams & Wilkins, 1936–1937, pp. 105–120; & by London: Dawsons, 1966.

————. On the nerves; giving an account of some experiments on their structure and functions, which lead to a new arrangement of the system. *Phil. Trans.*, 1821, *111*, 398–424.

———. Of the nerves which associate the muscles of the chest in the actions of breathing, speaking, and expression. *Phil. Trans.*, 1822, *112*, 284–312.

———. On the motions of the eye, in illustration of the uses of the muscles and nerves of the obit. *Phil. Trans.*, 1823, *113*, 166–186, 289–307.
———. On the nervous circle which connects the voluntary muscles with the brain. *Phil. Trans.*, 1826, 2, 163–173.

———. Lectures on the nervous system. *Lond. med. Gaz.*, 1827, 553–556, 617–622, 681–686, 745–747.

———. On the nerves of the face ; being a second paper on that subject. *Phil. Trans.*, 1829, 317–330, & *J. Physiol.*, 1830, *10*, 1–35, 189–196.

———. *The hand: Its mechanism and vital endowments as evincing design.* (9th ed.) London: Bell, 1874. (1833)

———. On the functions of some parts of the brain, and on the relations between the brain and nerves of motion and sensation. *Phil. Trans.*, 1834, *124*, 471–484.

———. *A familiar treatise on the five senses.* London: Washburne, 1841.

Bodenheimer, *Biology* ; Clarke & O'Malley, *Brain* ; Dember, *Perception* ; Dennis, *Psychology* ; Fulton & Wilson, *Physiology* ; Hall, *Source Book* ; Herrnstein & Boring, *Source Book* ; Hunter & Macalpine, *Psychiatry* ; Parsons, *Society* ; Sahakian, *Psychology*

RUTH (FULTON) BENEDICT
1887-1948
American Anthropologist (16)

Benedict, Ruth. *An anthropologist at work: Writings of Ruth Benedict.* Ed. by Margaret Mead. Boston: Houghton Mifflin, 1959.   **B C**

———. Psychological types in the cultures of the Southwest. *Proc. 23rd Int. Cong. Americanists,* 1928, 572–581.

———. Configurations of culture in North America. *Amer. Anthrop.*, 1932, *34*, 1–27.

———. Anthropology and the abnormal. *J. gen. Psychol.*, 1934, *10*, 59–82. Reprinted in L. Y. Rabkin & J. E. Carr (Eds.), *Sourcebook in abnormal psychology.* Boston: Houghton Mifflin, 1967, pp. 9–19.

———. *Patterns of culture.* Boston: Houghton Mifflin, 1934. (Reprinted 1961)

———. Continuities and discontinuities in cultural conditioning. *Psychiatry,* 1938, *1*, 161–167. Reprinted in C. Kluckhohn & H. A. Murray (Eds.), *Personality in nature, society and culture.* (2nd ed.) New York: Knopf, 1953, pp. 522–531. (1948)

———. Religion. In F. Boas (Ed.), *General anthropology.* Boston: Heath, 1938, pp. 627–665.

———, & Weltfish, G. *The races of mankind.* (Rev. ed.) New York: Viking Press, 1945. (1940) (Reprinted 1959)

———. *The chrysanthemum and the sword: Patterns of Japanese culture.* Boston: Houghton Mifflin, 1946.

———. Child rearing in certain European countries. *Amer. J. Orthopsychiat.*, 1949, *19*, 342–350.

Fried, *Anthropology* ; Goldschmidt, *Mankind* ; O'Brien & Schrag, *Sociology* ; Parsons, *Society*

FRIEDRICH EDUARD BENEKE
1798-1854
German Philosopher (17)

Beneke, F. E. *Psychologisch-pädagogische Abhandlungen und Aufsätze.* Ed. by M. Moltke. Leipzig: Siegismund & Volkening, 1877.   **C**

———. *Erfahrungsseelenlehre als Grundlage alles Wissens in ihren Hauptzügen dargestellt.* Amsterdam: Bonset, 1965. (1820)

———. *Neue Grundlegung zur Metaphysik.* Berlin: Mittler, 1822.

———. *Grundlegung zur Physik der Sitten.* Berlin: Mittler, 1822.

————. *Psychologische Skizzen.* (2 vols.) Göttingen: Vandenhoeck & Ruprecht, 1825–1827.

————. *Schutzschrift für meine Grundlegung zur Physik der Sitten.* Leipzig: Reclam, 1823.

————. *Das Verhältnis von Seele und Leib.* Amsterdam: Bonset, 1965. (1826)

————. *Kant und die philosophische Aufgabe unserer Zeit.* Berlin: Mittler, 1832.

————. *Die Philosophie in ihrem Verhältnisse zur Erfahrung, zur Spekulation und zum Leben dargestellt.* Berlin: Mittler, 1833.

————. *Lehrbuch der Psychologie als Naturwissenschaft.* (4th ed.) Berlin: Mittler, 1877. (1833) (Reprinted 1964)

————. *Erziehungs- und Unterrichtslehre.* (4th ed.) Berlin: Mittler, 1876. (1835–1836)

————. *System der Metaphysik und Religionsphilosophie, aus den natürlichen Grundverhältnissen des menschlichen Geistes.* Berlin: Dümmler, 1840.

————. *System der Logik als Kunstlehre des Denkens.* Berlin: Dümmler, 1842.

————. *Lehrbuch der Psychologie als Naturwissenschaft.* (2nd ed.) Amsterdam: Bonset, 1964. (1845)

————. *Die neue Psychologie.* Berlin: Mittler, 1845.

————. *Pragmatische Psychologie, oder Seelenlehre in der Anwendung auf das Leben.* (2 vols. in 1) Berlin: Mittler, 1850.

————. *Lehrbuch der pragmatischen Psychologie oder der Seelenlehre in der Anwendung auf das Leben.* Berlin: Mittler, 1853.

Rabkin & Carr, *Abnormal* ; Rand, *Classical Psychologists* ; Rand, *Moralists*

JEREMY BENTHAM
1748-1832
English Philosopher (22)

Bentham, J. *The works for Jeremy Bentham.* (11 vols.) Ed. by J. Bowring. Edinburgh: Tait, 1828–1843. (Reprinted 1962)   **Bl C**

————. Bentham's theory of fictions. *(Essay on logic* and *Fragment on ontology.)* Ed. by C. K. Ogden. London: Kegan Paul, 1932. (Reprinted 1959)   **C**

————. *The correspondence of Jeremy Bentham, 1752–1780.* (3 vols.) Ed. by T. L. S. Sprigge. London: Athlone Press, 1968.   **B C**

————. *The collected works of Jeremy Bentham.* (Ult. 38 vols.) Ed. by J. H. Burns, London: Athlone Press, 1968–   **C**

————. *An introduction to the principles of morals and legislation.* Ed by J. H. Burns & H. L. A. Hart. London: Athlone Press, 1970. (1789)

————. *Panopticon: Or, the inspection-house.* (3 vols.) London: Payne, 1791. Reprinted in *Works,* Vol. 4, *op. cit.,* pp. 37–172.

————. A table of springs of action. (1815) In P. McReynolds (Ed.), *Four early works on motivation.* Gainesville, Fla.: Scholars' Facsimiles & Reprints, 1969, pp. 477–512. Also in *Works,* Vol. 1, *op. cit.,* pp. 195–219.

————. Chrestomathia. (1816) In *Works.* Vol. 8, *op. cit.,* pp. 1–191.

————. The rationale of reward. (1825) In *Works,* Vol. 2, *op. cit.,* pp. 189–266.

————. Rationale of judicial evidence. (1827) In *Works,* Vols. 6, 7, *op. cit.,* pp. 189–585, 1–644.

————. *Deontology: Or the science of morality.* (2 vols.) Ed. by J. Bowring. London: Longman, Rees, Orme, Browne, Green, & Longman, 1834. (Reprinted 1971)

————. Logical arrangements, or instruments of invention and discovery employed. (1838) In *Works,* Vol. 3, *op. cit.,* pp. 285–295.

————. Essay on logic. (1843) In *Works,* Vol. 8, *op. cit.,* pp. 213-293.

————. Essay on language. (1843) In *Works,* Vol. 8, *op. cit.,* pp. 294–338.

————. *The limits of jurisprudence defined, being part two of an introduction to the principles of morals and legislation.* Intro. by C. W. Everett. Westport, Conn.: Greenwood Press, 1971, (1945)

Brinton, *Age Reason*; Hunter & Macalpine, *Psychiatry*; Murphy, *Western*; Rand, *Moralists*

(ISAAC) MADISON BENTLEY
(1870-1955)
American Psychologist (21)

Bentley, M. The memory image and its qualitative fidelity. *Amer. J. Psychol.*, 1899–1900, *11*, 1–48.

——. The synthetic experiment. *Amer. J. Psychol.*, 1899–1900, *11*, 405–425.

——. Psychology of mental arrangement. *Amer. J. Psychol.*, 1902, *13*, 269–293.

——. A critique of "fusion." *Amer. J. Psychol.*, 1903, *14*, 324–336.

——, & Titchener, E. B. Ebbinghaus' explanation of beats. *Amer. J. Psychol.*, 1904, *15*, 62–71.

——, & Sabine, G. H. A study in tonal analysis. I. *Amer. J. Psychol.*, 1905, *16*, 484–498.

Day, Lucy M., & ——. A note on learning in Paramecium. *J. anim. Behav.*, 1911, *1*, 67–73.

Barnholt, Sarah E., & ——. Thermal intensity and the area of the stimulus. *Amer. J. Psychol.*, 1911, *22*, 325–332.

——. A preface to social psychology. *Psychol. Monogr.*, 1916, *21*, No. 92, pp. 1–25.

——. The psychological antecedents of phrenology. *Psychol. Monogr.*, 1916, *21*, No. 92, pp. 102–115.

——. *The new field of psychology: The psychological functions and their government.* New York: Appleton-Century, 1933. (1924)

——. The major categories of psychology. *Psychol. Rev.*, 1926, *33*, 71–105.

Weber, O. F., & ——. The relation of instruction to the psychosomatic functions. *Psychol. Monogr.*, 1926, *35*, No. 163, pp. 1–15.

——. Qualitative resemblance among odors. *Psychol. Monogr.*, 1926, *35*, No. 163, pp. 144–151.

——. The psychologies called "structural": Historical derivation. In C. Murchison (Ed.), *Psychologies of 1925.* (3rd ed.) Worcester, Mass.: Clark University Press, 1928, pp. 383–393. (1926)

——. The work of the structuralists. In C. Murchison (Ed.), *Psychologies of 1925.* (3rd ed.) Worcester, Mass.: Clark University Press, 1928, pp. 395–404. (1926)

——. The psychological organism. In C. Murchison (Ed.), *Psychologies of 1925.* (3rd ed.), Worcester, Mass.: Clark University Press, 1928, pp. 405–412. (1926)

——. Environment and context. *Amer J. Psychol.*, 1927, *39*, 54–61.

——. Is "emotion" more than a chapter heading? In M. L. Reymert (Ed.), *Feelings and emotions: The Wittenberg symposium.* Worcester, Mass.: Clark University Press, 1928, pp. 17–23.

Mikesell, W. H., & ——. Configuration and brightness contrast. *J. exp. Psychol.*, 1930, *13*, 1–23.

——. A psychology for psychologists. In C. Murchison (Ed.), *Psychologies of 1930.* Worcester, Mass.: Clark University Press, 1930, pp. 95–114.

——, & Gundlach, R. The dependence of tonal attributes upon phase. *Amer. J. Psychol.*, 1930, *42*, 519–543.

——. Psychology's family relations among the sciences. *Science,* 1931, *73*, 113–117.

——. Mind, body, and soul in medical psychology. *Amer. J. Psychol.*, 1933, *45*, 577–591.

——, & Varon, Edith J. An accessory study of "phonetic symbolism." *Amer. J. Psychol.*, 1933, *45*, 76–86.

——. Madison Bentley. In C. Murchison (Ed.), *A history of psychology in autobiography.* Vol. 3. Worcester, Mass.: Clark University Press, 1936, pp. 53–67.   **B**

——. The psychologist's uses of neurology. *Amer. J. Psychol.*, 1937, *49*, 233–264.

———— The nature and uses of experiment in psychology. *Amer. J. Psychol.*, 1937, *50*, 452–469.

————. The theater of living in animal psychology. *Amer. J. Psychol.*, 1944, *57*, 1–48.

————. Suggestions toward a psychological history of the hominids. *Amer. J. Psychol.*, 1947, *60*, 479–501.

————. Forecast, timing and other primary factors in the government of certain biomechanical systems. *Amer. J. Psychol.*, 1952, *65*, 329–345.

Beardslee, *Perception*; Moore & Hartmann, *Industrial Psychology*; Peterson, *Combination Tones*

VITTORIO BENUSSI
1878-1927
Italian-Austrian Psychologist (20)

Benussi, W. Ueber den Einfluss der Farbe auf die Grösse der Zöllnerschen Täuschung. *Z. Psychol.*, 1902, *29*, 264–351, 385–433.

————. Zur Psychologie des Gestalterfassens. In A. Meinong (Ed.), *Untersuchungen zur Gegenstandstheorie und Psychologie.* Leipzig: Barth, 1904, pp. 304–448.

————. Ein neuer Beweis für die spezifische Helligkeit der Farben. In A. Meinong (Ed.), *Untersuchungen zur Gegenstandstheorie und Psychologie.* Leipzig: Barth, 1904, pp. 473–480.

————. Experimentelles über Vorstellungsinadäquatheit. I. II. *Z. Psychol.*, 1906, *42*, 22–55; 1907, *45*, 188–230.

————. Zur experimentellen Analyse des Zeitvergleichs. I. Zeitgrösse und Betonungsgestalt. *Arch. ges. Psychol.*, 1907, *9*, 366–449.

————. Ueber Aufmerksamkeitsrichtung beim Raum- und Zeitvergleich. *Z. Psychol.*, 1909, *51*, 73–107.

————. Ueber die Grundlagen des Gewichtseindruckes. *Arch. ges. Psychol.*, 1910, *17*, 1–185.

————. Ueber die Motive der Scheinkörperlichkeit bei umkehrbaren Zeichnungen. *Arch. ges. Psychol.*, 1911, *20*, 363–396.

————. Stroboskopische Scheinbewegungen und geometrischoptische Gestalttäuschungen. *Arch. ges. Psychol.*, 1912, *24*, 31–62.

————. *Psychologie der Zeitauffassung.* Heidelberg: Winter 1913.

————. Gesetze der inadäquaten Gestaltauffassung. *Arch. ges. Psychol.*, 1914, *32*, 396–419.

————. Die Atmungssymptome der Lüge. *Arch. ges. Psychol.*, 1914, *31*, 244–273.

————. Die Gestaltwahrnehmungen. *Z. Psychol.*, 1914, *69*, 255–292.

————. (Review) Koffka-Kenkel. Beiträge zur Psychologie der Gestalt- und Bewegungserlebnisse. *Zeitschr. f. Psychol.* Abt. 1. Bd. 67. S. 353–449. Februar 1914. *Arch. ges. Psychol.*, 1914, *32*, 50–57.

————. Versuche zur Analyse taktil-erweckter Scheinbewegungen. *Arch. ges. Psychol.*, 1917, *36*, 59–135.

————. Ueber Scheinbewegungskombination. *Arch. ges. Psychol.*, 1918, *37*, 233–282.

————. *La suggestione e l'ipnosi come mezzo di analisi psichica reale.* Bologna: Zanichelli, 1925.

————. Recherches expérimentales sur la perception de l'espace. I: La méthode haplodiplocinescopique. II: Le phénomène de Panum. *J. Psychol. norm. path.*, 1925, *22*, 625–666; 1928, *25*, 464–506.

————. Sur l'autonomie fonctionnelle émotive (à propos d'un compte-rendu de M. H. Wallon). *J. Psychol. norm. path.*, 1927, *24*, 341–344.

————. Zur experimentellen Grundlegung hypnosuggestiver Methoden psychischer Analyse. *Psychol. Forsch.*, 1927, *9*, 197–276.

HENRI BERGSON
1859-1941
French Philosopher (22)

Bergson, H. *Mind energy, lectures and essays.* (6th ed.) Trans. by H. W. Carr. New York: Holt, 1920. (1909)   **C**

————. *The creative mind.* Trans. by Mabelle L. Andison. New York: Philosophical Library, 1946. (1934) (Reprinted 1965)   **C**

————. *Ecrits et paroles.* (3 vols.) Ed. by R. M. Mossé-Bastide. Paris: Presses Universitaires de France, 1957–1959.   **C**

————. *Oeuvres. Edition du centenaire.* (2nd ed.) Annotated by A. Robinet. Paris: Presses Universitaires de France, 1963. (1959)   **C Bl**

————. *De la simulation inconsciente dans l'état d'hypnotisme. Rev. phil.,* 1886, *22,* 525–531.

————. *Time and free will: An essay on the immediate data of consciousness.* Trans. by F. L. Pogson. New York: Macmillan, 1910. (1889)   **Bl**

————. *Matter and memory.* Trans. by Nancy M. Paul & W. S. Palmer. New York: Macmillan, 1911. (1896)

————. *Laughter: An essay on the meaning of the comic.* Trans. by C. Brereton & F. Rothwell. London: Macmillan, 1911. (1900)

————. *The world of dreams.* Trans. by W. Baskin. New York: Philosophical Library, 1958. (1901)

————. An introduction to metaphysics. (1903) In *The creative mind, op. cit.,* pp. 159–200.

————. *Creative evolution.* Trans. by A. Mitchell, New York: Holt, 1911. (1907)

————. Philosophical intuition. (1911) In *The creative mind, op. cit.,* pp. 107–129.

————. On the pragmatism of William James. (1911) In *The creative mind, op. cit.,* pp. 209–219.

————. The philosophy of Claude Bernard. (1913) Trans. by A. C. Klebs. *Bull. hist. Med.,* 1936, *4,* 15–21. Reprinted in *The creative mind, op. cit.,* pp. 201–208.

————. *Duration and simultaneity.* (2nd ed.) Trans. by L. Jacobson. Indianapolis, Ind.: Bobbs-Merrill, 1965. (1922)

————. *The two sources of morality and religion.* Trans. by R. A. Audra & C. Brereton. New York: Holt, 1935. (1932)

Dampier, *Literature* ; Hall, *Source Book* ; Park & Burgess, *Sociology* ; Rand, *Classical Philosophers*

GEORGE BERKELEY
1685-1753
English Philosopher (25)

Berkeley, G. *Essay, principles, dialogues, with selections from other writings.* Ed. by Mary W. Calkins. New York: Scribner's, 1929. (Reprinted 1959)   **C**

————. *The works of George Berkeley, Bishop of Cloyne.* Ed. by A. A. Luce & T. E. Jessop. (9 vols.) London: Nelson, 1948–1957.   **B C**

————. *Philosophical writings.* Ed. by T. E. Jessop. Austin, Tex.: University of Texas Press, 1953.   **C**

————. *Works on vision.* Ed. by C. M. Turbayne. Indianapolis, Ind.: Bobbs-Merrill, 1963.   **C**

————. *Principles, dialogues, and philosophical correspondence.* Ed. by C. M. Turbayne. Indianapolis, Ind.: Bobbs-Merrill, 1965.   **C**

————. *An essay towards a new theory of vision.* (1709) In *Works,* Vol. 1, *op. cit.,* pp. 159–239.

————. *A treatise concerning the principles of human knowledge.* (2nd ed.) (1710) In *Works,* Vol. 2, *op. cit.,* pp. 19–113.

————. *Three dialogues between Hylas and Philonous.* (1713) In *Works,* Vol. 2, *op. cit.,* pp. 163–263.

————. *De Motu ; sive, de motus principio & natura, et de causa communicationis motuum.* (1721) In *Works,* Vol. 4, *op. cit.,* pp. 11–30. Eng. trans. pp. 31–52.

————, & Johnson, S. *Philosophical correspondence between Berkeley and Samuel Johnson, 1729–30.* In *Works,* Vol. 2, *op. cit.,* pp. 271–294.   **B**

————. *Alicphron: Or, the minute philosopher: Containing an apology for the Christian religion against those who are called free-thinkers.* (1732) In *Works,* Vol. 3, *op. cit.,* pp. 31–337.

————. The theory of vision vindicated and explained. (1733) In *Works*, Vol. 1, *op. cit.*, pp. 249–276.

――――. *The analyst: Or, a discourse addressed to infidel mathematicians.* (1734) In *Works*, Vol. 4, *op. cit.*, pp. 63–102.

――――. *Siris: A chain of philosophical reflexions and enquiries concerning the virtues of tar-water, and divers other subjects.* (1744) In *Works*, Vol. 5, *op. cit.*, pp. 25–164.

――――. *Philosophical commentaries, generally called the commonplace book.* (1891) Ed. by A. A. Luce. London: Nelson, 1944. Reprinted in *Works*, Vol. 1, *op. cit.*, pp. 7–104.

Ackermann, *Theories*; Dennis, *Psychology*; Herrnstein & Boring, *Source Book*; Hutchins, *Great Books*; Lawrence & O'Connor, *Phenomenology*; Margolis, *Introduction*; Newman, *Mathematics*; Rand, *Classical Philosophers*; Rand, *Classical Psychologists*; Sahakian, *Psychology*; Slotkin, *Anthropology*; Smith, *Source Book*

CLAUDE BERNARD
1813-1878
French Physiologist (25)

Bernard, C. *Oeuvres* (19 vols.) Ed. by E. Renan et al. Paris: Baillière, 1855–1881.   **C**

――――. *Pensées. Notes détachées.* Ed. by L. Delhoume. Paris: Ballière, 1937.   **C**

――――. *Philosophie, manuscrit inédit.* Ed. by J. Chevalier. Paris: Boivin, 1938.   **C**

――――. *Principes de médicine expérimentale.* Ed. by L. Delhoume. Paris: Presses Universitaires de France, 1947.   **C**

――――. *Esquisses et notes de travail inédites, recueillies et commentées par Léon Binet.* Paris: Masson, 1952.   **C**

――――. Recherches anatomiques et physiologiques sur la corde du tympan, pour servir à l'histoire de l'hémiplégie-faciale. *Ann. méd.-psychol.*, 1843, *1*, 408, 439.

――――. Recherches expérimentales sur les fonctions du nerf spinal, étudié spécialement dans

ses rapports avec le pneumogastrique. *Arch. gén. Méd.*, 1844, 4th ser., *4*, 397–426, *5*, 51–93.

――――. De l'origine du sucre dans l'économie animale. *Arch. gén. Méd.*, 1848, 4th ser., *18*, 303–319.

――――. *Leçons de physiologie expérimentale appliquée à la médecine.* (2 vols.) Paris: Baillière, 1854–1855.

――――. *Leçons sur les effets des substances toxiques et médicamenteuses.* Paris: Baillière, 1857.

――――. *Leçons sur la physiologie et la pathologie du système nerveux.* (2 vols.) Paris: Baillière, 1858.

――――. *Leçons sur les propriétés physiologiques et les altérations pathologiques des liquides de l'organisme.* (2 vols.) Paris: Baillière. 1859.

――――. Du rôle des actions réflexes paralysantes dans le phénomène des sécrétions. *J. anat. Physiol.*, 1864, *1*, 507–513.

――――. *An introduction to the study of experimental medicine.* Trans. by H. C. Greene. New York: Collier, 1961. (1865)

――――. *Rapport sur les progrès et la marche de la physiologie générale en France.* Paris: Imprimerie Impériale, 1867.

――――. *Leçons de pathologie expérimentale.* (2nd ed.) Paris: Baillière, 1880. (1872)

――――. *De la physiologie générale.* Brussels: Culture et Civilisation, 1965. (1872)

――――. Des fonctions du cerveau. *Rev. deux Mondes*, 1872, *98*, 373–385.

――――. *Leçons sur la chaleur animale, sur les effets de la chaleur et sur la fièvre, etc.* Paris: Baillière, 1876.

――――. *La science expérimentale.* (4th ed.) Paris: Baillière, 1906. (1878)

――――. *Leçons sur les phénomènes de la vie communs aux animaux et aux végétaux.* (2 vols.) Paris: Vrin, 1966. (1878–1879)

――――. *Leçons de physiologie opératoire.* Paris: Baillière, 1879.

――――. *The Cahier rouge of Claude Bernard.*

Trans. by H. H. Hoff, & Lucienne & R. Guillemin. In F. Grande & M. B. Visscher (Eds.). *Claude Bernard and experimental medicine.* Cambridge: Schenkman, 1967, pp. 1–120.

Bodenheimer, *Biology*; Clarke & O'Malley, *Brain*; Clendening, *Source Book*; Fulton & Wilson, *Physiology*; Gabriel & Fogel, *Biology*; Hall, *Source Book*; Rook, *Origins*; Schwartz & Bishop, *Moments Discovery*

HIPPOLYTE BERNHEIM
1840-1919
French Hypnotist (23)

Bernheim, H. *Contribution à l'étude des localisations cérébrales.* Paris: Berger-Levrault & Baillière, 1878.

———. *De la suggestion dans l'état hypnotique.* Paris: Doin, 1884.

———. *Hypnosis and suggestion in psychotherapy: A treatise on the nature and uses of hypnotism.* (2nd ed.) Trans. by C. A. Herter. New Hyde Park, N.Y.: University Books, 1964. (1884–1886)

———. *De la suggestion et de ses applications à la thérapeutique.* (2nd ed.) Paris: Doin, 1888. (1886)

———. De la suggestion envisagée au point de vue pédagogique. *Rev. hypno.,* 1886–1887, *1,* 129–139.

———. De l'influence hypnotique et de ses degrés. *Rev. hypno.,* 1886–1887, *1,* 225–232.

———. Correspondance à la critique de M. Binet sur le livre de M. Bernheim. *Rev. phil.,* 1887, *23,* 93–98.

———. Des hallucinations rétroactives provoquées sans hypnotisme et des faux témoignages. *Rev. hypno.,* 1887–1888, *2,* 4–13.

———. De l'action médicamenteuse à distance. *Rev. hypno.,* 1887–1888, *2,* 161–165.

———. Considérations générales sur la suggestion. *Rev. hypno.,* 1887–1888, *2,* 198–202.

———. L'hypnotisme et l'Ecole de Nancy. *Gazette Hôp.,* 1888, *61,* 337–339.

———. De l'amnésie rétroactive dans le sommeil provoqué. *Rev. hypno.,* 1889–1890, *4,* 12–14.

———. Des hallucinations négatives suggérées. *Rev. hypno.,* 1889, *3,* 161–165.

———. Les suggestions criminelles. *Rev. hypno.,* 1889–1890, *4,* 260–267, 293–301.

———. Hypnotisme et hystérie. Réponse à Monsieur le Dr. Babinski. *Gazette Hebd. Méd. Chir.,* 1891, *28,* 385–386.

———. Hypnotisme et hystérie. Dernier mot à propos de la conférence de M. Babinski. *Gazette Hebd. Méd. Chir.,* 1891, *28,* 409-410.

———. *Hypnotisme, suggestion, psychothérapie. Etudes nouvelles.* Paris: Doin, 1891.

———. Hypnotismus und Suggestion. *Z. Hypno.,* 1892–1893, *1,* 115–122.

———. *L'hypnotisme et la suggestion dans leurs rapports avec la médecine légale.* Nancy: Crépin-Leblond, 1897.

———. Conception nouvelle et étiologie de l'hystérie. *Bull. méd.,* 1902, *89,* 937–943.

———. *Hypnotisme et suggestion, hystérie, psychonévroses, neurasthénie, psychothérapie.* (3rd ed.) Paris: Doin, 1910. (1903)

———. *Conception du mot hystérie. Critique des doctrines actuelles.* Paris: Doin, 1905.

———. Conception pathogénique des états dits neurasthéniques, psychasthéniques, psychoneurasthéniques liés à une dyscrasie toxique souvent constitutionelle et native. *Rev. méd.,* 1909, *29,* 257–270.

———. *Jubilé du Professeur H. Bernheim.* Nancy: Arts Graphiques, 1910. **B**

———. Définition et valeur thérapeutique de l'hypnotisme. *Rev. Psychiat. Psychol. exp.,* 1911, *15,* 402–415. Reprinted in C. E. Shorer, The later Bernheim: A translation. *J. hist. Behav. Sci.,* 1968, *4,* 28–39.

Claparède, E., & ———. Definition, psychologische Interpretation und therapeutischer

Wert des Hypnotismus. *Jb. Psychol. Neurol.,* 1912, *19,* 276–299.

———. Sommeil et somnambulisme. *l'Encéphale,* 1912, *7,* 305–315, 417–428.

———. L'hypnotisme. Ses évolutions diverses. Son état actuel. *Arch. int. Neurol.,* 1913, *2,* 69–76.

———. *L'aphasie. Conception psychologique et clinique.* Paris: Doin, 1914.

Goshen, *Documentary;* Tinterow, *Hypnosis*

DANIEL BERNOULLI
1700-1782
Swiss Mathematician (11)

Euler, L., & Bernoulli, D. Der Briefwechsel zwischen Leonhard Euler und Daniel Bernoulli. Ed. by G. Eneström. *Bibliotheca math.,* 1906– 1907, *7,* 126–156. **B C**

———. *Versuch einer neuen Theorie der Wertbestimmung von Glücksfällen.* Trans. by A. Pringsheim. Leipzig: Duncker & Humblot, 1896. (1730–1731)

———. *Hydrodynamics.* Trans. by T. Carmody & H. Kobus. New York: Dover, 1968. (1738)

———. Exposition of a new theory on the measurement of risk. (1738) Trans. by L. Sommer. *Econometrica,* 1954, *22,* 23–36.

———. The most probable choice between several discrepant observations and the formation therefrom of the most likely induction. Trans. by C. G. Allen from the essay in *Acta Acad. Petrop.* (1777) *Biometrika,* 1961, *48,* 3–13. Trans. in E. S. Pearson & M. G. Kendall (Eds.), *Studies in the history of statistics and probability.* London: Griffin, 1970, pp. 157–167.

———. Versuch einer neuen Theorie der Bewegung der Muskeln. *Phys. med. Abh. Akad. Wiss. Petersburg,* Riga, 1782, *1,* 3–28.

———. Versuch in Ansehung des Sehnerves. *Phys. med. Abh. Akad. Wiss. Petersburg,* Riga, 1782, *1,* 28–32.

Miller, *Mathematics;* Newman, *Mathematics.*

JULIUS BERNSTEIN
1839-1917
German Physiologist (12)

Bernstein, J. Zur Theorie des Fechner'schen Gesetzes der Empfindung. *Arch. anal. Physiol.,* 1868, 388–393.

———. Ueber den zeitlichen Verlauf der negativen Schwankung des Nervenstromes. *Arch. ges. Physiol.,* 1868, *1,* 173–207.

———. *Untersuchungen über den Erregungsvorgang im Nerven- und Muskelsysteme.* Heidelberg: Winter, 1871.

———. *The five senses of man.* (No trans. given.) New York: Macmillan, 1876. (1875)

———. *Die fünf Sinne des Menschen.* (2nd ed.) Leipzig: Internationale wissenschaftliche Bibliothek, 1889. (1875)

———. Ueber die Höhe des Muskeltones bei elektrischer und chemischer Reizung. *Arch. ges. Physiol.,* 1875, *11,* 191–206.

———. Ueber die Ermüdung und Erholung der Nerven. *Arch. ges. Physiol.,* 1877, *15,* 289–327.

———. Die Erregungszeit der Nervenendorgane in den Muskeln. In E. Du Bois-Reymond (Ed.), *Archiv für Physiologie.* Leipzig: Veit, 1882, pp. 329–346.

———. Ueber die specifische Energie des Hörnerven, die Wahrnehmung binauraler (diotischer) Schwebungen und die Beziehungen der Hörfunktion zur statischen Funktion des Ohrlabyrinths. *Arch. ges. Physiol.,* 1894, *57,* 475– 494.

———. Ueber das angebliche Hören labyrinthloser Tauben. *Arch. ges. Physiol.,* 1895, *61,* 113–122.

———. Ueber die Latenzdauer der Muskelzukung. *Arch. ges. Physiol.,* 1897, *67,* 207–218.

———. *Lehrbuch der Physiologie des thierischen Organismus, im Speciellen des Menschen.* Stuttgart: Enke, 1900.

———. Untersuchungen zur Thermodynamik der

biolektrischen Ströme. *Arch. ges. Physiol.*, 1902, *92*, 521–562.

———, & Tschermak, A. Ueber die Frage: Präexistenztheorie oder Alternationstheorie des Muskelstromes. *Arch. ges. Physiol.*, 1904, *103*, 67–83.

———. Ueber die Temperaturcoeffizienten der Muskelenergie. *Arch. ges. Physiol.*, 1908, *122*, 129–195.

———. *Elektrobiologie ; die Lehre von den elektrischen Vorgängen im Organismus auf moderner Grundlage dargestellt.* Brunswick: Vieweg, 1912.

Clarke & O'Malley, *Brain*

FRIEDRICH WILHELM BESSEL
1784–1846
German Astronomer-Mathematician (23)

Bessel, F. W. *Astronomische Beobachtungen auf der Königlichen Universitäts-Sternwarte in Königsberg.* (21 vols.) Königsberg: Leupold, 1815–1844.   **C**

———. *Astronomische Untersuchungen.* (2 vols.) Königsberg: Bornträger, 1841–1843.   **C**

———. *Populäre Vorlesungen.* Ed. by N. C. Schumacher. Hamburg: n.p., 1848.   **C**

———. *Abhandlungen von Friedrich Wilhelm Bessel.* (3 vols.) Ed. by R. Engelmann. Leipzig: Engelmann, 1875–1876.   **B Bl C**

———, & Bessel, F. W. *Briefwechsel zwischen Gauss und Bessel.* Ed. by G. F. J. A. v. Auwers. Leipzig: Engelmann, 1880. (Reprinted 1969)   **B C**

———. Untersuchungen über die Bahn des Olbersschen Kometen. *Ahb. Akad. Berlin*, math. Kl., 1812–1813, 117–160. (1816)

———. Ueber den Ort des Polarsterns. *Berlin. Astron. Jb.*, 1818, 233–240. (1815)

———. *Persönliche Gleichung bei Durchgangsbeobachtungen.* (1822) Reprinted in *Abhandlungen*, Vol. 3, *op. cit.*, pp. 300–304.

———. Ueber eine Kritik der Greenwicher Beobachtungen im Philosophical Magazine. (1825) Reprinted in *Abhandlungen*, Vol. 3, *op. cit.*, pp. 460–462.

———. Ueber die Bestimmung des Gesetzes einer periodischen Erscheinung. *Astron. Nachr.*, 1828, *6*, 333–348. Reprinted in *Abhandlungen*, Vol. 2, *op. cit.*, pp. 364–372.

———. Betrachtung über die Methode der Vervielfältigung der Beobachtungen. *Astron. Nachr.*, 1834, *9*, 269–290. Reprinted in *Abhandlungen*, Vol. 3, *op. cit.*, pp. 306–317.

———. *Untersuchungen über die Länge des einfachen Secundenpendels.* Berlin: K. Akademie der Wissenschaften, 1838. Reprinted in *Abhandlungen*, Vol. 3, *op. cit.*, pp. 139–209.

———. Untersuchungen über die Wahrscheinlichkeit der Beobachtungsfehler. *Astron. Nachr.*, 1838, *15*, 369–404. Reprinted in *Abhandlungen*, Vol. 2, *op. cit.*, pp. 372–391.

———. Lebensabriss. (1875) In *Abhandlungen*, Vol. 1, *op. cit.*, pp. xi–xxxi.   **B**

Smith, *Source Book*

ALBRECHT BETHE
1872-1954
German Physiologist (16)

Bethe, A. Ueber die Erhaltung des Gleichgewichts. *Biol. Zbl.*, 1894, *14*, 95–114.

———. Die otocyste von Mysis. *Zool. Jb. Abt. Anat.*, 1895, *8*, 544–564.

———. Das Nervensystem von Cacinus Maenus. Ein anatomisch-physiologischer Versuch. *Arch. mikr. Anat.*, 1897, *50*, 460–546, 589–639 ; 1898, *51*, 382–452.

———. Vergleichende Untersuchungen über die Functionen des Centralnervensystems der Arthropoden. *Arch. ges. Physiol.*, 1897, *68*, 449–545.

———. Die anatomischen Elemente des Nervensystems und ihre physiologische Bedeutung. *Biol. Zbl.*, 1898, *18*, 843–874.

————. Dürfen wir den Ameisen und Bienen psychische Qualitäten zuschreiben? *Arch. ges. Physiol.*, 1898, *70*, 15–100.

Beer, T., ————, & Uexküll, J. v. Vorschläge zu einer objektivierenden Nomenklatur in der Physiologie des Nervensystems. *Biol. Zbl.*, 1899, *19*, 517–521 ; also *Zbl. Physiol.*, 1899, *13*, 137–141. Reprinted in E. Dzendolet, Behaviorism and sensation in the paper by Beer, Bethe and von Uexküll. (1899) *J. hist Behav. Sci.*, 1967, *3*, 256–261.

————. Die Locomotion des Haifisches (Scyllium) und ihre Beziehungen zu den einzelnen Gehirntheilen und zum Labyrinth. *Arch. ges. Physiol.*, 1899, *76*, 470–493.

————. Ueber die Neurofibrillen in den Ganglionzellen von Wirbelthieren und ihre Beziehungen zu den Golginetzen. *Arch. mikr. Anat.*, 1900, *55*, 513–558.

————. *Allgemeine Anatomie und Physiologie des Nervensystems.* Leipzig: Thieme, 1903.

————, & Happel, P. Die Zerlegung der Muskelzuckung in Teilfunktionen. I. Die Kurven der isotonischen Zuckung des curarisierten Sartorius nebst Bemerkungen über Latenzzeit und Geschwindigkeit der Kontraktionswelle. *Arch. ges. Physiol.*, 1923, *201*, 157–181.

————. Untersuchungen über die elastischen Eigenschaften der Muskeln bei verschiedenen funktionellen Zuständen. I. Mitt. Einführung und neue Methode zur Bestimmung der Zug-Elastizität. *Arch. ges. Physiol.*, 1924, *205*, 63–75.

————. Plastizität und Zentrelehre. In A. Bethe *et al.* (Eds.), *Handbuch der normalen und pathologischen Physiologie.* Vol. 15, Part 2. Berlin: Springer-Verlag, 1931, pp. 1175–1222.

————, & Fischer, A. Die Anpassungsfähigkeit (Plastizität) des Nervensystems. In A. Bethe *et al.* (Eds.), *Handbuch der normalen und pathologischen Physiologie,* Vol. 15, Part 2. Berlin: Springer-Verlag, 1931, pp. 1045–1130.

————. Rhythmik und Periodik, besonders im Hinblick auf die Bewegungen des Herzens und der Meduse. *Arch. ges. Physiol.*, 1937, *239*, 41–73.

————. *Allgemeine Physiologie.* Berlin: Springer-Verlag, 1952.

MARIE FRANÇOIS XAVIER BICHAT
1771-1802
French Physiologist (17)

Bichat, M. F. X. Mémoire sur les rapports qui existent entre les organes à la forme symétrique et ceux à forme irrégulière. *Mém. Soc. méd. émulation*, 1798, *2*, 477–487.

————. Mémoire sur la membrane synoviale des articulations. *Mém. Soc. méd. émulation*, 1798, *2*, 351–370.

————. Dissertation sur les membranes et sur leurs rapports généraux d'organisation. *Mém. Soc. méd. émulation*, 1798, *2*, 371–385.

————. *Physiological researches upon life and death.* (2nd ed.) Trans. by F. Gold. Boston: Richardson & Lord, 1827. (1800)

————. *Recherches physiologiques sur la vie et la mort.* (4th ed.) Paris: Béchet, 1822. (1800)

————. *A treatise on the membranes in general, and on different membranes in particular.* (New ed.) Trans. by J. G. Coffin. Boston: Cummings & Hilliard, 1813. (1800)

————. *Traité des membranes en général et de diverses membranes en particulier.* (3rd ed.) Paris: Gabon, 1816. (1800)

————. *Anatomie générale, appliquée à la physiologie et à la médicine.* (New ed.) (4 vols. in 8) Ed. by P. A. Béclard. Paris: Brosson, 1821. (1801)

————. *General anatomy, applied to physiology and medicine.* Trans. by G. Hayward. (3 vols.) Boston: Richardson & Lord, 1822. (1801)

————. *Traité d'anatomie descriptive.* (5 vols.) Paris: Gabon & Brosson, 1801–1803.

————. *Anatomie pathologique. Dernier cours de Xavier Bichat d'après un manuscrit autographe de P. A. Béchard avec une notice sur la vie et les travaux de Bichat par F. G. Boisseau.* Paris: Baillière, 1825.

Bodenheimer, *Biology* ; Hall, *Source Book*

ALFRED BINET
1857–1911
French Psychologist (27)

Binet, A. *The experimental psychology of Alfred Binet: Selected papers*. Ed. by R. H. Pollack & Margaret W. Brenner. New York: Springer, 1969. **C**

————. De la fusion des sensations semblables. *Rev. phil.*, 1880, *10*, 284–294. Trans. in *The experimental psychology of Alfred Binet, op. cit.*, pp. 3–12.

————. Le raisonnement dans les perceptions. *Rev. phil.*, 1883, *15*, 406–432.

————, & Féré, C. L'hypnotisme chez les hystériques: Le transfert. *Rev. phil.*, 1885, *19*, 1–25.

————, & Féré, C. La polarisation psychique. *Rev. phil.*, 1885, *19*, 369–402.

————, & Delboeuf, J. L. R. Les diverses écoles hypnotiques. *Rev. phil.*, 1886, *22*, 532–538.

————, & Féré, C. *The psychology of reasoning: Based on experimental researches in hypnotism.* (2nd ed.) Trans. by A. G. Whyte. Chicago: Open Court, 1901. (1886)

————. La perception de l'étendue par l'oeil. *Rev. phil.*, 1886, *21*, 113–121. Trans. in *The experimental psychology of Alfred Binet, op. cit.*, pp. 147–155.

————, & Féré, C. *Animal magnetism.* (4th ed.) (No trans. given.) New York: Appleton, 1901. (1887)

————. Le fétichisme dans l'amour. *Rev. phil.*, 1887, *24*, 143–167, 252–275.

————. L'intensité des images mentales. *Rev. phil.*, 1887, *23*, 473–497.

————, & Féré, C. Recherches expérimentales sur la physiologie des mouvements chez les hystériques. *Arch. Physiol. norm. path.*, 1887 (3rd ser.), 320–373.

————. *The psychic life of microorganisms: A study in experimental psychology.* Trans. by T. McCormack. Chicago: Open Court, 1903. (1888)

————. On double consciousness. Chicago: Open Court, 1889. Reprinted in part in French trans. in Various, *Centenaire de Th. Ribot et Jubilé de la Psychologie Scientifique Française*. Paris: Imprimerie moderne, 1939, pp. 109–113.

————. Recherches sur les mouvements chez quelques jeunes enfants. *Rev. phil.*, 1890, *29*, 297–309. Trans. in *The experimental psychology of Alfred Binet., op. cit.*, pp. 156–167.

————. La perception des longueurs et des nombres chez quelques petits enfants. *Rev. phil.*, 1890, *30* 68–81. Trans. in *The experimental psychology of Alfred Binet, op. cit.*, pp. 79–92.

————. Perceptions d'enfants. *Rev. phil.*, 1890, *30*, 582–611. Trans. in *The experimental psychology of Alfred Binet, op. cit.*, pp. 93–126.

————. La perception de la durée dans les réactions simples. *Rev. phil.*, 1892, *33*, 650–659. Trans. in *The experimental psychology of Alfred Binet, op. cit.*, pp. 168–178.

————. *Alterations in personality.* Trans. by Helen G. Baldwin. New York: Appleton, 1896. (1892)

————. Mnemonic virtuosity: A study of chess players. (1893) Trans. by Marianne L. Simmel & S. E. Barron. *Genet. Psychol. Monogr.*, 1966, *74*, 127–162.

Charcot, J. M., & ————. Un calculateur du type visuel. *Rev. phil.*, 1893, *35*, 590–594.

———— (in collab. with P. Courtier & V. Henri). *Introduction à la psychologie expérimentale.* Paris: Alcan, 1894.

————, & Henneguy, L. *La psychologie des grands calculateurs et joueurs d'échecs.* Paris: Hachette, 1894.

————, & Henri, V. La mémoire des mots. *Année psychol.*, 1894, *1*, 1–23.

————, & Henri, V. La mémoire des phrases. *Année psychol.*, 1894, *1*, 24–59.

————. Reverse illusions of orientation. *Psychol. Rev.*, 1894, *1*, 337–350.

————, & Henri, V. Recherches sur le développement de la mémoire visuelle des enfants. *Rev. phil.*, 1894, *37*, 348–350. Trans. in *The experi-*

mental psychology of Alfred Binet, op. cit., pp. 127–129.

———, & Henri, V. De la suggestibilité naturelle chez les enfants. *Rev. phil.,* 1894, *38,* 337–347.

———. La peur chez les enfants. *Année psychol.,* 1895, *2,* 223–254. Trans. in *The experimental psychology of Alfred Binet, op. cit.,* pp. 179–194.

———, & Henri, V. La psychologie individuelle. *Année psychol.,* 1895, *2,* 411–465.

———. La mesure des illusions visuelles chez les enfants. *Rev. phil.,* 1895, *40,* 11–25. Trans. in *The experimental psychology of Alfred Binet, op. cit.,* pp. 130–144.

———. Psychologie individuelle: La description d'un objet. *Année psychol.,* 1896, *3,* 296–332.

———. Connais toi-même. *Rev. rev.,* 1896, *19,* 419–424.

———, & Vaschide, N. La psychologie à l'école primaire. *Année psychol.,* 1897, *4,* 1–14.

———, & Vaschide, N. Corrélation des épreuves physiques. *Année psychol.,* 1897, *4,* 142–172.

———. La mesure en psychologie individuelle. *Rev. phil.,* 1898, *46,* 113–123.

———, & Henri, V. *La fatigue intellectuelle.* Paris: Schleicher, 1898.

———. Attention et adaptation. *Année psychol.,* 1899, *6,* 248–404.

———. *La suggestibilité.* Paris: Schleicher, 1900.

———. Recherches sur la technique de la mensuration de la tête vivante. *Année psychol.,* 1900, *7,* 314–368.

———. Recherches de céphalométrie sur des enfants d'élite et arriérés des écoles primaires de Paris. *Année psychol.,* 1900, *7,* 412–429.

———. Influence de l'exercice et de la suggestion sur la position de seuil. *Année psychol.,* 1902, *9,* 235–245. Trans. in *The experimental psychology of Alfred Binet, op. cit.,* pp. 13–22.

———. Le seuil de la sensation double ne peut pas être fixé scientifiquement. *Année psychol.,* 1902, *9,* 247–252. Trans. in *The experimental psychology of Alfred Binet, op. cit.,* pp. 22–27.

———. La pensée sans images. *Rev. phil.,* 1903, *55,* 138–152. Trans. in *The experimental psychology of Alfred Binet, op. cit.,* pp. 207–221.

———. De la sensation à l'intelligence. *Rev. phil.,* 1903, *56,* 449–467, 592–618. Trans. in *The experimental psychology of Alfred Binet, op. cit.,* pp. 28–73.

———. *L'étude expérimentale de l'intelligence.* Paris: Schleicher, 1903. (Reprinted 1922)

———. La création littéraire ; portrait psychologique de M. Paul Hervieu. *Année psychol.,* 1904, *10,* 1–62.

———. Sommaire des travaux en cours à la société de psychologie de l'enfant. *Année psychol.,* 1904, *10,* 116–130.

———. La Commission ministérielle pour les anormaux. *Bull. Soc. lib. Étud. psychol. Enf.,* 1904, *18,* 506.

———. *The mind and the brain.* Trans. by F. Legge. London: Kegan Paul, 1907. (1905)

———. La science du témoignage. *Année psychol.,* 1905, *11,* 128–136.

———, & Simon, T. Sur la nécessité d'établir un diagnostic scientifique des états inférieurs de l'intelligence. *Année psychol.,* 1905, *11,* 163–190.

———, & Simon, T. Méthodes nouvelles pour le diagnostic du niveau intellectuel des anormaux. *Année phychol.,* 1905, *11,* 191–244.

———, & Simon, T. Application des méthodes nouvelles au diagnostic du niveau intellectuel chez des enfants normaux et anormaux d'hospice et d'école primaire. *Année psychol.,* 1905, *11,* 245–336.

———. *Les révélations de l'écriture d'après un contrôle scientifique.* Paris: Alcan, 1906.

———. Pour la philosophie de la conscience. *Année psychol.,* 1906, *12,* 113–136.

———, Vaney, M., & Simon, T. Recherches de pédagogie scientifique. *Année psychol.,* 1906, *12,* 233–274.

———, & Simon, T. *Les enfants anormaux: Guide pour l'admission des enfants anormaux dans les classes de perfectionnement.* Paris: Colin, 1907.

———, & Simon, T. *Mentally defective children.* Trans. by W. B. Drummond. New York: Longmans, Green, 1914. (1907)

———. Les nouvelles classes de perfectionnement. *Bull. Soc. Lib. Étud. psychol. Enf.*, 1907, *41*, 170–183.

———, & Simon, T. *The development of intelligence in children.* Trans. by Elizabeth S. Kite. Baltimore, Md.: Williams & Wilkins, 1916. (1908)

———. Une enquête sur l'évolution de l'enseignement philosophique. *Année psychol.*, 1908, *14*, 152–231.

———. Essai de chiromancie expérimentale. *Année psychol.*, 1908, *14*, 390–404.

———. Allocution du Président. *Bull. Soc. lib. Étud. psychol. Enf.*, 1908, *43*, 37–52.

———, & Simon, T. *The intelligence of the feebleminded.* Trans. by Elizabeth S. Kite. Baltimore, Md.: Williams & Wilkins, 1916. (1908, 1909)

———. *Les idées modernes sur les enfants.* Paris: Flammarion, 1909.

———. Le mystère de la peinture. *Année psychol.*, 1909, *15*, 300–315.

———, & Simon, T. Peut-on enseigner la parole aux sourds-muets? *Année psychol.*, 1909, *15*, 373–396.

———. Les signes physiques de l'intelligence chez les enfants. *Année psychol.*, 1910, *16*, 1–30.

———, & Binet, Alice. Rembrandt d'après un nouveau mode de critique d'art. *Année psychol.*, 1910, *16*, 31–50.

———, & Simon, T. Définitions des principaux états mentaux l'aliénation. I: L'hystérie. II: La folie avec conscience. III: La folie maniaque-dépressive. IV: La folie systématisée. V: Les démences. VI: L'arriération. VII: Conclusions. *Année psychol.*, 1910, *16*, 61–371.

———. Le diagnostic judiciaire par la méthode des associations. *Année psychol.*, 1910, *16*, 372–383.

———, & Simon, T. *A method of measuring the development of the intelligence of young children.* Trans. by Clara H. Town. Chicago: Medical Book, 1913. (1911)

———. Qu'est-ce qu'une émotion: Qu'est-ce qu'un acte intellectuel? *Année psychol.*, 1911, *17*, 1–47.

———. Nouvelles recherches sur la mesure du niveau intellectuel chez les enfants d'école. *Année psychol.*, 1911, *17*, 145–201.

———, & Simon, T. Réponse à quelques critiques. *Année psychol.*, 1911, *17*, 270–277.

———, & Simon, T. La confusion mentale. *Année psychol.*, 1911, *17*, 278–300.

———, & Simon, T. La législation des aliénés. *Année psychol.*, 1911, *17*, 351–362.

———, & Simon, T. Parallèle entre les classifications des aliénistes. *Année psychol.*, 1911, *17*, 363–388.

———, & Lorde, A. *Théâtre de la peur.* Paris: Librairie théâtrale, 1924.

Beck & Molish, *Reflexes;* Dember, *Perception;* Dennis, *Psychology;* Dennis, *Readings Developmental;* Hameline, *Anthologie;* Herrnstein & Boring, *Source Book;* Kessen, *Child;* Park & Burgess, *Sociology;* Rosenblith & Allinsmith, *Causes Behavior;* Sahakian, *Psychology;* Shor, *Hypnosis*

WALTER VAN DYKE BINGHAM
1880-1952
American Psychologist (23)

Bingham, W. V. D. Studies in melody. *Psychol. Monogr.*, 1909–1910, *12*, No. 50.

———. Psychology applied. *Sci. Mon.*, N.Y., 1923, *16*, 141–159.   **B**

———. On the possibility of an applied psychology. *Psychol. Rev.*, 1923, *30*, 289–305.

———, & Davis, W. T. Intelligence test scores and business success. *J. appl. Psychol.*, 1924, *8*, 1–22.

————, & Freyd, M. *Procedures in employment psychology: A manual for developing scientific methods of vocational selection.* Chicago: Shaw, 1926.

————, & Slocombe, C. S. Men who have accidents: Individual differences among motormen and bus operators. *Personnel J.,* 1927, *6,* 251–257.

————, Moore, B. V., & Gustad, J. W. *How to interview.* (4th rev. ed.) New York: Harper, 1959. (1931)

————. Psychology in industry. In E. M. East (Ed.), *Biology in human affairs.* New York: McGraw-Hill, 1931, pp. 123–162.

————. Classifying and testing for clerical jobs. *Personnel J.,* 1935, *14,* 163–172.

————. The future of industrial psychology. *J. consult. Psychol.,* 1937, *1,* 9–11.

————. *Aptitudes and aptitude testing.* New York: Harper, 1937.

————. Halo, invalid and valid. *J. appl. Psychol.,* 1939, *23,* 221–228.

————. Industrial psychology and government. *J. appl. Psychol.,* 1940, *24,* 1–9.

————, *et al.* Report of the committee on classification of Military Personnel Advisory to the Adjutant General's Office. *Science,* 1941, *93,* 572–574.

————. Psychological services in the United States Army. *J. consult. Psychol.,* 1941, *5,* 221–224.

————. Personnel classification testing in the Army. *Science,* 1944, *100,* 275–280.

————. Inequalities in adult capacity—from military data. *Science,* 1946, *104,* 147–152.

————. Military psychology in war and peace. *Science,* 1947, *106,* 155–160.

————. Psychologists in industry. *Amer. Psychologist,* 1948, *3,* 321–323.

————. Emotions in the factory. In M. L. Reymert (Ed.), *Feelings and emotions: The Moose-* *heart symposium.* New York: McGraw-Hill, 1950, pp. 495–501.

————. Expectancies. *Année psychol.,* 1951, *51,* 549–555.

————. Walter Van Dyke Bingham. In E. G. Boring *et al.* (Eds.), *A history of psychology in autobiography.* Vol. 4. Worcester, Mass.: Clark University Press, 1952, pp. 1–26. **B**

————. Psychology as a science, as a technology and as a profession. *Amer. Psychologist,* 1953, *8,* 115–118.

Moore & Hartmann, *Industrial Psychology*

LUDWIG BINSWANGER
1881-1966
Swiss Psychiatrist (19)

Binswanger, L. *Ausgewählte Vorträge und Aufsätze.* Vol. 1: *Zur phänomenologischen Anthropologie.* Vol. 2: *Zur Problematik der psychiatrischen Forschung und zum Problem der Psychiatrie.* Bern: Francke, 1947, 1955. (1942–1955) **C**

————. *Being-in-the-world: Selected papers.* Trans. with intro. by J. Needleman. New York: Basic Books, 1963. **C**

————. On the psychogalvanic phenomenon in association experiments. In C. G. Jung, *et. al., Studies in word-association: Experiments in diagnosis of psychopathological conditions carried out at the psychiatric clinic of the University of Zurich.* Trans. by M. D. Eder. New York: Moffat-Yard, 1919, pp. 446–530. (1918)

————. *Einführung in die Probleme der allgemeinen Psychologie.* Amsterdam: Bonset, 1965. (1922)

————. Zum Problem von Sprechen und Denken. *Schweiz. Arch. Neurol. Psychiat.,* 1926, *18,* 247–283.

————. *Wandlungen in der Auffassung und Deutung des Traumes. Von den Griechen bis zur Gegenwart.* Berlin: Springer-Verlag, 1928.

————. Dream and existence. (1930) Reprinted in *Being-in-the-world, op. cit.,* pp. 222–248.

————. *Ueber Ideenflucht.* Zurich: Füssli, 1933.

————. Freud's conception of man in the light of anthropology. (1936). Reprinted in *Being-in-the-world, op. cit.,* pp. 149–181.

————. Freud and the Magna Charta of clinical psychiatry. (1936) Reprinted in *Being-in-the-world, op. cit.,* pp. 182–205.

————. On the relationship between Husserl's phenomenology and psychological insight. *Phil. phenomenol. Res.,* 1941, *2,* 199–210.

————. *Grundformen und Erkenntnis menschlichen Daseins.* (4th ed.) Munich: Reinhardt, 1964. (1942)

————. The case of Ellen West: An anthropological-clinical study. Trans. by W. M. Mendel & J. Lyons. (1944) In R. May, E. Angel, & H. F. Ellenberger (Eds.), *Existence: A new dimension in psychiatry and psychology.* New York: Basic Books, 1958, pp. 237–364.

————. Insanity as life-historical phenomenon and as mental disease: The case of Ilse. Trans. by E. Angel. (1945) In R. May, E. Angel, & H. F. Ellenberger (Eds.), *Existence: A new dimension in psychiatry and psychology.* New York: Basic Books, 1958, pp. 214–236.

————. The existential analysis school of thought. Trans. by E. Angel. (1946) In R. May, E. Angel, & H. F. Ellenberger (Eds.), *Existence: A new dimension in psychiatry and psychology.* New York: Basic Books, 1958, pp. 191–213.

————. *Henrik Ibsen und das Problem der Selbstrealisation in der Kunst.* Heidelberg: Schneider, 1949.

————. Heidegger's analytic of existence and its meaning in psychiatry. (1949) Reprinted in *Being-in-the-world, op. cit.,* pp. 206–221.

————. The case of Lola Voss. (1949) Reprinted in *Being-in-the-world, op. cit.,* pp. 266–301.

————. Existential analysis and psychotherapy. (1954) In *Progress in psychotherapy.* Vol. 1. Ed. by Frieda Fromm-Reichmann & J. L. Moreno. New York: Grune & Stratton, 1956, pp. 144–148.

————. Zur Theorie und Praxis der Psychotherapie Schizophrener. *Z. psychosom. Med.,* 1955, *1,* 253–260.

————. *Sigmund Freud: Reminiscences of a friendship.* New York: Grune & Stratton, 1957. (1956) **B**

————. *Drei Formen missglückten Daseins: Verstiegenheit, Verschrobenheit, Manieriertheit.* Tübingen: Niemeyer, 1956.

————. Der Heilweg der analytischen Psychologie C. G. Jungs. *Heilw. Tiefenpsychol.,* 1956, 35–48.

————. *Der Mensch in der Psychiatrie.* Pfüllingen: Neske, 1957.

————. *Schizophrenie.* Pfüllingen: Neske, 1957.

————. Introduction to schizophrenia. (1957) Reprinted in *Being-in-the-world, op. cit.,* pp. 249–265.

————. Daseinsanalyse, Psychiatrie, Schizophrenie. *Schweiz. Arch. Neurol. Psychiat.,* 1958, *81,* 1–8.

————. *Melancholie und Manie.* Pfüllingen: Neske, 1960.

————. *Wahn. Beiträge zu seiner phänomenologischen und daseinsanalytischen Erforschung.* Pfüllingen: Neske, 1965.

Matson, *Being*; Sahakian, *Psychology*

CHARLES BIRD
1893-1957
American Psychologist (11)

Bird, C. The relative importance of maturation and habit in the development of an instinct. *J. genet. Psychol.,* 1925, *32,* 68–91.

————. The effect of maturation upon the pecking instinct of chicks. *J. genet. Psychol.,* 1926, *33,* 212–234.

————. The influence of the press upon the accuracy of report. *J. abnorm. soc. Psychol.,* 1927, *22,* 123–129.

————. An improved method for detecting cheating in objective examinations. *J. educ. Res.,* 1929, *19,* 341–348.

————. *Effective study habits*. New York: Century, 1931.

Berman, Isabel R., & ————. Sex differences in speed of reading. *J. appl. Psychol.*, 1933, *17*, 221–226.

————. Maturation and practice: Their effects upon the feeding reactions of chicks. *J. comp. Psychol.*, 1933, *16*, 343–366.

————, & Beers, F. S. Maximum and minimum inner speech in reading. *J. appl. Psychol.*, 1933, *17*, 182–187.

————, & Andrew, Dorothy M. Concerning the length of new-type examinations. *J. educ. Psychol.*, 1936, *27*, 641–654.

————. & Andrew, Dorothy M. The comparative validity of new-type questions. *J. educ. Psychol.*, 1937, *28*, 241–258.

Andrew, Dorothy M., & ————. A comparison of two new-type questions: Recall and recognition. *J. educ. Psychol.*, 1938, *29*, 175–193.

Andrew, Dorothy M., & ————. The stability of new-type questions. *J. educ. Psychol.*, 1938, *29*, 501–512.

————. *Social psychology*. New York: Appleton-Century, 1940.

————, & Bird, Dorothy M. *Learning more by effective study*. New York: Appleton-Century, 1945.

————, Monachesi, E. D., & Burdick, H. Infiltration and the attitudes of white and Negro parents and children. *J. abnorm. soc. Psychol.*, 1952, *47*, 688–699.

————, Monachesi, E. D., & Burdick, H. Studies of group tensions. II: The effect of parental discouragement of play activities upon the attitudes of white children toward Negroes. *Child Developmt.*, 1952, *23*, 295–306.

————, Monachesi, E. D., & Burdick, H. Studies of group tensions. III: Methods of validating a questionnaire concerning White-Negro relationships by means of voluntary statements. *Hum. Relat.*, 1953, *6*, 99–111.

————, & Monachesi, E. D. Prejudice and dis-

content. *J. abnorm. soc. Psychol.*, 1954, *49*, 29–35.

Hockbaum, G., Darley, J. G., Monachesi, E. D., & ————. Socioeconomic variables in a large city. *Amer. J. Sociol.*, 1955, *61*, 31–38.

(PAUL) EUGEN BLEULER
1857-1939
Swiss Psychiatrist (25)

Bleuler, E. Zur Auffassung der subcorticalen Aphasien. *Neurol. Zbl.*, 1882, *11*, 562–563.

————. *Der geborene Verbrecher*. Munich: Lehmann, 1896.

————. Affectivity, suggestibility, paranoia. Utica, N.Y.: State Hosp. Press, 1912. Also *State Hosp. Bull.*, 1912, *4*, 481–601. (1906)

————. *Affektivität, Suggestibilität, Paranoia*. (2nd ed.) Halle: Marhold, 1926.

————. Freud'sche Mechanismen in der Symptomatologie von Psychosen. *Psychiat. Neurol. Wochenschr.*, 1906, *8*, 323–324, 338–339.

————. Die Psychologie des Trinkers. *Int. Monatssch. Erforsch. Alkohol. bekämpf. Trinks.*, 1910, *20*, 393–400, 441–448.

————. Die Psychoanalyse Freuds. *Jb. Psychoanal. Psychopath. Forsch.*, 1910, *2*, 623–730.

————. *Dementia praecox or the group of schizophrenias*. Trans. by J. Zinkin. New York: International Universities Press, 1950. (1911) (Reprinted 1964)

————. Antwort auf die Bemerkungen Jungs zur Theorie des Negativismus. *Jb. Psychoanal. Psychopath. Forsch.*, 1912, *3*, 475–578.

————. *Die Psychoanalyse Freuds*. Leipzig: Deuticke, 1911.

————. The theory of schizophrenic negativism. Trans. by W. A. White. *J. nerv. ment. Dis.*, 1912, *39*, 50–57, 133–139, 195–202, 274–279.

————. Autistic thinking. *Amer. J. Insan.*, 1912–1913, *69*, 873–886.

————. Zur Theorie der Sekundärempfindungen. *Z. Psychol.*, 1913, *65*, 1–39.

———. *Textbook of psychiatry.* New York: Dover, 1951. (1916)   **Bl**

———. *Lehrbuch der Psychiatrie.* Ed. by M. Bleuler. (11th ed.) Berlin: Springer-Verlag, 1968. (1916)

———. Upon the significance of assocation experiments. In C. G. Jung, *Studies in word-association.* New York: Moffat-Yard, 1919, pp. 1–7. (1918)

———. Consciousness and association. In C. G. Jung, *Studies in word-association.* New York: Moffat-Yard, 1919, pp. 266–296. (1918)

———. *Autistic undisciplined thinking in medicine and how to overcome it.* Trans. by E. Harms. Darien, Conn.: Hafner, 1970. (1919)

———. Ueber unbewusstes psychisches Geschehen. *Z. Neurol.,* 1921, *64,* 122–135.

———. *Naturgeschichte der Seele und ihres Bewusstwerdens. Eine Elementarpsychologie.* Berlin: Springer-Verlag, 1921.

———. Biologische Psychologie. *Z. ges. Neurol. Psychiat.,* 1923, *83,* 554–585.

———. Die Lokalisation der Psyche. *Allg. Z. Psychiat.,* 1924, *80,* 305–311.

———. *Die Psychoide als Prinzip der organischen Entwicklung.* Berlin: Springer-Verlag, 1925.

———. Primäre und sekundäre Symptome der Schizophrenie. *Z. ges. Neurol. Psychiat.,* 1930, *124,* 601–646.

———. Psyche and psychoid. *Psychiat. Quart.,* 1930, *4,* 35–48.

———. Mechanismus - Vitalismus - Mnemismus. *Abh. Theor. Organ. Entwickl.,* 1931, No. 6.

———. Mnemismus, Psychoide. *Schweiz. Arch. Neurol. Psychiat.,* 1934, *33,* 177–191.

———. Bewusstheit und Unbewusstes. *Scientia,* 1938, *63,* 144–156.

———. Mnemistic biology and psychology. *J. nerv. ment. Dis.,* 1938, *87,* 169–201.

Rabkin & Carr, *Abnormal* ; Rapaport, *Thought* ; Sahakian, *Psychology* ; Shipley, *Classics*

MAGNUS (GUSTAV) BLIX
1849-1904
Swedish Physiologist (14)

Blix, M. *Oftalmetriska Studies.* Upsala: Berling, 1880.

———. Experimentelle Beiträge zur Lösung der Frage über die specifische Energie der Hautnerven. I, II. *Z. Biol.,* 1884, *20,* 141–156 ; 1885, *21,* 145–160. (1882)

———. Die Länge und die Spannung des Muskels. *Skand. Arch. Physiol.,* 1892, *3,* 295–318 ; 1893, *4,* 399–409 ; 1895, *5,* 150–172, 173–206.

———. Ueber gleichfarbige (isochromatische) Induktion. *Skand. Arch. Physiol.,* 1895, *5,* 13–19.

———. Studien über Muskelwärme. *Skand. Arch. Physiol.,* 1902, *12,* 52–128.

———. Neue Registrierapparate. *Arch. ges. Physiol.,* 1902, *90,* 405–420.

———. Ueber die sogenannte poggendorffsche optische Täuschung. *Skand. Arch. Physiol.,* 1902, *13,* 193–228.

———. Zur Frage über die menschliche Arbeitskraft. *Skand. Arch. Physiol.,* 1903, *15,* 122–146.

CHARLES BLONDEL
1876-1939
French Psychologist (11)

Blondel, C. *La conscience morbide.* (2nd ed.) Paris: Alcan, 1928. (1913)

———. *La psycho-physiologie de Gall, ses idées directrices.* Paris: Alcan, 1914.

———. Les volitions. In G. Dumas (Ed.), *Traité de psychologie.* Vol. 2. Paris: Alcan, 1924, pp. 333–425.

———. La personnalité. In G. Dumas (Ed.), *Traité de psychologie.* Vol. 2. Paris: Alcan, 1924, pp. 522–574.

———. *La psychanalyse.* Paris: Alcan, 1924.

———. Psychologie pathologique et sociologie. *J. Psychol. norm. path.,* 1925, *22,* 326–359.

──. *La mentalité primitive*. Paris: Stock, 1926.

──. The morbid mind. *Psyche*, 1926, (24), 73–86.

──. La psychologie selon Comte, Durkheim et Tarde. I: Le point de vue d'Auguste Comte. II: Le point de vue de Durkheim. III: Le point de vue de Tarde. *J. Psychol. norm. path.*, 1927, *24*, 381–399, 493–519, 591–609.

──. *The troubled conscience and the insane mind*. Intro. by E. G. Crookshank. London: Kegan Paul, Trench, & Trübner, 1928.

──. *Introduction à la psychologie collective*. Paris: Colin, 1928.

──. L'âme primitive d'après M. Lévy-Bruhl. *Rev. Métaphys. Morale*, 1928, *35*, 381–407.

──. La psychologie des sentiments de M. Pierre Janet. *Rev. Métaphys. Morale*, 1933, *40*, 511–536.

──. L'activité automatique et l'activité synthétique. In G. Dumas (Ed.), *Nouveau traité de psychologie*. Vol. 4. Paris: Alcan, 1934, pp. 341–385.

──. Les volitions. In G. Dumas (Ed.), *Nouveau traité de psychologie*. Vol. 6. Paris: Alcan, 1938, pp. 317–397.

──. La personnalité. In G. Dumas (Ed.), *Nouveau traité de psychologie*. Vol. 7. Book 1, Fasc. 3. Paris: Alcan, 1948, pp. 97–135.

Hameline, *Anthologie*

FRANZ BOAS
1858-1942
German-American Anthropologist (19)

Boas, F. *Race, language, and culture*. New York: Macmillan, 1940. (Reprinted 1966)   C

──. *Race and democratic society*. New York: Augustin, 1945.   C

──. Ueber eine neue Form des Gesetzes der Unterschiedsschwelle. *Arch. ges. Physiol.*, 1881, *26*, 493–500.

──. Ueber die Grundaufgabe der Psychophysik. *Arch. ges. Physiol.*, 1882, *28*, 566–576.

──. Ueber die verschiedenen Formen des Unterschiedsschwellenwerthes. *Arch. ges. Physiol.*, 1882, *27*, 214–222.

──. Ueber die Berechnung der Unterschiedsswellenwerthe nach der Methode der richtigen und falschen Fälle. *Arch. ges. Physiol.*, 1882, *28*, 84–94.

──. Die Bestimmung der Unterschiedsempfindlichkeit nach der Methode der übermerklichen Unterschiede. *Arch. ges. Physiol.*, 1882, *28*, 562–566.

──. Ueber den Unterschiedsschwellenwerth als ein Maas der Intensität psychischer Vorgänge. *Phil. Monat.*, 1882, *18*, 367–375.

──. The central Eskimo. In *U.S. Bureau of American ethnology. Sixth Annual Rep., 1884–1885*. Washington: 1888, 399–669. (Reprinted 1964)

──. Anthropological investigations in schools. *J. genet. Psychol.*, 1891, *1*, 225–228.

──. Growth. (1892–1939) In *Race, language, and culture, op. cit.*, pp. 103–130.

──. The limitations of the comparative method of anthropology. *Science*, 1896, *4*, 901–908. Reprinted in *Race, language, and culture, op. cit.*, pp. 270–280.

Farrand, L., & ──. Physical characteristics of the tribes of British Columbia. In twelfth and final report on the northwestern tribes of Canada. *Rep. Brit. Ass. Adv. Sci.*, 1898, 628–644.

──. The history of anthropology. *Science*, 1904, *20*, 513–524.

──. The measurement of variable quantities. *Arch. Psychol.*, N.Y., 1906, No. 5.

──. Psychological problems in anthropology. *Amer. J. Psychol.*, 1910, *21*, 371–384.

──. *The mind of primitive man*. (Rev. ed.) New York: Macmillan, 1938. (1911)

──. Introduction. In F. Boas (Ed.), *Handbook of American Indian languages*. Washington,

D.C.: Smithsonian Institution, 1911, pp. 1–83. Reprinted in part as Linguistics and ethnology in D. Hymes (Ed.), *Language in culture and society: A reader in linguistic and anthropology.* New York: Harper & Row, 1964, pp. 15–26.

———. The methods of ethnology. *Amer. Anthrop.,* 1920, *22,* 311–321. Reprinted in F. de Laguna (Ed.), *Selected papers from the American anthropologist, 1888–1920.* Evanston, Ill.: Row, Peterson, 1960, pp. 877–887 ; & in *Race, language, and culture, op. cit.,* pp. 281–289.

———. Evolution or diffusion. *Amer. Anthrop.,* 1924, *26,* 340–344. Reprinted in *Race, language, and culture, op. cit.,* pp. 290–304.

———. Anthropology and statistics. In W. F. Ogburn & A. Goldenweiser (Eds.), *The social sciences and their interrelations.* Boston: Houghton Mifflin, 1927, pp. 114–120.

———. *Primitive art.* Irvington-on-Hudson, N.Y.: Capital Publishing, 1951. (1927)

———. *Anthropology and modern life.* (Rev. ed.) New York: Norton, 1932. (1928)

———. Some problems of methodology in the social sciences. In L. D. White (Ed.), *The new social science.* Berkeley, Calif.: University of California Press, 1930, pp. 84–98. Reprinted in *Race, language, and culture, op. cit.,* pp. 260–264.

———. Race and progress. *Science,* 1931, *74,* 1–8. Reprinted in *Race, language, and culture, op. cit.,* pp. 3–17.

———. The aims of anthropological research. *Science,* 1932, *76,* 605–613. Reprinted in *Race, language, and culture, op. cit.,* pp. 243–259.

———. History and science in anthropology: A reply. *Amer. Anthrop.,* 1936, *38,* 137–141. Reprinted in *Race, language, and culture, op. cit.,* pp. 305–315.   **B**

——— (Ed.), *General anthropology.* Boston: Heath, 1938.

Count, *Race ;* Goldschmidt, *Mankind ;* Kroeber, *Source Book* ; Parsons, *Society ;* Thomas, *Source Book*

CHARLES BONNET
1720-1793
Swiss Biologist (20)

Bonnet, C. *Oeuvres d'histoire naturelle et de philosophie de Charles Bonnet.* (18 vols.) Neuchâtel: Fausche, 1779–1783.   **C**

———. *Mémoires autobiographiques.* Ed. by R. Savioz. Paris: Vrin, 1948.   **B C**

———. *Traité d'insectologie.* (2 vols.) Paris: Durand, 1745. (1743)

———. *Recherches sur l'usage des feuilles dans les plantes, et sur quelques autres sujets relatifs à l'histoire de la végétation.* Göttingen: Luzac, 1754.

———. *Essai de psychology, ou considérations sur les opérations de l'âme, sur l'habitude et sur l'éducation.* London: n.p., 1754. (Reprinted 1968)

———. *Essai analytique sur les facultés de l'âme.* (2nd ed.) (2 vols.) Copenhagen: Philibert, 1775. (1760) (Reprinted 1968)

———. *Considérations sur les corps organisés.* (3rd ed.) (2 vols.) Amsterdam: Rey, 1776. (1762)

———. *The contemplation of nature.* (2 vols.) London: Longmans, Becket & Hondt, 1766. (1764)

———. *Contemplation de la nature.* (2nd ed.) (2 vols.) Amsterdam: Rey, 1769. (1764) (Reprinted 1968)

———. *La palingénésie philosophique, ou idées sur l'état passé et sur l'état futur des êtres vivans.* (2 vols.) Geneva: Philibert & Chirol, 1770. (1769)

Bodenheimer, *Biology* ; Hall, *Source Book* ; Rand, *Classical Psychologists*

WILLIAM FREDERICK BOOK
1873-1940
American Psychologist (12)

Book, W. F. *The psychology of skill, with special reference to its acquisition in typewriting.* New York: Gregg, 1925. (1908)

———. The role of the teacher in the most expeditious and economic learning. *J. educ. Psychol.*, 1910, *1*, 183–199.

———. On the genesis and development of conscious attitudes (Bewustseinslagen). *Psychol. Rev.*, 1910, *17*, 381–398.

———. *Vocational education and the public schools.* Indianapolis, Ind.: Burford, 1913.

———. Variations in mental ability and its distribution among the school population of an Indiana county. *Bull. Exten. Div. Indiana Univer.*, 1918, *4*, No. 4, 100–140.

———. An efficient method for measuring the results of instruction in colleges and schools. *Bull. Exten. Div. Indiana Univer.*, 1921, *6*, No. 12.

———, & Norvell, L. The will to learn, an experimental study of incentives. *J. genet. Psychol.*, 1922, *29*, 305–362.

———. *The intelligence of high school seniors: As revealed by a state-wide mental survey.* New York: Macmillan, 1922.

———, Beard, A. S., & Chambers, O. R. Studies in observational learning. *Bull. Exten. Div. Indiana Univer.*, 1922, *7*, No. 12, 43–133.

———. *Learning to typewrite, with a discussion of the psychology and pedagogy of skill.* New York: Gregg, 1925.

———. *Learning how to study and work effectively: A contribution to the psychology of personal efficiency.* Boston: Ginn, 1926.

———. How to develop an interest in one's tasks and work. *J. educ. Psychol.*, 1927, *18*, 1–10.

———. *How to succeed in college.* Baltimore, Md.: Warwick & York, 1927.

———. Newer personnel practices in colleges. *Personnel J.*, 1928, *7*, 38–53

———, & Meadows, J. L. Sex differences in 5925 high school seniors in ten psychological tests. *J. appl. Psychol.*, 1928, *12*, 56–81.

———. How a special disability in spelling was diagnosed and corrected. *J. appl. Psychol.*, 1929, *13*, 378–393.

———, & Harter, R. S. Mistakes which pupils make in spelling. *J. educ. Res.*, 1929, *19*, 106–118.

———. The development of higher orders of perceptual habits in reading. *J. educ. Res.*, 1930, *21*, 161–176.

———. *Economy and technique of learning.* New York: Heath, 1932.

GEORGE BOOLE
1815-1864
Irish Mathematican (15)

Boole, C. *Collected logical works.* (2 vols.) La Salle, Ill.: Open Court, 1952. (1916)   C

———. *Studies in logic and probability.* Ed. by R. Rhees. London: Watts, 1952.   C

———. *The mathematical analysis of logic: Being an essay towards a calculus of deductive reasoning.* Oxford: Blackwell, 1951. (1847) Reprinted in *Collected logical works,* Vol. 1, *op. cit.*

———. *The claims of science, especially as founded in its relations to human nature. A lecture delivered in Queen's College, Cork, at the opening of the third session in Oct. 1851.* London: Taylor, Walton, & Mayberry, 1851.

———. *An investigation of the laws of thought on which are founded the mathematical theories of logic and probabilities.* New York: Dover, 1951. (1854) Reprinted in *Collected logical works,* Vol. 2, *op. cit.*

———. On the application of the theory of probabilities to the question of the combination of testimonies or judgments. *Trans. Roy. Soc. Edinb.*, 1857, *21*, 597–652.

———. *A treatise on differential equations.* (5th ed.) Rev. by I. Todhunter. New York: Chelsea, 1959. (1859)

———. *A treatise on the calculus of finite differences.* (3rd ed.) New York: Stechert, 1926. (1860) (Reprinted 1960)

———. On the theory of probabilities. *Proc. Roy. Soc.*, 1862–1863, *12*, 179–184. Reprinted in *Collected works,* Vol. 1, *op. cit.*, pp. 386–424.

Newman, *Mathematics*

BENJAMIN BIENAIME BOURDON
1860-1943
French Psychologist (13)

Bourdon, B. L'évolution phonétique du langage. *Rev. phil.,* 1888, *26,* 335–369.

———. Les résultats des théories contemporaines sur l'association des idées. *Rev. phil.,* 1891, *31,* 561–610.

———. *L'expression des émotions et des tendances dans le langage.* Paris: Alcan, 1892.

———. Recherches sur la succession des phénomènes psychologiques. *Rev. phil.,* 1893, *35,* 225–260.

———. La sensation de plaisir. *Rev. phil.,* 1893, *36,* 225–237.

———. Influence de l'âge sur la mémoire immédiate. *Rev. phil.,* 1894, *38,* 148–167.

———. Observations comparatives sur la reconnaissance, la discrimination et l'association. *Rev. phil.,* 1895, *40,* 153–185.

———. Recherches sur les phénomènes intellectuels. *Année psychol.,* 1895, *2,* 54–69.

———. Expériences sur la perception visuelle de la profondeur. *Rev. phil.,* 1897, *43,* 29–55.

———. L'application de la méthode graphique à l'étude de l'intensité de la voix. *Année psychol.,* 1897, *4,* 369–378.

———. Recherches sur l'habitude. *Année psychol.,* 1901, *8,* 327–340.

———. *La perception visuelle de l'espace.* Paris: Schleicher, 1902.

———. Contribution à l'étude de l'individualité dans les associations verbales. *Phil. Stud.,* 1902, *19,* 49–62.

———. Sur la distinction des sensations des deux yeux. *Année psychol.,* 1902, *9,* 41–56.

———. La perception de la verticalité de la tête et du corps. *Rev. phil.,* 1904, *57,* 462–492.

———, & Dide, M. Un cas d'amnésie continue. *Année psychol.,* 1904, *10,* 84–115.

———. L'état actuel de la question du sens musculaire. *Rev. scient.,* 1904, *2,* 97–100, 134–137.

———, & Dide, M. Etat de la sensibilité tactile dans 3 cas d'hémiplégie organique. *Année psychol.,* 1905, *11,* 40–68.

———. Influence de l'intensité lumineuse sur certaines phases de l'excitation rétinienne. *Bull. Soc. sci. méd. Ouest,* 1905, *14,* 83–90.

———. Influence de la force centrifuge sur la perception de la verticale. *Année psychol.,* 1906, *12,* 84–94.

———. L'effort. *Rev. phil.,* 1906, *61,* 1–14.

———. Sur le rôle de la tête dans la perception de l'espace. *Rev. phil.,* 1906, *61,* 526–529.

———. Recherches tachistoscopiques. *Année psychol.,* 1910, *16,* 51–60.

———. Recherches sur les sensations de rotation. *Bull. Soc. sci. méd. Ouest,* 1911, *20,* 72–117.

———. La perception des mouvements de nos membres. *Année psychol.,* 1912, *18,* 33–48.

———. La perception des grandeurs. *Rev. phil.,* 1912, *74,* 433–448.

———. Recherches sur la perception des mouvements rectilignes de tout le corps. *Année psychol.,* 1914, *20,* 1–16.

———. La doctrine dualiste. *Rev. phil.,* 1915, *80,* 1–20.

———. Recherches sur les perceptions spatiales auditives. *Année psychol.,* 1914–1919, *21,* 79–109.

———. Les sensations. In G. Dumas (Ed.), *Traité de psychologie.* Vol. 1. Paris: Alcan, 1923, pp. 318–401.

———. La perception. In G. Dumas (Ed.), *Traité de psychologie.* Vol. 2. Paris: Alcan, 1924, pp. 3–43.

———. Quelques expériences sur les perceptions spatiales auditives. *Année psychol.,* 1925, *26,* 72–78.

———. La perception et la pensée verbales. *J. Psychol. norm. path.,* 1925, *22,* 721–727.

———. *L'intelligence.* Paris: Alcan, 1926.

———. Benjamin Bourdon: Heredity, environment, and education. In C. Murchison (Ed.). *A history of psychology in autobiography.* Vol. 2. Worcester, Mass.: Clark University Press, 1932, pp. 1–16. **B**

———. Les sensations. In G. Dumas (Ed.), *Nouveau traité de psychologie.* Vol. 2. Paris: Alcan, 1932, pp. 83–218.

———. Sur la fonction des canaux semi-circulaires de l'oreille chez l'homme. *Bull. Soc. sci. Bretagne,* 1933, *10,* No. 1–2, 1–5.

———. Couleur et profondeur. *J. Psychol. norm. path.,* 1935, *32,* 673–686.

———. La perception. In G. Dumas (Ed.), *Nouveau traité de psychologie.* Vol. 5. Paris: Alcan, 1936, pp. 1–84.

———. Quelques expériences sur le mouvement visuel. In Various, *Centenaire de Th. Ribot et Jubilé de la Psychologie Scientifique Française.* Paris: Imprimerie moderne, 1939, pp. 287–298.

———. La théorie des sensations chez Descartes. *J. Psychol. norm. path.,* 1939, *36,* 321–343.

Hameline, *Anthologie*

HENRY PICKERING BOWDITCH
1840-1911
American Physiologist (12)

Bowditch, H. P. Ueber die Eigenthümlichkeiten der Reizbarkeit welche die Muskelfasern des Herzens zeigen. *Arb. Physiol.,* Leipzig, 1871, *6,* 139–176. Also in *Ber. Verh. kön. sächs. Ges. Wiss. Leipzig,* Math.-phys. Kl., 1871, *23,* 652–689.

———. The growth of children. *8th Ann. Rep. Mass. State Bd. Hlth.,* Boston, 1877, 275–325.

———. The growth of children: A supplementary investigation. *10th Ann. Rep. Mass. State Bd. Hlth.,* Boston, 1879, 33–62.

———, & Southard, W. F. A comparison of sight and touch. *J. Physiol.,* 1880–1882, *3,* 232–245.

———. The relation between growth and disease. *Trans. Amer. Med. Ass.,* 1881, *32,* 371–377.

———, & Hall, G. S. Optical illusions of motion. *J. Physiol.,* 1882, *3,* 297–307.

———. Note on the nature of nerve-force. *J. Physiol.,* 1885, *6,* 133–135.

———. The reinforcement and inhibition of the knee-jerk. *Boston med. surg. J.,* 1888, *98,* 542–546.

———. Ueber den Nachweis der Unermüdlichkeit der Säugethiernerven. *Arch. Physiol.,* 1890, 505–508.

———, & Warren, J. W. The knee-jerk and its physiological modifications. *J. Physiol.,* 1890, *11,* 25–64.

———. The growth of children studied by Galton's method of percentile grades, *22nd Ann. Rep. Mass. State Bd. Hlth.,* Boston, 1891, 479–522.

———. Physiology of vision. In W. H. Howell (Ed.), *An American textbook of physiology.* Philadelphia: Saunders, 1900–1901. (1896)

———. The medical school of the future. *Phila. med. J.,* 1900, *5,* 1011–1018.

Fulton & Wilson, *Physiology*

JAMES BRAID
1795?-1860
English Hypnotist (21)

Braid, J. *Satanic agency and mesmerism reviewed, in a letter to the Rev. H. Mc. Neile, A. M. of Liverpool, in reply to a sermon preached by him in St. Jude's Church, Liverpool, on Sunday, April 10th, 1842. Manchester.* Liverpool: Simms & Dinham, Galt & Anderson, & Willmer & Smith, 1842.

———. [Neurypnology, or the rationale of nervous sleep.] *Braid on hypnotism: The beginnings of modern hypnosis.* (Rev. ed.) Biographical & bibliographical intro. by A. E. Waite. New York: Julian Press, 1960. (1843) **B Bl**

———. Observations on mesmeric and hypnotic phenomena. *Med. Times,* 1844, *10,* 31–32, 47.

———. Ueber die Unterschiede des nervösen und des gewöhnlichen Schlafes. (1845) In W. T.

Preyer (Ed.), *Der Hypnotismus.* Vienna: Urban & Schwarzenberg, 1882, pp. 177–208.

———. Mr. Braid on hypnotism. *Lancet*, 1845, *1*, 627–628.

———. *The power of the mind over the body: An experimental inquiry into the nature and cause of the phenomena attributed by Baron Reichenbach and others to a "New imponderable."* London: Churchill, 1846.

———. *Observations on trance: Or, human hybernation.* London: Churchill, 1850.

———. Electro-biological phenomena, considered physiologically and psychologically. *Mon. J. Med. Sci.*, June 1851.

———. *Magic, witchcraft, animal magnetism, hypnotism and electrobiology: Being a digest of the latest views of the author on these subjects, embracing Observations on J. C. Colguhoun's History of magic, etc.* (3rd ed., greatly enlarged) London: Churchill, 1852.

———. *Hypnotic therapeutics illustrated by cases.* Edinburgh: Murray & Gibb, 1853.

———. *The physiology of fascination and the critics criticised.* Manchester: Grant, 1855.

———. *Observations of the nature and treatment of certain forms of paralysis.* London: Richards, 1855.

———. Ueber den Hypnotismus. (1860) In W. Preyer, *Die Entdeckung des Hypnotismus.* Berlin: Pätel, 1881, pp. 59–96.

Dennis, *Psychology*; Hunter & Macalpine, *Psychiatry*; Reeves, *Body Mind*; Tinterow, *Hypnosis*

FRANZ BRENTANO
1838-1917
German-Austrian Philosopher (27)

Brentano, F. *Untersuchungen zur Sinnespsychologie.* Leipzig: Duncker & Humblot, 1907.
                                                      C

———. *The true and the evident.* Ed. by R. M. Chisholm. New York: Humanities Press, 1966. (1930)   C

———. *Von der mannigfachen Bedeutung des Seienden nach Aristoteles.* Hildesheim: Olms, 1960. (1862)

———. *Die Psychologie des Aristoteles, insbesondere seine Lehre vom "Nous Poetikos."* Darmstadt: Wissenschaftliche Buchgesellschaft, 1967. (1867)

———. *Psychologie vom empirischen Standpunkte.* (2 vols.) Ed. by O. Kraus. Leipzig: Duncker & Humblot, 1924–1925. (1874) (Reprinted 1959)

———. *The origins of the knowledge of right and wrong.* Trans. by R. M. Chisholm & E. H. Schneewind, New York: Humanities Press, 1969. (1889)

———. *Vom Ursprung sittlicher Erkenntis.* (4th ed.) Ed. by O. Kraus. Hamburg: Meiner, 1955. (1889)

———. *Das Genie: Vortrag gehalten im Saale des Ingenieur- und Architektenvereins in Wien.* Leipzig: Duncker & Humblot, 1892.

———. Ueber ein optisches Paradoxon. *Z. Psychol.*, 1892, *3*, 349–358; 1893, *5*, 61–82.

———. *Ueber die Zukunft der Philosophie.* (2nd ed.) Ed. & intro. by O. Kraus. Leipzig: Meiner, 1929. (1893)

———. Zur Lehre von den optischen Täuschungen. *Z. Psychol.*, 1893, *6*, 1–7.

———. Ueber das phänomenale Grün. (1893) In *Untersuchungen, op. cit.,* pp. 3–49.

———. *Die vier Phasen der Philosophie und ihr augenblicklicher Stand.* (1894) Ed. & intro. by O. Kraus. Leipzig: Meiner, 1926.

———. Ueber Individuation, multiple Qualität und Intensität sinnlicher Erscheinungen. (1896) In *Untersuchungen, op. cit.,* pp. 53–98.

———. Von der psychologischen Analyse der Tonqualitäten in ihre eigentlichersten Elemente. (1966) In *Untersuchungen, op. cit.,* pp. 101–125.

———. *Aristoteles' Lehre vom Ursprung des menschlichen Geistes.* Leipzig: Veit, 1911.

———. *Von der Klassifikation der psychischen Phänomene.* Leipzig: Duncker & Humblot, 1911.

———. *Psychologie vom empirischen Standpunkt.* Vol. 2. *Von der Klassifikation der psychischen Phänomene, mit neuen Abhandlungen aus dem Nachlass.* Ed. by O. Kraus. Leipzig: Meiner, 1925. (1911)

———. *Aristoteles und seine Weltanschauung.* Leipzig: Quelle & Meyer, 1911.

———. *Zur Lehre vom Raum und Zeit. Kant-Stud.,* 1920, *24,* 1–23.

———. *Versuch über die Erkenntnis.* Ed. by A. Kastil. Leipzig: Weiner, 1925.

———. *Vom sinnlichen und poetischen Bewusst-sein.* Vol. III. *Psychologie.* Ed. by O. Kraus. Leipzig: Meiner, 1928.

———. *Vom Dasein Gottes.* Ed. by A. Kastil. Leipzig: Meiner, 1929.

———. *Wahrheit und Evidenz.* Ed. & intro. by O. Kraus. Leipzig: Meiner, 1930.

———. Briefe Franz Brentanos an Hugo Berg-mann. Ed. by H. Bergmann. *Phil. phenomenol. Res.,* 1946–1947, *7,* 83–158.   **B**

———. *Grundlegung und Aufbau der Ethik.* Ed. by Franziska Meyer-Hillebrand. Bern: Francke, 1952.

———. *Religion und Philosoph*ie. Ed. by Fran-ziska Meyer-Hillebrand. Bern: Francke, 1954.

———. *Die Lehre vom richtigen Urteil.* Ed. by Franziska Meyer-Hillebrand. Bern: Francke, 1956.

———. *Grundzüge der Aesthetik.* Ed. by Fran-ziska Meyer-Hillebrand. Bern: Francke, 1959.

———. *Geschichte der griechischen Philosophie.* Ed. by Franziska Meyer-Hillebrand. Bern: Francke, 1963.

Chisholm, *Realism* ; Herrnstein & Bor-ing, *Source Book* ; Sahakian, *Psychology*

———. *A history of psychology.* (3 vols.) Lon-don: Allen, 1912–1921. (Reprinted 1970)

———. *Brett's history of psychology.* (Abridged) Ed. by R. S. Peters. New York: Macmillan, 1953. (1912–1921)

———. *Government of man: An introduction to ethics and politics.* London: Bell, 1913.

———. The present status of psychological science in different countries: Canada. *Scand. Sci. Rev.,* 1924, *3,* 208–215.

———. Francis Joseph Gall and the state of medicine at the end of the 18th century. *Canad. med. Ass. J.,* 1927, *17,* 352–355.

———. *Psychology, ancient and modern.* In *Our debt to Greece and Rome* series. New York: Longmans, 1928. (Reprinted 1963)

———. Historical development of the theory of emotions. In M. L. Reymert (Ed.), *Feelings and emotions: The Wittenberg symposium.* Wor-cester, Mass.: Clark University Press, 1928, pp. 388–397.

———. History of psychology. In *Encyclopaedia Britannica.* Vol. 18. (14th ed.) New York: En-cyclopaedia Britannica, 1929, pp. 706–720.

———. Associationism and "Act" psychology: A historical retrospect. In C. Murchison (Ed.), *Psychologies of 1930.* Worcester, Mass.: Clark University Press, 1930, pp. 39–55.

———. Goethe's place in the history of science. *Univer. Toronto Quart.,* 1932, *1,* 279–299.

———. William James and the American ideals. *Univer. Toronto Quart.,* 1937, *6,* 159–173.

———. The psychology of William James in rela-tion to philosophy. In Various, *In commemora-tion of William James 1842–1942.* New York: Columbia University Press, 1942, pp. 81–94.

GEORGE SIDNEY BRETT
1879-1944
English-Canadian Psychologist (18)

Brett, G. S. *The philosophy of Gassendi.* London: Macmillan, 1908.

JOSEF BREUER
1842-1925
Austrian Psychoanalyst (23)

Breuer, J. *Studien über den Vestibularapparat.* Vienna: Gerold, 1904.   **C**

———. Die Selbststeuerung der Athmung durch den Nervus vagus. *Sitzber. kön. Akad. Wiss., Wien,* Math.-naturw. Kl., 1868, *58*(2), 909–937.

———. Ueber die Bogengänge des Labyrinths. *Allg. Wien med. Z.,* 1873, *18,* 598, 606.

———. Ueber die Function der Bogengänge des Ohrlabyrinthes. *Wien. med. Jb.,* 1874, *4,* 72–124.

———. Beiträge zur Lehre vom statischen Sinne (Gleichgewichtorgan, Vestibularapparat des Ohrlabyrinthes). *Wien. med. Jb.,* 1875, *5,* 87–156.

———. Neue Versuche an den Ohrbogengängen. *Arch. ges. Physiol.,* 1888–1889, *44,* 135–152.

———. Ueber die Function der Otolithen-Apparate. *Arch. ges. Physiol.,* 1809, *48,* 195–306.

———, & Freud, S. On the psychical mechanism of hysterical phenomena (1893). *Int. J. Psycho-Anal.,* 1956, *37,* 8–13. Reprinted in S. Freud, *Collected papers.* Vol. 1. Ed. by E. Jones & J. Strachey. New York: Basic Books, 1959, pp. 24–41.

———, & Freud, S. *Studies on hysteria.* Trans. by J. Strachey. New York: Basic Books, 1957. (1895)

———. Ueber Bogengänge und Raumsinn. *Arch. Anat. Physiol., Physiol. Abt.,* 1897, *68,* 29–111, 596–648.

———, & Kreidl, A. Ueber die scheinbare Drehung des Gesichtsfeldes während der Einwirkung einer Centrifugalkraft. *Arch. ges. Physiol.,* 1898, *70,* 494–510.

———. Bemerkungen zu Dr. H. Abels Abhandlung, "Ueber Nachempfindungen im Gebiete des kinästhetische und statischen Sinnes." *Z. Psychol.,* 1907, *45,* 78–84.

———. Ueber das Gehörorgan der Vögel. *Sitzber. kais. Akad. Wiss. Wien,* Math.-naturw. Kl., 1907, *116,* Pt. 3, 249–292.

———. Ueber Ewalds Versuch mit dem "pneumatischen Hammer" (Bogengangapparat). *Z. Sinnesphysiol.,* 1908, *42,* 373–378.

———, & Freud, S. On the theory of hysterical attacks. (1940) Reprinted in S. Freud, *Collected papers.* Vol. 5. Ed. by E. Jones & J. Strachey. New York: Basic Books, 1959, pp. 27–30.

———. Autobiography. Ed. & trans. by C. P. Oberdorf. *Int. J. Psycho-Anal.,* 1953, *34,* 64–67.
B

Shipley, *Classics* ; Vetter, *Personality*

PERCY WILLIAMS BRIDGMAN
1882-1961
American Physicist (24)

Bridgman, P. W. *Collected experimental papers of P. W. Bridgman.* (7 vols.) Cambridge: Harvard University Press, 1964.   **C**

———. The technique of high pressure experimenting. *Amer. Acad. Arts Sci. Proc.,* 1914, *49,* 627–643.

———. The electrical resistance of metals under pressure. *Amer. Acad. Arts Sci. Proc.,* 1917, *52,* 571–646.

———. *Dimensional analysis.* (Rev. ed.) New Haven: Yale University Press, 1931. (1922)

———. *The logic of modern physics.* New York: Macmillan, 1927.

———. On the nature and the limitations of cosmical inquiries. *Sci. Mon.,* N.Y., 1933, *37,* 385–397.

———. *The nature of physical theory.* Princeton, N.J.: Princeton University Press, 1936. (Reprinted 1964)

———. Operational analysis. *Phil. Sci.,* 1938, *5,* 114–131.

———. Science: Public or private? *Phil. Sci.,* 1940, *7,* 36–48.

———. Some general principles of operational analysis. *Psychol. Rev.,* 1945, *52,* 246–249.

———. Rejoinders and second thoughts. *Psychol. Rev.,* 1945, *52,* 281–284.

———. The potential intelligent society of the future. In F. S. C. Northrop (Ed.), *Ideological differences and world order.* New Haven: Yale University Press, 1949, pp. 229–249.

———. The operational aspect of meaning. *Synthèse,* 1950–1951, *8,* 251–259.

—. *Reflections of a physicist.* New York: Philosophical Library, 1950.   **B**

—. The nature of some of our physical concepts. *Brit. J. Phil. Sci.,* 1951, *1,* 257–272; *2,* 25–44, 142–160.

—. Remarks on the present state of operationalism. *Sci. Mon.,* N.Y., 1954, *79,* 224–226.

—. Science and common sense. *Sci. Mon.,* N.Y., 1954, *79,* 32–39.

—. Probability, logic and ESP. *Science,* 1956, *123,* 15–17.

—. Determinism in modern science. (1958) In S. Hook (Ed.), *Determinism and freedom in the age of modern science.* New York: Collier, 1961, pp. 57–75.

—. *The way things are.* Cambridge: Harvard University Press, 1959.

—. Some comments on dimensions of mind. (1960) In S. Hook (Ed.), *Dimensions of mind.* New York: Collier, 1961, pp. 90–92.

—. Significance of the Mach principle. *Amer. J. Physics,* 1961, *29,* 32–36.

Mueller, *American Philosophy;* Strain, *Philosophies Education*

ABRAHAM ARDEN BRILL
1874-1948
American Psychoanalyst (18)

Brill, A. A. *Psychoanalysis: Its theories and practical application.* (3rd ed.) Philadelphia: Saunders, 1922. (1912)   **C**

—. Psychological factors in dementia praecox: An analysis. *J. abnorm. Psychol.,* 1908, *3,* 219–239.

—. A contribution to the psychopathology of everyday life. *Psychotherapy,* 1909, *2*(9), 5–21.

—. Psychoanalytic fragments from a day's work. *J. abnorm. Psychol.,* 1913–1914, *8,* 310–321.

—. *Fundamental conceptions of psychoanalysis.* New York: Harcourt, Brace, 1921.

—. The application of psychoanalysis to psychiatry. *J. nerv. ment. Dis.,* 1928, *68,* 561–577.

—. Unconscious insight: Some of its manifestations. *Int. J. Psycho-Anal.,* 1929, *10,* 145–161.

—. Introduction. In S. Freud, *The basic writings of Sigmund Freud.* Ed. by A. A. Brill. New York: Random House, 1938, pp. 3–32.   **B**

—. The introduction and development of Freud's work in the United States. *Amer. J. Sociol.,* 1939–1940, *45,* 318–325.

—. A psychoanalyst scans his past. *J. nerv. ment. Dis.,* 1942, *95,* 537–549.   **B**

—. The Freudian epoch. In Various, *The march of medicine.* New York: Columbia University Press, 1943, pp. 68–99.

—. *Freud's contribution to psychiatry.* New York: Norton, 1944. (Reprinted 1962)   **B**

—. Psychoanalytic fragments. *Psychoanal. Rev.,* 1944, *31,* 121–127.

—. *Lectures on psychoanalytic psychiatry.* New York: Knopf, 1946. (Reprinted 1955)

PAUL BROCA
1824-1880
French Neurologist (24)

Broca, P. *Mémoires sur le cerveau de l'homme et des primates.* Paris: Reinwald, 1888.   **C**

—. *Mémoires d'anthropologie.* (5 vols.) Paris: Reinwald, 1871–1888.   **C**

—. *Correspondance de Paul Broca (1841–1857).* (2 vols.) Paris: Schmidt, 1886.   **B C**

—. *Propriétés et fonctions de la moëlle épinière; Rapport sur quelques expériences de M. Brown-Séquard.* Paris: Baillière, 1856. (1855)

—. *Sur le siège de la faculté du langage articulé, avec deux observations d'aphémie (perte de la parole).* Paris: Masson, 1861.

———. Sur le volume et la forme du cerveau suivant les individus et suivant les races. *Bull. Soc. anthrop.,* Paris, 1861, *2,* 139–204.

———. Perte de la parole, ramollissement chronique et destruction partielle du lobe antérieur gauche du cerveau. *Bull. Soc. anthrop.,* Paris, 1861, *2,* 235–238. Trans. in *J. Neurosurg.,* 1964, *21,* 424–431, & in R. H. Wilkins (Ed.), *Neurosurgical classics.* New York: Johnson Reprint, 1965, pp. 63–64.

———. Remarques sur le siège de la faculté du langage articulé, suivies d'une observation d'aphémie (perte de la parole). *Bull. Soc. anat.,* 1861, *6,* 330–357. Trans. by G. von Bonin in *Some papers on the cerebral cortex.* Springfield, Ill.: Thomas, 1960, pp. 49–72.

———. Nouvelle observation d'aphémie produite par une lésion de la moitié postérieure des deuxième et troisième circonvolutions frontales gauches. *Bull. Soc. anat.,* 1861, *6,* 398–407. Trans. in R. H. Wilkins (Ed.), *Neurosurgical classics.* New York: Johnson Reprint, 1965, pp. 64–68.

———. La linguistique et l'anthropologie. *Bull. Soc. anthrop.,* Paris, *3,* 264–319.

———. Localisation des fonctions cérébrales. Siège de la faculté du langage articulé. *Bull. Soc. anthrop.,* Paris, 1863, *4,* 200–208.

———. Remarques sur le siège, le diagnostic et la nature de l'aphémie. *Bull. Soc. anat.,* 1863, *8* (2nd ser.), 379–385, 393–399.

———. Review of the proceedings of the anthropological society of Paris. *Anthrop. Rev.,* London, 1863, *1,* 274–310.

———. *Instructions générales de la Société d'anthropologie de Paris pour les recherches anthropologiques à faire sur le vivant.* (2nd ed.) Paris: Masson, 1879. (1865)

———. L'intelligence des animaux et le règne humain. *Bull. Soc. anthrop.,* Paris, 1865, *6,* 656–670 ; 1866, *1* (2nd ser.), 53–79.

———. Sur la faculté générale du langage, dans ses rapports avec la faculté du langage articulé. *Bull. Soc. anthrop.,* Paris, 1865, *1* (2nd ser.), 377–382.

Bonamy, C., ———, & Beau, E. *Atlas d'anatomie descriptive du corps humain.* (4 vols.) Paris: Masson, 1866.

———. The progress of anthropology in Europe and America. *J. Anthrop. Inst.,* N.Y., 1871, *1,* 24–40.

———. *Instructions craniologiques et craniométriques de la Société d'anthropologie de Paris.* Paris: Masson, 1875.

———. *Sur la topographie cranio-cérébrale.* Paris: Leroux, 1876.

———. *Sur la trépanation du crâne et les amulettes crâniennes à l'époque néolithique.* Paris: Leroux, 1877.

———. *De la différence fonctionnelle des deux hémisphères cérébraux.* Paris: Masson, 1877.

———. *Sur l'angle orbito-occipital.* Paris: Leroux, 1877.

———. Recherches sur les centres olfactifs. *Rev. anthrop.,* 1879, *2,* 385–455.

———. *Etude des variations craniométriques.* Paris: Hennuyer, 1880.

Clarke & O'Malley, *Brain* ; Count, *Race* ; Herrnstein & Boring, *Source Book* ; Sahakian, *Psychology*

AUGUSTA FOX BRONNER (HEALY)
1881-1966
American Psychologist (11)

Bronner, Augusta F. A comparative study of the intelligence of delinquent girls. *Teach. Coll., Contr. Educ.,* 1914, No. 68.

Healy, W., & ———. An outline for institutional education and treatment of young offenders. *J. educ. Psychol.,* 1915, *6,* 301–316.

———. Attitude as it affects performance on tests. *Psychol. Rev.,* 1916, *23,* 303–331.

Healy, W., & ———. Youthful offenders: A comparative study of two groups, each of 1,000 recidivists. *Amer. J. Sociol.*, 1916–1917, *22*, 38–52.

————. *The psychology of special abilities and disabilities.* Boston: Little, Brown, 1917.

————. Apperceptive abilities. *Psychol. Rev.*, 1921, *28*, 270–279.

Healy, W., & ————. *Delinquents and criminals: Their making and unmaking. Studies of two American cities.* New York: Macmillan, 1926.

————, Healy, W., Lowe, Gladys W., & Shimberg, Myra E. *A manual of individual mental tests and testing.* Boston: Little, Brown, 1927.

Healy, W., ————, Baylor, M. H., & Murphy, J. P. *Reconstructing behavior in youth: A study of problem children in foster families.* New York: Knopf, 1929.

Healy, W., ————, & Bowers, Anna M. *The structure and meaning of psychoanalysis, as related to personality and behavior.* New York: Knopf, 1930.

————. Psychiatric concepts of the early Greek philosophers. *Amer. J. Orthopsychiat.*, 1932, *2*, 103–113.

Healy, W., & ————. *New light on delinquency and its treatment.* New Haven: Yale University Press, 1936.

Healy, W., & ————. *Treatment and what happened afterward.* Boston: Judge Baker Guidance Center, 1939.

————. Treatment and what happened afterward. (A second report.) *Amer. J. Orthopsychiat.*, 1944, *14*, 28–36.

Healy, W., & ————. The child guidance clinic: Birth and growth of an idea. In G. Lowrey (Ed.), *Orthopsychiatry: 1923–1948: Retrospect and prospect.* New York: American Orthopsychiatric Association, 1948, pp. 14–49.   **B**

————. Behavior clinics. In V. C. Branham & S. B. Kutash (Eds.), *Encyclopedia of criminology.* New York: Philosophical Library, 1949, pp. 30–39.

Healy, W., & ————. Orthopsychiatry: An overview. *Amer. J. Orthopsychiat.*, 1955, *25*, 472–474.

THOMAS BROWN
1778-1820
Scottish Philosopher (22)

Brown, T. *Observations on the Zoonomia of Erasmus Darwin.* Edinburgh: Mundell, 1798.

————. *Inquiry into the relation of cause and effect.* (Formerly, *Observations on the nature and tendency of the doctrine of Mr. Hume concerning the relation of cause and effect.*) (4th ed.) London: Bohn, 1835. (1804) (Reprinted 1971)

————. *Lectures on the philosophy of the human mind.* Memoir by D. Welsh. (20th ed.) London: Tegg, 1860. (1820)   **Bl**

Dember, *Perception* ; Dennis, *Psychology* ; Herrnstein & Boring, *Source Book* ; Murphy, *Western* ; Rand, *Classical Psychologists* ; Sahakian, *Psychology*

WARNER BROWN
1882-1956
American Psychologist (11)

Brown, W. Time in English verse rhythm. *Arch. Psychol.*, N.Y., 1908, No. 10.

————. The judgment of difference with special reference to the doctrine of the threshold in the case of lifted weights. *Univ. Calif. Publ. Psychol.*, 1910, *1*, 1–71.

————. Temporal and accentual rhythm. *Psychol. Rev.*, 1911, *18*, 336–346.

————. The judgment of very weak sensory stimuli, with special reference to the absolute threshold of sensation for common salt. *Univ. Calif. Publ. Psychol.*, 1914, *1*, 199–268.

————. Habit interference in card sorting. *Univ. Calif. Publ. Psychol.*, 1914, *1*, 269–321.

————. Practice in associating number-names with number systems. *Psychol. Rev.*, 1915, *22*, 77–80.

————. Incidental memory in a group of persons. *Psychol. Rev.*, 1915, *22*, 81–85.

————. Practice in associating color-names with colors. *Psychol. Rev.*, 1915, *22*, 45–55.

———. Practice in grading and identifying shades of gray. *Psychol. Rev.*, 1915, *22*, 519–526.

———. To what extent is memory measured by a single recall? *J. exp. Psychol.*, 1923, *6*, 377–382.

———, & Whitell, F. Yerkes' multiple choice method with human adults. *J. comp. Psychol.*, 1923, *3*, 305–326.

Wong, H., & ———. Effects of surroundings upon mental work as measured by Yerkes' multiple choice method. *J. comp. Psychol.*, 1923, *3*, 319–326.

———. Whole and part methods in learning. *J. educ. Psychol.*, 1924, *15*, 229–233.

———. Effects of interval on recall. *J. exp. Psychol.*, 1924, *7*, 469–474.

———. Auditory and visual cues in maze learning. *Univ. Calif. Publ. Psychol.*, 1932, *5*(6), 115–122.

———. Spatial integrations in a human maze. *Univ. Calif. Publ. Psychol.*, 1932, *5*(6), 123–134.

———. Growth of memory images. *Amer. J. Psychol.*, 1935, *47*, 90–102.

———. Reorientation in a multiple path maze. *Univ. Calif. Publ. Psychol.*, 1937, *5*(7), 135–160.

———, & Gilhousen, H. C. *College psychology.* New York: Prentice-Hall, 1950. (Reprinted 1970)

WILLIAM BROWN
1881-1952
English Psychologist (11)

Brown, W. Some experimental results in the correlation of mental abilities. *Brit. J. Psychol.*, 1909–1910, *3*, 296–322.

———. An objective study of mathematical intelligence. *Biometrika*, 1910, *7*, 352–367.

———, & Thomson, G. H. *The essentials of mental measurement.* (4th ed.) New York: Macmillan, 1940. (1911)

———. The effects of 'observational errors' and other factors upon correlation coefficients in psychology. *Brit. J. Psychol.*, 1913–1914, *6*, 223–238.

———. *Psychology and psychotherapy.* (5th ed.) London: Arnold, 1944. (1921)

———. *Suggestion and mental analysis: An outline of the theory and practice of mind cure.* New York: Doran, 1922.

———. *Mind and personality: An essay in psychology and philosophy.* New York: Putnam, 1927.

———. *Science and personality.* New Haven: Yale University Press, 1929.

———. The mathematical and experimental evidence for the existence of a central intellective factor (g). *Brit. J. Psychol.*, 1932–1933, *23*, 171–179.

———, & Stephenson, W. A test of the theory of two factors. *Brit. J. Psychol.*, 1932–1933, *23*, 352–370.

———, & Stephenson, W. Professor Godfrey Thomson's note. *Brit. J. Psychol.*, 1933–1934, *24*, 209–212.

———. *Psychological methods of healing: An introduction to psychotherapy.* London: University of London Press, 1938.

———. *War and the psychological conditions of peace.* (2nd ed.) London: Black, 1942. (1939)

———. The psychology of modern Germany. *Brit. J. Psychol.*, 1944, *34*, 43–59.

———. *Personality and religion.* London: University of London Press, 1946.

Drever, *Sourcebook*

CHARLES EDOUARD BROWN-SÉQUARD
1817?-1894
French Physiologist (14)

Brown-Séquard, C. E. *Notice sur les travaux scientifiques.* Paris: Masson, 1878.   **B Bl C**

———. Correspondance avec d'Arsonval. In L. Delhoume (Ed.), *De Claude Bernard à d'Arsonval.* Paris: Baillière, 1939.   **B C**

———. *Recherches et expériences sur la physiologie de la moëlle épinière.* Paris: Rignoux, 1846.

———. De la transmission des impressions sensitives par la moëlle épinière. *C. r. Soc. Biol. Paris,* 1849, *1,* 192–194.

———. De la transmission croisée des impressions sensitives par la moëlle épinière. *C. r. Soc. Biol. Paris,* 1851, *2,* 33–34.

———. Experimental researches applied to physiology and pathology. *Med. Exam.,* Phila., 1852, *8,* 481–504.

———. *Experimental researches applied to physiology and pathology.* New York: Baillière, 1853.

———. *Recherches expérimentales sur la transmission croisée des impressions dans la moëlle épinière.* Paris: Masson, 1855.

———. *Experimental and clinical researches on the physiology and pathology of the spinal cord and other parts of the nervous centers.* Richmond, Va.: Colin, 1855.

———. *Recherches expérimentales sur la physiologie des capsules surrénales.* Paris: Rignoux, 1856.

———. *Researches on epilepsy: Its artificial production in animals, and its etiology, nature and treatment in man.* Boston: Clapp, 1857.

———. *Course of lectures on the physiology and pathology of the central nervous system.* Philadelphia: Collins, 1860.

———. Recherches sur la transmission des impressions de tact, de chatouillement, de douleur, de température et de contraction (sens musculaire) dans la moëlle épinière. *J. physiol.,* 1863, *6,* 124–145, 232–248, 581–646.

———. *Lectures on the diagnosis and treatment of functional nervous affections.* Philadelphia: Lippincott, 1868.

———. Nouvelles recherches sur l'épilepsie due à certaines lésions de la moëlle épinière et des nerfs rachidiens. *Arch. physiol.,* 1869, *2,* 211–220, 422–441, 496–503.

———. *Leçons sur les nerfs vasomoteurs, l'épilepsie et sur les actions réflexes normales et morbides.* Paris: Masson, 1872.

———. Introduction à une série de mémoires sur la physiologie et pathologie des diverses parties de l'encéphale. *Arch. physiol.,* 1877, *4,* 409–423, 655–694.

———. Dual character of the brain. *Smithsonian Miscell, Coll.,* 1878, *15,* Art. 3.

———. *Doctrines relatives aux principales actions des centres nerveux.* Paris: Masson, 1879.

———. Faits nouveaux relatifs à la mise en jeu ou à l'arrêt des propriétés motrices ou sensitives de diverses parties du centre cérébrorachidien. *Arch. physiol.,* 1879, *6,* 494–499.

———. Recherches cliniques et expérimentales sur les entrecroisements des conducteurs servant aux mouvements volontaires. *Arch. physiol.,* 1889, *1,* 5th ser., 219–245.

———. Recherches sur la localisation des conducteurs des impressions sensitives dans les diverses parties de l'encéphale, et sur la pathogénie des anesthésies du centre encéphalique. *Arch. physiol.,* 1889, *1,* 5th ser., 484–498.

———. Expérience démontrant la puissance dynamogénique chez l'homme d'un liquide extrait de testicules d'animaux. *Arch. physiol.,* 1889, *1,* 5th ser., 651–658.

———. De quelques règles générales relatives à l'inhibition. *Arch. physiol.,* 1889, *1,* 5th ser., 751–761.

———. Localisation prétendue de fonctions diverses dans les centres nerveux et surtout dans certaines parties des organes auditifs. *Arch. physiol.,* 1892, *4,* 5th ser., 366–368.

———. Le sommeil normal, comme le sommeil hypnotique, est le résultat d'une inhibition de l'activité intellectuelle. *Arch. physiol.,* 1899, *1,* 6th ser., 333–335.

Clark & O'Malley, *Brain*; Fulton & Wilson, *Physiology*

ERNST WILHELM VON BRUCKE
1819-1892
German-Austrian Physiologist (20)

Brücke, E. W. V. Ueber die stereoscopischen Erscheinungen und Wheatstones Angriff auf die Lehre von den identischen Stellen der Netzhäute. *Arch. Anat. Physiol. wiss. Med.,* 1841, 459–476.

————. Ueber die physiologische Bedeutung der stabförmigen Körper und der Zwillingszapfen in den Augen der Wirbelthiere. *Arch. Anat. Physiol. wiss. Med.,* 1844, 444–451.

————. Anatomische Untersuchungen über die sogenannten leuchtenden Augen bei den Wirbelthieren. *Arch. Anat. Physiol. wiss. Med.,* 1845, 387–406.

————. Ueber den Musculus Cramptonianus und den Spannmuskel der Choroidea. *Arch. Anat. Physiol. wiss. Med.,* 1846, 370–378.

————. *Anatomische Beschreibung des menschlichen Augapfels.* Berlin: Reimer, 1847.

————. Ueber das Leuchten der menschlichen Augen. *Arch. Anat. Physiol. wiss. Med.,* 1847, 225–227.

————. Untersuchungen über subjective Farben. *Denkschr. Akad. Wiss. Wien,* Math.-naturw. Kl., 1852, *3,* 95–108.

————. *Grundzüge der Physiologie und Systematik der Sprachlaute für Linguisten und Taubstummenlehrer.* (2nd ed.) Vienna: Gerold, 1876. (1856)

————. Beiträge zur Lehre von der Verdauung. *Sitzber. Akad. Wiss. Wien,* Math.-naturw. Kl., 1861, *43*(2), 601–623.

————. Ueber Ergänzungsfarben und Contrastfarben. *Sitzber. Akad. Wiss. Wien,* Math.-naturw. Kl., 1865, *51*(2), 461–501.

————. *Die Physiologie der Farben für die Zwecke der Kunstgewerbe.* (2nd ed.) Leipzig: Hirzel, 1887, (1866)

————. *Die physiologischen Grundlagen der neuhochdeutschen Verskunst.* Vienna: Gerold, 1871.

————. *Vorlesungen über Physiologie.* (5th ed.) (2 vols. in 1) *Physiologie der Nerven und der Sinnesorgane und Entwickelungsgeschichte.* Vienna: Braumüller, 1885–1887. (1873–1874)

————. *Bruchstücke aus der Theorie der bildenden Künste.* Leipzig: Internationale wissenschaftliche Bibliothek, 1877.

————. Ueber willkürliche und krampfhafte Bewegungen. *Sitzber. Akad. Wiss. Wien,* Math.-naturw. Kl., 1877, *76*(3), 237–279.

————. *Principes scientifiques des beaux-arts.* Paris: Baillière, 1878.

————. Ueber einige Empfindungen im Gebiete der Sehnerven. *Sitzber. Akad. Wiss. Wien,* Math.-naturw. Kl., 1878, *77*(3), 39–71.

————. Ueber einige Consequenzen der Young-Helmholtz'schen Theorie. *Sitzber. Akad. Wiss. Wien,* Math.-naturw. Kl., 1879, *80*(3), 18–72; 1881, *84*(3), 425–458.

————. *Schönheit und Fehler der menschlichen Gestalt.* (2nd ed.) Vienna: Braumüller, 1893. (1891)

LEON BRUNSCHVICG
1869-1944
French Philosopher (11)

Brunschvicg, L. *Le génie de Pascal.* Paris: Hachette, 1932. (1924) **B C**

————. *Ecrits philosophiques.* (3 vols.) Paris: Presses Universitaires de France, 1951–1958. **C**

————. *La modalité du jugement.* (2nd ed.) Paris: Alcan, 1934. (1897)

————. *Spinoza et ses contemporains.* (3rd ed.) Paris: Alcan, 1923. (1905)

————. *Introduction à la vie de l'esprit.* (3rd ed.) Paris: Alcan, 1920. (1905)

————. *Les étapes de la philosophie mathématique.* (3rd ed.) Paris: Alcan, 1929. (1912)

————. *L'expérience humaine et la causalité physique.* (3rd ed.) Paris: Presses Universitaires de France, 1949. (1922)

———. *Le progrès de la conscience dans la philosophie occidentale.* (2nd ed.) (3 vols.) Paris: Presses Universitaires de France, 1953. (1927)

———. *De la connaissance de soi.* Paris: Alcan, 1931.

———. *Blaise Pascal.* Paris: Vrin, 1953. (1932)

———. *Les âges de l'intelligence.* Paris: Alcan, 1934.

———. *René Descartes.* Paris: Rieder, 1937.

———. *La raison et la religion.* Paris: Alcan, 1939.

———. *Descartes et Pascal: Lecteurs de Montaigne.* Paris: Brentano, 1944.

———. *Héritage de mots, héritage d'idées.* (2nd ed.) Paris: Presses Universitaires de France, 1950. (1945)

EGON BRUNSWIK
1903-1955
Austrian-American Psychologist (26)

Brunswik, E. Zur Entwicklung der Albedowahrnehmung. *Z. Psychol.,* 1929, *109,* 40–115.

———, & Kardos, L. Das Duplizitätsprinzip in der Theorie der Farbenwahrnehmung. *Z. Psychol.,* 1929, *111,* 307–320.

———, & Kindermann, H. Eidetik bei taubstummen Jugendlichen. *Z. angew. Psychol.,* 1929, *34,* 244–274.

———. Prinzipienfragen der Gestalttheorie. In E. Brunswik, Charlotte Bühler, Hildegard Hetzer, et al. *Beiträge zur Problemgeschichte der Psychologie: Festschrift zu Karl Bühlers 50. Geburtstag.* Jena: Fischer, 1929, pp. 78–149.

———. Die Zugänglichkeit von Gegenständen für die Wahrnehmung und deren quantitative Bestimmung. *Arch. ges. Psychol.,* 1932, *88,* 377–418.

———. *Wahrnehmung und Gegenstandswelt: Grundlegung einer Psychologie vom Gegenstand her.* Leipzig: Deuticke, 1934. Excerpts reprinted in *The psychology of Egon Brunswik.* Ed. by K. R. Hammond. New York: Holt, Rinehart & Winston, 1966, pp. 515–534.

———. *Experimentelle Psychologie in Demonstrationen.* Vienna: Springer-Verlag, 1935.

Tolman, E. C., & ———. The organism and the causal texture of the environment. *Psychol. Rev.,* 1935, *42,* 43–77. Reprinted in *The Psychology of Egon Brunswik, op. cit.,* pp. 457–486.

———, & Reiter, Lotte. Eindruckscharaktere schematisierter Gesichter. *Z. Psychol.,* 1937, *142,* 67–134.

———. Psychology as a science of objective relations. *Phil. Sci.,* 1938, *4,* 227–260.

———. Die Eingliederung der Psychologie in die exakten Wissenschaften. *Einheitswissenschaften,* 1938, *6,* 17–34.

———. Probability as a determiner of rat behavior. *J. exp. Psychol.,* 1939, *25,* 175–197.

———. The conceptual focus of some psychological systems. In *J. unif. Sci.,* 1939, *8,* 36–49. Reprinted in M. H. Marx (Ed.), *Theories in contemporary psychology.* New York: Macmillan, 1963, pp. 226–237.

———. Thing constancy as measured by correlation coefficients. *Psychol. Rev.,* 1940, *47,* 69–78.

———. Distal focussing of perception: Size constancy in a representative sample of situations. *Psychol. Monogr.,* 1944, No. 254.

———. Organismic achievement and environmental probability. *Psychol. Rev.,* 1943, *50,* 255–272. Reprinted in M. H. Marx (Ed.), *Psychological theory: Contemporary readings.* New York: Macmillan, 1959, pp. 188–203.

———. *Perception and the representative design of psychological experiments.* (2nd ed.) Berkeley, Calif.: University of California Press, 1956. (1947)

———. Discussion: Remarks on functionalism in perception. *J. Pers.,* 1949–1950, *18,* 56–65.

———, & Herma, H. Probability learning of perceptual cues in the establishment of a weight illusion. *J. exp. Psychol.,* 1951, *41,* 281–290.

————, & Kamiya, J. Ecological cue-validity of "proximity" and of other Gestalt factors. *Amer. J. Psychol.*, 1953, *66*, 20–32.

————. Reasoning as a universal behavior model and a functional differentiation between "perception" and "thinking." (1966) In *The psychology of Egon Brunswik, op. cit.*, pp. 487–494.

————. In defense of probabilistic functionalism: A reply. *Psychol. Rev.*, 1955, *62*, 236–242.

————. The conceptual framework of psychology. In O. Neurath *et al.* (Eds.), *International encyclopedia of unified science.* Vol. 1, No. 10. Chicago: University of Chicago Press, 1955, pp. 655–760.

————. Representative design and probabilistic theory in a functional psychology. *Psychol. Rev.*, 1955, *62*, 193–217.

————. Historical and thematic relations of psychology to other sciences. *Sci. Mon.*, N.Y., 1956, *83*, 151–161. Reprinted in *The psychology of Egon Brunswik, op. cit.*, pp. 495–513.

————. Scope and aspects of the cognitive problem. In Various, *Contemporary approaches to cognition: A symposium held at the University of Colorado.* Cambridge: Harvard University Press, 1957, pp. 5–31.

————. Ontogenetic and other developmental parallels to the history of science. In H. Evans (Ed.), *Men and moments in the history of science.* Seattle, Wash.: University of Washington Press, 1959, pp. 3–21.

Beck & Molish, *Reflexes*

WILLIAM LOWE BRYAN
1860-1955
American Psychologist (16)

Bryan, W. L. On the development of voluntary motor ability. *Amer. J. Psychol.*, 1892, *5*, 123–204. (Also Worcester: Blanchard, 1892)

————. Review of recent experimental literature. *Psychol. Rev.*, 1894, *1*, 101–107.

————, & Harter, N. Studies in the physiology and psychology of the telegraphic language. *Psychol. Rev.*, 1897, *4*, 27–53.

————, & Harter, N. Studies on the telegraphic language: The acquisition of a hierarchy of habits. *Psychol. Rev.*, 1899, *6*, 346–375.

————. Theory and practice: President's address. *Psychol. Rev.*, 1904, *11*, 71–82.

————, Lindley, E. H., & Harter, N. On the psychology of learning a life occupation. *Ind. Univ. Publ. Sci. Ser.*, 1941, No. 11.

Pressey, *Casebook*

GEORGES LOUIS LECLERC DE BUFFON
1707-1788
French Biologist (13)

Buffon, G. L. L. d. *Oeuvres complètes de Buffon.* (12 vols.) Ed. by P. Flourens. Paris: Garnier, 1853–1855.   **C**

————. *Oeuvres complètes.* (New ed.) (14 vols.) Intro. by J. J. Lanesson; assembled & annotated by M. Nadault de Buffon. Paris: Le Vasseur, 1884–1885.   **C**

————. *Oeuvres philosophiques de Buffon.* Ed. by J. Piveteau. Paris: Presses Universitaires de France, 1957.   **Bl C**

————. Dissertation sur les couleurs accidentelles. *Mém. Acad. roy. Sci. Paris,* 1743, 147–158.

————. Dissertation sur les causes du strabisme ou des yeux louches. *Mém. Acad. roy. Sci. Paris,* 1743, 231–248.

————. *Natural history, general and particular.* (3rd ed.) (9 vols.) Trans. by W. Smellie. London: Strahan, 1791. (1749–1788)

————. Histoire naturelle. (1749–1788) In *Oeuvres complètes,* Vols. 1–6, *op. cit.*

————. *Discours sur le style.* (2nd ed.) Ed. by R. Nollet. Paris: Hachette, 1951. (1753)

————. *Les époques de la nature.* Intro. & ed. by J. Roger. Paris: Mémoires du Muséum, 1962. (1778)

Brinton, *Age Reason* ; Count, *Race* ; Hall, *Source Book* ; Slotkin, *Anthropology*

KARL BUHLER
1879-1963
German-Austrian Psychologist (26)

Bühler, K. *Die Uhren der Lebewesen und Fragmente aus dem Nachlass.* Ed. by G. Lebzeltern ; pref. by H. Rohracher. Vienna: Böhlaus, 1969.
Bl C

——. Tatsachen und Probleme zu einer Psychologie der Denkvorgänge. I. Ueber Gedanken : II. Ueber Gedankenzusammenhänge. III. Ueber Gedankenerinnerungen. *Arch. ges. Psychol.,* 1907, *9,* 297–365 ; 1908, *12,* 1–23, 24–92.

——. Antwort auf die von W. Wundt erhobenen Einwände gegen die Methode der Selbstbeobachtung an experimentell erzeugten Erlebnissen. *Arch. ges. Psychol.,* 1908, *12,* 93–123.

——. Zur Kritik der Denkexperimente. *Z. Psychol.,* 1909, *51,* 108–118.

——. Aufmerksamkeit. In E. Korschelt *et al.* (Eds.), *Handwörterbuch der Naturwissenschaften.* Vol. 1. Jena: Fischer, 1912, pp. 732–741.

——. Denken. In E. Korschelt *et. al.* (Eds.), *Handwörterbuch der Naturwissenschaften.* Vol. 2. Jena: Fischer, 1912, pp. 889–896.

——. *Die Gestaltwahrnehmungen. I. Experimentelle Untersuchungen zur psychologischen und ästhetischen Analyse der Raum- und Zeitanschauung.* Stuttgart: Spemann, 1913.

——. Zeitsinn und Raumsinn. In E. Korschelt *et al.* (Eds.), *Handwörterbuch der Naturwissenschaften.* Vol. 10. Jena: Fischer, 1915, pp. 726–748.

——. *Die geistige Entwicklung des Kindes.* Jena: Fischer, 1918. (Reprinted 1930)

——. *The mental development of the child.* (5th ed.) Trans. by O. Oeser. New York: Harcourt, 1930. (1918)

——. (With collab. of Lotte Schenk-Danzinger.) *Abriss der geistigen Entwicklung des Kleinkindes.* (9th ed.) Heidelberg: Quelle & Meyer, 1967. (1919)

——. Eine Bemerkung zu der Diskussion über die Psychologie des Denkens. *Z. Psychol.,* 1919, *82,* 97–101.

——. Replik. *Z. Psychol.,* 1920, *83,* 95.

——. *Handbuch der Psychologie.* Part I. *Die Struktur der Wahrnehmungen.* Vol. I. *Die Erscheinungsweisen der Farben.* Jena: Fischer, 1922.

——. Ueber den Begriff der sprachlichen Darstellung. *Psychol. Forsch.,* 1923, *3,* 282–294.

——. Die Krise der Psychologie. *Kant-Stud.,* 1926, *31,* 455–526. (Reprinted 1929)

——. Les Lois générales d'évolution dans le langage de l'enfant. *J. Psychol. norm. path.,* 1926, *23,* 597–607.

——. Die "Neue Psychologie" Koffkas. *Z. Psychol.,* 1926, *99,* 145–159.

——. *Die Krise der Psychologie.* (3rd ed.) Stuttgart: Fischer, 1965. (1927)

——. Displeasure and pleasure in relation to activity. In M. L. Reymert (Ed.), *Feelings and emotions: The Wittenberg symposium.* Worcester, Mass.: Clark University Press, 1928, pp. 195–199.

——. Das Ganze der Sprachtheorie, ihr Aufbau und ihre Teile. *Ber. Kongr. dtsch. Ges. Psychol.,* Hamburg, 1932, *12,* 95–122.

——. Axiomatik der Sprachwissenschaften. *Kant-Stud.,* 1933, *38,* 19–20.

——. Zur Geschichte der Ausdruckstheorie. *Z. Psychol.,* 1933, *129,* 246–261.

——. *Ausdruckstheorie: Das System an der Geschichte aufgezeigt.* (2nd ed.) Pref. by A. Wellek. Stuttgart: Fischer, 1968. (1934)

——. *Theorie der Sprache.* (2nd ed.) Stuttgart: Fischer, 1968. (1934)

——. Forschung zur Sprachtheorie: Einleitung. *Arch. ges. Psychol.,* 1935, *94,* 401–412.

——. *Die Zukunft der Psychologie und die Schule.* Vienna: Jugend & Volk, 1936.

Bühler, Charlotte, ——, & Lefever, D. W. *Development of the basic Rorschach score with a manual of directions.* Los Angeles, Calif.: Authors, 1949.

——. The skywise and neighborwise navigation of ants and bees. *Acta Psychol.,* 1951–1952, *8,* 225–263.

———. Der Atemfaktor in tierischen Geruchs-spuren. *Jb. Psychol. Psychother.,* 1953, *1,* 479–483.

———. Menschliche Fernorientierung: Eine psychophysische Analyse an zwei Beispielen (Columbus und Lindbergh). *Jb. Psychol. Psychother.,* 1954, *2,* 242–258.

———. The essentials of contact navigation. *Acta Psychol.,* 1954, *10,* 278–316.

———. *Das Gestaltprinzip im Leben des Menschen und der Tiere.* Bern: Huber, 1960.

———. Christian von Ehrenfels und Albert Einstein. In F. Weinhandl (Ed.), *Gestalthaftes Sehen.* Darmstadt: Wissenschaft Buchgesellschaft, 1960, pp. 86–91.

Rapaport, *Thought*

WILLIAM HENRY BURNHAM
1855-1941
American Psychologist (13)

Burnham, W. H. Memory, historically and experimentally considered. *Amer. J. Psychol.,* 1888–1889, *2,* 39–90, 225–270, 431–464, 568–622.

———. The study of adolescence. *J. genet. Psychol.,* 1891, *1,* 174–195.

———. Individual differences in the imagination of children, *J. genet. Psychol.,* 1892, *2,* 204–225.

———. Retroactive amnesia: Illustrative cases and a tentative explanation. *Amer. J. Psychol.,* 1903, *14* (part 2), 118–132.

———. The history of education. In W. H. Burnham & H. Suzzallo. *The history of education as a professional subject.* New York: Teachers College, Columbia University, 1908, pp. 3–27.

———. Attention and interest. *Amer. J. Psychol.,* 1908, *19,* 14–18.

———. The problem of fatigue. *Amer. J. Psychol.,* 1908, *19,* 385–399.

———. The hygiene of instruction. *Addr. Proc. Nat. Educ. Ass.,* 1910, *48,* 900–906.

———. The group as a stimulus to mental activity. *Science,* 1910, *31*(N.S.), 761–767.

———. Arithmetic and school hygiene. *J. genet. Psychol.,* 1911, *18,* 54–73.

———. Oxygen supply as a condition of efficient brain activity. *J. educ. Psychol.,* 1911, *2,* 421–428.

———. *Bibliographies on educational psychology.* Worcester, Mass.: Clark University Press, 1913. **Bl**

———. Orderly association as a condition of efficient brain activity. *J. genet. Psychol.,* 1913, *20,* 360–390.

———. A health examination at school entrance. *J. genet. Psychol.,* 1914, *21,* 219–241.

———. Mental hygiene and the conditioned reflex. *J. genet Psychol.,* 1917, *24,* 449–488.

———. *Bibliographies on educational subjects: The history of education.* Worcester, Mass.: Clark University Press, 1917.

———. The significance of stimulation in the development of the nervous system. *Amer. J. Psychol.,* 1917, *28,* 38–56.

———. The hygiene of sleep. *J. genet. Psychol.,* 1920, *27,* 1–35.

———. The significance of the conditioned reflex in mental hygiene. *Ment. Hyg.,* N.Y., 1921, *5,* 673–706.

———. *The normal mind: An introduction to mental hygiene and the hygiene of school instruction.* New York: Appleton, 1924.

———. *Great teachers and mental health.* New York: Appleton, 1926.

———. Personality differences and mental health. *J. genet. Psychol.,* 1929, *36,* 361–389.

———. *The wholesome personality: A contribution to mental hygiene.* New York: Appleton, 1932.

PIERRE JEAN GEORGES CABANIS
1757-1808
French Philosopher (22)

Cabanis, P. J. G. *Oeuvres complètes.* (5 vols.) Ed. by F. Thurot. Paris: Bossange, 1823–1825. **C**

――――. *Oeuvres philosophiques.* (2 vols.) Ed. by C. Lehec & J. Cazeneuve. Paris: Presses Universitaires de France, 1956.   **C**

――――. *An essay on the certainty of medicine.* Trans. by R. La Roche. Philadelphia: Desilver, 1823. (1798) Reprinted in *Oeuvres philosophiques,* Vol. 1, *op. cit.,* pp. 32–103.

――――. *Journal de la maladie et de la mort d'Honoré-Gabriel-Victor Riquetti Mirabeau.* Paris: Grabit, 1791.

――――. *Considérations générales sur l'étude de l'homme et sur les rapports de son organisation physique avec ses facultés intellectuelles et morales.* Paris: Thurot, 1796–1798. (Reprinted 1802)

――――. *Corps législatif. Conseil des cinq-cents: Rapport par Cabanis au nom des commissions d'instruction publique et des instructions républicaines et réunies sur l'organisation des écoles de médecine. Séance du 29 brumaire an VII.* Paris: Imprimerie Nationale, 1799.

――――. Rapports du physique et du moral de l'homme. (2nd ed.) (1802) In *Oeuvres philosophiques,* Vol. 1, *op. cit.,* pp. 105–631.

――――. Coup d'oeil sur les révolutions et sur la réforme de la médecine. (1804) In *Oeuvres philosophiques,* Vol. 2, *op. cit.,* pp. 65–254.

――――. Lettre à M. F. sur les causes premières. (1806–1807) In *Oeuvres philosophiques,* Vol. 2, *op. cit.,* pp. 255–298.

――――. Notice sur Benjamin Franklin. (1825) In *Oeuvres philosophiques,* Vol. 2, *op. cit.,* pp. 341–367.

MARY WHITON CALKINS
1863-1930
American Psychologist (20)

Calkins, Mary W. A suggested classification of cases of association. *Phil. Rev.,* 1892, *1,* 389–402.

――――. Statistics of dreams. *Amer. J. Psychol.,* 1893, *5,* 311–343.

――――. A statistical study of pseudo-chromesthe-sia and mental-forms. *Amer. J. Psychol.,* 1893, *5,* 439–464.

――――. Notes on Fichte's "Grundlage der Wissenschaftslehre." *Phil. Rev.,* 1894, *3,* 459–462.

――――. Association: An essay analytic and experimental. *Psychol. Monogr.,* 1896, *1,* No. 2.

――――. Community of ideas of men and women. *Psychol. Rev.,* 1896, *3,* 426–430.

――――. Kant's conception of the Leibniz space and time doctrine. *Phil. Rev.,* 1897, *6,* 356–369.

――――. Short studies in memory and in association. I. A study of immediate and of delayed recall of the concrete and of the verbal. II. The tendency to mental combinations. III. Association with childhood experience. *Psychol. Rev.,* 1898, *5,* 451–462.

――――. Time as related to causality and to space. *Mind,* 1899, *8*(N.S.), 216–232.

――――. Attributes of sensation. *Psychol. Rev.,* 1899, *6,* 506–514 ; 1904, *11,* 221–222.

――――. Psychology as science of selves. *Phil. Rev.,* 1900, *9,* 490–501.

――――. Elements of conscious complexes. *Psychol. Rev.,* 1900, *7,* 377–389.

――――. An attempted experiment in psychological aesthetics. *Psychol. Rev.,* 1900, *7,* 580–591.

――――. *An introduction to psychology.* (2nd ed.) New York: Macmillan, 1905. (1901)

――――. The limits of genetic and of comparative psychology. *Brit. J. Psychol.,* 1904–1905, *1,* 261–285.

――――. A reconciliation between structural and functional psychology. (President's address.) *Psychol. Rev.,* 1906, *13,* 61–80.

――――. Psychology: What is it about? *J. Phil.,* 1907, *4,* 673–683.

――――. *The persistent problems of philosophy.* (5th ed.) New York: Macmillan, 1925. (1907)

――――. The ego and empirical psychology. *Psychol. Bull.,* 1908, *5,* 27–30.

――――. Psychology as science of self. I. Is the self body or has it body? II. The nature of self. III. The description of consciousness. *J. Phil.*, 1908, *5*, 12–20, 64–68, 113–121.

———. Self and soul. *Phil. Rev.*, 1908, *17*, 272–280.

———. *A first book in psychology.* (4th ed.) New York: Macmillan, 1914. (1909)

———. The abandonment of sensationalism in psychology. *Amer. J. Psychol.*, 1909, *20*, 269–277.

———. Professor Titchener on the thought processes. *Psychol. Bull.*, 1910, *7*, 293–297.

———. The self in recent psychology. *Psychol. Bull.*, 1912, *9*, 25–30.

———. The self in scientific psychology. *Amer. J. Psychol.*, 1915, *26*, 495–524.

———. A clue to Holt's treatment of the Freudian wish. *J. Phil.*, 1917, *14*, 441–442.

———. The case of self against soul. *Psychol. Rev.*, 1917, *24*, 278–300.

———. The equivocal position of the "presentation" in the psychology of James Ward. *Psychol. Bull.*, 1920, *17*, 429–432.

———. The truly psychological behaviorism. *Psychol. Rev.*, 1921, *28*, 1–18.

———. Fact and inference in Raymond Wheeler's doctrine of will and self-activity. *Psychol. Rev.*, 1921, *28*, 356–373.

———. McDougall's treatment of experience. *Brit. J. Psychol.*, 1922–1923, *13*, 337–343.

———. The foundations of psychology. *J. Phil.*, 1923, *20*, 5–15.

———. Converging lines in contemporary psychology. *Brit. J. Psychol.*, 1925–1926, *16*, 171–179.

———. Critical comments on the "Gestalt-Theorie." *Psychol. Rev.*, 1926, *33*, 135–158.

———. The self in recent psychology. *Psychol. Bull.*, 1927, *24*, 205–215.

———. Self-awareness and meaning. *Amer. J. Psychol.*, 1927, *38*, 441–448.

———. The ambiguous concept: Meaning. *Amer. J. Psychol.*, 1927, *39*, 7–22.

———. Value—primarily a psychological conception. *J. Phil. Stud.*, 1928, *3*, 413–426.

———. Analysis: Chemical or psychological? *Psychol. Rev.*, 1929, *36*, 348–352.

———. Mary Whiton Calkins. In C. Murchison (Ed.), *A history of psychology in autobiography.* Vol. 1. Worcester, Mass.: Clark University Press, 1930, pp. 31–62.   **B**

———, & Gamble, Eleanore A. McC. The self-psychology of the psychoanalysts. *Psychol. Rev.*, 1930, *37*, 277–304.

———. The case against behaviorism. *Sewanee Rev.*, 1930, *38*, 199–209.

Herrnstein & Boring, *Source Book*

WALTER BRADFORD CANNON
1871-1945
American Physiologist (27)

Davenport, C. B., & Cannon, W. B. On the determination of the direction and rate of movement of organisms by light. *J. Physiol.*, 1897, *21*, 22–32.

———. The movements of the stomach studied by means of Röntgen rays. *Amer. J. Physiol.*, 1898, *1*, 359–382.

———. *A laboratory course in physiology.* (9th ed.) Cambridge: Harvard University, 1936. (1910)

———. *The mechanical factors of digestion.* London: Arnold, 1911.

———. The interrelations of emotions as suggested by recent physiological researches. *Amer. J. Psychol.*, 1914, *25*, 256–282.

———. *Bodily changes in pain, hunger, fear and rage.* (2nd ed.) New York: Appleton, 1929. (1915)

———. The physiological basis of thirst. *Proc. Roy. Soc.*, London, 1918, *90B*, 283–301.

———. The isolated heart as an indicator of adrenal secretion induced by pain, asphyxia and excitement. *Amer. J. Physiol.,* 1919, *50,* 399–432.

———, & Rapport, D. Further observations on the denervated heart in relation to adrenal secretion. *Amer. J. Physiol.,* 1921, *58,* 308–337.

———, & Rapport, D. The reflex center for adrenal secretion and its response to excitatory and inhibitory influences. *Amer. J. Physiol.,* 1921, *58,* 338–352.

———. *Traumatic shock.* New York: Appleton, 1923.

———, McIver, M. A., & Bliss, S. W. A sympathetic and adrenal mechanism for mobilizing sugar in hypoglycemia. *Amer. J. Physiol.,* 1924, *69,* 46–66.

———, & Britton, S. W. Pseudaffective medulliadrenal secretion. *Amer. J. Physiol.,* 1925, *72,* 283–294.

———, Lewis, J. T., & Britton, S. W. Studies on the conditions of activity in endocrine glands: XVII. A lasting preparation of the denervated heart for detecting internal secretion, with evidence for accessory accelerator fibers from the thoracic sympathetic chain. *Amer. J. Physiol.,* 1926, *77,* 326–352.

———, Querido, A., Britton, S. W., & Bright, E. M. Studies on the conditions of activity in endocrine glands. XXI. The role of adrenal secretion in the chemical control of body temperature. *Amer. J. Physiol.,* 1927, *79,* 466–507.

———. The James-Lange theory of emotions: A critical examination and an alternative theory. *Amer. J. Psychol.,* 1927, *39,* 106–124.

———, Newton, H. F., Bright, E. M., Menkin, V., & Moore, R. M. Some aspects of the physiology of animals surviving complete exclusion of sympathetic nerve impulses. *Amer. J. Physiol.,* 1928, *89,* 84–107.

———. Neural organization for emotional expression. In M. L. Reymert (Ed.), *Feelings and emotions: The Wittenberg symposium.* Worcester, Mass.: Clark University Press, 1928, pp. 257–269.

———. The autonomic nervous system: An interpretation. (The Linacre lecture, 1930.) *Lancet,* 1930, *1,* 1109–1115.

———. Again the James-Lange and the thalamic theories of emotion. *Psychol. Rev.,* 1931, *38,* 281–295.

———, & Bacq, Z. M. A hormone produced by sympathetic action on smooth muscle. *Amer. J. Physiol.,* 1931, *96,* 392–412.

———. *The wisdom of the body.* New York: Norton, 1932.

———, & Rosenblueth, A. Sympathin E and sympathin I. *Amer. J. Physiol.,* 1933, *104,* 557–574.

———. Chemical mediators of autonomic nerve impulses. *Science,* 1933, *78,* 43–48.

Rosenblueth, A., & ———. Direct electrical stimulation of denervated autonomic effectors. *Amer. J. Physiol.,* 1934, *108,* 384–396.

———. Hunger and Thirst. In C. Murchison (Ed.), *A handbook of general experimental psychology.* Worcester, Mass.: Clark University Press, 1934, pp. 247–263.

Rosenblueth, A., & ———. The chemical mediation of sympathetic vasodilator nerve impulses. *Amer. J. Physiol.,* 1935, *112,* 33–40.

Rosenblueth, A., & ———. The adequacy of the chemical theory of smooth muscle excitation. *Amer. J. Physiol.,* 1936, *116,* 414–429.

———. *Digestion and health.* New York: Norton, 1936.

———. The role of emotion in disease. *Ann. Int. Med.,* 1936, *9,* 1453–1465.

———, & Rosenblueth, A. *Autonomic neuroeffector systems.* New York: Macmillan, 1937. (Reprinted 1971)

———. The body physiologic and the body politic. *Science,* 1941, *93,* 1–10.

———. *The body as a guide to politics.* London: Watts, 1942.

———. *The way of an investigator: A scientist's experiences in medical research.* New York: Norton, 1945.

B

———. *International relations in science.* Waltham, Mass.: Chronica Botanica, 1945.

———, & Rosenblueth, A. *The supersensitivity of denervated structures: A law of denervation.* New York: Macmillan, 1949. (Reprinted 1971)

Arnold, *Emotion ;* Dennis, *Psychology ;* Fulton & Wilson, *Physiology ;* Russell, *Motivation ;* Sahakian, *Psychology*

ANTON JULIUS CARLSON
1875-1956
American Pychologist (12)

Carlson, A. J. *The psychology of the Leibnizian monad: A critique.* Rock Island, Ill.: Lutheran Augustana Book Concern, 1899.

———. Further evidence of the direct relation between the rate of conduction in a motor nerve and the rapidity of contraction in the muscle. *Amer. J. Physiol.,* 1906, *15,* 136–143.

———. Contributions to the physiology of the stomach. I: The character of the movements of the empty stomach in man. II: The relation between the contractions of the empty stomach and the sensation of hunger. III: The contractions of the empty stomach inhibited reflexly from the mouth. IV: The influence of the contractions of the empty stomach in man on the vaso-motor center, on the rate of the heart-beat, and on the reflex excitability of the spinal cord. V: The influence of stimulation of the gastric mucosa on the contractions of the empty stomach (hunger contractions) in man. VI: A study of the mechanism of the hunger contraction of the empty stomach by experiment on dogs. VII: The inhibitory reflexes from the gastric mucosa. *Amer. J. Physiol.,* 1912, *31,* 151–168, 175–192, 212–222, 318–327 ; 1913, *32,* 245–263, 369–388, 389–397.

———. *The control of hunger in health and disease.* Chicago: University of Chicago Press, 1916.

———, & Jacobson, E. The influence of relaxation upon the knee jerk. *Amer. J. Physiol.,* 1925, *73,* 324–328.

———, & Johnson, C. A. Effects of hunger contractions on the knee jerk. *Amer. J. Physiol.,* 1928, *84,* 189–191.

———, & Johnson, V. *The machinery of the body.* (4th ed.) Chicago: University of Chicago Press, 1953. (1937)

———. Science versus life. *Science,* 1941, *93,* 93–100.

———. The conditioned reflex therapy of alcohol addiction. *Quart. J. stud. Alcohol.,* 1944, *5,* 212–215.

WILLIAM BENJAMIN CARPENTER
1813-1885
English Physiologist (14)

Carpenter, W. B. *Nature and man: Essays, scientific and philosophical.* London: Kegan Paul, Trench, 1888. (Reprinted 1970)   **B Bl C**

———. *Principles of physiology, general and comparative.* (3rd ed.) London: Churchill, 1851. (1839)

———. *Principles of human physiology.* (8th ed.) Ed. by H. Power. Philadelphia: Lea, 1876. (1842)

———. *Manual of physiology.* (4th ed.) London: Churchill, 1865. (1846)

———. *The microscope and its revelations.* (8th ed.) Ed. by W. H. Dallinger. Philadelphia: Blakiston, 1901. (1856)

———. On the unconscious activity of the brain. *Proc. Roy. Inst.,* 1869, *5,* 338–345.

———. Physiology of will. *Contemp. Rev.,* 1871, *17,* 192–217.

———. On mind and will in nature. *Contemp. Rev.,* 1872, *20,* 738–762.

———. Man the interpreter of nature. (1872) Reprinted in G. Basalla *et al.* (Eds.), *Victorian science: A self portrait from The Presidential Addresses of the British Association for the Advancement of Science.* Garden City, N.Y.: Doubleday, 1970, pp. 111–135, & in *Nature and man, op. cit.,* pp. 185–210.

———. *Principles of mental physiology, with their applications to the training and discipline of the mind and the study of its morbid conditions*. (4th ed.) New York: Appleton, 1900. (1874)

———. On the doctrine of human automatism. (1875) Reprinted in *Nature and man, op. cit.*, pp. 261–283.

———. *Mesmerism, spiritualism, &c., historically & scientifically considered*. New York: Appleton, 1877.

———. The force behind nature. (1880) In *Nature and man, op. cit.*, pp. 350–364.

———. The argument from design in the organic world, reconsidered in its relation to the doctrines of evolution and natural selection. (1884) In *Nature and man, op. cit.*, pp. 409–463.

HARVEY A. CARR
1873-1954
American Psychologist (23)

Carr, H. A. The pendular whiplash illusion of motion. *Psychol. Rev.*, 1907, *14*, 169–180.

———, & Watson, J. B. Orientation in the white rat. *J. comp. Neurol. Psychol.*, 1908, *18*, 27–44.

———. Unusual illusions occurring in psycholeptic attacks of hysterical origin. *J. abnorm. Psychol.*, 1908, *2*, 260–271.

———. Visual illusions of depth. *Psychol. Rev.*, 1909, *16*, 219–256.

———. The autokinetic sensation. *Psychol. Rev.*, 1910, *17*, 42–75.

———. Some novel experiences. *Psychol. Rev.*, 1912, *19*, 60–65.

———. Principles of selection in animal learning. *Psychol. Rev.*, 1914, *21*, 157–165.

———. Head's theory of cutaneous sensitivity. *Psychol. Rev.*, 1916, *23*, 262–278.

———. The distribution and elimination of errors in the maze. *J. anim. Behav.*, 1917, *7*, 145–160.

———. Maze studies with the white rat. I. Normal animals. II. Blind animals. III. Anosomic animals. *J. anim. Behav.*, 1917, *7*, 259–306.

———. The alternation problem: A preliminary study. *J. anim. Behav.*, 1917, *7*, 365–384.

———. The nature of mental process. *Psychol. Rev.*, 1917, *24*, 181–187.

———. The relation between emotion and its expression. *Psychol. Rev.*, 1917, *24*, 369–375.

———. Length of time interval in successive association. *Psychol. Rev.*, 1919, *26*, 335–353.

———, & Freeman, A. S. Time relationships in the formation of associations. *Psychol. Rev.*, 1919, *26*, 465–473.

———, & Koch, Helen. The influence of extraneous controls in the learning process. *Psychol. Rev.*, 1919, *26*, 287–293.

———, & Hardy, M. C. Some factors in the perception of relative motion: A preliminary experiment. *Psychol. Rev.*, 1920, *27*, 24–37.

———. The influence of visual guidance in maze learning. *J. exp. Psychol.*, 1921, *4*, 399–417.

———. *Psychology: A study of mental activity*. New York: Longmans, Green, 1925.

———. The reliability of the maze experiment. *J. comp. Psychol.*, 1926, *6*, 85–93.

———. The interpretation of the animal mind. *Psychol. Rev.*, 1927, *34*, 87–106.

———. An interpretation of the Weber-Fechner Law. *Psychol. Rev.*, 1927, *34*, 313–319.

———. The differentia of an emotion. In M. L. Reymert (Ed.), *Feelings and emotions: The Wittenberg symposium*. Worcester, Mass.: Clark University Press, 1928, pp. 228–235.

———. Functionalism. In C. Murchison (Ed.), *Psychologies of 1930*. Worcester, Mass.: Clark University Press, 1930, pp. 59–78.

———. The laws of association. *Psychol. Rev.*, 1931, *38*, 212–228.

———. *An introduction to space perception*. New York: Longmans, Green, 1935.

———. Harvey A. Carr. In C. Murchison (Ed.), *A history of psychology in autobiography*. Vol. 3. Worcester, Mass.: Clark University Press, 1936, pp. 69–82.   **B**

———. The search for certainty. *Psychol. Rev.*, 1937, *44*, 274–296.

———. The law of effect: A round table discussion. I. *Psychol. Rev.*, 1938, *45*, 191–199.

———, & Kingsbury, F. A. The concept of ability. *Psychol. Rev.*, 1938, *45*, 354–376.

———, & Kingsbury, F. A. The concept of traits. *Psychol. Rev.*, 1938, *45*, 497–524.

———. The reliability vs. the validity of test scores. *Psychol. Rev.*, 1938, *45*, 435–440.

———, & Kingsbury, F. A. The concept of the individual. *Psychol. Rev.*, 1939, *46*, 359–382.

Valentine, *Experimental*

HULSEY CASON
1893-1950
American Psychologist (11)

Cason, H. The conditioned pupillary reaction. *J. exp. Psychol.*, 1922, *5*, 108–146.

———. The conditioned eyelid reaction. *J. exp. Psychol.*, 1922, *5*, 153–196.

———. Purposive psychology and the conditioned reflex. *Psychol. Rev.*, 1924, *31*, 253–255.

———. Criticisms of the laws of exercise and effect. *Psychol. Rev.*, 1924, *31*, 397–417.

———, & Cason, Eloise B. Association tendencies and learning ability. *J. exp. Psychol.*, 1925, *8*, 167–189.

———. The physical basis of the conditioned response. *Amer. J. Psychol.*, 1925, *36*, 371–393.

———. General aspects of the conditioned response. *Psychol. Rev.*, 1925, *32*, 298–316.

———. The conditioned reflex or conditioned response as a common activity of living organisms. *Psychol. Bull.*, 1925, *22*, 445–472.

———. Specific serial learning: A study of backward association and a study of remote forward association. *J. exp. Psychol.*, 1926, *9*, 195–227, 299–324.

———. Common annoyances: A psychological study of every-day aversions and irritations. *Psychol. Monogr.*, 1930, *40*, No. 182.

———. The pleasure-pain theory of learning. *Psychol. Rev.*, 1932, *39*, 440–466.

———. An interacting-pattern theory of the affectivities. *Psychol. Rev.*, 1933, *40*, 282–291.

———, & Katcher, N. An attempt to condition breathing and eyelid responses to a subliminal electric stimulus. *J. exp. Psychol.*, 1933, *16*, 831–842.

———, & Cason, E. B. Affectivity in relation to breathing and gross bodily movement. *J. gen. Psychol.*, 1933, *9*, 130–156.

———. Dr. Hilgard on the conditioned eyelid reaction. *J. exp. Psychol.*, 1934, *17*, 894–899.

Silverman, A., & ———. Incidental memory for pleasant, unpleasant, and indifferent words. *Amer. J. Psychol.*, 1934, *46*, 315–320.

———. The role of verbal activities in the conditioning of human subjects. *Psychol. Rev.*, 1934, *41*, 563–571.

———. The nightmare dream. *Psychol. Monogr.*, 1935, *46*, No. 209.

———. An attempt to condition hand withdrawal responses in human subjects. *J. exp. Psychol.*, 1935, *18*, 307–317.

———. Backward conditioned eyelid reactions. *J. exp. Psychol.*, 1935, *18*, 599–611.

———. Sensory conditioning. *J. exp. Psychol.*, 1936, *19*, 572–591.

———. The concepts of learning and memory. *Psychol. Rev.*, 1937, *44*, 54–61.

———. Dr. Kellogg on the definition of learning. *Psychol. Rev.*, 1938, *45*, 101–105.

———. The concept of the psychopath. *Amer. J. Orthopsychiat.*, 1948, *18*, 297–308.

Valentine, *Experimental*

JAMES McKEEN CATTELL
1860-1944
American Psychologist (26)

Cattell, J. M. *James McKeen Cattell: Man of science.* Vol. I: *Psychological research.* Vol. II: *Addresses and formal papers.* Ed. by A. T.

Poffenberger. Lancaster, Pa.: Science Press, 1947. **C**

———. Ueber die Zeit der Erkennung und Benennung von Schriftzeichen, Bildern und Farben. *Phil. Stud.*, 1885, *2*, 635–650. Trans. in *James McKeen Cattell*, Vol. 1, *op. cit.*, pp. 13–25.

———. The time it takes to see and name objects. *Mind*, 1886, *11*, 63–65. Reprinted in *James McKeen Cattell*, Vol. 1, *op. cit.*, pp. 107–109.

———. Psychometrische Untersuchungen. *Phil. Stud.*, 1886, *3*, 305–335, 452–492; 1888, *4*, 241–250.

———. The time taken up by cerebral operations: I: Apparatus and methods. II: The reaction time. III: The perception time. IV: The willtime. V: The influence of attention, fatigue and practice on the duration of cerebral operations. *Mind*, 1886, *11*, 220–230, 230–242, 377–392, 524–534, 534–538. Parts I & II reprinted in *James McKeen Cattell*, Vol. 1, *op. cit.*, pp. 41–94.

———. Experiments on the association of ideas. *Mind*, 1887, *12*, 68–74. Reprinted in *James McKeen Cattell*, Vol. 1, *op. cit.*, pp. 95–102.

———. The psychological laboratory at Leipsic. *Mind*, 1888, *13*, 37–51. Reprinted in *James McKeen Cattell*, Vol. 2, *op. cit.*, pp. 7–20.

———, & Bryant, Sophie. Mental association investigated by experiment. *Mind*, 1889, *14*, 230–250. Reprinted in *James McKeen Cattell*, Vol. 1, *op. cit.*, pp. 110–131.

———. Mental tests and measurements. *Mind*, 1890, *15*, 373–381. Reprinted in *James McKeen Cattell*, Vol. 1, *op. cit.*, pp. 132–141.

———. Psychology at the University of Pennsylvania. *Amer. J. Psychol.*, 1890, *3*, 281–283.

———. On the origin of music. *Mind*, 1891, *16*, 386–388.

Fullerton, G. S., & ———. *On the perception of small differences with special reference to the extent, force and time of movement.* Philadelphia, Pa.: University of Pennsylvania Press, 1892. Reprinted in *James McKeen Cattell*, Vol. 1, *op. cit.*, pp. 142–251.

———. Aufmerksamkeit und Reaction. *Phil. Stud.*, 1893, *8*, 403–406. Trans. in *James McKeen Cattell*, Vol. 1, *op. cit.*, pp. 252–255.

———. Mental measurement. *Phil. Rev.*, 1893, *2*, 316–332. Reprinted in *James McKeen Cattell*, Vol. 2, *op. cit.*, pp. 33–45.

———. On errors of observation. *Amer. J. Psychol.*, 1893, *5*, 285–293. Reprinted in *James McKeen Cattell*, Vol. 1, *op. cit.*, pp. 256–264.

———. Tests of the senses and faculties. *Educ. Rev.*, N.Y., 1893, *5*, 257–265. Reprinted in *James McKeen Cattell*, Vol. 2, *op. cit.*, pp. 26–32.

———, & Dolley, C. S. On reaction-times and the velocity of the nervous impulse. *Psychol. Rev.*, 1894, *1*, 159–168, & in *Proc. Nat. Acad. Sci.*, 1896, *7*, 393–415. Reprinted in *James McKeen Cattell*, Vol. 1, *op. cit.*, pp. 265–301.

———. Address of the President before the American Psychological Association, 1895. *Psychol. Rev.*, 1896, *3*, 134–148. Reprinted in *James McKeen Cattell*, Vol. 2, *op. cit.*, pp. 52–64.

———, & Farrand, L. Physical and mental measurements of the students of Columbia University. *Psychol. Rev.*, 1896, *3*, 618–648. Reprinted in *James McKeen Cattell*, Vol. 1, *op. cit.*, pp. 305–330.

———, Farrand, L., & Baldwin, J. M. Note on reaction-types. *Psychol. Rev.*, 1897, *4*, 297–299.

———. The perception of light. *System. Dis. Eye*, 1897, *1*, 505–538. Reprinted in *James McKeen Cattell*, Vol. 2, *op. cit.*, pp. 65–102.

———. The advance of psychology. *Proc. Amer. Ass. Adv. Sci.*, 1898, *47*, 3–15. Reprinted in *James McKeen Cattell*, Vol. 2, *op. cit.*, pp. 106–116.

———. The psychological laboratory. *Psychol. Rev.*, 1898, *5*, 655–658.

———. On relations of time and space in vision. *Psychol. Rev.*, 1900, *7*, 325–343. Reprinted in *James McKeen Cattell*, Vol. 1, *op. cit.*, pp. 338–354.

———. The American Association for the Advancement of Science. *Science*, 1901, *13*, 961–

969. Reprinted in *James McKeen Cattell*, Vol. 2, *op. cit.*, pp. 117–126.

——. The time of perception as a measure of differences in perception. *Phil. Stud.*, 1902, *19*, 63–68. Reprinted in *James McKeen Cattell*, Vol. 1, *op. cit.*, pp. 355–359.

——. Statistics of American psychologists. *Amer. J. Psychol.*, 1903, *14*, 310–328. Reprinted in *James McKeen Cattell*, Vol. 1, *op. cit.*, pp. 360–375.

——. A statistical study of eminent men. *Pop. Sci. Mon.*, 1903, *62*, 359–377. Reprinted in *James McKeen Cattell*, Vol. 2, *op. cit.*, pp. 165–184.

——. The conceptions and methods of psychology. *Pop. Sci. Mon.*, 1904, *66*, 176–186. Reprinted in *James McKeen Cattell*, Vol. 2, *op. cit.*, pp. 197–207.

——. A statistical study of American men of science. *Science*, 1906, *24*, 658–665, 699–707, 732–742. Reprinted in *James McKeen Cattell*, Vol. 1, *op. cit.*, pp. 388–426.

—— (Ed.), *American men of science: A biographical directory*. (7th ed.) Lancaster, Pa.: Science Press, 1944. (1906)

——. Reactions and perceptions. In *Essays philosophical and psychological in honor of William James by his colleagues at Columbia University*. New York: Longmans, Green, 1908, pp. 569–584. Reprinted in *James McKeen Cattell*, Vol. 2, *op. cit.*, pp. 215–221.

——. A further statistical study of American men of science. *Science*, 1910, *32*, 633–648, 672–688. Reprinted in *James McKeen Cattell*, Vol. 1, *op. cit.*, pp. 427–477.

——. Research and teaching in the university. *Science*, 1914, *40*, 628–630.

——. Families of American men of science. *Pop. Sci. Mon.*, 1915, *86*, 504–515; *Sci. Mon.*, N.Y., 1917, *4*, 248–262; *5*, 368–377. Reprinted in *James McKeen Cattell*, Vol. 1, *op. cit.*, pp. 478–519.

——. The order of scientific merit. *Science*, 1922, *56*, 541–547. Reprinted in *James McKeen Cattell*, Vol. 1, *op. cit.*, pp. 520–529.

——. The interpretation of intelligence tests. *Sci. Mon.*, N.Y., 1924, *18*, 508–516. Reprinted in *James McKeen Cattell*, Vol. 2, *op. cit.*, pp. 372–380.

——. The scientific men of the world. *Sci. Mon.*, N.Y., 1926, *23*, 468–471. Reprinted in *James McKeen Cattell*, Vol. 1, *op. cit.*, pp. 530–534.

——. Some psychological experiments. *Science*, 1926, *63*, 1–8, 29–35. Reprinted in *James McKeen Cattell*, Vol. 2, *op. cit.*, pp. 381–406.

——. The origin and distribution of scientific men. *Science*, 1927, *66*, 513–516. Reprinted in *James McKeen Cattell*, Vol. 1, *op. cit.*, pp. 535–542.

——. Early psychological laboratories. *Science*, 1928, *67*, 543–548. Reprinted in M. L. Reymert (Ed.), *Feelings and emotions: The Wittenberg symposium*. Worcester, Mass.: Clark University Press, 1928, pp. 427–433, & in *James McKeen Cattell*, Vol. 2, *op. cit.*, pp. 431–440.

——. Psychology in America. *Sci. Mon.*, N.Y., 1930, *30*, 114–126; *Science*, 1929, *70*, 335–347. Reprinted in *James McKeen Cattell*, Vol. 2, *op. cit.*, pp. 441–484.

——. The usefulness of psychology. *Science*, 1930, *72*, 284–287. Reprinted in *James McKeen Cattell*, Vol. 2, *op. cit.*, pp. 485–489.

——. Retrospect: Psychology as a profession. *J. consult. Psychol.*, 1937, *1*, 1–3. Reprinted in *J. consult. Psychol.*, 1946, *10*, 289–291, & in *James McKeen Cattell*, Vol. 2, *op. cit.*, pp. 496–499.

——. The founding of the association and of the Hopkins and Clark Laboratories. *Psychol. Rev.*, 1943, *50*, 61–64. Reprinted in *James McKeen Cattell*, Vol. 2, *op. cit.*, pp. 500–503.

Anastasi, *Individual Differences*; Dennis, *Psychology*; Herrnstein & Boring, *Source Book*; Jenkins & Paterson, *Individual Differences*; Moore & Hartmann, *Industrial Psychology*; Sahakian, *Psychology*; Shipley, *Classics*

JEAN-MARTIN CHARCOT
1825-1893
French Neurologist (27)

Charcot, J.-M. *Oeuvres complètes. Leçons sur les maladies du système nerveux.* (9 vols.) Paris: Bureaux du Progrès Médical, 1888–1894. **C**

————. *A propos de six cas d'hystérie chez l'homme.* Paris: Théraplix, 1969. **C**

————. *Clinical lectures on the diseases of old age.* Trans. by L. H. Hunt. New York: Wood, 1881. (1866–1867)

————. *Clinical lectures on senile and chronic diseases.* (2nd ed.) Trans. by W. S. Tuke. London: New Sydenham Society, 1881. (1867)

————. *Leçons sur les maladies du système nerveux faites à la Salpêtrière.* Ed. by D. M. Bourneville. (2nd ed.) (3 vols.) Paris: Delahaye, 1875–1887. (1872–1883)

————. *Klinische Vorträge über Krankheiten des Nervensystems.* (2 vols.) According to Dr. Bourneville's ed., & trans. by B. Fetzer. Stuttgart: Metzler, 1874–1878.

————. *Leçons sur les localisations dans les maladies du cerveau et de la moëlle épinière faites à la Faculté de Médecine de Paris.* (2nd ed.) Paris: Bureaux du Progrès Médical, 1876–1880. (1875)

————. *Lectures on localization in diseases of the brain.* Trans. by E. P. Fowler. New York: Wood, 1878. (1876)

————. *Lectures on the diseases of the nervous system.* (2nd ser.) (3 vols.) Trans. by G. Sigerson. London: New Sydenham Society, 1877–1889. (1879) (Reprinted 1962)

————, & Magnan, V. Inversion du sens génital et autres perversions sexuelles. *Arch. Neurol.,* 1882, *3,* 53–60 ; *4,* 296–322.

————. *Lectures on the localisation of cerebral and spinal diseases.* Trans. by W. B. Hadden. London: New Sydenham Society, 1883.

————. L'hypnotisme en thérapeutique ; guérison d'une contracture hystérique. *Rev. hypno.,* 1886–1887, *1,* 296–301, 321–327.

————. *Leçons du mardi à la Salpêtrière. Policlinique, 1887–1889.* (2 vols.) Paris: Bureaux du Progrès Médical, 1887–1889.

————, & Richer, P. *Les démoniaques dans l'art.* Paris: Delahaye & Lecrosnier, 1887.

————. *Traité de médecine.* (6 vols.) Paris: Masson, 1891–1894.

————. Sur un cas d'amnésie rétro-antérograde, probablement d'origine hystérique. *Rev. méd.,* 1892, *12,* 81–96.

————. Sur les divers états nerveux déterminés par l'hypnotisation chez les hystériques. *C. r. Acad. Sci.,* 1882, *94*(1), 403–405.

————, & Marie, P. Hysteria mainly hystero-epilepsy. In D. H. Tuke (Ed.), *Dictionary of psychological medicine.* Vol. 1. London: Churchill, 1892, pp. 627–641.

————, & Tourette, G. d. l. Hypnotism in the hysterical. In D. H. Tuke (Ed.), *Dictionary of psychological medicine.* Vol. 1. London: Churchill, 1892, pp. 606–610.

————. *Clinique des maladies du système nerveux.* (2 vols.) Ed. by G. Guinon. Paris: Bureaux du Progrès Médical, 1892–1893.

————, & Binet, A. Un calculateur du type visuel. *Rev. phil.,* 1893, *35,* 590–594.

————. The faith-cure. *New Rev.,* 1893, *8,* 18–31.

————, & Pitres, A. *Les centres moteurs corticaux chez l'homme.* Paris: Rueff, 1895.

————. Sur quelques points controversés de la doctrine des localisations cérébrales. *Arch. Clin. Bordeaux,* 1895, *3,* 389–427.

————. *La foi qui guérit.* Paris: Alcan, 1897.

Clendening, *Source Book* ; Goshen, *Documentary ;* Sahakian, *Psychology ;* Shipley, *Classics*

EDOUARD CLAPAREDE
1873-1940
Swiss Psychologist (26)

Claparède E. *Causeries psychologiques, 1ère série.* Geneva: Kündig, 1933. **C**

————. *Causeries psychologiques. 2ème série.* Geneva: Kündig, 1935. **C**

————. *Causeries psychologiques. 3ème série.* Geneva: Naville, 1937. **C**

Flournoy, T., & ————. Enquête sur l'audition colorée. *Arch. Sci. phys. nat.,* 1892, *28,* 505–508.

————. *Du sens musculaire à propos de quelques cas d'hémiataxie post-hémiplégique.* Geneva: Eggimann, 1897.

————. Contributions to the history of psychology: V. Translation of "stereognostic perception" by E. Claparède. (1898) Trans. by Gloria F. Wolinsky & Elizabeth Ayer. *Percept. mot. Skills,* 1967, *24,* 35–41.

————. Revue générale sur l'agnosie. *Année psychol.,* 1899, *6,* 74–143.

————. Avons-nous des sensations spécifiques de la position des membres? *Année psychol.,* 1900, *7,* 249–263.

————. Expériences sur la vitesse du soulèvement des poids de volumes différents. *Arch. Psychol.,* Geneva, 1901–1902, *1,* 69–94.

————. L'obsession de la rougeur, à propos d'un cas d'éreuthophobie. *Arch. Psychol.,* Geneva, 1901–1902, *1,* 307–334 ; 1902–1903, *2,* 60–61.

————. Essai d'une nouvelle classification des associations d'idées. *Arch. Psychol.,* Geneva, 1901–1902, *1,* 335–380.

————. La psychologie dans ses rapports avec la médecine. *Rev. méd. Suisse Rom.,* 1901, *21,* 597–609.

————. La faculté d'orientation lointaine (sens de direction – sens du retour). *Arch. Psychol.,* Geneva, 1902–1903, *2,* 133–180.

————. *L'association des idées.* Paris: Doin, 1903.

————. The consciousness of animals. *Int. Quart.,* 1903, *4,* 296–315.

————. Esquisse d'une théorie biologique du sommeil. *Arch. Psychol.,* Geneva, 1904–1905, *4,* 245–349. (Also Geneva: Kündig, 1905)

————. *Expériences collectives sur le témoignage (témoignage simple — appréciation — confrontation).* Geneva: Kündig, 1905.

————. *Psychologie de l'enfant et pédagogie expérimentale.* (Posthumous ed.) (2 vols.) Neuchâtel: Delachaux & Niestlé, 1946. (1905)

————. *Experimental pedagogy and the psychology of the child.* (4th ed.) Trans. by Mary Louch & H. Holman. London: Arnold, 1913. (1905)

————. L'agrandissement et la proximité apparents de la lune à l'horizon. *Arch. Psychol.,* Geneva, 1905–1906, *5,* 121–148, 254–257.

————. The value of biological interpretation for abnormal psychology. *J. abnorm. Psychol.,* 1906, *1,* 83–92.

————. La psychologie judiciaire. *Année psychol.,* 1906, *12,* 275–302.

————. La fonction du sommeil. *Riv. sci.,* 1907, *2,* 141–158.

————, Fehr, H., & Flournoy, T. *Enquête sur la méthode de travail des mathématiciens.* Geneva: Georg, 1908.

————. *Classification et plan des méthodes psychologiques.* Geneva: Kündig, 1908.

————, & Baade, W. Recherches expérimentales sur quelques processus psychiques simples dans un cas d'hypnose. *Arch. Psychol.,* Geneva, 1908–1909, *8,* 288–294.

————. *La psychologie animale de Charles Bonnet.* Geneva: Georg, 1909.

————. Die Methoden der tierpsychologischen Beobachtungen und Versuche. *Ber. III. Kongr. exper. Psychol.,* 1909, 22–58. (Also Leipzig: Barth, 1909)

————. William James (1842–1910). *Arch. Psychol.,* Geneva, 1910–1911, *10,* 96–105.

————. La question de la "mémoire" affective. *Arch. Psychol.,* Geneva, 1910–1911, *10,* 361–377.

————. Recognition and "me-ness." (1911) In D. Rapaport (Ed.), *Organization and pathology of thought.* New York: Columbia University Press, 1951, pp. 58–75.

————. Les chevaux savants d'Elberfeld. *Arch. Psychol.,* Geneva, 1912, *12,* 263–304.

————. Rousseau et la signification de l'enfance. *Ann. suisse Hyg. scol.,* 1912, *13,* 525–537.

————, & Bernheim, H. Definition, psychologische Interpretation und therapeutischer Wert des Hypnotismus. *J. Psychol. Neurol.,* 1912, *19,* 276–299.

————. J. J. Rousseau et la conception fonctionnelle de l'enfance. *Rev. Métaphys. Morale,* 1912, *20,* 391–416.

————. La question du sommeil. *Année psychol.,* 1912, *18,* 419–459.

————. *La pédagogie de John Dewey.* Neuchâtel: Delachaux & Niestlé, 1913.

————. Encore les chevaux d'Elberfeld. *Arch. Psychol., Geneva,* 1913, *13,* 244–284. (Also Geneva: Kündig, 1913)

————. Tests de développement et tests d'aptitude. *Arch. Psychol.,* Geneva, 1914, *14,* 101–107.

————. Expériences sur la mémoire des associations spontanées. *Arch. Psychol.,* Geneva, 1915, *15,* 306–313.

————. Profils psychologiques gradués d'après l'ordination des sujets. *Arch. Psychol.,* Geneva, 1916–1917, *16,* 70–81.

————. *L'école sur mesure.* Lausanne: Payot, 1953. (1920)

————. Théodore Flournoy, sa vie et son oeuvre (1854–1920). *Arch. Psychol.,* Geneva, 1921–1923, *18,* 1–125.

————. *Problems and methods of vocational guidance.* Geneva: International Labour Office, 1922.

Dumas, G., & ————. L'orientation et l'équilibre. In G. Dumas (Ed.), *Traité de psychologie.* Vol. 1. Paris: Alcan, 1923, pp. 572–605.

————. *Comment diagnostiquer les aptitudes des écoliers?* Paris: Flammarion, 1924.

————. The nature of general intelligence and ability. *Brit. J. Psychol.,* 1923–1924, *14,* 236–242.

————. Note sur la localisation du moi. *Arch. Psychol.,* Geneva, 1924–1925, *19,* 172–182.

————. Les temps de réaction et la psychologie appliquée. *Arch. Psychol.,* Geneva, 1924–1925, *19,* 277–284.

————. The psychology of the child at Geneva and the J. J. Rousseau Institute. *J. genet. Psychol.,* 1925, *32,* 92–104.

————. Does the will express the entire personality? In C. M. Campbell (Ed.), *Problems of personality.* London: Kegan Paul, 1925, pp. 37–43.

————. Pedagogical tendencies. *Monist,* 1926, *36,* 477–486.

————. Feelings and emotions. In M. L. Reymert (Ed.), *Feelings and emotions: The Wittenberg symposium.* Worcester, Mass.: Clark University Press, 1928, pp. 124–139.

————. Opinions et travaux divers relatifs à la théorie biologique du sommeil et de l'hystérie. *Arch. Psychol.,* Geneva, 1928–1929, *21,* 113–174.

————. Le sommeil et la veille. *J. Psychol. norm. path.,* 1929, *26,* 433–493.

————. Edouard Claparède. In C. Murchison (Ed.), *A history of psychology in autobiography.* Vol. 1. Worcester, Mass.: Clark University Press, 1930, pp. 63–97. **B**

————. Esquisse historique des Congrès Internationaux de Psychologie. Remerciement au nom des congressistes étrangers. *Ninth Int. Congress Psychol., Proc. Papers.* Princeton, N.J.: Psychological Review, 1930, pp. 33–47.

————. L'émotion "pure." *Arch. Psychol.,* Geneva, 1930–1931, *22,* 333–347.

————. *L'éducation fonctionnelle.* Neuchâtel: Delachaux & Niestlé, 1931.

————. Point de vue du psychologue et point de vue du sujet. *Arch. Psychol.,* Geneva, 1931–1932, *23,* 1–24.

————. La genèse de l'hypothèse: Etude expérimentale. *Arch. Psychol.,* Geneva, 1933–1934, *24,* 1–155.

————. *La genèse de l'hypothèse: Etude expérimentale.* Geneva: Kündig, 1934.

————. *Le sentiment d'infériorité chez l'enfant.*

Geneva: Université de Genève, Institut des sciences de l'éducation, 1934.

———. Le sommeil et la veille. In G. Dumas (Ed.), *Nouveau traité de psychologie*. Vol. 4. Paris: Alcan, 1934, pp. 455–522.

———. Die Jugendkunde und pädagogische Psychologie in Genf. *Z. Jugendk.*, 1935, *5*, 76–84.

———. Rousseau et l'origine du langage. *Ann. Soc. Rousseau*, 1936, No. 24.

———. La psychologie fonctionnelle. *Acta Psychol.*, Geneva, 1936, *1*, 65–76.

———. Some major laws of conduct. *Amer. J. Psychol.*, 1937, *50*, 68–78.

———. Simples souvenirs. In Various, *Centenaire de Th. Ribot et Jubilé de la Psychologie Scientifique Française*. Paris: Imprimerie moderne, 1939, pp. 139–150.   **B**

———. *Morale et politique ou les vacances de la probité*. Neuchâtel: Baconnière, 1947. (1940)

———. *L'orientation lointaine*. Paris: Presses Universitaires de France, 1943.

———. Autobiographie. (1946) In P. Bovet (Ed.), *Le développement mental*. Neuchâtel: Delachaux & Niestlé, 1946, pp. 34–42.   **B**

Arnold, *Emotion ;* Hameline, *Anthologie ;* Rapaport, *Thought*

GEORGE ELLETT COGHILL
1872-1941
American Anatomist (20)

Coghill, G. E. Cranial nerves of Triton taeniatus. *J. comp. Neurol.*, 1906, *16*, 247–264.

———. The development of the swimming movement in amphibian embryos. *Anat. Rec.*, 1908, *2*, 148.

———. The reaction to tactile stimuli and the development of the swimming movement in embryos of Diemyctylus torosus Eschscholtz. *J. comp. Neurol.*, 1909, *19*, 83–105.

———. The primary ventral roots and somatic motor column of Amblystoma. *J. comp. Neurol.*, 1913, *23*, 121–143.

———. Correlated anatomical and physiological studies of the growth of the nervous system of Amphibia. I. The afferent system of the trunk of Amblystoma. II. The afferent system of the head of Amblystoma. III. The floor plate of Amblystoma. IV. Rates of proliferation and differentiation in the central nervous system of Amblystoma. V. The growth of the pattern of the motor mechanism of Amblystoma punctatum. VI. The mechanism of integration in Amblystoma punctatum. VII. The growth of the pattern of the association mechanism of the rhombencephalon and spinal cord of Amblystoma punctatum. VIII. The development of the pattern of differentiation in the cerebrum of Amblystoma punctatum. IX. The mechanism of association of Amblystoma punctatum. X. Corollaries of the anatomical and physiological study of Amblystoma from the age of earliest movement to swimming. XI. The proliferation of cells in the spinal cord as a factor in the individuation of reflexes of the hind leg of Amblystoma punctatum cope. XII. Quantitative relations of the spinal cord and ganglia correlated with the development of reflexes of the leg in Amblystoma punctatum cope. *J. comp. Neurol.*, 1914, *24*, 161–233 ; 1916, *26*, 247–340 ; 1924, *37*, 37–69, 71–120 ; 1926, *40*, 47–94 ; 1926, *41*, 95–152 ; 1926, *42*, 1–16 ; 1928, *45*, 227–247 ; 1930, *51*, 311–375 ; 1931, *53*, 147–168 ; 1933, *57*, 327–358 ; 1936, *64*, 135–167.

———. The early development of behavior in Amblystoma and in man. *Arch. Neurol. Psychiat.*, Chicago, 1929, *21*, 989–1009.

———. *Anatomy and the problem of behavior*. New York: Hafner, 1964. (1929)

———. The genetic interrelation of instinctive behavior and reflexes. *Psychol. Rev.*, 1930, *37*, 264–266.

———. The development of half centers in relation to the question of antagonism in reflexes. *J. gen. Psychol.*, 1930, *4*, 335–338.

———. The structural basis of the integration of behavior. *Proc. Nat. Acad. Sci.*, 1930, *16*, 637–643.

──────. Individuation versus integration in the development of behavior. *J. gen. Psychol.,* 1930, *3,* 431–435.

──────. Growth of a localized functional center in a relatively equipotential nervous organ. *Arch. Neurol. Psychiat.,* Chicago, 1933, *30,* 1086–1091.

──────. The neuro-embryologic study of behavior: Principles, perspective and aim. *Science,* 1933, *78,* 131–138.

──────. Integration and motivation of behavior as problems of growth. *J. genet. Psychol.,* 1936, *48,* 3–19.

──────. Space-time as a pattern of psycho-organismal mentation. *Amer. J. Psychol.,* 1938, *51,* 759–763.

──────. Early embryonic somatic movements in birds and in mammals other than man. *Monog. Soc. Res. Child Developmt,* 1940, *5,* No. 2.

──────. Flexion spasms and mass reflexes in relation to the ontogenetic development of behavior. *J. comp. Neurol.,* 1943, *79,* 463–486.

SAMUEL TAYLOR COLERIDGE
1772-1834
English Philosopher (11)

Coleridge, S. T. *Confession of an inquiring spirit.* Ed. by H. N. Coleridge. Boston: Munroe, 1841. (1840)   **C**

──────. *The complete works of S. T. Coleridge.* (7 vols.) Ed. by W. G. T. Shedd. New York: Harper, 1854.   **C**

──────. *Anima Poetae: From the unpublished note-books of Samuel Taylor Coleridge.* Ed. by E. H. Coleridge. New York: Houghton Mifflin, 1895.   **B C**

──────. *Coleridge on logic and learning, with selections from the unpublished manuscripts.* Ed. by Alice D. Snyder. New Haven: Yale University Press, 1929. (Reprinted 1970)   **C**

──────. *The philosophical lectures (1808–1819),* hitherto unpublished. Ed. by Kathleen Coburn. New York: Philosophical Library, 1949.   **C**

──────. *Inquiring spirit: A new presentation of Coleridge from his published and unpublished prose writings.* Ed. by Kathleen Coburn. New York: Pantheon Books, 1951.   **C**

──────. *Coleridge on the Seventeenth Century.* Ed. by Roberta F. Brinkley. Durham, N.C.: Duke University Press, 1955. (Reprinted 1969)   **C**

──────. *Collected letters.* (3 vols. in 6) Ed. by E. L. Griggs. London: Oxford University Press, 1956–1971.   **C**

──────. *The notebooks of Samuel Taylor Coleridge.* (2 vols. in 4 so far) Ed. by Kathleen Coburn. New York: Pantheon Books, 1957–   **C**

──────. *The collected works of Samuel Taylor Coleridge.* (Ult. 16 vols. in 24) Ed. by Kathleen Coburn. Princeton, N.J.: Princeton University Press, 1968–   **B Bl C**

──────. *The friend.* (2nd ed.) (3 vols.) Ed. by Barbara Rooke. London: Routledge & Kegan Paul, 1969. (1808–1810) In *Collected works,* Vol. 4 (1, 2), *op. cit.*   **B**

──────. *Biographia Literaria: Or biographical sketches of literary life and opinions.* Ed. by G. Watson. New York: Dutton, 1962. (1817)

──────. *Aids to reflection.* (7th ed.) Ed. by H. N. Coleridge. New York: Stanford & Swords, 1850. (1825)

──────. *Hints towards the formation of a more comprehensive theory of life.* Ed. by S. B. Watson. Philadelphia: Lea & Blanchard, 1898. (1848) (Reprinted 1970)

──────. On the definitions of life hitherto received. Hints toward a more comprehensive theory. (1848) In *Miscellanies, aesthetic and literary: to which is added the theory of life.* Pref. by S. B. Watson. London: Bell, 1885, pp. 349–430.

──────. *Treatise on method as published in the Encyclopedia Metropolitana.* Ed. by Alice D. Snyder. London: Constable, 1934. (1849)

JAN AMOS COMENIUS
(Czech: Jan Amos Komensky)
1592-1670
Czech Educator (15)

Comenius, J. A. *The great didactic of John Amos Comenius.* (Abridged) Trans. by M. W. Keatinge. New York: McGraw-Hill, 1931. (1657)
C

——. *Grosse Didaktik in neuer Uebersetzung.* Ed. by A. Fletner. Düsseldorf: Bondi, 1954. (1657)
C

——. *Opera didactica omnia.* (3 vols.) Prague: Czechoslovak Academy of Sciences, 1957. (1657)
C

——. *Spisy Jana Amosa Komenského.* (6 vols.) Ed. by J. Kvacala. Prague: Nakladem Ceské Akademie, 1897–1902.
C

——. *Die Mutterschule.* Ed. by K. Würzburger. Zurich: Zwingli, 1943. (1921)
C

——. *De rerum humanarum emendatione consultatio catholica.* (2 vols.) Prague: Czechoslovak Academy of Sciences, 1966.
C

——. *John Amos Comenius on education.* Intro. by J. Piaget. New York: Teachers College Press, 1967.
C

——. *Ausgewählte Werke.* (3 vols.) Ed. by K. Schaller & D. Tschizewskij. Hildesheim: Olms, 1968.
C

——. *The labyrinth of the world and the paradise of the heart.* Trans. by M. Spinka. Chicago: National Union of Czechoslovak Protestants in America, 1942. (1623)

——. *The school of infancy.* Ed. by E. M. Eller. Chapel Hill, N.C.: University of North Carolina Press, 1956. (1633)

——. *A reformation of schooles.* Trans. by S. Hartlib. Menston: Scholar Press, 1969. (1642)

——. *The analytic didactic of Comenius.* Trans. by V. Jelinek. Chicago: University of Chicago Press, 1953. (1657)

——. *The Orbis Pictus.* Ed. by C. W. Bardeen. Syracuse, N.Y.: Bardeen, 1887. (1657)

——. *Orbis sensualium pictus.* (Facsimile of 3rd London ed.) Sydney: Sydney University Press, 1967. (1657)

Nash, *Models;* Price, *Education;* Ulich, *Educational Wisdom*

(ISADORE) AUGUSTE
(MARIE FRANCOIS) COMTE
1798-1857
French Philosopher (25)

Comte, A. *Lettres d'Auguste Comte à M. Valat.* Ed. by P. Valat. Paris: Dunod, 1870.   B C

——. *Lettres d'Auguste Comte à John Stuart Mill.* Paris: Leroux, 1877. (1841–1846)   B C

——. *Oeuvres.* (12 vols.) (Ed. not given) Paris: Anthropos, 1968–1971. (1851–1856)   C

——. *Opuscules de philosophie sociale 1819–1828.* Paris: Leroux, 1883.   C

——. *Confessions and testament of Auguste Comte and his correspondence with Clotilde de Vaux.* Ed. by A. Crompton. Liverpool: Young & Sons, 1910. (1884)   C

——, & Mill, J. S. *Lettres inédites de John Stuart Mill à Auguste Comte publiées avec les réponses de Comte.* Ed. by L. Lévy-Bruhl. Paris: Alcan, 1899.   B C

——. *Passages from the letters of Auguste Comte.* Trans. by J. K. Ingram. London: Black, 1901. (Reprinted 1970)   B C

——. *Correspondance inédite d'Auguste Comte.* (4 vols.) Paris: Société Positiviste, 1903–1904.   B C

——. *Lettres inédites à C. de Blignières.* Ed. by P. Arbousse-Bastide. Paris: Vrin, 1932.   B C

——. *Nouvelles lettres inédites.* Ed. by P. E. de Berredo-Carneiro. Paris: Archives Positivistes, 1939.   B C

——. *Oeuvres choisies.* Intro. by H. Gouhier. Paris: Aubier, 1952.   C

——. *Sociologie: Textes choisis.* (2nd ed.) Paris: Presses Universitaires de France, 1963. (1957)   C

————. *Introduction to positive philosophy.* Ed., intro., & rev. trans. by F. Ferre. Indianapolis, Ind.: Bobbs-Merrill, 1970. (1830)

————. *Cours de philosophie positive.* (4th ed.) (6 vols.) Brussels:Culture et Civilisation, 1972. (1830–1842)

————. *The positive philosophy of Auguste Comte.* (3rd ed.) (3 vols.) Trans. & condensed by Harriet Martineau. London: Bell, 1896. (1830–1842) (Reprinted 1970)

————. *A discourse on the positive spirit.* Trans. by E. S. Beesly. London: Reeves, 1903. (1844) (Reprinted 1970)

————. *A general view of positivism.* Trans. by J. H. Bridges. New York: Speller, 1957. (1848)

————. *Calendrier positiviste ou système général de commémoration publique.* Brussels: Culture et Civilisation, 1969. (1849)

————. *System of positive polity.* (4 vols.) Trans. by R. Congreve. New York: Franklin, 1966. (1851–1854)

————. *Système de politique positive ou traité de sociologie, instituant la religion de l'humanité.* (4 vols.) Brussels: Culture et Civilisation, 1969. (1851–1854)

————. *Religion of humanity: Subjective synthesis or universal system of the conceptions adapted to the normal state of humanity.* London: Kegan Paul, Trench & Truebner, 1891. (1856)

————. *The catechism of positive religion.* Trans. by R. Congreve. London: Chapman, 1858. (1852)

Coser, *Sociological Thought;* Gardiner, *Philosophy;* Park & Burgess, *Sociology;* Parsons, *Society;* Rand, *Classical Philosophers*

ETIENNE BONNOT DE CONDILLAC
1714-1780
French Philosopher (25)

Condillac, E. B. d. *Oeuvres de Condillac, revues, corrigées par l'auteur. imprimées sur ses manuscrits autographes, et augmentées de la langue des calculs, ouvrage posthume.* (23 vols.) Ed. by G. Arncoux *et al.* Paris: Houel, 1798.　**C**

————. *Oeuvres philosophiques de Condillac.* (3 vols.) Ed. by G. Le Roy. Paris: Presses Universitaires de France, 1947–1951.　**Bl C**

————. *Lettres inédites à Gabriel Cramer.* Ed. by G. Le Roy. Paris: Presses Universitaires de France, 1953.　**B C**

————. *An essay on the origin of human knowledge: Being a supplement to Mr. Locke's essay on the human understanding.* Trans. by T. Nugent. London: Nourse, 1756. (1746) Reprinted in French in *Oeuvres philosophiques,* Vol. 1, *op. cit.,* pp. 1–118.

————. *Traité des systèmes, où l'on en démêle les inconvénients et les avantages.* Paris: Libraires Associés, 1787. (1749) Reprinted in *Oeuvres philosophiques,* Vol. 1, *op. cit.,* pp. 119–217.

————. *Condillac's treatise on the sensations.* Trans. by Geraldine Carr. London: Favil Press, 1930. (1754) Reprinted 1971, & in French in *Oeuvres philosophiques,* Vol. 1, *op. cit..* pp. 219–335.

————. *Traité des animaux, où, après avoir fait des observations critiques sur le sentiment de Descartes, et sur celui de M. de Buffon, on entreprend d'expliquer leurs principales facultés.* (1755) Reprinted in *Oeuvres philosophiques,* Vol. 1, *op. cit.,* pp. 337–379.

————. *De l'art de raisonner.* (1775) Reprinted in *Oeuvres philosophiques,* Vol. 1, *op. cit.,* pp. 617–714.

————. *De l'art de penser.* (1775) Reprinted in *Oeuvres philosophiques,* Vol. 1, *op. cit.,* pp. 715–776.

————. *Dissertation on freedom.* (1755) In *Treatise on the sensations, op. cit.,* pp. 243–250.

————. *The logic of Condillac.* Trans. by J. Neef. Philadelphia: Private publ., 1809. (1780) Reprinted in French in *Oeuvres de Condillac,* Vol. 22, *op. cit.*

————. *La langue des calculs.* Paris: Houel, 1797–1798. Reprinted in *Oeuvres de Condillac,* Vol. 23, *op. cit.*

Murphy, *Western ;* Rand, *Classical Phi-losophers ;* Rand, *Classical Psychologists ;* Reeves, *Body Mind ;* Sahakian, *Psychology*

MARIE JEAN ANTOINE CONDORCET
(Marie Jean Antoine Nicholas de Caritat, Marquis de Condorcet)
1743-1794
French Philosopher (20)

Condorcet, M. J. A. *Oeuvres de Condorcet.* (12 vols.) Ed. by A. Condorcet-O'Connor & F. Arago. Stuttgart: Frommann, 1968. (1847–1849)   **C**

———. *Correspondance inédite de Condorcet et Turgot, 1770–1779.* Ed. by C. Henry. Paris: Charavay, 1883.   **B C**

———. *Eloges des Académiciens de l'Académie Royale des Sciences morts depuis 1666 jusqu'en 1699.* Paris: Singer-Polignac, 1968. (1773)

———. *Eloge de Mariotte.* (1773) In *Eloges des Académiciens, op. cit.,* pp. 49–66.

———. *Eloge de Huyghens.* (1773) In *Eloges des Académiciens, op. cit.,* pp. 104–134.

———. *Eloge de D'Alembert.* (1784) Reprinted in *Oeuvres complètes de D'Alembert.* Vol. 1. Geneva: Slatkine, 1967, pp. i–xxviii.

———. *Life of Voltaire.* (No trans. given) Philadelphia: Spotswood, 1792. (1785)

———. *Essai sur l'application de l'analyse à la probabilité des décisions rendues à la pluralité des voix.* Paris: Imprimerie Royale, 1785.

———. *Life of M. Turgot.* (No trans. given) London: Johnson, 1787. (1786)

———. *Rapport et projet de décret sur l'organisation générale de l'instruction publique.* (1792) (New ed.) Ed. by G. Compayré. Paris: Hachette, 1883. Reprinted in *Oeuvres,* Vol. 7, *op. cit.,* pp. 449–573.

———. *Tableau général de la science qui a pour objet l'application du calcul aux sciences morales et politiques.* (1793) Reprinted in *Oeuvres,* Vol. 1, *op. cit.,* pp. 539–573.

———. *Sketch for a historical picture of the progress of the human mind.* Trans. by June Barraclough, & intro. by S. Hampshire. London: Weidenfeld & Nicolson, 1955. (1795)

———. *Eléments du calcul des probabilités, et son application aux jeux de hasard, à la loterie, et aux jugements des hommes.* Paris: Royez, 1805.

———. Observations on the twenty-ninth book of the spirit of laws. In [A. L. C. Destutt de Tracy] *A commentary and review of Montesquieu's Spirit of laws.* Philadelphia: Duane, 1811, pp. 261–287.

———. *Esquisse d'un tableau historique des progrès de l'esprit humain.* Rev. by O. H. Prior ; new ed. by Y. Belaval. Paris: Vrin, 1970.

Brinton, *Age Reason ;* Slotkin, *Anthropology*

CHARLES HORTON COOLEY
1864-1929
American Sociologist (13)

Cooley, C. H. *Sociological theory and social research, being the selected papers of Charles Horton Cooley.* New York: Holt, 1930.
                                          B Bl C

———. Genius, fame, and the comparison of races. *Ann. Amer. Acad. Pol. Soc. Sci.,* 1897, *9,* 1–42. Reprinted in *Sociological theory and social research, op. cit.,* pp. 121–159.

———. *Human nature and the social order.* (Rev. ed.) In Charles H. Cooley, *Two major works: Social organization and human nature and the social order.* Glencoe, Ill.: Free Press, 1956. (1902)

———. A study of the early use of self-words by a child. *Psychol. Rev.,* 1908, *15,* 339–357. Reprinted in *Sociological theory and social research, op. cit.,* pp. 229–247.

———. *Social organization: A study of the larger mind.* In *Two major works, op. cit.* (1909)

————. *Social process.* Intro. by R. C. Hinkle. Carbondale, Ill.: Southern Illinois University Press, 1966. (1918)

————. Heredity or environment. *J. appl. Soc.,* 1926, *10,* 303–307.

————. *Life and the student: Roadside notes on human nature, society, and letters.* New York: Knopf, 1927. **B**

Borgatta, *Present-day Sociology;* Coser, *Sociological Theory;* Coser, *Sociological Thought;* Goldschmidt, *Mankind;* McNall, *Sociological Perspectives;* Park & Burgess, *Sociology;* Parsons, *Society;* Ross, *Social Order*

EMILE COUE
1857-1926
French Hypnotist (18)

Coué, E., & Orton, J. L. *Conscious auto-suggestion.* London: Fisher, Unwin (n. d.)

————. *La maîtrise de soi-même par l'auto-sug-gestion consciente.* (New ed.) Nancy: Author, 1923. (1921)

————. Self mastery through conscious auto-suggestion. (1921) In E. Coué & C. H. Brooks, *Better and better every day.* New York: Barnes & Noble, 1961, pp. 9–81.

————. Autosuggestion. *J. ment. Sci.,* 1923, *69,* 137–140.

————. *My method, including American impressions.* Garden City, N.Y.: Doubleday, Page, 1923.

————. *How to practice suggestion and auto-suggestion.* New York: American Library Service, 1923.

VICTOR COUSIN
1792-1867
French Philosopher (15)

Cousin, V. *Philosophical essays.* Trans. by G. Ripley. London: Hamilton & Adams, 1839. (1819–1820) **C**

————. *Philosophie écossaise.* (4th ed.) Paris: Lévy, 1864. (1819–1820) **C**

————. *Fragments philosophiques.* (4th ed.) (2 vols.) Paris: Ladrange, 1847. (1826) **C**

————. *Oeuvres complètes.* (16 vols. in 12) Paris: Ladrange, 1846–1851. **C**

————. *Lectures on the true, the beautiful, the good.* (3rd ed.) Trans. by O. W. Wight. New York: Appleton, 1893. (1818)

————. *Du vrai, du beau et du bien.* (31st ed.) Paris: Perrin, 1926. (1818)

————. *The philosophy of Kant.* Ed. by A. G. Henderson. London: Chapman, 1854. (1819–1820)

————. *Philosophie sensualiste au dix-huitième siècle.* (5th ed.) Paris: Didier, 1866. (1819–1820)

————. *Introduction to the history of philosophy.* Trans. by H. G. Linberg. Boston: Hillard, Gray, Little & Wilkins, 1832. (1828)

————. *Histoire générale de la philosophie.* (11th ed.) Paris: Perrin, 1884. (1828)

————. *Cours de l'histoire de la philosophie.* (Rev. ed.) (3 vols. in 2) Paris: Didier, 1841. (1828–1829)

————. *Elements of psychology included in a critical examination of Locke's Essay on the human understanding, and additional pieces.* (4th ed.) Trans. by C. S. Henry. New York: Iveson & Phinney, 1856. (1834)

————. Nouvelles considérations sur le sommeil, les songes et le somnambulisme. Mémoire posthume de M. Maine de Biran. *Acad. Roy. Sci. Mor. Pol.,* 1837, *1,* Ser. 2, 5–77.

————. *Cours de l'histoire de la philosophie moderne.* (New ed.) (5 vols.) Paris: Ladrange, 1846. (1841)

————. *Course of the history of modern philosophy.* (2 vols.) Trans. by O. W. Wight. New York: Appleton, 1852. (1841) (Reprinted 1970)

————. *Etudes sur Pascal.* (6th ed.) Paris: Didier, 1876. (1842)

————. Un fragment inédit de Pascal: Discours sur la passion de l'amour. *Rev. Deux Mondes,* Sept. 1843, 990–1007.

------. *Fragments de philosophie cartésienne.* (5th ed.) Paris: Didier, 1866. (1845)

BENEDETTO CROCE
1866-1952
Italian Philosopher (15)

Croce, B. *The philosophy of the spirit.* (4 vols.) Trans. by D. Ainslie. London: Macmillan, 1909–1921.   **C**

------. *Politics and morals.* Trans. by S. J. Catiglione. London: Allen & Unwin, 1946. (1928) (Reprinted 1970)   **C**

------. *My philosophy, and other essays on the moral and political problems of our time.* Selected by R. Klibansky, & trans. by E. F. Carritt. London: Allen & Unwin, 1949.   **C**

------. *Historical materialism and the economics of Karl Marx.* Trans. by C. M. Meredith. New York: Macmillan, 1914. (Also New York: Russell & Russell, 1966) (1900)

------. *Logic as the science of pure concept.* (3rd ed.) Trans. by D. Ainslie. New York: Macmillan, 1917. (1909)

------. *Aesthetic: As science of expression and general linguistic.* (2nd ed.) Trans. by D. Ainslie. London: Macmillan, 1929. (1909)

------. *Philosophy of Giambattista Vico.* Trans. by R. G. Collingwood. New York: Macmillan, 1913. (1911)

------. *The essence of aesthetic.* Trans. by D. Ainslie. London: Heinemann, 1921. (1913)

------. *What is living and what is dead of the philosophy of Hegel.* Trans. by D. Ainslie. London: Macmillan, 1915. (1913)

------. *The conduct of life.* Trans. by A. Livingston. Freeport, N.Y.: Books for Libraries, 1967. (1915)

------. *History: Its theory and practice.* Trans. by D. Ainslie. New York: Harcourt, Brace, 1921. (1917)

------. *An autobiography.* (2nd ed.) Trans. by R. G. Collingwood. Oxford: Clarendon Press, 1945. (1918)   **B**

------. *Goethe.* Trans. by J. Schlosser. Zurich: Amaltheaverlag, 1920. (1919)

------. Benedetto Croce. In R. Schmidt (Ed.), *Die Philosophie der Gegenwart in Selbstdarstellungen.* Vol. 4. Leipzig: Meiner, 1923, pp. 1–46.
                                                            B Bl

WILLIAM JOHN CROZIER
1892-1955
American Physiologist (18)

Crozier, W. J., & Parker, G. H. Recent developments in biology. In *Development of Harvard University, 1869–1929.* Cambridge: Harvard University Press, 1930, pp. 394–399.

------. Chemoreception. In C. Murchison (Ed.), *A handbook of general experimental psychology.* Worcester, Mass.: Clark University Press, 1934, pp. 987–1036.

------, & Hoagland, H. The study of living organisms. In C. Murchison (Ed.), *A handbook of general experimental psychology.* Worcester, Mass.: Clark University Press, 1934, pp. 3–108.

------. On the variability of critical illumination for flicker fusion and intensity discrimination. *J. gen. Physiol.,* 1936, *19,* 503–523.

------, Wolf, E., & Zerrahn-Wolf, Gertrud. On critical frequency and critical illumination for response to flickered light. *J. gen. Physiol.,* 1936, *20,* 211–228.

------, Wolf, E., & Zerrahn-Wolf, Gertrud. Intensity and critical frequency for visual flicker. *J. gen. Physiol.,* 1938, *21,* 203–222.

------, Wolf, E., & Zerrahn-Wolf, Gertrud. On the duplexity theory of visual response in vertebrates. I. *Proc. Nat. Acad. Sci.,* 1938, *24,* 125–130.

------, Wolf, E., & Zerrahn-Wolf, Gertrud. Specific constants for visual excitation. II. *Proc. Nat. Acad. Sci.,* 1938, *24,* 221–224.

------, & Wolf, E. On the duplexity theory of visual response in vertebrates. II. *Proc. Nat. Acad. Sci.,* 1938, *24,* 538–541.

------, & Wolf, E. Specific constants for visual

excitation. III. *Proc. Nat. Acad. Sci.*, 1938, *24*, 542–545.

————, & Wolf, E. The flicker response contour for the gecko (rod retina). *J. gen. Physiol.*, 1939, *22*, 555–566.

————, & Wolf, E. The flicker response contour for the frog. *J. gen. Physiol.*, 1939, *23*, 229–238.

————. The theory of the visual threshold. I. Time and intensity. *Proc. Nat. Acad. Sci.*, 1940, *26*, 54–60.

————, & Wolf, E. Temperature and the critical intensity for response to visual flicker. IV. On the invariance of critical thermal increments, and the theory of the response contour. *Proc. Nat. Acad. Sci.*, 1940, *26*, 60–65.

————. On the law for minimal discrimination of intensities. *Proc. Nat. Acad. Sci.*, 1940, *26*, 382–389.

————, & Wolf, E. Theory and measurement of visual mechanisms. VI. Wave length and flash duration in flicker. *J. gen. Physiol.*, 1941, *25*, 89–110.

————, & Wolf, E. Theory and measurement of visual mechanisms. VIII. The form of the flicker contour. *J. gen. Physiol.*, 1942, *25*, 369–379. Reprinted in R. D. Luce (Ed.), *Readings in mathematical psychology*. Vol. 2. New York: Wiley, 1965, pp. 310–320.

————, & Wolf, E. Theory and measurement of visual mechanisms. XI. On flicker with subdivided fields. *J. gen. Physiol.*, 1944, *27*, 401–432.

————, & Wolf, E. Theory and measurement of visual mechanisms. XII. On visual duplexity. *J. gen. Physiol.*, 1944, *27*, 513–528.

Miller, *Mathematics*

(BARON) GEORGES (JEAN-LEOPOLD-NICOLAS-FREDERIC) CUVIER
1769-1832
French Biologist (12)

Cuvier, G. *Lettres de Georges Cuvier à C. M. (i.e., H.) Pfaff, 1788–1792, sur l'histoire natu-*

relle, la politique, et la littérature. Trans. by L. Marchant. Paris: Masson, 1858.   **B C**

————. *Tableau élémentaire de l'histoire naturelle des animaux.* Brussels: Culture et Civilisation, 1969. (1798)

————. *Lectures on comparative anatomy.* (2 vols.) Trans. by W. Ross. London: Longman & Rees, 1802. (1800–1805)

————. *Leçons d'anatomie comparée.* Ed. by C. Duméril & G. L. Duvernoy. Brussels: Culture et Civilisation, 1969. (1800–1805)

————. Rapport sur un mémoire de MM. Gall et Spurzheim, relatif à l'anatomie du cerveau. *Ann. Muséum*, 1808, *11*, 329–375.

————. *Rapport historique sur les progrés des sciences naturelles depuis 1789, et sur leur état actuel.* Brussels: Culture et Civilisation, 1969. (1810)

————. *Recherches sur les ossements fossiles de quadrupèdes, où l'on rétablit les caractères de plusieurs espèces d animaux que les révolutions du globe paroissent avoir détruites.* (4 vols.) Brussels: Culture et Civilisation, 1969. (1812)

————. *Discours sur les révolutions de la surface du globe, et sur les changements qu'elles ont produits dans le règne animal.* Brussels: Culture et Civilisation, 1969. (1812)

————. *A discourse on the revolutions of the surface of the globe, and the changes thereby produced in the animal kingdom.* Trans. unspecified. Philadelphia: Carey & Lea, 1831. (1812)

————. Réflexions sur la marche actuelle des sciences et sur leurs rapports avec la société. (1816) In *Recueil des éloges historiques lus dans les séances publiques de l'Institut de France.* Vol. 3. (New ed.) Paris: Didot, 1861, pp. 251–270.

————. *Le règne animal distribué d'après son organisation, pour servir de base à l'histoire naturelle des animaux et d'introduction à l'anatomie comparée.* Brussels: Culture et Civilisation, 1969. (1817)

————. *The animal kingdom, arranged after its organization, forming a natural history of* animals, and an introduction to comparative anatomy. (2nd ed.) Trans. unspecified. Additions by W. B. Carpenter & J. O. Westwood. Boston: Estes & Lauriat, 1878. (1817)

———. Instinct. In F. G. Levrault (Ed.), *Dictionnaire des sciences naturelles.* Vol. 23. Paris: Le Normant, 1822, pp. 528–554.

———. *Histoire des sciences naturelles, depuis leur origine jusqu'à nos jours, chez tous les peuples connus.* (5 vols.) Ed. by M. de Saint-Agy. Brussels: Culture et Civilisation, 1969. (1841–1845)

Bodenheimer, *Biology ;* Count, *Race*

JOHN DALTON
1766-1844
English Chemist (23)

Dalton, J., et al. *Foundations of atomic theory, comprising papers and abstracts.* Edinburgh: Livingstone, 1948.   **C**

———. *Meteorological observations and essays.* (2nd ed.) Manchester: Harrison & Crossfield, 1834. (1793)

———. Extraordinary facts relating to the vision of colours: With observations. *Mem. Lit. Phil. Soc. Manchester,* 1798, *5,* 28–45.

———. On the absorption of gases by water and other liquids. *Mem. Lit. Phil. Soc. Manchester,* Ser. 2, 1805, *1,* 271–287. Reprinted in *Foundations of atomic theory, op. cit.,* pp. 15–26.

———. Experimental enquiry into the proportion of the several gases or elastic fluids, constituting the atmosphere. *Mem. Lit. Phil. Soc. Manchester,* Ser. 2, 1805, *1,* 244–258. Reprinted in *Foundations of atomic theory, op. cit.,* pp. 5–15.

———. *A new system of chemical philosophy.* London: Dawsons, 1953. (1808–1827)

———. On respiration and animal heat. *Mem. Lit. Phil. Soc. Manchester,* Ser. 2, 1813, *2,* 15–44.

Dennis, *Psychology ;* Hall, *Nature's Laws ;* Schwartz & Bishop, *Moments Discovery*

CHARLES (ROBERT) DARWIN
1809-1882
English Biologist (27)

Darwin, C. *The life and letters of Charles Darwin.* (2 vols.) Ed. by F. Darwin. New York: Appleton, 1887.   **B Bl C**

———. *The autobiography of Charles Darwin 1809–1882.* Ed. by Nora Barlow. London: Collins, 1958. (1887)   **B C**

———. Darwin's *Notebooks on transmutation of species.* Pt. I. First notebook (July 1837–February 1838). Pt. II. Second notebook (February–July 1838). Pt. III. Third notebook (July 15, 1838–October 2, 1838). Pt. IV. Fourth notebook (October 1838–July 10, 1839). Pt. V. Agenda and corrigenda. Pt. VI. Pages excised by Darwin. Ed. & intro. with notes by G. De Beer et al. *Bull. Brit. Mus. (Nat. Hist.) Hist. Ser.,* 1960, *2,* 23–73, 75–118, 119–150, 153–183 ; 1961, *2,* 185–200 ; 1967, *3,* 131–176.   **C**

———. *Charles Darwin and the voyage of the Beagle.* Ed. by Nora Barlow. New York: Philosophical Library, 1946. (1945) (1840–1848)   **B**

———, & Wallace, A. R. *Evolution by natural selection.* Ed. with intro. by G. De Beer. Cambridge: Cambridge University Press, 1958. (1858)

———. I. On the natural means of selection ; on the comparison of domestic races and true species. II. Abstract of a letter from Charles Darwin to Professor Asa Gray. *J. Linn. Soc.,* 1858, *3,* 46–53. Reprinted in C. Darwin & A. R. Wallace, *Evolution by natural selection, op. cit.,* pp. 259–267.

———. *On the origin of species.* (6th ed.) New York: Macmillan, 1927. (1859) (Reprinted 1969)

———. *The origin of species: A variorum text.* Ed. by M. Peckham. Philadelphia: University of Pennsylvania Press, 1959. (1859)

———. *On the origin of the species.* A facsimile of the 1st ed., with intro. by E. Mayr. Cambridge: Harvard University Press, 1964. (1859)

———. *The movements and habits of climbing*

plants. (2nd ed., rev.) New York: Appleton, 1893. (1865) (Reprinted 1969)

————. *The variation of animals and plants under domestication.* (2 vols.) New York: Appleton, 1896. (1868) (Reprinted 1969)

————. *The descent of man and selection in relation to sex.* (2nd ed.) New York: Appleton, 1930. (1871) (Rerinted 1969)

————. *The expression of the emotions in man and animals.* Ed. by F. Darwin. Chicago: University of Chicago Press, 1965. (1872) (Reprinted 1969)

————. *Insectivorous plants.* (2nd ed., rev.) Ed. by F. Darwin. London: Murray, 1888. (1875) (Reprinted 1969)

————. *The effects of cross and self fertilisation in the vegetable kingdom.* New York: Appleton, 1892. (1876)

————. *The different forms of flowers on plants of the same species.* New York: Appleton, 1896. (1877) (Reprinted 1969)

————. A biographical sketch of an infant. *Mind,* 1877, *2,* 285–294.

————. Preliminary notice. (1879) In E. Kraus, *Erasmus Darwin.* (2nd ed.) London: Murray, 1887, pp. 1–107.

————, & Darwin, F. *Power of movement in plants.* New York: Appleton, 1880. (Reprinted 1969)

————. A posthumous essay on instinct. In G. J. Romanes, *Mental evolution in animals: With a posthumous essay on instinct by Charles Darwin.* New York: Appleton, 1885, pp. 355–384.

Beck & Molish, *Reflexes;* Bodenheimer, *Biology;* Count, *Race;* Dampier, *Literature;* Dennis, *Readings Developmental;* Drever, *Sourcebook;* Fulton & Wilson, *Physiology;* Gabriel, *Biology;* Grinder, *Genetic Psychology;* Gruber, *Creative Thinking;* Hall, *Source Book;* Herrnstein & Boring, *Source Book;* Hutchins, *Great Books;* Kessen, *Child;* Kroeber, *Source Book;* Murphy, *Western;* Park & Burgess, *Sociology;* Parsons, *Society;* Rook, *Origins;* Russell, *Motivation;* Sahakian, *Psychology;* Schwartz & Bishop, *Moments Discovery*

ERASMUS DARWIN
1731-1802
English Biologist (16)

Darwin, E. *The essential writings of Erasmus Darwin.* Ed., with linking commentary, by D. King-Hele. London: MacGibbon & Kee, 1968.
C

————. *The botanic garden.* (7th ed.) London: Johnson, 1824. (1789, 1791) (Reprinted 1972)

————. *Zoonomia: or, the laws of organic life.* (3rd ed.) (4 vols.) London: Johnson, 1801. (1794, 1796)

————. *A plan for the conduct of female education in boarding schools.* Derby: Johnson, 1797. (Reprinted 1968)

————. *Phytologia; or the philosophy of agriculture and gardening.* London: Johnson, 1800. (Reprinted 1969)

————. *The temple of nature; or, the origin of society; a poem with philosophical notes.* (3rd ed.) London: Jones, 1825. (1803) (Reprinted 1972)

Hunter & Macalpine, *Psychiatry;* Slotkin, *Anthropology*

CHARLES BENEDICT DAVENPORT
1866-1944
American Geneticist (11)

Davenport, C. B., & Cannon, W. B. On the determination of the direction and rate of movement of organisms by light. *J. Physiol.,* 1897, *21,* 22–32

————. *Experimental morphology.* (2 vols.) New York: Macmillan, 1897, 1899.

————, & Lewis, F. T. Phototaxis of Daphnia. *Science,* 1899, *9,* 368.

Davenport, Gertrude C., & ————. Heredity and eye-color in man. *Science,* 1907, *26,* 589–592.

Davenport, Gertrude C., & ————. Heredity of skin pigmentation in man. *Amer. Naturalist,* 1910, *44,* 641–672, 705–731.

———. *Heredity in relation to eugenics.* New York: Holt, 1911.

———, & Weeks, D. F. A first study of inheritance of epilepsy. *J. nerv. ment. Dis.,* 1911, *38,* 641–670.

———. Heredity of skin color in Negro-white crosses. *Carnegie Inst. Wash. Publ.,* 1913, No. 188.

———. The feebly inhibited: (A) Nomadism or the wandering impulse with special reference to heredity. (B) Inheritance of temperament. *Carnegie Inst. Wash. Publ.,* 1915, No. 236.

———. Inheritance of stature. *Genetics,* 1917, *2,* 313–389.

———. Heredity of constitutional mental disorders. *Psychol. Bull.,* 1920, *17,* 300–310.

———. *Body-build and its inheritance.* Carnegie Institute of Washington Publ. No. 329. Washington, D.C.: Carnegie Institution, 1923.

———, & Nelson, L. A. Heredity and culture as factors in body-build. *Publ. Health Rep.,* 1925, *40,* 2601–2605.

———. Human metamorphosis. *Amer. J. phys. Anthrop.,* 1926, *9,* 205–232.

———. Human growth curve. *J. gen. Physiol.,* 1926–1927, *10,* 205–216.

———. The mingling of races. In E. V. Cowdry (Ed.), *Human biology and racial welfare.* New York: Hoeber, 1930, pp. 553–565.

———. Individual vs. mass studies in child growth. *Proc. Amer. phil. Soc.,* 1931, *70,* 381–389.

———. Body-build and its inheritance. *Proc. Ass. Res. nerv. ment. Dis.,* 1933, *14,* 21–27.

———. Causes of retarded and incomplete development. *Proc. Amer. Ass. ment. Def.,* 1936, *41,* 208–214.

———. Interpretation of certain infantile growth curves. *Growth,* 1937, *1,* 279–283.

Count, *Race ;* Park & Burgess, *Sociology*

WALTER FENNO DEARBORN
1878-1955
American Psychologist (12)

Dearborn, W. F. Retinal local signs. *Psychol. Rev.,* 1904, *11,* 297–307.

———. Experiments in learning. *J. educ. Psychol.,* 1910, *1,* 373–388.

———. *Formen des Infantilismus mit Berücksichtigung ihrer klinischen Unterscheidung.* Jena: Fischer, 1913.

———, Anderson, I. E., & Christiansen, A. O. Form board and construction tests of mental ability. *J. educ. Psychol.,* 1916, *7,* 445–458.

———, & Brewer, J. M. Methods and results of a class experiment in reading. *J. educ. Psychol.,* 1918, *9,* 63–82.

———. Intelligence and its measurement. A symposium. *J. educ. Psychol.,* 1921, *12,* 210–212.

———, & Lincoln, E. A. A class experiment in learning. *J. educ. Psychol.,* 1922, *13,* 330–340.

Shaw, E. A., Lincoln, E. A., & ———. A series of form board and performance tests of intelligence. *Harvard Monogr. Educ.,* 1923, *1,* No. 4.

Lord, E. E., Carmichael, L., & ———. Special disabilities in learning to read and write. *Harvard Monogr. Educ.,* 1925, *2,* No. 1.

———. *Intelligence tests: Their significance for school and society.* Boston: Houghton Mifflin, 1928.

———, & Long, H. H. On comparing IQ's at different age levels on the same scale. *J. educ. Res.,* 1928, *18,* 265–274.

———, & Smith, C. W. The results of rescoring five hundred thirty Dearborn tests. *J. educ. Psychol.,* 1929, *20,* 177–183.

———, & Cattell, Psyche. The intelligence and achievement of private school pupils. *J. educ. Psychol.,* 1930, *21,* 197–211.

———. *Difficulties in learning.* Chicago: University of Chicago Press, 1932.

———. The mental and physical development of school children. *School & Soc.,* 1935, *41,* 585–593.

————. The use of the tachistoscope in diagnostic and remedial reading. *Psychol. Monogr.*, 1936, *47*, No. 212, pp. 1–19.

————, & Rothney, J. W. M. *Scholastic, economic, and social backgrounds of unemployed youth*. Cambridge: Harvard University Press, 1938.

————, & Anderson, I. H. Aniseikonia as related to disability in reading. *J. exp. Psychol.*, 1938, *23*, 559–577.

————, Rothney, J. W. M., & Shuttleworth, F. K. Data on the growth of public school children. *Monogr. Soc. Res. Child Developmt*, 1938, *3*, No. 1.

Anderson, I. H., & ————. Reading ability as related to college achievement. *J. Psychol.*, 1941, *11*, 387–396.

————, & Rothney, J. W. M. *Predicting the child's development*. Cambridge: Sci-Art, 1941.

Carmichael, L., & ————. *Reading and visual fatigue*. Boston: Houghton Mifflin, 1947.

OVIDE JEAN DECROLY
1871-1932
Belgian Psychologist (11)

Decroly, O. *Etudes de psychogenèse ; observations, expériences et enquêtes sur le développement des aptitudes de l'enfant*. Brussels: Lamertin, 1932.   **C**

————, & Degand, J. Les tests de Binet et Simon pour la mesure de l'intelligence ; contribution critique. *Arch. Psychol.*, Geneva, 1906–1907, *6*, 27–130.

————, & Degand, J. Contribution à la pédagogie de la lecture et de l'écriture. Comment un enfant sourd-muet apprit à lire par la méthode naturelle. *Arch. Psychol.*, Geneva, 1906–1907, *6*, 339–353.

————, & Degand, J. Expériences de mémoire visuelle verbale et de mémoire des images chez des enfants normaux et anormaux. *Année psychol.*, 1907, *13*, 122–132.

————. La psychologie, la pathologie et le traitement des enfants anormaux. *Bull. Soc. méd. ment. Belg.*, 1907, 448–461.

————, & Degand, J. La mesure de l'intelligence chez les enfants: 2ème contribution critique. La méthode de De Sanctis. *Int. Arch. Schulzhyg.*, 1907, *4*, 230–303.

————, & Degand, J. La mesure de l'intelligence chez des enfants normaux, d'après les tests de MM. Binet et Simon: Nouvelle contribution critique. *Arch. Psychol.*, Geneva, 1909–1910, *9*, 81–108.

————, & Degand, J. Contribution à la psychologie de la lecture. *Arch. Psychol.*, Geneva, 1910, *9*, 177–191.

————. La psychologie du dessin. *J. Neurol. Psychiat.*, 1912, *17*, 421–424.

————, & Degand, J. Observations relatives à l'évolution des notions de quantités continues et discontinues chez l'enfant. *Arch. Psychol.*, Geneva, 1912, *12*, 81–121.

————. Le développement de l'aptitude graphique. *J. Neurol. Psychiat.*, 1912, *17*, 441–453.

————, & Degand, J. Observations relatives au développement de la notion du temps chez une petite fille de la naissance à 5 ans ½. *Arch. Psychol.*, Geneva, 1913, *13*, 113–161.

————. Epreuve nouvelle pour l'examen mental et son application aux enfants anormaux. (1913) *Année psychol.*, 1914, *20*, 140–159.

————, & Monchamp, A. *L'initiation à l'activité intellectuelle et motrice par les jeux éducatifs. Contribution à la pédagogie des jeunes enfants et des irréguliers*. (3rd ed.) Neuchâtel: Delachaux & Niestlé, 1924. (1914)

————, & Boon, G. *Vers l'école rénovée*. Paris: Nathan, 1921.

————. L'intelligence et sa mesure. *Ann. Bull. Soc. Roy. Sci. méd. nat. Bruxelles*, 1921, *75*, 138–152.

————. Les méthodes non verbales d'examen mental. *Année psychol.*, 1923, *24*, 70–82.

————. Les tests individuels et les tests simultanés. *Année psychol.*, 1923, *24*, 128–133.

————. Le principe de la globalisation appliqué à l'éducation du langage parlé et écrit. *Arch. Psychol.*, Geneva, 1926–1927, *20*, 324–346.

———. Essai d'application du test de Ballard dans les écoles belges. *Année psychol.*, 1926, *27*, 57–93.

———. Quelques considérations sur le mensonge envisagé comme manifestation de l'instinct de défense. *J. Neurol. Psychiat.*, 1928, *28*, 465–486.

———, & Buyse, R. *La pratique des tests mentaux.* Paris: Alcan, 1928.

———. *La fonction de globalisation et son application à l'enseignement.* Brussels: Lamertin, 1929.

———, & Wauthier, M. L. Contribution à l'étude des tests du caractère. *J. Psychol. norm. path.*, 1929, *26*, 201–250.

———, & Decroly, J. La démence chez l'enfant. *J. Neurol. Psychiat.*, 1929, *29*, 461–479.

———, & Decroly, D. J. La démence de l'idiotie chez l'enfant. *J. Neurol. Psychiat.*, 1930, *30*, 32–38.

———. *Le développement du langage parlé chez l'enfant.* Brussels: Centrale du P. E. S. de Belgique, 1930.

———, & Decroly, J. Démence et idiotie chez l'enfant (anormal). *J. Neurol. Psychiat.*, 1930, *30*, 359–383.

———. La valeur du quotient intellectuel chez les enfants anormaux. *J. Neurol. Psychiat.*, 1930, *30*, 885–889.

———. *Comment l'enfant arrive à parler.* (2 vols in 1) Ed. by J. E. Segars. Brussels: Centrale du P.E.S. de Belgique, 1934.

———. *L'exploration du langage de l'enfant. Epreuves de compréhension, d'imitation et d'expression.* Ed. by J. Jadot-Decroly & S. E. Segars. Brussels: Centre National d'Education, 1936.

EDMUND BURKE DELABARRE
1863-1945
American Psychologist (12)

Delabarre, E. B. On the seat of optical after-images. *Amer. J. Psychol.*, 1889, *2*, 326–328.

———. *Ueber Bewegungsempfindungen.* Freiburg: Epstein, 1891.

———. The influence of muscular states on consciousness. *Mind*, 1892, *1* (N.S.), 379–396.

———. Les laboratoires de psychologie en Amérique. *Année psychol.*, 1894, *1*, 209–245.

———. Interpretation of the phenomena of double consciousness. *Progress of the world*, 1895, *1*(3), 21–26.

———, Logan, R. R., & Reed, A. O. The force and rapidity of reaction movements. *Psychol. Rev.*, 1897, *4*, 615–631.

———. A method of recording eye-movements. *Amer. J. Psychol.*, 1898, *9*, 572–574.

———. Conditions affecting the judgment of the direction of lines. *Psychol. Rev.*, 1900, *7*, 142.

———. The relation of mental content to nervous activity. *Amer. J. Insan.*, 1900, *57*, 645–660.

———. Accuracy of perception of verticality and the factors that influence it. *J. Phil.*, 1904, *1*, 85–94.

———. Influence of surrounding objects on the apparent direction of a line. In J. H. Tufts *et al.* (Eds.), *Studies in philosophy and psychology: A commemorative volume by former students of Charles Edward Garman.* Boston: Houghton Mifflin, 1906, pp. 239–295.

———. Formal discipline and the doctrine of common elements. *Education*, 1909, *29*, 585–600.

HENRI DELACROIX
1873-1937
French Psychologist (15)

Delacroix, H. Avenarius, Esquisse de l'empiriocriticisme. *Rev. Métaphys. Morale*, 1897, *5*, 764–769; 1898, *6*, 61–102.

———. L'art de la vie intérieure. *Rev. Métaphys. Morale*, 1902, *10*, 164–183.

———. Les variétés de l'expérience religieuse par William James. *Rev. Métaphys. Morale*, 1903, *11*, 642–669.

————. *Etudes d'histoire et de psychologie du mysticisme.* Paris: Alcan, 1908.

————. Le mysticisme et la religion. *Scientia,* 1917, *21,* 462–475; *22,* 27–38.

————. *La psychologie de Stendhal.* Paris: Alcan, 1918.

————. Psychologie du langage. *Rev. phil.,* 1918, *85,* 1–27.

————, & Meyerson, I. Troubles du sentiment et de la notion d'espace. *J. Psychol. norm. path.,* 1920, *17,* 377–384.

————. Le sentiment esthétique. *J. Psychol. norm. path.,* 1920, *17,* 385–414.

————. De l'automatisme dans l'imitation. *J. Psychol. norm. path.,* 1921, *18,* 97–139.

————. L'inspiration prophétique. Le prophète. *J. Psychol. norm. path.,* 1921, *18,* 781–803.

————. *La religion, et la foi.* Paris: Alcan, 1922.

Dagnan, J., ————, & Dumas, G. *L'association des idées.* In G. Dumas (Ed.), *Traité de psychologie.* Vol. 1. Paris: Alcan, 1923, pp. 820–845.

————. Linguistique et psychologie. *J. Psychol. norm. path.,* 1923, *20,* 798–825.

————. *Le langage et la pensée.* (2nd ed.) Paris: Alcan, 1930. (1924)

————. Les souvenirs. In G. Dumas (Ed.), *Traité de psychologie.* Vol. 2. Paris: Alcan, 1924, pp. 44–112.

————. Les opérations intellectuelles. In G. Dumas (Ed.), *Traité de psychologie.* Vol. 2. Paris: Alcan, 1924, pp. 113–226.

Dumas, G., Belot, G., & ————. Les sentiments complexes. In G. Dumas (Ed.), *Traité de psychologie.* Vol. 2. Paris: Alcan, 1924, pp. 227–332.

————. Maine de Biran et l'Ecole médico-psychologique. *Bull. Soc. franç. Phil.,* 1924, *24,* 51–63.

————. Remarques sur "Une Grande Mystique." *J. Psychol. norm. path.,* 1925, *22,* 545–584.

————. *L'analyse psychologique de la fonction linguistique.* Oxford: Clarendon Press, 1926.

————. *Psychologie de l'art: Essai sur l'activité artistique.* Paris: Alcan, 1927.

————. L'aphasie selon Henry Head. *J. Psychol. norm. path.,* 1927, *24,* 285–322.

————. La mémoire affective. *J. Psychol. norm. path.,* 1931, *28,* 321–344.

————, Cassirer, E., & Jordan, L. *Psychologie du langage.* Paris: Alcan, 1933.

————. Au seuil du langage. *J. Psychol. norm. path.,* 1933, *30,* 9–17.

————. *L'enfant et le langage.* Paris: Alcan, 1934.

————. *Les grandes formes de la vie mentale.* Paris: Alcan, 1934.

————. L'association des idées. In G. Dumas (Ed.), *Nouveau traité de psychologie.* Vol. 4. Paris: Alcan, 1934, pp. 137–160.

————. La fabrication du nombre. *J. Psychol. norm. path.,* 1934, *31,* 5–26.

————. *Le temps et les souvenirs: Le rêve et la rêverie.* Paris: Alcan, 1936.

————. Les opérations intellectuelles. In G. Dumas (Ed.), *Nouveau traité de psychologie.* Vol. 5. Paris: Alcan, 1936, pp. 85–182.

————. La croyance. In G. Dumas (Ed.), *Nouveau traité de psychologie.* Vol. 5. Paris: Alcan, 1936, pp. 185–304.

————. Les souvenirs. In G. Dumas (Ed.), *Nouveau traité de psychologie.* Vol. 5. Paris: Alcan, 1936, pp. 305–404.

————. *Les grands mystiques chrétiens.* Paris: Alcan, 1938.

————. Les sentiments esthétiques et l'art. In G. Dumas (Ed.), *Nouveau traité de psychologie.* Vol. 6. Paris: Alcan, 1938, pp. 253–316.

————. L'invention et le génie. In G. Dumas (Ed.), *Nouveau traité de psychologie.* Vol. 6. Paris: Alcan, 1938, pp. 447–544.

JOSEPH REMI LEOPOLD DELBOEUF
1831-1896
Belgian Psychologist (24)

Delboeuf, J. *Eléments de psychophysique, générale et spéciale.* Paris: Baillière, 1883.   **C**

————. Etude psychophysique: Recherches théoriques et expérimentales sur la mesure des sensations et spécialement des sensations de lumière et de fatigue. *Mém. Acad. Sci. Belg.,* 1873, *23,* No. 5. Reprinted in modified and abridged form in *Eléments de psychophysique, op. cit.,* pp. 1–105.

————. Théorie générale de la sensibilité. *Mém. Acad. Sci. Belg.,* 1875, *26,* No. 3. Reprinted in abridged form in *Eléments de psychophysique, op. cit.,* pp. 145–249.

————. *La psychologie comme science naturelle ; son présent et son avenir.* Brussels: Muquardt, 1876.

————. La loi psychophysique. Hering et Fechner. *Rev. phil.,* 1877, *3,* 225–263.

————. Le rôle des sens dans la formation de l'idée d'espace. Pourquoi les sensations visuelles sont-elles étendues? *Rev. phil.,* 1877, *4,* 167–184.

————. La loi psychophysique et le nouveau livre de Fechner. *Rev. phil.,* 1878, *5,* 34–63, 127–157.

————. Psychologie comparée: Le sens des couleurs chez les animaux d'après Grant-Allen. *Rev. Sci.,* 1879, *23,* 1101–1110.

————. Le sommeil et les rêves. *Rev. phil.,* 1879, *8,* 349–356, 494–520 ; 1880, *9,* 129–169, 413–437, 632–647.

————. Sur la fusion des sensations semblables. *Rev. phil.,* 1880, *10,* 644–648.

————. *Examen critique de la loi psychophysique: Sa base et sa signification.* Paris: Baillière, 1883.

————. Un nouveau centre de vision dans l'oeil humain. *Rev. Sci.,* 1883, *32,* 167–170.

————. L'intelligence des animaux. *Rev. Sci.,* 1884, *34,* 670 ; 1885, *36,* 596–597 ; 1886, *37,* 3–10.

————. *Le sommeil et les rêves considérés principalement dans leurs rapports avec les théories de la certitude et de la mémoire.* Paris: Baillière, 1885.

————. La mémoire chez les hypnotisés. *Rev. phil.,* 1886, *21,* 441–472.

————. De l'influence de l'imitation et de l'éducation dans le somnambulisme provoqué. *Rev. phil.,* 1886, *22,* 146–171.

————. Une visite à la Salpêtrière. *Rev. Belg.,* 1886, *54,* 121–147, 258–275.

Binet, A., & ————. Les diverses écoles hypnotiques. *Rev. phil.,* 1886, *22,* 532–538.

————. Les suggestions à echéance. *Rev. hypno.,* 1886–1887, *1,* 166–170.

————. De l'origine des effets curatifs de l'hypnotisme: Etude de psychologie expérimentale. *Bull. Acad. Roy. Sci. Belg.,* 1887, *13,* 773–812. (Also Paris: Brochüre, 1887)

————. De la prétendue veille somnambulique. *Rev. phil.,* 1887, *23,* 113–142, 262–285.

————. De l'analogie entre l'état hypnotique et l'état normal. *Rev. hypno.,* 1887–1888, *2,* 289–292.

————. *L'hypnotisme et la liberté des représentations publiques.* Paris: Desoër, 1888.

————. Origine des effets curatifs instantanés de l'hypnotisme sur les maladies chroniques. *Rev. hypno.,* 1889, *3,* 66–69.

————. Des hallucinations négatives suggérées. *Rev. hypno.,* 1889, *3,* 202–205.

————. *Le magnétisme animal, à propos d'une visite à l'école de Nancy.* Paris: Alcan, 1889.

————. *Magnétiseurs et médecins.* Paris: Baillière, 1890.

————. *De l'étendue de l'action curative de l'hypnotisme. L'hypnotisme appliqué aux altérations de l'organe visuel.* Paris: Alcan, 1890.

————. Pourquoi mourons-nous? *Rev. phil.,* 1891, *31,* 225–257, 408–427.

————. *L'hypnotisme devant les chambres législatives belges.* Paris: Alcan, 1892.

———. Einige psychologische Betrachtungen über den Hypnotismus gelegentlich eines durch Suggestion geheilten Falles von Mordmanie. *Z. Hypno.,* 1892, *1,* 43–48, 84–90.

———. De l'appréciation du temps par les somnambules. *Proc. Soc. psychic. Res.,* 1892, *8,* 414–421.

———. Sur une nouvelle illusion d'optique. *Rev. sci.,* 1893, *51,* 237–241.

———. Die verbrecherischen Suggestionen. *Z. Hypno.,* 1893–1894, *2,* 177–198, 221–240, 247–268.

Herrnstein & Boring, *Source Book*

SANTE DE SANCTIS
1862-1935
Italian Psychologist (13)

De Sanctis, S. *Lo studio sperimentale dell'attenzione.* Poggibonzi: Capelli, 1895. (1894)

———. Contributo alla conoscenza del *Corpo mammillare* nell'uomo. *Ric. Lab. anat. norm. Univ. Roma,* 1894, *4,* 125–135.

——— (with Maria Montessori). *Sulle cosidette allucinazioni antagonistiche.* Rome: Alighieri, 1897.

———. Sui rapporti etiologici tra sogni e pazzia. Deliri e psicosi da sogni. *Riv. quind. psicol.,* 1897–1898, *1,* 310–321.

———. Studien über die Aufmerksamkeit. *Z. Psychol.,* 1898, *17,* 205–214.

———. Die Träume, medizinisch-psychologische *Untersuchungen.* Trans. by O. Schmidt. Halle: Marhold, 1901. (1899)

———. *I sogni. Studi clinici e psicologici di un alienista.* Turin: Bocca, 1899.

———. *La ricerca psicologica nella grafica infantile. I designi dei bambini.* Rome: Alighieri, 1901.

———, & Neyroz, U. Experimental investigations concerning the depth of sleep. Trans. by H. C. Warren. *Psychol. Rev.,* 1902, *9,* 254–282.

———. Le problème de la conscience dans la psychologie moderne. *Arch. Psychol.,* Geneva, 1903–1904, *3,* 379–388.

———. *Die Mimik des Denkens.* Trans. by J. Bresler. Halle: Marhold, 1906. (1904)

———. Types et degrés d'insuffisance mentale. (1906) *Année psychol.,* 1906, *12,* 70–83.

———. Mental development and the measurement of the level of intelligence. *J. educ. Psychol.,* 1911, *2,* 498–507.

———. *Patologie e profilassi mentali.* Milan: Vallardi, 1912.

———. L'interpretazione dei sogni. *Riv. Psicol.,* 1914, *10,* 358–375.

———. *Educazione dei deficienti.* Milan: Vallardi, 1915.

———. Psicologia della vocazione. *Riv. Psicol.,* 1919, *15,* 30–69.

———. *Psychologie des Traumes.* In G. Kafka (Ed.) *Handbuch der vergleichenden Psychologie.* Vol. 3. *Die Funktionen des abnormen Seelenslebens.* Munich: Reinhardt, 1922, pp. 231–329.

———. *Religious conversations: A bio-psychological study.* Trans. by H. Augier. New York: Harcourt, Brace, 1927. (1924)

———. *La neuropsichiatria infantile.* Rome: Stock, 1925.

———. Suggestione e ricerca psicologita. *Arch. It psicol.,* 1925, *4,* 60–76.

———. Mental work. *J. genet. Psychol.,* 1926, *33,* 119–134.

———. Intuitions in children. *J. genet. Psychol.* 1928, *35,* 18–25.

———. *Psicologia sperimentale.* Vol. 1. *Psicologia generale.* Vol. 2. *Psicologia applicata.* Rome: Stock, 1929–1930.

———. Principi e applicazione della psicologia de lavoro. *Atti VII convegno psicol. sper. e psico tecn.,* 1929, Torino, 17–38.

————. La criminalità per tendenza. *Giustizia penale*, 1933, *39*, 1–28.

————. The psychophysiology of the dream. *J. Pers.*, 1933–1934, *2*, 269–287.

————. Psicologia e psicopatologia. *Riv. Psicol.*, 1934, *30*, 1–12.

————. So-called "reactions" in characterology and psychiatry. *J. Pers.*, 1934–1935, *3*, 40–53.

————. La tecnica psicologica per la conoscenza e per l'emenda dei minori traviati e delinquenti. *Riv. Psicol.*, 1935, *31*, 1–29.

————. Sante De Sanctis. In C. Murchison (Ed.), *A history of psychology in autobiography*. Vol. 3. Worcester, Mass.: Clark University Press, 1936, pp. 83–120.   **B**

RENE DESCARTES
1596-1650
French Philosopher (27)

Descartes, R. *Oeuvres de Descartes*. (13 vols.) Ed. by C. Adam & P. Tannery. Paris: Vrin, 1964– (1897–1913)   **C**

————. *The philosophical works of Descartes*. (2 vols.) Trans. by Elizabeth S. Haldane & G. R. T. Ross. New York: Dover, 1955. (1911)   **C**

————, & Huyghens, C. *Correspondence of Descartes and Constantijn Huyghens, 1635–1647*. Ed. by L. Roth, & pref. by C. Adam. Oxford: Clarendon Press, 1926.   **B C**

————. *Sélections*. Ed. by R. M. Eaton. New York: Scribner's, 1927. (Reprinted ca. 1970)   **C**

————. *Correspondance*. (8 vols.) Intro. & ed. by C. Adam & G. Milhaud. Paris: Presses Universitaires de France, 1936–1963.   **B C**

————. *Descartes' philosophical writings*. Trans. by N. K. Smith. London: Macmillan, 1952.   **C**

————. *Discourse on method and meditations*. Trans. by A. Wollaston. Baltimore, Md.: Penguin Books, 1960.   **B C**

————. *Philosophical essays: Discourse on method ; Meditations: Rules for the direction of the mind*. Trans. by L. J. Lafleur. Indianapolis, Ind.: Bobbs-Merrill, 1964.   **C**

————. Dioptric. (1637) Excerpt in *Philosophical writings, op. cit.*, pp. 167–179.

————. *Discours de la méthode*. Comm. by E. Gilson. Paris: Vrin, 1925. (1637) (Reprinted 1966)

————. Discourse on the method of rightly conducting the reason. (1637) In *The philosophical works*, Vol. 1, *op. cit.*, pp. 81–130.

————. *The geometry*. Trans. by D. E. Smith & Marcia L. Latham. Chicago: Open Court, 1925. (1637) (Reprinted 1954)

————. Meditations on first philosophy. (1641) In *The philosophical works*, Vol. 1, *op. cit.*, pp. 133–199.

————. *Objections against the meditations and replies*. (1641) In *The philosophical works*, Vol. 2, *op. cit.*, pp. 1–344.

————. Selections from the principles of philosophy. (1644) In *The philosophical works*, Vol. 1, *op. cit.*, pp. 203–302.

————. Letter to Marquis of Newcastle. (1646) In *Selections, op. cit.*, pp. 355–357.   **B**

————. Notes directed against a certain programme. (1647) In *The philosophical works*, Vol. 1, *op. cit.*, pp. 431–450.

————. Letter to Henry More. (1649) In *Selections, op. cit.*, pp. 358–360.   **B**

————. The passions of the soul. (1649) In *The philosophical works*, Vol. 1, *op. cit.*, pp. 329–428.

————. *Les passions de l'âme*. Ed. by Geneviève Rodis-Lewis. Paris: Vrin, 1955. (1649)

————. Passions of the soul. (Abridged.) (1649) In *Essential works of Descartes*. Trans. by L. Blair. New York: Bantam Books, 1961, pp. 108–210.

————. Treatise on man. (1662) (Excerpt) In *Selections, op. cit.*, pp. 350–354.

————. Rules for the direction of the mind. (1701) In *The philosophical works*, Vol. 1, *op. cit.*, pp. 1–77.

————. *Lettres sur la morale, correspondance avec la princesse Elisabeth, Chanut et la reine Christine*. Ed. by Y. Chevalier. Paris: Boivin, 1935. (Reprinted 1955)

————. *Descartes' philosophical letters*. Trans. & ed. by A. Kenny. Oxford: Clarendon Press, 1970.

————. *Treatise of man*. Ed., trans., & comm. by T. S. Hall. Cambridge: Harvard University Press, 1972.

Ackermann, *Theories;* Bodenheimer, *Biology;* Brinton, *Age Reason;* Clarke & O'Malley, *Brain;* Dennis, *Psychology;* Fulton & Wilson, *Physiology;* Hall, *Nature's Laws;* Hall, *Source Book;* Herrnstein & Boring, *Source Book;* Hunter & Macalpine, *Psychiatry;* Hutchins, *Great Books;* Lawrence & O'Connor, *Phenomenology*; Margolis, *Introduction*; Matson, *Being;* Murphy, *Western;* Newman, *Mathematics;* Popkin, *Philosophy;* Rand, *Classical Philosophers;* Rand, *Classical Psychologists;* Reeves, *Body Mind;* Sahakian, *Psychology;* Schwartz & Bishop, *Moments Discovery;* Slotkin, *Anthropology;* Smith, *Source Book;* Ulich, *Educational Wisdom*

MAX DESSOIR
1867-1947
German Psychologist (18)

Dessoir, M. *Psychologische Skizzen (under the pseudonym Edmund W. Rells)*. Leipzig: Abel, 1893. **C**

————. *Psychologische Briefe*. Rev. ed. of *Vom Diesseits der Seele*. Berlin: Wedding-Verlag, 1948. (1923) **C**

————. *Bibliographie des modernen Hypnotismus*. Berlin: Duncker, 1888. **Bl**

————. *Das Doppel-Ich. Schriften der Gesellschaft für Experimentalpsychologie in Berlin*. (2nd ed.) Leipzig: Günther, 1896. (1890)

————. *Erster Nachtrag zur Bibliographie des modernen Hypnotismus*. Berlin: Duncker, 1890.

————. *Experimentelle Psychopathologie. Vtljsch. wiss. Phil.*, 1891, *15*, 59–106, 190–209.

————. Ueber den Hautsinn. *Arch. Anat. Physiol., Physiol. Abt.*, 1892, 175–339.

————. *Geschichte der neueren deutschen Psychologie. Von Leibniz bis Kant*. (3rd ed.) (2 vols.) Berlin: Duncker, 1902. (1894) Reprinted in 1 vol., 1964.

————. Zur Psychologie der Vita sexualis. *Allg. Z. Psychiat.*, 1894, *50*, 941–975.

————. Der Fall Piper. *Psychische Stud.*, 1900, *27*, 179–185.

————, & Menzer, P. (Eds.), *Philosophisches Lesebuch*. (4th ed.) Stuttgart: Enke, 1917. (1903)

————. Anschauung und Beschreibung. *Arch. syst. Phil.*, 1904, *10*, 20–65.

————. *Aesthetik und allgemeine Kunstwissenschaft in den Grundzügen dargestellt*. (2nd ed.) Stuttgart: Enke, 1923. (1906)

————. Das Unterbewusstsein. *Z. Psychother. med. Psychol.*, 1909, *1*, 193–211.

————. *Outlines of the history of psychology*. Trans. by D. Fisher. New York: Macmillan, 1912. (1911)

————. *Kriegspsychologische Betrachtungen*. Leipzig: Hirzel, 1916.

————. *Von jenseits der Seele: Die Geheimwissenschaften in kritischer Betrachtung*. (6th ed.) Stuttgart: Enke, 1931. (1917)

————. Kant und die Psychologie. *Kant-Stud.*, 1924, *29*, 98–120.

————. Character types. *J. Pers.*, 1934–1935, *3*, 214–221.

————. *Einleitung in die Philosophie*. (2nd ed.) Stuttgart: Enke, 1946. (1936)

————. *Buch der Erinnerung*. (2nd ed.) Stuttgart: Enke, 1947. (1946) **B**

————. *Das Ich, der Traum, der Tod*. (2nd ed.) Stuttgart: Enke, 1951. (1947)

ANTOINE LOUIS CLAUDE DESTUTT DE TRACY
1754-1836
French Philosopher (11)

Destutt de Tracy, A. L. C. *Projet d'éléments d'idéologie à l'usage des écoles centrales.* Paris: Didot, 1801.

———. *Analyse raisonnée de l'Origine de tous les cultes, ou, Religion universelle; ouvrage publié en l'an III, par Depuis.* Paris: Courcier, 1804.

———. *Eléments d'idéologie.* (2nd ed.) (5 vols. in 4) Paris: Lévi, 1825–1827. (1804–1818)

———. *Discours prononcés dans la séance publique tenue par la classe de la langue et de la littérature françaises de l'Institut de France.* Paris: Baudouin, 1808.

———. *Commentaire sur l'Esprit des lois de Montesquieu.* Paris: Desoër, 1819. (1811)

———. *A commentary and review of Montesquieu's Spirit of laws.* Philadelphia: Duane, 1811.

———. *Principes logiques, ou Recueil de faits relatifs à l'intelligence humaine.* Paris: Courcier, 1817.

———. A treatise on political economy. Book I. *(A treatise on political economy; to which is prefixed a supplement to a preceding work on the understanding; or elements of ideology; with an analytical table, and an introduction on the faculty of the will.)* Trans. by T. Jefferson. Detroit, Mich.: Center for Health Education, 1973. (1817)

———. *De l'amour.* Intro. by G. Chinard. Paris: Les Belles-Lettres, 1926. (1819)

———. Le mémoire de Berlin. (1806) *Rev. phil.,* 1932, *58,* 161–187. **B**

HUGO DE VRIES
1848-1935
Dutch Geneticist (16)

De Vries, H. *Opera e periodicis collata.* (7 vols.) Utrecht: Oosthoek, 1918–1927. **C**

———. Zur Mechanik der Bewegung von Schlingpflanzen. *Arb. bot. Inst. Würzburg,* 1874, *1,* 317–342. Reprinted in *Opera,* Vol. 1, *op. cit.,* pp. 224–252.

———. Sur les unités des caractères spécifiques et leur application à l'étude des hybrides. *Rev. gén. Bot.,* 1900, *12,* 257–271. Reprinted in *Opera,* Vol. 6, *op. cit.,* pp. 256–269.

———. Das Spaltungsgesetz der Bastarde. Vorläufige Mitteilung. *Ber. Deutsch. Bot. Ges.,* 1900, *18,* 83–90. Reprinted in *Opera,* Vol. 6, *op. cit.,* pp. 208–215, & trans. in C. Stern & Eva R. Sherwood (Eds.), *The origin of genetics. A Mendel source book.* San Francisco, Calif.: Freeman, 1966, pp. 107–117.

———. *Die Mutationen und die Mutationsperioden bei der Entstehung der Arten.* Leipzig: Veit, 1901.

———. *Die Mutations-Theorie. Versuche und Beobachtungen über die Entstehung von Arten im Pflanzenreich. Vol. I. Die Entstehung der Arten durch Mutation. Vol. II. Elementare Bastardlehre.* Leipzig: Veit, 1901, 1903.

———. *The mutation theory: Experiments and observations on the origin of species in the vegetable kingdom. Vol. 1. The origin of species by mutation.* Trans. by J. B. Farmer & A. D. Darbishire. Chicago: Open Court, 1909–1910. (1901) (Reprinted 1969)

———. The origin of species by mutation. *Science,* 1902, *15*(N.S.), 721–729.

———. *Befruchtung und Bastardierung.* Leipzig: Veit, 1903. Reprinted in *Opera,* Vol. 6, *op. cit.,* pp. 339–353.

———. *Species and varieties: Their origin by mutation.* (2nd ed.) Ed. by D. T. MacDougal. Chicago: Open Court, 1906. (1905)

———. *Plant-breeding: Comments on the experiments of Nilsson and Burbank.* (2nd ed.) Chicago: Open Court, 1919. (1907)

———. *Intracellular pangenesis.* Trans. by C. Stuart Gager. Chicago: Open Court, 1910. Reprinted in German in *Opera,* Vol. 5, *op. cit.,* pp. 1-149.

———. *Gruppenweise Artbildung unter spezieller*

Berücksichtigung der Gattung Oenothera. Berlin: Bornträger, 1913.

———, & Boedijn, K. On the distribution of mutant characters among the chromosomes of Oenothera Lamarckiana. *Genetics,* 1923, *8,* 233–238. Reprinted in *Opera,* Vol. 7, *op. cit.,* pp. 509–515.

———. *Letters from H. de Vries and C. Correns to H. F. Roberts.* (1924) Reprinted in C. Stern & Eva R. Sherwood (Eds.), *The origin of genetics. A Mendel source book.* San Francisco, Calif.: Freeman, 1966, pp. 133–134. **B**

Rook, *Origins* ; Schwartz & Bishop, *Moments Discovery*

JOHN DEWEY
1859-1952
American Philosopher (27)

Dewey, J. *The influence of Darwin on philosophy and other essays in contemporary thought.* New York: Holt, 1910. **C**

———. *Essays in experimental logic.* New York: Dover, 1953. (1916) **C**

———. *Characters and events: Popular essays in social and political philosophy.* (2 vols.) Ed. by J. Ratner. New York: Holt, 1929. **C**

———. *Philosophy and civilization.* New York: Capricorn Books, 1963. (1931) **C**

———. *Intelligence in the modern world: John Dewey's philosophy.* Ed. by J. Ratner. New York: Random House, 1939. **C**

———. *Education today.* Ed. by J. Ratner. New York: Putnam's, 1940. **C**

———. *Dewey on education: Selections.* Intro. & notes by M. S. Dworkin. New York: Teachers College Press, 1959. **C**

———. *On experience, nature, and freedom: Representative selections.* Ed. by R. J. Bernstein. Indianapolis, Ind.: Bobbs-Merrill, 1960. **C**

———. *Philosophy, psychology, and social practice.* Ed. by J. Ratner. New York: Putnam's, 1968. (1963) **C**

———, & Bentley, A. F. *John Dewey and Arthur F. Bentley: A philosophical correspondence, 1932–1951.* Ed. by J. Ratner & J. Altman. New Brunswick, N.J.: Rutgers University Press, 1964. **B C**

———. *The early works, 1882–1898.* Vol. 2. *1887. Psychology.* Carbondale, Ill.: Southern Illinois University Press, 1967. **C**

———. *The early works, 1882–1898.* Vol. 1. *1882–1888. Early essays and Leibniz's "New essays concerning human understanding."* Pref. by F. Bowers. Carbondale, Ill.: Southern Illinois University Press, 1969. **C**

———. *The early works, 1882–1898.* Vol. 3. *1889–1892. Early essays and outlines of a critical theory of ethics.* Carbondale, Ill.: Southern Illinois University Press, 1969. **C**

———. *The early works, 1882–1898.* Vol. 4. *1893–1894. Early essays and the study of ethics: A syllabus.* Carbondale, Ill.: Southern Illinois University Press, 1971. **C**

———. The new psychology. *Andover Rev.,* 1884, *2,* 278–289. Reprinted in *Philosophy, psychology, and social practice, op. cit.,* pp. 49–63, & in *Early works,* Vol. 1, *op. cit.,* pp. 48–60.

———. Kant and philosophic method. *J. specul. Phil.,* 1884, *18,* 162–174. Reprinted in *Philosophy, psychology, and social practice, op. cit.,* pp. 35–48, & in *Early works,* Vol. 1, *op. cit.,* pp. 34–47.

———. Soul and body. *Biblio. Sacra,* 1886, *43,* 239–263. Reprinted in *Philosophy, psychology, and social practice, op. cit.,* pp. 63–86, & in *Early works,* Vol. 1, *op. cit.,* pp. 93–115.

———. The psychological standpoint. *Mind,* 1886, *11,* 1–19. Reprinted in *Philosophy, psychology, and social practice, op. cit.,* pp. 87–108, & in *Early works,* Vol. 1, *op. cit.,* pp. 122–143.

———. Psychology as philosophic method. *Mind,* 1886, *11,* 153–173. Reprinted in *Philosophy, psychology, and social practice, op. cit.,* pp. 109–141, & in *Early works,* Vol. 1, *op. cit.,* pp. 144–167.

———. *Psychology.* (3rd ed.) New York: Harper, 1891. (1887) Reprinted in *Early works,* Vol. 2, *op. cit.*

———. Illusory psychology. *Mind,* 1887, *12,* 83–88. Reprinted in *Early works,* Vol. 1, *op. cit.,* pp. 168–175.

———. On some current conceptions of the term "self." *Mind,* 1890, *15,* 58–74. Reprinted in *Philosophy, psychology, and social practice, op. cit.,* pp. 160–179, & in *Early works,* Vol. 3, *op. cit.,* pp. 56–74.

———. The ego as cause. *Phil. Rev.,* 1894, *3,* 337–341. Reprinted in *Philosophy, psychology, and social practice, op. cit.,* pp. 203–208, & in *Early works,* Vol. 4, *op cit.,* pp. 91–95.

———. The psychology of infant language. *Psychol. Rev.,* 1894, *1,* 63–66. Reprinted in *Philosophy, psychology, and social practice, op. cit.,* pp. 209–213, & in *Early works,* Vol. 4, *op. cit.,* pp. 66–69.

———. The theory of emotion. I. Emotional attitudes. II. The significance of emotions. *Psychol. Rev.,* 1894, *1,* 553–569; 1895, *2,* 13–32. Reprinted in *Philosophy, psychology, and social practice, op. cit.,* pp. 214–251, & in *Early works,* Vol. 4, *op. cit.,* pp. 152–188.

———. The reflex arc concept in psychology. *Psychol. Rev.,* 1896, *3,* 357–370. Reprinted in *Philosophy, psychology, and social practice, op. cit.,* pp. 253–266, & in W. Dembler (Ed.), *Visual Perception: The nineteenth century.* New York: Wiley, 1964, pp. 193–206.

———. The psychology of effort. *Psychol. Rev.,* 1897, *6,* 43–56. Reprinted in *Philosophy, psychology, and social practice, op. cit.,* pp. 267–280.

———. *Psychology and philosophic method.* Berkeley, Calif.: University of California Press, 1899.

———. *The school and society.* (Rev. ed.) Chicago: University of Chicago Press, 1961. (1900)

———. Psychology and social practice. *Psychol. Rev.,* 1900, *7,* 105–124. Reprinted in *Philosophy, psychology, and social practice, op. cit.,* pp. 295–315.

———. Interpretation of savage mind. *Psychol. Rev.,* 1902, *9,* 217–230. Reprinted in *Philosophy, psychology, and social practice, op. cit.,* pp.

281–294, & in *Philosophy and civilization, op. cit.,* pp. 173–187.

———. *Logical conditions of a scientific treatment of mortality.* Chicago: University of Chicago Press, 1903.

———. The philosophical work of Herbert Spencer. *Phil. Rev.,* 1904, *13,* 159–175. Reprinted in *Characters and events,* Vol. 1, *op. cit.,* pp. 45–62.

———, & Tufts, J. H. *Ethics.* (Rev. ed.) New York: Holt, 1932. (1908)

———. *How we think: A restatement of the relation of reflective thinking to the educative process.* (Rev. ed.) Boston: Heath, 1933. (1910)

———. Reply to Professor Royce's critique of instrumentalism. *Phil. Rev.,* 1912, *21,* 69–81.

———. *Interest and effort in education.* New York: Houghton Mifflin, 1913.

———. The logic of judgments of practice. *J. Phil.,* 1915, *12,* 533–543.

———, & Dewey, Evelyn. *Schools of tomorrow.* New York: Dutton, 1915.

———. The pragmatism of Peirce. *J. Phil.,* 1916, *13,* 709–715.

———. The need for social psychology. *Psychol. Rev.,* 1917, *24,* 266–277.

———. The motivation of Hobbes's political philosophy. In *Studies in the history of ideas.* Vol. 1. New York: Columbia University Press, 1918, pp. 88–115.

———. *Reconstruction in philosophy.* (Enlarged ed.) Boston: Beacon Press, 1948. (1920)

———. *Human nature and conduct: An introduction to social psychology.* New York: Random House, 1930. (1922)

———. The naturalistic theory of perception by the senses. *J. Phil.,* 1925, *22,* 596–605.

———. *Experience and nature.* (2nd ed.) La Salle, Ill.: Open Court, 1958. (1925)

———. Body and mind. *Ment. Hyg.,* N.Y., 1928, *12,* 1–17. Reprinted in *Philosophy and civilization, op. cit.,* pp. 299–317.

———. *The quest for certainty.* New York: Minton, Balch, 1929. (Reprinted 1960)

———. *The sources of a science of education.* New York: Liveright, 1929.

———. *Individualism, old and new.* New York: Minton, Balch, 1930.

———. From absolutism to experimentalism. In G. P. Adams & W. P. Montague (Eds.), *Contemporary American philosophy: Personal statements.* Vol 2. New York: Macmillan, 1930, pp. 13–27.   **B**

———. Conduct and experience. In C. Murchison (Ed.), *Psychologies of 1930.* Worcester, Mass.: Clark University Press, 1930, pp. 409–422.

———. *A common faith.* New Haven: Yale University Press, 1934.

———. *Art as experience.* New York: Putnam's, 1959. (1934)

———. Unity of science as a social problem. In O. Neurath *et al.* (Eds.), *International encyclopedia of unified science.* Vol. 1, No. 1, Chicago: University of Chicago Press, 1938, pp. 29–38.

———. *Experience and education.* New York: Macmillan, 1938.

———. *Logic: The theory of inquiry.* New York: Holt, 1938.

———. Experience, knowledge, and value: A rejoinder. (1939) In P. A. Schilpp (Ed.), *The philosophy of John Dewey.* (2nd ed.) New York: Tudor, 1951, pp. 515–608.

———. *Freedom and culture.* New York: Putnam's, 1939.

———. Nature in experience. *Phil. Rev.,* 1940, *49,* 244–258. Reprinted in *On experience, nature, and freedom, op. cit.,* pp. 244–260.

———. The vanishing subject in the psychology of William James. *J. Phil.,* 1940, *37,* 589–599.

———. Objectivity-subjectivity of modern philosophy. *J. Phil.,* 1941, *38,* 533–542.

———. The philosophy of Whitehead. In P. A. Schilpp (Ed.), *The philosophy of Alfred North Whitehead.* Evanston, Ill.: Northwestern University Press, 1941, pp. 641–661.

———. William James as empiricist. In *In Commemoration of William James, 1842–1942.* New York: AMS Press, 1967, pp. 48–57. (1941)

———. How is mind to be known? *J. Phil.,* 1942, *39,* 29–35.

———. Anti-naturalism in extremis. In Y. H. Krikorian (Ed.), *Naturalism and the human spirit.* New York: Columbia University Press, 1944, pp. 1–16.

———, Hook, S., & Nagel, E. Are naturalists materialists? *J. Phil.,* 1945, *42,* 515–530.

———, & Bentley, A. F. *Knowing and the known.* Boston: Beacon Press, 1949.

Cubberley, *Public Educators;* Dember, *Perception;* Dennis, *Psychology;* Fisch, *Philosophical;* Grob, *American Ideas;* Herrnstein & Boring, *Source Book;* Kurtz, *American Thought;* Madden, *Scientific Thought;* Mann & Kreyche, *Reflections Man;* Margolis, *Introduction;* Matson, *Being;* Mueller, *American Philosophy;* Nash, *Models;* Park & Burgess, *Sociology;* Price, *Education;* Rorty, *Pragmatic Philosophy;* Sahakian, *Psychology;* Strain, *Philosophies Education;* Thomas, *Source Book*

DENIS DIDEROT
1713-1784
French Philosopher (19)

Diderot, D. *Oeuvres philosophiques.* Ed. by P. Vernière. Paris: Garnier, 1956. (1772)   **C**

———. *Oeuvres complètes.* (20 vols.) Ed. by J. Assézat & M. Tourneux. Paris: Garnier, 1875–1877. (Reprinted 1968)   **C**

———. *Diderot's early philosophical works.* Trans. by Margaret Jourdain. Chicago: Open Court, 1916.   **C**

———. *Dialogues.* Trans. by Francis Bireel. New York: Brentano, 1927.   **C**

———. *Correspondance inédite.* Ed. by A. Babelon. Paris: Gallimard, 1931.   **B C**

———. *Diderot, interpreter of nature: Selected writings.* Trans. by Jean Stewart & J. Kemp.

New York: International Publisher, 1963. (1938)   **C**

——. *Oeuvres choisies.* (7 vols.) Paris: Editions Sociales, 1952–1964.   **C**

——. *Diderot's selected writings.* Ed. by L. G. Crocker. New York: Macmillan, 1966.   **C**

——. *Pensées philosophiques.* Geneva: Droz, 1965. (1746) Selection reprinted in *Oeuvres choisies,* Vol. 1, *op. cit.*

——. Mémoires sur différents sujets de mathématiques. (1748) In *Oeuvres complètes,* Vol. 9, *op. cit.,* pp. 73–82.

——. *Lettre sur les aveugles.* (2nd ed.) Ed. by R. Niklans. Geneva: Droz, 1963. (1749) Selections reprinted in *Oeuvres choisies,* Vol. 1, *op. cit.,* & trans. in *Diderot's selected writings, op. cit.,* pp. 14–39.

——. *Diderot: Lettre sur les sourds et muets.* Ed. by P. H. Meyer. Geneva: Droz, 1965. (1751)

——, & Alembert, J. L. R. d'. *The "Encyclopédie of Diderot and d'Alembert: Selected articles.* Ed. by J. Lough. Cambridge: Cambridge University Press, 1954. (1751–1772)

——, & Alembert, J. L. R. d'. *Encyclopédie ou dictionnaire raisonné des sciences, des arts et des métiers.* (35 vols.) Stuttgart-Bad Canstatt: Frommann, 1966. (1751–1772)

——, Alembert, J. L. R. d', *et al. Encyclopedia: Selections.* Trans. by Nelly S. Hoyt & T. Cassirer. Indianapolis, Ind.: Bobbs-Merrill, 1965. (1751–1772)

——. *Pensées sur l'interprétation de la nature.* (1754) In *Oeuvres complètes,* Vol. 2, *op. cit.,* pp. 9–62, & in *Oeuvres choisies,* Vol. 2, *op. cit.,* pp. 35–108.

——. Réfutation suivie de l'ouvrage d'Helvétius intitulé l'homme. (1774–1775) In *Oeuvres complètes,* Vol. 2, *op. cit.,* pp. 263–456.

Grimm, F. M. v., & ——. Rapport des commissaires chargés par le roi de l'examen du magnétisme animal. (1784) *Corresp. litt.,* 1813, *3* (3), 10–20.

——. Le rêve de d'Alembert. Entretien entre d'Alembert et Diderot et suite de l'entretien. (1830) In *Oeuvres choisies,* Vol. 3, *op. cit.,* pp. 1–104.

——. *Eléments de physiologie.* Ed. by J. Mayer. Paris: Didier, 1964. (1875)

Brinton, *Age Reason*; Torrey, *Les Philosophes*

WILHELM DILTHEY
1833-1911
German Philosopher (22)

Dilthey, W. *Gesammelte Schriften.* (12 vols.) Ed. by H. Mehl *et al.* Stuttgart: Teubner, 1914–1958. (Variously reprinted)

——. Ueber das Studium der Geschichte der Wissenschaften vom Menschen, der Gesellschaft und dem Staat. (1875) In *Gesammelte Schriften,* Vol. 5, *op. cit.,* pp. 31–73.

——. Einleitung in die Geisteswissenschaften. (5th ed.) (1883) In *Gesammelte Schriften,* Vol. 1, *op. cit.*

——. Dichterische Einbildungskraft und Wahnsinn. (1886) In *Gesammelte Schriften,* Vol. 6, *op. cit.,* pp. 90–102.

——. Die Einbildungskraft des Dichters. Bausteine für eine Poetik. (1887) In *Gesammelte Schriften,* Vol. 6, *op. cit.,* pp. 103–241.

——. Ideen über eine beschreibende und zergliedernde Psychologie. *Sitzber. Akad. Wiss.,* Berlin, 1894, *2,* 1309–1407. Reprinted in *Gesammelte Schriften,* Vol. 5, *op. cit.,* pp. 139–240.

——. Die Jugendgeschichte Hegels. (1905) In *Gesammelte Schriften,* Vol. 4, *op. cit.,* pp. 1–187. (1905)

——. (Ueber vergleichende Psychologie.) Beiträge zum Studium der Individualität. (1895–1896) In *Gesammelte Schriften,* Vol. 5, *op. cit.,* pp. 241–316.

——. I. Der psychische Strukturzusammenhang. (1905) In *Gesammelte Schriften,* Vol. 7, *op. cit.,* pp. 1–24.

——. Das Wesen der Philosophie. (1907) In *Gesammelte Schriften,* Vol. 5, *op. cit.,* pp. 339–

416. Trans. as *The essence of philosophy* by S. A. & W. T. Emery. Chapel Hill, N.C.: University of North Carolina Press, 1954.

———. II. Der Aufbau der geschichtlichen Welt in den Geisteswissenschaften. (1910) In *Gesammelte Schriften,* Vol. 7, *op. cit.,* pp. 77–188. Partial trans. in *Meaning in history.* Ed. by H. P. Rickman. London: Allen & Unwin, 1961. Reprinted as *Pattern and meaning in history,* 1961. (1905–1910)

———. III. Plan der Fortsetzung zum Aufbau der geschichtlichen Welt in den Geisteswissenschaften. (1910) In *Gesammelte Schriften,* Vol. 7, *op. cit.,* pp. 189–291.

———. Die Typen der Weltanschauung und ihre Ausbildung in den metaphysischen Systemen. (1911) In *Gesammelte Schriften,* Vol. 8, *op. cit.,* pp. 75–118. Trans. as *Dilthey's philosophy of existence. Introduction to Weltanschauungslehre.* Trans. & intro. by W. Kluback & M. Weinbaum. London: Vision Press, 1967.

———. Leibniz und sein Zeitalter. (1926) In *Gesammelte Schriften,* Vol. 3, *op. cit.,* pp. 1–80.

———. *Pädagogik.* Leipzig: Teubner, 1934. Reprinted in *Gesammelte Schriften,* Vol. 9, *op. cit.,* pp. 1–231.

DOROTHEA (originally Dorothy) LYNDE DIX
1802-1887
American Lay Person (11)

Dix, Dorothea L. *Memorial: To the Legislature of Massachusetts.* Boston: Munroe & Francis, 1843. (Reprinted 1904)

———. *Memorial to the Honorable the Legislature of the State of New York.* Albany, N.Y.: n.p., 1844.

———. *Memorial soliciting a state hospital for the insane submitted to the Legislature of New Jersey, January 23, 1845.* (2nd ed.) Trenton, N.J.: n.p., 1845.

———. *Memorial soliciting a state hospital for the insane submitted to the Legislature of New Jersey, February 2, 1845.* Trenton, N.J.: n.p., 1845.

———. *Remarks on prisons and prison discipline in the United States.* Boston: Monroe & Francis, 1845. (Reprinted 1962)

———. *Memorial soliciting a state hospital for the insane submitted to the Legislature of Pennsylvania, February 3, 1856.* Philadelphia: Ashmead, 1845.

———. *Memorial soliciting an appropriation for the state hospital for the insane, at Lexington; and also urging the necessity for establishing a new hospital in the Green River Country.* Frankfort, Ky.: Hodges, 1846.

———. *Memorial soliciting enlarged and improved accommodations for the insane of the State of Tennessee, by the establishment of a new hospital.* Printed by Order of the General Assembly, November, 1847. Nashville, Tenn.: Whig & Politician, 1847.

———. Memorial of Miss Dix, to the Honorable the Senate and House of Representatives of the State of Illinois. (1847) In *Reports of the Illinois State Hospital for the Insane, 1847–1862.* Chicago: Fulton, 1863, pp. 9–31.

———. Memorial of D. L. Dix, Praying a grant of land for the relief and support of the indigent curable and incurable insane in the U.S., June 27, 1848. *U.S. Senate, Miscellaneous Documents,* No. 150.

———. *Memorial soliciting a state hospital for the insane.* Montgomery, Ala.: Advertiser & Gazette, 1849.

———. *Memorial soliciting adequate appropriations for the construction of a state hospital for the insane, in the state of Mississippi. February 1850. Printed by the order of the Legislature.* Jackson, Miss.: Fall & Marshall, 1850.

Gosher, *Documentary;* Hunter & Macalpine, *Psychiatry*

RAYMOND DODGE
1871-1942
American Psychologist (20)

Erdmann, B., & Dodge, R. *Die psychologischen Untersuchungen über das Lesen auf experimenteller Grundlage.* Halle: Niemeyer, 1898.

Erdmann, B., & ———. Zur Erläuterung unserer tachistoskopischen Versuche. *Z. Psychol.*, 1900, *22*, 241–267.

———. Visual perception during eye movement. *Psychol. Rev.*, 1900, *7*, 454–465.

———, & Cline, T. S. The angle velocity of eye movement. *Psychol. Rev.*, 1901, *8*, 145–157.

———. Five types of eye movements in the horizontal meridian plane of the field of regard. *Amer. J. Physiol.*, 1903, *8*, 307–329.

———. The participation of the eye movements in the visual perception of motion. *Psychol. Rev.*, 1904, *11*, 1–14.

———. The illusion of clear vision during eye movement. *Psychol. Bull.*, 1905, *2*, 193–199.

———. An experimental study of visual fixation. *Psychol. Monogr.*, 1907, *8*, No. 35.

———. A systematic exploration of a normal knee-jerk. *Z. allg. Physiol.*, 1910, *12*, 1–58.

———. A working hypothesis for inner psychophysics. *Psychol. Rev.*, 1911, *18*, 167–185.

———. The theory and limitations of introspection. *Amer. J. Psychol.*, 1912, *23*, 214–229.

———. Mental work: A study in psychodynamics. *Psychol. Rev.*, 1913, *20*, 1–42.

———. The refractory phase of the protective wink reflex: The primary fatigue of a human nervous arc. *Amer. J. Psychol.*, 1913, *24*, 1–7.

———, & Benedict, F. G. *Psychological effects of alcohol: An experimental investigation of the effects of moderate doses of ethyl alcohol on a related group of neuro-muscular processes in man.* Washington, D.C.: Carnegie Institution, 1915.

———. The laws of relative fatigue. *Psychol. Rev.*, 1917, *24*, 89–113.

———. The latent time of compensatory eye movements. *J. exp. Psychol.*, 1921, *4*, 247–269.

———. Habituation to rotation. *J. exp. Psychol.*, 1923, *6*, 1–35.

———. Thresholds of rotation. *J. exp. Psychol.*, 1923, *6*, 107–137.

———. Adequacy of reflex compensatory eye movements, including the effects of neural rivalry and competition. *J. exp. Psychol.*, 1923, *6*, 169–181.

———. The problem of inhibition. *Psychol. Rev.*, 1926, *33*, 1–12.

———. Theories of inhibition. *Psychol. Rev.*, 1926, *33*, 106–122.

———. Theories of inhibition. II. The refractory phase hypothesis of inhibition. *Psychol. Rev.*, 1926, *33*, 167–187.

———, & Bott, E. A. Antagonistic muscle action in voluntary flexion and extension. *Psychol. Rev.*, 1927, *34*, 241–272.

Travis, R. C., & ———. Sensori-motor consequences of passive rotary and rectilinear oscillation of the body. *Proc. Nat. Acad. Sci.*, 1927, *13*, 843–846.

———. *Elementary conditions of human variability: A study of the variation of successive responses to similar stimuli at different levels of the cerebro-spinal system of a human subject.* New York: Columbia University Press, 1931. (1927)

———. Protopraxic and epicritic stratification of human adjustment. *Amer. J. Psychol.*, 1927, *39*, 145–157.

———, & Travis, R. C. Experimental analysis of the sensori-motor consequences of passive oscillation, rotary, and rectilinear. *Psychol. Monogr.*, 1928, *38*, No. 175.

Gatti, A., & ———. Ueber die Unterschiedsempfindlichkeit bei Reizung eines einzelnen, isolierten Tastorgans. *Arch. ges. Psychol.*, 1929, *69*, 405–426.

Gatti, A., & ———. Ueber die Deformation der Haut in einer Reihe von Druckwerten. *Arch. ges. Psychol.*, 1929, *71*, 481–492.

———. Raymond Dodge. In C. Murchison (Ed.), *A history of psychology in autobiography.* Vol. 1. Worcester, Mass.: Clark University Press, 1930, pp. 99–121.   **B**

———. Fundamental steps in the development of adaptive behavior of the eyes. *J. gen. Psychol.*, 1930, *4*, 3–14.

——. *Conditions and consequences of human variability*. New Haven: Yale University Press, 1931.

——, & Kahn, E. *The craving for superiority*. New Haven: Yale University Press, 1931.

——. Anticipatory reaction. *Science*, 1933, *78*, 197–203.

——. Constructive reactionism: Knowledge of reality from a psycho-physiological viewpoint. *Psychol. Rev.*, 1934, *41*, 98–102.

Park & Burgess, *Sociology*

HENRY HERBERT DONALDSON
1857-1938
American Neurologist (15)

Donaldson, H. H. On the temperature sense. *Mind*, 1885, *10*, 399–416.

Hall, G. S., & ——. Motor sensations on the skin. *Mind*, 1885, *10*, 557–572.

——. On the relation of neurology to psychology. *Amer. J. Psychol.*, 1888, *1*, 209–221.

——. Anatomical observations on the brain and several sense-organs of the blind deaf-mute, Laura Dewey Bridgman, etc. *Amer. J. Psychol.*, 1890, *3*, 293–341 ; 1892, *4*, 248–294.

——, & Bolton, T. L. The size of several cranial nerves in man as indicated by the areas of their cross-sections. *Amer. J. Psychol.*, 1892, *4*, 224–229.

——. The extent of the visual area of the cortex in man as deduced from the study of Laura Bridgman's brain. *Amer. J. Psychol.*, 1892, *4*, 503–513.

——. *The growth of the brain: A study of the nervous system in relation to education*. New York: Scribners, 1895.

——. The education of the nervous system. *Educ. Rev.*, 1895, *9*, 105–121.

——. Observations on the weight and length of the central nervous system and of the legs in bullfrogs of different sizes. *J. comp. Neurol.*, 1898, *8*, 314–335.

——. President's address (Studies on the growth of the mammalian nervous system). *J. nerv. ment. Dis.*, 1911, *38*, 257–266.

——. The rat: Data and reference tables for the albino rat (Mus Norvegicus Albinus) and the Norway rat (Mus Norvegicus). (2nd ed.) *Mem. Wistar Inst. Anat. Biol.*, 1924, No. 6. (1915)

——. A comparison of growth changes in the nervous system of the rat with corresponding changes in the nervous system of man. *Proc. Nat. Acad. Sci.*, 1918, *4*, 280–283.

—— (with assist. of Myrtelle M. Canavan). A study of the brains of three scholars. *J. comp. Neurol.*, 1928, *46*, 1–95.

King, Helen D., & ——. Life processes and size of the body and organs of the gray Norway rat during ten generations in captivity. *Amer. Anat. Mem.*, 1929, *14*, 1–106.

——. The brain problem—in relation to weight and form. *Amer. J. Psychiat.*, 1932, *12*, 197–214.

——, & Meeser, Ruth E. On the effects of exercise carried through seven generations on the weight of the musculature and on the composition and weight of several organs of the albino rat. *Amer. J. Anat.*, 1932, *50*, 359–396.

——, & Meeser, Ruth E. On the effect of exercise beginning at different ages on the weight of the musculature and of several organs of the albino rat. *Amer. J. Anat.*, 1933, *53*, 403–411.

——. The nervous skeleton. Presidential address before the American Neurological Association, Atlantic City, June 3, 1937. *Trans. Amer. Neurol. Ass.*, 1937, *63*, 1–9.

Dennis, *Psychology*

F(RANCISCUS) C(ORNELIS) DONDERS
1818-1889
Dutch Ophthalmologist (19)

Donders, F. C. Physiologische en pathologische aantekeningen van gemengden aard: De bewegingen van het menschelijk oog. *Ned. Lancet*, 1846, *2*, 104–138, 345–380, 432–463, 537–568, 641–655.

———. *Physiologie des Menschen.* Leipzig: Hirzel, 1859. (1856)

———. Ueber die Natur der Vocale. *Arch. holländ. Beitr. Nat. Heilk.,* 1858, *1,* 157–162.

———. Beiträge zur Kenntnis der Refractions- und Accomodationsanomalien. *Arch. Ophthalm.,* 1860, *6,* 62–106, 210–243 ; 1860, *7,* 155–204.

———. *On the anomalies of accommodation and refraction of the eye.* Trans. by W. D. Moore. London: New Sydenham Society, 1864.

———. *An essay on the nature and consequences of anomalies of refraction.* Trans., rev., & ed. by C. A. Oliver. Philadelphia: Blakiston, 1899. (1864)

———. Zur Klangfarbe der Vocale. *Ann. Phys. Chem.,* 1864, *123,* 527–528.

———. On the rapidity of thought and of the determination of the will. (1865) Trans. by W. D. Moore. *Brit. For. Med.-Chir. Rev.,* 1866, *38,* 168–170.

———. Deux instruments pour la mesure du temps nécessaire pour les actes psychiques. *Arch. néerl. Sci. Ex. Natur.,* 1867, *2,* 247–250.

———. Das binoculare Sehen und die Vorstellung von der dritten Dimension. *Arch. Ophthalm.,* 1867, *13,* 1–48.

———. Twee werktuigen, tot bepaling van den tijd, voor psychische processen benoodigd. *Onderzoek. Physiol. Labor. Utrecht,* 1867–1868, *2,* 21–25 ; also *Ned. Arch. Gen.-Natuurk.,* 1868, *3,* 105–109. Trans. by W. G. Koster. *Acta Psychol.,* 1969, *30,* 432–435.

———. Over de snelheid van psychische processen. *Onderzoek. Physiol. Labor. Utrecht,* 1868–1869, *2,* 92–120. Trans. by W. G. Koster. *Acta Psychol.,* 1969, *30,* 412–431. Also Die Schnelligkeit psychischer Processe. *Arch. Anat. Physiol.,* 1868, *6,* 657–681, & La vitesse des actes physiques. *Arch. néerl. Sci. Ex. Natur.,* 1868, *3,* 296–317.

———. Proces Verbaal van de gewone Vergadering der Koninklijke Akademie van Wetenschappen. Afdeeling Natuurkunde op saturdag 24 Junij 1865. Trans. by W. G. Koster. *Acta Psychol.,* 1969, *30,* 409–411.

———. *De physiologie der spraakklanken.* Utrecht: Post, 1870.

———. Die Projection der Gesichtserscheinungen nach den Richtungslinien. *Arch. Ophthalm.,* 1871, *17,* 1–68.

———. Versuch einer genetischen Erklärung der Augenbewegungen. *Arch. ges. Physiol.,* 1876, *13,* 373–421.

———. Korte beschrijving van eenige werktuigen en toestellen tot de collectie van het Physiologische Laboratorium en het Ned. Gasthuis voor Ooglijders behoorende. *Onderzoek. Physiol. Labor. Utrecht,* 1877, *4,* 8–30. Trans. in part by W. G. Koster. *Acta Psychol.,* 1969, *30,* 436–438.

———. Ueber Farbensysteme. *Arch. Ophthalm.,* 1881, *27* (1), 155–223.

———. Sur les systèmes chromatiques. *Ann. ocul.,* 1881, *6,* 109–144, 197–220.

———. Noch einmal die Farbensysteme. *Arch. Ophthalm.,* 1884, *30* (1), 15–90.

———. Farbengleichungen. *Arch. Physiol.,* 1884, *8,* 518–552.

Clarke & O'Malley, *Brain* ; Clendening, *Source Book*

JUNE ETTA DOWNEY
1875-1932
American Psychologist (14)

Downey, June E. A musical experiment. *Amer. J. Psychol.,* 1897, *9,* 63–69.

———. Control processes in modified handwriting: An experimental study. *Psychol. Monogr.,* 1908, *9,* No. 37.

———. Automatic phenomena of muscle-reading. *J. Phil.,* 1908, *5,* 650–658.

———. Muscle-reading: A method of investigating involuntary movements and mental types. *Psychol. Rev.,* 1909, *16,* 257–301.

———. Judgments on the sex of handwriting. *Psychol. Rev.,* 1910, *17,* 205–216.

———. Literary self-projection. *Psychol. Rev.,* 1912, *19,* 299–311.

———. *Graphology and the psychology of handwriting.* Baltimore, Md.: Warwick & York, 1919.

———. The Will-Profile. *Univer. Wyo. Bull.,* Vol. 16, No. 4b. *Dept. Psychol. Bull.,* 1919, No. 3.

———. Ratings for intelligence and for Will-Temperament. *School & Soc.,* 1920, *12,* 292–294.

———. Some volitional patterns revealed by the Will-Profile. *J. exp. Psychol.,* 1920, *3,* 281–301.

———. Testing the Will-Temperament Tests. *School & Soc.,* 1922, *16,* 161–168.

———. *The will-temperament and its testing.* Yonkers-on-Hudson, N.Y.: World Book, 1923.

———. Jung's "psychological types" and will-temperament patterns. *J. abnorm. soc. Psychol.,* 1924, *18,* 345–349.

———. *The kingdom of the mind.* New York: Macmillan, 1927.

Uhrbrock, R. S., & ———. A non-verbal Will-Temperament Test. *J. appl. Psychol.,* 1927, *11,* 95–105.

———. Individual differences in reaction to the word-in-itself. *Amer. J. Psychol.,* 1927, *39,* 323–342.

———, & Uhrbrock, R. S. Reliability of the Group Will-Temperament Tests. *J. educ. Psychol.,* 1927, *18,* 26–39.

———. Observations on the validation of the Group Will-Temperament Test. *J. educ. Psychol.,* 1927, *18,* 592–600.

———. *Creative imagination: Studies in the psychology of literature.* New York: Harcourt, Brace, 1929.

———. Familial trends in personality. *J. Pers.,* 1932–1933, *1,* 35–47.

JAMES DREVER
1873-1950
Scottish Psychologist (23)

Drever, J. *Instinct in man: A contribution to the psychology of education.* (2nd ed.) Cambridge: Cambridge University Press, 1921. (1917)

———. Instinct and the unconscious. V. *Brit. J. Psychol.,* 1919–1920, *10,* 27–34.

———. *The psychology of everyday life.* (5th ed.) London: Methuen, 1927. (1921)

———. *The psychology of industry.* (Rev. ed.) London: Methuen, 1926. (1921)

———. *An introduction to the psychology of education.* London: Arnold, 1922.

———. The classification of the instincts. II. *Brit. J. Psychol.,* 1923–1924, *14,* 248–255.

———. "Conscious" and "unconscious" in psychology. *J. abnorm. soc. Psychol.,* 1924–1925, *19,* 327–332.

———, & Collins, Mary. *A first laboratory guide in psychology.* London: Methuen, 1926.

Collins, Mary, & ———. *An introduction to experimental psychology.* London: Methuen, 1926.

———, & Collins, Mary. *Performance tests of intelligence.* Edinburgh: Oliver & Boyd, 1936. (1928)

———. In what sense can we speak of primary colours? *Brit. J. Psychol.,* 1930–1931, *21,* 360–367.

———. James Drever. In C. Murchison (Ed.), *A history of psychology in autobiography.* Vol. 2. Worcester, Mass.: Clark University Press, 1932, pp. 17–34.   **B**

———. The present position in psychology. *Philosophy,* 1932, *7,* 311–319.

———. Instinct as impulse. Is the doctrine of instincts dead? A symposium. IV. *Brit. J. Psychol.,* 1942, *12,* 88–96.

———. An autobiography. *Occup. Psychol.,* London, 1948, *22,* 20–30.   **B**

———. *A dictionary of psychology.* (Rev. ed.) New York: Penguin Books, 1964. (1952)

Moore & Hartmann, *Industrial Psychology*

HANS ADOLF EDUARD DRIESCH
1867-1941
German Biologist (18)

Driesch, H. A. E. *Lebenserinnerungen: Aufzeichnungen eines Forschers und Denkers in entscheidender Zeit.* Ed. by Ingeborg Tetaz-Driesch. Basel: Reinhardt, 1951. (1932) **B C**

——. *Philosophische Gegenwartsfragen.* Leipzig: Hirzel, 1933.

——. Tektonische Studien an Hydroidpolypen. *Jena Z. Naturwiss.,* 1890, *24,* 189–226, 657–688; 1891, *25,* 467–479.

——. *Die mathematisch-mechanische Betrachtung morphologischer Probleme der Biologie.* Jena: Fischer, 1891.

——. Entwicklungsmechanische Studien. I. Der Werth der beiden ersten Furchungszellen in der Echinodermenentwicklung. Experimentelle Erzeugung von Theil- und Doppelbildungen. II. Ueber die Beziehungen des Lichtes zur ersten Etappe der thierischen Formbildung. III. Die Verminderung des Furchungsmaterials und ihre Folgen (Weiteres über Theilbildungen). IV. Experimentelle Veränderungen des Typus der Furchung und ihre Folgen (Wirkungen von Wärmezufuhr und von Druck). V. Von der Furchung doppeltbefruchteter Eier. VI. Ueber einige allgemeine Fragen der theoretischen Morphologie. *Z. wiss. Zool.,* 1892, *53,* 160–184; 1893, *55,* 1–62.

——. *Die Biologie als selbständige Grundwissenschaft.* Leipzig: Engelmann, 1893.

——. Zur Verlagerung der Blastomeren des Echinideies. *Anat. Anz.,* 1893, *8,* 348–357.

——. Zur Theorie der tierischen Formbildung. *Biol. Zbl.,* 1893, *13,* 296–312.

——. *Analytische Theorie der organischen Entwicklung.* Leipzig: Engelmann, 1894.

——. Entwicklungsmechanische Studien. VII. Exogastrula und Anenteria (über die Wirkung von Wärmezufuhr auf die Larvenentwicklung der Echinideien). VIII. Ueber Variation der Mikromerenbildung (Wirkung von Verdünnung des Meereswassers). IX. Ueber die Vertretbarkeit der "Anlagen" von Ektoderm und Entoderm. X. Ueber einige allgemeine entwicklungsmechanische Ergebnisse. *Mitt. zool. Stat. Neapel,* 1895, *11,* 221–254.

——. Die Maschinentheorie des Lebens. *Biol. Zbl.,* 1896, *16,* 353–368.

——. Ueber den Werth des biologischen Experiments. *Arch. Entwicklungsmech.,* 1897, *5,* 133–142.

——. *Die Lokalisation morphogenetischer Vorgänge, ein Beweis vitalistischen Geschehens.* Leipzig: Engelmann, 1899.

——. *Die organischen Regulationen.* Leipzig: Engelmann, 1901.

——. *Die "Seele" als elementarer Naturfaktor.* Leipzig: Engelmann, 1903.

——. *Naturbegriffe und Naturteile.* Leipzig: Engelmann, 1904.

——. *Der Vitalismus als Geschichte und als Lehre.* (2nd ed.) Leipzig: Barth, 1922. (1905)

——. *The history and theory of vitalism.* Trans. by C. K. Ogden. London: Macmillan, 1914. (1905)

——. *The science and philosophy of the organism.* (2nd ed.) (2 vols.) London: Black, 1929. (1908)

——. Philosophie des Organischen: (3rd ed.) Leipzig: Reinicke, 1923. (1908)

——. *Zwei Vorträge zur Naturphilosophie.* Leipzig: Engelmann, 1910.

——. *Ordnungslehre, ein System des nichtmetaphysischen Teiles der Philosophie.* (Rev. ed.) Jena: Diederichs, 1923. (1912)

——. *The problem of individuality.* New York: Macmillan, 1914.

——. Ueber die grundsätzliche Unmöglichkeit einer "Vereinigung" von universeller Teleologie und Mechanismus. *Sitzber. Heidelb. Akad. Wiss.,* Phil.-hist. Kl., 1914, No. 1. (Also Heidelberg: Winter, 1914)

——. *Mind and body. A criticism of psychophysical parallelism.* (3rd ed.) Trans. by T. Besterman. New York: Dial Press, 1927. (1916)

Bl

————. *Das Problem der Freiheit.* (2nd ed.) Darmstadt: Reichl, 1920. (1917)

————. *Wirklichkeitslehre, ein metaphysischer Versuch.* (2nd ed.) Leipzig: Reinicke, 1922. (1917)

————. Critical remarks on some modern types of psychology. *J. genet. Psychol.,* 1917, *34,* 3–13.

————. *Logische Studien über Entwicklung.* (2 vols.) Heidelberg: Winter, 1918–1919. (Also in *Sitzber. Heidelberger Akad. Wiss.,* Phil.-hist. Kl., 1918, *9,* iii ; 1919, *10,* xviii.)

————. *Wissen und Denken. Ein Prolegomenon zu aller Philosophie.* (2nd ed.) Leipzig: Reinicke, 1922. (1919)

————. *Das Ganze und die Summe.* Leipzig: Reinicke, 1921.

————. Hans Adolf Eduard Driesch. In R. Schmidt (Ed.), *Die Philosophie der Gegenwart in Selbstdarstellungen.* Vol. 1. (2nd ed.) Leipzig: Meiner, 1923, pp. 49–78.   **B Bl**

————. *Metaphysik.* Breslau: Hirt, 1924.

————. *Relativitätstheorie und Philosophie.* Karlsruhe: Braun, 1924.

————. *The crisis in psychology.* Princeton, N.J.: Princeton University Press, 1925.

————. "Physische Gestalten" und Organismen. *Ann. Phil.,* 1925, *5,* 1–11.

————. Kritisches zur Ganzheitslehre. *Ann. Phil.,* 1925, *5,* 281–304.

————. *Grundprobleme der Psychologie.* (2nd ed.) Leipzig: Reinicke, 1929. (1926)

————. *Metaphysik der Natur.* Munich: Oldenbourg, 1927.

————. *Man and the universe.* Trans. by W. H. Johnston. London: Allen & Unwin, 1929. (1928)

————. *Der Mensch und die Welt.* (2nd ed.) Zurich: Rascher, 1945. (1928)

————. Zur vitalistischen Begriffsbildung. *Arch. Entwicklungsmech.,* 1929, *116,* 1–6.

————. *Philosophische Forschungswege. Ratschläge und Warnungen.* Leipzig: Reinicke, 1930.

————, & Woltereck, H. (Eds.), *Das Lebensproblem im Lichte der modernen Forschung.* Leipzig: Quelle & Meyer, 1931.

————. *Parapsychologie: Die Wissenschaft von den "okkulten" Erscheinungen: Methodik und Theorie.* (3rd ed.) Zurich: Rascher, 1952. (1932)

————. The experiment: Is it the only and is it a reliable way to establish psychological facts? *J. Pers.,* 1932–1933, *1,* 181–194.

————. *Die Maschine und der Organismus.* Leipzig: Barth, 1935.

————. Der Begriff des Ganzen in der Psychologie. *Z. Rassenk.,* 1936, *4,* 27–32.

————. Der Weg der theoretischen Biologie. *Z. ges. Naturw.,* 1938, *6,* 209–232.

————. *Alltagsrätsel des Seelenlebens.* (2nd ed.) Zurich: Rascher, 1954. (1939)

Gabriel & Fogel, *Biology* ; Hall, *Source Book*

EMIL DU BOIS-REYMOND
1818-1896
German Physiologist (23)

Du Bois-Reymond, E. *Untersuchungen über thierische Electricität.* (2 vols. in 3) Berlin: Reimer, 1848, 1849, 1884.   **C**

————. *Gesammelte Abhandlungen zur allgemeinen Muskel- und Nervenphysik.* (2 vols.) Leipzig: Veit, 1875–1877.   **C**

————. *Reden.* (2nd ed.) Ed. by Estelle Du Bois-Reymond. Leipzig: Veit, 1912. (1886–1887)   **C**

————, & Ludwig, C. *Zwei grosse Naturforscher des 19. Jahrhunderts. Ein Briefwechsel zwischen Emil Du Bois-Reymond und Carl Ludwig.* Ed. by Estelle Du Bois-Reymond & P. Diepgen. Leipzig: Barth, 1927.   **B C**

————. Vorläufiger Abriss einiger Untersuchungen über den sogenannten Froschström und über die elektromotorischen Fische. *Anal. Physik Chem.,* 1843, *58,* 1–30.

———. Note sur la loi qui préside à l'irritation électrique des nerfs et sur la modification du courant musculaire par l'effet de la contraction. *Ann. Chim. Phys.*, 1850, *30*, 178–188.

———. *On Signor Carlo Matteucci's letter to H. Bence Jones.* London: Churchill, 1853.

———. Gedächtnissrede auf Johannes Müller. *Abh. Preuss. Akd. Wiss.* Berlin, 1860, *4*, 25–190.

B

———. *Beschreibung einiger Vorrichtungen und Versuchsweisen zu elektrophysiologischen Zwecken.* Berlin: Dümmler, 1863.

———. On the time required for the transmission of volition and sensation through the nerves; a lecture. In H. B. Jones (Ed.), *Croonian lectures on matter and force.* London: Churchill, 1868, pp. 97–132.

———. *Voltaire in seiner Beziehung zur Naturwissenschaft.* Berlin: Dümmler, 1868.

———. *Ueber die Grenzen der Naturerkenntnis.* (5th ed.) Leipzig: Veit, 1903. (1875–1877)

———. Rede: Offentliche Sitzung vom 28. Januar 1875. *Monatsber. kön. preuss. Akad. Wiss.,* Berlin, 1875, 85–112.

———. *Culturgeschichte und Naturwissenschaft.* Leipzig: Veit, 1878.

———. *Ueber die Grenzen des Naturkennens.* (1872) In *Ueber die Grenzen des Naturkennens & Die sieben Welträthsel.* Leipzig: Veit, 1891, pp. 13–66.

———. The seven world-problems. (1880) *Pop. Sci. Mon.,* 1881–1882, *20*, 433–447.

———. *Untersuchungen am Zitteral (Gymnotus electricus).* Leipzig: Veit, 1881.

———. *Ueber die Uebung.* Berlin: Hirschwald, 1881.

———. Vorläufiger Bericht über die von Prof. Fritsch in Aegypten und am Mittelmeer angestellten neuen Untersuchungen an elektrischen Fischen. In E. Du Bois-Reymond (Ed.), *Archiv für Physiologie.* Leipzig: Veit, 1882, pp. 61–75.

———. *Goethe und kein Ende.* Leipzig: Veit, 1883.

———. On secondary electromotive phenomena in muscles, nerves, and electrical organs. *Sitzber. kön.-preuss. Akad. Wiss. Berlin,* 1883, *16*, 343–404. Reprinted in J. Burdon-Sanderson (Ed.), *Translations of foreign biological memoirs.* Oxford: Clarendon Press, 1887, pp. 161–225.

———. Ueber Brückes Theorie des körperlichen Sehens. *Z. Psychol.,* 1891, *2*, 427–437.

———. *Maupertuis.* Leipzig: Veit, 1893.

———. Allgemeine Physiologie der glatten Muskeln. In W. Nagel (Ed.), *Handbuch der Physiologie des Menschen.* Vol. 4. Brunswick: Vieweg, 1909, pp. 544–563.

———. Spezielle Bewegungslehre mit Ueberblick über die Physiologie der Gelenke. In W. Nagel (Ed.), *Handbuch der Physiologie des Menschen.* Vol. 4. Brunswick: Vieweg, 1909, pp. 564–628.

Bodenheimer, *Biology* ; Clarke & O'Malley, *Brain* ; Fried, *Anthropology*

GEORGES DUMAS
1866-1946
French Psychologist (21)

Dumas, G. *La vie affective.* Paris: Presses Universitaires de France, 1948.   **C**

———. *Les états intellectuels dans la mélancolie.* Paris: Alcan, 1895.

———. *Théorie psychologique de l'espace.* Paris: Alcan, 1895.

———. Recherches expérimentales sur l'excitation et la dépression. *Rev. phil.,* 1897, *43*, 623–634.

———. L'état mental d'Auguste Comte. *Rev. phil.,* 1898, *45*, 30–60, 151–180, 387–414.

———. *La tristesse et la joie.* Paris: Alcan, 1900.

———. Les obsessions et la psychasthénie d'après le Dr. Pierre Janet. *Rev. phil.,* 1903, *56*, 293–312.

———. Le sourire: Etude psychophysiologique. *Rev. phil.,* 1904, *58*, 1–23, 136–151.

———. *Psychologie des deux messies positivistes: Saint-Simon et Auguste Comte.* Paris: Alcan, 1905.

————. *Le sourire: Psychologie et physiologie.* (2nd ed.) Paris: Presses Universitaires de France, 1948. (1906)

————. Qu'est-ce que la psychologie pathologique? *J. Psychol. norm. path.,* 1908, *5,* 9–22.

————. Qu'est-ce que la psychologie pathologique? *J. Psychol. norm. path.,* 1915, *11,* 73–87.

————, & Aimé, H. *Névroses et psychoses de guerre chez les austro-allemands.* Paris: Alcan, 1919.

————. *Troubles mentaux et troubles nerveux de guerre.* Paris: Alcan, 1919.

————. L'interpsychologie. *J. Psychol. norm. path.,* 1920, *17,* 515–537.

————, & Piéron, H. L'excitation et le mouvement. In G. Dumas (Ed.), *Traité de psychologie.* Vol. 1. Paris: Alcan, 1923, pp. 233–317.

Barat, L., ————, & Dugas, L. Les états affectifs. In G. Dumas (Ed.), *Traité de psychologie.* Vol. 1. Paris: Alcan, 1923, pp. 402–501.

————, & Claparède, E. L'orientation et l'équilibre. In G. Dumas (Ed.), *Traité de psychologie.* Vol. 1. Paris: Alcan, 1923, pp. 572–605.

————. L'expression des émotions. In G. Dumas (Ed.), *Traité de psychologie.* Vol. 1. Paris: Alcan, 1923, pp. 606–690.

————. Le rire et les larmes. In G. Dumas (Ed.), *Traité de psychologie.* Vol. 1. Paris: Alcan, 1923, pp. 691–732.

Dagnan, J., Delacroix, H., & ————. L'association des idées. In G. Dumas (Ed.), *Traité de psychologie.* Vol. 1. Paris: Alcan, 1923, pp. 820–845.

————. Avant-propos d'un traité de psychologie. *Rev. phil.,* 1923, *95,* 5–37.

————. Psychologie de l'hystérie. *J. Psychol. norm. path.,* 1923, *20,* 895–920.

————, Belot, G., & Delacroix, H. Les sentiments complexes. In G. Dumas (Ed.), *Traité de psychologie.* Vol. 2. Paris: Alcan, 1924, pp. 227–332.

————. L'interpsychologie. In G. Dumas (Ed.), *Traité de psychologie.* Vol. 2. Paris: Alcan, 1924, pp. 739–764.

————. La pathologie mentale. In G. Dumas (Ed.), *Traité de psychologie.* Vol. 2. Paris: Alcan, 1924, pp. 811–1006.

————. La psychologie pathologique. In G. Dumas (Ed.), *Traité de psychologie.* Vol. 2. Paris: Alcan, 1924, pp. 1007–1070.

————. Un nouveau chapitre de psychologie. In G. Dumas (Ed.), *Traité de psychologie.* Vol. 2. Paris: Alcan, 1924, pp. 1071–1120.

————. Conclusion. In G. Dumas (Ed.), *Traité de psychologie.* Vol. 2. Paris: Alcan, 1924, pp. 1121–1158.

————. Le choc émotionnel. Réactions glandulaires et vasculaires. *J. Psychol. norm. path.,* 1928, *25,* 130–164.

————. Introduction à la psychologie. In G. Dumas (Ed.), *Nouveau traité de psychologie.* Vol. 1. Paris: Alcan, 1930, pp. 335–366.

————. La mimique des aveugles. *Bull. Acad. méd.,* 1932, *107,* 607–610.

————, & Piéron, H. L'excitation et le mouvement. In G. Dumas (Ed.), *Nouveau traité de psychologie.* Vol. 2. Paris: Alcan, 1932, pp. 3–58.

————. Le désagréable et l'agréable. In G. Dumas (Ed.), *Nouveau traité de psychologie.* Vol. 2. Paris: Alcan, 1932, pp. 211–250.

————. La douleur et le plaisir. In G. Dumas (Ed.), *Nouveau traité de psychologie.* Vol. 2. Paris: Alcan, 1932, pp. 251–296.

————. Les chocs émotionnels. In G. Dumas (Ed.), *Nouveau traité de psychologie.* Vol. 2. Paris: Alcan, 1932, pp. 297–348.

————. Le choc émotionnel. Les émotions. In G. Dumas (Ed.), *Nouveau traité de psychologie.* Vol. 2. Paris: Alcan, 1932, pp. 349–443.

————. Les besoins. In G. Dumas (Ed.), *Nouveau traité de psychologie.* Vol. 2. Paris: Alcan, 1932, pp. 444–497.

————. L'expression des émotions: Historique et méthodes. In G. Dumas (Ed.), *Nouveau traité de psychologie.* Vol. 3. Paris: Alcan, 1933, pp. 41–83.

———. L'expression des émotions: Les expressions préalables. In G. Dumas (Ed.), *Nouveau traité de psychologie*. Vol. 3. Paris: Alcan, 1933, pp. 84–120.

———. L'expression des émotions: Réactions émotionnelles communes. In G. Dumas (Ed.), *Nouveau traité de psychologie*. Vol. 3. Paris: Alcan, 1933, pp. 210–292.

———. L'expression des émotions: Les mimiques motrices et sécrétoires. In G. Dumas (Ed.), *Nouveau traité de psychologie*. Vol. 3. Paris: Alcan, 1933, pp. 295–338.

———. L'expression des émotions: La mimique vocale. In G. Dumas (Ed.), *Nouveau traité de psychologie*. Vol. 3. Paris: Alcan, 1933, pp. 339–357.

———. La symbolisation. In G. Dumas (Ed.), *Nouveau traité de psychologie*. Vol. 4. Paris: Alcan, 1934, pp. 264–338.

———. Discours de M. Georges Dumas. In Various, *Centenaire de Th. Ribot et Jubilé de la Psychologie Scientifique Française*. Paris: Imprimerie moderne, 1939, pp. 37–46.

———. Prophétisme et suggestion. In Various, *Mélanges Pierre Janet*. Paris: d'Artrey, 1939, pp. 75–86.

———. *Le surnaturel et les dieux d'après les maladies mentales*. Paris: Presses Universitaires de France, 1946.

Arnold, *Emotion*

KARL DUNCKER
1903-1940
German Psychologist (18)

Duncker, K. A qualitative (experimental and theoretical) study of productive thinking (solving of comprehensible problems). *J. genet. Psychol.*, 1926, *33*, 642–708.

———. Der Behaviorismus—die amerikanische Psychologie. *Pädag. Zbl.*, 1927, *12*, 1–13.

———. Ueber induzierte Bewegung. Ein Beitrag zur Theorie optisch wahrgenommener Bewegung. *Psychol. Forsch.*, 1929, *12*, 180–259. Ab-

stracted & trans. in W. D. Ellis (Ed.), *A source book of Gestalt psychology*. London: Routledge & Kegan Paul, 1938, pp. 161–172.

———. Behaviorismus und Gestaltpsychologie. *Erkenntnis*, 1933, *3*, 162–176.

———. *Zur Psychologie des produktiven Denkens*. Berlin: Springer-Verlag, 1935. (Reprinted 1963)

———. On problem-solving. (1935) Trans. by Lynne S. Lees, *Psychol. Monogr.*, 1945, *58*, No. 270.

———. Lernen und Einsicht im Dienst der Zielerreichungen. *Acta Psychol.*, 1936, *1*, 77–82.

———. Some preliminary experiments on the mutual influence of pains. *Psychol. Forsch.*, 1937, *21*, 311–326.

———. Experimental modification of children's food preferences through social suggestion. *J. abnorm. soc. Psychol.*, 1938, *33*, 489–507.

———. The influence of past experience upon perceptual properties. *Amer. J. Psychol.*, 1939, *52*, 255–265.

———. Ethical relativity? (An enquiry into the psychology of ethics). *Mind*, 1939, *48*, 39–57.

———, & Krechevsky, I. On solution-achievement. *Psychol. Rev.*, 1939, *46*, 176–185.

———. On pleasure, emotion, and striving. *Phil. phenomenol. Res.*, 1941, *1*, 391–430.

———. Phenomenology and epistemology of consciousness of objects. Trans. by Luise Haessler. *Phil. phenomenol. Res.*, 1947, 7, 505–542.

Gruber, *Creative Thinking* ; Mandler & Mandler, *Thinking*

KNIGHT DUNLAP
1875-1949
American Psychologist (22)

Dunlap, K. The effect of imperceptible shadows on the judgment of distance. *Psychol. Rev.*, 1900, 7, 435–453.

———. The complication experiment and related phenomena. *Psychol. Rev.*, 1910, *17*, 157–191.

————. Reactions to rhythmic stimuli with attempt to synchronize. *Psychol. Rev.,* 1910, *17,* 399–416.

————. Difference-sensibility for rate of discrete impressions. *Psychol. Rev.,* 1912, *19,* 32–59.

————. The case against introspection. *Psychol. Rev.,* 1912, *19,* 404–413.

————. The nature of perceived relations. *Psychol. Rev.,* 1912, *19,* 415–446.

————. Color theory and realism. *Psychol. Rev.,* 1915, *22,* 99–103.

————. Thought-content and feeling. *Psychol. Rev.,* 1916, *23,* 49–70.

————. "Scientific prepossession" and antiscientific animus. *J. Phil.,* 1919, *16,* 156–160.

————. Are there any instincts? *J. abnorm. Psychol.,* 1919, *14,* 307–311.

————. *Mysticism, Freudianism, and scientific psychology.* St. Louis, Mo.: Mosby, 1920.

————. The social need for scientific psychology. *Sci. Mon.,* N.Y., 1920, *11,* 502–517.

————. Light-spot adaptation. *Amer. J. Physiol.,* 1921, *55,* 201–211.

————. The identity of instinct and habit. *J. Phil.,* 1922, *19,* 85–94.

————. The foundations of social psychology. *Psychol. Rev.,* 1923, *30,* 81–102.

————. Instinct and desire. *J. abnorm. soc. Psychol.,* 1925, *20,* 170–173.

————. Adaptation of nystagmus to repeated caloric stimulation in rabbits. *J. comp. Psychol.,* 1925, *5,* 485–493.

————. *Social psychology.* Baltimore, Md.: Williams & Wilkins, 1925.

————. *The theoretical aspect of psychology.* In C. Murchison (Ed.), *Psychologies of 1925.* (3rd ed.) Worcester, Mass.: Clark University Press, 1928, pp. 309–329. (1926)

————. The experimental methods of psychology. In C. Murchison (Ed.), *Psychologies of 1925.* (3rd ed.) Worcester, Mass.: Clark University Press, 1928, pp. 331–351. (1926)

————. The applications of psychology to social problems. In C. Murchison (Ed.), *Psychologies of 1925.* (3rd ed.) Worcester, Mass.: Clark University Press, 1928, pp. 353–379. (1926)

————. The use and abuse of abstractions in psychology. *Phil. Rev.,* 1927, *36,* 462–487.

————. The development and function of clothing. *J. gen. Psychol.,* 1928, *1,* 64–78.

————. A revision of the fundamental law of habit formation. *Science,* 1928, *67,* 360–362.

————. Emotion as a dynamic background. In M. L. Reymert (Ed.), *Feelings and emotions: The Wittenberg symposium.* Worcester, Mass.: Clark University Press, 1928, pp. 150–160.

————. Response psychology. Part 8. Reaction psychology. In C. Murchison (Ed.), *Psychologies of 1930.* Worcester, Mass.: Clark University Press, 1930, pp. 309–323.

————. Knight Dunlap. In C. Murchison (Ed.), *A history of psychology in autobiography.* Vol. 2. Worcester, Mass.: Clark University Press, 1932, pp. 35–61.   **B**

————. Are emotions teleological constructs? *Amer. J. Psychol.,* 1932, *44,* 572–576.

————. *Habits, their making and unmaking.* New York: Liveright, 1932.

————. The susceptibility of rats to electric shock. *J. comp. Psychol.,* 1933, *15,* 199–207.

————. *Civilized life.* Baltimore. Md.: Williams & Wilkins, 1935.

————. *Elements of psychology.* St. Louis, Mo.: Mosby, 1936.

————. The postulate of common content. *Psychol. Rev.,* 1940, *47,* 306–321.

————. The method and problems of social psychology. *Psychol. Rev.,* 1940, *47,* 471–485.

————. The historical method in psychology. *J. gen. Psychol.,* 1941, *24,* 49–62.

————. The technique of negative practice. *Amer. J. Psychol.,* 1942, *55,* 270–273.

————. *Religion, its functions in human life: A study of religion from the point of view of psychology.* New York: McGraw-Hill, 1946.

Moore & Hartmann, *Industrial Psychology*

EMILE DURKHEIM
1858-1917
French Sociologist (23)

Durkheim, E. *Education and sociology.* Trans. by S. D. Fox. Glencoe, Ill.: Free Press, 1956. (1922)   C

————. *Sociology and philosophy.* Trans. by D. F. Pocock, & intro. by J. G. Peristiany. Glencoe, Ill.: Free Press, 1953. (1924)   C

————. *Professional ethics and civil morals.* Trans. by Cornelia Brookfield. London: Routledge & Kegan Paul, 1957. (1950)   Bl C

————. *Emile Durkheim: Selections from his work.* Ed. by G. Simpson. New York: Crowell, 1963.   C

————. *Journal sociologique.* Ed., intro., & notes by J. Duvignaud. Paris: Presses Universitaires de France, 1969.   C

————. *La science sociale et l'action.* Ed. & intro. by J.-C. Filloux. Paris: Presses Universitaires de France, 1970.   C

————. Suicide et natalité. Etude de statistique morale. *Rev. phil.,* 1888, *26,* 446–463.

————. *Montesquieu and Rousseau: Forerunners of sociology.* Trans. by R. Manheim. Ann Arbor, Mich.: University of Michigan Press, 1960. (1892, 1918)

————. *The division of labor in society.* (1st & 5th ed.) Trans. by G. Simpson. New York: Macmillan, 1933. (1893) (Reprinted 1965)

————. *The rules of sociological method.* (8th ed.) Trans. by Sarah A. Solovay & J. H. Mueller. Chicago: University of Chicago Press, 1938. (1895) (Reprinted 1950)

————. *Suicide, a study in sociology.* Trans. by J. A. Spaulding & G. Simpson. Glencoe, Ill.: Free Press, 1951. (1897)

————. Prefaces to *L'année sociologique.* Prefaces to Vols. I, II ; 1898, 1899. In K. H. Wolff (Ed.), *Emile Durkheim, 1858–1917: A collection of essays, with translations and bibliography.* Columbus, Ohio: Ohio State University Press, 1960, pp. 341–353. (Reprinted 1961)

————, & Mauss, M. *Primitive classification.* Ed. by R. Needham. Chicago: University of Chicago Press, 1967. (1903)

————. La sociologia ed il suo dominio scientifico. *Riv. Ital. Sociol.,* 1906, *4,* 127–148. Trans. in K. H. Wolff (Ed.), *Emile Durkheim, op. cit.,* pp. 354–375.

————. *The elementary forms of the religious life.* Trans. by J. W. Swain. New York: Macmillan, 1915. (1912)

————. Le dualisme de la nature humaine et ses conditions sociales. *Scientia,* 1914, *15,* 206–221. Trans. in K. H. Wolff (Ed.), *Emile Durkheim, op. cit.,* pp. 325–340.

————. Le contrat social de Rousseau. *Rev. Métaphys., Morale,* 1918, *25,* 1–23, 129–161.

————. La pédagogie de Rousseau. *Rev. Métaphys. Morale,* 1919, *26,* 153–180.

————. *Moral education: A study in the theory and application of the sociology of education.* Trans. by H. Schnwer, & ed. by E. K. Wilson. New York: Free Press, 1961. (1925)

————. *Socialism and Saint-Simon.* Trans. by Charlotte Sattler, & intro. by A. W. Gouldner. Yellow Springs, Ohio: Antioch Press, 1958. (1928) (Reprinted 1962)

————. *L'évolution pédagogique en France.* (2 vols.) Paris: Alcan, 1938.

————. *Pragmatisme et sociologie. Lectures 1–5, 13–14.* Paris: Vrin, 1955. Trans. in K. H. Wolff (Ed.), *Emile Durkheim, op. cit.,* pp. 386–436.

Borgatta, *Present-day Sociology* ; Coser & Rosenberg, *Sociological Theory* ; Park & Burgess, *Sociology* ; Parsons, *Society* ; Ross, *Social Order*

JOHANNES GREGORIUS
DUSSER DE BARENNE
1885-1940
Dutch-American Physiologist (13)

Dusser de Barenne, J. G. Die Strychnineinwirkung auf das Zentralnervensystem. *Fol. Neurobiol.,* 1912, *6,* 277–286 ; 1913, *7,* 549–561.

———. Experimental researches on sensory localizations in the cerebral cortex. *Quart. J. exp. Physiol.,* 1915–1916, *9,* 355–390.

———. Recherches expérimentales sur les fonctions du système nerveux central, faites en particulier sur deux chats dont le néopallium avait été enlevé. *Arch. Néerl. Physiol.,* 1919, *4,* 31–123.

———, & Magnus, R. Beiträge zum Problem der Körperstellung. *Arch. ges. Physiol.,* 1920, *180,* 75–89.

———. Die Funktionen des Kleinhirns: Physiologie und allgemeine Neuropathologie. In G. Alexander & O. Marburg (Eds.), *Handbuch der Neurologie des Ohres.* Vol. 1. Vienna: Urban & Schwarzenberg, 1923, pp. 589–672.

———. Untersuchungen über die Aktionsströme der quergestreiften Muskulatur bei der Enthirnungsstarre der Katze und der Willkür-Kontraktion des Menschen. *Skand. Arch. Physiol.,* 1923, *43,* 107–119.

———. Experimental researches on the sensory localization in the cerebral cortex of the monkey (Macacus). *Proc. roy. Soc.,* 1924, *96B,* 272–291.

———, & Burger, G. C. E. A method for the graphic registration of oxygen consumption and carbon dioxide output by respiratory exchange in decerebrate rigidity. *J. Physiol.,* 1924, *59,* 17–29.

———. On a release-phenomenon in electrical stimulation of the "motor" cerebral cortex. *Science,* 1931, *73,* 213–214.

———. Corticalization of function and functional localization in the cerebral cortex. *Arch. Neurol. Psychiat.,* Chicago, 1933, *30,* 884–890.

———, & McCulloch, W. S. An "extinction" phenomenon on stimulation of the cerebral cortex, *Proc. Soc. exp. Biol.,* N. Y., 1934, *32,* 524–527.

———. The labyrinthine and postural mechanisms. In C. M. Murchison (Ed.), *A handbook of general experimental psychology.* Worcester, Mass.: Clark University Press, 1934, pp. 204–246.

———. Central levels of sensory integration. *Proc. Ass. Res. nerv. ment. Dis.,* 1934, *15,* 274–288.

———, & McCulloch, W. S. Some effects of laminar coagulation upon the local action potentials of the cerebral cortex of the monkey. *Amer. J. Physiol.,* 1936, *114,* 692–694.

———. Physiologie der Grosshirnrinde. In O. Bumke & O. Foerster (Eds.), *Handbuch der Neurologie.* Vol. 2. Berlin: Springer-Verlag, 1937, pp. 268–319.

———, & McCulloch, W. S. Local stimulatory inactivation within the cerebral cortex, the factor for extinction. *Amer. J. Physiol.,* 1937, *118,* 510–524.

———, & McCulloch, W. S. Functional organization in the sensory cortex of the monkey (Macaca mulatta). *J. Neurophysiol.,* 1938, *1,* 69–85.

———, & McCulloch, W. S. Sensorimotor cortex, nucleus caudatus and thalamus opticus. *J. Neurophysiol.,* 1938, *1,* 364–377.

———, & McCulloch, W. S. Physiological delimitation of neurones in the central nervous system. *Amer. J. Physiol.,* 1939, *127,* 620–628.

———, & McCulloch, W. S. Factors for facilitation and extinction in the central nervous system. *J. Neurophysiol.,* 1939, *2,* 319–355.

———, Garol, H. W., & McCulloch, W. S. The "motor" cortex of the chimpanzee. *J. Neurophysiol.,* 1941, *4,* 287–303.

———, & McCulloch, W. S. Functional interdependence of sensory cortex and thalamus. *J. Neurophysiol.,* 1941, *4,* 304–310.

———, & McCulloch, W. S. Suppression of motor response obtained from area 4 by stimulation of area 4s. *J. Neurophysiol.*, 1941, *4*, 311–323.

———, Garol, H. W., & McCulloch, W. S. Functional organization of sensory and adjacent cortex of the monkey. *J. Neurophysiol.*, 1941, *4*, 324–330.

Clarke & O'Malley, *Brain*

HERMANN EBBINGHAUS
1850-1909
German Psychologist (27)

———. *Ueber die Hartmann'sche Philosophie des Unbewussten.* Düsseldorf: Dietz, 1873.

———. *Memory: A contribution to experimental psychology.* Trans. by H. A. Ruger and Clara E. Bussenius. New York: Teachers College, Columbia University, 1913. (1885) (Reprinted 1964)

———. *Ueber das Gedächtnis.* Amsterdam: Bonset, 1966. (1885)

———. Die Gesetzmässigkeit des Helligkeitskontrastes. *Sitzber. preuss. Akad. Wiss. Berlin,* 1887, 995–1009.

———. Ueber den Grund der Abweichungen von dem Webers'chen Gesetz bei Lichtempfindungen. *Arch. ges. Physiol.,* 1889, *45,* 113–133.

———. Ueber Nachbilder im binocularen Sehen und die binocularen Farbenerscheinungen überhaupt. *Arch. ges. Physiol.,* 1890, *46,* 498–508.

———. Ueber negative Empfindungswerte. *Z. Psychol.,* 1890, *1,* 320–334, 463–485.

———. Theorie des Farbensehens. *Z. Psychol.,* 1893, *5,* 145–238.

———. Ueber erklärende und beschreibende Psychologie. *Z. Psychol.,* 1896, *9,* 161–205.

———. *Grundzüge der Psychologie.* (3rd ed.) (2 vols.) Ed. by E. Dürr. Leipzig: Veit, 1911, 1913. (1897, 1908) (Vol. 1, 2nd ed., reprinted 1968)

———. Ueber eine neue Methode zur Prüfung geistiger Fähigkeiten und ihre Anwendung bei Schulkindern. *Z. Psychol.,* 1897, *13,* 401–459.

———. Die Psychologie jetzt und vor hundert Jahren. In *Fourth International Congress of Psychology.* Paris: Alcan, 1901, pp. 49–60.

———. *Abriss der Psychologie.* (9th ed.) Ed. by K. Bühler. Berlin: De Gruyter, 1932. (1908)

———. *Psychology: An elementary text-book.* Trans. by M. Meyer. Boston: Heath, 1908.

Beck & Molish, *Reflexes* ; Dennis, *Psychology ;* Herrnstein & Boring, *Source Book ;* Wrenn, *Contributions*

JONATHAN EDWARDS
1703-1758
American Philosopher (11)

Edwards, J. *The works of President Edwards with a memoir of his life.* (10 vols.) Ed. by S. E. Dwight. New York: Carvill, 1829–1830.
B Bl C

———. *The works of President Edwards: A reprint of the Worcester edition, with valuable additions and a copious general index.* (4 vols.) New York: Levitt, Trow, 1844.　　**C**

———. *Jonathan Edwards: Representative selections.* (Rev. ed.) Ed. by C. H. Faust & T. H. Johnson. Cincinnati, Ohio: American Book, 1962. (1935)　　**C**

———. *Puritan sage: Collected writings of Jonathan Edwards.* Ed. by V. Ferm. New York: Library Publishers, 1953.　　**B C**

———. *The philosophy of Jonathan Edwards from his private notebooks.* Ed. by H. G. Townsend. Eugene, Ore.: University of Oregon Press, 1955. (Reprinted 1970)　　**C**

———. *The works of Jonathan Edwards.* (4 vols.; others to come) Gen. ed. P. Miller. New Haven: Yale University Press, 1957– .　　**C**

———. The great awakening. Ed. C. C. Goen. Gen. ed. P. Miller. *The works of Jonathan Edwards,* Vol. 4. New Haven: Yale University Press, 1972.

———. *Religious affections.* Ed. by J. E. Smith. Gen. ed. P. Miller, *The works of Jonathan Edwards.* Vol. 2. New Haven: Yale University Press, 1959. (1746)

―――. *Freedom of the will.* Ed. by P. Ramsey. Gen. ed. P. Miller, *The works of Jonathan Edwards.* Vol. 1. New Haven: Yale University Press, 1957. (1754) (Reprinted 1968)

―――. *Original sin.* Ed. by C. A. Holbrook. Gen. ed. P. Miller, *The works of Jonathan Edwards.* Vol. 3. New Haven: Yale University Press, 1970. (1758)

―――. *The nature of true virtue.* Foreword by W. K. Frankena. Ann Arbor, Mich.: University of Michigan Press, 1960. (1765)

―――. *Charity and its fruits: Christian love as manifestation of the heart and life.* London: Banner of Truth Trust, 1969. (1852)

―――. *Images of shadows of divine things.* Ed. by P. Miller. New Haven: Yale University Press, 1948.

Brinton, *Age Reason*; Grob & Beck, *American Ideas*; Kurtz, *American Thought*; Mueller, *American Philosophy*

CHRISTIAN VON EHRENFELS
1859-1932
Austrian Philosopher (26)

Ehrenfels, C. v. *Metaphysische Ausführungen im Anschlusse an Emil Du Bois-Reymond.* Vienna: Gerold, 1886.

―――. Ueber Fühlen und Wollen. *Sitzber. Akad. Wiss.*, 1887, *114*, 523–636.

―――. Ueber Gestaltqualitäten. *Vtljsch. wiss. Phil.*, 1890, *14*, 249–292. Reprinted with comments in *Das Primzahlengesetz entwickelt und dargestellt auf Grund der Gestalttheorie.* Leipzig: Reisland, 1922. Both reprinted in F. Weinhandl (Ed.), *Gestalthaftes Sehen: Ergebnisse und Aufgaben der Morphologie: Zum hundertjahr. Geburtstag von Chr. v. Ehrenfels.* Darmstadt: Wissenschaft Buchgesellschaft, 1960, pp. 11–43, 47–60.

―――. Zur Philosophie der Mathematik. *Vtljsch. wiss. Phil.*, 1891, *15*, 285–347.

―――. Von der Wertdefinition zum Motivationsgesetz. *Arch. syst. Phil.*, 1896, *2*, 103–124.

―――. The ethical theory of value. *Int. J. Ethics*, 1896, *6*, 371–384.

―――. *System der Werttheorie.* (2 vols.) Leipzig: Reisland, 1897, 1898.

―――. Die Intensität der Gefühle. Eine Entgegnung auf Franz Brentanos neue Intensitätslehre. *Z. Psychol.*, 1897, *16*, 49–70.

―――. Entgegnung auf H. Schwarz' Kritik der empiristischen Willenspsychologie und des Gesetzes der relativen Glücksförderung. *Vtljsch. wiss. Phil.*, 1899, *23*, 261–284.

―――. *Sexualethik.* Wiesbaden: Bergmann, 1907. (1901)

―――. Die sexuale Reform. *Politischanthrop Rev.*, 1903–1904, *2*, 970–994.

―――. *Grundbegriffe der Ethik.* Wiesbaden: Bergmann, 1907.

―――. Die konstitutive Verderblichkeit der Monogamie und die Unentbehrlichkeit einer Sexualreform. *Arch. Rassen-Gesell. Biol.*, 1908, *4*, 615–651, 803–830.

―――. Leitziele zur Rassenbewertung. *Arch Rassen-Gesell. Biol.*, 1911, *8*, 59–71.

―――. *Kosmogonie.* Jena: Diederichs, 1916.

―――. *Höhe und Reinheit der Gestalt.* (1916) Reprinted in F. Weinhandl (Ed.), *Gestalthaftes Sehen, op. cit.*, pp. 44–46.

―――. Die Sexualmoral der Zukunft. *Arch Rassen-Gesell. Biol.*, 1929, *22*, 292–303.

―――. On Gestalt-qualities. (1932) *Psychol Rev.*, 1937, *44*, 521–524.

JOHN ELLIOTSON
1791-1868
English Hypnotist (22)

Elliotson, J. (Ed.), J. F. Blumenbach, *Human physiology.* (5th ed.) London: Longmans Orme, Brown, Green, & Longmans, 1840.

―――. *Numerous cases of surgical operation without pain in mesmeric state; with remarks* Philadelphia: Lea & Blanchard, 1843.

————. The cerebral development and character of the murderers Hocker and Connor. *Zooist,* 1845, *3,* 120–140.

————. The cerebral development of the murderer Benjamin Ellison. *Zooist,* 1845, *3,* 258–281.

————. *The Harveian oration.* London: Baillière, 1846.

————. The London College of Physicians and Mesmerists. *Zooist,* 1848–1849, *6,* 399–405.

————. An account of the head of Rush, the Norfolk murderer. *Zooist,* 1849, *7,* 107–121.

————. *Mesmerism in India. Second half-yearly report of the Calcutta Mesmeric Hospital from 1st March to 1st September, 1849, containing accounts of formidable and numerous painless surgical operations, and of the successful administration of mesmerism in insanity and other diseases. To which is added remarks on the conduct of the English medical journalists and nearly the whole of the medical profession, in reference to the greatest of medical blessings; with some hints to the public on the employment of mesmerism and on mesmerisers.* (2nd ed.) London: Baillière, 1850. (1850)

————. On the brains of Manning and his wife, the Bermondsey murderers. *Zooist,* 1852, *9,* 334–356.

Hunter & Macalpine, *Psychiatry*; Tinterow, *Hypnosis*

(HENRY) HAVELOCK ELLIS
1859-1939
English Psychologist (23)

Ellis, H. *Studies in the psychology of sex.* (3rd ed.) (9 vols.) New York: Random House, 1936. (1897 ff.) **C**

————. *On life and sex: Essays of love and virtue.* (2 vols. in 1) Garden City, N.Y.: Garden City Publishing, 1937. (1921–1931) **C**

————. *Sex and marriage: Eros in contemporary life.* Ed. by J. Gawsworth. New York: Random House, 1952. (1951) **C**

————. *Man and woman: A study of human secondary sexual characteristics.* (6th ed.) London: Black, 1926. (1884)

————. *The new spirit.* (4th ed.) Boston: Houghton Mifflin, 1926. (1890)

————. On dreaming of the dead. *Psychol. Rev.,* 1895, *2,* 458–461.

————. A note on hypnagogic paramnesia. *Mind,* 1897, *6*(N.S.), 283–287.

————. *Affirmations.* (2nd ed.) London: Constable, 1915. (1898)

————. The stuff that dreams are made of. *Pop. Sci. Mon.,* 1899, *54,* 721–735.

————. The evolution of modesty. *Psychol. Rev.,* 1899, *6,* 134–145.

————. Mescal: A study of a divine plant. *Pop. Sci. Mon.,* 1902, *61,* 52–71.

————. *A study of British genius.* (Rev. ed.) Boston: Houghton Mifflin, 1926. (1904)

————. *The world of dreams.* (Rev. ed.) Boston: Houghton Mifflin, 1926. (1911)

————. *The task of social hygiene.* Boston: Houghton Mifflin, 1912.

————. *The dance of life.* Boston: Houghton Mifflin, 1933. (1923)

————. *Impressions and comments, third (and final) series, 1920–1923.* Boston: Houghton Mifflin, 1924.

————. The conception of narcissism. *Psychoanal. Rev.,* 1927, *14,* 129–153. Reprinted in M. H. Sherman (Ed.), *Psychoanalysis in America: Historical perspectives.* Springfield, Ill.: Thomas, 1965, pp. 403–430.

————. *The colour-sense in literature.* London: Ulysses Book Shop, 1931.

————. *Psychology of sex: A manual for students.* New York: Long & Smith, 1933.

————. Foreword. (1936) In *Studies in the psychology of sex,* Vol. 1, *op. cit.,* pp. ix–xxiii. **B**

————. *My life.* (New ed.) London: Spearman, 1967. (1939) **B**

Krich, *Sexual Revolution*

EMIL EMMERT
1844-1911
Swiss Ophthalmologist (17)

Emmert, E. *Gesichtswahrnehmungen und Sinnestäuschungen.* Bern: Jent & Reinert, 1873.

————. *Ueber Refractions- und Akkomodationsverhältnisse des menschlichen Auges.* Bern: Haller, 1876.

————. *Ueber funktionelle Störungen des menschlichen Auges im allgemeinen sowie speciell nach Schultersuchungen in den Cantonen Bern, Solathum und Neunberg nebst Angabe der Hülfsmittel dagegen.* Bern: Haller, 1876.

————. Grössenverhältnisse der Nachbilder. *Klin. Monatsbl. Augenheilk.,* 1881, *19,* 443–450.

————. Zur Gradeinteilung der Ophthalmometer und Perimeter. *Arch. Augenheilk.,* 1910, *67,* 327–341.

HORACE BIDWELL ENGLISH
1892-1961
American Psychologist (14)

English, H. B. An experimental study of mental capacities of school children, correlated with social status. *Psychol. Monogr.,* 1917, *23,* No. 100, pp. 266–331.

————. In aid of introspection. *Amer. J. Psychol.,* 1921, *32,* 404–414.

————. Dynamic psychology and the problem of motivation. *Psychol. Rev.,* 1921, *28,* 239–248.

————. Is a synthesis of psychological schools to be found in a personalistic act-psychology? *Psychol. Rev.,* 1926, *33,* 298–307.

————. *A student's dictionary of psychological terms.* (4th ed.) New York: Harper, 1934. (1928)

————. Three cases of the "conditioned fear response." *J. abnorm. soc. Psychol.,* 1929–1930, *24,* 221–225.

————. The ghostly tradition and the descriptive categories of psychology. *Psychol. Rev.,* 1933, *40,* 498–513.

————, Welborn, E. L., & Killian, C. D. Studies in substance memorization. *J. gen. Psychol.,* 1934, *11,* 233–260.

————. Organization of the American association of applied psychologists. *J. consult. Psychol.,* 1938, *2,* 7–16.

Edwards, A. L., & ————. The effect of the immediate test on verbatim and summary retention. *Amer. J. Psychol.,* 1939, *52,* 372–375.

Edwards, A. L., & ————. Reminiscence in relation to differential difficulty. *J. exp. Psychol.,* 1939, *25,* 100–108.

————, & Edwards, A. L. Reminiscence, substance learning, and initial difficulty—a methodological study. *Psychol. Rev.,* 1939, *46,* 253–263.

————, & Edwards, A. L. Studies in substance learning and retention. IX. The effect of maturity level on verbatim and summary retention. *J. gen Psychol.,* 1939, *21,* 271–276.

————, & Raimy, V. C. *Studying the individual school child: A manual of guidance.* New York: Holt, 1941.

————. Fundamentals and fundamentalism in the preparation of applied psychologists. *J. consult. Psychol.,* 1941, *5,* 1–13.

————, & Edwards, A. L. Practice as cause of reminiscence. *Psychol. Rev.,* 1941, *48,* 524–529.

————. Reminiscence—reply to Dr. Buxton's critique. *Psychol. Rev.,* 1942, *49,* 505–512.

————. *Learning as psychotechnology: A study guide.* Columbus, Ohio: Ohio State University, 1949.

————. Educational psychology. In J. P. Guilford (Ed.), *Fields of psychology.* (2nd ed.) New York: Van Nostrand, 1950, pp. 115–169.

————. Learning: There ain't no such animal. *J. educ. Psychol.,* 1952, *43,* 321–330.

————. *The historical roots of learning theory.* Garden City, N.Y.: Doubleday, 1954.

————, & English, Ava C. *A comprehensive dictionary of psychological and psychoanalytical terms: A guide to usage.* New York: McKay, 1958.

———. *Dynamics of child development.* New York: Holt, 1961.

———. Education of the emotions. *J. hum. Psychol.,* 1961, *1,* 101–109.

BENNO ERDMANN
1851-1921
German Psychologist (12)

Erdmann, B. *Die Axiome der Geometrie.* Leipzig: Voss, 1877.

———. Hume und Kant um 1762. *Arch. Gesch. Phil.,* 1888, *1,* 62–77, 216–230.

———. *Logik.* (2nd ed.) Halle: Niemeyer, 1907. (1892)

———. Zur Theorie der Beobachtung. *Arch. syst. Phil.,* 1895, *1,* 14–33, 145–164.

———. Die psychologischen Grundlagen der Beziehungen zwischen Sprechen und Denken. *Arch. syst. Phil.,* 1896, *2,* 355–418, *3,* 31–48; 1897, *3,* 150–173; 1901, *7,* 147–176, 316–371, 439–491.

———, & Dodge, R. *Die psychologischen Untersuchungen über das Lesen auf experimenteller Grundlage.* Halle: Niemeyer, 1898.

———, & Dodge, R. Zur Erläuterung unserer tachistoskopischen Versuche. *Z. Psychol.,* 1900, *22,* 241–267.

———. *Umrisse zur Psychologie des Denkens.* (2nd ed.) Tübingen: Mohr, 1908. (1900)

———. *Immanuel Kant.* Bonn: Cohen, 1904.

———. *Historische Untersuchungen über Kants Prolegomena.* Halle: Niemeyer, 1904.

———. The content and validity of the causal law. Parts I, II. *Phil. Rev.,* 1905, *14,* 138–165, 290–307.

———. *Wissenschaftliche Hypothesen über Leib und Seele.* Cologne: Du Mont-Schauberg, 1908.

———. *Betrachtungen über die Deutung und Wertung der Lehre Spinozas.* Berlin: Weidmann, 1910.

———. *Erkennen und Verstehen.* (2nd ed.) Berlin: Reimer, 1913. (1912)

———. *Die Funktionen der Phantasie im wissenschaftlichen Denken.* Berlin: Paetel, 1913.

———. *Grundzüge der Reproduktionspsychologie.* Berlin: De Gruyter, 1920.

———. Die philosophischen Grundlagen von Helmholtz' Wahrnehmungstheorie. *Abh. preuss. Akad. Wiss.,* Phil.-hist. Kl., 1921, No. 1.

JAMES ESDAILE
1808-1859
English Hypnotist (20)

Esdaile, J. *Mesmeric feats.* Hooghly: n.p., 1845.

———. *Hypnosis in medicine and surgery. (Mesmerism in India.)* New York: Institute for Research in Hypnosis Publication Society, 1957. (1846)

———. *A record of cases treated in the Mesmeric Hospital Calcutta from November, 1846, to May, 1847, with reports of the official visitors.* Calcutta: Ridsdale, 1847.

———. *Review of my reviewers.* Calcutta: n.p., 1848.

———. Letter to J. Elliotson. In J. Elliotson, *Mesmerism in India. Second half-yearly report of the Calcutta Mesmeric Hospital from 1st March to 1st September, 1849, containing accounts of formidable and numerous painless surgical operations, and of the successful administration of mesmerism in insanity and other diseases. To which is added remarks on the conduct of the English medical journalists and nearly the whole of the medical profession, in reference to the greatest of medical blessings; with some hints to the public on the employment of mesmerism and on mesmerisers.* (2nd ed.) London: Baillière, 1850. (1850)

———. *Natural and mesmeric clairvoyance with its practical application of mesmerism in surgery and medicine.* London: Baillière, 1852.

Tinterow, *Hypnosis*

JEAN ETIENNE ESQUIROL
1772-1840
French Psychiatrist (18)

Esquirol, J. E. *Passions considérées comme causes, symptômes et moyens curatifs de l'aliénation mentale.* (2 vols.) Paris: Annuaire médico-chirurgical des hôpitaux, 1805.

————. Délire. Démence. Démonomanie. Eroromanie. Folie. Fureur. Idiotisme. Hallucination. Lypémanie. Manie. Maison d'aliénés. Monomanie. Suicide. In *Dictionnaire des sciences médicales.* Vol. 60. Paris: Crapart & Panckoucke, 1812-1822.

————. *Des établissements des aliénés en France, et des moyens d'améliorer le sort de ces infortunés.* Paris: Hazard, 1819. (1818)

————. Observations d'hallucinations. *Rec. périod. Soc. méd.,* 1819, *66,* 289-305.

————. Notice sur le village de Gheel. *Rev. méd.,* 1822, *7,* 137-154.

————. Introduction à l'étude des aliénations mentales. *Rev. méd.,* 1822, *8,* 31-38.

————. Notes. In J. C. Hoffbauer, *Médecine légale relative aux aliénés et aux sourds-muets ou les lois appliquées aux désordres de l'intelligence.* Trans. from German by A. M. Chambeyron. Paris: Baillière, 1827.

————. *Note sur la monomanie homicide.* Paris: Baillière, 1827.

————. Remarques sur la statistique des aliénés et sur le rapport du nombre des aliénés à la population. Analyse de la statistique des aliénés de la Norvège. *Ann. Hyg. publ. Méd. lég.,* 1830, *4,* 332-359.

————. *Observations on the illusion of the insane and on the medicolegal question of their confinement.* Trans. by W. Liddell. London: Renshaw & Rush, 1833. (1832)

————. Mémoire historique et statistique sur la maison royale de Charenton. Paris: Renouard 1835.

————. *Examen du projet de loi sur les aliénés.* Paris: Baillière, 1838.

————. *Des maladies mentales considérées sous les rapports médical, hygiénique et médico-légal.* (2 vols. + atlas) Paris: Baillière, 1838.

————. *Mental maladies: A treatise on insanity.* Trans. with addit. by B. K. Hunt. New York: Hafner, 1965. (1838)

————. Notes. In W. C. Ellis, *Traité de l'aliénation mentale.* Paris: Rouvier, 1840.

————, *et al.* (Reports of consultations.) In C. C. Marc, *De la folie considérée dans ses rapports avec les questions médico-judiciaires.* (2 vols.) Paris: Baillière, 1840, Vol. 1, pp. 52-56, 514-516; Vol. 2, pp. 149-154, 302-303, 674-682, 684-689, 696-698.

Goshen, *Documentary*; Hunter & Macalpine, *Psychiatry*; Shipley, *Classics*

LEONHARD EULER
1707-1783
Swiss-Russian Mathematician (12)

Euler, L., Bernoulli, J. I., & Bernoulli, D. Der Briefwechsel zwischen Leonhard Euler, Johann I. und Daniel Bernoulli. Ed. by G. Eneström. *Biblioth. Math.,* 1903, *4,* 344-388; 1904, *5,* 248-291; 1905, *6,* 16-87. **C**

————, & Bernoulli, D. Der Briefwechsel zwischen Leonhard Euler und Daniel Bernoulli. Ed. by G. Eneström. *Biblioth. Math.,* 1906-1907, *7,* 126-156. **C**

————. *Opera omnia.* (Ult. 72 vols.) I. *Opera mathematica.* (29 vols.) II. *Opera mechanica et astronomica.* (Ult. 31 vols.) III. *Opera physica, miscellanea, epistolae.* (Ult. 12 vols.) Berlin: Teubner; Zurich: Fussli; Berlin: Springer-Verlag, 1911– **C**

————. *Correspondance mathématique et physique de quelques célèbres géomètres du XVIIIe siècle.* (2 vols.) Ed. by P. H. Fuss. London: Johnson, 1968. (1843) **B C**

————. *Die Berliner und die Petersburger Akademie der Wissenschaften im Briefwechsel Leonhard Euler.* (2 vols.) Ed. by A. P. Jukevič & E. Winter. Berlin: Akademie-Verlag, 1959-1961. **B C**

———, & Goldbach, C. *Leonhard Euler und Christian Goldbach: Briefwechsel 1729–1764.* Ed. by A. P. Jukevič & E. Winter. Berlin: Akademie-Verlag, 1965.   **C**

———. *Mechanik, oder analytische Darstellung von der Bewegung.* (2 vols.) Ed. by J. P. Wohlfers. Greifswald: Koch, 1848–1850. (1736)

———. *Tentamen novae theoriae musicae ex certissimis harmoniae principiis dilucide expositae.* St. Petersburg: Ex Typographia Academiae Scientiarum, 1739.

———. *Letter of Euler to a German princess, on different subjects in physics and philosophy.* Trans. by H. Hunter. New York: Harper, 1872. (1770)

———. *Elements of algebra.* Trans. by J. Hewlett. London: Longmans, Orme, 1840. (1770)

———. Observationes in praecedentem dissertationem illustr. Bernoulli. *Mem. Acta Acad. Petrop.,* 1777, Part 1, 24–33. (1778) Trans. in E. S. Pearson & G. M. Kendall (Eds.), *Studies in the history of statistics and probability.* London: Griffin, 1970, pp. 167–172.

———. *Introduction à l'analyse infinitésimale.* (2 vols.) Trans. by J. B. Labey. Paris: Barrois, 1796–1797.

Smith, *Source Book*

JULIUS RICHARD EWALD
1855-1921
German Physiologist (17)

Ewald, J. R. *Der normale Athmungsdruck und seine Curve.* Strassburg: Fischbach, 1880.

———. Zur Physiologie der Bogengänge: Fortsetzung über Bewegungen der Perilymphs. *Arch. ges. Physiol.,* 1887, *41,* 463–483 ; 1889, *44,* 319–326.

———. Technische Hilfsmittel zur physiologischen Untersuchung. I. Stromwender. II. Eine neue Anwendung der Pohlschen Wippe. *Arch. ges. Physiol.,* 1888, *42,* 467–482.

———. Das Kopfschwingen. *Arch. ges. Physiol.,* 1889, *44,* 326–345.

———. Ueber motorische Störungen nach Verletzungen der Bogengänge. *Zbl. med. Wiss.,* 1890, *28,* 114–116, 130–132.

———. Die Abhängigkeit des galvanischen Schwindels vom innern Ohr. *Zbl. med. Wiss.,* 1890, *28,* 753–755.

———. Bedeutung des Ohres für normale Muskelkontraktion. *Zbl. Physiol.,* 1892, *5,* 4–6.

———. *Physiologische Untersuchungen über das Endorgan des Nervus Octavus.* Wiesbaden: Bergmann, 1892.

———. Die centrale Entstehung von Schwebungen zweier monotisch gehörter Töne. *Arch. ges. Physiol.,* 1894, *57,* 80–88.

———. Zur Physiologie des Labyrinths. III. Das Hören labyrinthloser Tauben. *Arch. ges. Physiol.,* 1894, *59,* 258–275.

———. Zur Physiologie des Labyrinths. IV. Die Beziehungen des Grosshirns zum Tonuslabyrinth. *Arch. ges. Physiol.,* 1895, *60,* 492–508.

———. Zur Physiologie des Labyrinths. V. Die Beziehungen des Tonuslabyrinths zur Totenstarre und über die Nysten'sche Reihe. *Arch. ges. Physiol.,* 1896, *63,* 521–541.

———. Ueber die Beziehungen zwischen der excitablen Zone des Grosshirns und dem Ohrlabyrinth. *Ber. klin. Wochensch.,* 1896, *33,* 929–932.

Goltz, F., & ———. Der Hund mit verkürztem Rückenmark. *Arch. ges. Physiol.,* 1896, *63,* 362–400.

———. Ueber künstliche Reizung der Grosshirnrinde. *Deutsch. med. Wochensch.,* 1898, No. 39.

———. *Neue Hörtheorie.* Bonn: Strauss, 1899.

———. Zur Physiologie des Labyrinths. VI. Eine neue Hörtheorie. *Arch. ges. Physiol.,* 1899, *76,* 147–188.

———. Zur Physiologie des Labyrinths. VII. Die Erzeugung von Schallbildern in der Camera acustica. *Arch. ges. Physiol.,* 1903, *93,* 485–500.

———. Die Wirkung des Radiums auf das Labyrinth. *Z. Physiol.,* 1905, *19,* 297–298.

———, & Jäderholm, G. A. Auch alle Geräusche geben, wenn sie intermittiert werden, Intermittenztöne. *Arch. ges. Physiol.,* 1906, *115,* 555–563.

———, & Jäderholm, G. A. Die Herabsetzung der subjektiven Tonhöhe durch Steigerung der objektiven Intensität. *Arch. ges. Physiol.,* 1908, *124,* 29–36.

———. Ueber die neuen Versuche, die Angriffsstellen der von Tönen ausgehenden Schallwellen im Ohre zu lokalisieren. *Arch. ges. Physiol.,* 1910, *131,* 188–198.

———. *Schematische Darstellung der Lage der Bogengänge.* Wiesbaden: Bergmann, 1914.

———. *Das Strassburger physiologische Praktikum.* Leipzig: Barth, 1914.

———. Schallbildertheorie und Erkenntnistheorie. *Z. Sinnesphysiol.,* 1922, *53,* 213–217.

SIGMUND EXNER
1846-1926
Austrian Physiologist (18)

Exner, S. Ueber die zu einer Gesichtswahrnehmung nötige Zeit. *Sitzber. Akad. Wiss. Wien,* Math.-naturw. Kl., 1868, *58*(2), 601–632.

———. Ueber einige neue subjective Gesichtserscheinungen. *Arch. ges. Physiol.,* 1868, *1,* 375–394.

———. Bemerkungen über intermittirende Netzhautreizung. *Arch. ges. Physiol.,* 1870, *3,* 214–240.

———. Ueber den Erregungsvorgang im Sehnervenapparate. *Sitzber. Akad. Wiss. Wien,* Math.-naturw. Kl., 1872, *65*(3), 59–70.

———. Experimentelle Untersuchung der einfachsten psychischen Processe. *Arch. ges. Physiol.,* 1873, *7,* 601–660; 1874, *8,* 526–537; 1875, *11,* 403–432, 581–602.

———. Kleine Mittheilungen physiologischen Inhaltes. Ein Versuch über Trochleariskreuzung. Mennière'sche Krankheit bei Kaninchen. Ein Schulversuch aus der Muskelphysiologie. Ueber die Lymphwege des Ovariums, zum Theil nach Untersuchungen von Dr. A. Bukel aus Boston. *Sitzber. Akad. Wiss. Wien,* Math.-naturw. Kl., 1874, *70*(3), 151–161.

———. Ueber das Sehen von Bewegungen und die Theorie des zusammengesetzten Auges. *Sitzber. Akad. Wiss. Wien,* Math.-naturw. Kl., 1875, *72*(3), 156–190.

———. Zur Lehre von den Gehörsempfindungen. *Arch. ges. Physiol.,* 1876, *13,* 228–252.

———. Fortgesetzte Studien über die Endigungsweise der Geruchnerven. *Sitzber. Akad. Wiss. Wien,* Math.-naturw. Kl., 1877, *76*(3), 171–221.

Eckhard, C., & ———. Physiologie des Rückenmarks und Gehirns. In L. Hermann (Ed.), *Handbuch der Physiologie.* Vol. 2, Part 2. Leipzig: Vogel, 1879.

———. Weitere Untersuchungen über die Regeneration in der Netzhaut und über Druckblindheit. *Arch. ges. Physiol.,* 1879, *20,* 614–626.

———. *Untersuchungen über die Lokalisation der Funktionen in der Grosshirnrinde des Menschen.* Vienna: Braumüller, 1881.

———. Zur Kenntnis vom feineren Baue der Grosshirnrinde. *Sitzber. Akad. Wiss. Wien,* Math.-naturw. Kl., 1881, *83*(3), 151–167.

———. Zur Frage nach der Rindenlokalisation beim Menschen. *Arch. ges. Physiol.,* 1882, *27,* 412–421.

———. Zur Kenntnis der motorischen Rindenfelder. *Sitzber. Akad. Wiss. Wien,* Math.-naturw. Kl., 1882, *84*(3), 185–190.

———. Zur Kenntnis von der Wechselwirkung der Erregungen im Zentralnervensystem. *Arch. ges. Physiol.,* 1882, *28,* 487–506.

———. Die Innervation des Kehlkopfes. *Sitzber. Akad. Wiss. Wien,* Math.-naturw. Kl., 1884, *89*(3), 63–118.

———. Notiz zu der Frage von der Faservertheilung mehrerer Nerven in einem Muskel. *Arch. ges. Physiol.,* 1885, *36,* 572–576.

———. Ueber die Funktionsweise der Netzhautperipherie und den Sitz der Nachbilder. *Arch. Ophthalm.,* 1886, *32*(1), 233–252.

———. Ueber neuere Forschungsresultate, die Lokalisation in der Hirnrinde betreffend. *Wien. med. Wochensch.,* 1886, *36,* 1629–1633, 1665–1669, 1699–1704.

———. Gegenbemerkung "eine neue Urtheils-täuschung im Gebiete des Gesichtssinnes" betreffend. *Arch. ges. Physiol.*, 1887, *40*, 323–330.

———. Ueber optische Eigenschaften lebender Muskelfasern. *Arch. ges. Physiol.*, 1887, *40*, 360–393.

———, & Paneth, J. Das Rindenfeld des Facialis und seine Verbindungen bei Hund und Kaninchen. *Arch. ges. Physiol.*, 1887, *41*, 349–358.

———. Bemerkungen über die Innervation des Musculus crico-thyreoideus. *Arch. ges. Physiol.*, 1888, *43*, 22–29.

———. Ueber optische Bewegungsempfindungen. *Biol. Zbl.*, 1888–1889, *8*, 437–448.

———. Das Verschwinden der Nachbilder bei Augenbewegungen. *Z. Psychol.*, 1890, *1*, 47–51.

———. *Die Physiologie der facettirten Augen von Krebsen und Insecten.* Leipzig: Deuticke, 1891.

———. Ueber Sensomobilität. *Arch. ges. Physiol.*, 1891, *48*, 592–613.

———. *Entwurf zu einer physiologischen Erklärung der psychischen Erscheinungen.* Vienna: Deuticke, 1894.

———. Ueber autokinetische Empfindungen. *Z. Psychol.*, 1896, *12*, 313–330.

———. Studien auf dem Grenzgebiete des localisirten Sehens. *Arch. ges. Physiol.*, 1898, *73*, 117–171.

———. Zur Kenntnis des zentralen Sehaktes. *Z. Psychol.*, 1904, *36*, 194–212.

———. *Ueber das Orientierungsvermögen der Brieftauben.* Vienna: Hölder, 1906.

———. Bemerkungen zur Frage nach der Vererbung erworbener psychischer Eigenschaften. *Ber. IV. Kongr. exper. Psychol.*, 1911, 203–210.

———. Ueber phonetische Untersuchungsmethoden. *Wien. med. Wochensch.*, 1914, *64*, 1931–1937.

———. Ueber den Klang einiger Sprachen. *Wien. med. Wochensch.*, 1920, *70*, 1235–1237, 1315–1317.

JEAN HENRI FABRE
1823-1915
French Biologist (20)

Fabre, J. H. *The life of the fly: With which are interspersed some chapters of autobiography.* Trans. by A. T. de Mattos. New York: Dodd, Mead, 1913. (1879–1907) **B C**

———. *The life and love of the insect.* Trans. by A. T. de Mattos. London: Black, 1918. (1879–1907) **C**

———. *Souvenirs entomologiques.* (10 vols.) Paris: Delagrave, 1922–1924. (1879–1907) **C**

———. *The wonders of instincts.* Eng. trans. papers from *Souvenirs entomologiques,* by A. T. de Mattos & B. Miall. New York: Century, 1918. (1879–1907)

———. *Social life in the insect world.* Trans. by B. Miall. New York: Century, 1912. (Reprinted 1937) **C**

———. *Souvenirs entomologiques. Etudes sur l'instinct et les moeurs des insectes.* (11 vols.) Paris: Delagrave, 1914–1924. **C**

———. *The insect world of J. Henri Fabre.* Ed. by E. W. Teale. New York: Dodd, Mead, 1949. **C**

———. *Animal life in field and garden.* Trans. by Florence C. Bicknell. New York: Century, 1921. (1901) **C**

———. *Les inventeurs et leurs inventions: Histoire élémentaire des principales découvertes dans l'ordre des sciences physiques.* Paris: Delagrave, 1881.

———, & Darwin, C. Ueber den Orientierungssinn der Mörtelbienen. *Kosmos,* 1908, *5*, 360.

Hall, *Source Book*

MICHAEL FARADAY
1791-1867
English Physicist (15)

Faraday, M. *Experimental researches in electricity.* (3 vols.) London: Quaritch, 1839–1855. (Reprinted 1966) **C**

——. *Experimental researches in chemistry and physics*. Brussels: Culture et Civilisation, 1969. (1859) **C**

——. *Faraday's diary, being the various philosophical notes of experimental investigation*. (8 vols.) Ed. by T. Martin. London: Bell, 1922–1936. **C**

——. *Diary*. (2 vols.) London: Bell, 1932. **B C**

——. *The selected correspondence of Michael Faraday*. Vol. 1. *1812–1848*. Vol. 2. *1849–1866*. Ed. by L. P. Williams (with assist. of Rose Mary Fitzgerald & O. Stallybrass). Cambridge: Cambridge University Press, 1971. **B C**

——. On a peculiar class of optical deceptions. *J. roy. Inst.*, 1831, *1*, 205–223.

——. *On the various forces of nature and their relation to each other*. (New ed.) Ed. by W. Croakes. London: Chatto & Windus, 1894. (1873)

Dampier, *Literature*; Hutchins, *Great Books*

DEAN FARNSWORTH
1902-1959
American Psychologist (12)

Farnsworth, D. The Farnsworth-Munsell 100 hue and dichotomous tests for color vision. *J. opt. Soc. Amer.*, 1943, *33*, 568–578.

——, Reed, J. D., & Shilling, C. W. *The effect of certain illuminants on scores made on pseudo-isochromatic tests*. New London, Conn.: Naval Medical Research Lab., 1948.

——, Sperling, H., & Kimble, Priscilla F. A battery of pass-fail tests for detecting degree of color deficiency. *USN Submar. Med. Res. Lab. Rep*. 1949, *8*, No. 147, pp. 39–68.

Sexton, Mary, Malone, Florence L., & ——. The effect of ultraviolet radiation from fluorescent lights on dark adaptation and visual acuity. *USN Submar. Med. Res. Lab. Rep.*, 1950, *9*, No. 169, pp. 301–317.

——. Color vision. In D. H. Freyer & E. R. Henry (Eds.), *Handbook of applied psychology*. Vol. 1. New York: Rinehart, 1950, pp. 309–311.

Judd, D. B., Plaza, L., & ——. Tritanopia with abnormally heavy ocular pigmentation. *J. opt. Soc. Amer.*, 1950, *40*, 833–841.

——. Inspection goggle for checking visible quality of lighting for dark adaptation. *USN Submar. Med. Res. Lab. Rep.*, 1951, *10*, No. 170, pp. 1–17.

Malone, Florence L., Sexton, Mary S., & ——. The detectability of yellows, yellow-reds, and reds in air-sea rescue. *USN Submar. Med. Res. Lab. Rep.*, 1951, *10*, No. 170, pp. 177–185.

Sexton, Mary S., Malone, Florence L., & ——. The relative detectability of red purples, reds, and yellow-reds in air-sea rescue. *USN Submar. Med. Res. Lab. Rep.*, 1952, *11*(12).

——. Developments in submarine and small vessel lighting. *USN Submar. Med. Res. Lab. Rep.*, 1952, *11*(26), pp. 1–6.

Willis, Marion P., & ——. Comparative evaluation of anomaloscopes. *USN Submar. Med. Res. Lab. Rep.*, 1952, *11*, No. 190.

——, & Hillmann, Beverly. A comparison of specifications for dark adaptation red. *USN Submar. Med. Res. Lab. Rep.*, 1953, *12*, No. 219.

Hillmann, Beverly, Connolly, K., & ——. Color perception of small stimuli with central vision. *USN Submar. Med. Res. Lab. Rep.*, 1954, *13*, No. 18.

——. An introduction to the principles of color deficiency. *USN Submar. Med. Res. Lab. Rep.*, 1954, *13*(15), No. 254.

Mueller, G., Fooks, G., Sperling, H. G., ——, & Wundt, H. W. Dark adaptation and the near ultraviolet. *USN Submar. Med. Res. Lab. Rep.*, 1955, *14*(8), No. 268.

——. Tritanomalous vision as a threshold function. *USN Submar. Med. Res. Lab. Rep.*, 1956 *15*, No. 3.

Kalmus, H., & ——. Impairment and recovery of taste following irradiation of the oropharynx. *J. Laryngol. Otol.*, 1959, *73*, 180–182.

——. Let's look at those isochromatic lines again. *Vision Res.*, 1961, *1*, 1–5.

LIVINGSTON FARRAND
1867-1939
American Psychologist (11)

Farrand, L. Review of recent literature on idiocy and imbecility. *Psychol. Rev.*, 1894, *1*, 636–638.

Cattell, J. McK., & ———. Physical and mental measurements of the students of Columbia University. *Psychol. Rev.*, 1896, *3*, 618–648. Reprinted in J. McK. Cattell, *James McKeen Cattell*. Vol. 1. Ed. by A. T. Poffenberger. Lancaster, Pa.: Science Press, 1947, pp. 305–330.

———. Review of recent literature on ethnology. *Psychol. Rev.*, 1896, *3*, 558–562.

———, Cattell, J. McK., & Baldwin, J. M. Note on "Reaction types." *Psychol. Rev.*, 1897, *4*, 297–299.

———. American Psychological Association. *Science*, 1897, *5*(N.S.), 206–215 ; 1900, *11*(N.S.), 132–135 ; 1901, *13*(N.S.), 211–214.

———, & Boas, F. Physical characteristics of the tribes of British Columbia. In twelfth and final report on the northwestern tribes of Canada. *Rep. Brit. Ass. Adv. Sci.*, 1898, 628–644.

Anastasi, *Individual Differences*

FRANKLIN FEARING
1892-1962
American Psychologist (12)

Fearing, F. The value of psychological tests in psychiatric diagnoses. *J. abnorm. Psychol.*, 1919, *14*, 190–196.

———. The factors influencing static equilibrium: An experimental study of the influence of height, weight, and position of the feet on amount of sway, together with an analysis of the variability in the records of one reagent over a long period of time. *J. comp. Psychol.*, 1924, *4*, 91–121.

———. The factors influencing static equilibrium: An experimental study of the effects of practice upon amount and direction of sway. *J. comp. Psychol.*, 1924, *4*, 163–183.

———. Some extra-intellectual factors in delinquency. *J. Delinq.*, 1924, *8*, 145–153.

———. The experimental study of the Romberg sign. *J. nerv. ment. Dis.*, 1925, *61*, 449–465.

———. Factors influencing static equilibrium: An experimental study of the effect of controlled and uncontrolled attention upon sway. *J. comp. Psychol.*, 1925, *5*, 1–24.

———. Post-rotational head nystagmus in adult pigeons. *J. comp. Psychol.*, 1926, *6*, 115–131.

———. Motor automatisms and reflex action. *Psychol. Bull.*, 1926, *23*, 457–481.

———. A critique of the experimental studies of cortical inhibition with special reference to the knee-jerk. *J. comp. Psychol.*, 1927, *7*, 285–296.

———. Psychological studies of historical personalities. *Psychol. Bull.*, 1927, *24*, 521–539.

———. The history of the experimental study of the knee-jerk. *Amer. J. Psychol.*, 1928, *40*, 92–111.

———. René Descartes: A study in the history of the theories of reflex action. *Psychol. Rev.*, 1929, *36*, 375–388.

———. Jan Swammerdam: A study in the history of comparative and physiological psychology of the 17th century. *Amer. J. Psychol.*, 1929, *41*, 442–455.

———. *Reflex action: A study in the history of physiological psychology.* Baltimore, Md.: Williams & Wilkins, 1930. (Reprinted 1970)

———. The experimental study of attitude, meaning, and the processes antecedent to action by N. Ach and others in the Würzburg Laboratory. In S. A. Rice (Ed.), *Methods in social science*. Chicago: University of Chicago Press, 1931, pp. 715–729.

———, & Mowrer, O. H. The effect of general anaesthesia upon the experimental reduction of vestibular nystagmus. *J. gen. Psychol.*, 1934, *11*, 133–144.

———, & Ross, Georgia. Behavior factors affecting body temperature in pigeons. I. General level of activity as modified by anaesthesia and visual controls. II. General level of activity as modified by deprivation and ingestion of food with particular reference to the "hunger drive." *J. comp. Psychol.,* 1936, *22,* 219–230, 231–239.

————. The retention of the effects of repeated elicitation of the post-rotational nystagmus in pigeons. I. The retention of the effects of "massed" stimulation. *J. comp. Psychol.,* 1940, *30,* 31–40.

————. The retention of the effects of repeated elicitation of the post-rotational nystagmus in pigeons. II. The retention of the effects of "distributed" stimulation. *J. comp. Psychol.,* 1941, *31,* 47–56.

————, & Krise, E. M. Conforming behavior and the J-curve hypothesis. *J. soc. Psychol.,* 1941, *14,* 109–118.

————, & Fearing, F. M. Factors in the appraisal interview considered with particular reference to the selection of public personnel. *J. Psychol.,* 1942, *14,* 131–153.

————. Influence of the movies on attitudes and behavior. *Ann. Amer. Acad. polit. soc. Sci.* 1947, *254,* 70–79.

————. Group behavior and the concept of emotion. In M. L. Reymert, *Feelings and emotions: The Mooseheart symposium.* New York: McGraw-Hill, 1950, pp. 448–458.

Spiegelman, M., Terwilliger, C., & ————. The content of comic strips: A study of a mass medium of communication. *J. soc. Psychol.,* 1952, *35,* 37–57.

————. Toward a psychological theory of human communication. *J. Pers.,* 1953, *22,* 71–88.

Spiegelman, M., Terwilliger, C., & ————. The content of comics: Goals and means to goals of comic strip characters. *J. soc. Psychol.,* 1953, *37,* 189–203.

GUSTAV THEODOR FECHNER
1801-1887
German Philosopher (27)

Fechner, G. T. *Gedichte.* (Dr. Mises) Leipzig: Breitkopf & Härtel, 1841.   C

————. *Räthselbüchlein von Dr. Mises.* (4th ed.) Leipzig: Breitkopf & Härtel, 1876. (1850)   C

————. *Kleine Schriften.* (Dr. Mises) Leipzig: Breitkopf & Härtel, 1913. (1875)   C

————. *Zwei Abhandlungen. Ueber die Frage des Weberschen Gesetzes und Periodicitäts-Gesetzes im Gebiete des Zeitsinnes. Ueber die Methode der richtigen und falschen Fälle in Anwendung auf die Massbestimmungen der Feinheit oder extensiven Empfindlichkeit des Raumsinnes.* (2 vols in 1) Leipzig: Hirzel, 1887. (Reprinted 1966)   C

————, Preyer, W., & Vierordt, K. v. *Wissenschaftliche Briefe von Gustav Theodor Fechner und W. Preyer nebst einem Briefwechsel zwischen K. von Vierordt und Fechner.* Ed. by W. Preyer. Hamburg: Voss, 1890.   B C

————. *Kollektivmasslehre.* Ed. by G. F. Lipps. Leipzig: Engelmann, 1897.   C

————. *Ausgewählte Schriften.* Berlin: Borngräber, 1907.   C

————. *Religion of a scientist: Selections from Gustav Th. Fechner.* Ed. & trans. by W. Lowrie. New York: Pantheon Books, 1946.   C

————. *Seele und Welt. Eine kleine Auswahl aus den Schriften von Gustav Theodor Fechner.* Klagenfurt: Kaiser, 1947.   C

————. *Praemissae ad theoriam organismi generalem. Specimeni i assumpto socio M. Gul. Drobisch. Leipzig: Staritii, 1823.*

————. The comparative anatomy of angels: A sketch by Dr. Mises: 1825. Trans. by Hildegard Corbet & Marilyn E. Marshall. *J. hist. Behav. Sci.,* 1969, *5,* 135–151.

————. *Massbestimmungen über die galvanische Kette.* Leipzig: Brockhaus, 1831.

————. *The little books of life after death.* (5th ed.) Intro. by W. James, & trans. by Mary Wadsworth. Boston: Little, Brown, 1904. (1836) (Reprinted 1943)

————. Ueber die subjectiven Komplementärfarben. *Ann. Phys. Chem.,* 1838, *44*(6), 221–245, *44*(7), 513–535.

————. Ueber eine Scheibe zur Erzeugung subjektiver Farben. *Ann. Phys. Chem.,* 1838, *45,* 227–232.

———. Ueber die subjektiven Nach- und Neben-bilder. *Ann. Phys. Chem.,* 1840, *50*(6), 193–221, *50*(7), 427–470.

———. *Ueber das höchste Gut.* Leipzig: Breit-kopf & Härtel, 1846. (Reprinted 1923)

———. *Nanna: Oder über das Seelenleben der Pflanzen.* (5th ed.) Leipzig: Voss, 1921. (1848)

———. Ueber das Lustprinzip des Handelns. *Z. Phil. phil. Krit.,* 1848, *19*(N.S.), 1–30, 163–194.

———. Ueber die mathematische Behandlung organischer Gestalten und Processe. *Ber. sächs. Ges. Wiss. Leipzig,* Math.-phys. Kl., 1849, *1*, 50–64.

———. *Zend-Avesta: Oder über die Dinge des Himmels und des Jenseits, vom Standpunkt der Naturbetrachtung.* (3rd ed.) (2 vols.) Leipzig: Voss, 1906. (1851)

———. Ueber die Erkenntnis Gottes in der Natur aus der Natur. *Z. Phil. phil. Krit.,* 1852, *21*, 193–209.

———. Zur Kritik der Grundlagen von Herbarts Metaphysik. *Z. Phil. phil. Krit.,* 1853, *23*, 70–102.

———. *Ueber die physikalische und philosophi-sche Atomenlehre.* (2nd ed.) Leipzig: Mendels-sohn, 1864. (1855)

———. *Professor Schleiden und der Mond.* Leip-zig: Gumprecht, 1856.

———. Das psychische Mass. *Z. Phil. phil. Krit.,* 1858, *32*, 1–24.

———. *Ueber ein wichtiges psychophysiches Ge-setz und dessen Beziehung zur Schätzung der Sterngrössen.* Leipzig: Hirzel, 1859. Also in *Abh. sächs. Ges. Wiss. Leipzig,* Math.-phys. Kl., 1859, *4*, 455–532.

———. *Elements of psychophysics.* Vol. 1. Trans. by H. E Adler, & ed. by E. G. Boring & D. H. Howes. New York: Holt, Rinehart, & Winston, 1966. (1860)

———. *Elemente der Psychophysik.* (2 vols.) Leipzig: Breitkopf & Härtel, 1860. Reprinted with notes & bibliography, 1889. (Reprinted 1964)

———. *Ueber einige Verhältnisse des binocularen Sehens.* Leipzig: Hirzel, 1860. Also *Abh. sachs. Ges. Wiss. Leipzig,* Math.-phys. Kl., 1861, *5*, 337–564.

———. Ueber die Contrastempfindung. *Ber. sächs. Ges. Wiss. Leipzig,* Math.-phys. Kl., 1860, *12*, 71–145.

———. Einige Bemerkungen gegen die Abhand-lung Prof. Osanns über Ergänzungsfarben. *Ber. sächs. Ges. Wiss. Leipzig,* Maths.-phys. Kl., 1860, *12*, 146–165.

———. *Ueber die Seelenfrage. Ein Gang durch die sichtbare Welt, um die unsichtbare zu fin-den.* (3rd ed.) Leipzig: Voss, 1928 (1861)

———. Ueber die Correctionen bezüglich der Genauigkeitsbestimmung der Beobachtungen, der Bestimmung der Schwankungen meteorolo-gischer Einzelwerthe um ihren Mittelwerth, und der psychophysischen Massbestimmungen nach der Methode der mittleren Fehler. *Ber. sächs. Ges. Wiss. Leipzig,* Math.-phys. Kl. 1861, *13*, 56–113.

———. Ueber den seitlichen Fenster- und Kerzen-versuch. *Ber. sächs. Ges. Wiss. Leipzig,* Math.-phys. Kl., 1862, *14*, 27–56.

———. *Die drei Motive und Gründe des Glaubens.* (2nd ed.) Leipzig: Breitkopf & Härtel, 1910. (1863)

———. *Zur Deutungsfrage und Geschichte der Holbein'schen Madonna.* Leipzig: Weigel, 1866.

———. Die historischen Quellen und Verhand-lungen über die Holbein'sche Madonna. *Arch. zeichn. Künste,* 1866, *12*, 193–266. Also Leip-zig: Weigel, 1866.

———. *Ueber die Aechtheitsfrage der Holbein' schen Madonna.* Leipzig: Breitkopf & Härtel, 1871.

———. *Zur experimentalen Aesthetik. Abh. sächs. Ges. Wiss.,* Math.-phys. Kl., 1871, *9*(6), 553–635. (Also Leipzig: Hirzel, 1871)

———. *Bericht über das auf der Dresdner Hol-bein-Ausstellung ausgelegte Album.* Leipzig: Breitkopf & Härtel, 1872.

———. *Einige Ideen zur Schöpfungs- und Entwick-elungsgeschichte der Organismen.* Leipzig: Breitkopf & Härtel, 1873.

———. Ueber die Bestimmung des wahrscheinlichen Fehlers eines Beobachtungsmittels durch die Summe der einfachen Abweichungen. *Ann. Phys.*, 1874, Jubelband, 66–81.

———. Ueber den Ausgangswerth der kleinsten Abweichungssumme, dessen Bestimmung, Verwendung und Verallgemeinerung. *Abh. sächs. Ges. Wiss. Leipzig*, Math.-phys. Kl., 1878, *11*, 1–76. (1874)

———. *Vorschule der Aesthetik.* (2nd ed.) (2 vols.) Leipzig: Breitkopf & Härtel, 1897–1898. (1876) (Reprinted 1925)

———. *In Sachen der Psychophysik.* Leipzig: Breitkopf & Härtel, 1877. (Reprinted 1968)

———. *Die Tagesansicht gegenüber der Nachtansicht.* (3rd ed.) Leipzig: Breitkopf & Härtel, 1919. (1879)

———. Ueber die Aufgaben der Psychophysik. *Allg. Z.*, Munich, 1882, Nos. 339, 340.

———. *Revision der Hauptpunkte der Psychophysik.* Leipzig: Breitkopf & Härtel, 1882. (Reprinted 1965)

———. Ueber die Frage des Weber'schen Gesetzes und Periodicitätsgesetzes im Gebiete des Zeitsinns. *Abh. sächs. Ges. Wiss. Leipzig*, Math.-phys. Kl., 1884 *13*(1), 1–108. (Also Leipzig: Hirzel, 1884.) (Reprinted 1966)

———. Ueber die Methode der richtigen und falschen Fälle in Anwendung auf die Massbestimmungen der Feinheit oder extensive Empfindlichkeit des Raumsinnes. *Abh. sächs. Ges. Wiss. Leipzig*, Math.-phys. Kl. 1884, *13*(2), 109–312. (Also Leipzig: Hirzel, 1884)

———. Ueber die Methode der richtigen und falschen Fälle in Anwendung auf die Massbestimmungen der Feinheit des Raumsinnes oder der sog. extensiven Empfindlichkeit der Haut *Z. Biol.*, 1885, *21*, 527–569.

———. In Sachen des Zeitsinnes und der Methode der richtigen und falschen Fälle, gegen Estel und Lorenz. *Phil. Stud.*, 1886, *3*, 1–37.

———. Ueber die psychischen Massprincipien und das Weber'sche Gesetz. *Phil. Stud.*, 1888, *4*, 161–230.

———. Ueber negative Empfindungswerte. (Briefliche Mitteilungen an W. Preyer.) *Z. Psychol.*, 1890, *1*, 29–46, 108–120.

Dennis, *Psychology*; Herrnstein & Boring, *Source Book*; Miller, *Mathematics*; Rand, *Classical Psychologists*

OTTO FENICHEL
1898-1946
Austrian-American Psychoanalyst (15)

Fenichel, O. *The collected papers of Otto Fenichel: First series.* New York: Norton, 1953. **C**

———. *The collected papers of Otto Fenichel: Second series.* New York: Norton, 1954. **C**

———. Psychoanalyse und Metaphysik. *Imago*, 1923, *9*, 318–343. Trans. in *Collected papers*, Vol. 1, *op. cit.*, pp. 8–26.

———. Ueber organlibidinöse Begleiterscheinungen der Thiebabwehr. *Int. Z. ärztl. Psychoanal.*, 1928, *14*, 45–64. Trans. in *Collected papers*, Vol. 1, *op. cit.*, pp. 128–146.

———. Zur prägenitalen Vorgeschichte des Oedipuskomplexes. *Int. Z. ärztl. Psychoanal.*, 1930, *16*, 319–342. Trans. in *Collected papers*, Vol. 1, *op. cit.*, pp. 181–203.

———. *Outline of clinical psychoanalysis.* Trans. by B. D. Lewin & G. Zilboorg. New York: Norton, 1934. (1931)

———. Psychoanalyse der Politik. *Psychoanal. Bewegung*, 1932, *4*, 255–268.

———. Psychoanalysis as the nucleus of a future dialectical-materialistic psychology (1934) *Amer. Imago*, 1967, *24*, 290–311.

———. Zur Kritik des Todestriebes. *Imago*, 1935, *21*, 458–466. Trans. in *Collected papers*, Vol. 1, *op. cit.*, pp. 363–372.

———. Ego disturbances and their treatment. *Int. J. Psycho-Anal.*, 1938, *19*, 416–438. Reprinted in *Collected papers*, Vol. 2, *op. cit.*, pp. 109–128.

———. *Problems of psychoanalytic technique.* Trans. by D. Brunswick. Albany, N.Y.: Psychoanalytic Quarterly Press, 1939.

——. Zur Oekonimik der Pseudologia phantastica. *Int. Z. ärztl. Psychoanal.*, 1939, *24*, 21–32.

——. The ego and the effects. *Psychoanal. Rev.*, 1941, *28*, 49–60. Reprinted in *Collected papers*, Vol. 2, *op. cit.*, pp. 215–227.

——. *The psychoanalytic theory of neurosis.* New York: Norton, 1945.

——. Elements of a psychoanalytic theory of anti-Semitism. In E. Simmel (Ed.), *Antisemitism: A social disease.* New York: International Universities Press, 1946, pp. 11–32. Reprinted in *Collected papers*, Vol. 2, *op. cit.*, pp. 335–348.

——. Some remarks on Freud's place in the history of science. *Psychoanal. Quart.*, 1946, *15*, 279–284. Reprinted in *Collected papers*, Vol. 2, *op. cit.*, pp. 362–366.

Rapaport, *Thought*

CHARLES FERE
1852-1907
French Psychiatrist (18)

Féré, C. *Etude des troubles fonctionnels de la vision.* Paris: Alcan, 1882.

——. *Contribution à l'étude des troubles fonctionnels de la vision par lésions cérébrales.* Paris: Delahaye & Lecrosnier, 1882.

Binet, A., & ——. Les paralysies par suggestion *Rev. sci.*, 1884, *34*(2), 45–49.

Binet, A., & ——. Note sur le somnambulisme partiel et les localisations cérébrales. *C. r. Soc. Biol.*, 1884, *36*, 491–492.

Binet, A., & ——. L'hypnotisme chez les hystériques: Le transfert. *Rev. phil.*, 1885, *19*, 1–25.

Binet, A., & ——. Hypnotisme et responsabilité. *Rev. phil.*, 1885, *19*, 265–272.

Binet, A., & ——. La théorie physiologique de l'hallucination. *Rev. sci.*, 1885, *35*(1), 49–53.

——. Nerve troubles as foreshadowed in the child. *Brain*, 1885, *8*, 230–238.

Binet, A., & ——. *The psychology of reasoning: Based on experimental researches in hypnotism.* Trans. by A. G. Whyte. London: Kegan Paul, 1901. (1886)

——. *Traité élémentaire d'anatomie médicale du système nerveux.* Paris: Delahaye & Lecrosnier, 1886.

Binet, A., & ——. Expériences sur les images associées. *Rev. phil.*, 1886, *21*, 159–163.

——. Sensation et mouvement. Contribution à la psychologie du foetus. *Rev. phil.*, 1886, *21*, 247–264.

Binet, A., & ——. Recherches expérimentales sur la physiologie des mouvements chez les hystériques. *Arch. physiol.*, 1887, *10*, 320–373.

——. A contribution to the pathology of dreams and of hysterical paralysis. *Brain*, 1887, *9*, 488–493. (Reprinted Paris, 1887)

——. *Sensation et mouvement. Etudes expérimentales de psycho-mécanique.* (2nd ed.) Paris: Alcan, 1900. (1887)

Binet, A., & ——. *Animal magnetism.* (4th ed.) (Trans. not given.) New York: Appleton, 1901. (1887)

——. *Dégénérescence et criminalité.* Paris: Alcan, 1895. (1888)

——. *Du traitement des aliénés dans les familles.* Paris: Décembre-Alonnier, 1889.

——. *Les épilepsies et les épileptiques.* Paris: Alcan, 1890.

——. *The pathology of emotions: Physiological and clinical studies.* Trans. by R. Park. London: University Press, 1899. (1892)

——. *La famille névropathique.* (2nd ed.) Paris: Alcan, 1898. (1894)

——. Morbid heredity. *Pop Sci. Mon.*, 1895, *47*, 388–399.

——. La physiologie dans les métaphores. *Rev. phil.*, 1895, *40*, 352–359.

——. Le langage réflexe. *Rev. phil.*, 1896, *41*, 39–43.

———. L'antithèse dans l'expression des émotions. *Rev. phil.,* 1896, *42,* 498–501.

———. La main, l'appréhension et le toucher. *Rev. phil.,* 1896, *41,* 621–636.

———. Les perversions sexuelles chez les animaux. *Rev. phil.,* 1897, *43,* 494–503.

———. Influence de l'éducation de la motilité volontaire sur la sensibilité. *Rev. phil.,* 1897, *44,* 591–604.

———. *Les phobies épileptiques.* Paris: Dentu, 1899.

———. *Sexual degeneration in mankind and in animals.* (10th ed.) Trans. by U. van Der Horst. New York: Falstaff Press, 1932. (1899)

———. *Anomalies des organes génitaux.* Paris: Alcan, 1901.

———. Recherches expérimentales sur la fatigue par des excitations de l'odorat. *Nouv. Icon. Salpêtrière,* 1901, *14,* 327–353.

———. Influence de l'alcool et du tabac sur le travail. *Arch. Neurol.,* 1901, *12,* 369–384, 463–475.

———. Etudes expérimentales sur le travail chez l'homme et sur quelques conditions qui influent sur sa valeur. *J. anat. Physiol.,* 1901, *37,* 1–79.

———. Les variations de l'excitabilité dans la fatigue. *Année psychol.,* 1901, *7,* 69–81.

———. Etude expérimentale de l'influence des excitations agréables et des excitations désagréables sur le travail. *Année psychol.,* 1901, *7,* 82–129.

———. L'excitabilité comparée des deux hémisphères cérébraux chez l'homme. *Année psychol.,* 1900, *7,* 143–160.

———. L'influence du rythme sur le travail. *Année psychol.,* 1901, *8,* 49–106.

———. L'alternance de l'activité des deux hémisphères cérébraux. *Année psychol.,* 1902, *8,* 107–149.

———. L'influence de quelques poisons nerveux sur le travail. *Année psychol.,* 1901, *8,* 151–184.

———. *Travail et plaisir.* Paris: Alcan, 1904.

Shor, *Hypnosis*

SANDOR FERENCZI
1873-1933
Hungarian Psychoanalyst (19)

Ferenczi, S. *First contributions to psychoanalysis.* Trans. by E. Jones. London: Hogarth, 1952. (1916) (In other editions, titled *Contributions to psychoanalysis* and *Sex in psychoanalysis.*)
C

———. *Populäre Vorträge über Psychoanalyse.* Vienna: Internationaler Psychoanalytischer Verlag, 1922.
C

———. *Further contributions to the theory and technique of psychoanalysis.* (2nd ed.) Trans. by Jane I. Suttie *et al.,* & comp. by J. Rickman. London: Hogarth, 1950. (1926) (In another edition, titled *Theory and technique of psychoanalysis.*)
Bl C

———. *Bausteine zur Psychoanalyse.* (4 vols.) Bern: Huber, 1939.
Bl C

———. *Final contributions to the problems and methods of psychoanalysis.* Ed. by M. Balint, & trans. by E. Mosbacher *et al.* New York: Basic Books, 1955. (In another edition, titled *Problems and methods of psychoanalysis.*)
C

———. On the psychological analysis of dreams. *Amer. J. Psychol.,* 1910, *21,* 309–328.

———. On obscene words. (1911) In *First contributions, op. cit.,* pp. 132–153.

———. On transitory symptom-constructions during the analysis. (1912) In *First contributions, op. cit.,* pp. 193–212.

———. Belief, disbelief and conviction. (1913) In *Further contributions, op. cit.,* pp. 437–450.

———. Stages in the development of the sense of reality. (1913) In *First contributions, op. cit.,* pp. 213–239.

———. *Hysterie und Pathoneurosen.* Leipzig: Internationale Psychoanalytische Bibliothek, 1919.

———. Concerning the role of homosexuality in the pathogenesis of paranoia. (1920) Reprinted in *First contributions, op. cit.,* pp. 154–186.

————, & Rank, O. *The development of psycho-analysis*. Trans. by Caroline Newton. New York: Nervous & Mental Diseases Publishing, 1925. (1923)

————. *Thalassa: A theory of genitality*. Trans. by H. A. Bunker, Jr. Albany, N.Y.: Psycho-analytic Quarterly Press, 1938. (1924)

————. Psychoanalysis of sexual habits. *Int. J. Psycho-Anal.*, 1925, *6*, 372–404. Reprinted in *Further contributions, op. cit.*, pp. 259–297.

————. Present-day problems in psychoanalysis. *Arch. Psycho-Anal.*, 1927, *1*, 522–530. Reprinted in *Final contributions, op. cit.*, pp. 29–40.

————. Interprétation et traitement psychanalytique de l'impuissance psychosexuelle chez l'homme. (1908) *Rev. fr. psychanal.*, 1930–1931, *4*, 230–244.

————. Freud's influence on medicine. In S. Lorand (Ed.), *Psychoanalysis today*. New York: International Universities Press, 1944, pp. 1–11. (1933) Reprinted in *Final contributions, op. cit.*, pp. 143–155.

————. Ten letters to Freud. *Int. J. Psycho-Anal.*, 1949, *30*, 243–250.   **B**

Rosenblith & Allinsmith, *Causes Behavior*;
Shor, *Hypnosis*

SAMUEL WEILLER FERNBERGER
1887-1956
American Psychologist (18)

Fernberger, S. W. On the relation of the methods of just perceptible differences and constant stimuli. *Psychol. Monogr.*, 1913, *14*, No. 61.

————. The elimination of the two extreme values of the comparison stimuli in the method of constant stimuli. *Psychol. Rev.*, 1914, *21*, 335–355.

————. The effect of the attitude of the subject upon the measure of sensitivity. *Amer. J. Psychol.*, 1914, *25*, 538–543.

————. The influence of mental and physical work on the formation of judgments in lifted weight experiments. *J. exp. Psychol.*, 1916, *1*, 508–532.

————. On the number of articles of psychological interest published in the different languages. *Amer. J. Psychol.*, 1917, *28*, 141–150.

————. An introspective analysis of the process of comparing. *Psychol. Monogr.*, 1919, *26*, No. 117.

————. Possible effects of the imaginal type of the subject on aphasic disturbances. *Amer. J. Psychol.*, 1919, *30*, 327–336.

————. Interdependence of judgments within the series for the method of constant stimuli. *J. exp. Psychol.*, 1920, *3*, 126–150.

————. Further statistics of the American Psychological Association. *Psychol. Bull.*, 1921, *18*, 569–572.

————. A preliminary study of the range of visual apprehension. *Amer. J. Psychol.*, 1921, *32*, 121–133.

————. An experimental study of the "stimulus error." *J. exp. Psychol.*, 1921, *4*, 63–76.

————. Behavior versus introspective psychology. *Psychol. Rev.*, 1922, *29*, 409–413.

————. False suggestion and the Piderit model. *Amer. J. Psychol.*, 1928, *40*, 562–568.

————. Statistical analyses of the members and associates of the American Psychological Association, Inc. in 1928: A cross section of American professional psychology. *Psychol. Rev.*, 1928, *35*, 447–465.

————. Publications of American psychologists. *Psychol. Rev.*, 1930, *37*, 526–544.

————. Can an emotion be accurately judged by its facial expression alone? *J. crim. Law Criminol.*, 1930, *20*, 554–565.

————. The use of equality judgments in psychophysical procedures. *Psychol. Rev.*, 1930, *37*, 107–112.

————. On absolute and relative judgments in lifted weight experiments. *Amer. J. Psychol.*, 1931, *43*, 560–578.

————. Instructions and the psychophysical limen. *Amer. J. Psychol.*, 1931, *43*, 361–376.

———. The American Psychological Association: A historical summary, 1892–1930. *Psychol. Bull.,* 1932, *29,* 1–89.

———. A psychological cycle. *Amer. J. Psychol.,* 1937, *50,* 207–217.

———. Publications, politics and economics. *Psychol. Bull.,* 1938, *35,* 84–90.

———. The scientific interests and scientific publications of the members of the American Psychological Association, Inc. *Psychol. Bull.,* 1938, *35,* 261–281.

———. The American Psychological Association, 1892–1942. *Psychol. Rev.,* 1943, *50,* 33–60.

———. Some European psychological laboratories —1951. *Amer. J. Psychol.,* 1952, *65,* 619–626.

———. The prestige and impact of various psychologists on psychology in America. *Amer. J. Psychol.,* 1954, *67,* 288–298.

———. On the number of articles of psychological interest published in the different languages: 1946–1955. *Amer. J. Psychol.,* 1956, *69,* 304–309.

CLARENCE ERROL FERREE
1877-1942
American Psychologist (11)

Ferree, C. E. An experimental examination of the phenomena usually attributed to fluctuation of attention. *Amer. J. Psychol.,* 1906, *17,* 81–120.

———. The intermittence of minimal visual sensations. *Amer. J. Psychol.,* 1908, *19,* 58–129.

———. The streaming phenomenon. *Amer. J. Psychol.,* 1908, *19,* 484–503.

———, & Rand, Gertrude. Colored after-image and contrast sensations from stimuli in which no color is sensed. *Psychol. Rev.,* 1912, *19,* 195–239.

———. Description of a rotary campimeter. *Amer. J. Psychol.,* 1912, *23,* 449–453.

———. The fluctuation of liminal visual stimuli of point area. *Amer. J. Psychol.,* 1913, *24,* 378–409.

———, & Rand, Gertrude. A preliminary study of the deficiencies of the method of flicker for the photometry of lights of different color. *Psychol. Rev.,* 1915, *22,* 110–162.

———, & Rand, Gertrude. A spectroscopic apparatus for the investigation of the color sensitivity of the retina, central and peripheral. *J. exp. Psychol.,* 1916, *1,* 247–283.

———, & Rand, Gertrude. A simple daylight photometer. *Amer. J. Psychol.,* 1916, *27,* 335–340.

———, & Rand, Gertrude. A new method of heterochromatic photometry: A reply to Dr. Johnson. *Psychol. Rev.,* 1917, *24,* 159–173.

———, & Rand, Gertrude. Some areas of color blindness of an unusual type in the peripheral retina. *J. exp. Psychol.,* 1917, *2,* 295–303.

———, & Rand, Gertrude. Lighting in its relation to the eye. *Proc. Amer. Phil. Soc.,* 1918, *57,* 440–478.

———, & Rand, Gertrude. Some experiments on the eye with different illuminants. I. *Trans. Illum. Eng. Soc.,* 1918, *13,* 50–82; 1919, *14,* 107–132.

———, & Rand, Gertrude. Chromatic thresholds of sensation from center to periphery of the retina and their bearing on color theory. I. II. *Psychol. Rev.,* 1919, *26,* 16–41, 150–163.

———, Rand, Gertrude, & Haupt, I. A. A method of standardizing the color value of the daylight illumination of an optics room. *Amer. J. Psychol.,* 1920, *31,* 77–87.

———, & Rand, Gertrude. The absolute limits of color sensitivity and the effect of intensity of light on the apparent limits. *Psychol. Rev.,* 1920, *27,* 1–23.

———, & Rand, Gertrude. The limits of color sensitivity: Effects of brightness of pre-exposure and surrounding field. *Psychol. Rev.,* 1920, *27,* 377–398.

———, & Rand, Gertrude. The effect of varying the intensity of light on the disagreement of flicker and equality-of-brightness photometry for lights of different composition. *Amer. J. Psychol.,* 1925, *36,* 171–177.

———, & Rand, Gertrude. The effect of speed of rotation of the disc on the disagreement of flicker and equality-of-brightness photometry for lights of different composition and intensity. *Amer. J. Psychol.*, 1925, *36*, 178–187.

———, & Rand, Gertrude. The agreement of flicker and equality-of-brightness photometry when the same lengths of exposure are used in both methods. *Amer. J. Psychol.*, 1925, *36*, 188–191.

———, & Rand, Gertrude. The effect of relation to background on the size and shape of the form field for stimuli of different sizes. *Amer. J. Ophthalm.*, 1931, *14*, 1018–1029.

———, & Rand, Gertrude. Visibility of objects as affected by color and composition of light. Part I. With lights of equal luminosity or brightness. *Personnel J.*, 1931, *9*, 475–492.

———, Rand, Gertrude, & Hardy, C. An important factor in space perception in the peripheral field of vision. *Amer. J. Psychol.*, 1933, *45*, 228–247.

Moore & Hartmann, *Industrial Psychology*

PAUL JOHANN ANSELM VON FEUERBACH
1775-1833
German Philosopher (14)

Feuerbach, P. J. A. v. *Kleine Schriften vermischten Inhalts.* Nuremberg: Otto, 1833.   **C**

———. *Anselm Ritter v. Feuerbachs Leben und Werke.* (2 vols.) Ed. by L. Feuerbach. Leipzig: Wigand, 1852.   **B C**

———. *Kritik des natürlichen Rechts.* Altona: Verlagsgesellschaft, 1796.

———. *Anti-Hobbes ; oder über die Grenzen der höchsten Gewalt und das Zwängerecht der Bürger gegen den Oberherrn.* Erfurt: Henning, 1798.

———. *Ueber Philosophie und Empirie in ihrem Verhältnisse zur positiven Rechtswissenschaft.* Landshut: Attenkofer, 1804.

———. *Narratives of remarkable criminal trials.* Trans. by Lady Duff-Gordon. New York: Harper, 1846. (1808)

———. *Betrachtungen über das Geschworenen Gericht.* Landshut: Krull, 1813.

———. *Aktenmässige Darstellung merkwürdiger Verbrechen.* (3rd ed.) (2 vols.) Frankfurt: Heyer, 1849. (1828–1829)

———. *Caspar Hauser. An account of an individual kept in a dungeon, separated from all communication with the world, from early childhood to about the age of seventeen.* Trans. by H. G. Linberg. Boston: Allen & Ticknor, 1832. (1832)

JOHANN GOTTLIEB FICHTE
1762-1814
German Philosopher (16)

Fichte, J. G. *J. G. Fichtes nachgelassene Werke.* (3 vols.) Ed. by J. H. Fichte. Berlin: De Gruyter, 1962. (1834–1835)

———. *Sämtliche Werke.* (8 vols.) Ed. by J. H. Fichte. Berlin: Veit, 1845–1846. (Reprinted 1965)   **Bl C**

———. *Fichte's popular works.* (4th ed.) (2 vols.) Trans. with memoir by W. Smith. London: Truebner, 1889. (1845–1849)   **C**

Schiller, J. C. F. v., & ———. *Schillers und Fichtes Briefwechsel.* Berlin: Veit, 1847.   **B C**

———, & Schelling, F. W. J. v. *Fichtes und Schellings philosopher Briefwechsel aus dem Nachlasse beider.* Ed. by I. H. Fichte & K. F. A. Schelling. Stuttgart: Cotta, 1856.   **C**

———. *Ausgewählte Werke.* (6 vols.) Ed. by F. Medicus. Darmstadt: Wissenschaftliche Buchgesellschaft, 1954. (1908–1912)   **C**

———. *Briefwechsel.* (2 vols.) Ed. by H. Schulz. Hildesheim: Olms, 1967. (1925)   **C**

———. *Werke. Gesamtausgabe.* (Ult. 26 vols.) Ed. by R. Lauth & H. Jacob. Stuttgart: Frommann, 1964– .   **C**

———. *Grundlage der gesamten Wissenschaftslehre.* Hamburg: Meiner, 1961. (1794)

————. The vocation of the scholar. (1794) In *Fichte's popular works,* Vol. 1, *op. cit.,* pp. 149–205.

————. *The science of knowledge (Wissenschafts-lehre) with the first and second introductions.* Ed. & trans. by P. Heath & J. Lachs. New York: Appleton-Century-Crofts, 1970. (1794–1795)

————. *Grundlage des Naturrechts nach Principien der Wissenschaftslehre.* (2 vols.) Jena: Gabler, 1796–1797. Reprinted in *Sämtliche Werke,* Vol. 3, *op. cit.,* pp. 1–385.

————. *Erste und zweite Einleitung in Die Wissenschaftslehre.* Hamburg: Meiner, 1961. (1797)

————. *Das System der Sittenlehre nach den Principien der Wissenschaftlehre.* Jena: Gabler, 1798. Reprinted in *Sämtliche Werke,* Vol. 4, *op. cit.,* pp. 1–365, & reprinted 1969.

————. *Die Bestimmung des Menschen.* (2nd ed.) Berlin: Voss, 1838. (1800) Reprinted in *Sämtliche Werke,* Vol. 2, *op. cit.,* pp. 165–319.

————. Fichte's criticism on Schelling. (1806) Trans. by A. E. Kroeger. *J. specul. Phil.,* 1878, *12,* 160–170, 316–326.

————. *Addresses to the German nation.* Trans. by R. F. Jones & G. H. Turnbull, & intro. by G. A. Kelly. New York: Harper & Row, 1968. (1808)

————. *The science of rights.* Trans. by A. E. Kroeger. London: Truebner, 1889. (1812)

————. *Erste Wissenschaftslehre von 1804, aus dem Nachlass hrsg. von Hans Gliwitzky, mit einem Strukturvergleich zwischen der W. L. 1804[1] und der W. L. 1804[2] von Joachim Widmann.* Stuttgart: Kohlhammer, 1969.

Gardiner, *Philosophy*; Rand, *Classical Philosophers*; Rand, *Moralists*

(SIR) RONALD AYLMER FISHER
1890-1962
English Statistician (20)

Fisher, R. A. *Contributions to mathematical statistics.* New York: Wiley, 1950.　**B C**

————. On an absolute criterion for fitting frequency curves. *Messenger Math.,* 1912, *41*(N.S.), 155–160.

————. Frequency-distribution of the values of the correlation coefficient in samples from an indefinitely large population. *Biometrika,* 1915, *10,* 507–521.

————. The correlation between relatives on the supposition of Mendelian inheritance. *Trans. Roy. Soc. Edinburgh,* 1918, *52,* 399–433.

————. A mathematical examination of the methods of determining the accuracy of an observation by the mean error, and by the mean square error. *Mon. Not. R. Astr. Soc.,* 1920, *80,* 758–770.

————. On the mathematical foundations of theoretical statistics. *Phil. Trans.,* 1921, *222A,* 309–368.

————. The goodness of fit of regression formulae and the distribution of regression coefficients. *J. Roy. Stat. Soc.,* 1922, *85,* 597–612.

————. The distribution of the partial correlation coefficient. *Metron,* 1924, *3*(3–4), 329–332.

————. Theory of statistical estimation. *Proc. Camb. Phil. Soc.,* 1925, *22,* 700–725. Reprinted in *Contributions to mathematical statistics, op. cit.,* pp. 11.699a–11.725. (1923–1925)

————. *Statistical methods for research workers.* (13th ed.) New York: Hafner, 1963. (1925)　**Bl**

————. Applications of "Student's" distribution. *Metron,* 1926, *5*(3), 90–104.

————. The general sampling distribution of the multiple correlation coefficient. *Proc. Roy. Soc.,* London, 1928, *121A,* 654–673. Reprinted in *Contributions to mathematical statistics, op. cit.,* pp. 14.653–14.763.

————. *The genetical theory of natural selection.* (2nd ed.) Oxford: Oxford University Press, 1930. (1929) (Reprinted 1958)

————. Moments and product moments of sampling distributions. *Proc. Lond. Math. Soc.,* 1929. *30,* 199–238. Reprinted in *Contributions to mathematical statistics, op. cit.,* pp. 20.198a–20.237.

———. Tests of significance in harmonic analysis. *Proc. Roy. Soc., London,* 1929, *125A,* 54–59.

———. *The social selection of human fertility.* New York: Oxford University Press, 1932.

———. Immer, F. R., & Tedin, O. The genetical interpretation of statistics of the third degree in the study of quantitative inheritance. *Genetics,* 1932, *17,* 107–124.

———. The concepts of inverse probability and fiducial probability referring to unknown parameters. *Proc. Roy. Soc.,* London, 1933, *139A,* 343–348.

———. The amount of information supplied by records of families as a function of the linkage in the population samples. *Ann. Eugen.,* Cambridge, 1934, *6,* 66–70.

———. The use of simultaneous estimation in the evaluation of linkage. *Ann. Eugen.,* Cambridge, 1934, *6,* 71–76.

———. The effect of methods of ascertainment upon the estimation of frequencies. *Ann. Eugen.,* Cambridge, 1934, *6,* 13–25.

———. Randomization and an old enigma of card play. *Math. Gazette,* 1934, *18,* 294–297.

———. The logic of inductive inference. *J. Roy. Stat. Soc.,* 1935, *98,* 39–82.

———. *The design of experiments.* (8th ed.) New York: Hafner, 1966. (1935) **B**

———. The fiducial argument in statistical inference. *Ann. Eugen.,* Cambridge, 1935, *6,* 391–398.

Barbacki, S., & ———. A test of the supposed precision of systematic arrangements. *Ann. Eugen.,* Cambridge, 1936, *7,* 189–193.

———. Has Mendel's work been rediscovered? *Ann. Sci.,* 1936, *1,* 115–137. Reprinted in C. Stern & Eva R. Sherwood (Eds.), *The origin of genetics: A Mendel source book.* San Francisco, Calif.: Freeman, 1966, pp. 139–172.

———, & Yates, F. *Statistical tables for biological, agricultural and medical research.* (6th ed.) New York: Hafner, 1964. (1938)

———. The sampling distribution of some statistics obtained from non-linear equations. *Ann. Eugen.,* Cambridge, 1939, *9,* 238–249.

———. The comparison of samples with possibly unequal variances. *Ann. Eugen.,* Cambridge, 1939, *9,* 174–180.

———. Gene frequencies in a cline determined by selection and diffusion. *Biometrics,* 1950, *6,* 353–361.

———. Standard calculations of evaluating a blood-group system. *Heredity,* 1951, *5,* 95–102.

———. A combinatorial formulation of multiple linkage test. *Nature,* 1951, *167,* 520.

———. Sequential experimentation. *Biometrics,* 1952, *8,* 183–187.

———. The analysis of variance with various binomial transformations. *Biometrics,* 1954, *10,* 130–139, 140–151.

———. Statistical methods and scientific induction. *J. Roy. Stat. Soc.,* 1955, *17B,* 69–78.

———. On a test of significance in Pearson's Biometrika tables. *J. Roy. Stat. Soc.,* 1956, *18B,* 56–60.

———. *Statistical methods and scientific inference.* (2nd ed.) Edinburgh: Oliver & Boyd, 1959. (1956)

———. The underworld of probability. *Sankhyā,* 1957, *18,* 201–210.

———. Mathematical probability in the natural sciences. *Technometrics,* 1959, *1,* 21–29.

———. Scientific thought and the refinement of human reasoning. *J. oper. res. soc.,* Japan, 1960, *3*(1, 2), 1–10.

Newman, *Mathematics*

PAUL MORRIS FITTS
1912-1965
American Psychologist (16)

Fitts, P. M. Perseveration of non-rewarded behavior in relation to food-deprivation and work-requirement. *J. genet. Psychol.,* 1940, *57,* 165–191.

Flanagan, J. C., & ———. Psychological testing program for the selection and classification of air crew officers. *Air Surg. Bull.,* 1944, *1*(6), 1–5.

———. German applied psychology during World War II. *Amer. Psychologist,* 1946, *1,* 151–161.

———, & Jones, R. E. Psychological aspects of instrument display. I. Analysis of 270 "pilot-error" experiencès in reading and interpreting aircraft instruments. (1947) In H. W. Sinaiko (Ed.), *Selected papers on human factors in the design and use of control systems.* New York: Dover, 1961, pp. 359–396.

———, & Jones, R. E. *Analysis of factors contributing to 460 "pilot-error" experiences in operating aircraft controls.* Wright-Patterson Air Force Base, Dayton, Ohio: Aero Medical Laboratory, Air Material Command, July 1947. Reprinted in H. W. Sinaiko (Ed.), *Selected papers on human factors in the design and use of control systems.* New York: Dover, 1961, pp. 332–358.

——— (Ed.), *Psychological research on equipment design. AAF aviation psychology reports. No. 19.* Washington, D.C.: United States Government Printing Office, 1947.

———. Psychological research on equipment designs in the AAF. *Amer. Psychologist,* 1947, *2,* 93–98.

———. Engineering psychology and equipment design. In S. S. Stevens (Ed.), *Handbook of experimental psychology.* New York: Wiley, 1951, pp. 1287–1340.

———, & Simon, C. W. Some relations between stimulus patterns and performance in a continuous dual-pursuit task. *J. exp. Psychol.,* 1952, *43,* 428–436.

———, & Seeger, C. M. S-R compatibility: Spatial characteristics of stimulus and response codes. *J. exp. Psychol.,* 1953, *46,* 199–210.

———. The information capacity of the human motor system in controlling the amplitude of movement. *J. exp. Psychol.,* 1954, *47,* 381–391.

———, & Deininger, R. L. S-R compatibility: Correspondence among paired elements within stimulus and response codes. *J. exp. Psychol.,* 1954, *48,* 483–492.

Noble, M., ———, & Warren, C. E. The frequency response of skilled subjects in a pursuit tracking task. *J. exp. Psychol.,* 1955, *49,* 249–256.

———, Weinstein, M., Rappaport, M., Anderson, N., & Leonard, J. A. Stimulus correlates of visual pattern recognition: A probability approach. *J. exp. Psychol.,* 1956, *51,* 1–11.

———. Engineering psychology. *Annu. rev. Psychol.,* 1958, *9,* 267–294.

———. Factors in complex skill training. In R. Glaser (Ed.), *Training research and education.* Pittsburgh, Pa.: University of Pittsburgh Press, 1962, pp. 177–197.

———, Peterson, J. R., & Wolpe, G. Cognitive aspects of information processing. II. Adjustments to stimulus redundancy. *J. exp. Psychol.,* 1963, *65,* 423–432.

———. Engineering psychology. In S. Koch (Ed.), *Psychology: A study of a science.* Study 2. *Empirical substructures and relations with other sciences.* Vol. 5. *The process areas, the person, and some applied fields: Their place in psychology and science.* New York: McGraw-Hill, 1963, pp. 908–933.

———, & Peterson, J. R. Information capacity of discrete motor responses. *J. exp. Psychol.,* 1964, *67,* 103–112.

———. Perceptual-motor skill learning. In A. W. Melton (Ed.), *Categories of human learning.* New York: Academic Press, 1964, pp. 243–285.

———. Cognitive aspects of information processing. III. Set for speed versus accuracy. *J. exp. Psychol.,* 1966, *71,* 849–857.

———, & Posner, M. I. *Human performance.* Belmont, Calif.: Brooks Cole, 1967.

PAUL EMIL FLECHSIG
1847-1929
German Psychiatrist (13)

Flechsig, P. E. *Die Leitungsbahnen im Gehirn und Rückenmark des Menschen auf Grund entwickelungsgeschichtlicher Untersuchungen dargestellt.* Leipzig: Engelmann, 1876.

————. Ueber "Systemerkrankungen" im Rückenmark. *Arch. Heilk.,* 1877–1878, *18,* 101–141,
289–343, 461–483, *19,* 53–90, 441–447.

————. Zur Anatomie und Entwickelungsgeschichte der Leitungsbahnen im Grosshirn des
Menschen. *Arch. Anat. Physiol.,* 1881, 12–75.

————. *Die körperlichen Grundlagen der Geistes-
störungen.* Leipzig: Veit, 1882.

————. *Plan des menschlichen Gehirns.* Leipzig:
Veit, 1883.

————. Erwiderung auf Prof. Aug. Forels Bemerkungen "Zur Acusticusfrage." *Neurol. Zbl.,*
1887, *6,* 33–34.

————. Zur Entwickelungsgeschichte der Assozia-
tionssysteme im menschlichen Gehirn. *Ber.
sächs. Akad. Wiss.,* Math.-phys. Kl., 1894, *46,*
164–167.

————. *Gehirn und Seele.* (2nd ed.) Leipzig:
Veit, 1896. (1894)

————. Ueber die Assoziationszentren des
menschlichen Gehirns. *Dritter Int. Congr.
Psychol.,* 1895, 49–67.

————. *Die Grenzen geistiger Gesundheit und
Krankheit.* Leipzig: Veit, 1896.

————. *Die Lokalisation der geistigen Vorgänge,
insbesondere der Sinnesempfindungen des Menschen.* Leipzig: Veit, 1896.

————. Ueber Projektions- und Assoziationszentren des menschlichen Gehirns. *Névraxe,*
1900, *2,* 60–69.

————. Developmental (myelogenetic) localisation
of the cerebral cortex in the human subject.
Lancet, 1901, *2,* 1027–1029.

————. Einige Bemerkungen über die Untersuchungsmethoden der Grosshirnrinde, insbesondere des Menschen. *Ber. sächs. Akad. Wiss.,*
Math.-phys. Kl., 1904, *56,* 50–104, 177–248.

————. Brain physiology and theories of volition.
(1905) Reprinted in & trans. by G. v. Bonin
(Ed.), *Some papers on the cerebral cortex*
Springfield, Ill.: Thomas, 1960, pp. 181–200.

————. *Anatomie des menschlichen Gehirns und
Rückenmarks auf myelogenetischer Grundlage.*
(2 vols.) Leipzig: Thieme, 1920.   **Bl**

————. *Meine myelogenetische Hirnlehre. Mit
biographischer Einleitung.* Berlin: Springer-
Verlag, 1927.   **B Bl**

Clarke & O'Malley, *Brain*

PIERRE JEAN MARIE FLOURENS
1794-1867
French Physiologist (24)

Flourens, P. J. M. *Recueil des éloges historiques
lus dans les séances publiques de l'Académie
des Sciences.* (3 vols.) Paris: Garnier, 1856–
1862.   **C**

————. Recherches physiques sur les propriétés
et les fonctions du système nerveux dans les
animaux vertébrés. *Arch. gén. Méd.,* 1823, *2,*
321–370.

————. *Recherches expérimentales sur les propriétés et les fonctions du système nerveux
dans les animaux vertébrés.* (2nd ed.) Paris:
Baillière, 1842. (1824) Selections reprinted in &
trans. by G. v. Bonin (Ed.), *Some papers on the
cerebral cortex.* Springfield, Ill.: Thomas, 1960,
pp. 3–21.

————. *Expériences sur le système nerveux.* Paris:
Crevot, 1825.

————. Nouvelles expériences sur le système nerveux. *Mém. Acad. roy. Sci.,* 1830, *9,* 478–497.

————. Expériences sur les canaux semi-circulaires
de l'oreille chez les oiseaux. *Mém. Acad. roy.
Sci.,* 1830, *9,* 455–466.

————. Expériences sur les canaux semi-circulaires de l'oreille chez les mammifères. *Mém.
Acad. roy. Sci.,* 1830, *9,* 467–477.

————. *Histoire des travaux de Georges Cuvier.*
(3rd ed.) Paris: Garnier, 1858. (1834)

————. *Phrenology examined.* (2nd ed.) Trans. by
D. de L. Meigs. Philadelphia: Hogan & Thompson, 1846. (1842)

————. *Histoire des travaux et des idées de
Buffon.* (2nd ed.) Paris: Hachette, 1850. (1844)

————. *Cours de physiologie comparée.* Paris:
Baillière, 1856.

————. *De la vie et de l'intelligence.* (2nd ed.) Paris: Garnier, 1858. (1858)

————. *Eloge historique de François Magendie.* Paris: Garnier, 1858. **B**

————. *De la raison, du génie, et de la folie.* Paris: Garnier, 1861.

————. *Psychologie comparée.* (2nd ed.) Paris: Garnier, 1864. (1861)

————. Nouvelles expériences sur l'indépendance respective des fonctions cérébrales. *C. r. Acad. Sci.,* 1861, *52,* 673–675.

————. *Ontologie naturelle; ou, étude philosophique des êtres.* Paris: Garnier, 1861.

————. *De la phrénologie et des études vraies sur le cerveau.* Paris: Garnier, 1863.

————. *Examen du livre de M. Darwin sur l'origine des espèces.* Paris: Garnier, 1864.

————. *De l'unité de composition et du débat entre Cuvier et Geoffroy Saint-Hilaire.* Paris: Garnier, 1865.

Clarke & O'Malley, *Brain*; Dennis, *Psychology*; Fulton & Wilson, *Physiology*; Herrnstein & Boring, *Source Book*

THEODORE FLOURNOY
1854-1920
Swiss Psychologist (11)

Flournoy, T. *Esprits et médiums. Mélanges de métaphysique et de psychologie.* Geneva: Kündig, 1911. **C**

James, W., & ————. *The letters of William James and Théodore Flournoy.* Ed. by R. C. LeClair. Madison, Wisc.: University of Wisconsin Press, 1966. **B C**

————. *Spiritism and psychology.* Trans. by H. Carrington. New York: Harper, 1911. (1911)

————. *Métaphysique et psychologie.* (2nd ed.) Geneva: Georg, 1919. (1890)

————. Activité psychique et physiologie générale. *Rev. phil.,* 1891, *31,* 506–509.

————, & Claparède, E. Enquête sur l'audition colorée. *Arch. Sci. phys. nat.,* 1892, *28,* 505–508.

————. *Des phénomènes de synopsie.* Paris: Alcan, 1893.

————. De l'action du milieu sur l'idéation. *Année psychol.,* 1894, *1,* 180–190.

————. Illusions de poids. De l'influence de la perception visuelle des corps sur leur poids apparent. *Année psychol.,* 1894, *1,* 198–208.

————. Note sur les temps de lecture et d'omission. *Année psychol.,* 1895, *2,* 45–53.

————. *Observations sur quelques types de réaction simple.* Geneva: Eggimann, 1896.

————. Strange personifications. (1895) *Pop. Sci. Mon.,* 1897, *51,* 112–116.

————. *From India to the planet Mars: A study of a case of somnambulism.* Trans. by D. B. Vermilye. New York: Harper, 1900. (Reprinted 1963)

————. Le cas de Charles Bonnet; hallucinations visuelles chez un vieillard opéré de la cataracte. *Arch. Psychol.,* Geneva, 1901–1902, *1,* 1–23.

————. Nouvelles observations sur un cas de somnambulisme avec glossolalie. *Arch. Psychol.,* Geneva, 1901–1902, *1,* 101–255.

————. Les principes de la psychologie religieuse. *Arch. Psychol.,* Geneva, 1902–1903, *2,* 33–57.

————. Observations de psychologie religieuse. *Arch. Psychol.,* Geneva, 1902–1903, *2,* 327–366.

————. Note sur un songe prophétique réalisé. *Arch. Psychol.,* Geneva, 1904–1905, *4,* 58–72, 226–227.

————. Sur le panpsychisme comme explication des rapports de l'âme et du corps. *Arch. Psychol.,* Geneva, 1904–1905, *4,* 129–144.

Claparède, E., Fehr, H., & ————. *Enquête sur la méthode de travail des mathématiciens.* Geneva: Georg, 1908.

————. *The philosophy of William James.* Trans. by E. B. Holt & W. James, Jr. New York: Holt, 1917. (1911)

———. Une mystique moderne. *Arch. Psychol.,* Geneva, 1915, *15,* 1–224.

———. L'idée centrale de la Critique de la Raison pure. *Arch. Psychol.,* Geneva, 1921–1923, *18,* 126–134.

JOHN CARL FLUGEL
1884-1955
English Psychologist (16)

Flugel, J. C. *Men and their motives: Psychoanalytic studies.* New York: International Universities Press, 1947. (1934)   **C**

———. *Studies in feeling and desire.* London: Duckworth, 1955.   **C**

———, & McDougall, W. Further observations on the variation of the intensity of visual sensation with the duration of the stimulus. *Brit. J. Psychol.,* 1909–1910, *3,* 178–207.

———. The influence of attention in illusions of reversible perspective. *Brit. J. Psychol.,* 1912–1913, *5,* 357–397.

———. Some observations on local fatigue in illusions of reversible perspective. *Brit. J. Psychol.,* 1913–1914, *6,* 60–77.

———, & McDougall, W. Some observations on psychological contrast. *Brit. J. Psychol.,* 1914–1915, *7,* 349–385.

———. Freudian mechanisms as factors in moral development. *Brit. J. Psychol.,* 1915–1917, *8,* 477–509.

———. On local fatigue in the auditory system. *Brit. J. Psychol.,* 1920–1921, *11,* 105–134.

———. *The psycho-analytic study of the family.* London: Hogarth Press, 1921.

———. On the biological basis of sexual repression and its sociological significance. *Brit. J. med. Psychol.,* 1921, *1,* 225–280.

———. Quantitative study of feeling and emotion in everyday life. *Brit. J. Psychol.,* 1924–1925, *15,* 318–355. Reprinted in *Studies in feeling and desire, op. cit.,* pp. 155–194.

———. Sexual and social sentiments. *Brit. J. med. Psychol.,* 1927, *7,* 139–176. Reprinted in *Men and their motives, op. cit.,* pp. 44–101.

———. Practice, fatigue and oscillation: A study of work at high pressure. *Brit. J. Psychol. Monogr.,* 1928, *4*(13), 1–92.

———. Clothes symbolism and clothes ambivalence. *Int. J. Psycho-Anal.,* 1929, *10,* 205–217.

———. Psychoanalysis: Its status and promise. In C. Murchison (Ed.), *Psychologies of 1930.* Worcester, Mass.: Clark University Press, 1930, pp. 374–394.

———. *The psychology of clothes.* London: Hogarth Press, 1930. (Reprinted 1970)

———. *An introduction to psychoanalysis.* London: Gollancz, 1932.

———. *A hundred years of psychology 1833–1933. With an additional part: 1933–1963 by Dr. J. West.* New York: Basic Books, 1964. (1933)

———. Psychoanalysis and hormic psychology. *J. Pers.,* 1936–1937, *5,* 160–167.

———. Feeling and hormic theory. *J. Pers.,* 1939, *7,* 211–229.

———. Sublimation: Its nature and conditions. *Brit. J. educ. Psychol.,* 1942, *12,* 10–25, 97–107, 162–166.

———. *Man, morals and society: A psychoanalytical study.* New York: International Universities Press, 1945. (Reprinted 1970)

———. *Population, psychology and peace.* London: Watts, 1947.

———. L'appétit vient en mangeant. Some reflections on the self-sustaining tendencies. *Brit. J. Psychol.,* 1948, *38,* 171–190.

———. The death instinct, homeostasis and allied concepts: Some problems and implications. *Int. J. Psycho-Anal.,* 1953, *34, Suppl.,* 43–71.

———. Humor and laughter. In G. Lindzey (Ed.), *Handbook of social psychology.* Vol. 2. Cambridge: Addison-Wesley, 1954, pp. 709–734.
Drever, *Sourcebook*

AUGUST FOREL
1848-1931
Swiss Anatomist (16)

Forel, A. *Gesammelte hirnanatomische Abhandlungen mit einem Aufsatz über die Aufgaben der Neurobiologie.* Munich: Reinhardt. 1907.
C

———. *Briefe, Correspondance, 1864–1927.* Ed. by H. H. Walser. Bern: Huber, 1968. **B Bl C**

———. *Les fourmis de la Suisse.* (2nd ed.) La Chaux-de-Fonds: Imprimerie Coopérative, 1920. (1874)

———. Untersuchungen über die Haubenregion und ihre oberen Verknüpfungen im Gehirne des Menschen und einiger Säugethiere, mit Beiträgen zu den Methoden der Gehirnuntersuchung. *Arch. Psychiat. Nervenkr.,* 1877, 7, 393–495.

———. *Das Gedächtnis und seine Abnormitäten.* Zurich: Füssli, 1885.

———. *The sense of insects.* Trans. by M. Yearsley. London: Methuen, 1908. (1887)

———. Einige hirnanatomische Betrachtungen und Ergebnisse. *Arch. Psychiat. Nervenkr.,* 1887, *18,* 162–198.

———. Quelques remarques sur la suggestion. *Rev. hypno.,* 1889, *3,* 296–307.

———. *Hypnotism or suggestion and psychotherapy.* (5th ed.) Trans. by H. W. Armit. New York: Allied Publications, 1949. (1889)

———. *Der Hypnotismus oder die Suggestion und die Psychotherapie; ihre psychologische, psychophysiologische und medizinische Bedeutung mit Einschluss der Psychoanalyse, sowie der Telepathiefrage; ein Lehrbuch für Studierende sowie für weitere Kreise.* (12th ed.) Stuttgart: Enke, 1923. (1889)

———. Suggestionslehre und Wissenschaft. *Z. Hypno.,* 1892–1893, *1,* 1–10, 33–42, 73–83.

———. Suggestibilität und Geistesstörung. *Z. Hypno.,* 1892–1893, *1,* 336–339.

———. *Gehirn und Seele.* (13th ed.) Leipzig: Kröner, 1922. (1894)

———. Nochmals das Bewusstsein. *Z. Hypno.,* 1894–1895, *3,* 65–69.

———. Activité cérébrale et conscience. *Rev. phil.,* 1895, *40,* 468–475.

———. Un aperçu de psychologie comparée. *Année psychol.,* 1895, *2,* 18–44.

———. Der Unterschied zwischen der Suggestibilität und der Hysterie. Was ist Hysterie? *Z. Hypno.,* 1896–1897, *5,* 89–94.

———. Selbst-Biographie eines Falles von Mania acuta. *Arch. Psychiat. Nervenkr.,* 1901, *34,* 960–997.

———. *Hygiene der Nerven und des Geistes im gesunden und kranken Zustand.* (7th ed.) Stuttgart: Moritz, 1922. (1903)

———. *The sexual question: A scientific psychological, hygienic and sociological study.* (2nd ed.) Trans. by C. F. Marshall. Brooklyn, N.Y.: Physicians & Surgeons Book, 1922. (1905)

———. *The social world of the ants compared with that of man.* (2 vols.) Trans. by C. K. Ogden. New York: Boni, 1930. (1910)

———. Subjektive und induktive Selbstbeobachtung über psychische und nervöse Tätigkeit nach Hirnthrombose. *J. Psychol. Neurol.,* 1915, *21,* 417–440.

———. *August Forel. Die Medizin der Gegenwart in Selbstdarstellungen.* Vol. 6. Ed. by L. R. Grote. Leipzig: Meiner, 1927, pp. 53–87. **B Bl**

———. *Out of my life and work.* Trans. by B. Miall. New York: Norton, 1937. (1935) **B**
Clarke & O'Malley, *Brain*; Tinterow, *Hypnosis*

(FRANÇOIS MARIE) CHARLES FOURIER
1772-1837
French Philosopher (14)

Fourier, C. *Selections from the works of Fourier.* Trans. by Julia Franklin, & intro. by C. Gide. London: Swan Sonnenschein, 1901. (Reprinted 1970) **C**

———. *Oeuvres complètes de Charles Fourier.* (Ult. 12+ vols.) Intro. by S. D. Oleszkiewiez. Paris: Editions Anthropos, 1966– **C**

———. *The utopian vision of Charles Fourier, selected texts on work, love and passionate attraction.* Trans. & ed. by J. Beecher & R. Bienvenu. Boston: Beacon Press, 1971.   **C**

———. *Harmonian man: Selected writings of Charles Fourier.* Ed. by M. Poster. Garden City, N.J.: Doubleday, 1971.   **C**

———. *The social destiny of man: Or, theory of the four movements.* (2 vols.) Ed. by A. Brisbane. New York: Dewitt, 1857, (1808)   **C**

———. *Theory of social organization.* Intro. by A. Brisbane. New York: Somerby, 1876. (1822) (Reprinted 1970)

———. *Traité de l'association domestique-agricole.* (2 vols.) Paris: Bossange, 1822.

———. *Le nouveau monde industriel et sociétaire ; Ou, invention du procédé d'industrie attrayante et naturelle distribuée en séries passionnées.* Paris: Bossange, 1829. (Reprinted 1970)

———, *La fausse industrie morcelée, répugnante, mensongère, et l'antidote: L'industrie naturelle, combinée, attrayante, véridique donnant quadruple produit.* (2 vols.) Paris: Bossange, 1835–1836.

———. *The passions of the human soul, and their influence on society and civilization.* (2 vols.) Trans. by H. Doherty. New York: Kelley, 1968. (1851)

BENJAMIN FRANKLIN
1706-1790
American Philosopher (13)

Franklin, B. *The writings of Benjamin Franklin.* (10 vols.) Ed. by A. H. Smyth. New York: Macmillan, 1905–1907.   **B C**

———. *Educational views of Benjamin Franklin.* Ed. by T. Woody. New York: McGraw-Hill, 1931.   **C**

———. *The ingenious Dr. Franklin: Selected Scientific letters of Benjamin Franklin.* Ed. by N. G. Goodman. Philadelphia: University of Pennsylvania Press, 1931.   **B C**

———. *Benjamin Franklin: Representative selections with introduction, bibliography and notes.* Ed. by F. L. Mott & C. E. Jorgenson. New York: American Book, 1936.   **B C**

———. *Benjamin Franklin's autobiographical writings.* Ed. by C. Van Doren. New York: Viking Press, 1945.   **B C**

———. *The papers of Benjamin Franklin.* (Ult. 40 vols.) Ed. by L. W. Labaree *et al.* New Haven: Yale University Press, 1959–   **B C**

———. *Benjamin Franklin on education.* Ed. by J. H. Best. New York: Teachers College Press, 1962.   **C**

———. *A dissertation on liberty and necessity, pleasure and pain.* New York: Facsimile Text Society, 1930. (1725) Reprinted in I. W. Riley, *American Philosophy: The early schools.* New York: Dodd, Mead, 1907, pp. 571–580, & in J. Parton, *Life and times of Benjamin Franklin.* Vol. 1. New York: Mason, 1964, pp. 605–617.

———. *Benjamin Franklin's experiments: A new edition of Benjamin Franklin's "Experiments and observations on electricity."* Ed. by I. B. Cohen. Cambridge: Harvard University Press, 1941. (1751)

———. *Some account of the Pennsylvania Hospital.* Intro. by I. B. Cohen. Baltimore, Md.: Johns Hopkins Press, 1954. (1754)

———. *Report of Dr. Franklin and others charged by the king of France, with examination of the animal magnetism, as now practised in Paris.* Trans. by W. Godwin. London: Johnson, 1785. (1784)

———. *The autobiography.* Ed. by L. W. Labaree *et al.* New Haven: Yale University Press, 1964. (1789)   **B**

———. *Benjamin Franklin: A biography in his own words.* New York: Newsweek, 1972.   **B**

Brinton, *Age Reason* ; Grob & Beck, *American Ideas* ; Hunter & Macalpine, *Psychiatry* ; Kurtz, *American Thought* ; Mueller, *American Philosophy* ; Schwartz & Bishop, *Moments Discovery* ; Slotkin, *Anthropology* ; Tinterow, *Hypnosis* ; Ulich, *Educational Wisdom*

SHEPHERD IVORY FRANZ
1874-1933
American Psychologist (20)

Franz, S. I. After-images. *Psychol. Monogr.,* 1899, *3,* No. 12.

――――. On the method of estimating the force of voluntary contractions and on fatigue. *Amer. J. Physiol.,* 1900, *4,* 348–372.

――――. On the functions of the cerebrum: The frontal lobes in relation to the production and retention of simple sensory-motor habits. *Amer. J. Physiol.,* 1902, *8,* 1–22.

――――. Psychological opportunity in psychiatry. *J. Phil.,* 1906, *3,* 561–567.

――――. On the functions of the cerebrum: The frontal lobes. *Arch. Psychol.,* N.Y., 1907, No. 2.

White, W. A., & ――――. The use of association tests in determining mental contents. *Govt. Hosp. Insane Bull.,* 1909, *1,* 55–71.

――――. On sensations following nerve division. *J. comp. Neurol.,* 1909, *19,* 107–124, 215–236.

――――. On the association functions of the cerebrum. *J. Phil.,* 1910, *7,* 673–683.

――――, & Lafora, G. R. On the functions of the cerebrum: The occipital lobes. *Psychol. Monogr.,* 1911, *13,* No. 56.

――――. On the functions of the cerebrum: Concerning the lateral portions of the occipital lobes. *Amer. J. Physiol.,* 1911, *28,* 308–317.

――――. On the functions of the post-central cerebral convolutions. *J. comp. Neurol.,* 1911, *21,* 115–127.

――――. *Handbook of mental examination methods.* (2nd ed.) New York: Macmillan, 1919. (1912)

――――. New phrenology. *Science,* 1912, *35,* 321–328.

――――. The accuracy of localization of touch stimuli in different bodily segments. *Psychol. Rev.,* 1913, *20,* 107–128.

―――― (With assist. of J. D. Strout). I. Symptomatical differences associated with similar cerebral lesions in the insane. II. Variations in the distribution of the motor centers. *Psychol. Monogr.,* 1915, *19,* No. 81.

――――. The scientific productivity of American professional psychologists. *Psychol. Rev.,* 1917, *24,* 197–219.

――――, & Lashley, K. S. The retention of habits by the rat, after destruction of frontal portion of the cerebrum. *Psychobiology,* 1917, *1,* 3–18. Reprinted in K. S. Lashley, *The neuropsychology of Lashley.* Ed. by F. A. Beach *et al.* New York: McGraw-Hill, 1960, pp. 72–81.

Lashley, K. S., & ――――. The effect of cerebral destructions upon habit-formation and retention in the albino rat. *Psychobiology,* 1917, *1,* 71–139.

――――. Cerebral-mental relations. *Psychol. Rev.,* 1921, *28,* 81–95.

――――. Psychology and psychiatry. *Psychol. Rev.,* 1922, *29,* 241–249.

――――. Conceptions of cerebral functions. *Psychol. Rev.,* 1923, *30,* 438–446.

――――. *Nervous and mental re-education.* New York: Macmillan, 1924.

――――. The abnormal individual. In C. Murchison (Ed.), *The foundations of experimental psychology.* Worcester, Mass.: Clark University Press, 1929, pp. 809–831.

――――. Shepherd Ivory Franz. In C. Murchison (Ed.), *A history of psychology in autobiography.* Vol. 2. Worcester, Mass.: Clark University Press, 1932, pp. 89–113.　**B**

――――. *Persons, one and three: A study in multiple personalities.* New York: McGraw-Hill, 1933.

Dennis, *Psychology* ; Herrnstein & Boring, *Source Book*

FRANK NUGENT FREEMAN
1880-1961
American Psychologist (11)

Freeman, F. N. Experimental analysis of the writing movement. *Psychol. Monogr.,* 1914, *17,* No. 75, pp. 1–46.

———. *Experimental education*. Boston: Houghton Mifflin, 1916.

———. *The psychology of the common branches*. Boston: Houghton Mifflin, 1916.

———. Discussion: A critique of the Yerkes-Bridges-Hardwick comparison of the Binet-Simon and point scales. *Psychol. Rev.*, 1917, *24*, 484–490.

———. *How children learn*. Boston: Houghton Mifflin, 1917.

———. Intelligence and its measurement: A symposium. *J. educ. Psychol.*, 1921, *12*, 133–136.

———. The interpretation and application of the intelligence quotient. *J. educ. Psychol.*, 1921, *12*, 3–13.

Holzinger, K. J., & ———. The interpretation of Burt's regression equation. *J. educ. Psychol.*, 1925, *16*, 577–582.

Holzinger, K. J., & ———. Rejoinder on Burt's regression equation. *J. educ. Psychol*, 1926, *17*, 384–386.

———. *Mental tests*. (Rev. ed.) Boston: Houghton Mifflin, 1939. (1926)

———, Holzinger, K. J., & Mitchell, B. C. The influence of environment on the intelligence, school achievement, and conduct of foster children. *Yearb. Nat. Soc. Stud. Educ.*, 1928, *27*(1), 102–217.

———. The individual in school. II. Special abilities and their measurement. In C. Murchison (Ed.), *The foundations of experimental psychology*. Worcester, Mass.: Clark University Press, 1929, pp. 705–737.

———. The effect of environment on intelligence. *School & Soc.*, 1930, *31*, 623–632.

Newman, H. H., ———, & Holzinger, K. J. *Twins: A study of heredity and environment*. Chicago: University of Chicago Press, 1937.

———, & Flory, C. D. Growth in intellectual ability as measured by repeated tests. *Monogr. Soc. Res. Child Developmt.*, 1937, 2, No. 2.

———. Intellectual growth based on longitudinal studies. *Bull. Sch. Educ. Ind. Univer.*, 1938, *14*, No. 4, 33–34.

———. The meaning of intelligence. *Yearb. Nat. Soc. Stud. Educ.*, 1940, *39*(1), 11–20.

———. Cooperative research with adequate support. *J. educ. Res.*, 1941, *34*, 321–326.

———. The monopoly of objective tests. *High Points*, 1946, *28*, 7–15.

ELSE FRENKEL-BRUNSWIK
1908-1958
Austrian-American Psychologist (19)

Frenkel-Brunswik, Else. Atomismus und Mechanismus in der Assoziationspsychologie. *Z. Psychol.*, 1931, *123*, 193–258.

———, & Weisskopf, Edith. *Wunsch und Pflicht im Aufbau des menschlichen Lebens*. Vienna: Gerold, 1937.

———. Mechanisms of self-deception. *J. soc. Psychol.*, 1939, *10*, 409–420.

———. Psychoanalysis and personality research. *J. abnorm. soc. Psychol.*, 1940, *35*, 176–197.

———. Motivation and behavior. *Genet. Psychol. Monogr.*, 1942, *26*, 121–265.

———, & Sanford, R. N. Some personality factors in anti-Semitism. *J. Psychol.*, 1945, *20*, 271–291.

———. A study of prejudice in children. *Hum. Relat.*, 1948, *1*, 295–306.

———. Dynamic and cognitive categorization of qualitative material. I. General problems and the thematic apperception test. II. Interviews of the ethnically prejudiced. *J. Psychol.*, 1948, *25*, 253–260, 261–277.

———. Intolerance of ambiguity as an emotional and perceptual personality variable. *J. Pers.*, 1949, *18*, 108–143. Reprinted in J. S. Bruner & D. Krech (Eds.), *Perception and Personality: A symposium*. Durham, N.C.: Duke University Press, 1949, pp. 108–143 ; & in H. Brand (Ed.), *The study of personality: A book of readings*, New York: Wiley, 1954, pp. 509–538.

———. Personality theory and perception. In R. R. Blake & G. V. Ramsey (Eds.), *Perception: An approach to personality*. New York: Ronald Press, 1951, pp. 356–419.

————. Interaction of psychological and sociological factors in political behavior. *Amer. Polit. Sci. Rev.*, 1952, *46*, 44–65.

————, & Havel, Joan. Prejudice in the interviews of children. I. Attitudes toward minority groups. *J. genet. Psychol.*, 1953, *82*, 91–136.

————. Social research and the problem of values: A reply. *J. abnorm. soc. Psychol.*, 1954, *49*, 466–471.

————. Environmental controls and the impoverishment of thought. In C. J. Friedrich (Ed.), *Totalitarianism*. Cambridge: Harvard University Press, 1954, pp. 171–202.

————. Psychoanalysis and the unity of science. *Daedalus*, 1954, *80*, 271–350.

————. Meaning of psychoanalytic concepts and confirmation of psychoanalytic theories. *Sci. Mon.*, N.Y., 1954, *79*, 293–300.

————. Perspectives in psychoanalytic theory. In H. P. David & H. v. Bracken (Eds.), *Perspectives in personality theory*. New York: Basic Books, 1957, pp. 159–182.

Beardslee, *Perception*

SIGMUND FREUD
1856-1939
Austrian Psychoanalyst (27)

Freud, S. *Collected papers*. (5 vols.) Ed. by E. Jones & J. Strachey. New York: Basic Books, 1959. (1924–1950)   **C**

————. *The origins of psychoanalysis: Letters to Wilhelm Fliess, drafts and notes: 1887–1902.* Ed. by Marie Bonaparte, Anna Freud, & E. Kris. New York: Basic Books, 1954. (1950)   **B C**

————. *The standard edition of the complete psychological works of Sigmund Freud.* (23 vols.) Ed. & trans. by J. Strachey *et al.* London: Hogarth Press, 1953–1966.   **B Bl C**

————. *Letters of Sigmund Freud.* Ed. by E. L. Freud, & trans. by Tania & J. Stern. New York: Basic Books, 1960.   **B C**

————. *Psychoanalysis and faith: The letters of Sigmund Freud and Oskar Pfister.* Ed. by H. Meng & E. L. Freud. New York: Basic Books, 1963.   **B C**

————, & Abraham, K. *A psychoanalytic dialogue: The letters of Sigmund Freud and Karl Abraham, 1907–1926.* Ed. by Hilda C. Abraham & E. L. Freud. New York: Basic Books, 1966. (1965)   **B C**

————. *Brautbriefe. Briefe an Martha Bernays aus den Jahren 1882–1886.* Ed. & intro. by E. L. Freud. Frankfurt: Fischer, 1968.   **B C**

————, & Zweig, A. *The letters of Sigmund Freud and Arnold Zweig.* Ed. by E. L. Freud, & trans. by Prof. & Mrs. W. D. Robson-Scott. New York: Harcourt, Brace, & World, 1970.   **C**

————. Observations of a severe case of hemi-anaesthesia in a hysterical male. (1886) Reprinted in *Complete works*, Vol. 1, *op. cit.*, pp. 23–31.

————. *On aphasia: A critical study.* Trans. by E. Stengel. New York: International Universities Press, 1953. (1891)

————. A case of successful treatment by hypnotism with some remarks on the origin of hysterical symptoms through "counterwill." (1892–1893) Reprinted in *Complete works*, Vol. 1, *op. cit.*, pp. 115–128, & in *Collected papers*, Vol. 5, *op. cit.*, pp. 33–46.

Breuer, J., & ————. On the psychical mechanism of hysterical phenomena. (1893) Reprinted in *Collected papers*, Vol. 3, *op. cit.*, pp. 24–41.

Breuer, J., & ————. *Studies on hysteria.* Trans. by J. Strachey. New York: Basic Books, 1957. (1893, 1895) Reprinted in *Complete works*, Vol. 2, *op. cit.*, pp. vii–xxx.

————. The neuro-psychoses of defence. (1894) Reprinted in *Complete works*, Vol. 3, *op. cit.*, pp. 41–61.

————. *The interpretation of dreams.* (8th ed.) Trans. by J. Strachey. New York: Basic Books, 1955. (1900) Also in *Complete works*, Vols. 4, 5, *op. cit.*

————. *The psychopathology of everyday life: Forgetting, slips of the tongue, bungled actions, superstitions and errors.* (11th ed.) (1904) Reprinted in *Complete works*, Vol. 6, *op. cit.*

———. Freud's psycho-analytic procedure. (1904) Reprinted in *Complete works,* Vol. 7, *op. cit.,* pp. 247–254, & in *Collected papers,* Vol. 1, *op. cit.,* pp. 264–271.

———. *Jokes and their relation to the unconscious.* Trans. & ed. by J. Strachey. New York: Norton, 1963. (1905) Reprinted in *Complete works,* Vol. 8, *op. cit.*

———. *Three essays on the theory of sexuality.* (4th ed.) Ed. by J. Strachey. New York: Basic Books, 1962. (1905) Reprinted in *Complete works,* Vol. 7, *op. cit.,* pp. 123–243.

———. Fragment of an analysis of a case of hysteria. (1905) Reprinted in *Complete works,* Vol. 7, *op. cit.,* pp. 1–122, & in *Collected papers,* Vol. 3, *op. cit.,* pp. 13–146.

———. Delusions and dreams in Jensen's *Gradiva.* (1907) Reprinted in *Complete works,* Vol. 9, *op. cit.,* pp. 7–95.

———. On the sexual theories of children. (1908) Reprinted in *Complete works,* Vol. 9, *op. cit.,* pp. 209–226.

———. Character and anal erotism. (1908) Reprinted in *Complete works,* Vol. 9, *op. cit.,* pp. 169–175.

———. Analysis of a phobia in a five-year-old boy. (1909) Reprinted in *Complete works,* Vol. 10, *op. cit.,* pp. 1–147, & in *Collected papers,* Vol. 3, *op. cit.,* pp. 149–287.

———. The origin and development of psycho-analysis. *Amer. J. Psychol.,* 1910, *21,* 181–218. Strachey trans. reprinted in *Complete works,* Vol. 11, *op. cit.,* pp. 8–55. **B**

———. Psycho-analytic notes on an autobiographical account of a case of paranoia (dementia paranoides). (1911) Reprinted in *Complete works,* Vol. 12, *op. cit.,* pp. 1–82, & in *Collected papers,* Vol. 3, *op. cit.,* pp. 387–466.

———. Formulations on the two principles of mental functioning. (1911) Reprinted in *Complete works,* Vol. 12, *op. cit.,* pp. 213–226, & in *Collected papers,* Vol. 4, *op. cit.,* pp. 13–21.

———. A note on the unconscious in psychoanalysis. (1912) Reprinted in *Complete works,* Vol. 12, *op. cit.,* pp. 255–266, & in *Collected papers,* Vol. 4, *op. cit.,* pp. 22–29.

———. The dynamics of transference. (1912) Reprinted in *Complete works,* Vol. 12, *op. cit.,* pp. 97–108, & in *Collected papers,* Vol. 2, *op. cit.,* pp. 312–322.

———. *Totem and taboo.* Trans. by J. Strachey. London: Routledge & Kegan Paul, 1950. (1913) Reprinted in *Complete works,* Vol. 13, *op. cit.,* pp. vii–162.

———. The claims of psycho-analysis to scientific interest. (1913) Reprinted in *Complete works,* Vol. 13, *op. cit.,* pp. 163–190.

———. On beginning the treatment (further recommendations on the technique of psychoanalysis). I. (1913) Reprinted in *Complete works,* Vol. 12, *op. cit.,* pp. 121–144, & in *Collected papers,* Vol. 1, *op. cit.,* pp. 342–365.

———. *On the history of the psycho-analytic movement.* (Rev. ed.) Ed. by J. Strachey, & trans. by Joan Rivière. New York: Norton, 1966. (1914) Reprinted in *Complete works,* Vol. 14, *op. cit.,* pp. 1–66, & in *Collected papers,* Vol. 1, *op. cit.,* pp. 287–359.

———. On narcissism: An introduction. (1914) Reprinted in *Complete works,* Vol. 14, *op. cit.,* pp. 67–102, & in *Collected papers,* Vol. 4, *op. cit,.* pp. 30–59.

——— Remembering, repeating and working-through (further recommendations on the technique of psycho-analysis). II. (1914) Reprinted in *Complete works,* Vol. 12, *op. cit.,* pp. 145–156, & in *Collected papers,* Vol. 2, *op. cit.,* pp. 366–376.

———. Instincts and their vicissitudes. (1915) Reprinted in *Complete works,* Vol. 14, *op. cit.,* pp. 109–140, & in *Collected papers,* Vol. 4, *op. cit.,* pp. 69–83.

———. Observations on transference-love (further recommendations on the technique of psycho-analysis). III. (1915) Reprinted in *Complete works,* Vol. 12, *op. cit.,* pp. 156–173, & in *Collected papers,* Vol. 2, *op. cit.,* pp. 377–391.

———. Repression. (1915) Reprinted in *Complete works,* Vol. 14, *op. cit.,* pp. 141–158, & in *Collected papers,* Vol. 4, *op. cit.,* pp. 84–97.

———. The unconscious. (1915) Reprinted in *Complete works,* Vol. 14, *op. cit.,* pp. 159–215, & in *Collected papers,* Vol. 4, *op. cit.,* pp. 98–136.

———. *The complete introductory lectures on psycho-analysis.* Trans. & ed. by J. Strachey. London: Allen & Unwin, 1971. (1916–1917, 1933) Reprinted in *Complete works,* Vols. 15, 16, 22, *op. cit.*

———. Mourning and melancholia. (1917) Reprinted in *Complete works,* Vol. 14, *op. cit.,* pp. 237–260, & in *Collected papers,* Vol. 4, *op. cit.,* pp. 152–170.

———. From the history of an infantile neurosis. (1918) Reprinted in *Complete works,* Vol. 17, *op. cit.,* pp. 1–123, & in *Collected papers,* Vol. 3, *op. cit.,* pp. 473–605.

———. "A child is being beaten": A contribution to the study of the origin of sexual perversion. (1919) Reprinted in *Complete works,* Vol. 17, *op. cit.,* pp. 175–204, & in *Collected papers,* Vol. 2, *op. cit.,* pp. 172–201.

———. *Beyond the pleasure principle.* Trans. by J. Strachey. London: Hogarth Press, 1950. (1920) Reprinted in *Complete works,* Vol. 18, *op. cit.,* pp. 1–64.

———. *Group psychology and the analysis of the ego.* Trans. by J. Strachey. London: Hogarth Press, 1948. (1921) Reprinted in *Complete works,* Vol. 18, *op. cit.,* pp. 65–143.

———. *The ego and the id.* London: Hogarth Press, 1947. (1923) Reprinted in *Complete works,* Vol. 19, *op. cit.,* pp. 1–66.

———. *An autobiographical study.* (2nd ed.) Trans. by J. Strachey. London: Hogarth Press, 1935. (1925) Reprinted in *Complete works,* Vol. 20, *op. cit.,* pp. 1–74. **B**

———. The resistances to psycho-analysis. (1925) Reprinted in *Complete works,* Vol. 19, *op. cit.,* pp. 211–224, & in *Collected papers,* Vol. 5, *op. cit.,* pp. 163–174.

———. A note upon the "mystic writing-pad." (1925) Reprinted in *Complete works,* Vol. 19, *op. cit.,* pp. 225–232, & in *Collected papers,* Vol. 5, *op. cit.,* pp. 175–180.

———. Some physical consequences of the anatomical distinction between the sexes. (1925) Reprinted in *Complete works,* Vol. 19, *op. cit.,* pp. 241–258, & in *Collected papers,* Vol. 5, *op. cit.,* pp. 186–197.

———. Inhibitions, symptoms and anxiety. (1926) Reprinted in *Complete works,* Vol. 20, *op. cit.,* pp. 75–178.

———. The question of lay analysis: Conversations with an impartial person. (1926) Reprinted in *Complete works,* Vol. 20, *op. cit.,* pp. 177–258.

———. *The future of an illusion.* Trans. by W. D. Robson-Scott. London: Hogarth Press, 1928. (1927) Reprinted in *Complete works,* Vol. 21, *op. cit.,* pp. 1–56.

———. *Civilization and its discontents.* Trans. by Joan Rivière. London: Hogarth Press, 1930. Reprinted in *Complete works,* Vol. 21, *op. cit.,* pp. 57–145.

———. Analysis terminable and interminable. (1937) Reprinted in *Complete works,* Vol. 23, *op. cit.,* pp. 209–253, & in *Collected papers,* Vol. 5, *op. cit.,* pp. 316–357.

———. *Moses and monotheism: Three essays.* Trans. by Katherine Jones. New York: Knopf, 1939. (1939) Reprinted in *Complete works,* Vol. 23, *op. cit.,* pp. 1–56.

———. *An outline of psychoanalysis.* New York: Norton, 1949. (1940) Reprinted in *Complete works,* Vol. 23, *op. cit.,* pp. 141–207.

———. The project for a scientific psychology. (1950) In *The origins of psychoanalysis, op. cit.,* pp. 347–445. Reprinted in *Complete works,* Vol. 1, *op. cit.,* pp. 281–397.

———. Report on my studies in Paris and Berlin. (1956) Reprinted in *Complete works,* Vol. 1, *op. cit.,* pp. 1–15. **B**

———, & Bullitt, W. C. *Thomas Woodrow Wilson: A psychoanalytic psychological study.* Boston: Houghton Mifflin, 1966.

Beck & Molish, *Reflexes*; Bindra & Stewart, *Motivation*; Dennis, *Readings Developmental*; Drever, *Sourcebook*; Goshen, *Documentary*; Gruber, *Creative*

Thinking; Hutchins, *Great Books*; Kessen, *Child*; Krech, *Sexual Revolution*; Lawrence & O'Connors, *Phenomenology*; Lindzey & Hall, *Personality*; Matson, *Being*; Nash, *Models*; Parsons, *Society*; Perez, *Readings*; Rabkin & Carr, *Abnormal*; Rapaport, *Thought*; Russell, *Motivation*; Sahakian, *Personality*; Sahakian, *Psychology*; Shipley, *Classics*; Tinterow, *Hypnosis*; Vetter, *Personality*

MAX VON FREY
1852-1932
German Physiologist (23)

Frey, M. v. *Die Gefühle und ihr Verhältnis zu den Empfindungen.* Leipzig: Georg, 1894.

———. Beiträge zur Physiologie des Schmerzsinnes. *Ber. sächs. Ges. Wiss. Leipzig,* Math.-phys. Kl., 1894, *46,* 185–196, 283–296; 1895, *47,* 166–184.

———. Beiträge zur Sinnesphysiologie der Haut. *Z. Biol.,* 1895, *47,* 166–184, & *Ber. sächs. Ges. Wiss. Leipzig,* Math.-phys. Kl., 1897, *49,* 462–468.

———. Untersuchungen über die Sinnesfunktionen der menschlichen Haut. Vol. 1. Druckempfindung und Schmerz. *Abh. sächs. Ges. Wiss. Leipzig,* Math.-phys. Kl., 1897, *23,* 169–266.

———. Ueber den Ortsinn der Haut. *Ber. Würzb. Phys. Med.,* 1899, 97–103.

———, & Kiesow, F. Ueber die Funktion der Tastkörperchen. *Z. Psychol.,* 1899, *20,* 126–163.

———, & Metzner, R. Die Raumschwelle der Haut bei Successivreizung. *Z. Psychol.,* 1902, *29,* 161–182.

———. *Vorlesungen über Physiologie.* (3rd ed.) Berlin: Springer-Verlag, 1920. (1904)

———. The distribution of afferent nerves in the skin. *J. Amer. med. Ass.,* 1906, *47,* 645–648.

———. Allgemeine Physiologie der quergestreiften Muskeln. In W. Nagel (Ed.), *Handbuch der Physiologie des Menschen.* Vol. 4. Brunswick: Vieweg, 1909, pp. 427–543.

———. Physiologie der Sinnesorgane der menschlichen Haut. I. Temperatursinn. *Erg. Physiol.,* 1910, *9,* 351–369.

———. Der laugige Geruch. *Arch. ges. Physiol.,* 1910, *136,* 275–281.

———. Die Wirkung gleichzeitiger Druckempfindungen aufeinander. *Z. Biol.,* 1911, *56,* 574–598.

———. Physiologie der Sinnesorgane der menschlichen Haut. II. Drucksinn. *Erg. Physiol.,* 1913, *13,* 96–124.

———, & Pauli, R. Die Stärke und Deutlichkeit einer Druckempfindung unter der Wirkung eines begleitenden Reizes. *Z. Biol.,* 1913, *50,* 497–516.

———. Studien über den Kraftsinn. *Z. Biol.,* 1914, *63,* 129–154.

———. Beobachtungen an Hautflächen mit geschädigten Innervation. *Z. Biol.,* 1914, *63,* 335–376.

———. Neue Untersuchungen über die Sinnesleistungen der menschlichen Haut. *Fortschr. Psychol.,* 1914, *2,* 207–225.

———, & Goldman, A. Der zeitliche Verlauf der Einstellung bei den Druckempfindungen. *Z. Biol.,* 1915, *65,* 183–202.

———. Die Vergleichung von Gewichten mit Hilfe des Kraftsinns. *Z. Biol.,* 1915, *65,* 203–224.

———. Physiologische Versuche über das Vibrationsgefühl. *Z. Biol.,* 1915, *65,* 417–427.

———. Die physiologischen und psychologischen Grundlagen der Gewichtsschätzung. *Arch. Anthrop.,* 1915, *13,* 342–347.

———, & Meyer, O. B. Versuche über die Wahrnehmung geführter Bewegungen. *Z. Biol.,* 1918, *68,* 301–338.

———. Weitere Beobachtungen über die Wahrnehmung von Bewegungen nach Gelenkresektion. *Z. Biol.,* 1919, *69,* 322–330.

———. Ueber die zur eben merklichen Erregung des Drucksinns erforderlichen Energiemengen. *Z. Biol.,* 1919, *70,* 133–147.

—, & Webels, W. Ueber die der Hornhaut und Bindehaut des Auges eigentümlichen Empfindungsqualitäten. *Z. Biol.,* 1922, *74,* 173–190.

—. Verspätete Schmerzempfindungen. *Z. ges. Neurol. Psychiat.,* 1922, *79,* 324–333.

—. Versuche über schmerzerregende Reize. *Z. Biol.,* 1922, *76,* 1–24.

—. Ueber Wandlungen der Empfindungen bei formal verschiedener Reizung einer Art von Sinnesnerven. *Psychol. Forsch.,* 1923, *3,* 209–218. Abstracted & trans. in W. D. Ellis (Ed.), *A source book of Gestalt psychology.* London: Routledge & Kegan Paul, 1938, pp. 193–195.

—. Ueber die Beziehungen zwischen Kitzel-, Berührungs- und Druckempfindung. *Skand. Arch. Physiol.,* 1923, *43,* 93–100.

—, Rein, H., & Strughold, H. Beiträge zur Frage tiefen Drucksinns. *Z. Biol.,* 1925, *82,* 359–377.

—, & Goldman, A. Die Tangoreceptoren des Menschen. In A. Bethe, G. v. Bergmann, G. Emleden, & A. Ellingen (Eds.), *Handbuch der normalen und pathologischen Physiologie.* Vol. II, Part 1. Berlin: Springer-Verlag, 1926, pp. 94–130.

—, & Strughold, H. Weitere Untersuchungen über das Verhalten von Hornhaut und Bindehaut des menschlichen Auges gegen Berührungsreize. *Z. Biol.,* 1926, *84,* 321–334.

—. Fortgesetzte Untersuchungen über die sinnesphysiologischen Grundlagen der Bewegungswahrnehmungen. *Z. ges. Neurol. Psychiat.,* 1926, *104,* 821–832.

—. Mechanism of temperature sensations. *Amer. J. Physiol.,* 1930, *94,* 505–506.

Herrnstein & Boring, *Source Book*

GUSTAV FRITSCH
1838-1927
German Anatomist (18)

Fritsch, G., & Hitzig, E. Ueber die elektrische Erregbarkeit des Grosshirns. *Arch. Anat. Physiol.,* 1870, 300–332. Reprinted in E. Hit-

zig, *Untersuchungen über das Gehirn*: *Abhandlungen physiologischen und pathologischen Inhalts.* Berlin: Hirschwald, 1874, pp. 1–31 ; in E. Hitzig, *Physiologische und klinische Untersuchungen über das Gehirn: Gesammelte Abhandlungen.* (2nd ed.) Berlin: Hirschwald, 1904, pp. 8–35 ; trans. by G. v. Bonin in *Some papers on the cerebral cortex,* Springfield, Ill.: Thomas, 1960, pp. 73–96 ; & trans. in R. H. Wilkins (Ed.), *Neurosurgical classics.* New York: Johnson Reprint, 1965, pp. 16–27.

—. Vergleichende Untersuchungen menschlicher Augen. *Sitzber. preuss. Akad. Wiss.,* 1900, 636–653.

—. Vergleichende Untersuchungen der Fovea centralis des Menschen. *Anat. Anz.,* 1907, *30,* 462–464, *31,* 415–416.

—. Ueber den Bau und die Bedeutung der histologischen Elemente in der Netzhaut des Auges besonders am Ort des deutlichsten Sehens, bei verschiedenen Menschenrassen. *Anat. Anz.,* 1908, *32* (Suppl.), 141–145.

—. *Ueber Bau und Bedeutung der Area centralis des Menschen.* Berlin: Reimer, 1908.

—. Beiträge zur Histologie des Auges vor Pteropus. *Z. wiss. Zool.,* 1911, *98,* 288–296.

—. Der Ort des deutlichen Sehens in der Netzhaut der Vögel. *Arch. mikrosk. Anat.* 1911, *78,* 245–270.

—. Der Ort des deutlichen Sehens in der Netzhaut der Vögel. Nachtrag. *Z. wiss. Zool.* 1914, *110,* 76–86.

Clarke & O'Malley, *Brain* ; Herrnstein & Boring, *Source Book* ; Count, *Race*

FRIEDRICH FROBEL
1782-1852
German Educator (13)

Fröbel, F. *Friedrich Froebel's pedagogics of the kindergarten, or his ideas concerning the play and playthings.* Trans. by Josephine Jarvis. New York: Appleton, 1904. (1861) (Reprinted 1970

—. *Education by development: The second part of the pedagogics of the kindergarten*

Trans. by Josephine Jarvis. New York: Appleton, 1899. (1861) (Reprinted 1970)   **C**

———. *Gesammelte pädagogische Schriften*. (3 vols.) Ed. by W. Lange. Berlin: Enslin, 1862–1874.   **C**

———. *Froebel letters*. Ed. by A. H. Heinemann. Boston: Lee & Shepard, 1893. (Reprinted 1970)   **B C**

———. *The student's Froebel*. (2 parts) Ed. & trans. by W. H. Herford. London: Pitman, 1911–1915.   **C**

———. *Froebel's chief writings on education*. Ed. & trans. by S. S. F. Fletcher & J. Welton. New York: Longmans, Green, 1912.   **Bl C**

———. *Ausgewählte Schriften*. Vol. 1. *Kleine Schriften und Briefe*. Vol. 2. *Menschenerziehung*. Ed. by Erika Hoffmann. Godesberg: Küpper, 1951.   **Bl C**

———. *Friedrich Froebel: A selection from his writings*. Ed. by Irene M. Lilley. Cambridge: Cambridge University Press, 1967.   **C**

———. *Education of man*. (Abridged) Ed. & trans. by W. N. Hailmann. New York: Appleton, 1912. (1826) Excerpts reprinted in *Friedrich Froebel: A selection from his writings, op. cit.*, pp. 48–67, 81–92, 121–159, & condensed version in *Froebel's chief writings on education, op. cit.*, pp. 31–169.

———. *Autobiography of Friedrich Froebel*. Ed., trans., & annotated by Emilie Michaelis & H. K. Moore. Syracuse, N.Y.: Bardeen, 1889. (1828) (Reprinted 1971)   **B Bl**

———. *Brief an die Frauen in Keilhau*. Ed. by B. Gumlich. Weimar: Böhlau, 1935. (1831) Excerpts trans. in *Friedrich Froebel: A selection from his writings, op. cit.*, pp. 44–67.

Ulich, *Educational Wisdom*

JOSEPH FROBES
1866-1947
German-Dutch Psychologist (16)

Fröbes, J. Ein Beitrag über die sogenannten Vergleichungen übermerklicher Empfindungsunterschiede. *Z. Psychol.*, 1904, *36*, 241–268, 344–380.

———. *Psychologia speculativa in usum scholarum*. (2nd ed.) (2 vols.) Freiburg: Herder, 1927. (1906, 1911)

———. *Lehrbuch der experimentellen Psychologie*. (3rd ed.) (2 vols.) Freiburg: Herder, 1935, 1929. (1915)

———. Aus der Vorgeschichte der psychologischen Optik. *Z. Psychol.*, 1920, *85*, 1–36.

———. Dynamische Psychologie. *Scholastik*, 1928, *3*, 219–238.

———. Die Bedeutung des Lehrbuches in der Psychologie und eine Kritik darüber. *Z. Psychol.*, 1930, *116*, 368–380.

———. Eine neue Erklärung der Willensfreiheit. *Scholastik*, 1932, *7*, 67–81.

———. Zur Frage der höheren Gefühle, eine Erwiderung. *Scholastik*, 1932, *7*, 561–563.

———. *Brevior cursus psychologiae speculativae*. Paris: Lethielleux, 1933.

———. Naturwissenschaftliche und geisteswissenschaftliche Psychologie. *Scholastik*, 1934, *9*, 58–79.

———. Joseph Fröbes. In C. Murchison (Ed.), *A history of psychology in autobiography*. Vol. 3. Worcester, Mass.: Clark University Press, 1936, pp. 121–152.   **B**

———. *Tractatus logicae formalis*. Rome: Universitas Gregoriana, 1940.

———. Wesen und Wert der Graphologie (Ein Ueberblick). *Scholastik.*, 1940, *15*, 76–87.

———. *Compendio de psicologia experimental*. (2nd ed.) Madrid: Rivadeneyra, 1948. (1941)

———. Typen des Charakters. *Scholastik*, 1949, *20–24*, 518–543.

FRIEDA FROMM-REICHMANN
1889-1957
German-American Psychoanalyst (12)

Fromm-Reichmann, Frieda. *Psychoanalysis and psychotherapy: Selected papers of Frieda Fromm-Reichmann*. Ed. by D. M. Bullard. Chicago: University of Chicago Press, 1959. **C**

—. Contributions to the psychogenesis of migraine. *Psychoanal. Rev.,* 1937, *24,* 26–33. Reprinted in *Psychoanalysis and psychotherapy, op. cit.,* pp. 283–289.

—. Transference problems in schizophrenics. *Psychoanal. Quart.,* 1939, *8*(4), 412–426. Reprinted in S. S. Tomkins (Ed.), *Contemporary psychopathology: A source book.* Cambridge: Harvard University Press, 1947, pp. 371–380, & in *Psychoanalysis and psychotherapy, op. cit.,* pp. 117–128.

—. Recent advances in psychoanalytic therapy. *Psychiatry,* 1941, *4,* 161–164. Reprinted in *Psychoanalysis and psychotherapy, op. cit.,* pp. 49–54.

—. Remarks on the philosophy of mental disorder. *Psychiatry,* 1946, *9,* 293–308. Reprinted in *Psychoanalysis and psychotherapy, op. cit.,* pp. 3–24.

—. Intensive psychotherapy of manic-depressives. *Grenzgeb. Neurol.,* 1949, *9,* 158–165. Reprinted in *Psychoanalysis and psychotherapy, op. cit.,* pp. 221–226.

—. *Principles of intensive psychotherapy.* Chicago: University of Chicago Press, 1950.

—. Some aspects of psychoanalytic psychotherapy with schizophrenics. In *Psychotherapy with schizophrenics.* New York: International Universities Press, 1952, pp. 89–111. Reprinted in *Psychoanalysis and psychotherapy, op. cit.,* pp. 176–193.

—. Psychotherapy of schizophrenia. *Amer. J. Psychiat.,* 1954, *111,* 410–419. Reprinted in *Psychoanalysis and psychotherapy, op. cit.,* pp. 194–209.

—, et al. An intensive study of twelve cases of manic-depressive psychosis. *Psychiatry,* 1954, *17,* 103–137. Reprinted in *Psychoanalysis and psychotherapy, op. cit.,* pp. 227–276.

—. Psychoanalytic and general dynamic conceptions of theory and of therapy: Differences and similarities. *J. Amer. Psychoanal. Ass.,* 1954, *2,* 711–721. Reprinted in *Psychoanalysis and psychotherapy, op. cit.,* pp. 105–113.

—. Psychiatric aspects of anxiety. In Clara Thompson, M. Mazer, & E. Witenberg (Eds.),

An outline of psychoanalysis. New York: Random House, 1955, pp. 113–133. Reprinted in *Psychoanalysis and psychotherapy, op. cit.,* pp. 306–324, & in L. Y. Rabkin & J. E. Carr (Eds.), *Sourcebook in abnormal psychology.* Boston: Houghton Mifflin, 1967, pp. 131–139.

—. Notes on the history and philosophy of psychotherapy. In Frieda Fromm-Reichmann & J. L. Moreno (Eds.), *Progress in psychotherapy.* Vol. 1. New York: Grune & Stratton, 1956, pp. 1–23. Reprinted in *Psychoanalysis and psychotherapy, op. cit.,* pp. 25–46.

—. Basic problems in the psychotherapy of schizophrenia. *Psychiatry,* 1958, *21,* 1–6. Reprinted in *Psychoanalysis and psychotherapy, op. cit.,* pp. 210–217.

—. Loneliness. *Psychiatry,* 1959, *22,* 1–15. Reprinted in part in *Psychoanalysis and psychotherapy, op. cit.,* pp. 325–336.

Rabkin & Carr, *Abnormal*

GEORGE STUART FULLERTON
1859-1925
American Psychologist (14)

Fullerton, G. S. *On sameness and identity.* Philadelphia: University of Pennsylvania Press, 1890.

—, & Cattell, J. McK. *On the perception of small differences with special reference to the extent, force and time of movement.* Philadelphia: University of Pennsylvania Press, 1892. Reprinted in A. T. Poffenberger (Ed.), *James McKeen Cattell.* Vol. 1. Lancaster, Pa.: Science Press, 1947, pp. 142–251.

—. The psychological standpoint. *Psychol. Rev.,* 1894, *1,* 113–133.

—. Psychology and physiology. *Psychol. Rev.,* 1895, *3,* 1–20.

—. The "knower" in psychology. *Psychol. Rev.,* 1897, *4,* 1–26.

—. The criterion of sensation. *Psychol. Rev.,* 1900, *7,* 159–171.

—. The world as mechanism. *Psychol. Rev.,* 1902, *9,* 1–26.

———. The atomic self. *Psychol. Rev.,* 1902, *9,* 231–253.

———. The influence of Darwin on the mental and moral sciences. *Proc. Amer. phil. Soc.,* 1909, *48,* 25–38.

JOHN FARQUHAR FULTON
1899-1960
American Physiologist (14)

Fulton, J. F. Lapicque's investigations on the chronaxie of excitable tissues. *Nature,* 1924, *113,* 427–430.

———. The influence of initial tension upon the magnitude and duration of the mechanical response in skeletal muscle. *Proc. Roy. Soc.,* 1924, *96B,* 475–490.

———. The influence of tension upon the electrical responses of muscle to repetitive stimuli. *Proc. Roy. Soc.,* 1925, *97B,* 406–423.

———. Some observations upon the electrical responses and shape of the isometric twitch of skeletal muscle (intact). *Proc. Roy. Soc.,* 1925, *97B,* 424–436.

———. The relation between the durations of the isometric twitch and of the after-action of tetanus. *Proc. Roy. Soc.,* 1925, *97B,* 431–443.

———, & Liddell, E. G. T. Observations on ipsilateral contraction and "inhibitory" rhythm. *Proc. Roy. Soc.,* 1925, *98B,* 214–227.

———. Fatigue and plurisegmental innervation of individual muscle fibres. *Proc. Roy. Soc.,* 1925, *98B,* 493–505.

———. The latent period of skeletal muscle. *Quart. J. exp. Physiol.,* 1925, *15,* 349–366.

———. On the summation of contractions in skeletal muscle. *Amer. J. Physiol.,* 1925, *75,* 211–234.

———. The influence of shortening on the size of the action current and the duration of the mechanical response of skeletal muscle. *Amer. J. Physiol.,* 1925, *75,* 235–260.

———. The inseparability of mechanical and electrical responses in skeletal muscle. *Amer. J. Physiol.,* 1925, *75,* 261–266.

———. *Muscular contraction and the reflex control of movement.* Baltimore, Md.: Williams & Wilkins, 1926.

———, & Pi-Suñer, J. A note concerning the probable function of various afferent end-organs in skeletal muscle. *Amer. J. Physiol.,* 1928, *83,* 554–562.

———. *The history of the physiology of muscle.* Baltimore, Md.: Williams & Wilkins, 1930.

———, & Wilson, L. G. (Eds.), *Selected readings in the history of physiology.* (2nd ed.) Springfield, Ill.: Thomas, 1966. (1930)

———. A note on the history of the word physiology. *Yale J. Biol. Med.,* 1930–1931, *3,* 59–62.

———. *Physiology.* New York: Hoeber, 1931.

———. A bibliography of the Honourable Robert Boyle. *Proc. Oxford Bibliog. Soc.,* 1931, *3,* 1–160.

———. The rise of the experimental method: Bacon and the Royal Society of London. *Yale J. Biol. Med.,* 1930–1931, *3,* 299–320.

———. The functional activity of single units in the central nervous system. *Science,* 1931, *73,* 685–692.

———, & Keller, A. D. *The sign of Babinski: A study of the evolution of cortical dominance in primates.* Springfield, Ill.: Thomas, 1932.

———. A note on the definition of the "motor" and "premotor" eras. *Brain,* 1935, *58,* 311–316.

———, & Jacobsen, C. F. The functions of the frontal lobes of the brain, a comparative study of apes, monkeys and man. *Fiziol. Zh. SSSR,* 1935, *19,* 359–370.

Spence, K. W., & ———. The effects of occipital lobectomy on vision in the chimpanzee. *Brain,* 1936, *59,* 35–50.

———. *Sir Kenelm Digby: Writer, bibliophile and protagonist of William Harvey.* New York: Oliver, 1937. (Reprinted 1970)

———. *Physiology of the nervous system.* (3rd ed.) New York: Oxford University Press, 1949. (1938)

————. *Harvey Cushing, a biography*. Springfield, Ill.: Thomas, 1946.

————, & Thomson, Elizabeth H. *Benjamin Siliman, 1779–1864, pathfinder in American science*. New York: Schuman, 1947.

————. *Aviation medicine in its preventive aspects: An historical survey*. London: Oxford University Press, 1948.

————. *Functional localization in relation to frontal lobotomy*. London: Oxford University Press, 1949.

————. *Functional localization in the frontal lobes and cerebellum*. Oxford: Clarendon Press, 1949.

————. *Humanism in an age of science*. New York: Schuman, 1950.

————. *Vesalius four centuries later. Medicine in the eighteenth century*. Lawrence, Kan.: University of Kansas Press, 1950.

————. *The great medical bibliographers: A study in humanism*. Philadelphia: University of Pennsylvania Press, 1951.

————. *Frontal lobotomy and affective behavior: A neurophysiological analysis*. New York: Norton, 1951.

————. *The frontal lobes and human behaviour*. Liverpool: University Press of Liverpool, 1952.

————. *The historical contribution of physiology to neurology*. In E. A. Underwood (Ed.), *Science, medicine, and history: Essays in honor of Charles Singer*. Vol. 2. London: Oxford University Press, 1953, pp. 537–544.

————. *Les fondements physiologiques de l'activité mentale*. *J. Psychol. norm. path.*, 1956, *53*, 129–140.

————. *Historical reflections on the backgrounds of neurophysiology: Inhibition, excitation, and integration of activity*. In C. M. Brooks & P. F. Cranefield (Eds.), *The historical development of physiological thought*. New York: Hafner, 1959, pp. 67–79.

GALILEO GALILEI
1564-1642
Italian Astronomer-Mathematician (22)

Galileo, G. *Edizione nazionale delle opere di Galileo Galilei*. (2nd ed.) (20 vols. in 21) Ed. by A. Favoro. Florence: Barbera, 1966. (1890–1909). (Reprinted 1929–1939) **B Bl C**

————. *Discoveries and opinions of Galileo*. Trans. by S. Drake. New York: Doubleday, 1957. **C**

————. *Il pensiero di Galileo Galilei. Una antologia dagli scritti*. Ed. by P. Rossi. Turin: Loescher, 1968. **C**

————. *On motion*. (1590) In *Galileo on motion and on mechanics*. Trans. by I. E. Drabkin. Madison, Wisc.: University of Wisconsin Press, 1960, pp. 13–114.

————. *On mechanics*. (1600) In *Galileo on motion and on mechanics*. Trans. by S. Drake. Madison, Wisc.: University of Wisconsin Press, 1960, pp. 147–182.

————. *The starry messenger*. (1610) In *Discoveries and opinions of Galileo, op. cit.*, pp. 21–58.

————. *Excerpts from letters on sunspots*. (1613) In *Discoveries and opinions of Galileo, op. cit.*, pp. 87–144.

————. *The essayer*. (1623) In *The controversy on the comets of 1618*. Trans. by S. Drake. Philadelphia: University of Pennsylvania Press, 1960, pp. 151–336.

————. *Dialogue concerning the two chief world systems*. Trans. by S. Drake. Berkeley, Calif.: University of California Press, 1967. (1632)

————. *Dialogues concerning two new sciences*. Trans. by H. Crew & A. de Salvio. New York: Macmillan, 1914. (1638) (Reprinted 1955)

Bodenheimer, *Biology*; Dampier, *Literature*; Dennis, *Psychology*; Hall, *Nature's Laws*; Hutchins, *Great Books*; Newman, *Mathematics*; Popkin, *Philosophy*; Schwartz & Bishop, *Moments Discovery*; Smith, *Source Book*; Ulich, *Educational Wisdom*

FRANZ JOSEPH GALL
1758-1828
Austrian-French Physiologist (24)

Gall, F. J. *Sur les fonctions du cerveau et sur celle de chacune de ses parties, avec des observations sur la possibilité de reconnaître les instincts, les penchants, les talents, et les dispositions morales et intellectuelles des hommes et des animaux par la configuration de leur cerveau et de leur tête.* (6 vols.) Paris: Baillière, 1822–1825. **C**

————. *Works: On the functions of the brain and each of its parts, with observations on the possibility of determining the instincts, propensities, and talents, on the moral and intellectual dispositions of men and animals by the configuration of the brain and head.* (6 vols.) Trans. by W. Lewis [and/or I. Ray]. Boston: Marsh, Capen & Lyon, 1835. (1822–1825) **C**

————. *Vollständige Geisteskunde, oder auf Erfahrung gestützte Darstellung der geistigen und moralischen Fähigkeiten und ihrer körperlichen Bedingungen. Ein unentbehrliches Handbuch für Erzieher, Aerzte, Rechtsgelehrte, Gesetzgeber, Polizeibeamte, Geistliche, Künstler, Eltern und Geschäftsleute, die Menschenkenntnis nöthig haben. Freie Uebersetzung der sechs Bände von Galls Organologie. Mit einer Steindrucktafel.* Nuremberg: Leuchs, 1829. (1822–1825) **C**

————. *Philosophisch-medizinische Untersuchungen über Natur und Kunst, im kranken und gesunden Zustande des Menschen.* (2nd ed.) (2 vols.) Leipzig: Baumgärtner, 1800. (1791)

————, & Spurzheim, J. G. *Recherches sur le système nerveux en général et sur celui du cerveau en particulier, mémoire présenté à l'Institut de France, le 14 mars 1808, suivi d'observations sur le rapport qui en a été fait à cette compagnie par ses commissaires.* Paris: Schoell & Nicolle, 1809. (Reprinted 1967)

————, & Spurzheim, J. G. *Anatomie et physiologie du système nerveux en général, et du cerveau en particulier, avec des observations sur la possibilité de reconnaître plusieurs dispositions intellectuelles et morales de l'homme et des animaux, par la configuration de leurs têtes.* (4 vols.) Paris: Schoell, 1810–1819.

Clarke & O'Malley, *Brain*; Herrnstein & Boring, *Source Book*

FRANCIS GALTON
1822-1911
English Psychologist (27)

Galton, F. *Inquiries into human faculty and its development.* (3rd ed.) London: Dent, 1907. (1883) (Reprinted 1952) **C**

————. *Essays in eugenics.* London: Eugenic Society, 1909. **C**

————. Hereditary talent and character. *Macmillan's Mag.*, 1865, *12*, 157–166, 318–327.

————. *Hereditary genius: An inquiry into its laws and consequences.* (2nd ed.) New York: Horizon Press, 1952. (1869)

————. *English men of science: Their nature and nurture.* New York: Appleton, 1875. (1874) (Reprinted 1970)

————. Statistical inquiries into the efficacy of prayer. *Fortn. Rev.*, 1872, *12*, 125–135.

————. On the causes which operate to create scientific men. *Fortn. Rev.*, 1873, *13*, 345–351.

————. A theory of heredity. *J. Anthrop. Inst.*, 1876, *5*, 329–348.

————. The history of twins, as a criterion of the relative powers of nature and nurture. *J. Anthrop. Inst.*, 1876, *5*, 391–406.

————. Typical laws of heredity. *Proc. Roy. Inst. Gr. Brit.*, 1879, *8*, 282–301. (1877)

————. Psychometric facts. *Nineteenth Cent.*, 1879, *5*, 425–433.

————. Psychometric experiments. *Brain*, 1879, *2*, 149–162.

————. The geometric mean in vital and social statistics, *Proc. Roy. Soc.*, London, 1879, *29*, 365–367.

————. Statistics of mental imagery. *Mind*, 1880, *5*, 301–318.

————. The visions of sane persons. *Proc. Roy. Inst. Gr. Brit.*, 1881, *9*, 644–655.

————. The anthropometric laboratory. *Fortn. Rev.*, 1882, *31*, 332–338.

————. *Record of family faculties.* London: Macmillan, 1884.

————. *Life history album.* (2nd ed.) London: Macmillan, 1903. (1884)

————. Free-will, observations and inferences. *Mind*, 1884, *9*, 406–413.

————. Measurement of character. *Fortn. Rev.*, 1884, *36*, 179–185.

————. Some results of the anthropometric laboratory. *J. Anthrop. Inst.*, 1885, *14*, 275–287.

————. Regression towards mediocrity in hereditary stature. *J. Anthrop. Inst.*, 1885–1886, *15*, 246–263.

————. Family likeness in stature. *Proc. Roy. Soc.*, London, 1886, *40*, 42–63.

————. Family likeness in eye colour. *Proc. Roy. Soc.*, London, 1886, *40*, 402–416.

————. Co-relations and their measurement, chiefly from anthropometric data. *Proc. Roy. Soc.*, London, 1898, *45*, 135–145.

————. *Natural inheritance.* New York: Macmillan, 1894. (1889)

————. *Finger prints.* London: Macmillan, 1892. (Reprinted 1965)

————. The just-perceptible difference. *Proc. Roy. Inst. Gr. Brit.*, 1893, *14*, 13–26.

————. Arithmetic by smell. *Psychol. Rev.*, 1894, *1*, 61–62.

————. Note to the memoir by Prof. Karl Pearson on spurious correlation. *Proc. Roy. Soc.*, London, 1897, *60*, 498–502.

————. The average contribution of each ancestor to the total heritage of the offspring. *Proc. Roy. Soc.*, London, 1897, *61*, 401–413.

————. The possible improvement of the human breed under the existing conditions of law and sentiment. *Nature*, 1901, *64*, 659–665.

————. Eugenics: Its definition, scope, and aims. *Amer. J. Sociol.*, 1904–1905, *10*, 1–6.

————. Distribution of successes and of natural ability among the kinsfolk of fellows of the Royal Society. *Nature*, 1904, *70*, 354–356.

————. Studies in eugenics. *Amer. J. Sociol.*, 1905–1906, *11*, 11–25.

————. Grades and deviates. *Biometrika*, 1906–1907, *5*, 400–406.

————. *Memories of my life.* London: Methuen, 1908. **B**

Anastasi, *Individual Differences*; Dampier, *Literature*; Dennis, *Psychology*; Dennis, *Readings Developmental*; Goshen, *Documentary*; Hall, *Source Book*; Herrnstein & Boring, *Source Book*; Jenkins & Paterson, *Individual Differences*; Kroeber, *Source Book*; Newman, *Mathematics*; Park & Burgess, *Sociology*; Sahakian, *Psychology*; Shor, *Hypnosis*; Wiseman, *Intelligence*

LUIGI (or ALOISIO) GALVANI
1737-1798
Italian Physiologist (20)

Galvani, L. *Opere edite ed inedite del Professore Luigi Galvani.* Ed. by S. Gherardi. Bologna: Dall'Olmo, 1841. **Bl C**

————. *Memorie e esperimenti inediti con la iconografia di lui e un saggio di bibliografia degli scritti.* Bologna: Capelli, 1937. **C**

————. *Abhandlung über die Kräfte der Elektricität bei der Muskelbewegung.* Ed. by A. J. Eittingen. Leipzig: Engelmann, 1894. (1791).

————. *Commentary on the effects of electricity on muscular motion.* Ed. & trans. by Margaret G. Foley. Norwalk, Conn.: Burndy, 1954. (1791)

————. De viribus electricitatis. (1791) In *Opere*, *op. cit*, pp. 59–129.

————. *Commentary on the effect of electricity on muscular motion.* Trans. by R. M. Green. Cambridge: Licht, 1953. (1791)

———. Memorie sulla elettricità animale di Luigi Galvani . . . al celebre abate Lazzaro Spallanzani. (1797) In *Opere, op. cit.,* pp. 299–434.

Clarke & O'Malley, *Brain* ; Clendening, *Source Book* ; Fulton & Wilson, *Physiology*

PIERRE GASSENDI
1592-1655
French Philosopher (11)

Gassendi, P. *Opera omnia.* (6 vols.) Ed. by H. L. H. de Montmort. Stuttgart-Bad Canstatt: Frommann, 1968. (1658)   **C**

———. *Abrégé de la philosophie de Mr. Gassendi.* Ed. by F. Bernier. Paris: Michallet, 1675.   **C**

———. *Selected works.* Trans. & extensive comments by C. B. Brush. New York: Johnson Reprint, 1972.   **C**

———. *Lettres familières à François Luillier pendant l'hiver 1632–1633.* Intro., notes, & index by B. Rochot. Paris: Vrin, 1944.   **B C**

———. *Dissertations en forme de paradoxes contre les Aristotéliciens.* Ed. & trans. by B. Rochot. Paris: Vrin, 1959. (1624)

———. The fifth set of objections. (1641) In *The philosophical works of Descartes.* Vol. 2. (2nd ed.) Trans. by Elizabeth S. Haldane & G. R. T. Ross, Cambridge: Cambridge University Press, 1931, pp. 135–203. (Reprinted 1955)

———. *Recherches métaphysiques.* Ed. & trans. by B. Rochot. Paris: Vrin, 1962. (1644)   **Bl**

———. *De vita et moribus Epicuri libri octo.* Amsterdam: Rodopi, 1968. (1647)

———. *Syntagma philosophiae Epicuri cum refutationibus dogmatum quae contra fidem Christianam ab eo asserta sunt.* The Hague: Vlacq, 1659. (1649)

———. *Three discourses of happiness, virtue and liberty.* Coll. & trans. by M. Bernier. London: Churchill, 1699. (1694)

Popkin, *Philosophy*

CARL FRIEDRICH GAUSS
1777-1855
German Mathematician (22)

Gauss, C. F. *Werke.* (12 vols.) Ed. by E. Shering *et al.* Göttingen: Perthes ; Leipzig: Teubner ; Berlin: Springer-Verlag, 1863–1933.   **C**

Humboldt, A. v., & ———. *Briefe zwischen A. v. Humboldt und Gauss.* Ed. by K. Bruhns. Leipzig: Engelmann, 1877.   **B C**

———, & Bessel, F. W. *Briefwechsel zwischen Gauss und Bessel.* Ed. by G. F. A. v. Auwers. Leipzig: Engelmann, 1880. (Reprinted 1969)
B C

———. *Gauss's work (1803–1826) on the theory of least squares.* Trans. by H. F. Trotter. Princeton, N.J.: Princeton University Press, 1957. (1885)

———. *Inaugural lecture on astronomy and papers on the foundations of mathematics.* Trans. by G. W. Dunnington. Baton Rouge, La.: Louisiana State University Press, 1937. **C**

———. *Disquisitiones arithmeticae.* Trans. by A. A. Clarke. New Haven: Yale University Press, 1966. (1801)

———. *Theory of motion of the heavenly bodies moving about the sun in conic sections.* Trans. by C. H. Davis. New York: Dover, 1963. (1809)

———. Bestimmung der Genauigkeit der Beobachtungen. *Z. Astr. verwand. Wiss.,* 1816, *1,* 187–197. Reprinted in *Werke,* Vol. 4, *op. cit.,* pp. 109–117.

———. Theoria combinationis observationum erroribus minimis obnoxiae. *Comment. Soc. Göttingen,* 1823, *5,* 33–90. Reprinted in *Werke,* Vol. 4, *op. cit.,* pp. 1–53.

———. *General investigations of curved surfaces.* Trans. by A. Hiltebeitel & J. Morehead. Hewlett, N.Y.: Raven Press, 1965. (1825, 1827)

———. Supplementum theoriae combinationis observationum erroribus minimis obnoxiae. *Comment. Soc. Göttingen,* 1828, *6,* 57–98. Reprinted in *Werke,* Vol. 4, *op. cit.,* pp. 57–93.

————. General theory of terrestrial magnetism. (1839) In R. Taylor (Ed.), *Scientific memoirs, selected from the transactions of foreign academies of science, and learned societies, and from foreign journals.* Vol. 2. New York: Johnson, 1966, pp. 184–251.

————. General propositions relating to attractive and repulsive forces acting in the inverse ratio of the square of the distance. (1840) In R. Taylor (Ed.), *Scientific memoirs, selected from the transactions of foreign academies of science, and learned societies, and from foreign journals.* Vol. 3. New York: Johnson, 1966, pp. 153–196.

Smith, *Source Book*

ADHEMAR GELB
1887-1936
German Psychologist (15)

Gelb, A. Theoretisches über "Gestaltqualitäten." *Z. Psychol.,* 1911, *58,* 1–58.

————, & Goldstein, K. Psychologische Analysen hirnpathologischer Fälle auf Grund von Untersuchungen Hirnverletzter. I. Zur Psychologie des optischen Wahrnehmungs- und Erkennungsvorganges. *Z. ges. Neurol. Psychiat.,* 1918, *41,* 1–143. Reprinted in A. Gelb & K. Goldstein (Eds.), *Psychologische Analysen hirnpathologischer Fälle.* Vol. 1. Leipzig: Barth, 1920, pp. 1–142, & abstracted & trans. in W. D. Ellis (Ed.), *A source book of Gestalt psychology.* London: Routledge & Kegan Paul, 1938, pp. 315–325.

————, & Goldstein, K. Psychologische Analysen hirnpathologischer Fälle auf Grund von Untersuchungen Hirnverletzter. VII. Ueber Gesichtsfeldbefunde bei abnormer "Ermüdbarkeit" des Auges (sog. "Ringskotome"). (1918) *Arch. Ophthalm.,* 1922, *109,* 387–403.

————, & Goldstein, K. Das röhrenförmige Gesichtsfeld: Nebst einer Vorrichtung für perimetrische Gesichtsfelduntersuchungen in verschiedenen Entfernungen. In A. Gelb & K. Goldstein (Eds.), *Psychologische Analysen hirnpathologischer Fälle.* Vol. 1. Leipzig: Barth, 1920, pp. 143–156.

Goldstein, K., & ————. Psychologische Analysen hirnpathologischer Fälle auf Grund von Untersuchungen Hirnverletzter. II. Ueber den Einfluss des vollständigen Verlustes des optischen Vorstellungsvermögens auf das taktile Erkennen. *Z. Psychol.,* 1920, *83,* 1–94. Reprinted in A. Gelb & K. Goldstein (Eds.), *Psychologische Analysen hirnpathologischer Fälle.* Vol. 1. Leipzig: Barth, 1920, pp. 157–250.

————. Psychologische Analysen hirnpathologischer Fälle auf Grund von Untersuchungen Hirnverletzter. V. Ueber den Wegfall der Wahrnehmung von "Oberflächenfarben." *Z. Psychol.,* 1920, *84,* 193–257. Reprinted in A. Gelb & K. Goldstein (Eds.), *Psychologische Analysen hirnpathologischer Fälle.* Vol. 1. Leipzig: Barth, 1920, pp. 354–418.

————. Ueber eine eigenartige Sehstörung ("Dysmorphopsie") infolge von Gesichtsfeldeinengung. Ein Beitrag zur Lehre von den Beziehungen zwischen "Gesichtsfeld" und "Sehen." *Psychol. Forsch.* 1923, *4,* 38–63.

————, & Goldstein, K. Psychologische Analysen hirnpathologischer Fälle auf Grund von Untersuchungen Hirnverletzter. X. Ueber Farbennamenamnesie, nebst Bemerkungen über das Wesen der amnestischen Aphasie überhaupt und die Beziehung zwischen Sprache und dem Verhalten zur Umwelt. XI. Zur Frage nach der gegenseitigen funktionellen Beziehung der geschädigten und der ungeschädigten Sehsphäre bei Hemianopsie. *Psychol. Forsch.,* 1924–1925, *6,* 127–186, 187–199.

————. Die psychologische Bedeutung pathologischer Störungen der Raumwahrnehmung. *Ber IX. Kong. exp. Psychol.,* Leipzig, 1926, 23–80.

————. Die "Farbenkonstanz" der Sehdinge. In A. Bethe *et al.* (Eds.), *Handbuch der normalen und pathologischen Physiologie.* Vol. 12, Part 1. Berlin: Springer-Verlag, 1929, pp. 594–678. Abstracted & trans. in W. D. Ellis (Ed.), *A source book of Gestalt psychology.* London: Routledge & Kegan Paul, 1938, pp. 196–209.

————. Die Erscheinungen des simultanen Kontrastes und der Eindruck der Feldbeleuchtung I. *Z. Psychol.,* 1932, *127,* 42–59.

————. Zur medizinischen Psychologie und philosophischen Anthropologie. *Acta Psychol.* 1937, *3,* 193–271.

AGOSTINO (EDOARDO) GEMELLI
1878-1959
Italian Psychologist (22)

Gemelli, A. *Il problema della conoscenza e le scuole critica, positiva e neocritica.* Cantonzavo: Tip del Sud, 1899.

——. *Psicologie e biologie.* (3rd ed.) Florence: Fiorentina, 1913. (1908)

——. *Le dottrine moderne della delinquenza.* (3rd ed.) Milan: Vita e Pensiero, 1920. (1908)

——. L'introspezione sperimentale nello studio pensiero e della volontà. *Riv. Psicol.,* 1911, *7,* 466–508 ; 1912, *8,* 48–71.

——. *L'enigma della vita e i nuovi orizzonti della biologia.* Florence: Fiorentina, 1914.

——. *Il metodo degli equivalenti.* Florence: Fiorentina, 1914.

——. *Il nostro soldato: Saggi di psicologia militare.* Milan: Treves, 1917.

——. Sull'applicazione dei metodi psico-fisici all'esame dei candidati all'aviazione militare. *Riv. Psicol.,* 1917, *13,* 157–190.

——, Tessier, G., & Galli, A. Le percezione della posizione del nostro corpo e dei suoi spostamenti. (Contributo alla psicofisiologia dell'aviatore.) *Arch. ital. Psicol.,* 1920, *1,* 107–182.

——. *Nuovi orizzonti della psicologia sperimentale.* (2nd ed.) Milan: Vita e Pensiero, 1923. (1921)

——. Ueber das Entstehen von Gestalten. Beitrag zur Phänomenologie der Wahrnehmung. *Arch. ges. Psychol.,* 1928, *65,* 207–268.

——. Contribution à l'étude de la perception. Recherches expérimentales et vues générales. *J. Psychol. norm. path.,* 1928, *25,* 97–129.

——. Recherches sur le diagnostic de l'habilité motrice. *Rev. sci. travail,* 1929, *1,* 181–197.

——. Sur la valeur des temps de réaction simple surtout en rapport à leur application à la sélection personnelle. *Arch. ital. Biol.,* 1929, *81,* 159–171.

——. L'abità manuale. *Arch. sci. Biol.,* 1929, *14,* 76–124.

——. Agostino Edoardo Gemelli. In R. Schmidt (Ed.), *Die Philosophie der Gegenwart in Selbstdarstellungen.* Vol. 7. Leipzig: Meiner, 1929, pp. 43–67.   **B Bl**

——. Recherches sur la nature de l'habilité manuelle. *J. Psychol. norm. path.,* 1929, *26,* 163–200.

——. Sulla natura e sulla genesi del carattere. *Quad. Psichiat.,* 1930, *8,* 41–61.

——. I problemi attuali della psicologia nella industria nazionale. *Pubbl. Univ. Cattol. S. Cuore,* 1931, *6,* 369–393.

——. Problèmes de psychologie expérimentale dans l'étude des exercices physiques. *J. Psychol. norm. path.,* 1931, *28,* 183–213.

——. Ricerche sulla diagnosi dell'abilità motrice. *Pubbl. Univ. Cattol. S. Cuore,* 1931, *6,* 431–445.

——. Sulla natura e sulla genesi del carattere. *Pubbl. Univ. Cattol. S. Cuore,* 1931, *6,* 175–201.

——, & Ponzo, M. I fattori psicofisici predisponenti all'infortunio stradale e le prospettive di organizzazione psicotecnica preventiva. *Atti 2 Cong. Soc. Ital. med. soc.,* 1932, 1934.

——, & Pastori, G. Elektrische Analyse der Sprache. II. Untersuchungen über die Gestaltung der Wörter und Phrasen. *Psychol. Forsch.,* 1933, *18,* 191–217.

——. La misura in psicologia. *Riv. Fil. neoscolast.,* 1934, *26,* 522–540.

——, & Pastori, G. Analyse électrique du langage. I. Recherches sur la nature des voyelles. *Arch. néerl. phon. expér.,* 1934, *10.*

——. *L'analisi elettroacustica del linguaggio.* (2 vols.) Milan: Vita e Pensiero, 1934.

——. Il punto di vista della neoscolastica di fronte alla moderna psicologia. *Riv. Fil. neoscolast.,* 1934, *26* (Suppl.), 1–25.

——. Ueber das Wesen und die Entstehung des Charakters. *Int. Z. Indiv.-Psychol.,* 1935, *13,* 7–30.

——Neue Beobachtungen über das Wesen der Wahrnehmung. *Acta Psychol.,* 1936, *1,* 83–98.

————. La psicologia della percezione. *Riv. Fil. neo-scolast.*, 1936, *28*, 15–46.

————. *Metodi, compiti e limiti della psicologia nello studio e nella prevenzione della delinquenza.* Milan: Vita e Pensiero, 1936.

————. Observations sur le phonème au point de vue de la psychologie. *Acta Psychol.*, 1938–1939, *4*, 83–112.

————. Die Psychotechnik in der italienischen korporativen Auffassung der Gesellschaft. *Industr. Psychotech.*, 1938, *15*, 1–10.

————. Introduzione allo studio dei progressi della fisiologia e psicologia in Italia, negli ultimi cento anni. In Various, *Un secolo di progresso scientificó italiano, 1839–1939.* Vol. IV. Rome: Società Italiana per il Progresso delle Scienze, 1939, pp. 149–154.

————, & Banissoni, F. Speranze e preoccupazioni degli psicologi italiani in tema di insegnamento della psicologia nelle università italiane e nei vari tipi di scuole dell'ordine superiore. *Arch. Psicol. Neurol. Psychiat.*, 1941, *2*, 796–821.

————. Funzioni e strutture psichiche. *Riv. Psicol.*, 1942, *21*, 57–89.

————. *La psicologia al servizio dell'orientamento professionale nelle scuole.* Bologna: Zanichelli, 1943.

————. *L'orientamento professionale dei giovani nelle scuole.* (2nd ed.) Milan: Università Cattolica del Sacro Cuore, 1947. (1943)

————. Biologia e psicologia. *Contr. Lab. Psicol.*, Milano, 1944, *12*, 89–107.

————, & Sidlauskaite, E. *La psicologia della età evolutiva.* (5th ed.) Milan: Giuffrè, 1956. (1945)

————. *La personalità del delinquente, nei suoi fondamenti biologici e psicologici.* (2nd ed.) Milan: Giuffrè, 1949. (1946)

————, & Zunini, G. *Introduzione alla psicologia.* (4th ed.) Milan: Università Cattolica del Sacro Cuore, 1954. (1947)

————. Le mécanisme de l'influence des mouvements de la tête sur la localisation des sons. *Acta Psychol.*, 1949, *6*, 27–32.

————. La strutturazione psicologica del linguaggio studiata mediante l'analisi elettroacustica. *Pontificia acad. scient. scriptavaria*, 1950, No. 8.

————. Le psychologue devant les problèmes de la psychiatrie. *Psyché*, 1951, *6*, 66–85.

———— (With collab. of C. Colombi & R. F. Schupfer). L'enregistrement électrique des mouvements oculogyres et ses applications. *Année psychol.*, 1951, *51*, 185–200.

————. Agostino Gemelli. In E. G. Boring *et al.* (Eds.), *A history of psychology in autobiography.* Vol. 4. Worcester, Mass.: Clark University Press, 1952, pp. 97–121.

————. Percezione e personalità. *Cont. Lab. Psicol. Sacro Cuore*, Milan, 1952, Ser. 15, 1–15.

————. Le aporie della moderna psicologia. *Riv. Fil., neo-scholast.*, 1954, *46*, 97–115.

————. *Psychoanalysis today.* New York: Kenedy, 1955. (1954)

————. *Psicologia e religione nella concezione analitica di C. G. Jung.* Milan: Vita e Pensiero, 1955.

————, & Cappellini, A. The influence of the subject's attitude in perception. *Acta Psychol.*, 1958, *14*, 12–23.

————. The visual perception of movement. *Amer. J. Psychol.*, 1958, *71*, 291–297.

ARNOLD (LUCIUS) GESELL
1880-1961
American Psychologist (25)

Gesell, A. *Studies in child development.* New York: Harper, 1948.

————. Accuracy in handwriting as related to school intelligence and sex. *Amer. J. Psychol.*, 1905, *16*, 1–13.

————. Mental and physical correspondence in twins. *Sci. Mon.*, N.Y., 1922, *14*, 305–344, 415–428.

————. *The retarded child: How to help him.* Bloomington, Ind.: Public School Publishing, 1925. (Reprinted 1970)

———. *The mental growth of the pre-school child: A psychological outline of normal development from birth to the sixth year, including a system of developmental diagnosis.* New York: Macmillan, 1925.

———. *Infancy and human growth.* New York: Macmillan, 1928.

———. Maturation and infant behavior pattern. *Psychol. Rev.,* 1929, *36,* 307–319.

———, & Thompson, Helen. Learning and growth in identical infant twins: An experimental study by the method of co-twin control. *Genet. Psychol. Monogr.,* 1929, No. 6, 1–124.

———. The individual in infancy. In C. Murchison (Ed.), *The foundations of experimental psychology.* Worcester, Mass.: Clark University Press, 1929, pp. 628–660.

———. Maturation and the patterning of behaviour. In C. Murchison (Ed.), *Handbook of child psychology.* (2nd ed.) Worcester, Mass.: Clark University Press, 1933, pp. 209–235. (1931)

———, Thompson, Helen, & Amatruda, Catherine S. *Infant behavior: Its genesis and growth.* New York: McGraw-Hill, 1934.

———. *An atlas of infant behavior: A systematic delineation of the forms and early growth of human behavior patterns.* Vol. 1. *Normative series.* (With Helen Thompson & Catherine S. Amatruda.) Vol. II. *Naturalistic series.* (With Alice V. Keliher, Frances L. Ilg, & Jessie J. Carlson.) New Haven: Yale University Press. 1934.

———. Cinemanalysis: A method of behavior study. *J. genet. Psychol.,* 1935, *47,* 3–16.

———, & Halverson, H. M. The development of the thumb opposition in the human infant. *J. genet. Psychol.,* 1936, *48,* 339–361.

———. Clinical mongolism in colored races, with report of case of Negro mongolism. *J. Amer. Med. Ass.,* 1936, *106,* 1146–1150.

———, & Blake, E. M. Twinning and ocular pathology. *Arch. Ophthalm.,* 1936, *15,* 1050–1071.

———, & Ilg, Frances L. *Feeding behavior of infants: A pediatric approach to the mental hygiene of early life.* Philadelphia: Lippincott, 1937.

——— (with Louise B. Ames). Early evidences of individuality in the human infant. *Sci. Mon.,* N.Y., 1937, *45,* 217–225.

———, & Thompson, Helen. (Assisted by Catherine S. Amatruda.) *The psychology of early growth, including norms of infant behavior and a method of genetic analysis.* New York: Macmillan, 1938.

———, Castmer, B. M., Thompson, Helen, & Amatruda, Catherine S. *Biographies of child development: The mental growth careers of eighty-four infants and children.* New York: Hoeber, 1939.

———, et al. *First five years of life: A guide to the study of the preschool child.* New York: Harper, 1940.

———, & Ames, Louise B. The ontogenetic organization of prone behavior in human infancy. *J. genet. Psychol.,* 1940, *56,* 247–263.

———, & Thompson, Helen. Twins T and C from infancy to adolescence: A biogenetic study of individual differences by the method of co-twin control. *Genet. Psychol. Monogr.,* 1941, *24,* 3–121.

———. *Wolf child and human child.* New York: Harper, 1941.

———, & Amatruda, Catherine S. *Developmental diagnosis: Normal and abnormal child development: Clinical methods and pediatric applications.* (2nd rev. ed.) New York: Hoeber, 1947. (1941)

———, & Halverson, H. M. The daily maturation of infant behavior: A cinema study of postures, movements and laterality. *J. genet. Psychol.,* 1942, *61,* 3–32.

———. Genius, giftedness and growth. In *March of medicine; the New York Academy of Medicine Lectures to the Laity, 1942.* New York: Columbia University Press, 1943, pp. 100–140.

———, & Ilg, Frances L. (In collab. with Janet Learned & Louise B. Ames.) *Infant and child in the culture of today.* New York: Harper, 1943.

———, & Amatruda, Catherine S. *Embryology of behavior: The beginnings of the human mind.* New York: Harper, 1945. (Reprinted 1970)

———. *How a baby grows: A story in pictures.* New York: Harper, 1945.

———, & Ilg, Frances L. (In collab. with Louise B. Ames & Glenna E. Bullis.) *The child from five to ten.* New York: Harper, 1946.

———. The ontogenesis of infant behavior. In L. Carmichael (Ed.), *Manual of child psychology.* (2nd ed.) New York: Wiley, 1954, pp. 335–373. (1946)

———, & Ames, Louise B. The development of handedness. *J. genet. Psychol.,* 1947, *70,* 155–175.

———, Ilg, Frances L., & Bullis, Glenna E. *Vision: Its development in infant and child.* New York: Hoeber, 1949.

———, & Ames, Louise B. Tonic-neck-reflex and symmetro-tonic behavior; developmental and clinical aspects. *J. Pediat.,* 1950, *36,* 165–176.

———. Child vision and developmental optics. *Année psychol.,* 1951, *51,* 379–385.

———. Developmental diagnosis of infant behavior. *Postgrad. Med.,* 1951, *10,* 289–294.

———. *Infant development: The embryology of early human behavior.* New York: Harper, 1952.

———. Arnold Gesell. In E. G. Boring *et al.* (Eds.), *A history of psychology in autobiography.* Vol. 4. Worcester, Mass.: Clark University Press, 1952, pp. 123–142.   **B**

———, Ilg, Frances L., & Ames, Louise B. *Youth: The years from ten to sixteen.* New York: Harper, 1956.

Kessen, *Child*; Sahakian, *Psychology*; Skain, *Philosophies Education*

ARNOLD GEULINCX
1624-1669
Flemish Philosopher (11)

Geulincx, A. *Arnoldi Geulincx antverpiensis opera philosophica.* (3 vols.) Ed. by J. P. N. Land. The Hague: Nijhoff, 1891–1893.   **B C**

———. Quaestiones quodlibeticae in ultramque partem disputatae. (1653) In *Opera philosophica,* Vol. 1, *op. cit.,* pp. 68–147.

———. Logica fundamentis suis, a quibus hactenus collapsa fuerat, restituta. (1662) In *Opera philosophica,* Vol. 1, *op. cit.,* pp. 165–454.

———. Methodus inveniendi argumenta, quae solertia quibusdam dicitur. (1663) In *Opera philosophica,* Vol. 2, *op. cit.,* pp. 3–111.

———. Ethica. (1665) In *Opera philosophica,* Vol. 3, *op. cit.,* pp. 1–271. Trans. in *Ethik, oder über die Kardinaltugenden (Fleiss, Gehorsam, Gerechtigkeit und Demut).* Ed. by G. Schmitz. Hamburg: Meiner, 1948.

———. Metaphysica vera et metaphysica ad mentem peripateticam. (1691) In *Opera philosophica,* Vol. 2, *op. cit.,* pp. 138–310.

———. Annotata latiora in principia philosophiae Renate Descartes. (1691) In *Opera philosophica,* Vol. 3, *op. cit.,* pp. 361–521.

HENRY HERBERT GODDARD
1866-1957
American Psychologist (19)

Goddard, H. H. The Binet and Simon tests of intellectual capacity. *Train. Sch. Bull.,* 1908, *5*(10), 3–9.

———. Four hundred feeble-minded children classified by the Binet method. *J. genet. Psychol.,* 1910, *17,* 388–397.

———. A measuring scale for intelligence. *Train. Sch. Bull.,* 1910, *6,* 146–154.

———, & Hill, H. F. Feeble-mindedness and criminality. *Train. Sch. Bull.,* 1911, *8,* 3–6.

———, & Hill, H. F. Delinquent girls tested by the Binet Scale. *Train. Sch. Bull.,* 1911, *8,* 50–56.

———. Two thousand normal children measured by the Binet measuring scale of intelligence. *J. genet. Psychol.,* 1911, *18,* 232–259.

———. *The Kallikak family: A study in the heredity of feeble-mindedness.* New York: Macmillan, 1913.

———. Standard method for giving the Binet test. *Train. Sch. Bull.,* 1913, *10,* 23–30.

———. *Feeble-mindedness: Its causes and consequences.* New York: Macmillan, 1914.

———. *School training of defective children.* Yonkers-on-Hudson, N.Y.: World Book, 1914.

———. The adaptation board as a measure of intelligence. *Train. Sch. Bull.,* 1915, *11,* 182–188.

———. *The criminal imbecile: An analysis of three remarkable murder cases.* New York: Macmillan, 1915.

———. *Psychology of the normal and subnormal.* New York: Dodd, Mead, 1919.

———. *Human efficiency and levels of intelligence.* Princeton, N.J.: Princeton University Press, 1920.

———. *Juvenile delinquency.* New York: Dodd, Mead, 1921.

———. *Two souls in one body? A case of dual personality.* London: Rider, 1927.

———. *School training of gifted children.* Yonkers-on-Hudson, N.Y.: World Book, 1928.

———. In defense of the Kallikak study. *Science,* 1942, *95,* 574–576.

———. In the beginning. *Train. Sch. Bull.,* 1943, *40,* 154–161.   **B**

———. What is intelligence? *J. soc. Psychol.,* 1946, *24,* 51–69.

———. *Our children in the atomic age.* Mellott, Ind.: Hopkins Syndicate, 1948.

Sahakian, *Psychology*

JOHANN WOLFGANG VON GOETHE
1749-1832
German Philosopher (25)

Humboldt, W. v., & Goethe, J. W. v. *Goethes Briefwechsel mit den Gebrüdern von Humboldt. 1795–1832.* Ed. by F. T. Bratranek. Leipzig: Brockhaus, 1876.   **B C**

Schiller, F., & ———. *Selections from the correspondence between Schiller and Goethe.* Ed. with intro. & notes by J. P. Robertson. Boston: Ginn, 1898.   **C**

———. *Sämtliche Werke.* Jubiläums-Ausgabe. (40 vols.) Ed. by E. v. d. Hellen. Stuttgart: Cotta, 1902–1907.   **B C**

Schiller, F., & ———. *Der Briefwechsel zwischen Schiller und Goethe.* (3 vols.) Ed. by H. G. Gräf & A. Leitzmann. Leipzig: Insel, 1912. (1911)   **C**

———. *Die Schriften zur Naturwissenschaft.* (9 vols.) Ed. by Deutsche Akademie der Naturforscher zu Halle. Weimar: Böhlaus, 1947–1959.   **C**

———. Rameaus Neffe: Ein Dialog von Diderot aus dem Manuskript übersetzt und mit Anmerkungen begleitet. (1805) Reprinted in *Sämtliche Werke,* Vol. 34, *op. cit.,* pp. 49–196.

———. *Faust.* Trans. & intro. by C. E. Passage. Indianapolis, Ind.: Bobbs-Merrill, 1965. (1808–1832)

———. *Theory of colours.* Trans. by C. L. Eastlake. Cambridge: MIT Press, 1970. Also *Goethe's color theory.* Trans. & ed. by H. Aach. New York: Van Nostrand-Reinhold, 1971. (1810) Reprinted in German in *Sämtliche Werke,* Vol. 40, *op. cit.,* pp. 60–322.

———. Aus meinem Leben: Dichtung und Wahrheit. (1811–1814) Reprinted in *Sämtliche Werke,* Vols. 22–25, *op. cit.*   **B**

———. *Poetry & truth from my own life.* (2 vols.) Rev. trans. by Minna Steele Smith, & intro. by K. Breul. London: Bell, 1913. (1811–1814)   **B**

———. Maximen und Reflexionen. (1821–1829) Reprinted in *Sämtliche Werke,* Vol. 39, *op. cit.,* pp. 58–116.

———. *Wilhelm Meister, apprenticeship and travels.* Trans. by R. O. Moon. London: Foulis, 1947. (1828, 1829) Reprinted in German in *Sämtliche Werke,* Vols. 17–20, *op. cit.*

———. Annalen. (1830) Reprinted in *Sämtliche Werke,* Vol. 30, *op. cit.*   **B**

———. Principes de philosophie zoologique. (1830–1832) Reprinted in *Sämtliche Werke,* Vol. 39, *op. cit.,* pp. 218–248.

Gruber, *Creative Thinking*; Hall, *Source Book*; Hutchins, *Great Books*; Slotkin, *Anthropology*

ALFRED GOLDSCHEIDER
1858-1935
German Physiologist (18)

Goldscheider, A. *Gesammelte Abhandlungen.* Vol. I. *Physiologie der Hautsinnesnerven.* Vol. II. *Physiologie des Muskelsinnes.* Leipzig: Barth, 1898.   **C**

———. *Die Lehre von den specifischen Energieen der Sinnesnerven.* Berlin: Hirschwald, 1881. Reprinted in *Gesammelte Abhandlungen,* Vol. I, *op. cit.,* pp. 1–52.

———. Die specifische Energie der Gefühlsnerven der Haut. *Monatsh. prac. Dermatol.,* 1884, *3,* 283–300. Reprinted in *Gesammelte Abhandlungen.* Vol. I, *op. cit.,* pp. 77–93.

———. Die specifische Energie der Temperaturnerven. *Monatsh. prac. Dermatol.,* 1884, *3,* 198–208, 225–241. Reprinted in *Gesammelte Abhandlungen,* Vol. I, *op. cit.,* pp. 53–76.

———. Ueber Wärme-, Kälte- und Druckpunkte. *Verhandl. physiol. Ges. Berlin,* 1885, *10,* 21–26. Reprinted in *Gesammelte Abhandlungen,* Vol. I, *op. cit.,* pp. 100–106.

———. Neue Thatsachen über die Hautsinnesnerven. *Arch. Anat. Physiol.,* Leipzig, 1885, 1–110. Reprinted in *Gesammelte Abhandlungen,* Vol. I, *op. cit.,* pp. 107–218.

———. Histologische Untersuchungen über die Endigungweise der Hautsinnesnerven beim Menschen. *Arch. Anat. Physiol.,* Suppl. vol., 1886, *5,* 191–227. Reprinted in *Gesammelte Abhandlungen,* Vol. I, *op. cit.,* pp. 219–249.

———. Zur Dualität des Temperatursinnes. *Arch. ges. Physiol.,* 1886, *39,* 96–120. Reprinted in *Gesammelte Abhandlungen,* Vol. I, *op. cit.,* pp. 275–296.

———. Untersuchungen über den Muskelsinn. *Arch. Physiol.,* 1889, 369–502, Suppl., 141–218. Reprinted in *Gesammelte Abhandlungen,* Vol. II, *op. cit.,* pp. 97–281.

Gad, J., & ———. Ueber die Summation von Hautreizen. *Z. klin. Med.,* 1892, *20,* 339–373. Reprinted in *Gesammelte Abhandlungen,* Vol. I, *op. cit.,* pp. 397–432.

———. Zur Physiologie und Pathologie der Handschrift. *Arch. Psychiat.,* 1892, *24,* 503–525.

———. *Ueber den Schmerz in physiologischer und klinischer Hinsicht.* Berlin: Hirschwald, 1894.

———. *Die Bedeutung der Reize für Pathologie und Therapie im Lichte der Nervenlehre.* Leipzig: Barth, 1898.

———, & Flatau, E. *Normale und pathologische Anatomie der Nervenzellen.* Berlin: Fischer, 1898.

———. *Anleitung zur Uebungsbehandlung der Ataxie.* (2nd ed.) Leipzig: Thieme, 1904. (1899)

———. *Diagnostik der Krankheiten des Nervensystems.* Berlin: Fischer, 1911.

———. Beiträge zur Lehre von der Hautsensibilität. *Z. klin. Med.,* 1912, *75,* 1–14, 387–410.

———. Ueber die Empfindung der Hitze. *Z. klin. Med.,* 1912, *75,* 1–14.

———. Revision der Lehre vom Temperatursinn. *Ber. V. Kongr. exper. Psychol.* Leipzig: Barth, 1912, pp. 222–227.

———. Weitere Mitteilungen zur Physiologie der Sinnesnerven der Haut. *Arch. ges. Physiol.,* 1917, *168,* 36–88.

———. *Das Schmerzproblem.* Berlin: Springer-Verlag, 1920.

———. *Thermoreceptoren.* In A. Bethe *et al.* (Eds.), *Handbuch der normalen und pathologischen Physiologie.* Vol. 8, Pt. 1. Berlin: Springer-Verlag, 1926, pp. 131–180.

———. Schmerz. In A. Bethe *et al.* (Eds.), *Handbuch der normalen und pathologischen Physiologie.* Vol. 8, Pt. 1. Berlin: Springer-Verlag, 1926, pp. 181–202.

———. *Therapie innerer Krankheiten.* Berlin: Springer-Verlag, 1929.

KURT GOLDSTEIN
1878-1965
German-American Neurologist (26)

Goldstein, K. *Selected papers/Ausgewählte Schriften.* Ed. by A. Gurwitsch, Else M. Goldstein Haudek, & W. E. Haudek. Intro. by A. Gurwitsch. The Hague: Nijhoff, 1971.   **C**

———. Merkfähigkeit, Gedächtnis und Assoziation. Ein Beitrag zur Psychologie des Gedächtnisses auf Grund von Untersuchungen Schwachsinniger. *Z. Psychol.,* 1906, *41,* 38–47, 117–144.

———. Zur Frage der amnestischen Aphasie und ihrer Abgrenzung gegenüber der transkortikalen und glossopsychischen Aphasie. *Arch. Psychiat. Nervenkr.,* 1906, *41,* 911–950. Reprinted in *Selected papers, op. cit.,* pp. 12–57.

———. Zur Lehre von der motorischen Apraxie. *J. Psychol. Neurol.,* 1908, *11,* 168–187, 270–283.

———. Zur Theorie der Halluzinationen. Studien über normale und pathologische Wahrnehmung. *Arch. Psychiat. Nervenkr.,* 1908, *44,* 584–655, 1036–1106.

———. Ueber Aphasie. *Beih. med. Klin.,* 1910, *6,* 1–32.

———. Zur pathologischen Anatomie der Dementia praecox. *Arch. Psychiat. Nervenkr.,* 1910, *46,* 1062–1090.

———. Ueber Apraxie. *Beih. med. Klin.,* 1911, *7,* 271–302.

———. a) Rechtsseitige Hemiplegie, Aphasie, und linksseitige Apraxie. b) Gehirn einer Patientin mit rechtsseitiger Hemiplegie, Aphasie, ideatorischer Apraxie und Agnosie. c) Gehirn eines Mannes mit vollständiger Aufhebung der Sensibilität auf einer Seite (rechts) und Augenmuskellähmungen auf der anderen und der

gleichen Seite. *Deutsch. med. Wochensch.,* 1913, *39,* 1074–1075.

———. Ueber die Störungen der Grammatik bei Hirnkrankheiten. *Monatssch. Psychiat. Neurol.,* 1913, *34,* 540–568.

———. Weitere Bemerkungen zur Theorie der Hallucinationen. *Z. ges. Neurol. Psychiat.,* 1913, *14,* 502–544.

———. Ueber kortikale Sensibilitätsstörungen. *Z. ges. Neurol. Psychiat.,* 1916, *33,* 494–517.

———. Die transkortikalen Aphasien. *Erg. Neurol. Psychiat.,* 1917, *2,* 349–629.

Gelb, A., & ———. Psychologische Alanysen hirnpathologischer Fälle auf Grund von Untersuchungen Hirnverletzter. I. Zur Psychologie des optischen Wahrnehmungs- und Erkennungsvorganges. *Z. ges. Neurol. Psychiat.,* 1918, *41,* 1–143. Reprinted in A. Gelb & K. Goldstein (Eds.), *Psychologische Analysen hirnpathologischer Fälle.* Vol. 1. Leipzig: Barth, 1920, pp. 1–142, & abstracted & trans. in W. D. Ellis (Ed.), *A source book of Gestalt psychology.* London: Routledge & Kegan Paul, 1938, pp. 315–325.

———, & Reichmann, F. Ueber kortikale Sensibilitätsstörungen, besonders am Kopfe. *Z. ges. Neurol. Psychiat.,* 1919, *53,* 49–79.

———, & Gelb, A. Psychologische Analysen hirnpathologischer Fälle auf Grund von Untersuchungen Hirnverletzter. II. Ueber den Einfluss des vollständigen Verlustes des optischen Vorstellungsvermögens auf das taktile Erkennen. *Z. Psychol.,* 1920, *83,* 1–94. Reprinted in A. Gelb & K. Goldstein (Eds.), *Psychologische Analysen hirnpathologischer Fälle.* Vol. 1. Leipzig: Barth, 1920, pp. 157–250.

Gelb, A., & ———. Das röhrenförmige Gesichtsfeld: Nebst einer Vorrichtung für perimetrische Gesichtsfelduntersuchungen in verschiedenen Entfernungen. In A. Gelb & K. Goldstein (Eds.), *Psychologische Analysen hirnpathologischer Fälle.* Vol. 1. Leipzig: Barth, 1920, pp. 143–156.

———. Psychologische Methoden zur Untersuchung der Hautsinne. In E. Abderhalden

(Ed.), *Handbuch der biologischen Arbeitsmethoden.* Vol. 6. Berlin: Urban & Schwarzenberg, 1922, pp. 477–546.

————. Zur Anatomie und Physiologie des Gehirns, Lokalisationslehre. In H. Oppenheim, K. Goldstein, R. Cassirer, M. Nonne, & B. Pfeiffer (Eds.), *Lehrbuch der Nervenkrankheiten für Aerzte und Studierende.* Vol. 2. (7th ed.) Berlin: Karger, 1923, pp. 927–1025.

————. Zur Frage der Restitution nach umschriebenem Hirndefekt. *Schweiz. Arch. Neurol. Psychiat.*, 1923, *13*, 283–296.

————. Ueber die Abhängigkeit der Bewegungen von optischen Vorgängen. (Bewegungsstörungen bei Seelenblinden.) *Monatssch. Psychiat. Neurol.*, 1923, *54*, 141–194.

————. Ueber gleichartige funktionelle Bedingtheit der Symptome bei organischen und psychischen Krankheiten; im besonderen über den funktionellen Mechanismus der Zwangsvorgänge. *Monatssch. Psychiat. Neurol.*, 1924, *57*, 191–209.

Gelb, A., & ————. Psychologische Analysen hirnpathologischer Fälle auf Grund von Untersuchungen Hirnverletzter. X. Ueber Farbennamenamnesie, nebst Bemerkungen über das Wesen der amnestischen Aphasie überhaupt und die Beziehung zwischen Sprache und dem Verhalten zur Umwelt. XI. Zur Frage nach der gegenseitigen funktionellen Beziehung der geschädigten und der ungeschädigten Sehsphäre bei Hemianopsie. *Psychol. Forsch.*, 1924–1925, *6*, 127–186, 187–199. Part 1 reprinted in *Selected papers, op. cit.*, pp. 58–125.

————. Zur Theorie der Funktion des Nervensystems. *Arch. Psychiat.*, 1925, *74*, 370–405.

————. Das Symptom, seine Entstehung und Bedeutung für unsere Auffassung vom Bau und von der Funktion des Nervensystems. *Arch. Psychiat. Nervenkr.*, 1925, *76*, 84–108. Reprinted in *Selected papers, op. cit.*, pp. 126–153.

————, & Rosenthal-Veit, O. Ueber akustische Lokalisation und deren Beeinflussbarkeit durch andere Sinnesreize. *Psychol. Forsch.*, 1926, *8*, 318–335.

————. Ueber Aphasie. *Schweiz. Arch. Neurol. Psychiat.*, 1926, *19*, 3–38, 292–322. Reprinted in *Selected papers, op. cit.*, pp. 154–230.

————. Die Beziehungen der Psychoanalyse zur Biologie. *Bericht über den II. allgemeinen ärztlichen Kongress für Psychotherapie in Bad Nauheim.* Leipzig: Hirzel, 1927, pp. 15–52.

————. Das Kleinhirn. In A. Bethe *et al.* (Eds.), *Handbuch der normalen und pathologischen Physiologie.* Vol. 10. Berlin: Springer-Verlag, 1927, pp. 222–317.

————. Die Lokalisation in der Grosshirnrinde. Nach Erfahrungen am kranken Menschen. In A. Bethe *et al.* (Eds.), *Handbuch der normalen und pathologischen Physiologie.* Vol. 10. Berlin: Springer-Verlag, 1927, pp. 600–842.

————. Beobachtungen über die Veränderungen des Gesamtverhaltens bei Gehirnschädigung. *Monatssch. Psychiat. Neurol.*, 1928, *68*, 217–242.

————. Zum Problem der Angst. *Allg. ärztl. Z. Psychother. Psych. Hyg.*, 1929, *2*, 409–436. Reprinted in *Selected papers, op. cit.*, pp. 231–262.

————. Zum Problem der Tendenz zum ausgezeichneten Verhalten. Zugleich ein Beitrag zur Symptomatologie der Kleinhirn- und Stirnhirnläsion. *Deutsch. Z. Nervenkr.*, 1929, *109*, 1–61.

————, & Rosenthal, O. Zum Problem der Wirkung der Farben auf den Organismus. (Auf Grund von Untersuchungen der Farbeinwirkung auf Abweichen, Grössen- und Zeitschätzung, etc., bei Cerebellar- und Frontalhirnerkrankung.) *Schweiz. Arch. Neurol. Psychiat.*, 1930, *26*, 3–26.

————. Ueber die Plastizität des Organismus auf Grund von Erfahrungen am nervenkranken Menschen. In A. Bethe *et al.* (Eds.), *Handbuch der normalen und pathologischen Physiologie.* Vol. 15. Berlin: Springer-Verlag, 1931, pp. 1133–1174.

————. Ueber Zeigen und Greifen. *Nervenarzt*, 1931, *4*, 453–466. Reprinted in *Selected papers, op. cit.*, pp. 263–281.

————, & Cohn, H. Die Allgemeinerscheinungen bei Hirngeschwülsten in ihrer Bedeutung für die Diagnostik. *Erg. ges. Med.*, 1932, *17*, 257–330.

——. L'analyse de l'aphasie et l'étude de l'essence du langage. *J. Psychol. norm. path.*, 1933, *30*, 430–496. Reprinted in *Selected papers, op. cit.*, pp. 282–344.

——. Ueber Täuschungen des Tastsinnes unter pathologischen Umständen. *Z. Psychol.*, 1933, *129*, 282–290.

——. *The organism: A holistic approach to biology, derived from pathological data in man.* New York: American Book, 1939. (1934) (Reprinted 1963)

——. Ueber monokuläre Doppelbilder. (Ihre Entstehung und Bedeutung für die Theorie von der Funktion des Nervensystems.) *Jb. Psychiat.*, 1934, *51*, 16–38.

——. The problem of the meaning of words based on the observations of aphasic patients. *J. Psychol.*, 1936, *2*, 301–316. Reprinted in *Selected papers, op. cit.*, pp. 345–359.

——, & Katz, S. The psychopathology of Pick's disease. *Arch. Neurol. Psychiat.*, 1937, *38*, 473–490.

——, & Bolles, Marjorie. A study of the impairment of "abstract behavior" in schizophrenic patients. *Psychiat. Quart.*, 1938, *12*, 42–65.

——. The significance of special mental tests for diagnosis and prognosis in schizophrenia. *Amer. J. Psychiat.*, 1939, *96*, 575–587.

——. *Human nature in the light of psychopathology.* Cambridge: Harvard University Press, 1940. (Reprinted 1963)

——, & Scheerer, M. Abstract and concrete behavior: An experimental study with special tests. *Psychol. Monogr.*, 1941, *53*, No. 239. Excerpt reprinted in *Selected papers, op. cit.*, pp. 365–399.

——. *After-effects of brain injuries in war: Their evaluation and treatment.* Foreword by D. Denny-Brown. New York: Grune & Stratton, 1942.

——. The significance of psychological research in schizophrenia. *J. nerv. ment. Dis.*, 1943, *97*, 261–279. Reprinted in S. S. Tomkins (Ed.),

Contemporary psychopathology. Cambridge: Harvard University Press, 1943, pp. 302–318.

——. Concerning rigidity. *J. Pers.*, 1943, *11*, 209–226.

——. Methodological approach to the study of schizophrenic thought disorder. In J. S. Kasanin (Ed.), *Language and thought in schizophrenia.* Berkeley, Calif.: University of California Press, 1944, pp. 17–39. (Reprinted 1964)

Hanfmann, Eugenia, Rickers-Ovsiankina, Maria, & ——. Case Lanuti: Extreme concretization of behavior due to damage of the brain cortex. *Psychol. Monogr.*, 1944, *57*, No. 264.

Scheerer, M., Rothmann, Eva, & ——. A case of "Idiot Savant." An experimental study of personality organization. *Psychol. Monogr.*, 1945, *58*, No. 269.

——. An organismic approach to the problem of motivation. *Trans. N.Y. Acad. Sci.*, 1947, Ser. 2, *9*, 218-230. Reprinted in *Selected papers, op. cit.*, pp. 409-421.

——. *Language and language disturbances: Aphasic symptom complexes and their significance for medicine and theory of language.* New York: Grune & Stratton, 1948.

——. On emotions: Considerations from the organismic point of view. *J. Psychol.*, 1951, *31*, 37–49. Reprinted in *Selected papers, op. cit.*, pp. 425–438.

——. *Thinking and speaking. A symposium.* Ed. by G. Révész. Amsterdam: North Holland Publishing, 1954, pp. 175–196.

——. The concept of transference in treatment of organic and functional nervous disease. *Acta psychother., psychosom., orthopaed.*, 1954, *2*, 334–353.

——. Bemerkungen zum Problem "Sprechen und Denken" auf Grund hirnpathologischer Erfahrungen. *Acta Psychol.*, 1954, *10*, 175–196. Reprinted in *Selected papers, op. cit.*, pp. 443–465.

——. The smiling of the infant and the problem of understanding the "other." *J. Psychol.*, 1957, *44*, 175–191. Reprinted in *Selected papers, op. cit.*, pp. 466–484.

———. Notes on the development of my concepts. *J. indiv. Psychol.,* 1959, *15,* 5–14. Reprinted in *Selected papers, op. cit.,* pp. 1–12. **B**

———. Concerning the concreteness in schizophrenia. *J. abnorm. soc. Psychol.,* 1959, *59,* 146–148.

———. Sensoritonic theory and the concept of self-realization. In B. Kaplan & S. Wapner (Eds.), *Perspectives in psychological theory.* New York: International Universities Press, 1960, pp. 115–123.

———. Stress and the concept of self-realization. In S. Z. Klausner (Ed.), *The quest for self-control.* New York: Free Press, 1965, pp. 341–355.

———. Kurt Goldstein. In E. G. Boring & G. Lindzey (Eds.), *A history of psychology in autobiography.* Vol. 5. New York: Appleton-Century-Crofts, 1967, pp. 145–166. **B**

Lindzey & Hall, *Personality* ; Rabkin & Carr, *Abnormal* ; Sahakian, *Personality* ; Sahakian, *Psychology* ; Vetter, *Personality*

CAMILLO GOLGI
1844-1926
Italian Anatomist (14)

Golgi, C. *Opera omnia.* (4 vols.) Milan: Hoepli, 1903, 1930. **C**

———. Contribuzione alla fina anatomia degli organi centrali del sistema nervoso. (1871) In *Opera omnia,* Vol. 1, *op. cit.,* pp. 5–69.

———. Sulla fina struttura dei bulbi alfattoria. (1875) In *Opera omnia,* Vol. 1, *op. cit.,* pp. 113–132.

———. Di una nuova reazione apparentemente nera delle cellule nervose cerebrali ottenuta col bicloruro di mercurio. (1878) In *Opera omnia,* Vol. 1, *op. cit.,* pp. 143–148.

———. Considerazioni anatomiche sulla dottrina delle localizzazioni cerebrali. (1882). In *Opera omnia,* Vol. 1, *op. cit.,* pp. 261–293.

———. Sulla fina anatomia degli organi centrali del sistema nervoso. (1882–1885) In *Opera omnia,* Vols. 1, 2, *op. cit.,* pp. 295–536.

———. Sulla fina anatomia degli organi centrali del sistema nervoso. Milan: Hoepli, 1886.

———. Untersuchungen über den feineren Bau des centralen und peripherischen Nervensystems. Trans. by R. Teuschen. Jena: Fischer, ca. 1894. (1886)

———. Modificazione del metodo di colorazione degli elementi nervosi col cloruro di mercurio. (1891) In *Opera omnia,* Vol. 2, *op. cit.,* pp. 607–619.

———. La rete nervosa diffusa degli organi centrali del sistema nervoso. Suo significato fisiologico. (1891) In *Opera omnia,* Vol. 2, *op. cit.,* pp. 579–605.

———. Du nouveau sur la structure des cellules nerveuses des ganglions spinaux. *Arch. ital. Biol.,* 1899, *31,* 273–280.

———. The neuron doctrine—theory and facts. (1906) In Nobel Foundation (Ed.), *Nobel lectures: Physiology or medicine, 1901–1921.* New York: American Elsevier, 1967, pp. 189–217.

———. La doctrine de neuron. Théorie et faits. *Nordiskt med. Arch.,* 1907, *40,* 1–26.

———. Une méthode pour la prompte et facile démonstration de l'appareil réticulaire interne des cellules nerveuses. *Arch. ital. Biol.,* 1908, *49,* 269–274.

———. La moderna evoluzione delle dottrine e delle conoscenze sulla vita. II. I problemi fondamentali psicofisiologici. *Scientia,* 1914, *16,* 364–383.

Clarke & O'Malley, *Brain*

FRIEDRICH LEOPOLD GOLTZ
1834-1902
German Physiologist (12)

Goltz, F. L. *Beiträge zur Lehre von den Funktionen der Nervenzentren des Frosches.* Berlin: Hirschwald, 1869. **C**

———. *Gesammelte Abhandlungen.* Bonn: Strauss, 1881. **C**

———. Ueber Reflexionen von und zum Herzen. *Königsb. med. Jb.,* 1862, *3,* 271–274.

———. Ueber die physiologische Bedeutung der Bogengänge des Ohrlabyrinths. *Arch. ges. Physiol.*, 1870, *3*, 172–192.

———. Ueber die Funktionen des Lendenmarks des Hundes. *Arch. ges. Physiol.*, 1873, *8*, 460–498.

———, & Freusberg, A. Ueber gefässerweiternde Nerven. *Arch. ges. Physiol.*, 1874, *9*, 174–199.

———, & Freusberg, A. Ueber den Einfluss des Nervensystems auf die Vorgänge während der Schwangerschaft und des Gebärakts. *Arch. ges. Physiol.*, 1874, *9*, 552–565.

———, & Gergens, E. Ueber die Verrichtungen des Grosshirns. *Arch. ges Physiol.*, 1876, *13*, 1–44 ; 1876, *14*, 412–443.

———, & Mering, J. v. Ueber die Verrichtungen des Grosshirns. 3. *Arch. ges. Physiol.*, 1879, *20*, 1–54.

———, Mering, J. v., & Ewald, R. Ueber die Verrichtungen des Grosshirns. 4. *Arch. ges. Physiol.*, 1881, *26*, 1–49.

———, & Ferrier, D. On the localisation of function in the cortex cerebri. *Int. Med. Congr.*, London, 1881, *1*, 218–243.

———. Ueber Lokalisationen der Funktionen des Grosshirns. *Verh. Dritten Congr. inn. Med.*, Wiesbaden, 1884, *3*, 261–275.

———. Ueber die moderne Phrenologie. *Deutsch. Rundsch.*, 1885, *45*, 263–283, 361–375.

———. Ueber die Verrichtungen des Grosshirns. *Arch. ges. Physiol.*, 1889, *42*, 419–467. Reprinted in & trans. by G. v. Bonin (Ed.), *Some papers on the cerebral cortex*. Springfield, Ill.: Thomas, 1960, pp. 118–158.

———. Der Hund ohne Grosshirn. *Arch. ges. Physiol.*, 1892, *51*, 570–614.

———, & Ewald, J. R. Der Hund mit verkürztem Rückenmark. *Arch. ges. Physiol.*, 1896, *63*, 362–400.

———. Beobachtungen an einem Affen mit verstümmeltem Grosshirn. *Arch. ges. Physiol.*, 1899, *76*, 411–426.

Clarke & O'Malley, *Brain*

FLORENCE LAURA GOODENOUGH
1886-1959
American Psychologist (20)

Goodenough, Florence L. A new approach to the measurement of intelligence of young children. *J. genet. Psychol.*, 1926, *33*, 185–211.

———. Racial differences in the intelligence of school children. *J. exp. Psychol.*, 1926, *9*, 388–397.

———. *Measurement of intelligence by drawings.* Yonkers-on-Hudson, N.Y.: World Book, 1926.

———, & Leahy, Alice M. The effect of certain family relationships upon the development of personality. *J. genet. Psychol.*, 1927, *34*, 45–71.

———. The relationship of the intelligence of pre-school children to the education of their parents. *School & Soc.*, 1927, *26*, 54–56.

———. The consistency of sex differences in mental traits at various ages. *Psychol. Rev.*, 1927, *34*, 440–462.

———. *The Kuhlmann-Binet tests for children of pre-school age: A critical study and evaluation.* Minneapolis, Minn.: University of Minnesota Press, 1928.

———. Measuring behavior traits by means of repeated short samples. *J. juv. Res.*, 1928, *12*, 230–235.

———. A preliminary report on the effect of nursery-school training upon the intelligence test scores of young children. *Yearb. Nat. Soc. Stud. Educ.*, 1928, *27*(1), 361–369.

———. The relation of the intelligence of pre-school children to the occupation of their fathers. *Amer. J. Psychol.*, 1928, *40*, 284–294.

———. The emotional behavior of young children during mental tests. *J. juv. Res.*, 1929, *13*, 204–219.

———. Interrelationships in the behavior of young children. *Child Developmt.*, 1930, *1*, 29–47.

———. *Anger in young children.* Minneapolis, Minn.: University of Minnesota Press, 1931.

---. The expression of the emotions in infancy. *Child Developmt.*, 1931, *2*, 96–101.

---. The measurement of mental growth. In C. Murchison (Ed.), *Handbook of child psychology.* (2nd ed.) Worcester, Mass.: Clark University Press, 1933, pp. 303–328. (1931)

---, & Anderson, J. E. *Experimental child study.* New York: Appleton-Century-Crofts, 1931.

---. Expression of the emotions in a blind-deaf child. *J. abnorm. soc. Psychol.*, 1932, *27*, 328–333.

---. Trends in modern psychology. *Psychol. Bull.*, 1934, *31*, 81–97.

---, & Tyler, Leona E. *Developmental psychology.* (3rd ed.) New York: Appleton-Century-Crofts, 1959. (1934)

---. The development of the reactive process from early childhood to maturity. *J. exp. Psychol.*, 1935, *18*, 431–450.

---. Look to the evidence! A critique of recent experiments on raising the I.Q. *Educ. Meth.*, 1939, *19*, 73–79.

---, & Maurer, Katherine M. The mental development of nursery school children compared with that of non-nursery school children. *Yearb. Nat. Soc. Stud. Educ.*, 1940, *39*(2), 161–178.

---, & Maurer, Katherine M. The relative potency of the nursery school and the statistical laboratory in boosting the I.Q. *J. educ. Psychol.*, 1940, *31*, 541–549.

---. Can we influence mental growth? A critique of recent experiments. *Educ. Rec.*, 1940, *21*, Suppl. 13, 120–143.

---. New evidence on environmental influence on intelligence. *Yearb. Nat. Soc. Stud. Educ.*, 1940, *39*(1), 307–365.

---. Some special problems of nature-nurture research. Ed. by G. M. Whipple. *Yearb. Nat. Soc. Stud. Educ.*, 1940, *39*(1), 367–384.

---. Month of birth as related to socio-economic status of parents. *J. genet. Psychol.*, 1941, *59*, 65–76.

---. Studies of the 1937 revision of the Stanford-Binet scale. I. Variability of the IQ at successive age-levels. *J. educ. Psychol.*, 1942, *32*, 241–251.

---, & Maurer, Katherine M. *The mental growth of children from age two to fourteen years: A study of the predictive value of the Minnesota Pre-school Scales.* Minneapolis, Minn.: University of Minnesota Press, 1942.

---, & Harris, D. B. Intellectual growth in childhood. *Rev. educ. Res.*, 1947, *17*, 306–316.

---. The appraisal of child personality. *Psychol. Rev.*, 1949, *36*, 123–131.

---. *Mental testing: Its history, principles and applications.* New York: Rinehart, 1949. (Reprinted 1968)

---, & Harris, D. B. Studies in the psychology of children's drawings: II. 1928–1949. *Psychol. Bull.*, 1950, *47*, 369–433.

---. (With assist. of Lois M. Rynkiewicz.) *Exceptional children.* New York: Appleton-Century-Crofts, 1956.

Beck & Molish, *Reflexes*

WILLIAM SEALY GOSSET ("STUDENT")
1876-1937
English Statistician (13)

[Gosset, W. S.] *"Student's" collected papers.* Ed. by E. S. Pearson & J. Wishart. London: Cambridge University Press, 1942.   **Bl C**

[---.] On the error of counting with a haemacytometer. *Biometrika*, 1906–1907, *5*, 351–360. Reprinted in *Collected papers, op. cit.*, pp. 1–10.

[---.] The probable error of a correlation coefficient. *Biometrika*, 1908–1909, *6*, 302–310. Reprinted in *Collected papers, op. cit.*, pp. 35–42.

[---.] The probable error of a mean. *Biometrika*, 1908–1909, *6*, 1–25. Reprinted in *Collected papers, op. cit.*, pp. 11–34.

[---.] The distribution of means of samples which are not drawn at random. *Biometrika*,

1909–1910, *7*, 210–214. Reprinted in *Collected papers, op. cit.,* pp. 43–48.

[————.] The correction to be made to the correlation ratio for grouping. *Biometrika,* 1913, *9*, 316–329. Reprinted in *Collected papers, op. cit.,* pp. 53–57.

[————.] An explanation of deviations from Poisson's law in practice. *Biometrika,* 1918–1919, *12*, 211–215.

[————.] An experimental determination of the probable error of Dr. Spearman's correlation coefficients. *Biometrika,* 1921, *13*, 263–282. Reprinted in *Collected papers, op. cit.,* pp. 70–89.

[————.] New tables for testing the significance of observations. *Metron,* 1925, *5*(3), 105–120. Reprinted in *Collected papers, op. cit.,* pp. 115–120.

[————.] Errors of routine analysis. *Biometrika,* 1927, *19*, 151–164. Reprinted in *Collected papers, op. cit.,* pp. 135–149.

[————.] On the z-test. *Biometrika,* 1931, *23*, 407–408. Reprinted in *Collected papers, op. cit.,* pp. 179–180.

[————.]. The Lanarkshire milk experiment. *Biometrika,* 1931, *23*, 398–406. Reprinted in *Collected papers, op. cit.,* pp. 169–178.

[————.] Evolution by selection: The implications of Winter's selection experiment. *Eugen. Rev.,* Cambridge, 1933, *24*, 293–296. Reprinted in *Collected papers, op. cit.,* pp. 181–185.

[————.] Comparison between balanced and random arrangements of field plots. *Biometrika,* 1938, *29*, 361–379. Reprinted in *Collected papers, op. cit.,* pp. 199–215.

KARL GROOS
1861-1946
German Psychologist (16)

Groos, K. *Das Spiel, zwei Vorträge.* I. *Der Lebenswert des Spiels.* II. *Das Spiel als Katharsis.* Jena: Fischer, 1922.   **C**

————. *Das philosophische System von Karl Groos. Eigene Gesamtdarstellungen.* Berlin: Junker & Dünnhaupt, 1934.   **C**

————. *Seele, Welt und Gott.* Stuttgart: Kohlhammer, 1952.   **C**

————. *Der ästhetische Genuss.* Giessen: Ricker, 1902. (1892)

————. *The play of animals.* Trans. by Elizabeth L. Baldwin, & ed. by J. M. Baldwin. New York: Appleton, 1898. (1896)

————. *Die Spiele der Tiere.* (3rd ed.) Jena: Fischer, 1930. (1896)

————. Zum Problem der unbewussten Zeitschätzung. *Z. Psychol.,* 1896, *9,* 321–330.

————. *The play of man.* Trans. by Elizabeth L. Baldwin, & pref. by J. M. Baldwin. New York: Appleton, 1901. (1898)

————. Experimentelle Beiträge zur Psychologie des Erkennens. *Z. Psychol.,* 1901, *26,* 145–167.

————. *Das Seelenleben des Kindes.* (6th ed.) Berlin: Reuther & Reichard, 1923. (1903)

————, & Groos, Marie. Die optischen Qualitäten in der Lyrik Schillers. *Z. Aesth. allg. Kunstwiss.,* 1909, *4,* 559–571.

————, & Groos, Marie. Die akustischen Phänomene in der Lyrik Schillers. *Z. Aesth. allg. Kunstwiss.,* 1910, *5,* 545–570.

————, & Netto, J. Psychologisch-statistische Untersuchungen über die visuellen Sinneseindrücke in Shakespeares lyrischen und epischen Dichtungen. *Englische Stud.,* 1911, *43,* 27–51.

————. Das anschauliche Vorstellen beim poetischen Gleichnis. *Z. Aesth. allg. Kunstwiss.,* 1914, *9,* 186–207.

————. *Bismarck im eigenen Urteil ; psychologische Studien.* Stuttgart: Cotta, 1920.

————. *Fürst Metternich ; eine Studie zur Psychologie der Eitelkeit.* Stuttgart: Cotta, 1922.

————. Karl Groos. In R. Schmidt (Ed.), *Die Philosophie der Gegenwart in Selbstdarstellungen.* (2nd ed.) Vol. 2. Leipzig: Meiner, 1923, pp. 103–119.

————. *Der Aufbau der Systeme: eine formale Einführung in die Philosophie.* Leipzig: Meiner, 1924.

———. Ueber wissenschaftliche Einfälle. *Z. Psychol.*, 1924, *95*, 1–26.

———. Enkapsis. Ein Beitrag zur Strukturphilosophie. *Z. Psychol.*, 1926, *98*, 273–303.

———. Die "Stimme des Gewissens." Zwei psychologische Stichproben. *Z. Psychol.*, 1928, *108*, 321–330.

———. Die Verwertung der Eidetik als Kunstmittel in Jack Londons Roman "Martin Eden." *Z. angew. Psychol.*, 1929, *33*, 417–438.

———. *Zur Psychologie und Metaphysik des Werterlebens.* Berlin: Junker & Dünnhaupt, 1932.

———. Karl Groos. In C. Murchison (Ed.), *A history of psychology in autobiography.* Vol. 2. Worcester, Mass.: Clark University Press, 1932, pp. 115–152.   **B**

———. Zum Problem der Tiersprache. *Z. Psychol.*, 1935, *134*, 225–235.

———. *Die Unsterblichkeitsfrage.* Berlin: Junker & Dünnhaupt, 1936.

———. Vererbte Gewohnheit? *Ned. Tijdschr. Psychol.*, 1936, *4*, 85–95.

———. Ueber das Nachahmen. *Z. Psychol.*, 1939, *145*, 358–389.

———. Seele und Raum. *Z. deutsch. Kulturphil.*, 1939, *5*, 107–117.

———. Das Wesen und die Formen der Bewusstheit. *Z. Psychol.*, 1940, *149*, 1–30.

HANS WALTER GRUHLE
1880-1958
German Psychiatrist (12)

Gruhle, H. W. *Verstehen und Einfühlen: Gesammelte Schriften.* Berlin: Springer-Verlag, 1953.   **C**

———. *Die Ursachen der jugendlichen Verwahrlosung und Kriminalität.* Berlin: Springer-Verlag, 1912.

———. Ergographische Studien. *Psychol. Arb.*, 1912–1914, *6*, 339–418.

———. *Psychologie des Abnormen.* In G. Kafka (Ed.), *Handbuch der vergleichenden Psychologie.* Vol. 3. *Die Funktionen des abnormen Seelenslebens.* Munich: Reinhardt, 1922, pp. 1–151.

———. Ueber die Fortschritte in der Erkenntnis der Epilepsie in den Jahren 1910–1920 und über das Wesen dieser Krankheit. *Zbl. ges. Neurol.*, 1923, *34*, 1–97.

———. Historische Bemerkungen zum Problem: Charakter und Körperbau. *Z. Neurol.*, 1923, *84*, 444–449.

———. Swedenborgs Träume. Ein Beitrag zur Phänomenologie seiner Mystik. *Psychol. Forsch.*, 1924, *5*, 273–320.

———. Konstitution und Charakter. *Naturwissenschaften*, 1924, *12*, 969–975.

———. Der Körperbau der Normalen. *Arch. Psychiat.*, 1926, *77*, 1–32.

———. *Grundriss der Psychiatrie.* (15th ed.) Berlin: Springer-Verlag, 1948. (1937)

———. *Selbstmord.* Leipzig: Thieme, 1940.

———. Das Verstehen des Verbrechers. *Nervenarzt*, 1942, *15*, 53–58.

———. *Das Porträt. Eine Studie zur Einführung in den Ausdruck.* Freiburg: Zähringer, 1948.

———. *Verstehende Psychologie (Erlebnislehre): Ein Lehrbuch.* (2nd ed.) Stuttgart: Thieme, 1956. (1948)

———. Ichqualität und Impulserlebnis. *Psychol. Forsch.*, 1949, *23*, 1–9.

———. Kritik der Psychoanalyse. *Stud. Gen.*, 1950, *3*, 369–392.

———. *Geschichtsschreibung und Psychologie.* Bonn: Bouvier, 1953.

———. Sprechen und Denken. *Acta Psychol.*, 1954, *10*, 197–204.

———. *Gutachtentechnik.* Berlin: Springer-Verlag, 1955.

PAUL GUILLAUME
1878-1962
French Psychologist (16)

Guillaume, P. Le problème de la perception de l'espace et la psychologie de l'enfant. *J. Psychol. norm. path.*, 1924, *21,* 112–134.

———. La théorie de la forme. *J. Psychol. norm. path.*, 1925, *22,* 768–800.

———. *Imitation in children.* (2nd ed.) Trans. by Elaine P. Halperin. Chicago: University of Chicago Press, 1971. (1925)

———. Les débuts de la phrase dans le langage de l'enfant. *J. Psychol. norm. path.*, 1927, *24,* 1–25, 26–77.

———. Le développement des éléments formels dans le langage de l'enfant. *J. Psychol. norm. path.*, 1927, *24,* 203–229.

———, & Meyerson, I. Recherches sur l'usage de l'instrument chez les singes. *J. Psychol. norm. path.*, 1930, *27,* 177–236.

———. *Psychologie.* Paris: Alcan, 1931.

———. A propos d'une explication psychologique. *J. Psychol. norm. path.*, 1932, *29,* 657–672.

———. L'objectivité en psychologie. *J. Psychol. norm. path.*, 1932, *29,* 682–743.

———, & Meyerson, I. Recherches sur l'usage de l'instrument chez les singes. III. L'intermédiaire indépendant de l'objet. *J. Psychol. norm. path.*, 1934, *31,* 497–554.

———. *La formation des habitudes.* (Rev. ed.) Paris: Presses Universitaires de France, 1947. (1936)

———. L'appréhension des figures géométriques. *J. Psychol. norm. path.*, 1937, *34,* 675–710.

———. La psychologie d'Henri Delacroix. *J. Psychol. norm. path.*, 1937, *34,* 593–605.

———. *La psychologie de la forme.* Paris: Flammarion, 1937.

———. La théorie de la forme et la notion de valeur d'après M. Köhler. *J. Psychol. norm. path.*, 1939, *36,* 274–286.

———. *La psychologie de l'enfant.* Paris: Hermann, 1940.

———. *La psychologie animale.* (3rd ed.) Paris: Colin, 1964. (1940)

———. *Introduction à la psychologie.* (13th ed.) Paris: Vrin, 1964. (1942)

———. *Manuel de psychologie.* Paris: Presses Universitaires de France, 1943.

———. "La perception de la causalité" d'Albert Michotte. *J. Psychol. norm. path.*, 1947, *40,* 112–128.

———. Sur la mémoire musicale. *Année psychol.,* 1951, *51,* 413–422.

———. La compréhension des dessins. *J. Psychol. norm. path.*, 1953, *46,* 278–298.

———. Cinquante ans de psychologie animale. *J. Psychol. norm. path.*, 1954, *47–51,* 233–242.

———. Cybernétique et psychologie. *J. Psychol. norm. path.*, 1954, *47–51,* 360–378.

———. Cybernétique et psychologie. II. Machines et systèmes physiques. *J. Psychol. norm. path.*, 1954, *47–51,* 486–499.

Hameline, *Anthologie*

EDWIN RAY GUTHRIE
1886-1959
American Psychologist (26)

Guthrie, E. R. *The paradoxes of Mr. Russell: With a brief account of their history.* Lancaster, Pa.: New Era Printing, 1915.

———. Russell's theory of types. *J. Phil.,* 1915, *12,* 381–385.

———. The field of logic. *J. Phil.,* 1916, *13,* 152–158.

Smith, S., & ———. *General psychology in terms of behavior.* New York: Appleton, 1921.

Smith, S., & ———. Exhibitionism. *J. abnorm. soc. Psychol.,* 1922, *17,* 206–209.

———. Purpose and mechanism in psychology. *J. Phil.,* 1924, *21,* 673–682.

———. Measuring student opinion of teachers. *School & Soc.,* 1927, *25,* 175–176.

———. Measuring introversion and extroversion. *J. abnorm. soc. Psychol.*, 1927–1928, *22*, 82–88.

———, & Morrill, H. The fusion of non-musical intervals. *Amer. J. Psychol.*, 1928, *40*, 624–625.

———. Conditioning as a principle of learning. *Psychol. Rev.*, 1930, *37*, 412–428. Reprinted in part in M. H. Marx (Ed.), *Psychological theory: Contemporary readings.* New York: Macmillan, 1951, pp. 428–438.

———. On the nature of psychological explanations. *Psychol. Rev.*, 1933, *40*, 124–137.

———. Association as a function of time interval. *Psychol. Rev.*, 1933, *40*, 355–367.

———. Discussion: Pavlov's theory of conditioning. *Psychol. Rev.*, 1934, *41*, 199–206.

———. Reward and punishment. *Psychol. Rev.*, 1934, *41*, 450–460.

———. *The psychology of learning.* (Rev. ed.) New York: Harper, 1952. (1935) (Reprinted 1960)

———. Tolman on associative learning. *Psychol. Rev.*, 1937, *44*, 525–528.

Yacorzinski, G., & ———. A comparative study of involuntary and voluntary conditioned responses. *J. gen. Psychol.*, 1937, *16*, 235–257.

———. *The psychology of human conflict.* New York: Harper & Row, 1938. (Reprinted 1962)

———. The effect of outcome on learning. *Psychol. Rev.*, 1939, *46*, 480–485.

———. Association and the law of effect. *Psychol. Rev.*, 1940, *47*, 127–148.

———. The principle of associative learning. In F. P. Clarke & M. C. Nahm (Eds.), *Philosophical essays in honor of Edgar Arthur Singer, Jr.* Philadelphia: University of Pennsylvania Press, 1942, pp. 100–114. (Reprinted 1969)

———. Conditioning: A theory of learning in terms of stimulus, response and association. *Yearb. Nat. Soc. Stud. Educ.*, 1942, *41*(2), 17–60.

———. Psychology of war time. *Marriage and family living*, 1943, *5*, 56–57.

———. Personality in terms of associative learning. In J. McV. Hunt (Ed.), *Personality and the behavior disorders: A handbook based on experimental and clinical research.* Vol. 1. New York: Ronald Press, 1944, 49–68.

———. Psychological facts and psychological theory. *Psychol. Bull.*, 1946, *43*, 1–20.

———. Recency or effect?—A reply to Captain O'Connor. *Harvard educ. Rev.*, 1946, *16*, 286–289.

———, & Horton, G. P. *Cats in a puzzle box.* New York: Rinehart, 1946.

———. The evaluation of teaching. *Educ. Rec.*, 1949, *30*, 109–115.

———, & Edwards, A. L. *Psychology: A first course in human behavior.* New York: Harper, 1949.

———, & Powers, F. F. *Educational Psychology.* New York: Ronald Press, 1950.

———. The status of systematic psychology. *Amer. Psychologist*, 1950, *5*, 97–101.

———. *The state university: Its function and its future.* Seattle, Wash.: University of Washington Press, 1959.

———. Association by contiguity. In S. Koch (Ed.), *Psychology: A study of a science.* Study 1. *Conceptual and systematic.* Vol. 2. *General systematic formulations, learning, and special processes.* New York: McGraw-Hill, 1959, pp. 158–195.

Boe & Church, *Punishment;* O'Brien & Schrag, *Sociology*

ERNST HEINRICH HAECKEL
1834-1919
German Biologist (15)

Haeckel, E. H. *Biologische Studien.* (3 vols.) Leipzig: Engelmann, 1870–1877. **C**

———. *Gemeinverständliche Werke.* (6 vols.) Ed. by H. Schmidt. 1 & 2. *Natürliche Schöpfungsgeschichte.* 3. *Die Welträtsel.* 4. *Die Lebenswunder.* 5. *Vorträge und Abhandlungen.* 6. *Reisen, Indische Reisebriefe aus Insulinde.* Leipzig: Kröner, 1924. **C**

———. *Ernst und Agnes Haeckel. Ein Briefwechsel.* Ed. by K. Huschker. Jena: Urbana, 1950. **B C**

———. Der Briefwechsel zwischen Thomas Henry Huxley und Ernst Haeckel. Ed. by G. Uschmann & Ilse John. *Wiss. Z. Friedrich-Schiller Univ. Jena,* 1959–1960, *9,* 7–33. **B C**

———. *Generelle Morphologie der Organismen.* (2 vols.) Berlin: Reimer, 1866.

———. *Natürliche Schöpfungsgeschichte.* (10th ed.) Berlin: Reimer, 1902. (1868)

———. *The history of creation, or the development of the earth and its inhabitants by the action of natural causes.* (4th ed.) (2 vols.) Trans. by E. R. Lankester. London: Kegan Paul, Trench, & Truebner, 1899, (1868)

———. *Anthropogenie.* (6th ed.) (2 vols.) Leipzig: Engelmann, 1910. (1874)

———. *The evolution of man: A popular exposition of the principle points of human ontogeny and phylogeny.* (3rd ed.) (2 vols.) New York: Appleton, 1896. (1874)

———. Ueber die Individualität des Thierkörpers. *Jena. Z. Naturwiss.,* 1878, *12,* 1–20.

———. *Freedom in science and teaching.* New York: Appleton, 1879. (1878)

———. *Das System der Medusen.* (2 vols.) Jena: Fischer, 1879–1881.

———. *Die Naturanschauung von Darwin, Goethe, und Lamarck.* Jena: Fischer, 1882.

———. *The confession of faith of a man of science.* Trans. by J. Gilchrist. London: Black, 1903. (1893) **B**

———. *Die systematische Phylogenie. Entwurf eines natürlichen Systems den Organismen auf Grund ihrer Stammesgeschichte.* (3 vols.) Berlin: Reimer, 1894–1896.

———. *The last link: Our present knowledge of the descent of man.* (2nd ed.) London: Black, 1899. (1898)

———. *The riddle of the universe, at the close of the nineteenth century.* Trans. by J. McCabe.

New York: Harper, 1900. (1899) (Reprinted 1968)

———. *The wonders of life.* Trans. by J. McCabe. New York: Harper, 1905. (1904) (Reprinted in German, 1970)

———. *Die Natur als Künstlerin.* Berlin: Vita, 1913.

———. *Kristallseelen.* Leipzig: Kröner, 1917.

———. *Italienfahrt. Briefe an die Braut 1859–1860.* Leipzig: Röhler & Umelang, 1921.

———. *The story of the development of a youth. Letters to his parents 1852–1856.* New York: Harper, 1923.

———. *Himmelhoch jauchzend.* Dresden: Reissner, 1927.

———. *Haeckel und Allmers. Die Geschichte einer Freundschaft in Briefen der Freunde.* Ed. by R. Koop. Bremen: Geist, 1941. **B**

Count, *Race* ; Drever, *Sourcebook ;* Grinder, *Genetic Psychology* ; Hall, *Source Book*

G(RANVILLE) STANLEY HALL
1844-1924
American Psychologist (27)

Hall, G. S. *Letters of G. Stanley Hall to Jonas Gilman Clark.* Ed. by N. Rush. Worcester, Mass.: Clark University Library, 1948. **B C**

———. *Health, growth and heredity.* Ed. by C. E. Strickland & C. Burgess. New York: Teachers College Press, 1965. **C**

———. Philosophy in the United States. *Mind,* 1879, *4,* 89–105.

———. *Aspects of German culture.* Boston: Osgood, 1881.

Bowditch, H. P., & ———. Optical illusions of motion. *J. Physiol.,* 1882, *3,* 297–307.

———. The moral and religious training of children. *Princeton Rev.,* 1882, *10,* 26–48.

———. Reaction-time and attention in the hypnotic state. *Mind,* 1883, *8,* 170–182.

————. The contents of children's minds. *Princeton Rev.*, 1883, *11*, 249–272.

————, & Donaldson, H. H. Motor sensations on the skin. *Mind*, 1885, *10*, 557–572.

————. The new psychology. *Andover Rev.*, 1885, *3*, 120–135, 239–248.

————. A sketch of the history of reflex action. *Amer. J. Psychol.*, 1890, *3*, 71–86.

————. Notes on the study of infants. *J. genet. Psychol.*, 1891, *1*, 127–138.

————. The contents of children's minds on entering school. *J. genet. Psychol.*, 1891, *1* 139–173.

————. Laboratory of the McLean Hospital, Somerville, Massachusetts. *Amer. J. Insan.*, 1894–1895, *51*, 358–364.

Dunton, L., Münsterberg, H., Harris, W. T., & ————. *The old psychology and the new: Addresses before the Massachusetts schoolmasters' club, April 27, 1895*. Boston: New England Publishing, 1895.

———— Psychological education. *Amer. J. Insan.*, 1896, *53*, 228–241.

————. A study of fears. *Amer. J. Psychol.*, 1897, *8*, 147–249.

————. Some aspects of the early sense of self. *Amer. J. Psychol.*, 1898, *9*, 351–395.

————. A study of anger. *Amer. J. Psychol.*, 1899, *10*, 516–591.

————. Note on early memories. *J. genet. Psychol.*, 1899, *6*, 485–512.   B

————. Confessions of a psychologist. *J. genet. Psychol.*, 1901, *8*, 92–143.   B

————. *Adolescence: Its psychology and its relations to physiology, anthropology, sociology, sex, crime, religion and education.* (2 vols.) New York: Appleton, 1904. (Reprinted 1968)

————. *Youth, its education, regimen and hygiene.* (Condensation of *Adolescence*.) New York: Appleton, 1907. (1904)

————. Mental science. *Science,* 1904, *20*(N.S.), 481–490.

————. The affiliation of psychology with philosophy and with the natural sciences. *Science,* 1906, *23*(N.S.), 297–301.

————. A glance at the phyletic background of genetic psychology. *Amer. J. Psychol.*, 1908, *19*, 149–212.

————. Evolution and psychology. In American Association for the Advancement of Science, *Fifty years of Darwinism.* New York: Holt, 1909, pp. 251–267. Reprinted in part in *Health, growth and heredity, op. cit.*, pp. 40–50.

————. *Founders of modern psychology.* New York: Appleton, 1912.

————. A synthetic genetic study of fear. Chaps. 1, 2. *Amer. J. Psychol.*, 1914, *25*, 149–200, 321–392.

————. The Freudian methods applied to anger. *Amer. J. Psychol.*, 1915, *26*, 438–443.

————. A reminiscence. *Amer. J. Psychol.*, 1917, *28*, 297–300.   B

————. *Jesus the Christ, in the light of psychology.* (2 vols.) New York: Doubleday, 1917.

————. *Recreations of a psychologist.* New York: Appleton, 1920.   B

————. *Morale: The supreme standard of life and conduct.* New York: Appleton, 1920.

————. Preface. In S. Freud, *A general introduction to psycho-analysis.* New York: Boni & Liveright, 1920, pp. v–vii.

————. *Senescence: The last half of life.* New York: Appleton, 1922.

————. *Life and confessions of a psychologist.* New York: Appleton, 1923.   B Bl

Cubberley, *Public Educators* ; Dennis, *Psychology* ; Dennis, *Readings Developmental* ; Grinder, *Genetic Psychology* ; Herrnstein & Boring, *Source Book* ; Kessen, *Child* ; Sahakian, *Psychology* ; Shipley, *Classics* ; Strain, *Philosophies Education*

MARSHALL HALL
1790-1857
English Physiologist (21)

Hall, M. *Memoirs of Marshall Hall.* Ed. by his widow. London: Bentley, 1861. **B C**

———. *The principles of diagnosis.* (2nd ed.) New York: Appleton, 1835. (1817)

———. On the nervous circle which connects the voluntary muscles with the brain. *Phil. Trans.,* 1826, *116*(2), 163–173.

———. *A critical and experimental essay on the circulation of the blood, especially as observed in the minute and capillary vessels of the batrachia and of fishes.* London: Sherwood, Gilbert & Piper, 1831.

———. On a particular function of the nervous system. *Proc. Zool. Soc.,* 1832, *2,* 190–192.

———. On the reflex function of the medulla oblongata and the medulla spinalis. *Phil. Trans.,* 1833, *123,* 635–665.

———. *Memoirs on the nervous system. I. The reflex function of the medulla oblongata and medulla spinalis. II. The true spinal marrow, and the excito-motory system of the nerves.* London: Sherwood, Gilbert & Piper, 1837.

———. *Diseases and derangements of the nervous system.* London: Baillière, 1841.

———. *Gulstonian lectures.* London: Baillière, 1842.

———. *New memoir on the nervous system.* London: Baillière, 1843.

———. Sur la division du système nerveux en système cérébral, système spinal et système ganglionnaire, *C. r. hebdomad. séances Acad. Sci.,* 1847, *24,* 619–622.

———. *Synopsis of the diastaltic nervous system: Or the system of the spinal marrow, and its reflex arcs; as the nervous agent in all the functions of ingestion and of egestion in the animal economy.* London: Mallett, 1850.

———. Recherches expérimentales sur le système nerveux. *C. r. hebdomad. séances Acad. Sci.,* 1851, *32,* 633–634, 832–834, 879.

———. *Synopsis of cerebral and spinal seizures of inorganic origin and of paroxysmal form as a class; and of their pathology as involved in the structures and actions of the neck.* London: Mallett, 1851.

Clarke & O'Malley, *Brain*; Fulton & Wilson, *Physiology*

ALBRECHT VON HALLER
1708-1777
Swiss Physiologist (17)

Haller, A. v. *Mémoires sur la nature sensible et irritable des parties du corps animal.* (4 vols.) Lausanne: Bousquet, 1756–1760. **C**

———. *Opera minora emendata.* (3 vols.) Lausanne: Grasset, 1762–1768. **C**

———. *Tagebuch seiner Beobachtungen über Schriftsteller und über sich selbst.* (2 vols.) Bern: Heller, 1787. **B C**

———. *Gedichte.* Ed. by L. Hirzel. Frauenfeld: Huber, 1917. (1882) **C**

———. *Albrecht von Haller & Giambattista Morgagni. Briefwechsel 1745–1768.* Ed. by E. Hintzche. Bern: Huber, 1964. **B C**

———. *Icones anatomicae,* (3 vols.) Göttingen: Vandenhoeck, 1743–1756.

———. *First lines of physiology.* (3rd ed.) (2 vols. in 1) Intro. by L. S. King. New York: Johnson Reprint, 1966. (1747)

———. *Réflexions sur le système de la génération de M. de Buffon.* Geneva: Barillot, 1751.

———. De partibus corporis humani sentientibus et irritabilibus. (1752) In *Opera minora, op. cit.,* pp. 329–502.

———. De partibus corporis humani sensibilibus et irritabilibus. *Comment. Soc. reg. sci. Götting.,* 1753, *2,* 114–158.

———. *A dissertation on the sensible and irritable parts of animals.* Intro. by O. Temkin. Baltimore, Md.: Johns Hopkins Press, 1936. (1753)

———. *Opuscula pathologica, partim recusa, partim inedita, quibus sectiones cadaverum mor-*

bosorum potissimum continentur. Accedunt experimenta de respiratione, quarta parte aucta. Lausanne: Bousquet, 1755. (Reprinted 1768)

————. *Deux mémoires sur le mouvement du sang et sur les effets de la saignée fondés sur des expériences faites sur des animaux.* Lausanne: Bousquet, 1756.

————. *Elementa physiologiae corporis humani.* (2 vols.) Lausanne: Bousquet, 1757–1766.

————. *Bibliotheca botanica.* (2 vols.) Zurich: Orell, Gessner & Fuessli, 1771–1772.

————. *Bibliotheca anatomica.* (2 vols.) Hildesheim: Olms, 1969. (1774–1777) **B**

————. *Bibliotheca chirurgica.* Basel: Schweighauser, 1774; Bern: Haller, 1775. (Reprinted 1968)

————. *Bibliotheca medicinae practicae.* (4 vols.) Basel: Schweighauser, 1776; Bern: Haller, 1778. (Reprinted 1968)

————. *Briefwechsel zwischen A. v. Haller und Eberhard Friedrich von Gemmingen.* Ed. by H. Fischer. Tübingen: Literarischer Verein in Stuttgart, 1899.

————. Albrecht von Hallers Briefe an Johannes Gesner. Ed. by H. E. Sigerist. *Abh. Ges. Wiss. Göttingen,* Math.-phys. Kl., 1923, *11,* No. 2. **B**

————. *Albrecht Hallers Tagebuch seiner Studienreise nach London, Paris, Strassburg und Basel, 1727–1728.* (2nd enl. & annot. ed.) Ed. by E. Hintzsche. Bern: Huber, 1968. **B**

Bodenheimer, *Biology;* Clarke & O'Malley, *Brain;* Clendening, *Source Book;* Fulton & Wilson, *Physiology;* Hall, *Source Book*

(SIR) WILLIAM HAMILTON
1788-1856
Scottish Philosopher (21)

Hamilton, W. Dissertations, historical, critical and supplementary. (1846–1863) In T. Reid, *Philosophical Works.* Vol. II. Hildesheim, Olms, 1967, pp. 741–991. **C**

————. *Discussions on philosophy and literature, education and university reform: Chiefly from the Edinburgh Review.* New York: Harper, 1856. (1852) **C**

————. *Philosophy.* Arranged & ed. by O. W. Wight. New York: Appleton, 1859. (Reprinted 1971) **C**

————. *The metaphysics of Sir William Hamilton, collected, arranged, & abridged by Francis Bowen.* Cambridge: Sever & Francis, 1865. (1859) **C**

————. *Lectures on metaphysics and logic.* Vols. 1, 2. *Metaphysics.* (7th ed.) Vols. 3, 4. *Logic.* (3rd ed.) Ed. by H. L. Mansel & J. Veitch. Boston: Allyn, 1876. (1859) **C**

————. Philosophy of perception. *Edinb. Rev.,* 1830, *52,* 158–207.

Drever, *Sourcebook;* Hunter & Macalpine, *Psychiatry;* Robinson, *Scottish Philosophy*

DAVID HARTLEY
1705-1757
English Philosopher (24)

Hartley, D. *Original letters from . . . Dr. Hartley.* Ed. by R. Warner. London: Publisher unknown, 1872. (1817)

————. *Various conjectures on the perception, motion, and generation of ideas.* Trans. by R. E. A. Palmer. Los Angeles: Andrews Clark Memorial Library, University of California, 1959. (1746)

————. Enquiry into the origin of the human appetites and affections. Lincoln: Publisher unknown, 1747.

————. *Observations on man, his frame, his duty and his expectations.* Intro. by T. L. Huguelet. Gainesville, Fla.: Scholars' Facsimiles & Reprints, 1966. (1749)

————. *Hartley's theory of the human mind, on the principles of association of ideas; with essays relating to the subject of it.* (2nd ed.) Ed. by J. Priestley. London: Johnson, 1790. (1749) (Reprinted 1971)

————. *Observations on man. To which is prefixed a sketch of the life and character of Dr. Hartley by his son David Hartley.* Ed. by D. Hartley, Jr. (6th rev. ed.) (2 vols.) London: Tegg, 1834. (1749)   **Bl**

Dennis, *Psychology;* Herrnstein & Boring, *Source Book;* Hunter & Macalpine, *Psychiatry;* Mandler & Mandler, *Thinking;* Murphy, *Western;* Rand, *Classical Psychologists;* Rand, *Moralists;* Reeves, *Body Mind;* Sahakian, *Psychology*

(KARL ROBERT) EDUARD VON HARTMANN
1842-1905
German Philosopher (15)

Hartmann, E. v. *Gesammelte Studien und Aufsätze gemeinverständlichen Inhalts.* Berlin: Duncker, 1876.   **C**

————. *Schellings philosophisches* [sic] *System.* Leipzig: Haacke, 1907. (1869)

————. *Philosophy of the unconscious: Speculative results according to the inductive method of physical science.* (9th ed.) Trans. by W. C. Coupland. New York: Harcourt, Brace, 1931. (1869)

————. *Philosophie des Unbewusstseins.* (12th ed.) (3 vols.) Ed. by A. Drews. Leipzig: Kröner, 1923. (1869)

————. *Das Unbewusste vom Standpunkte der Physiologie und Descendenztheorie.* Berlin: Naumburg, 1872.

————. The true and the false in Darwinism. Trans. by H. J. D'Árcy. *J. specul. Phil.,* 1877, *11,* 244–251, 392–399.

————. *Das sittliche Bewusstsein.* (2nd ed.) Leipzig: Haacke, 1889. (1879)

————. *Zur Geschichte und Begründung des Pessimismus.* (2nd ed.) Berlin: Duncker, 1891. (1880)

————. *The religion of the future.* Trans. by E. Dare. London: Stewart, 1886. (1882)

————. *Spiritism.* Trans. by C. Fullerton. London: Psychological Press, n.d. (1885)

————. *Lotzes Philosophie.* Leipzig: Friedrich, 1888.

————. *Das Grundproblem der Erkenntnistheorie.* Leipzig: Friedrich, 1889.

————. Wundts System der Philosophie. *Preuss. Jb.,* 1890, *66,* 1–31, 123–132.

————. *Kants Erkenntnistheorie und Metaphysik in den vier Perioden ihrer Entwickelung.* Leipzig: Friedrich, 1894.

————. *Die moderne Psychologie: Eine kritische Geschichte der deutschen Psychologie in der zweiten Hälfte des neunzehnten Jahrhunderts.* Leipzig: Haacke, 1901.

————. Die Ginalität in ihrem Verhältnis zur Kausalität. *Phil. Stud.,* 1903, *18,* 505–514.

————. *Das Problem des Lebens.* Bad Sachsa: Haacke, 1906.

————. *System der Philosophie im Grundriss.* (8 vols.) Bad Sachsa: Haacke, 1907–1909.

————. Grundriss der Psychologie. (1908) In *System der Philosophie im Grundriss.* Vol. 3, *op. cit.*

————. *Philosophie des Schönen.* Ed. by R. Müller-Freienfels. Berlin: Volksverband der Bücherfreunde, 1924.

WILLIAM HARVEY
1578-1657
English Physiologist (20)

Harvey, W. *On the motion of the heart and blood in animals.* Rev. ed. by L. Bowie, intro. by M. Graubard, & trans. by T. Willis. Chicago: Regnery, 1962.   **C**

————. *The works of William Harvey, M.D.* Trans. by T. Willis. London: Sydenham Society, 1847. (Reprinted 1962)   **C**

————. *Circulation of the blood: Two anatomical essays by William Harvey, together with nine letters written by him, the whole translated from the Latin and slightly annotated by Kenneth J. Franklin.* Oxford: Blackwell, Scientific Publications, 1958.   **C**

――――. *Lectures on the whole of anatomy: An annotated translation of Prelectiones Anatomiae Universalis.* Ed. by C. D. O'Malley, F. N. L. Poynter, & K. F. Russell. Berkeley, Calif.: University of California Press, 1961. (1616)

――――. *Anatomical lectures: Prelectiones Anatomiae Universalis, De Musculis.* Ed. with intro., trans., & notes by Gweneth Whitteridge. Edinburgh: Livingstone, 1964. (1616)

――――. *De motu locali animalium, 1627.* Ed., trans., & intro. by Gweneth Whitteridge. Cambridge: Cambridge University Press, 1959. (1627)

――――. *Movement of the heart and blood in animals, an anatomical essay.* Trans. by K. J. Franklin. Oxford: Blackwell, 1957. (1628) (Reprinted 1965)

――――. *Exercitatio anatomica de motu cordis et sanguinis in animalibus.* (5th ed.) Trans. & annot. by C. D. Leake. Springfield, Ill.: Thomas, 1970. (1628)   **B Bl**

Bodenheimer, *Biology*; Brinton, *Age Reason*; Clendening, *Source Book*; Fulton & Wilson, *Physiology*; Hall, *Nature's Laws*; Hall, *Source Book*; Hunter & Macalpine, *Psychiatry*; Hutchins, *Great Books*; Rook, *Origins*; Schwartz & Bishop, *Moments Discovery*

HENRY HEAD
1861-1940
English Neurologist (25)

Head, H. (With W. H. R. Rivers, G. Holmes, J. Sherren, T. Thompson, & G. Riddoch.) *Studies in neurology.* (2 vols.) London: Oxford University Press, 1920.   **C**

――――. Ueber die negativen und positiven Schwankungen des Nervenstromes. *Arch. ges. Physiol.,* 1887, *40,* 207–273.

――――. On disturbances of sensation with especial reference to the pain of visceral disease. *Brain,* 1893, *16,* 1–133; 1894, *17,* 339–480; 1896, *19,* 153–276.

――――. Certain mental changes that accompany visceral disease. *Brain,* 1901, *24,* 345–429.

――――, & Sherren, J. The consequences of injury to the peripheral nerves in man. *Brain,* 1905, *28,* 116–340. Reprinted in *Studies in neurology,* Vol. 1, *op. cit.,* pp. 166–224.

――――, Rivers, W. H. R., & Sherren, J. The afferent nervous system from a new aspect. *Brain,* 1905, *28,* 99–116. Reprinted in *Studies in neurology,* Vol. 1, *op. cit.,* pp. 55–65.

――――, & Rivers, W. H. R. A human experiment in nerve division. *Brain,* 1908, *31,* 323–450. Reprinted in *Studies in neurology,* Vol. 1, *op. cit.,* pp. 225–329.

――――. Occupation-neuroses. In T. C. Allbutt & H. D. Rolleston (Eds.), *A system of medicine, by many writers.* Vol. 8. (New ed.) New York: Macmillan, 1910.

――――, & Holmes, G. Sensory disturbances from cerebral lesions. *Brain,* 1911–1912, *34,* 102–271. Also abridged in *Lancet,* 1912, *182,* 1–4, 79–83. 144–153. Reprinted in *Studies in neurology,* Vol. 2, *op. cit.,* pp. 533–638.

――――. Hughlings Jackson on aphasia and kindred affections of speech; together with a complete bibliography of Dr. Jackson's publications on speech and a reprint of some of the most important parts. *Brain,* 1915, *38,* 1–190.

――――, & Riddoch, G. Automatic bladder, excessive sweating and some other reflex conditions in gross injuries of the spinal cord. *Brain,* 1917, *40,* 188–263. Reprinted in *Studies in neurology,* Vol. 2, *op. cit.,* pp. 467–530.

――――. Sensation and the cerebral cortex. *Brain,* 1918, *41,* 58–253. Reprinted in *Studies in neurology,* Vol. 2, *op. cit.,* pp. 639–800.

――――. Epilogue. (1920) In *Studies in neurology,* Vol. 2, *op. cit.,* pp. 801–809.

――――. Aphasia and kindred disorders of speech. *Brain,* 1920, *43,* 87–165.

――――. Aphasia: An historical review. *Brain,* 1920, *43,* 390–411.

――――. Release of function in the nervous system. Croonian Lecture. *Proc. roy. Soc.,* London, 1920–1921, *92B,* 184–209.

――――. Disorders of symbolic thinking and expression. *Brit. J. Psychol.,* 1920–1921, *11,* 179–193.

―――. Speech and cerebral localization. *Brain,* 1923, *46,* 355–528.

―――. The conception of nervous and mental energy. II. "Vigilance": A physiological state of the nervous system. *Brit. J. Psychol.,* 1923–1924, *14,* 126–147.

―――. *Aphasia and kindred disorders of speech.* (2 vols.) Cambridge: Cambridge University Press, 1926. (Reprinted 1963)

Herrnstein & Boring, *Source Book*

WILLIAM HEALY
1869-1963
American Psychiatrist (17)

Healy, W., & Fernald, Grace M. Tests for practical mental classification. *Psychol. Monogr.,* 1911, *13,* No. 54.

―――. A pictorial completion text. *Psychol. Rev.,* 1914, *21,* 189–203.

―――, & Bronner, Augusta F. An outline for institutional education and treatment of young offenders. *J. educ. Psychol.,* 1915, *6,* 301–316.

―――. *Honesty: A study of the causes and treatment of dishonesty among children.* Indianapolis, Ind.: Bobbs-Merrill, 1915.

―――, & Healy, Mary T. *Pathological lying, accusation and swindling: A study in forensic psychology.* Boston: Little, Brown, 1915. (Reprinted 1969)

―――. *The individual delinquent: A text-book of diagnosis and prognosis for all concerned in understanding offenders.* Boston: Little, Brown, 1915.

―――, & Bronner, Augusta F. Youthful offenders: A comparative study of two groups, each of 1,000 recidivists. *Amer. J. Sociol.,* 1916–1917, *22,* 38–52.

―――. *Mental conflicts and misconduct.* Montclair, N.J.: Patterson Smith, 1969. (1917)

―――. Pictorial completion test II. *J. appl. Psychol.,* 1921, *5,* 225–239.

―――. *The practical value of scientific study of juvenile delinquents.* Washington, D.C.: U.S. Government Printing Office, 1922.

―――, & Bronner, Augusta F. *Delinquents and criminals: Their making and unmaking: Studies of two American cities.* New York: Macmillan, 1926.

Bronner, Augusta F., ―――, Lowe, Gladys M., & Shimberg, Myra E. *A manual of individual mental tests and testing.* Boston: Little, Brown, 1927.

―――, Bronner, Augusta F., Baylor, M. H., & Murphy, J. P. *Reconstructing behavior in youth: A study of problem children in foster homes.* New York: Knopf, 1929.

―――, Bronner, Augusta F., & Bowers, Anna M. *The structure and meaning of psychoanalysis, as related to personality and behavior.* New York: Knopf, 1930.

Alexander, F., & ―――. *Roots of crime: Psychoanalytic studies.* New York: Knopf, 1935.

―――, & Bronner, Augusta F. *New light on delinquency and its treatment.* New Haven: Yale University Press, 1936.

―――. *Personality in formation and action.* New York: Norton, 1938.

―――, & Bronner, Augusta F. *Treatment and what happened afterward.* Boston: Judge Baker Guidance Center, 1939.

―――, & Alper, B. S. *Criminal youth and the Borstal system.* New York: Commonwealth Fund, 1941.

―――, *et al.* Psychiatry and delinquency. Round table discussion. *Amer. J. Orthopsychiat.,* 1949, *19,* 317–341.

―――, & Bronner, Augusta F. The child guidance clinic: Birth and growth of an idea. In L. G. Lowrey (Ed.), *Orthopsychiatry 1923–1948: Retrospect and prospect.* New York: American Orthopsychiatric Association, 1948, pp. 14–49.

B

―――, & Bronner, Augusta F. Orthopsychiatry: An over-view. *Amer. J. Orthopsychiat.,* 1955, *25,* 472–474.

Beck & Molish, *Reflexes*

SELIG HECHT
1892-1947
American Physiologist (22)

Hecht, S. The photochemical nature of the photosensory process. *J. gen. Physiol.*, 1919–1920, *2*, 229–246.

———. Intensity and the process of photoreception. *J. gen. Physiol.*, 1919–1920, *2*, 337–347.

———. The dark adaption of the human eye. *J. gen. Physiol.*, 1919–1920, *2*, 499–518.

———. Photochemistry of visual purple. I. The kinetics of the decomposition of visual purple by light. *J. gen. Physiol.*, 1920–1921, *3*, 1–13.

———. Photochemistry of visual purple. II. The effect of temperature on the bleaching of visual purple by light. *J. gen. Physiol.*, 1920–1921, *3*, 285–290.

———. Time and intensity in photosensory stimulation. *J. gen. Physiol.*, 1920–1921, *3*, 367–374.

———. The relation between the wave-length of light and its effect on the photosensory process. *J. gen. Physiol.*, 1920–1921, *3*, 375–390.

———. The nature of foveal dark adaptation. *J. gen. Physiol.*, 1921–1922, *4*, 113–139.

———. Sensory adaptation and the stationary state. *J. gen. Physiol.*, 1922–1923, *5*, 555–580.

———. Photochemistry of visual purple. III. The relation between the intensity of light and the rate of bleaching of visual purple. *J. gen. Physiol.*, 1923–1924, *6*, 731–740.

———. Intensity discrimination and the stationary state. *J. gen. Physiol.*, 1923–1924, *6*, 355–373.

———. On the binocular fusion of colors and its relation to theories of color vision. *Proc. Nat. Acad. Sci.*, 1928, *14*, 237–241.

———, Wolf, E., & Wald, G. D. The visual acuity of insects. *Amer. J. Physiol.*, 1929, *90*, 381–382.

———. Vision. II. The nature of the photoreceptor process. In C. Murchison (Ed.), *The foundations of experimental psychology*. Worcester, Mass.: Clark University Press, 1929, pp. 216–272, & in C. Murchison (Ed.), *A handbook of general experimental psychology*. Worcester, Mass.: Clark University Press, 1934, pp. 704–828.

———. The development of Thomas Young's theory of color vision. *J. opt. Soc. Amer.*, 1930, *20*, 231–270.

———. The interrelations of various aspects of color vision. *J. opt. Soc. Amer.*, 1931, *21*, 615–639.

———, & Wolf, E. Intermittent stimulation by light. I. The validity of Talbot's law for *Mya*. *J. gen. Physiol.*, 1931–1932, *15*, 369–389.

———. A theory of visual intensity discrimination. *J. gen. Physiol.*, 1934–1935, *18*, 767–789.

———, Haig, C., & Wald, C. The dark adaptation of retinal fields of different size and location. *J. gen. Physiol.*, 1935–1936, *19*, 321–337.

———. Intensity discrimination and its relation to the adaptation of the eye. *J. Physiol.*, 1936, *86*, 15–21.

———, & Schlaer, S. The color vision of dichromats. I. Wave-length discrimination, brightness distribution, and color mixture. II. Saturation as the basis for wave-length discrimination and color mixture. *J. gen. Physiol.*, 1936–1937, *20*, 57–82, 83–93.

———. The instantaneous visual threshold after light adaptation. *Proc. Nat. Acad. Sci.*, 1937, *23*, 227–233.

———. Rods, cones, and the chemical basis of vision. *Physiol. Rev.*, 1937, *17*, 239–290.

———. *La base chimique et structurale de la vision*. Paris: Hermann, 1938.

———. The nature of the visual process. *Bull. N.Y. Acad. Med.*, 1938, *14*, 21–45.

———, & Mintz, E. U. The visibility of single lines at various illuminations and the retinal basis of visual resolution. *J. gen. Physiol.*, 1938–1939, *22*, 593–612.

———, Schlaer, S., & Pirenne, M. H. Energy at the threshold of vision. *Science*, 1941, *93*, 585–587

———, Schlaer, S., & Pirenne, M. H. Energy quanta and vision. *J. gen. Physiol.*, 1941–1942, *25*, 819–840.

———. The quantum relations of vision. *J. opt. Soc. Amer.*, 1942, *32*, 42–49.

———. Energy and vision. *Amer. Scientist*, 1944, *32*, 159–177. Reprinted in G. A. Baitsell (Ed.), *Science in progress*. Series IV. New Haven: Yale University Press, 1945, pp. 75–97.

———, & Hsia, Y. Dark adaptation following light adaption to red and white lights. *J. opt. Soc. Amer.*, 1945, *35*, 261–267.

———, & Hsia, Y. Colorblind vision. I. Luminosity losses in the spectrum for dichromats. *J. gen. Physiol.*, 1947–1948, *31*, 141–152.

———, Ross, S., & Mueller, C. G. The visibility of lines and squares at high brightnesses. *J. opt. Soc. Amer.*, 1947, *37*, 500–507.

———. Brightness, visual acuity and colour blindness. *Documenta Ophthalm.*, 1949, *3*, 289–306.

Miller, *Mathematics* ; Teevan, *Vision*

GEORG WILHELM FRIEDRICH HEGEL
1770-1831
German Philosopher (18)

Schelling, F. W. J. v., & Hegel, G. W. F. *Briefe von und an Hegel*. (2 vols.) Ed. by K. Hegel. Leipzig: Duncker & Humblot, 1887.   **C**

———. *Sämtliche Werke*. (18+ vols.) Ed. first by G. Lasson & later by J. Hoffmeister. Hamburg: Meiner, 1905– .   **C**

———. *Sämtliche Werke*. (20 vols.) Ed. by H. Glockner. Stuttgart: Frommann, 1948–1964. (1927–1930)   **C**

———. *On Christianity: Early theological writings*. Trans. by T. M. Knox. Gloucester, Mass.: Smith, 1961. (1948)   **C**

———. *The philosophy of Hegel*. Ed. by C. J. Friedrich. New York: Random House, 1953.   **C**

———. *Hegel's political writings*. Trans. by T. M. Knox. Oxford: Clarendon Press, 1964.   **C**

———. Gesammelte Werke. Ed. Deutsche Forschungsgemeinschaft. (Ult. 18+ vols.) Hamburg: Meiner, 1968–   **C**

———. *The phenomenology of mind*. (2nd ed.) Trans. by J. J. B. Baillie. New York: Macmillan, 1931. (1807)

———. *Phänomenologie des Geistes*. (6th ed.) Ed. by J. Hoffmeister. Hamburg: Meiner, 1952. (1807)

———. *Hegel's science of logic*. (2nd ed.) New York: Humanities Press, 1969. (1812–1816)

———. *Philosophy of mind*. (From the *Encyclopedia of the philosophical sciences*, Part 3.) Trans. by W. Wallace. Oxford: Clarendon Press, 1894. (1817) (Reprinted 1970)

———. *The philosophy of right*. Trans. by T. M. Knox. London: Oxford University Press, 1942. (1821)

———. *Hegel's philosophy of nature, being part 2 of Encyclopaedia of the philosophical sciences*. Ed. & trans. by A. V. Miller ; foreword by J. N. Findlay. Oxford: Clarendon Press, 1970. (1830)

———. *Lectures on the philosophy of religion, together with a work on the proofs of the existence of God*. (2nd ed.) (3 vols.) Trans. by E. B. Speirs & J. B. Sanderson. London: Kegan Paul, Trench & Truebner, 1895. (1832) (Reprinted 1962)

———. *Lectures on the history of philosophy*. (3 vols.) Trans. by Elizabeth S. Haldane & Frances H. Simson. London: Kegan Paul, Trench & Truebner, 1892–1896. (1833–1836) (Reprinted 1955)

———. *The philosophy of fine art*. (4 vols.) Trans. by F. P. B. Osmaston. London: Bell, 1920. (1835, 1837, 1838)

———. *Hegel's philosophy of nature*. (3 vols.) Ed., intro., & trans. by M. J. Petry. London: Allen & Unwin, 1970. (1842)

———. *Reason in history: A general introduction to the philosophy of history*. (2nd ed.) Ed. by R. S. Hartman. New York: Liberal Arts Press, 1953. (1839)

Gardiner, *Philosophy* ; Hutchins, *Great Books* ; Mann & Kreyche, *Reflections Man* ; Parsons, *Society* ; Rand, *Classical Philosophers* ; Rand, *Moralists*

WILLY HELLPACH
1877-1955
German Psychologist (12)

Hellpach, W. *Universitas litterarum. Gesammelte Aufsätze. Zum 70. Geburtstag im Namen von Freunden und Kollegen.* Ed. by G. Hess & W. Witte, with contrib. by C. Oehme, B. de Rudder, A. Wellek, & W. Witte. Stuttgart: Enke, 1948.   **C Bl**

————. *Studien zur Ethnophysiognomik und Ethophysiognomik.* Heidelberg: Winter, 1951.   **C**

————. Die Farbenempfindung in indirektem Sehen. *Phil. Stud.,* 1900, *15,* 524–578.

————. *Die Grenzwissenschaften der Psychologie.* Leipzig: Dürr, 1902.

————. Psychologie und Nervenheilkunde. *Phil. Stud.,* 1902, *19,* 192–242.

————. *Grundlinien einer Psychologie der Hysterie.* Leipzig: Engelmann, 1904.

————. *Nervenleben und Weltanschauung.* Wiesbaden: Bergmann, 1905.

————. Ueber die Anwendung psychopathologischer Erkenntnisse auf gesellschaftliche und geschichtliche Erscheinungen. *Ann. Naturphil.,* 1906, *3,* 321–348.

————. Grundgedanken zur Wissenschaftslehre der Psychopathologie. I. Der Gegenstand der Psychopathologie. *Arch. ges. Psychol.,* 1906, *7,* 143–226.

————. *Die geistigen Epidemien.* Frankfurt: Literar-Anstalt, 1907.

————. Unbewusstes oder Wechselwirkung. *Z. Psychol.,* 1908, *48,* 238–258, 321–384.

————. *Geopsyche. Die Menschenseele unter dem Einfluss von Wetter und Klima, Boden und Landschaft.* (7th ed.) Stuttgart: Enke, 1965. (1911)

————. Was heisst "Stoffwechsel bei geistiger Arbeit"? *Z. angew. Psychol.,* 1912, *5,* 561–565.

————. Vom Ausdruck der Verlegenheit. Ein Versuch zur Sozialpsychologie der Gemütsbewegungen. *Arch. ges. Psychol.,* 1913, *27,* 1–62.

————, & Lang, R. *Gruppenfabrikation.* Berlin: Springer-Verlag, 1922.

————. *Prägung. 12 Abhandlungen aus Leben und Lehre der Erziehung.* Leipzig: Quelle & Meyer, 1928.

————. Psychologie der Umwelt. In E. Abderhalden (Ed.), *Handbuch der biologischen Arbeitsmethoden.* Vol. 6. *Methoden der experimentellen Psychologie.* Part C/I. *Methoden der angewandten Psychologie.* Vienna: Urban & Schwarzenberg, 1928, pp. 109–218.

————. *Sozialpsychologie. Ein Elementarlehrbuch für Studierende und Praktizierende.* (3rd ed.) Stuttgart: Enke, 1951. (1933)

————. Die Bewusstseins-Unbewusstseins-Polarität der Seele. *Arch ges. Psychol.,* 1936, *96,* 221–239.

————. *Einführung in die Völkerpsychologie.* (3rd ed.) Stuttgart: Enke, 1951. (1938)

————. Technik und Psyche. *Industr. Psychotech.,* 1938, *15,* 267–277.

————. *Mensch und Volk der Grosstadt.* (2nd ed.) Stuttgart: Enke, 1952. (1939)

————. *Das Wellengesetz unseres Lebens.* Hamburg: Wegner, 1942.

————. *Deutsche Physiognomik. Grundlegung einer Naturgeschichte der Nationalgesichter.* (2nd ed.) Berlin: De Gruyter, 1949. (1942)

————. Mensch und Volk der Alpen (Rasse und Stamm—Begabung und Charakter—Gemeinschaftssinn und Kulturanteil). *Wien. klin. Wochensch.,* 1942, *55,* 181–185, 208–213.

————. *Völkerentwicklung und Völkergeschichte unterm Walten und Wirken von bindendem Gesetz und schöpferischer Freiheit im Völkerseelenleben.* Stuttgart: Hippokrates, 1944.

————. *Sinne und Seele, 12 Gänge in ihrem Grenzdickicht.* Stuttgart: Enke, 1946.

————. *Klinische Psychologie.* (With contrib. by B. de Rudder, *Klinische Psychologie des Kindesalters,* & by W. Witte, *Klinische Möglichkeiten experimenteller Psychodiagnostik.*) (2nd enl. ed.) Stuttgart: Thieme, 1949. (1946)

————. *Das Magethos.* Stuttgart: Hippokrates, 1947.

————. *Grundriss der Religionspsychologie (Glaubenseelenkunde).* Stuttgart: Enke, 1951.

————. *Beiträge zur Individual- und Sozialpsychologie der historischen Dialektik.* Heidelberg: Winter, 1952.

————. *Universelle Psychologie eines Genius—Goethe. Der Mensch und Mitmensch. Das Geschöpf im Schöpfer.* Meisenheim: Weskultur-Verlag, 1952.

————. *Kulturpsychologie. Eine Darstellung der seelischen Ursprünge und Antriebe, Gestaltungen und Zerrüttungen, Wandlungen und Wirkungen menschlischer Wertordnungen und Güterschöpfungen.* Stuttgart: Enke, 1953.

————. *Der Sozialorganismus. Menschengemeinschaften als Lebewesen.* (2nd rev. ed.) Cologne: Westdeutscher Verlag, 1953.

————. *Der deutsche Charakter.* Bonn: Athenäum, 1954.

————. Körperschaden und Seelenleid. *Nervenarzt,* 1954, *25,* 68–72.

HERMANN LUDWIG FERDINAND VON HELMHOLTZ
1821-1894
German Physiologist (27)

Helmholtz, H. L. F. v. *Vorträge und Reden.* (5th ed.) (2 vols.) Brunswick: Vieweg, 1903. (1865)   **C**

————. *Popular lectures on scientific subjects.* (5th ed.) (2 vols.) Trans. by E. Atkinson, P. H. Pye-Smith, *et al.* New York: Longmans, Green, 1904. (1881)   **C**

————. *Popular scientific lectures.* Ed. & selected by M. Kline. New York: Dover, 1962. (1881)   **C**

————. *Wissenschaftliche Abhandlungen.* (3 vols.) Leipzig: Barth, 1882–1895.   **C**

————. *Counting and measuring.* Trans. by Charlotte L. Bryan. New York: Van Nostrand, 1930. (1887)   **C**

————. *Schriften zur Erkenntnistheorie.* Ed. by P. Herts & M. Schlick. Berlin: Springer-Verlag, 1921.   **C**

————. *Helmholtz on perception: Its physiology and development.* Ed. by R. M. & Roslyn P. Warren. New York: Wiley, 1968.   **C**

————. *Selected writings of Hermann von Helmholtz.* Ed. by R. Kahl. Middletown, Conn.: Wesleyan University Press, 1971.   **C Bl**

————. *Ueber die Erhaltung der Kraft.* Berlin: Reimer, 1847. Reprinted in *Wissenschaftliche Abhandlungen,* Vol. 1, *op. cit.,* pp. 12–75 ; as sep. vol., 1966 ; & in trans. in *Selected writings, op. cit.,* pp. 3–55.

————. Ueber die Fortpflanzungsgeschwindigkeit der Nervenreizung. *Verh. könig. preuss. Akad. Wiss.,* Berlin, 1850, 14–15 ; *Arch. Anat. Physiol. wiss. Med.,* 1850, 71–73 ; *Ann. Chem.,* 1855, *43,* 367–379. Reprinted in *Wissenschaftliche Abhandlungen,* Vol. 3, *op. cit.,* pp. 1–3.

————. Messungen über den zeitlichen Verlauf der Zuckung animalischer Muskeln und die Fortpflanzungsgeschwindigkeit der Reizung in den Nerven. *Arch. Anat. Physiol. wiss. Med.,* 1850, 276–364. Reprinted in *Wissenschaftliche Abhandlungen,* Vol. 2, *op. cit.,* pp. 764–843.

————. Ueber die Methoden, kleinste Zeittheile zu messen, und ihre Anwendung für physiologische Zwecke. *Königsberger naturwiss. Unterhalt.,* 1851, *2*(2), 169–189. Reprinted in *Wissenschaftliche Abhandlungen,* Vol. 2, *op. cit.,* pp. 862–880.

————. *Beschreibung eines Augenspiegels zur Untersuchung der Netzhaut im lebenden Auge.* Berlin: Förstner, 1851. Reprinted in *Wissenschaftliche Abhandlungen,* Vol. 2, *op. cit.,* pp. 229–260, & in trans. by T. H. Shastid in R. H. Wilkins (Ed.), *Neurosurgical classics.* New York: Johnson Reprint, 1965, pp. 279–293.

————. Messungen über Fortpflanzungsgeschwindigkeit der Reizung in den Nerven. *Arch. Anat. Physiol. wiss. Med.,* 1852, 199–216. Reprinted in *Wissenschaftliche Abhandlungen,* Vol. 2, *op. cit.,* pp. 844–861.

————. Ueber die Theorie der zusammengesetzten Farben. *Ann. Phys. Chem.,* 1852, *87,* 45–66 ; &

Arch. Anat. Physiol. wiss. Med., 1852, 461–482. Reprinted in *Wissenschaftliche Abhandlungen,* Vol. 2, *op. cit.,* pp. 3–23.

————. Ueber die Natur der menschlichen Sinnesempfindungen, Habilitation. *Königsberger naturwiss. Unterhalt.,* 1852, *3,* 1–20. Reprinted in *Wissenschaftliche Abhandlungen,* Vol. 2, *op. cit.,* pp. 591–609.

————. *Ueber Goethes naturwissenschaftliche Arbeiten.* New York: Holt, 1889. (1853) Reprinted in *Vorträge und Reden,* Vol. 1, *op. cit.,* pp. 23–45, & trans. in *Popular scientific lectures, op. cit.,* pp. 1–21, & in *Selected writings, op. cit.,* pp. 56–74.

————. Ueber die Akkomodation des Auges. *Arch. Ophthalm.,* 1854, *1*(2), 1–74. Reprinted in *Wissenschaftliche Abhandlungen,* Vol. 2, *op. cit.,* pp. 283–345.

————. *Ueber das Sehen des Menschen.* Leipzig: Voss, 1855. Reprinted in *Vorträge und Reden,* Vol. 1, *op. cit.,* pp. 85–117.

————. Ueber die Zusammensetzung von Spektralfarben. *Ann. Phys. Chem.,* 1855–1856, *94,* 1–28. Reprinted in *Wissenschaftliche Abhandlungen,* Vol. 2, *op. cit.,* pp. 45–70.

————. Ueber die Kombinationstöne. *Ann. Phys. Chem.,* 1855–1856, *94,* 497–540. Reprinted in *Wissenschaftliche Abhandlungen,* Vol. 1, *op. cit.,* pp. 263–302.

————. *Treatise on physiological optics.* (3rd ed.) (3 vols.) Ed. by J. P. C. Southall. Rochester, N.Y.: Optical Society of America, 1924. (1856–1869) (Reprinted 1962)

————. On the physiological causes of harmony in music. (1857) *Scientific lectures, op. cit.,* pp. 22–58; in *Helmholtz on perception, op. cit.,* pp. 27–60; in *Selected writings, op. cit.,* pp. 74–108, & in German in *Vorträge und Reden,* Vol. 1, *op. cit.,* pp. 119–155.

————. Ueber Integrale der hydro-dynamischen Gleichungen, welche den Wirbelbewegungen entsprechen. *J. reine angew. Math.,* 1858, *55,* 25–55. Reprinted in *Wissenschaftliche Abhandlungen,* Vol. 1, *op. cit.,* pp. 101–134.

————. Die Klangfarbe der Vokale. *Ann. Phys. Chem.,* 1859, *108,* 280–290. Reprinted in *Wissenschaftliche Abhandlungen,* Vol. 1, *op. cit.,* pp. 397–407.

————. The relation of the natural sciences to science in general. (1862) An academic discourse delivered at Heidelberg on November 22, 1862. In *Selected writings, op. cit.,* pp. 122–143. Reprinted in German in *Vorträge und Reden,* Vol. 1, *op. cit.,* pp. 157–185.

————. Ueber die arabisch-persische Tonleiter. *Verh. natur.-hist.-med. Vereins Heidelberg,* 1862, *2,* 216–217. Reprinted in *Wissenschaftliche Abhandlungen,* Vol. 1, *op. cit.,* pp. 424–426.

————. *On the sensations of tone.* (4th ed.) Trans. by A. J. Ellis. New York: Dover, 1954. (1863)

————. Versuche über die Fortpflanzungsgeschwindigkeit der Reizung in den motorischen Nerven des Menschen. (Zusammen mit N. Baxt, Petersburg.) *Monatsber. könig. preuss. Akad. Wiss.,* Berlin, 1867, 228–234.

————. The recent progress of the theory of vision. (1868) *Popular scientific lectures, op. cit.,* pp. 93–155; *Helmholtz on perception, op. cit.,* pp. 61–136; *Selected writings, op. cit.,* pp. 144–222, & in German in *Vorträge und Reden,* Vol. 2, *op. cit.,* pp. 265–365.

————. *Die Mechanik der Gehörknöchelchen und des Trommelfells.* Bonn: Cohen, 1869.

————. The aim and progress of physical science (1869). The opening address delivered at the Naturforscherversammlung in Innsbrück in 1869. In *Selected writings, op. cit.,* pp. 223–254. Reprinted in German in *Vorträge und Reden,* Vol. 3, *op. cit.,* pp. 367–398.

————. The origin and meaning of geometrical axioms. I. Trans. by E. Atkinson. (1870) *Mind,* 1876, *1,* 301–321. Rev. trans. in *Selected writings, op. cit.,* pp. 246–265.

————. Ueber die Schallschwingungen in der Schnecke des Ohres. *Verh. natur.-hist.-med. Vereins Heidelberg,* 1871, *5,* 33–38. Reprinted in *Wissenschaftliche Abhandlungen,* Vol. 2, *op. cit.,* pp. 582–588.

————, & Baxt, N. Ueber die Zeit, welche nöthig ist, damit ein Gesichtseindruck zum Bewusstsein kommt. Berliner Monatsber., 8. Juni 1871 pp 333–337. Reprinted in *Wissenschaftliche Abhandlungen*, Vol. 2, *op. cit.*, pp. 947–952.

———. The relation of optics to painting. (1871) The substance of a series of lectures delivered in Cologne, Düsseldorf, Berlin, and Bonn, 1871. In *Selected writings, op. cit.*, pp. 297–329. Reprinted in German in *Vorträge und Reden*, Vol. 2, *op. cit.*, pp. 93–135.

———. *Die Thatsachen in der Wahrnehmung*. Berlin: Hirschwald, 1878. Reprinted in *Vorträge und Reden*, Vol. 2, *op. cit.*, pp. 213–247, & trans. in *Helmholtz and perception, op. cit.*, pp. 207–246, & in *Selected writings, op. cit.*, pp. 366–408.

———. The origin and meaning of geometric axioms. II. *Mind*, 1878, *3*, 212–225. Reprinted in *Selected writings, op. cit.*, pp. 360–365, 339–408, & in German in *Wissenschaftliche Abhandlungen*, Vol. 2, *op. cit.*, pp. 640–660.

———. An epistemological analysis of counting and measurement. (1887) An essay contributed to the Festschrift honoring Eduard Zeller in 1887. In *Selected writings, op. cit.*, pp. 437–465. Reprinted in German in *Wissenschaftliche Abhandlungen*, Vol. 3, *op. cit.*, pp. 356–391.

———. Zur Geschichte des Prinzips der kleinsten Action, *Sitzber. Akad. Wiss.*, Berlin, 1887, 225–236. Reprinted in *Wissenschaftliche Abhandlungen*, Vol. 3, *op. cit.*, pp. 249–263.

———. Die Störung der Wahrnehmung kleinster Helligkeitsunterschiede durch das Eigenlicht der Netzhaut. *Z. Psychol.*, 1890, *1*, 5–17. Reprinted in *Wissenschaftliche Abhandlungen*, Vol. 3, *op. cit.*, pp. 392–406.

———. Autobiographisches. Tischrede bei der Feier des 70. Geburtstages. (1891) In *Vorträge und Reden*, Vol. 1, *op. cit.*, pp. 1–21, & trans. in *Selected writings, op. cit.*, pp. 466–478. **B**

———. Versuch einer erweiterten Anwendung des Fechner'schen Gesetzes im Farbensystem. *Z. Psychol.*, 1891, *2*, 1–30. Reprinted in *Wissenschaftliche Abhandlungen*, Vol. 3, *op. cit.*, pp. 407–437.

———. Versuch das psychophysische Gesetz auf die Farbenunterschiede trichromatischer Augen anzuwenden. *Z. Psychol.*, 1892, *3*, 1–20.

———. Kürzeste Linien im Farbensystem. *Z. Psychol.*, 1892, *3*, 108–122.

———. *Goethes Vorahnungen kommender naturwissenschaftlicher Ideen*. Berlin; Pätel, 1892. Reprinted in *Vorträge und Reden*, Vol. 2, *op. cit.*, pp. 335–361, & trans. in *Selected writings, op. cit.*, pp. 479–500.

———. Ueber den Ursprung der richtigen Deutung unserer Sinneseindrücke. *Z. Psychol.*, 1894, *7*, 81–96. Reprinted in *Wissenschaftliche Abhandlungen*, Vol. 3, *op. cit.*, pp. 536–553, & trans. in *Helmholtz on perception, op. cit.*, pp. 249–260, & in *Selected writings, op. cit.*, pp. 501–512.

Clarke & O'Malley, *Brain*; Dember, *Perception*; Dennis, *Psychology*; Fulton & Wilson, *Physiology*; Hall, *Source Book*; Herrnstein & Boring, *Source Book*; Hirst, *Perception*; MacAdam, *Color Science*; Murphy, *Western*; Newman, *Mathematics*; Rand, *Classical Psychologists*; Shipley, *Classics*; Teevan, *Vision*

CLAUDE ADRIEN HELVETIUS
1715-1771
French Philosopher (15)

Helvétius, C. A. *Oeuvres complètes*. Ed. by Y. Belaval. (14 vols. in 7) Hildesheim: Olms, 1967–1969. (1795) **C**

———. *Notes de la main d'Helvétius, publiées d'après un manuscrit inédit*. Ed. by A. Keim. Paris: Alcan, 1907. **C**

———. *Choix de textes*. Ed. by J. B. Séverac. Paris: Michaud, 1911. **C**

———. *Essays on the mind and its several faculties*. (Trans. anon.) London: Richardson, Sherwood, Neely, & Jones, 1809. (1758)

———. *De l'esprit*. Paris: Ladrigue, 1843. (1758) Also in *Oeuvres complètes*, Vols. 1–6, *op. cit.*

———. *A treatise on man: His intellectual faculties and his education*. Trans. by W. Hooper. (2 vols.) London: Vernor, Hood, & Sharpe, 1810 (1772), & in *Oeuvres complètes*, Vols. 7–12, *op. cit.* **Bl**

———. *Le vrai sens du système de la nature.* London: La Haye, 1774.

———. *Lettres d'Helvétius.* (1795) In *Oeuvres complètes,* Vol. 14, *op. cit.,* pp. 7–109.

———. Lettres relatives au livre de l'esprit. (1795) In *Oeuvres complètes,* Vol. 13, *op. cit.,* pp. 129–148.

———. *Two letters of Helvétius on merits of Montesquieu's Spirit of laws.* Philadelphia: Diane, 1811.

Brinton, *Age Reason*; Rand, *Moralists*; Torrey, *Les Philosophes*

VIVIAN ALLEN CHARLES HENMON
1877-1950
American Psychologist (11)

Henmon, V. A. C. The time of perception as a measure of differences in sensations. *Arch. Psychol.,* N.Y., 1906, No. 8. Also New York: Science Press, 1906.

———. The relation of the time of a judgment to its accuracy. *Psychol. Rev.,* 1911, *18,* 186–201.

———. The relation between mode of presentation and retention. *Psychol. Rev.,* 1912, *19,* 79–96.

———, & Wells, F. L. Concerning individual differences in reaction times. *Psychol. Rev.,* 1914, *21,* 153–156.

———. The relation between learning and retention and amount to be learned. *J. exp. Psychol.,* 1917, *2,* 476–484.

———. The measurement of ability in Latin. I: Vocabulary. II: Sentence tests. III: Vocabulary and sentence tests. *J. educ. Psychol.,* 1917, *8,* 515–538, 589–599; 1920, *11,* 121–136.

———. Air service tests of aptitude for flying. *J. appl. Psychol.,* 1919, *3,* 103–109.

———. An experimental study of the value of word study. *J. educ. Psychol.,* 1921, *12,* 98–102.

———. Intelligence and its measurement: A symposium. *J. educ. Psychol.,* 1921, *12,* 195–198.

———. The measurement of intelligence. *School & Soc.,* 1921, *13,* 151–158.

———, & Streetz, R. A comparative study of four group scales for primary grades. *J. educ. Res.,* 1922, *5,* 185–194.

———, & Livingstone, W. F. Comparative variability at different ages. *J. educ. Psychol.,* 1922, *13,* 17–29.

———. Some limitations of educational tests. *J. educ. Res.,* 1923, *7,* 185–198.

———. Prognosis tests in the modern foreign languages. In Various, *Prognosis tests in the modern foreign languages.* New York: Macmillan, 1929, pp. 3–31.

———. *Achievement tests in the modern foreign languages.* New York: Macmillan, 1929.

———. Some significant results of the Modern Foreign Language Study. *J. educ. Res.,* 1929, *19,* 79–91.

———. *Individual differences: Their measurement and significance.* Chicago: University of Chicago Press, 1932.

———. The function, value, and future of educational research in colleges and universities. *J. educ. Res.,* 1934, *27,* 493–502.

Valentine, *Experimental*

HANS HENNING
1885-1946
German Psychologist (20)

Henning, H. *Analyse moderner Erkenntnistheorien mit besonderer Berücksichtigung des Realitätsproblems.* Strassburg: Bongard, 1912. **C**

———. *Ernst Mach als Philosoph, Physiker und Psycholog.* Leipzig: Barth, 1915.

———. *Der Geruch: Ein Handbuch für die Gebiete der Psychologie, Physiologie, Zoologie, Botanik, Chemie, Physik, Neurologie, Ethnologie, Sprachwissenschaft, Literatur, Aesthetik, und Kulturgeschichte.* Leipzig: Barth, 1924. Also in *Z. Psychol.,* 1915, *73,* 161–257; 1916, *74,* 305–434, *75,* 177–230, *76,* 1–127.

——. Physiologie und Psychologie des Geruchs. *Ergeb. Physiol.*, 1919, *17*, 572–627.

——. Experimentelle Untersuchungen zur Denkpsychologie. I. Die assoziative Mischwirkung, das Vorstellen von noch nie Wahrgenommenen und deren Grenzen. *Z. Psychol.*, 1919, *81*, 1–96.

——. Physiologie und Psychologie des Geschmacks. *Ergeb. Physiol.*, 1921, *19*, 1–78.

——. Assoziationsgesetz und Geruchsgedächtnis. *Z. Psychol.*, 1922, *89*, 38–80.

——. Ein neuartiger Tiefeneindruck. Die Versuchsanordnung des Rasterdiapositivs. *Z. Psychol.*, 1923, *92*, 161–176.

——. Eine neuartige Komplexsynästhesie und Komplexordnung. *Z. Psychol.*, 1923, *92*, 149–160.

——. Eine Testprüfung des Willens. *Prakt. Psychol.*, 1923, *4*, 97–104.

——. Das Urbild. *Z. Psychol.*, 1924, *94*, 273–277.

——. *Psychologie der Gegenwart.* (2nd ed.) Leipzig: Kröner, 1931. (1925)

——. *Die Aufmerksamkeit.* Berlin: Urban & Schwarzenberg, 1925.

——. Psychologie der chemischen Sinne. In A. Bethe *et al.* (Eds.), *Handbuch der normalen und pathologischen Physiologie.* Vol. 11. Berlin: Springer-Verlag, 1926, pp. 393–405.

——. Zur Psychologie der höheren Säuger. Experimentelles und Kritisches über das spezifisch Tierhafte. *Z. Psychol.*, 1927, *105*, 273–301.

——. Charaktertests. *Industr. Psychotech.*, 1927, *4*, 270–273.

——. Experimentelle Charakterprüfungen. *Psychol. Med.*, 1927, *3*, 19–28.

——. Ueber innere Hemmung. *Z. Psychol.*, 1928, *106*, 23–57.

——. Ziele und Möglichkeiten der experimentellen Charakterprüfung. *J. Charakterol.*, 1929, *6*, 213–273.

VICTOR HENRI
1872-1940
French Psychologist (16)

Henri, V. Recherches sur la localisation des sensations tactiles. *Arch. Physiol.*, 1893, *5*, 619–627.

——. Les laboratoires de psychologie expérimentale en Allemagne. *Rev. phil.*, 1893, *36*, 608–622.

Binet, A., & ——. Recherches sur le développement de la mémoire visuelle des enfants. *Rev. phil.*, 1894, *37*, 348–350. Trans. in R. H. Pollack & Margaret W. Brenner (Eds.), *The experimental psychology of Alfred Binet: Selected papers.* New York: Springer, 1968, pp. 127–129.

Binet, A., & ——. De la suggestibilité naturelle chez les enfants. *Rev. phil.*, 1894, *38*, 337–347.

Binet, A., & ——. La mémoire des mots. *Année psychol.*, 1894, *1*, 1–23.

Binet, A., & ——. La mémoire des phrases. *Année psychol.*, 1894, *1*, 24–59.

Binet, A. (In collab. with P. Courtier & ——) *Introduction à la psychologie expérimentale.* Paris: Alcan, 1894.

——. Recherches sur la localisation des sensations tactiles. *Année psychol.*, 1895, *2*, 168–192.

——. Revue générale sur les sens de lieu de la peau. *Année psychol.*, 1895, *2*, 295–362.

Binet, A., & ——. La psychologie individuelle. *Année psychol.*, 1895, *2*, 411–465.

——. A review of "Experimentelle Studien zur Individual-Psychologie." *Année psychol.*, 1895, *2*, 795–797.

——. Le calcul des probabilités en psychologie. *Année psychol.*, 1895, *2*, 466–500.

——, & Tawney, G. Ueber die Trugwahrnehmung zweier Punkte bei der Berührung eines Punktes der Haut. *Phil. Stud.*, 1895, *11*, 394–405.

——. Etude sur le travail psychique et physique. *Année psychol.*, 1896, *3*, 232–278.

——. Travaux de psychophysique. *Rev. phil.*, 1896, *42*, 55–79.

———, & Henri, Catherine. Enquête sur les premiers souvenirs de l'enfance. *Année psychol.,* 1896, *3,* 184–198.

———. *Ueber die Raumwahrnehmungen des Tastsinnes: Ein Beitrag zur experimentellen Psychologie.* Berlin: Reuther & Reichard, 1898.

Binet, A., & ———. *La fatigue intellectuelle.* Paris: Schleicher, 1898.

———. Education de la mémoire. *Année psychol.,* 1901, *8,* 1–48.

———, & Larguier des Bancels, J. Photochimie de la rétine. *J. Physiol.,* 1911, *13,* 841–856.

———, & Larguier des Bancels, J. Sur l'interprétation des lois de Weber et de Jost (recherches sur les réactions des Cyclopes.) *Arch. Psychol.,* Geneva, 1912, *12,* 329–334.

Herrnstein & Boring, *Source Book*

JOHANN FRIEDRICH HERBART
1776-1841
German Philosopher (27)

Herbart, J. F. *Sämtliche Werke* (2nd ed.) (13 vols.) Ed. by G. Hartenstein. Leipzig: Voss, 1883–1893. (1850–1852) C

———. *Ungedruckte Briefe von und an Herbart.* Ed. by R. Zimmerman. Vienna: Braumüller, 1877. B C

———. *Johann Friedrich Herbart. Sämtliche Werke in chronologischer Reihenfolge.* (19 vols.) Ed. by K. Kehrbach & O. Flügel. Aalen: Scientia Verlag, 1964. (1887–1912) B C

——— *ABC of sense perception and minor pedagogical works.* Ed. by W. J. Eckoff. New York: Appleton, 1896. C

———. *Letters and lectures on education.* Trans. by H. M. & Emmie Felkin. Syracuse, N.Y.: Bardeen, 1898. C

———. *Pädagogische Schriften.* (3 vols.) Ed. by W. Asmus. Düsseldorf: Küpper, 1964–1965. C

———. *Kleinere Abhandlungen zur Psychologie, 1811–1840.* Amsterdam: Bonset, 1969. C

———. *The science of education: Its general*

principles deduced from its aim and the aesthetic revelation of the world. Trans. by H. M. & Emmie Felkin. Boston: Heath, 1902. (1804–1806). In German in *Sämtliche Werke in chronologischer Reihenfolge,* Vol. 2, *op. cit.,* pp. 1–139.

———. Hauptpunkte der Metaphysik. (1806) In *Sämtliche Werke in chronologischer Reihenfolge,* Vol. 2, *op. cit.,* pp. 175–216.

———. *Ueber philosophisches Studium,* Göttingen: Dietrich, 1807.

———. Psychologische Bemerkungen zur Tonlehre. (1811) In *Sämtliche Werke in chronologischer Reihenfolge,* Vol. 3, *op. cit.,* pp. 97–118.

———. Theoriae de attractione elementorum principia metaphysica. (1812) In *Sämtliche Werke in chronoligischer Reihenfolge,* Vol. 3. *op. cit.,* pp. 155–200.

———. Psychologische Untersuchung über die Stärke einer gegebenen Vorstellung als Funktion ihrer Dauer betrachtet. (1812) In *Sämtliche Werke in chronologischer Reihenfolge,* Vol. 3. *op. cit.,* pp. 119–145.

———. Ueber die dunkle Seite der Pädagogik. (1812) Reprinted in *Sämtliche Werke in chronologischer Reihenfolge,* Vol. 3, *op. cit,* pp 147–154.

———. Lehrbuch zur Einleitung in die Philosophie. (1813) In *Sämtliche Werke in chronologischer Reihenfolge,* Vol. 4, *op. cit.,* pp.1–294.

———. *A text-book in psychology: An attempt to found the science of psychology on experience, metaphysics, and mathematics.* (2nd ed.) Ed. by W. T. Harris & trans. by Margaret K. Smith New York: Appleton, 1891. (1816) In German in *Sämtliche Werke in chronologischer Reihenfolge,* Vol. 4, *op. cit.,* pp. 295–379.

———. *Lehrbuch zur Psychologie.* (2nd ed. Königsberg: Unzer, 1834. (1816) In *Sämtliche Werke in chronologischer Reinhenfolge,* Vol. 4 *op. cit.,* pp. 295–622.

———. Ueber einige Beziehungen zwischer Psychologie und Staatswissenschaft. (1821) Re printed in *Sämtliche Werke in chronologischer Reihenfolge,* Vol. 5, *op. cit.,* pp. 25–70.

———. *Psychologie als Wissenschaft, neu gegründet auf Erfahrung, Metaphysik und Mathematik.* (2 vols.) Amsterdam: Bonset, 1968. (1824–1825) In *Sämtliche Werke in chronologischer Reihenfolge,* Vol. 5, *op. cit.,* pp. 179–434; Vol. 6, pp. 1–340.

———. Allgemeine Metaphysik nebst den Anfängen der philosophischen Naturlehre. (1828–1829) In *Sämtliche Werke in chronologischer Reihenfolge.* Vols. 7 & 8, *op. cit.*

———. Kurze Enzyklopädie der Philosophie aus praktischen Gesichtspunkten entworfen. (1831) In *Sämtliche Werke in chronologischer Reihenfolge,* Vol. 9, *op. cit.,* pp. 17–338.

———. Briefe über die Anwendung der Psychologie auf die Pädagogik. (1831) Reprinted in *Sämtliche Werke in chronologischer Reihenfolge,* Vol. 9, *op. cit.,* pp. 339–462.

———. Psychologische Untersuchung. (2 vols.) (1839, 1840) In *Sämtliche Werke in chronologischer Reinhenfolge,* Vol. 11, *op. cit.,* pp. 45–343.

———. *Umriss pädagogischer Vorlesungen.* Göttingen: Dietrich, 1841.

———. Outlines of educational doctrine. Trans. by A. F. Lange. New York: Macmillan, 1901. (1876–1878). In German in *Sämtliche Werke in chronologischer Reihenfolge,* Vol. 10, *op. cit.,* pp. 65–296.

———. Possibility and necessity of applying mathematics in psychology. (n.d.) Trans. by H. Haanel. *J. spec. Phil.,* 1877, *11*, 251–264.

———. Drei Briefe von Johann Friedrich Herbart. *Phil. Stud.,* 1888–1889, *5*, 321–326. **B**

Miller, *Mathematics;* Murphy, *Western*; Rand, *Classical Psychologists;* Sahakian, *Psychology*; Shipley, *Classics*; Ulich, *Educational Wisdom*

JOHANN GOTTFRIED VON HERDER
1744–1803
German Philosopher (11)

Herder, J. G. v. *Sämtliche Werke.* (33 vols.) Ed. by B. Suphan. Hildesheim: Olms, 1967–1968. (1877–1913) **C**

———. *Herder.* (5th ed.) Ed. by E. Kühnemann. Berlin: Union Deutsche Verlagsgesellschaft, 1913. (1895) **C**

———. *Mensch und Welt.* Comp. by E. Ruprecht. Jena: Diederichs, 1942. **C**

———. *Sprachphilosophie. Schriften.* Ed. by E. Heintel. Hamburg: Meiner, 1960. **C**

———. *Herder on social and political culture.* Trans. by F. M. Barnard. Cambridge: Cambridge University Press, 1969. **C**

———. Essay on the origin of language. (1772) Trans. by A. Gode. In Anon., *On the origin of language.* New York: Ungar, 1966, pp. 85–166.

———. *Vom Erkennen und Empfinden der menschlichen Seele. Bemerkungen und Träume.* Leipzig: Hartknoch, 1778. In *Sämtliche Werke,* Vol. 8, *op. cit.,* pp. 165–235. **B**

———. *Outlines of a philosophy of the history of man.* (2nd ed.) Trans. by T. O. Churchill. New York: Bergman, 1966. (1784–1791)

———. *Reflections on the philosophy of the history of mankind.* Abridged & intro. by F. E. Manuel, & trans. by T. O. Churchill. Chicago: University of Chicago Press, 1968. (1784–1791)

———. *Metakritik zur Kritik der reinen Vernunft.* Vol. I. *Verstand und Erfahrung.* Vol. II. *Vernunft und Sprache.* Leipzig: Hartknoch, 1799.

———. *Kalligone. Vom Angenehmen und Schönen.* (3 vols.) Leipzig: Hartknoch, 1800.

———. *Stimmen der Völker in Liedern.* Leipzig: Reclam, 1880. (1828)

Slotkin, *Anthropology*

EWALD HERING
1834–1918
German Physiologist (27)

Hering, E., *Fünf Reden von Ewald Hering.* Ed. by H. E. Hering. Leipzig: Engelmann, 1921. **C**

———. *Wissenschaftliche Abhandlungen.* (2 vols.) Ed. by M. Le Blanc & M. Gildemeister. Leipzig: Thieme, 1931. **C**

———. *Beiträge zur Physiologie.* (5 parts) Leipzig: Engelmann, 1861–1864.

———. Die Selbststeuerung der Athmung durch den Nervus vagus. Mittheilung über eine von Dr. Joseph Breuer im physiologischen Institut der k.k. Josephs-Akademie ausgeführte Untersuchung. *Sitzber. Akad. Wiss. Wien,* Math.-naturw. Kl., 1868, *57*(2), 672–677.

———. *Die Lehre vom binocularen Sehen.* Leipzig: Engelmann, 1868.

———. Bemerkungen zu der Abhandlung von Donders über das binoculare Sehen. *Arch. Ophthalm.,* 1868, *14,* 1–12.

———. *Memory: Lectures on the specific energies of the nervous system.* (4th ed.) Chicago: Open Court, 1913. (1870)

———. *Ueber das Gedächtnis als eine allgemeine Funktion der organisierten Materie.* (1870) Reprinted in *Fünf Reden von Ewald Hering, op. cit.,* pp. 5–31.

———. *Zur Lehre vom Lichtsinne.* (Rev. ed.) Vienna: Gerold, 1878. (1872–1875)

———. Zur Lehre von der Beziehung zwischen Leib und Seele. I. Mittheilung. Ueber Fechners psychophysisches Gesetz. *Sitzber. Akad. Wiss. Wien,* Math-naturw. Kl., 1876. *72*(3) 310–348.

———. Grundzüge einer Theorie des Temperatursinns. *Sitzber. Akad. Wiss. Wien,* Math.-naturw. Kl., 1877, *75,* 101–135.

———. *Spatial sense movements of the eye.* Trans. by C. Radde. Baltimore, Md.: American Academy of Optometry, 1942. (1879) (Reprinted 1971)

———. *Der Raumsinn und die Bewegungen des Auges.* In L. Hermann (Ed.), *Handbuch der Physiologie,* Vol. 3, Part 1. Leipzig: Vogel, 1879, pp. 343–601.

———. *Der Temperatursinn.* In L. Hermann (Ed.), *Handbuch der Physiologie,* Vol. 3, Part 2. Leipzig: Vogel, 1880, pp. 415–448.

———. *Zur Erklärung der Farbenblindheit aus der Theorie der Gegenfarben.* Prague: Tempsky, 1880.

———. Beiträge zur allgemeinen Nerven- und Muskelpsychologie. IX. Ueber Nervenreizung durch den Nervenstrom. *Sitzber. Akad. Wiss. Wien,* Math.-naturw. Kl., 1822, *85*(3), 237–275. English trans. in J. Burdon-Sanderson (Ed.), *Translations of foreign biological memoirs.* Vol. 5. Oxford: Clarendon Press, 1887, pp. 167–225.

———. Beiträge zur allgemeinen Nerven- und Muskelpsychologie. XIII Ueber der Bois-Reymonds Untersuchung der sekundär-electromotorischen Erscheinungen am Muskel. *Sitzber. Akad. Wiss. Wien,* Math.-naturw. Kl. 1883, *88*(3), 445–471. English trans. in J. Burdon-Sanderson (Ed.), *Translations of foreign biological memoirs.* Vol. 5. Oxford: Clarendon Press, 1887, pp. 227–251.

———. Beiträge zur allgemeinen Nerven- und Muskelphysiologie. XI. Ueber positive Nachschwankung des Nervenstromes nach elektrischer Reizung. *Sitzber. Akad. Wiss. Wien,* Math.-naturw. Kl., 1884, *89*(3), 137–158, 219–237. English trans. in J. Burdon-Sanderson (Ed.), *Translations of foreign biological memoirs.* Vol. 5. Oxford: Clarendon Press, 1887, pp. 253–273.

———. Ueber die spezifischen Energieen des Nervensystems. (1884) Reprinted in *Fünf Reden von Ewald Hering, op. cit.,* pp. 33–51.

———. Ueber individuelle Verschiedenheiten des Farbensinnes. *Lotos Jb. Naturwiss.,* 1885, *34,* 142–198.

———. Ueber Sigmund Exners neue Urtheilstäuschung auf dem Gebiete des Gesichtssinnes. *Arch. ges. Physiol.,* 1886, *39,* 159–170.

———. Ueber Holmgrens vermeintlichen Nachweis der Elementarempfindungen des Gesichtssinns. *Arch. ges. Physiol.,* 1887, *40,* 1–20.

———. Ueber die Theorie des simultanen Kontrastes von Helmholtz. *Arch. ges. Physiol.,* 1887, *40,* 172–191, *41,* 1–29, 358–367; 1888, *43,* 1–21.

———. Beleuchtung eines Angriffes auf die Theorie der Gegenfarben. *Arch. ges. Physiol.,* 1887, *41,* 29–46.

———. Ueber den Begriff "Urtheilstäuschung" in der physiologischen Optik und über die Wahrnehmung simultaner und successiver Helligkeitsunterschiede. *Arch. ges. Physiol.,* 1887, *41,* 91–106.

———. Ueber Newtons Gesetz der Farbenmischung. *Lotos Jb. Naturwiss.,* 1887, *35,* 177–268.

———. Eine Vorrichtung zur Farbenmischung, zur Diagnose der Farbenblindheit und zur Untersuchung der Kontrasterscheinungen. *Arch. ges. Physiol.,* 1888, *42,* 119–144.

———. Zur Theorie der Vorgänge in der lebendigen Substanz. (1888) Reprinted in *Fünf Reden von Ewald Hering, op. cit.* pp. 53–103, & in English trans. in *Brain,* 1897, *20,* 232–258.

———. Ueber die von v. Kries wider die Theorie der Gegenfarben erhobenen Einwände. I. Ueber die Unabhängigkeit der Farbengleichungen von den Erregbarkeitsänderungen des Sehorgans. II. Ueber successive Lichtinduktion und sogenannte negative Nachbilder. III. Ueber die sogenannten Ermüdungserscheinungen. *Arch. ges. Physiol.,* 1888, *42,* 488–506, *43,* 264–288, 329–346.

———. Ueber die Hypothesen zur Erklärung der peripheren Farbenblindheit. *Arch. Ophthalm.,* 1889, *35*(4), 63–83 ; 1890, *36*(1), 264.

———. Zur Diagnostik der Farbenblindheit. *Arch. Ophthalm.,* 1890, *36*(1), 217–233.

———. Die Untersuchung einseitiger Störungen des Farbensinnes mittels binocularer Farbengleichungen. *Arch. Ophthalm.,* 1890, *36*(3), 1–23.

———. Beitrag zur Lehre vom Simultankontrast. *Z. Psychol.,* 1890, *1,* 18–28.

———. Eine Methode zur Beobachtung des Simultankontrastes. *Arch. ges. Physiol.,* 1890, *47,* 236–242.

———. Prüfung der sogenannten Farbendreiecke mit Hülfe des Farbensinns excentrischer Netzhautstellen. *Arch. ges Physiol.,* 1890, *47,* 417–438.

———. Ueber Ermüdung und Erholung des Sehorgans. *Arch. Ophthalm.,* 1891, *37*(3), 1–36 ; 1892, *38*(2), 252–258 ; 1893, *39*(2), 274–290.

———. Untersuchung eines total Farbenblinden. *Arch. ges. Physiol.,* 1891, *49,* 563–608.

———. Ueber den Einfluss der Macula Lutea auf spectrale Farbengleichungen. *Arch. ges. Physiol.,* 1893, *54,* 277–312.

———. Ueber einen Fall von Gelb-Blaublindheit. *Arch. ges. Physiol.,* 1894, *57,* 308–332.

———. Ueber das sogenannte Purkinje'sche Phänomen. *Arch. ges. Physiol.,* 1895, *60,* 519–542.

———. Ueber angebliche Blaublindheit der Zapfen-Sehzellen. *Arch. ges. Physiol.,* 1895, *61,* 106–112.

———. Zur Theorie der Nerventätigkeit. (1899) Reprinted in *Fünf Reden von Ewald Hering, op. cit.,* pp. 105–131.

———. Ueber die von der Farbenempfindlichkeit unabhängige Aenderung der Weissempfindlichkeit. *Arch. ges. Physiol.,* 1903, *94,* 533–554.

———. *Outlines of a theory of the light sense.* Trans. by L. M. Hurvich & Dorothea Jameson. Cambridge : Harvard University Press, 1964. (1905, 1907, 1911)

———. Antwortrede. (1906) In *Fünf Reden von Ewald Hering, op. cit.,* pp. 133–140.

———. Das Purkinje'sche Phänomen im zentralen Bezirke des Sehfeldes. *Arch. Ophthalm.,* 1916, *90,* 1–12.

Herrnstein & Boring, *Source Book* ; Rand, *Classical Psychologists* ; Reeves, *Body Mind ;* Teevan, *Vision*

CHARLES JUDSON HERRICK
1868-1960
American Physiologist (16)

Herrick, C. J. The organs and sense of taste in fishes. *U.S. Fish. Comm. Bull.,* 1902, *22,* 237–272.

———. The morphological subdivision of the brain. *J. comp. Neurol.,* 1908, *18,* 393–408.

———. The morphology of the forebrain in *Amphibia* and *Reptilia*. *J. comp. Neurol.*, 1910, *20*, 413–446.

———. Some reflections on the origin and significance of the cerebral cortex. *J. anim. Behav.*, 1913, *3*, 222–236.

———. *An introduction to neurology*. (5th ed.) Philadelphia: Saunders, 1931. (1915)

———, & Coghill, G. E. The development of reflex mechanisms in *Amblystoma*. *J. comp. Neurol.*, 1915, *25*, 65–85.

———. Introspection as a biological method. *J. Phil.*, 1915, *12*, 543–551.

———. A sketch of the origin of the cerebral hemispheres. *J. comp. Neurol.*, 1921, *32*, 429–454.

———. Origin and evolution of the cerebellum. *Arch. Neurol. Psychiat.*, Chicago, 1924, *11*, 621–652.

———. *Neurological foundations of animal behavior*. New York: Holt, 1924.

———. The natural history of purpose. *Psychol. Rev.*, 1925, *32*, 417–430.

———. Morphogenetic factors in the differentiation of the nervous system. *Physiol. Rev.*, 1925, *5*, 112–130.

———. *Fatalism or freedom, a biologist's answer*. New York: Norton, 1926.

———. *Brains of rats and men*. Chicago: University of Chicago Press, 1926.

———. Anatomical patterns and behavior patterns. *Physiol. Zoöl.*, 1929, *2*, 439–448.

———. *The thinking machine*. (2nd ed.) Chicago: University of Chicago Press, 1932. (1929)

———. Localization of function in the nervous system. *Proc. Nat. Acad. Sci.*, 1930, *16*, 643–650.

———. The order of nature. *Monist*, 1930, *40*, 182–192.

———. The evolution of cerebral localization patterns. *Science*, 1933, *78*, 439–444.

———. The amphibian forebrain. VI. *Necturus*. *J. comp. Neurol.*, 1933, *58*, 1–288.

———. The amphibian forebrain. VII. The architectural plan of the brain. *J. comp. Neurol.*, 1933, *58*, 481–506.

———. The amphibian forebrain. VIII. Cerebral hemispheres and pallial primordia. *J. comp. Neurol.*, 1933, *58*, 737–762.

———. Morphogenesis of the brain. *J. Morphol.*, 1933, *54*, 233–258.

———. The amphibian forebrain. IX. Neuropil and other interstitial nervous tissue. *J. comp. Neurol.*, 1934, *59*, 93–116.

———. The amphibian forebrain. X. Localized functions and integrating functions. *J. comp. Neurol.*, 1934, *59*, 239–266.

———. The hypothalamus of *Necturus*. *J. comp. Neurol.*, 1934, *59*, 375–430.

———. Neurobiological foundations of modern humanism. *Proc. Inst. Med.*, Chicago, 1936, *11*, 86–99.

———. A neurologist makes up his mind. *Sci. Mon.*, N.Y., 1939, *49*, 99–110.

———. The natural history of experience. *Phil. Sci.*, 1945, *12*, 57–71.

———. Seeing and believing. *Sci. Mon.*, N.Y., 1947, *64*, 253–260.

———. *The brain of the tiger salamander, Amblystoma tigrinum*. Chicago: University of Chicago Press, 1948.

———. *George Ellett Coghill, naturalist and philosopher*. Chicago: University of Chicago Press, 1949.

———. One hundred volumes of the Journal of Comparative Neurology. *J. comp. Neurol.*, 1954, *100*, 717–756.

———. Psychology from a biologist's point of view. *Psychol. Rev.*, 1955, *62*, 333–340.

———. *The evolution of human nature*. Austin Texas: The University of Texas Press, 1956.

———. Medical teaching by a non-medical specialist. In D. J. Ingle (Ed.), *A dozen doctors Autobiographical sketches*. Chicago: University of Chicago Press, 1963, pp. 25–40.

MELVILLE JEAN HERSKOVITS
1895-1963
American Anthropologist (13)

Herskovits, M. J. A test of the Downey Will-Temperament Test. *J. appl. Psychol.*, 1924, *8*, 75–88.

——. *The Negro and the intelligence tests.* Hanover, N.H.: Sociological Press, 1927.

——. *The American Negro: A study in racial crossing.* New York: Knopf, 1928.

Willey, M. H., & ——. Psychology and culture. *Psychol. Bull.*, 1929, *24*, 253–283.

——, & Herskovits, Frances S. *Rebel destiny, among the Bush Negroes of Dutch Guiana.* New York: Whittlesey House, 1934.

——. Freudian mechanisms in Negro psychology. In E. E. Evans-Prichard *et al.* (Eds.), *Essays presented to C. G. Seligman.* London: Kegan Paul, 1934, pp. 75–84.

——. Social history of the Negro. In C. Murchison (Ed.), *A handbook of social psychology.* Worcester, Mass.: Clark University Press, 1935, pp. 207–267.

——. Applied anthropology and the American anthropologists. *Science*, 1936, *83*, 215–222.

——. *Life in a Haitian valley.* New York: Octagon Books, 1964. (1937)

——. *Dahomey, an ancient West African Kingdom.* (2 vols.) New York: Augustin, 1937.

——. African gods and Catholic saints in New World Negro belief. *Amer. Anthrop.*, 1937, *39*, 635–643.

——. *Acculturation: The study of culture contact.* Gloucester, Mass.: Smith, 1958. (1938)

——. *Economic anthropology: A study in comparative economics.* (2nd ed.) New York: Knopf, 1952. (1940)

——. Some comments on the study of cultural contact. *Amer. Anthrop.*, 1941, *43*(1), 1–10.

——. *The myth of the Negro past.* New York: Harper, 1941. (Reprinted 1958)

——. The process of cultural change. In R. Linton (Ed.), *The science of man in the world crisis.* New York: Columbia University Press, 1945, pp. 143–170.

——. *Man and his works: The science of cultural anthropology.* New York: Knopf, 1948.

——. *Cultural anthropology.* (Abridged version of *Man and his works*), 1955. (1948) New York: Knopf, 1948. **Bl**

——. The hypothetical situation, a technique of field research. *Southwest. J. Anthrop.*, 1950, *6*, 32–40.

——. Some psychological implications of Afro-American studies. In S. Tax (Ed.), *Acculturation in the Americas.* Chicago: University of Chicago Press, 1952, pp. 152–160.

——. Tender and tough minded anthropology and the study of values in culture. *Southwest. J. Anthrop.*, 1951, *7*, 22–31.

——. *Franz Boas: The science of man in the making.* New York: Scribner's, 1953.

——. Some problems of method in ethnography. In R. F. Spencer (Ed.), *Method and perspective in anthropology: Papers in honor of Wilson D. Wallis.* Minneapolis, Minn.: University of Minnesota Press, 1954, pp. 3–24.

——, & Herskovits, Frances S. *Dahomean narrative: A cross-cultural analysis.* Evanston, Ill.: Northwestern University Press, 1958.

——. On cultural and psychological reality. In J. H. Rohrer & M. Sherif (Eds.), *Social psychology at the crossroads.* New York: Harper, 1959, pp. 145–163. (Reprinted 1970).

——, & Bascom, W. R. The problem of stability and change in African culture. In W. Bascom & M. J. Herskovits (Eds.), *Continuity and change in African culture.* Chicago: University of Chicago Press, 1962, pp. 1–14.

——. *The human factor in changing Africa.* New York: Knopf, 1962.

Segall, M. H., Campbell, D. T., & ——. *The influence of culture on visual perception.* Indianapolis, Ind.: Bobbs-Merrill, 1966.

Goldschmidt, *Mankind*

GERARDUS HEYMANS
1857-1930
Dutch Psychologist (17)

Heymans, G. *Gesammelte kleinere Schriften zur Philosophie und Psychologie.* (3 vols.) The Hague: Nijhoff, 1927.　　　　**C**

————. Erkenntnistheorie und Psychologie. *Phil. Monatsh.,* 1889, *25,* 1–28. Reprinted in *Gesammelte Schriften,* Vol. 1, *op. cit.,* pp. 123–149.

————. Einige Bemerkungen über die sogenannte empiristische Periode Kants. *Arch. ges. Phil.,* 1889, *2,* 572–591. Reprinted in *Gesammelte Schriften,* Vol. 3, *op. cit.,* pp. 150–167.

————. Zur Parallelismusfrage. *Z. Psychol.,* 1897, *17,* 62–105. Reprinted in *Gesammelte Schriften,* Vol. 3, *op. cit.,* pp. 255–298.

————. *Die Gesetze und Elemente des wissenschaftlichen Denkens.* (3rd ed.) (2 vols.) Leipzig: Barth, 1915. (1890)

————. Quantitative Untersuchungen über das "optische Paradoxon." *Z. Psychol.,* 1896, *9,* 221–255, 420. Reprinted in *Gesammelte Schriften,* Vol. 2, *op. cit.,* pp. 1–34.

————. Quantitative Untersuchungen über die Zöllner'sche und die Loeb'sche Täuschung. *Z. Psychol.,* 1897, *14,* 101–139. Reprinted in *Gesammelte Schriften,* Vol. 2, *op. cit.,* pp. 35–71.

————. Untersuchungen über psychische Hemmung. *Z. Psychol.,* 1899, *21,* 321–359; 1901, *26,* 305–382; 1904, *34,* 15–28; 1906, *41,* 28–37, 86–116; 1909, *53,* 401–415. Reprinted in *Gesammelte Schriften,* Vol. 2, *op. cit.,* pp. 72–250.

————. Zur Psychologie der Komik. *Z. Psychol.,* 1899, *20,* 164–173. Reprinted in *Gesammelte Schriften,* Vol. 2, *op. cit.,* pp. 606–615.

————. Ueber Unterschiedsschwellen bei Mischungen von Kontrastfarben. *Z. Psychol,* 1903, *32,* 38–49. Reprinted in *Gesammelte Schriften,* Vol. 2, *op. cit.,* pp. 251–262.

————. Eine Enquête über Dépersonalisation und "fausse reconnaissance." *Z. Psychol.,* 1904, *36,* 321–343. Reprinted in *Gesammelte Schriften,* Vol. 3, *op. cit.,* pp. 1–24.

————, & Wiersma, E. Beiträge zur speziellen Psychologie auf Grund einer Massenuntersuchung. *Z. Psychol.,* 1906, *42,* 81–127, 258–301; 1906, *43,* 321–373; 1907, *45,* 1–43; 1908, *46,* 321–333; 1908, *49,* 414–439; 1909, *51,* 1–72; 1912, *62,* 1–59; 1918, *90,* 76–89. Reprinted in *Gesammelte Schriften,* Vol. 3, *op. cit.,* pp. 41–414.

————. Weitere Daten über Dépersonalisation und "fausse reconnaissance." *Z. Psychol.,* 1906, *43,* 1–17. Reprinted in *Gesammelte Schriften,* Vol. 3, *op. cit.,* pp. 25–40.

————. Ueber einige psychische Korrelationen. *Z. angew. Psychol.,* 1908, *1,* 313–381. Reprinted in *Gesammelte Schriften,* Vol. 3, *op. cit.,* pp. 415–489.

————. *Die Psychologie der Frauen.* (2nd ed.) Heidelberg: Winter, 1924. (1910)

————. *Einführung in die Metaphysik auf Grundlage der Erfahrung.* (2nd ed.) Leipzig: Barth, 1920. (1911)

————. Des méthodes dans la psychologie spéciale. *Année psychol.,* 1911, *17,* 64–79. Reprinted in *Gesammelte Schriften,* Vol. 3, *op. cit.,* pp. 490–506.

————, & Brugmans, H. J. F. W. Intelligenzprüfungen mit Studierenden. *Z. angew. Psychol.,* 1913, *7,* 317–331.

————. In Sachen des psychischen Monismus. *Z. Psychol.,* 1913, *63,* 241–285, *64,* 1–33; 1916, *75,* 54–77, *76,* 217–231; 1918, *79,* 211–227. Reprinted in *Gesammelte Schriften,* Vol. 3, *op. cit.,* pp. 299–463.

————. *Einführung in die Ethik auf Grundlage der Erfahrung.* Leipzig: Barth, 1914.

————, .& Wiersma, E. Verschiedenheiten der Altersentwicklung bei männlichen und weiblichen Mittelschülern. *Z. angew. Psychol.,* 1916, *11,* 441–464.

Brugmans, H. J. F. W., & ————. Versuche über Benennungs- und Lesezeiten. *Z. Psychol.,* 1917, *77,* 92–110.

————. *Ueber die Anwendbarkeit des Energiebegriffes in der Psychologie.* Leipzig: Barth, 1921.

————, & Brugmans, H. J. F. W. Spezielle Psychologie der Träume. *Z. angew. Psychol.,* 1921, *18,* 201–224.

————. Gerardus Heymans. In R. Schmidt (Ed.), *Die Philosophie der Gegenwart in Selbstdarstellungen.* Vol. 3. Leipzig: Meiner, 1922, pp. 1–52. Reprinted in *Gesammelte Schriften,* Vol 1, *op. cit.,* pp. 1–54.   **B Bl**

————. Ueber "verstehende Psychologie." *Z. Psychol.,* 1927, *102,* 6–34.

————. *Einführung in die spezielle Psychologie.* Leipzig: Barth, 1932. (1929)

————. Gerardus Heymans. In C. Murchison (Ed.), *A history of psychology in autobiography.* Vol. 2. Worcester, Mass.: Clark University Press, 1932, pp. 153–195.   **B**

EDUARD HITZIG
1838-1907
German Psychiatrist (18)

Hitzig, E. *Untersuchungen über das Gehirn: Abhandlungen physiologischen und pathologischen Inhalts.* Berlin: Hirschwald, 1874.   **C**

————. *Physiologische und klinische Untersuchungen über das Gehirn: Gesammelte Abhandlungen.* (2nd ed.) Berlin: Hirschwald, 1904. (1903)   **C**

Fritsch, G., & ————. Ueber die elektrische Erregbarkeit des Grosshirns. *Arch. Anat. Physiol.,* 1870, 300–332. Reprinted in Hitzig, E., *Untersuchungen über das Gehirn, op. cit.,* pp. 1–31, & in Hitzig, E., *Physiologische und klinische Untersuchungen über das Gehirn, op. cit.,* pp. 8–35; trans. by G. von Bonin in *Some papers on the cerebral cortex.* Springfield, Ill.: Thomas, 1960, pp. 73–96, & in R. H. Wilkins (Ed.), *Neurosurgical classics.* New York: Johnson Reprint, 1965, pp. 16–27.

————. Ueber die beim Galvanisieren des Kopfes entstehenden Störungen der Muskelinnervation und der Vorstellungen vom Verhalten im Raume. *Arch. Physiol.,* Leipzig, 1871, *38,* 716–770. Reprinted in *Untersuchungen über das Gehirn, op. cit.,* pp. 196–247, & in *Physiologische und klinische Untersuchungen über das Gehirn, op. cit.,* pp. 336–385.

————. Untersuchungen zur Physiologie des Gehirns. *Arch. Anat. Physiol.,* 1873, 397–435. Reprinted in *Untersuchungen über das Gehirn, op. cit.,* pp. 32–62, & in *Physiologische und klinische Untersuchungen über das Gehirn, op. cit.,* pp. 36–62.

————. Kritische und experimentelle Untersuchungen zur Physiologie des Grosshirns im Anschluss an die Untersuchungen des Herrn Professor D. Ferrier in London. (1874) In *Untersuchungen über das Gehirn, op. cit.,* pp. 63–113, & in *Physiologische und klinische Untersuchungen über das Gehirn, op. cit.,* pp. 114–158.

————. Bemerkungen zu der vorstehenden Abhandlung. (1874) In *Untersuchungen über das Gehirn, op. cit.,* pp. 248–260.

————. *Ueber den Querulantewahnsinn, seine nosologische Stellung und seine forensische Bedeutung.* Leipzig: Vogel, 1895.

————. *Der Schwindel.* (2nd ed.) Ed. by J. R. Ewald & R. Wollenberg. Vienna: Hölder, 1911. (1898)

————. Les centres de projection et d'association du cerveau humain. *Congr. Int. Méd. C.r.,* 1900, *7,* 75–100.

————. Hughlings Jackson and the cortical motor centres in the light of physiological research. *Brain,* 1900, *23,* 545–581.

————. Alte und neue Untersuchungen über das Gehirn. 1. Ueber die nach Verletzungen des Hinterhirns auftretenden Störungen der Bewegung und Empfindung. *Arch. Psychiat. Nervenkr.,* 1901, *34,* 1–38. Reprinted in *Physiologische und klinische Untersuchungen über das Gehirn: Gesammelte Abhandlungen, op. cit.,* pp. 1–22.

————. Alte und neue Untersuchungen über das Gehirn. 2. Der Versuch Loebs, *Arch. Psychiat. Nervenkr.,* 1901, *35,* 275–392, 575–611. Reprinted in *Physiologische und klinische Untersuchungen über das Gehirn: Gesammelte Abhandlungen, op. cit.,* pp. 23–36.

————. Alte und neue Untersuchungen über das Gehirn. 3. Historisches, Kritisches und Experimentelles über Methoden und Theorien der

Grosshirnforschung. *Arch. Psychiat. Nervenkr.*, 1903, *36*, 1–96. Reprinted in *Physiologische und klinische Untersuchungen über das Gehirn: Gesammelte Abhandlungen, op. cit.*, pp. 37–154.

――――. Einige Bemerkungen zu der Arbeit C. von Monakows "Ueber den gegenwärtigen Stand der Frage nach der Lokalisation im Grosshirn." *Arch. Psychiat. Nervenkr.*, 1903, *36*, 905–913.

――――. Alte und neue Untersuchungen über das Gehirn. 4. Ueber die Beziehungen der Rinde und der subcorticalen Ganglienzellschicht des Hundes. *Arch. Psychiat. Nervenkr.*, 1903, *37*, 299–467, 849–1013. Reprinted in *Physiologische und klinische Untersuchungen über das Gehirn: Gesammelte Abhandlungen, op. cit.*, pp. 155–618.

――――. Einleitung. (1903) In *Physiologische und klinische Untersuchungen über das Gehirn. op. cit.*, pp. 1–7.

――――. *Welt und Gehirn: Ein Essay.* Berlin: Hirschwald, 1905.

Clarke & O'Malley, *Brain ;* Herrnstein & Boring, *Source Book*

THOMAS HOBBES
1588-1679
English Philosopher (24)

Hobbes, T. *The English works of Thomas Hobbes.* (11 vols.) Ed. by W. Molesworth. Aalen: Scientia, 1962. (1839–1845)   **C**

――――. *Opera philosophica quae Latine scripsit omnia.* (5 vols.) Ed. by W. Molesworth. Aalen: Scientia, 1961. (1839–1845)   **C**

――――. *The metaphysical system of Hobbes in twelve chapters from elements of philosophy concerning body together with briefer extracts from human nature and Leviathan.* (2nd ed.) Ed. by Mary W. Calkins. La Salle, Ill.: Open Court, 1963. (1905)   **C**

――――. *Selections.* Ed. by F. J. E. Woodbridge. New York: Scribner's, 1930. (Reprinted 1959)   **C**

――――. *Body, man, and citizen: Selections from Thomas Hobbes.* Ed. by R. Peters. New York: Collier, 1962.   **C**

――――. Philosophical rudiments concerning government and society. (1642) In *English works,* Vol. 2, *op. cit.*, pp. 1–319.

――――. The third set of objections. (1642) In *The philosophical works of Descartes.* Vol. 2. (2nd ed.) Trans. by Elizabeth S. Haldane & G. R. T. Ross. Cambridge: Cambridge University Press, 1931, pp. 60–78. (Reprinted 1955)

――――. *De Cive or the citizen.* Ed. by S. Lamprecht. New York: Appleton, 1949. (1642)

――――. *The elements of law: Natural and politic.* Ed. by F. Tonnies. Cambridge: Cambridge University Press, 1928. (1650) (Reprinted 1971)

――――. Human nature: Or the fundamental elements of policy. (1650) In *English Works,* Vol. 4, *op. cit.*, pp. 1–76.

――――. *Leviathan.* Ed. by E. Rhys. New York: Dutton, 1931. (1651)

――――. *Leviathan.* Ed. by M. Oakeshott. Oxford: Blackwell, 1947. (1651) (Reprinted 1962).

――――. Leviathan or, the matter, form, and power of commonwealth, ecclesiastical and civil. (1651) In *English works,* Vol. 3, *op. cit.*, pp. 1–714.

――――. Of liberty and necessity. (1654) In *English works,* Vol. 4, *op. cit.*, pp. 239–278.

――――. De Corpore Politico. (1655) In *English works,* Vol. 4, *op. cit.*, pp. 77–228.

――――. Elements of philosophy: The first section, concerning body. (1653) In *English works,* Vol. 1, *op. cit.*, pp. 1–532.

――――. The questions concerning liberty, necessity and chance, clearly stated and debated between D. Bramhall, Bishop of Derry, and Thomas Hobbes of Malmesbury. (1656) In *English works,* Vol. 5, *op. cit.*, pp. 1–455.

――――. Behemoth. (1679) In *English works,* Vol. 6, *op. cit.*, pp. 161–418.

――――. A dialogue between a philosopher and a student of the common laws of England. (1681) In *English works,* Vol. 6, *op. cit.*, pp. 1–160.

――――. Vita. (1681) In *Opera Latine,* Vol. 1, *op. cit.*, pp. 8–21.   **B**

Brinton, *Age Reason;* Dennis, *Psychology*; Herrnstein & Boring, *Source Book*; Hunter & Macalpine, *Psychiatry*; Hutchins, *Great Books*; Lawrence & O'Connor, *Phenomenology*; Mandler & Mandler, *Thinking*; Margolis, *Introduction*; Matson, *Being*; Murphy, *Western*; Parsons, *Society*; Rand, *Classical Philosophers*; Rand, *Classical Psychologists*; Rand, *Moralists*; Sahakian, *Psychology*; Slotkin, *Anthropology*

LEONARD TRELAWNEY HOBHOUSE
1864-1929
English Sociologist (19)

Hobhouse, L. T. *Sociology and philosophy: A centenary collection of essays and articles.* Ed. by M. Ginsberg. Cambridge: Harvard University Press, 1966.   **C**

————. *The labour movement.* (3rd ed.) New York: Macmillan, 1912. (1893)

————. *The theory of knowledge: A contribution to some problems of logic and metaphysics.* (3rd ed.) London: Methuen, 1921. (1896)

————. Some problems of conception. *Mind,* 1897, *6*(N.S.), 145–163.

————. *Mind in evolution.* (3rd ed.) London: Macmillan, 1926. (1901)

————. Faith and the will to believe. *Proc. Aristot. Soc.,* 1904, *4*(N.S.), 87–110.

————. *Morals in evolution: A study in comparative ethics.* (7th ed.) London: Chapman & Hall, 1951. (1906) (Reprinted 1969)

————. Value and limitation of eugenics. *Sociol. Rev.,* 1911, *4*, 281–302.

————. *Social evolution and political theory.* New York: Columbia University Press, 1911.

————. *Development and purpose: An essay towards a philosophy of evolution.* (2nd ed.) New York: Macmillan, 1927. (1913)

————, Wheeler, G. C., & Ginsberg, M. *The material culture and social institutions of the simpler peoples, an essay in correlation.* New York: Humanities Press, 1965. (1915)

————. Are physical, biological and psychological categories irreducible? *Proc. Aristot. Soc.,* 1917–1918, *18*, 468–478.

————. *The metaphysical theory of the state.* New York: Macmillan, 1918.

————. *The rational good: A study in the logic of practice.* London: Watts, 1947. (1921)

————. The philosophy of development. In J. H. Muirhead (Ed.), *Contemporary British philosophy: Personal statements.* 1st series. New York: Macmillan, 1924, pp. 149–188.

————. *Social development: Its nature and conditions.* London: Allen & Unwin, 1966. (1924)

————. The place of mind in nature. *Proc. Aristot. Soc.,* 1926, Suppl. 6, 112–126.

————. Friede und Ordnung bei den primitivsten Völkern innerhalb der Gruppe. *Z. Völkerpsychol. Soziol.,* 1929, *5*, 40–56.

————. Das Verhältnis zwischen Gruppen und Stämmen bei den primitivsten Völkern. *Z. Völkerpsychol. Soziol.,* 1929, *5*, 172–192.

————. Comparative psychology. In *Encyclopaedia Britannica.* Vol. 6. (14th ed.) Chicago: Encyclopaedia Britannica, 1938, pp. 167–170.

Park & Burgess, *Sociology*

HARALD HOFFDING
1843-1931
Danish Philosopher (24)

Höffding, H. Zur Psychologie der Gefühle. *Phil. Monatsh.,* 1880, *16*, 416–457.

————. *Outlines of psychology.* Trans. by Mary E. Lowndes. New York: Macmillan, 1891. (1882)

————. *Psychologie in Umrissen auf Grundlage der Erfahrung.* (5th ed.) Trans. by F. Bendixen. Leipzig: Altenburg, 1914. (1882)

————. Die psychologische Bedeutung der Wiederholung. *Vtljsch. wiss. Phil.,* 1883, 7, 296–328.

————. Wiedererkennen, Association und psychische Aktivität. *Vtljsch. wiss. Phil.,* 1889, *13*, 420–458; 1890, *14*, 27–40, 167–205, 293–316.

————. Psychische und physische Aktivität. *Vtljsch. wiss. Phil.,* 1891, *15,* 233–250.

————. *Søren Kierkegaard als Philosoph.* Trans. by A. Dorner & C. Schrempf. Stuttgart: Frommann, 1922. (1892)

————. Zur Theorie des Wiedererkennens. Eine Replik. *Phil. Stud.,* 1893, *8,* 86–96.

————. *Jean Jacques Rousseau and his philosophy.* (2nd ed.) Trans. by W. Richards & L. E. Saidla. New Haven: Yale University Press, 1930. (1896) (Reprinted 1970)

————. *A history of modern philosophy from the close of the Renaissance to our own day.* (2 vols.) Trans. by B. E. Meyer. New York: Macmillan, 1900. (1894) (Reprinted 1955)

————. La base psychologique des jugements logiques. (1899) *Rev. phil.,* 1901, *52,* 345–378, 501–539.

————. *The philosophy of religion.* Trans. from German ed. by B. E. Meyer. New York: Macmillan, 1906. (1901)

————. *The problems of philosophy.* Trans. by G. M. Fisher. New York: Macmillan, 1905. (1902)

————. A philosophical confession. *J. Phil.,* 1905, *2,* 85–92.

————. The present state of psychology and its relations to the neighboring sciences. *Psychol. Rev.,* 1905, *12,* 67–77.

————. Le concept de la volonté. (1906) *Rev. Métaphys. Morale,* 1907, *15,* 1–17.

————. *Philosophes contemporains.* Trans. from German by A. Tremesaygues. Paris: Alcan, 1907.

————. The influence of the conception of evolution on modern philosophy. In A. C. Seward (Ed.), *Darwin and modern science.* Cambridge: Cambridge University Press, 1909, pp. 446–464.

————. *Der menschliche Gedanke, seine Formen und seine Aufgaben.* Leipzig: Reisland, 1911. (1910)

————. Rousseau et la religion. *Rev. Métaphys. Morale,* 1912, *20,* 275–293.

————. *La philosophie de Bergson, exposé et critique.* Paris: Alcan, 1916. (1914)

————. *Humor als Lebensgefühl (Der Grosse Humor). Eine psychologische Studie.* (2nd ed.) Trans. by H. Goebel. Leipzig: Reisland, 1930. (1916)

————. *Erlebnis und Deutung.* Trans. by E. v. Magnus. Stuttgart: Frommann, 1923. (1918)

————. Harald Höffding. In R. Schmidt (Ed.), *Die Philosophie der Gegenwart in Selbstdarstellungen.* Vol. 4. Leipzig: Meiner, 1923, pp. 75–97. **B Bl**

————. *Spinozas Ethica: Analyse und Charakteristik.* Heidelberg: Winter, 1924. (1918)

————. *Erkenntnistheorie und Lebensauffassung.* Leipzig: Reisland, 1926. (1925)

————. Zur Stellung der Erkenntnistheorie in unserer Zeit. *Kant-Stud.,* 1930, *35,* 480–495.

————. Harald Höffding. In C. Murchison (Ed.), *A history of psychology in autobiography.* Vol. 2. Worcester, Mass.: Clark University Press, 1932, pp. 197–205. **B**

HARRY LEVI HOLLINGWORTH
1880-1956
American Psychologist (20)

Hollingworth, H. L. Vicarious functioning of irrelevant imagery. *J. Phil.,* 1911, *8,* 688–692.

————. The influence of caffeine on the speed and quality of performance in typewriting. *Psychol. Rev.,* 1912, *19,* 66–73.

————. The influence of caffeine on mental and motor efficiency. *Arch. Psychol.,* N.Y., 1912, No. 22.

Strong, Margaret H., & ————. The influence of form and category on the outcome of judgment. *J. Phil.,* 1912, *9,* 513–520.

————. Characteristic differences between recall and recognition. *Amer. J. Psychol.,* 1913, *24,* 532–544.

————. Experimental studies in judgment. *Arch. Psychol.*, N.Y., 1913, No. 29.

————. Correlation of abilities as affected by practice. *J. educ. Psychol.*, 1913, *4*, 405–414.

————. Individual differences before, during and after practice. *Psychol. Rev.*, 1914, *21*, 1–8.

————. Variations in efficiency during the working day. *Psychol. Rev.*, 1914, *21*, 473–491.

Cogan, L. C., Conklin, A. M., & ————. An experimental study of self-analysis, estimates of associates, and results of tests. *School & Soc.*, 1915, *2*, 171–179.

————. *Vocational psychology: Its problems and methods.* New York: Appleton, 1916.

————, & Poffenberger, A. T., Jr. *The sense of taste.* New York: Moffat, Yard, 1917.

. *The psychology of functional neuroses.* New York: Appleton, 1920.

————. *Judging human character.* New York: Appleton, 1922.

————. The definition of judgment. *Psychol. Rev.*, 1925, *32*, 337–361.

————. *Mental growth and decline: A survey of developmental psychology.* New York: Appleton, 1927.   **Bl**

————. *Psychology: Its facts and principles.* New York: Appleton, 1928.

————. General laws of redintegration. *J. gen. Psychol.*, 1928, *1*, 79–90.

————. Sensuous determinants of psychological attitude. *Psychol. Rev.*, 1928, *35*, 93–117.

————. *Vocational psychology and character analyses.* New York: Appleton, 1929.

————. *Abnormal psychology: Its concepts and theories.* New York: Ronald Press, 1930.

————. *The psychology of the audience.* New York: American Book, 1935.

————. *Psychology and ethics: A study of the sense of obligation.* New York: Ronald Press, 1949.

Moore & Hartmann, *Industrial Psychology*

LETA STETTER HOLLINGWORTH
1886-1939
American Psychologist (12)

Hollingworth, Leta S. Variability as related to sex differences in achievement. *Amer. J. Sociol.*, 1914, *19*, 510–530.

————, & Winferd, A. The psychology of special disability in spelling. *Teach. Coll. Contrib. Educ.*, 1918, No. 88.

————. *The psychology of subnormal children.* New York: Macmillan, 1920.

————. *Special talents and defects: Their significance for education.* New York: Macmillan, 1923.

————. *Gifted children: Their nature and nurture.* New York: Macmillan, 1926.

————. *The psychology of the adolescent.* New York: Appleton, 1928.

————. The child of special gifts or special deficiencies. In C. Murchison (Ed.), *A handbook of child psychology.* (2nd ed.) Worcester, Mass.: Clark University Press, 1933, pp. 842–854. (1931)

————. The adolescent child. In C. Murchison (Ed.), *A handbook of child psychology.* (2nd ed.) Worcester, Mass.: Clark University Press, 1933, pp. 882–908. (1931)

————, & Kaunitz, Ruth M. The centile status of gifted children at maturity. *J. genet. Psychol.*, 1934, *45*, 106–120.

Lorge, I., & ————. Adult status of highly intelligent children. *J. genet. Psychol.*, 1936, *49*, 215–226.

————. The significance of deviates. I. Review of research. *Yearb. Nat. Soc. Stud. Educ.*, 1940, *39*(1), 43–66.

————. *Children above 180 IQ. Stanford-Binet— Origin and development.* Yonkers-on-Hudson, N.Y.: World Book, 1942.

Pressey, *Casebook*

EDWIN BISSELL HOLT
1873-1946
American Psychologist (22)

Holt, E. B. Eye-movement and central anaesthesia. *Psychol. Monogr.*, 1903, *4*, No 17, pp. 3–45.

———. The illusion of resolution-stripes on the color-wheel. *Psychol. Monogr.*, 1903, *4*, No. 17, pp. 167–204.

———. The classification of psycho-physic methods. *Psychol. Rev.*, 1904, *11*, 343–369.

———. Eye movements during dizziness. *Harvard Psychol. Stud.*, 1906, *2*, 57–66.

———. On ocular nystagmus and the localization of sensory data during dizziness. *Psychol. Rev.*, 1909, *16*, 377–398.

———. *The concept of consciousness*. London: Allen, 1914.

———. *The Freudian wish and its place in ethics*. New York: Holt, 1915. (Reprinted 1966)

———. Response and cognition. *J. Phil.*, 1915, *12*, 365–373, 393–409. Reprinted in *The Freudian wish, op. cit.*, pp. 153–208.

———. *Animal drive and the learning process. An essay toward radical empiricism*. New York: Holt, 1931.

———. The argument for sensationism as drawn from Dr. Berkeley. *Psychol. Rev.*, 1934, *41*, 509–533.

———. The whimsical condition of social psychology and of mankind. In H. Kallen & S. Hook (Eds.), *American philosophy today and tomorrow*. New York: Furman, 1935, pp. 171–202.

———. Eight steps in neuro-muscular integration. In Various, (*Problems of nervous physiology and behavior.*) Tiflis: Akademiya Nauk. Georgia, 1936, pp. 25–36.

———. Materialism and the criterion of the psychic. *Psychol. Rev.*, 1937, *44*, 33–53.

———. William James as psychologist. In *In commemoration of William James, 1842–1942*. New York: AMS Press, 1967, pp. 34–47. (1942)

Chisholm, *Realism* ; Herrnstein & Boring, *Source Book* ; Park & Burgess, *Sociology* ; Russell, *Motivation*

KARL JOHN HOLZINGER
1892-1954
American Psychologist (13)

Holzinger, K. J. On scoring multiple response tests. *J. educ. Psychol.*, 1924, *15*, 445–447.

———. *Statistical tables for students in education and psychology*. Chicago: University of Chicago Press, 1925.

Spearman, C., & ———. The sampling error in the theory of two factors. *Brit. J. Psychol.*, 1925, *15*, 17–19.

———, & Clayton, B. Further experiments in the application of Spearman's prophecy formula. *J. educ. Psychol.*, 1925, *16*, 289–299.

Spearman C., & ———. Note on the sampling error of tetrad differences. *Brit. J. Psychol.*, 1925–1926, *16*, 86–88.

———. *Statistical methods for students in education*. Boston: Ginn, 1928.

Freeman, F. N., ———, & Mitchell, B. C. The influence of environment on the intelligence, school achievement, and conduct of foster children. *Yearb. Nat. Soc. Stud. Educ.*, 1928, 27(1), 102–217.

———, & Church, A. E. R. On the means of samples from a U-shaped population. *Biometrika*, 1928, *20A*, 361–388.

———. On tetrad differences with overlapping variables. *J. educ. Psychol.*, 1929, *20*, 91–97.

———. The relative effect of nature and nurture influences on twin differences. *J. educ. Psychol.*, 1929, *20*, 241–248.

———. *Statistical résumé of the Spearman two-factor theory*. Chicago: University of Chicago Press, 1930.

———. Thorndike's C.A.V.D. is full of G. *J. educ. Psychol.*, 1931, *22*, 161–166.

———, & Swineford, F. Uniqueness of factor patterns. *J. educ. Psychol.*, 1932, *23*, 247–258.

———. Recent research on unitary mental traits. *J. Pers.*, 1935–1936, *4*, 335–343.

Newman, H. H., Freeman, F. N., & ———. *Twins: A study of heredity and environment*. Chicago: University of Chicago Press, 1937.

———, & Swineford, F. The bifactor method. *Psychometrika*, 1937, *2*, 41–54.

———, & Harman, H. H. Relationships between factors obtained from certain analyses. *J. educ. Psychol.*, 1937, *28*, 321–345.

———. Reply to special review of "Twins." *Psychol. Bull.*, 1938, *35*, 436–444.

———, & Harman, H. H. Comparison of two factorial analyses. *Psychometrika*, 1938, *3*, 45–60.

———, & Swineford, F. A study in factor analysis: The stability of a bifactor solution. *Supp. Educ. Monogr.*, No. 48. Chicago: Dept. of Educ., University of Chicago, 1939.

———. A synthetic approach to factor analysis. *Psychometrika*, 1940, *5*, 235–250.

———, & Harman, H. H. *Factor analysis: A synthesis of factorial methods*. Chicago: University of Chicago Press, 1941.

———. Why do people factor? *Psychometrika*, 1942, *7*, 147–156.

———. Factoring test scores and implications for the method of averages. *Psychometrika*, 1944, *9*, 155–168.

———. A simple method of factor analysis. *Psychometrika*, 1944, *9*, 257–262.

———. Interpretation of second order factors. *Psychometrika*, 1945, *10*, 21–25.

———. A comparison of the principal-axis and centroid factors. *J. educ. Psychol.*, 1946, *37*, 449–472.

———. Applications of the simple method of factor analysis. *J. educ. Psychol.*, 1949, *40*, 129–142.

ERICH VON HORNBOSTEL
1877-1935
German Psychologist (16)

Hornbostel, E. v. Melodischer Tanz. *Z. int. Musik Ges.*, 1904, *4*, 482–488.

———. Ueber vergleichende akustische und musikpsychologische Untersuchungen. *Z. angew. Psychol.*, 1910, *3*, 465–487.

Stumpf, C., & ———. Ueber die Bedeutung ethnologischer Untersuchungen für die Psychologie und Aesthetik der Tonkunst. *Ber. IV. Kong. exper. Psychol.*, Leipzig, 1911, pp. 256–269.

———, & Wertheimer, M. Ueber die Wahrnehmung der Schallrichtung. *Sitzber. preuss. Akad. Wiss.*, 1920, 388–396.

———. Ueber optische Inversion. *Psychol. Forsch.*, 1922, *1*, 130–156.

———. Beobachtungen über ein- und zweiohriges Hören. *Psychol. Forsch.*, 1923, *4*, 64–114.

———. The psychophysiology of monotic and diotic hearing. *Proc. VII. Int. Cong. Psychol.*, Cambridge, 1924, 377–381.

———. The unity of the senses. (1925) *Psyche*, 1926, No. 28, 83–89.

———. Das räumliche Hören. In A. Bethe *et al.* (Eds.), *Handbuch der normalen und pathologischen Physiologie*. Vol. 11. Berlin: Springer-Verlag, 1926, pp. 602–618.

———. Psychologie der Gehörserscheinungen. In A. Bethe *et al.* (Eds.), *Handbuch der normalen und pathologischen Physiologie*. Vol. 11. Berlin: Springer-Verlag, 1926, pp. 701–730.

Abraham, O., & ———. Zur Psychologie der Tondistanz. *Z. Psychol.*, 1926, *98*, 233–249.

———. Laut und Sinn. In *Sprachwissenschaftliche und andere Studien. Festschrift für Meinhof*. Hamburg: Friedrickson, 1927, pp. 329–348.

———. Neue Beiträge zur physiologischen Hörtheorie. *Jber. ges. Physiol.*, 1928, 753–771.

———. Gestaltpsychologisches zur Heilkritik. In *Festschrift für G. Adler*. Leipzig: Hirzel, 1930, pp. 12–16.

———. Ueber Verschiebung der Tonhöhe. *Folia oto-laryngologica*, 1931, *21*, 100–106.

———. Ueber Geruchshelligkeit. *Arch. ges. Physiol.*, 1931, *227*, 517–538.

KAREN HORNEY
1885-1952
German-American Psychoanalyst (23)

Horney, Karen. *The collected works of Karen Horney*. (2 vols.) New York: Norton, 1963.
C

————. *Feminine psychology*. Ed. by H. Kelman. New York: Norton, 1967. **C**

————. On the genesis of the castration complex in women. (1923) *Int. J. Psycho-Anal.*, 1924, 5, 50–65. Reprinted in *Feminine psychology, op. cit.*, pp. 37–53.

————. The flight from womanhood: The masculinity complex in women, as viewed by men and by women. *Int. J. Psycho-Anal.*, 1926, 7, 324–339. Reprinted in *Feminine psychology, op. cit.*, pp. 54–70.

————. The problem of the monogamous ideal. *Int. J. Psycho-Anal.*, 1928, 9, 318–331. Reprinted in *Feminine psychology, op. cit.*, pp. 84–98.

————. The dread of women. *Int. J. Psycho-Anal.*, 1932, 13, 348–360. Reprinted in *Feminine psychology, op. cit.*, pp. 133–146.

————. The denial of the vagina. *Int. J. Psycho-Anal.*, 1933, 14, 57–70. Reprinted in *Feminine psychology, op. cit.*, pp. 214–233.

————. Personality changes in female adolescents. *Amer. J. Orthopsychiat.*, 1935, 5, 19–26. Reprinted in *Feminine psychology, op. cit.*, pp. 234–244.

————. The problem of feminine masochism. *Psychoanal. Rev.*, 1935, 22, 241–257. Reprinted in *Feminine psychology, op. cit.*, pp. 214–233.

————. Culture and neurosis. *Amer. sociol. Rev.*, 1936, 1, 221–235.

————. *The neurotic personality of our time*. New York: Norton, 1937.

————. What is a neurosis? *Amer. J. Sociol.*, 1939, 45, 426–432.

————. *New ways in psychoanalysis*. New York: Norton, 1939.

————. *Self-analysis*. New York: Norton, 1942.

————. *Our inner conflicts: A constructive theory of neurosis*. New York: Norton, 1945.

————. What does the analyst do? (1946) In *Are you considering psychoanalysis?* New York: Norton, 1946, pp. 187–209.

————. How do you progress after analysis? (1946) In *Are you considering psychoanalysis?* New York: Norton, 1946, pp. 235–257.

————. The value of vindictiveness. *Amer. J. Psychoanal.*, 1948, 8, 3–12.

————. *Neurosis and human growth: The struggle toward self-realization*. New York: Norton, 1950.

————. On feeling abused. *Amer. J. Psychoanal.*, 1951, 11, 5–12. Reprinted in H. Kelman (Ed.), *Advances in psychoanalysis*. New York: Norton, 1964, pp. 29–46.

————. The paucity of inner experiences. *Amer. J. Psychoanal.*, 1952, 12, 3–9. Reprinted in H. Kelman (Ed.), *Advances in psychoanalysis*. New York: Norton, 1964, pp. 47–64.

Lindzey & Hall, *Personality*; Sahakian, *Personality*; Vetter, *Personality*

CARL IVER HOVLAND
1912-1961
American Psychologist (23)

Hovland, C. I. Inhibition of reinforcement and phenomena of experimental extinction. *Proc. Nat. Acad. Sci.*, 1936, 22, 430–433.

————. The generalization of conditioned responses. III. Extinction, spontaneous recovery, and disinhibition of conditioned and of generalized responses. *J. exp. Psychol.*, 1937, 21, 47–62.

————. The generalization of conditioned responses. I. The sensory generalization of conditioned responses with varying frequencies of tone. *J. gen. Psychol.*, 1937, 17, 125–148. Reprinted in J. F. Hall (Ed.), *Readings in the psychology of learning*. New York: Lippincott, 1967, pp. 327–346.

———. The generalization of conditioned responses. IV. The effects of varying amounts of reinforcement upon the degree of generalization of conditioned responses. *J. exp. Psychol.*, 1937, *21*, 261–276.

———. The generalization of conditioned responses. II. The sensory generalization of conditioned responses with varying intensities of tone. *J. genet. Psychol.*, 1937, *51*, 279–291.

———. Experimental studies in rote-learning theory. I. Reminiscence following learning by massed and by distributed practice. *J. exp. Psychol.*, 1938, *22*, 201–224.

———, & Sears, R. R. Experiments on motor conflict. I. Types of conflict and their modes of resolution. *J. exp. Psychol.*, 1938, *23*, 477–493.

Hull, C. L., ———, Ross, R. T., Hall, M., Perkins, D. T., & Fitch, F. B. *Mathematico-deductive theory of rote learning: A study in scientific methodology.* New Haven: Yale University Press, 1940.

———, & Sears, R. R. Minor studies of aggression. VI. Correlation of lynchings with economic indices. *J. Psychol.*, 1940, *9*, 301–310.

———, Lumsdaine, A. A., & Sheffield, F. D. *Studies in social psychology in World War II.* Vol. 3. *Experiments on mass communication.* Princeton: Princeton University Press, 1949.

———. Human learning and retention. In S. S. Stevens (Ed.), *Handbook of experimental psychology.* New York: Wiley, 1951, pp. 613–689.

———, & Weiss, W. The influence of source credibility on communication effectiveness. *Publ. Opin. Quart.*, 1951–1952, *15*, 635–650.

———, & Mandell, W. An experimental comparison of conclusion-drawing by the communicator and by the audience. *J. abnorm. soc. Psychol.*, 1952, *47*, 581–588.

———, & Sherif, M. Judgmental phenomena and scales of attitude measurement; item displacement in Thurstone scales. *J. abnorm. soc. Psychol.*, 1952, *47*, 822–832.

———. A "communication analysis" of concept learning. *Psychol. Rev.*, 1952, *59*, 461–472.

———, & Kurtz, K. H. Experimental studies in rote-learning theory. X. Pre-learning syllable familiarization and the length-difficulty relationship. *J. exp. Psychol.*, 1952, *44*, 31–39. Reprinted in J. F. Hall (Ed.), *Readings in the psychology of learning.* New York: Lippincott, 1967, pp. 404–416.

———, & Weiss, W. Transmission of information concerning concepts through positive and negative instances. *J. exp. Psychol.*, 1953, *45*, 175–182.

Kelman, H. C., & ———. "Reinstatement" of the communicator in delayed measurement of opinion change. *J. abnorm. soc. Psychol.*, 1953, *48*, 327–335.

———, Janis, I. L., & Kelley, H. H. *Communication and persuasion: Psychological studies of opinion change.* New Haven: Yale University Press, 1953.

———. Effects of the mass media of communication. In G. Lindzey (Ed.), *Handbook of social psychology.* Vol. 2. Cambridge: Addison-Wesley, 1954, pp. 1062–1103.

Kelley, H. H., ———, Schwartz, M., & Abelson, R. P. The influence of judges' attitudes in three methods of attitude scaling. *J. soc. Psychol.*, 1955, *42*, 147–158.

Kurtz, K. H., & ———. Concept learning with differing sequences of instances. *J. exp. Psychol.*, 1956, *51*, 239–243.

———, & Pritzker, H. A. Extent of opinion change as a function of amount of change advocated. *J. abnorm. soc. Psychol.*, 1957, *54*, 257–261.

———, Harvey, O. J., & Sherif, M. Assimilation and contrast effects in reactions to communication and attitude change. *J. abnorm. soc. Psychol.*, 1957, *55*, 244–252.

———, et al. *The order of presentation in persuasion.* New Haven: Yale University Press, 1957.

Sherif, M., Taub, D., & ———. Assimilation and contrast effects of anchoring stimuli on judgments. *J. exp. Psychol.*, 1958, *55*, 150–155.

Janis, I. L., ———, et al. *Personality and persuasibility.* New Haven: Yale University Press, 1959.

———. Reconciling conflicting results derived from experimental and survey studies of attitude change. *Amer. Psychologist,* 1959, *14,* 8–17.

Morrisett, L., & ———. A comparison of three varieties of training in human problem solving. *J. exp. Psychol.,* 1959, *58,* 52–55.

Rosenberg, M. J., ———, et al. *Attitude organization and change. An analysis of consistency among attitude components.* New Haven, Yale University Press, 1960.

———. Computer simulation of thinking. *Amer. Psychologist,* 1960, *15,* 687–693.

Hunt, E. B., & ———. Order of consideration of different types of concepts. *J. exp. Psychol.,* 1960, *59,* 220–225.

Sherif, M., & ———. *Social judgment: Assimilation and contrast effects in communication and attitude change. Yale studies in attitude and communication.* Vol. 4. New Haven: Yale University Press, 1961.

Shepard, R. N., ———, & Jenkins, H. M. Learning and memorization of classifications. *Psychol. Monogr.,* 1961, *75,* No. 517.

Hunt, E. B., & ———. Programming a model of human concept formulation. *Proc. West, Jt. Computer Conf.,* 1961, *19,* 145–155. Reprinted in E. Feigenbaum & J. Feldman (Eds.), *Computers and thought.* New York: McGraw-Hill, 1963, pp. 310–325.

CLARK LEONARD HULL
1884-1952
American Psychologist (27)

Hull, C. L., & Montgomery, R. B. An experimental investigation of certain alleged relations between character and handwriting. *Psychol. Rev.,* 1919, *26,* 63–74.

———. Quantitative aspects of the evolution of concepts. *Psychol. Monogr.,* 1920, *28,* No. 123.

———, & Lugoff, L. S. Complex signs in diagnostic free association. *J. exp. Psychol.,* 1921, *4,* 111–136.

———. The influence of tobacco smoking on mental and motor efficiency. *Psychol. Monogr.,* 1924, *33,* No. 150.

———. *Aptitude testing.* Yonkers-on-Hudson, N.Y.: World Book, 1928.

———. Hypnotism in scientific perspective. *Sci. Mon.,* N.Y., 1929, *29,* 154–162.

———. A functional interpretation of the conditioned reflex. *Psychol. Rev.,* 1929, *36,* 498–511. Reprinted in M. Marx (Ed.), *Psychological theory: Contemporary readings.* New York: Macmillan, 1959, pp. 399–410.

———. Quantitative methods of investigating waking suggestion. *J. abnorm. soc. Psychol.,* 1929, *24,* 153–169.

———. Quantitative methods of investigating hypnotic suggestion. I. II. *J. abnorm. soc. Psychol.,* 1930–1931, *25,* 200–223, 390–417.

———. Simple trial-and-error learning: A study in psychological theory. *Psychol. Rev.,* 1930, *37,* 241–256.

———. Knowledge and purpose as habit mechanisms. *Psychol. Rev.,* 1930, *37,* 511–525.

Baernstein, H. D., & ———. A mechanical model of the conditioned reflex. *J. gen. Psychol.,* 1931, *5,* 99–106.

———, & Krueger, R. C. An electrochemical parallel to the conditioned reflex. *J. gen. Psychol.,* 1931, *5,* 262–269.

———. Goal attraction and directing ideas conceived as habit phenomena. *Psychol. Rev.,* 1931, *38,* 487–506.

———. The goal gradient hypothesis and maze learning. *Psychol. Rev.,* 1932, *39,* 25–43.

———. Differential habituation to internal stimuli in the albino rat. *J. comp. Psychol.,* 1933, *16,* 255–273.

———. *Hypnosis and suggestibility: An experimental approach.* New York: Appleton-Century, 1933. (Reprinted 1968)

Bass, M. J., & ———. The irradiation of a tactile conditioned reflex in man. *J. comp. Psychol.*, 1934, *17*, 47–65.

———. The rat's speed-of-locomotion gradient in the approach to food. *J. comp. Psychol.*, 1934, *17*, 393–422.

———. The concept of the habit-family hierarchy and maze learning: I. II. *Psychol. Rev.*, 1934, *41*, 33–54, 134–152.

———. Learning. II. The factor of the conditioned reflex. In C. Murchison (Ed.), *A handbook of general experimental psychology*. Worcester, Mass.: Clark University Press, 1934, pp. 382–455.

———. The influence of caffeine and other factors on certain phenomena of rote learning. *J. gen. Psychol.*, 1935, *13*, 249–274.

———. Thorndike's Fundamentals of learning. *Psychol. Bull.*, 1935, *32*, 807–823.

———. The mechanism of the assembly of behavior segments in novel combinations suitable for problem solution. *Psychol. Rev.*, 1935, *42*, 219–245.

———. The conflicting psychologies of learning—a way out. *Psychol. Rev.*, 1935, *42*, 491–516.

———. Mind, mechanism, and adaptive behavior. *Psychol. Rev.*, 1937, *44*, 1–32.

———. Logical positivism as a constructive methodology in the social sciences. *Erkenntnis*, 1938, *6*, 35–38.

———, & Spence, K. W. "Correction" vs. "noncorrection" method of trial-and-error learning in rats. *J. comp. Psychol.*, 1938, *25*, 127–145.

———. The goal-gradient hypothesis applied to some "field-force" problems in the behavior of young children. *Psychol. Rev.*, 1938, *45*, 271–299.

———. The problem of stimulus equivalence in behavior theory. *Psychol. Rev.*, 1939, *46*, 9–30.

———. Modern behaviorism and psychoanalysis. *Trans. N.Y., Acad. Sci.*, 1939, *1*, Ser. II, 78–82.

———. Simple trial-and-error learning: An empirical investigation. *J. comp. Psychol.*, 1939, *27*, 233–258.

———, Hovland, C. I., Ross, R. T., Hall, M., Perkins, D. T., & Fitch, F. B. *Mathematico-deductive theory of rote learning: A study in scientific methodology*. New Haven: Yale University Press, 1940.

———. Explorations in the patterning of stimuli conditioned to the G.S.R. *J. exp. Psychol.*, 1940, *27*, 95–110.

———. Conditioning: Outline of a systematic theory of learning. *Yearb. Nat. Soc. Stud. Educ.*, 1942, *41*(2), 61–95.

———. The problem of intervening variables in molar behavior theory. *Psychol. Rev.*, 1943, *50*, 273–291. Reprinted in M. Marx (Ed.), *Psychological theory: Contemporary readings*. New York: Macmillan, 1951, pp. 203–216.

———. A postscript concerning intervening variables. *Psychol. Rev.*, 1943, *50*, 540.

———. *Principles of behavior: An introduction to behavior theory*. New York: Appleton-Century, 1943.

———. Value, valuation, and natural science methodology. *Phil. Sci.*, 1944, *11*, 125–141.

———. The place of innate individual and species differences in a natural-science theory of behavior. *Psychol. Rev.*, 1945, *52*, 55–60.

———. The discrimination of stimulus configurations and the hypothesis of afferent neural interaction. *Psychol. Rev.*, 1945, *52*, 133–142.

———. Moral values, behaviorism, and the world crisis. *Trans. N.Y. Acad. Sci.*, 1945, *7*, 90–94.

Felsinger, J. M., Gladstone, A. I., Yamaguchi, H. G., & ———. Reaction latency (s_tR) as a function of the number of reinforcements (N). *J. exp. Psychol.*, 1947, *37*, 214–228.

Gladstone, A. I., Yamaguchi, H. G., ———, & Felsinger, J. M. Some functional relationships of reaction potential (sE_R) and related phenomena. *J. exp. Psychol.*, 1947, *37*, 510–526.

———. The problem of primary stimulus generalization. *Psychol. Rev.*, 1947, *54*, 120–134.

———, Felsinger, J. M., Gladstone, A. I., & Yamaguchi, H. G. A proposed quantification of habit strength. *Psychol. Rev.*, 1947, *54*, 237–254.

Yamaguchi, H. G., ———, Felsinger, J. M., & Gladstone, A. I. Characteristics of dispersions based on the pooled momentary reaction potentials ($s\bar{E}_R$) of a group. *Psychol. Rev.*, 1948, *55*, 216–238.

———. Reactively heterogeneous compound trial-and-error learning with distributed trials and serial reinforcement. *J. exp. Psychol.*, 1948, *38*, 17–28.

———. Stimulus intensity dynamism (V) and stimulus generalization. *Psychol. Rev.*, 1949, *56*, 67–76.

———. Behavior postulates and corollaries— 1949. *Psychol. Rev.*, 1950, *57*, 173–180.

———. Simple qualitative discrimination learning. *Psychol. Rev.*, 1950, *57*, 303–313.

Wilcoxon, H. C., Hays, R., & ———. A preliminary determination of the functional relationship of effective reaction potential ($s\bar{E}_R$) to the ordinal number of Vincentized extinction reactions (ń). *J. exp. Psychol.*, 1950, *40*, 194–199.

———. A primary social science law. *Sci. Mon.*, N.Y., 1950, *71*, 221–228.

———. *Essentials of behavior.* New Haven: Yale University Press, 1951.

———, Livingston, J. R., Rouse, R. O., & Barker, A. N. True, sham and esophageal feeding as reinforcements. *J. comp. physiol. Psychol.*, 1951, *44*, 236–245.

———. Clark L. Hull. In E. G. Boring *et al.* (Eds.), *A history of psychology in autobiography.* Vol. 4. Worcester, Mass.: Clark University Press, 1952, pp. 143–162. **B**

———. *A behavior system: An introduction to behavior theory concerning the individual organism.* New Haven: Yale University Press, 1952. (Reprinted 1964)

Bincha & Stewart, *Motivation*; Dennis, *Psychology*; Matson, *Being*; Miller, *Mathematics*; Moore & Hartmann, *Industrial Psychology*; Parsons, *Society*; Perez, *Readings*; Pressey, *Casebook*; Russell, *Motivation*; Sahakian, *Psychology*; Shipley, *Classics*; Shor, *Hypnosis*; Valentine, *Experimental*; Wiseman, *Intelligence*; Wrenn, *Contributions*

WILHELM VON HUMBOLDT
1767-1835
German Philosopher (17)

Humboldt, W. v. Briefe an eine Freundin. (15th ed.) Ed. by Charlotte Diede. Leipzig: Brockhaus, 1925 (1849) **B C**

Goethe, J. W. v., ———, & Humboldt, A. v. *Goethes Briefwechsel mit den Gebrüdern von Humboldt. 1795–1832.* Ed. by F. T. Brockhaus. Leipzig: Brockhaus, 1876. **C**

———. *Gesammelte Schriften.* (15 vols.) Ed. by Königliche Preussische Akademie der Wissenschaften. Berlin: Behr, 1903–1936. (Reprinted 1968) **C**

———, & Humboldt, Caroline. *Wilhelm und Caroline von Humboldt in ihren Briefen.* (7 vols.) Ed. by Anna v. Sydow. Berlin: Mittler, 1906–1919. **B C**

———. *Briefe.* Munich: Hanser, 1952. **B C**

———. *Humanist without portfolio.* Trans. by Marianne Cowan. Detroit, Mich.: Wayne State University Press, 1963. **C**

———. Tagebücher. (1788–1835) In *Gesammelte Schriften,* Vols. 14, 15, *op. cit.* **B**

———. Ueber die Gesetze der Entwicklung der menschlichen Kräfte. (1791) In *Gesammelte Schriften.* Vol. 1, *op. cit.,* pp. 86–96. Fragment trans. in *Humanist without portfolio, op. cit.*

———. *The limits of state action.* Ed. by J. W. Burow. Cambridge: Cambridge University Press, 1969. (1792)

———. Plan einer vergleichenden Anthropologie. (1795) In *Gesammelte Schriften,* Vol. 1, *op. cit.,* pp. 377–410. Fragment trans. in *Humanist without portfolio, op. cit.*

———. Das achtzehnte Jahrhundert (1796–1797). In *Gesammelte Schriften,* Vol. 2, *op. cit.,* pp. 1–112. Fragment trans. in *Humanist without portfolio, op. cit.*

———. Betrachtungen über die Weltgeschichte. (1814) In *Gesammelte Schriften,* Vol. 3, *op. cit.,* pp. 350–359. Fragment trans. in *Humanist without portfolio, op. cit.*

———. Bruchstück einer Selbstbiographie. (1816) In *Gesammelte Schriften,* Vol. 15, *op. cit.,* pp. 451–460. Trans. in *Humanist without portfolio, op. cit,* pp. 395–403. **B**

———. Ueber den National-Charakter der Sprachen. (1822) In *Gesammelte Schriften,* Vol. 4, *op. cit.,* pp. 420–435.

———. *Ueber die Verschiedenheit des menschlichen Sprachbaues und ihren Einfluss auf die geistige Entwickelung des Menschengeschlechts.* Bonn: Dümmler, 1960. (1836)

———. *Linguistic variability and intellectual development.* Trans. by G. C. Buck & F. A. Raven. Philadelphia: University of Pennsylvania Press, 1971. (1836)

———. *Ueber die Kawi-Sprache auf der Insel Java, nebst einer Einleitung über die Verschiedenheit des menschlichen Sprachbaues und ihren Einfluss auf die geistige Entwickelung des Menschengeschlechts.* (3 vols.) Berlin: Drukkerei der Königlichen Akademie der Wissenschaften, 1836–1839.

———. *The sphere and duties of government.* Trans. by J. Coulthard. London: Chapman, 1854. (1852) (Reprinted 1967)

DAVID HUME
1711-1776
Scottish Philosopher (27)

Hume, D. *The philosophical works of David Hume.* Ed. by T. H. Green & T. H. Grose. (4 vols.) Aalen: Scientia, 1964. (1874–1875) **C**

———. *Essays moral, political, and literary.* (3rd ed.) (2 vols.) Ed. by T. H. Green & T. H. Grose. New York: Longmans, 1912. (Reprinted 1969) (1875) **C**

———. *Letters of David Hume to William Strahan.* Ed. by C. B. Hill. Oxford: Clarendon Press, 1888. (Reprinted 1970) **B C**

———. *David Hume selections.* Ed. by C. W. Hendel, Jr. New York: Scribner's, 1927. **C**

———. *The letters of David Hume.* (2 vols.) Ed. by J. Y. T. Greig. Oxford: Oxford University Press, 1932. **B C**

———. *New Letters of David Hume.* Ed. by R. Klibansky & E. C. Mossner. Oxford: Oxford University Press, 1954. **B C**

———. *David Hume on human nature and the understanding.* Ed. by A. Flew. New York: Crowell-Collier, 1962. **C**

———. A treatise of human nature. Ed. by E. C. Mossner. Baltimore, Md.: Penguin Books, 1969. (1739–1740) Also in *Philosophical works,* Vols. 1, 2, *op. cit.,* pp. 1–347, 3–415.

———. Appendix to the treatise of human nature. (1740) In *Philosophical works,* Vol. 2, *op. cit.,* pp. 551–560.

———. *An abstract of a treatise of human nature.* (1740) In *David Hume on human nature and understanding, op. cit.,* pp. 287–302.

———. On the rise and progress of the arts and sciences. (1741, 1742) In *Philosophical works,* Vol. 3, *op. cit.,* pp. 124–155.

———. Of national characters. (1741, 1742) In *Philosophical works,* Vol. 3, *op. cit.,* pp. 224–244.

———. An enquiry concerning human understanding. (1748) In *Philosophical works,* Vol. 4, *op. cit.,* pp. 1–135.

———. *Enquiries concerning the human understanding and concerning the principles of morals.* Ed. by L. A. Selby-Bigge. Oxford: Clarendon Press, 1955. (1748, 1751)

———. *An enquiry concerning human understanding.* Ed. by T. J. McCormack & Mary W. Calkins. La Salle, Ill.: Open Court, 1963. (1748)

———. *An inquiry concerning the principles of morals.* (Posth. ed.) Ed. by C. W. Hendel. New York: Liberal Arts Press, 1957. (1751) Reprinted in *Philosophical works,* Vol. 4, *op. cit.,* pp. 169–287.

———. A dissertation on the passions. (1757) In *Philosophical works,* Vol. 4, *op. cit.,* pp. 139–166.

———. The natural history of religion. (1757) In *Philosophical works,* Vol. 4, *op. cit.,* pp. 309–363.

———. Essay I—Of the immortality of the soul. (1777) In *Philosophical works,* Vol. 4, *op. cit.,* pp. 399–406.

———. Essay II—Of suicide. (1777) In *Philosophical works,* Vol. 4, *op. cit.,* pp. 406–414.

———. My own life. (1777) In *Philosophical works,* Vol. 1, *op. cit.,* pp. iii–xv. In *Hume on human nature and the understanding, op. cit.,* pp. 304–310, and in *Letters of David Hume to William Strahan, op. cit.,* pp. xvii–xxiv.   **B**

———. Dialogues concerning natural religion. (1779) In *Philosophical works,* Vol. 2, *op. cit.,* pp. 419–548.

———. *Dialogues concerning natural religion.* Ed. by N. K. Smith. New York: Hafner, 1957. (1779)

Ackermann, *Theories;* Brinton, *Age Reason*; Herrnstein & Boring, *Source Book;* Hirst, *Perception;* Hunter & Macalpine, *Psychiatry;* Hutchins, *Great Books;* Madden, *Scientific Thought;* Mandler and Mandler, *Thinking;* Mann & Kreyche, *Reflections Man;* Margolis, *Introduction;* Murphy, *Western;* Parsons, *Society;* Rand, *Classical Philosophers;* Rand, *Classical Psychologists;* Rand, *Moralists;* Reeves, *Body Mind;* Robinson, *Scottish Philosophy;* Sahakian, *Psychology;* Schneider, *Scottish Moralists*

GEORGE HUMPHREY
1889-1966
English Psychologist (17)

Humphrey, G. The conditioned reflex and the Freudian wish. *J. abnorm. Psychol.,* 1919–1920, *14,* 388–392.

———. Education and Freudianism. I: The Freudian mechanisms and the conditioned reflex. II: The child's unconscious mind. *J. abnorm. Psychol.,* 1920–1921, *15,* 350–386, 387–402.

———. Imitation and the conditioned reflex. *J. genet. Psychol.,* 1921, *28,* 1–21.

———. The conditioned reflex and the elementary social reaction. *J. abnorm. soc. Psychol.,* 1922–1923, *17,* 113–119.

———. The theory of Einstein and the Gestalt-Psychologie: A parallel. *Amer. J. Psychol.,* 1924, *35,* 353–359.

———. The psychology of Gestalt, some educational implications. *J. educ. Psychol.,* 1924, *15,* 401–412.

———. Is the conditioned reflex the unit of habit? *J. abnorm. soc. Psychol.,* 1925–1926, *20,* 10–16.

———. The effect of sequences of indifferent stimuli on a reaction of the conditioned response type. *J. abnorm. soc. Psychol.,* 1927–1928, *22,* 194–212.

———. The conditioned reflex and the laws of learning. *J. educ. Psychol.,* 1928, *19,* 424–430.

———. Extinction and negative adaptation. *Psychol. Rev.,* 1930, *37,* 361–363.

———. Learning and the living system. *Psychol. Rev.,* 1930, *37,* 497–510.

———. *The nature of learning in its relation to the living system.* London: Kegan Paul, Trench, & Truebner, 1933.

———. A note on system-theory. *Psychol. Rev.,* 1937, *44,* 346–348.

———, & Marcuse, F. New methods of obtaining neurotic behavior in rats. *Amer. J. Psychol.,* 1939, *52,* 616–619.

——— (Ed.), *Directed thinking.* New York: Dodd, Mead, 1948.

———. *On psychology to-day.* Oxford: Clarendon Press, 1949.

———. *Thinking: An introduction to its experimental psychology.* New York: Wiley, 1951.

———. Five years in the Oxford chair. *Brit. J. Psychol.,* 1953, *44,* 381–383.   **B**

——— (Ed.), *Social psychology through experiment.* London: Methuen, 1962.

———, & Coxen, R. V. *The chemistry of thinking.* Springfield, Ill.: Thomas, 1963.

———. Wilhelm Wundt. The great master. In B. B. Wolman (Ed.), *Historical roots of contemporary psychology.* New York: Harper & Row, 1968, pp. 275–297.

WALTER SAMUEL HUNTER
1889-1954
American Psychologist (25)

Hunter, W. S. The delayed reaction in animals and children. *Behavior Monogr.*, 1913, *2*, No. 6. (Also New York: Holt, 1913.)

————. The question of form perception. *J. anim. Behav.*, 1913, *3*, 329–333.

————. The auditory sensitivity of the white rat. *J. anim. Behav.*, 1914, *4*, 215–222; 1915, *5*, 312–329.

————. The after-effect of visual motion. *Psychol. Rev.*, 1914, *21*, 245–277.

————. Retinal factors in visual after-movement. *Psychol. Rev.*, 1915, *22*, 479–489.

————. A reformulation of the law of association. *Psychol. Rev.*, 1917, *24*, 188–196.

————. The delayed reaction in a child. *Psychol. Rev.*, 1917, *24*, 74–87.

————, & Yarbrough, J. U. The interference of auditory habits in the white rat. *J. anim. Behav.*, 1917, *7*, 49–65.

————. Some notes on the auditory sensitivity of the white rat. *Psychobiology*, 1918, *1*, 339–351.

————. *General psychology.* (Rev. ed.) Chicago: University of Chicago Press, 1923. (1919)

————. The temporal maze and kinesthetic sensory processes in the white rat. *Psychobiology*, 1920, *2*, 1–17.

————. The modification of instinct from the standpoint of social psychology. *Psychol. Rev.*, 1920, *27*, 247–269.

————. Correlation studies with the maze in rats and humans. *Comp. Psychol. Monogr.*, 1922, *1*, 37–56.

————. Habit interference in the white rat and in human subjects. *J. comp. Psychol.*, 1922, *2*, 29–59.

————. The problem of consciousness. *Psychol. Rev.*, 1924, *31*, 1–31.

————. The symbolic process. *Psychol. Rev.*, 1924, *31*, 478–497.

————, & Randolph, V. Further studies on the reliability of the maze with rats and humans. *J. comp. Psychol.*, 1924, *4*, 431–442.

————. General anthroponomy and its systematic problems. *Amer. J. Psychol.*, 1925, *36*, 286–302.

————. The subject's report. *Psychol. Rev.*, 1925, *32*, 153–170.

————. A reply to Professor Carr on "The reliability of the maze experiment." *J. comp. Psychol.*, 1926, *6*, 393–398.

————. Psychology and anthroponomy. In C. Murchison (Ed.), *Psychologies of 1925*. (3rd ed.) Worcester, Mass.: Clark University Press, 1928, pp. 83–107. (1926)

————. Further data on the auditory sensitivity of the white rat. *J. genet. Psychol.*, 1927, *34*, 177–186.

————. The behavior of the white rat on inclined planes. *J. genet. Psychol.*, 1927, *34*, 299–332.

————. The behavior of raccoons in a double alternation temporal maze. *J. genet. Psychol.*, 1928, *35*, 374–388.

————. *Human behavior.* Chicago: University of Chicago Press, 1928.

————. Learning. II. Experimental studies of learning. In C. Murchison (Ed.), *The foundations of experimental psychology*. Worcester, Mass.: Clark University Press, 1929, pp. 564–627.

————. The sensory control of the maze habit in the white rat. *J. genet. Psychol.*, 1929, *36*, 505–537.

————. Anthroponomy and psychology. In C. Murchison (Ed.), *Psychologies of 1930*. Worcester, Mass.: Clark University Press, 1930, pp. 281–300.

————. A further consideration of the sensory control of the maze habit in the white rat. *J. genet. Psychol.*, 1930, *38*, 3–19.

————. A consideration of Lashley's theory of the equipotentiality of cerebral action. *J. gen. Psychol.*, 1930, *3*, 455–468.

————. Lashley on "cerebral control versus reflexology." *J. gen. Psychol.*, 1931, *5*, 230–234.

——, & Nagge, J. The white rat and the double alternation temporal maze. *J. genet. Psychol.*, 1931, *39*, 303–319.

——. The psychological study of behavior. *Psychol. Rev.*, 1932, *39*, 1–24.

——. Basic phenomena in learning. *J. gen. Psychol.*, 1933, *8*, 299–317.

——. Learning. IV. Experimental studies of learning. In C. Murchison (Ed.), *A handbook of general experimental psychology*. Worcester, Mass.: Clark University Press, 1934, pp. 497–570.

——, & Hudgins, C. V. Voluntary activity from the standpoint of behaviorism. *J. gen. Psychol.*, 1934, *10*, 198–204.

—— Conditioning and maze learning in the rat. *J. comp. Psychol.*, 1935, *19*, 417–424.

——. Conditioning and extinction in the rat. *Brit. J. Psychol.*, 1935–1936, *26*, 135–148.

——. Learning curves for conditioning and maze learning. *J. exp. Psychol.*, 1936, *19*, 121–128.

——. H. A. Carr on the problem of reliability. *Psychol. Rev.*, 1937, *44*, 529–532.

——. Muscle potentials and conditioning in the rat. *J. exp. Psychol.*, 1937, *21*, 611–624.

——. An experiment on the disinhibition of voluntary responses. *J. exp. Psychol.*, 1938, *22*, 419–428.

——, & Sigler, Marian. The span of visual discrimination as a function of time and intensity of stimulation. *J. exp. Psychol.*, 1940, *26*, 160–179.

——. On the professional training of psychologists. *Psychol. Rev.*, 1941, *48*, 498–523.

——. Psychology in the war. *Amer. Psychologist*, 1946, *1*, 479–492.

——. Some observations on the status of psychology. In *Miscellanea psychologica. Albert Michotte*. Louvain: *Institut supérieur de Philosophie*, 1947, pp. 39–48.

——, & Bartlett, Susan C. Double alternation behavior in young children. *J. exp. Psychol.*, 1948, *38*, 558–567.

——. Walter S. Hunter. In E. G. Boring *et al.* (Eds.), *A history of psychology in autobiography*. Vol. 4. Worcester, Mass.: Clark University Press, 1952, pp. 163–187. **B**

——. Research interests in psychology. *Amer. J. Psychol.*, 1952, *65*, 627–632.

Dennis, *Psychology ;* Valentine, *Experimental*

EDMUND HUSSERL
1859-1938
German Philosopher (26)

Husserl, E. *Phenomenology and the crisis of philosophy: Philosophy as rigorous science* (1911) & *Philosophy and the crisis of European man* (1936–1954). Trans. by Q. Lauer. New York: Harper, 1965. **C**

——. *Erfahrung und Urteil-Untersuchungen zur Genalogie der Logik*. (2nd ed.) Ed. by L. Landgrebe. Hamburg: Claasen, 1954. (1939) **C**

——. *Husserliana: Gesammelte Werke*. (Ult. 30 vols.) Ed. by H. L. Van Breda. The Hague: Nijhoff, 1950– **C**

——. *Ueber den Begriff der Zahl. Psychologische Analysen*. Halle: Heynemann, 1887. Reprinted in *Husserliana*, Vol. XII, *op. cit.*, pp. 289–339.

——. *Philosophie der Arithmetik*. Vol 1. *Logische Studien und psychologische Untersuchungen*. Halle: Pfeffer, 1891. Reprinted in *Husserliana*, Vol. XII, *op. cit.*, pp. 1–283.

——. *The phenomenology of internal time-consciousness*. Trans. by J. S. Churchill, & ed. by M. Heidegger. Bloomington, Ind.: Indiana University Press, 1964. (1893–1917) Also in German in *Husserliana*, Vol. X, *op. cit.*, pp. 3–134.

——. *Logical investigations*. Trans. by J. N. Findlay. New York: Humanities Press, 1970. (1900–1901)

———. *The idea of phenomenology.* Trans. by W. P. Alston & G. Naknikian. The Hague: Nijhoff, 1964. (1907) Reprinted in German in *Husserliana,* Vol. II, *op. cit.*

———. *Ideas: General introduction to pure phenomenology.* Trans. by W. R. B. Gibson. New York: Macmillan, 1952. (1913) Reprinted in German in *Husserliana,* Vol. III, *op. cit.*

———. *Erste Philosophie.* Vol. 1: *Kritische Ideengeschichte.* Vol. 2: *Theorie der phänomenologischen Reduktion.* Ed. by R. Boehm. In *Husserliana,* Vols. VII, VIII, *op. cit.,* 1956, 1959. (1923, 1924)

———. *Phänomenologische Psychologie.* (1925, 1928) In *Husserliana,* Vol. IX, *op. cit.,* 1962, pp. 1–234.

———. *Formal and transcendental logic.* Trans. by D. Cairns. The Hague: Nijhoff, 1970. (1929)

———. *Phenomenology.* (1929) Trans. by R. E. Palmer. *J. Brit. soc. Phenomenol.,* 1971, *2,* 77–90.

———. *The crisis of European sciences and transcendental phenomenology: An introduction to phenomenological philosophy.* Trans. & intro. by D. Carr. Evanston, Ill.: Northwestern University Press, 1970. (1935–1937) Also in German in *Husserliana,* Vol. VI, *op. cit.,* pp. 1–276.

———. *Paris lectures.* (2nd ed.) Trans. by P. Koestenbaum. The Hague: Nijhoff, 1967. (1950) Also in German in *Husserliana,* Vol. I, *op. cit.,* pp. 1–39.

———. *Cartesian meditations: An introduction to phenomenology.* Trans. by D. Cairns. The Hague: Nijhoff, 1964. (1950) Also in German in *Husserliana,* Vol. I, *op. cit.,* pp. 41–183.

———. *Ideen zu einer reinen Phänomenologie und phänomenologischen Philosophie.* Book 2: *Phänomenologische Untersuchungen zur Konstitution.* Book 3: *Die Phänomenologie und die Fundamente der Wissenschaften.* Ed. by M. Biemel. In *Husserliana,* Vols. IV, V, *op. cit.,* 1952.

Chisholm, *Realism* ; Lawrence & O'Connor, *Phenomenology* ; Sahakian, *Psychology*

THOMAS HENRY HUXLEY
1825-1895
English Biologist (18)

Huxley, T. H. *American addresses, with a lecture on the study of biology.* New York: Appleton, 1877. (Reprinted 1970)   **C**

———. *Collected essays.* (9 vols.) Hildesheim: Olms, 1970. (1893–1894)   **C**

———. *The scientific memoirs of Thomas Henry Huxley.* (5 vols.) Ed. by M. Foster & E. R. Lankester. New York: Macmillan, 1898–1903.   **C**

———. *Life and letters of Thomas Henry Huxley.* (2nd ed.) (2 vols.) Ed. by L. Huxley. London: Macmillan, 1913. (1900) (Reprinted 1968)   **B C**

———. *The essence of T. H. Huxley: Selections from his writings.* Ed. by C. Bibby. New York: St. Martin's Press, 1967   **C**

———. *T. H. Huxley on education.* Ed. by C. Bibby. Cambridge: Cambridge University Press, 1971.   **C**

———. *Autobiographical fragments.* (1840–1895) In *The essence of T. H. Huxley, op. cit.,* pp. 1–26.

———. *Darwiniana.* (1859–1888) Reprinted in *Collected essays,* Vol. 2, *op. cit.*

———. *On the origin of species or, the causes of the phenomena of organic nature.* Ann Arbor, Mich.: University of Michigan Press, 1968. (1863)

———. *Evidence as to man's place in nature.* New York: Appleton, 1890. (1863) Reprinted in *Collected Essays,* Vol. 7. *op. cit.,* pp. 1–208.

———. *On the physical basis of life.* New Haven: Chatfield, 1870. (1869) (Reprinted 1970)

———. *A manual of the anatomy of vertebrated animals.* London: Churchill, 1871.

——— Joseph Priestley. (1874) Reprinted in *Collected essays,* Vol. 3, *op. cit.,* pp. 1–37.

———. On the hypothesis that animals are automata, and its history. *Fortn. Rev.,* 1874, *22,* 555–580. Reprinted in *Collected essays,* Vol. 1, *op. cit.,* pp. 199–250, & in part in *The essence of T. H. Huxley, op. cit.,* pp. 37–38, 69–71.

————. Hume, with helps to the study of Berkeley. (1878) Reprinted in *Collected essays,* Vol. 6, *op. cit.*

————. On sensation and the unity of structure of sensiferous organs. (1879) Reprinted in *Collected essays,* Vol. 6, *op. cit.,* pp. 288–319.

————. Science and morals. (1886) Reprinted in *Collected essays,* Vol. 9, *op. cit.,* pp. 117–146.

————. Agnosticism. (1889) Reprinted in *Collected essays,* Vol. 5, *op. cit.,* pp. 209–262.

————. On the natural inequality of men. (1890) Reprinted in *Collected essays,* Vol. 1, *op. cit.,* pp. 290–335.

————. The Aryan question and prehistoric man. (1890) Reprinted in *Collected essays,* Vol. 7, *op. cit.,* pp. 271–328.

————. Possibilities and impossibilities. (1891) Reprinted in *Collected essays,* Vol. 5, *op. cit.,* pp. 192–208.

————. Evolution and ethics (1893) Reprinted in *Collected essays,* Vol. 9, *op. cit.,* pp. 46–116.

————. Autobiography. (1894) Reprinted in *Collected essays,* Vol. 1, *op. cit.,* pp. 1–17. **B**

Count, *Race ;* Grinder, *Genetic Psychology ;* Hall, *Source Book ;* Kroeber, *Source Book ;* Nash, *Models*

CHRISTIAN HUYGENS
1629-1695
Dutch Astronomer-Mathematician (14)

Huygens, C. *Oeuvres complètes.* (22 vols.) Ed. by Société Hollandaise des Sciences. The Hague: Nijhoff, 1888–1950. (Reprinted 1967) **B Bl C**

————. *Dioptrique.* (1653–1692) In *Oeuvres complètes,* Vol. 13, Parts 1, 2, *op. cit.*

————. *Horologium oscillatorium.* Brussels: Culture et Civilisation, 1966. (1673)

————. Pièces et fragments concernant la question de l'existence et de la perceptibilité du "mouvement absolu." (ca. 1688) In *Oeuvres complètes,* Vol. 16, *op. cit.,* pp. 213–233.

————. *Treatise on light.* Trans. by S. P. Thompson. Chicago: University of Chicago Press, 1945. (1690) Also in H. Crew (Ed.), *The wave theory of light.* New York: American Book, 1900, pp. 1–41.

————. *Traité de la lumière, où sont expliquées les causes de ce qui luy arrive dans la réflexion, et dans la réfraction.* Brussels: Culture et Civilisation, 1967. (Also London: Dawsons, 1966) (1690)

————. *The celestial worlds discovered.* London: Cass, 1968. (1698)

Hall, *Nature's Laws ;* Hutchins, *Great Books ;* Schwartz & Bishop, *Moments Discovery*

JEAN (MARC GESPARD) ITARD
1775-1838
French Psychiatrist (23)

Itard, J. M. G. *An historical account of the discovery and education of a savage man, or of the first developments, physical and moral, of the young savage caught in the woods near Aveyron, in the year 1798.* London: Phillips 1802. (1801) (Reprinted 1970)

————. *Rapports et mémoires sur le sauvage d'Aveyron.* Paris: Alcan, 1804. (1801)

————. *The wild boy of Aveyron.* Trans. by G & Muriel Humphrey. New York: Century 1932. (1801, 1806)

————. *Rapport fait à son Excellence le Ministre de l'Intérieur sur les nouveaux développement et l'état actuel du sauvage d'Aveyron.* Paris: Marcel, 1807.

————. *Traité des maladies d'oreille et de l'audition.* (2 vols.) Paris: Méquignon-Marvis, 1821

————. Mémoire sur quelques fonctions involontaires des appareils de la locomotion, de la préhension et de la voix. *Arch. gén. méd* 1825, *8,* 385–407.

————. De la parole considérée comme moyen de développement de la sensibilité organique. *Rev méd. franç.,* 1828, *2,* 359–370.

Clendening, *Source Book ;* Dennis, *Reading Developmental*

JOHN HUGHLINGS JACKSON
1835-1911
English Neurologist (21)

Jackson, J. H. *Neurological fragments.* London: Oxford University Press, 1925. **B Bl C**

——. *Selected writings of John Hughlings Jackson.* (2 vols.) Ed. by J. Taylor. London: Staples Press, 1958. (1931) **Bl C**

——. Loss of speech; its association with valvular disease of the heart and with hemiplegia on the right side. *London Hosp. Rep.,* 1864, *1,* 388–471.

——. Notes on the physiology and pathology of language—remarks on those cases of disease of the nervous system in which defect of expression is the most striking symptom. (1866) Reprinted in *Selected writings,* Vol. 2, *op. cit.,* pp. 121–128.

——. Notes on the physiology and pathology of the nervous system. (1868) Reprinted in *Selected writings,* Vol. 2, *op. cit.,* pp. 215–237.

——. Observations on the physiology of language. (1868) Reprinted in *Brain,* 1915, *38,* 59–64.

——. A study of convulsions. (1870) Reprinted in *Selected writings,* Vol. 1, *op. cit.,* pp. 8–36.

——. Hunterian oration on the physiological aspect of education. (1872) Reprinted in *Selected writings,* Vol. 2, *op. cit.,* pp. 265–269.

——. On the anatomical and physiological localisation of movements in the brain. (1873) Reprinted in *Selected writings,* Vol. 1, *op. cit.,* pp. 37–76.

——. On the nature of the duality of the brain. (1874) Reprinted in *Selected writings,* Vol. 2, *op. cit.,* pp. 129–145.

——. Contemporary mental disorders after epileptic paroxysms. (1875) Reprinted in *Selected writings,* Vol. 1, *op. cit.,* pp. 119–134.

——. Intellectual warnings of epileptic seizures. (1876) Reprinted in *Selected writings,* Vol. 1, *op. cit.,* pp. 274–275.

——. Ophthalmology in relation to general medicine. (1877) Reprinted in *Selected writings,* Vol. 2, *op. cit.,* pp. 300–319.

——. On affections of speech from disease of the brain. *Brain,* 1878, *1,* 304–330. Reprinted in *Selected writings,* Vol. 2, *op. cit.,* pp. 155–170.

——. Affections of speech from diseases of the brain. *Brain,* 1879, *2,* 203–222, 323–356. Reprinted in *Selected writings,* Vol. 2, *op. cit.,* pp. 171–204.

——. On psychology and the nervous system. *Med. Press Circ.,* 1879, *2,* 199–201, 239–241, 283–285, 409–411, 429–430.

——. Remarks on dissolution of the nervous system, as exemplified in certain post-epileptic conditions. (1881) Reprinted in *Selected writings,* Vol. 2, *op. cit.,* pp. 3–28.

——. On some implications of dissolution of the nervous system. (1882) Reprinted in *Selected writings,* Vol. 2, *op. cit.,* pp. 29–44.

——. Croonian lectures on evolution and dissolution of the nervous system (1884) Reprinted in *Selected writings,* Vol. 2, *op. cit.,* pp. 45–75.

——. Remarks on evolution and dissolution of the nervous system. (1887) Reprinted in *Selected writings,* Vol. 2, *op. cit.,* pp. 76–118.

——. An address on the psychology of joking. (1887–1888). Reprinted in *Selected writings,* Vol. 2, *op. cit.,* pp. 359–364.

——. Factors of insanities. (1894) Reprinted in *Selected writings,* Vol. 2, *op. cit.,* pp. 411–421.

—— The relations of different divisions of the central nervous system to one another and to parts of the body. *Lancet,* 1898, *1,* 79–87; *Brit. Med. J.,* 1898, *1,* 65–69. Reprinted in *Selected writings,* Vol. 2, *op. cit.,* pp. 422–443.

Beck & Molish, *Reflexes;* Clarke & O'Malley, *Brain;* Fulton & Wilson, *Physiology;* Herrnstein & Boring, *Source Book;* Shipley, *Classics*

ERICH RUDOLF JAENSCH
1883-1940
German Psychologist (25)

Jaensch, E. R. *Ueber den Aufbau der Wahrneh-mungswelt und die Grundlagen der menschlichen Erkenntnis.* Vol. 1. *Ueber den Aufbau der Wahrnehmungswelt. Eine Untersuchung über Grundlagen und Ausgangspunkte unseres Welt-bildes, durchgeführt mit den Forschungsmitteln der Jugendpsychologie, angewandt auf erkennt-nistheoretische, naturphilosophische und päda-gogische Fragen.* (2nd ed.) Leipzig: Barth, 1927. (1923)   C

————. *Untersuchungen über Grundfragen der Akustik und Tonpsychologie.* Leipzig: Barth, 1929.   C

————, et al. *Ueber Grundfragen der Farben-psychologie, zugleich ein Beitrag zur Theorie der Erfahrung.* Leipzig: Barth, 1930.   C

————. *Ueber den Aufbau der Wahrnehmungs-welt und die Grundlagen der menschlichen Erkenntnis.* Vol. 2. *Ueber die Grundlagen der menschlichen Erkenntnis.* Leipzig: Barth, 1931.   C

————. *Neue Wege der Lichtbiologie (unter funktionellem und ganzheitlichem Betrach-tungsgesichtspunkt. Eine experimentelle Unter-suchung über die Duplizität unseres Sehorgans nach Tages- und Dämmerungssehen, ihre Bedeutung für das Verständnis der Formen der Farbenanomalie und Farbenblindheit, der indi--viduellen Unterschiede des Farbensehens und Zusammenhangs zwischen Lichtsinn und Per-sönlichkeit).* Leipzig: Barth, 1933.   C

————. *Eidetische Anlage und kindliches Seelen-leben. Studien und Abhandlungen zur Grund-legung der Eidetik und Jugendanthropologie.* Leipzig: Barth, 1934.   C

————. Ueber die Beziehungen von Zeitschät-zung und Bewegungsempfindung. *Z. Psychol.,* 1906, *41,* 257–279.

————. Ueber Täuschungen des Tastsinns. (Im Hinblick auf die geometrisch-optischen Täu-schungen.) *Z. Psychol.,* 1906, *41,* 280–294, 382–422.

————. Zur Analyse der Gesichtswahrnehmungen.

Experimentell-psychologische Untersuchungen nebst Anwendung auf die Pathologie des Sehens. *Z. Psychol.,* 1909, Suppl. 4. (Also Leip-zig: Barth, 1909) (Reprinted 1970)

————. Ueber die Wahrnehmung des Raumes. Eine experimentell-psychologische Untersu-chung nebst Anwendung auf Aesthetik und Erkenntnislehre. *Z. Psychol.,* 1911, Suppl. 6. (Also Leipzig: Barth, 1911) (Reprinted 1970)

————. Ueber Grundfragen der Farbenpsycho-logie. *Ber. VI. Kong. exp. Psychol. in Göttingen.* Leipzig: Barth, 1914, pp. 45–56.

————. *Einige allgemeinere Fragen der Psycho-logie und Biologie des Denkens erläutert an der Lehre vom Vergleich.* Leipzig: Barth, 1920.

————. *Eidetic imagery and typological methods of investigation.* (2nd ed.) Trans. by O. Oeser. New York: Harcourt, Brace, 1934. (1925)

————. Die typologische Methode in der Psychologie und ihre Bedeutung für die Ner-venheilkunde. *Deutsch. Z. Nervenheilk.,* 1925, *88,* 193–206.

————, & Jaensch, W. Einfache psychische Vor-gänge und somatische Korrelationserscheinun-gen nach sportlicher Leistung und im Training. *Sitzber. Ges. Bef. ges. Naturwiss. Marburg,* 1925, 49–65.

————. Die Psychologie in Deutschland und die inneren Richtlinien ihrer Forschungsarbeit. In *Jahrbücher der Philosophie.* Vol. 8. Berlin: Mittler, 1927, pp. 93–168.

————. Ueber Eidetik und typologische For-schungsmethode. *Z. Psychol.,* 1927, *102,* 35–56

————, & Schweicher, J. *Die Streitfrage zwischen Assoziations- und Funktionspsychologie, geprüft nach eidetischer Methode.* Berlin: Elsner, 1927

————. Psychological and psychophysical in-vestigations of types in their relation to the psychology of religion. In M. L. Reymert (Ed.) *Feelings and emotions: The Wittenberg sym posium.* Worcester, Mass.: Clark University Press, 1928, pp. 355–371.

————. *Neue Wege der Erziehungslehre und Jugendkunde. Zur philosophischen Grundlegung der Pädagogik.* (2nd ed.) Erfurt: Stenger, 1935 (1928)

————. Ueber Methoden der psychologischen Typenforschung. *Z. Psychol.,* 1928, *108,* 1–16.

————. *Grundformen menschlichen Seins. Mit Berücksichtigung ihrer Beziehungen zu Biologie und Medizin, zu Kulturphilosophie und Pädagogik.* Berlin: Elsner, 1929.

————. *Wirklichkeit und Wert in der Philosophie und Kultur der Neuzeit. Prolegomena zur philosophischen Forschung auf der Grundlage philosophischer Anthropologie nach empirischer Methode.* Berlin: Elsner, 1929.

————, & Grünhut, L. *Ueber Gestalttheorie und Gestaltpsychologie.* Langensalza: Beyer, 1929.

————. Zur Grundlegung der Wertlehre als Wirklichkeitswissenschaft und zur Abwehr des Irrealismus. *Arch. ges. Psychol.,* 1930, 77, 609–648.

————. Grundsätzliches zur Typenforschung und empirisch vorgehenden philosophischen Anthropologie. *Z. Psychol.,* 1930, *116,* 107–116.

————. Ueber den Aufbau des Bewusstseins (unter besonderer Berücksichtigung der Kohärenzverhältnisse). *Z. Psychol.,* 1930, Suppl. 16. (Also Leipzig: Barth, 1930) (Reprinted 1970)

————, & Schnieder, E. *Der Berufstypus des Schauspielers im Zusammenhang mit den allgemeinen Kunst- und Kulturfragen der Gegenwart. Ein Beitrag zur Integrationstypologie.* Leipzig: Barth, 1932.

————. Auseinandersetzungen in Sachen der Eidetik und Typenlehre. VII. Das Verhältnis der Integrationstypologie zu anderen Formen der Typenlehre, insbesondere zur Typenlehre Kretschmers. *Z. Psychol.,* 1932, *125,* 113–148.

————. Auseinandersetzungen in Sachen der Eidetik und Typenlehre. VIII. Weiteres zur Auseinandersetzung der Integrationstypologie mit der Typenlehre Kretschmers. *Z. Psychol.,* 1932, *126,* 51–85.

————. *Die Lage und die Aufgaben der Psychologie, ihre Sendung in der deutschen Bewegung und an der Kulturwende.* Leipzig: Barth, 1933.

————. *Neue Wege der Lichtbiologie unter funktionellem und ganzheitlichem Betrachtungsgesichtspunkt.* Leipzig: Barth, 1933.

————. Zur Auseinandersetzung der Typenlehre Kretschmers und der Integrationstypologie. *Z. Psychol.,* 1933, *130,* 370–376.

————. *Eidetische Anlage und kindliches Seelenleben. Studien und Abhandlungen zur Grundlegung der Eidetik der Jugendanthropologie.* Leipzig: Barth, 1934.

————. *Der Kampf der deutschen Psychologie.* Langensalza: Beltz, 1934.

————. Farbensystem und Aufbau der psychophysischen Person. I. II. III. *Z. Psychol.,* 1934, *132,* 193–201, 202–210, 211–238.

————. Gemeinschaftsbildung und Staatsauffassung aus dem Gesichtspunkt der psychologischen Typenforschung. Sammelreferat. In *Ber. 14. Kongr. Dtsch. Ges. Psychol.* Jena: Fischer, 1935, pp. 145–172.

————. Tuberkulose und Seelenleben mit einem Beitrag zur schizophreniefrage. W. Ponndorf zum 70. Geburtstag. *Z. Psychol.,* 1935, *135,* 1–19.

————. Wege der Jugendanthropologie. Forschungsrichtung und Arbeitsergebnisse des Marburger Instituts. *Z. pädag. Psychol. Jugendkd.,* 1935, *5,* 14–24.

————. Wege und Ziele der Psychologie in Deutschland. *Amer. J Psychol.,* 1937, *50,* 1–22.

————. Gefühl und Empfindung. *Ber. 15. Kongr. dtsch. Ges. Psychol.* Jena: Fischer, 1937, 65–70.

————. Die Psychologie und die Wandlungen im deutschen Idealismus. *Ber. 15. Kongr. dtsch. Gesell. Psychol.* Jena: Fischer, 1937, 257–280.

————. Die biologisch fundierte psychologische Anthropologie, ihre Stellung zur Rassenkunde und Kulturphilosophie, ihr Gegensatz zur unbiologischen Anthropologie. *Z. Psychol.,* 1936, *137,* 1–50.

————. Lage und Aufgabe der Psychologie im neuen Reich. *Z. Psychol.,* 1936, *138,* 209–238.

————. Zur Neugestaltung des deutschen Studententums und der Hochschule. *Z. angew. Psychol.,* 1937, Suppl. No. 74. (Also Leipzig: Barth, 1937)

———. Der Gengetypus. Psychologisch-anthropologische Grundlagen deutscher Kulturphilosophie, ausgehend von dem, was wir überwinden wollen. *Z. angew. Psychol.*, 1938, Suppl. No. 75. (Also Leipzig: Barth, 1938)

———. *Das Wahrheitsproblem bei der völkischen Neugestaltung von Wissenschaft und Erziehung.* Lagensalza: Beyer, 1939.

———. Wozu Psychologie? *Ber. 16. Kongr. dtsch. Gesell. Psychol.* Leipzig: Barth, 1939, 7–30.

———. Der Kampf der deutschen Psychologie und der Geisteskampf der -Bewegung. *Z. Psychol.*, 1939, *145*, 273–280.

———. Neues und Grundsätzliches in den Aufgaben der Wahrnehmungspsychologie. *Z. Psychol.*, 1939, *146*, 193–228.

———. Vom Umbruch der Psychologie und der Wissenschaft überhaupt. *Z. Psychol.*, 1939, *147*, 1–9.

———, & Althoff, F. *Mathematisches Denken und Seelenform.* Leipzig: Barth, 1939.

Sahakian, *Psychology*

WALTER JAENSCH
1889-
German Psychiatrist (11)

Jaensch, W. Ueber Wechselbeziehungen von optischen, zerebralen und somatischen Stigmen bei Konstitutionstypen. *Z. Neurol. Psychiat.*, 1920, *29*, 104–115.

Jaensch, E. R., & ———. Ueber die Verbreitung der eidetischen Anlage im Jugendalter. *Z. Psychol.*, 1921, *87*, 91–96.

———. Ueber psychophysische Konstitutionstypen. *Z. ges. Neurol. Psychiat.*, 1925, *97*, 374–386.

Jaensch, E. R., & ———. Einfache psychische Vorgänge und somatische Korrelationserscheinungen nach sportlicher Leistung und im Training. *Sitzber. Ges. Bef. ges. Naturwiss. Marburg*, 1925, 49–65.

———. Ueber die Verbreitung eidetischer Phänomene und ihnen zugrunde liegender psychophysischer Konstitutionstypen. *Klin. Woch.*, 1926, *5*, 406–410.

———. *Grundzüge einer Physiologie und Klinik der psychophysischen Persönlichkeit.* Berlin: Springer-Verlag, 1926.

———, & Wittneben, W. Gesammelte Arbeiten zur Casuistik und Therapie von Entwicklungs- und Differenzierungsstörungen I. W. Wittneben, Casuistik und Therapie archikapillären Zustandsbilder bei Jugendlichen. *Z. Kinderforsch.*, 1926, *32*, 359–414.

———. Die Hautkapillarmikroskopie am Lebenden. In E. Aberhalden (Ed.), *Handbuch der biologischen Arbeitsmethoden.* Section 9, Pt. 3, No. 5. Berlin: Urban & Schwarzenberg, 1930, pp. 865–940.

———. *Körperform, Wesensart und Rasse. Skizzen zu einer medizinisch-biologischen Konstitutionslehre.* Leipzig: Thieme, 1934.

———, & Gundermann, O. *Klinische Rassenhygiene und Eugenik. Ein Beitrag zur Frage ihrer Grenzen auf Grundlage konstitutionsbiologischer Untersuchungen mittels Kapillarmikroskopie am Lebenden.* Berlin: Schötz, 1934.

———. *Leibesübungen und Körperkonstitution.* Berlin: Metzner, 1935.

———, *et al. Körperformung, Rasse, Seele und Leibesübungen.* (2 vols. in 1) Berlin: Metzner, 1936.

———, & Hoffmann, A. Rasse, Konstitution und Höchstleistung bei den Siegern des II. Olympia. *Münch. med. Wochenschr.*, 1937, *84*, Part 1, 16–22.

———. Unser Standort in Wissenschaft, Leben und Weltanschauung. *Konstitution Klinik*, 1938, *1*, 1–11.

———. Unfertige Konstitutionen bei Jugendlichen und Konstitutionstherapie. *Z. pädag. Psychol.*, 1938, *39*, 30–36.

———, & Pulnermüller, K. *Konstitutionstherapie und Entwicklungsstörungen.* Stuttgart: Enke, 1939.

WILLIAM JAMES
1842-1910
American Philosopher (27)

James, W. *The will to believe and other essays in popular philosophy*. New York: Longmans, Green, 1897. (Reprinted 1956)   **C**

————. *On some of life's ideals: On a certain blindness in human beings: what makes a life significant*. New York: Holt, 1912 (1899)   **C**

————. *On vital reserves*. New York: Holt, 1911.   **C**

————. *Memories and studies*. Ed. by H. James. New York: Greenwood Press, 1968. (1911)   **B C**

————. *Collected essays and reviews*. New York: Longmans, Green, 1920.   **C**

————. *The letters of William James*. (2 vols.) Ed. by H. James. Boston: Atlantic Monthly Press, 1920.   **B C**

————. *As William James said*. Ed. by Elizabeth P. Aldrich. New York: Vanguard, 1942.   **C**

————. *Essays in pragmatism*. Ed. by Alburey Castell. New York: Hafner, 1948.   **C**

————. *William James: A selection from his writings*. Ed. by Margaret Knight. Baltimore, Md.: Penguin Books, 1950.   **C**

————. *William James: Philosopher and man*. Comp. by C. H. Compton. New York: Scarecrow Press, 1957.   **C**

————. *William James on psychical research*. Ed. by G. Murphy & R. O. Ballou. New York: Viking Press, 1960.   **C**

————. *The selected letters of William James*. Intro. by Elizabeth Hardwick. New York: Farrar, Straus, & Cudahy, 1961.   **C**

————, & Flournoy, T. *The letters of William James and Theodore Flournoy*. Ed. by R. C. LeClair. Madison, Wisc.: University of Wisconsin Press, 1966.   **B C**

————. *Essays in radical empiricism, and a pluralistic universe*. Gloucester, Mass.: Smith, 1967.   **C**

————. *The writings of William James: A comprehensive edition; including annotated bibliography of the writings of William James*. Ed. by J. J. McDermott. New York: Random House, 1967.   **C**

————. *The moral philosophy of William James*. Ed. by J. K. Roth. New York: Crowell, 1969.   **C**

————. Remarks on Spencer's definition of mind as correspondence. *J. spec. Phil.*, 1878, *12*, 1–18.

————. Are we automata? *Mind*, 1879, *4*, 1–22.

————. Great men, great thoughts and the environment. *Atlantic Mon.*, 1880, *46*, 441–459. Reprinted in *The will to believe and other essays, op. cit.*, pp. 216–254.

————. The sense of dizziness in deaf-mutes. *Mind*, 1881, *6*, 412–413.

————. On some Hegelisms. *Mind*, 1882, *7*, 186–208. Reprinted in *The will to believe and other essays, op. cit.*, pp. 263–298. (Reprinted 1956)

————. On some omissions of introspective psychology. *Mind*, 1884, *9*, 1–26.

————. What is an emotion? *Mind*, 1884, *9*, 188–205.

Lange, C. G., & ————. *The emotions*. Ed. by K. Dunlap. Baltimore, Md.: Williams & Wilkins, 1922. (1884, 1890) (Reprinted 1967)

————. The dilemma of determinism. *Unitar. Rev.*, 1884, *22*, 193–224. Reprinted in *The will to believe and other essays, op. cit.*, pp. 145–183.

————. On the function of cognition. *Mind*, 1885, *10*, 27–44.

————. The perception of space. *Mind*, 1887, *12*, 321–353.

————. Reaction-time in the hypnotic trance. *Proc. Amer. Soc. psychic. Res.*, 1887, *1*, 246–248.

————. What the will effects. *Scribner's Mag.*, 1888, *3*, 240–250.

————. *The principles of psychology*. (2 vols.) New York: Holt, 1890. (Reprinted 1950)

————. The hidden self. *Scribner's Mag.*, 1890, *7*, 361–373.

————. A plea for psychology as a "natural science." *Phil. Rev.*, 1892, *1*, 146–153.

————. *Psychology: Briefer course.* New York: Holt, 1892. (Reprinted 1962)

————. The physical basis of emotion. *Psychol. Rev.*, 1894, *1*, 516–529. Reprinted in *Collected essays and reviews, op. cit.,* pp. 346–370.

————. Professor Wundt and feelings of innervation. *Psychol. Rev.*, 1894, *1*, 70–73.

————. The knowing of things together. *Psychol. Rev.*, 1895, *2*, 105–124.

————. *Human immortality: Two supposed objections to the doctrine.* (2nd ed.) Boston: Houghton Mifflin, 1899. (1898)

————. *Talks to teachers on psychology: And to students on some of life's ideals.* New York: Holt, 1899. (Reprinted 1958)

————. *The varieties of religious experience: A study in human nature.* New York: Longmans, Green, 1902. (Reprinted 1963)

————. Does consciousness exist? *J. Phil.*, 1904, *1*, 477–491. Reprinted in *Essays in radical empiricism, op. cit.,* pp. 1–38.

————. The Chicago school. *Psychol. Bull.*, 1904, *1*, 1–5.

————. The experience of activity. *Psychol. Rev.*, 1905, *12*, 1–17. Reprinted in *Essays in radical empiricism, op. cit.,* pp. 155–188.

————. *Pragmatism: A new name for some old ways of thinking.* New York: Longmans, Green, 1907.

————. The energies of men. *Phil. Rev.*, 1907, *16*, 1–20. Reprinted in *On vital reserves, op. cit.,* pp. 3–39.

————. Report on Mrs. Piper's Hodgson-control. *Proc. Amer. Soc. psychic. Res.*, 1909, *3*, 470–589.

————. *A pluralistic universe.* New York: Longmans, Green, 1909. (Reprinted 1967)

————. *The meaning of truth: A sequel to "pragmatism."* New York: Longmans, Green, 1909. (Reprinted 1970)

————. *Some problems of philosophy.* London: Longmans, Green, 1911.

Arnold, *Emotion;* Beck & Molish, *Reflexes;* Dennis, *Psychology;* Drever, *Sourcebook;* Fisch, *Philosophers;* Grob & Beck, *American Ideas;* Herrnstein & Boring, *Source Book;* Hutchins, *Great Books;* Mann & Kreyche, *Reflections Man;* Margolis, *Introduction;* Matson, *Being;* Mueller, *American Philosophy;* Murphy, *Western;* Park & Burgess, *Sociology;* Rand, *Classical Philosophers;* Rand, *Classical Psychologists;* Reeves, *Body Mind;* Rorty, *Pragmatic Philosophy;* Russell, *Motivation;* Sahakian, *Psychology;* Shipley, *Classics*

PIERRE JANET
1859-1947
French Psychologist (27)

Janet, P. Note sur quelques phénomènes de somnambulisme. (1886) Trans. by B. S. Kopell as: M. Pierre Janet, Report on some phenomena of somnambulism. *J. hist. Behav. Sci.*, 1968, *4*, 124–131.

————. Deuxième note sur le sommeil provoqué à distance et la suggestion mentale pendant l'état somnambulistique. (1886) Trans. by B. S. Kopell as: Second observation of sleep provoked from a distance and the mental suggestion during the somnambulistic state. *J. hist. Behav. Sci.*, 1968, *4*, 258–267.

————. Les actes inconscients et le dédoublement de la personnalité pendant le somnambulisme provoqué. *Rev. phil.*, 1886 (II), *21*, 577–592.

————. L'anesthésie systématisée et la dissociation des phénomènes psychologiques. *Rev. phil.*, 1887 (II), *23*, 449–472.

————. Les actes inconscients et la mémoire pendant le somnambulisme. *Rev. phil.*, 1888 (I), *25*, 238–279.

————. *L'automatisme psychologique.* (10th ed.) Paris: Alcan, 1930. (1889)

————. Etude sur un cas d'aboulie et d'idées fixes. *Rev. phil.*, 1891 (I), *31*, 258–287, 382–407.

————. *The mental state of hystericals: A study of mental stigmata and mental accidents.* Trans. by Caroline R. Corson. New York: Putnam, 1901. (1893–1894)

————. *L'état mental des hystériques, les stigmates mentaux.* (2nd ed.) Paris: Alcan, 1911. (1893)

————. *Etat mental des hystériques. Les accidents mentaux.* (2nd ed.) Paris: Alcan, 1922. (1894)

————. Histoire d'une idée fixe. *Rev. phil.,* 1894, *37,* 121–168.

————. J. M. Charcot, son oeuvre psychologique. *Rev. phil.,* 1895, *39,* 569–604.

————. Un cas de possession et l'exorcisme moderne. *Bull. Univer. Lyon,* 1895, *8,* 41–57.

————. *Notes sur quelques spasmes des muscles du tronc chez les hystériques.* Paris: Alcan-Lévy, 1895.

————. Résumé historique des études sur le sentiment de la personnalité. *Rev. sci.,* 1896, *5,* 98–103.

————. L'Influence somnambulique et le besoin de direction. *Rev. phil.,* 1897 (I), *43,* 113–143. Also in *Névroses et idées fixes.* Vol. 2. Paris: Alcan, 1898, pp. 423–480.

————. Traitement psychologique de l'hystérie. In A. Robin (Ed.), *Traité de thérapeutique appliquée.* Fasc. 15. Paris: Rueff, 1898, pp. 140–216.

————. *Névroses et idées fixes.* (2 vols.) Paris: Alcan, 1898.

————, & Raymond, F. *Les obsessions et la psychasthénie.* (2 vols.) Paris: Alcan, 1903. (Reprinted 1926)

————. L'amnésie et la dissociation des souvenirs par l'émotion. *J. Psychol. norm. path.,* 1904, *1,* 417–453.

————. The psycholeptic crises. *Boston Med. Surg. J.,* 1905, *4,* 93–100.

————. Mental pathology. *Psychol. Rev.,* 1905, *12,* 98–117.

————. On the pathogenesis of some impulsions. *J. abnorm. Psychol.,* 1906–1907, *1,* 1–17.

————. *The major symptoms of hysteria.* (2nd ed.) New York: Macmillan, 1924. (1907)

————. *Les névroses.* Paris: Flammarion, 1909.

Jastrow, J., Münsterberg, H., Ribot, T., ————, Hart, B., & Prince, M. *Subconscious phenomena.* Boston: Badger, 1910.

————. La kleptomanie et la dépression mentale. *J. Psychol. norm. path.,* 1911, *8,* 97–103.

————. La psycho-analyse. (Rapport au XVIIe Congrès international de médecine de Londres.) *J. Psychol. norm. path.,* 1914, *11,* 97–130.

————. Psychoanalysis. *J. abnorm. Psychol.,* 1914–1915, *9,* 1–35, 153–187.

————. L'oeuvre philosophique de Th. Ribot. *J. Psychol. norm. path.,* 1915, *13,* 268–282.

————. Valeur de la psycho-analyse de Freud. *Rev. Psychothér, psychol. appl.,* 1915, *29,* 82–83.

————. *Les médications psychologiques.* (3 vols.) Paris: Alcan, 1919.

————. *Psychological healing: A historical and clinical study.* (2 vols.) Trans. by E. & C. Paul. London: Allen & Unwin, 1925. (1919)

————. Les oscillations et l'activité mentale. *J. Psychol. norm. path.,* 1920, *17,* 31–44 ; 1921, *28,* 140–145.

————. La tension psychologique, ses degrés, ses oscillations. *Brit. J. med. Psychol.,* 1920–1921, *1,* 1–15, 144–164, 209–224.

————. Alcoholism in relation to mental depression. *J. Amer. Med. Ass.,* 1921, *77,* 1462–1467.

————. A case of psychasthenic delirium. *Amer. J. Psychiat.,* 1922, *1,* 319–322.

————. *La médecine psychologique.* (2 vols.) Paris: Flammarion, 1923.

————. La tension psychologique et ses oscillations. In G. Dumas (Ed.), *Traité de psychologie.* Vol. 1. Paris: Alcan, 1923, pp. 919–952.

————. *Principles of psychotherapy.* Trans. by H. M. & E. R. Guthrier. New York: Macmillan, 1924.

————. L'atonie et l'asthénie psychologiques. *Brit. J. med. Psychol.,* 1924, *4,* 1–11.

————. Les états de consolation et les extases. *J. Psychol. norm. path.,* 1925, *22,* 369–420.

————. Les sentiments de joie dans l'extase. *J. Psychol. norm. path.,* 1925, *22,* 465–499.

————. *Psychologie expérimentale. Compte-rendu du cours de M. Janet, Collège de France.* Paris: Chahine, 1926.

————. *Psicología de los sentimientos.* Mexico, DF: Sociedad de Edición y Libreria Franco-Americana, 1926.

————. *De l'angoisse à l'extase.* Vol. 1: *Un délire religieux: La croyance.* Vol. 2: *Les sentiments fondamentaux.* Paris: Alcan, 1926, 1928.

————. A propos de la schizophrénie. *J. Psychol. norm. path.,* 1927, *24,* 477–492.

————. Le sentiment du vide. *J. Psychol. norm. path.,* 1927, *24,* 861–887.

————. *La pensée intérieure et ses troubles.* Paris: Chahine, 1927.

————. *L'évolution de la mémoire et la notion du temps* (Compte-rendu intégral des conférences d'après les notes sténographiques.) Paris: Chahine, 1928.

————. Fear of action as an essential element in the sentiment of melancholia. In M. L. Reymert (Ed.), *Feelings and emotions: The Wittenberg symposium.* Worcester, Mass.: Clark University Press, 1928, pp. 297–309.

————. *L'évolution psychologique de la personnalité.* Paris: Chahine, 1930.

————. L'analyse psychologique. In C. Murchison (Ed.), *Psychologies of 1930.* Worcester, Mass.: Clark University Press, 1930, pp. 369–373.

————. Pierre Janet. In C. Murchison (Ed.), *A history of psychology in autobiography.* Vol. 1. Worcester, Mass.: Clark University Press, 1930, pp. 123–133.

———— *La force et la faiblesse psychologiques.* Paris: Maloine, 1932.

————. L'hallucination dans le délire de persécution. *Rev. phil.,* 1932, *57,* 61–98, 279–331.

————. *L'amour et la haine.* Paris: Maloine, 1932.

————. La tension psychologique et ses oscillations. In G. Dumas (Ed.), *Nouveau traité de psychologie.* Vol. 4. Paris: Alcan, 1934, pp. 386–411.

————. *Les débuts de l'intelligence.* Paris: Flammarion, 1935.

————. *L'intelligence avant le langage.* Paris: Flammarion, 1936.

————. La psychologie de la croyance et le mysticisme. *Rev. Métaphys. Morale,* 1936, *43,* 327–358, 507–532; 1937, *44,* 369–410.

————. Le langage inconsistant. *Theoria,* 1937, *3,* 57–71.

————. La psychologie de la conduite. *Encyclopédie française,* 1938, *8,* 8°-08-11-8°-08-16.

————. Discours de M. Pierre Janet. In Various, *Centenaire de Th. Ribot et Jubilé de la Psychologie Scientifique Française.* Paris: Imprimerie moderne, 1939, pp. 27–36. **B**

————. Perspectives de l'application de la psychologie à l'industrie. *Premier cycle d'étude de psychologie industrielle.* Fasc. No. 1. *Psychologie et travail.* Paris: Cégos, 1943, pp. 3–8.

————. Autobiographie psychologique. *Etud. phil.,* 1946, *2*(N.S.), 81–87.

Goshen, *Documentary;* Hameline, *Anthologie;* Sahakian, *Psychology;* Shor, *Hypnosis*

JOSEPH JASTROW
1863-1944
American Psychologist (22)

Peirce, C. S., & Jastrow, J. On small differences of sensation. *Mem. Nat. Acad. Sci.,* 1884, *3,* 73–83. Reprinted in A. W. Burks (Ed.), *Collected papers of Charles Sanders Peirce.* Vol. 7. *Science and philosophy.* Cambridge: Harvard University Press, 1958, pp. 13–27.

Hall, G. S., & ————. Studies of rhythm. (I) *Mind,* 1886, *11,* 55–62.

————. The perception of space by disparate senses. *Mind,* 1886, *11,* 539–554.

———. The psychology of deception. *Pop. Sci. Mon.*, 1888, *34*, 145–157.

———. The psycho-physic law and star magnitudes. *Amer. J. Psychol.*, 1888, *1*, 112–127.

———. A critique of psycho-physic methods. *Amer. J. Psychol.*, 1888, *1*, 271–309.

———. *The time-relations of mental phenomena.* New York: Hodges, 1890.

——— (with assist. of F. Whitton). The perception of space by disparate senses. *Amer. J. Psychol.*, 1890, *3*, 49–54.

———. Psychology at the University of Wisconsin. *Amer. J. Psychol.*, 1890, *3*, 273–276.

———. A statistical study of memory and association. *Educ. Rev.*, N.Y., 1891, *2*, 442–452.

——— (with assist. of G. W. Morehouse). A novel optical illusion. *Amer. J. Psychol.*, 1891–1892, *4*, 201–208.

——— (with assist. of W. B. Cairnes). The psychophysic series and the time sense. *Amer. J. Psychol.*, 1891–1892, *4*, 213–217.

——— (with assist. of Helen West). A study of Zöllner's figures and other related illusions. *Amer. J. Psychol.*, 1891–1892, *4*, 381–398.

——— (with assist. of Helen West). A study of involuntary movements. *Amer. J. Psychol.*, 1891–1892, *4*, 398–407.

——— (with assist. of G. W. Morehouse). Some anthropometric and psychologic tests on college students—a preliminary survey. *Amer. J. Psychol.*, 1891–1892, *4*, 420–428.

———. On the judgment of angles and positions of lines. *Amer. J. Psychol.*, 1892, *5*, 214–248.

——— (with assist. of T. D. Carter & E. P. Sherry). A further study of involuntary movement. *Amer. J. Psychol.*, 1892, *5*, 223–231.

———. Community and the association of ideas: A statistical study. *Psychol. Rev.*, 1894, *1*, 152–158.

———. Community of ideas of men and women. *Psychol. Rev.*, 1896, *3*, 68–71.

———, Baldwin, J. M., & Cattell, J. McK.

Physical and mental tests. *Psychol. Rev.*, 1898, *5*, 172–179.

———. The psychology of invention. *Psychol. Rev.*, 1898, *5*, 307–309.

———. Practical aspects of psychology. *Educ. Rev.*, N.Y., 1899, *17*, 135–153.

———. *Fact and fable in psychology.* Boston: Houghton Mifflin, 1900.

———. Some currents and undercurrents in psychology. *Psychol. Rev.*, 1901, *8*, 1–26.

———. Helen Keller: A psychological autobiography. *Pop. Sci. Mon.*, 1903, *63*, 71–83.

———. *The subconscious.* Boston: Houghton Mifflin, 1906.

———, Münsterberg, H., Ribot, T., Janet, P., Hart, B., & Prince, M. *Subconscious phenomena.* Boston: Badger, 1910.

———. The professorial question. *Science,* 1910, *32*, 112–114.

———. *Character and temperament.* New York: Appleton, 1915.

———. Antecedents of the study of character and temperament. *Pop. Sci. Mon.*, 1915, *86*, 590–613.

———. Varieties of psychological experience. *Psychol. Rev.*, 1917, *24*, 249–265.

———. *The psychology of conviction: A study of beliefs and attitudes.* Boston: Houghton Mifflin, 1918.

———. Contributions of Freudism to psychology. IV. The neurological concept of behavior. *Psychol. Rev.*, 1924, *31*, 203–218.

———. The reconstruction of psychology. *Psychol. Rev.*, 1927, *34*, 169–195.

———. Concepts and "isms" in psychology. *Amer. J. Psychol.*, 1927, *39*, 1–6.

———. *Keeping mentally fit: A guide to everyday psychology.* Garden City, N.Y.: Greenberg, 1928.

———. The place of emotion in modern psychology. In M. L. Reymert (Ed.), *Feelings and emotions: The Wittenberg symposium.* Worcester, Mass.: Clark University Press, 1928, 24–38.

———. *Piloting your life: The psychologist as helmsman.* New York: Emerson, 1930.

———. Joseph Jastrow. In C. Murchison (Ed.), *A history of psychology in autobiography.* Vol. 1. Worcester, Mass.: Clark University Press, 1930, pp. 135–162.   **B**

———. *Effective thinking.* New York: Simon & Schuster, 1931. (Republished as *Managing your mind.* New York: Greenberg, 1935)

———. *The house that Freud built.* New York: Greenberg, 1932. (Republished as *Freud, his dream and sex theories.* New York: World Publishing, 1940)

———. *Wish and wisdom: Episodes in the vagaries of belief.* New York: Appleton-Century, 1935.

———. *Sanity first, the art of sensible living.* New York: Greenberg, 1935. (Republished as *Getting more out of life.* New York: Emerson, 1940)

———. Has psychology failed? *Amer. Scholar,* 1935, *4,* 261–269.

———. *The betrayal of intelligence: A preface to debunking.* New York: Greenberg, 1938.

———. American psychology in the '80's and '90's. *Psychol. Rev.,* 1943, *50,* 65–67.

Dennis, *Readings Developmental* ; Moore & Hartmann, *Industrial Psychology*

HERBERT SPENCER JENNINGS
1868-1947
American Biologist (25)

Jennings, H. S. Studies on reactions to stimuli in unicellular organisms. I: Reactions to chemical, osmotic and mechanical stimuli in the ciliate infusoria. *J. Physiol.,* 1897, *21,* 258–322. II: The mechanism of the motor reactions of Paramecium. *Amer. J. Physiol.,* 1899, *2,* 311–341. III: Reactions to localized stimuli in Spirostomum and Stentor. *Amer. Naturalist,* 1899, *33,* 373–389. IV: Laws of chemotaxis in Para-mecium. *Amer. J. Physiol.,* 1899, *2,* 355–393. V: On the movements and motor reflexes of the Flagellata and Ciliata. *Amer. J. Physiol.,* 1900, *3,* 229–260. VI: On the reactions of Chilomonas to organic acids. *Amer. J. Physiol.,* 1900, *3,* 397–403. VII: The manner in which bacteria react to stimuli, especially to chemical stimuli. *Amer. J. Physiol.,* 1901, *5,* 31–37 (with J. H. Crosby). VIII: On the reactions of infusoria to carbonic and other acids, with especial reference to the causes of the gatherings spontaneously formed. *Amer. J. Physiol.,* 1902, *6,* 233–250 (with E. M. Moore). IX: On the behavior of fixed infusoria (Stentor and Vorticella), with special reference to the modifiability of protozoan reactions. *Amer. J. Physiol.,* 1902, *8,* 23–60. X: The movements and reactions of pieces of infusoria. *Biol. Bull.,* 1902, *3,* 225–234 (with Clara Jamieson).

———. The psychology of a protozoan. *Amer. J. Psychol.,* 1899, *10,* 503–515.

———. *Reactions to heat and cold in the ciliate infusoria. Contributions to the study of the behavior of the lower organisms.* Washington, D.C.: Carnegie Institution, 1904.

———. The behavior of Paramecium. Additional features and general relations. *J. comp. neurol. Psychol.,* 1904, *14,* 441–510.

———. The basis for taxis and certain other terms in the behavior of infusoria. *J. comp. neurol. Psychol.,* 1905, *15,* 138–143.

———. *Behavior of the lower organisms.* New York: Columbia University Press, 1906. (Reprinted 1962)

———. Behavior of the Starfish Asterias Forrei de Loriol. *Univ. Cal. Pub. Zool.,* 1907, *4,* 53–185.

———. Recent works on the behavior of the higher animals. *Amer. Naturalist,* 1908, *42,* 355–360.

———. The interpretation of the behavior of the lower organisms. *Science,* 1908, *27,* 698–710.

———. Animal behavior. *Amer. Naturalist,* 1908, *42,* 754–760.

———. Heredity, variation and evolution in protozoa. *Proc. Amer. Phil. Soc.,* 1908, *47,* 393–547.

———. The work of J. von Uexküll on the physiology of movements and behavior. *J. comp. neurol. Psychol.,* 1909, *19,* 313–336.

———. Diverse ideals and divergent conclusions in the study of behavior in lower organisms. *Amer. J. Psychol.,* 1910, *21,* 349–370.

———. Heredity and personality. *Science,* 1911, *34,* 902–910.

———, & Lashley, K. S. Biparental inheritance of size in Paramecium. *J. exp. Zool.,* 1913, *15,* 193–200.

———, & Lashley, K. S. Biparental inheritance and the question of sexuality in Paramecium. *J. exp. Zool.,* 1913, *14,* 393–466.

———. Mechanism and vitalism. *Phil. Rev.,* 1918, *27,* 577–596.

———. Experimental determinism and human conduct. *J. Phil.,* 1919, *16,* 180–183.

———. Heredity and environment. *Sci. Mon., N.Y.,* 1924, *19,* 225–238.

———. The inheritance of acquired characters. *Forum,* 1926, *76,* 702–711.

———. *Some implications of emergent evolution: Diverse doctrines of evolution—their relation to the practice of science and of life.* Hanover, N.H.: Sociological Press, 1927.

———. *The biological basis of human nature.* New York: Norton, 1930.

———. *Genetics.* New York: Norton, 1935.

———. *The beginnings of social behavior in unicellular organisms.* Philadelphia: University of Pennsylvania Press, 1941.

Herrnstein & Boring, *Source Book*

WILLIAM STANLEY JEVONS
1835-1882
English Logician (11)

Jevons, W. S. *Methods of social reform and other papers.* Ed. by Harriet A. Jevons. London: Macmillan, 1883.   **C**

———. *Letters and journal of W. Stanley Jevons.* Ed. by Harriet A. Jevons. London: Macmillan, 1886.   **B Bl C**

———. *The principles of economics: A fragment of a treatise on the industrial mechanism of society, and other papers.* New York: Kelley, 1965. (1905)   **C**

———. *Pure logic, or the logic of quality apart from quantity: With remarks on Boole's system and on the relation of logic and mathematics.* New York: Macmillan, 1890. (1864)   **C**

———. *The substitution of similars, the true principle of reasoning, derived from a modification of Aristotle's dictum.* London: Macmillan, 1869.

———. On the mechanical performance of logical inference. *Phil. Trans.,* 1870, *160,* 497–518.

———. *Elementary lessons in logic, deductive and inductive.* (2nd ed.) New York: Macmillan, 1881. (1870)

———. *The theory of political economy.* (4th ed.) New York: Macmillan, 1924. (1871)

———. On a general system of numerically definite reasoning. *Mem. Lit. Phil. Soc. Manchester,* Ser. 3, 1871, *4,* 330–352.

———. The power of numerical discrimination. *Nature,* 1871, *3,* 281–282.

———. Who discovered the quantification of the predicate? *Contemp. Rev.,* 1873, *21,* 821–824.

———. *The principles of science: A treatise on logic and scientific method.* (2nd ed.) Macmillan, 1905. (1874) (Reprinted 1958)

———. J. S. Mill's philosophy tested. *Contemp. Rev.,* 1877–1878, *31,* 167–182 ; 256–275 ; 1878, *32,* 88–89 ; 1879, *36,* 521–528. Reprinted in *Pure logic, op. cit.,* pp. 199–267.

———. *Studies in deductive logic, a manual for students.* (3rd ed.) New York: Macmillan, 1896. (1880)

———. *The state in relation to labour.* (4th ed.) London: Macmillan, 1910. (1882)

———. *Investigations in currency and finance.* (2nd ed.) London: Macmillan, 1909. (1884)

Miller, *Mathematics ;* Newman, *Mathematics*

FRIEDRICH JODL
1849-1914
German-Austrian Philosopher (11)

Jodl, F. *Vom wahren und vom falschen Idealismus.* Leipzig: Kröner, 1914.　　　**C**

———. *Vom Lebenswege.* (2 vols.) Ed. by W. Börner. Stuttgart: Cotta, 1916–1917.　　**C**

———. *Kritik des Idealismus.* Ed. by C. Siegel & W. Schmied-Kowarzik. Leipzig: Akademische Verlagsgesellschaft, 1920.　　**C**

———. *Leben und Philosophie David Humes.* Halle: Pfeffer, 1872.

———. *Die Kulturgeschichtsschreibung.* Halle: Pfeffer, 1878.

———. *Geschichte der Ethik in der neueren Philosophie.* Stuttgart: Cotta, 1882–1889.

———. *Volkswirtschaftslehre und Ethik.* Berlin: Habel, 1885.

———. On the origin and import of the idea of causality. *Monist,* 1895–1896, *6,* 516–533.

———. *Lehrbuch der Psychologie.* (New ed.) (2 vols.) Ed. by H. K. F. Henning. Stuttgart: Cotta, 1925. (1896)

———. *Geschichte der Ethik als philosophischer Wissenschaft.* (2 vols.) Stuttgart: Cotta, 1930. (1906–1912)

———. *Der Monismus und die Kulturprobleme der Gegenwart.* Leipzig: Kröner, 1911.

———. *Aesthetik der bildenden Künste.* (2nd ed.) Stuttgart: Cotta, 1920. (1917)

———. *Allgemeine Ethik.* Stuttgart: Cotta, 1918.

———. *Geschichte der neueren Philosophie.* Ed. by K. Roretz. Vienna: Rikola, 1924.

SAMUEL JOHNSON
1696-1772
American Philosopher (12)

Johnson, S. *Samuel Johnson, President of King's College: His career and writings.* (4 vols.) Ed. by H. & Carol Schneider. New York: Columbia University Press, 1929.　**B Bl C**

———. *Some historical remarks concerning the collegiate school of Conn. in New Haven.* New Haven: Bibliographical Press, 1933. (1717)

———. *Elementa philosophica.* (2nd ed.) Philadelphia: Franklin, 1752. (1746) Reprinted in *Samuel Johnson,* Vol. 2, *op. cit.,* pp. 357–515.

———. *Ethics elementa.* Boston: Rogers & Fowle, 1746.

———. *The Christian indeed.* New Haven: Green, 1768.

———. Memoirs of the life of the Rev. S. Johnson and several things relating to the state both of religion and learning in his times. (1765–1770) In *Samuel Johnson.* Vol. 1, *op. cit.,* pp. 1–50.　　**B**

Berkeley, G., & ———. Philosophical correspondence between Berkeley and Samuel Johnson, 1729–30. In Berkeley, G., *The works of George Berkeley, Bishop of Cloyne.* Ed. by A. A. Luce & T. E. Jessop. Vol. 2. London: Nelson, 1949, pp. 265–294 ; & in *Samuel Johnson,* Vol. 2, *op. cit.,* pp. 261–284.

Kurtz, *American Thought ;* Mueller, *American Philosophy*

(ALFRED) ERNEST JONES
1879-1958
English Psychoanalyst (22)

Jones, E. *Papers on psycho-analysis.* (5th ed.) London: Baillière, Tindall & Cox, 1948. (1912) (Reprinted 1961)　　**C**

———. *Essays in applied psycho-analysis.* (2 vols.) London: Hogarth Press, 1951. (1923) (Reprinted 1964)　　**C**

———. Rationalisation in every-day life. *J. abnorm. Psychol.,* 1908, *3,* 161–169.

———. Freud's theory of dreams. *Amer. J. Psychol.,* 1910, *21,* 283–308. Reprinted in *Papers on psycho-analysis, op. cit.,* pp. 217–250.

———. The Oedipus-Complex as an explanation of Hamlet's mystery: A study in motive. *Amer. J. Psychol.,* 1910, *21,* 72–113.

———. Freud's psychology. *Psychol. Bull.*, 1910, 7, 109–128. Reprinted in *Papers on psycho-analysis, op. cit.*, pp. 1–23.

———. The action of suggestion in psychotherapy. *J. abnorm. Psychol.*, 1911, 5, 217–254.

———. Professor Janet on psycho-analysis: A rejoinder. *J. abnorm. Psychol.*, 1914–1915, 9, 400–410.

———. The significance of the unconscious in psychopathology. *Rev. Neurol. Psychiat.*, 1914, 12, 474–481.

———. The theory of symbolism. (1916) In *Papers on psycho-analysis, op. cit.*, pp. 87–144.

———. Why is the "unconscious" unconscious? *Brit. J. Psychol.*, 1917–1919, 9, 230–256.

———. Some problems of adolescence. *Brit. J. Psychol.*, 1922–1923, 13, 31–47.

———. *Social aspects of psycho-analysis.* London: Williams & Norgate, 1924.

———. Mother-right and the sexual ignorance of savages. *Int. J. Psycho-Anal.*, 1925, 6, 109–130. Reprinted in *Essays in applied psycho-analysis*, Vol. 2, *op. cit.*, pp. 145–173.

———The psychology of religion. *Brit. J. Med. Psychol.*, 1926, 6, 264–269.

———. The origin and structure of the Super-ego. *Int. J. Psycho-Anal.*, 1926, 7, 303–311.

———. The early development of female sexuality. *Int. J. Psycho-Anal.*, 1927, 8, 459–472.

———. Psychoanalysis and folk lore. *Scientia*, 1934, 55, 209–220. Reprinted in *Essays in applied psycho-analysis*, Vol. 2, *op. cit.*, pp. 1–21.

———. Psychoanalysis and the instincts. *Brit. J. Psychol.*, 1936, 26, 273–288. Reprinted in *Papers on psycho-analysis, op. cit.*, pp. 153–172.

———. *Hamlet and Oedipus.* Garden City, N.Y.: Doubleday, 1955. (1949)

———. *On the nightmare.* New York: Liveright, 1951.

———. *The life and work of Sigmund Freud.* (3 vols.) New York: Basic Books, 1953–1957. **B**

———. The early history of psycho-analysis. *J. ment. Sci.*, 1954, 100, 198–210.

———. *Sigmund Freud: Four centenary addresses.* New York: Basic Books, 1956.

———. *Free associations: Memories of a psycho-analyst.* New York: Basic Books, 1959. **B**

Jung, C., & ———. *Conversations with Carl Jung and reactions from Ernest Jones.* (Recorded by R. I. Evans.) Princeton, N.J.: Van Nostrand, 1964.

ADOLPH JOST
(ca. 1870-ca. 1920)
German Psychologist (16)

Jost, A. Die Assoziationsfestigkeit in ihrer Abhängigkeit der Verteilung der Wiederholungen. *Z. Psychol.*, 1897, 14, 436–472.

CHARLES HUBBARD JUDD
1873-1946
American Psychologist (22)

Judd, C. H. Ueber Raumwahrnehmungen im Gebiete des Tastsinnes. *Phil. Stud.*, 1896, 12, 409–463.

———. Some facts of binocular vision. *Psychol. Rev.*, 1897, 4, 374–389.

———. An optical illusion. *Psychol. Rev.*, 1898, 5, 286–294.

———. Visual perception of the third dimension. *Psychol. Rev.*, 1898, 5, 388–400.

———. Binocular factors in monocular vision. *Science*, 1898, 7, 269–271.

———. Retinal images and binocular vision. *Science*, 1898, 7, 425–426.

———. A study of geometrical illusions. *Psychol. Rev.*, 1899, 6, 241–261.

———. An experimental study of writing-movements. *Phil. Stud.*, 1902, 19, 243–259.

———. Practice and its effects on the perception of illusions. *Psychol. Rev.*, 1902, 9, 27–39.

——. *Genetic psychology for teachers.* New York: Appleton, 1903.

——, McAllister, C. N., & Steele, W. M. General introduction to a series of studies of eye movements by means of kinetoscopic photographs. *Psychol. Monogr.,* 1905, 7, No. 29, pp. 1–16.

——. The Müller-Lyer illusion. *Psychol. Monogr.,* 1905, 7, No. 29, pp. 55–81.

——. Practice without knowledge of results. *Psychol. Monogr.,* 1905, 7, No. 29, pp. 185–198.

——. Movement and consciousness. *Psychol. Monogr.,* 1905, 7, No. 29, pp. 199–226.

——. The relation of special training to general intelligence. *Educ. Rev.,* 1908, 36, 28–42.

——. Evolution and consciousness. *Psychol. Rev.,* 1910, 17, 77–97.

——. *Psychology of high school subjects.* Boston: Ginn, 1915.

——. *Introduction to the scientific study of education.* Boston: Ginn, 1918.

——, & Buswell, G. T. Silent reading: A study of various types. *Univ. Chicago Suppl. Educ. Monogr.,* 1922, No. 23. (Reprinted 1959)

——. *The psychology of social institutions.* New York: Macmillan, 1926.

——. *Psychology of secondary education.* Boston: Ginn, 1927.

——. Psychological analysis of the fundamentals of arithmetic. *Univ. Chicago Suppl. Educ. Monog.,* 1927, No. 31.

——. Reduction of articulation. *Amer. J. Psychol.,* 1927, 39, 313–322.

——. Charles H. Judd. In C. Murchison (Ed.), *A history of psychology in autobiography.* Vol. 2. Worcester, Mass.: Clark University Press, 1932, pp. 207–235. **B**

——. *Education and social process.* New York: Harcourt, Brace, 1934.

——. *Psychology: General introduction.* (2nd ed.) Boston: Ginn, 1917. (1907)

——. *Education as cultivation of the higher mental processes.* New York: Macmillan, 1936.

——. *Educational psychology.* Boston: Houghton Mifflin, 1939.

Cubberley, *Public Educators;* Park & Burgess, *Sociology*

CARL GUSTAV JUNG
1875-1961
Swiss Psychiatrist (27)

Jung, C. G. *Collected papers on analytical psychology.* (2nd ed.) Ed. by Constance E. Long. London: Baillière, Tindall & Cox, 1917. **C**

——. *Contributions to analytical psychology.* Trans. by C. F. & H. G. Baynes. New York: Harcourt, Brace, 1928. **C**

——. *Two essays on analytical psychology.* Trans. by C. F. & H. G. Baynes. New York: Dodd Mead, 1928. Reprinted in *Collected works,* Vol. 7, *vide infra.* **C**

Wilhelm, R., & ——. *The secret of the golden flower.* Trans. by C. F. Baynes. New York: Harcourt, Brace, 1931. (1929) **C**

——. *Modern man in search of a soul.* Trans. by W. S. Dell & Cary F. Baynes. New York: Harcourt, Brace & World, 1933. **C**

——. *The integration of personality.* Trans. by S. Dell. New York: Farrar & Rinehart, 1939. **C**

——. *Essays on contemporary events.* Trans. by Various. London: Kegan Paul, 1947. **C**

——, & Pauli, W. *The interpretation of nature and the psyche.* Trans. by R. F. C. Hull. New York: Pantheon Books, 1955. (1952) **C**

——. *Psychological reflections: A new anthology of his writings, 1905–1961.* (2nd ed.) Ed. by Jolande Jacobi & R. F. C. Hull. New York: Pantheon Books, 1961. (1953) **C**

——. *The collected works of C. G. Jung.* (Ult. 19 vols.) Ed. by H. Read *et al.,* & trans. by R. F. C. Hull. Princeton, N.J.: Princeton University Press, 1954– **C**

————. *Basic writings*. Ed. by Violet S. De Laszlo. New York: Random House, 1959. **C**

————. *The portable Jung*. Ed. by J. Campbell. New York: Viking Press, 1971. **B Bl C**

————. On the psychology and pathology of so-called occult phenomena. (1902) Reprinted in *Collected works*, Vol. 1, *op. cit.*, pp. 1–88, & in *Collected papers, op. cit.*, pp. 1–93.

————, & Riklin, F. The associations of normal subjects. (1904) Reprinted in *Studies in word-association, vide infra*, pp. 8–172, & to be reprinted in *Collected works*, Vol. 2, *op. cit.*

————. Cryptomnesia. (1905) Trans. in *Collected works*, Vol. 1, *op. cit.*, pp. 95–106.

————. On psychophysical relations of the associative experiment. (1906) *J. abnorm. Psychol.*, 1906–1907, *1*, 249–257. To be reprinted in *Collected works*, Vol. 2, *op. cit.*

————, et al. *Studies in word-association: Experiments in diagnosis of psychopathological conditions carried out at the psychiatric clinic of the University of Zurich*. Trans. by M. D. Eder. New York: Moffat-Yard, 1919. (1906–1909) Jung studies reprinted in *Collected works*, Vol. 2, *op. cit.*

————. *The psychology of dementia praecox*. Trans. by A. A. Brill. New York: Mental & Nervous Disease Publishing, 1936. (1907) Reprinted in *Collected works*, Vol. 3, *op. cit.*, pp. 1–151.

Ricksher, C., & ————. Further investigations on the galvanic phenomenon and respiration in normal and insane individuals. *J. abnorm. Psychol.*, 1907–1908, *2*, 189–217. Reprinted in *Collected works*, Vol. 2, *op. cit.*

————. The content of the psychoses. (1908) Trans. in *Collected works*, Vol. 3, *op. cit.*, pp. 153–178, & in *Collected papers, op. cit.*, pp. 312–351.

————. The analysis of dreams. (1909) Trans. in *Collected works*, Vol. 4, *op. cit.*, pp. 25–34.

————. The association method. *Amer. J. Psychol.*, 1910, *21*, 219–269. Reprinted in *Collected papers, op. cit.*, pp. 94–155, & to be reprinted in *Collected works*, Vol. 2, *op. cit.*

————. *Symbols of transformation: An analysis of the prelude to a case of schizophrenia*. (4th ed.) (2 vols.) Trans. by R. F. C. Hull. New York: Harper, 1962. (1912) Trans. in *Collected works*, Vol. 5, *op. cit.*

————. On the psychology of the unconscious. (5th ed.) (1912) Trans. in *Collected works*, Vol. 7, *op. cit.*, pp. 1–119.

————. General aspects of psychoanalysis. (1913) Trans. in *Collected works*, Vol. 4, *op. cit.*, pp. 229–251, & in *Collected papers, op. cit.*, pp. 206–225.

————. The theory of psychoanalysis. (1913) Trans. in *Collected works*, Vol. 4, *op. cit.*, pp. 83–226.

————. Some crucial points in psychoanalysis: A correspondence between Dr. Jung and Dr. Loÿ. (1914) Trans. in *Collected works*, Vol. 4, *op. cit.*, pp. 252–289, & in *Collected papers, op. cit.*, pp. 236–277. **B**

————. On psychological understanding. (1915) Reprinted in *Collected works*, Vol. 3, *op. cit.*, pp. 179–193.

————. General aspects of dream psychology. (1916) Trans. in *Collected works*, Vol. 8, *op. cit.*, pp. 237–280.

————. The transcendent function. (1916) Trans. in *Collected works*, Vol. 8, *op. cit.*, pp. 67–91.

————. The relations between the ego and the unconscious. (1916) Trans. in *Collected works*, Vol. 7, *op. cit.*, pp. 123–227, & in *Two essays on analytical psychology, op. cit.*, pp. 125–269.

————. Instinct and the unconscious. III. *Brit. J. Psychol.*, 1919–1920, *10*, 15–23. Reprinted in *Collected works*, Vol. 8, *op. cit.*, pp. 129–138.

————. The therapeutic value of abreaction. *Brit. J. Psychol.*, 1921, *11*, 13–22. Reprinted in *Collected works*, Vol. 16, *op. cit.*, pp. 129–138, & in *Contributions to analytical psychology, op. cit.*, pp. 282–294.

————. *Psychological types, or the psychology of individuation*. Trans. by H. G. Baynes. New York: Harcourt, Brace, 1924. (1921) Reprinted in diff. trans. in *Collected works*, Vol. 6, *op. cit.*

———. On the relation of analytical psychology to the poetic art. (1922) Reprinted in *Collected works*, Vol. 15, *op. cit.*, pp. 65–83, & in *Contributions to analytical psychology*, *op. cit.*, pp. 225–249.

———. Mind and earth. (1927) Trans. in *Collected works*, Vol. 10, *op. cit.*, pp. 29–49, & in *Contributions to analytical psychology*, *op. cit.*, 99–140.

———. The structure of the psyche. (1927) Reprinted in *Collected works*, Vol. 8, *op. cit.*, pp. 159–234.

———. On psychic energy. (1928) Trans. in *Collected works*, Vol. 8, *op. cit.*, pp. 3–66, & in *Contributions to analytical psychology*, *op. cit.*, pp. 1–76.

———. Freud and Jung: Contrasts. (1929) Trans. in *Collected works*, Vol. 4, *op. cit.*, pp. 333–340, & in *Modern man in search of a soul*, *op. cit.*, pp. 132–142.

———. Commentary on "The secret of the golden flower." (1929) Trans. in *Collected works*, Vol. 13, *op. cit.*, pp. 1–56, & in Wilhelm, R., & Jung, C. G., *The secret of the golden flower*, *op. cit.*, & in later editions (pagination varies).

———. The significance of consultation and heredity in psychology. (1929) Trans. in *Collected works*, Vol. 8, *op. cit.*, pp. 107–113.

———. Introduction to Kranefeldt's "Secret ways of the mind." (1930) Trans. in *Collected works*, Vol. 4, *op. cit.*, pp. 324–332.

———. Psychotherapists or the clergy. (1932) Trans. in *Collected works*, Vol. 11, *op. cit.*, pp. 327–347, & in *Modern man in search of a soul*, *op. cit.*, pp. 255–282.

———. Sigmund Freud in his historical setting. *J. Pers.*, 1932, *1*, 48–55. Trans. in *Collected works*, Vol. 15, *op. cit.*, pp. 33–40.

———. A study in the process of individuation. (1934) Reprinted in *Collected works*, Vol. 9, Part 1, *op. cit.*, pp. 290–354, & in *Integration of the personality*, *op. cit.*, pp. 30–52.

———. Archetypes of the collective unconscious. (1935) Reprinted in *Collected works*, Vol. 9, Part 1, *op. cit.*, pp. 3–41, & in *Integration of the personality*, *op. cit.*, pp. 52–85.

———. The state of psychotherapy today. (1934) Trans. in *Collected works*, Vol. 10, *op. cit.*, pp. 157–173.

———. Principles of practical psychotherapy. (1935) Trans. in *Collected works*, Vol. 16, *op. cit.*, pp. 3–35.

———. The concept of the collective unconscious. (1936) Reprinted in *Collected works*, Vol. 9, Part 1, *op. cit.*, pp. 42–53.

———. Psychological factors determining human behavior. (1936) Reprinted in *Collected works*, Vol. 8, *op. cit.*, pp. 114–125.

———. *Analytical psychology: Its theory and practice.* New York: Random House, 1968. (1936)

———. Psychology and religion. (1937) Reprinted in *Collected works*, Vol. 11, *op. cit.*, pp. 3–105.

———. Conscious, unconscious, and individuation. (1939) Reprinted in *Collected works*, Vol. 9, Part 1, *op. cit.*, pp. 275–289.

———. On the psychogenesis of schizophrenia. *J. ment. Sci.*, 1939, *85*, 999–1011. Reprinted in *Collected works*, Vol. 3, *op. cit.*, pp. 233–249.

———. In memory of Sigmund Freud. (1939) Reprinted in *Collected works*, Vol. 15, *op. cit.*, pp. 41–49.

———, & Kerenyi, C. *Essays on a science of mythology: The myth of the divine child and the mysteries of Eleusis.* Trans. by R. F. C. Hull. Princeton, N.J.: Princeton University Press, 1959–1963. (1941) Reprinted in *Collected works*, Vol. 9, Part 1, *op. cit.*, pp. 149–203.

———. Psychology and alchemy. (2nd ed.) (1944) Trans. in *Collected works*, Vol. 12, *op. cit.*

———. The phenomenology of the spirit in fairytales. (1946) Trans. in *Collected works*, Vol. 9, Part 1, *op. cit.*, pp. 207–254.

———. Psychology of the transference interpreted in conjunction with a set of alchemical illustrations. (1946) Trans. in *Collected works* Vol. 16, *op. cit.*, pp. 163–321.

———. On the nature of the psyche. (1947) Trans. in *Collected works*, Vol. 8, *op. cit.*, pp. 159–234.

————. Aion: Researches into the phenomenology of the self. (2nd ed.) (1951) Trans. in *Collected works,* Vol. 9, Part 2, *op. cit.*

————. Synchronicity: An acausal connecting principle. (1952) Trans. in *Collected works,* Vol. 8, *op. cit.,* pp. 417–519, & in C. G. Jung & W. Pauli, *The interpretation of nature and the psyche, op. cit.,* pp. 5–146.

————. Answer to Job. Trans. by R. F. C. Hull. London: Routledge & Kegan Paul, 1954. (1952) Reprinted in *Collected works,* Vol. 11, *op. cit.,* pp. 355–470.

————. Mysterium coniunctionis: An inquiry into the separation and synthesis of psychic opposites in alchemy. (2 vols.) (1955–1956) Trans. in *Collected works,* Vol. 14, *op. cit.*

————. Recent thoughts on schizophrenia. (1957) Reprinted in *Collected works,* Vol. 3, *op. cit.,* pp. 250–255.

————. *The undiscovered self (present and future).* Trans. by R. F. C. Hull. Boston: Little, Brown, 1958. (1957) Reprinted in *Collected works,* Vol. 10, *op. cit.,* pp. 245–305.

————. *Flying saucers: A modern myth of things seen in the skies.* Trans. by R. F. C. Hull. New York: Harcourt, Brace, 1959. (1958) Reprinted in *Collected works,* Vol. 10, *op. cit.,* pp. 307–433.

————. Schizophrenia. (1958) Trans. in *Collected works,* Vol. 3, *op. cit.,* pp. 256–271.

————. A psychological view of conscience. (1958) Trans. in *Collected works,* Vol. 10, *op. cit.,* pp. 437–455.

————. *Memories, Dreams, Reflections* (Expanded version). New York: Pantheon Books, 1973. (1961) **B**

————. *Erinnerungen, Träume, Gedanken.* Ed. by Aniela Jaffé. Zurich: Rascher, 1962. (Reprinted in trans. 1963) **B**

————, & Jones, E. *Conversations with Carl Jung and reactions from Ernest Jones.* Recorded by R. I. Evans. Princeton, N.J.: Van Nostrand, 1964. **B**

————. *C. G. Jung: Letters.* Selected & ed. by G. Adler in collab. with Aniela Jaffé. Princeton, N.J.: Princeton University Press, 1973. **B**

Beck & Molish, *Reflexes ;* Drever, *Sourcebook ;* Gruber, *Creative Thinking ;* Lindzey & Hall, *Personality ;* Matson, *Being ;* Sahakian, *Personality ;* Sahakian, *Psychology ;* Shipley, *Classics ;* Vetter, *Personality*

GUSTAV KAFKA
1883-1953
German Psychologist (14)

Kafka, G. Versuch einer kritischen Darstellung der neueren Anschauungen über das Ich-problem. *Arch. ges. Psychol.,* 1910, *19,* 1–241.

————. Ueber Grundlagen und Ziele einer wissenschaftlichen Tierpsychologie. *Arch. ges. Psychol.,* 1913, *29,* 1–15.

————. *Einführung in die Tierpsychologie auf experimenteller und ethologischer Grundlage.* I. *Die Sinne der Wirbellosen.* Leipzig: Barth, 1914.

————. Tierpsychologie. In G. Kafka (Ed.), *Handbuch der vergleichenden Psychologie.* Vol. 1. *Die Entwicklungsstufen des Seelenlebens.* Munich: Reinhardt, 1922, pp. 9–144.

————. Zum Begriff des "Psychischen" und seiner Entwicklungsgeschichte. *Arch. ges. Psychol.,* 1924, *48,* 193–212.

————. Ein Aussageversuch mit Kriminalbeamten. *Z. angew. Psychol.,* 1928, *31,* 173–201.

————. "Verstehende Psychologie" und Psychologie des Verstehens. *Arch. ges. Psychol.,* 1928, *65,* 7–40.

————. Zur Psychologie des Ekels. *Z. angew. Psychol.,* 1929, *34,* 1–46.

————. The change in the concepts of "world" and "surrounding-world." *J. gen. Psychol.,* 1936, *14,* 438–460.

————. Grundsätzliches zur Ausdruckspsychologie. *Acta Psychol.,* 1937, *3,* 273–314.

————. Zur Revision des Typusbegriffes. *Z. Psychol.,* 1938, *144,* 109–133.

————. Neue Notiz über einem im Traum angestellten Versuch, den Traum selbst zu analysieren. *Z. Psychol.,* 1943, *155,* 255–258.

————. Die metaphysischen Voraussetzungen der Psychologie. *Proc. Xth Int. Congr. Phil. Amsterdam 1948*, 1949, *1*, 240–243.

————. Ueber das Erlebnis des Lebensalters. *Acta Psychol.*, 1949, *6*, 178–189.

————. *Was sind Rassen?* Munich: Federmann, 1949.

————. Ueber Uraffekte. *Acta Psychol.*, 1950, *7*, 256–278.

————. Die Angst vor der Transzendenz. *Phil. Jb.*, 1950, *60*, 139–150.

————. Psychagogik und Psychotherapie. *Acta Psychol.*, 1951, *8*, 25–34.

————. Forschungsaufgaben der Psychologie in der Gegenwart. *Phil. Jb.*, 1951, *61*, 393–407.

————. Ueber die irrationalen Wurzeln des Judenhasses. *Jb. Psychol. Psychother.*, 1953, *1*, 289–320.

IMMANUEL KANT
1724-1804
German Philosopher (25)

Kant, I. *Kant's introduction to logic, and his essay on the mistaken subtilty of the four figures.* Trans. by T. K. Abbott. London: Longmans, Green, 1885. (Reprinted 1970) **C**

————. *Kant's cosmogony as in his essay on the retardation of the rotation of the earth and his natural history and theory of heavens.* Trans. by W. Hastie. Glasgow: Maclehose, 1900. **C**

————. *Kants gesammelte Schriften.* (23 vols.) Ed. by Königliche Preussische Akademie der Wissenschaften. Berlin: Reimer, 1902–1955. (Reprinted in part 1968–   ) **C**

————. *Werke.* (11 vols.) Ed. by E. Cassirer *et al.* Berlin: Cassirer, 1922–1923. **C**

————. *Lectures on ethics.* Trans. by L. Infield. New York: Harper & Row, 1963. (1924) **C**

————. *Selections.* Ed. by T. M. Greene. New York: Scribner's, 1929. **C**

————. *Immanuel Kant reader.* Ed. & trans. by R. B. Blakney. New York: Harper, 1960. **C**

————. *Philosophical correspondence, 1759–99.* Ed. and trans. by A. Zweig. Chicago: University of Chicago Press, 1967. **B C**

————. *Selected pre-critical writings and correspondence with Beck.* Trans. by G. B. Kerferd & D. E. Walford. New York: Barnes & Noble, 1968. **B C**

————. *Universal natural history and theory of the heavens.* New intro. by M. K. Munitz, & trans. by W. Hastie. Ann Arbor, Mich.: University of Michigan Press, 1969. (1755) Reprinted in German in *Werke*, Vol. 1, *op. cit.*, pp. 219–370.

————. *Observations on the feeling of the beautiful and sublime.* Trans. by J. T. Goldthwait. Berkeley, Calif.: University of California Press, 1965. (1764) Reprinted in German in *Werke*, Vol. 2, *op. cit.*, pp. 243–300.

————. Träume eines Geistersehers, erläutert durch Träume der Metaphysik. (1766) Reprinted in *Werke*, Vol. 2, *op. cit.*, pp. 329–390.

————. On the form and principles of the sensible and intelligible world. (1770) In *Selected pre-critical writings, op. cit.*, pp. 45–92. Reprinted in Latin in *Werke*, Vol. 2, *op. cit.*, pp. 401–436.

————. *Critique of pure reason.* (2nd ed.) Trans. by N. K. Smith. London: Macmillan, 1933. (1781) Reprinted in German in *Werke*, Vol. 3, *op. cit.*

————. *Critique of pure reason.* Intro. by A. D. Lindsay. Trans. by J. M. D. Meiklejohn. New York: Dutton, 1964. (1781) Reprinted in German in *Werke*, Vol. 3, *op. cit.*

————. *Prolegomena to any future metaphysics.* Trans. by L. W. Beck. New York: Liberal Arts Press, 1950. (1783) Reprinted in German in *Werke*, Vol. 4, *op. cit.*, pp. 1–139.

————. Rezensionen von J. G. Herders Ideen zur Philosophie der Geschichte der Menschheit. Parts 1, 2. (1785) Reprinted in *Werke*, Vol. 4, *op. cit.*, pp. 177–200.

————. *The moral law: Kant's groundwork of the metaphysics of morals.* Trans. & analysed by H. J. Paton. New York: Barnes & Noble, 1967. (1785) Reprinted in German in *Werke*, Vol. 4, *op. cit.*, pp. 241–324.

———. *The metaphysical foundations of natural science.* Trans by J. Ellington. Indianapolis, Ind.: Bobbs-Merrill, 1968. (1786) Reprinted in German in *Werke,* Vol. 4, *op. cit.,* pp. 367–478.

———. *The critique of practical reason.* Trans. by T. K. Abbott. New York: Longmans, Green, 1959. (1788) Reprinted in German in *Werke,* Vol. 5, *op. cit.,* pp. 1–176.

———. *First introduction to the critique of judgment.* Trans. by J. Haden. Indianapolis, Ind.: Bobbs-Merrill, 1965. (1788) Reprinted in German in *Werke,* Vol. 5, *op. cit.,* pp. 177–231.

———. *Kant's critique of teleological judgment. The critique of judgment.* Trans. & ed. by J. C. Meredith. Oxford: Clarendon Press, 1928. (1790) Reprinted in German in *Werke,* Vol. 5, *op. cit.,* pp. 233–568.

———. *Ueber eine Entdeckung nach der alle neue Kritik der reinen Vernunft durch eine ältere entbehrlich gemacht werden soll.* (1790) Reprinted in *Werke,* Vol. 6, *op. cit.,* pp. 7–71.

———. *Ueber das Organ der Seele.* (1796) Reprinted in *Werke,* Vol. 6, *op. cit.,* pp. 515–521.

———. *Der Streit der Fakultäten* (1798) Reprinted in *Werke,* Vol. 7, *op. cit.,* pp. 311–431.

———. *Anthropologie in pragmatischer Hinsicht.* (2nd ed.) (1798) Reprinted in *Werke,* Vol. 8, *op. cit.,* pp. 1–228, & in part trans. by A. E. Kroeger in *J. specul. Phil.,* 1875, *9,* 16–27, 239–245, 406–416 ; 1876, *10,* 319–323 ; 1877, *11,* 310–317, 353–363 ; 1879, *13,* 281–289 ; 1880, *14,* 154–169 ; 1881, *15,* 62–66 ; 1882, *16,* 47–52, 395–413.

———. *The classification of mental disorders.* (Excerpt from *Anthropologie in pragmatischer Hinsicht.*) Trans. & ed. by C. T. Sullivan. Doylestown, Pa.: Doylestown Foundation, 1964. (1798)

———. *The educational theory of Immanuel Kant.* (Lecture-notes on pedagogy.) Trans. by E. F. Buchner. Philadelphia: Lippincott, 1904. (1803) Reprinted in German in *Werke,* Vol. 8, *op. cit.,* pp. 453–508.

———. *Preisschrift über die Fortschritte der Metaphysik seit Leibniz und Wolff.* (1804) Reprinted in *Werke,* Vol. 8, *op. cit.,* pp. 233–321.

Ackermann, *Theories ;* Brinton, *Age Reason ;* Count, *Race ;* Herrnstein & Boring, *Source Book ;* Hutchins, *Great Books ;* Lawrence & O'Connor, *Phenomenology ;* Madden, *Scientific Thought ;* Margolis, *Introduction ;* Price, *Education ;* Rand, *Classical Philosophers ;* Rand, *Moralists ;* Sahakian, *Psychology ;* Slotkin, *Anthropology*

THEODORE KARWOSKI
1896-1957
American Psychologist (11)

Karwoski, T., & Christensen, E. O. A test for art appreciation. *J. educ. Psychol.,* 1926, *17,* 187–194.

———. Variations toward purple in the visual after-image. *Amer. J. Psychol.,* 1929, *41,* 625–636.

———. The memory value of size. *J. exp. Psychol.,* 1931, *14,* 539–554.

———. Psychophysics and mescal intoxication. *J. gen. Psychol.,* 1936, *15,* 212–220.

Serrat, W. D., & ———. An investigation of the effect of auditory stimulation on visual sensitivity. *J. exp. Psychol.,* 1936, *19,* 604–611.

Butler, J. R., & ———. *Human psychology.* New York: Pitman, 1936.

———, & Crook, M. N. The bleaching effect. *J. gen. Psychol.,* 1937, *16,* 259–264.

———, & Crook, M. N. Studies in the peripheral retina. I. The Purkinje after-image. *J. gen. Psychol.,* 1937, *16,* 323–356.

———, & Odbert, H. S. Color-music. *Psychol. Monogr.,* 1938, *50,* No. 222.

———, & Warrener, H. Studies in the peripheral retina. II. The Purkinje after-image on the near foveal area of the retina. *J. gen. Psychol.,* 1942, *26,* 129–151.

Odbert, H. S., ———, & Eckerson, A. B. Studies in synesthetic thinking. I. Musical and verbal association of color and mood. *J. gen. Psychol.,* 1942, *26,* 153–173.

————, Odbert, H. S., & Osgood, C. E. Studies in synesthetic thinking. II. The roles of form in visual responses to music. *J. gen. Psychol.*, 1942, *26*, 199–222.

————, & Perry, W. B. Studies in the peripheral retina. III. The Purkinje after-image bulge. *J. gen. Psychol.*, 1943, *29*, 63–85.

————, Gramlich, F. W., & Arnott, P. Psychological studies in semantics. I. Free association reactions to words, drawings, and objects. *J. soc. Psychol.*, 1944, *20*, 233–247.

————, & Berthold, F., Jr. Psychological studies in semantics. II. Reliability of free association tests. *J. soc. Psychol.*, 1945, *22*, 87–102.

————, & Schacter, J. Psychological studies in semantics. III. Reaction times for similarity and difference. *J. soc. Psychol.*, 1948, *28*, 103–120.

————, & Lloyd, V. V. Studies in vision. V. The role of chromatic aberration in depth perception. *J. gen. Psychol.*, 1951, *44*, 159–173.

————, & Wayner, M., Jr. Studies in vision. IV. The interactions of rods and cones in after-sensations. *J. gen. Psychol.*, 1951, *44*, 215–233.

Stagner, R., & ————. *Psychology*. New York: McGraw-Hill, 1952.

————. The cognitive processes. In A. A. Roback (Ed.), *Present-day psychology: An original survey of departments, branches, methods and phases, including clinical and dynamic psychology*. New York: Philosophical Library, 1955, pp. 77–102.

DAVID KATZ
1884-1953
German Psychologist (25)

Katz, D. Ein Beitrag zur Kenntnis der Kinderzeichnungen. *Z. Psychol.*, 1906, *41*, 241–256.

————. Experimentelle Beiträge zur Psychologie des Vergleichs im Gebiete des Zeitsinns. *Z. Psychol.*, 1906, *42*, 302–340, 414–450.

————. *The world of colour.* (2nd ed.) Trans. by R. B. MacLeod & C. W. Fox. London: Kegan Paul, Trench & Truebner, 1935. (1911) (Reprinted 1970)

————. Die Erscheinungsweisen der Farben und ihre Beeinflussung durch die individuelle Erfahrung. *Z. Psychol.*, 1911, Suppl. 7. (Also Leipzig: Barth, 1911) (Reprinted 1970)

Révész, G., & ————. Zur Kenntnis des Lichtsinnes der Nachtvögel. *Z. Sinnespsychol.*, 1913, *48*, 165–170.

————. *Studien zur Kinderpsychologie.* Leipzig: Quelle & Meyer, 1913.

————. *Psychologie und mathematischer Unterricht.* Leipzig: Teubner, 1913.

————. *Die Erscheinungsweisen der Tasteindrücke.* Rostock: Kommissionsverlag-Warkenten, 1920.

Révész. G., & ————. Experimentelle Studien zur vergleichenden Psychologie. *Z. angew. Psychol.*, 1921, *18*, 307–320.

————. *Zur Psychologie des Amputierten und seiner Prothese.* Leipzig: Barth, 1921.

————, & Toll, A. Die Messung von Charakter und Begabungsunterschieden bei Tieren (Versuche mit Hühnern.) *Z. Psychol.*, 1923, *93*, 287–311.

————. Der Aufbau der Tastwelt. *Z. Psychol.*, 1925, Suppl. 11. (Also Leipzig: Barth, 1925) (Reprinted 1970)

————, & Katz, Rosa. *Conversations with children.* London: Kegan Paul, Trench & Truebner, 1936. (1927)

————. Sammelreferat über Arbeiten aus dem Gebiet der Farbenwahrnehmung. 1 & 2. *Psychol. Forsch.*, 1928, *11*, 136–156, 172; 1929, *13*, 260–279.

————. Psychologische Probleme des Hungers und Appetits, insbesondere beim Kinde. *Z. Kinderforsch.*, 1928, *34*, 158–197.

————, & Katz, Rosa. Psychologische Untersuchungen über Hunger und Appetit. *Arch. ges. Psychol.*, 1928, *65*, 269–320.

————. The development of conscience in the child as revealed by his talks with adults. In M. L. Reymert (Ed.), *Feelings and emotions: The Wittenberg symposium*. Worcester, Mass.: Clark University Press, 1928, pp. 332–343.

———. *The world of colour.* Trans. by R. B. MacLeod & C. W. Fox. London: Paul, 1935. (1930)

———. *The vibratory sense and other lectures.* University of Maine Studies, Second Series, No. 14. Orono, Me.: University of Maine Press, 1930.

———. *Hunger und Appetit: Untersuchungen zur medizinischen Psychologie.* Leipzig: Barth, 1932.

———. Some fundamental laws of psychology of needs: Hunger, *J. Pers.,* 1935, *3,* 312–326.

———. *Animals and men: Studies in comparative psychology.* New York: Longmans, Green, 1937. (Reprinted 1971)

———. *Gestalt psychology: Its nature and significance.* (2nd ed.) Trans. by R. Tyson. New York: Ronald Press, 1950. (1942)

———. Gestaltgesetze des Körpererlebnisses. *Acta Paediat.,* 1943, *30,* 389–405.

———. *Gestaltpsychologie.* (4th ed.) Rev. by W. Metzger, M. Stadler, & H. Crabus. Basel: Schwabe, 1969. (1944)

———. *Psychological atlas.* Trans. by F. Gaynor. New York: Philosophical Library, 1948. (1945) (Reprinted 1968)

———, & Künnapas, T. Propriozeptiver Reflex und Willenshandlung. *Acta Paediat.,* 1946, *33,* 1–12.

———. *Mensch und Tier. Studien zur vergleichenden Psychologie.* Zurich: Conzett & Huber, 1948.

———. The scriptochronograph. *Quart. J. exp. Psychol.,* 1948, *1,* 53–56.

———. Gestalt laws of mental work. *Brit. J. Psychol.,* 1948–1949, *39,* 175–183.

———, & MacLeod, R. B. The mandible principle in muscular action. *Acta Psychol.,* 1949, *6,* 33–39.

———, & Seichter, H. Graphological experiments with the scriptochronograph. *Acta Psychol.,* 1950, *7,* 279–287.

———. Connective inhibitions during thought processes. In M. L. Reymert (Ed.), *Feelings and emotions: The Mooseheart symposium.* New York: McGraw-Hill, 1950, pp. 203–210.

———. Some graphological experiments with the scriptochronograph. *Année psychol.,* 1951, *51,* 585–591.

———. David Katz. In E. G. Boring *et al.* (Eds.), *A history of psychology in autobiography.* Vol. 4. Worcester, Mass.: Clark University Press, 1952, pp. 189–211.   **B**

———. Der sozialpsychologische Faktor als Organisator unseres Gedächtnisses. *Schweiz. Z. Psychol.,* 1952, *11,* 252–265.

———. *Studien zur experimentellen Psychologie.* Basel: Schwabe, 1953.

———. Gehobene Gewichte. Variationen eines alten Themas der experimentellen Psychologie. *Wiener Z. Phil., Psychol., Pädag.,* 1953, *20,* 219–223.

———. Zur Frage der Problemfindung in der Psychologie. *Jb. Psychol. Psychother.,* 1953, *1,* 484–489.

———. Psychologie des Sicherheitsmarginals. *Acta Psychol.,* 1953, *9,* 255–273.

———. Fünf Jahrzehnte im Dienst der psychologischen Forschung: Autobiographische Aufzeichnungen und Bibliographie. (Expanded version of autobiography of 1952, with bibliography.) *Psychol. Beitr.,* 1954, *1,* 470–491.

B Bl

Beardslee, *Perception*

TRUMAN LEE KELLEY
1884-1961
American Psychologist (21)

Kelley, T. L. Comparable measures. *J. educ. Psychol.,* 1914, *5,* 589–595.

———. *Educational guidance: An experimental study in the analysis and prediction of ability of high school pupils.* New York: Columbia University Teachers College, 1914.

———. Principles underlying the classifications of men. *J. appl. Psychol.,* 1919, *3,* 50–67.

———. A new measure of dispersion. *Quart. Publ. Amer. Stat. Ass.,* 1920–1921, *17,* 743–749.

———. Certain properties of index numbers. *Quart. Publ. Amer. Stat. Ass.,* 1921, *17,* 826–841.

———. The reliability of test scores. *J. educ. Res.,* 1921, *3,* 370–379.

———. The principles and techniques of mental measurement. *Amer. J. Psychol.,* 1923, *34,* 408–432.

———. *Statistical method.* (2nd ed.) New York: Macmillan, 1924. (1923)

———. The applicability of the Spearman-Brown formula for the measurement of reliability. *J. educ. Psychol.,* 1925, *16,* 300–303.

———. *The influence of nurture upon native differences.* New York: Macmillan, 1926.

———. *Interpretation of educational measurements.* Yonkers-on-Hudson, N. Y.: World Book, 1927.

———. *Crossroads in the mind of man.* Stanford, Calif.: Stanford University Press, 1928.

Berks, Barbara S., & ———. Comments upon statistical hazards in nature-nurture investigations. *Yearb. Nat. Soc. Stud. Educ.,* 1928, *27*(1); 33–38.

———, & Shen, E. General statistical principles. In C. Murchison (Ed.), *The foundations of experimental psychology.* Worcester, Mass.: Clark University Press, 1929, pp. 832–854.

———, & Shen, E. The statistical treatment of certain typical problems. In C. Murchison (Ed.), *The foundations of experimental psychology.* Worcester, Mass.: Clark University Press, 1929, pp. 855–883.

———, & McNemar, Q. Doolittle versus Kelley-Salisbury iteration method for computing multiple regression coefficients. *J. Amer. Stat. Ass.,* 1929, *24,* 164–169.

———. *Scientific method: Its function in research and in education.* New York: Macmillan, 1932. (1929)

———. *The inheritance of mental traits.* In C. Murchison (Ed.), *Psychologies of 1930.* Worcester, Mass.: Clark University Press, 1930, pp. 423–443.

———, & Krey, A. C. *Tests and measurements in the social sciences.* New York: Scribner's, 1934.

———. *Essential traits of mental life: The purposes and principles underlying the selection and measurement of independent mental factors, together with computational tables.* Cambridge: Harvard University Press, 1935.

———. An unbiassed correlation ratio measure. *Proc. Nat. Acad. Sci.,* 1935, *21,* 554–559.

———. *The Kelley statistical tables.* New York: Macmillan, 1938.

———. Mental factors of no importance. *J. educ. Psychol.,* 1939, *30,* 139–142.

———. *Talents and tasks: Their conjunction in a democracy for wholesome living and national defense.* Cambridge: Harvard University Press, 1940.

———. The future psychology of mental traits. *Psychometrika,* 1940, *5,* 1–15.

———. The reliability coefficient. *Psychometrika,* 1942, *7,* 75–83.

———. The evidence for periodicity in short time series. *J. Amer. Stat. Ass.,* 1943, *38,* 319–326.

———. *Fundamentals of statistics.* Cambridge: Harvard University Press, 1947.

Jenkins & Paterson, *Individual Differences;* Wiseman, *Intelligence*

CHESTER ELIJAH KELLOGG
1888-1948
American Psychologist (13)

Kellogg, C. E., & Yerkes, R. M. A graphic method of recording maze reactions. *J. anim. Behav.,* 1914, *4,* 50–55.

———. Alternation and interference of feelings. *Psychol. Monogr.,* 1915, *18,* No. 79.

———. Relative values of intelligence tests and matriculation examinations as means of estimating probable success in college. *School & Soc.*, 1929, *30*, 893–896.

————. A social-psychological version of the aesthetic attitude. *J. soc. Psychol.*, 1930, *1*, 429–434.

————, & Morton, N. W. Abilities and unemployment. *Personnel J.*, 1934, *13*, 169–175.

————, & Morton, N. W. Revised Beta examination. *Personnel J.*, 1934, *13*, 94–100.

————. The problem of principal components. I. Derivation of Hotelling's method from Thurstone's. *J. educ. Psychol.*, 1936, *27*, 512–520.

————. The problem of principal components. II. The argument for communalities. *J. educ. Psychol.*, 1936, *27*, 581–590.

————. Dr. J. B. Rhine and extra-sensory perception. *J. abnorm. soc. Psychol.*, 1936, *31*, 190–193.

————. The problems of matching and sampling in the study of extra-sensory perception. *J. abnorm. soc. Psychol.*, 1937, *32*, 462–479.

————. New evidence (?) for "extra-sensory perception." *Sci. Mon.*, N.Y., 1937, *45*, 331–341.

————. A note in reply to Mr. Charles E. Stuart. *J. abnorm. soc. Psychol.*, 1938, *33*, 521–526.

————. The statistical techniques of ESP. *J. gen. Psychol.*, 1938, *19*, 383–390.

————. A correction for Thurstone's multiple factor analysis. *Canad. J. Psychol.*, 1948, *2*, 137–139.

GEORGE ALEXANDER KELLY
1905-1967
American Psychologist (17)

Kelly, G. A. *Clinical psychology and personality: The selected papers of George Kelly.* Ed. by B. Maher. New York: Wiley, 1969. **B Bl C**

————. The practical effectiveness of certain types of recommendations made by a psychological clinic. *J. gen. Psychol.*, 1938, *19*, 211–217.

————. A method of diagnosing personality in the psychological clinic. *Psychol. Rec.*, 1938, *2*, 95–111.

————. The assumption of an originally homogeneous universe and some of its statistical implications. *J. Psychol.*, 1938, *5*, 201–208.

Howard, A. R., & ————. A theoretical approach to psychological movement. *J. abnorm. soc. Psychol.*, 1954, *49*, 399–404.

————. The psychology of personal constructs. Vol. 1: *A theory of personality.* Vol. 2: *Clinical diagnosis and psychotherapy.* New York: Norton, 1955.

————. Man's construction of his alternatives. In G. Lindzey (Ed.), *Assessment of human motives.* New York: Rinehart, 1958, pp. 33–64. Reprinted in *Clinical psychology and personality, op. cit.,* pp. 66–93.

————. The theory and technique of assessment. *Annu. rev. Psychol.*, 1958, *9*, 323–352.

————. Suicide: The personal construct point of view. In E. S. Schneidman & N. L. Farberow (Eds.), *The cry for help.* New York: McGraw-Hill, 1961, pp. 255–280.

————. Europe's matrix of decision. In M. R. Jones (Ed.), *Nebraska symposium on motivation, 1962.* Lincoln, Neb.: University of Nebraska Press, 1962, pp. 83–123.

————. Discussion: Aldous, the personable computer. In S. Tomkins & S. Messick (Eds.), *Computer simulation of personality: Report of the Princeton Conference.* New York: Wiley, 1963, pp. 221–229.

————. Nonparametric factor analysis of personality theories. *J. indiv. Psychol.*, 1963, *19*, 115–147. Reprinted in *Clinical psychology and personality, op. cit.,* pp. 301–332.

————. Personal construct theory as a line of inference. *J. Psychol.*, Pakistan, 1964, *1*, 80–93.

————. The language of hypothesis: Man's psychological instrument. *J. indiv. Psychol.*, 1964, *20*, 137–152. Reprinted in *Clinical psychology and personality, op. cit.,* pp. 147–162.

————. The strategy of psychological research. *Bull. Brit. Psychol. Soc.*, 1965, *18*, 1–15. Reprinted in *Clinical psychology and personality, op. cit.,* pp. 114–132.

———. The threat of aggression. *J. hum. Psychol.,* 1965, *5,* 195–201. Reprinted in *Clinical psychology and personality, op. cit.,* pp. 281–288.

———. Sin and psychotherapy. (1962) In O. H. Mowrer (Ed.), *Morality and mental health.* Chicago: Rand McNally, 1966, pp. 365–381. Reprinted in *Clinical psychology and personality, op. cit.,* pp. 165–188 ; & in W. E. Vinacke (Ed.), *Readings in general psychology.* New York: American Book, 1968, pp. 123–139.

———. A psychology of the optimal man. In A. R. Mahrer (Ed.), *Goals of psychotherapy.* New York: Appleton-Century-Crofts, 1966, pp. 238–258.

———. The autobiography of a theory. (1969) In *Clinical psychology and personality, op. cit.,* pp. 46–65.   **B**

———. A brief introduction to personal construct theory. In *Readings for a cognitive theory of personality.* Ed. by J. C. Mancuso. New York: Holt, Rinehart & Winston, 1970, pp. 27–58. Reprinted in D. Bannister (Ed.), *Perspectives in personal construct theory.* New York: Academic Press, 1970, pp. 1–29.

———. Behaviour is an experiment. In D. Bannister (Ed.), *Perspectives in personal construct theory.* New York: Academic Press, 1970, pp. 255–269.

JOHANNES KEPLER
1571-1630
German Astronomer-Mathematician (19)

Kepler, J. *Johannes Kepler in seinen Briefen.* (2 vols.) Ed. by M. Caspar & W. v. Dyck. Munich: Oldenbourg, 1930.   **B Bl C**

———. *Gesammelte Werke.* (18 vols.) Ed. by W. v. Dyck & M. Caspar. Munich: Beck, 1937–1969.   **B Bl C**

———. *Ad vitellionem paralipomena quibus astronomiae pars optica traditur.* Frankfurt: Marnium et haeredes Austriae, 1604. (Reprinted 1968)

———. De modo visionis. In A. C. Crombie, Kepler: De modo visionis. A translation from the Latin of Ad Vitallionem paralipomena, V,

2, and related passages on the formation of the retinal image. (1604) In Various, *Mélanges Alexandre Koyré: I. L'aventure de la science.* Paris: Hermann, 1964, pp. 135–172.

———. Astronomia pars optica. (1604) In *Gesammelte Werke,* Vol. 2, *op. cit.*

———. Neue Astronomie (Astronomia nova). (1609) In *Gesammelte Werke,* Vol. 3, *op. cit.*

———. *Astronomia nova aitiologetos.* Brussels: Culture et Civilisation, 1968. (1609)

———. *Kepler's conversation with Galileo's sidereal messenger.* Trans. & ed. by E. Rosen. New York: Johnson, 1965. (1610)

———. *Dioptrik.* Leipzig: Engelmann, 1909, (1611)

———. Epitome of Copernican astronomy. Books 4 & 5. Trans. by C. G. Wallis. In *Great books of the Western world.* Vol. 16. Chicago: Encyclopaedia Britannica, 1939, pp. 839–1004. (1618–1621)

———. The harmonies of the world. Part V. Trans. by C. G. Wallis. In *Great books of the Western world.* Vol. 16. Chicago: Encyclopaedia Britannica, 1952, pp. 1005–1085. (1619)

———. *Kepler's Somnium: The dream, or posthumous work on lunar astronomy.* Trans. with commentary by E. Rosen. Madison, Wisc.: University of Wisconsin Press, 1967. (1634)

Hall, *Nature's Laws ;* Herrnstein & Boring, *Source Book ;* Hutchins, *Great Books ;* Newman, *Mathematics ;* Popkin, *Philosophy ;* Schwartz & Bishop, *Moments Discovery*

FEDERICO KIESOW
1858-1940
German-Italian Psychologist (19)

Kiesow, F. Beiträge zur physiologischen Psychologie des Geschmackssinnes. *Phil. Stud ,* 1894, *10,* 329–368, 523–561 ; 1896, *12,* 255–278, 464–473.

———. Ueber die Wirkung des Cocain und der Gymnemasäure auf die Schleimhaut der Zunge und des Mundraums. *Phil. Stud.,* 1894, *9,* 510–527.

————. Versuche mit Mossos Sphygmomano-meter über die durch psychische Erregungen hervorgerufenen Veränderungen des Blutdrucks beim Menschen. *Phil. Stud.,* 1895, *11,* 41–60.

————. Untersuchungen über Temperaturempfin-dungen. *Phil. Stud.,* 1895, *11,* 135–145.

————. Investigation of cutaneous sensibility. *Psychol. Rev.,* 1896, *3,* 188–191.

————. Sur l'excitation du sens de pression produite par des déformations constantes de la peau. *Arch. ital. Biol.,* 1896–1897, *26,* 417–442.

————. Zur Psychophysiologie der Mundhöhle. *Phil. Stud.,* 1898, *14,* 567–588.

————. Schmeckversuche an einzelnen Papillen. *Phil. Stud.,* 1898, *14,* 591–615.

————. Contributo alla psico-fisiologia della cavita orale. *Arch. ital. Otol.,* 1899, *9,* 129–146.

————. Sur la méthode pour étudier les senti-ments simples. *Arch. ital. Biol.,* 1899, *32,* 159–164.

Frey, M. v., & ————. Ueber die Funktion der Tastkörperchen. *Z. Psychol.,* 1899, *20,* 126–163.

————. Contributo alla psico-fisiologia del senso tattile. *Gior. R. Acad. Med., Turino,* 1900, *63,* 1–8.

————, & Hahn, R. Beobachtungen über die Emp-findlichkeit der hinteren Teile des Mundraumes für Tast-, Schmerz-, Temperatur- und Ge-schmacksreize. *Z. Psychol.,* 1901, *26,* 383–417.

————, & Hahn, R. Ueber Geschmacksempfin-dungen im Kehlkopf. *Z. Psychol.,* 1902, *27,* 80–94.

————. Ueber Verteilung und Empfindlichkeit der Tastpunkte. *Phil. Stud.,* 1902, *19,* 260–309.

————. Zur Psychophysiologie der Mundhöhle nebst Beobachtungen über Funktionen des Tast- und Schmerzapparates und einige Bemer-kungen über die wahrscheinlichen Tastorgane der Zungenspitze und des Lippenrots. *Z. Psychol.,* 1903, *33,* 424–443.

————. Zur Frage nach der Fortpflanzungsge-schwindigkeit der Erregung in sensiblen Nerven des Menschen. *Z. Psychol.,* 1903, *33,* 444–452.

————. Ein Beitrag zur Frage nach den Reaktions-zeiten der Geschmacksempfindungen. *Z. Psy-chol.,* 1903, *33,* 453–461.

————. Ueber die einfachen Reaktionszeiten der taktilen Belastungsempfindung. *Z. Psychol.,* 1904, *35,* 8–49.

————. Ueber die Tastempfindlichkeit der Kör-peroberfläche für punktuelle mechanische Reize (Nachtrag). *Z. Psychol.,* 1904, *35,* 234–251.

————. Ueber einige geometrisch-optische Täu-schungen. *Arch. ges. Psychol.,* 1906, *6,* 289–305.

————. Ueber sogenannte "frei steigende" Vor-stellungen und plötzlich auftretende Aenderun-gen des Gemütszustandes. Sind die Verbin-dungsglieder, welche hierbei in Frage kommen, unbewusst oder unbemerkt? *Arch. ges. Psychol.,* 1906, *6,* 357–390.

————. Kurze Zusammenfassung des Inhalts der vorstehenden Arbeit. *Arch. ges. Psychol.,* 1910, *16,* 346–351.

————. Beobachtungen über die Reaktionszeiten momentaner Schalleindrücke. *Arch. ges. Psy-chol.,* 1910, *16,* 352–375.

————, & Ponzo, M. Beobachtungen über die Reaktionszeiten der Temperaturempfindungen. *Arch. ges. Psychol.,* 1910, *16,* 376–396.

————. Beobachtungen über die Reaktionszeiten der schmerzhaften Stichempfindung, nebst einigen Vorbemerkungen über die Entwicklung unserer Kenntnis von den Schmerzempfin-dungen seit J. Müller und E. H. Weber. *Arch. ges. Psychol.,* 1910, *18,* 265–304.

————, & Ponzo, M. Observations sur les temps de réaction pour les sensations thermiques. *Arch. ital. Biol.,* 1911, *56,* 216–224.

————. Ueber die Versuche von E. H. Weber und M. Scabodföldi. *Arch. ges. Psychol.,* 1911–1912, *22,* 50–104.

————. Sul concetto di senso e sulla classifica-zione delle sensazioni. *Riv. Psicol. norm. pat.,* 1912, *8,* 136–152.

————. Osservazioni sopra il rapporto tra due oggetti visti separatamente coi due occhi. *Arch. ital. Psicol.,* 1920–1921, *1,* 3–38, 239–290.

———. Ueber Metallglanz im stereoskopischen Sehen. *Arch. ges. Psychol.,* 1922, *43,* 1–10.

———. Ueber die taktile Unterschiedsempfindlichkeit bei suczessiver Reizung einzelner Empfindungsorgane. *Arch. ges. Psychol.,* 1922, *43,* 11–23.

———. Ueber bilaterale Mischung von Licht- und Geruchsempfindungen. *Arch. néerl. Physiol.,* 1922, *7,* 281–284.

———. Scienza della natura e psicologia empirica. *Arch. ital. Psicol.,* 1923, *2,* 73–104 ; 1925, *4,* 1–19.

———. Si verificano nei bambini e nei fanciulli immagini consecutive contrarie? Contributo allo studio dei fenomeni eidetici. *Arch. ital. Psicol.,* 1924, *3,* 121–132.

———. Zur Frage nach der Gültigkeit des Weber'schen Gesetzes im Gebiete der Tastempfindungen. *Arch. ges. Psychol.,* 1924, *47,* 1–13.

———. Ueber die Vergleichung linearer Strecken und ihre Beziehung zum Weber'schen Gesetze. *Arch. ges. Psychol.,* 1925, *52,* 61–90, *53,* 433–446.

———. Zur Kritik der Eidetik. *Arch. ges. Psychol.,* 1925, *53,* 447–484.

———. Sul confronto di tratti lineari e sua relazione con la legge di Weber. *Arch. ital. Psicol.,* 1925, *4,* 20–44, 157–169 ; 1926, *4,* 20–44 ; 1928, *7,* 38–60.

———. Ueber die schmerzfreie Zone der Wangenschleimhaut. *Arch. ges. Psychol.,* 1926, *55,* 37–46.

———. Kritische Bemerkungen zur Eidetik, nebst an Eidetikern und Nichteidetikern angestellten Beobachtungen. *Arch. ges. Psychol.,* 1927, *59,* 339–460.

———. The problem of the condition of arousal of the pure sensation of cutaneous pain. *J. gen. Psychol.,* 1928, *1,* 199–212.

———. The feeling-tone of sensation. In M. L. Reymert (Ed.), *Feelings and emotions: The Wittenberg symposium.* Worcester, Mass.: Clark University Press, 1928, 89–103.

———. Sulla frequenza dei sogni gustativi ed olfattivi. *Arch. ital. Psicol.,* 1929, *7,* 226–231.

———. Autobiography. In C. Murchison (Ed.), *History of psychology in autobiography.* Vol. 1. Worcester, Mass.: Clark University Press, 1930, pp. 163–190.

———. Ueber die Entstehung der Braunempfindung. *Neue psychol. Stud.,* 1930, *6*(1), 119–130.

B

ALFRED CHARLES KINSEY
1894-1956
American Biologist (21)

Kinsey, A. C. *Methods in biology.* Philadelphia: Lippincott, 1937.

———. Homosexuality: Criteria for a hormonal explanation of the homosexual. *J. clin. Endocrinol.,* 1941, *1,* 424–428.

———, Pomeroy, W. B., & Martin, C. E. *Sexual behavior in the human male.* Philadelphia: Saunders, 1948.

———, Pomeroy, W. B., Martin, C. E., & Gebhard, P. H. Concepts of normality and abnormality in sexual behavior. In P. H. Hoch & J. Zubin (Eds.), *Psychosexual development in health and disease.* New York: Grune & Stratton, 1949, pp. 11–32.

———, Pomeroy, W. B., Martin, C. E., & Gebhard, P. H. *Sexual behavior in the human female.* Philadelphia: Saunders, 1953.

———, et al. The Cochran-Mosteller-Tukey report on the Kinsey study: A symposium. *J. Amer. Stat. Ass.,* 1955, *50,* 811–829.

Dennis, *Readings Developmental ;* Wrenn, *Contributions*

EDWIN ASBURY KIRKPATRICK
1862-1937
American Psychologist (11)

Kirkpatrick, E. A. *Inductive psychology: An introduction to the study of mental phenomena.* New York: Kellogg, 1895. (1893)

———. An experimental study of memory. *Psychol. Rev.,* 1894, *1,* 602–609.

———. The development of voluntary movement. *Psychol. Rev.,* 1899, *6,* 275–281.

———. Individual tests of school children. *Psychol. Rev.,* 1900, *7,* 274–280.

———. *Fundamentals of child study.* (4th ed.) New York: Macmillan, 1929. (1903)

———. A broader basis for psychology necessary. *J. Phil.,* 1907, *4,* 542–546.

———. *Genetic psychology.* New York: Macmillan, 1909.

———. *Individual in the making.* Boston: Houghton Mifflin, 1911.

———. An experiment in memorizing versus incidental learning. *J. educ. Psychol.,* 1914, *5,* 405–412.

———. *Fundamentals of sociology.* Boston: Houghton Mifflin, 1916.

———. Intelligence tests in Massachusetts normal schools. *School & Soc.,* 1922, *15,* 55–60.

LUDWIG KLAGES
1872-1956
German-Swiss Psychologist (15)

Klages, L. *Mensch und Erde. 10 Abhandlungen.* (6th ed.) Stuttgart: Kröner, 1956. (1920) **C**

———. *Zur Ausdruckslehre und Charakterkunde. Gesammelte Abhandlungen.* Heidelberg: Kampmann, 1927. Reprinted in part in *Sämtliche Werke,* Vol. 6, *vide infra.* **C**

———. *Sämtliche Werke.* (Ult. 10 vols.) Ed. by E. Frauchiger *et al.* Bonn: Bouvier, 1964.
B Bl C

———. *The science of character.* Trans. by W. H. Johnston. (5th & 6th ed.) Cambridge: Sci-Art, 1932. (1910)

———. *Die Grundlagen der Charakterkunde.* (13th ed.) Bonn: Bouvier, 1966. (1910)

———. *Grundlegung der Wissenschaft vom Ausdruck.* (9th ed.) (2 vols.) Bonn: Bouvier, 1970. (1913) Earlier edition reprinted in *Sämtliche Werke,* Vol. 6, *op. cit.,* pp. 315–665.

———. *Handschrift und Charakter. Gemeinverständlicher Abriss der graphologischen Technik.* (26th ed.) Bonn: Bouvier, 1968. (1917) Reprinted in earlier edition in *Sämtliche Werke,* Vol. 7, *op. cit.,* pp. 285–540.

———. Bemerkungen über die Schranken des Goethe'schen Menschen. (1917) Reprinted in *Mensch und Erde, op. cit.,* pp. 62–75.

———. *Vom Wesen des Bewusstseins. Aus einer lebenswissenschaftlichen Vorlesung.* (4th ed.) Munich: Barth, 1955. (1921)

———. *Vom kosmogonischen Eros.* (7th ed.) Bonn: Bouvier, 1968. (1922)

———. *Einführung in die Psychologie der Handschrift.* (2nd ed.) Heidelberg: Kampmann, 1928. (1924) Reprinted in *Sämtliche Werke,* Vol. 7, *op. cit.,* pp. 541–591.

———. *Die psychologischen Errungenschaften Nietzsches.* (3rd ed.) Bonn: Bouvier, 1958. (1926)

———. *Vorschule der Charakterkunde.* (3rd ed.) Leipzig: Barth, 1942. (1928)

———. *Der Geist als Widersacher der Seele.* (4th ed.) (3 vols. in 4.) Bonn: Bouvier, 1960. (1929–1932) Reprinted in *Sämtliche Werke,* Vol. 1, *op. cit.*

———. *Graphologisches Lesebuch.* (5th ed.) Munich: Barth, 1954. (1930) Reprinted in *Sämtliche Werke,* Vol. 8, *op. cit.,* pp. 337–406.

———. *Goethe als Seelenforscher.* (3rd ed.) Zurich: Hirzel, 1949. (1932)

———. *Graphologie.* (4th ed.) Heidelberg: Quelle & Meyer, 1949. (1932) Reprinted in *Sämtliche Werke,* Vol. 8, *op. cit.,* pp. 407–475.

———. *Vom Wesen des Rhythmus.* (2nd ed.) Leipzig: Gropengiesser, 1944. (1933)

———. *Vom Sinn des Lebens.* Ed. by H. Kern. Hamburg: Saucke, 1940.

———. *Ursprünge der Seelenforschung.* (2nd ed.) Stuttgart: Reclam, 1952. (1942)

———. Randbemerkungen zu Pophals "Psychophysiologie der Spannungserscheinungen in der

Handschrift." *Z. angew. Psychol.,* 1942, *63,* 38–99. Reprinted in *Sämtliche Werke,* Vol. 8, *op. cit.,* pp. 477–536.

———. *Rhythmen und Runen. Nachlass.* Leipzig: Barth, 1944.

———. Wie finden wir die Seele des Nebenmenschen? (Behaviorismus und Physiognomik.) *Kongressber. Berufsverb. Dtsch. Psychologen,* Bonn, 1948, *2,* 65–88. (Also Hamburg: Nolte, 1948.)

———. *Die Sprache als Quelle der Seelenkunde.* Zurich: Hirzel, 1948.

———. *Was die Graphologie nicht kann. Ein Brief.* Zurich: Speer, 1949. Reprinted in *Sämtliche Werke,* Vol. 8, *op. cit.,* pp. 537–559.

———. Vom Traumbewusstsein. Hamburg: Saucke, 1952..

———. Von den Mitteln zur Beglaubigung graphologischer Befunde. (Wiederabdruck aus den *Graphologischen Monatsheften,* 1906.) *Z. Menschenkd.,* 1956, *20,* 331–338.

Arnold, *Emotion*

MELANIE KLEIN
1882-1960
German-English Psychoanalyst (17)

Klein, Melanie. *Contributions to psycho-analysis, 1921–1945.* Intro. by E. Jones. London: Hogarth Press, 1948.   **C**

———. The development of a child. *Int. J. Psycho-Anal.,* 1923, *4,* 419–474. (1921) Reprinted in *Contributions to psycho-analysis, op. cit.,* pp. 13–67.

———. Criminal tendencies in normal children. *Brit. J. Med. Psychol.,* 1927, 7, 177–192.

———, *et al.* Symposium on child-analysis. *Int. J. Psycho-Anal.,* 1927, *8,* 339–380. Reprinted in *Contributions to psycho-analysis, op. cit.,* pp. 152–184.

———. Early stages of the Oedipus conflict and of super-ego formation. (1928) In *Contributions to psycho-analysis, op. cit.,* pp. 202–214.

———. Personification in the play of children (1929). In *Contributions to psycho-analysis, op. cit.,* pp. 215–226.

———. The importance of symbol-formation in the development of the ego. (1930) In *Contributions to psycho-analysis, op. cit.,* pp. 236–250.

———. The psychotherapy of the psychoses. (1930) In *Contributions to psycho-analysis, op. cit.,* pp. 251–253.

———. *The psycho-analysis of children.* (3rd ed.) Trans. by A. Strachey. London: Hogarth Press, 1959. (1932)

———. The early development of conscience in the child. (1933) In *Psycho-analysis today.* New York: International Universities Press, 1944, pp. 64–74.

———, & Rivière, Joan. *Love, hate and reparation.* New York: Norton, 1964. (1937)

———. A contribution to the psycho-genesis of manic-depressive states. (1937) In *Contributions to psycho-analysis, op. cit.,* pp. 282–310.

———. Mourning and its relation to manic-depressive states. (1940) In *Contributions to psycho-analysis, op. cit.,* pp. 311–338.

———. The Oedipus complex in the light of early anxieties. (1945) In *Contributions to psycho-analysis, op. cit.,* pp. 339–390.

———. On the theory of anxiety and guilt. (1948) In Joan Rivière (Ed.), *Developments in psycho-analysis.* London: Hogarth Press, 1970, pp. 271–291.

———. On observing the behavior of young infants. (1952) In Joan Rivière (Ed.), *Developments in psychoanalysis, op. cit.,* pp. 237–270.

———. Notes on some schizoid mechanisms. (1952) In Joan Rivière (Ed.), *Developments in psychoanalysis, op. cit.,* pp. 237–270, 292–320.

————. Some theoretical conclusions regarding the emotional life of the infant. (1952) In Joan Rivière (Ed.), *Developments in psychoanalysis, op. cit.,* pp. 198–236.

————. The origins of transference. *Int. J. Psycho-Anal.,* 1952, *33,* 433–438.

————. The psychoanalytic play technique. *Amer. J. Orthopsychiat.,* 1955, *25,* 223–237.

————. On identification. In Melanie Klein *et al.* (Eds.), *New directions in psycho-analysis: The significance of infant conflict in the pattern of adult behaviour.* New York: Basic Books, 1957, pp. 309–345.

————. The psycho-analytic play technique: Its history and significance. In Melanie Klein *et al.* (Eds.), *New directions in psycho-analysis: The significance of infant conflict in the pattern of adult behaviour.* New York: Basic Books, 1957, pp. 3–22.

————. *Envy and gratitude: A study of unconscious sources.* New York: Basic Books, 1957.

————. *Narrative of a child analysis.* New York: Basic Books, 1961.

GUSTAV OTTO KLEMM
1884-1939
German Psychologist (20)

Klemm, G. O. Versuche mit dem Komplikationspendel. *Psychol. Stud.,* 1907, *2,* 324–357.

————. Untersuchungen über den Verlauf der Aufmerksamkeit bei einfachen und mehrfachen Reizen. *Psychol. Stud.,* 1908, *4,* 283–352.

————. Lokalisation von Sinneseindrücken bei disparaten Nebenreizen. *Psychol. Stud.,* 1909, *5,* 73–161.

————. *A history of psychology.* Trans. by E. C. Wilm & R. Pintner. New York: Scribner's, 1914. (1911)

————. Untersuchungen über die Lokalisation von Schallreizen. 1: Der Einfluss der Intensität auf die Tiefenlokalisation. 2: Versuche mit einem monotischen Beobachter. *Psychol. Stud.,* 1913, *8,* 226–270, 497–565.

Wirth, W., & ————. Ueber den Anstieg der inneren Tastempfindung. *Psychol. Stud.,* 1913, *8,* 485–496.

————. Untersuchungen über die Lokalisation von Schallreizen. 3: Ueber den Anteil des beidohrigen Hörens. 4: Ueber den Einfluss des binauralen Zeitunterschiedes. *Arch. ges. Psychol.,* 1918, *38,* 71–114; 1920, *40,* 117–146.

————. *Sinnestäuschungen.* Leipzig: Dürr, 1919.

————. Ueber die Korrelation verschiedenartiger Auffassungsleistungen bei Eignungsprüfungen. *Arch. ges. Psychol.,* 1921, *42,* 79–90.

————. Zur Geschichte des Leipziger psychologischen Instituts. In *Wilhelm Wundt, eine Würdigung.* (2nd ed.) Erfurt: Stenger, 1924, pp. 92–101.

————. Wahrnehmungsanalyse. In E. Abderhalden (Ed.), *Handbuch der biologischen Arbeitsmethoden.* Vol. 6: *Methoden der experimentellen Psychologie.* Part B/1. Berlin: Urban & Schwarzenberg, 1925, pp. 1–106.

————, & Olsson, E. Ueber den Einfluss mechanischer und sinnvoller Hilfen bei Gedächtnisleistungen. *Z. pädag. Psychol.,* 1925, *26,* 188–194.

————. *Psychologie und Berufsberatung.* Leipzig: Arbeitsamt, 1927.

————. Die angewandte Psychologie in der Landwirtschaft. *Vortragsfol. Leipziger Oekonom. Soz.,* 1927, pp. 109–119.

————. Eignungsprüfungen an messtechnischem Personal. In E. Abderhalden (Ed.), *Handbuch der biologischen Arbeitsmethoden.* Vol. 6: *Methoden der experimentellen Psychologie.* Part C/I. Vienna: Urban & Schwarzenberg, 1928, pp. 565–619.

————. Erfahrungen bei einer Eignungsprüfung an Kriminalbeamten. *Neue psychol. Stud.,* 1929, *5(1),* 1–22.

————. Zufall oder Geschicklichkeit? *Neue psychol. Stud.,* 1929, *5(1),* 23–64.

———. Ueber die Atmungssymptome bei Untersuchungsgefangenen. *Neue psychol. Stud.,* 1929, *5*(1), 111–132.

———. Gedanken über Leibesübungen. *Neue psychol. Stud.,* 1930, *5*(2), 145–169.

Benscher, Ilse, & ———. Korrelationstheoretisches zur Ganzheit. *Neue psychol. Stud.,* 1930, *5*(2), 169–196.

———. Streifzüge durch die Psychotechnik (Eignungspsychologie). In Arbeitsamt Leipzig (Ed.), *Aus der Praxis der Berufsberatung.* Leipzig: Wolf, 1930, pp. 269–310.

———. *Pädagogische Psychologie.* Breslau: Hirt, 1933.

——— Die psychologischen Grundfragen der Technik. Sammelbericht. *Ber. Kongr. dtsch. Ges. Psychol., 1933,* 1934, *13,* 63–76.

———. Otto Klemm. In C. Murchison (Ed.), *A history of psychology in autobiography.* Vol. 3. Worcester, Mass.: Clark University Press, 1936, pp. 153–180. **B**

———. Die Entdeckung der Bewegungsgestalt. *Arbeitsschule,* 1936, *50,* 8–16.

———. Verantwortung. *Amer. J. Psychol.,* 1937, *50,* 157–165.

Ehrhardt, A., & ———. Rasse und Leistung auf Grund von Erfahrungen im Felde der Eignungsuntersuchung. *Z. angew. Psychol.,* 1937, *53,* 1–18.

———. Zwölf Leitsätze zu einer Psychologie der Leibesübungen. *Neue psychol. Stud.,* 1938, *9*(4), 383–398.

———. Der Kugelstoss. Bericht über eine Untersuchung A. Vogels. *Z. angew. Psychol.,* 1938, *54,* 81–91.

———. Gedanken über seelische Anpassung. *Arch. ges. Psychol.,* 1938, *100,* 387–400.

CLYDE KAY MABEN KLUCKHOHN
1905-1960
American Anthropologist (18)

Kluckhohn, C. K. M. *Culture and behavior: Collected essays of Clyde Kluckhohn.* Ed. by R.

Kluckhohn. Riverside, N.Y.: Free Press, 1962. (Reprinted 1965) **Bl C**

———. *To the foot of the rainbow.* New York: Century, 1927. **B**

———. *Beyond the rainbow.* Boston: Christopher, 1933.

———. Some reflections on the method and theory of the Kulturkreislehre. *Amer. Anthrop.,* 1936, *38,* 157–196.

———. Theoretical bases for an empirical method of studying the acquisition of culture by individuals. *Man,* 1939, *39,* 98–103. Reprinted in *Culture and behavior, op. cit.,* pp. 244–254.

———. On certain recent applications of association coefficients to ethnological data. *Amer. Anthrop.,* 1939, *41,* 345–377.

———. The place of theory in anthropological studies. *Phil. Sci.,* 1939, *6,* 328–344.

———, & Spencer, Katherine. *A bibliography of the Navaho Indians.* New York: Augustin, 1940.

———. Patterning as exemplified in Navaho culture. In L. Spier *et al.* (Eds.), *Language, culture and personality: Essays in memory of Edward Sapir.* Menasha, Wisc.: Sapir Memorial Publication Fund, 1941, pp. 109–130. (Reprinted 1960)

———. Myths and rituals: A general theory. *Harvard Theol. Rev.,* 1942, *35,* 45–79.

———, & Mowrer, O. H. "Culture and personality": A conceptual scheme. *Amer. Anthrop.,* 1944, *46,* 1–29. Reprinted as "Determinants and components of personality" in A. Weider & D. Wechsler (Eds.), *Contributions toward medical psychology.* Vol. 1. New York: Ronald Press, 1953, pp. 105–135.

Mowrer, O H., & ———. Dynamic theory of personality. In J. McV. Hunt (Ed.), *Personality and the behavior disorders.* Vol. 1. New York: Ronald Press, 1944, pp. 69–135.

———. The influence of psychiatry on anthropology in America during the past one hundred years. In J. K. Hall *et al.* (Eds.), *One hundred years of American psychiatry.* New York: Columbia University Press, 1944, pp. 589–617.

Gottschalk, L., ———, & Angell, R. The personal document in history, anthropology, and sociology. New York: *Social Science Res. Council Bull.,* 1945, No. 53. (Reprinted 1960)

———, & Kelly, W. H. The concept of culture. In R. Linton (Ed.), *The science of man in the world crisis.* New York: Columbia University Press, 1945, pp. 78–106. Reprinted in *Culture and behavior, op. cit.,* pp. 19–73.

———, & Leighton, Dorothea C. *The Navaho.* Cambridge: Harvard University Press, 1946.

———. Some aspects of Navaho infancy and early childhood. In G. Roheim (Ed.), *Psychoanalysis and the social sciences.* Vol. 1. New York: International Universities Press, 1947, pp. 37–86. Reprinted in part in I. T. Sanders (Ed.), *Societies around the world.* Lexington, Ky.: University of Kentucky Press, 1948, pp. 149–160.

Leighton, Dorothea, & ———. *Children of the people: The Navaho individual and his development.* Cambridge: Harvard University Press, 1947.

Murray, H. A., & ———. Outline of a conception of personality. In C. Kluckhohn & H. A. Murray (Eds.), *Personality in nature, society and culture.* (2nd ed.) New York: Knopf, 1953, pp. 3–49. (1948)

———, & Murray, H. A. Personality formation: The determinants. In C. Kluckhohn & H. A. Murray (Eds.), *Personality in nature, society and culture.* (2nd ed.) New York: Knopf, 1953, pp. 53–67. (1948)

———. An anthropologist looks at psychology. *Amer. Psychologist,* 1948, *3,* 439–442.

———. Needed refinements in the biographical approach. In S. S. Sargent & M. W. Smith (Eds.), *Culture and personality.* New York: Viking Fund, 1949, pp. 75–92.

———. *Mirror for man: The relation of anthropology to modern life.* New York: McGraw-Hill, 1949.

———. The limitations of adaptation and adjustment as concepts for understanding cultural behavior. In J. Romano (Ed.), *Adaptation.* Ithaca, N.Y.: Cornell University Press, 1949,

pp. 96–113. Reprinted in *Culture and behavior, op. cit.,* pp. 255–264.

———. Values and value-orientations in the theory of action: An exploration in definition and classification. In T. Parsons & E. A. Shils (Eds.), *Toward a general theory of action.* Cambridge: Harvard University Press, 1951, pp. 388–433.

———. The study of culture. In D. Lerner & H. Lasswell (Eds.), *The policy sciences.* Stanford, Calif.: Stanford University Press, 1951, pp. 86–101.

Kroeber, A. L., & ———. *Culture: A critical review of concepts and definitions.* Cambridge: Peabody Museum, 1952.

———. Universal categories of culture. In A. L. Kroeber (Ed.), *Anthropology today: An encyclopedic inventory.* Chicago: University of Chicago Press, 1953, pp. 507–523. Reprinted in F. W. Moore (Ed.), *Readings in cross-cultural methodology.* New Haven: Human Relations Area Files Press, 1961, pp. 89–105.

———. Culture and behavior. In G. Lindzey (Ed.), *Handbook of social psychology.* Vol. 2. Cambridge: Addison-Wesley, 1954, pp. 921–976.

———. Physical anthropology. *Amer. Anthrop.,* 1955, *57,* 1280–1295.

———. Implicit and explicit values in the social sciences related to human growth and development. *Merrill-Palmer Quart.,* 1955, *1,* 131–140.

Gerard, R. W., ———, & Rapaport, A. Biological and cultural evolution. *Behav. Sci.,* 1956, *1,* 6–34.

———. The impact of Freud on anthropology. *Bull. N.Y. Acad. Med.,* 1956, *32,* 903–907. Reprinted in I. G. Sarason (Ed.), *Psychoanalysis and the study of behavior.* Princeton, N.J.: Van Nostrand, 1965, pp. 88–93.

———. Toward a comparison of value-emphases in different cultures. In L. D. White (Ed.), *The state of the social sciences.* Chicago: University of Chicago Press, 1956, pp. 116–132.

———. Developments in the field of anthropology

in the twentieth century. *J. World hist.*, 1957, *3*, 754–777.

―――. The scientific study of values and contemporary civilization. *Proc. Amer. Phil. Soc.*, 1958, *102*, 469–476.

―――. Anthropology and psychology. *Acta Psychol.*, 1959, *15*, 63–75.

Albert, Ethel M., & ―――― (with assist. of R. LeVine, W. Seulowitz, & Miriam Gallaher. *A selected bibliography on values, ethics, and esthetics in the behavioral sciences and philosophy, 1920–1958*. Glencoe, Ill.: Free Press, 1959.

―――. Common humanity and diverse cultures. In D. Lerner (Ed.), *Human meaning of the social sciences*. New York: Meridian, 1959, pp. 245–284.

―――. *Anthropology and the classics*. Providence, R.I.: Brown University Press, 1961.

Coser & Rosenberg, *Sociological Theory* ; Goldschmidt, *Mankind* ; Ross, *Social Order*

KURT KOFFKA
1886-1941
German-American Psychologist (27)

Koffka, K. Untersuchungen an einem protanomalen System. *Z. Sinnesphysiol.*, 1908, *43*, 123–145.

―――. Experimental-Untersuchungen zur Lehre vom Rhythmus. *Z. Psychol.*, 1909, *52*, 1–109.

―――. Ueber latente Einstellung. *IV. Kongr. exper. Psychol. in Innsbrück*, 1910, 239–241.

―――. Ein neuer Versuch eines objektiven Systems der Psychologie. *Z. Psychol.*, 1912, *61*, 266–278.

―――. *Zur Analyse der Vorstellungen und ihrer Gesetze. Eine experimentelle Untersuchung.* Leipzig: Quelle & Meyer, 1912. Reprinted in part in Jean M. Mandler & G. Mandler (Eds.), *Thinking: From association to Gestalt*. New York: Wiley, 1964, pp. 236–250.

―――. Psychologie der Wahrnehmung. *Geisteswissenschaften*, 1914, *26*, 711–716, 796–800.

―――. Beiträge zur Psychologie der Gestalt- und Bewegungserlebnisse. III. Zur Grundlegung der Wahrnehmungs-Psychologie. Eine Auseinandersetzung mit V. Benussi. *Z. Psychol.*, 1915, *73*, 11–90. Abstracted & trans. in W. D. Ellis (Ed.), *A sourcebook of Gestalt psychology* London: Routledge & Kegan Paul, 1938, pp 371–378.

―――. Probleme der experimentellen Psychologie I. Die Unterschiedsschwelle. *Naturwissenschaften*, 1917, *7*, 1–5, 23–28.

―――. Beiträge zur Psychologie der Gestalt. IV Zur Theorie einfachster gesehener Bewegungen Ein physiologisch-mathematischer Versuch. *Z Psychol.*, 1919, *82*, 257–292.

―――. Probleme der experimentellen Psychologie II. Ueber den Einfluss der Erfahrung auf die Wahrnehmung. *Naturwissenschaften*, 1919, *7* 597–605.

―――. *The growth of the mind: An introduction to child psychology.* (2nd ed.) Trans. by R. M Ogden. London: Routledge & Kegan Paul 1928. (1921) (Reprinted 1959)

―――. Perception: An introduction to the *Gestalttheorie*. *Psychol. Bull.*, 1922, *19*, 531–585.

―――. Zur Theorie der Erlebniswahrnehmung *Ann. Phil.*, 1922, *3*, 375–399.

―――. Ueber die Untersuchungen an den sogenannten optischen Anschauungsbildern. *Psychol Forsch.*, 1923, *3*, 124–167.

―――. Ueber die Messung der Grösse von Nach bildern. *Psychol. Forsch.*, 1923, *3*, 219–230.

―――. Ueber Feldbegrenzung und Felderfüllung *Psychol. Forsch.*, 1923, *4*, 176–203.

―――. Théorie de la forme et psychologie de l'enfant. *J. Psychol. norm. path.*, 1924, *21* 102–112.

―――. Introspection and the method of psychol ogy. *Brit. J. Psychol.*, 1924–1925, *15*, 149–161

―――. Psychologie. In M. Dessoir (Ed.), *Lehr buch der Philosophie. Vol. 2. Die Philosophie in ihren Einzelgebieten.* Berlin: Ullstein, 1925 pp. 497–603.

——. Mental development. In C. Murchison (Ed.), *Psychologies of 1925.* (3rd ed.) Worcester, Mass.: Clark University Press, 1928, pp. 129–143. (1926)

——. Ueber das Sehen von Bewegung. Bemerkungen zu der Arbeit von Higginson. *Psychol. Forsch.,* 1926, *8,* 222–235.

——. Die Krisis in der Psychologie: Bemerkungen zu dem Buch gleichen Namens von Hans Driesch. *Naturwissenschaften,* 1926, *14,* 581–586.

——. Bemerkungen zur Denkpsychologie. *Psychol. Forsch.,* 1927, *9,* 163–184.

——. On the structure of the unconscious. In *The unconscious, a symposium.* Ed. by E. Dummer. New York: Knopf, 1927, pp. 43–68.

——. Psychologie der Wahrnehmung. *VIIIth Int. Congr. Psych. held at Groningen: Proceedings and papers.* Groningen: Noordhoff, 1927, pp. 159–165.

——. On Gestalt theory. *Smith Alumn. Quart.,* 1928, 142–147.

——. Some problems of space perception. In C. Murchison (Ed.), *Psychologies of 1930.* Worcester, Mass.: Clark University Press, 1930, pp. 161–187.

——. Die Wahrnehmung von Bewegung. In A. Bethe *et al.* (Eds.), *Handbuch der normalen und pathologischen Physiologie.* Vol. 12, Part 2. Berlin: Springer-Verlag, 1931, pp. 1166–1214.

——. Psycnologie der optischen Wahrnehmung. In A. Bethe *et al.* (Eds.), *Handbuch der normalen und pathologischen Physiologie.* Vol. 12, Part 2. Berlin: Springer-Verlag, 1931, pp. 1215–1271.

——, & Mintz, A. Beiträge zur Psychologie der Gestalt. XIX. On the influence of transformation and contrast on colour- and brightness-thresholds. *Psychol. Forsch.,* 1931, *14,* 183–198.

——, & Sturm, M. Beiträge zur Psychologie der Gestalt. XX A study of the movement after-image. *Psychol. Forsch.,* 1931, *14,* 269–293.

——, & Harrower, Molly R. Beiträge zur Psychologie der Gestalt. XXI. Colour and or-

ganization. I. II. *Psychol. Forsch.,* 1931, *15,* 145–192, 194–274.

——. A new theory of brightness constancy: A contribution to a general theory of vision. In *Report of a joint discussion on vision by the physical and optical societies.* Cambridge: Physical Society, 1932, pp. 182–188.

——. Les notions d'héréditaire et d'acquis en psychologie. *J. Psychol. norm. path.,* 1932, *29,* 5–19.

——. Beiträge zur Psychologie der Gestalt. XXIII. Some remarks on the theory of colour constancy. *Psychol. Forsch.,* 1932, *16,* 329–355.

——. On problems of colour perception. *Acta Psychol.,* 1935, *1,* 129–134.

——. *Principles of Gestalt psychology.* New York: Harcourt, Brace, 1935.

——. The ontological status of value. In H. Kallen & S. Hook (Eds.), *American philosophy today and tomorrow.* New York: Furman, 1935, pp. 275–309.

——. Problems in the psychology of art. Art: A Bryn Mawr symposium. *Bryn Mawr Not. Monogr.,* 1940, *9,* 180–273.

Beardslee, *Perception ;* Hirst, *Perception ;* Mandler & Mandler, *Thinking ;* Sahakian, *Psychology ;* Shipley, *Classics*

WOLFGANG KOHLER
1887-1967
German-American Psychologist (27)

Köhler, W. *The selected papers of Wolfgang Köhler.* Ed. by Mary Henle with trans. by H. E. Adler, E. Goldmeier & Mary Henle. New York: Liveright, 1971. (Reprinted 1971) **Bl C**

——. Akustische Untersuchungen. I, II, III, & IV. *Z. Psychol.,* 1909, *54,* 241–289 ; 1910, *58,* 59–140 ; 1913, *64,* 92–105 ; 1915, *72,* 1–192.

——. Ueber unbemerkte Empfindungen und Urteilstäuschungen. *Z. Psychol.,* 1913, *66,* 51–80. Trans. in *Selected papers, op. cit.,* pp. 13–39.

———. Optische Untersuchungen am Schimpansen und am Haushuhn. *Abh. preuss. Akad. Wiss. Berlin,* Phys.-math. Kl., 1915, No. 3.

———. *The mentality of apes.* (2nd ed.) Trans. by Ella Winter. New York: Harcourt, Brace, 1925. (1917) (Reprinted 1959)

———. Intelligenzprüfungen an Anthropoiden. *Abh. preuss. Akad. Wiss. Berlin.* Phys.-math. Kl., 1917, No. 1.

———. Die Farbe der Sehdinge beim Schimpansen und beim Haushuhn. *Z. Psychol.,* 1917, 77, 248–255.

———. Nachweis einfacher Strukturfunktionen beim Schimpansen und beim Haushuhn: Ueber eine neue Methode zur Untersuchung des bunten Farbensystems. *Abh. preuss. Akad. Wiss. Berlin,* Phys.-math. Kl., 1918, No. 2. Abstracted & trans. in W. D. Ellis (Ed.), *A source book of Gestalt psychology.* London: Routledge & Kegan Paul, 1938, pp. 217–227.

———. *Die physischen Gestalten in Ruhe und im stationären Zustand.* Brunswick: Vieweg, 1920. (2nd ed., Erlangen, 1924.) Abstracted, trans., & reprinted in W. D. Ellis (Ed.), *A source book of Gestalt psychology.* London: Routledge & Kegan Paul, 1938, pp. 17–54.

———. Die Methoden der psychologischen Forschung an Affen. In E. Abderhalden (Ed.), *Handbuch der biologischen Arbeitsmethoden.* Berlin: Urban & Schwarzenberg, 1921. Div. 6, Part D, pp. 69–120. Parts trans. in *Selected papers, op. cit.,* pp. 197–223.

———. Gestaltprobleme und Anfänge einer Gestalttheorie. *Jahresber. ges. Physiol. exp. Pharmakol.,* 1924, 3, 512–539. Abstracted & trans. in W. D. Ellis (Ed.) *A source book of Gestalt psychology.* London: Routledge & Kegan Paul, 1938, pp. 55–70.

———. Zur Psychologie des Schimpansen. *Psychol. Forsch.,* 1922, 1, 2–46. Trans. in *The mentality of apes* (2nd ed.), *op. cit.,* pp. 271–329.

———. Ueber eine neue Methode zur psychologischen Untersuchung von Menschenaffen. *Psychol. Forsch.,* 1922, 1, 390–397. Trans. in *Selected papers, op. cit.,* pp. 224–233.

———. Zur Theorie der stroboskopischen Bewegung. *Psychol. Forsch.,* 1923, 3, 397–406.

———. Zur Theorie des Sukzessivvergleichs und zur Zeitfehler. *Psychol. Forsch.,* 1923, 4, 115–175.

———. An aspect of Gestalt psychology. *J. genet. Psychol.,* 1925, 32, 691–723, & in C. Murchison (Ed.), *Psychologies of 1925.* (3rd ed.) Worcester, Mass.: Clark University Press, 1928, pp. 163–195. Reprinted in *Selected papers, op. cit.,* pp. 40–61.

———. Komplextheorie und Gestalttheorie. Antwort auf G. E. Müllers Schrift gleichen Namens. *Psychol. Forsch.,* 1925, 6, 358–416. Abstracted & trans. in W. D. Ellis (Ed.), *A source book of Gestalt psychology.* London: Routledge & Kegan Paul, 1938, pp. 379–388.

———. Zur Komplextheorie. *Psychol. Forsch.,* 1926, 8, 236–243.

———. Zum Problem der Regulation. *Arch. Entwicklungsmech.,* 1927, 112, 315–332. Trans. in *Selected papers, op. cit.,* pp. 305–326.

———. Bemerkungen zur Gestalttheorie: Im Anschluss an Rignanos Kritik. *Psychol. Forsch.,* 1928, 11, 188–234. Abstracted & trans. in W. D. Ellis (Ed.), *A source book of Gestalt psychology.* London: Routledge & Kegan Paul, 1938, pp. 389–396.

———. Intelligence in apes. In C. Murchison (Ed.), *Psychologies of 1925.* (3rd ed.) Worcester, Mass.: Clark University Press, 1928, pp. 145–161.

———. *Gestalt psychology: An introduction to new concepts in modern psychology.* (Rev. ed.) New York: Liveright, 1947. (1929) (Reprinted 1959, 1970)

———. *Psychologische Probleme.* (Enlarged ed.) Berlin: Springer-Verlag, 1933. (1929)

———. Ein altes Scheinproblem. *Naturwissenschaften,* 1929, 17, 395–401. Trans. in *Selected papers, op. cit.,* pp. 125–141.

———. La perception humaine. *J. Psychol. norm. pathol.,* 1930, 27, 5–30. Reprinted in trans. in *Selected papers, op. cit.,* pp. 142–167.

————. Some tasks of Gestalt psychology. In C. Murchison (Ed.), *Psychologies of 1930*. Worcester, Mass.; Clark University Press, 1930, pp. 143–160.

————. Das Wesen der Intelligenz. In A. Keller (Ed.), *Kind und Umwelt, Anlage und Erziehung*. Leipzig: Deuticke, 1930, pp. 132–146. Trans. in *Selected papers, op. cit.*, pp. 168–188.

————. The new psychology and physics. *Yale Rev.*, 1930, *19*, 560–576. Reprinted in *Selected papers, op. cit.*, pp. 237–251.

————. Zur Boltzmann'schen Theorie des zweiten Hauptsatzes. *Erkenntnis*, 1932, *2*, 336–353.

————. Zur Psychophysik des Vergleichs und des Raumes. *Psychol. Forsch.*, 1933, *18*, 343–360.

————, & Restorff, Hedwig v. Analyse von Vorgängen im Spurenfeld. II. Zur Theorie der Reproduktion. *Psychol. Forsch.*, 1935, *21*, 56–112.

————. Psychological remarks on some questions of anthropology. *Amer. J. Psychol.*, 1937, *50*, 271–288. Reprinted in Mary Henle (Ed.), *Documents of Gestalt psychology*. Berkeley, Calif.: University of California Press, 1961, pp. 203–221 ; & in *Selected papers, op. cit.*, pp. 376–397.

————. *The place of value in a world of facts*. New York: Liveright, 1938. (Reprinted 1966)

————. *Dynamics in psychology*. New York: Liveright, 1940. (Reprinted 1960)

————. On the nature of associations. *Proc. Amer. Phil. Soc.*, 1941, *84*, 489–502.

————. Value and fact. *J. Phil.*, 1944, *41*, 197–212. Reprinted in *Selected papers, op. cit.*, pp. 356–375.

————, & Wallach, H. Figural after-effects: An investigation of visual processes. *Proc. Amer. Phil. Soc.*, 1944, *88*, 269–357.

————, & Emery, D. A. Figural after-effects in the third dimension of visual space. *Amer. J. Psychol.*, 1947, *60*, 159–201.

————, & Held, R. The cortical correlate of pattern vision. *Science*, 1949, *110*, 414–419.

————. Psychology and evolution. *Acta Psychol.*, 1950, *7*, 288–297. Reprinted in Mary Henle (Ed.), *Documents of Gestalt psychology*. Berkeley, Calif.: University of California Press, 1961, pp. 67–75.

————. Relational determination in perception. In L. A. Jeffress (Ed.), *Cerebral mechanisms in behavior*. New York: Wiley, 1951, pp. 200–230. (Reprinted 1967)

————, Held, R., & O'Connell, D. N. An investigation of cortical currents. *Proc. Amer. Phil. Soc.*, 1952, *96*, 290–330.

————. The scientists from Europe and their new environment. In Neumann, F. L. *et al.*, *The cultural migration*. Philadelphia: University of Pennsylvania Press, 1953, pp. 112–137. Reprinted in *Selected papers, op. cit.*, pp. 413–435.

————. Direction of processes in living systems. *Sci. Mon.*, N.Y., 1955, *80*, 29–32. Reprinted in *Selected papers, op. cit.*, pp. 327–334.

————, & Adams, Pauline A. Perception and attention. *Amer. J. Psychol.*, 1958, *71*, 489–503. Reprinted in Mary Henle (Ed.), *Documents of Gestalt psychology*. Berkeley, Calif.: University of California Press, 1961, pp. 146–163.

————. The present situation in brain physiology. *Amer. Psychologist*, 1958, *13*, 150–154. Reprinted in Mary Henle (Ed.), *Documents of Gestalt psychology*. Berkeley, Calif.: University of California Press, 1961, pp. 97–106.

————. Psychologie und Naturwissenschaft. *Acta Psychol.*, 1959, *15*, 37–50. Trans. in *Selected papers, op. cit.*, pp. 252–273.

————. Gestalt psychology today. *Amer. Psychologist*, 1959, *14*, 727–734. Reprinted in Mary Henle (Ed.), *Documents of Gestalt psychology*. Berkeley, Calif.: University of California Press, 1961, pp. 1–15.

————. The mind-body problem. In S. Hook (Ed.), *Dimensions of mind*. New York: New York University Press, 1960, pp. 3–23. Reprinted in *Selected papers, op. cit.*, pp. 62–82.

————. Unsolved problems in the field of figural after-effects. *Psychol. Rec.*, 1965, *15*, 63–83. Reprinted in *Selected papers, op. cit.*, pp. 274–302.

————. A task for philosophers. In P. K. Feyerabend & G. Maxwell (Eds.), *Mind, matter, and method: Essays in philosophy and science in honor of Herbert Feigl.* Minneapolis, Minn.: University of Minnesota Press, 1966, pp. 70–91. Reprinted in *Selected papers, op. cit.,* pp. 83–107.

————. Gestalt psychology. *Psychol. Forsch.,* 1967, *31,* xviii–xxx. Trans. in D. L. Krantz (Ed.), *Schools of psychology: A symposium.* New York: Appleton-Century-Crofts, 1969, pp. 69–85; & in *Selected papers, op. cit.,* pp. 108–122.

————. *The task of Gestalt psychology.* Princeton, N.J.: Princeton University Press, 1969. (Reprinted 1972)

> Beardslee, *Perception;* Beck & Molish, *Reflexes;* Dennis, *Psychology;* Gruber, *Creative Thinking;* Herrnstein & Boring, *Source Book;* Parsons, *Society;* Perez, *Readings;* Sahakian, *Psychology;* Shipley, *Classics;* Wrenn, *Contributions*

ARTHUR KONIG
1856-1901
German Physicist (16)

König, A. *Gesammelte Abhandlungen zur physiologischen Optik.* Leipzig: Barth, 1903.   C

————. Zur Kenntnis dichromatischer Farbensysteme. *Ann. Phys. Chem.,* 1844, *22,* 567–578. Reprinted in *Gesammelte Abhandlungen, op. cit.,* pp. 11–22.

————, & Dieterici, C. Ueber die Empfindlichkeit des normalen Auges für Wellenlänge-Unterschiede des Lichtes. *Ann. Phys. Chem.,* 1884, *22,* 579–589. Reprinted in *Gesammelte Abhandlungen, op. cit.,* pp. 23–33.

————. Zur Kritik einer Abhandlung von Herrn E. Hering: Ueber individuelle Verschiedenheiten des Farbensinnes. *Cbl. prakt. Augenhlk.,* 1885, *9,* 260–265. Reprinted in *Gesammelte Abhandlungen, op. cit.,* pp. 37–43.

————, & Dieterici, C. Die Grundempfindungen und ihre Intensitätsverteilung im Spectrum. *Sitzber. Akad. Wiss.,* Berlin, 1886, 805–829.

Reprinted in *Gesammelte Abhandlungen, op. cit.,* pp. 60–87.

————. The modern development of Thomas Young's theory of colour vision. *Rep. Brit. Ass.,* Birmingham meeting, 1886, 431–439. Trans. in *Gesammelte Abhandlungen, op. cit.,* pp. 88–107.

————. Ueber Newtons Gesetz der Farbenmischung und darauf bezügliche Versuche des Hrn. Eugen Brodhun. *Sitzber. Akad. Wiss.,* Berlin, 1887, 311–317. Reprinted in *Gesammelte Abhandlungen, op. cit.,* pp. 108–115.

————, & Brodhun, E. Experimentelle Untersuchung über die psychophysische Fundamentalform in Bezug auf den Gesichtssinn. *Sitzber. Akad. Wiss.,* Berlin, 1888, 917–931. Reprinted in *Gesammelte Abhandlungen, op. cit.,* pp. 116–139.

————. Ueber den Helligkeitswert der Spectralfarben bei verschiedener absoluter Intensität. In *Beiträge zur Psychologie und Physiologie der Sinnesorgane.* Hamburg: Voss, 1891, pp. 309–388. Reprinted in *Gesammelte Abhandlungen, op. cit.,* pp. 144–213.

————, & Dieterici, C. Die Grundempfindungen in normalen und anormalen Farbensysteme und ihre Intensitätsverteilung im Spectrum. *Z. Psychol.,* 1893, *4,* 241–347. Reprinted in *Gesammelte Abhandlungen, op. cit.,* pp. 214–321.

————. Eine bisher noch nicht beobachtete Form angeborener Farbenblindheit (Pseudo-Monochaomasie). *Z. Psychol.,* 1894, *7,* 161–171.

————. Ueber den menschlichen Sehpurpur und seine Bedeutung für das Sehen. *Sitzber. Akad. Wiss.,* Berlin, 1894, Part 2, 577–598. Reprinted in *Gesammelte Abhandlungen, op. cit.,* pp. 338–363.

————. Ueber die Anzahl der unterscheidbaren Spektralfarben und Helligkeitsstufen. *Z. Psychol.,* 1895, *8,* 375–380. Reprinted in *Gesammelte Abhandlungen, op. cit.,* pp. 367–372.

————. Quantitative Bestimmungen an complementären Spectralfarben. *Sitzber. Akad. Wiss.,* Berlin, 1896, 945–949. Reprinted in *Gesammelte Abhandlungen, op. cit.,* pp. 373–377.

————. Die Abhängigkeit der Farben- und Helligkeitsgleichungen von der absoluten Intensität. *Sitzber. Akad. Wiss.,* Berlin, 1897, 871–882. Reprinted in *Gesammelte Abhandlungen, op. cit.,* pp. 416–429.

————. Ueber "Blaublindheit." *Sitzber. Akad. Wiss.,* Berlin, 1897, 718–731. Reprinted in *Gesammelte Abhandlungen, op. cit.,* pp. 396–415.

————. Die Abhängigkeit der Sehschärfe von der Beleuchtungsintensität. *Sitzber. Akad. Wiss.,* Berlin, 1897, 559–575. Reprinted in *Gesammelte Abhandlungen, op. cit.,* pp. 378–395.

————. Bemerkungen über angeborene totale Farbenblindheit. *Z. Psychol.,* 1899, *20,* 425–434.

KONSTANTIN (N.) KORNILOV
1879-1957
Russian Psychologist (13)

Kornilov, K. N. (*Behavior of children of preschool age.*) (3rd ed.) Moscow: Giz, 1927. (1917)

————. Dynamometrische Methode der Untersuchung der Reaktionen. *Arch. ges. Physiol.,* 1921, *40,* 59–78.

————. (*Study on human reactions: Reactology.*) Moscow: Giz, 1922.

————. (The dialectical method in psychology.) *Pod. Znamenem Marksizma,* 1924, (1), 107–113.

————. (Contemporary psychology and Marxism.) *Pod. Znamenem Marksizma,* 1924, (1), 41–45. (4), 86–114.

————. (The mechanical materialism in contemporary psychology: A reply to V. Struminsky.) *Pod. Znamenem Marksizma,* 1926 (4/5), 185–212.

————. (*A textbook of psychology in the light of dialectical materialism.*) (5th ed.) Moscow: Giz, 1931. (1927)

————. (The present state of psychology in the U.S.S.R.) *Pod. Znamenem Marksizma,* 1927, (10/11), 195–217.

————. (The comparative significance of scientific investigation in the line of psychology and pedology from the standpoint of Marxism.) *Zh. Psikhol. Pedol. Psikhotekhn.,* 1928, *1,* 5–28.

————. (*Scientific principles in psychology.*) Moscow: Uchpedgiz, 1929.

————. (The present-day mechanist standpoint on the law of conservation of psychic energy.) *Psikhologiya,* 1929, *2,* 3–15.

————. Psychology in the light of dialectic materialism. In C. Murchison (Ed.), *Psychologies of 1930.* Worcester, Mass.: Clark University Press, 1930, pp. 243–278.

————. (Concerning the total of psychological discussions.) *Psikhologiya,* 1931, *4,* 44–78.

————, Smirnov, A. A., & Teplov, B. M. (Eds.), (*Psychology.*) (3rd ed.) Moscow: Uchpedgiz, 1948. (1938)

————. (The value of methods of scientific investigation in the field of psychology.) *Met. Izuch. Reb.,* 1935, 87–100.

————. Einführung in die Psychologie. (2nd ed.) Berlin: Volk und Wissenschaften, 1950. (1942)

————. (*Psychology: A textbook for colleges of education.*) Moscow: Uchpedgiz, 1946.

————. (*Training of will and character.*) Moscow: Trudrezervizdat, 1950.

————. (On the tasks of Soviet psychology.) *Vop. Psikhol.,* 1955, *1*(4), 16–28.

————. (Principles for studying the psychology of the personality of Soviet man.) *Vop. Psikhol.,* 1957, *3,* 131–141.

EMIL KRAEPELIN
1856-1926
German Psychiatrist (27)

Kraepelin, E. *Arbeiten aus der deutschen Forschungsanstalt für Psychiatrie in München.* (3 vols.) Berlin: Springer-Verlag, 1920–1921.

C

————. Ueber psychische Schwäche. Eine Studie. *Arch. Psychiat.,* 1882, *13,* 382–426.

Kraepelin — 240 —

————. Ueber die Einwirkung einiger medikamentöser Stoffe auf die Dauer einfacher psychischer Vorgänge. *Phil. Stud.*, 1881–1883, *1*, 417–462, 573–605.

————. *Psychiatrie.* (4th ed.) Leipzig: Meiner, 1893. (1883)

————. *Psychiatrie. Ein Lehrbuch für Studierende und Aerzte.* (8th ed.) (4 vols.) Leipzig, Barth, 1909–1913. (1883)

————. *Clinical psychiatry: A textbook for students and physicians.* (7th ed.) Trans. & abstracted by A. R. Diefendorf. New York: Macmillan, 1915. (1883)

————. *Dementia praecox and paraphrenia.* (Section on dementia praecox from 8th German ed. of *Text-book of psychiatry*.) Trans. by R. Mary Barclay, & intro. by E. Harms. Huntington, N.Y.: Krieger, 1971. (1883)

————. Zur Psychologie des Komischen. *Phil. Stud.*, 1883–1885, *2*, 128–160, 327–361.

————. Zur Frage der Gültigkeit des Weber'schen Gesetzes bei Lichtempfindungen. *Phil. Stud.*, 1883–1885, *2*, 306–326.

————. Nachtrag zu der Arbeit über die Gültigkeit des Weber'schen Gesetzes bei Lichtempfindungen. *Phil. Stud.*, 1883–1885, *2*, 651–654.

————. Zur Kenntnis der psychophysischen Methoden. *Phil. Stud.*, 1890–1891, *6*, 493–513.

————. *Ueber die Beeinflussung einfacher psychischer Vorgänge durch einige Arzneimittel.* Jena: Fischer, 1892.

————. *Ueber geistige Arbeit.* (3rd ed.) Jena: Fischer, 1901. (1894)

————. Der psychologische Versuch in der Psychiatrie. *Psychol. Arb.*, 1895–1896, *1*, 1–91.

Hoch, A., & ————. Ueber die Wirkung der Theebestandtheile auf körperliche und geistige Arbeit. *Psychol. Arb.*, 1895–1896, *1*, 378–488.

Rivers, W., & ————. Ueber Ermüdung und Erholung. *Psychol. Arb.*, 1895–1896, *1*, 627–678.

————. *Zur Hygiene der Arbeit.* Jena: Fischer, 1896.

————. *Zur Ueberbürdungsfrage.* Jena: Fischer, 1898.

————. Neuere Untersuchungen über die psychischen Wirkungen des Alkohols. *Münchener medizin. Wochensch.*, 1899, *46*, 1365–1369.

Cron, L., & ————. Ueber die Messung der Auffassungsfähigkeit. *Psychol. Arb.*, 1899, *2*, 203–325.

————. *Die psychiatrischen Aufgaben des Staates.* Jena: Fischer, 1900.

————. *Einführung in die psychiatrische Klinik.* (3 vols.) (4th ed.) Leipzig: Barth, 1921. (1901)

Kürz, E., & ————. Ueber die Beeinflussung psychischer Vorgänge durch regelmässigen Alkoholgenuss. *Psychol. Arb.*, 1901, *3*, 417–457.

Oseretskowsky, A., & ————. Ueber die Beeinflussung der Muskelleistung durch verschiedene Arbeitsbedingungen. *Psychol. Arb.*, 1901, *3*, 587–690.

————. *Lectures on clinical psychiatry.* Rev. & ed. by T. Johnstone. New York: Hafner, 1968. (1901)

————. Die Arbeitskurve. *Phil. Stud.*, 1902, *19*, 459–507.

————. Ueber Ermüdungsmessungen. *Arch. ges. Psychol.*, 1903, *1*, 9–30.

Hylan, J. P., & ————. Ueber die Wirkung kurzer Arbeitszeiten. *Psychol. Arb.*, 1904, *4*, 454–494.

————. Zur Entartungsfrage. *Z. Nervenheilk.*, 1908, *19*, 745–751.

————. Ueber Sprachstörungen im Traume. *Psychol. Arb.*, 1910, *5*, 1–104.

————. Ueber Hysterie. *Z. Neurol.*, 1913, *18*, 261–280.

————. Ein Forschungsinstitut für Psychiatrie. *Z. Neurol.*, 1916, *32*, 1–38.

————. *One hundred years of psychiatry.* New York: Citadel, 1962. (1917)

————. *Ziele und Wege der psychiatrischen Forschung.* Berlin: Springer-Verlag, 1918.

————. Die Erforschung psychischer Krankheitsformen. *Z. Neurol.*, 1919, *51*, 224–246.

————. Arbeitspsychologie. *Naturwissenschaften,* 1920, *8,* 855–859.

————. Wilhelm Wundt. *Z. Neurol.,* 1920, *61,* 351–362.

————. Arbeitspsychologische Untersuchungen. *Z. Neurol.,* 1921, *70,* 230–240.

————. Wesen und Ursachen der Homosexualität. *Z. pädag. Psychol.,* 1922, *23,* 51–56.

————. Zur Kenntnis des Drucksinnes der Haut. *Psychol. Arb.,* 1922, *7,* 413–441.

————. Gedanken über die Arbeitskurve. *Psychol. Arb.,* 1922, *7,* 535–537, 547.

————. Bemerkungen zu der vorstehenden Arbeit. *Psychol. Arb.,* 1923–1925, *8,* 181–185.

————. Fortsetzung der Ermüdigungsmessungen bei einem Kind. *Psychol. Arb.,* 1923–1925, *8,* 204–216.

————. Arbeitpsychologische Ausblicke. *Psychol. Arb.,* 1923–1925, *8,* 431–450.

————. *Irrenfürsorge und Wissenschaft.* Berlin: Springer-Verlag, 1925.

Goshen, *Documentary;* Sahakian, *Psychology;* Shipley, *Classics*

ERNST KRETSCHMER
1888-1964
German Psychiatrist (26)

Kretschmer, E. *Psychotherapeutische Studien.* Stuttgart: Thieme, 1949.   **C**

————. *Gestalten und Gedanken.* Stuttgart: Thieme, 1963.   **B Bl C**

————. *Mensch und Lebensgrund: Gesammelte Aufsätze.* Ed. by W. Kretschmer. Tübingen: Rainer, 1966.   **Bl C**

————. *Die Ideale und die Seele. Ein psychologischer Neuerungsversuch.* Leipzig: Haacke, 1900.

————. Wahnbildung und manisch-depressives Symptomkomplex. *Allg. Z. Psychiat.,* 1914, *71,* 397–464. (Also Berlin: Reimer, 1914)

————. Hysterische Erkränkung und hysterische Gewöhnung. *Z. ges. Neurol. Psychiat.,* 1917, *37,* 64–91.

————. *Der sensitive Beziehungswahn. Ein Beitrag zur Paranoiafrage und zur psychiatrischen Charakterlehre.* (4th ed.) Ed. by W. Kretschmer. Heidelberg: Springer-Verlag, 1966. (1918)

————. Ueber psychogene Wahnbildungen bei traumatischer Hirnschwäche. *Z. ges. Neurol. Psychiat.,* 1919, *45,* 272–300.

————. Zur Kritik des Unbewussten. *Z. ges. Neurol. Psychiat.,* 1919, *46,* 368–387.

————. Seele und Bewusstsein. Kritisches zur Verständigung mit Bleuler. *Z. ges. Neurol. Psychiat.,* 1920, *53,* 97–102.

————. *Körperbau und Charakter: Untersuchungen zum Konstitutionsproblem und zur Lehre von den Temperamenten.* (25th ed.) Ed. by W. Kretschmer. Berlin: Springer-Verlag, 1967. (1921)

————. *Physique and character: An investigation of the nature of constitution and of the theory of temperament.* (2nd rev. ed.) Trans. by W. J. H. Sprott. New York: Harcourt, Brace, 1925. (1921) (Reprinted 1970)

————. *A text-book of medical psychology* (2nd ed.) Trans. by E. B. Strauss. London: Hogarth Press, 1952. (1922)

————. *Medizinische Psychologie.* (12th ed.) Stuttgart: Thieme, 1963. (1922)

————. Konstitution und Rasse. *Z. ges. Neurol. Psychiat.,* 1923, *82,* 139–147.

————. *Hysteria, reflex and instinct* (prob. 6th ed.) Trans. by Vlasta & W. Baskin. New York: Philosophical Library, 1960. (1923)

————, & Kehrer, F. *Die Veranlagung zu seelischen Störungen.* Berlin: Springer-Verlag, 1924.

————. Lebensalter und Umwelt in ihrer Wirkung auf den Konstitutionstypus. *Z. ges. Neurol. Psychiat.,* 1926, *101,* 278–292.

————. *Ueber Hysterie.* (2nd ed.) Leipzig: Thieme, 1927. (1923)

————. Experimentelle Typenpsychologie, sinnes-

und denkpsychologische Resultate. *Z. ges. Neurol. Psychiat.,* 1928, *113,* 776–796.

―――. *The psychology of men of genius.* Trans. by R. B. Cattell. New York: Harcourt, Brace, 1931. (1929) (Reprinted 1970)

―――. *Geniale Menschen.* (5th ed.) Berlin: Springer-Verlag, 1958. (1929)

―――. Breeding of the mental endowments of genius. *Psychiat. Quart.,* 1930, *4,* 74–80.

―――. The experimental method treated as an instrument of psychological investigation. *J. Pers.,* 1932–1933, *1,* 175–180.

―――, & Enke, W. *Die Persönlichkeit der Athletiker.* Leipzig: Thieme, 1936.

―――. Heredity and constitution in the aetiology of psychic disorders. *Brit. Med. J.,* 1937(2), 403–406.

―――. Structure of personality in psychotherapy. *Brit. Med. J.,* 1937(2), 518–522.

―――. Methodisches zur Konstitutionsstatistik. *Z. menschl. Vererbgs.-Konstit.-Lehre,* 1950–1951, *30,* 359–363.

―――. Der triebhafte Verbrecher und seine Diagnostik. *Arch. Psychiat. Nervenkr.,* 1953–1954, *191,* 1–23.

―――. Schizophrenien und Pubertätskrisen und ihre seelische Führung. *Monatssch. Psychiat. Neurol.,* 1953, *125,* 562–571.

―――. Konstitutionelle Entwicklungsphysiologie, ihre experimentelle und arbeitswissenschaftliche Erforschung. *Z. menschl. Vererbgs.-Konstit.-Lehre,* 1953–1954, *32,* 337–344.

―――. Sigmund Freud im Licht der Geschichte. *Z. Psychother. med. Psychol.,* 1957, Suppl., 1–6.

―――. Die somatopsychischen Funktionssysteme der Schizophrenen in ihrer existentiellen und therapeutischen Bedeutung. *Acta Psychother.,* 1960, *8,* 188–200.

Drever, *Sourcebook;* Sahakian, *Psychology*

JOHANNES VON KRIES
1853-1928
German Physiologist (25)

Kries, J. v. *Abhandlungen zur Physiologie der Gesichtsempfindungen.* (5 vols.) Leipzig: Barth, 1897–1925.

―――, & Auerbach, F. Die Zeitdauer einfachster psychischer Vorgänge. *Arch. Anat. Physiol.,* 1877, 297–378.

―――. Beitrag zur Physiologie der Gesichtsempfindungen. *Arch. Anat. Physiol.,* 1878, 503–524.

―――. Ueber die Messung intensiver Grösser und über das sogenannte psychophysiche Gesetz. *Vtljsch. wiss. Phil.,* 1882, *6,* 257–294.

―――. *Die Gesichtsempfindungen und ihre Analyse.* Leipzig: Veit, 1882.

―――. Bemerkungen zu der Arbeit von Aubert "Die Helligkeit des Schwarz und Weiss." *Arch. ges. Physiol.,* 1884, *33,* 249–251.

―――, & Brauneck, H. Ueber einen Fundamentalsatz aus der Theorie der Gesichtsempfindungen. *Arch. Anat. Physiol.,* 1885, 79–84.

―――. Zur Kenntnis der willkürlichen Muskeltätigkeit. *Arch. Anat. Physiol., physiol. Abth.,* 1886 (suppl.), 1–16.

―――. *Die Principien der Wahrscheinlichkeitsrechnung.* Freiburg: Mohr, 1886.

―――. Entgegnung an Herrn E. Hering. *Arch. ges. Physiol.,* 1887, *41,* 389–397.

―――. Ueber Unterscheidungszeiten. *Vtljsch. wiss. Phil.,* 1887, *11,* 1–23.

―――. Ueber Erkennen der Schallrichtung. *Z. Psychol.,* 1890, *1,* 235–251.

―――. Beiträge zur Lehre vom Augenmass. In A. König (Ed.), *Beiträge zur Psychologie und Physiologie der Sinnesorgane.* Hamburg: Voss, 1891, pp. 173–193.

―――. Ueber das absolute Gehör. *Z. Psychol.,* 1892, *3,* 257–279.

―――. Ueber den Einfluss der Adaptation auf Licht und Farbenempfindung und über di

Funktion der Stäbchen. (1894) *Ber. naturf. Ges. Freiburg*, 1895, *9*, 61–70.

————. Ueber die Natur gewisser mit den psychischen Vorgängen verknüpfter Gehirnzustände. *Z. Psychol.*, 1895, *8*, 1–33.

————. Ueber die Funktion der Netzhautstäbchen. *Z. Psychol.*, 1896, *9*, 81–123.

————, & Nagel, W. A. Ueber den Einfluss von Lichtstärke und Adaptation auf das Sehen des Dichromaten (Grünblinden). *Z. Psychol.*, 1896, *12*, 1–38.

————. Ueber die Wirkung kurzdauernder Lichtreize auf das Sehorgan. *Z. Psychol.*, 1896, *12*, 81–101.

————. Ueber das Purkinje'sche Phänomen und sein Fehlen auf der Fovea centralis. *Zbl. Physiol.*, 1896, *10*, 1–3.

————. Ueber die dichromatischen Farbensysteme (Partielle Farbenblindheit). (1896) *Zbl. Physiol.*, 1897, *10*, 148–152; 1919, *56*, 137–152.

————. Ueber die funktionellen Verschiedenheiten des Netzhautzentrums und der Nachbartheile. *Arch. Ophthalm.*, 1896, *42*(3), 95–133.

————. Ueber Farbensysteme. *Z. Psychol.*, 1897, *13*, 241–324, 473.

————. Ueber die Farbenblindheit der Netzhautperipherie. *Z. Psychol.*, 1897, *15*, 247–279.

————. Ueber die absolute Empfindlichkeit der verschiedenen Netzhautteile in dunkeladaptierten Augen. *Z. Psychol.*, 1897, *15*, 327–351.

————. *Ueber die materiellen Grundlagen der Bewusstseinserscheinungen.* Freiburg: Lehmann, 1898.

————. Normal and anomalous colour systems. (1899) In Helmholtz, H. L. F., *Treatise on physiological optics*. Vol. 2 (3rd ed.) *The sensations of vision*. Ed. by J. P. C. Southall. Rochester, N.Y.: Optical Society of America, 1924, pp. 395–425.

————. Ueber die anomalen trichromatischen Farbensysteme. *Z. Psychol.*, 1899, *19*, 63–69.

————. Kritische Bemerkungen zur Farbentheorie. *Z. Psychol.*, 1899, *19*, 175–191.

————, & Nagel, W. A. Weitere Mittheilungen über die funktionelle Sonderstellung des Netzhautzentrums. *Z. Psychol.*, 1900, *23*, 161–186.

————. Ueber die Abhängigkeit der Dämmerungswerthe vom Adaptationsgrade. *Z. Psychol.*, 1901, *25*, 225–238.

————. Ueber die Wirkung kurzdauernder Reize auf das Sehorgan. *Z. Psychol.*, 1901, *28*, 239–243.

————. Ueber die Wahrnehmung des Flimmerns durch normale und durch total farbenblinde Personen. *Z. Psychol.*, 1903, *32*, 113–117.

————. Die Gesichtsempfindungen. In W. Nagel (Ed.), *Handbuch der Physiologie des Menschen*. Vol. 3: *Gesichtssinn*. Brunswick: Vieweg, 1905, pp. 109–282.

————. Zur Psychologie der Sinne. In W. Nagel (Ed.), *Handbuch der Physiologie des Menschen*. Vol. 3. Brunswick: Vieweg, 1905, pp. 16–29.

————. Ueber das Binokularsehen exzentrischer Netzhautteile. *Z. Sinnesphysiol.*, 1909, *44*, 165–181.

————. Appendix 1: Concerning the spatial configuration in vision; with special reference to the question of innate dispositions and experience. (1910) In Helmholtz, H. L. F., *Treatise on physiological optics*. Vol. 3 (3rd ed.). Ed. by J. P. C. Southall. Rochester, N.Y.: Optical Society of America, 1925, pp. 560–652.

————. Ueber einen Fall von einseitiger angeborener Deuteranomalie (Grünschwäche). *Z. Sinnesphysiol.*, 1918, *50*, 137–152.

————. Ueber das stereophotometrische Verfahren zur Helligkeitsvergleichung ungleichfarbiger Lichter. *Naturwissenschaften*, 1923, *11*, 461–470.

————. Zur physiologischen Farbenlehre. *Klin. Monatsbl. Augenhk.*, 1923, *70*, 577–628.

————. *Allgemeine Sinnesphysiologie.* Leipzig: Vogel, 1923.

————. Theories of vision. (1924) In Helmholtz, H. L. F., *Treatise on physiological optics*. Vol. 2 (3rd ed.) *The sensations of vision*. Ed. by J. P. C. Southall. Rochester, N.Y.: Optical Society of America, 1924, pp. 426–454.

———. *Goethe als Psycholog.* Tübingen: Mohr, 1924.

———. Notes, 27–32. (1924) In Helmholtz, H. L. F., *Treatise on physiological optics.* Vol. 3 (3rd ed.). Ed. by J. P. C. Southall. Rochester, N.Y.: Optical Society of America, 1924, pp. 127–154, 232–242, 270–281, 369–400, 488–493, 528–531.

———. *Immanuel Kant und seine Bedeutung für die Naturforschung der Gegenwart.* Berlin: Springer-Verlag, 1924.

———. Ueber einige Aufgaben der Farbenlehre. *Z Tech. Phys.*, 1924, *5*, 327–349.

———. Appendix 2: On the theory of binocular instruments. (1925) In Helmholtz, H. L. F. *Treatise on physiological optics.* Vol. 3 (3rd ed.). Ed. by J. P. C. Southall. Rochester, N.Y.: Optical Society of America, 1925, pp. 652–688.

———. Zur Theorie des Tages- und Dämmerungssehens. In A. Bethe *et al.* (Eds.), *Handbuch der normalen und pathologischen Physiologie.* Vol. 12. Part 1. Berlin: Springer-Verlag, 1929, pp. 679–713.

MacAdam, *Color Science*

ERNST KRIS
1900-1957
Austrian-American Psychoanalyst (11)

Kris, E. *Psychoanalytic explorations in art.* New York: International Universities Press, 1952.
C

Hartmann, H., ———, & Loewenstein, R. M. *Papers on psychoanalytic psychology.* New York: International Universities Press, 1964.
C

———, & Kurz, O. *Die Legende vom Künstler.* Vienna: Krystallverlag, 1934.

———. Zur Psychologie älterer Biographik (dargestellt an der des bildenden Künstlers). *Imago*, 1935, *21*, 320-344. Trans. in *Psychoanalytic explorations in art, op. cit.*, pp. 64–84.

———. On inspiration. *Int. J. Psycho-Anal.*, 1939, *20*, 377–389.

———. The "danger" of propaganda. *Amer. Imago*, 1941, *2*, 3–42.

———. Approaches to art. (1941–1946) In *Psychoanalytic explorations in art, op. cit.*, pp. 13–63.

———, & Speier, H. *German radio propaganda; report on home broadcasts during the war.* London: Oxford University Press, 1944.

Hartmann, H., & ———. The genetic approach in psychoanalysis. *Psychoanal. Stud. Child*, 1945, *1*, 11–30.

Hartmann, H., ———, & Loewenstein, R. M. Comments on the formation of psychic structure. *Psychoanal. Stud. Child*, 1946, *2*, 11–38.

———, & Leites, N. Trends in twentieth century propaganda. In G. Roheim (Ed.), *Psychoanalysis and the social sciences.* Vol. 1. New York: International Universities Press, 1947, pp. 393–409.

———. On preconscious mental processes. *Psychoanal. Quart.*, 1950, *19*, 540–560.

———. The nature of psychoanalytic propositions and their validation. In S. Hook & M. R. Konvitz (Eds.), *Freedom and experience*, Ithaca, N.Y.: Cornell University Press, 1947, pp. 239–259. Reprinted in M. Marx (Ed.), *Psychological theory: Contemporary readings.* New York: Macmillan, 1951, pp. 323–351.

———. *On the origins of psychoanalysis.* New York: Basic Books, 1953. (1950)

———. The significance of Freud's earliest discoveries. *Int. J. Psycho-Anal.*, 1950, *31*, 108–116.

———. Notes on the development and on some current problems of psychoanalytic child psychology. *Psychoanal. Stud. Child*, 1950, *5*, 24–46.

———. Ego psychology and interpretation in psychoanalytic therapy. *Psychoanal. Quart.*, 1951, *20*, 15–30.

———. Neutralization and sublimation: Observations on young children. *Psychoanal. Stud. Child*, 1955, *10*, 30–46.

———. The personal myth: A problem in

psychoanalytic techniques. *J. Amer. Psycho-anal. Assoc.,* 1956, *4,* 653–681.

———. The recovery of childhood memories in psychoanalysis. *Psychoanal. Stud. Child,* 1956, *11,* 54–88.

———. On some vicissitudes of insight in psychoanalysis. *Int. J. Psycho-Anal.,* 1956, *37,* 445–455.

———. Decline and recovery in the life of a three-year-old, or data in psychoanalytic perspective on the mother-child relationship. *Psychoanal. Stud. Child,* 1962, *17,* 175–215.

Rapaport, *Thought ;* Vetter, *Personality*

OSWALD KROH
1887-1955
German Psychologist (12)

Kroh, O. Ueber Farbenkonstanz und Farben-trransformation. *Z. Sinnesphysiol.,* 1921, *52,* 181–216, 235–273.

———. *Eine einzigartige Begabung und ihre psychologische Analyse.* Göttingen: Vandenhoeck & Rupprecht, 1922.

———. *Subjektive Anschauungsbilder bei Jugendlichen.* Göttingen: Vandenhoeck & Rupprecht, 1922.

———. *Die Phasen der Jugendentwicklung: Entwicklungspsychologie des Grundschulkindes.* (2nd ed.) Berlin: Beltz, 1960. (1926)

———, & Scholl, R. Ueber die teilinhaltliche Beachtung von Form und Farbe beim Haushuhn. *Z. Psychol.,* 1926, *100,* 260–273.

———. Weitere Beiträge zur Psychologie des Haushuhns. *Z. Psychol.,* 1927, *103,* 203–227.

———. *Die Psychologie des Grundschulkindes.* (9th & 10th ed.) Langensalza: Beyer, 1931. (1928)

———. *Entwicklungspsychologie des Grundschulkindes.* (13th ed.) Langensalza: Beyer, 1944. (1928)

———. Die Anfänge der psychischen Entwicklung des Kindes in allgemeinpsychologischer Beleuchtung. *Z. Psychol.,* 1929, *100,* 325–343.

——— (with G. Bayer *et al.*). Experimentelle Beiträge zur Typenkunde. Vol. 1. *Z. Psychol.,* 1929, Suppl. 14. (Also Leipzig: Barth, 1929) (Reprinted 1970)

——— (with P. Lamparter & H. Lamparter). Experimentelle Beiträge zur Typenkunde. Vol. 3. *Z. Psychol.,* 1932, Suppl. 22. (Also Leipzig: Barth, 1932) (Reprinted 1970)

———. *Psychologie der Oberstufe.* (6th ed.) Langensalza: Beyer, 1940 (1932)

———. Die Gesetzhaftigkeit geistiger Entwicklung. *Z. pädag. Psychol.,* 1936, *37,* 1–15, 49–65, 97–108.

———. Das Schichtenproblem in entwicklungsgeschichtlicher Beleuchtung. *Arch. ges. Psychol.,* 1937, *98,* 203–216.

———. Pädagogische Psychologie im Dienste völkischer Erziehung. *Z. pädag. Psychol.,* 1937, *38,* 1–13.

———. Vom Auftrag deutscher Erziehungspsychologie. *Z. pädag. Psychol.,* 1940, *41,* 1–8.

———. Abschliessende Bemerkungen zur Diskussion Lamparter-Wellek. *Z. Psychol.,* 1941–1942, *151,* 322–331.

———. Zum Ausbau der Prüfungsordnung für Diplomspsychologen. *Z. Psychol.,* 1943, *155,* 1–15.

———. Missverständnisse um die Psychologie. *Deutschlands Erneuerung,* 1943, *27,* 21–37.

———. Zur Prinzipienlehre des pädagogischen Geschehens. *Z. pädag. Psychol.,* 1943, *44,* 1–19.

———. Von Wahr- und Wachträumen. Zur Frage nach dem Sinn des Traumes. *Z. Psychol.,* 1944, *156,* 66–84.

———. Vom Wesen und Aufgabenbereich der pädagogischen Psychologie. *Int. Z. Erziehung,* 1944, *13,* 161–174.

———. Zur Psychologie des Schulanfängers. *Pädagogik,* 1948, *3,* 63–83.

———. Vom Einfluss der gesellschaftlichen Verhältnisse auf die Charakterentwicklung. *Psychol. Rundsch.,* 1949–1950, *1,* 26–36.

———. Die Eidetik in neuer Beleuchtung. *Psychol. Rundsch.,* 1950, *1,* 257–265.

———. *Revision der Erziehung.* (5th ed.) Heidelberg: Quelle & Meyer, 1960. (1952)

———. Allgemeinpsychologische Folgerungen aus kindespsychologischen Erkenntnissen. *Stud. Gen.,* 1952, *5,* 267–279.

———. Erziehung aus mitmenschlicher Verantwortung. *Pädag. Bl.,* 1953, *4,* 1–5.

———. Sexualerziehung aus sozialethischer Verantwortung. *Jb. Psychol. Psychother.,* 1953, *1,* 489–512.

———. Vom Auftrag der Psychologie in der Krise der Gegenwart. *Psychol. Rundsch.,* 1955, *6,* 29–32.

———. Der Einfluss der geänderten gesellschaftlichen Verhältnisse auf das Erziehungsdenken der letzten Jahrzehnte. *Bildung u. Erziehung,* 1955, *8,* 489–505.

———. Die Bedeutung der modernen Persönlichkeitsforschung für die Erziehung. *Jb. Psychol. Psychother.,* 1955, *3,* 272–279.

———. Aufgaben und Methoden der allgemeinen Entwicklungspsychologie. In O. W. Haseloff & H. Stachowiak (Eds.), *Moderne Entwicklungspsychologie.* Berlin: Lüttke, 1956, pp. 15–23.

———. Psychologische Probleme des Schulkindalters. (1956) In O. W. Haseloff & H. Stachowiak (Eds.), *Moderne Entwicklungspsychologie, op. cit.,* pp. 69–78.

———. Das Leib-Seele-Problem in entwicklungspsychologischer Sicht. *Studium Gen.,* 1956, *9,* 249–273.

———. Die psychologischen und pädagogischen Veröffentlichungen. *Jb. Psychol. Psychother.,* 1956, *4,* 338–345.

FELIX (E.) KRUEGER
1874-1948
German Psychologist (20)

Krueger, F. *Zur Philosophie und Psychologie der Ganzheit: Schriften aus den Jahren 1918–1940.* Ed. by E. Heuss. Berlin: Springer-Verlag, 1953.
C

———. *Ist Philosophie ohne Psychologie möglich?* Munich: Ackermann, 1896.

———. *Der Begriff des absolut Wertvollen als Grundbegriff der Moralphilosophie.* Leipzig: Teubner, 1898.

———. Beobachtungen an Zweiklängen. *Phil. Stud.,* 1900, *16,* 307–379, 568–664.

———. Zur Theorie der Combinationstöne. *Phil. Stud.,* 1901, *17,* 185–310.

———. *Das Bewusstsein der Konsonanz. Eine psychologische Analyse.* Leipzig: Engelmann, 1903.

———. Differenztöne und Konsonanz. *Arch. ges. Psychol.,* 1903, *1,* 20–275; 1903, *2,* 1–80.

———, & Spearman, C. E. Die Korrelation zwischen verschiedenen geistigen Leistungsfähigkeiten. *Z. Psychol.,* 1906, *44,* 50–114.

———. *Beziehungen der experimentellen Phonetik zur Psychologie.* Leipzig: Barth, 1907. (1906)

———. Die Theorie der Konsonanz. Eine psychologische Auseinandersetzung vornehmlich mit C. Stumpf und Th. Lipps. *Psychol. Stud.,* 1906, *1,* 305–387; 1907, *2,* 205–255; 1908, *4,* 207–282; 1910, *5,* 294–411.

———. *Mitbewegungen beib Singen, Sprechen und Hören.* Leipzig: Breitkopf & Härtel, 1910.

———. Consonance and dissonance. *J. Phil.,* 1913, *10,* 158–160.

———. Magical factors in the first development of human labor. *Amer. J. Psychol.,* 1913, *24,* 256–261.

———. New aims and tendencies in psychology. *Phil. Rev.,* 1913, *22,* 251–264.

———. *Ueber Entwicklungspsychologie, ihre sachliche und geschichtliche Notwendigkeit.* Leipzig: Engelmann, 1915.

———. Die Tiefendimension und die Gegensätzlichkeit des Gefühlslebens. In *Festschrift zu Johannes Volkelts 70. Geburtstag.* Munich: Beck, 1918, pp. 265–286. Reprinted in *Zur Philosophie und Psychologie der Ganzheit, op. cit.,* pp. 177–194.

———. *Selbstbesinnung in deutscher Not. Rede an die aus dem Felde Zurückgekehrten der Universität Leipzig.* Stuttgart: Enke, 1919.

———. *Wilhelm Wundt als deutscher Denker.* (2nd ed.) Erfurt: Stenger, 1924. (1922)

———. *Der Strukturbegriff in der Psychologie.* Jena: Fischer, 1931. (1924) Reprinted in *Zur Philosophie und Psychologie der Ganzheit, op. cit.*, pp. 125–145.

———. Zur Entwicklungspsychologie des Rechts. *Arb. Z. Entw.-Psychol.*, 1926, *7*, 737–778.

———. Zur Einführung. Ueber psychische Ganzheit. *Neue Psychol. Stud.*, 1926, *1*, 5–121. Reprinted in *Zur Philosophie und Psychologie der Ganzheit, op. cit.*, pp. 33–124.

———. *Das Wesen der Gefühle. Entwurf einer systematischen Theorie.* (5th ed.) Leipzig: Akademische Verlagsgesellschaft, 1937. (1928) Reprinted in *Zur Philosophie und Psychologie der Ganzheit, op. cit.*, pp. 195–221.

———. *Wissenschaften und der Zusammenhang des Wirklichen.* Munich: Beck, 1928.

———. The essence of feeling: Outline of a systematic theory. In M. L. Reymert (Ed.), *Feelings and emotions: The Wittenberg symposium.* Worcester, Mass.: Clark University Press, 1928, pp. 58–88.

———. Die Arbeit des Menschen als philosophisches Problem. *Bl. deutsch. Phil.*, 1929, *3*, 159–192.

———. *Die Aufgaben der Psychologie an den deutschen Hochschulen.* Jena: Fischer, 1932.

———. Das Problem der Ganzheit. *Bl. deutsch. Phil.*, 1932, *6*, 111–139. Reprinted in *Zur Philosophie und Psychologie der Ganzheit, op. cit.*, pp. 151–177.

———. Zweckmässigkeit, Sinn und Wert. *Bl. deutsch. Phil.*, 1934, *7*, 459–466.

———. *Zur Psychologie des Gemeinschaftslebens.* Jena: Fischer, 1935.

———. Gefühlsartiges im tierischen Verhalten. In *Z. Tierpsychol.*, 1937, *1*, 97–128. Reprinted in *Zur Philosophie und Psychologie der Ganzheit, op. cit.*, pp. 222–259.

———. Der strukturelle Grund des Fühlens und des Wollens. *XV. Kongr. Dtsch. Ges. Psychol.*, Jena, 1937, 181-189. Reprinted in *Zur Philosophie und Psychologie der Ganzheit, op. cit.*, pp. 260–267.

———. Entwicklungspsychologie der Ganzheit. In *Riv. Psicol.*, 1939, *2*, 427–461 ; 1940, *3*, 88–125. Reprinted in *Zur Philosophie und Psychologie der Ganzheit, op. cit.*, pp. 268–325.

———. Otto Klemm und das Psychologische Institut der Universität Leipzig. *Z. angew. Psychol.*, 1939, *56*, 253–346. (Also Leipzig: Barth, 1939)

———. *Lehre von dem Ganzen. Seele, Gemeinschaft und das Göttliche.* Bern: Huber, 1948.

B

Arnold, *Emotion*

FREDERICK KUHLMANN
1876-1941
American Psychologist (11)

Kuhlmann, F. Experimental studies in mental deficiency: Three cases of imbecility (Mongolian) and six cases of feeble-mindedness. *Amer. J. Psychol.*, 1904, *15*, 391–446.

———. The place of mental imagery and memory among mental functions. *Amer. J. Psychol.*, 1905, *16*, 337–356.

———. On the analysis of the memory consciousness: A study in the mental imagery and memory of meaningless visual figures. *Psychol. Rev.*, 1906, *13*, 316–348.

———. On the analysis of memory consciousness for pictures of familiar objects. *Amer. J. Psychol.*, 1907, *18*, 389–420.

———. Problems in the analysis of the memory consciousness, *J. Phil.*, 1907, *4*, 5–14.

———. Some preliminary observations on the development of instincts and habits in young birds. *Psychol. Monogr.*, 1909, *11*, No. 44, pp. 49–84.

———. On the analysis of auditory memory consciousness. *Amer. J. Psychol.*, 1909, *20*, 194–218.

————. Binet and Simon's system for measuring the intelligence of children. *J. Psycho-Asthen.,* 1911, *15,* 76–92.

————. A revision of the Binet-Simon system for measuring the intelligence of children. *J. Psycho-Asthen. Monogr. Suppl.,* 1912, No. 1.

————. The results of grading thirteen hundred feeble-minded children with the Binet-Simon tests. *J. educ. Psychol.,* 1913, *4,* 261–268.

————. Zur Psychologie der Schrift des Kindes. *Z. pädag. Psychol.,* 1914, *15,* 488–491.

————. What constitutes feeble-mindedness? *J. Psycho-Asthen.,* 1915, *19,* 214–236.

————. Distribution of the feeble-minded in society. *J. crim. Law Criminol.,* 1916, *7,* 205–218.

————. Part played by the state institutions in the care of the feeble-minded. *J. Psycho-Asthen.,* 1916, *21,* 3–24.

————. A further extension and revision of the Binet-Simon Scale. *J. crim. Law Criminol.,* 1918, *8,* 890–901.

————. The results of repeated mental re-examinations of 639 feeble-minded over a period of ten years. *J. appl. Psychol.,* 1921, *5,* 195–224.

————. *Handbook of mental tests: A further revision and extension of the Binet-Simon Scale.* Baltimore, Md.: Warwick & York, 1922.

————, *et al.* Mental deficiency, feeble-mindedness, and defective delinquency. *Proc. Amer. Ass. Stud. Feeble-Mind.,* 1924, *29,* 58–76.

————. The Kuhlmann-Anderson Intelligence Tests compared with seven others. *J. appl. Psychol.,* 1928, *12,* 545–594.

————. A new scale of intelligence tests with some new measures. *Proc. Amer. Ass. ment. Def.,* 1938, *43,* 47–55.

————. One hundred years of special care and training. *Amer. J. ment. Def.,* 1940, *45,* 8–24.

————. Definition of mental deficiency. *Amer. J. ment. Def.,* 1941, *46,* 206–213.

————. Types of total scores on mental tests with special reference to a median score on a Binet-type scale. *J. consult. Psychol.,* 1941, 5, 279–286.

————. Retrogressive trends in clinical psychology. *J. consult. Psychol.,* 1941, *5,* 97–104.

————. Our changing fashions in methods of research. *Amer. J. Psychol.,* 1942, *55,* 569–573.

————, & Odoroff, M. E. Verification of the Heinis mental growth curve on results with the Stanford-Binet tests. *J. Psychol.,* 1942, *13,* 355–364.

————. Classification and licensing of psychologists. *Amer. J. Psychol.,* 1943, *56,* 120–129.

OSWALD KULPE
1862-1915
German Psychologist (27)

Külpe, O. Zur Theorie der sinnlichen Gefühle. *Vtljsch. wiss. Phil.,* 1887, *11,* 424–482 ; 1888, *12,* 50–80.

————. Die Lehre vom Willen in der neueren Psychologie. *Phil. Stud.,* 1888–1889, *5,* 179–244, 381–446. (Also Leipzig: Engelmann, 1888.)

————. Ueber die Gleichzeitigkeit und Ungleichzeitigkeit. *Phil. Stud.,* 1890–1891, *6,* 514–535 ; 1892, *7,* 147–168.

————. Das Ich und die Aussenwelt. *Phil. Stud.,* 1892, *7,* 394–413 ; 1893, *8,* 311–341.

————. Anfang und Aussicht der Experimente. *Arch. Ges. Phil.,* 1893, *6,* 170–189, 449–467.

————. *Outlines of psychology: Based upon the results of experimental investigation.* (3rd ed.) Trans. by E. B. Titchener. New York: Macmillan, 1909. (1893)

————, & Kirschmann, A. Ein neuer Apparat zur Kontrolle zeitmessender Instrumente. *Phil. Stud.,* 1893, *8,* 145–172.

————. Aussichten der experimentellen Psychologie. *Phil. Monatsschr.,* 1894, *30,* 281–294.

————. *Introduction to philosophy: A handbook for students of psychology, logic, ethics, aes-*

thetics and general philosophy. Trans. by W. B. Pillsbury & E. B. Titchener. New York: Macmillan, 1907, (1895)

————. *Einleitung in die Philosophie.* (7th ed.) Leipzig: Hirzel, 1915. (1895)

————. Zur Lehre von der Aufmerksamkeit. *Z. Phil. phil. Krit.,* 1897, *110,* 7–38.

————. Ueber die Beziehungen zwischen körperlichen und seelischen Vorgängen. *Z. Hypno.,* 1898, *7,* 97–120.

————. Ueber den assoziativen Faktor des ästhetischen Eindrucks. *Vtljsch. wiss. Phil.,* 1899, *23,* 145–183.

————. Zu Gustav Theodor Fechners Gedächtnis. *Vtljsch. wiss. Phil.,* 1901, *25,* 190–217.   **B**

————. Ueber die Objektivirung und Subjektivirung von Sinneseindrücken. *Phil. Stud.,* 1902, *19,* 508–556.

————. The problem of attention. *Monist,* 1902, *13,* 38–68.

————. Zur Frage nach der Beziehung der ebenmerklichen zu den übermerklichen Unterschieden. *Phil. Stud.,* 1902, *18,* 328–346.

————. *Die Philosophie der Gegenwart in Deutschland.* (6th ed.) Leipzig: Hirzel, 1913. (1902)

————. Ein Beitrag zur experimentellen Aesthetik. *Amer. J. Psychol.,* 1903, *14,* 479–495.

————. Versuche über Abstraktion. *Ber. I. Kongr. exp. Psychol.,* 1904, 56–68.

————. Der gegenwärtige Stand der Experimental-Aesthetik. *Ber. II. Kongr. exp. Psychol.,* Würzburg, 1906. Leipzig: Barth, 1907, pp. 1–57.

————. *Immanuel Kant. Darstellung und Würdigung.* (5th ed.) Ed. by A. Messer. Leipzig: Teubner, 1921. (1907)

————. Ein Beitrag zur Gefühlslehre. *III. Int. Kongr. exp. Psychol.,* 1908, 1909, 546–555.

————. Zur Psychologie der Gefühle. *VI. Kongr. int. Psychol.,* 1910 (1909), 183–196.

————. *Erkenntnistheorie und Naturwissenschaft.* Leipzig: Hirzel, 1910.

————. Pour la psychologie du sentiment. *J. Psychol. norm. path.,* 1910, *7,* 1–13.

————. *Psychologie und Medizin.* Leipzig: Engelmann, 1912.

————. Ueber die moderne Psychologie des Denkens. *Int. Monatsschr. Wiss., Kunst Technik,* 1912, *6,* 1070–1110.

————. *Die Realisierung: Ein Beitrag zur Grundlegung der Realwissenschaften.* (3 vols.) Vols. 2 & 3 ed. by A. Messer. Leipzig: Hirzel, 1912–1923.

————. *Die Ethik und der Krieg.* Leipzig: Hirzel, 1915.

————. Ernst Neumann und die Aesthetik. *Z. pädag. Psychol.,* 1915, *16,* 232–238.

————. Antwort. *Z. pädag. Psychol.,* 1915, *17,* 169–170.

————. *Vorlesungen über Psychologie.* (2nd ed.) Ed. by K. Bühler. Leipzig: Hirzel, 1922. (1920)

————. *Grundlagen der Aesthetik.* Ed. by S. Behn. Leipzig: Hirzel, 1921.

Beck & Molish, *Reflexes;* Mandler & Mandler, *Thinking*

GEORGE TRUMBULL LADD
1842-1921
American Psychologist (24)

Ladd, G. T. *Elements of physiological psychology.* New York: Scribner's, 1887.

————, & Woodworth, R.S. *Elements of physiological psychology.* (Rev. ed.) New York: Scribner's, 1911. (1887)

————. On body and mind. *Mind,* 1888, *13,* 627–629.

————. *Introduction to philosophy.* New York: Scribner's, 1890.

————. Influence of modern psychology upon theological opinion. *Andover Rev.,* 1890, *14,* 557–578.

————. *Outlines of physiological psychology.* New York: Scribner's, 1890.

————. A contribution to the psychology of visual dreams. *Mind*, 1892, *1*, 299–304.

————. Psychology as so-called "natural science." *Phil. Rev.*, 1892, *1*, 24–53.

————. *Primer of psychology.* New York: Longmans, Green, 1894.

————. Direct control of the retinal field. *Psychol. Rev.*, 1894, *1*, 351–355.

————. Is psychology a science? *Psychol. Rev.*, 1894, *1*, 392–395.

————. *Psychology: Descriptive and explanatory: A treatise of the phenomena, laws, and development of human mental life.* New York: Scribner's, 1894.

————. *Philosophy of mind.* New York: Scribner's, 1895.

————. The consciousness of identity and so-called double consciousness. *Psychol. Rev.*, 1895, *2*, 159–161.

————. Consciousness and evolution. *Psychol. Rev.*, 1896, *3*, 296–300.

————. *Philosophy of knowledge.* New York: Scribner's, 1897. (Reprinted 1970)

————. *Outlines of descriptive psychology: A textbook of mental science for colleges and normal schools.* New York: Scribner's, 1898.

————. A color illusion. *Stud. Yale psychol. Lab.*, 1898, *6*, 1–5.

————. *A theory of reality.* New York: Scribner's, 1899.

————. *Essays on the higher education.* New York: Scribner's, 1899.

————. On certain hindrances to the progress of psychology in America. *Psychol. Rev.*, 1899, *6*, 121–133.

————. *Philosophy of conduct.* New York: Scribner's, 1902.

————. Legal aspects of hypnotism. *Yale Law Rev.*, 1902, *11*, 173–194.

————. Direct control of the "retinal field": Report of three cases. *Psychol. Rev.*, 1903, *10*, 139–149.

————. Brief critique of "psychological parallelism." *Mind*, 1903, *12*(N.S.), 374–380.

————. Suggestions from two cases of cerebral surgery without anesthetics. *Pop. Sci. Mon.*, 1909, *74*, 562–567.

————. *The teacher's practical philosophy.* New York: Funk & Wagnalls, 1911.

————. The ontological problem of psychology. *Phil. Rev.*, 1911, *20*, 363–385.

————. Rationalism and empiricism. *Mind*, 1913, *22*, 1–13.

————. The study of man. *Science*, 1913, *37*, 275–290.

————. A defence of idealism. *Mind*, 1914, *23*, 473–488.

————. *The secret of personality.* New York: Longmans, Green, 1918.

————. A case of multiple personality. *Yale Rev.*, 1919, *8*, 318–333.

Sahakian, *Psychology*

CHRISTINE LADD-FRANKLIN
1847-1930
American Psychologist (22)

Ladd-Franklin, Christine. *Colour and colour theories.* New York: Harcourt, Brace, 1929.
C

————. A method for the experimental determination of the horopter. *Amer. J. Psychol.*, 1887, *1*, 99–111.

————. On some characteristics of symbolic logic. *Amer. J. Psychol.*, 1889, *2*, 543–567.

————. Eine neue Theorie der Lichtempfindungen. *Z. Psychol.*, 1892, *4*, 211–221. Reprinted in *Colour and colour theories, op. cit.*, pp. 219–230.

————. On theories of light-sensation. *Mind*, 1893, *2*(N.S.), 473–489. Reprinted in *Colour and colour theories, op. cit.*, pp. 72–91.

————. Intuition and reason. *Monist*, 1893, *3*, 211–219.

————. Professor Ebbinghaus' theory of colour vision. *Mind*, 1894, *3*(N.S.), 98–104.

————. Colour-sensation theory. *Psychol. Rev.*, 1894, *1*, 169–171.

————. Normal night-blindness of the fovea. *Psychol. Rev.*, 1895, *2*, 137–148. Reprinted in *Colour and colour theories, op. cit.*, pp. 92–104.

————. The inverted image on the retina. *Science*, 1896, *3*, 201–203, 517.

————. The colour-vision of approaching sleep. *Psychol. Rev.*, 1897, *4*, 641-643.

————. The extended Purkinje phenomenon (for gray lights). *Psychol. Rev.*, 1898, *5*, 309–312.

————. (Review) Helmholtz' "Physiologische Optik." *Psychol. Rev.*, 1898, *5*, 416–420.

————. Professor Muller's theory of the light-sense. *Psychol. Rev.*, 1899, *6*, 70–85.

————. The dissimilarity in function of the rods and the cones of the retina. *Psychol. Rev.*, 1900, *7*, 600–606. Reprinted in *Colour and colour theories, op. cit.*, pp. 105–113.

————. Ebbinghaus's theory of color-vision. *Science*, 1901, *14*, 30–31.

————. On colour theories and chromatic sensations. *Psychol. Rev.*, 1916, *23*, 237–249. Reprinted in *Colour and colour theories, op. cit.*, pp. 132–147.

————. Practical logic and color theories. *Psychol. Rev.*, 1922, *29*, 180–200. Reprinted in *Colour and colour theories, op. cit.*, pp. 165–186.

————. Tetrachromatic vision and the genetic theory of color. *Amer. J. physiol. Opt.*, 1923, *4*, 403–415.

————. L'état actuel du problème de la nature des sensations de couleur. *Année psychol.*, 1924, *25*, 1–17.

————. The nature of the color sensations (1924). In Helmholtz, H. L. F., *Treatise on physiological optics*. Vol. 2. *The sensations of vision*. Ed. by J. P. C. Southall. Rochester, N.Y.: Optical Society of America, 1924, pp. 455–468. Reprinted in *Colour and colour theories, op. cit.*, pp. 148–164.

Sahakian, *Psychology*; Teevan, *Vision*

JEAN BAPTISTE PIERRE ANTOINE DE MONET LAMARCK
1744-1829
French Biologist (23)

Lamarck, J. B. P. A. *The Lamarck manuscripts at Harvard*. Ed. by W. M. Wheeler & T. Barbour. Cambridge: Harvard University Press, 1933.
C

————. *Inédits de Lamarck d'après les manuscrits conservés à la Bibliothèque centrale du Muséum d'Histoire naturelle de Paris*. Ed. by M. Vachon, G. Rousseau, & Y. Laissus. Paris: Masson, 1971.
C

————. *Recherches sur les causes des principaux faits physiques, et particulièrement sur celles de la combustion, de l'élévation de l'eau dans l'état de vapeurs ; de la chaleur produite par le frottement des corps solides entre eux ; de la chaleur qui se rend sensible dans des décompositions subites, dans les effervescences et dans le corps de beaucoup d'animaux pendant la durée de leur vie ; de la causticité, de la saveur et de l'odeur de certains composés ; de la couleur des corps ; de l'origine des composés et de tous les minéraux ; enfin l'entretien de la vie des êtres organiques, de leur accroissement, de leur état de vigeur, de leur dépérissement et de leur mort.* (2 vols.) Paris: Maradan, 1794.
C

————. *Mémoires de physique et d'histoire naturelle, établis sur des bases de raisonnement indépendantes de toute théorie, avec l'exposition de nouvelles considérations sur la cause générale des dissolutions ; sur la matière de feu, sur la couleur des corps ; sur la formation des composés ; sur l'origine des minéraux ; et sur l'organisation des corps vivants.* Paris: Agasse, 1797.

————. *Gall's system.* (ca. 1800) In *The Lamarck manuscripts at Harvard, op. cit.*, pp. 103–139.

————. *Système des animaux sans vertèbres, ou tableau général des classes, des ordres et des genres de ces animaux.* Brussels: Culture et Civilisation, 1969, (1801)

————. *Recherches sur l'organisation des corps vivants et particulièrement sur son origine, sur la cause de son développement et des progrès de sa composition (et sur celle qui, tendant continuellement à la détruire, dans chaque in-*

dividu, amène nécessairement sa mort. Paris: Author (Maillard), 1802.

―――. *Hydrogeology.* Trans. by A. V. Carozzi. Urbana, Ill.: University of Illinois Press, 1964. (1802)

―――. Discours d'ouverture (An VIII, An X, An XI et 1806). In A. Giard (Ed.), *Bulletin scientifique de la France et de la Belgique.* Vol. 40. Paris: Danel, 1907.

―――. *Zoological philosophy: An exposition with regard to the natural history of animals.* Trans. by H. Elliot. New York: Hafner, 1963. (1809)

―――. *Philosophie zoologique.* (2 vols.) Brussels: Culture et Civilisation, 1969. (1809)

―――. *Histoire naturelle des animaux sans vertèbres, présentant les caractères généraux et particuliers de ces animaux, leur distribution, leurs classes, leurs familles, leurs genres, et la citation des principales espèces qui s'y rapportent; précédée d'une Introduction offrant la détermination des caractères essentiels de l'animal, sa distinction du végétal et des autres corps naturels, enfin, l'exposition des principes fondamentaux de la zoologie.* (7 vols.) Paris: Verdière, 1815–1822. (Reprinted 1969)

―――. Idea and imagination. (1817) In *The Lamarck manuscripts at Harvard, op. cit.,* pp. 140–174.

―――. Faculté. In Anon, *Nouveau dictionnaire d'histoire naturelle.* Vol. 11. Paris: Déterville, 1817, pp. 8–18.

―――. Fonctions organiques. (1817) In *Nouveau dictionnaire,* Vol. 11, *op. cit.,* pp. 593–596.

―――. Habitude. (1817) In *Nouveau dictionnaire,* Vol. 14, *op. cit.,* pp. 129–138.

―――. Homme. (1817) In *Nouveau dictionnaire,* Vol. 15, *op. cit.,* pp. 270–276.

―――. Jugement. (1817) In *Nouveau dictionnaire,* Vol. 16, *op. cit.,* pp. 570–579.

―――. Intelligence. (1817) In *Nouveau dictionnaire,* Vol. 16, *op. cit.,* pp. 344–360.

―――. Instinct. (1817) In *Nouveau dictionnaire,* Vol. 16, *op. cit.,* pp. 331–343.

―――. Imagination. (1817) In *Nouveau dictionnaire,* Vol. 16, *op. cit.,* pp. 126–132.

―――. Idée. (1817) In *Nouveau dictionnaire,* Vol. 16, *op. cit.,* pp. 78–94.

―――. *Système analytique des connaissances positives de l'homme restreintes à celles qui proviennent directement ou indirectement de l'observation.* Paris: Author, 1820. (Reprinted 1970)

Bodenheimer, *Biology;* Count, *Race;* Dampier, *Literature;* Grinder, *Genetic Psychology;* Hall, *Source Book;* Rook, *Origins;* Schwartz & Bishop, *Moments Discovery*

JULIEN OFFRAY DE LA METTRIE
1709-1751
French Philosopher (26)

La Mettrie, J. O. d. *Oeuvres philosophiques* (2 vols. in 1) Hildesheim: Olms, 1970. (1774) **C**

―――. *La Mettrie: Textes choisis.* Ed. by Marcelle Tisserand. Paris: Editions Sociales, 1954. **C**

―――. *Traité du vertige avec la description d'une catalepsie hystérique* . . . Rennes: Garnier, 1837. (1737)

―――. *Essai sur l'esprit et les beaux esprits.* Amsterdam: Bernard, 1740.

―――. *Institutions de médecine de Mr. Herman Boerhaave.* (2nd ed.) (8 vols.) Paris: Huart, Briasson, Durand, 1743–1750.

―――. Traité de l'âme. (1745) In *Oeuvres philosophiques,* Vol. 1, *op. cit.,* pp. 1–185.

―――. La volupté par Mr. le Chevalier de M. (1745) In *Oeuvres philosophiques,* Vol. 2, *op. cit.,* pp. 195–267.

―――. The natural history of the soul: Extracts. (1745) In *Man a machine, vide infra,* pp. 151–161.

―――. Abrégé des systèmes. (ca. 1747) In *Oeuvres philosophiques,* Vol. 1, *op. cit.,* pp. 189–226.

―――. *Man a machine.* Trans. by Gertrude C.

Bussey & Mary W. Calkins. La Salle, Ill.: Open Court, 1912. (1748)

————. *L'Homme-Plante*. Ed. by F. L. Rougier. New York: Columbia University Institute of French Studies, 1936. (1748)

————. L'homme machine. (1748) In *Oeuvres philosophiques*, Vol. 1, *op. cit.*, pp. 269–356.

————. Les animaux plus que machines. (1750) In *Oeuvres philosophiques*, Vol. 2, *op. cit.*, pp. 23–80.

————. Epître à mon esprit *ou* L'anonyme persiflé. (1774) In *Oeuvres philosophiques*, Vol. 2, *op. cit.*, pp. 181–193.

Bodenheimer, *Biology;* Herrnstein & Boring, *Source Book;* Matson, *Being;* Sahakian, *Psychology;* Torrey, *Les Philosophes*

CARNEY LANDIS
1897-1962
American Psychologist (16)

Landis, C. Studies of emotional reactions. I. A preliminary study of facial expression. *J. exp. Psychol.*, 1924, 7, 325–341.

————. Studies of emotional reactions. II. General behavior and facial expression. *J. comp. Psychol.*, 1924, 4, 447–509.

————, Gullette, Ruth, & Jacobsen, C. Criteria of emotionality. *J. genet. Psychol.*, 1925, 32, 209–234.

————, & Gullette, Ruth. Studies of emotional reactions. III. Systolic blood pressure and inspiration-expiration ratios. *J. comp. Psychol.*, 1925, 5, 221–253.

————. Studies of emotional reactions. V. Severe emotional upset. *J. comp. Psychol.*, 1926, 6, 221–242.

————. Electrical phenomena of the body during sleep. *Amer. J. Physiol.*, 1927, 81, 6–19.

————, & De Wick, H. N. The electrical phenomena of the skin (psychogalvanic reflex). *Psychol. Bull.*, 1929, 26, 64–119.

————. Emotion. II. The expressions of emotion. In C. Murchison (Ed.), *The foundations of experimental psychology*. Worcester, Mass.: Clark University Press, 1929, pp. 488–523.

————. Psychology and the psychogalvanic reflex. *Psychol. Rev.*, 1930, 37, 381–398.

————, & Hunt, W. A. Adrenalin and emotion. *Psychol. Rev.*, 1932, 39, 467–485.

————. Electrical phenomena of the skin (galvanic skin response). *Psychol. Bull.*, 1932, 29, 693–752.

————. An attempt to measure emotional traits in juvenile delinquency. In K. S. Lashley (Ed.), *Studies in dynamics of behavior*. Chicago: University of Chicago Press, 1932, pp. 265–323.

————. Emotion. II. The expressions of emotion. In C. Murchison (Ed.), *A handbook of general experimental psychology*. Worcester, Mass.: Clarke University Press, 1934, pp. 312–351.

————, & Hunt, W. A. The conscious correlates of the galvanic skin response. *J. exp. Psychol.*, 1935, 18, 505–529.

————, & Page, J. D. *Modern society and mental disease*. New York: Farrar & Rinehart, 1938.

————, & Hunt, W. A. *The startle pattern*. New York: Rinehart, 1939. (Reprinted 1967)

————, *et al. Sex in development*. New York: Hoeber, 1940. (Reprinted 1970)

————. Psychoanalytic phenomena. *J. abnorm. soc. Psychol.*, 1940, 35, 17–28.

————, & Bolles, M. Marjorie. *Personality and sexuality of the physically handicapped woman*. New York: Hoeber, 1942.

————, & Bolles, M. Marjorie. *Textbook of abnormal psychology*. (Rev. ed.) New York: Macmillan, 1950. (1946)

————. A modern dynamic psychology. *J. comp. physiol. Psychol.*, 1947, 40, 135–141.

————, Zubin, J., & Mettler, F. A. The functions of the human frontal lobe. *J. Psychol.*, 1950, 30, 123–138.

————. Determinants of the critical flicker-fusion threshold. *Physiol. Rev.*, 1954, 34, 259–286.

————. *Varieties of psychopathological experience.* Ed. by F. A. Mettler. New York: Holt, 1964.

Valentine, *Experimental*

CARL GEORG LANGE
1834-1900
Danish Physiologist (14)

Lange, C. G., & James, W. *The emotions.* Ed. by K. Dunlap. Baltimore, Md.: Williams & Wilkins, 1922. (1884, 1893) (Reprinted 1967)

————. *Om sindsbevaegelser, et psyko-fysiologisk studie.* Leipzig: Thomas, 1887. (1885)

————. *Ueber Gemütsbewegungen.* Trans. by H. Kurella. Leipzig: Thomas, 1887. (1885)

————. *Die Gemütsbewegungen, ihr Wesen und ihr Einfluss auf körperliche, besonders auf krankhafte Lebenserscheinungen.* (2nd ed.) Würzburg: Kabitzsch, 1910. (1885)

————. *Periodische Depressionszustände und ihre Pathogenesis auf dem Boden der harnsauren Diathese.* Hamburg: Voss, 1896.

Rand, *Classical Psychologists*; Sahakian, *Psychology*

(GUSTAV) LUDWIG LANGE
1863-1936
German Psychologist (12)

Lange, L. Ueber die wissenschaftliche Fassung des Galilei'schen Beharrungsgesetzes. *Phil. Stud.,* 1883–1885, *2,* 266–297.

————. Nochmals über das Beharrungsgesetz. *Phil. Stud.,* 1883–1885, *2,* 539–545.

————. Die geschichtliche Entwicklung des Bewegungsbegriffes und ihr voraussichtliches Endergebniss. Ein Beitrag zur historischen Kritik der mechanischen Principien. *Phil. Stud.,* 1886, *3,* 337–419, 643–691.

————. Ein Chronograph nebst Controllapparat für sehr genaue Zeitmessungen. *Phil. Stud.,* 1887–1888, *4,* 457–470.

————. Neue Experimente über den Vorgang der einfachen Reaktion auf Sinneseindrücke. *Phil. Stud.,* 1887–1888, *4,* 479–510.

————. Ueber das Massprincip der Psychophysik und den Algorithmus der Empfindungsgrössen. *Phil. Stud.,* 1894, *10,* 125–139.

————. Das Inertialsystem vor dem Forum der Naturforschung. Kritisches und Antikritisches. *Phil. Stud.,* 1902, *20,* 1–71.

HERBERT SIDNEY LANGFELD
1879-1958
American Psychologist (20)

Langfeld, H. S. Titchener's system of psychology. *Monist,* 1911, *21,* 624–630.

————. Voluntary movement under positive and negative instruction. *Psychol. Rev.,* 1913, *20,* 459–478.

————. A study in simultaneous and alternating finger movements. *Psychol. Rev.,* 1915, *22,* 453–478.

————. Concerning the image. *Psychol. Rev.,* 1916, *23,* 180–189.

————, & Allport, F. H. *An elementary laboratory course in psychology.* Boston: Houghton Mifflin, 1916.

————. The differential limen for finger span. *J. exp. Psychol.,* 1917, *2,* 416–430.

————. The judgment of emotions from facial expressions. *J. abnorm. Psychol.,* 1918, *13,* 172–184.

————. Judgment of facial expression and suggestion. *Psychol. Rev.,* 1918, *25,* 488–494.

————. *The aesthetic attitude.* New York: Harcourt, Brace, 1920.

————. Apparent visual movement with a stationary stimulus. *Amer. J. Psychol.,* 1927, *39,* 343–355.

————. Consciousness and motor response. *Psychol. Rev.,* 1927, *34,* 1–9.

————. The role of feeling and emotion in aesthetics. In M. L. Reymert (Ed.), *Feelings and emotions: The Wittenberg symposium*. Worcester, Mass.: Clark University Press, 1928, pp. 346–354.

———. A response interpretation of consciousness. *Psychol. Rev.*, 1931, *38*, 87–108.

———. The historical development of response psychology. *Science*, 1933, *77*, 243–250.

———. The place of aesthetics in social psychology. *Brit. J. Psychol.*, 1936–1937, *27*, 135–147.

Boring, E. G., ———, & Weld, H. P. *Foundations of psychology*. New York: Wiley, 1948.

———. Heredity and experience. *Année psychol.*, 1951, *51*, 11–25.

———. The development of American psychology. *Scientia*, 1951, *86*, 264–269.

LOUIS LAPICQUE
1866-1952
French Physiologist (18)

Lapicque, L. *La chronaxie*. Paris: Masson, 1925.
———. Plan d'une théorie physique du fonctionnement des centres nerveux. *C. r. soc. biol.*, 1907, *63*, 787–790 ; 1913, *74*, 1012–1014.

———. Sur la théorie de l'excitation électrique. *J. Physiol. Path. gén.*, 1907, *10*, 601-616.

———. Définition expérimentale de l'excitabilité. *C. r. soc. biol.*, 1909, *67*, 280–283.

———. Essai d'une nouvelle théorie physiologique de l'émotion. *J. Psychol. norm. path.*, 1911, *8*, 1–8.

———. Excitabilité des nerfs itératifs, théorie de leur fonctionnement. *C. r. acad. sci., Paris*, 1912, *155*, 70–72.

———, & Legendre, R. Changement d'excitabilité des nerfs conditionné par une altération de leur gaine de myéline. *C. r. acad. sci., Paris*, 1914, *158*, 803–805.

———, & Legendre, R. Altérations des fibres nerveuses myéliniques sous l'action des anesthésiques et de divers poisons nerveux. *J. Physiol. Path. gén.* 1922, *21*, 163–172.

———. Le poids du cerveau et l'intelligence. In G. Dumas (Ed.), *Traité de psychologie*. Vol. 1. Paris: Alcan, 1923, pp. 73–93.

———, & Lapicque, M. Nouvelle démonstration de l'égalité des chronaxies entre le muscle strié et son nerf moteur. *C. r. acad. sci., Paris*, 1925, *180*, 1056–1058.

———. Un chapitre d'histoire de la physiologie. La conception de la durée dans l'excitation au XIXᵉ siècle. *J. Psychol. norm. path.*, 1925, *22*, 97–127.

———. *L'excitabilité en fonction du temps. La chronaxie, sa signification et sa mesure*. Paris: Presses Universitaires de France, 1926.

———. Physiologie générale du système nerveux. In G. Dumas (Ed.), *Nouveau traité de psychologie*. Vol. 1. Paris: Alcan, 1930, pp. 147–222.

———. La chronaxie et sa signification physiologique. I. *Scientia*, 1932, *52*, 223–233.

———. Alpha and gamma curves in slow muscles. *J. Physiol.*, 1933, *78*, 381–403.

———. La chronaxie en biologie générale. *Biol. Rev.*, 1935, *10*, 483–514.

———. *La chronaxie et ses applications physiologiques*. Paris: Hermann, 1938.

———. Organisation quantitative de la commande des muscles volontaires. *J. Psychol. norm. path.*, 1940–1941, *37–38*, 433–445.

———, & Lapicque, M. L'excitabilité rythmogène comme seconde espèce d'excitabilité dans le muscle strié. *Bull. biol.*, 1943, *37*, 718–720.

———. *La machine nerveuse*. Paris: Flammarion, 1943.

———. *L'isochronisme neuromusculaire et l'excitabilité rythmogène*. Paris: Hermann, 1946.

———. Sur la conscience psychologique considérée comme intégrale d'éléments cellulaires de conscience. *C. r. acad. sci., Paris*, 1952, *234*, 1511–1514.

Fulton & Wilson, *Physiology*

PIERRE SIMON DE LAPLACE
1749-1827
French Astronomer-Mathematician (17)

Laplace, P. S. *Oeuvres complètes*. (14 vols.) Published under the auspices of The Acad. of Science by MM. les secrétaires perpétuels. Paris: Gauthier-Villars, 1878–1912. **B Bl C**

————. Mémoire sur la probabilité des causes par les évènements. *Mémoires présentés à l'Académie des Sciences*, 1774, *6*, 621–656. Reprinted in *Oeuvres complètes*, Vol. 8, *op. cit.*, pp. 27–65.

————. Mémoire sur les probabilités. *Mémoires présentés à l'Académie des Sciences*. (1781) In *Oeuvres complètes*, *op. cit.*, Vol. 9, pp. 383–485.

————. *Exposition du système du monde*. (5th ed.) Paris: Bachelier, 1824. (1796)

————. *The system of the world*. (2 vols.) Trans. by H. H. Harte. London: Longmans, 1830. (1796)

————. *Mécanique céleste*. (Celestial mechanics.) (4 vols.) Trans. by N. Bowditch. Boston: Hillard Gray, 1829–1839. (1799–1823)

————. *Traité de mécanique céleste*. (5 vols.) Brussels: Culture et Civilisation, 1967. (1799–1823)

————. Mémoire sur les approximations des formules qui sont fonctions de très grands nombres et sur leurs applications aux probabilités. *Mémoires de l'Institut*, 1809, 353–415, 539–565. Reprinted in *Oeuvres complètes*, Vol. 10, *op. cit.*, pp 209–301.

————. Mémoire sur les intégrales définies et leur application aux probabilités. *Mémoires de l'Institut*, 1810, 279–347.

————. *Théorie analytique des probabilités*. Brussels: Culture et Civilisation, 1967. (1812)

————. *Essai philosophique sur les probabilités*. Brussels: Culture et Civilisation, 1967. (1814)

————. *A philosophical essay on probabilities*. (6th ed.) Trans. by F. W. Truscott & F. L. Emory. New York: Dover, 1951. (1814)

Dampier, *Literature ;* Madden, *Scientific Thought ;* Newman, *Mathematics ;* Schwartz & Bishop, *Moments Discovery ;* Smith, *Source Book*

KARL SPENCER LASHLEY
1890-1958
American Psychologist (27)

Lashley, K. S. *The neuropsychology of Lashley*. Ed. by F. A. Beach *et al.* New York: McGraw-Hill, 1960. **Bl C**

————. Visual discrimination of size and form in the albino rat. *J. anim. Behav.*, 1912, *2*, 310–331.

————, & Watson, J. B. Notes on the development of a young monkey. *J. anim. Behav.*, 1913, *3*, 114–139.

————, & Watson, J. B. An historical and experimental study of homing. *Carnegie Publ.*, 1915, *211*, 9–60.

————. Reflex secretion of the human parotid gland. *J. exp. Psychol.*, 1916, I, 461–493. Reprinted in *The neuropsychology of Lashley*, *op. cit.*, pp. 28–51.

Franz, S. I., & ————. The retention of habits by the rat after destruction of frontal portion of the cerebrum. *Psychobiology*, 1917, *1*, 3–18. Reprinted in *The neuropsychology of Lashley*, *op. cit.*, pp. 72–81.

————, & Franz, S. I. The effect of cerebral destruction upon habit-formation and retention in the albino rat. *Psychobiology*, 1917, *1*, 71–140.

————. The effect of strychnine and caffeine upon rate of learning. *Psychobiology*, 1917, *1*, 141–170.

————. Modifiability of the preferential use of the hands in the rhesus monkey. *J. anim. Behav.*, 1917, *7*, 178–186.

————. Studies of cerebral function in learning. *Psychobiology*, 1920, *2*, 55–135.

————. Studies of cerebral function in learning. II. The effects of long-continued practice upon localization. *J. comp. Psychol.*, 1921, *1*, 453–468. Reprinted in *The neuropsychology of Lashley*, *op. cit.*, pp. 94–106.

————. Studies of cerebral function in learning. III. The motor areas. *Brain*, 1921, *44*, 255–286.

————. Studies of cerebral function in learning. IV. Vicarious function after destruction of the visual areas. *Amer. J. Physiol.*, 1922, *59*, 44–71.

————. The behavioristic interpretation of consciousness. *Psychol. Rev.*, 1923, *30*, 237–272, 329–353.

————. Studies of cerebral function in learning. V. The retention of motor habits after destruction of the so-called motor areas in primates. *Arch. Neurol. Psychiat.*, Chicago, 1924, 249–276. Reprinted in *The neuropsychology of Lashley, op. cit.*, pp. 107–138.

————. Contributions of Freudism to psychology. III. Physiological analysis of the libido. *Psychol. Rev.*, 1924, *31*, 192–202.

————. Studies of cerebral function in learning. VI. The theory that synaptic resistance is reduced by the passage of the nerve impulse. *Psychol. Rev.*, 1924, *31*, 369–375. Reprinted in *The neuropsychology of Lashley, op. cit.*, pp. 136–141.

————. Studies of cerebral function in learning. VII. The relation between cerebral mass, learning and retention. *J. comp. Neurol.*, 1926, *41*, 1–58.

————, & McCarthey, Dorothea A. The survival of the maze habit after cerebellar injuries. *J. comp. Psychol.*, 1926, *6*, 423–433. Reprinted in *The neuropsychology of Lashley, op. cit.*, pp. 155–163.

————. Learning. I. Nervous mechanisms in learning. In C. Murchison (Ed.), *The foundations of experimental psychology*. Worcester, Mass.: Clark University Press, 1929, pp. 524–563. Reprinted as Learning. III. Nervous mechanisms in learning. In C. Murchison (Ed.), *A handbook of general experimental psychology*. Worcester, Mass.: Clark University Press, 1934, pp. 456–496.

————, & Ball, Josephine. Spinal conduction and kinesthetic sensitivity in the maze habit. *J. comp. Psychol.*, 1929, *9*, 71–105. Reprinted in *The neuropsychology of Lashley, op. cit.*, pp. 164–190.

————. *Brain mechanisms and intelligence: A quantitative study of injuries to the brain.* Chicago: University of Chicago Press, 1930. (Reprinted 1963)

————. The mechanism of vision. I. A method for rapid analysis of pattern-vision in the rat. II. The influence of cerebral lesions upon the threshold of discrimination for brightness in the rat. III. The comparative visual acuity of pigmented and albino rats. *J. genet. Psychol.*, 1930, *37*, 453–460, 461–480, 481–484. Part I reprinted in *The neuropsychology of Lashley, op. cit.*, pp. 210–216.

————. Basic neural mechanisms in behavior. *Psychol. Rev.*, 1930, *37*, 1–24. Reprinted in *The neuropsychology of Lashley, op. cit.*, pp. 191–209.

————. The mechanism of vision. IV. The cerebral areas necessary for pattern vision in the rat. *J. comp. Neurol.*, 1931, *53*, 419–478.

————. Mass action in cerebral function. *Science*, 1931, *73*, 245–254.

————. The mechanism of vision. V. The structure and image-forming power of the rat's eye. *J. comp. Psychol.*, 1932, *13*, 173–200.

————. Integrative functions of cerebral cortex. *Physiol. Rev.*, 1933, *13*, 1–42. Reprinted in *The neuropsychology of Lashley, op. cit.*, pp. 217–255.

————. The mechanism of vision. VIII. The projection of the retina upon the cerebral cortex of the rat. *J. comp. Neurol.*, 1934, *60*, 57–79. Reprinted in *The neuropsychology of Lashley, op. cit.*, pp. 256–270.

————. Studies of cerebral function in learning. XI. The behavior of the rat in latch-box situations. *Comp. Psychol. Monogr.*, 1935, *11*, 5–40. Reprinted in *The neuropsychology of Lashley, op. cit.*, pp. 278–302.

————. The mechanism of vision. XII. Nervous structures concerned in the acquisition and retention of habits based on reactions to light. *Comp. Psychol. Monogr.*, 1935, *11*, 43–79. Reprinted in *The neuropsychology of Lashley, op. cit.*, pp. 303–327.

————. Functional determinants of cerebral localization. *Arch. Neurol. Psychiat.*, Chicago, 1937, *38*, 371–387. Reprinted in *The neuropsychology of Lashley, op. cit.*, pp. 328–344.

———. The thalamus and emotion. *Psychol. Rev.,* 1938, *45,* 42–61. Reprinted in *The neuropsychology of Lashley, op. cit.,* pp. 345–360.

———. Conditional reactions in the rat. *J. Psychol.,* 1938, *6,* 311–324. Reprinted in *The neuropsychology of Lashley, op. cit.,* pp. 361–371.

———. Experimental analysis of instinctive behavior. *Psychol. Rev.,* 1938, *45,* 445–471. Reprinted in *The neuropsychology of Lashley, op. cit.,* pp. 372–392.

———. Factors limiting recovery after central nervous lesions. *J. nerv. ment. Dis.,* 1938, *88,* 733–755.

———. Coalescence of neurology and psychology. *Proc. Amer. Phil. Soc.,* 1941, *84,* 461–470.

———. An examination of the "continuity theory" as applied to discriminative learning. *J. gen. Psychol.,* 1942, *26,* 241–265. Reprinted in *The neuropsychology of Lashley, op. cit.,* pp. 421–431.

———, & Wade, M. The Pavlovian theory of generalization. *Psychol. Rev.,* 1946, *53,* 72–87.

———. Structural variation in the nervous system in relation to behavior. *Psychol. Rev.,* 1947, *54,* 325–334.

———. In search of the engram. In *Physiological mechanisms in animal behaviour:* Society of experimental biology symposium No. 4. Cambridge: Cambridge University Press, 1950, pp. 454–482. Reprinted in *The neuropsychology of Lashley, op. cit.,* pp. 478–505; in T. K. Landauer (Ed.), *Readings in physiological psychology: The bodily basis of behavior.* New York: McGraw-Hill, 1967, pp. 287–313; & in C. R. Evans & A. D. J. Robertson (Eds.), *Key papers: Brain physiology and psychology.* Berkeley, Calif.: University of California Press, 1966, pp. 2–31.

———, Chow, K. L., & Semmes, Josephine. An examination of the electrical field theory of cerebral integration. *Psychol. Rev.,* 1951, *58,* 123–136.

———. The problem of serial order in behavior. In L. A. Jeffress (Ed.), *Cerebral mechanisms in behavior.* New York: Wiley, 1951, pp. 112–136.

Reprinted in S. Saporta (Ed.), *Psycholinguistics: A book of readings.* New York: Holt, Rinehart & Winston, 1961, pp. 180–198; & in *The neuropsychology of Lashley, op. cit.,* pp. 506–528.

———. Cerebral organization and behavior. In H. C. Solomon, S. Cobb, & W. Penfield (Eds.). *The brain and human behavior.* Baltimore, Md.: Williams & Wilkins, 1958, pp. 1–18. Reprinted in *The neuropsychology of Lashley, op. cit.,* pp. 529–543.

Clarke & O'Malley, *Brain ;* Dennis, *Psychology ;* Herrnstein & Boring, *Source Book ;* Valentine, *Experimental*

ANTOINE LAURENT LAVOISIER
1743-1794
French Chemist (16)

Lavoisier, A. L. *Oeuvres de Lavoisier.* (6 vols.) Ed. by E. Grimaux *et al.* New York: Johnson, 1965. (1862–1893)   **C**

———. Opuscules, physiques et chimiques. (1774) In *Oeuvres,* Vol. 1, *op. cit.,* pp. 437–655.

———. Mémoire sur la nature du principe qui se combine avec les métaux pendant leur calcination, & qui en augmente le poids. *Observations Phys.,* 1775, *5,* 429–433 ; *Mém. acad. sci.* 1778, 520. Trans. in J. B. Conant (Ed.), *Case histories in experimental science.* Vol. 1. Cambridge: Harvard University Press, 1948, pp. 78–84.

———. Réflexions sur la phlogistique pour servir de développement à la théorie de la combustion et de la calcination, publiées en 1777. Reprinted in *Oeuvres,* Vol. 2, *op. cit.,* pp. 623–655.

———. Expériences sur la respiration des animaux, et sur les changements qui arrivent à l'air en passant par leur poumon. *Mém. acad. sci.,* 1777, pp. 185–195. (1780) Reprinted in *Oeuvres,* Vol. 2, *op. cit.,* pp. 174–183.

———. Mémoire sur la combustion en général. *Mém. acad. sci.,* 1777, pp. 592–600. (1780) Reprinted in *Oeuvres,* Vol. 2, *op. cit.,* pp. 225–233.

———, & Laplace, P. S. d. Mémoire sur la chaleur. *Mém. acad. sci.,* 1780, 355–408. (1784)

Reprinted in *Oeuvres*, Vol. 2, *op. cit.*, pp. 283–333.

———. Mémoire sur la formation de l'acide, nommé air fixe ou acide crayeux, et que je désignerai désormais sous le nom d'acide du charbon. *Mém. acad. sci.*, 1784, 448–467. (1784) Reprinted in *Oeuvres*, Vol. 2, *op. cit.*, pp. 403–422.

———. Sur le magnétisme animal. (1784) In *Oeuvres*, Vol. 3, *op. cit.*, pp. 499–527.

———. *Méthode de nomenclature chimique.* Paris: Cuchet, 1787.

———. Traité élémentaire de chimie. (1782) In *Oeuvres*, Vol. 1, *op. cit.*, pp. 1–435.

———. *Traité élémentaire de chimie, présenté dans un ordre nouveau, et d'après les découvertes modernes.* (2 vols.) Brussels: Culture et Civilisation, 1965. (1789)

———. *Elements of chemistry, in a new systematic order, containing all the modern discoveries.* (3rd ed.) Trans. by R. Kerr. Edinburgh: Creech, 1796. (1790)

———, & Séguin, A. Second mémoire sur la respiration. *Ann. Chimie*, 1814, *91*, 318–334.

Bodenheimer, *Biology;* Dampier, *Literature;* Fulton & Wilson, *Physiology;* Gabriel & Fogel, *Biology;* Hall, *Nature's Laws;* Hall, *Source Book;* Schwartz & Bishop, *Moments Discovery*

MORITZ LAZARUS
1824-1903
German Philosopher (13)

Lazarus, M. *Ideale Fragen in Reden und Vorträgen.* Berlin: Hofmann, 1878.   **C**

———. *Das Leben der Seele in Monographien über seine Erscheinungen und Gesetze.* (3rd ed.) (3 vols.) Berlin: Dümmler, 1883–1887. (1856–1857)   **Bl**

———, & Steinthal, H. Einleitende Gedanken zur Völkerpsychologie, als Einladung zu einer Zeitschrift für Völkerpsychologie und Sprachwissenschaft. *Z. Völkerpsychol.*, 1860, *1*, 1–73.

———. Ueber die Verdichtung des Denkens in der Geschichte. *Z. Völkerpsychol.*, 1862, *2*, 54–62.

———. Ueber das Verhältnis des Einzelnen zur Gesamtheit. *Z. Völkerpsychol.*, 1862, *2*, 393–458.

———. Einige synthetische Gedanken zur Völkerpsychologie. *Z. Völkerpsychol.*, 1865, *3*, 1–95.

———. Ueber die Ideen in der Geschichte. *Z. Völkerpsychol.*, 1865, *3*, 385–486.

———. Zur Lehre von den Sinnestäuchungen. *Z. Völkerpsychol.*, 1868, *5*, 113–152.

———. *Ein psychologischer Blick in unsere Zeit.* Berlin: Dümmler, 1872.

———. *Geist und Sprache.* Berlin: Dümmler, 1878.

———. *Unser Standpunkt.* Berlin: Stuhr, 1881.

———. *Ueber die Reize des Spiels.* Berlin: Dümmler, 1883.

———. *Treu und Frei.* Leipzig: Winter, 1887.

———. *Der Prophet Jeremias.* New York: Stechert, 1894.

———. *Die Ethik des Judentums, dargestellt.* (2 vols.) Frankfurt: Kauffmann, 1898–1911.

———. *Moritz Lazarus' Lebenserinnerungen.* Berlin: Reimer, 1906.

———. *Aus meiner Jugend: Autobiographie.* Frankfurt: Kauffmann, 1913.   **B**

GUSTAVE LE BON
1841-1931
French Sociologist (24)

Le Bon, G. Application de la psychologie à la classification des races. *Rev. phil.*, 1886, *22*, 593–619.

———. *L'Equitation actuelle et ses principes, recherches expérimentales.* Paris: Flammarion, 1913. (1892)

———. *Les monuments de l'Inde.* Paris: Firmin-Didot, 1893.

------. *Lois psychologiques de l'évolution des peuples.* (3rd ed.) Paris: Alcan, 1898. (1894)

------. Rôle du caractère dans la vie des peuples. *Rev. sci.,* 1894, *4e S.I,* 33–38, 73–82, 193–204.

------. Le rôle des idées dans l'évolution des peuples. *Rev. sci.,* 1894, *4e S.I.* 653–658, 678–682.

------. Les bases psychologiques du dressage. *Rev. phil.,* 1894, *38,* 596–610.

------. *The crowd: A study of the popular mind.* Intro. by R. K. Merton. New York: Viking Press, 1960. (1895)

------. *The psychology of socialism.* Wells, Vt.: Fraser, 1965. (1898)

------. Les projets de réforme de l'enseignement. *Rev. phil.,* 1901, *52,* 233–260.

------. *La psychologie de l'éducation.* Paris: Flammarion, 1902.

------. *Evolution of matter.* New York: Scribner's, 1906. (1905)

------. *L'évolution des forces.* Paris: Flammarion, 1907.

------. *La psychologie politique et la défense sociale.* Paris: Flammarion, 1910 (Reprinted 1966)

------. *Les opinions et les croyances.* Paris: Flammarion, 1911.

------. *The psychology of revolution.* Trans. by B. Miall. London: Allen & Unwin, 1913. (1912)

------. *Aphorisme du temps présent.* Paris: Flammarion, 1913.

------. *The psychology of the great war.* Trans. by E. Andrews. London: Fisher & Unwin, 1916. (1916)

------. *The world in revolt: A psychological study of our times.* Trans. by B. Miall. London: Unwin, 1921. (1920)

------. *The world unbalanced.* New York: Longmans, 1924. (1923)

------. La vie inconsciente et la vie collective dans la psychologie moderne. *Psychol. et vie,* 1932, *6,* 1–3.

Borgatta, *Present-day Sociology;* Park & Burgess, *Sociology;* Sahakian, *Psychology*

ANTON VAN LEEUWENHOEK
1632-1723
Dutch Biologist (16)

Leeuwenhoek, A. v. *Arcana naturae detecta.* (2 vols.) Brussels: Culture et Civilisation, 1966. (1695–1697)   **B C**

------. *Opera Omnia.* (4 vols.) Hildesheim: Olms, 1968. (1715–1722)   **C**

------. *The collected letters of A. van Leeuwenhoek.* (Ult. 17 vols.) Ed. by a committee of the Royal Dutch Academy of Scientists. Amsterdam: Swets & Zeitlinger, 1939– . Vols. 1–7, 1939–1965; Vol. 8, 1967; Vol. 9, 1969.   **B C**

------. A specimen of some observations made by a microscope, contrived by M. Leeuwenhoeck [sic] in Holland, lately communicated by Dr. Regnerus de Graaf. *Phil. Trans.,* 1673, *8,* 6037–6038. Reprinted in *Collected papers,* Vol. 1, *op. cit.,* pp. 28–39.

------. More observations from Mr. Leewenhook [sic]. *Phil. Trans.,* 1674, *9,* 178–182. Reprinted in *Collected papers,* Vol. 1, *op. cit.,* pp. 136–167.

------. Microscopical observations concerning the optic nerve. *Phil. Trans.,* 1675, *10,* 378–380. Reprinted in *Collected papers,* Vol. 1, *op. cit.,* pp. 188–203.

------. Other microscopical observations, made by the same, about the texture of the blood, the sap of some plants, the figure of sugar and salt, and the probable cause of the difference of their tasts [sic]. *Phil. Trans.,* 1675, *10,* 380–385. Reprinted in *Collected papers,* Vol. 1, *op. cit.,* pp. 296–327.

------. An abstract of a letter of Mr. Anthony Leeuwenhoeck [sic] Fellow of the R. Society; concerning the parts of the brain of several animals; the chalk stones of the gout, the leprosy; and the scales of eeles. *Phil. Trans.,* 1684–1685, *15,* 883–895. Reprinted in *Collected papers,* Vol. 4, *op. cit.,* pp. 253–299.

------. An extract of a letter from Mr. Anthony Leeuwenhoeck, [sic] F. of the R.S. to a S. of the R. Society. *Phil. Trans.,* 1685, *15,* 963–979. Reprinted in *Collected papers,* Vol. 5, *op. cit.,* pp. 2–67.

——. *On the circulation of the blood.* (1688) Latin facsimile with intro. by A. Schierbeek. Nieuwkoop: de Graaf, 1962. (1695)

——. *Part of a letter . . . concerning the eyes of beetles, &c. Phil. Trans.,* 1698, *20,* 169–175.

Bodenheimer, *Biology;* Clendening, *Source Book;* Fulton & Wilson, *Physiology;* Gabriel & Fogel, *Biology;* Hall, *Source Book;* Rook, *Origins;* Schwartz & Bishop, *Moments Discovery*

ALFRED GEORG LUDWIG LEHMANN
1858-1921
Danish Psychologist (16)

Lehmann, A. Versuch einer Erklärung des Einflusses des Gesichtswinkels auf die Auffassung von Licht und Farbe, bei direktem Sehen. *Arch. ges. Physiol.,* 1885, *36,* 580–639.

——. Ueber die Anwendung der Methode der mittleren Abstufungen auf den Lichtsinn. *Phil. Stud.,* 1886, *3,* 497–533.

——. Ueber Photometrie mittelst rotirender Scheiben. *Phil. Stud.,* 1887–1888, *4,* 231–240.

——. Ueber Wiedererkennen. Versuch einer experimentellen Bestätigung der Theorie der Vorstellungsassociationen. *Phil. Stud.,* 1888–1889, *5,* 96–156.

——. Kritische und experimentelle Studien über das Wiedererkennen. *Phil. Stud.,* 1892, *7,* 169–212.

——. *Die Hauptgesetze des menschlichen Gefühlslebens: Eine experimentelle und analytische Untersuchung über die Natur und das Auftreten der Gefühlszustände nebst einem Beitrage zu deren Systematik.* (2nd ed.) Leipzig: Reisland, 1914. (1892)

——. Ueber die Beziehung zwischen Athmung und Aufmerksamkeit. *Phil. Stud.,* 1894, *9,* 66–95.

Hansen, F. C., & ——. Ueber unwillkürliches Flüstern. *Phil. Stud.,* 1895, *11,* 471–530.

——. *Die körperlichen Aeusserungen psychischer Zustände.* (2 vols.) Leipzig: Reisland, 1899. (1898)

——. *Aberglaube und Zauberei.* (2nd ed.) Stuttgart: Enke, 1908. (1898)

——. Ueber die Helligkeitsvariationen der Farben. *Phil. Stud.,* 1902, *20,* 72–115.

——. *Die körperlichen Aeusserungen psychischer Zustände.* Vol. 3: *Elemente der Psychodynamik.* Leipzig: Reisland, 1905.

——. Beiträge zur Psychodynamik der Gewichtsempfindungen. *Arch. ges. Psychol.,* 1906, *6,* 425–499.

——. *Lehrbuch der psychologischen Methodik.* Leipzig: Reisland, 1906.

——. Ueber zwei verschiedene Formen der Halladaptation der Netzhaut. *Folia neuro-biologica,* 1909, *3,* 1–10.

——. Ueber die Schwingungen der Basilarmembran und die Helmholtzsche Resonanztheorie. *Folia neuro-biologica,* 1910, *4,* 116–132.

——. *Stofskifte ved sjaelelig virksomhed.* (With a résumé in English) Copenhagen: Høst, 1918.

——. *Om størst udbytte af legemligt og aandelight arbejde.* (2 vols.) Copenhagen: Frimodt, 1919.

Arnold, *Emotion*

GOTTFRIED WILHELM VON LEIBNIZ
1646-1716
German Philosopher (26)

Leibniz, G. W. v. *Deutsche Schriften.* (2 vols.) Ed. by G. E. Guhrauer. Hildesheim: Olms, 1966. (1838–1840)   **B C**

——. *God. Guil. Leibnitii: Opera philosophica.* Ed. by J. E. Erdmann. Berlin: Weichleri, 1840.   **C**

——. *Gesammelte Werke. Folge I: Geschichte.* (4 vols.) Ed. by G. H. Pertz. Hildesheim: Olms, 1966. (1843–1847)   **C**

——, & Wolff, C. *Briefwechsel zwischen Leibniz und Christian Wolff.* Ed. by C. I. v Gerhardt. Hildesheim: Olms, 1971. (1860)   **B C**

——. *Die philosophischen Schriften von Gottfried Wilhelm Leibniz.* (7 vols.) Ed. by C. I. v. Gerhardt. Hildesheim: Olms, 1960–1961. (1875–1890)   **C**

———. *Der Briefwechsel von G. W. von Leibniz in der Königlichen öffentlichen Bibliothek zu Hannover.* Ed. by E. Bodemann. Hildesheim: Olms, 1965. (1889)   **B C**

———. *Philosophical works.* Ed. & trans. by G. M. Duncan. New Haven: Tuttle, Moorehouse, & Taylor, 1908. (1890)   **C**

———. *Opuscules et fragments inédits de Leibniz.* (1903) Ed. by L. Couturat. Hildesheim: Olms, 1966.   **C**

———. *The early mathematical manuscripts of Leibniz.* Ed. by J. M. Child. Chicago: Open Court, 1924. (Reprinted 1970)   **C**

———. *Sämtliche Schriften und Briefe,* (Ult. 40 vols.) Ed. by the Preussische Akademie der Wissenschaften, Darmstadt: Reich, 1923–   **C**

———. *Philosophical writings.* Trans. & ed. by Mary Morris. London: Dent, 1934.   **C**

———. *Textes inédits d'après les manuscrits de la bibliothèque provinciale de Hanovre* (2 vols.) Ed. by G. Grua. Paris: Presses Universitaires de France, 1948.   **C**

———. *Theodicy: Essays on the goodness of God, the freedom of man, and the origin of evil.* Trans. by E. M. Huggard, & ed. by A. Farrer. London: Routledge & Kegan Paul, 1951. (Reprinted 1970)   **C**

———. *Selections.* Ed. by P. P. Wiener. New York: Scribner's, 1951.   **C**

Malebranche, N., & ———. *Relations personnelles, présentées avec les textes complets des auteurs et de leurs correspondants.* Ed. by A. Robinet. Paris: Vrin, 1955.   **B C**

———. *Philosophical papers and letters.* (2 vols.) Trans. by L. E. Loemker. Chicago: University of Chicago Press, 1956.   **C**

———. *Discourse on metaphysics, correspondence with Arnauld, the monadology.* Trans. by G. R. Montgomery, & revised by A. R. Chandler. La Salle, Ill.: Open Court, 1962.   **C**

———. *Monadology and other philosophical essays.* Trans. by P. & Anne M. Schrecker. Indianapolis: Bobbs-Merrill, 1965.   **C**

———, & Clarke, S. *The Leibniz-Clarke correspondence.* Ed. by H. G. Alexander. Manchester: Manchester University Press, 1956. (Reprinted 1965)   **B C**

———. *Logical papers: A selection.* Trans. by G. H. R. Parkinson. Oxford: Clarendon Press, 1966.   **C**

———. *Reise-Journal, 1687–1688.* Hildesheim: Olms, 1966.   **B C**

———, & Arnauld, A. *The Leibniz-Arnauld correspondence.* Trans. by H. T. Mason. New York: Barnes & Noble, 1967.   **B C**

———. Reflections on knowledge, truth, and ideas. (1684) In *Selections, op. cit.,* pp. 283–290.

———. Discourse on metaphysics. (1686) In *Selections, op. cit.,* pp. 290–345.

———. *Metaphysische Abhandlung.* Ed. by H. Herring. Hamburg: Meiner, 1958. (1686)

———. On a general principle, useful for the explanation of laws of nature. (1687) In *Selections, op. cit.,* pp. 65–70.

———. New system of nature. (1695) Trans. by A. E. Kroeger. *J. specul. Phil.,* 1871, *5,* 209–219.

———. On substance as active force rather than mere extension. (1699) In *Selections, op. cit.,* pp. 156–181.

———. On the doctrine of a universal spirit. Trans. by A. E. Kroeger. *J. specul. Philos.,* 1871, *5,* 118–129. (1702)

———. Refutation of Spinoza. (ca. 1708). In *Selections, op. cit.,* pp. 485–497.

———. Remarks on the opinion of Malebranche that *we see all things in God,* with reference to Locke's examination of it. (ca. 1708) In *Selections, op. cit.,* pp. 497–503.

———. The theodicy: Abridgement. (1710). In *Selections, op. cit.,* pp. 509–522.

———. The monadology. (1714) In *Selections, op. cit.,* pp. 533–552.

———. Metaphysical foundations of mathematics. (1715) In *Selections, op. cit.,* pp. 201–216.

———. On the doctrine of Malebranche. (1715) In *Selections, op. cit.,* pp. 552–558.

———. On Newton's mathematical principles of philosophy. (Letters to Samuel Clarke, 1715–1716.) In *Selections, op. cit.,* pp. 216–280.

———. *New essays concerning human understanding.* (3rd ed.) Trans. by A. G. Langley. LaSalle, Ill.: Open Court, 1949. (1765), & in *Selections, op. cit.,* pp. 367–480.

Brinton, *Age Reason;* Popkin, *Philosophy;* Rand, *Classical Philosophers;* Rand, *Classical Psychologists;* Reeves, *Body Mind;* Sahakian, *Psychology;* Slotkin, *Anthropology;* Smith, *Source Book*

GOTTHOLD EPHRAIM LESSING
1729-1781
German Philosopher (11)

Lessing, G. E. *The dramatic works.* Trans. by E. Bell. London: Bell, 1895. **C**

———. *Selected prose works.* Trans. by E. C. Beasley & Helen Zimmern. London: Bell, 1900. **C**

———. *Laokoon, and how the ancients represented death.* Trans. by Helen Zimmern & E. C. Beasley. London: Bell, 1914. **C**

———. *Werke.* (25 vols.) Ed. by J. Petersen & W. v. Olshausen. Berlin: Bong, 1925–1935. **C**

———. *Laocoön, Nathan the wise and Minna von Barnhelm.* New York: Dutton, 1930. **C**

———. *Lessings gesammelte Werke.* (10 vols.) Ed. by P. Rilla. Berlin: Aufbau-Verlag, 1954–1958. **C**

———. *Lessing's theological writings.* Trans. by H. Chadwick. Stanford, Calif.: Stanford University Press, 1957. (1956) **C**

———. *Gesammelte Werke.* (2 vols.) Ed. by W. Stammler. Munich: Hauser, 1959. **C**

———. *Gesammelte Werke.* (23 vols.) Ed. by K. Lachmann & F. Muncker. Berlin: De Gruyter, 1968. **C**

———. *Hamburgische Dramaturgie.* Ed. by G. Waterhouse. Cambridge: Cambridge University Press, 1926. (1767)

———. *Die Erziehung des Menschengeschlechts.* Berlin: Voss, 1780.

———. *The education of the human race.* Trans. by F. W. Robertson. London: Paul, 1881. (1780)

Brinton, *Age Reason;* Slotkin, *Anthropology*

JAMES HENRY LEUBA
1868-1946
American Psychologist (15)

Leuba, J. H. A new instrument for Weber's law, with indications of a law of sense-memory. *Amer. J. Psychol.,* 1892–1893, *5,* 370–384.

———. A study in the psychology of religious phenomena. *Amer. J. Psychol.,* 1896, *7,* 309–385.

———. The psycho-physiology of the moral imperative. *Amer. J. Psychol.,* 1897, *8,* 528–559.

———. On the validity of the Griesebach method of determining fatigue. *Psychol. Rev.,* 1899, *6,* 573–598.

———. The contents of religious consciousness. *Monist,* 1901, *11,* 536–573.

———. Introduction to a psychological study of religion. *Monist,* 1901, *11,* 195–225.

———. The field and the problems of the psychology of religion. *Amer. J. rel. Psychol. Educ.,* 1904, *1,* 155–167.

———. Professor Wm. James' interpretation of religious experience. *Int. J. Ethics,* 1904, *14,* 323–339.

———. *A psychological study of religion: Its origin, function and future.* New York: Macmillan, 1912. (Reprinted 1969)

———. Sociology and psychology: The conception of religion and magic and the place of psychology in sociological studies: A discussion of the views of Durkheim and of Hubert and Mauss. *Amer. J. Sociol.,* 1913, *19,* 323–342.

———. *The belief in God and immortality. A psychological, anthropological and statistical study.* Chicago: Open Court, 1921. (1916)

———. *The psychological origin and the nature of religion.* London: Constable, 1921.

———. Contributions of Freudism to psychology. II. Freudian psychology and scientific inspiration. *Psychol. Rev.*, 1924, *31*, 184–191.

———. *The psychology of religious mysticism.* New York: Harcourt, Brace, 1925. (1924)

———. Les grands mystiques chrétiens, l'hystérie et la neurasthénie. *J. Psychol. norm. path.*, 1925, *22*, 236–251.

———. Invisible presences. *Atl. Mon.*, 1927, *139*, 71-81.

———. Morality among the animals. *Harper's Mag.*, 1928, *157,* 97–103.

———. *God or man?* New York: Holt, 1933.

———. The making of a psychologist of religion. In V. T. Ferm (Ed.), *Religion in transition.* London: Allen & Unwin, 1937, pp. 173–200.

LUCIEN LEVY-BRUHL
1857-1939
French Anthropologist (23)

Lévy-Bruhl, L. *Les carnets de Lucien Lévy-Bruhl.* Paris: Presses Universitaires de France, 1949.
C

———. *L'idée de responsabilité.* Paris: Hachette, 1884.

———. *L'Allemagne depuis Leibniz.* Paris: Hachette, 1890.

———. Nicholas Malebranche. *Open Court,* 1898, *12,* 543–556.

———. Maine de Biran. *Open Court,* 1899, *13,* 458–464.

———. *History of modern philosophy in France.* Trans. by G. Coblence. Chicago: Open Court, 1899. (Reprinted 1924)

———. *The philosophy of Auguste Comte.* Trans. by Kathleen de Beaumont-Klein. New York: Putnam, 1903. (1900)

———. *La philosophie d'Auguste Comte.* (6th ed.) Paris: Alcan, 1921. (1900)

———. *Ethics and moral science.* Trans. by Elizabeth Lee. London: Constable, 1950. (1903) (Reprinted 1971)

———. L'orientation de la pensée philosophique de David Hume. *Rev. Mét. Mor.,* 1909, *17,* 596–619.

———. *How natives think.* Trans. by Lilian A. Clare. New York: Knopf, 1926. (1910)

———. *Primitive mentality.* Trans. by Lilian A. Clare. New York: Macmillan, 1923. (1922)

———. *The "soul" of the primitive.* Trans. by Lilian A. Clare. New York: Macmillan, 1928. (1927) (Reprinted 1966)

———. *Primitives and the supernatural.* Trans. by L. A. Clare. London: Allen & Unwin, 1936. (1931)

———. Le temps et l'espace du monde mythique. *Scientia,* 1935, *57,* 139–149.

———. *La mythologie primitive. Le monde mythique des Australiens et des Papous.* Paris: Alcan, 1935.

———. *L'expérience mystique et les symboles chez les primitifs.* Paris: Alcan, 1938.

GEORGE HENRY LEWES
1817-1878
English Philosopher (11)

Lewes, G. H. *The biographical history of philosophy, from its origin in Greece down to the present day.* (2nd ed.) New York: Appleton, 1871. (1845, 1846)

———. *Comte's philosophy of the sciences ; being an exposition of the principles of the Cours de philosophie positive of Auguste Comte.* London: Bell, 1890. (1853)

———. *The life of Goethe.* (2nd ed.) London: Smith, Elder, 1864. (1856)

———. *The physiology of common life.* (2 vols.) New York: Appleton, 1860.

———. *Aristotle: A chapter from the history of a science, including analyses of Aristotle's scientific writings.* London: Smith & Elder, 1864.

———. Auguste Comte. *Fortn. Rev.,* 1866, *3,* 385–410.

———. Sensation in the spinal cord. *Nature,* 1874, *9,* 83–84.

———. *Problems of life and mind.* First series. *The foundation of a creed.* (5 vols.) Boston: Osgood, 1874–1875.

———. Psychological principles. (1874) In *Problems of life and mind*, Vol. 1, *op. cit.*, pp. 99–180.

———. What is sensation? *Mind*, 1876, *1*, 157–161.

———. Consciousness and unconsciousness. *Mind*, 1877, *2*, 156–167.

———. *The physical basis of mind, with illustrations: Being the second series of problems of life and mind.* Boston: Osgood, 1877.

———. Motor-feelings and the muscular sense. *Brain*, 1878, *1*, 14–28.

———. *Problems of life and mind.* Third series. Problem the first. *The study of psychology: Its object, scope and method.* Boston: Houghton, Osgood, 1879.

———. *Problems of life and mind.* Third series. Problem the second. *Mind as a function of the organism.* Problem the third. *The sphere of sense and logic of feeling.* Problem the fourth. *The sphere of intellect and logic of signs.* Boston: Houghton, Osgood, 1879–1880.

KURT LEWIN
1890-1947
German-American Psychologist (26)

Lewin, K. *A dynamic theory of personality: Selected papers.* Trans. by D. K. Adams & K. E. Zener. New York: McGraw-Hill, 1935. **C**

———. *Resolving social conflicts: Selected papers on group dynamics.* Ed. by Gertrud W. Lewin. New York: Harper & Row, 1948. **C**

———. *Field theory in social science: Selected theoretical papers.* Ed. by D. Cartwright. New York: Harper, 1951. **C**

———. Krieglandschaft. *Z. angew. Psychol.*, 1917, *12*, 440–447.

———. Die psychische Tätigkeit bei der Hemmung von Willensvorgängen und das Grundgesetz der Assoziation. *Z. Psychol.*, 1917, 77, 212–247.

———. *Der Begriff der Genese in Physik, Biologie und Entwicklungsgeschichte.* Berlin: Springer-Verlag, 1922.

———. Das Problem der Willensmessung und das Grundgesetz der Assoziation. I. II. *Psychol. Forsch.*, 1922, *1*, 191–302 ; 1922, *2*, 65–140.

———. Ueber die Umkehrung der Raumlage auf den Kopf stehender Worte und Figuren in der Wahrnehmung. *Psychol. Forsch.*, 1923, *4*, 210–261.

———. *Vorsatz Wille und Bedürfnis mit Vorbemerkungen über die psychischen Kräfte und Energien und die Struktur der Seele.* Berlin: Springer-Verlag, 1926. Abstracted, trans., & reprinted in W. D. Ellis (Ed.), *A source book of Gestalt psychology.* London: Routledge & Kegan Paul, 1938, pp. 283–299 ; & in *A dynamic theory of personality, op. cit.*, pp. 43–65.

———, & Sakuma, K. Die Sehrichtung monocularer und binocularer Objekte bei Bewegung und das Zustandekommen des Tiefeneffekts. *Psychol. Forsch.*, 1925, *6*, 298–357.

———. Idee und Aufgabe der vergleichenden Wissenschaftslehre. *Sonderdr. Sympos.*, 1926, *2*, 61–93.

———. Untersuchungen zur Handlungs- und Affektpsychologie. III, IV. *Psychol. Forsch.*, 1927, *9*, 1–158.

———. Gesetz und Experiment in der Psychologie. *Symposium*, 1927, *1*, 375–421.

———. *Die Entwicklung der experimentellen Willenpsychologie und die Psychotherapie.* Leipzig: Hirzel, 1929.

———. The conflict between Aristotelian and Galilean modes of thought in contemporary psychology. *J. gen. Psychol.*, 1931, *5*, 141–177. Reprinted in *A dynamic theory of personality, op. cit.*, pp. 1–42.

———. *Die psychologische Situation bei Lohn und Strafe.* Leipzig: Hirzel, 1931. Reprinted in *A dynamic theory of personality, op. cit.*, pp. 114–170.

———. Environmental forces. In C. Murchison (Ed.), *Handbook of child psychology*. (2nd rev. ed.) Worcester, Mass.: Clark University Press, 1933, pp. 590–623. (1931) Reprinted in *A dynamic theory of personality, op. cit.*, pp. 66–113.

———. Vectors, cognitive processes, and Mr. Tolman's criticism. *J. gen. Psychol.*, 1933, *8*, 318–345.

———. Der Richtungsbegriff in der Psychologie. Der spezielle und allgemeine hodologische Raum. *Psychol. Forsch.*, 1934, *19*, 249–299.

———. Psycho-sociological problems of a minority group. *J. Pers.*, 1935, *3*, 175–187. Reprinted in *Resolving social conflicts, op. cit.*, pp. 145–158.

———. Some social psychological differences between the United States and Germany. *J. Pers.*, 1936, *4*, 265–273. Reprinted in *Resolving social conflicts, op. cit.*, pp. 3–33.

———. *Principles of topological psychology*. Trans. by F. & Grace Heider. New York: McGraw-Hill, 1936.

———. *The conceptual representation and measurement of psychological forces*. Durham, N.C.: Duke University Press, 1938. (Reprinted 1968)

———, Lippitt, R., & White, R. Patterns of aggressive behavior in experimentally created "social climates." *J. soc. Psychol.*, 1939, *10*, 271–299.

———. Field theory and experiment in social psychology: Concepts and methods. *Amer. J. Sociol.*, 1939, *44*, 868–897. Reprinted in *Field theory in social science, op. cit.*, pp. 130–154; &, in part, in M. Marx (Ed.), *Psychological theory: Contemporary readings*. New York: Macmillan, 1959, pp. 527–542.

———, Formalization and progress in psychology. *Univer. Iowa Stud. child Welf.*, 1940, *16*, No. 3, 7–42. Reprinted in *Field theory in social science, op. cit.*, pp. 1–29.

Barker, R., Dembo, Tamara, & ———. Frustration and regression: An experiment with young children. *Univer. Iowa Stud. child Welf.*, 1941, *18*, No. 1. Reprinted in part in *Field theory in social science, op. cit.*, pp. 87–129.

———. Field theory of learning. *Yearb. Nat. Soc. stud. Educ.*, 1942, *41*(2), 215–242. Reprinted in *Field theory in social science, op. cit.*, pp. 60–86.

———. Forces behind food habits and methods of change. *Nat. Res. Counc. Bull.*, 1943, No. 108, 35–65. Reprinted in part in *Field theory in social science, op. cit.*, pp. 174–187.

———. Defining the "field at a given time." *Psychol. Rev.*, 1943, *50*, 292–310. Reprinted in M. Marx (Ed.), *Psychological theory: Contemporary readings*. New York: Macmillan, 1959, pp. 299–315, & in *Field theory in social science, op. cit.*, pp. 43–59.

———. Dembo, Tamara, Festinger, L., & Sears, Pauline S. Level of aspiration. In J. McV. Hunt (Ed.), *Personality and the behavior disorders*. Vol. 1. New York: Ronald Press, 1944, pp. 333–378.

———. Constructs in psychology and psychological ecology. *Univer. Iowa Stud. child Welf.*, 1944, *20*, 1–29. Reprinted in *Field theory in social science, op. cit.*, pp. 30–42.

———. Action research and minority problems. *J. soc. Issues*, 1946, *2*, 34–46. Reprinted in *Resolving social conflicts, op. cit.*, pp. 201–216.

———. Behavior and development as a function of the total situation. In L. Carmichael (Ed.): *Manual of child psychology*. New York: Wiley, 1946, pp. 791–844. Reprinted in *Field theory in social science, op. cit.*, pp. 238–303.

———. Frontiers in group dynamics. *Hum. Relat.*, 1947, *1*, 5–41. Reprinted in *Field theory in social science, op. cit.*, pp. 188–237.

———. Frontiers in group dynamics. II. Channels of group life: Social planning and action research. *Hum. Relat.*, 1947, *1*, 143–153.

———. Studies in group decision. In D. Cartwright & A. Zander (Eds.), *Group dynamics: Research and theory*. Evanston, Ill.: Row, Peterson, 1953, pp. 287–301.

Beck & Molish, *Reflexes;* Lindzey & Hall, *Personality;* Miller, *Mathematics;* Parsons, *Society;* Rapaport, *Thought;* Russell, *Motivation;* Sahakian, *Personality;* Sahakian, *Psychology;* Shipley, *Classics;* Vetter, *Personality;* Wrenn, *Contributions*

AMBROISE AUGUSTE LIEBEAULT
1823-1904
French Hypnotist (21)

Liébeault, A. A. *Du sommeil et des états analogues, considérés surtout au point de vue de l'action morale sur le physique.* Paris: Masson, 1866. (Reprinted 1969)

———. *Ebauche de psychologie.* Paris: Masson, 1873.

———. *Etude sur le zoomagnétisme.* Paris: Masson, 1883.

———. Confession d'un médecin hypnotiseur. *Rev. hypno.*, 1886–1887, *1*, 105–110, 143–148.

———. Classification des degrés du sommeil provoqué. *Rev. hypno.*, 1886–1887, *1*, 199–204.

———. Traitement par suggestion hypnotique de l'incontinence d'urine chez les adultes et les enfants au-dessus de trois ans. *Rev. hypno.*, 1886–1887, *1*, 71–77.

———. Emploi de la suggestion hypnotique pour l'éducation des enfants et des adolescents. *Rev. hypno.*, 1889, *3*, 195–201.

———. *Thérapeutique suggestive. Son mécanisme propriétés diverses du sommeil provoqué et des états analogues.* Paris: Doin, 1891.

———. Streifzüge in das Gebiet der passiven Zustände, des Schlafes und der Träume. *Z. Hypno.*, 1892–1893, *1*, 129–138, 155–163, 202–211, 223–234, 264–273.

———. Hypnotismus and Suggestionstherapie. *Z. Hypno.*, 1892–1893, *1*, 11–16.

———. Criminelle hypnotische Suggestionen. *Z. Hypno.*, 1894–1895, *3*, 193–206, 225–229.

———. Das Wachen, ein aktiver Seelenzustand. Der Schlaf, ein passiver Seelenzustand. Physiologische passive Zustände, beziehentlich pathologische, welche dem Schlaf analog sind. Suggestion. *Z. Hypno.*, 1894–1895, *3*, 22–28, 33–46.

JOHANNES LINDWORSKY
1875-1939
German-Czech Psychologist (15)

Lindworsky, J. *Das schlussfolgernde Denken.* Freiburg: Herder, 1916.

———. Wahrnehmung und Vorstellung. *Z. Psychol.*, 1918, *80*, 201–225.

———. *Der Wille.* (3rd ed.) Leipzig: Barth, 1923. (1919)

———. Zur Psychologie der Begriffe. *Phil. Jb.*, 1919, 1–14.

———. *Experimental psychology.* (4th ed.) Trans. by H. R. DeSilva. New York: Macmillan, 1931. (1921)

———. Beiträge zur Lehre von den Vorstellungen. *Arch. ges. Psychol.*, 1922, *42*, 91–96.

———. Psychische Vorzüge und Mängel bei der Lösung von Denkaufgaben. *Z. angew. Psychol.*, 1921, *18*, 50–98.

———. *The training of the will.* (3rd ed.) Trans. by A. Steiner & E. A. Fitzpatrick. Milwaukee, Wisc.: Bruce, 1929. (1922)

———. Beiträge zur Lehre von den Vorstellungen. *Arch. ges. Psychol.*, 1922, *42*, 91–96.

———. *Willensschule.* (5th ed.) Ed. by H. v. Thurn. Paderborn: Schönigh, 1953. (1923)

———. Umrissskizze zu einer theoretischen Psychologie. *Z. Psychol.*, 1922, *89*, 313–357.

———. Zur Theorie des binokularen Einfachsehens und verwandter Erscheinungen. *Z. Psychol.*, 1924, *94*, 134–145.

———. Revision einer Relationstheorie. *Arch. ges. Psychol.*, 1924, *48*, 248–289.

———. Methoden der Phantasieforschung. In E. Abderhalden (Ed.), *Handbuch der biologischen Arbeitsmethoden.* Vienna: Urban & Schwarzenberg, 1925, pp. 131–156.

———. Methoden der Denkforschung. In E. Abderhalden (Ed.), *Handbuch der biologischen Arbeitsmethoden.* Vienna: Urban & Schwarzenberg, 1925, pp. 157–184.

———. Eine versteckte, aber bedeutsame Gedächtniseigenschaft. *Z. pädag. Psychol.*, 1925, *26*, 23–29.

———. Die Psychoanalyse vom Standpunkt der Psychologie. *Z. Kinderforsch.*, 1925, *30*, 229–238.

———. *Exerzitien und Charakterbildung.* Innsbrück: Marian, 1926.

———. *Theoretische Psychologie im Umriss.* (4th ed.) Leipzig: Barth, 1932. (1927)

———. *Theoretical psychology.* Trans. by H. R. de Silva. St. Louis, Mo.: Herder, 1932. (1927)

———. Orientierende Untersuchungen über höhere Gefühle. *Arch. ges. Psychol.*, 1928, *61*, 197–260.

———. Zum Problem der Gestalttäuschungen. *Arch. ges. Psychol.*, 1929, *71*, 391–408.

———. Denken und Fühlen. Eine Ergänzung zu "Orientierende Untersuchungen über höhere Gefühle." *Arch. ges. Psychol.*, 1931, *82*, 430–439.

———. Zur jüngsten experimentellen Willensuntersuchung. *Arch. ges. Psychol.*, 1932, *86*, 533–538.

———. *Erfolgreiche Erziehung.* Freiburg: Herder, 1933.

———. *Das Seelenleben des Menschen. Eine Einführung in die Psychologie.* Bonn: Hanstein, 1934.

———. Psychotechnik und Ergebnisse der neueren Willensforschung. *Industr. Psychotech.*, 1934, *12*, 371–374.

———. Consciousness versus mechanisms in the theory of perception. *J. gen. Psychol.*, 1934, *11*, 369–378,

———. *The psychology of asceticism.* Trans. by E. A. Hering. London: Edwards, 1936. (1935)

Bl

CAROLUS LINNAEUS
(Latinized form of Carl von Linnē)
1707-1778
Swedish Biologist (19)

Linnaeus, C. *A selection of the correspondence of Linnaeus, and other naturalists, from the original manuscripts.* (2 vols.) Ed. by J. E. Smith. London: Longman, Hurst, Rees, Orme & Brown, 1821. **B C**

———. *Systema Natura.* Lugduni: Batavorum, 1735. (Reprinted 1963)

———. *The "Critical Botanica" of Linnaeus.* Trans. by A. Hart. London: Roy. Society, 1938. (1736)

———. An oration concerning the necessity of travelling in one's own countrey. (1741) In B. Stillingfleet (Ed.), *Miscellaneous tracts relating to natural history, husbandry and physick.* (4th ed.) London: Dodsley, Leigh, Sothby & Payne, 1791, pp. 1–35. (Reprinted 1970)

———. *Species Plantarum: A facsimile of the first edition, 1753.* (2 vols.) London: Ray, 1957-1959. (1753)

———. *Reflections on the study of Nature.* London: Nicol, 1785. (1754)

———. Odores Medicamentorum, *Amoenitates Academicae*, 1756, *3*, 183–201.

———. *A general system of nature, through the three grand kingdoms of animals, vegetables, and minerals, systematically divided into their several classes, orders, genera, species, and varieties, with their habitations, manners, economy, structure, and peculiarities.* (7 vols.) London: Lackington, Allen, 1806. (1758–1759) (Reprinted 1968)

———. *A dissertation on the sexes of plants.* Trans. by J. E. Smith. London: Smith, 1786. (1759)

———. Dissertation on inserts. In Anon. *Select dissertations from the Amoenitates Academicae.* Vol. 1. Trans. by F. J. Brand. London: Robinson & Robson, 1781, pp. 309–343. (Reprinted 1970)

Bodenheimer, *Biology;* Dampier, *Literature;* Hall, *Source Book;* Schwartz & Bishop, *Moments Discovery;* Slotkin, *Anthropology*

RALPH LINTON
1893-1953
American Anthropologist (19)

Linton, R. *The Tanala: A hill tribe of Madagas-car.* Field museum of natural history, publica-tion No. 317, Anthropological Series, Vol. 22. Chicago: The Museum, 1933.

———. *The study of man: An introduction.* New York: Appleton-Century, 1936.

———. Culture, society and the individual. *J. abnorm. soc. Psychol.,* 1938, *33,* 425–436.

———. The effects of culture on mental and emotional processes. *Res. Publ. Ass. nerv. ment. Dis.,* 1939, *19,* 293–304.

———. Acculturation and the processes of culture change. In R. Linton (Ed.), *Acculturation in seven American Indian tribes.* New York: Appleton-Century, 1940, pp. 463–482.

———. The process of culture transfer. (1940) In *Acculturation in seven American Indian tribes, op. cit.,* pp. 483–500.

———. The distinctive aspects of acculturation. (1940) In *Acculturation in seven American Indian tribes, op. cit.,* pp. 501–520.

———. Psychology and anthropology. *J. soc. Phil.,* 1940, *5,* 127–142.

———. Age and sex categories. *Amer. soc. Rev.,* 1942, *7,* 589–603.

———. *The cultural background of personality.* New York: Appleton-Century, 1945.

———. The scope and aims of anthropology. In R. Linton (Ed.), *The science of man in the world crisis.* New York: Columbia University Press, 1945, pp. 3–18.

———. Present world conditions in cultural per-spective. (1945) In *The science of man in the world crisis, op. cit.,* pp. 201–221.

Kardiner, A. (With collab. of R. Linton, Cora Du Bois, & J. West.) *The psychological frontiers of society.* New York: Columbia University Press, 1945.

———. The concept of national character. In A. H. Stanton & S. E. Perry (Eds.), *Personality and political crisis.* Glencoe, Ill.: Free Press, 1951, pp. 133–150.

———. The problem of universal values. In R. F. Spencer (Ed.), *Method and perspective in anthropology: Papers in honor of Wilson D. Wallis.* Minneapolis, Minn.: University of Min-nesota Press, 1954, pp. 145–168.

———. *The tree of culture.* New York: Knopf, 1955.

———. *Culture and mental disorders.* Ed. by G. Devereux. Springfield, Ill.: Thomas, 1956.

Borgatta, *Present-day Sociology;* Coser & Rosenberg, *Sociological Theory;* Fried, *Anthropology;* Goldschmidt, *Man-kind;* Hoebel & Jennings, *Anthropology;* O'Brien & Schrag, *Sociology;* Parsons. *Society;* Ross, *Social Order*

THEODOR LIPPS
1851-1914
German Psychologist (23)

Lipps, T. *Psychological studies.* (2nd ed.) Trans. by H. C. Sanborn. Baltimore, Md.: Williams & Wilkins, 1926. (1885)   **C**

———. *Psychologische Untersuchungen.* (2 vols.) Leipzig: Engelmann, 1912–1913.   **C**

———. *(Die) Grundtatsachen des Seelenlebens.* Bonn: Cohen, 1912. (1883)

———. Ueber eine falsche Nachbildlokalisation und damit Zusammenhängendes. *Z. Psychol.,* 1890, *1,* 60–74.

———. Zur Psychologie der Kausalität. *Z. Psy-chol.,* 1890, *1,* 252–299.

———. *Der Streit über die Tragödie.* (2nd ed.) Leipzig: Voss, 1915. (1891)

———. Aesthetische Faktoren der Raumanschau-ung. In A. König (Ed.), *Beiträge zur Psycho-logie und Physiologie der Sinnesorgane.* Ham-burg: Voss, 1891, pp. 217–307.

———. Die Raumanschauung und die Augen-bewegungen. *Z. Psychol.,* 1892, *3,* 123–171.

———. Optische Streitfragen. *Z. Psychol.,* 1892, *3,* 493–504.

---. *Grundzüge der Logik.* Leipzig: Voss, 1893.

---. Zur Lehre von den Gefühlen, insbesondere den ästhetischen Elementargefühlen. *Z. Psychol.,* 1895, *8,* 321–361.

---. Die geometrisch-optischen Täuschungen. *Z. Psychol.,* 1896, *12,* 39–59, 275.

---. Der Begriff des Unbewussten in der Psychologie. *III. Int. Congr. Psychol.,* 1896, 146–163.

---. Zur Psychologie der Suggestion. *Z. Hypno.,* 1897, *6,* 94–119, 154–159.

---. Bemerkung zu Heymanns' Artikel "Quantitative Untersuchungen über die Zöllner'sche und die Loeb'sche Täuschung." *Z. Psychol.,* 1897, *15,* 132–138.

---. Raumästhetik und geometrisch-optische Täuschungen. *Z. Psychol.,* 1898, *18,* 405–441. (Also Leipzig: Barth, 1897) (Reprinted 1966)

---. *Suggestion und Hypnose.* Munich: Straub, 1898.

---. *Komik und Humor.* Hamburg: Voss, 1898.

---. Tonverwandtschaft und Tonverschmelzung. *Z. Psychol.,* 1899, *19,* 1–40.

---. Zu den Gestaltqualitäten. *Z. Psychol.,* 1900, *22,* 383–385.

---. Aesthetische Einfühlung. *Z. Psychol.,* 1900, *22,* 415–450.

---. *Das Selbstbewusstsein: Empfindung und Gefühl.* Wiesbaden: Bergmann, 1901.

---. *Psychologie, Wissenschaft und Leben.* Munich: Franz, 1901.

---. Psychische Vorgänge und psychische Kausalität. *Z. Psychol.,* 1901, *25,* 161–203.

---. *Vom Fühlen, Wollen und Denken. Versuch einer Theorie des Willens.* (3rd rev. ed.) Leipzig: Barth, 1926. (1902)

---. *Einheiten und Relationen. Eine Skizze zur Psychologie der Apperception.* Leipzig: Barth, 1902.

---. Zur Theorie der Melodie. *Z. Psychol.,* 1902, *27,* 225–263.

---. Einige psychologische Streitpunkte. *Z. Psychol.,* 1902, *28,* 145–178.

---. *Aesthetik: Psychologie des Schönen und der Kunst.* (3rd ed.) (3 vols.) Leipzig: Voss, 1923. (1903–1906)

---. Einfühlung, innere Nachahmung, und Organempfindungen. *Arch. ges. Psychol.,* 1903, *1,* 185–204.

---. *Leitfaden der Psychologie.* (3rd ed.) Leipzig: Engelmann, 1909. (1903)

---. Fortsetzung der "Psychologischen Streitpunkte." *Z. Psychol.,* 1903, *31,* 47–78.

---. *Inhalt und Gegenstand. Psychologie und Logik.* Munich: Franz, 1905.

---. Weiteres zur "Einführung." *Arch. ges. Psychol.,* 1905, *4,* 465–519.

---. Zur Verständigung über die geometrisch-optischen Täuschungen. *Z. Psychol.,* 1905, *38,* 241–258.

---. *Naturwissenschaft und Weltanschauung.* (2nd ed.) Heidelberg: Winter, 1907. (1906)

---. *Ueber einfachste Form der Raumkunst.* Munich: Franz, 1906.

---. Ueber Urteilsgefühle. *Arch. ges. Psychol.,* 1906, *7,* 1–32.

---. Zur "ästhetischen Mechanik." *Z. Aesth.,* 1906, *1,* 1–29.

---. Die Wege der Psychologie. *Arch. ges. Psychol.,* 1906, *6,* 1–21.

---. Psychologie und Aesthetik. *Arch. ges. Psychol.,* 1907, *9,* 91–116.

JOHN LOCKE
1632–1704
English Philosopher (27)

Locke, J. *The works of John Locke.* (10 vols.) Aalen: Scientia Verlag, 1963. (1823)   **C**

---. *Selections.* Ed. by S. P. Lamprecht. New York: Scribner's, 1928.   **C**

———. *The educational writings of John Locke.* Ed. by J. L. Axtell. London: Cambridge University Press, 1968.   **C**

———. A defence of Mr. Locke's opinion concerning personal identity. In *Works,* Vol. 3, *op. cit.,* pp. 177–201.

———. *Essays on the law of nature.* Ed., trans., & intro. by W. v. Leyden. Oxford: Clarendon Press, 1954. (1663).

———. *An essay concerning the understanding, knowledge, opinion, and assent.* (Draft B.) Ed. by B. Rand. Cambridge: Harvard University Press, 1931. (1671)

———. *An early draft of Locke's essay together with excerpts from his journal.* Ed. by R. Aaron & J. Gibb. Oxford: Clarendon Press, 1936. (1671)

———. *Two treatises of government.* Ed. by P. Laslett. London: Cambridge University Press, 1960. (1690)

———. *An essay concerning human understanding.* (2 vols.) Ed. by A. C. Fraser. London: Oxford University Press, 1894. (1690) (Reprinted 1959)

———. *An essay concerning human understanding.* (2 vols.) Ed. by J. W. Yolton. New York: Dutton, 1961. (1690)

———. Some thoughts concerning education. (1693) In *Works,* Vol. 9, *op. cit.,* pp. 1–210.

———. A discourse of miracles. (1706) In *Works,* Vol. 9, *op. cit.,* pp. 256–265.

———. An examination of P. Malebranche's opinion of seeing all things in God. (1706) In *Works,* Vol. 9, *op. cit.,* pp. 211–255.

———. *Of the conduct of the understanding.* Ed. by F. W. Garforth. New York: Teachers College Press, Columbia University, 1966. (1706)

———. Some familiar letters between Mr. Locke, and several of his friends. (1708) In *Works, op. cit.,* Vol. 9, pp. 285–472 ; Vol. 10, pp 1–145. **B**

———. Elements of natural philosophy. (1750?) In *Works,* Vol. 3, *op. cit.,* pp. 301–330.

———. Medical notes in his journals, 1675–1698. In K. Dewhurst, *John Locke (1632–1704),*

physician and philosopher: *A medical biography,* London: Wellcome Historical Medical Library, 1963, pp. 62–223.

Brinton, *Age Reason ;* Dennis, *Psychology ;* Herrnstein & Boring, *Source Book ;* Hirst, *Perception ;* Hunter & Macalpine, *Psychiatry ;* Hutchins, *Great Books ;* Kessen, *Child ;* Mandler & Mandler, *Thinking ;* Margolis, *Introduction ;* Matson, *Being ;* Murphy, *Western ;* Nash, *Models ;* Parsons, *Society ;* Price, *Education ;* Rand, *Classical Psychologists ;* Rand, *Moralists ;* Sahakian, *Psychology ;* Ulich, *Educational Wisdom*

JACQUES LOEB
1859-1924
German-American Physiologist (26)

Loeb, J. *Studies in general physiology.* (2 vols.) Chicago: University of Chicago Press, 1905.
                                                      C

———. *The mechanistic conception of life.* Ed. by D. Fleming. Cambridge: Harvard University Press, 1964. (1912)   **B C**

———. Die Sehstörungen nach Verletzung der Grosshirnrinde. Nach Versuchen am Hunde. *Arch. ges. Physiol.,* 1884, *33,* 76–172.

———. Beiträge zur Physiologie des Grosshirns. *Arch. ges. Physiol.,* 1886, *39,* 265–346.

———. Muskeltätigkeit als Mass psychischer Tätigkeit. *Arch. ges. Physiol.,* 1886, *39,* 592–597.

———. Ueber die optische Inversion ebener Linearzeichnungen bei einäugiger Betrachtung. *Arch. ges. Physiol.,* 1887, *40,* 274–282.

———. Untersuchungen über den Fühlraum der Hand. *Arch. ges. Physiol.,* 1887, *41,* 107–127.

———. Die Orientierung der Thiere gegen die Schwerkraft der Erde. *Sitzber. phys.-med. Ges.,* Würzburg, 1888, *1,* 5–10.

———. Untersuchungen über die Orientierung im Fühlraum der Hand und im Blickraum. *Arch. ges. Physiol.,* 1890, *46,* 1–46.

———. *Der Heliotropismus der Thiere und seine Ueberstimmung mit den Heliotropismus der*

Pflanzen. Würzburg: Hertz, 1890. Trans. in *Studies in general physiology,* Vol. 1, *op. cit.,* pp. 1–88.

————. Weitere Untersuchungen über den Heliotropismus der Thiere und seine Uebereinstimmung mit dem Heliotropismus der Pflanzen (heliotropische Krümmungen bei Thieren). *Arch. ges. Physiol.,* 1890, *47,* 391–416. Trans. in *Studies in general physiology,* Vol. 1, *op. cit.,* pp. 89–106.

Koranyi, A., & ————. Ueber Störungen der compensatorischen und spontanen Bewegungen nach Verletzung des Grosshirns. *Arch. ges. Physiol.,* 1891, *48,* 423–430.

————. Ueber Geotropismus bei Thieren. *Arch. ges. Physiol.,* 1891, *49,* 175–189. Trans. in *Studies in general physiology,* Vol. 1, *op. cit.,* pp. 176–190.

————. Ueber den Anteil der Hörnerven an den nach Gehirnverletzung auftretenden Zwangsbewegungen, Zwangslagen und associierten Stellungsänderungen der Bulbi und Extremitäten. *Arch. ges. Physiol.,* 1891, *50,* 66–83.

————. Ueber künstliche Umwandlung positiv heliotropischer Thiere in negativ heliotropische und umgekehrt. *Arch. ges. Physiol.,* 1893, *54,* 81–107. Trans. in *Studies in general physiology,* Vol. 1, *op. cit.,* pp. 265–294.

————. Beiträge zur Gehirnphysiologie der Würmer. *Arch. ges. Physiol.,* 1894, *56,* 247–269. Trans. in *Studies in general physiology,* Vol. 1, *op. cit.,* pp. 345–369.

————. Zur Physiologie und Psychologie der Actinien. *Arch. ges. Physiol.,* 1895, *59,* 415–420.

————. Ueber den Nachweis von Kontrastscheinungen im Gebiete der Raumempfindungen des Auges. *Arch. ges. Physiol.,* 1895, *60,* 509–518.

————, & Maxwell, S. S. Zur Theorie des Galvanotropismus. *Arch. ges. Physiol.,* 1896, *63,* 121–144.

————. Ueber den Einfluss des Lichtes auf die Organbildung bei Thieren. *Arch. ges. Physiol.,* 1896, *63,* 273–292.

————. On egg-structure and the heredity of instincts. *Monist.* 1896–1897, *7,* 481–493.

————. Zur Theorie der physiologischen Licht- und Schwerkraftwirkungen. *Arch. ges. Physiol.,* 1897, *66,* 439–466.

————. Assimilation and heredity. *Monist,* 1897–1898, *8,* 547–555.

————. *Comparative physiology of the brain and comparative psychology.* Trans. by Anne L. Loeb. New York: Putnam's, 1900. (1899) Reprinted in part in *The mechanistic conception of life, op. cit.,* pp. 65–75.

————. *Untersuchungen über künstliche Parthogenese und das Wesen des Befruchtungsvorgangs.* Ed. by E. Schwalbe. Leipzig: Barth, 1906.

————. *The dynamics of living matter.* New York: Macmillan, 1906. (1906)

————. Ueber die Erregung von positivem Heliotropismus durch Säure, insbesondere Kohlensäure, und von negativem Heliotropismus durch ultraviolette Strahlen. *Arch. ges. Physiol.,* 1906, *115,* 564–581.

————. Ueber die Summation heliotropischer und geotropischer Wirkungen bei den auf der Drehscheibe ausgelösten compensatorischen Kopfbewegungen. *Arch. ges. Physiol.,* 1907, *116,* 368–374.

————. Concerning the theory of tropisms. *J. exp. Zoöl.,* 1907, *4,* 151–156.

————. Experimental study of the influence of environment on animals. In A. C. Seward (Ed.), *Darwin and modern science.* Cambridge: Cambridge University Press, 1909, pp. 247–270. Reprinted in *The mechanistic conception of life, op. cit.,* pp. 195–227.

————. The significance of tropisms for psychology. Trans. by Grace B. Watkinson. *Pop. Sci. Mon.,* 1911, *79,* 105–125. Reprinted in *The mechanistic conception of life, op. cit.,* pp. 35–62.

————. The mechanistic conception of life. *Pop. Sci. Mon.,* 1912, *80,* 5–21. Reprinted in *The mechanistic conception of life, op. cit.,* pp. 3–31.

——. *The organism as a whole: From a psycho-chemical viewpoint.* New York: Putnam's, 1916.

——. *Forced movements, tropisms, and animal conduct.* Philadelphia: Lippincott, 1918.

Bodenheimer, *Biology;* Gabriel & Fogel, *Biology;* Herrnstein & Boring, *Source Book*

CESARE LOMBROSO
1835-1909
Italian Sociologist (20)

Lombroso, C. *Nouvelles recherches de psychiatrie et d'anthropologie criminelle.* Paris: Alcan, 1892. **C**

——. *Les applications de l'anthropologie criminelle.* Paris: Alcan, 1892. **C**

——. *Les conquêtes récentes de la psychiatrie.* Turin: Bocca, 1898. **C**

——. *Nuovi studi sul genio.* (2 vols.) Rome: Sandron, 1901-1902. **C**

——. *Genio e follia.* (4th ed.) Turin: Bocca. 1882. (1864)

——. *Antropometria di 400 delinquenti veneti. Rend. Inst. Lombroso,* 1872, 5, No. 12.

——. *L'uomo delinquente.* (5th ed.) (3 vols.) Turin: Bocca, 1896-1897. (1876)

——. *La fusion de la folie morale et du criminel-né: Réponse à M. Tarde. Rev. phil.,* 1885. 20, 178-180.

——. *Studi sull'ipnotismo.* Turin: Bocca, 1886.

——. *Palimsesti del carcere.* Turin: Bocca, 1888.

——. *The man of genius.* New York: Scribner's, 1891. (1889)

——. *L'uomo di genio.* (6th ed.) Turin: Bocca, 1894. (1889)

——. *Il delitto politico e le rivoluzioni.* Turin: Bocca, 1890.

——. Illustrative studies in criminal anthropology. *Monist,* 1890-1891, 1, 177-196, 336-343.

——. Innovation and inertia in the world of psychology. *Monist,* 1890-1891, 1, 344-361.

——. *L'anthropologie criminelle et ses récents progrès.* (3rd ed.) Paris: Alcan, 1896. (1891)

——, & Ottolenghi, S. Die Sinne der Verbrecher. *Z. Psychol.,* 1891, 2, 337-360.

——, & Ferrero, W. *Female offender.* New York: Barnes & Noble, 1952. (1893)

——. *L'antisémitisme.* (2nd ed.) Trans. by A. Marie & M. Hamel. Paris: Giard & Brière, 1899. (1894)

——. Die minderbesten Phänomene des Nichtbewusstseins. *Deutsch. Rev.,* 1894, 3, 23-41.

——. *Gli anarchici.* (2nd ed.) Turin: Bocca, 1895. (1894)

——. *Genio e degenerazione.* (2nd ed.) Palermo: Sandron, 1908. (1897)

——. The heredity of acquired characteristics. *Forum,* 1897, 24, 200-208.

——. *Le crime: Causes et remèdes.* (2nd ed.) Paris: Alcan, 1907. (1899)

——. *Crime, its causes and remedies.* Trans. by H. P. Horton. Boston: Little, Brown, 1918. (1899)

——. Insane characters in fiction and the drama. *Pop. Sci. Mon.,* 1899, 55, 53-62.

——. Cesare Lombroso, modern ethologist. (With transl. of "Organi e gesti umani acquisiti." *Riv. Sci. biol.,* 1899, 1, May-June.) *Rassegna,* 1970, 47(2), 7-16.

——. The determining of genius. *Monist,* 1901, 12, 49-64.

——. *Delitti vecchi e delitti nuovi.* Turin: Bocca, 1902.

——. Ueber die Entstehungsweise und Eigenart des Genies. *Jb. ges. Med.,* 1907, 294, 125-141, 225-233; 1908, 298, 20-25, 132-138.

——. Osservazioni sul mondo esterno e sull' io. Diario giovanile (1854-1857). *Arch. anthrop. crim.,* 1932, 52, 5-39. **B**

Sahakian, *Psychology*

IRVING LORGE
1905-1960
American Psychologist (14)

Lorge, I. Influence of regularly interpolated time intervals upon subsequent learning. *Teach. Coll. Contr. Educ.*, 1930, No. 438.

————. The efficacy of intensified reward and of intensified punishment. *J. exp. Psychol.*, 1933, *16*, 177–207.

————. Retests after ten years. *J. educ. Psychol.*, 1934, *25*, 136–141.

Thorndike, E. L., Bregman, Elsie O., ————, Metcalfe, Zaida F., Robinson, Eleanore E., & Woodyard, Ella. *Prediction of vocational success*. New York: Commonwealth Fund, 1934.

————. The chimera of vocational guidance. *Teach. Coll. Rec.*, 1934, *35*, 359–371.

————. Personality traits by fiat. I. The analysis of the total trait scores and keys of the Bernreuter personality inventory. *J. educ. Psychol.*, 1935, *26*, 273–278.

————. Personality traits by fiat. II. A correction *J. educ. Psychol.*, 1935, *26*, 652–654.

————, Bernholz, Elna, & Sells, S. B. Personality traits by fiat. II. The consistency of the Bernreuter personality inventory by the Bernreuter and by the Flanagan keys. *J. educ. Psychol.*, 1935, *26*, 427–434.

————, & Thorndike, E. L. The influence of delay in the after-effect of a connection. *J. exp. Psychol.*, 1935, *18*, 186–194.

————. Prestige, suggestion and attitudes. *J. soc. Psychol.*, 1936, *7*, 386–402.

————. The influence of the test upon the nature of mental decline as a function of age. *J. educ. Psychol.*, 1936, *27*, 100–110.

————. Irrelevant rewards in animal learning. *J. comp. Psychol.*, 1936, *21*, 105–128.

————, & Hollingworth, Leta S. Adult status of highly intelligent children. *J. genet. Psychol.*, 1936, *49*, 215–226.

————. Intelligence and personality as revealed in questionnaires and inventories. *Yearb. Nat. Soc. Stud. Educ.*, 1940, *39*(1), 275–281.

————, & Blau, R. D. Broad occupational groupings by estimated abilities. *Occupations*, 1942, *21*, 289–295.

Thorndike, E. L., & ————. *The teacher's word book of 30,000 words*. New York: Bureau of Publications, Teachers College, Columbia University, 1944.

————. Predicting readability. *Teach. Coll. Rec.*, 1944, *45*, 404–419.

————. Schooling makes a difference. *Teach. Coll. Rec.*, 1945, *46*, 483–492.

Feifel, H., & ————. Qualitative differences in the vocabulary responses of children. *J. educ. Psychol.*, 1950, *41*, 1–18.

Tuckman, J., & ————. The best years of life: A study in ranking. *J. Psychol.*, 1952, *34*, 137–149.

Tuckman, J., & ————. *Retirement and the industrial worker*. New York: Bureau of Publications, Teachers College, Columbia University, 1953.

————, Tuckman, J., Aikman, L., Spiegel, J., & Moss, Gilda. Solutions by teams and by individuals to a field problem at different levels of reality. *J. educ. Psychol.*, 1955, *46*, 17–24.

————, Tuckman, J., Aikman, L., Spiegel, J., & Moss, Gilda. Problem-solving by teams and by individuals in a field setting. *J. educ. Psychol.*, 1955, *46*, 160–166.

————, & Solomon, H. Two models of group behavior in the solution of eureka-type problems. *Psychometrika*, 1955, *20*, 139–148.

————. Gerontology (later maturity). *Annu. rev. Psychol.*, 1956, *7*, 349–364.

————, Tuckman, J., Aikman, L., Spiegel, J., & Moss, Gilda. The adequacy of written reports in problem solving by teams and by individuals. *J. soc. Psychol.*, 1956, *43*, 65–74.

————, & Solomon, H. Individual performance and group performance in problem solving related to group size and previous exposure to the problem, *J. Psychol.*, 1959, *48*, 107–114.

Tuckman, J., ————, & Zeman, F. D. The self-image in aging. *J. genet. Psychol.*, 1961, *99*, 317–321.

Tuckman, J., & ————. Individual ability as a determinant of group superiority. *Hum. Relat.*, 1962, *15*, 45–51.

RUDOLF HERMANN LOTZE
1817-1881
German Philosopher (25)

Lotze, H. *Kleine Schriften*. (3 vols.) Ed. by D. Peipers. Leipzig: Hirzel, 1885–1891. **B Bl C**

————. *Metaphysics, in three books: Ontology, cosmology and psychology*. (2nd ed.) (2 vols.) Ed. by B. Bosanquet. Oxford: Clarendon Press, 1887. (1841)

————. *Leben und Lebenskraft*. In R. Wagner (Ed.), *Handwörterbuch der Physiologie*. Vol. 1. Brunswick: Vieweg, 1842, pp. ix–lviii. **B Bl**

————. *Allgemeine Pathologie und Therapie als mechanische Naturwissenschaften*. (2nd ed.) Leipzig: Hirzel, 1848. (1842)

————. *Instinkt*. In R. Wagner (Ed.), *Handwörterbuch der Physiologie*. Vol. 2. Brunswick: Vieweg, 1844, pp. 191–209.

————. *Seele und Seelenleben*. In R. Wagner (Ed.), *Handwörterbuch der Physiologie*. Vol. 3, Part 1. Brunswick: Vieweg, 1846, pp. 142–264.

————. *Allgemeine Physiologie des menschlichen Körpers*. Leipzig: Weidmann, 1851.

————. *Medizinische Psychologie oder Physiologie der Seele*. *Leipzig:* Weidmann. 1852. (Reprinted 1966)

————. *Ueber die Stärke der Vorstellungen*. *Z. Phil. phil. Krit.*, 1853, *22*, 181–209.

————. *Microcosmus: An essay concerning man and his relation to the world*. (4th ed.) (2 vols.) Trans. by Elizabeth Hamilton & E. E. Constance Jones. Edinburgh: Clark, 1899. (1856–1864)

————. *Streitschriften*. Vol. 1. *In Bezug auf Prof. I. H. Fichtes Anthropologie*. Leipzig: Hirzel, 1857.

————. *Geschichte der Aesthetik in Deutschland*. Munich: Cotta, 1868.

————. *Das Evangelium der armen Seele*. Leipzig: Hirzel, 1871.

————. *Logic, in three books: Of thought, of investigation, and of knowledge*. (2nd ed.) (2 vols.) Ed. by B. Bosanquet. Oxford: Clarendon Press, 1888. (1874)

————. *Lotze's system of philosophy*. I. *Logic*. II. *Metaphysics*. (2nd ed.) (2 vols.) Ed. by B. Bosanquet. Oxford: Clarendon Press, 1887–1888. (1874–1879)

————. *Outlines of psychology: Dictated portions of lectures of Hermann Lotze*. (3rd ed.) Trans. by G. T. Ladd. Boston: Ginn, 1886. (1881)

————. *Grundzüge der Psychologie*. (5th ed.) Leipzig: Hirzel, 1894. (1881)

————. *Outlines of practical philosophy*. Trans. by G. T. Ladd. Boston: Ginn, 1885. (1882)

————. *Grundzüge der Logik und Encyklopädie der Philosophie*. (3rd ed.) Leipzig: Hirzel, 1891. (1883)

————. *Outlines of metaphysic*. Trans. by G. T. Ladd. Boston: Ginn, Heath, 1884.

————. *Grundzüge der Aesthetik: Diktate aus den Vorlesungen von Hermann Lotze*. (2nd ed.) Leipzig: Hirzel, 1888. (1884)

————. *Outlines of aesthetics*. Trans. by G. T. Ladd. Boston: Ginn, 1886. (1884) (Reprinted 1970)

> Dember, *Perception ;* Herrnstein & Boring, *Source Book ;* Rand, *Classical Philosophers ;* Rand, *Classical Psychologists*

CHAUNCEY McKINLEY LOUTTIT
1901-1956
American Psychologist (13)

Louttit, C. M. Reproductive behavior of the guinea pig. I. The normal mating behavior II. The ontogenesis of the reproductive behavior pattern. III. Modifications of the behavior pattern. *J. comp. Psychol.*, 1927, *7*, 247–263 ; 1929, *9*, 293–304, 305–315.

————. Bibliography of bibliographies on psychology, 1900–1927. *Bull. Nat. Res. Coun.*, 1928, No. 65.

————. The use of bibliographies in psychology. *Psychol. Rev.*, 1929, *36*, 341–347.

————. Racial comparisons of ability in immediate recall of logical and nonsense material. *J. soc. Psychol.*, 1931, *2*, 205–215.

———. Test performance of a selected group of part-Hawaiians. *J. appl. Psychol.*, 1931, *15*, 43–52.

———. Psychological journals: A minor contribution to the history of psychology. *Psychol. Rev.*, 1931, *38*, 455–460.

———. *Handbook of psychological literature.* Bloomington, Ind.: Principia Press, 1932.

———. The Dewey decimal system and psychology. *J. gen. Psychol.*, 1933, *9*, 234–238.

———, & Lockridge, Lillian L. Psychological journals. *Amer. J. Psychol.*, 1934, *46*, 147–148.

———, & Stackman, H. The relationship between Porteous maze and Binet test performance. *J. educ. Psychol.*, 1936, *27*, 18–25.

———, & Halls, Emily C. Survey of speech defects among public school children of Indiana. *J. speech Dis.*, 1936, *1*, 73–80.

———. *Clinical psychology of exceptional children.* (3rd ed.) New York: Harper, 1957. (1936)

———. The Indiana University Psychological Clinics. *Psychol. Rec.*, 1937, *1*, 449–458.

———. The place of clinical psychology in mental hygiene. *Ment. Hyg.*, N.Y., 1937, *21*, 373–388.

———. The nature of clinical psychology. *Psychol. Bull.*, 1939, *36*, 361–389.

———. Library classification for psychological literature. *Psychol. Rec.*, 1941, *4*, 350–364.

———. The mentally deficient in the national emergency. *Train. Sch. Bull.*, 1941, *37*, 157–162.

———. Psychological examining in the United States Navy: An historical summary. *Psychol. Bull.*, 1942, *39*, 227–239.

———. The mirror tracing test as a diagnostic aid for emotional instability. *Psychol. Rec.*, 1943, *5*, 279–286.

———. Psychology during the war and afterward. *J. consult. Psychol.*, 1944, *8*, 1–7.

———. The school as a mental hygiene factor. *Ment. Hyg.*, N.Y., 1947, *31*, 50–65.

———. & Browne, C. G. The use of psychometric instruments in psychological clinics. *J. consult. Psychol.*, 1947, *11*, 49–54.

———. Training for non-directive counseling: A critique. *J. clin. Psychol.*, 1948, *4*, 236–240.

Daniel, R. S., & ———. *Professional problems in psychology.* New York: Prentice-Hall, 1953.

JOHN (BARON AVEBURY) LUBBOCK
1834-1913
English Biologist (16)

Lubbock, J. *Scientific lectures.* (2nd ed.) New York: Macmillan, 1890. (1879)   C

———. *Essays and addresses, 1900–1903.* New York: Macmillan, 1903. (Reprinted 1966)   C

———. *Prehistoric times as illustrated by ancient remains and the manners and customs of modern savages.* (7th ed., rev.) New York: Holt, 1913. (1865) (Reprinted 1969)

———. The early condition of man. *Anthrop. Rev.*, 1868, *6*, 1–21.

———. *The origin of civilization and the primitive condition of man: Mental and social condition of savages.* (7th ed.) New York: Longmans, Green, 1912. (1870)

———. On the development of relationships. *J. Roy. Anthrop. Inst.*, 1872, *1*, 1–29.

———. *On the origin and metamorphoses of insects.* London: Macmillan, 1874.

———. Observations on ants, bees and wasps. *J. Linn. Soc.*, 1876, *12*, 110–139, 227–251, 445–514; 1879, *14*, 265–290, 607–626; 1881, *15*, 167–187, 362–387; 1883, *16*, 110–121; 1884, *17*, 41–52.

———. The habits of ants. *Fortn. Rev.*, 1877, *28*, 287–306; *Rev. Sci.*, 1877, *13*, 56–66.

———. *Fifty years of science.* London: Macmillan, 1882.   B

———. *Ants, bees and wasps. A record of observations on the social Hymenoptera.* (Rev. ed.) New York: Dutton, 1929. (1882)

———. On the sense of colour among some of the lower animals. *Nature*, 1882, *25*, 422–424; 1882, *27*, 618.

———. On the sense of color among some of the lower animals, I & II. *J. Linn. Soc.*, 1883, *16*, 121–127; 1884, *17*, 205–214.

———. *On the senses, instincts and intelligence of animals with special reference to insects.* (6th ed.) London: Kegan Paul, Trench & Truebner, 1899. (1888)

———. *Intelligence of animals with special reference to insects.* New York: Hill, 1904.

———. *Marriage, totemism, and religion: An answer to critics.* New York: Longmans, Green, 1911.

CARL FRIEDRICH WILHELM LUDWIG
1816-1895
German-Austrian Physiologist (14)

Du Bois-Reymond, E., & Ludwig, C. *Zwei grosse Naturforscher des 19. Jahrhunderts. Ein Briefwechsel zwischen Emil Du Bois-Reymond und Carl Ludwig.* Ed. by Estelle Du Bois-Reymond & P. Diepgen. Leipzig: Barth, 1927. **B C**

———. *Beiträge zur Lehre vom Mechanismus der Harnsekretion.* Marburg: Elwer, 1843.

———. Nieren und Harnbereitung. In R. Wagner (Ed.), *Handwörterbuch der Physiologie.* Vol. 2. Brunswick: Vieweg, 1844, pp. 628–640.

———. Ueber die Herznerven des Frosches. *Arch. Anat.,* 1848, 134–143.

———. Neue Versuche über die Beihilfe der Nerven zu der Speichelsekretion. *Mitth. Naturforsch. Ges.,* Zurich, 1850, *2,* 210–239.

———. Neue Versuche über die Beihilfe der Nerven zur Speichelabsonderung. *Z. rat. Med.,* 1851, *1,* 254–277.

———. *Lehrbuch der Physiologie des Menschen.* (2nd ed.) (2 vols.) Heidelberg: Winter, 1858–1861. (1852–1856)

Cyon, E. v., & ———. Die Reflexe eines der sensiblen Nerven des Herzens auf die motorischen der Blutgefässe. (1866). *J. Anat.,* 1867, *4,* 472–485.

———. *Rede zum Gedächtnis an Ernst Heinrich Weber.* Leipzig: Veit, 1878.

Fulton & Wilson, *Physiology*

JOHN THOMSON MacCURDY
1886-1947
English Psychologist (12)

MacCurdy, J. T. The productions in a manic-like state illustrating Freudian mechanisms. *J. abnorm. Psychol.,* 1914, *8,* 361–375.

———. Ethical aspects of psychoanalysis. *Bull. Johns Hopkins Hosp.,* 1915, *26,* 169–173.

———. *Psychology of war.* New York: Dutton, 1926. (1917)

———. *War neuroses.* London: Cambridge University Press, 1918.

———. *Problems in dynamic psychology: A critique of psychoanalysis and suggested formulations.* New York: Macmillan, 1923.

———. *The psychology of emotion.* New York: Harcourt, Brace, 1925.

———. A hypothetical mental constitution of compulsive thinkers. *Brit. J. Med. Psychol.,* 1926, *6,* 159–177.

———. *Common principles in psychology and physiology.* New York: Macmillan, 1928.

———. The biological significance of blushing and shame. *Brit. J. Psychol.,* 1930–1931, *21,* 174–182.

———. The general nature of association processes within the central nervous system. *Brit. J. Psychol.,* 1931–1932, *22,* 136–149.

———. *Mind and money.* London: Faber & Faber, 1932.

———. The relation of psychopathology to social psychology. In F. Bartlett *et al.* (Eds.), *The study of society: Methods and problems.* London: Routledge & Kegan Paul, 1939, pp. 46–69.

———. *The structure of morale.* New York: Macmillan, 1943.

ERNST MACH
1838-1916
Austrian Physicist (25)

Mach, E. *Popular scientific lectures.* (5th ed.) Trans. by T. J. McCormack. Chicago: Open Court, 1943. (1894) **C**

————. *Space and geometry in the light of physiological, psychological, and physical inquiry.* Trans. by T. J. McCormack. Chicago: Open Court, 1906. (1901–1903) (Reprinted 1960) **C**

————. *Die Geschichte und die Wurzel des Satzes von der Erhaltung der Arbeit. Zur Geschichte des Arbeitsbegriffs. Kultur und Mechanik. (1872–1915).* Amsterdam: Bonset, 1969. **Bl C**

————. Ueber das Sehen von Lagen und Winkeln durch die Bewegung des Auges. *Sitzber. Akad. Wiss. Wien,* math-naturw. Kl., 1861, 43(2), 215–224.

————. Zur Theorie des Gehörorgans. *Sitzber. Akad. Wiss. Wien,* math.-naturw. Kl., 1863, 48(2), 283–300.

————. Untersuchungen über den Zeitsinn des Ohres. *Sitzber. Akad. Wiss. Wien,* math-naturw. Kl., 1865, 51 (2), 133–150. (Reprinted in *Untersuch. Naturlehre des Menschen und der Thiere,* 1870, 10, pp. 181–200.)

————. Ueber die physiologische Wirkung räumlichen Vertheilter Lichtreizes. *Sitzber., Akad. Wiss. Wien.,* math.-naturw. Kl., 1866, 54 (2), 131–144, 393–408 ; 1868, 57, 11–19.

————. *Einleitung in die Helmholtz'sche Musiktheorie.* Graz: Leuschner & Lubensky, 1866.

————. Ueber die Abhängigkeit der Netzhautstellen von einander. *Prag. Sitzber.,* 1868, 10–11.

————. *History and root of the principle of the conservation of energy.* Trans. by P. E. B. Jourdain. Chicago: Open Court, 1962. (1872)

————. Physikalische Versuche über den Gleichgewichtssinn des Menschen. *Sitzber. Akad. Wiss. Wien.* math.-naturw. Kl., 1873, 68(2), 124–140.

————. *Optisch-akustische Versuche.* Prague: Calvé, 1873.

————, & Kessel, J. *Beiträge zur Topographie und Mechanik des Mittelohres.* Vienna: Gerold, 1874.

————. Versuche über den Gleichgewichtssinn, *Sitzber. Akad. Wiss. Wien,* math.-naturw. Kl., 1874, 69(2), 121–135.

————. *Grundlinien der Lehre von den Bewegungsempfindungen.* Amsterdam: Bonset, 1967. (1875)

————. *Die Mechanik in ihrer Entwicklung.* (9th ed.) Leipzig: Brockhaus, 1933. (1883)

————. *Science of mechanics.* (6th ed.) Trans. by T. McCormack. La Salle, Ill.: Open Court, 1960. (1883)

————. Zur Analyse der Tonempfindungen. *Sitzber. Akad. Wiss. Wien,* math.-phys. Kl., 1885, 92(2), 1283–1289.

————. *The analysis of sensations: And the relation of the physical to the psychical.* Trans. by C. M. Williams from first German ed. ; & rev. & suppl. by S. Waterlow from the 5th German ed. Chicago: Open Court, 1897. (1886) (Reprinted 1959)

————. *Die Analyse der Empfindungen und das Verhältnis des Physischen zum Psychischen.* (9th ed.) Jena: Fischer, 1922. (1886)

————. The analysis of the sensations: Antimetaphysical. *Monist,* 1890–1891, *1,* 48–68.

————. Some questions of psycho-physics. *Monist,* 1890–1891, *1,* 393–400.

————. On the part played by accident in invention and discovery. *Monist,* 1895–1896, *6,* 161–175. Reprinted in *Popular scientific lectures, op. cit.,* pp. 259–281.

————. *Die Principien der Wärmelehre. Historisch-kritisch entwickelt.* (2nd ed.) Leipzig: Barth, 1900. (1896) (Reprinted 1970)

————. On sensations of orientation. *Monist,* 1897, *8,* 79–96. Reprinted in *Popular scientific lectures, op. cit.,* pp. 282–308.

————. On some phenomena attending the flight of projectiles. (1897) Reprinted in *Popular scientific lectures, op. cit.,* pp. 309–337.

————. On physiological, as distinguished from geometrical, space. *Monist,* 1906, *11,* 321–338. Reprinted in *Space and Geometry, op. cit.,* pp. 5–37.

————. *Erkenntnis und Irrtum. Skizzen zur Psychologie der Forschung.* (5th ed.) Leipzig: Barth, 1926. (1905) (Reprinted 1968)

————. Sur le rapport de la physique avec la psychologie. *Année psychol.*, 1906, *12*, 303–318.

————. *Principles of physical optics: An historical and philosophical treatment.* Trans. by J. Anderson & A. F. A. Young. London: Methuen, 1926. (1921) (Reprinted 1959)

Gardiner, *Philosophy;* Herrnstein & Boring, *Source Book;* Newman, *Mathematics;* Rand, *Classical Psychologists;* Shipley, *Classics*

FRANCOIS MAGENDIE
1783-1855
French Physiologist (25)

Magendie, F. *Mémoire sur l'usage de l'épiglotte dans la déglutition, présenté à la première classe de l'Institut le 22 mars 1813. Suivi du rapport fait à la classe par MM. Pinel et Percey, et d'un mémoire sur les images qui se forment au fond de l'oeil.* Paris: Méquignon-Marvis, 1813.

————. *An elementary treatise on human physiology on the basis of the précis élémentaire de physiologie.* (5th ed.) New York: Harper, 1844. (1816–1817)

————. (Verbal communication in discovery of functions of dorsal and ventral spinal nerve roots.) Procès-verb., 1822. *C. r. Acad. Sci.*, 1820–1823, *7*, 348.

————. Expériences sur les fonctions des nerfs rachidiens. *J. Physiol. exp. Pathol.*, 1822, *2*, 276–279. (Experiments upon the functions of the roots of the spinal nerves.) Trans. by J. Shaw in *London med. phys. J.*, 1822, *48*, 343–344.

————. Expériences sur les fonctions des racines des nerfs qui naissent de la moëlle épinière. *J. physiol. exp. Pathol.*, 1822, *2*, 366–371.

————. *A memoir on some recent discoveries relating to the functions of the nervous system.* London: Nimm, 1828. (1823)

————. Note sur le siège du mouvement et du sentiment dans la moëlle épinière. *J. Physiol. exp. Pathol.*, 1823, *3*, 153–157.

————. Mémoire sur les fonctions de quelques parties du système nerveux. *J. Physiol. exp. Pathol.*, 1824, *4*, 399–417.

————. Le nerf olfactif est-il l'organe de l'odorat? Expériences sur cette question. *J. Physiol. exp. Pathol.*, 1824, *4*, 169–176.

————. Mémoire sur un liquide qui se trouve dans le crâne et le canal vertébral de l'homme et des animaux mammifères. *J. Physiol. exp. Pathol.*, 1825, *5*, 27–37.

————. Mémoire physiologique sur le cerveau. *J. Physiol. exp. Pathol.*, 1828, *8*, 211–229.

————. *Leçons sur les fonctions et les maladies du système nerveux.* (2 vols.) Paris: Ebard, 1839–1841.

————. Quelques nouvelles expériences sur les fonctions du système nerveux. *C. r. Acad. Sci.*, 1839, *8*, 865.

————. *Recherches physiologiques et cliniques sur le liquide céphalo-rachidien ou cérébro-spinal.* Paris: Méquignon-Marvis, 1842.

————. *Phénomènes physiques de la vie.* (4 vols.) Paris: Baillière, 1842.

————. (Reply to Flourens.) *C. r. Acad. Sci.*, 1847, *24*, 320.

Clarke & O'Malley, *Brain;* Fulton & Wilson, *Physiology;* Herrnstein & Boring, *Source Book;* Sahakian, *Psychology*

MAINE DE BIRAN
(Marie François Pierre Gonthier de Biran)
1766-1824
French Philosopher (24)

Maine de Biran, M. F. P. G. *Nouvelles considérations sur les rapports du physique et du moral de l'homme.* Ed. by V. Cousin. Paris: Ladrange, 1834.   **C**

————. *Oeuvres de Maine de Biran.* (14 vols.) Ed. by P. Tisserand & H. Gouhier. Paris: Presses Universitaires de France, 1920–1942.   **C**

————. *Journal.* (3 vols.) Ed. by H. Gouhier. Neuchâtel: Editions de la Baconnière, 1954–1957. (1927)   **B C**

———. *Oeuvres choisies.* Ed. by H. Gouhier. Paris: Aubier, 1942.   **B C**

———. *Mémoire sur la décomposition de la pensée.* (2 vols.) Rev. ed. *Oeuvres,* Vols. 3–4, *op. cit.* Paris: Presses Universitaires de France, 1954.   **C**

———. *De l'existence. Textes inédits.* Ed. by H. Gouhier. Paris: Vrin, 1966.   **C**

———. *Lettres inédites de Maine de Biran à Ampère.* Ed. by H. Gouhier. *Rev. int. phil.,* 1966, *20,* 3–26.   **B C**

———. *Maine de Biran and Pestalozzi:* Some unpublished letters. Ed. by F. C. T. Moore. *Rev. int. phil.,* 1966, *20,* 27–52.   **B C**

———. *The influence of habit on the faculty of thinking.* Trans. by Margaret D. Boehm. Baltimore, Md.: Williams & Wilkins, 1929. (1803) (Reprinted 1971)

———. *De l'aperception immédiate. Mémoire de Berlin, 1807.* Ed. by J. Echeverria. Paris: Vrin, 1963.

———. Sur les rapports du physique et du moral de l'homme. (1811) Extracts in F. C. T. Moore, *The psychology of Maine de Biran.* Oxford: Clarendon Press, 1970, pp. 196–211.

———. Essai sur les fondements de la psychologie. (1812) In *Oeuvres choisies, op. cit.,* pp. 67–153.

———. Rapports des sciences naturelles avec la psychologie ou la science des facultés de l'esprit humain. In *Oeuvres choisies, op. cit.,* pp. 157–207. (1813)

———. Notes sur la philosophie de Kant. (1816) In *Oeuvres choisies, op. cit.,* pp. 211–228.

Rand, *Classical Psychologists*

NICHOLAS DE MALEBRANCHE
1638-1715
French Philosopher (21)

Malebranche, N. d. *Correspondance avec J. J. Dortous de Mairan.* Ed. by J. Moreau. Paris: Vrin, 1947. (1841)   **B C**

———, & Leibniz, G. W. *Relations personnelles, présentées avec les textes complets des auteurs et de leurs correspondants.* Ed. by A. Robinet. Paris: Vrin, 1955.   **B Bl C**

———. *Oeuvres complètes de Malebranche.* (21 vols.) Ed. by A. Robinet. Paris: Vrin, 1967, 1970. (1958-1965).   **B C**

———. *Lumière et mouvement de l'esprit.* Ed. by J. Costilhes. Paris: Presses Universitaires de France, 1962.   **C**

———. *De la recherche de la vérité où l'on traite de la nature de l'esprit de l'homme et de l'usage qu'il en doit faire pour éviter l'erreur dans les sciences.* (6th ed.) (3 vols.) Ed. by Geneviève Rodis-Lewis. Paris: Vrin, 1962. (1674) Reprinted in *Oeuvres.* Vols. 1, 2, 3, *op. cit.*

———. *Conversations chrétiennes..* Ed. by A. Robinet, Paris: Vrin, 5, 1929. (1677) Reprinted in *Oeuvres,* Vol. 4, *op. cit.*

———. *Traité de la nature et de la grâce.* Ed. by Ginette Dreyfus. Paris: Vrin, 1958. (1680) Reprinted in *Oeuvres,* Vol. 5, *op. cit.*

———. *Traité de morale.* Ed. by M. Adam. Paris: Vrin, 1966. (1683) Reprinted by *Oeuvres,* Vol. 11, *op. cit.*

———. *A treatise of morality.* (2 vols.) Trans. by J. Shipton. London: Knapton, 1699. (1683)

———. *Méditations chrétiennes.* Ed. by H. Gouhier, Paris: Montaigne, 1928. (1683) Reprinted in *Oeuvres,* Vol. 10, *op. cit.*

———. *I: Entretiens sur la métaphysique et sur la religion. II: Entretiens sur la métaphysique et sur la religion suivis des entretiens sur la mort.* (2 vols.) Ed. & intro. by A. Cuvillier. Paris: Vrin, 1948. (1688) Reprinted in *Oeuvres,* Vols. 12, 13, *op. cit.*

———. *Dialogues on metaphysics and on religion.* Trans. by M. Ginsburg. London: Allen & Unwin, 1923. (1688)

———. *Des lois générales de la communication des mouvements.* (1692) In *Recherche,* Vol. 3, *op. cit.,* pp. 269–298.

———. *Treatise concerning the search after truth.* (2nd ed.) Trans. by T. Taylor. London: Bowyer, 1700. (1694)

———. Réflexions sur la lumière, les couleurs et la génération du feu. *Mém. Acad. Sci.,* 1699, 22–36.

———. *Entretiens d'un philosophe chrétien et d'un philosophe chinois.* Ed. by A. Le Moine. Marseille: Gec, 1936. (1708) Reprinted in *Oeuvres,* Vol. 15, *op. cit.*

———. *Réflexions sur la prémotion physique.* Paris: David, 1715.

Popkin, *Philosophy;* Rand, *Moralists*

BRONISLAW KASPAR MALINOWSKI
1884-1942
English Anthropologist (22)

Malinowski, B. *A scientific theory of culture and other essays.* Pref. by H. Cairns. Chapel Hill, N.C.: University of North Carolina Press, 1944.   **C**

———. *Magic, science and religion, and other essays.* Intro. by R. Redfield. Garden City, N.Y.: Doubleday, 1954. (1948)   **C**

———. *Sex, culture and myth.* New York: Harcourt, Brace, & World, 1962.   **C**

———. *The family among the Australian aborigines: A sociological study.* New York: Schocken, 1963. (1913)

———. Ethnology and study of society. *Economica,* 1922, *2,* 208–219.

———. *Argonauts of the Western Pacific: Native enterprise and adventure in Melanesian New Guinea.* New York. Dutton, 1922.

———. The psychology of sex and the foundation of kinship in primitive society. *Psyche,* 1923, *4,* 98–128.

———. Psychoanalysis and anthropology. *Psyche,* 1924, *4,* 293–332.

———. Forschungen in einer mutterrechtlichen Gemeinschaft. *Z. Völkerpsychol. Soziol.,* 1925, *1,* 45–53, 278–284.

———. Complex and myth in mother-right. *Psyche,* 1925, *5,* 194–216.

———. The role of myth in life. *Psyche,* 1926, *6,* 29–39.

———. *Crime and custom in savage society.* New York: Harcourt, Brace, 1926. (Reprinted 1961)

———. *Myth in primitive psychology.* New York: Norton, 1926. (1926)

———. The life of culture. (1926) In G. E. Smith *et al. Culture: The diffusion controversy.* New York: Norton, 1927, pp. 26–46.

———. Primitive law and order. *Nature,* 1926, *117* (suppl.), 9–16.

———. Prenuptial intercourse between the sexes in the Trobriand Island, N. W. Melanesia. *Psychoanal. Rev.,* 1927, *14,* 20–36.

———. *The father in primitive psychology.* New York: Norton, 1966. (1927)

———. *Sex and repression in savage society.* New York: Harcourt, 1927.

———. Practical anthropology. *Africa,* 1929, *2,* 22–38.

———. *The sexual life of savages in north-western Melanesia: An ethnographic account of courtship, marriage and family life among the natives of the Trobriand Islands in British New Guinea.* New York: Liveright, 1929. (Reprinted 1962)

———. Parenthood: The basis of social structure. In V. F. Calverton & S. D. Schmalhausen (Eds.), *The new generation: The intimate problems of modern parents and children.* New York: Macaulay, 1930, pp. 113–168.

———. The relations between the sexes in tribal life. In V. F. Calverton (Ed.), *The making of man: An outline of anthropology.* New York: Random House, 1931, pp. 565–585.

———. The work and magic of prosperity in the Trobriand Islands. *Mensch en Maatschappij,* 1933, *9,* 154–174.

———. *Coral gardens and their magic: A study of the methods of tilling the soil and of agricultural rites in the Trobriand Islands.* (2 vols.) New York: American Book, 1935.

———. *The foundations of faith and morals.* London: Oxford University Press, 1936.

———. Culture as a determinant of behavior. (1936) In E. D. Adrian *et al.* (Eds.), *Factors determining human behavior.* Cambridge: Harvard University Press, 1937, pp. 133–168.

———. The dilemma of contemporary linguistics. Review of M. M. Lewis, *Infant speech: A study of the beginnings of language. Nature,* 1937, *140,* 172–173. Reprinted in D. Hymes (Ed.), *Language in culture and society: A reader in linguistics and anthropology.* New York: Harper & Row, 1964, pp. 63–65.

———. A nation-wide intelligence service. In C. Madge & T. Harrison (Eds.), *First year's work, 1937–1938, by mass-observation.* London: Drummond, 1938, pp. 81-121.

———. The anthropology of changing African cultures. In *Methods of study of culture contact in Africa.* London: Oxford University Press, 1938, pp. 7–38.

———. The present state of studies in culture contact: Some comments on an American approach. *Africa,* 1939, *12,* 27–47.

———. The group and the individual in functional analysis. *Amer. J. Sociol.,* 1939, *44,* 938–964.

———. Man's culture and man's behavior. 1, 2. *Sigma Xi Quart.,* 1941, *29,* 182–196 ; 1942, *30,* 66–78.

———. The scientific approach to the study of man. In Ruth N. Anshen (Ed.), *Science and man.* New York: Harcourt, Brace, 1942, pp. 207–242.

———. (With pref. by Anna V. Malinowski.) *Freedom and civilization.* New York: Roy, 1944.

———. *The dynamics of culture change: An inquiry into race relations in Africa.* Ed. by Phyllis M. Kaberry. New Haven: Yale University Press, 1945.

———. *A diary in the strict sense of the term.* Intro. by R. Firth, trans. by N. Guterman, & pref. by Valetta Malinowski. New York: Harcourt, Brace, & World, 1967. **B**

Coser & Rosenberg, *Sociological Theory ;* Dennis, *Readings ;* Goldschmidt, *Mankind ;* Hoebel & Jennings, *Anthropology ;* Parsons, *Society.*

THOMAS ROBERT MALTHUS
1766-1834
English Philosopher (17)

Malthus, T. R. *An essay on the principle of population and a summary view of the principle of population.* Ed. & intro. by A. Glew. Harmondsworth: Penguin, 1971. **C**

———. *An essay on the principle of population, as it affects the future improvement of society, with remarks on the speculations of Mr. Godwin, M. Condorcet, and other writers.* (Facs. ed.) London: Macmillan, 1926. (1798)

———. *On population.* New York: Random House, 1960. (1798) (Reprinted 1963)

———. *An essay on population.* (5th ed.) (2 vols.) New York: Dutton, 1914. (1798)

———. Letter to Samuel Whitehead. (1807) Reprinted in D. V. Glass (Ed.), *Introduction to Malthus.* London: Cass, 1953, pp. 185–205.

———. *Observations on the effects of the corn laws.* Ed. by J. H. Hollander. Baltimore, Md.: Johns Hopkins Press, 1932. (1814)

———. *The nature and progress of rent.* Ed. by J. H. Hollander. Baltimore, Md.: Johns Hopkins Press, 1903. (1815)

———. *Principles of political economy considered with a view to their practical application.* (2nd ed.) New York: Kelley, 1964. (1820)

———. *A summary view of the principle of population.* (1830) Reprinted in D. V. Glass (Ed.), *Introduction to Malthus, op. cit.,* pp. 114–181.

Bodenheimer, *Biology ;* Dampier, *Literature ;* Hall, *Source Book ;* Parsons, *Society ;* Ross, *Social Order*

KARL MARBE
1869-1953
German Psychologist (24)

Marbe, K. Die Schwankungen der Gesichtsempfindungen. *Phil. Stud.,* 1893, *8,* 615–637.

———. Zur Lehre von den Gesichtsempfindungen, welche aus successiven Reizen resultiren. *Phil. Stud.,* 1894, *9,* 384–399.

———. Theorie des Talbot'schen Gesetzes. *Phil. Stud.*, 1896, *12*, 279–296.

———. Neue Versuche über intermittirende Gesichtsreize. *Phil. Stud.*, 1897–1898, *13*, 106–115.

———. Die stroboskopischen Erscheinungen. *Phil. Stud.*, 1898, *14*, 376–401.

———. *Naturphilosophische Untersuchungen zur Wahrscheinlichkeitslehre.* Leipzig: Engelmann, 1899.

Thumb, A., & ———. *Experimentelle Untersuchungen über die psychologischen Grundlagen der sprachlichen Analogiebildung.* Leipzig: Engelmann, 1901.

———. *Experimentell-psychologische Untersuchungen über das Urteil, eine Einleitung in die Logik.* Leipzig: Engelmann, 1901.

———. *Ueber den Rhythmus der Prosa.* Giessen: Ricker, 1904.

———. W. Wundts Stellung zu meiner Theorie der stroboskopischen Erscheinungen und zur systematischen Selbstwahrnehmung. *Z. Psychol.*, 1907, *46*, 345–362.

———. Ueber die Verwendung russender Flammen in der Psychologie und deren Grenzgebiete. *Z. Psychol.*, 1908, *49*, 206–217.

———. Ueber das Gedankenlesen und die Gleichförmigkeit des psychischen Geschehens. *Z. Psychol.*, 1910, *56*, 241–263.

———. *Theorie der kinematographischen Projektionen.* Leipzig: Barth, 1910.

———. *Die Bedeutung der Psychologie für die übrigen Wissenschaften und die Praxis.* Leipzig: Barth, 1912.

———. *Grundzüge der forensischen Psychologie.* Munich: Beck, 1913.

———. *Die Aktion gegen die Psychologie. Eine Abwehr.* Leipzig: Teubner, 1913.

———. Psychologisches Gutachten zum Prozess wegen des Mülheimer Eisenbahnunglücks. *Forschr. Psychol. Anwen.*, 1913, *1*, 339–375.

———. Das psychologische Institut der Universität Würzburg. *Forschr. Psychol. Anwen.*, 1914, *2*, 302–320.

———. Zur Psychologie des Denkens. *Forschr. Psychol. Anwen.*, 1913, *3*, 1-42.

———. *Die Gleichförmigkeit in der Welt.* (2 vols.) Munich: Beck, 1916–1919.

———. Ueber Persönlichkeit, Einstellung, Suggestion und Hypnose. *Z. ges. Neurol. Psychiat.*, 1925, *94*, 359–366.

———. Ueber Einstellung und Umstellung. *Z. angew. Psychol.*, 1925, *26*, 43–57.

———. *Praktische Psychologie der Unfälle und Betriebsschäden.* Munich: Oldenbourg, 1926.

———. *Der Psycholog als Gerichtsgutachter im Straf- und Zivilprozess.* Stuttgart: Enke, 1926.

———. Ueber Strafanstalt und Psychologie. *Z. Psychol.*, 1926, *99*, 375–382.

———. *Psychologie der Werbung.* Stuttgart: Poeschel, 1927.

———. Die Eignung für Zahnheilkunde und ihre psychotechnische Prüfung. *Deutsch. Zahnärztl. Woch.*, 1928, *31*(6).

———. Psychologie des Befehlens und Gehorchens. *Z. Psychol.*, 1929, *113*, 373–386.

———. Ein experimentelles Gerichtsgutachten über Intelligenz und Glaubwürdigkeit eines erwachsenen Mädchens. *Arch. Kriminol.*, 1929, *85*, 1–13.

———. Der Psycholog als gerichtlicher Sachverständiger. *Arch. Kriminol.*, 1930, *86*, 1–15, 208–220.

———. *Psychologie der Wertreklame.* Stuttgart: Enke, 1930.

———. Persönlichkeit und Aussage. *Mitt. Krim.-biol. Gesell.*, 1931, *3*, 89–128.

———. Psychologisches Gutachten anlässlich des Wiederaufnahmegesuchs im Eierprozess Jürges. *Arch. ges. Psychol.*, 1931, *82*, 241–252.

———. *Die gerichtspsychologische Begutachtung von Autounfällen und die Eignung zum Chauffeur.* Leipzig: Hirschfeld, 1932.

———. Theorie der motorischen Einstellung und Persönlichkeit. *Z. Psychol.*, 1933, *129*, 305–322.

———. Zum Geleit. *Industr. Psychotech.*, 1938, *15*, 257–259.

———. *Neue Untersuchungen zur Psychologie, Statistik und Biologie.* Leipzig: Becker & Erler, 1940.

———. Zur Bedeutung der Psychologie für die Statistik. *Z. angew. Psychol.*, 1942, *63*, 328–346.

———. Psychologie und Biologie in der Ausdehnung der Geburtenstatistik. *Z. angew. Psychol.*, 1943, *65*, 247–255.

———. Gedanken über den dreifachen Sinn des psychologischen Schichtenbildes und seine pädagogische Bedeutung. *Z. pädag. Psychol.*, 1943, *44*, 29–45.

———. *Selbstbiographie des Psychologen Geheimrat Prof. Dr. Karl Marbe in Würzburg.* Halle: Deutsche Akademie der Naturforscher, 1945. **B Bl**

Mandler & Mandler, *Thinking*

EDME MARIOTTE
1620-1684
French Physicist (22)

Mariotte, E. *Oeuvres de M. Mariotte, de l'Académie royale des sciences ; comprenant tous les traités de cet auteur, tant ceux qui avoient déjà paru séparément, que ceux qui n'avoient pas encore été publiés.* (2 vols.) The Hague: Neaulme. 1740 (Reprinted 1923) **C**

———. Nouvelle découverte touchant le veüe. (1668) In *Oeuvres*, Vol. 2, *op. cit.*, pp. 495–534.

———. A new discovery touching vision. *Phil. Trans.*, 1668, *3*, 668–669.

———. Sur l'organe de la vision. (1669) *Hist. Acad. Roy. Sci.*, Paris, 1733, *1*, 68–69.

———. The answer of Monsieur Mariotte to Monsieur Pecquet, about the opinion, that the choroeides is the principal organ of sight ; communicated to the publisher from Paris. . . . *Phil. Trans.*, 1670, *5*, 1023–1042.

———. *De la nature des couleurs.* Paris: Michallet, 1681. Reprinted in *Oeuvres*, Vol. 1, *op. cit.*, pp. 195–320.

———, & Perrault, M. An account of two letters of Mr. Perrault and Mr. Mariotte, concerning vision. *Phil. Trans.*, 1683, *13*, 265–267.

Dennis, *Psychology*

KARL MARX
1818-1883
German Philosopher (16)

Marx, K., & Engels, F. *Historisch-kritische Gesamtausgabe: Werke, Schriften, Briefe.* (Ult. 42 vols.) Ed. by D. Rayazanov & D. B. Goldenbach. Berlin: Marx-Engels Verlag, 1927 ff. **C**

———, & Engels, F. *Werke.* (Ult. 44 vols.) Berlin: Dietz, 1956– **C**

———. Economic and philosophical manuscripts. In E. Fromm (Ed.), *Marx's concept of man.* Trans. by T. B. Bottomore. New York: Ungar, 1961, pp. 87–196. **C**

———, & Engels, F. *Selected works.* New York: International Publishers, 1968. **C**

———. *Kritik des Hegel'schen Staatsrechts. Die Frühschriften.* Stuttgart: Kröner, 1953. (1843)

———, & Engels, F. *The German ideology.* New York: International Publishers. 1960. (1845–1846)

———. *The poverty of philosophy.* New York: International Publishers, 1963. (1847)

———, Engels, F., et al. *Principles of Communism.* Trans. by P. M. Sweezy. New York: Monthly Review Press, 1964. (1848)

———. *A contribution to the critique of political economy.* (2nd ed.) Trans. by N. I. Stone. New York: International Library Publishing, 1904. (1859)

———. *Capital: A critique of political economy* (3rd ed.) (3 vols.) Ed. by F. Engels & trans. by S. Moore & E. Aveling. New York: International Publishers, 1967. (1867)

———, & Engels, F. Theses on Feuerbach. (1888) In *The German ideology.* Trans. & ed. by S. Ryozanskaya. Moscow: Progress Publishers, 1964, pp. 27–95.

Coser, *Sociological Thought ;* Coser & Rosenberg, *Sociological Theory ;* Gardiner, *Philosophy ;* Hutchins, *Great Books ;* Mann & Kreyche, *Reflections Man ;* Nash, *Models ;* Parsons, *Society*

MATATARO MATSUMOTO
1865-1943
Japanese Psychologist (11)

Matsumoto, M. Researches in acoustic space. *Stud. Yale Psychol. Lab.,* 1897, *5,* 1–75.

————, & Motora, Y. *(Experimental studies on the legibility and rapidity of writing of the two kinds of Japanese alphabets.)* Tokyo: Education Dept., 1904.

————. *(Diary of a migratory bird.)* Tokyo: Jitsugyono Nipponsha, 1917.

————. (Psychological studies on the technical methods of the Chinese pictorial art.) *Geibun,* 1910, *1,* No. 3, 1–19.

————. *(Mental works.)* Tokyo: Rikugokan, 1914.

————. *(Lectures on experimental psychology.)* Tokyo: Kodokan, 1914.

————. *(Psychocinematics.)* Tokyo: Rikugokan, 1914.

————. *(Psychological interpretation of modern Japanese paintings.)* (Rev. ed.) Tokyo: Hokubunkan, 1927. (1915)

————. *(On the methods of psychology.) Jap. J. Psychol.,* 1923, *1*(1), 1–8.

————. *(Outlines of psychology.)* (Rev. ed.) Tokyo: Kaizosha, 1928. (1923)

————. *(Psychology of intelligence.)* Tokyo: Kaizosha, 1925.

————. (Psychological aspect of the progress of formative art.) *Jap. J. Psychol.,* 1926, *1*(5), 1–22.

————. *(Psychology of appreciation of paintings.)* Tokyo: Iwanamishoten, 1926.

————. (Intelligence of cultured races.) *Jap. J. Psychol.,* 1927, *2*(6), 1–25.

————. (The life of woman represented in antique Egyptian painting and drawings.) *Jap. J. Psychol.,* 1929, *4*(1), 31–44.

————. *(Art of various races.)* Tokyo: Kaizosha, 1930.

————. Die Entwicklung der Psychologie in Japan. *Z. angew. Psychol.,* 1931, *39,* 230–239.

————. (Female ghosts in arts.) *Jap. J. appl. Psychol.,* 1934, *2,* 301–311.

————. (A retrospect on the Japanese Journal of Psychology.) *Jap. J. Psychol.,* 1935, *10,* 695–700.

————. *(History of psychology.)* Tokyo: Kaizosha, 1937.

HENRY MAUDSLEY
1834-1918
English Psychiatrist (16)

Maudsley, H. *The pathology of mind.* (2nd ed.) New York: Appleton, 1895. (1867)

————. *The physiology of mind.* (3rd ed.) New York: Appleton, 1878. (1867)

————. *Body and mind: An enquiry into their connection and mutual influence, specially in reference to mental disorders.* (Rev. ed.) New York: Appleton, 1886. (1870)

————. *Responsibility in mental disease.* New York: Appleton, 1897. (1875)

————. *Body and will.* New York: Appleton, 1884.

————. *Natural causes and supernatural seemings.* London: Kegan Paul, Trench, & Truebner, 1897. (1886)

————. The physical conditions of consciousness. *Mind,* 1887, *12,* 489–515.

————. The double brain. *Mind,* 1889, *14,* 161–187.

————. The cerebral cortex and its work. *Mind,* 1890, *15,* 161–190.

————. Criminal responsibility in relation to insanity. *J. ment. Sci.,* 1895, *41,* 657–674.

————. The new psychology. *J. ment. Sci.,* 1900, *46,* 411–426.

————. *Life in mind and conduct.* London: Macmillan, 1902.

————. The physical basis of consciousness. *J. ment. Sci.,* 1909, *55,* 1–22.

————. *Organic to human: Psychological and sociological.* London: Macmillan, 1916.

———. *Religion and realities.* London: Bale, Sons & Danielsson, 1918.

———. War psychology: English and German. *J. ment. Sci.,* 1919, *65,* 65–87.

JAMES CLERK MAXWELL
1831-1879
English Physicist (19)

Maxwell, J. C. *Scientific papers.* (2 vols.) Ed. by W. D. Niven. London: Cambridge University Press, 1890. (Reprinted 1927, 1953)   **C**

———. Experiments on colour; as perceived by the eye with remarks on colour blindness. *Trans. Roy. Soc. Edinburgh,* 1855, *21*(2), 275–298; *Edinb. J.,* 1855, *1,* 359–360. Reprinted in *Scientific papers,* Vol. 1, *op. cit.,* pp. 126–154.

———. On the unequal sensibility of the foramen centrale to light of different colours. (1856) In *Scientific papers,* Vol. 1, *op. cit.,* p. 242.

———. On the theory of compound colours with reference to mixtures of blue and yellow light. *Rep. Brit. Ass.,* 1856, *2,* 12–13. Reprinted in *Scientific papers,* Vol. 1, *op. cit.,* pp. 243–245.

———. On the theory of colours in relation to colour blindness. *Trans. Roy. Scot. Soc. Arts,* 1856, *4,* 394–400. Reprinted in *Scientific papers,* Vol. 1, *op. cit.,* pp. 119–125.

———. On the theory of compound colours, and the relations of the colours of the spectrum. *Proc. Roy. Soc.,* 1860, *10,* 404–409, 484–486. *Phil. Trans.,* 1860, *150,* 57–84. *Phil. Mag.,* 1860, *21,* 141–146. *Cimento,* 1860, *12,* 33–37. *Rep. Brit. Ass.,* 1860, *2,* 16. Reprinted in *Scientific papers,* Vol. 1, *op. cit.,* pp. 410–444.

———. On the theory of three primary colours. Lecture at the Royal Institution of Great Britain. (1861) In *Scientific papers.* Vol. 1, *op. cit.,* pp. 445–450.

———. On colour-vision at different points of the retina. *Rep. Brit. Ass. Adv. Sci.,* 1870, *40,* Abstr., 40–41.

———. *Theory of heat.* (7th ed.) London: Longmans, Green, 1883. (1871)

———. *A treatise on electricity and magnetism.* (3rd ed.) (2 vols.) Ed. by J. J. Thompson. Oxford: Clarendon Press, 1904. (1873)

———. *Matter and motion.* New York: Van Nostrand, 1892. (1876)

MacAdam, *Color Science*

(GEORGE) ELTON MAYO
1880-1949
Australian-American Psychologist (11)

Mayo, E. Revery and industrial fatigue. *J. Personnel Res.,* 1924, *3,* 273–281.

———. The human effect of mechanization. *Pap. Proc. 42nd Ann. Meet. Amer. Econ. Ass.,* 1930, *20,* No. 1.

———. Changing methods in industry. *Personnel J.,* 1930, *8,* No. 5.

———. The work of Jean Piaget. *Ohio St. Univer. Bull.,* 1930, *35,* No. 3.

———. The Western Electric Company experiment. *Human Factor,* 1930, *6,* No. 1.

———. Psychology in industry. *Ohio St. Univer. Bull.,* 1930, *35,* No. 3.

———. Economic stability and the standard of living. *Harv. Bus. Sch. Alum. Bull.,* 1931, *7,* No. 6.

———. Supervision and morale. *J. Nat. Inst. Indust. Psychol.,* 1931, *5,* No. 5.

———. *The human problems of an industrial civilization.* New York: Macmillan, 1933. (Reprinted 1946)

———. The dynamic pose. *Harv. Bus. Sch. Alum. Bull.,* 1933, *9,* No. 3.

———. Human relations in industry. *Ment. Hlth. Obser.,* 1934, *2,* No. 4.

———, & Henderson, L. J. The effects of social environment. *J. Indust. Hyg. Toxicol.,* 1936, *18,* No. 7.

———. Psychiatry and sociology in relation to social disorganization. *Amer. J. Sociol.,* 1937, *42,* 825–831.

———. What every village knows. *Surv. Graph.,* 1937, *26,* No. 12.

————. Routine interaction and the problem of collaboration. *Amer. Sociol. Rev.,* 1939, *4,* 335–340.

————. Industrial research. *Harv. Bus. Sch. Alum. Bull.,* 1940, *16,* No. 2.

————. Foreword. In F. J. Roethlisberger (Ed.), *Management and morale.* Cambridge: Harvard University Press, 1941, pp. xv–xxii.

————. Research in human relations. *Personnel,* 1941, *17,* No. 4.

————. The fifth columnists of business. *Harv. Bus. Sch. Alum. Bull.,* 1941, *17,* No. 1.

————. The study of human problems of administration. *Harv. Bus. Sch. Alum. Bull.,* 1942, *18,* No. 3.

————, & Lombard, G. F. F. *Teamwork and labor turnover in the aircraft industry of southern California.* Boston: Harvard University Graduate School of Business Administration, 1957. (1944)

————. *The social problems of an industrial civilization.* Boston: Division of Research, Graduate School of Business Administration, Harvard University, 1945.   **Bl**

————. Group tensions in industry. In L. Bryson *et al.* (Eds.), *Approaches to national unity.* New York: Harper, 1945, pp. 46–60.

————. *Some notes on the psychology of Pierre Janet.* Cambridge: Harvard University Press, 1948.

  Moore & Hartmann, *Industrial Psychology*

JAMES McCOSH
1811-1894
Scottish-American Philosopher (13)

McCosh, J. *Realistic philosophy defended in a philosophic sense.* (2 vols.) New York: Macmillan, 1887.   **C**

————. *Typical forms and special ends in creation.* (2nd ed.) Edinburgh: Constable, 1857. (1856)

————. Sir William Hamilton's metaphysics. *Dubl. Univer. Mag.,* 1859, *54,* 152–166.

————. *The intuitions of the mind inductively investigated.* (2nd ed.) New York: Carter, 1882. (1860)

————. *The supernatural in relation to the natural.* New York: Carter, 1862.

————. The scepticism of Hume. *Brit. For. Evangel. Rev.,* 1865, *14,* 826–850.

————. *An examination of Mr. J. S. Mill's philosophy, being a defence of fundamental truth.* (2nd ed., with additions.) New York: Carter, 1875. (1866)

————. Mill's reply to his critics. *Brit. For. Evangel. Rev.,* 1868, *17,* 332–362. Also in *Amer. Presbyt. Theol. Rev.,* 1868, *6*(N.S.), 350–391.

————. *Philosophical papers.* (2nd ed.) New York: Macmillan, 1869. (1868)

————. *The laws of discursive thought.* (Rev. ed.) New York: Scribner's, 1891. (1870)

————. Berkeley's philosophy. *Presbyt. Quart. Princeton Rev.,* 1873, *2*(N.S.), 1–30.

————. *The development hypothesis: Is it sufficient?* New York: Carter, 1876. (1874)

————. *The Scottish philosophy, biographical, expository, critical, from Hutcheson to Hamilton.* New York: Carter, 1875. (Reprinted 1966)

————. *The emotions.* New York: Scribner's, 1880.

————. On causation and development. *Princeton Rev.,* 1881, *57,* 369–389.

————. *Development: What it can do and what it cannot do.* New York: Scribner's, 1883.

————. *A criticism of the critical philosophy.* New York: Scribner's, 1884.

————. *Agnosticism of Hume and Huxley, with a notice of the Scottish School.* New York: Scribner's, 1884.

————. *Locke's theory of knowledge, with a notice of Berkeley.* New York: Scribner's, 1884.

————. *Psychology of the cognitive powers.* (Rev. ed.) New York: Scribner's, 1906. (1866)

——. *Psychology: The motive powers ; emotions, conscience, will.* New York: Scribner's, 1894. (1887)

Kurtz, *American Thought ;* Robinson, *Scottish Philosophy*

WILLIAM McDOUGALL
1871-1938
English-American Psychologist (27)

McDougall, W. *Religion and the sciences of life, with other essays on allied topics.* London: Methuen, 1934.   **C**

——. *William McDougall: Explorer of the mind: Studies in psychical research.* Ed. by R. Van Over & Laura Oteri. New York: Garrett, 1967.   **C**

——. A contribution towards an improvement in psychological method. *Mind,* 1898, *7*(N.S.), 15–33, 159–178, 364–387.

——. Some new observations in support of Thomas Young's theory of light- and color-vision. *Mind,* 1901, *10*(N.S.), 52–97, 210–245, 347–382.

——. The nature of inhibitory processes within the nervous system. *Brain,* 1903, *26,* 153–191.

——. Hearing, smell, taste, cutaneous sensation, etc. In *Reports of the Cambridge Anthropological Expedition to Torres Straits.* Vol. 2. Cambridge: Cambridge University Press, 1903, pp. 141–223.

——. The sensations excited by a single momentary stimulation of the eye. *Brit. J. Psychol.,* 1904–1905, *1,* 78–113.

——. The variation of the intensity of visual sensation with the duration of the stimulus. *Brit. J. Psychol.,* 1904–1905, *1,* 151–189.

——. On a new method for the study of concurrent mental operations and of mental fatigue. *Brit. J. Psychol.,* 1904–1905, *1,* 435–445.

——. *Physiological psychology.* London: Dent, 1921. (1905)

——. An investigation of the colour sense of two infants. *Brit. J. Psychol.,* 1906–1908, *2,* 338–352.

——. *An introduction to social psychology.* (33rd ed.) London: Methuen, 1950. (1908)

Flugel, J. C., & ——. Further observations on the variation of the intensity of visual sensation with the duration of the stimulus. *Brit. J. Psychol.,* 1909–1910, *3,* 178–207.

——. Instinct and intelligence. *Brit. J. Psychol.,* 1909–1910, *3,* 250–266.

——. *Body and mind: A history and a defense of animism.* (8th ed.) London: Methuen, 1938. (1911) (Reprinted 1961)

——. *Psychology: The study of behavior.* London: Oxford University Press, 1959. (1912)

Flugel, J. C., & ——. Some observations on psychological contrast. *Brit. J. Psychol.,* 1914–1915, *7,* 349–385.

——. Instinct and the unconscious. VI. *Brit. J. Psychol.,* 1919–1920, *10,* 35–42.

Smith, May, & ——. Some experiments in learning and retention. *Brit. J. Psychol.,* 1919–1920, *10,* 199–209.

——. *The group mind: A sketch of the principles of collective psychology, with some attempt to apply them to the interpretation of national life and character.* (2nd ed.) New York: Putnam, 1927. (1920)

——. Belief as a derived emotion. *Psychol. Rev.,* 1921, *28,* 315–327.

——. The use and abuse of instinct in social psychology. *J. abnorm. soc. Psychol.,* 1921–1922, *16,* 285–333.

——. *Outline of psychology.* New York: Scribner's, 1923.

——. Purposive or mechanical psychology? *Psychol. Rev.,* 1923, *30,* 273–288.

——. Purposive striving as a fundamental category of psychology. *Sci. Mon., N.Y.,* 1924, *19,* 305–312.

——. Can sociology and social psychology dispense with instincts? *Amer. J. Sociol.,* 1923–1924, *29,* 657–673.

——. An experiment for the testing of the hypnosis of Lamarck. *Brit. J. Psychol.,* 1926–1927, *17,* 267–304.

―――. Men or robots? I. II. In C. Murchison (Ed.), *Psychologies of 1925*. (3rd ed.) Worcester, Mass.: Clark University Press, 1928, pp. 273–291, 293–305. (1926)

―――. The hypothesis of inhibition by drainage. *Psychol. Rev.*, 1926, *33*, 370–374.

―――. Pleasure, pain and conation. *Brit. J. Psychol.*, 1926–1927, *17*, 171–180.

―――. *Character and the conduct of life*. London: Methuen, 1927.

―――. Emotion and feeling distinguished. In M. L. Reymert (Ed.), *Feelings and emotions: The Wittenberg symposium*. Worcester, Mass.: Clark University Press, 1928, pp. 200–205.

―――. The confusion of the concept. *J. Phil. Stud.*, 1928, *3*, 427–442.

―――. The bearing of Professor Pavlov's work on the problem of inhibition. *J. gen. Psychol.*, 1929, *2*, 231–262.

―――. Second report on a Lamarckian experiment. *Brit. J. Psychol.*, 1929, *20*, 201–218.

Watson, J. B., & ―――. *The battle of behaviorism*. New York: Norton, 1929.

―――. *Modern materialism and emergent evolution*. New York: Van Nostrand, 1929.

―――. The chemical theory of temperament applied to introversion and extraversion. *J. abnorm. soc. Psychol.*, 1929–1930, *24*, 293–309.

―――. The hormic psychology. In C. Murchison (Ed.), *Psychologies of 1930*. Worcester, Mass.: Clark University Press, 1930, pp. 3–36.

―――. William McDougall. In C. Murchison (Ed.), *A history of psychology in autobiography*. Vol. 1. Worcester, Mass.: Clark University Press, 1930, pp. 191–223. **B**

―――. *Outline of abnormal psychology*. New York: Scribner's, 1932. (1926)

―――. *The energies of men: A study of the fundamentals of dynamic psychology*. New York: Scribner's, 1932.

―――. Experimental psychology and psychological experiment. *J. Pers.*, 1933, *1*, 195–213.

Rhine, J. B., & ―――. Third report of Lamarckian experiment. *Brit. J. Psychol.*, 1933, *24*, 213–235.

―――. *The frontiers of psychology*. New York: Appleton-Century, 1934.

―――. The dynamics of the Gestalt psychology. *J. Pers.*, 1935, *4*, 232–244, 319–334; 1936, *5*, 61–82, 131–148.

―――. *Psycho-analysis and social psychology*. London: Methuen, 1936.

―――. Organization of the affective life: A critical survey. *Acta Psychol.*, 1937, *2*, 233–346.

―――. *The riddle of life: A survey of theories*. London: Methuen, 1938.

―――. Fourth report on a Lamarckian experiment. *Brit. J. Psychol.*, 1938, *28*, 321–345, 365–395.

Arnold, *Emotion;* Bindra & Stewart, *Motivation;* Borgatta, *Present-day Sociology;* Herrnstein & Boring, *Source Book;* Moore & Hartmann, *Industrial Psychology;* Park & Burgess, *Sociology;* Parsons, *Society;* Russell, *Motivation;* Sahakian, *Psychology;* Shipley, *Classics*

JOHN ALEXANDER McGEOCH
1897-1942
American Psychologist (20)

McGeoch, J. A. The acquisition of skill. *Psychol. Bull.*, 1927, *24*, 437–466; 1929, *26*, 457–498; 1931, *28*, 413–466.

―――. Memory. *Psychol. Bull.*, 1928, *25*, 513–549; 1930, *27*, 514–563.

―――, & Melton, A. W. The comparative retention values of maze habits and of nonsense syllables. *J. exp. Psychol.*, 1929, *12*, 392–414.

―――. The influence of degree of learning upon retroactive inhibition. *Amer. J. Psychol.*, 1929, *41*, 252–262.

―――. The influence of associative value upon the difficulty of nonsense-syllable lists. *J. genet. Psychol.*, 1930, *37*, 421–426.

―――, & McDonald, W. T. Meaningful relation and retroactive inhibition. *Amer. J. Psychol.*, 1931, *43*, 579–588.

―――. The influence of four different interpolated activities upon retention. *J. exp. Psychol.*, 1931, *14*, 400–413.

―――. The comparative retention values of a maze habit, of nonsense syllables, and of rational learning. *J. exp. Psychol.*, 1932, *15*, 662–680.

―――. The influence of degree of interpolated learning upon retroactive inhibition. *Amer. J. Psychol.*, 1932, *44*, 695–708.

―――. Forgetting and the law of disuse. *Psychol. Rev.*, 1932, *39*, 352–370.

―――. The configurational psychology of learning as represented by R. H. Wheeler and F. T. Perkins, *Principles of mental development. J. appl. Psychol.*, 1933, *17*, 83–96.

―――, & Peters, H. N. An all-or-none characteristic in the elimination of errors during the learning of a stylus maze. *J. exp. Psychol.*, 1933, *16*, 504–523.

―――. Studies in retroactive inhibition. I. The temporal course of the inhibitory effects of interpolated learning. *J. gen. Psychol.*, 1933, *9*, 24–43.

―――. Studies in retroactive inhibition. II. Relationships between temporal point of interpolation, length of interval, and amount of retroactive inhibition. *J. gen. Psychol.*, 1933, *9*, 44–57.

―――. The psychology of human learning. A bibliography. *Psychol. Bull.*, 1933, *30*, 1–62.

―――. The formal criteria of a systematic psychology. *Psychol. Rev.*, 1933, *40*, 1–12.

―――. The direction and extent of intra-serial associations at recall. *Amer. J. Psychol.*, 1936, *48*, 221–245.

―――. Learning and retention of verbal materials. *Psychol. Bull.*, 1934, *31*, 381–407.

―――. The vertical dimensions of mind. *Psychol. Rev.*, 1936, *43*, 107–129.

―――, McKinney, F., & Peters, H. N. Studies in retroactive inhibition. IX. Retroactive inhibition, reproductive inhibition, and reminiscence. *J.exp-Psychol.*, 1937, *20*, 131–143.

―――. All-or-none versus gradual elimination of homogeneous cul-de-sac. *Amer. J. Psychol.*, 1937, *50*, 111–129.

―――. *The psychology of human learning.* (2nd ed.) Rev. by A. L. Irion. New York: Longmans, Green, 1952. (1942)

―――, & Underwood, B. J. Tests of the two-factor theory of retroactive inhibition. *J. exp. Psychol.*, 1943, *32*, 1–16.

DOUGLAS (MURRAY) McGREGOR
1906-1964
American Psychologist (12)

McGregor, D. *Leadership and motivation: Essays of Douglas McGregor.* Ed. by W. G. Bennis & E. H. Schain, with collab. of Caroline McGregor. Cambridge: MIT Press, 1966.

―――. Scientific measurement and psychology. *Psychol. Rev.*, 1935, *42*, 246–266.

―――. Sensitivity of the eye to the saturation of colors. *J. exp. Psychol.*, 1936, *19*, 525–546.

―――. The major determinants of the prediction of social events. *J. abnorm. soc. Psychol.*, 1938, *33*, 179–204.

―――. Motives as a tool of market research. *Harvard Bus. Rev.*, 1940, *19*(1), 42–51.

―――, & Knickerbocker, I. Industrial relations and national defense: A challenge to management. *Personnel*, 1941, *18*(1), 49–63.

Arensberg, C. M., & ―――. Determination of morale in an industrial company. *Appl. Anthro.*, 1942, *1*(2), 12-34.

Knickerbocker, I., & ―――. Union-management cooperation: A psychological analysis. *Personnel*, 1942, *19*(3), 520–539.

―――. Conditions of effective leadership in the industrial organization. *J. consult. Psychol.*, 1944, *8*, 55–63.

―――. The foreman's responsibilities in the industrial organization. *Personnel*, 1946, *22*(5), 296–304.

―――. The staff function in human relations. *J. soc. Issues*, 1948, *4*(3), 5–22.

———. Toward a theory of organized human effort in industry. In *Psychology of Labor-Management Relations, Proceedings of the Meeting.* Champaign, Ill: Industrial Relations Research Association, 1949, pp. 111–122.

———. The human side of enterprise. *Manag. Rev.,* 1957, *46*(11), 72–128. Reprinted in *Leadership and motivation, op. cit.,* pp. 3–20.

———. An uneasy look at performance appraisals. *Harvard Business Rev.,* 1957, *35*(3). Reprinted in *Leadership and motivation, op. cit.,* pp. 184–197.

———. The significance of Scanlon's contribution. In F. G. Lesieur (Ed.), *The Scanlon Plan: A frontier in labor-management cooperation.* New York: Wiley, 1958, pp. 7–15. Reprinted in *Leadership and motivation, op. cit.,* pp. 114–126.

———. *The human side of enterprise.* New York: McGraw-Hill, 1960.

———. New concepts of management. *Technol. Rev.,* 1961, *63,* No. 4, 25–27. Reprinted in *Leadership and motivation, op. cit.,* pp. 21–29.

———. Behavioral science—what's in it for management. National Industrial Conference Board, *Bus. Manag. Rec.,* 1963, *25,* 32–44.

———. The manager, human nature and human sciences. (1966) In *Leadership and motivation, op. cit.,* pp. 201–238.

———. Why not exploit behavioral science? (1966) In *Leadership and motivation, op. cit.,* pp. 239–275.

———. *The professional manager.* Ed. by Caroline McGregor & W. G. Bennis. New York: McGraw-Hill, 1967.

GEORGE HERBERT MEAD
1863-1931
American Philosopher (19)

Mead, G. H. *The philosophy of the present.* Ed. by A. E. Murphy. Chicago: Open Court, 1932.   **C**

———. *Mind, self, and society from the standpoint of a social behaviorist.* Ed. by C. W. Morris. Chicago: University of Chicago Press, 1934.   **C**

———. *Movements of thought in the nineteenth century.* Ed. by M. H. Moore. Chicago: University of Chicago Press, 1936.   **C**

———. *The philosophy of the act.* Ed. by C. W. Morris *et al.* Chicago: University of Chicago Press, 1938.   **C**

———. *On social psychology: Selected papers.* (Rev. ed.) Ed. by A. Strauss. Chicago: University of Chicago Press, 1964. (1956)   **C**

———. *Selected writings.* Ed. by A. J. Reck. Indianapolis, Ind.: Bobbs-Merrill, 1964. **Bl C**

———. *George Herbert Mead: Essays on his social philosophy.* Ed. by J. W. Petras. New York: Teachers College Press, 1968.   **C**

———. Suggestions toward a theory of the philosophical disciplines. *Phil. Rev.,* 1900, *9,* 1–17. Reprinted in *Selected writings, op. cit.,* pp. 6–24.

———. The definition of the psychical. In *The Decennial Publications of the University of Chicago.* First series. Vol. III. Chicago: University of Chicago Press, 1903, pp. 77–112. Reprinted in *Selected writings, op. cit.,* pp. 25–59.

———. The relations of psychology and philology. *Psychol. Bull.,* 1904, *1,* 375–391.

———. Concerning animal perception. *Psychol. Rev.,* 1907, *14,* 383–390. Reprinted in *Selected writings, op. cit.,* pp. 73–81.

———. Social psychology as counterpart to physiological psychology. *Psychol. Bull.,* 1909, *6,* 401–408. Reprinted in *Selected writings, op. cit.,* pp. 94–104.

———. What social objects must psychology presuppose? *J. Phil.,* 1910, *7,* 174–180. Reprinted in *Selected writings, op. cit.,* pp. 105–113.

———. Psychology of social consciousness implied in instruction. *Science,* 1910, *31,* 688–693. Reprinted in *Essays on his social philosophy, op. cit.,* pp. 35–41.

———. Social consciousness and the consciousness of meaning. *Psychol. Bull.,* 1910, *7,* 397–405. Reprinted in *Selected writings, op. cit.,* pp. 123–133.

―――. The mechanism of social consciousness. *J. Phil.*, 1912, *9*, 401–406. Reprinted in *Selected writings, op. cit.*, pp. 134–141.

―――. The social self. *J. Phil.*, 1913, *10*, 374–380. Reprinted in *Selected writings, op. cit.*, pp. 142–149.

―――. The psychology of punitive justice. *Amer. J. Sociol.*, 1917–1918, *23*, 577–602. Reprinted in *Essays on his social philosophy, op. cit.*, pp. 130–150.

―――. A behavioristic account of the significant symbol. *J. Phil.*, 1922, *19*, 157–163. Reprinted in *Selected writings, op. cit.*, pp. 240–247.

―――. Scientific method and the moral sciences. *Int. J. Ethics*, 1922–1923, *33*, 229–247. Reprinted in *Selected writings, op. cit.*, pp. 248–266, & in *Essays on his social philosophy, op. cit.*, pp. 83–96.

―――. The genesis of the self and social control. *Int. J. Ethics*, 1924–1925, *35*, 251–277. Reprinted in *Selected writings, op. cit.*, pp. 267–293.

―――. A pragmatic theory of truth. In *Studies in the nature of truth: University of California Publications in philosophy*, No. 11. Berkeley, Calif.: University of California Press, 1929, pp. 65–88. Reprinted in *Selected writings, op. cit.*, pp. 320–344.

―――. Bishop Berkeley and his message. *J. Phil.*, 1929, *26*, 421–430.

―――. The nature of the past. In J. Coss (Ed.), *Essays in honor of John Dewey*. New York: Holt, 1929, pp. 235–242. Reprinted in *Selected writings, op. cit.*, pp. 345–354.

―――Cooley's contribution to American social thought. *Amer. J. Sociol.*, 1929–1930, *35*, 693–706. Reprinted in *Essays on his social philosophy, op. cit.*, pp. 293–307.

―――. The philosophies of Royce, James, and Dewey, in their American setting. *Int. J. Ethics,* 1929–1930, *40*, 211–231. Reprinted in *Essays on his social philosophy, op. cit.*, pp. 109–124.

―――. The philosophy of John Dewey. *Int. J. Ethics*, 1935–1936, *46*, 64–81.

Borgatta, *Present-day Sociology ;* Coser, *Sociological Thought ;* Coser & Rosenberg, *Sociological Theory ;* Curtis, *Knowledge ;* Fried, *Anthropology ;* McNall, *Sociological Perspective ;* Mueller, *American Philosophy ;* Parsons, *Society* ; Ross, *Social Order.*

ALEXIUS VON MEINONG
1853-1920
Austrian Philosopher (24)

Meinong, A. v. *Gesammelte Abhandlungen.* (2 vols.) Ed. by A. Höfler *et al.* Leipzig: Barth, 1913, 1914.   **C**

―――. *Philosophen Briefe : Aus der wissenschaft lichen Korrespondenz von Alexius Meinong mit Fachgenossen seiner Zeit.* Ed. by R. Kindinger. Graz: Akademische Druck- und Verlagsanstalt, 1965.   **B C**

―――. *Gesamtausgabe. (Verbesserter und durch Zusätze aus dem bisher unveröffentlichten Nachlass vermehrter Nachdruck der Veröffentlichungen Meinongs.)* (7 vols.) Ed. by R. Haller & R. Kindinger. Graz: Akademische Druck- und Verlagsanstalt, 1968.   **C**

―――. Hume-Studien. I. *Zur Geschichte und Kritik des modernen Nominalismus.* II. *Zur Relationstheorie.* Vienna: Gerold's, 1877, 1882. Reprinted in *Gesammelte Abhandlungen*, Vol. 1, *op. cit.*, pp. 1–72, & Vol. 2. *op. cit.*, pp. 1–170.

―――. Ueber Sinnesermüdung im Bereiche des Weber'schen Gesetzes. *Vtljsch. wiss. Phil.*, 1888, *12*, 1–31. Reprinted in *Gesammelte Abhandlungen*, Vol. 1, *op. cit.*, pp. 79–106.

―――. Ueber Begriff und Eigenschaften der Empfindung. *Vtljsch. wiss. Phil.*, 1888, *12*, 324–354, 477–502 ; 1889, *13*, 1–31. Reprinted in *Gesammelte Abhandlungen*, Vol. I, *op. cit.*, pp. 111–185.

―――. Ueber Phantasie-Vorstellung und Phantasie. *Z. Phil. phil. Krit.* 1889, *95*, 161–244. Reprinted in *Gesammelte Abhandlungen*, Vol. 1, *op. cit.*, pp. 195–271.

―――. Zur Psychologie der Komplexionen und Relationen. *Z. Psychol.*, 1891, *2*, 245–265. Reprinted in *Gesammelte Abhandlungen*, Vol. 1, *op. cit.*, pp. 281–300.

————. *Psychologisch-ethische Untersuchungen zur Werttheorie.* Graz: Leuschner & Lubensky, 1894.

————. Beiträge zur Theorie der psychischen Analyse. *Z. Psychol.,* 1894, *6,* 340–385, 417–455. Reprinted in *Gesammelte Abhandlungen,* Vol. 1, *op. cit.,* pp. 307–388.

————. Ueber Werthaltung und Wert. *Arch. syst. Phil.,* 1895, *1,* 327–346.

————. Ueber die Bedeutung des Weber'schen Gesetzes. *Z. Psychol.,* 1896, *11,* 81-133, 230–285, 353–404. Reprinted in *Gesammelte Abhandlungen,* Vol. 2, *op. cit.,* pp. 217–370. (Also Leipzig: Voss, 1896)

————, & Witasek, S. Zur experimentellen Bestimmung der Tonverschmelzungsgrade. *Z. Psychol.,* 1897, *15,* 189–205.

————. Ueber Raddrehung, Rollung und Aberration: Beiträge zur Theorie der Augenbewegungen. *Z. Psychol.,* 1898, *17,* 161–204. Reprinted in *Gesammelte Abhandlungen,* Vol. 1, *op. cit.,* pp. 399–441.

————. Ueber Gegenstände höherer Ordnung und deren Verhältnis zur inneren Wahrnehmung. *Z. Psychol.,* 1899, *21,* 181–271. Reprinted in *Gesammelte Abhandlungen,* Vol. 2, *op. cit.,* pp. 379–409.

————. Abstrahiren und Vergleichen. *Z. Psychol.,* 1900, *24,* 34–82.

————. Ueber Annahmen. *Z. Psychol.,* 1902, Suppl. 2. (Also Leipzig: Barth, 1902) (Reprinted 1970)

————. Bemerkungen über den Farbenkörper und das Mischungsgesetz. *Z. Psychol.,* 1903, *33,* 1–80.

————. Ueber Gegenstandstheorie. In A. Meinong (Ed.), *Untersuchungen zur Gegenstandstheorie und Psychologie.* Leipzig: Barth, 1904, pp. 1–50. Reprinted in *Gesammelte Abhandlungen,* Vol. 2, *op. cit.,* pp. 483–530.

————. Ueber Urteilsgefühle: Was sie sind und sie nicht sind. *Arch. ges. Psychol.,* 1905, *6,* 21–58. Reprinted in *Gesammelte Abhandlungen,* Vol. 1, *op. cit.,* pp. 579–614.

————. *Ueber die Erfahrungsgrundlagen unseres Wissens.* Berlin: Springer-Verlag, 1906.

————. *Ueber die Stellung der Gegenstandstheorie im System der Wissenschaften.* Leipzig: Voigtländer, 1907.

————. Fur die Psychologie und gegen den Psychologismus in der allgemeinen Werttheorie. *Logos,* 1912, *3,* 1–14.

————. *Ueber Möglichkeit und Wahrscheinlichkeit.* Leipzig: Barth, 1915.

————. *Ueber emotionale Präsentation.* Vienna: Hölder, 1917.

————. *Zum Erweise des allgemeinen Kausalgesetzes.* Vienna: Hölder, 1918.

————. *Zur Grundlegung der allgemeinen Werttheorie.* Ed. by E. Mally. Graz: Leuschner & Lubensky, 1923.

————. In R. Schmidt (Ed.), *Die Philosophie der Gegenwart in Selbstdarstellungen.* (2nd ed.) Vol. 1, Leipzig: Meiner, 1923, pp. 101–160. **B Bl**

Chisholm, *Realism*

GEORG MEISSNER
1829-1905
German Physiologist (11)

Meissner, G. *Beiträge zur Anatomie und Physiologie der Haut.* Leipzig: Voss, 1853.

————. *Beiträge zur Physiologie des Sehorgans.* Leipzig: Engelmann, 1854.

————. Zur Lehre von den Bewegungen des Auges. *Arch. Ophthalm.,* 1855, *2,* 1–123.

————. Beiträge zur Anatomie und Physiologie der Gordiaceen. *Z. wiss. Zool.,* 1856, *7,* 1–144.

————. Untersuchungen über den Tastsinn. *Z. rat. Med.,* 1859, *7,* 92–118.

————. Ueber die Bewegungen des Auges. *Z. rat. Med.,* 1860, *8,* 1–18.

————. Ueber das electrische Verhalten der Oberfläche des menschlichen Körpers. *Z. rat. Med.,* 1861, *12,* 263–313.

————. Zur Kenntniss des electrischen Verhaltens des Muskels. *Z. rat. Med.,* 1861, *12,* 344–353.

Cohn, F., & ———. Ueber das electrische Verhalten des thätigen Muskels. *Z. rat. Med.*, 1862, *15*, 27–59.

———. *Untersuchungen über den Sauerstoff.* Hanover: Hahn, 1863.

GREGOR JOHANN MENDEL
1822-1884
Austrian Geneticist (21)

Mendel, G. Versuche über Pflanzenhybriden. *Verh. Naturf. Ver. Brunn*, 1865, *4*, 1–47. Reprinted as *Experiments in plant hybridization.* Trans. by the Royal Horticultural Society, London. Cambridge: Harvard University Press, 1925, & in R. M. Nardone (Ed.), *Mendel centenary: Genetics, development and evolution.* Washington, D.C.: Catholic University of America Press, 1968, pp. 134–168.

———. Ueber einige aus künstlicher Befruchtung gewonnenen Hieracium-Bastarde. *Verh. Naturf. Ver. Brunn*, 1869, *8*, 26–28. (1870) Reprinted in C. Stern & Eva R. Sherwood (Eds.), *The origin of genetics, vide infra*, pp. 49–55.

———. Letters of 3 July and 27 September, 1870. Trans. by L. K. & G. Piternick in The birth of genetics. *Genetics*, 1950 (Suppl.), *35*, 1–29, & in *The origin of genetics.* Ed. by C. Stern & Eva R. Sherwood. San Francisco: Freeman, 1966, & in R. M. Nardone, Ed. *Mendel Centenary op. cit.* Washington, D.C.: Catholic University of America Press, 1968, pp. 168–273.

———. Gregor Mendel's autobiography. Ed. by Anne Iltis. *J. Heredity*, 1954, *45*, 231–234. **B**

———. *Autobiographia juvenilia.* Ed. by J. Sajner. Brno: Universität Purkyniana, 1972. **B**

Bodenheimer, *Biology;* Dampier, *Literature;* Gabriel & Fogel, *Biology;* Newman, *Mathematics;* Rook, *Origins;* Schwartz & Bishop, *Moments Discovery*

DESIRE JOSEPH MERCIER
1851-1926
Belgian Philosopher (16)

Mercier, D. *La correspondance de Son Excellence le Cardinal Mercier avec le gouvernement*

général allemand pendant l'occupation 1914–1918. Ed. by F. Mayence. Paris: Gabalda, 1919.

———. *Cours de philosophie.* (11th ed.) (2 vols.) Vol. 2. *Psychologie.* Paris: Alcan, 1923. (1892)

———, *et al. A manual of modern scholastic philosophy.* (3rd ed.) (2 vols.) Trans. by T. L. & S. A. Parker. London: Kegan Paul, Trench & Truebner, 1932. (1892)

———. *La définition philosophique de la vie.* (2nd ed.) Louvain: Charpentier & Schoonjans, 1898. (1892)

———. *The origins of contemporary psychology.* (2nd ed.) Trans. by W. H. Mitchell. New York: Kenedy, 1918. (1897)

———. *Les suggestions criminelles. Rev. néoscolast.*, 1897, *4*, 408–415.

———. La philosophie de Herbert Spencer. *Rev. néo-scolast.*, 1898, *5*, 5–29.

———. Le positivisme et les vérités nécessaires des mathématiques. *Rev. néo-scolast.*, 1899, *6*, 12–29.

———. *The relation of experimental psychology to philosophy.* Trans. by E. J. Wirth. New York: Benziger, 1902. (1900)

———. L'induction scientifique. *Rev. néo-scolast.*, 1900, *7*, 422–454.

———. La nature du raisonnement. *Rev. phil.*, 1902, *2*, 165–179.

———. La dernière idole. *Rev. néo-scolast.*, 1903, *10*, 73–91.

———. La liberté d'indifférence et le déterminisme psychologique. *Rev. néo-scolast.*, 1904, *11*, 5–17.

MAURICE MERLEAU-PONTY
1908-1961
French Philosopher (16)

Merleau-Ponty, M. *Humanism and terror.* Trans. by J. O'Neill. Boston: Beacon Press, 1969. (1947) **C**

———. *Sense and non-sense.* (3rd ed.) Trans. by H. L. & Patricia A. Dreyfus. Evanston, Ill.: Northwestern University Press, 1964. (1948) **C**

——. *Signs*. Trans. by R. C. McCleary. Evanston, Ill.: Northwestern University Press, 1964. (1960)   **C**

——. *The primacy of perception: And other essays on phenomenological psychology, the philosophy of art, history and politics*. Ed. by J. M. Edie. Evanston, Ill.: Northwestern University Press, 1964.   **C**

——. *The essential writings of Merleau-Ponty*. Ed. by A. L. Fisher. New York: Harcourt, Brace, & World, 1969.   **Bl C**

——. *The structure of behavior*. Trans. by A. L. Fisher. Boston: Beacon, 1963. (1942) (Reprinted 1967)

——. *Phenomenology of perception*. Trans. by C. Smith. New York: Humanities Press, 1962. (1945)

——. Marxism and philosophy. (1946) In *Sense and non-sense, op. cit.*, pp. 125–136.

——. *Les aventures de la dialectique*. Paris: Gallimard, 1955. (1951)

——. What is phenomenology? Trans. by J. F. Bannan. *Cross Cur.*, 1956, *6*, 59–70.

——. Les sciences de l'homme et la phénoménologie. *Bull. psychol.*, 1964, *18*, 141–170.

——. *The visible and the invisible*. Trans. by Alphonse Lingis. Evanston, Ill.: Northwestern University Press, 1968. (1964)

Lawrence & O'Conner, *Phenomenology ;* Strain, *Philosophies Education*

MARIN MERSENNE
1588-1648
French Philosopher (11)

Mersenne, M. *Correspondance*. (10 vols.) (Editions du Centre National de la Recherche Scientifique.) Paris: Presses Universitaires de France, 1945–1967.   **B C**

——. *Quaestiones in genesim*. Paris: Cramoisy, 1623.

——. *L'impiété des déistes, athées, et libertins de ce temps, combattue, & renversée de point par raisons tirées de la philosophie, & de la théologie*. Paris: Bilaine, 1624.

——. *La vérité des sciences contre les Septiques ou Pyrrhoniens*. Paris: Du Bray, 1625. (Reprinted 1969)

——. *Les mécaniques de Galilée, mathématicien et ingénieur du Duc de Florence*. Paris: Guénon, 1634

——. *Questions inouyés ou récréation des sçavans. Qui contiennent beaucoup de choses concernant la théorie, la philosophie et les mathématiques*. Paris: Villery, 1634.

——. *Questions théologiques, physiques, morales, et mathématiques, où chacun trouvera du contentement, ou de l'exercice*. Paris: Guénon, 1634.

——. *Les préludes de l'harmonie universelle*. Paris: Guénon, 1634.

——. *Questions harmoniques*. Paris: Villery, 1634.

——. *Harmonie universelle: The books on instruments*. Trans. by R. E. Chapman. The Hague: Nijhoff, 1957. (1636–1637)

——. *Harmonicorum libri*. Paris: Baudry, 1636.

——. *Les nouvelles pensées de Galilée, mathématicien et ingénieur du Duc de Florence*. Paris: Guénon, 1639.

——. The second set of objections. (1641) In *The philosophical works of Descartes*. Vol. 2. (2nd ed.) Trans. by Elizabeth S. Haldane & G. R. T. Ross. Cambridge: Cambridge University Press, 1931, pp. 24–29. (Reprinted 1955)

——. *Cogitata physicomathematica*. Paris: Bertier, 1644.

FRANZ (or FRIEDRICH) ANTON
MESMER
1734-1815
Austrian-French Hypnotist (25)

Mesmer, F. A. *Mémoire sur la découverte du magnétisme animal*. With the *Précis historique écrit par M. Paradis en mars 1777*. Paris: Didot, 1779. (1774)

——. *Mesmerism by Doctor Mesmer (1779), being the first translation of Mesmer's historic*

"Mémoire sur la découverte du magnétisme animal" to appear in English. Trans. by V. R. Myers; intro. by G. Frankau. London: Mac-Donald, 1948. (1779)

———. *Le magnétisme animal.* Ed. by R. Amadou; comments & notes by F. A. Pattie & J. Vinchon. Paris: Payot, 1971. (1779)

———. *Précis historique des faits relatifs au magnétisme animal de M. Mesmer jusqu'en avril 1781.* Paris: Leroux, 1781; also London: Bollen, 1781.

———. *Abhandlung über die Entdeckung des tierischen Magnetismus.* Karlsruhe: Macklot, 1781.

———. *Aphorismes de M. Mesmer, dictés à l'assemblée de ses élèves, & dans lesquels on trouve ses principes, sa théorie & ses moyens de magnétiser; le tout formant un corps de doctrine, développé en trois cents quarante-quatre paragraphes, pour faciliter l'application des commentaires au magnétisme animal.* (3rd ed.) Ed. with notes by C. de Veaumorel. Paris: Bertrand, 1785. (1784)

———. *Lettres de M. Mesmer à M. Vicq-d'Azyr, et à MM. les auteurs du "Journal de Paris."* Brussels: no publ., 1784.

———. *Lettre de M. Mesmer à M. le comte de C.,* Paris: no publ., 1784.

———. *Memoir of F. A. Mesmer, doctor of medicine, on his discoveries: 1799.* Mount Vernon, N.Y.: Eden, 1957. (1799)   **B**

———. *Lettre sur l'origine de la petite vérole et le moyen de la faire cesser.* Paris: Imprimerie des sciences et arts, 1800.

———. Letter to the Royal College of Physicians, London, 1802. In J. Elliotson, *The Harveian Oration,* 1846. London: Baillière, 1846, pp. 68–70.

———. *Allgemeine Erläuterungen über den Magnetismus und Somnambulismus.* Halle: Waisenhausbuchhandlung, 1813.

Dennis, *Psychology;* Goshen, *Documentary;* Sahakian, *Psychology;* Shor, *Hypnosis;* Tinterow, *Hypnosis*

AUGUST MESSER
1867-1937
German Psychologist (18)

Messer, A. Die Behandlung des Freiheitsproblems bei John Locke. *Arch. Ges. Phil.,* 1898, *11,* 404–434, 465–490.

———. *Die Wirksamkeit der Apperzeption in den persönlichen Beziehungen des Schullebens.* Berlin: Reuther & Reichard, 1899.

———. *Kritische Untersuchungen über Denken, Sprechen und Sprachunterricht.* Berlin: Reuther & Reichard, 1900.

———. Zur Beurteilung des Eudämonismus. *Z. Phil. phil. Krit.,* 1901, *119,* 59–76.

———. *Kants Ethik, eine Einführung in ihre Hauptprobleme und Beiträge zu deren Lösung.* Leipzig: Veit, 1904.

———. Experimentell-psychologische Untersuchungen über das Denken. *Arch. ges. Psychol.,* 1906, *8,* 1–224.

———. Bemerkungen zu meinen "Experimentellpsychologischen Untersuchungen über das Denken." *Arch. ges. Psychol.,* 1907, *10,* 409–428.

———. *Empfindung und Denken.* Leipzig: Quelle & Meyer, 1820. (1908)

———. *Einführung in die Erkenntnistheorie.* (2nd ed.) Leipzig: Meiner, 1921. (1909)

———. *Das Problem der Willensfreiheit.* (2nd ed.) Göttingen: Vandenhoeck & Ruprecht, 1918. (1911)

———. Husserls Phänomenologie in ihrem Verhältnis zur Psychologie. *Arch. ges. Psychol.,* 1911–1912, *22,* 117–129; 1914, *32,* 52–67.

———. *Die Philosophie der Gegenwart.* (6th ed.) Leipzig: Quelle & Meyer, 1927. (1912)

———. *Geschichte der Philosophie vom Beginn der Neuzeit bis zum Ende des 18. Jahrhunderts.* (5th ed.) (3 vols.) Leipzig: Quelle & Meyer, 1921. (1912)

———. *Das Problem der staatsbürgerlichen Erziehung historisch und systematisch behandelt.* Leipzig: Nemnich, 1912.

———. Ueber den Begriff des "Aktes." *Arch. ges. Psychol.,* 1912, *24,* 245–275.

———. *Psychologie.* (5th ed.) Stuttgart: Meiner, 1928. (1914)

———. *Die Apperzeption als Grundbegriff der pädagogischen Psychologie.* Berlin: Reuther & Reichard, 1915.

———. Zur Psychologie des Krieges. *Preuss. Jb.,* 1915, *159,* 216–232.

———. Das freie literarische Schaffen in Kindheit und Jugend. *Z. pädag. Psychol.,* 1915, *16,* 37–48.

———. *Ethik.* Leipzig: Quelle & Meyer, 1918.

———. *Glauben und Wissen. Geschichte einer inneren Entwicklung.* (2nd ed.) Munich: Reinhardt, 1920. (1919)

———. *Sittenlehre.* Leipzig: Quelle & Meyer, 1920.

———. *Fichte: Seine Persönlichkeit und seine Philosophie.* Leipzig: Quelle & Meyer, 1920.

———. *Natur und Geist. Philosophische Aufsätze.* Osterwieck (Harz): Zickfeldt, 1920.

———. *Weltanschauung und Erziehung.* Osterwieck (Harz): Zickfeldt, 1921.

———. *Erläuterung zu Nietzsches Zarathustra.* Stuttgart: Strecker & Schröder, 1922.

———. August Messer. In R. Schmidt (Ed.), *Die Philosophie der Gegenwart in Selbstdarstellungen.* Vol. 3. Leipzig: Meiner, 1922, pp. 145–176.

———. *Der kritische Realismus.* Karlsruhe: Braun, 1923.

Mandler & Mandler, *Thinking*

ERNST MEUMANN
1862-1915
German Psychologist (23)

Meumann, E. *Vorlesungen zur Einführung in die experimentelle Pädagogik und ihre psychologischen Grundlagen.* (2nd ed.) (3 vols.) Leipzig: Engelmann, 1911–1914. (1907–1908)   **C**

———. Beiträge zur Psychologie des Zeitsinns. *Phil. Stud.,* 1893, *8,* 431–509; 1894, *9,* 264–306.

———. Untersuchungen zur Psychologie und Aesthetik des Rhythmus. *Phil. Stud.,* 1894, *10,* 249–322, 393–430.

———. Beiträge zur Psychologie des Zeitbewusstseins. *Phil. Stud.,* 1896, *12,* 127–254.

Zoneff, P., & ———. Ueber Begleiterscheinungen psychischer Vorgänge in Atem und Puls. *Phil. Stud.,* 1901, *18,* 1–113.

———. *Die Entstehung der ersten Wortbedeutungen beim Kinde.* (2nd ed.) Leipzig: Engelmann, 1908. (1902)

———. Zur Einführung. *Arch. ges. Psychol.,* 1903, *1,* 1–6.

———. *Handarbeit und Schularbeit: Experimente an Kindern der Volksschule.* Leipzig: Klinckhardt, 1904.

Ebert, E., & ———. Ueber einige Grundfragen der Psychologie der Uebungsphänomene im Bereich des Gedächtnisses, zugleich ein Beitrag zur Psychologie der formalen Geistesbildung. A: Untersuchung der Wirkung einseitig mechanischer Uebung auf die Gesamtgedächtnisfunktion. B: Ueber ökonomische Lernmethoden. *Arch. ges. Psychol.,* 1904, *4,* 1–232. Also Leipzig: Engelmann, 1904.

———. Zur Einführung. *Exp. Pädag.,* 1905, *1,* 1–15.

———. Intelligenzprüfungen an Kindern der Volksschule. *Exp. Pädag.,* 1905, *1,* 35–101.

———. Aesthetische Versuche mit Schulkindern. *Exp. Pädag.,* 1906, *3,* 74–88.

———. Zur Frage der Sensibilität der inneren Organe. *Arch. ges. Psychol.,* 1907, *9,* 26–62.

———. Ueber Organempfindungsträume und eine merkwürdige Traumerinnerung. *Arch. ges. Psychol.,* 1907, *9,* 63–70.

———. Ueber Assoziationsexperimente mit Beeinflussung der Reproduktionszeit: Eine Mitteilung. *Arch. ges. Psychol.,* 1907, *9,* 117–150.

———. *The psychology of learning. An experimental investigation of the economy and tech-*

nique of memory. Trans. by J. W. Baird. New York: Appleton, 1913. (1907–1908)

──────. *Oekonomie und Technik des Gedächtnisses.* (5th ed.) Amsterdam: Bonset, 1967. (1907–1908)

──────. Methoden zur Feststellung des Vorstellungstypus. 1907. *Exp. Pädag.,* 1907, *4,* 23–63.

──────. *Intelligenz und Wille.* (4th ed.) Leipzig: Quelle & Meyer, 1925. (1908)

──────. *Einführung in die Aesthetik der Gegenwart.* (4th ed.) Leipzig: Quelle & Meyer, 1930. (1908)

──────. Neuere Ansichten über das Wesen der Phantasie mit besonderer Berücksichtigung der Phantasie des Kindes. *Z. exp. Pädag.,* 1908, *6,* 109–141.

──────. Eine neue Untersuchung über den Selbstmord im Jugendalter. *Z. exp. Pädag.,* 1908, *6,* 158–180.

──────. Weiteres zur Frage der Sensibilität der inneren Organe. *Arch. ges. Psychol.,* 1909, *14,* 279–310.

──────. Ueber Lesen und Schreiben im Traume. *Arch. ges. Psychol.,* 1909, *15,* 380–400.

──────. Ueber einige optische Täuschungen. *Arch. ges. Psychol.,* 1909, *15,* 401–409.

──────. Weiteres zur Frage der Sensibilität der inneren Organe und der Beurteilung der Organempfindungen. *Arch. ges. Psychol.,* 1909–1910, *16,* 228–236.

──────. Der gegenwärtige Stand der Methodik der Intelligenzprüfungen (mit besonderer Rücksicht auf die Kinderpsychologie). *Z. exp. Pädag.,* 1910, *9,* 68–79.

──────. Experimentelle Pädagogik und Schulreform. *Z. pädag. Psychol.,* 1911, *12,* 1–13.

──────. Ueber den kombinatorischen Faktor bei Vorstellungstypen. *Z. pädag. Psychol.,* 1911, *12,* 115–120.

──────. Die gegenwärtige Lage der Pädagogik. *Z. pädag. Psychol.,* 1911, *12,* 193–206.

──────. Ueber Bekanntheits- und Unbekanntheitsqualität. *Arch. ges. Psychol.,* 1911, *20,* 36–44.

──────. Ueber eine neue Methode der Intelligenzprüfung und über den Wert der Kombinationsmethode. *Z. pädag. Psychol.,* 1912, *13,* 145–163.

──────. Die Untersuchung der sittlichen Entwicklung des Kindes und ihre pädagogische Bedeutung. *Z. pädag. Psychol.,* 1912, *13,* 193–213.

──────. Programm zur psychologischen Untersuchung des Zeichnens. *Z. pädag. Psychol.,* 1912, *13,* 353–380.

──────, & Goldschmidt, R. H. Anleitung zu praktischen Arbeiten in der Jugendkunde und experimentellen Pädagogik. *Z. pädag. Psychol.,* 1912, *13,* 516–521, 623–638.

──────. Die soziale Bedeutung der Intelligenzprüfungen. *Z. pädag. Psychol.,* 1913, *14,* 433–440.

──────. Thesen zur psychologischen Grundlegung der Probleme über Koedukation und Koinstruktion. *Z. pädag. Psychol.,* 1913, *14,* 504–513.

──────. Zur Frage der Erziehungsziele. *Z. pädag. Psychol.,* 1914, *15,* 1–9.

──────. *System der Aesthetik.* Leipzig: Quelle & Meyer, 1919. (1914)

──────. *Abriss der experimentellen Pädagogik.* (2nd ed.) Leipzig: Engelmann, 1920. (1914)

──────. Wesen und Bedeutung des Nationalgefühls. *Z. pädag. Psychol.,* 1915, *16,* 84–106.

──────. Ueber Volkserziehung auf nationaler Grundlage. *Z. pädag. Psychol.,* 1915, *16,* 161–185.

ADOLF MEYER
1866-1950
Swiss-American Psychiatrist (21)

Meyer, A. *The commonsense psychiatry of Dr. Adolf Meyer: Fifty-two selected papers.* Ed. with biog. narrative by A. Leif. New York: McGraw-Hill, 1948.   **C**

———. *The collected papers.* (4 vols.) Ed. by Eunice E. Winters. Baltimore, Md.: Johns Hopkins Press, 1950–1952.   **C**

———. *Psychobiology: A science of man.* Compiled & trans. by Eunice E. Winters & A. M. Bowers. Springfield, Ill.: Thomas, 1957.   **C**

———. Critical review of the data and general methods and deductions of modern neurology. *J. comp. Neurol.,* 1898, *8,* 113–148, 249–313. Reprinted in *Collected papers,* Vol. 1, *op. cit.,* pp. 77–148.

———. Recent literature on normal and abnormal association. *Psychol. Bull.,* 1905, *2,* 242–259.

———. Aphasia. *Psychol. Bull.,* 1905, *2,* 261–277. Reprinted in *Collected papers,* Vol. 1, *op. cit.,* pp. 334–347.

———. The relation of emotional and intellectual functions in paranoia and in obsessions. *Psychol. Bull.,* 1906, *3,* 255–274. Reprinted in *Collected papers,* Vol. 2, *op. cit.,* pp. 499–516.

———. Application of association studies. *Psychol. Bull.,* 1906, *3,* 275–280.

———. Interpretation of obsessions. *Psychol. Bull.,* 1906, *3,* 280–283. Reprinted in *Collected papers,* Vol. 2, *op. cit.,* pp. 633–635.

———. Aphasia. *Psychol. Bull.,* 1907, *4,* 180–194. Reprinted in *Collected papers,* Vol. 1, *op. cit.,* pp. 347–358.

———. Misconceptions at the bottom of "hopelessness of all psychology." *Psychol. Bull.,* 1907, *4,* 170–179. Reprinted in *Collected papers,* Vol. 2, *op. cit.,* pp. 573–580.

———. The problems of mental reaction-types, mental causes and diseases. *Psychol. Bull.,* 1908, *5,* 245–261. Reprinted in *Collected papers,* Vol. 2, *op. cit.,* pp. 591–603.

———. A discussion of some fundamental issues in Freud's psychoanalysis. *State Hosp. Bull.,* 1909–1910, *2,* 827–848. Reprinted in *Collected papers,* Vol. 2, *op. cit.,* pp. 604–617.

———. The dynamic interpretation of dementia praecox. *Amer. J. Psychol.,* 1910, *21,* 385–403.

Reprinted in *Collected papers,* Vol. 2, *op. cit.,* pp. 443–458.

———, Jellife, S. E., & Hoch, A. *Dementia praecox.* Boston: Badger, 1911.

———. Pathopsychology and psychopathology. *Psychol. Bull.,* 1912, *9,* 129–145. Reprinted in *Collected papers,* Vol. 2, *op. cit.,* pp. 640–653.

———. Conditions for a home of psychology in the medical curriculum. *J. abnorm. Psychol.,* 1913, *7,* 313–325. Reprinted in *Collected papers,* Vol. 3, *op. cit.,* pp. 29–37.

———. Growth of scientific understanding of mentality and its relationship to social work. *Proc. Fiftieth Ann. Sess. Nat. Conf. Soc. Work,* 1923, *50,* 192–199. Reprinted in *Collected papers,* Vol. 4, *op. cit.,* pp. 241–250.

———. Thirty-five years of psychiatry in the United States and our present outlook. *Amer. J. Psychiat.,* 1928, *8* (N.S.), 1–31. Reprinted in *Collected papers,* Vol. 2, *op. cit.,* pp. 1–23.

———. Organization of community facilities for prevention, care, and treatment of nervous and mental diseases. *Proc. First Int. Cong. Ment. Hyg.,* 1932, *1,* 237–257, 265–266. Reprinted in *Collected papers,* Vol. 4, *op. cit.,* pp. 266–280.

———. The psychobiological point of view. In M. Bentley & E. V. Cowdry (Eds.), *The problem of mental disorder.* New York: McGraw-Hill, 1934, pp. 51–70. Reprinted in *Collected papers,* Vol. 3, *op. cit.,* pp. 429–443.

———. The birth and development of the mental hygiene movement. *Ment. Hyg.,* 1935, *19,* 29–37. Reprinted in *Collected papers,* Vol. 4, *op. cit.,* pp. 281–287.

———. Remarks at twenty-fourth anniversary of the Henry Phipps Psychiatric Clinic, April 1937. In S. Katzenelbogen (Ed.), *Contributions dedicated to Dr. Adolf Meyer by his colleagues, friends and pupils.* Baltimore, Md.: Johns Hopkins Press, 1938, pp. 1, 18–20, 47–54, 95–115. Reprinted in *Collected papers,* Vol. 2, *op. cit.,* pp. 210–233.   **B**

———. The philosophy of psychiatry. *Psychiat. & the war,* 1942, pp. 359–377. Reprinted in *Collected papers,* Vol. 3, *op. cit.,* pp. 478–491.

MAX FREDERICK MEYER
1873-1967
German-American Psychologist (20)

Meyer, M. F. Ueber Kombinationstöne und einige hierzu in Beziehung stehende akustische Erscheinungen. *Z. Psychol.*, 1896, *11*, 177–229.

Stumpf, C., & ————. Schwingungszahlbestimmungen bei sehr hohen Tönen. *Ann. Physik.*, 1897, *61*, 760–779.

————. Ueber die Rauhigkeit tiefer Töne. *Z. Psychol.*, 1897, *13*, 75–80.

————. Zur Theorie der Differenztöne und der Gehörsempfindungen überhaupt. *Z. Psychol.*, 1898, *16*, 1–34.

————. Ueber die Unterschiedsempfindlichkeit für Tonhöhen. *Z. Psychol.*, 1898, *16*, 352–372.

————. Ueber die Intensität der Einzeltöne zusammengesetzter Klänge. *Z. Psychol.*, 1898, *17*, 1–14.

————. Ueber Tonverschmelzung und die Theorie der Konsonanz. *Z. Psychol.*, 1898, *17*, 401–421.

————. Nachtrag zu meiner Abhandlung "über Tonverschmelzung und die Theorie der Konsonanz." *Z. Psychol.*, 1898, *18*, 274–293.

————. Die Tonpsychologie, ihre bisherige Entwickelung und ihre Bedeutung für die musikalische Pädagogik. *Z. pädag. Psychol.*, 1899, *1*, 74–85, 180–189, 245–254.

————. Is the memory of absolute pitch capable of development by training? *Psychol. Rev.*, 1899, *6*, 514–516.

————. Ueber Beurteilung zusammengesetzter Klänge. *Z. Psychol.*, 1899, *20*, 13–33.

————. Zur Theorie des Hörens. *Arch. ges. Physiol.*, 1900, *78*, 346–362.

————. E. ter Kuile's Theorie des Hörens. *Arch. ges. Physiol.*, 1900, *81*, 61–75.

————. Elements of a psychological theory of melody. *Psychol. Rev.*, 1900, *7*, 241–273.

————. Remarks on C. Lloyd Morgan's paper, "Relation of stimulus to sensation." *Amer. J. Psychol.*, 1900, *11*, 530–533.

————. Contributions to a psychological theory of music. *Univer. Missouri Stud.*, 1901, *1*, No. 1.

————. On the attributes of sensations. *Psychol. Rev.*, 1904, *11*, 83–103.

————. An experimental course in esthetics. *Psychol. Rev.*, 1907, *14*, 345–356.

————. An introduction to the mechanics of the inner ear. *Univer. Missouri Stud.*, 1907, *2*, No. 1.

————. The significance of wave form for our comprehension of audition. *Amer. J. Psychol.*, 1907, *18*, 170–176.

————. The nervous correlate of pleasantness and unpleasantness. *Psychol. Rev.*, 1908, *15*, 201–216, 292–322.

————. The nervous correlate of attention. I. II. *Psychol. Rev.*, 1908, *15*, 358–372; 1909, *16*, 36–47.

————. *The fundamental laws of human behavior.* Boston: Badger, 1911.

————. The present status of the problem of the relation between mind and body. *J. Phil.*, 1912, *9*, 365–371.

————. The comparative value of various conceptions of nervous function based on mechanical analogies. *Amer. J. Psychol.*, 1913, *24*, 555–563.

————. Vorschläge zur akustischen Terminologie. *Z. Psychol.*, 1914, *68*, 115–119.

————. *Psychology of the other-one: An introductory text-book of psychology.* (2nd ed., rev.) Columbia, Mo.: Missouri Book, 1922. (1921)

————. The psychological effects of drugs. *Psychol. Bull.*, 1922, *19*, 173–182.

————, & Eppright, F. O. The equation of the learning function. *Amer. J. Psychol.*, 1923, *34*, 203–222.

————. Some nonsense about the "common path." *Psychol. Rev.*, 1925, *32*, 431–442.

————. *Abnormal psychology.* Columbia, Mo.: Lucas Brothers, 1927.

————. The hydraulic principles governing the function of the cochlea. *J. gen. Psychol.*, 1928, *1*, 239–265.

———. The presentative arts. In J. F. McDermott & K. B. Taft (Eds.), *Sex in the arts*. New York: Harper, 1932, pp. 212–232.

———. That whale among the fishes—the theory of emotions. *Psychol. Rev.*, 1933, *40*, 292–300.

———. Can teaching the deaf profit from philology? *Amer. Ann. Deaf*, 1934, *79*, 95–108.

———. A plea for the distinction between preoccupation and true learning. *J. abnorm. soc. Psychol.*, 1934–1935, *29*, 56–65.

———. Frequency, duration, and recency vs. double stimulation. *Psychol. Rev.*, 1934, *41*, 177–183.

———. Fitting into a silent world: The first six years of life. *Univer. Missouri Stud.*, 1934, *9*, No. 2.

———. Meyer's theory of the mechanics of the inner ear. *Amer. J. Psychol.*, 1949, *62*, 114–119.

———. *How we hear: How tones make music*. Boston: Branford, 1950.

———. Crucial experiments in cochlear mechanics. *Amer. J. Psychol.*, 1953, *66*, 261–269.

———. A test of the hydraulic theory of cochlear mechanics through multiple frequency beats. *Amer. J. Psychol.*, 1954, *67*, 39–55.

———. Auditory fatigue beyond and within the compass of the voice. *Amer. J. Psychol.*, 1954, *67*, 538–543.

———. A working model of the cochlea. *Amer. J. Psychol.*, 1959, *72*, 293–296.

THEODOR HERMANN MEYNERT
1833-1892
German-Austrian Neurologist (12)

Meynert, T. H. *Klinische Vorlesungen über Psychiatrie auf wissenschaftlichen Grundlagen für Studierende und Aerzte, Juristen und Psychologen*. Vienna: Braumüller, 1890.   **C**

———. *Sammlung von populär-wissenschaftlichen Vorträgen über den Bau und die Leistungen des Gehirns*. Vienna: Braumüller, 1892.   **C**

———. Studien über die Bestandteile der Vierhügel, soweit sie in den nächst unterhalb gelegenen Querschnitten der Brücke gegeben sind. *Z. wiss. Zool.*, 1867, *17*, 655–679.

———. *Der Bau der Gross-Hirnrinde und seine örtliche Verschiedenheit*. Leipzig: Engelmann, 1868.

———. Studien über die Bedeutung des zweifachen Rückenmarksursprungs aus dem Grosshirn. *Sitzber. Akad. Wiss. Wien*, Math.-naturw. Kl., 1870, *60*, 447–462.

———. Beiträge zur Kenntnis der zentralen Projektion der Sinnesoberflächen. *Sitzber Akad. Wiss. Wien*, Math.-naturw. Kl., 1870, *60*, 547–566.

———. Ueber Unterschiede im Gehirnbau des Menschen und der Säugetiere. *Mitth. anthrop. Ges. Wien*, 1871, *1*, 79–93. (1870)

———. *Zur Mechanik des Gehirnbaues*. Vienna: Braumüller, 1874.

———. *Skizzen über Umfang und Wissenschaftliche Anordnung der klinischen Psychiatrie*. Vienna: Braumüller, 1876.

———. *Psychiatry: A clinical treatise on diseases of the forebrain*. Part 1. Trans. by B. Sachs. New York: Putnam's, 1885. (1884) (Reprinted 1968)

———. Die anthropologische Bedeutung der frontalen Gehirnentwicklung. *Jb. Psychiat.*, 1887, *7*, 1–48.

———. Amentia, die Verwirrtheit. Akuter Wahnsinn, allgemeiner Wahnsinn, Manie, Tobsucht, Melancholie mit Aufregung, Melancholie mit Stumpfsinn der Autoren. *Jb. Psychiat.*, 1890, *9*, 1–112.

———. On the collaboration of parts of the brain. (1891) Reprinted in & trans. by G. v. Bonin (Ed.), *Some papers on the cerebral cortex*. Springfield, Ill.: Thomas, 1960, pp. 159–180.

———. Neue Studien über die Assoziationsbündel des Hirnmantels. *Sitzber. Akad. Wiss. Wien*, Math.-naturw. Kl., 1892, *101*, 361–380.

Clarke & O'Malley, *Brain*

(BARON) ALBERT EDWARD MICHOTTE
(VAN DEN BERCK)
1881-1965
Belgian Psychologist (26)

Michotte, A. E. et al. *Causalité, permanence et réalité phenoménales.* (Studia Psychologica.) Louvain: Publications Universitaires, 1962. **C**

—————. *Les signes régionaux. Nouvelles recherches expérimentales sur la répartition de la sensibilité tactile dans les états d'attention et d'inattention.* Louvain: Institut Supérieur de Philosophie, 1905.

—————. A propos de la méthode d'introspection dans la psychologie expérimentale. *Rev. néoscolast.,* 1907, *14,* 507–532.

—————, & Prüm, E. Etude expérimentale sur le choix volontaire et ses antécédents immédiats. *Arch. psychol.,* 1910–1911, *10,* 113–320. (Also Louvain: Institut Supérieur de Philosophie, 1910.)

—————, & Ransy, C. Contribution à l'étude de la mémoire logique. In *Etudes de Psychologie.* Vol. 1. Louvain: Institut Supérieur de Philosophie, 1912, pp. 1–96.

—————. Nouvelles recherches sur la simultanéité apparente d'impressions disparates périodiques (Expérience de "complication"). In *Etudes de psychologie.* Vol. 1. Louvain: Institut Supérieur de Philosophie, 1912, pp. 97–192.

—————. Note à propos de contributions récentes à la psychologie de la volonté. In *Etudes de psychologie.* Vol. 1. Louvain: Institut Supérieur de Philosophie, 1912, pp. 193–233.

—————, & Portych, T. Deuxième étude sur la mémoire logique. La reproduction après des intervalles temporels de différentes longueurs. In *Etudes de psychologie.* Vol. 2. Louvain: Institut Supérieur de Philosophie, 1913, pp. 237–364.

—————. Psychologie et philosophie. *Rev. néoscolast.,* 1936, *39,* 208–228.

—————. La psychologie expérimentale et le problème des aptitudes. In Various, *Mélanges Pierre Janet.* Paris: Editions d'Artrey, 1939, pp. 155–167.

—————. La causalité physique est-elle une donnée phénoménale? *Tijdschr. Phil.,* 1941, *3,* 290–328. Reprinted in *Causalité, permanence et réalité phénoménales, op. cit.,* pp. 91–127.

—————. *The perception of causality.* (2nd ed.) New York: Basic Books, 1963. (1946)

—————. Le caractère de "réalité" des projections cinématographiques. *Rev. Int. Filmol.,* 1948, *1,* 249–261. Reprinted in *Causalité, permanence et réalité phénoménales, op. cit.,* pp. 435–453.

—————. L'énigme psychologique de la perspective dans le dessin linéaire. *Bull. Classe lettr. Acad, roy. Belg.,* 5e série, 1948, *34,* 268–288. Reprinted in *Causalité, permanence et réalité phénoménales, op. cit.,* pp. 454–471.

—————. La préfiguration dans les données sensorielles de notre conception spontanée du monde physique. *Proc. XIIth Int. Cong. Psychol.* Edinburgh: Oliver & Boyd, 1950, pp. 20–22. Reprinted in *Causalité, permanence et réalité phénoménales, op. cit.,* pp. 541–544.

—————. A propos de la permanence phénoménale, faits et théories. *Acta Psychol.,* 1950, *7,* 298–322.

—————, & De Clerck, J. Structures perceptives circulaires correspondant à des formes géometriques angulaires. *Année psychol.,* 1951, *50,* 305–326.

—————. La perception de la fonction "outil." In *Essays in psychology dedicated to David Katz.* Upsala: Almqvist & Wiksells, 1951, pp. 193–213. Reprinted in *Causalité, permanence et réalité phénoménales, op. cit.,* pp. 145–167.

—————. Albert Michotte van den Berck. In E. G. Boring *et al.* (Eds.), *A history of psychology in autobiography.* Vol. 4. Worcester, Mass.: Clark University Press, 1952, pp. 213–236. **B**

—————. L'influence de l'expérience sur la structuration des données sensorielles dans la perception. In *La perception. Symposium de l'association de psychologie scientifique de langue française.* Paris: Presses Universitaires de France, 1955, pp. 31–45. Reprinted in *Causalité, permanence et réalité phénoménales, op. cit.,* pp. 545–560.

———. Perception et cognition. *Proc. XIVth Int. Cong. Psychol.* Amsterdam: North-Holland, 1955, pp. 70–91. Reprinted in *Causalité, permanence et réalité phénoménales, op. cit.,* pp. 561–587.

———, Knops, L., & Coen-Gelders, A. Etude comparative de diverses situations donnant lieu à des impressions d'entraînement.In*Rencontre Contributions à une psychologie humaine, dédiées au Professeur Buytendijk.* Utrecht: Spectrum, 1957, pp. 284–294. Reprinted in *Causalité, permanence et réalité phénoménales, op. cit.,* pp. 231–243.

———. Les variations de réalité apparente de la troisième dimension dans les perceptions visuelles. *Arch. Psicol. Neurol. Psychiat.,* 1957, *18,* 203–213. Reprinted in *Causalité, permanence et réalité phénoménales, op. cit.,* pp. 512–522.

———. Réflexions sur le rôle du langage dans l'analyse des organisations perceptives. *Act. XVe Congr. int. Psychol., Acta Psychol.,* 1959, *15,* 70–91. Reprinted in *Causalité, permanence et réalité phénoménales, op. cit.,* pp. 91–127.

———. Théorie de la causalité phénoménale: Nouvelles perspectives—1961. (1962) In *Causalité, permanence et réalité phénoménales, op. cit.,* pp. 9–90.

———, *et al.* Die amodalen Ergänzungen von Wahrnehmungsstrukturen. In W. Metzger (Ed.), *Handbuch der Psychologie.* Vol. 1. *Allgemeine Psychologie: I. Der Aufbau des Erkennens.* Part 1. *Wahrnehmung und Bewusstsein.* Göttingen: Verlag für Psychologie, 1966, pp. 978–1002.

———, & Thinès, G. (With assist. of G. Reinert.) Die Kausalitätswahrnehmung. In W. Metzger (Ed.), *Handbuch der Psychologie.* Vol. 1. *Allgemeine Psychologie: I. Der Aufbau des Erkennens.* Part 1. *Wahrnehmung und Bewusstsein.* Göttingen: Verlag für Psychologie, 1966, pp. 954–977.

Arnold, *Emotion ;* Beardslee, *Perception ;* Hameline, *Anthologie*

JAMES MILL
1773-1836
English Philosopher (27)

Mill, J, & Mill, J. S. *James & John Stuart Mill on Education.* Ed. by F. A. Cavenagh. London: Cambridge University Press, 1931. (Reprinted 1970) **C**

———. *James Mill on education.* Ed. by W. H. Burston. London: Cambridge University Press, 1969. **C**

———. *An essay on government.* Ed. by C. V. Shields. New York: Liberal Arts Press, 1955. (1824)

———. *Elements of political economy.* (3rd ed.) London: Bohn, 1844. (1826) (Reprinted 1965)

———. *Analysis of the phenomena of the human mind.* (2nd ed. of 1869) Ed. by J. S. Mill, with notes by J. S. Mill, A. Bain, A. Findlater, & G. Grote. New York: Kelley, 1967. (1829)

———. *A fragment on Mackintosh.* (2nd ed.) London: Longmans, Green, Reader & Dyer, 1870. (1835)

Dennis, *Psychology ;* Herrnstein & Boring, *Source Book ;* Mandler & Mandler, *Thinking ;* Price, *Education ;* Rand, *Classical Psychologists ;* Sahakian, *Psychology*

JOHN STUART MILL
1806-1873
English Philosopher (27)

Mill, J. S. *The spirit of the age.* Intro. by F. A. v. Hayek. Chicago: University of Chicago Press, 1942. (1831) **C**

———. *On the logic of the moral sciences.* Ed. by H. M. Magid. Indianapolis, Ind.: Bobbs-Merrill, 1965. (1843) **C**

———. *Dissertations and discussions: Political, philosophical & historical.* (4 vols.) Ed. by A. Bain. New York: Holt, 1887. (1859) **C**

———. *The ethics of John Stuart Mill.* Ed. by C. Douglas. London: Blackwood, 1897. (Reprinted 1970) **C**

Comte, A., & ———. *Lettres inédites de John Stuart Mill à Auguste Comte publiées avec les réponses de Comte.* Ed. by L. Lévy-Bruhl. Paris: Alcan, 1899. **B C**

———. *Letters of J. S. Mill.* Ed. by H. S. R. Elliott. New York: Longmans, Green, 1910. **B C**

———. *On liberty, representative government, the subjection of women.* Ed. by M. G. Fawcett. London: Oxford University Press, 1933. **C**

Mill, J., & ———. *James & John Stuart Mill on education.* Ed. by F. A. Cavenagh. London: Cambridge University Press, 1931. (Reprinted 1970) **C**

———. *John Stuart Mill's philosophy of scientific method.* Ed. by E. Nagel. New York: Hafner, 1950. **C**

———. *J. S. Mill's boyhood visit to France.* Intro. & ed. by Anna J. Mill. Toronto: University of Toronto Press, 1960. **C**

———. *The early draft of J. S. Mill's autobiography.* Ed. by J. Stillinger. Urbana, Ill.: University of Illinois Press, 1961. **B C**

———. *Essential works of John Stuart Mill.* Ed. by M. Lerner. New York: Bantam, 1961. **C**

———. *Essays on politics and culture.* Ed. by Gertrude Himmelfarb. New York: Doubleday, 1962. **C**

———. *Collected Works of John Stuart Mill.* (Ult. approx. 13 vols.) Gen. ed.: F. E. L. Priestley. Toronto: University of Toronto Press, 1963– **C**

———. *The earlier letters, 1812–1848.* (1963) In *Collected works,* Vols. 12, 13, *op. cit.* **B C**

———. *Mill's essay on literature and society.* Ed. by J. B. Schneewind. New York: Collier, 1965. **C**

———. *Mill's ethical writings.* Ed. by J. B. Schneewind. New York: Collier, 1965. **C**

———. *John Stuart Mill: A selection of his works.* Ed. by J. M. Robson. New York: St. Martin's Press, 1966. **C**

———. *On Bentham and Coleridge.* Ed. by F. R. Leavis. New York: Harper & Row, 1962. (1838, 1859)

———. *A system of logic, ratiocinative and inductive, being a connected view of the principles of evidence, and the methods of scientific investigation.* (8th ed.) New York: Harper, 1874. (1843) (Reprinted 1961)

———. *Essays on some unsettled questions of political economy.* London: London School of Economics and Political Science, 1948. (1844)

———. *Letter from John S. Mill, Esq., to the Editor.* (James Mill's relation to Bentham.) *Edinb. Rev.,* 1844, *79,* 267–271.

———. *Principles of political economy, with some of their applications to social philosophy.* (1848) In *Collected works,* Vols. 2, 3, *op. cit.*

———. *Philosophy of necessary truth and causation. New Engl.,* 1850, *7,* 160–186.

———. *Bain's psychology. Edinb. Rev.,* 1859, *110,* 287–321. Reprinted in *Dissertations and discussions,* Vol. 4, *op. cit.,* pp. 101–156.

———. *Auguste Comte and positivism.* Ann Arbor, Mich.: University of Michigan Press, 1961. (1865)

———. *An examination of Sir William Hamilton's philosophy.* (2 vols.) (6th ed.) New York: Longmans, 1889. (1865)

———. *The subjection of women.* (2nd ed.) New York: Stokes, 1911. (1869) (Reprinted 1970)

———. *De l'intelligence par H. Taine. Fortn. Rev.,* 1870, *14,* 121–124. Reprinted in *Dissertations and discussions,* Vol. 5, *op. cit.,* pp. 122–130.

———. *Berkeley's life and writings. Fortn. Rev.,* 1871, *16,* 505–524. Reprinted in *Three essays on religion, op. cit.,* pp. 261–302.

———. *Autobiography.* Ed. by H. J. Stillinger. Boston: Houghton Mifflin, 1969. (1873) **B**

———. *Three essays on religion.* New York: Holt, 1874. (Reprinted 1970)

———. *Nature, and utility of religion.* Ed. by G. Nakhnikian. Indianapolis, Ind.: Bobbs-Merrill, 1958. (1874)

———. *On social freedom.* Intro. by Dorothy Fosdick. New York: Columbia University Press, 1941. (1907)

Dember, *Perception ;* Dennis, *Psychology ;* Gardiner, *Philosophy ;* Herrnstein & Boring, *Source Book ;* Hutchins, *Great Books ;* Madden, *Scientific Thought ;* Margolis, *Introduction ;* Murphy, *Western ;* Parsons, *Society ;* Rand, *Classical Philosophers ;* Rand, *Moralists ;* Reeves, *Body Mind ;* Sahakian, *Psychology*

EMILIO MIRA Y LOPEZ
1896-1964
Spanish-Brazilian Psychiatrist (13)

Mira y Lopez, E. Investigación de la inteligencia en el laboratorio de psicologia profesional de Barcelona. *Arch. Neurobiol.*, Madrid, 1920, No. 1.

———. *Psicotécnica. Para la Enciclopedia Espasa.* Barcelona: Espasa, 1924.

———. Exploración de la afectividad. *Rev. méd. Barcelona*, 1930, *44*, 222–259.

———. Pruebas para el reconocimiento de la inteligencia abstracta. *Rev. Pedag.*, 1931, *10*, 49–56.

———. Psicosis tramáticos. *Ars. med.*, 1931, *7*, 256–262.

———. *Psicología jurídica.* Barcelona: Salvat, 1932.

———. Psicopedagogía de la sociabilidad. *Rev. Psicol. Pedag.*, 1933, *1*, 354–368.

———. La nueva concepción experimental de la conducta moral. *Arch. Neurobiol.*, Madrid, 1933, *13*, 1059–1080.

———. A new conception of moral behavior. *J. crim. Law Criminol.*, 1934, *24*, 860–879.

———. Sobre el valor del psicodiagnóstico de Rorschach. *Progressos Clin.*, 1935, *30*, 808–845.

———. *Manual de psiquiatría.* Barcelona: Salvat, 1935.

———. Fear. *Lancet*, 1939, *1*, 1395.

———. Psychological work during the Spanish war. *Occup. Psychol.*, 1939, *13*, 165–177.

———. La prueba del zigzag en neurópsiquiatria. *Rev. Neurópsiquiat.*, Lima, 1939, *2*, 503–521.

———. Myokinetic psychodiagnosis: A new technique for exploring the conative trends of personality. *Proc. roy. Soc. Med.*, 1940, *33*, 9–30.

———. *Problemas psicológicos actuales.* Buenos Aires: El Ateneo, 1940.

———. *Psicología evolutiva del niño y el adolescente.* Buenos Aires: El Ateneo, 1941.

———. Bases cientificas de la psicoterápia. *Rev. Psiquiat., Crim.*, Buenos Aires, 1941. *6*, 271–282.

———. *Psychiatry in war.* New York: Norton, 1943.

———. *Instantaneas psicologicas.* Buenos Aires: Bajel, 1943.

———. *Manual de orientación profesional.* Buenos Aires: Kapelusz, 1947.

———. *Cuatro gigantes del alma.* Buenos Aires: El Ateneo, 1947.

———. *Como estudiar y cómo aprender.* Buenos Aires: Kapelusz, 1948.

———, Mira, A., & Aliveira, A. Aplicoção do psicodiagnóstico miocinetico ao estudo da agressividade. *Arquivos Brasileiros de Psicotécnica*, 1949, *1*, 69–116.

———. Etude sur la validité du test psychodiagnostique myokinétique. *Année psychol.*, 1951, *50*, 575–584.

———, *et al.* Comparaison entre le type de caractère (Erlebnistypus) selon le test de Rorschach et le type somatique selon la classification de Sheldon. In F. Baumgartner (Ed.), *La psycho-technique dans le monde moderne.* Paris: Presses Universitaires de France, 1952, pp. 148–152.

———. *Psiquitría.* (3 vols.) Buenos Aires: El Ateneo, 1952, 1954, 1955.

———. *Psicología experimental.* Buenos Aires: Kapelusz, 1955.

———. *Psicologia de la vida moderna.* Buenos Aires: El Ateneo, 1963.

WALTHER MOEDE
1888-1958
German Psychologist (12)

Moede, W. Gedächtnis in Psychologie, Physiologie und Biologie. Kritische Beiträge zum Gedächtnisproblem. *Arch. ges. Psychol.,* 1911–1912, *22,* 312–389.

————. Die psychische Kausalität und ihre Gegner. *Arch. ges. Psychol.,* 1913, *26,* 155–180.

————. Der Wetteifer, seine Struktur und sein Ausmass: Ein Beitrag zur experimentellen Gruppen-Psychologie. *Z. pädag. Psychol.,* 1914. *15,* 353–368, 369–393.

————Die Massen- und Sozialpsychologie im kritischen Ueberblick. *Z. pädag. Psychol.,* 1915, *16,* 385–404.

————. *Die Untersuchung und Uebung des Gehirngeschädigten nach experimentellen Methoden.* Langensalza: Beyer, 1917.

————. *Die Berliner Begabtenschulen.* Langensalza: Hirzel, 1918.

————. *Die Experimentalpsychologie im Dienste des Wirtschaftslebens.* Berlin: Springer-Verlag, 1919.

————. Die psychotechnische Eignungsprüfung des industriellen Lehrlings. *Prakt. Psychol.,* 1919–1920, *1,* 6–18, 65–81.

————. Die psychotechnische Arbeitsstudie. *Prakt. Psychol.,* 1919–1920, *1,* 135–146.

————. *Experimentelle Massenpsychologie: Beiträge zur Experimentalpsychologie der Gruppe.* Leipzig: Hirzel, 1920.

————. Ergebnisse der industriellen Psychotechnik. *Prakt. Psychol.,* 1920–1921, *2,* 289–328.

————. Die Richtlinien der Leistungspsychologie. *Industr. Psychotech.,* 1927, *4,* 193–209.

————. *Lehrbuch der Psychotechnik.* Vol. 1. Berlin: Springer-Verlag, 1930.

————. Eignungsprüfung für kaufmännische Lehrlinge und Angestellte. *Industr. Psychotech.,* 1930, *7,* 1–17.

————. Zur Methodik der Menschenbehandlung. *Industr. Psychotech.,* 1930, *7,* 107–111, 208–214. (Also Berlin: Buchholz & Wiesswaege, 1930)

————. Fehldiagnosen in der Eignungsfeststellung und Fehlurteile in Prüfungen überhaupt. *Industr. Psychotech.,* 1931, *8,* 321–334.

————. *Arbeitstechnik. Die Arbeitskrafte: Schutz, Erhaltung, Steigerung.* Stuttgart: Enke, 1935.

————. Stand und Lage der angewandten Psychologie in Deutschland. *Amer. J. Psychol.,* 1937, *50,* 307–327.

————. *Eignungsprüfung und Arbeitseinsatz.* Stuttgart: Enke, 1943.

————. Wirtschaftspsychologie. In N. K. Ach (Ed.), *Lehrbuch der Psychologie.* Vol. 3. *Praktische Psychologie.* Bamberg: Buchner, 1944, pp. 80–121.

————. Verkehrspsychologie. In N. K. Ach (Ed.), *Lehrbuch der Psychologie.* Vol. 3. *Praktische Psychologie.* Bamberg: Buchner, 1944, pp. 276–305.

————. *Betriebliche Arbeitswissenschaft.* Essen: Gerandet, 1954.

————. *Psychologie des Berufs- und Wirtschaftslebens.* Berlin: De Gruyter, 1958.

Moore & Hartmann, *Industrial Psychology*

ALBERT MOLL
1862-1939
German Psychiatrist (13)

Moll, A. *The study of hypnosis: Historical, clinical and experimental research in the technique of hypnotic induction.* (5th ed.) Intro. by J. H. Conn. New York: Julian Press, 1958. (1889)

————. *Hypnotism.* (4th ed.) Trans. by A. F. Hobkirk. New York: Scribner's, 1909. (1889)

————. Hypnotismus. *Arch. Psychiat.,* 1889, *20,* 592–595.

————. *Die konträre Sexualempfindung.* (2nd ed.) Berlin: Fischer, 1893. (1891)

————. *Der Rapport in der Hypnose, Untersuchungen über den tierischen Magnetismus.* Leipzig: Meiner, 1892.

———. *Perversions of the sex instinct: A study of sexual inversion based on clinical data and official documents.* Trans. by M. Popkin. Newark, N.J.: Julian Press, 1931. (1893)

———. Probleme in der Homosexualität. *Z. Crim.-Anthrop.,* 1897, *1,* 157–189.

———. *Untersuchungen über die Libido sexualis.* Berlin: Kornfeld, 1897.

———. *Libido sexualis: Studies in the psychosexual laws of love verified by clinical sexual case histories.* Trans. by P. Berger. North Hollywood, Calif.: Brandon House, 1966. (1897)

———. *Das nervöse Weib.* Berlin: Fontane, 1898.

———. *Die konträre Sexualempfindung.* Berlin: Fischer, 1899.

———. *The sexual life of the child.* Trans. by E. Paul. New York: Macmillan, 1924. (1909)

———. *Berühmte Homosexuelle.* Wiesbaden: Bergmann, 1910.

———. Medizinische und psychologische Betrachtungen zum Prozess Franz. *Z. ärztl. Fortbildg.,* 1923, 151–155.

———. *Handbuch der Sexualwissenschaften.* (2nd ed.) (2 vols.) Leipzig: Vogel, 1926. (1912)

———. Homosexualität und sogenannter Eros. *Verh. int. Kongr. Sexualforschg.,* 1928, *1*(3), 136–147.

———. *Ein Leben als Arzt der Seele.* Dresden: Reissner, 1936.   **B**

Park & Burgess, *Sociology*

WILLIAM MOLYNEUX
1656-1698
Irish Astronomer (13)

Molyneux, W. (Letters) In J. Locke. Some familiar letters between Mr. Locke, and several of his friends. In J. Locke, *The works of John Locke,* Vol. 9. Aalen: Scientia Verlag, 1963, pp. 285–472. (1708)   **B**

———. Concerning the apparent magnitude of the *sun* and *moon,* or the apparent distance of two stars, when nigh the *horizon,* and when higher elevated. *Phil. Trans.,* 1687, *16,* 314–323.

———. *Dioptrica Nova: A treatise of Dioptricks.* London: Toake, 1692.

Herrnstein & Boring, *Source Book*

CONSTANTIN VON MONAKOW
1853-1930
Swiss Neurologist (12)

Monakow, C. v. *Gehirn und Gewissen: Psychobiologische Aufsätze.* Zurich: Margarten Verlag, Conzett & Huber, 1950.   **B Bl C**

———. Ueber einige durch Exstirpation zirkumskripter Hirnrindenregionen bedingte Entwickelungshemmungen des Kaninchengehirns. *Arch. Psychiat. Nervenk.,* 1882, *12,* 141-156.

———. Weitere Mitteilungen über durch Exstirpation zirkumskripter Hirnrindenregionen bedingte Entwickelungshemmungen des Kaninchengehirns. *Arch. Psychiat. Nervenk.,* 1882, *12,* 535–549.

———. Experimentelle und pathologisch-anatomische Untersuchungen über die optischen Centren und Bahnen. *Arch. Psychiat. Nervenk.,* 1889, *20,* 714–787; 1892, *23,* 609–671; 1893, *24,* 229–268.

———. Experimentelle und pathologisch-anatomische Untersuchungen über die Haubenregion, den Sehhügel und die Regio subthalamica, nebst Beiträgen zur Kenntnis früh erworbener Gross- und Kleinhirndefekte. *Arch. Psychiat. Nervenk.,* 1895, *27,* 1–128.

———. *Gehirnpathologie.* (2nd ed.) (2 vols.) Vienna: Hölder, 1905. (1897)

———. Zur Anatomie und Physiologie des unteren Scheitelläppchens. *Arch. Psychiat. Nervenk.,* 1898, *31,* 1–73.

———. Ueber die Projektions- und die Assoziationszentren im Grosshirn. *Monatssch. Psychiat.,* 1900, *8,* 405–426.

———. Ueber Aufbau und Lokalisation der Bewegungen beim Menschen. *Ber. IV. Kongr. exp. Psychol.,* 1911, 1–28.

———. Localization of brain functions. (1911) Reprinted in & trans. by G. v. Bonin (Ed.),

Some papers on the cerebral cortex. Springfield, Ill.: Thomas, 1960, pp. 231–250.

————. *Die Lokalisation im Grosshirn und der Abbau der Funktionen durch kortikale Herde.* Wiesbaden: Bergmann, 1914.

————. Gefühl, Gesittung und Gehirn. (1915) In *Gehirn und Gewissen, op. cit.,* pp. 97–230.

————. Psychiatrie und Biologie. *Schweiz. Arch. Neurol. Psychiat.,* 1919, *4,* 13–44, 236–276.

————. Betrachtungen über Gefühl und Sprache. *Schweiz. Arch. Neurol. Psychiat.,* 1922, *11,* 118–124.

————. *Fünfzig Jahre Neurologie.* Zurich: Füssli, 1924.

————. Die "Phänomenologie" in biologisch-psychologischer Beleuchtung. *Schweiz. Arch. Neurol. Psychiat.,* 1926, *19,* 124–151.

————. Die Syneidesis, das biologische Gewissen. (1927) In *Gehirn und Gewissen, op. cit.,* pp. 231–282.

————, & Mourgue, R. *Introduction biologique à l'étude de la neurologie et de la psychopathologie. Intégration et désintégration de la fonction.* Paris: Alcan, 1928.

————. Zur Krisis der Psychanalyse. *Schweiz. Arch. Neurol. Psychiat.,* 1929, *24,* 75–79.

————, & Mourgue, R. *Biologische Einführung in das Studium der Neurologie und Psychopathologie.* Stuttgart: Hippokrates, 1930.

————. Wahrheit, Irrtum, Lüge (Menschliches und biologisches). (1930) In *Gehirn und Gewissen, op. cit.,* pp. 283–340.

————. Religion und Nervensystem (Biologische Betrachtungen). (1930) In *Gehirn und Gewissen, op. cit.,* pp. 341–373.

————. Psychologie, Biologie und Neurose (Hysterie). *Hippokrates,* 1930, *2,* 394–434, 445–473.

————. *Vita mea. Mein Leben.* Ed. by A. W. Gubser & E. H. Ackerknecht. Bern: Hüber, 1970.　　　　　　　　　　　　　　**B**

Clarke & O'Malley, *Brain*

CHARLES DE SECONDAT MONTESQUIEU
(Charles de Secondat, Baron de La Brède et de Montesquieu)
1689-1755
French Philosopher (17)

Montesquieu, C. d. *Oeuvres de Montesquieu.* (7 vols.) Ed. by E. Laboulaye. Paris: Garnier, 1875–1879.　　　　　　　　　　　　　　**C**

————. *Mélanges inédits de Montesquieu.* Ed. by G. de Montesquieu. Bordeaux: Gounouilhou, 1892.　　　　　　　　　　　　　　**C**

————. *Pensées et fragments inédits.* (2 vols.) Ed. by G. de Montesquieu. Bordeaux: Gounouilhou, 1899.　　　　　　　　　　　**C**

————. *Correspondance de Montesquieu.* (2 vols.) Ed. by F. Gebelir & A. Morize. Paris: Champion, 1914.　　　　　　　　　　　**B C**

————. *Oeuvres complètes.* (2 vols.) Ed. by R. Caillois. Paris: Gallimard, 1949–1951.　　**C**

————. *Oeuvres complètes.* (3 vols.) Ed. by A. Masson. Paris: Nagel, 1950–1955.　　　**C**

————. *Oeuvres complètes.* Ed. by D. Oster. New York: Macmillan, 1964.　　　　　　　　**C**

————. *The Persian letters.* Ed. by G. R. Healy. Indianapolis, Ind.: Bobbs-Merrill, 1964. (1721)

————. *Considerations on the causes of the greatness of the Romans and their decline.* Trans. by D. Lowenthal. New York: Free Press, 1965. (1734)

————. *The spirit of laws.* Trans. by T. Nugent, rev. by J. V. Pritchard, Chicago: Encyclopaedia Britannica, 1952. (1748)

————. *De l'esprit des lois.* (2 vols.) Ed. by G. Truc. Paris: Garnier, 1961, 1962. (1748)

Brinton, *Age Reason;* Slotkin, *Anthropology;* Torrey, *Les Philosophes*

MARIA MONTESSORI
1870-1952
Italian Educator (21)

Montessori, Maria. *Child in the church: Essays on the religious education and the training of character.* Ed. by E. M. Standing. St. Louis, Mo.: Herder, 1929. (Reprinted 1965)   **C**

De Sanctis, S. (with ———.) *Sulle cosidette allucinazioni antagonistiche.* Rome: Alighieri, 1897.

———. *The Montessori method: Scientific pedagogy as applied to child education in "The children's houses."* Trans. by Anne E. George. New York: Stokes, 1912. (1909) (Reprinted 1964)

———. *Pedagogical anthropology.* Trans. by F. T. Cooper. New York: Stokes, 1913. (1910)

———. *A Montessori handbook: Dr. Montessori's own handbook.* Ed. by R. C. Orem. New York: Putnam's, 1966. (1914)

———. My system of education. *Nat. Educ. Ass.,* 1915, *53,* 64–73.

———. *The Montessori elementary material: The advanced Montessori method.* Trans. by A. Livingston. Cambridge: Bentley, 1964. (1917)

———. *Spontaneous activity in education: The advanced Montessori method.* Trans. by Florence Simmonds. Cambridge: Bentley, 1964. (1917)

———. *Peace and education.* Trans. by A. Livingston. Geneva: International Bureau of Education, 1932.

———. *Les étapes de l'éducation.* Paris: Brouwer, 1936.

———. *The secret of childhood.* (7th ed.) Trans. by M. J. Costelloe. Notre Dame, Ind.: Fides, 1966. (1936)

———. *The absorbent mind.* (2nd ed.) Trans. by C. A. Claremont. New York: Holt, Rinehart, & Winston, 1967. (1949)

———. *De l'enfant à l'adolescent.* (Trans. by Georgette J. J. Bernard.) Paris: Brouwer, 1949.

Strain, *Philosophies Education*

CONWY LLOYD MORGAN
1852-1936
English Psychologist (27)

Morgan, C. L. Instinct. *Nature,* 1884, *29,* 370–374, 405, 451–452.

———. *The springs of conduct: An essay in evolution.* London: Kegan Paul, 1885.

———. On the study of animal intelligence. *Mind,* 1886, *11,* 174–185.

———. *Animal life and intelligence.* Boston: Ginn, 1891. (1890)

———. Mental evolution. *Monist,* 1891–1892, *2,* 161–177.

———. *Animal sketches.* London: Arnold, 1891.

———. The limits of animal intelligence. *Nature,* 1892, *46,* 417.

———. The law of psychogenesis. *Mind,* 1892, *1*(N.S.), 72–93.

———. *An introduction to comparative psychology.* (2nd ed.) New York: Scribner's, 1904. (1894)

———. *Psychology for teachers.* New York: Scribner's, 1898. (1894)

———. Some definitions of instinct. *Nat. Sci.,* 1895, *6,* 321–329.

———. Animal automatism and consciousness. *Monist,* 1896–1897, *7,* 1–18.

———. *Habit and instinct.* London: Arnold, 1896.

———. The philosophy of evolution. *Monist,* 1897–1898, *8,* 481–501.

———. Instinct and intelligence in animals. *Nature,* 1898, *57,* 326–330.

———. Animal intelligence. *Nat. Sci.,* 1898, *13,* 265–272.

———. Animal intelligence: An experimental study. *Nature,* 1898, *58,* 249–250.

———. Mr. Herbert Spencer's biology. *Nat. Sci.,* 1898, *13,* 377–383.

———. Psychology and the ego. *Monist,* 1899–1900, *10,* 62–84.

———. The relation of stimulus to sensation in visual impressions. *Psychol. Rev.,* 1900, 7, 217–233.

———. *Animal behaviour.* London: Arnold, 1900.

———. Comparative and genetic psychology. *Psychol. Rev.*, 1905, *12*, 78–97.

———. The natural history of experience. *Brit. J. Psychol.*, 1909–1910, *3*, 1–20.

Myers, C. S., & ———. I. Instinct and intelligence. *Brit. J. Psychol.*, 1909–1910, *3*, 209–218.

———. II. Instinct and intelligence. *Brit. J. Psychol.*, 1909–1910, *3*, 219–229.

———. *Instinct and experience.* New York: Macmillan, 1912.

———. *Spencer's philosophy of science.* Oxford: Clarendon Press, 1913.

———. Psychical selection: Expression and impression. *Brit. J. Psychol.*, 1920–1921, *11*, 206–224.

———. Instinctive behaviour and enjoyment. *Brit. J. Psychol.*, 1921, *12*, 1–30.

———. *Emergent evolution.* (3rd ed.) New York: Holt, 1931. (1923)

———. A philosophy of evolution. In J. H. Muirhead (Ed.). *Contemporary British philosophy: Personal statements.* (1st ser.) New York: Macmillan, 1924, pp. 271–306.   **B**

———. *Life, mind and spirit.* New York: Holt, 1925.

———. *Mind at the crossways.* New York: Holt, 1930. (1929)

———. *The animal mind.* New York: Longmans, Green, 1930.

———. C. Lloyd Morgan. In C. Murchison (Ed.), *A history of psychology in autobiography.* Vol. 2. Worcester, Mass.: Clark University Press, 1932, pp. 237–264.   **B**

———. *The emergence of novelty.* London: Williams, 1933.

Beck & Molish, *Reflexes ;* Fried, *Anthropology ;* Herrnstein & Boring, *Source Book ;* Park & Burgess, *Sociology ;* Riopelle, *Problem Solving ;* Sahakian, *Psychology*

KARL FRIEDRICH MUENZINGER
1885-1958
American Psychologist (16)

Muenzinger, K. F. Physical and psychological reality. *Psychol. Rev.*, 1927, *34*, 220–233.

———. Plasticity and mechanization of the problem box habit in guinea pigs. *J. comp. Psychol.*, 1928, *8*, 45–69.

———. Koener, Luella, & Frey. Evelyn. Variability of an habitual movement in guinea pigs. *J. comp. Psychol.*, 1929, *9*, 425–436.

———, & Gentry, Evelyn. Tone discrimination in white rats. *J. comp. Psychol.*, 1931, *12*, 195–205.

———. The primary factors in learning. *Psychol. Rev.*, 1931, *38*, 347–358.

———, & Walz, F. C. An analysis of the electrical stimulus producing a shock. *J. comp. Psychol.*, 1932, *13*, 157–171.

———. Motivation in learning. I. Electric shock for correct response in the visual discrimination habit. *J. comp. Psychol.*, 1934, *17*, 267–277.

———. Motivation in learning. II. The function of electric shock for right and wrong responses in human subjects. *J. exp. Psychol.*, 1934, *17*, 439–448.

———. Mechanism, vitalism and the organismic hypothesis. *Phil. Sci.*, 1935, *2*, 518–520.

———, & Reynolds, H. E. Color vision in white rats. I. Sensitivity to red. *J. genet. Psychol.*, 1936, *48*, 58–71.

———, & Dove, C. C. Serial learning. I. Gradients of uniformity and variability produced by success and failure of single responses. *J. gen. Psychol.*, 1937, *16*, 403–413.

———, Poe, Emily, & Poe, C. F. The effect of vitamin deficiency upon the acquisition and retention of the maze habit in the white rat. II. Vitamin B2 (G). *J. comp. Psychol.*, 1937, *23*, 59–66.

———, & Fletcher, F. M. Motivation in learning. VII. The effect of an enforced delay at the point of choice in the visual discrimination habit. *J. comp. Psychol.*, 1937, *23*, 383–392.

————. Vicarious trial and error at a point of choice. I. A general survey of its relation to learning efficiency. *J. genet. Psychol.*, 1938, *53*, 75–86.

————, Bernstone, A. H., & Richards, L. Motivation in learning. VIII. Equivalent amount of electric shock for right and wrong response in a visual discrimination habit. *J. comp. physiol. Psychol.*, 1938, *26*, 177–186.

————. *Psychology, the science of behavior.* (Rev. ed.) New York: Harper, 1942. (1939)

————, & Conrad, D. G. Latent learning observed through negative transfer. *J. comp. Psychol.*, 1953, *46*, 1–8.

Boe & Church, *Punishment*

GEORG ELIAS MULLER
1850-1934
German Psychologist (26)

Müller, G. E. *Kleine Beiträge zur Psychophysik der Farbenempfindungen.* Leipzig: Barth, 1934.
C

————. *Zur Theorie der sinnlichen Aufmerksamkeit.* Leipzig: Edelmann, 1873.

————. *Zur Grundlegung der Psychophysik.* (2nd ed.) Berlin: Hoffmann, 1879. (1878)

————. Ueber die Massbestimmungen des Ortsinnes der Haut mittels der Methode der richtigen und falschen Fälle. *Arch. ges. Physiol.*, 1879, *19*, 191–235.

————, & Schumann, F. Ueber die psychologischen Grundlagen der Vergleichung gehobener Gewichte. *Arch. ges. Physiol.*, 1889, *45*, 37–112.

————, & Schumann, F. Experimentelle Beiträge zur Untersuchung des Gedächtnisses. *Z. Psychol.*, 1894, *6*, 81–190, 257–338.

————. Zur Psychophysik der Gesichtsempfindungen. *Z. Psychol.*, 1896, *10*, 1–82, 321–413; 1897, *14*, 1–76, 161–193.

————. Ueber die galvanischen Gesichtsempfindungen. *Z. Psychol.*, 1897, *14*, 329–374.

Martin, Lillian J., & ————. *Zur Analyse der Unterschiedsempfindlichkeit. Experimentelle Beiträge.* Leipzig: Barth, 1899.

————, & Pilzecker, A. Experimentelle Beiträge zur Lehre vom Gedächtnis. *Z. Psychol.*, 1900, Suppl. 1. (Also Leipzig: Barth, 1900) Reprinted 1970)

————. Zur Analyse der Gedächtnistätigkeit und des Vorstellungsverlaufes. *Z. Psychol.*, 1911–1917, Suppl. 5, 8, 9. (Also Leipzig: Barth, 1924) (Reprinted 1970)

————. Ueber die Lokalisation der visuellen Vorstellungsbilder. *Ber. V. Kong. exp. Psychol.*, 1912, 118–122.

————. Neue Versuche mit Rückle. *Z. Psychol.*, 1913, *67*, 193–213.

————. Ueber das Aubert'sche Phänomen. *Z. Sinnesphysiol.*, 1915, *49*, 109–146.

————. Zur Theorie des Stäbchenapparates und der Zapfenblindheit. *Z. Sinnesphysiol.*, 1922, *54*, 9–48, 102–145.

————. Ueber Jaenschs Zurückführung des Simultankontraktes auf zentrale Transformation. *Z. Psychol.*, 1923, *93*, 1–16.

————. *Komplextheorie und Gestalttheorie. Ein Beitrag zur Wahrnehmungspsychologie.* Göttingen: Vandenhoeck & Ruprecht, 1923.

————. *Darstellung und Erklärung der verschiedenen Typen der Farbenblindheit.* Göttingen: Vandenhoeck & Ruprecht, 1924.

————. *Abriss der Psychologie.* Göttingen: Vandenhoeck & Ruprecht, 1924.

————. Bermerkung zu W. Köhlers Artikel: "Komplextheorie und Gestalttheorie." *Z. Psychol.*, 1926, *99*, 1–15.

————. Ueber die Farbenempfindungen. Psychophysische Untersuchungen. *Z. Psychol.*, 1930, Suppl. 17, 18. (Also Leipzig: Barth, 1930)

————. Kleine Beiträge zur Psychophysik der Farbenempfindungen. *Z. Sinnesphysiol.*, 1931, *62*, 53–109.

————. Erklärung des Liebmann-Effektes und gewisser Versuchsresultate von Koffka und Harrower. *Psychol. Forsch.*, 1934, *19*, 237–244.

———. Ueber den dominierenden Einfluss der Kontur. *Psychol. Forsch.*, 1934, *19*, 245–249.

———. Ueber die Entstehung der elektrischen Gesichtsempfindungen. *Z. Sinnesphysiol.*, 1934, *65*, 274–292.

Mandler & Mandler, *Thinking*

JOHANNES MULLER
1801-1858
German Physiologist (25)

Müller, J. *Briefe von Johannes Müller an Anders Retzius von dem Jahre 1830 bis 1857.* Stockholm: Aftonbladets Aktiebolags Tryckeri, 1900.
B C

———. *Ueber die phantastischen Gesichtserscheinungen. Eine physiologische Untersuchung mit einer physiologischen Urkunde des Aristoteles über den Traum.* Munich: Fritsch, 1967. (1826)

———. *Beiträge zur vergleichenden Physiologie des Gesichtssinnes des Menschen und der Tiere.* Leipzig: Cnobloch, 1826.

———. Bestätigung des Bell'schen Lehrsatzes. *Notiz. Geb. Natur. Heilk.*, *Weimar*, 1831, *30*, 113–122.

———. Nouvelles expériences sur l'effet que produit l'irritation mécanique et galvanique sur les racines des nerfs spinaux. *Ann. sci. nat.*, Paris, 1831, *23*, 95–112.

———. *Handbuch der Physiologie des Menschen für Vorlesungen.* (2 vols.) (2nd ed.) Koblenz: Hölscher, 1837–1844. (1833–1840)

———. *Elements of physiology.* (2 vols.) Ed. by J. Bell & trans. by W. Baly. Philadelphia: Lea & Blanchard, 1843. (1833–1840)

———. *Elements of human physiology.* Trans. by W. Baly & ed. by T. S. Lambert. New York: Leavitt, 1852. (1833–1840)

———. Johannes Müller on the inverted image: A new and unabridged translation. (1840) Trans. by W. Riese & G. E. Arrington. *Amer. J. Ophthalm.*, 1959, *47*, 185–187.

———. *Elements of physiology.* (2nd ed.) (2 vols.) Trans. & notes by W. Baly. London: Taylor & Walton, 1840–1843.

———. *Physiology of the senses, voice, and muscular motion, with the mental faculties.* Trans. & notes by W. Baly. London: Taylor, Walton & Maberly, 1848.

Bodenheimer, *Biology;* Clarke & O'Malley. *Brain;* Dember, *Perception;* Dennis, *Psychology;* Fulton & Wilson, *Physiology;* Hall, *Source Book;* Herrnstein & Boring, *Source Book;* Rand, *Classical Psychologists;* Rook, *Origins;* Schwartz & Bishop, *Moments Discovery*

RICHARD MULLER-FREIENFELS
1882-1949
German Psychologist (15)

Müller-Freienfels, R. Zur Theorie der Gefühlstöne der Farbenempfindungen. *Z. Psychol.*, 1908, *46*, 241–274.

———. Individuelle Verschiedenheiten in der Kunst. *Z. Psychol.*, 1909, *50*, 1–61.

———. Affekte und Triebe im künstlerischen Geniessen. *Arch. ges. Psychol.*, 1910, *18*, 249–264.

———. Die assoziativen Faktoren im ästhetischen Geniessen. *Z. Psychol.*, 1910, *54*, 71–118.

———. Zur Psychologie der Erregungs- und Rauschzustände. *Z. Psychol.*, 1910, *57*, 161–194.

———. *Psychologie der Kunst: Eine Darstellung der Grundzüge.* Vol. 1. *Die Psychologie des Kunstgeniessens und des Kunstschaffens.* Leipzig: Teubner, 1912.

———. Nietzsche und der Pragmatismus. *Arch. ges. Phil.*, 1913, *26*, 339–358.

———. Der Einfluss der Gefühle und motorischen Faktoren auf Assoziation und Denken. *Arch. ges. Psychol.*, 1913, *27*, 381–430.

———. *Das Denken und die Phantasie.* (2nd ed.) Leipzig: Barth, 1925. (1914)

———. Studien zur Lehre vom Gedächtnis. *Arch. ges. Psychol.*, 1915, *34*, 65–105.

————. *Persönlichkeit und Weltanschauung.* (2nd ed.) Leipzig: Teubner, 1923. (1919)

————. *Philosophie der Individualität.* (2nd ed.) Leipzig: Meiner, 1923. (1921)

————. *Irrationalismus. Umrisse einer Erkenntnislehre.* Leipzig: Meiner, 1922.

————. *Psychologie der Künste.* In G. Kafka (Ed.), *Handbuch der vergleichenden Psychologie.* Vol. 2. *Die Funktionen des normalen Seelenslebens.* Munich: Reinhardt, 1922, pp. 183–336.

————. *Grundzüge einer Lebenspsychologie.* (2 vols.) Leipzig: Barth, 1924–1925.

————. *Die Seele des Alltags.* Berlin: Wegweiser, 1925.

————. *Mysteries of the soul.* Trans. by B. Miall. London: Allen & Unwin, 1929. (1927)

————. *Die Hauptrichtungen der gegenwärtigen Psychologie.* (3rd ed.) Leipzig: Quelle & Meyer, 1933. (1929)

————. *Allgemeine Sozial- und Kulturpsychologie.* Leipzig: Barth, 1930.

————. *Tagebuch eines Psychologen.* Leipzig: Seemann, 1931.

————. Studies in the social psychology of science. *J. soc. Psychol.,* 1933, *4,* 26–41.

————. *Psychologie der Kunst: Die Psychologie der einzelnen Künste.* Vol. 3. Munich: Reinhardt, 1933.

————. *Lebensnahe Charakterkunde.* Leipzig: Lindner, 1935.

————. *The evolution of modern psychology.* Trans. by W. B. Wolfe. New Haven: Yale University Press, 1935.

————. Zur Psychologie der Psychologie. *Acta psychol.,* 1936, *1,* 157–174.

————. *Kindheit und Jugend.* Leipzig: Quelle & Meyer, 1937.

————. Zur Psychologie der Psychologie. *Z. Psychol.,* 1938, *142,* 135–168.

————. *Du und die Psychologie. Menschenkenntnis und Menschenbehandlung.* Düsseldorf: Deutscher Bücherbund, 1960. (1940)

————. *Das Lachen und das Lächeln.* Bonn: Leuchtturm, 1948.

————. *Der Mensch und das Universum.* Munich: Nymphenburger, 1949.

————. *Schicksal und Zufall. Eine wissenschaftliche Erörterung ausserwissenschaftlicher Probleme.* Munich: Wissenschaftliche Editions-Gesellschaft, 1949.

FRANZ (CARL) MULLER-LYER
1857-1916
German Psychiatrist (19)

Müller-Lyer, F. C. Optische Urteilstäuschungen. *Arch. Physiol. Suppl.,* 1889, 263–270.

————. Zur Lehre von den optischen Täuschungen: Ueber Kontrast und Konfluxion. *Z. Psychol.,* 1895, *9,* 1–16.

————. Ueber Kontrast und Konfluxion. II. *Z. Psychol.,* 1896, *10,* 421–431.

————. Ueber den Einfluss des Lichtes auf die körperlichen und psychischen Funktionen. *Z. Hypno.,* 1899–1900, *9,* 257–274.

————. *Phasen der Kultur und Richtungslinien des Fortschritts. Soziologische Ueberblicke.* Munich: Lehmann, 1908.

————. *Die Entwicklungsstufen der Menschheit. Eine Gesellschaftlehre in Ueberlicken und Einzeldarstellungen.* Vol. 1. *Der Sinn des Lebens und die Wissenschafts-Grundlinien einer Volksphilosophie.* Munich: Lehmann, 1910.

————. *Die Entwicklungsstufen der Menschheit.* Vol. 3. *Formen der Ehe, der Familie und der Verwandtschaft.* Munich: Langen, 1924. (1911)

————. *The family.* Trans. by F. W. S. Browne. New York: Knopf, 1931. (1912)

————. Die phaseologische Methode in der Soziologie. *Vtljsch. wiss. Phil. Soziol.,* 1912, *36,* 241–255.

————. *The evolution of modern marriage.* Trans. by I. Wigglesworth. London: Allen & Unwin, 1930. (1913)

———. *Phasen der Liebe. Eine Soziologie des Verhältnisses der Geschlechten.* Munich: Langen, 1913.

———. *Soziologie des Leidens.* Munich: Langen, 1914.

———. Soziologie des Bevölkerungswesens. *Vtljsch. wiss. Phil. Soziol.,* 1915, *39,* 381–399.

———. *The history of social development.* Trans. by E. C. & H. A. Lake. London: Allen & Unwin, 1935 (1920).

HUGO MUNSTERBERG
1863-1916
German-American Psychologist (24)

Münsterberg, H. *Die Willenshandlung. Ein Beitrag zur physiologischen Psychologie.* Freiburg: Mohr, 1888.

———. *Beiträge zur experimentellen Psychologie.* (4 vols.) Freiburg: Mohr, 1889.

———. Die Assoziation successiver Vorstellungen. *Z. Psychol.,* 1890, *1,* 99–107.

———. Studies from the Harvard psychological laboratory. I. Memory, attention, psychophysics. *Psychol. Rev.,* 1894, *1,* 34–60.

———, & Campbell, W. W. The motor power of ideas. *Psychol. Rev.,* 1894, *1,* 441–453.

———, & Pierce, A. H. The localization of sound. *Psychol. Rev.,* 1894, *1,* 461–476.

Dunton, L., ———, Harris, W. T., & Hall, G. S. *The old psychology and the new: Addresses before the Massachusetts schoolmasters' club, April 27, 1895.* Boston: New England Publishing, 1895.

———. Die verschobene Schachbrettfigur. *Z. Psychol.,* 1897, *15,* 182–188.

———. Psychology and history. *Psychol. Rev.,* 1899, *6,* 1–31.

———. *Psychology and life.* Boston: Houghton Mifflin, 1899.

———. *Grundzüge der Psychologie.* (2nd ed.) Leipzig: Barth, 1918. (1900)

———. Psychological atomism. *Psychol. Rev.,* 1900, *7,* 1–17.

———. .The position of psychology in the system of knowledge. *Psychol. Monogr.,* 1903, *4,* No. 17, pp. 641–654.

———. *The Americans.* Trans. by E. B. Holt. London: Williams, 1905.

———. *Science and idealism.* New York: Houghton Mifflin, 1906.

———. *On the witness stand.* New York: Boardman, 1933. (1908)

———. *Psychology and the teacher.* New York: Appleton, 1909.

———. *Psychotherapy.* New York: Moffat Yard, 1909.

———. *American problems from the point of view of a psychologist.* Freeport, N.Y.: Books for Libraries Press, 1969. (1910)

Jastrow, J., ———, Ribot, T., Janet, P., Hart, B., & Prince, M. *Subconscious phenomena.* Boston: Badger, 1910.

———. *Psychologie und Wirtschaftsleben.* Leipzig: Barth, 1912.

———. *Psychology and industrial efficiency.* Boston: Houghton Mifflin, 1913.

———. *Grundzüge der Psychotechnik.* (2nd ed.) Leipzig: Barth, 1920. (1914)

———. *Psychology: General and applied.* New York: Appleton, 1914.

———. *The film: A psychological study.* Foreword by R. Griffith. (Formerly published as *The photoplay: A psychological study.*) New York: Dover, 1970. (1916)

Beck & Molish, *Reflexes ;* Moore & Hartmann, *Industrial Psychology ;* Park & Burgess, *Sociology*

CARL MURCHISON
1887-1961
American Psychologist (20)

Murchison, C. *Criminal intelligence.* Worcester, Mass.: Clark University Press, 1926.

———, (Ed.), *Psychologies of 1925*. (3rd ed.) Worcester, Mass.: Clark University Press, 1928. (1926)

———, (Ed.). *The case for and against psychical belief*. Worcester, Mass.: Clark University Press, 1927. (Reprinted 1970)

———, & Langer, S. Tiedemann's observations on the development of the mental faculties of children. *J. genet. Psychol.*, 1927, *34*, 205–230.

———. *Social psychology: The psychology of political domination*. Worcester, Mass.: Clark University Press, 1929.

———, (Ed.). *The foundations of experimental psychology*. Worcester, Mass.: Clark University Press, 1929. (Reprinted 1966)

———. *A history of psychology in autobiography*. Vol. 1. Worcester, Mass.: Clark University Press, 1930.

———, (Ed.). *Psychologies of 1930*. Worcester, Mass.: Clark University Press, 1930.

———, (Ed.). *A handbook of child psychology*. (2nd ed.) Worcester, Mass.: Clark University Press, 1933. (1931)

———. *A history of psychology in autobiography*. Vol. 2. Worcester, Mass.: Clark University Press, 1932.

———, (Ed.). *The psychological register*. Vol. 3. Worcester, Mass.: Clark University Press, 1932.

———, (Ed.). *A handbook of general experimental psychology*. Worcester, Mass.: Clark University Press, 1934.

———. The experimental measurement of a social hierarchy in *Gallus domesticus*. I. The direct identification and direct measurement of Social Reflex No. 1 and Social Reflex No. 2. *J. gen. Psychol.*, 1935, *12*, 3–39.

———. The experimental measurement of a social hierarchy in *Gallus domesticus*. II. The identification and inferential measurement of Social Reflex No. 1 and Social Reflex No. 2 by means of social discrimination. *J. soc. Psychol.*, 1935, *6*, 3–30.

———. The experimental measurement of a social hierarchy in *Gallus domesticus*. III. The direct and inferential measurement of Social Reflex No. 3. *J. genet. Psychol.*, 1935, *46*, 76–102.

———. The experimental measurement of a social hierarchy in *Gallus Domesticus*. IV. Loss of body weight under conditions of mild starvation as a function of social dominance. *J. gen. Psychol.*, 1935, *12*, 296–312. Reprinted in R. B. Zajonc (Ed.), *Animal social psychology: A reader of experimental studies*. New York: Wiley, 1969, pp. 287–294.

———, Pomerat, C. M., & Zarrow, M. X. The experimental measurement of a social hierarchy in *Gallus domesticus*. V. The post-mortem measurement of anatomical features. *J. soc. Psychol.*, 1935, *6*, 172–181.

———. The experimental measurement of a social hierarchy in *Gallus domesticus*. VI. Preliminary identification of social law. *J. gen. Psychol.*, 1935, *13*, 277–248.

———. Pareto and experimental social psychology. *J. soc. Phil.*, 1935, *1*, 53–63.

———, (Ed.). *A handbook of social psychology*. Worcester, Mass.: Clark University Press, 1935. (Reprinted 1967)

———. The time function in the experimental formation of social hierarchies of different sizes in *Gallus domesticus*. *J. soc. Psychol.*, 1936, *7*, 3–18.

———, (Ed.). *A history of psychology in autobiography*. Vol. 3. Worcester, Mass.: Clark University Press, 1936.

———. Recollections of a magic decade at Clark: 1925–35. *J. gen. Psychol.*, 1959, *61*, 3–12. **B**

Zajonc, *Animal Social*

CHARLES SAMUEL MYERS
1873-1946
English Psychologist (21)

Myers, C. S. *A psychologist's point of view*. London: Heinemann, 1933. **C**

———. A study of rhythm in primitive music. *Brit. J. Psychol.*, 1904–1905, *1*, 397–406.

Myers

———. Some observations on the development of the colour sense. *Brit. J. Psychol.*, 1906–1908, *2*, 353–362.

———. Instinct and intelligence. *Brit. J. Psychol.*, 1909–1910, *3*, 209–218.

———. Instinct and intelligence: A reply. *Brit. J. Psychol.*, 1909–1910, *3*, 267–270.

———, & Bartlett, F. C. *Textbook of experimental psychology.* (3rd ed.) London: Cambridge University Press, 1925. (1909)

———. A case of synaesthesia. *Brit. J. Psychol.*, 1911, *4*, 228–238.

———. *An introduction to experimental psychology.* (Rev. ed.) Cambridge: Cambridge University Press, 1912. (1911)

———. Are the intensity differences of sensation quantitative? I. *Brit. J. Psychol.*, 1913–1914, *6*, 137–154.

———, & Valentine, C. W. A study of the individual differences in attitude towards tones. *Brit. J. Psychol.*, 1914–1915, *7*, 68–111.

———. Instinct and the unconscious. II. *Brit. J. Psychol.*, 1919–1920, *10*, 8–14.

———. *Mind and work.* New York: Putnam's, 1921. (1920)

———. The revival of emotional memories and its therapeutic value. II. *Brit. J. Med. Psychol.*, 1920, *1*, 20–22.

———. Individual differences in listening to music. *Brit. J. Psychol.*, 1922–1923, *13*, 52–71.

———. Conceptions of fatigue and adaptation. *Psychol. Rev.*, 1925, *32*, 1–16.

———. *Industrial psychology.* New York: People's Institute, 1925.

———. *Psychological conceptions in other sciences: The Herbert Spencer Lecture delivered at Oxford, 14 May, 1929.* Oxford: Clarendon Press, 1929.

———. On the nature of mind. *Nature*, 1931, *128*, 744–747.

———. *Business rationalisation, its dangers and advantages considered from the psychological and social standpoints.* London: Pitman, 1932.

———. *The absurdity of any mind-body relation.* London: Oxford University Press, 1932.

Welch, H. J., & ———. *Ten years of industrial psychology: An account of the first decade of the National Institute of Industrial Psychology.* London: Pitman, 1932.

———. Human improvability. *Bristol med.-chir. F.*, 1932, *49*, 31–46.

———. The relation of acts and contents of consciousness. *Brit. J. Psychol.*, 1932–1933, *23*, 343–351.

———. A psychological regard of medical education. *Lancet*, 1933, *225*, 1075–1080.

———. The human factor in accidents. *Human Factor*, 1934, *8*, 266–279.

———. The help of psychology in the choice of a career. *Rep. Brit. Ass.*, 1935, 487–493.

———. Charles Samuel Myers. In C. Murchison (Ed.), *History of psychology in autobiography.* Vol. 3. Worcester, Mass.: Clark University Press, 1936, pp. 215–230. (Reprinted 1961) **B**

———. Some present-day trends in vocational psychology. *Brit. J. educ. Psychol.*, 1936, *6*, 225–232.

———. Conceptions of mental fatigue. *Amer. J. Psychol.*, 1937, *50*, 296–306.

———. *Shell shock in France 1914–1918.* Cambridge: Cambridge University Press, 1940. **B**

———, Freeman, F. N., & Viteles, M. S. *Modern psychology.* Philadelphia: University of Pennsylvania Press, 1941.

———. Aspects of modern psychology. *Science*, 1941, *94*, 75–81, 102–105.

———. Is the doctrine of instincts dead? A symposium. VI. Retrospect and prospect. *Brit. J. educ. Psychol.*, 1942, *12*, 148–155.

———. The comparative study of instincts. *Brit. J. Psychol.*, 1945–1946, *36*, 1–9.

Drever, *Sourcebook ;* Moore & Hartmann, *Industrial Psychology ;* Park & Burgess, *Sociology*

WILIBALD (A.) NAGEL
1870-1910
German Physiologist (12)

Nagel, W. A. *Die niederen Sinne der Insekten.* Tübingen: Pietzcker, 1892.

―――. Beobachtungen über den Lichtsinn augenloser Muscheln. *Biol. Zbl.,* 1894, *14,* 385-390.

―――. Ein Beitrag zur Kenntnis des Lichtsinnes augenloser Tiere. *Biol. Zbl.,* 1894, *14,* 810–813.

―――. Vergleichend physiologische und anatomische Untersuchungen über den Geruchs- und Geschmackssinn und ihre Organe mit einleitenden Betrachtungen aus der allgemeinen vergleichenden Sinnesphysiologie. *Bibl. Zool.,* 1894–1896, *18,* 1–207. (Also Stuttgart: Nägele, 1894)

―――. Experimentelle sinnesphysiologische Untersuchungen an Coelenteräten. *Arch. ges. Physiol.,* 1894, *57,* 495–552.

Kries, J. v., & ―――. Ueber den Einfluss von Lichtstärke und Adaptation auf das Sehen des Dichromaten. (Grünblinden). *Z. Psychol.,* 1896, *12,* 1–38.

―――. Ueber kompensatorische Raddrehungen der Augen. *Z. Psychol.,* 1896, *12,* 331–354.

―――. *Der Lichtsinn augenloser Tiere: Eine biologische Studie.* Jena: Fischer, 1896.

―――. Ueber Mischgerüche und die Komponentengliederung des Geruchssinnes. *Z. Psychol.,* 1897, *15,* 82–101.

―――. Ueber das Aubert'sche Phänomen und verwandte Täuschungen über die vertikale Richtung. *Z. Psychol.,* 1898, *16,* 373–398.

―――. *Der Farbensinn der Tiere.* Wiesbaden: Bergmann, 1899.

―――. *Die Diagnose der praktisch wichtigen angeborenen Störungen des Farbensinnes.* Wiesbaden: Bergmann, 1899.

Kries, J. v., & ―――, Weitere Mitteilungen über die funktionelle Sonderstellung des Netzhautzentrums. *Z. Psychol.,* 1900, *23,* 161–186.

―――, & Schaefer, K. L. Ueber das Verhalten der Netzhautzapfen bei Dunkeladaptation des Auges. *Z. Psychol.,* 1904, *34,* 271–284.

―――. (Ed.) *Handbuch der Physiologie des Menschen.* (5 vols.) Brunswick: Vieweg, 1905–1910.

―――. Allgemeine Einleitung zur Physiologie der Sinne. (1905) In *Handbuch,* Vol. 3, *op. cit.,* pp. 1–15.

―――. Der Gesichtssinn. 2. Die Wirkungen des Lichtes auf die Netzhaut. (1905) In *Handbuch,* Vol. 3, *op. cit.,* pp. 91–108.

―――. Der Geruchssinn. (1905) In *Handbuch,* Vol. 3, *op. cit.,* pp. 589–620.

―――. Der Geschmackssinn. (1905) In *Handbuch,* Vol. 3, *op. cit.,* pp. 621–646.

―――. Die Lage-, Bewegungs- und Widerstandsempfindungen. (1905) In *Handbuch,* Vol. 3, *op. cit.,* pp. 734–806.

―――. Fortgesetzte Untersuchungen zur Symptomatologie und Diagnostik der angeborenen Störungen des Farbensinns. *Z. Sinnesphysiol.,* 1906, *41,* 239–282, 319–337.

―――. Zur Nomenklatur des Farbensinnstörungen. *Z. Sinnesphysiol.,* 1907, *42,* 65–68.

―――. Der Farbensinn des Hundes. *Zbl. Physiol.,* 1908, *22,* 205–207.

―――. Ueber typische und atypische Farbensinnstörungen nebst einem Anhang: Erwiderung an Herrn Dr. A. Guttmann. *Z. Sinnesphysiol.,* 1908, *43,* 299–314.

―――. Physiologie der Stimmwerkzeuge. (1909) In *Handbuch,* Vol. 4, *op. cit.,* pp. 691–792.

―――. Adaptation, twilight vision and the duplicity theory. (1911) In H. L. F. Helmholtz, *Treatise on physiological optics.* (3rd ed.) Vol. 2. *The sensations of vision.* Ed. by J. P. C. Southall. Rochester, N.Y.: Optical Society of America, 1924, pp. 313–394.

ISAAC NEWTON
1642-1727
English Astronomer-Mathematician (26)

Newton, I. *Correspondence of Sir Isaac Newton and Professor Cotes ; Including letters of other eminent men, now first published from the originals in the library of Trinity College,*

Cambridge, together with an appendix containing other unpublished letters and papers by Newton; with notes, synoptical view of the philosopher's life, and a variety of details illustrative of his history, by J. Edleston. London: Parker, 1850. (Reprinted 1968) **B C**

——. *Theological manuscripts.* Ed. & intro. by H. McLachlan. Liverpool: University Press, 1950. **C**

——. *Newton's philosophy of nature.* Ed. by H. S. Thayer. New York: Hafner, 1953. **C**

——. *Isaac Newton's papers and letters on philosophy and related documents.* Ed. by L. B. Cohen & R. E. Schofield. Cambridge: Harvard University Press, 1958. **C**

——. *The correspondence of Isaac Newton.* Vols. I–IV. Ed. by H. W. Turnbull & J. F. Scott. London: Cambridge University Press, 1959–1967. **C**

——. *Unpublished scientific papers of Isaac Newton.* Cambridge: Cambridge University Press, 1962. **C**

——. *The mathematical works of Isaac Newton.* (2 vols.) Ed. by D. T. Whiteside. New York: Johnson Reprint, 1964–1967. **C**

——. *The mathematical papers of Isaac Newton.* (5 vols.) Ed. by D. T. Whiteside. London: Cambridge University Press, 1967–1972. **C**

——. *A letter of Mr. Isaac Newton, . . .* containing his new theory about light and colors. *Phil. Trans.,* 1671–1672, *6,* 3075–3087.

——. *Mr. Isaac Newton's answer to some considerations upon his doctrine of light and colors ; which doctrine was printed in Numb. 80 of these Tracts. Phil. Trans.,* 1672, *7,* 5084–5103.

——. *New theory about light and colours.* London: Dawsons, 1965. (1672)

——. *Sir Isaac Newton's mathematical principles of natural philosophy and his system of the world.* (2 vols.) (3rd ed.) Trans. by A. Motte & rev. by F. Cajori. Berkeley, Calif.: University of California Press, 1934. (1687)

——. *Optics.* Ed. by F. Cajori. New York: McGraw-Hill, 1931. (1704)

——. *Opticks or a treatise of the reflexions, refractions, inflexions and colours of light. Also two treatises on the species and magnitude of curvilinear figures.* Ed. by I. B. Cohen, with an analytical table of contents by D. H. Roller. New York: Dover, 1952. (1704)

——. *A treatise of the system of the world.* (2nd ed.) Intro. by I. B. Cohen. London: Dawsons, 1969. (1728)

Dampier, *Literature ;* Dennis, *Psychology ;* Hall, *Nature's Laws ;* Hall, *Source Book ;* Herrnstein & Boring, *Source Book ;* Hutchins, *Great Books ;* MacAdam, *Color Science;* Newman, *Mathematics;* Schwartz & Bishop, *Moments Discovery ;* Smith, *Source Book*

FRIEDRICH WILHELM NIETZSCHE
1844-1900
German Philosopher (20)

Nietzsche, F. W. *Friedrich Nietzsches gesammelte Briefe.* (5 vols. in 6) Leipzig: Insel, 1900–1909. **B C**

——. *Gesammelte Werke: Musarionausgabe.* (23 vols.) Munich: Musarion, 1920–1929. **C**

——. *The portable Nietzsche.* Trans. by W. Kaufmann. New York: Viking Press, 1954. **C**

——. *Basic writings of Nietzsche.* Ed. by W. Kaufmann. New York: Random House, 1968. **C**

——. *Selected letters of Friedrich Nietzsche.* Ed. by C. Middleton. Chicago: University of Chicago Press, 1969. **B C**

——. *The birth of tragedy.* (1872) In *Basic writings, op. cit.,* pp. 15–144.

——. *The use and abuse of history.* Trans. by Adrian Collins. Indianapolis, Ind.: Bobbs-Merrill, 1949. (1874)

——. *Schopenhauer as educator.* Trans. by J. W. Hillesheim & M. B. Simpson. Chicago: Regenery, 1965. (1874)

———. *Joyful wisdom.* Trans. by K. F. Reinhardt. New York: Ungar, 1960. (1882)

———. Thus spoke Zarathustra. (1883–1892) In *The portable Nietzsche, op. cit.,* pp. 121–439.

———. Beyond good and evil. Prelude to a philosophy of the future. (1886) In *Basic writings, op. cit.,* pp. 181–435.

———. On the genealogy of morals. (1887) In *Basic writings, op. cit.,* pp. 439–599.

———. The case of Wagner: A musician's problem. (1888) In *Basic writings, op. cit.,* pp. 603–653.

———. Twilight of the idols or, how one philosophizes with a hammer. (1889) In *The portable Nietzsche, op. cit.,* pp. 463–563.

———. Nietzsche contra Wagner. (1895) In *The portable Nietzsche, op. cit.,* pp. 661–683.

———. The antichrist. (1895) In *The portable Nietzsche, op. cit.,* pp. 565–656.

———. *The will to power.* Trans. by W. Kaufmann & R. G. Hollingdale, & ed. with notes by W. Kaufmann. New York: Random House, 1966. (1901)

———. Ecce homo (1908) In *Basic writings, op. cit.,* pp. 657–791.

Gardiner, *Philosophy* ; Matson, *Being* ; Murphy, *Western*

HENRY WIEGHORST NISSEN
1901-1958
American Psychologist (14)

Warden, C. J., & Nissen, H. W. An experimental analysis of the obstruction method of measuring animal drives. *J. comp. Psychol.,* 1928, *8,* 325–342.

———. The effects of gonadectomy, vasotomy, and injection of placental and orchic extracts on the sex behavior of the white rat. *Genet. Psychol. Monogr.,* 1929, *5,* No. 6, pp. 449–550.

———. A study of exploratory behavior in the white rat by means of the obstruction method. *J. genet. Psychol.,* 1930, *37,* 361–376. Reprinted in C. J. Warden (Ed.), *Animal motivation: Experimental studies on the albino rat.* New York: Columbia University Press, 1931, pp. 354–367..

———. A study of exploratory behavior in the white rat by means of the obstruction method. *J. genet. Psychol.,* 1930, *37,* 361–376.

———. A study of maternal behavior in the white rat by means of the obstruction method. *J. genet. Psychol.,* 1930, *37,* 361–376.

———. A field study of the chimpanzee. *Comp. Psychol. Monogr.,* 1931, No. 8.

———, Machover, S., & Kinder, Elaine F. A study of performance tests given to a group of native African negro children. *Brit. J. Psychol.,* 1934–1935, *25,* 308–355.

———, Riesen, A. H., & Nowlis, V. Delayed response and discrimination learning by chimpanzees. *J. comp. Psychol.,* 1938, *26,* 361–386.

Yerkes, R. M., & ———. Pre-linguistic sign behavior in chimpanzee. *Science,* 1939, *89,* 585–587.

———, & Harrison, R. Visual and positional cues in the delayed responses of chimpanzees. *J. comp. Psychol.,* 1941, *31,* 437–445.

———. Ambivalent cues in discriminative behavior of chimpanzees. *J. Psychol.,* 1942, *14,* 3–33.

———, & Yerkes, R. M. Reproduction in the chimpanzee: Report on forty-nine births. *Anat. Rec.,* 1943, *86,* 567–578.

———, Blum, Josephine S., & Blum, R. A. Analysis of matching behavior in chimpanzee. *J. comp. physiol. Psychol.,* 1948, *41,* 62–74. Reprinted in A. J. Riopelle (Ed.), *Animal problem solving: Selected readings.* Baltimore, Md.: Penguin Books, 1967, pp. 334–350.

———, Blum, Josephine S., & Blum, R. A. Conditional matching behavior in chimpanzee; implications for the comparative study of intelligence. *J. comp. physiol. Psychol.,* 1949, *42,* 339–356.

———. Description of the learned response in discrimination behavior. *Psychol. Rev.,* 1950, *57,* 121–131.

———. Phylogenetic comparison. In S. S. Stevens (Ed.), *Handbook of experimental psychology.* New York: Wiley, 1951, pp. 347–386.

———Analysis of a complex conditional reaction in chimpanzee. *J. comp. physiol. Psychol.*, 1951, *44*, 9–16. Reprinted in A. J. Riopelle (Ed.), *Animal problem solving: Selected readings.* Baltimore, Md.: Penguin Books, 1967, pp. 305–314.

———, Chow, K. L., & Semmes, Josephine. Effects of restricted opportunity for tactual, kinesthetic, and manipulative experience on the behavior of a chimpanzee. *Amer. J. Psychol.*, 1951, *64*, 485–507.

———. Further comment on approach-avoidance as categories of response. *Psychol. Rev.*, 1952, *59*, 161–167.

———. The nature of the drive as innate determinant of behavioral organization. *Nebraska symposium on motivation*, 1954. Lincoln, Nebr.: University of Nebraska Press, 1954, pp. 281–321.

Chow, K. L., & ———. Interlocular transfer of learning in visually naive and experienced infant chimpanzees. *J. comp. physiol. Psychol.*, 1955, *48*, 229–237.

> Riopelle, *Problem Solving;* Valentine, *Experimental*

C(HARLES) K(AY) OGDEN
1889-1957
English Psychologist (12)

Ogden, C. K., & Wood, J. *The foundations of aesthetics.* (2nd ed.) London: Allen & Unwin, 1925. (1922)

———, & Richards, I. A. *The meaning of meaning: A study of the influence of language upon thought and of the science of symbolism.* (8th ed.) New York: Harcourt, Brace, 1947. (1923)

———. *The meaning of psychology.* New York: Harper, 1926.

———. Forensic orthology: Back to Bentham. *Psyche,* 1928, No. 32, 3–18.

———. Bentham's philosophy of as-if. *Psyche,* 1928, No. 33, 4–14.

———. Bentham on invention. *Psyche,* 1929, No. *10, 102*–109.

———. *The A.B.C. of psychology.* (3rd ed.) London: Kegan Paul, 1934. (1929)

———. Introduction. In J. Bentham, *Bentham's theory of fictions.* London: Kegan Paul, 1932, pp. ix–clii.

———. *Jeremy Bentham, 1832–1932.* London: Kegan Paul, Trench, & Truebner, 1932.

———. *Opposition: A linguistic and psychological analysis.* Intro. by I. A. Richards. Bloomington, Ind.: Indiana University Press. 1967, (1932)

———. The magic of words. *Psyche,* 1934, *14,* 9–87.

———. Sound, sense, and intelligibility; an orthological interpretation of stress and rhythm. *Psyche,* 1935, *15,* 19–26.

———. *The system of basic English.* New York: Harcourt, Brace, 1937.

ROBERT MORRIS OGDEN
1877-1959
American Psychologist (20)

Ogden, R. M. A method of mapping retinal circulation by projection. *Amer. J. Psychol.*, 1901, *12*, 281–291.

———. Memory and the economy of learning. *Psychol. Bull.*, 1904, *1*, 177–184.

———. The pictorial representation of distance. *Psychol. Bull.*, 1908, *5*, 109–113.

———. A contribution to the theory of tonal consonance. *Psychol. Bull.*, 1909, *6*, 297–303.

———. Imageless thought. Résumé and critique. *Psychol. Bull.*, 1911, *8*, 183–197.

———. The unconscious bias of laboratories. *Psychol. Bull.*, 1911, *8*, 330–331.

———. Knowing and expressing. *J. genet. Psychol.*, 1911, *18*, 47–53.

——. The relation of psychology to philosophy and education. *Psychol. Rev.*, 1913, *20*, 179–193.

——. Experimental criteria for differentiating memory and imagination in projected visual images. *Psychol. Rev.*, 1913, *20*, 378–410.

——. *An introduction to general psychology.* New York: Longmans, Green, 1914.

——. The attributes of sound. *Psychol. Rev.* 1918, *25*, 227–241.

——. The tonal manifold. *Psychol. Rev.*, 1920, *27*, 136–146.

——. Are there any sensations? *Amer. J. Psychol.*, 1922, *33*, 247–254.

——. *Hearing.* New York: Harcourt, Brace, 1924. (Reprinted 1970)

——. The nature of intelligence, *J. educ. Psychol.*, 1925, *16*, 361–369.

——, & Freeman, F. S. *Psychology and education.* (2nd ed.) New York: Harcourt, Brace, 1932, (1926)

——. The Gestalt-hypothesis. *Psychol. Rev.*, 1928, *35*, 136–141.

——. The Gestalt psychology of learning. *J. genet. Psychol.*, 1930, *38*, 280–287.

——. Structural psychology and the psychology of Gestalt: The methods of E. B. Titchener compared with those of K. Koffka, W. Köhler, and M. Wertheimer. In S. A. Rice (Ed.), *Methods in social science.* Chicago: University of Chicago Press, 1931, pp. 109–117.

——. Insight. *Amer. J. Psychol.*, 1932, *44*, 350–356.

——. Thorndike's proof of the law of effect. *Science,* 1933, *77*, 240.

——. Gestalt psychology and behaviorism. *Amer. J. Psychol.*, 1933, *45*, 151–155.

——. Sociology and Gestalt psychology. *Amer. J. Psychol.*, 1934, *46*, 651–655.

——. Naïve geometry in the psychology of art. *Amer. J. Psychol.*, 1937, *49*, 198–216.

——. *The psychology of art.* New York: Scribner's, 1938.

——. Science and knowledge. *Phil. Rev.*, N. Y., 1942, *51*, 559–573.

——. Oswald Külpe and the Würzburg School. *Amer. J. Psychol.*, 1951, *64*, 4–19.

JOHANNES ORTH
1847-1923
German Psychologist (13)

Orth, J. Ueber die Entstehung und Vererbung individueller Eigenschaften. In *Festschrift Albert von Kölliker zur Feier seines siebenzigsten Geburtstag gewidmet von seinen Schülern.* Leipzig: Engelmann, 1887, pp. 157–183.

Mayer, A., & ——. Zur qualitativen Untersuchung der Assoziation. *Z. Psychol.*, 1901, *26*, 1–13. Trans. in Jean M. & G. Mandler (Eds.), *Thinking: From association to Gestalt.* New York: Wiley, 1964, pp. 135–143.

——. *Gefühl und Bewusstseinslage: Eine kritisch-experimentelle Studie.* Berlin: Reuther & Reichard, 1903.

Mandler & Mandler, *Thinking*

(SIR) JOHN HERBERT PARSONS
1868-1957
English Ophthalmologist (13)

Parsons, J. H. On dilatation of the pupil from stimulation of the cortex cerebri. *J. Physiol.*, 1900–1901, *26*, 366–379.

——. Degenerations following lesions of the retina in monkeys. *Brain*, 1902, *25*, 257b–269b.

——. The neurology of vision. *Lancet*, 1904, *1*, 1029–1034, 1102–1105.

——. *The pathology of the eye.* (4 vols.) London: Hodder, Stoughton, & Froude, 1904–1908.

——, & Elder, W. S. D. *Diseases of the eye.* (11th ed.) London: Churchill, 1948. (1907)

——. Discussion on the hygiene of reading and near vision. *Brit. Med. J.*, 1914, *2*, 359–362.

——. *An introduction to the study of colour vision.* (2nd ed.) Cambridge: Cambridge University Press, 1924. (1915)

——. *Mind and the nation: A précis of applied psychology.* London: Bales, Son, & Danielson, 1918.

——. The Bowman Lecture on the foundations of vision. *Lancet,* 1925, *2,* 123–129.

——. *An introduction to the theory of perception.* Cambridge: Cambridge University Press, 1927.

——. Color vision and its anomalies: An address delivered to the Wilmer Ophthalmological Institute, Baltimore, Oct. 16, 1929. *Brit. J. Ophthalm.,* 1930, *14,* 97–114.

——. The Thomas Young oration: Young's theory of colour vision (1801–1931). *Trans. Opt. Soc.,* London, 1930–1931, *32,* 165–183.

——. The electrical response of the eye to light. *Brit. J. Ophthalm.,* 1936, *20,* 1–15.

——. Light and vision. *Brit. J. Ophthalm.,* 1943, *27,* 321–330.

BLAISE PASCAL
1623-1662
French Philosopher (19)

Pascal, B. *Miscellaneous writings of Pascal.* Trans. by M. P. Faugère. London: Longmans, Brown, Green, & Longman, 1849. **B C**

——. *Pensées et opuscules.* Ed. by L. Brunschvicg. Paris: Hachette, 1934. (1867) **C**

——. *Oeuvres complètes.* Ed., intro., & notes by L. Brunschvicg *et al.* (14 vols.) Paris: Hachette, 1908–1925. **C**

——. *Pensées & The provincial letters.* Trans. by T. M. Crie & W. F. Trotter. New York: Random House, 1941. **C**

——. *Great shorter works of Pascal.* Trans. by E. Caillet & J. C. Blankenagel. Philadelphia: Westminster, 1948. **C**

——. Scientific treatises. Trans. by R. Schofield. In R. M. Hutchins (Ed.), *Pascal: Great books*

of the Western world. Vol. 33. Chicago: Encyclopaedia Britannica, 1952, pp. 353–487. **C**

——. *Oeuvres complètes.* Ed. by J. Chevalier. Paris: Gallimard, 1954. **B C**

——. *Pensées.* Trans. by A. J. Krailsheimer. Baltimore, Md.: Penguin Books, 1966. (1670)

——. *Pascal's Pensées.* Ed. in French and English by H. F. Stewart. London: Routledge & Kegan Paul, 1950. (1670)

Brinton, *Age Reason;* Hutchins, *Great Books;* Popkin, *Philosophy;* Slotkin, *Anthropology;* Smith, *Source Book*

DONALD GILDERSLEEVE PATERSON
1892-1961
American Psychologist (15)

Pintner, R., & Paterson, D. G. The Binet Scale and the deaf child. *J. educ. Psychol.,* 1915, *6,* 201–211; also in *Amer. Ann. Deaf,* 1915, *60,* 301–311.

Pintner, R., & ——. A class test with deaf children. *J. educ. Psychol.,* 1915, *6,* 591–600; also in *Amer. Ann. Deaf,* 1916, *61,* 264–275.

Pintner, R., & ——. The survey of a day-school for the deaf. *Amer. Ann. Deaf,* 1916, *61,* 417–433.

Pintner, R., & ——. A measurement of the language ability of deaf children. *Psychol. Rev.,* 1916, *23,* 413–436.

Pintner, R., & ——. The ability of deaf and hearing children to follow printed directions. *J. genet. Psychol.,* 1916, *23,* 477–497.

Pintner, R., & ——. Learning tests with deaf children. *Psychol. Monogr.,* 1916, *20,* No. 88.

Pintner, R., & ——. *A scale of performance tests.* New York: Appleton, 1917.

——. The vocational testing movement. *J. Personn. Res.,* 1923, *1,* 295–305.

——. The Scott Company's file clerk's test. *J. Personn. Res.,* 1923, *1,* 547–561.

——. Methods of rating human qualities. *Ann. Amer. Acad. Pol. Soc. Sci.,* 1923, *110,* 81–93.

————, & Tinker, M. A. Studies of typographical factors influencing speed of reading. I. Type form. II. Size of type. III. Length of line. IV. Effect of practice on equivalence of test forms. V. Simultaneous variation of type size and line length. VI. Black type versus white type. VII. Variations in color of print and background. VIII. Space between lines or leading. IX. Reduction in size of newspaper print. X. Styles of type face. XI. Role of set in typographical studies. XII. Printing surface. XIII. Methodological considerations. *J. appl. Psychol.*, 1928, *12*, 359–368 ; 1929, *13*, 120–130, 205–219 ; 1930, *14*, 211–217 ; 1931, *15*, 72–78, 241–247, 471–479 ; 1932, *16*, 388–397, 525–531, 605–613 ; 1935, *19*, 647–651 ; 1936, *20*, 128–131, 132–145.

————,, *et al. Minnesota Mechanical Ability Tests.* Minneapolis, Minn.: University of Minnesota Press, 1930.

————. *Physique and intellect.* New York: Century, 1930.

Harris, J. A., Scammon, R. E., ————, *et al. The measurement of man.* Minneapolis, Minn.: University of Minnesota Press, 1930.

————. *Research studies in individual diagnosis.* Minneapolis, Minn.: University of Minnesota Press, 1934.

————, & Darley, J. G. (with assist. of R. M Elliott). *Men, women and jobs: A study in human engineering.* Minneapolis, Minn.: University of Minnesota Press, 1936.

————, Schneidler, Gwendolen G., & Williamson, E. G. *Student guidance techniques: A handbook for counselors in high schools and colleges.* New York: McGraw-Hill, 1938.

————, & Tinker, M. A. *How to make type readable.* New York: Harper, 1940.

————. Applied psychology comes of age. *J. consult. Psychol.*, 1940, *4*, 1–9.

————, & Stone, C. H. Dissatisfaction with life work among adult workers. *Occupations*, 1942, *21*, 219–221.

————, & Tinker, M. A. The effect of typography upon the perceptual span in reading. *Amer. J. Psychol.*, 1947, *60*, 388–396.

————, & Jenkins, J. J. Communication between management and worker. *J. appl. Psychol.*, 1948, *32*, 71–80.

Yoder, D., ————, *et al. Local labor market research: A case study.* Minneapolis, Minn.: University of Minnesota Press, 1948.

————. The conservation of human talent. *Amer. Psychologist*, 1957, *12*, 134–144. Reprinted in D. Wolfle (Ed.), *The discovery of talent.* Cambridge: Harvard University Press, 1969, pp. 24–51.

Moore & Hartmann, *Industrial Psychology*

FREDERIC (M.) PAULHAN
1856-1931
French Psychologist (11)

Paulhan, F. L'erreur et la sélection. *Rev. phil.*, 1879, *8*, 72–86, 179–190, 291–306.

————. La personnalité. *Rev. phil.*, 1880, *10*, 49–67.

————. Les variations de la personnalité à l'état normal. *Rev. phil.*, 1882, *13*, 639–653.

————. L'obligation morale au point de vue intellectuel. *Rev. phil.*, 1883, *15*, 496–510.

————. Croyance et volonté. *Rev. phil.*, 1884, *18*, 675–684.

————. *Les caractères.* (5th ed.) Paris: Alcan, 1922. (1884)

————. *La physiologie de l'esprit.* Paris: Alcan, 1885.

————. Sur l'émotion esthétique . *Rev. phil.*, 1885, *19*, 652–667.

————. *The laws of feeling.* (4th ed.) Trans. by C. K. Ogden. New York: Harcourt, Brace, 1930. (1887)

————. La finalité comme propriété des éléments physiques. *Rev. phil.*, 1888, *26*, 105–140.

————. *L'activité mentale et les éléments de l'esprit.* (2nd ed.) Paris: Alcan, 1913. (1889)

————. L'art chez l'enfant. *Rev. phil.*, 1889, *28*, 596–606.

————. *Le nouveau mysticisme*. Paris: Alcan, 1891.

————. *Les types intellectuels: Esprits logiques et esprits faux*. Paris: Alcan, 1896.

————. *Psychologie de l'invention*. Paris: Alcan, 1900.

————. Les esprits synthétiques. *Rev. phil.*, 1900, *49*, 561–595.

————. La simulation dans le caractère. *Rev. phil.*, 1901, *52*, 600–625 ; 1902, *53*, 457–488 ; 1903, *56*, 337–365, 495–527.

————. *La volonté*. Paris: Doin, 1902.

————. *Analystes et esprits synthétiques*. Paris: Alcan, 1928. (1902)

————. La méthode analytique dans la détermination des caractères. *Rev. phil.*, 1902, *54*, 413–416.

————. Sur la mémoire affective. *Rev. phil.*, 1902, *54*, 545–569 ; 1903, *55*, 42–70.

————. *La fonction de la mémoire et le souvenir affectif*. Paris: Alcan, 1904.

————. Histoire d'un souvenir. *J. Psychol. norm. path.*, 1904, *1*, 321–331.

————. Herbert Spencer d'après son autobiographie. *Rev. phil.*, 1907, *64*, 145–158.

————. *La morale de l'ironie*. Paris: Alcan, 1909.

————. La logique de la contradiction. *Rev. phil.*, 1910, *69*, 113–143, 275–303. Also Paris: Alcan, 1911.

————. Les conditions générales de la connaissance. *Rev. phil.*, 1914, *77*, 581–610.

————. *Les transformations sociales des sentiments*. Paris: Flammarion, 1920.

————. Sur le psychisme inconscient. *J. Psychol. norm. path.*, 1921, *18*, 1–28, 146–165.

————. Tendances et faits psychologiques. *J. Psychol. norm. path.*, 1922, *19*, 385–411, 520–542.

————. L'influence psychologique et les associations du présentisme. I: Les traits de caractère subordonnés du présentiste. II: Quelques groupes de présentistes. *J. Psychol. norm. path.*, 1925, *22*, 193–235, 297–325.

————. Qu'est-ce que le sens des mots? *J. Psychol. norm. path.*, 1928, *25*, 289–329.

————. Le sens du rire. *Rev. phil.*, 1931, *56*, 5–47.

IVAN PETROVITCH PAVLOV
1849-1936
Russian Physiologist (27)

Pavlov, I. P. *(Twenty years of objective studies of the higher nervous activity (behavior) in animals: Conditioned reflexes.)* Moscow: Medgiz, 1951. (1923)   C

————. *Die höchste Nerventätigkeit (das Verhalten) von Tieren*. (3rd ed.) Trans. by G. Volborth. Munich: Bergmann, 1926. (1923)   C

————. *Conditioned reflexes: An investigation of the physiological activity of the cerebral cortex*. Trans. & ed. by G. V. Anrep. London: Oxford University Press, 1927. (1926) (Reprinted 1960)   Bl C

————. *Lectures on conditioned reflexes: Twenty-five years of objective study of the higher nervous activity (behaviour) of animals*. Vol. 1. Trans. by W. H. Gantt & G. Volborth. New York: International Publishers, 1928.   Bl C

————. *Pawlowsche Mittwochkolloquien. Protokolle und Stenogramme physiologischer Kolloquien*. (3 vols.) Berlin: Akademie-Verlag, 1955-1956. (1949)   C

————. *Vorlesungen über die Arbeit der Grosshirnhemisphären*. Trans. by G. W. Volborth. Leningrad: Medgiz, 1932.   C

————. *(The most recent reports of the physiology and pathology of the higher nervous activities.)* Leningrad: Akademia Nauk, 1933.   C

————. *Lectures on conditioned reflexes*. Vol. 2. *Conditioned reflexes and psychiatry*. Trans. by W. H. Gantt. New York: International Publishers, 1941.   C

————. *Drei Abhandlungen über die Tätigkeit der Grosshirnrinde aus den Jahren 1922, 1923 und 1925*. Ed. by A. Mette. Berlin: Volk & Gesundheit, 1952.   C

――――. *Ausgewählte Werke.* Berlin: Akademie-Verlag, 1953.   **C**

――――. *Sämtliche Werke* (6 vols. in 8.) Berlin: Akademie-Verlag, 1953–1955.   **C**

――――. *Selected works.* Ed. by J. Gibbons. Trans. by S. Belsky. Moscow: Foreign Languages Publishing House, 1955. [*Experimental psychology and other essays.* New York: Philosophical Library, 1957, is an edition of these papers with political allusions omitted.]   **Bl C**

――――. *Die Lehre I. P. Pavlovs und die philosophischen Fragen der Psychologie.* Ed. by Institute of Philosophy, Academy of Sciences, USSR. Berlin: Volk & Gesundheit, 1955.   **C**

――――. *Psychopathology and psychiatry: Selected works.* Ed. by Y. Popov & L. Roklin, & trans. by D. Myshne & S. Belsky. Moscow: Foreign Languages Publishing House, 1962.   **C**

――――. Essential works of Pavlov. Ed. by M. Kaplan. New York: Bantam, 1966.   **C**

――――. *(Correspondence of I. P. Pavlov.)* Ed. by N. M. Gureeva, E. S. Kuliabko & V. L. Merkulov. Leningrad: Nauka, 1970.   **B C**

――――. *The work of the digestive glands.* (2nd ed.) Trans. by W. H. Thompson. London: Griffin, 1910. (1897)

――――. Sur la sécrétion psychique des glandes salivaires (phénomènes nerveux complexes dans le travail de glandes salivaires). *Arch. int. Physiol.,* 1904, *1,* 119–135.

――――. Physiology of digestion. (1904) In Nobel Foundation (Ed.), *Nobel lectures: Physiology or medicine, 1901–1921.* New York: Elsevier, 1967, pp. 141–155.

――――. *Naturwissenschaft und Gehirn.* Trans. by G. W. Volborth. Wiesbaden: Bergmann, 1910.

――――. Des sciences naturelles et le cerveau. *J. Psychol. norm. path.,* 1912, *9,* 1–13.

――――. L'inhibition des réflexes conditionnels. *J. Psychol. norm. path.,* 1913, *10,* 1–15.

――――. Sur le centre de la faim. *J. Psychol. norm. path.,* 1921, *18,* 273–281.

――――. The identity of inhibition with sleep and hypnosis. *Sci. Mon.,* N.Y., 1923, *17,* 603–608.

――――. A brief outline of the higher nervous activity. In C. Murchison (Ed.), *Psychologies of 1930.* Worcester, Mass.: Clark University Press, 1930, pp. 207–221. Reprinted in *Lectures on conditioned reflexes,* Vol. 2, *op. cit.,* pp. 44–70.

――――. Essai de digression d'un physiologiste dans le domaine de la psychiatrie. *Arch. Int. pharmadocyn.,* 1930, *38,* 222–227.

――――. The reply of a physiologist to psychologists. *Psychol. Rev.,* 1932, *39,* 91–127. Reprinted in *Lectures on conditioned reflexes,* Vol. 2, *op. cit.,* pp. 117–145, & in *Selected works, op. cit.,* pp. 414–453.

――――. Die Physiologie der höchsten Nerventätigkeit. (1932) *Arch. Sci. biol.,* 1933, *18,* 15–29.

――――. Essai d'une interprétation physiologique de l'hystérie. *Encéphale,* 1933, *28,* 285–295.

――――, & Petrova, M. K. A contribution to the physiology of the hypnotic state of dogs. *J. Pers.,* 1933–1934, *2,* 189–200.

――――. An attempt at a physiological interpretation of obsessional neurosis and paranoia. *J. ment. Sci.,* 1934, *80,* 187–197.

――――. *(Experimental pathology of the higher nervous activity.)* Leningrad: Ogiz, 1935.

――――. Bequest of Pavlov to the academic youth of his country. Trans. by P. Kupalov. *Science,* 1936, *83,* 369.

――――. Autobiography, (n.d.) In *Selected works, op. cit.,* pp. 41–44.

Clarke & O'Malley, *Brain;* Dennis, *Psychology;* Fulton & Wilson, *Physiology;* Herrnstein & Boring, *Source Book;* Matson, *Being;* Parsons, *Society;* Perez, *Readings;* Sahakian, *Psychology;* Shipley, *Classics;* Wrenn, *Contributions*

KARL PEARSON
1857–1936
English Statistician (27)

Pearson, K. *The ethic of freethought, a selection of essays and lectures.* London: Black, 1901. (1888)   **C**

———. *The chances of death and other studies in evolution.* (2 vols.) New York: Arnold, 1897. **C**

———. *Early statistical papers.* Ed. by E. S. Pearson. Cambridge: Cambridge University Press, 1948. **C**

———. *The grammar of science.* (2nd ed.) London: Black, 1900. (1892)

———. *The grammar of science.* (3rd ed.) New York, Dutton, 1911. (1892) (Reprinted 1957)

———. Contributions to the mathematical theory of evolution. *Phil. Trans.,* 1894, *185A,* 71–110.

———. Contributions to the mathematical theory of evolution. II. Skew variation in homogenous material. *Phil. Trans.,* 1895, *186A,* 343–414.

———. Mathematical contributions to the theory of evolution. III. Regression heredity, and panmixia. *Phil. Trans.,* 1896, *187A,* 253–318. Reprinted in *Early statistical papers, op. cit.,* pp. 113–178.

Whiteley, A. M., & ———. Data for the problem in the evolution in man. *Proc. Roy. Soc.,* London, 1899, *65,* 126–152, 290–306.

———. On the criterion that a given system of deviations from the probable in the case of a correlated system of variables is such that it can be reasonably supposed to have arisen from random sampling. *Phil. Mag.,* 1900, *50,* 157–175. Reprinted in *Early statistical papers, op. cit.,* pp. 339–357.

———. Note on Francis Galton's problem. *Biometrika,* 1902, *1,* 390–399.

———. Inheritance of psychical and physical characters in man. *Nature,* 1903, *68,* 607–608.

———. The law of ancestral heredity. *Biometrika,* 1903, *2,* 211–229.

———, & Lee, Alice. On the laws of inheritance in man. I. Inheritance of physical characters. *Biometrika,* 1903, *2,* 357–462.

———. On the inheritance of the mental and moral characters in man, and its comparison with the inheritance of the physical characters. The Huxley lecture for 1903. *J. Anthrop. Inst. Gt. Brit.,* 1903, *33,* 179–237.

———. On the laws of inheritance in man. II. On the inheritance of the mental and moral characters in man, and its comparison with the inheritance of the physical characters. *Biometrika,* 1904, *3,* 131–190.

———. Mathematical contributions to the theory of evolution. XII. On a generalized theory of alternative inheritance, with special reference to Mendel's laws. *Phil. Trans.,* 1904, *203A,* 53–86.

———. On the criterion which may serve to test various theories of inheritance. *Proc. Roy. Soc.,* London, 1904, *73B,* 262–280.

———. Mathematical contributions to the theory of evolution. XIV. On the general theory of skew correlation and non-linear regression. *Drap. Co. Res. Mem., Biom. Ser. II,* 1905.

———. On the relationship of intelligence to size and shape of head, and to other physical and mental characters. *Biometrika,* 1906, *5,* 105–146.

Elderton, Ethel M., & ———. *A first study of the influence of parental alcoholism on the physique and ability of the offspring.* Univ. of London, Francis Galton Laboratory for National Eugenics, Eugenics Laboratory, Memoirs. Vol. 10. London: Dulau, 1910.

———. On the probability that two independent distributions of frequency are really samples from the same population. *Biometrika,* 1911, *8,* 250–254.

———. On the probable error of a coefficient of correlation as found from a fourfold table. *Biometrika,* 1913, *9,* 22–27.

———, & Jaederholm, G. A. *Mendelism and the problem of mental defect.* London: Dulau, 1914.

———. *The life, letters, and labours of Francis Galton.* (3 vols. in 4) Cambridge: University of Cambridge Press, 1914–1930.

——— (Ed.), *Tables for statisticians and biometricians.* (2 vols.) London: University College, Biometric Laboratory, 1931. (1914)

———. *On the handicapping of the first-born.* London: Dulau, 1914.

———. On the general theory of multiple contingency with special reference to partial contingency. *Biometrika*, 1916, *11*, 145–158.

———. The fundamental problem of practical statistics. *Biometrika*, 1920, *13*, 1–16.

———. Notes on the history of correlation, being a paper read to the Society of Biometricians and Mathematical Statisticians, June 14, 1920. *Biometrika*, 1920, *13*, 25–45. Reprinted in C. S. Pearson & M. G. Kendall (Eds.), *Studies in the history of statistics and probability*. London: Griffin, 1970, pp. 185–205.

———. *Tracts for computers*, No. II. *On the construction of tables and on interpolation: Part I. Univariate tables.* London: Cambridge University Press, 1920.

———. On the x^2 test of goodness of fit. *Biometrika*, 1922, *14*, 186–191. Further note. *Biometrika*, 1922, *14*, 418.

———. *Francis Galton, 1822–1922: A centenary appreciation.* London: Cambridge University Press, 1922.

———. *On the relationship of health to the psychical and physical characters in school children.* London: Cambridge University Press, 1923.

———. Historical note on the origin of the normal curve of errors. *Biometrika*, 1924, *16*, 402–404.

———, & Holzinger, K. Note on the sampling error of tetrad differences. *Brit. J. Psychol.*, 1925–1926, *16*, 86–88.

———. Researches on the mode of distribution of the constants of samples taken at random from a bivariate normal population. *Proc. Roy. Soc.*, 1926, *112A*, 1–14.

———. Laplace: Being extracts from the lectures delivered by Karl Pearson. *Biometrika*, 1929, *21*, 202–216.

———. On the inheritance of mental disease. *Ann. Eugen.*, Cambridge, 1930, *4*, 362–380.

———. On the nature of the relationship between two of "Student's" variates (z1 and z2) when samples are taken from a bivariate normal population. *Biometrika*, 1931, *23*, 405–422.

———. Some properties of "Student's" z: correlation, regression, and scedasticity of z with the mean and standard deviation of the sample. *Biometrika*, 1931, *23*, 1–9.

———. Further remarks on the "z" test. *Biometrika*, 1931, *23*, 408–415.

———, Stouffer, S. A., & David, F. N. Further applications in statistics of the Tm(x) Bessel function. *Biometrika*, 1932, *24*, 293–350.

———. Experimental discussion of the $(x^2 P)$ test for goodness of fit. *Biometrika*, 1932, *24*, 351–381.

———. On the probability that two independent distributions of frequency are really samples from the same parent population. *Biometrika*, 1932, *24*, 457–470.

———. On a method of determining whether a sample of size n supposed to have been drawn from a parent population having a known probability integral has probably been drawn at random. *Biometrika*, 1933, *25*, 379–410.

———. *Speeches delivered at a dinner held in University College, London, in honour of Professor Karl Pearson, 23 April, 1934.* Cambridge: privately printed, University Press, 1934.   **B**

———. Method of moments and method of maximum likelihood. *Biometrika*, 1936, *28*, 34–59.

———. The laws of chance in relation to thought and conduct: Gresham Lecture delivered in 1892. *Biometrika*, 1941, *32*, 89–100.

Anastasi, *Individual Differences*; Count, *Race*; Kroeber, *Source Book*

GEORGE WILLIAMS PECKHAM
1845-1914
American Biologist (12)

Peckham, G. W. Some observations on the mental powers of spiders. *J. Morphol.*, Boston, 1887, *1*, 383–419.

———, & Peckham, Elizabeth G. On the duration of memory in wasps. *Amer. Naturalist*, 1887, *21*, 1038–1040.

————. Observations on sexual selection in spiders of the family Attidae. *Occasion. Pap. Natur. Hist. Soc., Wisconsin,* 1889–1890, *1,* 3–60.

————, & Peckham, Elizabeth. Protective resemblances in spiders. *Occasion. Pap. Natur. Hist. Soc., Wisconsin,* 1889–1890, *1,* 61–113.

————, & Peckham, Elizabeth G. The sense of sight in spiders, with some observations on the color sense. *Trans. Wis. Acad. Sciences, Arts, Letters,* 1895, *10,* 231–261.

————, & Peckham, Elizabeth G. On the instincts and habits of the solitary wasps. *Wis. Geol. Nat. Hist. Survey Bull.,* 1898, No. 2.

————, & Peckham, Elizabeth G. Instinct or reason? *Amer. Naturalist,* 1900. *34,* 817–818.

————, & Peckham, Elizabeth. *Wasps, social and solitary.* Boston: Houghton Mifflin, 1905.

CHARLES SANTIAGO SANDERS PEIRCE
1839-1914
American Philosopher (19)

Peirce, C. S. *Chance, love, and logic: Philosophical essays.* Ed. by M. R. Cohen. New York: Harcourt, Brace, 1923. (Reprinted 1968) **C**

————. *Collected papers of Charles Sanders Peirce.* (8 vols. in 4) Ed. by C. Hartshorne, P. Weiss, & A. W. Burks. Cambridge: Harvard University Press, 1931–1958. **B Bl C**

————. *The philosophy of Peirce: Selected writings.* Ed. by J. Buchler. London: Routledge & Kegan Paul, 1940. (Reprinted 1955 as *Philosophical writings of Peirce*) **C**

————. *Charles S. Peirce's letters to Lady Welby.* Ed. by I. C. Lieb. New Haven: Whitlock, 1953. **B C**

————. *Essays in the philosophy of science.* Ed. by V. Tomas. Indianapolis, Ind.: Bobbs-Merrill, 1957. **C**

————. *Values in a universe of chance: Selected writings of Charles S. Peirce (1839–1914).* Ed. by P. P. Wiener. Stanford, Calif.: Stanford University Press, 1958. (Reprinted 1919) **C**

————. On an improvement in Boole's calculus of logic. *Proc. Amer. Acad. Arts Sci.,* 1867, *7,* 250–261. Reprinted in *Collected papers,* Vol. 3, *op. cit.,* pp. 1–19.

————. Philosophy of mind. (1867–1903) In *Collected papers,* Vol. 7, *op. cit.,* pp. 223–397.

————. Questions concerning certain faculties claimed for man. *J. spec. Phil.,* 1868, *2,* 103–114. Reprinted in *Collected papers,* Vol. 5, *op. cit.,* pp. 135–222, & in *Values in a universe of chance, op. cit.,* pp. 15–38.

————. *Some consequences of four incapacities. J. spec. Phil.,* 1868, *2,* 140–157. Reprinted in *Collected papers,* Vol. 5, *op. cit.,* pp. 156–189, & in *Values in a universe of chance, op. cit.,* pp. 39–72.

————. Review of the works of George Berkeley, D.D., formerly Bishop of Cloyne. Ed. by A. C. Fraser. *N. Amer. Rev.,* 1871, *113,* 449–472. Reprinted in *Collected papers,* Vol. 8, *op. cit.,* pp. 7–38, & in *Values in a universe of chance, op. cit.,* pp. 73–88.

————. On the theory of errors of observation. In *Report of the Superintendent of the United States Coast Survey showing the progress of the work for the fiscal year ending with June 1870,* Appendix 21. Washington: Government Printing Office, 1873, pp. 200–224.

————. The fixation of belief. *Pop. Sci. Mon.,* 1877, *12,* 1–15. Reprinted in *Values in a universe of chance, op. cit.,* pp. 91–112.

————. How to make our ideas clear. *Pop. Sci. Mon.,* 1877–1878, *12,* 286–302. Reprinted in *Collected papers,* Vol. 5, *op. cit.,* pp. 248–271 ; in *Values in a universe of chance, op. cit.,* pp. 113–136 ; & in *Essays in the philosophy of science, op. cit.,* pp. 31–56.

————. Photometric researches. *Ann. Astronom. Observ. Harvard Coll.,* 1878, No. 9.

————. On the algebra of logic. *Amer. J. Math.,* 1880, *3,* 15–57. Reprinted in *Collected papers,* Vol. 3, *op. cit.,* pp. 154–251.

————. A theory of probable inference. In C. S. Peirce (Ed.), *Studies in logic, by members of the Johns Hopkins University.* Boston: Little,

Brown, 1883, pp. 126–181. Reprinted in *Collected papers*, Vol. 2, *op. cit.*, pp. 694–754.

——, & Jastrow, J. On small differences of sensation. *Mem. Nat. Acad. Sci.*, 1884, *3*, 73–83. Reprinted in *Collected papers*, Vol. 7, *op. cit.*, pp. 13–27.

——. The architecture of theories. *Monist*, 1891, *1*, 161–176. Reprinted in *Collected papers*, Vol. 6, *op. cit.*, pp. 11–27, & in *Values in a universe of chance, op. cit.*, pp. 142–159.

——. The law of mind. *Monist*, 1891–1892, *2*, 533–559.

——. A detailed classification of the sciences. Section 1, Chap. 2, of *Minute logic*. (1902) In *Collected papers*, Vol. 1, *op. cit.*, pp. 83–137.

——. Critical analysis of logical theories. Chap. 1 of *Minute logic*, (1902) In *Collected papers*, Vol. 2, *op. cit.*, pp. 3–41.

——. Consciousness. Personal communication. (June 12, 1902) Reprinted in *Collected papers*, Vol. 8, *op. cit.*, pp. 195–198.

——. Pragmatism: The normative sciences. Lecture 1, delivered at Cambridge, Mass., 1903. In *Collected papers*, Vol. 5, *op. cit.*, pp. 13–28.

——. Three types of reasoning. Lecture 6, delivered at Cambridge, Mass., 1903. In *Collected papers*, Vol. 5, *op. cit.*, pp. 94–111.

——. The issues of pragmatism. *Monist*, 1905, *15*, 481–499. Reprinted in *Collected papers*, Vol. 5, *op. cit.*, pp. 293–313, & in *Values in a universe of chance, op. cit.*, pp. 203–223.

——. What pragmatism is. *Monist*, 1905, *15*, 161–181. Reprinted in *Collected papers*, Vol. 5, *op. cit.*, pp. 272–292, & in *Values in a universe of chance, op. cit.*, pp. 180–202.

——. Prolegomena to an apology for pragmaticism. *Monist*, 1906, *16*, 492–546. Reprinted in *Collected papers*, Vol. 4, *op. cit.*, pp. 411–463.

Ackerman, *Theories ;* Fisch, *Philosophers ;* Grob & Beck, *American Ideas ;* Madden, *Scientific Thought ;* Mann & Kreyche, *Reflections Man ;* Mueller, *American Philosophy ;* Newman, *Mathematics ;* Rorty, *Pragmatic Philosophy*

JOHANN HEINRICH PESTALOZZI
1746-1827
Swiss Educator (22)

Pestalozzi, J. H. *Pestalozzi-Bibliographie. Die Schriften und Briefe Pestalozzis nach der Zeitfolge. Schriften und Aufsätze über ihn nach Inhalt und Zeitfolge.* (3 vols.) Ed. by A. Israel. Berlin: Hoffmann, 1903–1904 (Suppl.), 1921–1923. (Reprinted 1963)   **Bl C**

——. *Pestalozzi's educational writings.* Trans. & ed. by J. A. Green with assist. of F. A. Collie. New York: Longmans, Green, 1912.   **C**

——. *Sämtliche Werke.* (Ult 21 vols.) Ed. by A. Buchenau, E., Spranger, & H. Stettbacher. Berlin: de Gruyter, 1927–1963.   **Bl C**

——. *Pestalozzi.* Ed. by L. F. Anderson. New York: McGraw-Hill, 1931.   **C**

——. *Werke. Gedenkausgabe.* (8 vols.) Ed. by P. Baumgartner. Zurich: Erlenbach, 1944–1949.   **C**

——. *Sämtliche Briefe.* (4 vols.) Ed. by A. Buchenau. Zurich: Füssli, 1946–1951.   **C**

——. *The education of man, aphorisms.* Trans. by H. & Ruth Norden. New York: Philosophical Library, 1951.   **C**

——. *Leonard and Gertrude.* Trans. & abridged by Eva Channing. Boston: Heath, 1906. (1781)

——. Leonard and Gertrude. (1781) In H. Bernard (Ed.), *Pestalozzi and Pestalozzianism.* (2nd ed.) New York: Brownell, 1859, pp. 9–134.

——. Christopher and Alice: Selections. (1782) In H. Barnard (Ed.), *Pestalozzi and Pestalozzianism, op. cit.*, pp. 151–154.

——. *How Gertrude teaches her children.* (5th ed.) Trans. by Lucy Holland & Frances C. Turner, & ed. by E. Cook, Syracuse, N.Y.: Bardeen, 1915. (1798)

——. *Letters on early education.* Syracuse, N.Y.: Bardeen, 1906. (1827)

Cubberley, *Public Educators ;* Kessen, *Child ;* Ulich, *Educational Wisdom*

EDUARD FRIEDRICH WILHELM PFLUGER
1829-1910
German Physiologist (18)

Pflüger, E. F. W. Die psychischen Funktionen der Medulla oblongata und spinalis. *Arch. Anat. Physiol.*, 1851, 484–494.

————. *Die sensorischen Funktionen des Rückenmarks der Wirbeltiere nebst einer neuen Lehre über die Leitungsgesetze der Reflexionen.* Berlin: Hirschwald, 1853.

————. *Untersuchungen über die Physiologie des Electrotonus.* Berlin: Hirschwald, 1859.

————. *Ueber die Eierstöcke der Säugetiere und der Menschen.* Leipzig: Engelmann, 1863.

————. Kritische und experimentelle Untersuchungen zur Theorie der Hemmungsnerven. In *Untersuchungen aus dem physiologischen Laboratorium zu Bonn.* Berlin: Hirschwald, 1865, pp. 1–52.

————. Ueber die elektrischen Empfindungen. (1865) In *Untersuchungen aus dem physiologischen Laboratorium zu Bonn, op. cit.,* pp. 144–172.

————. Ueber die Diffusion der Sauerstoffe, den Ort und die Gesetze der Oxydationprozesse im tierischen Organismus. *Arch. Physiol.*, 1872, *6*, 43–64, 190.

————. Theorie des Schlafes. *Arch. Physiol.*, 1875, *10*, 468–478.

————. *Die teleologische Mechanik der lebendigen Natur.* Bonn: Cohen, 1877.

————. *Wesen und Aufgaben der Physiologie.* Bonn: Strauss, 1878.

————. Ueber den Einfluss der Schwerkraft auf die Teilung der Zellen und auf die Entwicklung des Embryos. *Arch. ges. Physiol.*, 1883, *31*, 311–318, *32*, 1–79.

————. Das Glycogen und seine Beziehung zur Zuckerkrankheit. *Arch. ges. Physiol.*, 1903, *96*, 1–398. (Also Bonn: Cohen, 1905)

————. Ueber den elementaren Bau des Nervensystems. *Arch. ges. Physiol.*, 1906, *112*, 1–69.

Clarke & O'Malley, *Brain*

OSKAR PFUNGST
1874-1932
German Psychiatrist (14)

Pfungst, O. *Clever Hans: The horse of Mr. von Osten.* Ed. by R. Rosenthal, & trans. by C. L. Rahn. New York: Holt, Rinehart & Winston, 1965. (1911)

————. Zur Psychologie der Affen. In *Berichte V. Kongress experimentelle Psychologie.* Leipzig: Barth, 1912, pp. 200–205.

————. Ueber "sprechende" Hunde. In *Berichte V. Kongress experimentelle Psychologie.* Leipzig: Barth, 1912, pp. 241–245.

————. Versuche und Beobachtungen an jungen Wölfen. In *Berichte VI. Kongress experimentelle Psychologie.* Leipzig: Barth, 1914, pp. 127–132.

————. Neue Dressurergebnisse. *Jb. Psychol. Neurol.*, 1920–1921, *26*, 318–320.

HENRI PIERON
1881-1964
French Psychologist (27)

Piéron, H., & Vaschide, N. *La psychologie du rêve au point de vue médical.* Paris: Baillière, 1902.

————. Le temps d'association simple. *Rev. psychiat.*, 1903, *55*, 515–518.

————, Toulouse, E., & Vaschide, N. *Technique de psychologie expérimentale.* (2nd ed.) (2 vols.) Paris: Doin, 1911. (1904)

————. Du rôle du sens musculaire dans l'orientation de certaines espèces de fourmis. *Bull. Inst. gén. psychol.* Paris, 1904, *4*, 168–185.

————. Grandeur et décadence des rayons N. Histoire d'une croyance. *Année psychol.*, 1907, *13*, 143–169.

————. *L'évolution de la mémoire.* Paris: Flammarion, 1910.

————. *Le problème physiologique du sommeil.* Paris: Masson, 1913.

————. Recherches expérimentales sur les phénomènes de mémoire. *Année psychol.*, 1913, *19*, 91–193.

——. I: Des réflexes labyrinthiques provoqués par excitation unilatérale. II: Des réflexes toxiques relevant du fonctionnement normal ou de l'excitation bilatérale des labyrinthes. *C. r. Soc. biol.*, 1918, *81*, 540–544, 545–550.

——. De l'interprétation des troubles labyrinthiques qui se manifestent dans la réflectivité tonique dans la rotation et dans la marche. *C. r. Soc. biol.*, 1918, *81*, 661–675.

——. Nouvelles recherches sur l'analyse du temps de latence sensorielle et sur la loi qui relie ce temps à l'intensité de l'excitation. *Année psychol.*, 1920–1921, *22*, 58–142.

——. Le mécanisme d'apparition des couleurs subjectives de Fechner-Benham. *Année psychol.*, 1922, *23*, 1–49.

——. L'orientation auditive latéral. *Année psychol.*, 1922, *23*, 186–213.

——. Le problème des sensations de douleur. *J. Psychol. norm. path.*, 1923, *20*, 482–489.

——. Les problèmes psycho-physiologiques de la perception du temps. *Année psychol.*, 1923, *24*, 1–26.

——. *Thought and the brain.* Trans. by C. K. Ogden. New York: Harcourt, Brace, 1927. (1923)

Dumas, G., & ——. L'excitation et le mouvement. Les réflexes sus-élémentaires. In G. Dumas (Ed.), *Traité de psychologie.* Vol. 1. Paris: Alcan, 1923, pp. 233–317.

——. L'habitude et la mémoire. In G. Dumas (Ed.), *Traité de psychologie.* Vol. 1. Paris: Alcan, 1923, pp. 771–819.

——. La psychologie zoologique. In G. Dumas (Ed.), *Traité de psychologie.* Vol. 2. Paris: Alcan, 1924, pp. 635–702.

——. *Psychologie expérimentale.* Paris: Colin, 1927. (1925)

——. Recherches expérimentales sur la marge de variation du temps de latence de la sensation lumineuse (par une méthode de masquage). *Année psychol.*, 1925, *26*, 1–30.

——. Des données que fournit sur le mécanisme de l'excitation lumineuse: L'étude du temps de latence sensorielle. *Année psychol.*, 1925, *26*, 92–106.

——. Les problèmes de la perception et la psychophysiologie. *Année psychol.*, 1926, *27*, 1–22.

——. Les lois de l'excitabilité lumineuse des lamellibranches. Recherches sur la loi de variation des énergies liminaires chez Mya arenaria. *Bull. stat. biol. Arachon*, 1926, *23*, 25–56.

——. La psychologie comme science du comportement et le behaviorisme. *J. Psychol. norm. path.*, 1927, *24*, 93–98.

——. Excitation lumineuse intermittente et excitation alternante. Caractéristiques et lois. *Année psychol.*, 1927, *28*, 98–126.

——. *Principles of experimental psychology.* Trans. by J. H. Miner. New York: Harcourt, Brace, 1929. (1925)

——. *Les sensibilités cutanées.* (3 vols.) Paris: Chahine & Maloine, 1928–1932.

——. Emotion in animals and man. In M. L. Reymert (Ed.), *Feelings and emotions: The Wittenberg symposium.* Worcester, Mass.: Clark University Press, 1928, pp. 284–294.

——. Les lois générales de la sensation. *J. Psychol. norm. path.*, 1928, *25*, 507–545.

——. La dissociation des douleurs cutanées et la differentiation des conducteurs algiques. *Année psychol.*, 1929, *30*, 1–24.

——. De la sommation spatiale des impressions lumineuses au niveau de la fovéa. *Année psychol.*, 1929, *30*, 87–105.

——. La sensation chromatique. Données sur la latence propre et l'établissement des sensations de couleur. *Année psychol.*, 1931, *32*, 1–29.

——. Les bases sensorielles de la connaissance. *Année psychol.*, 1932, *33*, 1–14.

Durup, G., & ——. Recherches au sujet de l'interprétation du phénomène de Purkinje par des différences dans les courbes de sensation des récepteurs chromatiques. *Année psychol.*, 1932, *33*, 57–83.

. L'attention. In G. Dumas, (Ed.), *Nouveau traité de psychologie.* Vol. 4. Paris: Alcan, 1934, pp. 3–66.

. L'habitude et la mémoire. In G. Dumas (Ed.), *Nouveau traité de psychologie.* Vol. 4. Paris: Alcan, 1934, pp. 67–136.

. Le problème du mécanisme physiologique impliqué par l'échelon différentiel de sensation. *Année psychol.,* 1934, *35,* 217–236.

. Le toucher. In G. H. Roger & L. Binet (Eds.) *Traité de physiologie normale et pathologique.* Vol. 10(2). Paris: Masson, 1935, pp. 1055–1228.

. Recherches expérimentales sur la sensation vibratoire cutanée. *Année psychol.,* 1935, *36,* 82–102.

. La connaissance sensorielle et les problèmes de la vision. Paris: Hermann, 1936.

. L'évolution de la sensation lumineuse. *Amer. J. Psychol.,* 1937, *50,* 23–32.

, & Segal, J. Recherches sur la sensibilité tactile digitale par stimulation électrique du nerf cutané. *Année psychol.,* 1938, *39,* 89–135.

. Physiologie de la vision. In Bailliart, P., et al., *Traité d'ophthalmologie.* Vol. 2. Paris: Masson, 1939, pp. 497–768.

. La dissociation de l'adaptation lumineuse et de l'adaptation chromatique et ses conséquences théoriques. *Année psychol.,* 1939, *40,* 1–14.

. Le Laboratoire de Psychologie de la Sorbonne. In Various, *Centenaire de Th. Ribot et Jubilé de la Psychologie Scientifique Française.* Paris: Imprimerie moderne, 1939, pp. 185–196.

, & Segal, J. Sur un phénomène de facilitation rétroactive dans l'excitation électrique de branches nerveuses cutanées (sensibilité tactile). *J. neurophysiol.,* 1939, *2,* 178–191.

. Les problèmes de la sensibilité vibratoire. *J. Psychol. norm. path.,* 1940–1941, *37–38,* 521–525.

. Psychologie zoologique. In G. Dumas (Ed.), *Nouveau traité de psychologie.* Vol. 8(1), Paris: Alcan, 1941, pp. 1–255.

Galifret, Y., & . Etude des fréquences critiques de fusion pour des stimulations chromatiques intermittentes à brillance constante. *Année psychol.,* 1944–1945, *45–46,* 1–15.

. La sensation, guide de vie. Paris: Gallimard, 1945.

. The sensations, their functions, processes, and mechanisms. Trans. by M. H. Pirenne & B. C. Abbott. New Haven: Yale University Press, 1952. (1945)

. De l'actinie à l'homme. (2 vols.) Paris: Presses Universitaires de France, 1958–1959.

Galifret, Y., & . La transmission intra-rétinienne de l'excitation lumineuse. *Année psychol.,* 1948, *49,* 1–19.

. Les problèmes psychophysiologiques de la douleur. *Année psychol.,* 1948, *49,* 359–372.

. Des relations entre psychologie et physiologie et du domaine propre de la psychophysiologie. *J. Psychol. norm. path.,* 1948, *41,* 401–414.

(Ed.), *Traité de psychologie appliquée* (7 vols.) Paris: Presses Universitaires de France, 1949–1959.

. La psychologie différentielle. (1949) In *Traité de psychologie appliquée,* Vol. 1, *op. cit.,* pp. 1–123.

. Sensory affectivity. In M. L. Reymert (Ed.), *Feelings and emotions: The Mooseheart symposium.* New York: McGraw-Hill, 1950, pp. 76–83.

. Quels sont les déterminants de la prégnance perceptive? *Acta psychol.,* 1950, *7,* 337–351.

. Vocabulaire de la psychologie. (4th ed.) Paris: Presses Universitaires de France, 1968. (1951)

. Les problèmes fondamentaux de la psychophysique dans la science actuelle. Paris: Hermann, 1951.

. Henri Piéron. In E. G. Boring et al. (Eds.), *A history of psychology in autobiography.* Vol. 4. Worcester, Mass.: Clark University Press, 1952, pp. 257–278.

B

———. Histoire succincte des congrès internationaux de psychologie. *Année psychol.,* 1954, *54,* 397–405.

———, Heyer, G., Mme H. Piéron, & Sauvy, H. *Le niveau intellectuel des enfants d'âge scolaire.* (2 vols.) Preface by H. Laugier. Paris: Presses Universitaires de France, 1954–1955.

———. Le maniement de la perception. (1955) In *Traité de psychologie appliquée,* Vol. 5, *op. cit.,* pp. 959–1091.

———. Conditionnement et psychologie. In A. Fessard *et al.* (Eds.), *Le conditionnement et l'apprentissage.* Paris: Presses Universitaires de France, 1958, pp. 3–14.

———. Les échelles subjectives peuvent-elles fournir la base d'une nouvelle loi psychophysique? *Année psychol.,* 1959, *59,* 1–34.

———. Pierre Janet: Quelques souvenirs. *Psychol. franç.,* 1960, *5,* 81–92.

———. *La vision en lumière intermittente.* Paris: C.N.R.S., 1961.

———. *Examens et docimologie.* Paris: Presses Universitaires de France, 1963.

———. Discours d'Henri Piéron pour le 75e anniversaire du Laboratoire de Psychologie de la Sorbonne. *Année psychol.,* 1965, *65,* 6–15. **B**

———. Vision of intermittent light. Trans. by L. M. Hurvich & Dorothea Jameson. *Cont. sens. Physiol.,* 1965, *1,* 179–264.

———. *L'homme, rien que l'homme.* Paris: Presses Universitaires de France, 1967.

Huber, W., ———, & Vergote, A. *La psychanalyse, science de l'homme.* Brussels: Dessart, 1967.

Hameline, *Anthologie*

WALTER BOWERS PILLSBURY
1872-1960
American Psychologist (21)

Pillsbury, W. B. Some questions of the cutaneous sensibility. *Amer. J. Psychol.,* 1895, *7,* 42–57.

———. A study in apperception. *Amer. J. Psychol.,* 1897, *8,* 315–393.

———. Does the sensation of movement originate in the joint? *Amer. J. Psychol.,* 1901, *12,* 346–353.

———. The ego and empirical psychology. *Phil. Rev.,* 1907, *16,* 387–407.

———. *Attention.* New York: Macmillan, 1908.

Calkins, Mary W., & ———. The ego and empirical psychology. *Psychol. Bull.,* 1908, *5,* 27–30, 60–62.

———. Meaning and image. *Psychol. Rev.,* 1908, *15,* 150–158.

———. *The psychology of reasoning.* New York: Appleton, 1910. (Reprinted 1970)

———. *The essentials of psychology.* New York: Macmillan, 1911.

———. The place of movement in consciousness. *Psychol. Rev.,* 1911, *18,* 83–99.

———. *The fundamentals of psychology.* (3rd ed.) New York: Macmillan, 1934. (1916)

———, & Meader, C. L. *The psychology of language.* New York: Appleton, 1928.

———. The utility of emotions. In M. L. Reymert (Ed.), *Feelings and emotions: The Wittenberg symposium.* Worcester, Mass.: Clark University Press, 1928, pp. 116–123.

———. The psychology of Edward Bradford Titchener. *Phil. Rev.,* 1928, *37,* 95–108.

———. *The history of psychology.* New York: Norton, 1929. (Reprinted 1970)

———. Walter B. Pillsbury. In C. Murchison (Ed.), *A history of psychology in autobiography.* Vol. 2. Worcester, Mass.: Clark University Press, 1932, pp. 265–295. **B**

———. Knowledge in modern psychology. *Psychol. Rev.,* 1950, *57,* 328–333.

———. The concept in psychology. *Année psychol.,* 1951, *51,* 97–104.

ALFONS PILZECKER
1865-ca 1920
German Psychologist (15)

Pilzecker, A. *Die Lehre von der sinnlichen Aufmerksamkeit.* Munich: Straub, 1889.

Müller, G. E., & ———. Experimentelle Beiträge zur Lehre vom Gedächtnis, *Z. Psychol.,* 1900, Suppl. 1. (Also Leipzig: Barth, 1900.) (Reprinted 1970)

PHILIPPE PINEL
1745-1826
French Psychiatrist (25)

Pinel, P. Observations sur une espèce particulière de mélancolie qui conduit au suicide. *Méd. écl.,* 1791, *1,* 154–199.

———. Mémoire sur la manie périodique ou intermittente. *Mém. soc. méd. émul.,* 1797, *1,* 94–119.

———. Recherches et observations sur le traitement moral des aliénés. *Mém. soc. méd. émul.,* 1798, *2,* 215–255.

———. *Nosographie philosophique, ou la méthode de l'analyse appliquée à la médecine.* (6th ed.) (3 vols.) Paris: Brosson, 1818. (1798)

———. Observations sur les aliénés et leur division en espèces distinctes. *Mém. soc. méd. émul.,* 1800, *3,* 1–26.

———. *A treatise on insanity.* Trans. by D. D. Davis. New York: Hafner, 1962. (1801) Scattered excerpts in W. Riese, *The legacy of Philippe Pinel: An inquiry into thought on mental alienation.* New York: Springer, 1969.

———. Introduction to the first edition of Pinel's "Traité." (1801) In W. Riese, *The legacy of Philippe Pinel: An inquiry into thought on mental alienation.* New York: Springer, 1969, pp. 30–49.

———. Medical philosophical treatise on mental alienation. (Excerpts) (1801) *Occup. Ther.,* 1947, *26,* 63–68.

———. *La médecine clinique rendue plus précise et plus exacte par l'application de l'analyse.* (3rd ed.) Paris: Brosson, 1815. (1802)

———. Résultat d'observations pour servir de base aux rapports juridiques dans les cas d'aliénation mentale. *Mém. soc. méd. émul.,* 1817, *8,* 675–684.

———. Rapport sur un mémoire par M. Esquirol, ayant pour titre "hallucination." *J. Physiol.,* 1817, *85,* 229–235.

———. Documents sur Philippe Pinel, recueillis et commentés. Ed. by G. Bollotte. *Inform. psychiat.,* 1968, *44,* 823–844.

———. Pinel et la réforme de l'enseignement de l'art de guérir. Un manuscrit inédit. Ed. by G. Bollotte. *Inform. psychiat.,* 1970, *46,* 657–668.

———. Un manuscrit inédit de Pinel sur l'enseignement de la médecine. Ed. by G. Bollotte. *Inform. psychiat.,* 1971, *47,* 105–128.

Goshen, *Documentary;* Hunter & Macalpine, *Psychiatry;* Matson, *Being;* Shipley, *Classics*

RUDOLF PINTNER
1884-1942
American Psychologist (18)

Pintner, R., & Paterson, D. G. The Binet Scale and the deaf child. *J. educ. Psychol.,* 1915, *6,* 201–210; also in *Amer. Ann. Deaf,* 1915, *60,* 301–311.

———, & Paterson, D. G. A class test with deaf children. *J. educ. Psychol.,* 1915, *6,* 591–600; also in *Amer. Ann. Deaf,* 1916, *61,* 264–275.

———, & Paterson, D. G. A measurement of the language ability of deaf children. *Psychol. Rev.,* 1916, *23,* 413–436.

———, & Paterson, D. G. The survey of a day-school for the deaf. *Amer. Ann. Deaf,* 1916, *61,* 417–433.

———, & Paterson, D. G. Learning tests with deaf children. *Psychol. Monogr.,* 1916, *20,* No. 88.

———, & Paterson, D. G. The ability of deaf and hearing children to follow printed directions. *J. genet. Psychol.,* 1916, *23,* 477–497.

————, & Anderson, Margaret M. The Müller-Lyer illusion with children and adults. *J. exp. Psychol.*, 1916, *1*, 200–210.

————, & Anderson, Margaret M. *The picture completion test.* Baltimore, Md.: Warwick & York, 1917.

————, & Paterson, D. G. A comparison of deaf and hearing children in visual memory for digits. *J. exp. Psychol.*, 1917, *2*, 76–88.

————. The mentality of the dependent child, together with a plan for a mental survey of an institution. *J. educ. Psychol.*, 1917, *8*, 220–238.

————, & Paterson, D. G. Psychological tests ot deaf children. *Volta Rev.*, 1917, *19*, 661–667.

————, & Paterson, D. G. *A scale of performance tests.* (2nd ed.) New York: Appleton, 1921. (1917)

————. The value of mental tests in the classification of pupils. *Amer. Ann. Deaf*, 1918, *63*, 196–204.

————, & Toops, H. A. A revised directions test. *J. educ. Psychol.*, 1918, *9*, 123–142.

————. Intelligence as estimated from photographs. *Psychol. Rev.*, 1918, *25*, 286–296.

————. *The mental survey.* New York: Appleton, 1918.

————. A non-language group intelligence test. *J. appl. Psychol.*, 1919, *3*, 199–214.

————. Intelligence and its measurement: A symposium. *J. educ. Psychol.*, 1921, *12*, 139–143.

————, & Cunningham, Bess V. The problem of group intelligence tests for very young children. *J. educ. Psychol.*, 1922, *13*, 465–472.

————. *Intelligence testing: Methods and results.* (2nd ed.) New York: Holt, 1931. (1923)

Thomson, G. H., & ————. Spurious correlation and relationship between tests. *J. educ. Psychol.*, 1924, *15*, 433–444.

————. Results obtained with the non-language group test. *J. educ. Psychol.*, 1924, *15*, 473–483.

————. *Educational psychology: An introductory text.* New York: Holt, 1929.

————. The individual in school. I. General ability. In C. Murchison (Ed.), *The foundations of experimental psychology.* Worcester, Mass.: Clark University Press, 1929, pp. 661–704.

————. The feebleminded child. In C. Murchison (Ed.), *Handbook of child psychology.* (2nd rev. ed.) Worcester, Mass.: Clark University Press, 1933, pp. 802–841. (1931)

————. Intelligence and month of birth. *J. appl. Psychol.*, 1931, *15*, 149–154.

————. The influence of language background on intelligence tests. *J. soc. Psychol.*, 1932, *3*, 235–240.

————, & Forlano, G. The influence of month of birth on intelligence quotients. *J. educ. Psychol.*, 1933, *24*, 561–584.

————, Maller, J. B., Forlano, G., & Axelrod, H. The measurement of pupil adjustment. *J. educ. Res.*, 1934–1935, *28*, 334–346.

————, & Forlano, G. The birth month of eminent men. *J. appl. Psychol.*, 1934, *18*, 178–188.

————, & Stanton, Mildred. Repeated tests with CAVD Scale. *J. educ. Psychol.*, 1937, *28*, 494–500.

————, & Forlano, G. The influence of attitude upon scaling of attitude items. *J. soc. Psychol.*, 1937, *8*, 39–45.

————, & Maller, J. B. Month of birth and average intelligence among different ethnic groups. *J. genet. Psychol.*, 1937, *50*, 91–107.

————, Fusfeld, I. S., & Brunschwig, Lily. Personality tests of deaf adults. *J. genet. Psychol.*, 1937, *51*, 305–327.

————, & Arsenian, S. The relation of bilingualism to verbal intelligence and school adjustment. *J. educ. Res.*, 1937–1938, *31*, 255–263.

————, & Lev, J. The intelligence of the hard-of-hearing school child. *J. genet. Psychol.*, 1939, *55*, 31–48.

————, & Forlano, G. Season of birth and intelligence. *J. genet. Psychol.*, 1939, *54*, 353–358.

————, Eisenson, J., & Stanton, Mildred. *The psychology of the physically handicapped.* New York: Crofts, 1941.

————, & Forlano, G. Season of birth and intelligence. *J. genet. Psychol.*, 1942, *61*, 81–86.

————. Intelligence testing of partially sighted children. *J. educ. Psychol.*, 1942, *33*, 265–272.

————, & Forlano, G. Season of birth and mental differences. *Psychol. Bull.*, 1943, *40*, 25–35.

JOSEPH ANTOINE FERDINAND PLATEAU
1801-1883
Belgian Physiologist (18)

Plateau, J. A. F. *Dissertation sur quelques propriétés des impressions produites par la lumière sur l'organe de la vue.* Liège: Dessain, 1829.

————. Ueber einige Eigenschaften der vom Licht auf das Gesichtsorgan hervorgebrachten Eindrücke. *Ann. Phys. Leipzig*, 1830, *20*, 304–332.

————. Essai d'une théorie générale comprenant: 1. La persistance des impressions de la rétine; 2. Les couleurs accidentelles; 3. L'irradiation; 4. Les effets de la juxtaposition des couleurs, les ombres colorées. *Ann. Chimie*, 1835, *58*, 377–407.

————. L'irradiation. *Bull. Acad. sci. Bruxelles*, 1837, *4*, 355–358; 1839, *6*, 501–505.

————. Sur de nouvelles applications curieuses de la persistance des impressions de la rétine. *Bull. Acad. sci. Bruxelles*, 1849, *16*, 424–428, 588–611.

————. Sur la mesure des sensations physiques et sur la loi qui lie l'intensité de ces sensations à l'intensité de la cause excitante. *C.r. Acad. Sci.*, 1872, *75*, 677–680. Also in *Bull. Acad. roy. Belg.*, 1872, *33*, 376–388.

————. Bibliographie analytique des principaux phénomènes subjectifs de la vision, depuis les temps anciens jusqu'à la fin du XVIIIe siècle, suivie d'une bibliographie simple pour la partie écoulée du siècle actuel. *Mém. Acad. roy. soc.*, *Belg.*, 1878, *42*, (No. 1); 1882, *43* (No. II).

STEPHEN POLYAK
1889-1955
Yugoslavian-American Anatomist (12)

Polyak, S. Die Struktureigentümlichkeiten des Rückenmarkes bei den Chiropteren. (Zugleich ein Beitrag zu der Frage über die spinalen Zentren des Sympathicus.) *Z. Anat. Entw.*, 1924, *74*, 509–576.

————. The connections of the acoustic nerve. *J. Anat.*, 1926, *60*, 465–469.

————. Die Verbindungen der Area striata (intrahemisphärale, kommissurale, palliodienzephalische, palliotektale Fasern) bei der Katze und deren funktionelle Bedeutung. *Z. ges. Neurol. Psychiat.*, 1926, *100*, 545–563.

————. Untersuchungen am Oktavussystem der Säugetiere und an den mit diesem koordinierten motorischen Apparaten des Hirnstammes. *J. Psychol. Neurol.*, 1926, *32*, 170–231.

————. An experimental study of the association, callosal, and projection fibers of the cerebral cortex of the cat. *J. comp. Neurol.*, 1927, *44*, 197–258.

————. Ueber den allgemeinen Bauplan des Gehörsystem und über seine Bedeutung für die Physiologie, für die Klinik und für die Psychologie. *Z. ges. Neurol. Psychiat.*, 1927, *110*, 1–49.

————. Die zuführenden Bahnen des Vorderhirns und ihre Rindenbeziehungen auf Grund experimenteller Untersuchungen an Affen. *Z. ges. Neurol. Psychiat.*, 1930, *125*, 138–162.

————. *The main afferent fiber system of the cerebral cortex in primates.* Berkeley, Calif.: University of California Press, 1932.

————. A contribution to the cerebral representation of the retina. *J. comp. Neurol.*, 1933, *57*, 541–617.

————, & Hayashi, R. The cerebral representation of the retina in the chimpanzee. *Brain*, 1936, *59*, 51–60.

————. Minute structure of the retina in monkeys an in apes. *Arch. Ophthalm.*, 1936, *15*, 477–519.

————. *The retina.* Chicago: University of Chicago Press, 1941. (Corrected reprint, 1948)

———. Anatomy of the retina. *Biol. Symp.,* 1942, 7, 193–202.

———. Retinal structure and colour vision. *Doc. ophthalm.,* 1949, 3, 24–56.

———. Santiago Ramón y Cajal and his investigation of the nervous system. *J. comp. Neurol.,* 1953, 98, 1–7.

———. *The vertebrate visual system.* Ed. by H. Klüver. Chicago: University of Chicago Press, 1957.

MacAdam, *Color Science*

MARIO PONZO
1882-1960
Italian Psychologist (15)

Ponzo, M. Studio della localizzazione delle sensazioni cutanee di dolore. *Mem. r. Accad. sci. Torino,* 1909, Ser. 2, 61, 15–54.

———. Intorno ad alcune illusioni nel campo delle sensazioni tattili, sull'illusione di Aristotele e fenomeni analoghi. *Arch. ges. Psychol.,* 1910, 16, 307–345.

Kiesow, F., & ———. Beobachtungen über die Reaktionszeiten der Temperaturempfindungen. *Arch. ges. Psychol.,* 1910, 16, 376–396.

———. Recherches sur la localisation des sensations tactiles et des sensations dolorifiques. *Arch. ital. Biol.,* 1911, 55, 1–14.

Kiesow, F., & ———. Observations sur les temps de réaction pour les sensations thermiques. *Arch. ital. Biol.,* 1911, 56, 216–224.

———. Étude de la localisation des sensations thermiques de chaud et de froid. *Arch. ital. Biol.,* 1913, 60, 218–231.

———. Caractéristiques individuelles et familiales des courbes pneumographiques dans les réactions phonétiques. *Arch. ital. Biol.,* 1915, 64, 306–312.

———. *Alla ricerca delle attitudini nei giovani.* Turin: Paravia, 1929.

———. Principi e fattori del dinamismo psichico nelle ricerche della scuola di psicologia di Torino. *Arch. ital. Psicol.,* 1931, 9, 1–30.

Gemelli, A., & ———. I fattori psicofisici predisponenti all'infortunio stradale e le prospettive di organizzazione psicotecnica preventiva. *Atti 2 Cong. Soc. Ital. med. soc.,* 1932, 1934.

Angyal, A., & ———. Zur Systematik der Gewichtsempfindungen. *Arch. ges. Psychol.,* 1933, 88, 629–634.

———. Attualità e visioni del'avvenire nell'opera di Sante De Sanctis. *Riv. Psicol. norm. pat.,* 1936, 32, 1–26.

———. L'Istituto di Psicologia della R. Università di Roma nella nuova sede ed i suoi compiti. *Arch. Psicol. Neurol. Psichiat.,* 1939, 1, 10–27.

———. Contributi della scuola di Psicologia di Roma alla conoscenza dell'adottamento psicomotorio. *Arch. Psicol. Neurol. Psichiat.,* 1941, 2, 257–271.

———. Die Schule in Italien und das Problem der Eignungsbestimmung und Ausrichtung der Schüler. *Z. angew. Psychol.,* 1942, 63, 249–289.

———. La psicotecnica nella scuola e nel lavoro. Contributi dell'Istituto di psicologia dell'Università di Roma nel perioda 1940–1946. *Arch. Psicol. Neurol. Psichiat.,* 1947, 8, 83–136.

———. Psicologia dell'azione e comprensione della personalità. *Riv. Psicol. norm. pat.,* 1949, 45, 181–194.

———. La respiration et la personne. *Année psychol.,* 1951, 51, 461–483.

WALTHER POPPELREUTER
1886-1939
German Psychologist (16)

Poppelreuter, W. Ueber die Bedeutung der scheinbaren Grösse und Gestalt für die Gesichtsraumwahrnehmung. *Z. Psychol.,* 1910, 54, 311–361.

———. Beiträge zur Raumpsychologie. *Z. Psychol.,* 1911, 58, 200–262.

———. Ueber die Ordnung des Vorstellungsablaufes. I. *Arch. ges. Psychol.,* 1912, 25, 208–349.

———. Nachweis der Unzweckmässigkeit, die gebräuchlichen Assoziationsexperimente mit sinnlosen Silben nach dem Erlernungs- und Treffenverfahren zur exakten Gewinnung elementarer Reproduktionsgesetze zu verwenden. *Z. Psychol.*, 1912, *61*, 1–24.

———. *Ueber die Ordnung des Vorstellungsablaufes.* Leipzig: Engelmann, 1913.

———. Ueber den Versuch einer Revision der psychophysiologischen Lehre von der elementaren Assoziation und Reproduktion. *Monatsschr. Psychol. Psychiat. Neurol.*, 1915, *37*, 278–323.

———. *Erfahrungen und Anregungen zu einer Kopfschuss-Invalidenfürsorge.* Leipzig: Voss, 1915.

———. *Aufgaben und Organisation der Hirnverletzten-Fürsorge.* Leipzig: Voss, 1916.

———. *Die psychischen Schädigungen durch Kopfschuss im Kriege 1914/17. Vol. I: Die Störungen der niederen und höheren Sehleistungen durch Verletzungen des Okzipitalhirns. Vol. II: Die Herabsetzung der körperlichen Leistungsfähigkeit und des Arbeitswillens durch Hirnverletzung im Vergleich zu Normalen und Psychogenen.* Leipzig: Voss, 1917–1918.

———. *Die Arbeitsschauuhr: Ein Beitrag zur praktischen Psychologie.* Langensalza: Wend & Klauwell, 1918.

———. *Allgemeine methodische Richtlinien der praktisch-psychologischen Begutachtung.* Leipzig: Kröner, 1923.

———. Ueber die Gesetzlichkeit der praktischen körperlichen Arbeitskurve. *Prakt. Psychol.*, 1923, *4*, 363–383.

———. Zur Psychologie und Pathologie der optischen Wahrnehmung. *Z. ges. Neurol. Psychiat.*, 1923, *83*, 26–152.

———. Die Arbeitskurve in der Eignungsprüfung. *Industr. Psychotechn.*, 1926, *3*, 161–167.

———. Psychologische Begutachtung der Erwerbsbeschränkten. In E. Abderhalden (Ed.), *Handbuch der biologischen Arbeitsmethoden.* Vol. 6: *Methoden der experimentellen Psychologie.* Part C/I. *Methoden der angewandten Psychologie.* Vienna: Urban & Schwarzenberg, 1928, pp. 369–552.

———. Die Arbeitskurve in der Diagnostik von Arbeitstypen. *Psychotechn. Z.*, 1928, *3*, 35–51.

———. *Zeitstudie und Betriebsüberwachung im Arbeitsschaubild.* Munich: Oldenbourg, 1929.

———. Beitrag zur Analyse der Fahrer-Lenkertätigkeit und deren Begutachtung. *Psychotechn. Z.*, 1929, *4*, 53–64.

———. Zur Frage der Steigerung der industriellen Arbeitsfähigkeit durch Recresalzufuhr. *Arbeitsphysiologie*, 1930, *2*, 507–519.

———. Selbstbeobachtungen über die Wirkung jahrelanger Phosphatzufuhr. *Arbeitsphysiologie*, 1930, *3*, 605–611.

———, & Mathieu, J. Die Einhebelsteuerung von elektrischen Fördermaschinen. *Industr. Psychotechn.*, 1930, *7*, 378–381.

———. Die methodische Rolle der determinierenden Tendenzen" bei Begutachtungsexperimenten. *Arch. ges. Psychol.*, 1932, *83*, 386–396.

———. *Psychokritische Pädagogik, zur Ueberwindung von Scheinwissen, Scheinkönnen, Scheindenken, usw.* Munich: Beck, 1933.

———. *Hitler, der politische Psychologe.* Langensalza: Beyer, 1934.

NOAH PORTER
1811-1892
American Philosopher (11)

Porter, N. *Science and sentiment, with other papers, chiefly philosophical.* New York: Scribner's, 1882. (Reprinted 1971) **C**

———. The principles of mental philosophy. *Amer. Presb. Theol. Rev.*, 1864, *2*(N.S.), 276–303.

———. *The human intellect, with an introduction upon psychology and the soul.* (4th ed.) New York: Scribner's, 1887. (1868)

———. *The elements of intellectual science: A manual for schools and colleges: Abridged from the "Human intellect."* New York: Scribner's, 1871.

————. *The sciences of nature versus the science of man: A plea for the science of man.* New York: Dodd & Mead, 1871. Reprinted in J. L. Blau (Ed.), *American philosophic addresses, 1700–1900.* New York: Columbia University Press, 1946, pp. 455–485.

————. Philosophy in Great Britain and America: A supplementary sketch. In F. Ueberweg, *History of philosophy.* Vol. 2. (4th ed.) Trans. by N. Porter. New York: Scribner's, 1873, pp. 349–460.

————. Professor Huxley's exposition of Hume's philosophy. *Princeton Rev.,* 1879, *55,* 421–450. Reprinted in *Science and sentiment, op. cit.,* pp. 293–330.

————. *The elements of moral science: Theoretical and practical.* New York: Scribner's, 1885.

————. *The two-hundredth birthday of Bishop George Berkeley: A discourse given at Yale College on the 12th of March, 1885.* New York: Scribner's, 1885. (Reprinted 1970)

————. *Kant's ethics. A critical exposition.* Chicago: Griggs, 1886.

———— (Ed.), *Webster's International dictionary of the English language. Being the authentic edition of Webster's unabridged dictionary. Comprising the issues of 1864, 1879, and 1884.* Springfield, Mass.: Merriam, 1890.

Cubberley, *Public Educators;* Mueller, *American Philosophy;* Robinson, *Scottish Philosophy*

(THIERRY) WILHELM PREYER
1841-1897
German Physiologist (22)

Preyer, W. *Akustische Untersuchungen.* Jena: Fischer, 1879.   **C**

————. *Biologische Zeitfragen.* Berlin: Allgemeiner Verein für deutsche Literatur, 1889.

Fechner, G. T., ————, & Vierordt, K. v. *Wissenschaftliche Briefe von Gustav Theodor Fechner und W. Preyer, nebst einem Briefwechsel zwischen K. von Vierordt und Fechner.* Ed. by W. Preyer. Hamburg: Voss, 1890.   **B C**

————. Ueber anomale Farbenempfindungen und die physiologischen Grundfarben. *Arch. ges. Physiol.,* 1868, *1,* 299–329.

————. *Ueber die Erforschung des Lebens.* Jena: Mauke, 1873.

————. Ueber eine Wirkung der Angst bei Tieren. *Zbl. med. Wiss.,* 1873, *11,* 177–179.

————. *Ueber die Grenzen der Tonwahrnehmung.* Jena: Dufft, 1876.

————. *Ueber die Ursache des Schlafes.* Stuttgart: Enke, 1877.

————. *Elemente der reinen Empfindungslehre.* Jena: Dufft, 1877.

————. *Die Kataplexie und der tierische Hypnotismus.* Jena: Fischer, 1878.

————. Die akumetrische Verwendung des Bell'schen Telephons. *Sitzber. Jena Ges. Med. Naturw.,* 1879, 45–49.

————. Ueber den Farben- und Temperatursinn, mit besonderer Rücksicht auf Farbenblindheit. *Arch. ges. Physiol.,* 1881, *25,* 31–100.

————. *The mind of the child.* Part 1. *The senses and the will.* (2nd ed.) Trans. by H. W. Brown. New York: Appleton, 1909. (1881)

————. *The mind of the child.* Part 2. *The development of the intellect.* (2nd ed.) Trans. by H. W. Brown. New York: Appleton, 1909. (1881)

————. *Die Entdeckung des Hypnotismus.* Berlin: Paetel, 1881.

————. *Spezielle Physiologie des Embryo. Untersuchungen über die Lebenserscheinungen vor der Geburt.* Leipzig: Grieben, 1885. Partial trans. in Embryonic motility and sensitivity. Trans. by G. E. Coghill & W. K. Legner. *Monogr. Soc. Res. Child Developmt.,* 1937, *2,* No. 6.

————. *Die Erklärung des Gedankenlesens, nebst Beschreibung eines neuen Verfahrens zum Nachweise unwillkürlicher Bewegungen.* Leipzig: Gera, 1886.

————. *Die Bewegungen der Seesterne.* Berlin: Friedländer, 1887.

———. Die Wahrnehmung der Schallrichtung mittelst der Bogengänge. *Arch. ges. Physiol.,* 1887, *40,* 586–622.

———. *Der Hypnotismus.* Vienna: Urban & Schwarzenberg, 1890.

———. Ueber den Ursprung des Zahlbegriffes aus dem Tonsinn und über das Wesen der Primzahlen. In A. König (Ed.), *Beiträge zur Psychologie und Physiologie der Sinnesorgane.* Hamburg: Voss, 1891, pp. 1–36.

———. *Mental development in the child.* Trans. by H. W. Brown. New York: Appleton, 1893.

———. Die Empfindung als Funktion der Reizänderung. *Z. Psychol.,* 1894, *7,* 241–248.

———. *Zur Psychologie des Schreibens, mit besonderer Rücksicht auf individuelle Verschiedenheiten der Handschriften.* (2 vols.) Leipzig: Voss, 1919. (1895)

———. Die Psychologie des Kindes. *Verh. Dritten Int. Congr. Psychol. München,* 1896, 80–94.

———. La psychologie de l'enfant. *Rev. sci.,* 1896, *6,* 616–622.

———. Farbenunterscheidung und Abstraktion in der ersten Kindheit. *Z. Psychol.,* 1897, *14,* 321–328.

Dennis, *Psychology;* Dennis, *Reading Developmental;* Kessen, *Child*

JOSEPH PRIESTLEY
1733-1804
English-American Chemist (13)

Priestley, J. *The theological and miscellaneous works of Joseph Priestley.* (25 vols. in 26) Ed. by J. T. Rutt. London: Smallfield, 1817–1832. (Reprinted 1969)   **C**

———. *Writings on philosophy, science, and politics.* Ed. by J. A. Passmore. New York: Collier, 1965.   **C**

———. *A scientific autobiography of Joseph Priestley, (1733–1804): Selected scientific correspondence, with commentary.* Ed. by R. E. Schofield. Cambridge: M.I.T. Press, 1966.
B Bl C

———. *The history and present state of electricity.* (2nd ed.) London: Dodsley, Johnson, Payne & Cadell, 1769. (1767) (Reprinted 1966)

———. *The history and present state of discoveries relating to vision, light, and colours.* London: Johnson, 1772. (Reprinted 1966)

———. *Experiments and observations on different kinds of air.* London: Johnson, 1774. (Reprinted 1970)

———. *An examination of Dr. Reid's inquiry into human mind on the principles of common sense, Dr. Beattie's essay on the nature and immutability of truth, and Dr. Oswald's appeal to common sense in behalf of religion.* (2nd ed.) London: Johnson, 1775. (1774)

——— (Ed.), *Hartley's theory of the human mind. on the principle of the association of ideas; with essays relating to the subject of it.* (2nd ed.) London: Johnson, 1790. (1775) (Reprinted 1971)

———. *A free discussion of the doctrines of materialism and philosophical necessity, in a correspondence between Dr. Price and Dr. Priestley; to which are added, by Dr. Priestley, an introduction, explaining the nature of the controversy, and letters to several writers who have animadverted on his Disquisitions relating to matter and spirit, or his Treatise on Necessity.* London: Johnson & Cadell, 1778. (1775)

———. *Disquisitions relating to matter and spirit and the doctrine of philosophical necessity illustrated. . . . To which is added, an answer to the letters . . . on Hartley's theory of the mind, etc.* (2nd ed.) (2 vols.) Birmingham: Johnson, 1782. (1777)

———. *Letters to a philosophical unbeliever. Part I, containing an examination of the principal objections to the doctrines of natural religion and especially those contained in the writings of Mr. Hume.* Bath: Cruttwell, 1780.

———. *Discourses relating to the evidences of revealed religion.* Philadelphia: Thompson, 1796.

———. *The doctrine of phlogiston established, and that of the composition of water refuted.* (2nd ed.) Northumberland: Priestley, 1803. (1800)

———. Some thoughts concerning dreams. *N.Y. Med. Repos.*, 1802, *5*, 125–129.

———. *Autobiography of Joseph Priestley*. Ed. by J. Lindsay. Teaneck, N.J.: Fairleigh Dickinson University Press, 1971. (1806)   **B**

———. *Memoirs of Dr. J. Priestley to the year 1795 written by himself, with a continuation by his son, J. Priestley*. (2 vols.) London: Allenson, 1806–1807. (Reprinted 1904)   **B**

Bodenheimer, *Biology ;* Fulton & Wilson, *Physiology ;* Gabriel & Fogel, *Biology ;* Hall, *Nature's Laws ;* Hall, *Source Book ;* Schwartz & Bishop, *Moments Discovery ;* Slotkin, *Anthropology*

MORTON PRINCE
1854-1929
American Psychiatrist (23)

Prince, M. *Clinical and experimental studies in personality* (Rev. ed.) Ed. by A. A. Roback. Cambridge: Sci-Art, 1939. (1929)   **C**

———. *The nature of mind and human automatism*. Philadelphia: Lippincott, 1885.

———. Association neuroses: A study of the pathology of hysterical joint affections, neurasthenia and allied forms of neuro-mimesis. *J. nerv. ment. Dis.*, 1891, *16*, 257–282. Reprinted in *Clinical and experimental studies in personality, op. cit.*, pp. 117–143.

———. The identification of mind and matter. *Phil. Rev.*, 1904, *13*, 444–451.

———. *The dissociation of personality: A biographical study in abnormal psychology*. (2nd ed.) New York: Longmans, Green, 1925. (1905) (Reprinted 1969)

———. Some of the present problems of abnormal psychology. *Psychol. Rev.*, 1905, *12*, 118–143. Reprinted in *Clinical and experimental studies in personality, op. cit.*, pp. 351–372.

———. The psychology of sudden religious conversion. *J. abnorm. Psychol.*, 1906, *1*, 42–54.

———. Hysteria from the point of view of dissociated personality, *J. abnorm. Psychol.*, 1906, *1*, 170–187.

———, & Coriat, I. Cases illustrating the educational treatment of the psycho-neuroses. *J. abnorm. Psychol.*, 1907, *2*, 166–177.

———, & Peterson, F. Experiments in psycho-galvanic reactions from co-conscious (subconscious) ideas in a case of multiple personality. *J. abnorm. Psychol.*, 1908–1909, *3*, 114–131. Reprinted in *Clinical and experimental studies in personality, op. cit.*, pp. 332–350.

———. The psychological principles and field of psychotherapy. *J. abnorm. Psychol.*, 1909–1910, *4*, 72–98.

Jastrow, J., Münsterberg, H., Ribot, T., Janet, P., Hart, B., & ———. *Subconscious phenomena*. Boston: Badger, 1910.

———. The mechanism and interpretation of dreams. *J. abnorm. Psychol.*, 1910–1911, *5*, 139–195, 337–353. Reprinted in *Clinical and experimental studies in personality, op. cit.*, pp. 509–566.

———. The meaning of ideas as determined by unconscious settings. *J. abnorm. Psychol.*, 1912, *7*, 233–258. Reprinted in *Clinical and experimental studies in personality, op. cit.*, pp. 51–82.

———. *The unconscious: The fundamentals of human personality, normal and abnormal*. (2nd ed.) New York: Macmillan, 1921. (1914)

———. American neurology of the past—neurology of the future. *J. nerv. ment. Dis.*, 1915, *42*, 445–454.

———. The subconscious settings of ideas in relation to the pathology of the psychoneuroses. *J. abnorm. Psychol.*, 1916, *11*, 1–18. Reprinted in *Clinical and experimental studies in personality, op. cit.*, pp. 98–116.

———. *The creed of Deutschtum and other war essays including the psychology of the Kaiser*. Boston: Badger, 1918.

———. Miss Beauchamp: The theory of the psychogenesis of multiple personality. *J. abnorm. Psychol.*, 1920, *15*, 67–135. Reprinted in

Clinical and experimental studies in personality, op. cit., pp. 185–268.

――――. The problem of personality. *J. genet. Psychol.,* 1925, *32,* 266–292.

――――. Three fundamental errors of the behaviorists and the reconciliation of the purposive and mechanistic concepts. In C. Murchison (Ed.), *Psychologies of 1925.* (3rd. ed.) Worcester, Mass.: Clark University Press, 1928, pp. 199–220. (1926)

――――. Awareness, consciousness, co-consciousness, and animal intelligence from the point of view of the data of abnormal psychology. In C. Murchison (Ed.), *Psychologies of 1925.* (3rd ed.) Worcester, Mass.: Clark University Press, 1928, pp. 221–243. (1926)

――――. The problem of personality, how many selves have we? In C. Murchison (Ed.), *Psychologies of 1925.* (3rd ed.) Worcester, Mass.: Clark University Press, 1928, pp. 245–271. (1926)

――――. Can emotion be regarded as energy? In M. L. Reymert (Ed.), *Feelings and emotions: The Wittenburg symposium.* Worcester, Mass.: Clark University Press, 1928, pp. 161–169.

――――. An experimental study of the mechanism of hallucinations. (1929) In *Clinical and experimental studies in personality, op, cit.,* pp. 424–476.

Park & Burgess, *Sociology;* Shipley, *Classics*

GEORG PROCHASKA
1749-1820
Czech Physiologist (11)

Prochaska, G. *Lehrsätze aus der Physiologie des Menschen.* (3rd ed.) (2 vols.) Vienna; Beck. 1810–1811. (1797)   C

――――. *Opera minorum anatomici, physiologici et pathologici argumenti.* (2 vols.) Vienna: Wappler & Beck, 1800.   C

――――. *Disquisitio anatomico-physiologica organismi corporis humani.* Vienna: Haykul, 1812.
                                                   C

――――. *Controversae quaestiones physiologicae.* Vienna: Graeffer, 1778.

――――. *De structura nervorum.* Vienna: Graeffer, 1779. Reprinted in *Opera minorum,* Vol. 1, op. cit., pp. 273–404.

――――. *Adnotationum academicarum fasciculi tres.* (3 vols. in 1.) Prague: Gerle, 1780–1784.

――――. De functionibus systematis nervosi commentatio. (1784) In *Adnotationum academicarum,* Vol. 3, op. cit., pp. 1–164. Reprinted in *Opera minorum,* Vol. 2, op. cit., pp. 1–214.

――――. *A dissertation on the functions of the nervous system.* Trans. by T. Laycock. London: Sydenham Society, 1851. (1784)

――――. *Principles of human physiology.* Vol. 2. Trans. & annot. by K. Resler. Prague: Academia, 1971. (1797)

――――. Einige Nachrichten und Bemerkungen über die warmen Bäder in Piestan. *Medizin. Jhrbüch. kais. königl. öster. Staates,* 1813, 2(1), 65–78.

――――. Einige Nachrichten über die mit einem zweyten Fötus schwanger geborenen Kinder, oder über den Foetus in Foetu mit physiologischen Bemerkungen begleitet nebst einer Kupfertafel. *Medizin. Jhrbüch. kais. königl. öster. Staates,* 1814, 2(4), 67–104.

――――. Beobachtungen über die schädlichen Wirkungen der Quecksilberdünste und besonders das Zittern der Gliedmassen, welchem die mit jenem Metalle umgehenden Arbeiter unterworfen sind. *Medizin. Jhrbüch. kais. königl. öster. Staates,* 1814, 2(3), 95–113

――――. *Versuch einer empirischen Darstellung des polarischen Naturgesetzes und dessen Anwendung auf die Thätigkeiten der organischen und unorganischen Körper, mit einem Rückblick auf den thierischen Magnetismus.* Vienna: Camesina, 1815.

――――. *Physiologie oder Lehre von der Natur des Menschen.* Vienna: Beck, 1820.

Clarke & O'Malley, *Brain;* Fulton & Wilson, *Physiology;* Herrnstein & Boring, *Source Book*

JOHANNES EVANGELISTA PURKINJE
(Czech: Jan Evangelista Purkyne)
1787-1869
Czech Physiologist (24)

Purkinje, J. E. *Opera omnia.* (9 vols.) Ed. by V. Kruta *et al.* Prague: Czechoslovak Academy of Sciences, 1918–1965.   **C**

———. *Opera selecta.* Prague: Cura societatis Spolek Českých Lékařů Praha, 1948.   **C**

———. *Physiologie der Sinne* (2nd ed.) Prague: Calve, 1823. (1819)

———. *Neue Beiträge zur Kenntnis des Sehens in subjektiver Hinsicht.* (2nd ed.) Berlin: Reimer, 1825. (1819) Reprinted in *Opera omnia,* Vol. 1, *op. cit.*

———. *Beobachtungen und Versuche zur Physiologie der Sinnesorgane.* I. *Beiträge zur Kenntniss des Sehens in subjektiver Hinsicht.* (2nd ed.) Prague: Calve, 1823. (1819) Reprinted in *Opera selecta,* Vol. 1, *op. cit.,* pp. 57–162, & in *Opera omnia,* Vol. 1, *op. cit.,* pp. 1–56.

———. Beiträge zur näheren Kenntnis des Schwindels aus heaugnostischen Daten. *Med. Jb. österr. Staates,* 1820, 79–125. Reprinted in *Opera omnia,* Vol. 2, *op. cit.,* pp. 15–37.

———. Relation über einige Versuche zur Ausmittlung der Brechen erregenden Eigenschaft verschiedener Präparate der Ipecacuana-Wurzel. In A. M. Pleischl (Ed.), *Das chemische Laboratorium an der k. k. Universität zu Prag.* Prague: Sommer, 1820, pp. 149–156. Reprinted in *Opera omnia,* Vol. 2, *op. cit.,* pp. 7–12.

———. Physiological examination of the organ of vision and the integumentary system. (1823) Reprinted in trans. in H. J. John, Jan Evangelista Purkyně: Czech scientist and patiot, 1787–1869. *Mem. Amer. Phil. Soc.,* 1959, 49, 54–62.

———. Ueber das indirekte Sehen. *Schl. Provinzialbl.,* 1824, 6–10. Reprinted in *Opera omnia,* Vol. 2, *op. cit.,* pp. 42–44.

———. Ueber Dr. Johann Müllers Werk: Zur vergleichenden Physiologie des Gesichtssinnes der Menschen und Tiere. *Uebers. Arb.,* 1826, 38. Reprinted in *Opera omnia,* Vol. 2, *op. cit.,* pp. 64–67.

———. Ueber die physiologische Bedeutung des Schwindels und die Beziehung desselben zu den neusten Versuchen über die Hirnfunction. *Rist. Mag. ges. Heilk.,* 1827, 23, 284–310.

———. Ueber die Verdienste Berkeley's um die Theorie des Sehens. *Uebers. Arb.,* 1828, 50. Reprinted in *Opera omnia,* Vol. 2, *op. cit.,* pp. 70–71.

———. (On visually perceived space.) *Časopis ceského musea,* 1837, 11, 191–201. Reprinted in *Opera omnia,* Vol. 7, *op. cit.,* pp. 114–121.

———. (Additional psychological investigations on space perception.) *Časopis českého musea,* 1840, 14, 355–375. Reprinted in *Opera omnia,* Vol. 7, *op. cit.,* pp. 122–134.

———. Ueber die Sinne im Allgemeinen. In R. Wagner (Ed.), *Handwörterbuch der Physiologie.* Vol. 3, Part 1. Brunswick: Vieweg, 1846, pp. 352–359.

———. Wachen, Schlaf, Traum und verwandte Zustände. In R. Wagner (Ed.), *Handwörterbuch der Physiologie.* Vol. 3. Part 2. Brunswick: Vieweg, 1846, pp. 412–480.

———. Ueber das Bewusstsein als eigentümliches Phänomen des Geisteswesens in der irdischen Natur. (1847) Reprinted in *Opera omnia,* Vol. 2, *op. cit.,* pp. 111–112.

———. (Detailed reports on my older and newer publications, especially in natural sciences.) *Ziva,* 1857, No. 5; 1858, No. 6. Reprinted in *Opera selecta, op. cit.,* pp. 121–175.

———. (Experiments on hearing.) *Ziva,* 1859, 261–267. Trans. in John, H. J., Jan Evangelista Purkyně: Czech scientist and patriot, 1787–1869. *Mem. Amer. Phil. Soc.,* 1959, 49, 75–79.

———. Ueber die Verwertung der bisherigen Beobachtungen im Gebiete des subjektiven Sehens für Anatomie, Physiologie, Physik, Psychologie, Kunst und Gewerbe. *Sitzber. kön. böhm. Ges. Wiss.,* 1860, 34–37. Reprinted in *Opera omnia,* Vol. 3, *op. cit.,* pp. 111–114.

———. Akademia. *Ziva,* 1861, 9, Nos. 2 & 3. (Also Prague: Renn, 1861.) Reprinted in *Opera omnia,* Vol. 9, *op. cit.,* pp. 15–111.

———. Ueber die Richtung der Wahrnehmung des Schalles. *Versamml. deutsch. Naturf. Aerzte,* 1862, *37,* 66–67. Reprinted in *Opera omnia,* Vol. 3, *op. cit.,* pp. 117–118.

———. (Human individual mind.) *Krok,* 1864–1865, *1,* 7–12, 129–133, 257–260 ; 1865–1866, *2,* 1–5. Reprinted in *Opera omnia,* Vol. 9, *op. cit.,* pp. 193–206.

———. (Psychological fragments.) (no date) *J. Psotnícková,* 1955 (no pagination).

Clarke & O'Malley, *Brain*

(LAMBERT) ADOLPHE (JACQUES) QUETELET
1796-1874
Belgian Statistician (24)

Quételet, A. *Correspondances mathématiques et physiques.* (4 vols.) Brussels: Hauman, 1827–1830. ₁₁₈₇₅–1826)   **B C**

———. *Letters addressed to H.R.H. the Grand Duke of Saxe-Coburg and Gotha, on the theory of probabilities, as applied to the moral and political sciences.* Trans. by O. G. Downes. London: Layton, 1849. (1846)   **C**

———. *Astronomie élémentaire.* Paris: Hachette, 1834. (1826)

———. *Astronomie populaire.* Brussels: Remy, 1832. (1827)

———. *Positions de physique, ou résumé d'un cours de physique générale.* (3 vols.) Brussels: Tarlier, 1827–1829.

———. *Instructions populaires sur le calcul des probabilités.* Brussels: Hayez & Tarlier, 1828.

———. Recherches statistiques sur le Royaume des Pays Bas. *Nouv. mém. Acad. roy. Sci. Belles Lettres,* 1829, *5,* 28–57.

———. *Recherches sur la loi de la croissance de l'homme aux différents âges.* Brussels: Hayez, 1831.

———. *Recherches sur le penchant au crime aux différents âges.* (2nd ed.) Brussels: Hayez, 1833. (1831)

———. Recherches sur la loi de la croissance de l'homme. *Nouv. mém. Acad. roy. Sci. Belles Lettres,* 1832, *7,* 1–32.

———. Lettre à M. Villerme, sur la possibilité de mesurer l'influence des causes qui modifient les éléments sociaux. *Corr. math. phys.,* 1832, *7,* 321–348. Reprinted with short intro. by J. E. Esquirol in *Ann. Hyg. Publ.,* 1833, *9,* 309–336.

———. *Recherches sur le poids de l'homme aux différents âges.* Brussels: Hayez. 1833.

———. *A treatise on man and the development of his faculties.* (With new 1842 intro.) Trans. by R. Knox. New York: Franklin, 1968. (1835)

———. *A treatise on man and the development of his faculties.* (With new 1842 intro.) Trans. by R. Knox, & intro. by S. Diamond. Gainesville, Fla.: Scholars' Facsimiles & Reprints, 1969. (1835)

———. *De l'influence des saisons sur la mortalité aux différents âges dans la Belgique.* Brussels: Hayez, 1838.

———. Détermination des équations personnelles des observateurs. *Nouv. mém. Acad. Bruxelles,* 1843, *16*(1), 4.

———. Sur l'appréciation des documents statistiques, et en particulier sur l'appréciation des moyennes. *Bull. Acad. Roy. Belg. Sci. Lettres Beaux-arts,* 1845, *2,* 205–286.

———. *Du système social et des lois qui le régissent.* Paris: Guillaumin, 1848.

———. *Théorie des probabilités.* Brussels: Jamar, 1853.

———. *Histoire des sciences mathématiques et physiques chez les Belges.* Brussels: Hayez, 1864.

———. *Sciences mathématiques et physiques chez les Belges au commencement du XIXe siècle.* Brussels: Van Buggenhout, 1866.

———. *Physique sociale, ou essai sur le développement des facultés de l'homme.* (2 vols.) Brussels: Marquardt, 1869.

———. Des lois concernant le développement de l'homme. *Bull. Acad. roy. Belg. Sci. Lettres Beaux-arts,* 1870, *29,* 669–680.

———. *Anthropométrie, ou mesure des différentes facultés de l'homme.* Brussels: Marquardt, 1871.

———. *Tables de mortalité et leur développement.* Brussels: Hayez, 1872.

SANTIAGO RAMON Y CAJAL
1852-1934
Spanish Anatomist (25)

Ramón y Cajal, S. *Studies on vertebrate neurogenesis.* Trans. by L. Guth. Springfield, Ill.: Thomas, 1959. (1929)   **C**

———. *Obras literarias completas, con una nota preliminar de F.S.R.* (4th ed.) Madrid: Aguilar, 1961. (1947)   **C**

———. *The world of Ramón y Cajal with selections from his non-scientific writings.* Ed. by E. H. Craigie & W. C. Gibson. Springfield, Ill.: Thomas, 1968.   **C**

———. Estructura del cerebelo. *Gac. med. Catalana,* 1888, *11,* 449–457.

———. Estructura de los centros nerviosos de los aves. *Rev. trimest. Histol. norm. patol.,* 1888, *1,* 305–315.

———. Réponse à M. Golgi à propos des fibrilles collatérales de la moelle épinière, et de la structure générale de la substance grise. *Anat. Anz.,* 1890, *5,* 579–587.

———. Sur la structure de l'écorce cérébrale de quelques mammifères. *Cellule,* 1891, *7,* 123–176.

———. La rétine des vertébrés. *Cellule,* 1893, *9,* 119–258.

———. Algunas contribuciones al conocimiento de los ganglios del encefalo. *Anal. Soc. Espan. Hist. Nat.,* 1894, *23,* 195–237.

———. *Les nouvelles idées sur la structure du système nerveux chez l'homme et chez les vertébrés.* (2nd ed.) Ed. by M. Duval. Paris: Reinwald, 1895. (1894)

———. *Die Retina der Wirbelthiere. Untersuchungen mit der Golgi-Cajal'schen Chromsilbermethode und der Ehrlich'schen Methylenblaufärbung.* Wiesbaden: Bergmann, 1894.

———. Comparative study of the sensory areas of the human cortex. In W. Story & L. N. Wilson (Eds.), *Clark University, 1889–1899.* Worcester, Mass.: Clark University, 1899, pp. 311–382.

———. *Histologie du système nerveux de l'homme et des vertébrés.* (2 vols.) Trans. by L. Azoulay. Paris: Maloine, 1909–1911. (1897–1904) Excerpt reprinted & trans. by G. v. Bonin (Ed.), *Some papers on the cerebral cortex.* Springfield, Ill.: Thomas, 1960, pp. 251–282.

———. *Histology.* (10th ed.) Trans. by M. Fernán-Nuñez. Rev. by J. F. Tello-Muñoz. Baltimore, Md.: Wood, 1933. (1897)

———. *Precepts and counsels on scientific investigation. Stimulants of the spirit.* (6th ed.) Trans. by J. M. Sanchez-Peres, & ed. by C. B. Courville. Mountain View, Calif.: Pacific Press, 1951. (1899)

———. *Die Struktur des Chiasma opticum nebst einer allgemeinen Theorie der Kreuzung der Nervenbahnen.* Leipzig: Barth, 1899.

———. *Studies on the cerebral cortex (limbic structures).* Trans. by L. M. Kraft. Chicago: Yearbook Publishers, 1955. (1901–1902)

———. *Recollections of my life.* Trans. from 3rd Spanish ed. by E. H. Craigie & J. Cano. Cambridge, Mass.: MIT Press, 1937. (1901–1917)
                                              B Bl

———. *Studien über die Hirnrinde des Menschen.* (5 vols.) Trans. by J. Bresler. Leipzig: Barth, 1906.

———. The structure and connexions of neurons. (1906) In Nobel Foundation (Ed.), *Nobel lectures: Physiology or medicine, 1901–1921.* New York: Elsevier, 1967, pp. 220–253.

———. Die histogenetischen Beweise der Neuronentheorie von His und Forel. *Anat. Anz.,* 1907, *30,* 113–144.

———. *Studien über Nervenregeneration.* Leipzig: Barth, 1908.

———. *Neuron theory or reticular theory? Objective evidence of the anatomical unity of nerve cells.* Trans. by M. U. Purkiss & C. A. Fox. Madrid: Instituto "Ramon y Cajal," 1954. (1933)

————. *Degeneration and regeneration of the nervous system.* (2 vols.) Trans. by R. M. May. London: Oxford University Press, 1928. (1913, 1914) (Reprinted 1959)

————. *Publicaciones de la junta para el homenaje a Cajal. Libro en honor de D. S. Ramón y Cajal. Trabajos originales de sus admiradores y discipulos, extranjeros y nacionales.* (2 vols.) Madrid: Jimenz & Molena, 1922.

————, & Castro, F. D. *Elementos de técnica micrográfica del sistema nervioso.* Madrid: Tipografia artistica, 1933.

Clarke & O'Malley, *Brain*

OTTO RANK
1884-1939
Austrian-American Psychoanalyst (23)

Rank, O. *Sexualität und Schuldefühl.* Vienna: Internationaler Psychoanalytischer Verlag, 1926. (1912, 1923)   C

————. *Psychoanalytische Beiträge zur Mythenforschung aus den Jahren 1912–1914.* (2nd ed.) Vienna: Internationaler Psychoanalytischer Verlag, 1922. (1919)   C

————. *Will therapy and truth and reality.* Trans. by Jessie Taft. New York: Knopf, 1945. (1920–1931)   C

————. *Art and artist.* (3rd ed.) Trans. by C. F. Atkinson. New York: Knopf, 1932. (1907)

————. *Myth of the birth of the hero.* New York: Brunner, 1952. (1909)

————. *A dream that explains itself.* (1910) *Psychoanal. Rev.,* 1918, *5,* 230–234.

————. *Das Inzest-Motiv in Dichtung und Sage: Grundzüge einer Psychologie des dichterischen Schaffens.* (2nd ed.) Leipzig: Deuticke, 1926. (1912)

————. Die Nacktheit in Sage und Dichtung. *Imago,* 1913, *2,* 267–301, 409–446.

————, & Sachs, H. *The significance of psychoanalysis for the mental sciences.* New York: Nervous & Mental Disease Publishing, 1916. (1913) (Reprinted 1970)

————. *The double: A psychoanalytic study.* Trans. & ed. by H. Tucker, Jr. Chapel Hill, N.C.: University of North Carolina Press, 1971. (1914)

————. Homer: Psychologische Beiträge zur Entstehungsgeschichte des Volksepos. I. II. *Imago,* 1917, *5,* 133–169.

————. Die Don Juan-Gestalt. *Imago,* 1922, *8,* 142–196. (Reprinted 1924)

Ferenczi, S., & ————. *The development of psychoanalysis.* Trans. by Caroline Newton. New York: Nervous & Mental Disease Publishing, 1925. (1924) (Reprinted 1956)

————. *Eine Neurosenanalyse in Träumen.* Zurich: Internationaler Psychoanalytischer Verlag, 1924.

————. *Technik der Psychoanalyse.* (3 vols.) Vienna: Deuticke, 1926–1931.

————. *The practical bearing of psychoanalysis.* New York: National Committee for Mental Hygiene, 1927.

————. *Grundzüge einer genetischen Psychologie auf Grund der Psychoanalyse der Ich-Struktur.* (3 vols.) Vienna: Deuticke, 1927–1929.

————. *The trauma of birth.* New York: Brunner, 1952. (1929)

————. *Psychology and the soul.* Trans. by W. D. Turner. Philadelphia: University of Pennsylvania Press, 1950. (1930) (Reprinted 1961)

————. *Modern education: A critique of its fundamental ideas.* Trans. by Mabel E. Moxen. New York: Knopf, 1932. (Reprinted 1968)

————. *Beyond psychology.* New York: Dover, 1958. (1941)

PAUL RANSCHBURG
1870-1945
Hungarian Psychologist (12)

Ranschburg, P. Beiträge zur Frage der hypnotisch-suggestiven Therapie. *Z. Hypno.,* 1896, *4,* 269–302.

————, & Hajós, L. *Beiträge zur Psychologie des hysterischen Geisteszustandes. Kritisch-experimentelle Studien.* Leipzig: Deuticke, 1897.

————. Ueber quantitative und qualitative Veränderungen geistiger Vorgänge im hohen Greisenalter. *Allg. Z. Psychiat.,* 1900, *57,* 689–718.

————. Studien über die Merkfähigkeit der Normalen, Nervenschwachen und Geisteskranken. *Monatssch. Psychiat. Neurol.,* 1901, *9,* 241–260.

————. Apparat und Methode zur Untersuchung des (optischen) Gedächtnisses für medizinische und pädagogisch-psychologische Zwecke. *Monatssch. Psychiat. Neurol.,* 1901, *10,* 321–333.

————. Ueber Hemmung gleichzeitiger Reizwirkungen. Experimenteller Beitrag zur Lehre von den Bedingungen der Aufmerksamkeit. *Z. Psychol.,* 1902, *30,* 39–86. Summarization in *Psychol. Rev.,* 1903, *10,* 455–457.

————. *(The mind of the child.)* (2nd ed.) Budapest: Athenaeum, 1908. (1905)

————. Ueber die Bedeutung der Aehnlichkeit beim Erlernen, Behalten und bei der Reproduktion. *Jb. Psychol. Neurol.,* 1905, *5,* 560–578.

————. Ueber Art und Wert klinischer Gedächtnismessungen. *Klin. psychisch. nerv. Krankh.,* 1907, *2,* 365–404 ; 1908, *3,* 97–126 ; 1910, *5,* 89–194.

————. Zur physiologischen und pathologischen Psychologie der elementaren Rechenarten. I: Normale. 2: Schlussteil. *Z. exp. Pädag.,* 1908, *7,* 135–162 ; 1909, *9,* 251–263.

————. *Das kranke Gedächtnis.* Leipzig: Barth, 1911.

————. Die Ergebnisse der experimentellen Psychopathologie des Gedächtnisses. *Ber. IV. Kongr. exp. Psychol.* Leipzig: Barth, 1911, pp. 95–100.

————. Neuere Untersuchungen über die Hemmung gleichzeitiger Reizwirkungen. *Ber. V. Kongr. exp. Psychol.* Leipzig: Barth, 1912, pp. 126–133.

————. Die Gedächtnisschwäche (Mnemasthenie) und ihre Behandlung. *Deutsch. med. Wochensch.,* 1912, *38,* 2393–2397.

————. Ueber die Wechselwirkungen gleichzeitiger Reize im Nervensystem und in der Seele. *Z. Psychol.,* 1913, *66,* 161–248 ; *67,* 22–144.

————. Psychologische Methoden zur Erforschung des Verlaufes der Nervenerregung unter normalen und pathologischen Bedingungen. *Z. Psychopathol.,* 1914 (Suppl.), 9–29.

————. *(The human mind.)* (2 vols.) Budapest: Pantheon, 1923.

————. Zur Psychologie, Physiologie und Physik der normalen und pathologischen Bewusstseinserscheinungen. In *(Bekhtèrev 40th anniversary commemorative volume).* Leningrad: Gos. Psikhonevr. Akad., 1926, pp. 71–80.

————. *Die Lese- und Schreibstörungen des Kindesalters. Ihre Psychologie, Physiologie, Pathologie, heilpädagogische und medizinische Therapie.* Halle: Marhold, 1928.

————. (Psychology and natural science.) *Magyar Psychol. Szemle,* 1928, *1,* 9–41.

————. Experimentelle Beiträge zur Lehre von Gedächtnis, Urteil und Schlussfolgerung an Gesunden und Kranken. *Arch. ges. Psychol.,* 1930, *77,* 437–526.

————. Reflexologie und Psychologie. *Kwart. Psychol.,* 1932, *3–4,* 17–324. (Also Poznan: Gorski, 1932)

————. Behaviorismus und Psychologie. Zur Kritik der apsychologischen Psychologien. *Arch. ges. Psychol.,* 1932, *86,* 307–406.

————, & Schill, E. Ueber Alexie und Agnosie. *Z. ges. Neurol. Psychiat.,* 1932, *139,* 192–240.

————. Beiträge zum Verhalten der Reflexe, Automatismen und bewussten Funktionen in scheinbar unbewussten Zuständen. *Z. Psychol.,* 1933, *129,* 338–352.

————. Der Stand der jugendkundlichen Bestrebungen in Ungarn. *Z. Jugendk.,* 1935, *5,* 187–200.

————. Les bases somatiques de la mémoire. In Various, *Centenaire de Th. Ribot et Jubilé de la Psychologie Scientifique Française.* Paris: Imprimerie moderne, 1939, pp. 513–531.

DAVID RAPAPORT
1911-1960
Hungarian-American Psychologist (21)

Rapaport, D. *The collected papers of David Rapaport.* Ed. by M. M. Gill. New York: Basic Books, 1967. **B Bl C**

————. Freudian mechanisms and frustration experiments. *Psychoanal. Quart.,* 1942, *11,* 503–511. Reprinted in S. S. Tomkins (Ed.), *Contemporary psychopathology: A source book.* Cambridge: Harvard University Press, 1947, pp. 582–587.

————. *Emotions and memory.* (2nd unaltered ed.) New York: International Universities Press, 1950. (1942) (Reprinted 1961)

————, & Lewy, E. The psychoanalytic concept of memory and its relation to recent memory theories. *Psychoanal. Quart.,* 1944, *13,* 16–42. Reprinted in *Collected papers, op. cit.,* pp. 136–159.

————. Gill, M. M,, & Schafer, R. *Diagnostic psychological testing.* (Rev. ed.) Ed. by R. R. Holt. New York: International Universities Press, 1968. (1945, 1946)

————. On the psycho-analytic theory of thinking. *Int. J. Psycho-Anal.,* 1950, *31,* 161–170. Reprinted in *Collected papers, op. cit.,* pp. 313–328.

————. The conceptual model of psychoanalysis. *J. Pers.,* 1951, *20,* 56–81. Reprinted in *Collected papers, op. cit.,* pp. 405–431.

————. On the psycho-analytic theory of affects. *Int. J. Psycho-Anal.,* 1953, *34,* 177–198. Reprinted in *Collected papers, op. cit.,* pp. 476–512.

————. A theoretical analysis of the superego concept. (1957) In *Collected papers, op. cit.,* pp. 685–709.

————. Cognitive structures. In *Contemporary approaches to cognition: A symposium.* Cambridge: Harvard University Press, 1957, pp. 157–200. Reprinted in *Collected papers, op. cit.,* pp. 631–664.

————. The theory of ego autonomy: A generalization. *Bull. Menninger Clin.,* 1958, *22,* 13–35.

Reprinted in *Collected papers, op. cit.,* pp. 722–744.

————. The study of kibbutz education and its bearing on the theory of development. *Amer. J. Orthopsychiat.,* 1958, *28,* 587–597. Reprinted in *Collected papers, op. cit.,* pp. 710–721.

————. A historical survey of psychoanalytic ego psychology. *Psychol. Iss.,* 1959, *1,* 5–17. Reprinted in *Collected papers, op. cit.,* pp. 745–757.

————, & Gill, M. M. The points of view and assumptions of metapsychology. *Int. J. Psycho-Anal.,* 1959, *40,* 153–162. Reprinted in *Collected papers, op. cit.,* pp. 795–811.

————. The structure of psychoanalytic theory: A systematizing attempt. In S. Koch (Ed.), *Psychology: A study of a science.* Study 1. *Conceptual and systematic.* Vol. 3. *Formulations of the person and the social context.* New York: McGraw-Hill, 1959, pp. 55–183.

————. On the psychoanalytic theory of motivation. In M. R. Jones (Ed.), *Nebraska symposium on motivation,* 1960. Lincoln, Nebr.: University of Nebraska Press, 1960, pp. 173–247. Reprinted in *Collected papers, op. cit.,* pp. 853–915.

————. Psychoanalysis as a developmental psychology. In B. Kaplan & S. Wapner (Eds.), *Perspectives in psychological theory: Essays in honor of Heinz Werner.* New York: International Universities Press, 1960, pp. 209–255. Reprinted in *Collected papers, op. cit.,* pp. 820–852.

Shakow, D., & ————. The influence of Freud on American psychology. *Psychol. Iss.,* 1964, No. 13. (Reprinted 1968)

Arnold, *Emotion;* Beck & Molish, *Reflexes;* Rapaport, *Thought*

LORD (JOHN WILLIAM STRUTT, 3rd BARON) RAYLEIGH
1842-1919
English Physicist (18)

Strutt, J. W. (Rayleigh, Lord). *Scientific papers.* (6 vols.) Cambridge: Cambridge University Press, 1899–1920. (Reprinted 1964 in 6 vols. in 3) **C**

———. Some experiments on colour. *Nature*, 1871, *3*, 234–237, 264, 265. Reprinted in *Scientific papers*, Vol. 1, *op. cit.*, pp. 79–86.

———. On Mr. Venn's explanation of a gambling paradox. *Mind*, 1877, *2*, 409–410. Reprinted in *Scientific papers*, Vol. 1, *op. cit.*, pp. 336–337.

———. *The theory of sound.* (2nd ed.) (2 vols.) London: Macmillan, 1926. (1877, 1878) (Reprinted 1945) **B**

———. Experiments in colour. *Nature*, 1882, *25*, 64–66. Reprinted in *Scientific papers*, Vol. 1, *op. cit.*, pp. 542–550.

———. On defective colour-vision. *Rep. Brit. Ass. Advanc. Sci.*, 1890, *60*, 728–729. Reprinted in *Scientific Papers*, Vol. 3, *op. cit.*, pp. 380–381.

———. The limits of audition. *Proc. Roy. Inst. Gr. Br.*, 1897, *15*, 417–418. Reprinted in *Scientific papers*, Vol. 4, *op. cit.*, pp. 297–298.

———. On our perception of sound direction. *Phil. Mag.*, 1907, *13*, 214–232. Reprinted in *Scientific papers*, Vol. 5, *op. cit.*, pp. 347–363.

———. Acoustical notes: Sensation of right and left from a revolving magnet and telephones. *Phil. Mag.*, 1907, *13*, 316–319. Reprinted in *Scientific papers*, Vol. 5, *op. cit.*, pp. 364–366.

———. On the perception of the direction of sound. *Proc. Roy. Soc.*, London, 1909, *83A*, 61–64. Reprinted in *Scientific papers*, Vol. 5, *op. cit.*, pp. 522–525.

———. On colour vision at the ends of the spectrum. *Proc. Roy. Soc.*, London, 1910, *84A*, 204–205. Reprinted in *Scientific papers*. Vol. 5, *op. cit.*, pp. 569–572.

———. On the sensibility of the eye to variations of wave-length in the yellow region of the spectrum. *Proc. Roy. Soc.*, London, 1910, *84A*, 464–468. Reprinted in *Scientific papers*, Vol. 6, *op. cit.*, pp. 621–624.

———. The perception of sound. *Nature*, 1918, *102*, 225. Reprinted in *Scientific papers*, Vol. 6, *op. cit.*, p. 564.

THOMAS REID
1710-1796
Scottish Philosopher (25)

Reid, T. *Philosophical works.* (8th ed.) (2 vols.) Ed. with notes & supplementary dissertations by W. Hamilton, & intro. by H. M. Bracken. Hildesheim: Olms, 1967, (1846). **B C**

———. *The works of Thomas Reid with selections from unpublished letters.* Edinburgh: MacLachlan & Stewart, 1863. **B C**

———. *Philosophical orations of Thomas Reid.* Ed. by. W. R. Humphries. Aberdeen: The University Press, 1937. **C**

———. An essay on quantity; occasioned by reading a treatise, in which simple and compound ratios are applied to virtue and merit. *Phil. Trans.*, 1748, *45*, 505–520. Reprinted in *Works*, Vol. 2, *op. cit.*, pp. 715–719.

———. *An inquiry into the human mind.* (4th ed.) Ed. by T. Duggan. Chicago: University of Chicago Press, 1970, & in *Works*, Vol. 1, *op. cit.*, pp. 93–211. (1764)

———. Correspondence. (1764–1796) In *Works*, *op. cit.*, Vol. 1, pp. 39–91. **B**

———. *Essays on the intellectual powers of man.* Intro. by B. A. Brody. Cambridge: MIT Press, 1969. Also in *Philosophical works.* (8th ed.) Vol. 1, *op. cit.*, pp. 213–508. (1785)

———. *Essays on the active powers of the human mind.* Cambridge: MIT Press, 1969, & in *Works*, Vol. 2, *op. cit.*, pp. 511–679. (1788)

Herrnstein & Boring, *Source Book*; Hunter & Macalpine, *Psychiatry*; Johnston, *Scottish Philosophy*; Rand, *Classical Psychologists*; Rand, *Moralists*; Robinson, *Scottish Philosophy*; Sahakian, *Psychology*; Schneider, *Scottish Moralists*

GEZA REVESZ
1878-1955
Dutch Psychologist (23)

Révész, G. *Psychological works and papers.* Amsterdam: North-Holland Publishing Co., 1956. **C**

————. Wird die Lichtempfindlichkeit eines Auges durch Reizung des anderen Auges verändert? *Z. Psychol.,* 1905, *39,* 314–326.

————, & Katz, D. Experimentell-psychologische Untersuchungen mit Hühnern. *Z. Psychol.,* 1908, *50,* 93–116.

Liebermann, P. v., & ————. Experimentelle Beiträge zur Orthosymphonie und zum Falschören. *Z. Psychol.,* 1912, *63,* 286–324.

Liebermann, P. v., & ————. Ueber eine besondere Form des Falschhörens in tiefen Lagen. *Z. Psychol.,* 1912, *63,* 325–335.

————, & Katz, D. Zur Kenntnis des Lichtsinnes der Nachtvögel. *Z. Sinnespsychol.,* 1912, *48,* 165–170.

————. *Zur Grundlegung der Tonpsychologie.* Leipzig: Veit, 1913.

————. *The psychology of a musical prodigy.* Trans. by E. Nyiregyházi. London: Kegan Paul, Trench, & Truebner, 1925. (1916) (Reprinted 1970)

————. *Geschichte des Seelenbegriffes und der Seelenlokalisation.* Amsterdam: Bonset, 1966. (1917)

————. Prüfung der Musikalität. *Z. Psychol.,* 1920, *85,* 163–209.

————. *Das frühzeitige Auftreten der Begabung und ihre Erkennung.* Leipzig: Barth, 1921.

————, & Katz, D. Experimentelle Studien zur vergleichenden Psychologie. *Z. angew. Psychol.,* 1921, *18,* 307–320.

————. Zur Analyse der tierischen Handlung. Theoretische und experimentelle Beiträge zur vergleichenden Psychologie. *Arch. néerl. Physiol.,* 1922, *7,* 469–477.

————. Tierpsychologische Untersuchungen. (Versuche auf Hühner.) *Z. Psychol.,* 1922, *88,* 130–137.

————. Experiments on animal space perception. *Brit. J. Psychol.,* 1923–1924, *14,* 387–414.

————. Expériences sur la mémoire topographique et sur la découverte d'un système chez des enfants et des singes inférieurs. *Arch. psychol.,* Geneva, 1923, *18,* 323–342.

————. Recherches de physiologie comparée. Reconnaissance d'un principe. *Arch. néerl. Physiol.,* 1923, *8,* 1–13.

————. Experimental study in abstraction in monkeys. *J. comp. Psychol.,* 1925, *5,* 293–341.

Katz, D., & ————. Musikgenuss bei Gehörlosen. (Ein Beitrag zur Theorie des musikalischen Genusses.) *Z Psychol.,* 1926, *99,* 289–324. (Also Leipzig: Barth, 1926.)

————. Zur Geschichte der Zweikomponentenlehre in der Tonpsychologie. *Z. Psychol,* 1926, *99,* 325–356.

————. *Ueber taktile Agnosie.* Haarlem: Bohn, 1928.

————. Erfolgstatistische Untersuchungen in höheren Schulen. *Z. angew. Psychol.,* 1928, *31,* 300–309.

————. *Psychologie van het bedrijfsleven.* (2nd ed.) Haarlem: Bohn, 1935. (1930)

————. Prüfung der rechnerischen Fähigkeit und Fertigkeit an Schülern der höchsten Klassen der Grundschule. I. *Z. angew. Psychol.,* 1930, *36,* 104–134, 215–237.

————. Sozialpsychologische Beobachtungen an Affen. I. *Z. Psychol.,* 1930, *118,* 142–162.

————. Zur Psychologie der Furcht- und Angstzustände. *Z. angew. Psychol.,* 1931, Suppl. 59, 203–240.

————. *Das Schöpferisch-persönliche und das Kollektive in ihrem kultur-historischen Zusammenhang.* Tübingen: Mohr, 1933.

————. Gibt es einen Hörraum? *Acta Psychol.,* 1937, *3,* 137–192.

————. The problem of space with particular emphasis on specific sensory spaces. *Amer. J. Psychol.,* 1937, *50,* 429–444.

————. *Die Formenwelt des Tastsinnes.* (2 vols.) The Hague: Nijhoff, 1938.

————. De l'origine du langage. In Various, *Centenaire de Th. Ribot et Jubilé de la Psychologie Scientifique Française.* Paris: Imprimerie moderne, 1939, pp. 533–544.

————. The indivisibility of mathematical talent. *Acta Psychol.*, 1940, *5*, 1–21.

————. Denken, sprechen, arbeiten: Studie zur vergleichenden Menschen- und Tierpsychologie. *Arch. Psicol. Neurol. Psichiat.*, 1940, *1*, 755–770.

————. Bericht über die Tätigkeit des psychologischen Laboratoriums der Universität Amsterdam. *Acta Psychol.*, 1941, *5*, 50–70.

————. *Die menschliche Hand: Eine psychologische Studie.* Basel: Karger, 1944. (1941)

————. Die Beziehung zwischen mathematischer und musikalischer Begabung. (1943) *Schweiz. Z. Psychol.*, 1946, *5*, 269–281.

————. *Die Bedeutung der Psychologie für die Wissenschaft, für die Praxis und die akademische Ausbildung der Psychologen.* Bern: Francke, 1947. (1944)

————. *Introduction to the psychology of music.* Trans. by G. I. C. de Courcy. London: Longmans, Green, 1953. (1944)

————. *The origins and prehistory of language.* Trans. by J. Butler. New York: Longmans, Green, 1956. (1946)

————. *Ursprung und Vorgeschichte der Sprache.* Bern: Francke, 1946.

————. Colour mixture and sound mixture. *Acta Psychol.*, 1949, *6*, 3–26.

————. Le problème du génie. *Année psychol.*, 1951, *51*, 83–96.

————. *Psychology and art of the blind.* Trans. by H. A. Wolff. London: Longmans, Green, 1950. (Reprinted 1970)

————. *Talent und Genie; Grundzüge einer Begabungspsychologie.* (New ed.) Bern: Francke, 1952. (1951)

————. Zur Revision der Gestaltpsychologie. *Schweiz. Z. Psychol.*, 1953, *12*, 89–110.

————. Höheres Lebensalter und geistige Leistungskraft. *Universitas*, 1953, *8*, 685–690.

————. Gestaltbildung und Strukturerkenntnis. *Wiener Z. Phil. Psychol. Pädag.*, 1953, *4*, 268–273.

————. Grundprinzipien des menschlichen und tierischen Daseins. *Psychol. Forsch.*, 1953, *24*, 215–229.

————. Lassen sich die bekannten geometrisch-optischen Täuschungen auch im haptischen Gebiet nachweisen? *Jb. Psychol. Psychother.*, 1953, *1*, 464–178.

————. Denken und Sprechen. *Acta Psychol.*, 1954, *10*, 3–50.

————. *Het persoonlijke en sociale leven van de blinden.* Leiden: Stenfert, 1955.

————. Bibliography of works and papers. *Acta Psychol.*, 1956, *12*, 208–215.   **Bl**

————. Die Sprachfunktion der Hand. *Psychol. Beitr.*, 1956, 2, 254–265.

————. Psychologie des Händedrucks und der Weltsprache der Hände. *Universitas*, 1956, *11*, 143–148.

————. Optik und Haptik. Die Beziehung zwischen optischen und haptischen Wahrnehmungen. *Stud. gen.*, 1957, *10*, 3′/4–379.

————. *Die Trias: Analyse der dualen und trialen Systeme.* Munich: Bayerische Akademie Wissenschaft, 1957.

MARTIN LUTHER REYMERT
1883-1953
Norwegian-American Psychologist (14)

Reymert, M. L. *Psychology of the teacher.* Worcester, Mass.: Clark University Press, 1917.

————. The personal equation in motor capacities. *Scand. Sci. Rev.*, 1923, *2*, 177–222.

————. Ontogenetic aspects of "meaning." *Proc. 8th Int Cong., Groningen.* Groningen: Noordhoff, 1927, pp. 393–396.

————. The new psychological laboratory of Wittenberg College. *Amer. J. Psychol.*, 1928, *40*, 171.

———— (Ed.), *Feelings and emotions: The Wittenberg symposium.* Worcester, Mass.: Clark University Press, 1928.

——, & Hartman, Mildred L. A qualitative and quantitative analysis of a mental test. *Amer. J. Psychol.,* 1933, *45,* 87–105.

——, & Frings, J. Children's intelligence in relation to occupation of father. *Amer. J. Sociol.,* 1935–1936, *41,* 351–354.

——, & Speer, G. S. Does the Luria technique measure emotion or merely bodily tension? A re-evaluation of the method. *J. Pers.,* 1938–1939, *7,* 192–200.

——, & Hinton, R. T., Jr. The effect of a change to a relatively superior environment upon the IQ's of one hundred children. *Yearb. Soc. Stud. Educ.,* 1940, *39*(2), 255–280.

——, & Kohn, H. A. An objective investigation of suggestibility. *J. Pers.,* 1940–1941, *9,* 44–48.

——, & Meister, R. K. A comparison of the original and revised Stanford-Binet intelligence scales. *Educ. Psychol. Measmt,* 1941, *1,* 67–76.

——. The Mooseheart system of child guidance. *Nerv. child.,* 1941, *1,* 73–99.

——. The place of war toys in the present emergency. *J. genet. Psychol.,* 1944, *64,* 317–322.

——, & Rotman, Miriam. Auditory changes in children from ages ten to eighteen. *J. genet. Psychol.,* 1946, *68,* 181–187.

——. Play therapy at Mooseheart. *J. except. Child.,* 1946, *13,* 2–9.

——. The organization and administration of a child guidance clinic. In E. Harms (Ed.), *Handbook of child guidance.* New York: Child Care Publications, 1947, pp. 225–248.

—— (Ed.). *Feelings and emotions: The Mooseheart symposium.* New York: Hafner, 1967. (1948)

THEODULE ARMAND RIBOT
1839-1916
French Psychologist (26)

Ribot, T. A. *The diseases of will, memory and personality.* Trans. by J. Fitzgerald. New York: Humboldt, 1903. (Also Chicago: Open Court, 1903)   **C**

——. *English psychology.* (3rd ed.) Trans. by J. M. Baldwin. New York: Appleton, 1892. (1870)

——. *Quid David Hartley de consociatione idearum senserit.* Paris: Guingamp, 1872.

——. *Heredity: A psychological study of its phenomena, laws, causes, and consequences.* Trans. anon. New York: Appleton, 1875. (1873)

——. *L'hérédité, étude psychologique sur ses phénomènes, ses lois, ses causes, ses conséquences.* (2nd ed.) Paris: Ladrange, 1882. (1873)

——. *La philosophie de Schopenhauer.* (10th ed.) Paris: Alcan, 1905. (1874)

——. La durée des actes psychiques. *Rev. phil.,* 1876, *1,* 267–288.

——. La psychologie de Herbart. *Rev. phil.,* 1876, *2,* 68–85.

——. Les théories allemandes sur l'espace tactile. *Rev. phil.,* 1878, *6,* 130–145.

——. *German psychology of to-day: The empirical school.* (2nd ed.) Trans. by J. M. Baldwin, & pref. by J. McCosh. New York: Scribner's, 1886. (1879)

——. Les mouvements et leur importance psychologique. *Rev. phil.,* 1879, *8,* 371–386.

——. La psychologie physiologique. *Rev. sci.,* 1879, *16,* 820–826.

——. La mémoire comme fait biologique. *Rev. phil.,* 1880, *9,* 516–547.

——. Les désordres généraux de la mémoire. *Rev. phil.,* 1880, *10,* 181–214.

——. Les désordres partiels de la mémoire. *Rev. phil.,* 1880, *10,* 485–516.

——. The diseases of memory. (1881) In *The diseases of will, memory and personality, op. cit.,* pp. 1–48.

——. *Diseases of memory.* Trans. by W. H. Smith. New York: Appleton, 1882. (1881)

——. Les conditions organiques de la personnalité. *Rev. phil.,* 1883, *16,* 619–642.

——. The diseases of the will. (1883) In *The diseases of will, memory and personality, op. cit.*, pp. 1–45.

——. *The diseases of the will*. (8th ed.) Chicago: Open Court, 1894. (1883).

——. L'anéantissement de la volonté. *Rev. phil.*, 1883, *15*, 135–169.

——. Les bases affectives de la personnalité. *Rev. phil.*, 1884, *18*, 138–172.

——. Les bases intellectuelles de la personnalité. *Rev. phil.*, 1884, *18*, 410–446.

——. The diseases of personality. (1885) In *The diseases of will, memory and personality, op. cit.*, pp. 1–52.

——. Le mécanisme de l'attention. *Rev. phil.*, 1887, *24*, 378–394, 490–514.

——. *The psychology of attention*. Trans. by J. Fitzgerald. (3rd ed.) Chicago: Open Court, 1911. (1888)

——. *Psychologie de l'attention*. (4th ed.) Paris: Alcan, 1919. (1888)

——. Enquête sur les idées générales. *Rev. phil.*, 1891, *32*, 376–388.

——. Sur les diverses formes du caractère. *Rev. phil.*, 1892, *34*, 480–500.

——. Psychologie des états affectifs: La mémoire affective. *Rev. Cours Conf.*, 1894, *10*, 65–68.

——. Les états affectifs et la mémoire. *Rev. neurol.*, 1894, *2*, 33–39.

——. Pathological pleasures and pains. *Monist*, 1895–1896, *6*, 176–187.

——. Les caractères anormaux et morbides. *Année psychol.*, 1895, *2*, 1–17.

——. *La psychologie des sentiments*. (13th ed.) Paris: Alcan, 1930. (1896)

——. *The evolution of general ideas*. Trans. by F. A. Welby. Chicago: Open Court, 1899. (1897)

——. The intelligence of animals. Trans. by F. A. Welby. *Open Court*, 1899, *13*, 85–97.

——. The general ideas of infants and deaf-mutes. *Open Court*, 1899, *13*, 164–175.

——. *Essay on the creative imagination*. Trans. by A. H. N. Baron. Chicago: Open Court, 1906. (1900)

——. L'imagination créatrice affective. *Rev. phil.*, 1902, *53*, 598–630.

——. *La logique des sentiments*. Paris: Alcan, 1905.

——. *Essai sur les passions*. Paris: Alcan, 1906.

——. *Problèmes de psychologie affective*. Paris: Alcan, 1909.

Jastrow, J., Münsterberg, H., ——, Janet, P., Hart, B., & Prince, M. *Subconscious phenomena*. Boston: Badger, 1910.

——. Le problème de la pensée sans images et sans mots. *Rev. phil.*, 1913, *76*, 50–68.

——. *La vie inconsciente et les mouvements*. Paris: Alcan, 1914.

Hameline, *Anthologie*; Park & Burgess, *Sociology*

CHARLES RICHET
1850-1935
French Physiologist (17)

Richet, C. Du somnambulisme provoqué. *J. anat. Physiol.*, 1875, *11*, 348–378.

——. La douleur. *Rev. phil.*, 1877, *4*, 457–481.

——. *Recherches experimentales et cliniques sur la sensibilité*. Paris: Alcan, 1877.

——. *Physiology and histology of the cerebral convolutions*. Trans. by E. P. Fawler. New York: Wood, 1879. (1878)

——. De l'influence des mouvements sur les idées. *Rev. phil.*, 1879, *8*, 610–615.

——. Du somnambulisme provoqué. *Rev. phil.*, 1880, *10*, 337–374, 462–484.

——. *Physiologie des muscles et des nerfs*. Paris: Baillière, 1882.

——. La personnalité et la mémoire dans le somnambulisme. *Rev. phil.*, 1883, *15*, 225–242.

———. La suggestion mentale et le calcul des probabilités. *Rev. phil.,* 1884, *18,* 609–674.

———. *L'homme et l'intelligence. Fragments de philosophie.* Paris: Alcan, 1884.

———. La peur. *Rev. Deux Mondes,* 1886, *76*(4), 73–117.

———. Les origines & les modalités de la mémoire. Essai de psychologie générale. *Rev. phil.,* 1886, *21,* 561–590.

———. Les mouvements inconscients. *Rev. hypno.,* 1886–1887, *1,* 170–176, 209–213.

———. Expériences sur le sommeil à distance. *Rev. hypno.,* 1887–1888, *2,* 225–240.

———. *Essai de psychologie générale.* Paris: Alcan, 1887.

———. Les réflexes psychiques. *Rev. phil.,* 1888, *25,* 225–237, 387–422, 500–528.

———. Qu'est ce que la physiologie générale? *Rev. phil.,* 1891, *31,* 337–367.

———. L'amour. *Rev. Deux Mondes,* 1891, *104,* 135–167.

———. Etude biologique sur la douleur. *Rev. sci.,* 1896, *6* (4e sér.), 225–232.

———. Circulation cérébrale. In *Dictionnaire de physiologie.* Vol. 2. Paris: Alcan, 1897, pp. 745–788.

———. La fonction du cerveau. *Rev. sci.,* 1897, *8* (4e sér.), 641–649.

Broca, A., & ———. Période réfractoire dans les centres nerveux. *C. r. Acad. sci.,* 1897, *124,* 96–99, 573–577, 697–700.

———. Physiologie du cerveau: Résumé général. In *Dictionnaire de physiologie.* Vol. 3. Paris: Alcan, 1898, pp. 48–57.

———. Physiologie générale du cerveau: Excitabilité dynamique cérébrale; processus psychiques. In *Dictionnaire de physiologie.* Vol. 3. Paris: Alcan, 1898, pp. 1–48.

———. La forme et la durée de la vibration nerveuse et l'unité psychologique du temps. *Rev. phil.,* 1899, *45,* 337–350.

———. Douleur. In *Dictionnaire de physiologie.* Vol. 5. Paris: Alcan, 1902, pp. 173–193.

———. Méthode expérimentale. In *Dictionnaire de physiologie.* Vol. 5. Paris: Alcan, 1902, pp. 894–903.

———. Anaphylaxis. (1913) In Nobel Foundation (Ed.), *Nobel lectures: Physiology or medicine, 1901–1921.* New York: Elsevier, 1967, pp. 473–490.

———. La sélection humaine. Paris: Alcan, 1919.

———. *Traité de physiologie médico-chirurgicale.* (2 vols.) Paris: Alcan, 1921.

———. *Thirty years of psychical research.* Trans. by S. de Brath. New York: Macmillan, 1923. (1922)

———. *L'intelligence et l'homme: Etudes de psychologie et de physiologie.* (New ed.) Paris: Alcan, 1936. (1927)

———. *The impotence of man.* Trans. by L. Harvey. Boston: Stratford, 1929. (1927)

———. *Our sixth sense.* Trans. by F. Rothwell. London: Rider, 1929. (1928)

———, & Richet, C., Jr. *Physiologie de l'homme.* Paris: Rieder, 1931.

———. Les réflexes d'acquisition (réflexes conditionnels de Pavloff). *C. r. Acad. sci.,* 1931, *192,* 1172–1173.

———. *Souvenirs d'un physiologiste.* Soigny: Peyronnet, 1933. **B**

———. *Au secours!* Paris: Peyronnet, 1935.

EUGENIO RIGNANO
1870-1930
Italian Philosopher (15)

Rignano, E. *Essays in scientific synthesis.* Trans. by W. J. Greenstreet. Chicago: Open Court, 1918. (1906) **C**

———. *Problemi della psiche.* Bologna: Zanichelli, 1928. **C**

———. *Di un socialismo in accordo colla dottrina economica liberale.* Turin: Bocca, 1901.

———. *La sociologie dans le cours de philosophie positive d'Auguste Comte.* Paris: Giard & Brière, 1902.

———. *La psicologia contemporanea.* Madrid: Fè & Jubera, 1902.

———. *Un socialisme en harmonie avec la doctrine économique libérale.* Paris: Giard & Brière, 1904.

———. *Upon the inheritance of acquired characters, a hypothesis of heredity, development, and assimilation.* Trans. by B. C. H. Harvey. Chicago: Open Court, 1911. (1905)

———. *La question de l'héritage.* Paris: Bellais, 1905.

———. Ueber die mnemonische Entstehung und die mnemonische Natur affektiver Neigungen. *Arch. ges. Psychol.,* 1911, *20,* 1–33.

———. Die Entwicklung des Räsonnements. *Arch. ges. Psychol.,* 1914, *32,* 1–51.

———. *The psychology of reasoning.* Trans. by W. A. Holl. New York: Harcourt, Brace, 1923. (1920)

———. *Come funziona la nostra intelligenza.* Bologna: Zanichelli, 1922.

———. *Biological memory.* Trans. by E. W. MacBride. New York: Harcourt, Brace, 1926. (1922) (Reprinted 1971)

———. *Man not a machine: A study of the finalistic aspects of life.* Foreword by H. Driesch. London: Kegan Paul, 1926. (1925)

———. *The nature of life.* Trans. by N. Mallinson. New York: Harcourt, Brace, 1930. (1926)

———. *La teoria della forma della nuova scuola psicologica tedesca. La "Gestalt."* I, II, III. *Scientia,* 1927, *21,* 145–158, 215–228, 280–290.

———. *The aim of human existence.* Chicago: Open Court, 1929. (1927)

———. *Problèmes de psychologie et de morale.* Paris: Alcan, 1928.

———. The psychological theory of form. Trans. by H. C. Warren. *Psychol. Rev.,* 1928, *35,* 118–135.

———. Zur Gestalttheorie. Antwort auf Herrn Köhlers kritische Erwiderung. *Scientia,* 1928, *22,* 323–356.

———. Die Gestalttheorie. *Psychol. Forsch.,* 1928, *11,* 172–187.

———, & Becker, H. Sociology, its methods and laws. Trans. by H. Becker. *Amer. J. Sociol.,* 1929, *34,* 429–450, 605–622.

———, The concept of purpose in biology. *Mind,* 1931, *40,* 335–340.

(BARON) WILLIAM HALSE RIVERS RIVERS
1864-1922
English Psychologist (19)

Rivers, W. H. R. *Kinship and social organisation* (together with *The genealogical method of anthropological inquiry*). London: Athlone Press, 1968. (1914)   **C**

———. *Psychology and politics, and other essays.* New York: Harcourt, 1923.   **C**

———. Experimental psychology in relation to insanity. *J. ment. Sci.,* 1895, *41,* 591–599.

———. On the apparent size of objects. *Mind,* 1896, *5*(N.S.), 71–80.

———, & Kraepelin, E. Ueber Ermüdung und Erholung. *Psychol. Arb.,* 1896, *1,* 627–678.

———. Primitive colour vision. *Pop. Sci. Mon.,* 1901, *59,* 44–58.

———, & Seligmann, C. G. Colour vision. In A. C. Hadden (Ed.), *Reports of the Cambridge Anthropological expedition to the Torres Straits.* Vol. II. *Physiology and psychology.* Part I: *Introduction and vision.* London: Cambridge University Press, 1901, pp. 48–96.

———. Colour vision of the natives of Upper Egypt. *J. Anthrop. Inst. Great Britain,* 1901, *31,* 229–245.

———. Observations on the senses of the Todas. *Brit. J. Psychol.,* 1904–1905, *1,* 321–396.

Head, H., ———, & Sherren, J. The afferent nervous system from a new aspect. *Brain,* 1905, *28,* 99–115.

———. *The Todas.* New York: Macmillan, 1906. (Reprinted 1967)

———, & Head, H. A human experiment in nerve division. *Brain*, 1908, *31*, 323–450.

———. *The influence of alcohol and other drugs on fatigue* (Croonian lecture). London: Arnold, 1908.

———. Vision. In E. A. Schäfer (Ed.), *Text-book of physiology*. Vol. 2. New York: Macmillan, 1910, pp. 1026–1148.

———. The genealogical method of anthropological inquiry, *Soc. Rev.*, 1910, *3*, 1–12.

———. The ethnological analyses of culture. Presidential address to Section H of the British Association for the Advancement of Science. *Rep. Brit. Ass. Adv. Sci.*, 1911, *81*, 490–499.

———. Survival in sociology. *Soc. Rev.*, 1913, *6*, 293–305.

———. *The history of Melanesian society*. (2 vols.) Cambridge: Cambridge University Press, 1914. (Reprinted 1968)

———. Sociology and psychology. *Soc. Rev.*, 1916, *9*, 1–13.

———. Why is the "unconscious" unconscious? II. *Brit. J. Psychol.*, 1917–1919, *9*, 236–246.

———. Dreams and primitive culture. *Bull. John Rylands Libr., Manchester*, 1918, *4*, 387–410.

———. Instinct and the unconscious. I. *Brit. J. Psychol.*, 1919–1920, *10*, 1–7.

———. Psychology and medicine. *Brit. J. Psychol.*, 1919–1920, *10*, 183–193.

———. *Instinct and the unconscious*. (2nd ed.) Cambridge: Cambridge University Press, 1922. (1920)

———. *Mind and medicine*. New York: Longmans, Green, 1920.

———. Affect in the dream. *Brit. J. Psychol.*, 1921–1922, *12*, 113–124.

———. *History and ethnology*. New York: Macmillan, 1922.

———. *Conflict and dream*. New York: Harcourt, 1923.

———. *Social organization*. New York: Knopf, 1924. (Reprinted 1968)

———. *Medicine, magic and religion*. New York: Harcourt, Brace, 1924.

———. *Psychology and ethnology*. New York: Harcourt, Brace, 1926.

Drever, *Sourcebook ;* Park & Burgess. *Sociology ;* Thomas, *Source Book*

A(BRAHAM) (A)ARON ROBACK
1890-1965
American Psychologist (17)

Roback, A. A. *Psychology, with chapters on character analysis and mental measurement*. Cambridge: Sci-Art, 1923.

———. *Behaviorism and psychology*. Cambridge: Sci-Art, 1923.

———. *A bibliography of character and personality*. Cambridge: Sci-Art, 1927.

———. *The psychology of character, with a survey of temperament*. (3rd ed.) New York: Harcourt, Brace, 1931. (1927)

———. *Jewish influence in modern thought*. Cambridge: Sci-Art, 1929. (Reprinted 1970)

———. Writing slips and personality. *J. Pers.*, 1932–1933, *1*, 137–146.

———. *Self-consciousness and its treatment*. Cambridge: Sci-Art, 1933.

———. Personalysis: A study in method. *J. Pers.*, 1934, *3*, 144–156.

———. *Self-consciousness self-treated*. Cambridge: Sci-Art, 1936.

———. Fifty years of the dissociation school. *J. abnorm. soc. Psychol.*, 1936–1937, *31*, 131–137.

———. *Behaviorism at twenty-five*. Cambridge: Sci-Art, 1937.

———. *The psychology of common sense*. Cambridge: Sci-Art, 1939.

———. *William James, his marginalia, personality and contribution*. Cambridge: Sci-Art, 1942.

——. *A history of American psychology.* (Rev. ed.) New York: Collier, 1964. (1952)

——. *Destiny and motivation in language.* Cambridge: Sci-Art, 1954.

——. *Aspects of applied psychology and crime.* Cambridge: Sci-Art, 1964.

EDWARD STEVENS ROBINSON
1893-1937
American Psychologist (16)

Robinson, E. S. The compensatory function of make-believe play. *Psychol. Rev.,* 1920, *27,* 429–439.

——. Some factors determining the degree of retroactive inhibition. *Psychol. Monogr.,* 1920, *28,* No. 128.

——. The relative efficiencies of distributed and concentrated study in memorizing. *J. exp. Psychol.,* 1921, *4,* 327–343.

——, & Herrmann, S. O. Effects of loss of sleep. I. *J. exp. Psychol.,* 1922, *5,* 19–32.

——. & Richardson-Robinson, F. Effects of loss of sleep. II. *J. exp. Psychol.,* 1922, *5,* 93–100.

——, & Heron, W. T. Results of variations in length of memorized material. *J. exp. Psychol.,* 1922, *5,* 428–448.

——, & Darrow, C. W. Effect of length of list upon memory for numbers. *Amer. J. Psychol.,* 1924, *35,* 235–243.

——, & Heron, W. T. The warming-up effect. *J. exp. Psychol.,* 1924, *7,* 81–97.

——, & Brown, Martha A. Effect of serial position upon memorization. *Amer. J. Psychol.,* 1926, *37,* 538–552.

——, & Bills, A. G. Two factors in the work decrement. *J. exp., Psychol.,* 1926, *9,* 415–443.

——. Principles of the work decrement. *Psychol. Rev.,* 1926, *33,* 123–134.

——. The "similarity" factor in retroaction. *Amer. J. Psychol.,* 1927, *39,* 297–312.

——. Methods of practice equilibration. *Amer. J. Psychol.,* 1929, *41,* 153–156.

——. Association theory today: An essay in systematic psychology. New York: Century, 1932. (Reprinted 1964)

——, & Robinson, Florence R. Practice and the work decrement. *Amer. J. Psychol.,* 1932, *44,* 547–551.

——. *Man as psychology sees him.* New York: Macmillan, 1932.

——. Work of the integrated organisms. In C. Murchison (Ed.), *A handbook of general experimental psychology.* Worcester, Mass.: Clark University Press, 1934, pp. 571–650.

——. *Law and the lawyers.* New York: Macmillan, 1935.

——. Psychology and the law. *J. soc. Phil.,* 1936, *1,* 197–217.

GEZA ROHEIM
1891-1953
Hungarian-American Psychoanalyst (11)

Róheim, G. Das Selbst. *Imago,* 1921, *7,* 1–39, 142-179, 310–348, 453–504.

——. Primitive man and environment. *Int. J. Psycho-Anal.,* 1921, *2,* 157–178.

——. Ethnology and folk psychology (collective review). (1921) *Int. J. Psycho-Anal.,* 1922, *3,* 188–222.

——. Nach dem Tode des Urvaters. *Imago,* 1923, *9,* 83–121.

——. *Social anthropology.* New York: Boni Liveright, 1925. Also as *Australian totemism: A psychoanalytic study in anthropology.* London: Allen & Unwin, 1925. (Reprinted 1971)

——. Die wilde Jagd. *Imago,* 1926, *12,* 465–477.

——. La psychologie raciale et les origines du capitalisme chez les primitifs. *Rev. franç. psychoanal.,* 1929, *3,* 122–149.

——. Psychoanalysis and anthropology. (1932) In D. G. Haring (Ed.), *Personal character and cultural milieu: A collection of readings.* (Rev. ed.) Syracuse, N.Y.: Syracuse University Press, 1949, pp. 565–588. (Reprinted 1970)

———. Psycho-analysis of primitive cultural types. *Int. J. Psycho-Anal.,* 1932, *13,* 2–224.

———. *The riddle of the sphinx, or human origins.* Trans. by R. Money-Kyrle. London: Hogarth, 1934.

———. The study of character development and the ontogenetic theory of culture. In *Essays presented to C. G. Seligman.* London: Paul, Trench & Truebner, 1934, pp. 281–293.

———. The evolution of culture. *Int. J. Psycho-Anal.,* 1934, *15,* 387–418.

———. The nescience of the Aranda. *Brit. J. med. Psychol.,* 1938, *17,* 343–360.

———. Freud and cultural anthropology. *Psychoanal. Quart.,* 1940, *9,* 246–255.

———. Myth and folk-tale. *Amer. Imago,* 1941, *2,* 266–279.

———. The origin and function of culture. *Nerv. Ment. Dis. Monogr.,* 1942, No. 6. (Reprinted 1969)

———. *War, crime and the covenant.* Monticello, N.Y.: Medical Journal Press, 1945. (1943) (Reprinted 1970)

———. *The eternal ones of the dream ; a psychoanalytic interpretation of Australian myth and ritual.* New York: International Universities Press, 1970. (1945)

———. *Psychoanalysis and anthropology: Culture, personality and the unconscious.* New York: International Universities Press, 1968. (1950)

———. *The gates of the dream.* New York: International Universities Press, 1969. (1952)

———. Some aspects of Semitic monotheism. *Psychoanal. Soc. Sci.,* 1955, *4,* 169–222.

———. The western tribes of central Australia: Their sexual life. *Psychoanal. Soc. Sci.,* 1958, *5,* 221–245.

LUIGI ROLANDO
1773-1831
Italian Anatomist (15)

Rolando, L. *Anatomes physiologica comparata disquisitio in respirationis organa.* (2nd ed.) (2 vols.) Turin: Publ. unknown, 1819. (1801)

———. *Sulle cause da cui dipende la vita negli esseri organizzati.* Florence: Moücke, 1807.

———. *Saggio sopra la vera struttura del cervello dell'uomo e degli animali e sopra le funzioni del sistema nervoso.* (2nd ed.) (3 vols.) Turin: Marietti, 1828. (1809)

———. *Humani corporis fabricae ac functionum analysis adumbrata.* Vienna: Volke, 1817.

———. Essai sur la véritable structure du cerveau de l'homme et des animaux, et sur les fonctions du système nerveux. *J. Physiol.,* 1822, *96,* 151–169.

———. Expériences sur les fonctions du système nerveux. *J. physiol. exp. path.,* 1823, *3,* 95–114.

———. *Ricerche anatomiche sulla struttura della midolla spinale.* Turin: Stamp, 1824.

———. Osservazioni sul cervelletto. *Mem. Accad. Sci. Torino,* 1825, *29,* 163–188.

———. Della struttura degli emisferi cerebrali. *Mem. Accad. Sci. Torino,* 1830, *35,* 103–147.

Clarke & O'Malley, *Brain*

GEORGE JOHN ROMANES
1848-1894
English Biologist (25)

Romanes, G. J. *Essays,* Ed. by C. L. Morgan. New York: Longmans, Green, 1897.   **C**

———. Perception and instinct in the lower animals. *Nature,* 1873, *8,* 282–283.

———. Instinct and acquisition. *Nature,* 1875, *12,* 553–554.

———. Conscience in animals. *J. Sci.,* 1876, *6,* 145–157.

———. Observations on the locomotor system of Medusae. *Phil. Trans.,* 1877, *166,* 269–313 ; 1878, *167,* 659–752 ; 1881, *171,* 161–202.

————. ("Physicus") *A candid examination of theism.* Boston: Houghton, Osgood, 1878.

————. Animal intelligence. *Nineteenth Cent.,* 1878, *4,* 653–672.

————. Hypnotism. *Nineteenth Cent.,* 1880, *8,* 474–480. Reprinted in *Essays, op. cit.,* pp. 213–225.

————. Mental differences between men and women. *Nineteenth Cent.,* 1881, *21,* 654–672. Reprinted in *Essays, op. cit.,* pp. 113–151.

————. *Animal intelligence.* London: Kegan Paul, Trench, 1882. (Reprinted 1970)

————. *The scientific evidences of organic evolution.* London: Macmillan, 1882.

————. The fallacy of materialism. I. Body and mind. *Nineteenth Cent.,* 1882, *12,* 871–888.

————. *Mental evolution in animals: With a posthumous essay on instinct, by Charles Darwin.* New York: Appleton, 1885. (1883) (Reprinted 1969)

————. Mr. Lloyd Morgan on instinct. *Nature,* 1884, *29,* 379–381.

————. Instinct. *Nature,* 1884, *29,* 428, 477.

————. The Darwinian theory of instinct. *Nineteenth Cent.,* 1884, *16,* 434–450. Reprinted in *Essays, op. cit.,* pp. 1–24.

————. *Jelly-fish, star-fish, and sea-urchins: Being a research on primitive nervous systems.* New York: Appleton, 1893. (1885)

————. Experiments on the sense of smell in dogs. *Nature,* 1887, *36,* 273–274.

————. *Poems: 1879–1889.* London: Harrison, 1889.

————. *Mental evolution in man: Origin of human faculty.* London: Kegan Paul, Trench, 1889. (Reprinted 1970)

————. Anti-Darwinism fallacies. *Forum,* 1889, *7,* 513–520.

————. Origin of human faculty. *Brain,* 1889, *12,* 289–307. Reprinted in *Essays, op. cit.,* pp. 86–112.

————. Weismann's theory of heredity. *Contemp. Rev.,* 1890, *62,* 686–699. Also *Smithsonian Rep.,* 1890, 433–446.

————. Darwin's latest critics. *Nineteenth Cent.,* 1890, *27,* 823–832.

————. *Darwinism illustrated.* Chicago: Open Court, 1892.

————. *Darwin and after Darwin. I. Darwinian theory.* (3rd ed.) *II. Post-Darwinian questions: Heredity and utility. III. Post-Darwinian questions: Isolation and physiological selection.* Chicago: Open Court, 1916, 1914. (1892)

————. *An examination of Weismannism.* Chicago: Open Court, 1893.

————. *Mind and motion and monism.* Ed. by C. L. Morgan. (New ed.) New York: Longmans, 1896. (1895)

————. *Thoughts on religion.* Chicago: Open Court, 1895.

Grinder, *Genetic Psychology;* Herrnstein & Boring, *Source Book;* Riopelle, *Problem Solving;* Sahakian, *Psychology*

HERMANN RORSCHACH
1884-1922
Swiss Psychiatrist (26)

Rorschach, H. *Gesammelte Aufsätze.* Ed. by K. W. Bash. Bern: Huber, 1965. **B Bl C**

————. Pferdediebstahl in Dämmerzuständen. *Arch. Kriminalanthrop. Kriminalistik,* 1912, *49,* 175–180. Reprinted in *Gesammelte Aufsätze, op. cit.,* pp. 170–175.

————. Ueber "Reflexhalluzinationen" und verwandte Erscheinungen. *Z. ges. Neurol.,* 1912, *13,* 357–400. Reprinted in *Gesammelte Aufsätze, op. cit.,* pp. 105–149.

————. Ein Beispiel von misslungener Sublimierung und ein Fall von Namenvergessen. *Zbl. Psychoanal.,* 1912, *2,* 403–406. Reprinted in *Gesammelte Aufsätze, op. cit.,* pp. 154–158.

————. Reflexhalluzinationen und Symbolik. *Zbl. Psychoanal.,* 1912, *3,* 121–128. Reprinted in *Gesammelte Aufsätze, op. cit.,* pp. 162–170.

————. Analytische Bemerkungen über das Gemälde eines Schizophrenen. *Zbl. Psychoanal..* 1913, *3,* 270–272. Reprinted in *Gesammelte Aufsätze, op. cit.,* pp. 178–183.

————. Ueber die Wahl des Freundes beim Neurotiker. *Zbl. Psychoanal.,* 1913, *3,* 524–527. Reprinted in *Gesammelte Aufsätze, op. cit.,* pp. 153–188.

————. Analyse einer schizophrenen Zeichnung. *Zbl. Psychoanal.,* 1914, *4,* 53–58. Reprinted in *Gesammelte Aufsätze, op. cit.,* pp. 188–194.

————. Assoziationsexperiment, freies Assoziieren und Hypnose im Dienst der Hebung einer Amnesie. *Corr.-Bl. Schweiz. Aertze,* 1917, *47,* 898–905. Reprinted in *Gesammelte Aufsätze, op. cit.,* pp. 196–205.

————. Einiges über schweizerische Sekten und Sektengründer. *Schweiz. Arch. Neurol. Psychiatr.,* 1917, *1,* 254–258. Reprinted in *Gesammelte Aufsätze, op. cit.,* pp. 206–212.

————. Weiteres über schweizerische Sektenbildungen. *Schweiz. Arch. Neurol. Psychiat.,* 1919, *2,* 385–388. Reprinted in *Gesammelte Aufsätze, op. cit.,* pp. 212–216.

————. *Psychodiagnostics: A diagnostic test based on perception.* (2nd ed.) Trans. by P. Lemkau & B. Kronenberg. New York: Grune & Stratton, 1942. (1921)

————, & Oberholzer, E. The application of the interpretation of form to psychoanalysis. *J. nerv. ment. Dis.,* 1924, *60,* 225–248. (1923) Reprinted in *Psychodiagnostics, op. cit.,* pp. 184–216.

————. Zwei schweizerische Sektenstifter. *Imago,* 1927, *13,* 395–441. Reprinted in *Gesammelte Aufsätze, op. cit.,* pp. 256–299.

Beck & Molish, *Reflexes;* Sahakian, *Psychology;* Shipley, *Classics*

AARON JOSHUA ROSANOFF
1878-1943
American Psychiatrist (15)

Rosanoff, A. J. *Manual of psychiatry.* (7th ed.) Chicago: Wiley, 1938. (1905)

Kent, Grace H., & ————. A study of association in insanity. *Amer. J. Insan.,* 1910, *67,* 37–96, 317–390.

————, & Orr, F. I. A study of heredity in insanity in the light of the Mendelian theory. *Amer. J. Insan.,* 1911, *68,* 221–261.

————. The prevention of insanity: Hygiene of the mind. *State Hosp. Bull. N.Y.,* 1911, *4,* 359–378.

————. Exciting causes in psychiatry. *Amer. J. Insan.,* 1912, *69,* 351–401.

————. Dissimilar heredity in mental disease. *Amer. J. Insan.,* 1913, *70,* 1–105.

Rosanoff, Isabel R., & ————. A study of association in children. *Psychol. Rev.,* 1913, *20,* 43–89.

————. A study of eugenic forces. Particularly of social conditions which bring about the segregation of neuropathic persons in special institutions. *Amer. J. Insan.,* 1915, *72,* 223–257.

————. Intellectual efficiency in relation to insanity. *Amer. J. Insan.,* 1916, *73,* 43–77.

————, Martin, Helen E., & Rosanoff, Isabel R. A higher scale of mental measurement and its application to cases of insanity. *Psychol. Monogr.,* 1918, *25,* No. 109.

Mitchell, Ida, Rosanoff, Isabel R., & ————. A study of association in Negro children. *Psychol. Rev.,* 1919, *26,* 354–359.

————. A theory of personality based mainly on psychiatric experience. *Psychol. Bull.,* 1920, *17,* 281–299.

Rosanoff, Isabel R., & ————. A study of mental disorders in twins. *J. juv. Res.,* 1931, *15,* 268–270.

————. Sex-linked inheritance in mental deficiency. *Amer. J. Psychiat.,* 1931, *11,* 289–298.

————. Twins: A study of certain mental disorders. *Calif. West. Med.,* 1932, *37,* 101–105.

————, Handy, Leva M., Rosanoff, Isabel R., & Inman-Kane, Christine V. Sex factors in intelligence in twins. *J. nerv. ment. Dis.,* 1934, *80,* 125–137.

————, *et al.* The etiology of so-called schizophrenic psychoses with special reference to their occurrence in twins. *Amer. J. Psychiat.*, 1934, *91*, 247–286.

————. Handy, Leva M., & Rosanoff, I. A. Criminality and delinquency in twins. *J. crim. Law Criminol.*, 1934, *24*, 923–934.

————. Handy, Leva M., & Rosanoff, I. A. Etiology of epilepsy with special reference to its occurrence in twins. *Arch. Neurol. Psychiat.*, Chicago, 1934, *31*, 1165–1193.

————, Handy, Leva M., & Plesset, Isabel R. The etiology of manic-depressive syndromes with special reference to their occurrence in twins. *Amer. J. Psychiat.*, 1935, *91*, 725–762.

————. A theory of chaotic sexuality. *Amer. J. Psychiat.*, 1935, *91*, 35–41.

————, Handy, Leva M., & Plesset, Isabel R. The etiology of mental deficiency with special reference to its occurrence in twins: A chapter in the genetic history of human intelligence. *Psychol. Monogr.*, 1937, *48*, No. 216.

————, Handy, Leva A., & Plesset, Isabel R. Mental disorders in triplets. *Amer. J. Psychiat.*, 1939, *95*, 1139–1142.

————, Handy, Leva M., & Plesset, Isabel R. The etiology of child behavior difficulties, juvenile delinquency and adult criminality, with special reference to their occurrence in twins. *Psychiat. Monogr.*, 1941, No. 1.

EDWARD ALSWORTH ROSS
1866-1951
American Sociologist (11)

Ward, L. F., & Ross, E. A. The Ward-Ross correspondence, 1891–1912. Ed. by B. Stern. *Amer. Sociol. Rev.*, 1938, *3*, 362–401 ; 1946, *11*, 734–748 ; 1947, *12*, 703–720 ; 1948, *13*, 82–94 ; 1949, *14*, 88–119.   **B C**

————. The mob mind. *Pop. Sci. Mon.*, 1897, *51*, 390–397.

————. *Social control: A survey of the foundations of order.* Intro. by J. Weinberg, Gisela J. Hinkle, & R. C. Hinkle. Cleveland, Ohio: Case Western Reserve University Press, 1969. (1901)

————. The present problem of social psychology. *Amer. J. Sociol.*, 1904–1905, *10*, 456–472.

————. *Foundations of sociology.* (5th ed) New York: Macmillan. 1912. (1905)

————. *Sin and society.* Boston: Houghton Mifflin, 1907.

————. The nature and scope of social psychology. *Amer. J. Sociol.*, 1908, *13*, 577–583.

————. Rational imitation. *Amer. J. Sociol.*, 1908, *13*, 721–728.

————. *Social psychology: An outline and sourcebook.* New York: Macmillan, 1918. (1908)

————. What is social psychology? *Psychol. Bull.*, 1909, *6*, 409–411.

————. Individuation. *Amer. J. Sociol.*, 1920, *25*, 469–479.

————. *The principles of sociology.* (3rd ed.) New York: Appleton-Century-Crofts, 1938. (1920)

————. *The outlines of sociology.* New York: Century, 1923. (Reprinted 1971)

————. *The social trend.* New York: Century, 1923. (Reprinted 1970)

————. *Seventy years of it.* New York: Appleton, 1936.   **B**

————. *New-age sociology.* New York: Appleton-Century, 1940.

————. Fifty years of sociology in the United States. *Amer. J. Sociol.*, 1945, *50*, 489–492.

Borgatta, *Present-day Sociology*

JEAN-JACQUES ROUSSEAU
1712-1778
Swiss-French Philosopher (24)

Rousseau, J. J. *Minor educational writings.* Trans. by W. Boyd. London: Blackie, 1910. (Reprinted 1962)   **C**

————. *The political writings of Rousseau.* (2 vols.) Ed. by C. E. Vaughan. New York: Wiley, 1962. (1915)   **C**

————. *Correspondance générale de J.-J. Rousseau*. Ed. by T. Dufour & P. P. Plan. (20 vols.) Paris: Colin, 1924–1934.   **B C**

————. *Citizen of Geneva: Selections from the letters of Jean-Jacques Rousseau*. Ed. by C. W. Hendel. New York: Oxford University Press, 1937.   **B C**

————. *Oeuvres complètes*. (4 vols.) Ed. by B. Gagnebin & M. Raymond. (Sponsored by the Société J.-J. Rousseau.) Paris: Gallimard, 1959–1969.   **C**

————. *Correspondance complète*. (14 vols.) Ed. by R. A. Leigh. Geneva: Institut et Musée Voltaire, Les Délices, 1965–1971.   **B C**

————. *Religious writings [of] Rousseau*. Ed. by R. Grimsley. London: Clarendon Press, 1970.   **C**

————. *Discours sur les sciences et les arts*. Ed. by G. R. Havens. New York: The Modern Language Association of America, 1946. (1750)

————. *The first and second discourses*. Ed. by R. Masters. New York: St. Martins Press, 1964. (1750–1755)

————. *Essay on the origin of languages which treats of melody and musical imitation*. (ca. 1755) Trans. by J. Howran. In *On the origin of language*. New York: Ungar, 1966, pp. 3–74.

————. *Discours sur l'origine et les fondements de l'inégalité parmi les hommes*. Ed. by H. F. Muller & R. E. G. Vaillant. New York: Oxford University Press, 1922. (1755)

————. *Notes en réfutation de l'ouvrage d'Helvétius intitulé "De l'esprit."* (1758) In G. Lahure (Ed.), *Oeuvres complètes de J.-J. Rousseau*. Vol. 12. Paris: Hachette, 1906, pp. 298–304.

————. *Lettre à Monsieur d'Alembert sur les spectacles*. Ed. by M. Fuchs. Lille: Giard, 1948. (1758)   **B**

————. *La nouvelle Héloïse*. (4 vols.) Ed. by D. Mornet. Paris: Hachette, 1925. (1761)

————. *The social contract*. Trans. by M. Cranston. Baltimore, Md.: Penguin Books, 1968. (1762)

————. *Emile: Selections*. Trans. & ed. by W. Boyd. New York: Teachers College Press, 1962. (1762)

————. *Lettres écrites de la montagne*. Neuchâtel: Ides et Calendes, 1962. (1764)   **B**

————. *Les rêveries du promeneur solitaire*. Ed. by M. Raymond. Lille: Giard, 1948. (1782)

————. *The confessions of Jean-Jacques Rousseau*. Trans. & intro. by J. M. Cohen. Baltimore, Md.: Penguin Books, 1959. (1782)   **B**

Brinton, *Age Reason;* Hutchins, *Great Books;* Kessen, *Child;* Park & Burgess, *Sociology;* Parson, *Society;* Price, *Education;* Slotkin, *Anthropology;* Torrey, *Les Philosophes;* Ulich, *Educational Wisdom*

JOSIAH ROYCE
1855-1916
American Philosopher (16)

Royce, J. *Studies of good and evil: A series of essays upon the problems of philosophy and life*. New York: Appleton, 1898. (Reprinted 1964)   **C**

————. *Race questions, provincialism, and other American problems*. New York: Macmillan, 1908. (Reprinted 1967)   **C**

————. *William James and other essays on the philosophy of life*. New York: Macmillan, 1911. (Reprinted 1967)   **C**

————. *Fugitive essays*. Ed. by J. Loewenberg. Cambridge: Harvard University Press, 1920. (Reprinted 1968)   **C**

————. *Royce's logical essays: Collected logical essays of Josiah Royce*. Ed. by D. S. Robinson. Dubuque, Iowa: Brown, 1951.   **C**

————. *The basic writings of Josiah Royce*. (2 vols.) Ed. by J. J. McDermott. Chicago: University of Chicago Press, 1969.   **C**

————. *Letters of Josiah Royce*. Ed. by J. Clendenning. Chicago: University of Chicago Press, 1970.   **B C**

————. The nature of voluntary progress. *Berk. Quart.*, 1880, July, 161–189. Reprinted in *Fugitive essays, op. cit.*, pp. 96–132.

————. "Mind-stuff" and reality. *Mind*, 1881, *6*, 365–377.

————. Kant's relation to modern philosophic progress. *J. specul. Phil.*, 1881, *15*, 360–381.

————. How beliefs are made. *Californian*, 1882, *5*, 122–139. Reprinted in *Fugitive essays, op. cit.*, pp. 345–363.

————. *The religious aspect of philosophy: A critique of the bases of conduct and of faith.* New York: Houghton Mifflin, 1885. (Reprinted 1958)

————. *California, from the conquest in 1846 to the Second Vigilance Committee in San Francisco (1856): A study of American character.* Boston: Houghton Mifflin, 1886. (Reprinted 1948)

————. *The feud of Oakfield Creek: A novel of California life.* Boston: Houghton Mifflin, 1887.

————. Report of the Committee on Phantasms and Presentiments. *Proc. Amer. Soc. Psychic. Res.*, Mar. 1889, 350–428.

————. Hallucination of memory and 'telepathy.' *Mind*, 1888, *13*, 244–248.

————. Is there a science of education? *Educ. Rev.*, 1891, *1*, 15–25, 121–132.

————. *The spirit of modern philosophy.* Boston: Houghton Mifflin, 1892. (Reprinted 1967)

————. On certain psychological aspects of moral training. *Int. J. Ethics*, 1892–1893, *3*, 413–436.

————. Mental defect and disorder from the teacher's point of view. *Educ. Rev.*, 1893, *6*, 209–222, 322–331, 449–463.

————. Can psychology be founded upon the study of consciousness alone, or is physiology needed for the purpose? In *Proceedings of the International Congress of Education of the World's Columbian Exposition.* New York: National Educational Association, 1894, pp. 687–692.

————. The imitative functions, and their place in human nature. *Century Mag.*, 1894, *26*(N.S.), 137–145.

————. The external world and the social consciousness. *Phil. Rev.*, 1894, *3*, 513–545.

————. Preliminary report on imitation. *Psychol. Rev.*, 1895, *2*, 217–235.

————. Some observations on the anomalies of self-consciousness. *Psychol. Rev.*, 1895, *2*, 433–457, 574–584. Reprinted in *Studies in good and evil, op. cit.*, pp. 169–197.

————. Self-consciousness, social consciousness and nature. *Phil. Rev.*, 1895, *4*, 465–485, 577–602. Reprinted in *Studies in good and evil, op. cit.*, pp. 198–248, & in *The basic writings*, Vol. 1, *op. cit.*, pp. 423–461.

————. The new psychology and the consulting psychologist. *Forum*, 1898, *26*, 80–96.

————. The psychology of invention. *Psychol. Rev.*, 1898, *5*, 113–144.

————. *The world and the individual.* (2 vols.) New York: Macmillan, 1899, 1901. (Reprinted 1959)

————. *The conception of immortality.* Boston: Houghton Mifflin, 1900. (Reprinted 1968)

————. Recent logical inquiries and their psychological bearing. *Psychol. Rev.*, 1902, *9*, 105–133. Reprinted in *The basic writings, op. cit.*, Vol. 2, pp. 655–680.

————. *Outlines of psychology: An elementary treatise with some practical applications.* New York: Macmillan, 1903.

————. *The philosophy of loyalty.* New York: Macmillan, 1908.

————. James as a philosopher. *Science*, 1911, *34*, 33–45. Reprinted in *William James and other essays, op. cit.*, pp. 3–45, & in *The basic writings*, Vol. 1, *op. cit.*, pp. 205–222.

————. *The sources of religious insight.* New York: Scribner's, 1912. (Reprinted 1963)

————. Some relations between philosophy and science in the first half of the nineteenth century in Germany. *Science*, 1913, *38*, 567–584. Reprinted in part in *The basic writings*, Vol. 2, *op. cit.*, pp. 763–768.

———. Primitive ways of thinking: With special reference to negation and classification. *Open Court*, 1913, *27*, 577–598.

———. Some psychological problems emphasized by pragmatism. *Pop. Sci. Mon.*, 1913, *83*, 394–411.

———. Mind. In J. Hastings (Ed.), *Encyclopedia of religion and ethics*. Vol. 8. New York: Scribner's, 1916, pp. 649–657. Reprinted in *The basic writings*, Vol. 2, *op. cit.*, pp. 735–761.

———. Words of Professor Royce at the Walton Hotel at Philadelphia, December 29, 1915. *Phil. Rev.*, 1916, *25*, 507–514. Reprinted in *The basic writings*, Vol. 1, *op. cit.*, pp. 31–42. **B**

———. *Lectures on modern idealism*. Ed. by J. Loewenberg. New Haven: Yale University Press, 1919. (Reprinted 1964)

———. *Josiah Royce's seminar, 1913–1914: As recorded in the notebooks of Harry T. Costello*. Ed. by G. Smith. New Brunswick, N.J.: Rutgers University Press, 1963.

———. The two-fold nature of knowledge: Imitative and reflective. An unpublished manuscript of Josiah Royce. Ed. by P. Fuss. *J. hist. Phil.*, 1966, *4*, 326–337.

Borgatta, *Present-day Sociology*; Fisch, *Philosophers*; Kurtz, *American Thought*; Mueller, *American Philosophy*; Rand, *Classical Philosophers*

EDGAR JOHN RUBIN
1886-1951
Danish Psychologist (27)

Rubin, E. J. *Experimentale psychologia; collected scientific papers in German, English, and French*. Copenhagen: Munksgaard, 1949. **C**

———. Den kloge Hans. (Der kluge Hans.) *Tilskueren*, 1910, *2*, 180–189.

———. Beobachtungen über Temperaturempfindungen. *Z. Sinnesphysiol.*, 1912, *46*, 388–393.

———. *Synsoplevede figurer. Studier i psykologisk Analyse*. Copenhagen: Gyldendal, 1915.

———. Vorteile der Zweckbetrachtung für die Erkenntnis. *Z. Psychol.*, 1920, *85*, 210–223.

———. *Visuell wahrgenommene Figuren. Studien in psychologischer Analyse*. I. Copenhagen: Gyldendal, 1921. (Reprinted 1970)

———. Zur Psychophysik der Geradheit. *Z. Psychol.*, 1922, *90*, 67–105.

———. Visuell wahrgenommene wirkliche Bewegungen. Vorläufige Mitteilung. *Z. Psychol.*, 1927, *103*, 384–393.

———. Ueber Gestaltwahrnehmung. *Ber. VIII. int. Kongr. Psychol.*, 1927, 175–182.

———. Kritisches und experimentelles zur "Empfindungszeit" Fröhlichs. *Psychol. Forsch.*, 1930, *13*, 101–112.

———. Bemerkungen zur Erwiderung Fröhlichs. *Psychol. Forsch.*, 1930, *13*, 289–292.

———. Beobachtungen zur psychologischen Akustik. *Z. Psychol.*, 1931, *122*, 109–114.

———. Studien über psychophysiologische Verarbeitungszeit. I. Ein Phenomen bei visuell-wahrgenommener Bewegung. *Z. Psychol.*, 1932, *124*, 192–211.

———. L'inachèvement forcé de la connaissance dans la philosophie de Höffding. *J. Psychol. norm. path.*, 1932, *29*, 673–681.

———. Haptische Untersuchungen. *Acta Psychol.*, 1936, *1*, 285–380.

———. Some elementary time experiences. *Acta psychol.*, 1936, *1*, 206–211.

———. Taste. *Brit. J. Psychol.*, 1936-1937, *27*, 74–85.

———. Geräuschverschiebungsversuche. *Acta Psychol.*, 1939, *4*, 203–236.

———. Quelques expériences sur les rapports entre les domaines auditif et tactile vibratoire. *J. Psychol. normi. path.*, 1939, *35*, 19–26.

———. Some aspects of the relation between the apparent quickness of rotation discs and the brightness of their backgrounds. In Various,

Miscellanea psychologica Albert Michotte. Louvain: Publications Universitaires de Louvain, 1947, pp. 221–224.

——. Visual figures apparently incompatible with geometry. *Acta Psychol.,* 1950, *7,* 365–387.

Beardslee, *Perception*

SERGEI (L.) RUBINSTEIN
1889-1960
Russian Psychologist (12)

Rubinstein, S. L. (The problem of psychology in the works of K. Marx.) *Sov. Psikhotekh.,* 1934, *7*(1), 3–20.

——. *(Fundamentals of psychology.)* Moscow: n.p., 1935.

——. (Tolman's neo-behaviorism.) *Leningrad. Gosud. Pedag.,* 1938, *18,* 115–130.

——. (On the problem of the states of attention.) *Leningrad. Gosud. Pedag.,* 1939, *18,* 7–19.

——. *Grundlagen der allgemeinen Psychologie.* Trans. by H. Hartmann. (3rd ed.) Berlin: Volk & Wissenschaften, 1969. (1940)

——. (Thoughts on psychology.) *Leningrad. Gosud. Pedag.,* 1940, *34,* 5–15.

——. (Some remarks on psychology of the deaf and blind.) *Leningrad. Gosud. Pedag.,* 1941, *35,* 226–228.

——. (On the psychology of speech.) *Leningrad. Gosud. Pedag.,* 1941, *35,* 6–20.

——. (The psychological conception of the French sociological school.) *Leningrad. Gosud. Pedag.,* 1941, *35,* 289–304.

——. Soviet psychology in wartime. (1943) *Phil. phenomenol. Res.,* 1944, *5,* 181–189.

——. (Physiology and psychology in the scientific work of I. M. Sechenov.) *Sov. Pedag.,* 1945, *11,* 40–44.

——. (The problem of activity and consciousness in the system of Soviet psychology.) (UZMGY) Moscow: Ogiz, 1945, No. 90, 3–21.

——. Consciousness in the light of dialectical materialism. (1945) Trans. by N. J. Nelson. *Sci. Soc.,* 1946, *10,* 252–261.

——. Psychological science and education. (1945) Trans. by I. D. London. *Harv. educ. Rev.,* 1948, *18,* 158–170.

——. (Speech.) *Vop. Fil.,* 1947, *1,* 420–427.

——. Die Struktur des Psychischen. Parts 1, 2. *Pädagogik,* 1948, *3,* 399–419 ; 1949, *4,* 17–25.

——. (The teachings of I. P. Pavlov and problems of psychology.) In S. A. Petrushevsky (Ed.), *(The teachings of I. P. Pavlov and the philosophical problems of psychology.)* Moscow: Akademiya Nauk, 1952, pp. 194–228.

——. Questions of psychological theory. (1955) In B. Simon (Ed.), *Psychology in the Soviet Union.* Stanford, Calif.: Stanford University Press, 1957, pp. 264–278.

——. (The psychological views of I. M. Sechenov and Soviet psychological science.) (1955) Reprinted in S. L. Rubinstein (Ed.), *(I. M. Sechenov and materialist psychology.)* Moscow: Akademiya Nauk, 1957, pp. 7–30.

Smirnov, A. A., Leontiev, A. N., ——, & Teplov, B. M. (Eds.), *(Psychology: A textbook for teachers colleges.)* (2nd ed.) Moscow: Uchpedgiz, 1962. (1956)

——. (On the question of language, speech and thinking.) *Vop. Yazykozn.,* 1957, *2,* 42–48.

——. *Sein und Bewusstsein.* Berlin: Deutscher Verlag der Wissenschaften, 1965. (1957)

——. The principle of determinism and the psychological theory of thinking. In B. G. Anan'ev *et al.* (Eds.), *Psychological sciences in the U. S. S. R.* Vol. 1. Washington, D. C.: U. S. Joint Publications Research Service, 1961, pp. 421–477. (1957)

——. (Philosophy and psychology.) *Vop. Fil.,* 1957, *11*(1), 114–127.

——. *Das Denken und die Wege seiner Erforschung.* Berlin: Deutscher Verlag der Wissenschaften, 1968. (1958)

——. (Theoretical problems of psychology and the problem of personality.) *Vop. Fil.,* 1959, *13*(3), 3–30.

——. *Prinzipien und Wege der Entwicklung der Psychologie.* Berlin: Deutscher Verlag der Wissenschaften, 1959. (1959)

——. *(The thinking process and the laws of analysis, synthesis, and generalization: Experimental investigations.)* Moscow: Akademiya Nauk, 1960.

——. (The problem of aptitude and questions in psychological theory.) *Vop. Psikhol.,* 1960, *6*(3), 3–22.

——. (The pressing tasks in psychological investigations on thinking.) In E. V. Shorokhova (Ed.), *(Investigation on thought in Soviet psychology.)* Moscow: Nauka, 1966, pp. 225–235.

——. Psychology. In Various, *Social sciences in the USSR.* Paris: Mouton, 1965, pp. 120–126.

——. The individual and the world. (1969) *Sov. Stud. Phil.,* 1969–1970, *8*, 371–389.

CHRISTIAN ALBAN RUCKMICK
1886-1961
American Psychologist (17)

Ruckmick, C. A. The history and status of psychology in the United States. *Amer. J. Psychol.,* 1912, *23*, 517–531.

——. The use of the term "function" in English textbooks of psychology. *Amer. J. Psychol.,* 1913, *24*, 99–123.

——. The role of kinaesthesis in the perception of rhythm. *Amer. J. Psychol.,* 1913, *24*, 305–359.

——. Visual rhythm. In *Studies in psychology: Titchener commemorative volume.* Worcester, Mass.: Wilson, 1917, pp. 231–254.

——. Dynamical principles in recent psychology: William James. *Psychol. Monogr.,* 1921, *39*, No. 136, 3–5.

——. A preliminary study of the emotions. *Psychol. Monogr.,* 1921, *39*, No. 136, 30–35.

——. The psychology of pleasantness. *Psychol. Rev.,* 1925, *32*, 362–383.

——. A schematic classification of general psychology. *Psychol. Rev.,* 1926, *33*, 397–406.

——. The rhythmical experience from the

systematic point of view. *Amer. J. Psychol.,* 1927, *39*, 356–366.

——. *The mental life: A survey of modern experimental psychology.* (2nd ed.) New York: Longmans, Green, 1929. (1928)

——. Why we have emotions. *Sci. Mon.,* N.Y., 1929, *28*, 252–262.

——. A new classification of tone qualities. *Psychol. Rev.,* 1929, *36*, 172–180.

——. Emotions in terms of the galvanometric technique. *Brit. J. Psychol.,* 1930–1931, *21*, 149–159.

——. *The psychology of feeling and emotion.* New York: McGraw-Hill, 1936.

——. The psychological laboratory at the University of Iowa. *J. exp. Psychol.,* 1937, *21*, 687–697.

BENJAMIN RUSH
1745-1813
American Psychiatrist (15)

Rush, B. *Medical inquiries and observations.* (4 vols.) Philadelphia: Prichard & Hall, 1819. (1789–1793)   **C**

——. *Essays, literary, moral, and philosophical.* Philadelphia: Bradford, 1806. (1798)   **C**

——. *Sixteen introductory lectures, to courses of lectures upon the institutes and practice of medicine, with a syllabus of the latter: To which are added two lectures upon the pleasures of the senses and of the mind with an inquiry into their proximate cause.* Philadelphia: Bradford & Innskeep, 1811.   **C**

——. *The selected writings of Benjamin Rush.* Ed. by D. D. Runes. New York: Philosophical Library, 1947.   **C**

——. *The autobiography of Benjamin Rush: His "Travels through life," together with his Commonplace Book for 1789–1813.* Ed. by G. W. Corner. Princeton, N.J.: American Philosophical Society & Princeton University Press, 1948.   **B C**

———. *Letters of Benjamin Rush.* (2 vols.) Ed. by L. H. Butterfield. Princeton, N.J.: Princeton University Press, 1951. **B C**

———. On the different species of mania. (Date unknown) In *Selected writings, op. cit.,* pp. 212–219.

———. An enquiry into the effects of spirituous liquors upon the human body and their influence. (1784) Reprinted in M. Keller (Ed.), The first American medical work on the effects of alcohol. *Quart. J. Stud. Alcohol.,* 1943, *4,* 321–341, & in *Selected writings, op. cit.,* pp. 334–341.

———. On the mode of education proper in a republic. (1784) Reprinted in *Selected writings, op. cit.,* pp. 87–96.

———. An inquiry into the influence of physical causes upon the moral faculty. (1786) Reprinted in *Selected writings, op. cit.,* pp. 181–211.

———. Thoughts upon the amusements and punishments which are proper for schools. (1790) Reprinted in *Selected writings, op. cit.,* pp. 106–116.

———. An account of the state of the body and mind in old age, with observations on its diseases, and their remedies. (1793) Reprinted in *Selected writings, op. cit.,* pp. 342–357.

———. Observations intended to favor a supposition that the black color (as it is called) of the negroes is derived from the leprosy. (1797) Reprinted in *Trans. Amer. phil. Soc.,* 1799, *4,* 289–297.

———. On the different species of phobia. (1798) In *Selected writings, op. cit.,* pp. 220–226.

———. Three lectures upon animal life. (1799) Reprinted in *Selected writings, op. cit.,* pp. 133–180.

———. On the necessary connection between observation and reasoning in medicine. (1806) Reprinted in *Selected writings, op. cit.,* pp. 245–253.

———. On the influence of physical causes, in promoting an increase of the strength and activity of the intellectual faculties of man. (1811) In *Introductory lectures, op. cit.,* pp. 88–119.

———. On the utility of a knowledge of the faculties and operations of the human mind, to a physician. (1811) In *Introductory lectures, op. cit.,* pp. 256–273.

———. Two lectures upon the pleasures of the senses and of the mind; with an inquiry into their proximate cause. (1811) In *Introductory lectures, op. cit.,* pp. 397–455.

———. *Medical inquiries and observations upon the diseases of the mind.* New York: Hafner, 1962. (1812)

———. Inquiry into the influence of physical causes upon the moral faculty. Philadelphia: Haswell, Barrington, & Haswell, 1839. Reprinted in J. L. Blau (Ed.), *American philosophic addresses,* 1700–1900. New York: Columbia University Press, 1946, pp. 312–343, & in *Selected writings, op. cit.,* pp. 181–211.

Goshen, *Documentary;* Hunter & Macalpine, *Psychiatry;* Kurtz, *American Thought;* Shipley, *Classics;* Slotkin, *Anthropology*

HANNS SACHS
1881-1947
Austrian-American Psychoanalyst (13)

Sachs, H. *The creative unconscious: Studies in the psychoanalysis of art.* (2nd ed.) Ed. by A. A. Roback. Cambridge: Sci-Art, 1951. (1942) **C**

———. Traumdeutung und Menschenkenntnis. *Jb. psychoanal. Forsch.,* 1911, *3,* 568–587.

———. Ueber Naturgefühl. *Imago,* 1912, *1,* 119–131.

Rank, O., & ———. The significance of psychoanalysis for the mental sciences. New York: Nervous & Mental Disease Publishing, 1916. (1913) (Reprinted 1970)

———. Das Thema "Tod." *Imago,* 1914, *3,* 456–461.

———. Der Sturm. *Imago,* 1919, *5,* 203–242.

———. Zur Genese der Perversionen. *Int. Z. Psycho.-Anal.,* 1923, *9,* 172–182.

———. *Gemeinsame Tagträume.* Vienna: Internationaler Psychoanalytischer Verlag, 1924.

————. Kunst und Persönlichkeit. *Imago*, 1929, *15*, 1–14.

————. One of the motive factors in the formation of the super-ego in women. *Int. J. Psycho-Anal.*, 1929, *10*, 39–50.

————. Zur Psychologie des Films. *Psychoanal. Bewegung*, 1929, *1*, 122–126.

————. *Caligula.* Trans. by H. Senger. London: Matthews & Marott, 1931. (1930)

————. Edgar Poe. Bemerkungen zu Marie Bonapartes Biographie des Dichters. *Imago*, 1934, *20*, 485–492.

————. Psychotherapy and the pursuit of happiness. *Amer. Imago*, 1941, *2*, 356–364.

————. "The man Moses" and the man Freud. *Psychoanal. Rev.*, 1941, *28*, 156–162. Reprinted in M. H. Sherman (Ed.), *Psychoanalysis in America: Historical perspectives.* Springfield, Ill.: Thomas, 1965, pp. 47–55.

————. The community of daydreams. (1942) In *The creative unconscious, op. cit.*, pp. 11–54.

————. *Freud: Master and friend.* Cambridge: Harvard University Press, 1944. **B**

————. *Masks of love and life, the philosophical basis of psychoanalysis.* Cambridge: Sci-Art, 1948.

EDMUND CLARK SANFORD
1859-1924
American Psychologist (20)

Sanford, E. C. The relative legibility of the small letters. *Amer. J. Psychol.*, 1888, *1*, 402–435.

————. Personal equation. *Amer. J. Psychol.*, 1888–1889, *2*, 3–38, 271–298, 403–430.

————. A simple & inexpensive chronoscope. *Amer. J. Psychol.*, 1890, *3*, 174–181.

————. Notes on studies of the language of children. *J. genet. Psychol.*, 1891, *1*, 257–260.

————. On reaction-times when the stimulus is applied to the reacting hand. *Amer. J. Psychol.*, 1892, *5*, 351–355.

————. A laboratory course in physiological psychology. 5. The visual perception of space. *Amer. J. Psychol.*, 1893, *6*, 593–616.

————. *A course in experimental psychology.* I. Sensation and perception. Boston: Heath, 1894, 1898.

————. A laboratory course in physiological psychology. 6. Monocular perception of space. *Amer. J. Psychol.*, 1895, *7*, 412–424.

————. Mental growth and decay. *Amer. J. Psychol.*, 1902, *13*, 426–449.

————. Illustrations of the application of psychological principles to ethical problems. *J. genet. Psychol.*, 1902, *9*, 18–27.

————. On the guessing of numbers. *Amer. J. Psychol.*, 1903, *14*, 647–665.

————. The psychic life of fishes. *Int. Quart.*, 1903, *7*, 316–333.

————. Psychology and physics. *Psychol. Rev.*, 1903, *10*, 105–119.

————. Experimental pedagogy and experimental psychology. *J. educ. Psychol.*, 1910, *1*, 590–595.

————. Methods of research in education. *J. educ. Psychol.*, 1912, *3*, 303–315.

————. The function of the several senses in the mental life. *Amer. J. Psychol.*, 1912, *23*, 59–74.

————. Psychic research in the animal field. Der kluge Hans and the Elberfeld horses. *Amer. J. Psychol.*, 1914, *25*, 1–31.

FILLMORE HARGRAVE SANFORD
1914-1967
American Psychologist (16)

Sanford, F. H. Speech and personality: A comparative case study. *J. Pers.*, 1941–1942, *10*, 169–198.

————. Speech and personality. *Psychol. Bull.*, 1942, *39*, 811–845.

————. *Authoritarianism and leadership: A study of the follower's orientation to authority.* Philadelphia: Institute for Research in Human Relations, 1950.

——. The use of a projective device in attitude surveying. *Publ. Opin. Quart.,* 1950–1951, *14,* 697–709.

——. Leadership identification and acceptance. In H. Guetzkow (Ed.), *Groups, leadership, and men.* Pittsburgh, Pa.: Carnegie Press, 1951, pp. 158–176.

——. Public orientation to Roosevelt. *Publ. Opin. Quart.,* 1951, *15* 189–216.

——, & Hempbill, J. K. An evaluation of a brief course in psychology at the U.S. Naval Academy. *Educ. Psychol. Measmt.,* 1952, *12,* 194–216.

——. Research on military leadership. In J. C. Flanagan *et al.* (Eds.), *Current trends: Psychology in the world emergency.* Pittsburgh, Pa.: University of Pittsburgh Press, 1952, pp. 17–74.

——, & Rosenstock, I. M. Projective techniques on the doorstep. *J. abnorm. soc. Psychol.,* 1952, *47,* 3–16.

——. Creative health and the principle of *Habeas Mentem. Amer. Psychologist,* 1955, *10,* 829–835.

——. *Psychology: A scientific study of man.* San Francisco: Wadsworth, 1961.

——. Annual report of the executive secretary: 1951. *Amer. Psychologist,* 1959, *6,* 644–670.

——. Toward a sociology of psychology. *Amer. Psychologist,* 1952, *7,* 83–85.

EDWARD SAPIR
1884-1939
American Anthropologist (19)

Sapir, E. *Selected writings of Edward Sapir in language, culture, and personality.* Ed. by D. G. Mandelbaum. Berkeley, Calif.: University of California Press, 1949.   **C**

——. *Letters from Edward Sapir to Robert H. Lowie.* Intro. & notes by R. H. Lowie. No place: no publisher [Berkeley, Calif.: Luella Cole Lowie?], 1965.   **B C**

——. Language and environment. *Amer. Anthrop.,* 1912, *14,* 226–242. Reprinted in F. de Laguna (Ed.), *Selected papers from the Amer-*

ican Anthropologist, 1888–1920. Evanston, Ill.: Row Peterson, 1960, pp. 434–450, & in *Selected writings, op. cit.,* pp. 89–103.

——. *Abnormal types of speech in Nootka.* Canada Dept. Mines Biological Survey, Memoir 61. Anthropological Ser. No. 5. Ottawa: Government Printing Bureau, 1915.

——. *Time perspective in aboriginal American culture.* Canada Geological Survey Memoir, 90. Anthropological Ser. No. 13. Ottawa: Government Printing Bureau, 1916. Reprinted in *Selected writings, op. cit.,* pp. 389–462.

——, Do we need a superorganic? *Amer. Anthrop.,* 1917, *19*(N.S.), 441–447.

——. *Language: An introduction to the study of speech.* New York: Harcourt, Brace, 1921.

——. Culture, genuine and spurious. *Amer. J. Sociol.,* 1924, *29,* 401–429. Reprinted in *Selected writings, op. cit.,* pp. 308–331.

——. Sound patterns in language. *Language,* 1925, *1,* 37–51. Reprinted in *Selected writings, op. cit.,* pp. 37–45.

——. Speech as a personality trait. *Amer. J. Sociol.,* 1926–1927, *32,* 892–905.

——. The unconscious patterning of behavior in society. In E. S. Dummer (Ed.), *The unconscious: A symposium.* New York: Knopf, 1927, pp. 114–142. Reprinted in *Selected writings, op. cit.,* pp. 544–559.

——. Anthropology and sociology. In W. F. Ogburn & A. Goldenweiser (Eds.), *The social sciences and their interrelations.* Boston: Houghton Mifflin, 1927, pp. 97–113.

——. A study in phonetic symbolism. *J. exp. Psychol.,* 1929, *12,* 225–239.

——. Communication. *Encycl. soc. sci.,* 1931, *4,* 78–81. Reprinted in *Selected writings, op. cit.,* pp. 104–109.

——. Cultural anthropology and psychiatry. *J. abnorm. soc. Psychol.,* 1932, *27,* 229–242. Reprinted in *Selected writings, op. cit.,* pp. 509–521.

——. La réalité psychologique des phonèmes. *J. Psychol. norm. path.,* 1933, *30,* 247–265. Trans. in *Selected writings, op. cit.,* pp. 46–60.

————. The emergence of the concept of personality in a study of cultures. *J. soc. Psychol.*, 1934, *5*, 408–415. Reprinted in *Selected writings, op. cit.*, pp. 590–597.

————. The contribution of psychiatry to an understanding of behavior in society. *Amer. J. Sociol.*, 1936–1937, *42*, 862–870.

————. Why cultural anthropology needs the psychiatrist. *Psychiatry*, 1938, *1*, 7–12. Reprinted in *Selected writings, op. cit.*, pp. 569–577.

————, & Swadesh, M. American Indian grammatical categories. *Word*, 1946, *2*, 103–112. Reprinted in D. Hymes (Ed.), *Language in culture and society: A reader in linguistics and anthropology*. New York: Harper & Row, 1964, pp. 100–114.

Goldschmidt, *Mankind ;* Parsons, *Society*

ROBERT SAUDEK
1881-1935
English Psychologist (11)

Saudek, R. *Psychology of handwriting*. New York: Doran, 1925.

————. Reading, writing and guessing. *Psyche*, 1927, 34–42.

————. The methods of graphology. *Brit. J. med. Psychol.*, 1927, *7*, 221–259.

————. *Experiments with handwriting*. New York: Morrow, 1929. (1928)

————. Die pathologischen Merkmale der Handschrift. *Soc. Med.*, 1929, No. 12.

————. Das zentrale Nervensystem und der Schreibakt. *Jb. Charakterol.*, 1929, *6*, 275–305.

————. Experimental graphology. *Sci. Prog.*, 1929, *23*, 468–486.

————. *Ce que le cinéma nous enseigne sur les mouvements de l'écriture*. Paris: Société de Graphologie, 1930.

————. Betonung und Unterbetonung von Wortanfängen und Wortenden als charakterologische und psychopathologische Merkmale der Schrift. *Z. angew. Psychol.*, 1930, *37*, 99–134.

————. Zur Psychologie der amerikanischen Handschrift. *Zbl. Graphol.*, 1931, *2*, 239–274.

————. Writing movements as indications of the writer's social behavior. *J. soc. Psychol.*, 1931, *2*, 337–373.

————. Zur experimentellen Graphologie. *Psychol. Med.*, 1931, *4*, 229–244.

————. Zur psychodiagnostischen Ausdeutung des Schreibdrucks. *Z. angew. Psychol.*, 1931, *39*, 433–449.

————. The years of puberty in a public school. *J. Pers.*, 1932–1933, *1*, 17–34.

Seeman, E., & ————. The self-expression of identical twins in handwriting and drawing. *J. Pers.*, 1932–1933, *1*, 91–128.

Seeman, E., & ————. The handwriting of identical twins reared apart. *J. Pers.*, 1932–1933, *1*, 268–285.

————. *Anonymous letters: A study in crime and handwriting*. London: Methuen, 1933.

————. Bestimmung persönlicher Interessen durch Testpsychologie und graphologische Methoden. *Charakter*, 1934, *1*, 19–26.

————. A British pair of identical twins reared apart. *J. Pers.*, 1934–1935, *3*, 17–39.

MARTIN SCHEERER
1900-1961
German-American Psychologist (14)

Scheerer, M. *Die Lehre von der Gestalt: Ihre Methode und ihr psychologischer Gegenstand*. Berlin: Gruyter, 1931.

Goldstein, K., & ————. Abstract and concrete behavior: An experimental study with special tests. *Psychol. Monogr.*, 1941, *53*, No. 239.

————. Facts about memory. *Amer. Mercury*, 1944, *58*, 481–487.

————, Rothmann, Eva, & Goldstein, K. A case of "Idiot Savant": An experimental study of personality organization. *Psychol. Monogr.*, 1945, *58*, No. 269.

———. Problems of performance analysis in the study of personality. *Ann. N.Y. Acad. Sci.,* 1946, *46,* 653–675.

———. An experiment in abstraction: Testing form-disparity tolerance. *Confinia Neurol.,* 1949, *9,* 232–254.

———. Personality functioning and cognitive psychology. *J. Pers.,* 1953, *22,* 1–16.

———. Cognitive theory. In G. Lindzey (Ed.), *Handbook of social psychology.* Vol. 1. Cambridge: Addison-Wesley, 1945, pp. 91–142.

———. On the relationship between experimental and non-experimental methods in psychology. *Psychol. Rec.,* 1958, *8,* 109–116.

———. Spheres of meaning: An analysis of stages from perception to abstract thinking. *J. indiv. psychol.,* 1959, *15,* 50–61.

Reiff, R., & ———. *Memory and hypnotic age regression.* New York: International Universities Press, 1960.

———, & Huling, M. D. Cognitive embeddedness in problem solving: A theoretical and experimental analysis. In B. Kaplan & S. Wapner (Eds.), *Perspectives in psychological theory.* New York: International Universities Press, 1960, pp. 256–302.

Riopelle, *Problem Solving*

FRIEDRICH WILHELM JOSEPH VON SCHELLING
1775-1854
German Philosopher (15)

Fichte, J. G., & Schelling, F. W. J. v. *Fichtes und Schellings philosophischer Briefwechsel aus dem Nachlasse Beider.* Ed. by I. H. Fichte & K. F. A. Schelling. Stuttgart: Cotta, 1856. **B C**

———. *Sämmtliche Werke.* Ed. by C. F. A. Schelling. *Erste Abteilung* (10 vols.) *Zweite Abteilung* (4 vols.). 1856–1861. Stuttgart: Cotta, 1856–1861. **C**

———. *Aus Schellings Leben in Briefen.* Ed. by G. L. Plitt. (3 vols. in 2) Leipzig: Hirzel, 1869–1870. **B C**

———, & Hegel, G. W. F. *Briefe von und an Hegel.* (2 vols.) Ed. by K. Hegel. Leipzig: Duncker & Humblot, 1887. **B C**

———. *Werke.* Ed. by M. Schröter. (6 vols.) Munich: Becke & Oldenbourg, 1927–1956. **C**

———. *Von der Weltseele, eine Hypothese der höhern Physik zur Erklärung des allgemeinen Organismus.* Ed. by O. Weiss. Leipzig: Meiner, 1911. (1798) Reprinted in *Sämmtliche Werke,* Part 1, Vol. 2, *op. cit.,* pp. 345–583.

———. *Einleitung zu seinem Entwurf eines Systems der Naturphilosophie.* Leipzig: Gabler, 1799. Trans. in part by T. Davidson. *J. specul. Phil.,* 1867, *1,* 193–220. Reprinted in *Sämmtliche Werke,* Part 1, Vol. 3, *op. cit.,* pp. 269–326.

———. *System der transcendentalen Idealismus.* Ed. by O. Weiss. Leipzig: Meiner, 1911. (1800) Reprinted in *Sämmtliche Werke,* Part 1, Vol. 3, *op. cit.,* pp. 327–634.

———. Excerpts from the system of transcendental idealism. (1800) Trans. by A. Hofstadter. In A. Hofstadter & R. Kuhns (Eds.), *Philosophies of art and beauty.* New York: Random House, 1964, pp. 347–377. Reprinted in German in *Sämmtliche Werke,* Part 1, Vol. 3, *op. cit.,* pp. 327–634.

———. *Bruno oder über das göttliche und natürliche Princip der Dinge.* (2nd ed.) Ed. by O. Weiss. Leipzig: Meiner, 1911. (1802) Reprinted in *Sämmtliche Werke,* Part 1, Vol. 4, *op. cit.,* pp. 213–332.

———. *On university studies.* Trans. by Ella S. Morgan, & ed. by N. Guterman. Athens, Ohio: Ohio University Press, 1966. (1803) Reprinted in German in *Sämmtliche Werke,* Part 1, Vol. 5, *op. cit.,* pp. 207–352.

———. *Darlegung des wahren Verhältnisses der Naturphilosophie zu der verbesserten Fichte'-schen Lehre.* Tübingen: Cotta, 1806. Reprinted in *Sämmtliche Werke,* Part 1, Vol. 7, *op. cit.,* pp. 1–126.

———. *The philosophy of art: An oration on the relation between the plastic arts and nature.* Trans. by A. Johnson. London: Chapman, 1845. (1807) Reprinted in German in *Sämmtliche Werke,* Part 1, Vol. 7, *op. cit.,* pp. 289–329.

———. *Of human freedom.* Trans. by J. Gutmann. Chicago: Open Court, 1936. (1834) Reprinted in German in *Sämmtliche Werke,* Part 1, Vol. 7, *op. cit.,* pp. 331–416. **Bl**

———. *The ages of the world.* Ed. & trans. by F. de Wolfe Bolman, Jr. New York: Columbia University Press, 1942. (1854)

Rand, *Classical Philosophers*

FRIEDRICH SCHILLER
1759-1805
German Philosopher (13)

Schiller, F. *Schillers Briefe.* Ed. by F. Jonas. (7 vols.) Stuttgart: Deutsche Verlags-Anstalt, 1892–1896. **C**

———. *Works.* (7 vols.) Ed. by Various. London: Bell, 1897–1903. **C**

———. *Selections from the correspondence between Schiller and Goethe.* Ed., intro., & notes by J. G. Robertson. Boston: Ginn, 1898. **B C**

———, & Humboldt, W. v. *Briefwechsel zwischen Schiller und Wilhelm von Humboldt.* (3rd ed.) Ed. by H. G. Gräf & A. Leitzmann. Stuttgart: Cotta, 1900. **B C**

———. *Aesthetical and philosophical essays.* (2 vols.) Ed. by N. H. Dole. Boston: Niccolls, 1902. **C**

———. *Schillers sämtliche Werke, Säkularausgabe.* (16 vols.) Ed. by E. v. d. Hellen *et al.* Stuttgart: Cotta, 1904–1905. **C**

———. *Philosophische Schriften.* Leipzig: Insel, 1906. **C**

———, & Goethe, J. W. v. *Der Briefwechsel zwischen Schiller und Goethe.* Vols. 1–3. Ed. by H. G. Gräf & A. Leitzmann. Leipzig: Insel, 1912. (1911) **B C**

———. *Philosophische Briefe.* New ed. by Agnes Holthusen. Hamburg: Saucke, 1937. **C**

———. *Werke.* (35 vols.) (National-Ausgabe) Ed. by J. Petersen. Weimar: Böhlau, 1943–1964. **C**

———. *Naive and sentimental poetry* and *On the sublime* Trans., intro., & notes by J. A. Elias. New York: Ungar, 1966. **C**

———. *On the aesthetic education of man, in a series of letters.* Trans. by R. Snell. New Haven: Yale University Press, 1954. (1793–1794)

PAUL HARKAI SCHILLER
1908-1949
Hungarian-German Psychologist (13)

Schiller, P. H. Das Ranschburgische Phänomen und dessen Einfluss auf das Erkennen von Kraftfahrzeugkennzeichen. *Psychotechn. Z.,* 1932, *7,* 49–59.

———. Untersuchungen über Empfindung und Empfinden. 4. Das optische Verschmelzen in seiner Abhängigkeit von heteromodaler Reizung. *Z. Psychol.,* 1932, *125,* 249–288.

———. Die Rauhigkeit als intermodale Erscheinung. *Z. Psychol.,* 1932, *127,* 265–289.

———. Stroboskopische Alternativversuche. *Psychol. Forsch.,* 1932, *16,* 179–214.

———. (On the task of psychology.) *Athenaeum,* 1937, *23,* 256–274.

———. A configurational theory of puzzles and jokes. *J. gen. Psychol.,* 1938, *18,* 217–234.

———. Psychology and physiology. *J. gen. Psychol.,* 1940, *23,* 329–341.

———. Umwegversuche an Elritzen minnous. *Z. Tierpsychol.,* 1942, *5,* 101–130.

———. *Handeln und Erleben.* Berlin: Junker & Dünnhaupt, 1944.

———. Delayed response in the minnow. *J. comp. physiol. Psychol.,* 1948, *41,* 233–238.

———. *Aufgabe der Psychologie. Eine Geschichte ihrer Probleme.* Vienna: Springer-Verlag, 1948.

Bakay, Eva, & ———. Manipulative correction of visually presented figures. *Amer. J. Psychol.,* 1948, *61,* 487–501.

———. Delayed detour response in the octopus. *J. comp. physiol. Psychol.,* 1949, *42,* 220–225.

———. Analysis of detour behavior. IV. Congruent and incongruent detour behavior in cats. *J. exp. Psychol.,* 1950, *40,* 217–227.

———. Figural preferences in the drawings of a chimpanzee. *J. comp. physiol. Psychol.*, 1951, *44*, 101–111.

———, & Hartmann, G. W. Manipulative completion of bisected geometrical figures. *Amer. J. Psychol.*, 1951, *64*, 238–246.

———. Innate constituents of complex responses in primates. *Psychol. Rev.*, 1952, *59*, 177–191.

———. Innate motor action as a basis of learning: Manipulative patterns in the chimpanzee. In Claire H. Schiller (Ed.), *Instinctive behavior.* New York: International Universities Press, 1957, pp. 264–287.

Riopelle, *Problem Solving*

HAROLD SCHLOSBERG
1904-1964
American Psychologist (20)

Schlosberg, H. A study of the conditioned patellar reflex. *J. exp. Psychol.*, 1928, *11*, 468–494.

———. An investigation of certain factors related to ease of conditioning. *J. gen. Psychol.*, 1932, *7*, 328–342.

———. Conditioned responses in the white rat. *J. genet. Psychol.*, 1934, *45*, 303–335.

———. Conditioned responses in the white rat. II. Conditioned responses based upon shock to the foreleg. *J. genet. Psychol.*, 1936, *49*, 107–138.

Pfaffmann, C., & ———. The conditioned knee jerk in psychotic and normal individuals. *J. Psychol.*, 1936, *1*, 201–206.

———. The relationship between success and the laws of conditioning. *Psychol. Rev.*, 1937, *44*, 379–394.

Kappauf, W. F., & ———. Conditioned responses in the white rat. III. Conditioning as a function of the length of the period of delay. *J. genet. Psychol.*, 1937, *50*, 27–45.

Woodworth, R. S., & ———. *Experimental psychology.* (Rev. ed.) New York: Holt, 1960. (1938)

Hughes, B., & ———. Conditioning in the white rat. IV. The conditioned lid reflex. *J. exp. Psychol.*, 1938, *23*, 641–650.

———. A scale for the judgment of facial expressions. *J. exp. Psychol.*, 1941, *29*, 497–510.

———, & Katz, A. Double alternation lever-pressing in the white rat. *Amer. J. Psychol.*, 1943, *56*, 274–282.

———, & Solomon, R. L. Latency of response in a choice of discrimination. *J. exp. Psychol.*, 1943, *33*, 22–39.

Blackwell, H. R., & ———. Octave generalization, pitch discrimination, and loudness thresholds in the white rat. *J. exp. Psychol.*, 1943, *33*, 407–419.

Leavitt, H. J., & ———. The retention of verbal and motor skills. *J. exp. Psychol.*, 1944, *34*, 404–417.

McGinnies, E., & ———. The effects of electroshock convulsions on double alternation lever-pressing in the white rat. *J. exp. Psychol.*, 1945, *35*, 361–373.

———. The concept of play. *Psychol. Rev.*, 1947, *54*, 229–231.

———. A probability formulation of the Hunter-Sigler effect. *J. exp. Psychol.*, 1948, *38*, 155–167.

Dusen, F. V., & ———. Further study of the retention of verbal and motor skills. *J. exp. Psychol.*, 1948, *38*, 526–534.

Casperson, R. C., & ———. Monocular and binocular intensity thresholds for fields containing 1–7 dots. *J. exp. Psychol.*, 1950, *40*, 81–92.

———, & Heineman, C. The relationship between two measures of response strength. *J. exp. Psychol.*, 1950, *40*, 235–247.

———. A note on depth perception, size constancy, and related topics. *Psychol. Rev.*, 1950, *57*, 314–317.

———. The description of facial expressions in terms of two dimensions. *J. exp. Psychol.*, 1952, *44*, 229–237. Reprinted in D. K. Candland (Ed.), *Emotion: Bodily change; an enduring problem in psychology: Selected readings.* Princeton, N.J.: Van Nostrand, 1962, pp. 220–234.

White, C. T., & ———. Degree of conditioning of the GSR as a function of the period of delay. *J. exp. Psychol.*, 1952, *43*, 357–362.

———. Three dimensions of emotion. *Psychol. Rev.*, 1954, *61*, 81–88.

———, & Pratt, Cornelia H. The secondary reward value of inaccessible food for hungry and satiated rats. *J. comp. physiol. Psychol.*, 1956, *49*, 149–152.

Kling, J. W., & ———. The uniqueness of patterns of skin-conductance. *Amer. J. Psychol.*, 1961, *74*, 74–79.

ARTHUR SCHOPENHAUER
1788-1860
German Philosopher (22)

Schopenhauer, A. *Essay on the freedom of the will.* Trans. by K. Kalenda. Indianapolis, Ind.: Bobbs-Merrill, 1960. (1841) **Bl C**

———. *Sämmtliche Werke* (7 vols.) Ed. by A. Hubscher. Wiesbaden: Brockhaus, 1946–1950. (1873–1874) **C**

———. *Kleinere Schriften.* (2 vols. in 1) Berlin: Wahrschauer, 1891. **C**

———. *Selected essays.* Biog., intro. & trans. by E. B. Bax. London: Bell, 1891. **B C**

———. *The living thoughts of Schopenhauer.* Intro. by T. Mann. London: Cassell, 1939. **C**

———. *Schopenhauer-Brevier,* Ed. by V. R. Schmidt. Wiesbaden: Dieterich, 1955. **C**

———. *Philosophische Menschenkunde.* Ed. by A. Bäumler. Stuttgart: Kröner, 1957. **C**

———. *The will to live: Selected writings of Arthur Schopenhauer.* Ed. by R. Taylor. New York: Doubleday, 1962. **C**

———. *Essays and aphorisms.* Trans. & intro. by R. J. Hollingdale. New York: Penguin, 1970. **C**

———. *On the fourfold root of the principle of sufficient reason.* (4th ed.) Trans. by Mrs. Karl Hillebrand. London: Bell, 1891. (1813)

———. *Ueber das Sehen und die Farben.* (3rd ed.) Ed. by J. Frauenstädt. Leipzig: Brockhaus, 1870. (1816)

———. *The world as will and idea.* (3 vols.) Trans. by R. B. Haldane & J. Kemp. London: Truebner, 1883. (1818)

———. *The world as will and representation.* (3rd ed.) (2 vols.) Trans. by E. F. J. Payne. Indian Hills, Col.: Falcon's Wing Press, 1958. (1818) (Reprinted 1967)

———. *On the will in nature: An account of the corroborations received by the author's philosophy since its first appearance from the empirical sciences.* (4th ed.) Trans. by Mrs. Karl Hillebrand. London: Bell, 1891. (1836)

———. *On the basis of morality.* Trans. by E. F. J. Payne; intro. by R. Taylor. Indianapolis, Ind.: Bobbs-Merrill, 1965. (1841)

———. *Parerga und Paralipomena,* (2nd ed.) Ed. by J. Frauenstädt. Berlin: Hayn, 1891. (1851)

———. *Essays from the Parerga and Paralipomena.* Trans. by T. B. Saunders. London: Allen & Unwin, 1951. (1851)

Gardiner, *Philosophy;* Park & Burgess, *Sociology;* Rand, *Classical Philosophers;* Rand, *Moralists*

FRIEDRICH SCHUMANN
1863-1940
German Psychologist (19)

Müller, G. E., & Schumann, F. Ueber die psychologischen Grundlagen der Vergleichung gehobener Gewichte. *Arch. ges. Physiol.*, 1889, *45*, 37–112.

———. Ueber das Gedächtniss für Komplexe regelmässig aufeinander folgender, gleicher Schalleindrücke. *Z. Psychol.*, 1889, *1*, 75–80.

———. Ueber die Schätzung kleiner Zeitgrössen. *Z. Psychol.*, 1893, *4*, 1–69.

Müller, G. E., & ———. Experimentelle Beiträge zur Untersuchung des Gedächtnisses. *Z. Psychol.*, 1894, *6*, 81–190, 257–339.

――――. Zur Psychologie der Zeitanschauung. *Z. Psychol.*, 1898, *17*, 106–148.

――――. Zur Schätzung leerer, von einfachen Schalleindrücken begrenzter Zeiten. *Z. Psychol.*, 1898, *18*, 1–48.

――――. Beiträge zur Analyse der Gesichtswahrnehmungen. *Z. Psychol.*, 1900, *23*, 1–32 ; 1900, *24*, 1–33 ; 1902, *30*, 241–291, 321–339 ; 1904, *36*, 161–185. (Also Leipzig: Barth, 1904)

――――. Psychologie des Lesens. *Ber. II. Kong. exper. Psychol.*, 1907, 153–186.

――――. Ueber einige Hauptprobleme der Lehre von den Gesichtswahrnehmungen. *Ber. V. Kong. exper. Psychol.*, 1912, 179–183.

――――. Untersuchungen über die psychologischen Grundprobleme der Tiefenwahrnehmung. I. Die Repräsentation des leeren Raumes im Bewusstsein. Eine neue Empfindung. *Z. Psychol.*, 1920, *85*, 224–244.

――――. Das Erkennungsurteil. *Z. Psychol.*, 1922, *88*, 205–224.

――――. Die Lokalisierung bei Blickbewegungen. *Z. Psychol.*, 1932, *127*, 113–128.

WALTER DILL SCOTT
1869-1955
American Psychologist (11)

Scott, W. D. *The psychology of public speaking.* (2nd ed.) New York: Barnes & Noble, 1926. (1907)

――――. *The psychology of advertising: A simple exposition of the principles of psychology in their relation to successful advertising.* Boston: Small & Maynard, 1908.

――――. An interpretation of the psycho-analytic method in psychotherapy with a report of a case so treated. *J. abnorm. Psychol.*, 1908-1909, *3*, 371–377.

――――. Personal differences in suggestibility. *Psychol. Rev.*, 1910, *17*, 147–154.

――――. *Increasing human efficiency in business.* (Rev. ed.) New York: Macmillan, 1923. (1911)

――――. *Influencing men in business: The psychology of argument and discussion.* (3rd ed.) New York: Ronald Press, 1928. (1911)

――――. Changes in some of our conceptions and practices of personnel. *Psychol. Rev.*, 1920, *27*, 81–94.

――――. *The psychology of advertising in theory and practice.* New York: Dodd, Mead, 1921.

――――, Clothier, R. C., & Spriegel, W. R. *Personnel management.* (5th ed.) New York: McGraw-Hill, 1954. (1923)

Moore & Hartmann, *Industrial Psychology*

EDWARD WHEELER SCRIPTURE
1864-1945
American-Austrian Psychologist (23)

Scripture, E. W. Arithmetical prodigies. *Amer. J. Psychol.*, 1891, *4*, 1–59.

――――. The problem of psychology. *Mind*, 1891, *16*, 305–326.

――――. Vorstellung und Gefühl. Eine experimentelle Untersuchung über ihren Zusammenhang. *Phil. Stud.*, 1891, *6*, 536–542.

――――. Ueber den associativen Verlauf der Vorstellungen. *Phil. Stud.*, 1892, *7*, 50–146. (Also Leipzig, 1891)

――――. Zur Definition einer Vorstellung. *Phil. Stud.*, 1892, *7*, 213–221.

――――. Tests on school children. *Educ. Rev.* 1893, *5*, 52–61.

――――. Psychological measurements. *Phil. Rev.*, 1893, *2*, 677–689.

――――. On means and values for direct measurements. *Stud. Yale Psychol. Lab.*, 1894, *2*, 1–39.

――――, & Smith, H. F. Researches on the highest audible tone. *Stud. Yale Psychol. Lab.*, 1894, *2*, 105–113.

――――. Work at the Yale laboratory. *Psychol. Rev.*, 1894, *1*, 66–69.

――――. Thinking, feeling, doing. *Psychol. Rev.*, 1896, *3*, 196–197.

————. Researches on reaction-time. *Stud. Yale Psychol. Lab.*, 1896, *4*, 12–26.

————. Researches on voluntary effort. *Stud. Yale Psychol. Lab.*, 1896, *4*, 69–75.

————. Elementary course in psychological measurements. *Stud. Yale Psychol. Lab.*, 1896, *4*, 89–139.

————. *The new psychology.* New York: Scribner's, 1897.

————. Sources of the new psychology. *Pop. Sci. Mon.*, 1897, *51*, 98–105.

————. Researches in experimental phonetics. *Stud. Yale Psychol. Lab.*, 1899, *7*, 1–101.

————. *The elements of experimental phonetics.* New York: Scribner's, 1902. (Reprinted 1971)

————. Researches in experimental phonetics. (2nd ser.) *Stud. Yale Psychol. Lab.*, 1902, *10*, 49–81.

————. *Researches in experimental phonetics: The study of speech curves.* Washington, D.C.: Carnegie Institution, 1906.

————. Untersuchungen über die Vokale. *Z. Biol.*, 1906–1907, *30*, 141–219, 232–308.

————. *Stuttering and lisping.* (2nd ed.) New York: Macmillan, 1923. (1912)

————. What is psychoanalysis? *Med. Rec.* 1913, *83*, 737–740.

————. The study of English speech by new methods of phonetic investigation. *Proc. Brit. Acad.*, 1921–1923, *10*, 271–299.

————. Zur Psychophysik und Physiologie der Vokale. *Z. Sinnesphysiol.*, 1927, *58*, 195–208.

————. *Anwendung der graphischen Methode auf Sprache und Gesang.* Leipzig: Barth, 1927.

————. *Grundzüge der englischen Verswissenschaft.* Marburg: Elwertssche Verlagsbuchhandlung, 1929.

————. E. W. Scripture. In C. Murchison (Ed.), *A history of psychology in autobiography.* Vol. 3. Worcester, Mass.: Clark University Press, 1936, pp. 231–261. **B**

CARL EMIL SEASHORE
1866-1949
American Psychologist (24)

Seashore, C. E. *In search of beauty in music: A scientific approach to musical esthetics.* New York: Ronald Press, 1947. **C**

————. On monocular accommodation time. *Stud. Yale Psychol. Lab.*, 1893, *1*, 56–70.

————. Measurements of illusions and hallucinations in normal life. *Stud. Yale Psychol. Lab.*, 1895, *3*, 1–67.

————. Weber's law in illusions. *Stud. Yale Psychol. Lab.*, 1896, *4*, 62–68.

————. A new factor in Weber's law. *Psychol. Rev.*, 1897, *4*, 522–524.

————. Hearing-ability and discriminative sensibility for pitch. *Univer. Iowa Stud. Psychol.*, 1899, *2*, 55–63.

————. Suggestions for tests on school children. *Educ. Rev.*, 1901, *22*, 69–82.

————. A voice tonoscope. *Univer. Iowa Stud. Psychol.*, 1902, *3*, 18–28.

————. The experimental study of mental fatigue. *Psychol. Bull.*, 1904, *1*, 97–101.

————, & Kent, Grace H. Periodicity and progressive change in continuous mental work. *Psychol. Monogr.*, 1905, No. 28, 46–101.

————, & Seashore, R. H. *Elementary experiments in psychology.* (Rev. ed.) New York: Holt, 1935. (1908)

————. Measurement of pitch discrimination: A preliminary report. *Psychol. Monogr.*, 1910, No. 53, 21–63.

————. The measure of a singer. *Science*, 1912, *35*, 201–212.

————. *Psychology in daily life.* New York: Appleton, 1913.

————. Avocational guidance in music. *J. appl. Psychol.*, 1917, *1*, 342–348.

————. *The psychology of musical talent.* New York: Silver Burdett, 1919.

————. A survey of musical talent in the public schools. *Univer. Iowa Stud. Child Welf.*, 1920, *1*, No. 2.

————. The inheritance of musical talent. *Musical Quart.*, 1920, *6*, 586–598.

————. Introduction to psychology. New York: Macmillan, 1923.

————. Sectioning on the basis of ability. *Bull. Amer. Ass. Univer. Prof.*, 1926, *9*, 9–24.

————. *Learning and living in college: Psychology of individual differences applied to the organization and pursuit of higher education.* Iowa City, Iowa: The University of Iowa, 1927.

————. Phonophotography as a new approach to the psychology of emotion. In M. L. Reymert (Ed.), *Feelings and emotions: The Wittenberg symposium.* Worcester, Mass.: Clark University Press, 1928, pp. 206–214.

————. The present status of research in the psychology of music at the University of Iowa. *Univer. Iowa Stud. Ser. Aims Prog. Res.*, 1928, *2*, No. 4.

Meier, N., & ————. The Meier-Seashore art judgment test. *Univer. Iowa Bur. Res. Serv.*, 1929.

————. Carl Emil Seashore. In C. Murchison (Ed.), *A history of psychology in autobiography.* Vol. 1. Worcester, Mass.: Clark University Press, 1930, pp. 225–297. **B**

————. Introduction. In The vibrato. *Univer. Iowa Stud. Psychol. Music*, 1932, *1*, 7–13.

————, & Seashore, H. G. The place of phonophotography in the study of primitive music. *Science*, 1934, *79*, 485–487.

————. The discovery and guidance of musical talent. *Yearb. Nat. Soc. Stud. Educ.*, 1935, *34*, 447–461.

————. Psychology of the vibrato in voice and instrument. *Univer. Iowa Stud. Psychol. Music*, 1936, No. 317.

————. The objective recording and analysis of musical performance. *Univer. Iowa Stud. Psychol. Music*, 1936, No. 330.

————. New vantage grounds in the psychology of music. *Science*, 1936, *84*, 517–522.

————. *Psychology of music.* New York: Dover, 1967. (1938)

Saetveit, J. G., Lewis, D., & ————. Revision of the Seashore measures of musical talent. *Univer. Iowa Stud. Ser. Aims Prog. Res.*, 1940, *65*, No. 388.

————. *Why we love music.* Philadelphia, Pa.: Ditson, 1941.

————. *Pioneering in psychology.* Iowa City, Iowa: University of Iowa Press, 1942. **B Bl**

————. A scientific approach to musical aesthetics. *Brit. J. Psychol.*, 1942, *32*, 287–294.

————. Science in music. *Science*, 1942, *95*, 417–422.

HAROLD GUSTAV SEASHORE
1906-1965
American Psychologist (11)

Seashore, H. G. The hearing of the pitch and intensity in vibrato. In The vibrato. *Univer. Iowa Stud. Psychol. Music*, 1932, *1*, 213–235.

Tiffin, J., & ————. Summary of established facts in experimental studies on the vibrato up to 1932. In The vibrato. *Univer. Iowa Stud. Psychol. Music*, 1932, *1*, 344–382.

Seashore, C. E., & ————. The place of phonophotography in the study of primitive music. *Science*, 1934, *79*, 485–487.

————. An objective analysis of artistic singing. *Univer. Iowa Stud. Psychol. Music*, 1936, *4*, 12–157.

————, & Koch, G. Postural steadiness under conditions of muscular tension and fatigue. *Psychol. Rec.*, 1938, *2*, 319–332.

————, & Bavelas, A. The functioning of knowledge of results in Thorndike's line-drawing experiment. *Psychol. Rev.*, 1941, *48*, 155–164.

————, & Bavelas, A. A study of frustration in children. *J. genet. Psychol.*, 1942, *61*, 279–314.

————. The superiority of college students on the Minnesota Rate of Manipulation Test. *J. appl. Psychol.*, 1947, *31*, 249–253.

————. Validation of the study of values for two vocational groups at the college level. *Educ. psychol. Measmt.*, 1947, *7*, 757–763.

————. The improvement of performance on the Minnesota Rate of Manipulation Test when bonuses are given. *J. appl. Psychol.*, 1947, *31*, 254–259.

————, & Bennett, G. K. A test of stenography: Some preliminary results. *Personnel Psychol.*, 1948, *1*, 197–209.

————. Ethical problems of the industrial psychologist. *Personnel Psychol.*, 1949, *2*, 103–113.

Bennett, G. K., ————, & Wesman, A. G. *Validation of the differential aptitude tests, third research report.* New York: Psychological Corporation, 1949. (Also *J. Consult. Psychol.*, 1950, *14*, 161–162.)

————, Wesman, A., & Doppelt, J. The standardization of the Wechsler Intelligence Scale for Children. *J. consult. Psychol.*, 1950, *14*, 99–110.

————. Differences between verbal and performance IQs on the Wechsler Intelligence Scale for Children. *J. consult. Psychol.*, 1951, *15*, 62–67.

Bennett, G. K., ————, & Wesman, A. G. *The DAT—Fifth Research Report.* New York: Psychological Corporation, 1951.

Bennett, G. K., ————, & Wesman, A. G. Aptitude testing: Does it "prove out" in counseling practice? *Occupations*, 1952, *30*, 584–593.

————. A code of ethics for the psychologist. *Personnel*, 1953, *30*, 35–38.

————. Validation of clerical testing in banks. *Personnel Psychol.*, 1953, *6*, 45–56.

————. Tenth grade tests as predictors of twelfth grade scholarship and college entrance status. *J. counsel. Psychol.*, 1954, *1*, 106–115.

————. Cross-validation of equations for predicting CEEB-SAT scores from DAT scores. *J. counsel. Psychol.*, 1955, *2*, 229–230.

Bennett, G. K., ————, & Wesman, A. G. The differential aptitude tests: An overview. *Personnel Guid. J.*, 1956, *35*, 81–93.

IVAN MICHAILOVICH SECHENOV
1829-1905
Russian Physiologist (26)

Sechenov, I. M. *Etudes psychologiques.* Paris: Alcan, 1884. (1873)   C

————. *Selected physiological and psychological works.* Ed. by G. Gibbons, & trans. by S. Belsky *et al.* Moscow: Foreign Languages Publishing House, n.d. (1961) (Reprinted 1968)   C

————. *Selected works.* Trans. by A. A. Subkov *et al.* Moscow: State Publishing House for Biological and Medical Literature, 1935.   C

————. *Oeuvres philosophiques et psychologiques choisies.* Trans. by E. Bronina. Moscow: Foreign Languages Publishing House, 1957. (1947)   C

————. *(Selected works.* Vol. 1. *Physiology and psychology.* Vol. 2. *Physiology of the nervous system.)* Moscow: Akademiya Nauk, 1952, 1956.   C

————. *Reflexes of the brain: An attempt to establish the physiological basis of psychological processes.* Trans. by S. Belsky. Boston: MIT Press, 1965. (1863) (Also in *Selected physiological and psychological works, op. cit.,* pp. 31–139, & in *Selected works, op. cit.,* pp. 263–336)

————. *Physiologische Studien über die Hemmungsmechanismen für die Reflexthätigkeit des Rückenmarkes im Gehirne des Frosches.* Berlin: Hirschwald, 1863. Reprinted in *Selected works, op. cit.,* pp. 153–176.

————. Who is to elaborate the problems of psychology and how? (1873) In *Selected physiological and psychological works, op. cit.,* pp. 179–260, & in *Selected works, op. cit.,* pp. 337–391.

————. The elements of thought. (2nd ed.) (1878) In *Selected physiological and psychological works, op. cit.,* pp. 265–401, & in *Selected works, op. cit.,* pp. 403–489.

————. Galvanische Erscheinungen an dem verlängerten Marke des Frosches. *Arch. ges. Physiol.,* 1882, *27*, 524–566. Reprinted in *Selected works, op. cit.,* pp. 212–242.

———. Impressions and reality. (1890) In *Selected physiological and psychological works, op. cit.,* pp. 422–437, & in *Selected works, op. cit.,* pp. 392–402.

———. *(The physiology of nerve centers.)* Moscow: Uchpedgiz, 1952. (1891)

———. *Autobiographical notes.* Trans. by K. Hanes. Washington, D. C.: American Institute of Biological Sciences, 1965. (1907)   **B**

Clarke & O'Malley, *Brain ;* Herrnstein & Boring, *Source Book*

———. *Report on education.* (2nd ed.) Milwaukee, Wisc.: Doerflinger, 1880. (1875)

———. Recent progress in the training of idiots. *Proc. Amer. Ass. ment. Def.,* 1876–1886, 60–65.

———. *Medical thermometry and human temperature.* New York: Wood, 1876.

———. *Psycho-physiological training of an idiotic hand.* New York: Putnam, 1879.

Goshen, *Documentary*

EDOUARD SEGUIN
1812-1880
French-American Psychiatrist (18)

Seguin, E. *Rapport et mémoires sur l'éducation des enfants normaux et anormaux.* Paris: Progrès médical, 1895.   **C**

———. *L'éducation physiologique.* Paris: Flammarion, 1931.   **Bl C**

———. *Conseils à M.O. sur l'éducation de son fils.* Paris: Porthmann, 1839.

———. *Théorie et pratique de l'éducation des enfants arriérés et idiots.* Paris: Baillière, 1842.

———. *Hygiène et éducation des idiots.* Paris: Baillière, 1843.

———. *Traitement moral, hygiène et éducation des idiots et des autres enfants arriérés ou retardés dans leur développement.* Paris: Baillière, 1846.

———. *Jacob Rodrigues Péreire, notice sur sa vie et ses travaux.* Paris: Baillière, 1847.

———. Origin of the treatment and training of idiots. *Barnard's Amer. J. Educ.,* 1856, *2,* 145–152.

———. *Idiocy: And its treatment by the physiological method.* New York: Teachers College, Columbia University, 1907. (1866) (Reprinted 1971)

———. *New facts and remarks concerning idiocy.* New York: Wood, 1870.

OTTO SELZ
1881-1944
German Psychologist (17)

Selz, O. Die psychologische Erkenntnistheorie und das Transzendenzproblem. Untersuchungen zur Entstehung des Transzendenzproblems und zur Transzendenztheorie des älteren englischen Empirismus. *Arch. ges. Psychol.,* 1909–1910, *16,* 1–110.

———. Die experimentelle Untersuchung des Willensaktes. *Z. Psychol.,* 1910, *57,* 241–270.

———. Willensakt und Temperament. Eine Erwiderung auf N. Achs Widerlegung. *Z. Psychol.,* 1911, *59,* 113–122.

———. Experimentelle Untersuchungen über den Verlauf determinierter intellektueller Prozesse. *Ber. V. Kongr. exp. Psychol.* Leipzig: Barth, 1912, pp. 229–234.

———. Die Gesetze der produktiven Tätigkeit. *Arch. ges. Psychol.,* 1913, *27,* 367–380.

———. *Ueber die Gesetze des geordneten Denkverlaufs. Eine experimentelle Untersuchung.* I. Stuttgart: Spemann, 1913.

———. Ueber den Anteil der individuellen Eigenschaften der Flugzeugführer und Beobachter an Fliegerunfällen. *Z. angew. Psychol.,* 1919, *15,* 254–300.

———. Komplextheorie und Konstellationstheorie. *Z. Psychol.,* 1920, *83,* 211—234.

———. *Zur Psychologie des produktiven Denkens und des Irrtums.* Bonn: Cohen, 1922.

. *Die Gesetze der produktiven und reproduktiven Geistestätigkeit. Kurzgefasste Darstellung.* Bonn: Cohen, 1924.

. Ueber die Persönlichkeitstypen und die Methoden ihrer Bestimmung. *Ber. VIII. Kongr. exp. Psychol.* Leipzig: Barth, 1924, pp. 3–27.

. Veränderungen in den psychologischen Grundlagen der Pädagogik seit Herbart. *Z. pädag. Psychol.,* 1925, *26,* 337–346.

. Zur Psychologie der Gegenwart. Eine Anmerkung zu Koffkas Darstellung. *Z. Psychol.,* 1926, *99,* 160–196.

. Die Umgestaltung der Grundanschauungen vom intellektuellen Geschehen. *Kant-Stud.,* 1927, *32,* 273–280. Trans. in Jean M. Mandler & G. Mandler (Eds.), *Thinking: From association to Gestalt.* New York: Wiley, 1964, pp. 225–234.

. Ein Schulbeispiel zur Frage der Würdigung jugendlicher Zeugenaussagen. *Monatssch. Krim.-Psychol. Strafrechtsref.,* 1928, *19,* 641–658.

. Ueber die Abhängigkeitsbeziehungen zwischen Lernlast und Lernerfolg. *Z. Psychol.,* 1929, *109,* 191–209.

. Essai d'une nouvelle théorie psychologique de l'espace, du temps et de la forme. *J. Psychol. norm. path.,* 1929, *26,* 337–353.

. Von der Systematik der Raumphänomene zur Gestalttheorie. *Arch. ges. Psychol.,* 1930, *77,* 527–551.

. Die psychologische Strukturanalyse des Ortskontinuums und die Grundlagen der Geometrie. *Z. Psychol.,* 1930, *114,* 351–362.

. Ergebnisse einer Umfrage über Hochschulstudium und Examenvorbereitung. *Z. angew. Psychol.,* 1933, *45,* 172–181.

. Gestalten und Steigerungsphänomene. *Arch. ges. Psychol.,* 1934, *91,* 319–394.

. Versuche zur Hebung des Intelligenzniveaus. Ein Beitrag zur Theorie der Intelligenz und ihrer erziehlichen Beeinflussung. *Z. Psychol.,* 1935, *134,* 236–301.

. Les problèmes génétiques de la totalité et le problème phénoménologique de la construction des touts et des formes. *J. Psychol. norm. path.,* 1936, *33,* 88–113.

. Die Aufbauprinzipien der phänomenalen Welt. *Acta Psychol.,* 1941, *5,* 7–35.

. Die Analyse des phänomenalen Kontinuums. Ein Beitrag zu einer synthetischen Psychologie der Ganzen. *Acta Psychol.,* 1949, *6,* 91–125.

Mandler & Mandler, *Thinking*

ALEXANDER FAULKNER SHAND
1858-1936
English Psychologist (15)

Shand, A. F. The unity of consciousness. *Mind,* 1888, *13,* 231–243.

. The nature of consciousness. *Mind,* 1891, *16,* 206–222.

. An analysis of attention. *Mind,* 1894, *3* (N.S.), 449–473.

. Attention and will: A study in involuntary action. *Mind,* 1895, *4*(N.S.), 450–471.

. Character and the emotions. *Mind,* 1896, *5*(N.S.), 203–226.

. Types of will. *Mind,* 1897, *6*(N.S.), 289–325.

. Feeling and thought. *Mind,* 1898, *7*(N.S.), 477–505.

. M. Ribot's theory of the passions. *Mind,* 1907, *16*(N.S.), 477–505.

. *The foundations of character: Being a study of the tendencies of the emotions and sentiments.* (2nd ed.) London: Macmillan, 1926. (1914)

, McDougall, W., & Stout, G. F. Instinct and emotion. *Proc. Arist. Soc.,* 1915, *15,* 22–99.

. Emotion and value. *Proc. Arist. Soc.,* 1919, *19,* 208–235.

. Of impulse, emotion, and instinct. *Proc. Arist. Soc.,* 1920, *20,* 79–88.

———. Suspicion. *Brit. J. Psychol.*, 1922–1923, *13*, 195–214.

———. The conception of sexuality. *Brit. J. med. Psychol.*, 1925, *5*, 189–195.

Arnold, *Emotion*

JOHN FREDERICK SHEPARD
1881-1965
American Psychologist (11)

Shepard, J. F. Organic changes and feelings. *Amer. J. Psychol.*, 1906, *17*, 522–584.

Billings, M. L., & ———. The change of heart rate with attention. *Psychol. Rev.*, 1910, *17*, 217–228.

———, & Fogelsonger, H. M. Studies in association and inhibition. *Psychol. Rev.*, 1913, *20*, 290–311.

———, & Breed, F. S. Maturation and use in the development of an instinct. *J. anim. Behav.*, 1913, *3*, 274–285.

———. *The circulation and sleep*. New York: Macmillan, 1914.

CHARLES SCOTT SHERRINGTON
1857-1952
English Physiologist (27)

Sherrington, C. S. *Selected writings of Sir Charles Sherrington*. Ed. by D. Denny-Brown. New York: Hoeber, 1940. (1937)   **Bl C**

———. Note on the knee-jerk and the correlation of antagonistic muscles. *Proc. Roy. Soc.*, London, 1893, *52*, 556–564. Reprinted in *Selected writings, op. cit.*, pp. 237–244.

———. Further experimental note on the correlation of action of antagonistic muscles. *Proc. Roy. Soc.*, London, 1893, *53*, 407–420. Reprinted in *Selected writings, op. cit.*, pp. 244–256.

———. Experiments in examination of the peripheral distribution of the fibres of the posterior roots of some spinal nerves. *Phil. Trans.*, 1894, *184B*, 641–763. Extract reprinted in *Selected writings, op. cit.*, pp. 31–56.

———. On reciprocal action in the retina as studied by means of some rotating discs. *J. Physiol.*, 1897, *21*, 33–54.

———. On reciprocal innervation of antagonistic muscles. Third note. *Proc. Roy. Soc.*, London, 1897, *60*, 414–417. Reprinted in *Selected writings, op. cit.*, pp. 256–259.

———. Decerebrate rigidity, and reflex co-ordination of movements. *J. Physiol.*, 1898, *22*, 319–332. Reprinted in *Selected writings, op. cit.*, pp. 314–325, & in R. H. Wilkins (Ed.), *Neurosurgical classics*. New York: Johnson Reprint, 1965, pp. 155–161.

———. Cutaneous sensations. In E. A. Schäfer (Ed.), *Text-book of physiology*. Vol. 2. New York: Macmillan, 1900, pp. 920–1001.

———. The muscular sense. In E. A. Schäfer (Ed.), *Text-book of physiology*. Vol. 2. New York: Macmillan, 1900, pp. 1002–1025.

———. *The integrative action of the nervous system*. (2nd ed.) New Haven: Yale University Press, 1947. (1906)

———. On the proprioceptive system especially in its reflex aspect. *Brain*, 1906, *29*, 467–482. Extract reprinted in *Selected writings, op. cit.*, pp. 326–329.

———. On plastic tonus and proprioceptive reflexes. *Quart. J. exp. Physiol.*, 1909, *2*, 109–156. Reprinted in *Selected writings, op. cit.*, pp. 329–363.

———. Flexion-reflex of the limb crossed extension-reflex, and reflex stepping and standing. *J. Physiol.*, 1910, *40*, 28–121. Extracts reprinted in *Selected writings, op. cit.*, pp. 163–188, 364–372.

———. Postural activity of muscle and nerve. *Brain*, 1915, *38*, 191–234. Extract reprinted in *Selected writings, op. cit.*, pp. 374–385.

Leyton, A. S. F., & ———. Observations on the excitable cortex of the chimpanzee, orang-utan and gorillas. *Quart. J. exp. Physiol.*, 1917, *11*, 135–222. Reprinted in G. v. Bonin (Ed.), *Some papers on the cerebral cortex*. Springfield, Ill.: Thomas, 1960, pp. 283–381.

———. Observations on the sensual role of the proprioceptive nerve-supply of the extrinsic ocular muscles. *Brain,* 1918, *41,* 332–343. Reprinted in *Selected writings, op. cit.,* pp. 105–115.

———. Some aspects of animal mechanism. Presidential Address, *Brit. Ass. Rep.,* 1922, 1–15.

———. Problems of muscular receptivity. *Nature,* 1924, *113,* 732, 892–894, 924–932. Extract reprinted in *Selected writings, op. cit.,* pp. 385–396.

Liddell, E. G. T., & ———. Reflexes in response to stretch (myotatic reflexes). *Proc. Roy. Soc.,* London, 1924, *963B,* 212–242. Reprinted in C. D. Barnes & C. Kircher (Eds.), *Readings in neurophysiology.* New York: Wiley, 1968, pp. 8–38.

———. *The assaying of Brabantius and other verse.* London: Oxford University Press, 1925.

———. Remarks on some aspects of reflex inhibition. *Proc. Roy. Soc.,* London, 1925, *97B,* 515–545. Extract reprinted in *Selected writings, op. cit.,* pp. 443–460.

———. Some functional problems attaching to convergence. *Proc. Roy. Soc.,* London, 1929, *105B,* 332–362; & *Brit. med. J.,* 1929, *1,* 1136–1137. Reprinted in *Selected writings, op. cit.,* pp. 464–486.

———, & Fulton, J. F. Nervous integrations in man. In E. Cowdry (Ed.), *Human biology and racial welfare.* New York: Hoeber, 1930, pp. 246–265.

———. Quantitative management of contraction in lowest level co-ordination. Hughlings Jackson Lecture. *Brain,* 1931, *54,* 1–28. Reprinted in *Selected writings, op. cit.,* pp. 497–514.

Creed, R. S., Denny-Brown, D., Eccles, J. C., Liddell, E. G. T., & ———. *Reflex activity of the spinal cord.* Oxford: Clarendon Press, 1932.

———. *The brain and its mechanism.* New York: Macmillan, 1933.

———. *Man on his nature.* (2nd ed.) Cambridge: Cambridge University Press, 1963. (1941)

———. *Goethe on nature and on science.* 2nd ed.) Cambridge: Cambridge University Press, 1949. (1942)

———. Marginalia. In E. A. Underwood (Ed.), *Science, medicine, and history: Essays in honour of Charles Singer.* Vol. 2. London: Oxford University Press, 1953, pp. 545–553.

Beck & Molish, *Reflexes;* Clarke & O'Malley, *Brain;* Fulton & Wilson, *Physiology;* Shipley, *Classics*

BORIS SIDIS
1867-1923
American Psychologist (17)

Sidis, B. *The psychology of suggestion: A research into the subconscious nature of man and society.* New York: Appleton, 1898.

Gieson, I. V., & ———. Neuron energy and its psychomotor manifestations. *Arch. Neurol. Psycho-Path.,* 1898, *1*(1), 5–25.

———. The nature and principles of psychology. *Amer. J. Insan.,* 1899, *56,* 41–52.

———. *Psychopathological researches: Studies in mental dissociation.* New York: Stechert, 1902.

———, & Goodhart, S. P. *Multiple personality: An experimental investigation into the nature of human individuality.* New York: Appleton, 1904. (Reprinted 1968)

———. An inquiry into the nature of hallucination. *Psychol. Rev.,* 1904, *11,* 15–29, 104–137.

———. Are there hypnotic hallucinations? *Psychol. Rev.,* 1906, *13,* 239–257.

White, W. A., & ———. Mental dissociation in functional psychosis. In G. E. Stechert (Ed.), *Psycho-pathological researches in mental dissociation.* Boston: Badger, 1908, pp. 33–102.

White, W. A., & ———. Mental dissociation in alcoholic psychosis. In G. E. Stechert (Ed.), *Psycho-pathological researches in mental dissociation.* Boston: Badger, 1908, pp. 103–122.

White, W. A., & ———. Mental dissociation in psychic epilepsy. In G. E. Stechert (Ed.), *Psycho-pathological researches in mental dissociation.* Boston: Badger, 1908, pp. 122–279.

———. An experimental study of sleep. *J. abnorm. Psychol.,* 1908, *3,* 1–32.

————, & Kalmus, H. T. A study of galvanometric deflections due to psycho-physiological processes. *Psychol. Rev.*, 1908, *15*, 391–396 ; 1909, *16*, 1–35.

————. An experimental study of sleep. Boston: Badger, 1909.

————. The psychotherapeutic value of the hypnoidal state. *J. abnorm. Psychol.*, 1909, *4*, 151–171.

————. The nature and cause of the galvanic phenomenon. *J. abnorm. Psychol.*, 1910, *5*, 69–74.

————, & Nelson, L. The nature and causation of the galvanic phenomenon. *Psychol. Rev.*, 1910, *17*, 98–146.

————. The psychology of laughter. New York: Appleton, 1913.

————. Symptomatology, psychognosis and diagnosis of psychopathic diseases. Boston: Badger, 1914.

————. The foundations of normal and abnormal psychology. Boston: Badger, 1914.

————. The causation and treatment of psychopathic diseases. Boston: Badger, 1916.

————. Philistine and genius. Boston: Badger, 1917.

————. Psychopathic aphonia, stammering and catalepsy. *J. abnorm. Psychol.*, 1917, *12*, 100–113.

————. The source and aim of human progress. Boston: Badger, 1919.

————. Nervous ills: Their cause and cure. Boston: Badger, 1922.

THEODORE SIMON
1873-1961
French Psychologist (21)

Simon, T. Expériences de suggestion sur des débiles. *Année psychol.*, 1899, *6*, 441–484.

————. Documents relatifs à la corrélation entre le développement physique et la capacité intellectuelle. Paris: Carré & Nand, 1900.

————. Recherches céphalométriques sur les enfants arriérés de la colonie de Vaucluse. *Année psychol.*, 1900, *7*, 430–489.

————. L'interprétation des sensations tactiles chez les enfants arriérés. *Année psychol.*, 1900, *7*, 537–558.

Binet, A., & ————. Enquête sur le mode d'existence des sujets sortis d'une école d'arriérés. *Année psychol.*, 1905, *11*, 163–190.

Binet, A., & ————. Application des méthodes nouvelles au diagnostic du niveau intellectuel chez des enfants normaux et anormaux d'hospice et d'école primaire. *Année psychol.*, 1905, *11*, 245–336.

Binet, A., & ————. Les enfants anormaux: Guide pour l'admission des enfants anormaux dans les classes de perfectionnement. Paris: Colin, 1907.

Binet, A., & ————. The development of intelligence in children. Trans. by Elizabeth S. Kite. Baltimore, Md.: Williams & Wilkins, 1916. (1908)

Binet, A., & ————. The intelligence of the feebleminded. Trans. by Elizabeth S. Kite. Baltimore, Md.: Williams & Wilkins, 1916. (1908, 1909)

Binet, A., & ————. Peut-on enseigner la parole aux sourds-muets? *Année psychol.*, 1909, *15*, 373–396.

Binet, A., & ————. Définitions des principaux états mentaux de l'aliénation. I. L'hystérie. II. La folie avec conscience. III. La folie maniaque-dépressive. IV. La folie systématisée. V. Les démences. VI. L'arriération. VII. Conclusions. *Année psychol.*, 1910, *16*, 61–371.

Binet, A., & ————. Réponse à quelques critiques. *Année psychol.*, 1911, *17*, 270–277.

Binet, A., & ————. La confusion mentale. *Année psychol.*, 1911, *17*, 278–300.

Binet, A., & ————. La législation des aliénés. *Année psychol.*, 1911, *17*, 351–362.

Binet, A., & ————. Parallèle entre les classifications des aliénistes. *Année psychol.*, 1911, *17*, 363–388.

Binet, A., & ————. A method of measuring the development of the intelligence of young chil-

dren. Trans. by Clara H. Town. Chicago: Medical Book, 1913. (1911)

————. Alfred Binet. *Année psychol.*, 1912, *18*, 1–16.   **B**

Binet, A., & ————. *Mentally defective children.* Trans. by W. B. Drummond. New York: Longmans, Green, 1914.

————. Questionnaire for the observation of a young child from birth to two years of age. Trans. by M. L. Reymert. *J. genet. Psychol.*, 1920, *27*, 200–204.

————. Nouveaux tests collectifs d'intelligence. *Bull. Soc. A. Binet*, 1934, No. 298, 90–97.

————. Généralement appliqués aux enfants, les tests pour la mesure du développement de l'intelligence valent-ils pour les adultes? *Ann. méd.-psychol.*, 1936, *94*, 474–477.

————. Faut-il exprimer en années d'âge le niveau mental d'un adulte? *Ann. méd.-psychol.*, 1936, *94*, 477–480.

————. Quelques problèmes posés par les tests. In Various, *Centenaire de Th. Ribot et Jubilé de la Psychologie Scientifique Française*. Paris: Imprimerie moderne, 1939, pp. 551–563.

> Beck & Molish, *Reflexes;* Dennis, *Psychology;* Kessen, *Child;* Rosenblith & Allinsmith, *Causes Behavior;* Shipley *Classics*

WILLARD STANTON SMALL
1870-1943
American Psychologist (18)

Small, W. S. *Experimental studies of the mental processes of the rat.* Worcester, Mass.: Orpna, 1899.   **C**

————. Notes on the psychic development of the young white rat. *Amer. J. Psychol.*, 1899–1900, *11*, 80–100.

————. An experimental study of the mental processes of the rat. *Amer. J. Psychol.*, 1899–1900 *11*, 131–165.

————. Experimental study of the mental pro-

cesses of the rat. II. *Amer. J. Psychol.*, 1901, *12*, 206–239.

> Herrnstein & Boring, *Source Book*

ADAM SMITH
1723-1790
Scottish Philosopher (17)

Smith, A. *Essays on philosophical subjects.* Ed. by J. Black & J. Hutton. London: Cadell, Davies, & Creech, 1795. (Reprinted 1970)   **C**

————. *The works of Adam Smith.* (5 vols.) Ed. by D. Stewart. Aalen: Zeller, 1963. (1811–1812)   **C**

————. The theory of moral sentiments. (6th ed.) (1759) In *Works*, Vol. 1, *op. cit.*; in H. W. Schneider (Ed.), *Adam Smith's moral and political philosophy.* New York: Hafner, 1948, pp. 1–277; & in part in L. A. Selby-Bigge (Ed.), *British moralists.* Vol. 1. Oxford: Clarendon Press, 1897, pp. 257–336. (1959) (Reprinted 1965 & 1966)

————. *An inquiry into the nature and causes of the wealth of nations.* Ed. by E. Cannan. (6th ed.) (2 vols.) London: Methuen, 1950. (1776)

————. *Select chapters and passages from The wealth of nations.* New York: Macmillan, 1926. (1776)

————. The nature and causes of the wealth of nations. (4th ed.) (1776) In *Works*, Vols. 2, 3, 4, *op. cit.*

————. Of the external senses. (1795) In *Essays, op. cit.*, pp. 197–244. Reprinted in *Works*, Vol. 5, *op. cit.*, pp. 333–399.

————. The principles which lead and direct philosophical enquiries: illustrated by the history of astronomy. (1795) In *Essays, op. cit.*, pp. 3–93.

————. Of the nature of that imitation which takes place in what are called the imitative arts. (1795) In *Essays, op. cit.*, pp. 133–179.

> Brinton, *Age Reason;* Hutchins, *Great Books;* Moore & Hartmann, *Industrial Psychology;* Park & Burgess, *Sociology;* Parsons, *Society;* Rand, *Moralists;*

Robinson, *Scottish Philosophy ;* Schneider,
Scottish Moralists ; Slotkin, *Anthropology*

JAN CHRISTIAAN SMUTS
1870-1950
South African Philosopher (13)

Smuts, J. C. *Selections from the Smuts papers.* (4
vols.) Ed. by W. K. Hancock & Jean v. d.
Poel. Cambridge: Cambridge University Press,
1966.   **B C**

———. *Die holistische Welt.* Trans. by H. Min-
kowski. Berlin: Metzner, 1938. (1926)

———. *Holism and evolution.* (Rev. ed.) New
York: Viking Press, 1961. (1926)

———. The scientific world picture of today.
Rep. Brit. Ass. Adv. Sci., 1931, 1–18. Reprinted
in trans. in *Int. Z. indiv. Psychol.,* 1932, *10,* 244–
261.

GEORGE SAMUEL SNODDY
1882-1947
American Psychologist (11)

Snoddy, G. S. An experimental analysis of a case
of trial and error learning in the human subject.
Psychol. Monogr., 1920, *28,* No. 124.

———, & Hyde, G. E. *Mental survey of Utah
schools and adaptation of the Army Beta tests.*
Salt Lake City, Utah: University of Utah, 1921.

———. Learning and stability: A psychophysiological analysis of a case of motor learning with
clinical applications. *J. appl. Psychol.,* 1926, *10,*
1–36.

———. *Evidence for two opposed processes in
mental growth.* Lancaster, Pa.: Science Press,
1935.

———. The time factor in learning. *Bull. sch.
Educ. Ind. Univer.,* 1936, *12,* No. 4, 30–44.

———. A reply to Doré and Hilgard. *J. exp.
Psychol.,* 1938, *23,* 375–383.

———. Evidence for a universal shock factor in
learning. *J. exp. Psychol.,* 1945, *35,* 403–417.

Valentine, *Experimental*

ELMER ERNEST SOUTHARD
1876-1920
American Psychiatrist (11)

Southard, E. E. On the somatic sources of somatic
delusions. *J. abnorm. Psychol.,* 1912–1913, *7,*
326–339.

———. Report of the Director of the Psycho-
pathic Department of the Boston State Hospital.
In *Fourth annual report of the trustees of the
Boston State Hospital for the year ending
November 30, 1912* (Public Document No. 84).
Boston: Wright & Potter, 1913, pp. 28–37.

———. Contributions from the Psychopathic
Hospital, Boston, Massachusetts: Introductory
note. *Boston Med. Surg. J.,* 1913, *169,* 109–116.

———. The psychopathic hospital idea. *J. Amer.
Med. Ass.,* 1913, *61,* 1972–1974.

———. The mind twist and brain spot hypotheses
in psychopathology and neuropathology. *Psychol. Bull.,* 1914, *11,* 117–130.

———. Feeble-mindedness as a leading social
problem. *Boston Med. Surg. J.,* 1914, *170,* 781–
784.

———. On the application of grammatical categories to the analysis of delusions. *Phil. Rev.,*
N.Y., 1916, *25,* 424–455.

———. On descriptive analysis of manifest delusions from the subject's point of view. *J. abnorm. Psychol.,* 1916–1917, *11,* 189–202.

———. Alienists and psychiatrists: Notes on
divisions and nomenclature of mental hygiene.
Ment. Hyg., N.Y., 1917, *1,* 567–571.

———. Report of the Director of the Psychopathic Department of the Boston State Hospital. In *Eighth annual report of the trustees
of the Boston State Hospital for the year ending
November 30, 1916* (Public Document No. 84).
Boston: Wright & Potter, 1917, pp. 28–78.

———, & Solomon, H. C. *Neurosyphilis: Modern
systematic diagnosis and treatment.* Boston:
Leonard, 1917.

———. Mental hygiene and social work: Notes
on a course in social psychiatry for social
workers. *Ment. Hyg.,* N.Y., 1918, *2,* 388–406.

——. Shell shock and after (the Shattuck lecture). *Boston Med. Surg. J.*, 1918, *179*, 73–93.

——. Report of the Director of the Psychopathic Department of the Boston State Hospital. In *Ninth annual report of the trustees of the Boston State Hospital for the year ending November 30, 1917* (Public Document No. 84). Boston: Wright & Potter, 1918, pp. 27–76.

——. The empathic index in the diagnosis of mental diseases. *J. abnorm. Psychol.*, 1918–1919, *13*, 199–214.

——. The individual versus the family as the unit of interest in social work. *Ment. Hyg.*, N.Y., 1919, *3*, 436–444.

——. *Shell-shock and other neuropsychiatric problems presented in five hundred and eighty-nine case histories from the war literature, 1914–1918.* Boston: Leonard, 1919.

——. Cross sections of mental hygiene, 1844, 1869, 1894. Presidential Address at Seventy-fifth Annual Meeting of American Medico-Psychological Association, Philadelphia, Pa., June 18–20, 1919. *Amer. J. Insan.*, 1919, *76*, 91–111.

——. Sigmund Freud, pessimist. *J. abnorm. Psychol.*, 1919–1920, *14*, 197–216.

——. The movement for a mental hygiene of industry. *Ment. Hyg.*, N.Y., 1920, *4*, 43–64.

——, & Jarrett, Mary C. *The kingdom of evils.* New York: Macmillan, 1922.   **Bl**

DOUGLAS ALEXANDER SPALDING
1840?-1877
English Biologist (12)

Spalding, D. A. On instinct. *Nature*, 1872, *6*, 485–486.

——. Instinct: With original observations on young animals. *Macmillan's Mag.*, 1873, *27*, 282–293. Reprinted in *Brit. J. anim. Behav.*, 1954, *2*, 2–11.

——. Herbert Spencer's psychology. *Nature*, 1873, *7*, 298–300, 357–359.

——. Flight not an acquisition. *Nature*, 1873, *8*, 289.

——. The relation of mind and body. *Nature*, 1874, *9*, 178–179.

——. Lewes's "Problems of life and mind." *Nature*, 1874, *10*, 1–2.

——. Automatism of animals and men. *Nature*, 1874, *10*, 520.

——. Sully's "Sensation and intuition." *Nature*, 1874, *11*, 44–45.

——. Fiske's "Cosmic philosophy." *Nature*, 1875, *12*, 267–270.

——. Instinct and acquisition. *Nature*, 1875, *12*, 507–508.

——. Maudsley's "Physiology of mind." *Nature*, 1876, *14*, 541–543.

——. The first swallow at Menton. *Nature*, 1877, *15*, 488.

——. The physical basis of mind. *Nature*, 1877, *16*, 261–262.

CHARLES EDWARD SPEARMAN
1863-1945
English Psychologist (27)

Spearman, C. The proof and measurement of association between two things. *Amer. J. Psychol.*, 1904, *15*, 72–101.

——. "General intelligence" objectively determined and measured. *Amer. J. Psychol.*, 1904, *15*, 201–293.

——. Analysis of "localization" illustrated by a Brown-Séquard case. *Brit. J. Psychol.*, 1904–1905, *1*, 286–314.

——. Proof and disproof of correlation. *Amer. J. Psychol.*, 1905, *16*, 228–231.

——, & Krueger, F. Die Korrelation zwischen verschiedenen geistigen Leistungsfähigkeiten. *Z. Physiol. Sinnes.*, 1906, *44*, 50–114.

——. "Footrule" for measuring correlation. *Brit. J. Psychol.*, 1906–1908, *2*, 89–108.

——. The method of "right and wrong" cases ("constant stimuli") without Gauss's formulae. *Brit. J. Psychol.*, 1906–1908, *2*, 227–242.

————. Demonstration of formulae for true measurement of correlation. *Amer. J. Psychol.*, 1907, *18*, 161–169.

————. Correlation calculated from faulty data. *Brit. J. Psychol.*, 1909–1910, *3*, 271–295.

Hart, B., & ————. General ability, its existence and nature. *Brit. J. Psychol.*, 1912–1913, *5*, 51–84.

————. Correlations of sums or differences. *Brit. J. Psychol.*, 1912–1913, *5*, 417–426.

————. The theory of two factors. *Psychol. Rev.*, 1914, *21*, 101–115.

————. The heredity of abilities. *Eugen. Rev.*, Cambridge, 1914–1915, *6*, 595–606.

Hart, B., & ————. Mental tests of dementia. *J. abnorm. Psychol.*, 1914, *9*, 217–264.

————. Manifold sub-theories of "the two factors." *Psychol. Rev.*, 1920, *27*, 159–172.

————. Recent contributions to the theory of "two factors." *Brit. J. Psychol.*, 1922–1923, *13*, 26–30.

————. Further note on the "theory of two factors." *Brit. J. Psychol.*, 1922–1923, *13*, 266–270.

————. *The nature of "intelligence" and the principles of cognition.* (2nd ed.) New York: Macmillan, 1927. (1923)

————, & Holzinger, K. The sampling error in the theory of two factors. *Brit. J. Psychol.*, 1924–1925, *15*, 17–19.

————. The new psychology of shape. *Brit. J. Psychol.*, 1924–1925, *15*, 211–225.

————. Material versus abstract factors in correlation. *Brit. J. Psychol.*, 1926–1927, *17*, 322–326.

————. *The abilities of man: Their nature and measurement.* New York: Macmillan, 1927.

————. The origin of error. *J. gen. Psychol.*, 1928, *1*, 29–53.

————. A new method for investigating the springs of action. In M. L. Reymert (Ed.), *Feelings and emotions: The Wittenberg symposium.* Worcester, Mass.: Clark University Press, 1928, pp. 39–48.

————. The sub-structure of the mind. *Brit. J. Psychol.*, 1928, *18*, 249–261.

————. Pearson's contribution to the theory of two factors. *Brit. J. Psychol.*, 1928–1929, *19*, 95–101.

————. The uniqueness of "G." *J. educ. Psychol.*, 1929, *20*, 212–216.

————. Response to T. Kelley. *J. educ. Psychol.*, 1929, *20*, 561–568.

————. *Creative mind.* New York: Appleton, 1931. (1930)

————. C. Spearman. In C. Murchison (Ed.), *A history of psychology in autobiography.* Vol. 1. Worcester, Mass.: Clark University Press, 1930, pp. 299–333. **B**

————. "G" and after—a school to end schools. In C. Murchison (Ed.), *Psychologies of 1930.* Worcester, Mass.: Clark University Press, 1930, pp. 339–366.

————. Normality. In C. Murchison (Ed.), *Psychologies of 1930.* Worcester, Mass.: Clark University Press, 1930, pp. 444–459.

————. Our need of some science in place of the word "intelligence." *J. educ. Psychol.*, 1931, *22*, 401–410.

————. What the theory of factors is *not. J. educ. Psychol.*, 1931, *22*, 112–117.

————. The theory of "two factors" and that of "sampling." *Brit. J. educ. Psychol.*, 1931, *1*, 140–161.

————. Pitfalls in the use of "probable errors." *J. educ. Psychol.*, 1932, *23*, 481–488.

————. The factor theory and its troubles. II. Garbling the evidence. III. Misrepresentation of the theory. IV. Uniqueness of *G*. V. Adequacy of proof. Conclusion: Scientific value. *J. educ. Psychol.*, 1933, *24*, 521–524, 591–601 ; 1934, *25*, 142–153, 310–319, 383–391.

————. German science of character. I. Approach from experimental psychology. II. Approach from typology. *J. Pers.*, 1936–1937, *5*, 177–201 ; 1937, *6*, 36–50.

————. The confusion that is Gestalt-psychology. *Amer. J. Psychol.*, 1937–1938, *50*, 369–383.

——. *Psychology down the ages.* (2 vols.) London: Macmillan, 1937.

——. Proposed explanation of individual differences of ability by "sampling." *Brit. J. Psychol.,* 1938–1939, *29,* 182–191.

——. The factorial analysis of ability. II. Determination of factors. *Brit. J. Psychol.,* 1939, *30,* 78–83.

——. Theory of general factor. *Brit. J. Psychol.,* 1945–1946, *36,* 117–131.

——, & Wynn-Jones, L. *Human ability: A continuation of "The abilities of man."* London: Macmillan, 1950.

Anastasi, *Individual Differences;* Herrnstein & Boring, *Source Book;* Jenkins & Paterson, *Individual Differences;* Miller, *Mathematics;* Sahakian, *Psychology;* Wiseman, *Intelligence*

KENNETH WARTENBE SPENCE
1907-1967
American Psychologist (25)

Spence, K. W. *Behavior theory and learning: Selected papers.* Englewood Cliffs, N.J.: Prentice-Hall, 1960.   **C**

——. The order of eliminating blinds in maze learning by the rat. *J. comp. Psychol.,* 1932, *14,* 9–27. Reprinted in *Behavior theory and learning, op. cit.,* pp. 225–244.

——. Theoretical interpretations of learning. In F. A. Moss (Ed.), *Comparative psychology.* (2nd ed.) New York: Prentice-Hall, 1946, pp. 280–329. (1934)

——. Visual acuity and its relation to brightness in chimpanzee and man. *J. comp. Psychol.,* 1934, *18,* 333–361.

——, & Shipley, W. C. The factors determining the difficulty of blind alleys in maze learning by the white rat. *J. comp. Psychol.,* 1934, *17,* 423–436.

——, & Fulton, J. F. The effects of occipital lobectomy on vision in the chimpanzee. *Brain,* 1936, *59,* 35–50.

——. The nature of discrimination learning in animals. *Psychol. Rev.,* 1936, *43,* 427–449. Reprinted in *Behavior theory and learning, op. cit.,* pp. 269–291.

——. Analysis of the formation of visual discrimination habits in chimpanzee. *J. comp. Psychol.,* 1937, *23,* 77–100.

——, & Yerkes, R. M. Weight, growth and age in chimpanzees. *Amer. J. phys. Anthrop.,* 1937, *22,* 229–246.

——. Experimental studies of learning and the higher mental processes in infra-human primates. *Psychol. Bull.,* 1937, *34,* 806–850.

——. The differential response in animals to stimuli varying within a single dimension. *Psychol. Rev.,* 1937, *44,* 430–444. Reprinted in *Behavior theory and learning, op. cit.,* pp. 292–307.

Hull, C. L., & ——. "Correction" vs. "non-correction" method of trial-and-error learning in rats. *J. comp. Psychol.,* 1938, *25,* 127–145.

——. Gradual vs. sudden solution of discrimination problems by chimpanzees. *J. comp. Psychol.,* 1938, *25,* 213–224. Reprinted in *Behavior theory and learning, op. cit.,* pp. 326–338.

——. The solution of multiple choice problems by chimpanzees. *Comp. Psychol. Monogr.,* 1939, No. 75, 1–55.

——. Continuous versus non-continuous interpretations of discrimination learning. *Psychol. Rev.,* 1940, *47,* 271–288. Reprinted in *Behavior theory and learning, op. cit.,* pp. 308–325.

Bergmann, G., & ——. Operationism and theory in psychology. *Psychol. Rev.,* 1941, *48,* 1–14. Reprinted in M. H. Marx (Ed.), *Psychological theory: Contemporary readings.* New York: Macmillan, 1959, pp. 54–66, & in *Behavior theory and learning, op. cit.,* pp. 3–16.

——. Failure of transposition in size discrimination of chimpanzee. *Amer. J. Psychol.,* 1941, *54,* 223–229.

——. The basis of solution by chimpanzees of the intermediate size problem. *J. exp. Psychol.,* 1942, *31,* 257–271. Reprinted in *Behavior theory and learning, op. cit.,* pp. 339–358.

Bergmann, G., & ———. The logic of psychophysical measurement. *Psychol. Rev.,* 1944, *51,* 1–24. Reprinted in H. Feigl & May Brodbeck (Eds.), *Readings in the philosophy of science.* New York: Appleton-Century-Crofts, 1953, pp. 103–119.

———. The nature of theory construction in contemporary psychology. *Psychol. Rev.,* 1944, *51,* 47–68. Reprinted in M. H. Marx (Ed.), *Theories in contemporary psychology.* New York: Macmillan, 1963, pp. 162–178; in M. H. Marx (Ed.), *Psychological theory: Contemporary readings.* New York: Macmillan, 1959, pp. 68–86; & in *Behavior theory and learning, op. cit.,* pp. 17–38.

———. An experimental test of the continuity and non-continuity theories of discrimination learning. *J. exp. Psychol.,* 1945, *35,* 253–266.

———, & Lippitt, R. O. An experimental test of the sign-Gestalt theory of trial-and-error learning. *J. exp. Psychol.,* 1946, *36,* 491–502.

Buxton, C. E., & ———. *An appraisal of certain tests of pilot aptitude.* CAA Div. Res. Rep. No. 64, 1946; Publ. Bd. No. 50335. Washington, D.C.: U.S. Department of Commerce, 1947.

———. The role of secondary reinforcement in delayed reward learning. *Psychol. Rev.,* 1947, *54,* 1–8.

———. The postulates and methods of "behaviorism." *Psychol. Rev.,* 1948, *55,* 67–78. Reprinted in H. Feigl & May Brodbeck (Eds.), *Readings in the philosophy of science.* New York: Appleton-Century-Crofts, 1953, pp. 571–584; in M. H. Marx (Ed.), *Theories in contemporary psychology.* New York: Macmillan, 1963, pp. 272–286; in M. H. Marx (Ed.), *Psychological theory: Contemporary readings.* New York: Macmillan, 1959, pp. 171–186; & in *Behavior theory and learning, op. cit.,* pp. 39–56.

———, Bergmann, G., & Lippitt, R. O. A study of simple learning under irrelevant motivational-reward conditions. *J. exp. Psychol.,* 1950, *40,* 539–552. Reprinted in *Behavior theory and learning, op. cit.,* pp. 202–224.

———. Cognitive versus stimulus-response theories of learning. *Psychol. Rev.,* 1950, *57,* 159–172. Reprinted in *Behavior theory and learning, op. cit.,* pp. 245–265.

———, & Taylor, Janet A. Anxiety and strength of the UCS as determiners of the amount of eyelid conditioning. *J. exp. Psychol.,* 1951, *42,* 183–188.

———. Theoretical interpretations of learning. In S. S. Stevens (Ed.), *Handbook of experimental psychology.* New York: Wiley, 1951, pp. 690–729.

Taylor, Janet A., & ———. The relationship of anxiety level to performance in serial learning. *J. exp. Psychol.,* 1952, *44,* 61–64.

———. The nature of response in discrimination learning. *Psychol. Rev.,* 1952, *59,* 89–93. Reprinted in *Behavior theory and learning, op. cit.,* pp. 359–365.

———. Mathematical formulations of learning phenomena. *Psychol. Rev.,* 1952, *59,* 152–160. Reprinted in *Behavior theory and learning, op. cit.,* pp. 57–70.

———. Clark Leonard Hull: 1884–1952. *Amer. J. Psychol.,* 1952, *65,* 639–646.

———. Learning and performance in eyelid conditioning as a function of intensity of the UCS. *J. exp. Psychol.,* 1953, *45,* 57–63. Reprinted in *Behavior theory and learning, op. cit.,* pp. 148–160.

———, & Farber, I. E. Conditioning and extinction as a function of anxiety. *J. exp. Psychol.,* 1953, *45,* 116–119.

———, & Taylor, Janet A. The relation of conditioned response strength to anxiety in normal, neurotic, and psychotic subjects. *J. exp. Educ.,* 1953, *45,* 265–272.

———. Mathematical theories of learning. *J. gen. Psychol.,* 1953, *49,* 283–291.

———. Current interpretations of learning data and some recent developments in stimulus-response theory. In D. K. Adams *et al., Learning theory, personality theory, and clinical research: The Kentucky symposium.* New York: Wiley, 1954, pp. 1–21.

————, & Farber, I. E. The relation of anxiety to differential eyelid conditioning. *J. exp. Psychol.*, 1954, *47*, 127–134.

————. The relation of response latency and speed to the intervening variables and N in S–R theory. *Psychol. Rev.*, 1954, *61*, 209–216. Reprinted in *Behavior theory and learning, op. cit.*, pp. 113–124.

Taylor, Janet A., & ————. Conditioning level in the behavior disorders. *J. abnorm. soc. Psychol.*, 1954, *49*, 497–502.

————. *Behavior theory and conditioning.* New Haven: Yale University Press, 1956.

————, Farber, I. E., & McFann, H. H. The relation of anxiety (drive) level to performance in competitional and non-competitional paired-associates learning. *J. exp. Psychol.*, 1956, *52*, 296–305. Reprinted in *Behavior theory and learning, op. cit.*, pp. 185–201.

————, Taylor, J., & Ketchel, Rhoda. Anxiety (drive) level and degree of competition in paired-associates learning. *J. exp. Psychol.*, 1956, *52*, 306–310.

Farber, I. E., & ————. Effects of anxiety, stress and task variables on reaction time. *J. Pers.*, 1956, *25*, 1–18.

————. The empirical basis and theoretical structure of psychology. *Phil. Sci.*, 1957, *24*, 97–108. Reprinted in *Behavior theory and learning, op. cit.*, pp. 71–87.

————. A theory of emotionally based drive (D) and its relation to performance in simple learning situations. *Amer. Psychologist*, 1958, *13*, 131–141. Reprinted in *Behavior theory and learning, op. cit.*, pp. 125–147.

————. Haggard, D. F., & Ross, L. E. UCS intensity and the associative (habit) strength of the eyelid CR. *J. exp. Psychol.*, 1958, *55*, 404–411. Reprinted in *Behavior theory and learning, op. cit.*, pp. 161–174.

————. Behavior theory and selective learning. *Nebraska symposium on motivation, 1958.* Ed. by M. R. Jones. Lincoln, Nebr.: University of Nebraska Press, 1958, pp. 73–107.

————. The relation of learning theory to the technology of education. *Harvard educ. Rev.*, 1959, *29*, 84–95.

————. Performance in eyelid conditioning related to changes in muscular tension and physiological measures of emotionality. *J. exp. Psychol.*, 1959, *58*, 417–422. Reprinted in *Behavior theory and learning, op. cit.*, pp. 175–184.

————. Conceptual models of spatial and nonspatial selective learning. (1960) In *Behavior theory and learning, op. cit.*, pp. 366–392.

————. The roles of reinforcement and nonreinforcement in simple learning. (1960) In *Behavior theory and learning, op. cit.*, pp. 91–112.

————, & Trapold, M. A. Performance in eyelid conditioning as a function of reinforcement schedules and changes in them. *Proc. Nat. Acad. Sciences*, 1961, *47*, 1860–1868.

————, Rutledge, E. F., & Talbott, H. Effect of the number of acquisition trials and the presence or absence of the UCS on extinction of the human eyelid CR. *J. exp. Psychol.*, 1963, *66*, 286–291.

————, Homzie, M. J., & Rutledge, E. F. Extinction of the human eyelid CR as a function of the discriminability of the change from acquisition to extinction. *J. exp. Psychol.*, 1964, *67*, 545–552.

————, & Spence, Janet T. The relation of eyelid conditioning to manifest anxiety, extraversion, and rigidity. *J. abnorm. soc. Psychol.*, 1964, *68*, 144–149.

————. Anxiety (drive) level and performance in eyelid conditioning. *Psychol. Bull.*, 1964, *61*, 129–139.

————. Extinction of the human eyelid CR as a function of presence or absence of the UCS during extinction. *J. exp. Psychol.*, 1966, *71*, 642–648.

————, & Platt, J. R. UCS intensity and performance in eyelid conditioning. *Psychol. Bull.*, 1966, *65*, 1–10.

————, & Spence, Janet T. Sex and anxiety difference in eyelid conditioning. *Psychol. Bull.*, 1966, *65,* 137–142.

————. Cognitive and drive factors in the extinction of the conditioned eye blink in human subjects. *Psychol. Rev.*, 1966, *73,* 445–458.

————, & Platt, J. R. Effects of partial reinforcement on acquisition and extinction of the conditioned eyeblink in a masking situation. *J. exp. Psychol.*, 1967, *74,* 259–263.

Madden, *Scientific Thought ;* Zajonc, *Animal Social*

HERBERT SPENCER
1820-1903
English Philosopher (27)

Spencer, H. *Essays on education.* New York: Dutton, 1910. (1861) **C**

————. *Various fragments.* (Enlarged ed.) New York: Appleton, 1914. (1897) **C**

————. *Facts and comments.* New York: Appleton, 1902. **C**

————. *Education: Intellectual, moral, and physical.* Paterson, N.J.: Littlefield, 1963. **C**

————. *Herbert Spencer on education.* Ed. by A. M. Kazamias. New York: Teachers College Press, Teachers College, Columbia University, 1966. **C**

————. *The works of Herbert Spencer.* Ed. by O. Zeller, (21 vols.) Osnabrück: Zeller, 1966– 1967. **C**

————. Spencer, H. *Herbert Spencer: Structure, function and evolution.* Ed. & intro. essay S. Andreski. London: Joseph Press, 1971. **C**

————. *Principles of psychology.* (4th ed.) New York: Appleton, 1897. (1855)

————. *Social statics: The conditions essential to human happiness specified, and the first of them developed.* New York: Humanities Press, 1954. (1855)

———— *Social statics.* (Abridged & revised) New York: Appleton, 1892. (1855)

————. Progress: Its law and cause. (1857) Reprinted in *Essays,* Vol. 1, *op. cit.,* pp. 8–62.

————. Bain on the emotions and the will. (1860) Reprinted in *Essays,* Vol. 1, *op. cit.,* pp. 241– 264.

————. *First principles.* (6th ed.) New York: Appleton, 1900. (1862) (Reprinted 1958)

————. *Reason for dissenting from the philosophy of M. Comte.* (3rd ed.) London: Williams & Norgate, 1884. (1864)

————. *The principles of biology.* (Rev. ed.) (2 vols.) New York: Appleton, 1898, 1899. (1866, 1867)

————. Mill versus Hamilton. The test of truth. *Fortn. Rev.,* 1865, *5,* 531–550. Reprinted in *Essays,* Vol. 2, *op. cit.,* pp. 188–200.

————. (Classifier) *Descriptive sociology.* (18 vols.) Compiled by D. Duncan, R. Scheppig, & J. Collier. New York: Appleton, 1873–1881.

————. *The study of sociology.* Ann Arbor, Mich.: University of Michigan Press, 1961. (1873)

————. Replies to criticisms (of "Principles of psychology"). *Pop. Sci. Mon.,* 1873, *4,* 295–309.

————. Replies to the quarterly reviewers (of "Principles of psychology"). *Pop. Sci. Mon.,* 1873, *4,* 541–552.

————. Emotions in the primitive man. *Pop. Sci. Mon.,* 1875, *6,* 331–339.

————. The comparative psychology of man. *Mind,* 1876, *1,* 7–20. Reprinted in *Essays,* Vol. 1, *op. cit.,* pp. 351–370.

————. *The principles of sociology.* (3rd ed.) (3 vols. in 5) New York: Appleton, 1896. (1876)

————. *The evolution of society: Selections from Herbert Spencer's Principles of sociology.* Ed. by R. L. Carneiro. Chicago, Ill.: University of Chicago Press, 1967. (1876)

————. *The principles of ethics.* (2 vols.) New York: Appleton, 1914. (1879 & 1893)

————. Les institutions politiques. I. Préliminaires. *Rev. phil.,* 1880, *10,* 447–461.

──────. De l'organisation politique en général. *Rev. phil.*, 1880, *10*, 626–643.

──────. *The factors of organic evolution.* New York: Appleton, 1887. (1886) Reprinted in *Essays*, Vol. 1, *op. cit.*, pp. 389–466.

──────. *An epitome of the synthetic philosophy.* (5th ed.) Ed. by F. A. Collins. New York: Appleton, 1895. (1889)

──────. *The inheritance of acquired characters. Nature*, 1890, *41*, 414–415.

──────. *An autobiography.* (2 vols.) New York: Appleton, 1904. (1894)   **B**

   Borgatta, *Present-day Sociology;* Coser, *Sociological Thought;* Coser & Rosenberg, *Sociological Theory;* Dember, *Perception;* Drever, *Sourcebook;* Grinder, *Genetic Psychology;* Herrnstein & Boring, *Source Book;* Park & Burgess, *Sociology;* Parsons, *Society;* Rand, *Classical Philosophers;* Rand, *Moralists;* Thomas, *Source Book*

BENEDICT (or BARUCH) SPINOZA
1632-1677
Dutch Philosopher (24)

Spinoza, B. *Benedicti de Spinoza Opera quotquot reperta sunt.* (3rd ed.) (4 vols.) Ed. by J. Van Vloten & J. P. N. Land. The Hague: Nijhoff, 1913–1914. (1882–1883)   **C**

──────. *The chief works of Benedict de Spinoza.* (2 vols.) Trans. by R. H. M. Elwes. New York: Dover, 1951. (1883)   **C**

──────. *The correspondence of Spinoza.* Ed. by A. Wolf. New York: Russell & Russell, 1966. (1928)   **C**

──────. *The political works: The tractatus theologico-politicus* in part and *The tractatus politicus* in full. Ed. by A. G. Wernham. Oxford: Clarendon Press, 1958.   **C**

──────. *Short treatise on God, man and his wellbeing.* Trans. by A. Wolf. London: Black, 1910. (ca. 1662) (Reprinted 1963)

──────. Principles of the philosophy of René Descartes. In *Earlier philosophical writings.*

Trans. by F. A. Hayes. Indianapolis, Ind.: Bobbs-Merrill, 1963, pp. 13–103. (1663)

──────. *The principles of Descartes' philosophy.* Trans. by H. H. Britain. Chicago: Open Court, 1905. (1663)

──────. *Ethics preceded by On the improvement of the understanding.* Ed. by J. Gutmann. New York: Hafner, 1949. (1677)

──────. *On the improvement of the understanding.* Trans. by J. Katz. Indianapolis, Ind.: Bobbs-Merrill, 1958. (1677)

──────. *Ethics* and *On the correction of the understanding.* Trans. by A. Boyle. New York: Dutton, 1967. (1677)

──────. *Algebraic calculation of the rainbow 1687.* Facsimile of original Dutch text with intro. by G. ten Doesschate. Nieuwkoop: de Graaf, 1963. (1687)

   Hutchins, *Great Books;* Rand, *Classical Philosophers;* Rand, *Classical Psychologists;* Rand, *Moralists;* Reeves, *Body Mind;* Sahakian, *Psychology;* Slotkin, *Anthropology*

EDUARD SPRANGER
1882-1963
German Psychologist (25)

Spranger, E. *Kultur und Erziehung. Gesammelte pädagogische Aufsätze.* (4th ed.) Leipzig: Quelle & Meyer, 1928. (1919)   **C**

──────. *Gedanken zur Daseingestaltung aus Vorträgen.* Ed. by H. W. Bähr. Munich: Piper, 1965.   **C Bl**

──────. *Gesammelte Schriften.* (Ult. 11 vols.) Ed. by H. W. Bähr *et al.* Tübingen: Niemeyer, 1968–.   **C**

──────. *Die Grundlagen der Geschichtswissenschaft. Eine erkenntnistheoretisch-psychologische Untersuchung.* Berlin: Reuther & Reichard, 1905.

──────. Wilhelm von Humboldt und Kant. *Kant-Stud.*, 1908, *13*, 57–129.

──────. *Wilhelm von Humboldt und die Humani-*

tätsidee. (2nd ed.) Berlin: Reuther & Reichard, 1928. (1909)

———. *Wilhelm von Humboldt und die Reform des Bildungswesens.* (2nd ed.) Berlin: Reuther & Reichard, 1960. (1910)

———. *Wilhelm Dilthey.* Leipzig: Wiegandt, 1912.

———. *Types of men: The psychology and ethics of personality.* (5th ed.) Trans. by P. J. W. Pigors. Halle: Niemeyer, 1928. (1913) (Reprinted 1966)

———. *Lebensformen.* (8th ed.) Tübingen; Niemeyer, 1950. (1913)

———. *Begabung und Studium.* Leipzig: Teubner, 1938. (1917)

———. Goethe und die Metamorphose des Menschen. *Jb. Goethe-Ges.,* 1924, *10,* 219–238.

———. *Psychologie des Jugendalters.* (28th ed.) Heidelberg: Quelle & Meyer, 1966. (1924)

———. Was hat Pestalozzi unserer Zeit zu sagen? *Kindergarten,* 1925, *66,* 253–258.

———. Zur Psychologie des Pubertätsalters. *Arch. Kinderheilk.,* 1925, *76,* 241–253.

———. *Die Frage nach der Einhalt der Psychologie.* Berlin: de Gruyter, 1926.

———. Verstehen und Erklären. Thesen. In *VIIIth international congress of psychology held at Groningen.* Groningen: Noordhoff, 1927, pp. 147–158.

———, & Niffka, E. *Der jugendliche Mensch.* Eberswalde: Müller, 1932.

———. *Volk, Staat, Erziehung. Gesammelte Reden und Aufsätze.* Leipzig: Quelle & Meyer, 1932.

———. *Goethes Weltanschauung. Reden und Aufsätze.* (2nd ed.) Leipzig: Insel, 1949. (1933)

———. Grundgedanken der geisteswissenschaftlichen Psychologie. *Erziehung,* 1933, *9,* 209–223, 257–269.

———. *Aus Friedrich Fröbels Gedankenwelt.* (4th ed.) Heidelberg: Quelle & Meyer, 1964. (1938)

———. Goethe über die letzten Fragen des Lebens. Eine Ansprache. *Goethe-Kalender,* 1941, *34,* 1–35.

———. *Schillers Geistesart, gespiegelt in seinen philosophischen Schriften und Gedichten.* Berlin: Preussische Akademie der Wissenschaften, 1941.

———. Goethe über die Phantasie. *Viermonatsschr. Goeth-Ges.,* Weimar, 1944, *9,* 5–23.

———. *Lebenserfahrung.* Tübingen: Wunderlich, 1945.

———. Kulturpathologie? In *Reden bei der feierlichen Eröffnung des Sommersemesters am 23. April 1947.* Tübingen: Mohr, 1947, pp. 18–40.

———. *Die Magie der Seele.* (2nd ed.) Tübingen: Mohr, 1949. (1947)

———. *Pestalozzis Denkformen.* (2nd ed.) Heidelberg: Quelle & Meyer, 1959. (1947)

———. *Goethe über sich selbst.* Tübingen: Neomarius, 1949.

———. J. G. Herder: Ahnung und Erfüllung. Gedächtnisrede. In F. Martine (Ed.), *Vom Geist der Dichtung. Gedächtnisschrift für Rudolf Petsch.* Hamburg: Hoffmann & Campe, 1949, pp. 31–48.

———. *Pädagogische Perspektiven, Beiträge zu Erziehungsfragen der Gegenwart.* (6th ed.) Heidelberg: Quelle & Meyer, 1969. (1951)

———. *Gedenkrede zu Friedrich Fröbels 100. Todestag.* Heidelberg: Quelle & Meyer, 1953.

———. Zur Psychologie der Bildsamkeit des Erwachsenen. Eine Skizze. In F. Arnold (Ed.), *Bildungsfragen der Gegenwart.* Stuttgart: Klotz, 1953, pp. 71–88.

———. *Kulturfragen der Gegenwart.* (4th ed.) Heidelberg: Quelle & Meyer, 1964. (1953)

———. *Mein Konflikt mit der Hitlerregierung.* Tübingen: Laupp, 1955. **B**

———. *Der geborene Erzieher.* (5th ed.) Heidelberg: Quelle & Meyer, 1968. (1958)

———. *Das Gesetz der ungewollten Nebenwirkungen in der Erziehung.* (2nd ed.) Heidelberg: Quelle & Meyer, 1965. (1962)

Strain, *Philosophisches Education*

JOHANN GASPAR SPURZHEIM
1776-1832
Austrian-French Physiologist (21)

Gall, F. J., & Spurzheim, J. G. *Recherches sur le système nerveux en géneral, et sur celui du cerveau en particulier, mémoire présenté à l'Institut de France, le 14 mars 1808, suivi d'observations sur le rapport qui en a été fait à cette compagnie par ses commissaires.* Paris: Schoell & Nicolle, 1809. (Reprinted 1967)

Gall, F. J., & ———. *Anatomie et physiologie du système nerveux en général, et du cerveau en particulier, avec des observations sur la possibilité de reconnâitre plusieurs dispositions intellectuelles et morales de l'homme et des animaux, par la configuration de leurs têtes.* (4 vols.) Paris: Schoell, 1810–1819.

———. *The physiognomical system of doctors Gall and Spurzheim; founded on anatomical and physiological examination of the nervous system in general, and of the brain in particular, and indicating the dispositions and manifestations of the mind.* (2nd ed.) London: Baldwin, Cradock & Joy, 1815. (1815)

———. *Outlines of phrenology: Being also a manual of reference for the marked bust.* (4th ed.) Boston: Marsh, Capen & Lyon, 1836. (1815)

———. *Phrenology, or the doctrine of the mental phenomena.* (2 vols.) (1st Amer. ed. from 3rd London ed.) Boston: Marsh, Capen & Lyon, 1832, 1833. (1815)

———. *Phrenology, or the doctrine of the mental phenomena.* (Rev. ed. from 2nd Amer. ed.) Intro. by C. Elder. Philadelphia: Lippincott, 1908. (1815)

———. *Outlines of the physiognomical system of doctors Gall and Spurzheim.* London: Baldwin, Cradock & Joy, 1815.

———. *Observations on the deranged manifestations of the mind or insanity.* Intro. by A. A. Walsh. (1st Amer. ed. of 1833) Gainsville, Fla.: Scholars' Facsimiles & Reprints, 1970. (1817)

———. *Examination of the objections made in Britain against the doctrines of Gall and Spurzheim,* and bound with *Phrenology article of the*

Foreign Quarterly Review, by R. Chenevix, with notes by J. G. Spurzheim. Boston: Marsh, Capen & Lyon, 1833. (1817, 1830)

———. *Essai philosophique sur la nature morale et intellectuelle de l'homme.* Paris: Treuttel & Würtz, 1820.

———. *A view of the elementary principles of education, founded on the study of the nature of man.* (5th Amer. ed.) Boston: Marsh, Capen & Lyon, 1836. (1822)

———. *A view of the philosophical principles of phrenology.* (3rd ed.) London: Treuttel, Würtz & Richter, n.d. (ca. 1845). (1825)

———. *Philosophical catechism of the natural laws of man.* (3rd ed.) Boston: Marsh, Capen & Lyon, 1833. (1825)

———. *The anatomy of the brain, with a general view of the nervous system.* Trans. by R. Willis. London: Highley, 1926.

———. *Phrenology, in connexion with the study of physiognomy. Part I. Characters.* London: Treuttel, Würtz & Richter, 1826.

———. *Phrenology in connexion with the study of physiognomy.* (4th ed.) Boston: Marsh, Capen & Lyon, 1836. (1826) **B**

———. *Appendix to "The anatomy of the brain" containing a paper read before The Royal Society on the 14th of May, 1829, and some remarks on Mr. Charles Bell's animadversions on phrenology.* London: Treuttel, Würtz & Richter, 1830.

Clarke & O'Malley, *Brain;* Goshen, *Documentary;* Hunter & Macalpine, *Psychiatry*

EDWIN DILLER STARBUCK
1866-1947
American Psychologist (12)

Starbuck, E. D. A study of conversion. *Amer. J. Psychol.,* 1896, *8,* 268–308.

———. Some aspects of religious growth. *Amer. J. Psychol.,* 1897, *9,* 70–124.

―――. Contributions to the psychology of religion. *Amer. J. Psychol.*, 1898, *9*, 70–124.

―――. *The psychology of religion: An empirical study of the growth of religious consciousness.* New York: Scribner's, 1901. (1899)

―――. The feelings and their place in religion. *Amer. J. Rel. Psychol. Educ.*, 1904, *1*, 168–186.

―――. *Child mind and child religion.* Chicago: University of Chicago Press, 1908.

―――. The intimate senses as sources of wisdom. *J. Rel.*, 1921, *1*, 129–145.

―――. Fundamentals of character training. *Proc. Addr. Nat. Educ. Ass.*, 1924, *62*, 159–165.

―――. Life and confessions of G. Stanley Hall; some notes on the psychology of genius. *J. Phil.*, 1924, *21*, 141–153.

―――. G. Stanley Hall as a psychologist. *Psychol. Rev.*, 1925, *32*, 103–120.

―――. The challenging epochs in the life of a child. *Proc. Addr. Nat. Educ. Ass.*, 1926, *64*, 147–152.

―――. An empirical study of mysticism. *Proc. Sixth Int. Cong. Phil.*, 1927, 87–94.

―――. (Prize Essay) In Various, *Moral training in the public schools.* Boston: Ginn, 1927, pp. 89–121.

―――, & Shuttleworth, F. K. *A guide to literature for character training.* Vol. I. *Fairy tale, myth, and legend.* Vol. II. *Fiction.* Vol. III. *Biography.* New York: Macmillan, 1928, 1930, 1931.

―――. Religious psychology and research methods. *Rel. Educ.*, 1929, *24*, 874–876.

―――. *Look to this day!* Los Angeles: Southern California Press, 1945.   **B Bl**

HEYMANN STEINTHAL
(more properly HAJIM STEINTHAL)
1823-1899
German Philosopher (12)

Steinthal, H. *Gesammelte kleine Schriften.* Berlin: Harrwitz & Gossmann, 1880.   **C**

―――. *Die Sprachwissenschaft Wilh. von Humboldts und die Hegelsche Philosophie.* Berlin: Dümmler, 1848.

―――. *Die Klassifikation der Sprachen dargestellt als die Entwickelung der Sprachidee.* Berlin: Dümmler, 1850.

―――. *Charakteristik der hauptsächlichsten Typen des Sprachbaues.* (Rev. of *Die Klassifikation der Sprachen.*) (3rd ed.) Rev. by F. Mistelli. Berlin: Dümmler, 1893. (1850)

―――. *Der Ursprung der Sprache: Im Zusammenhange mit den letzten Fragen alles Wissens.* (4th ed.) Berlin: Dümmler, 1888. (1851)

―――. *Die Entwickelung der Schrift.* Berlin: Dümmler, 1852.

―――. *Grammatik, Logik und Psychologie. Ihre Principien und ihr Verhältniss zueinander.* Hildesheim: Olms, 1968. (1855)

―――. *Geschichte der Sprachwissenschaft bei den Griechen und Römern mit besonderer Rücksicht auf die Logik.* (2nd ed.) Berlin: Dümmler, 1863. (1855) (Reprinted 1971)

―――. *Philologie, Geschichte und Psychologie in ihren gegenseitigen Beziehungen.* Berlin: Dümmler, 1864. (1855)

Lazarus, M., & ―――. Einleitende Gedanken zur Völkerpsychologie als Einladung zu einer Zeitschrift für Völkerpsychologie und Sprachwissenschaft. *Z. Völkerpsychol.*, 1860, *1*, 1–73.

―――. Zur Charakteristik der semitischen Völker. *Z. Völkerpsychol.*, 1860, *1*, 328–345.

―――. *Die Mande-Negersprachen, psychologisch und phonetisch betrachtet.* Berlin: Dümmler, 1867.

―――. Zum Ursprung der Sprache. *Z. Völkerpsychol.*, 1868, *5*, 73–82.

―――. *Abriss der Sprachwissenschaft.* (2 vols.) Berlin: Harrwitz & Gossmann, 1871–1881.

―――. *Einleitung in die Psychologie und Sprachwissenschaft.* (2nd ed.) Berlin: Harrwitz & Gossmann, 1881. (1871)

―――. Wie einer den Nagel auf den Kopf trifft. *Z. Völkerpsychol.*, 1874, *8*, 216–249.

——. *Allgemeine Ethik.* Berlin: Reimer, 1885.

——. Der Begriff der Völkerpsychologie. *Z. Völkerpsychol.*, 1887, *17*, 233–264.

——. An den Leser. *Z. Volkskunde*, 1891, *1*, 10–17.

WILHELM STEKEL
1868-1940
Austrian Psychoanalyst (16)

Stekel, W. *Twelve essays on sex and psychoanalysis.* Trans. by S. A. Tannenbaum. New York: Cosmopolis Press, 1922. **C**

——. *Fortschritte der Sexualwissenschaft und Psychanalyse.* (3 vols.) Vienna: Deuticke, 1924–1928. **C**

——. *Conditions of nervous anxiety and their treatment.* (3rd ed.) Trans. by Rosalie Gabler. New York: Dodd, Mead, 1923. (1908)

——. *Poetry and neurosis.* (1909) Trans. by J. S. v. Teslaar. *Psychoanal. Rev.*, 1923, *10*, 73–96, 190–208, 316–328, 457–466; *11*, 48–60.

——. *Die Sprache des Traumes. Eine Darstellung der Symbolik und Deutung des Traumes in ihren Beziehungen zur kranken und gesunden Seele für Aerzte und Psychologen.* (3rd ed.) Wiesbaden: Bergmann, 1927. (1911)

——. *Sex and dreams, the language of dreams.* Trans. by J. S. v. Teslaar. Boston: Badger, 1922. (1911)

——. *Die Träume der Dichter. Eine vergleichende Untersuchung der unbewussten Triebkräfte bei Dichtern, Neurotikern und Verbrechern.* Wiesbaden: Bergmann, 1912.

——. *The beloved ego: Foundations of the new study of the psyche.* Trans. by Rosalie Gabler. New York: Moffat, Yard, 1921. (1913)

——. *Auto-erotism: A psychiatric study of onanism and neurosis.* Trans. by J. S. v. Teslaar. New York: Liveright, 1950. (1917)

——. *Bi-sexual love: The homosexual neuroses.* Trans. by J. S. v. Teslaar. Boston: Badger, 1922. (1917)

——. *Obsessions: Their cause and treatment.* (1910) Trans. by S. A. Tannenbaum. *Amer. J. Urol. Sex,* 1918, *14*, 147–165.

——. *Sleep, the will to sleep and insomnia.* (1915) Trans. by S. A. Tannenbaum. *Amer. J. Urol. Sex,* 1918, *14*, 385–416.

——. *Frigidity in woman in relation to her love life.* (2 vols.) Trans. by J. S. v. Teslaar. New York: Boni & Liveright, 1926. (1920)

——. *The depths of the soul.* Trans. by S. A. Tannenbaum. New York: Moffat, Yard, 1922. (1921)

——. *Psychoanalysis and suggestion therapy.* Trans. by J. S. v. Teslaar. New York: Moffat, Yard, 1923.

——. *Sexual aberrations; the phenomena of fetishism in relation to sex.* (2 vols.) Trans. by S. Parker. New York: Liveright, 1952. (1923)

——. *Peculiarities of behavior.* (2 vols.) Trans. by J. S. v. Teslaar. New York: Liveright, 1924.

——. *Sadism and masochism: The psychology of hatred and cruelty.* Trans. by Louise Brink. (2 vols.) New York: Liveright, 1929. (1925)

——. *Zwang und Zweifel.* (2 vols.) Vienna: Urban & Schwarzenberg, 1927–1929.

——. *A primer for mothers.* Trans. by F. Ilmer. New York: Macaulay, 1931.

——. *Marriage at the crossroads.* Trans. by A. D. Garman. New York: Godwin, 1931. (1931)

——, & Frohman, B. S. Analysis of a key dream. *Psychoanal. Rev.*, 1931, *18*, 379–393.

——. *Erziehung der Eltern.* Vienna: Weidmann, 1934.

——. *Fortschritte und Technik der Traumdeutung.* Vienna: Weidmann, 1935.

——. *Technique of analytical psychotherapy.* London: Lane, 1939. (1938)

——. *The autobiography of Wilhelm Stekel: The life story of a pioneer psychoanalyst.* Ed. by E. A. Guthiel. New York: Liveright, 1950. **B**

Rapaport, *Thought*

(LOUIS) WILLIAM STERN
1871-1938
German Psychologist (26)

Stern, W. *Person und Sache.* (3 vols.) Leipzig: Barth, 1923-1924. **C**

——. Die Wahrnehmung von Bewegungen vermittelst des Auges. *Z. Psychol.,* 1894, *7,* 321–386.

——. Die Wahrnehmung von Tonveränderungen. *Z. Psychol.,* 1896, *11,* 1–30; 1899, *21,* 360–387; 1899, *22,* 1–12.

——. Psychische Präsenzzeit. *Z. Psychol.,* 1897, *13,* 325–349.

——. *Psychologie der Veränderungsauffassung.* (2nd ed.) Breslau: Preuss & Junger, 1906. (1898)

——. *Ueber Psychologie der individuellen Differenzen. (Ideen zu einer differentiellen Psychologie.)* Leipzig: Barth, 1900.

——. Die psychologische Arbeit des neunzehnten Jahrhunderts insbesondere in Deutschland. *Z. pädag. Psychol.,* 1900, *2,* 239–352, 413–436.

——. Der Tonvariator. *Z. Psychol.,* 1902, *30,* 422–432.

——. Angewandte Psychologie. *Beit. Psychol. Aussage,* 1903, *1,* 4–45.

——. Aussagestudium. *Beit. Psychol. Aussage,* 1903, *1,* 46–78.

——. Die Aussage als geistige Leistung und als Verhörsprodukt. *Beit. Psychol. Aussage,* 1903, *1,* 269–418. (Also Leipzig: Barth, 1904)

——, & Stern, Clara. *Erinnerung, Aussage und Lüge in der ersten Kindheit.* (3rd ed.) Leipzig: Barth, 1922. (1905)

——. Wirklichkeitsversuche. *Beit. Psychol. Aussage,* 1905, *2,* 1–31.

——. Ueber Schätzungen, insbesondere. Zeit- und Raumschätzungen. *Beit. Psychol. Aussage,* 1905, *2,* 32–72.

——, & Stern, Clara. *Die Kindersprache: Eine psychologische und sprachtheoretische Untersuchung.* (4th ed.) Leipzig: Barth, 1927. (1907)

——. Sammlungen freier Kinderzeichnungen. *Z. angew. Psychol.,* 1908, *1,* 179–187.

——. & Stern, Clara. *Monographien über die seelische Entwicklung des Kindes.* (4th ed.) (2 vols.) Leipzig: Barth, 1928–1931. (1909)

——. Die Entwickelung der Raumwahrnehmung in der ersten Kindheit. *Z. angew. Psychol.,* 1909, *2,* 412–423.

——. Abstracts of lectures on the psychology of testimony and on the study of individuality. *Amer. J. Psychol.,* 1910, *21,* 270–282.

——. Helen Keller. Persönliche Eindrücke. *Z. angew. Psychol.,* 1910, *3,* 321–333.

——. *Die differentielle Psychologie in ihren methodischen Grundlagen.* (2nd ed.) Leipzig: Barth, 1921. (1911)

——. *Psychology of early childhood up to the sixth year of age.* (6th ed., German) Trans. by Anna Barwell. New York: Holt, 1930. (1914)

——. *Psychologie der frühen Kindheit.* (8th ed.) Leipzig: Quelle & Meyer, 1952. (1914)

——. *The psychological methods of testing intelligence.* Trans. by G. M. Whipple. Baltimore, Md.: Warwick & York, 1914.

——. *Jugendliches Seelenleben und Krieg.* Leipzig: Barth, 1915.

——. Die Psychologie und der Personalismus. *Z. Psychol.,* 1917, *78,* 1–54. (Also Leipzig: Barth, 1917)

——. *Die Intelligenz der Kinder und Jugendlichen und die Methoden ihrer Untersuchung.* (4th ed.) Leipzig: Barth, 1928. (1920)

——. *Die Psychologie und die Schülerauslese.* Leipzig: Barth, 1920.

——. Die menschliche Persönlichkeit und ihr psychisches Leben. *Z. pädag. Psychol.,* 1920, *21,* 1–23.

——. Vom Ichbewusstsein des Jugendlichen. *Z. pädag. Psychol.,* 1922, *23,* 8–16.

——. Das Ernstspiel der Jugendzeit. *Z. pädag. Psychol.,* 1924, *25,* 241–252.

——. William Stern. In R. Schmidt (Ed.), *Die Philosophie der Gegenwart in Selbstdarstellungen.* Vol. 6. Leipzig: Meiner, 1925, pp. 129–184. Trans. in C. Murchison (Ed.), *A history of psychology in autobiography*. Vol. 1. Worcester, Mass.: Clark University Press, 1930, pp. 335–388.

———. Theory of constancy of intelligence. Trans. by H. Klüver. *Psychol. Clin.*, 1925, *16*, 110–118.

———. *Anfänge der Reifezeit. Ein Knabentagebuch in psychologischer Bearbeitung*. (2nd ed.) Leipzig: Quelle & Meyer, 1929. (1925)

———. *Neue Beiträge zur Theorie und Praxis der Intelligenzprüfung*. Leipzig: Barth, 1925.

———. *Probleme der Schülerauslese*. Leipzig: Quelle & Meyer, 1926.

———. *Sittlichkeitsvergehen an höheren Schulen*. Leipzig: Quelle & Meyer, 1928.

———. "Ernstspiel" and the affective life: A contribution to the psychology of personality. In M. L. Reymert (Ed.), *Feelings and emotions: The Wittenberg symposium*. Worcester, Mass.: Clark University Press, 1928, pp. 324–331.

———. La psychologie de la personnalité et la méthode de tests. *J. Psychol. norm. path.*, 1928, *25*, 5–18.

———. *Studien zur Personwissenschaft*. Part I. *Personalistik als Wissenschaft*. (2nd ed.) Leipzig: Barth, 1932. (1930)

———. Personalistik der Erinnerung. *Z. Psychol.*, 1930, *118*, 350–381.

———. On the nature and structure of character. *J. Pers.*, 1934–1935, *3*, 270–289.

———. *General psychology from the personalistic standpoint*. Trans. by H. D. Spoerl. New York: Macmillan, 1938. (1935)

———. *Allgemeine Psychologie auf personalistischen Grundlagen*, (2nd ed.) The Hague: Nijhoff, 1950. (1935)

———. Raum und Zeit als personale Dimensionen. *Acta Psychol.*, 1936, *1*, 220–232.

———. Cloud pictures: A new method for testing imagination. *J. Pers.*, 1937, *6*, 132–146.

———. Ein Test zur Prüfung der kindlichen Phantasietätigkeit. *Z. Kinderpsychiat.*, 1938, *5*, 5–11.

———. The psychology of testimony. *J. abnorm. soc. Psychol.*, 1939, *34*, 3–20.

Herrnstein & Boring, *Source Book;* Matson, *Being;* Sahakian, *Psychology;* Shipley, *Classics*

DUGALD STEWART
1753-1828
Scottish Philosopher (23)

Stewart, D. *Philosophical essays*. (3rd ed.) Ed. by W. Hamilton. Edinburgh: Constable, 1818. (1810) Reprinted in *Works*, Vol. 5, *vide infra*.
C

———. *Collected works*. (11 vols.) Ed. by W Hamilton. Westmead: Gregg, 1971. (1854–1860)
C

———. *Elements of the philosophy of the human mind*. (2 vols.) Cambridge: Munroe, 1833. (1792, 1813) Reprinted in *Works*, Vols. 2, 3, 4, *op. cit.*, & New York: Garland, 1971.

———. Outlines of moral philosophy. (1793) In *Works*, Vols. 2, 8, *op. cit.*

———. Account of the life and writings of Adam Smith, LL.D. (1793) In A. Smith, *Adam Smith*. Vol. 5. Aalen: Zeller, 1963, pp. 403–552, & in *Works*, Vol. 10, *op. cit.*, pp. 2–98.

———. Account of the life and writings of Thomas Reid, D.D., F.R.S.E. (1802) In T. Reid, *Philosophical works*. (8th ed.) Vol. 1. Ed. with notes & suppl. dissertations by W. Hamilton, & intro. by H. M. Bracken. Hildesheim: Olms, 1967, pp. 3–38, & in *Works*, Vol. 10, *op. cit.*, pp. 243–328.

———. Dissertation first: Exhibiting a general view of the progress of metaphysical and ethical philosophy, since the revival of letters in Europe. (1824) In *Encyclopaedia Britannica*. (8th ed.) Vol. 1. *Dissertations*. Boston: Little, Brown, 1860, pp. 1–289, & in *Works*, Vol. 1, *op. cit.*, pp. 1–197.

———. *The philosophy of the active and moral powers of man*. (9th ed.) Rev. by J. Walker. Philadelphia: Butler, 1866. (1828) Reprinted in *Works*, Vols. 6, 7, *op. cit.*

Fried, *Anthropology;* Hunter & Macalpine, *Psychiatry ;* Johnson, *Scottish Philosophy ;* Robinson, *Scottish Philosophy ;*
Schneider, *Scottish Moralists*

CHRISTIAN (H.) STOELTING
1864-1943
American Layman (12)

Stoelting, C. H. *Apparatus, tests and supplies for
psychology, psychometry, psychotechnology,
psychiatry, neurology, anthropology, phonetics,
physiology, and pharmacology.* Chicago: Stoelting, 1930.

CALVIN PERRY STONE
1892-1954
American Psychologist (16)

Stone, C. P. The congenital sexual behavior of the
young male albino rat. *J. comp. Psychol.,* 1922,
2, 95–153.

———. Further study of sensory functions in the
activation of sexual behavior in the young male
albino rat. *J. comp. Psychol.,* 1923, *3,* 469–473.

———. A note on "feminine" behavior in
adult male rats. *Amer. J. Physiol.,* 1924, *68,*
39–41.

———. The awakening of copulatory ability in
the male albino rat. *Amer. J. Physiol.,* 1924,
68, 407–424.

———. Delay in the awakening of copulatory
ability in the male albino rat incurred by
defective diets. I. Quantitative deficiency. II.
Qualitative deficiency. *J. comp. Psychol.,* 1924,
4, 195–224 ; 1925, *5,* 177–203.

———. The family resemblance of female rats
with respect to (1) the ages of first oestrus, and
(2) the body weights. *Amer. J. Physiol.,* 1926,
77, 625–637.

———. The retention of copulatory ability in
male rats following castration. *J. comp.
Psychol.,* 1927, *7,* 369–387.

———, & Nyswander, Dorothy B. The reliability
of rat learning scores from the Multiple-T maze

as determined by four different methods. *J.
genet. Psychol.,* 1927, *34,* 497–524.

———, & Sturman-Hulbe, Mary. Food vs. sex
as incentives for male rats on the maze-learning problem. *Amer. J. Psychol.,* 1927, *38,* 403–
408.

Burlingame, Mildred, & ———. Family resemblance in maze-learning ability in white rats.
Yearb. Nat. Soc. Stud. Educ., 1928, *27*(1), 89–99.

———, & Lindley, S. Some effects of inanition
on animal behavior. *Psychol. Bull.,* 1928, *25,*
12–23.

———. The age factor in animal learning. I. Rats
in the problem box and the maze. *Genet.
Psychol. Monogr.,* 1929, *5,* 1–130.

———. The age factor in learning. II. Rats on a
multiple light discrimination box and a difficult
maze. *Genet. Psychol. Monogr.,* 1929, *6,* 125–
202.

———. The retention of copulatory activity in
male rabbits following castration. *J. genet.
Psychol.,* 1932, *40,* 296–305.

McNemar, Q., & ———. The sex difference in
rats on three learning tasks. *J. comp. Psychol.,*
1932, *14,* 171–180.

———. Wildness and savageness in rats of different strains. In K. S. Lashley (Ed.), *Studies in
dynamics of behavior.* Chicago: University of
Chicago Press, 1932, pp. 3–55.

———. Motivation. In F. A. Moss (Ed.), *Comparative psychology.* (2nd ed.) New York:
Prentice-Hall, 1946, pp. 65–97. (1934)

———. Learning. I. The factor of maturation. In
C. Murchison (Ed.), *A Handbook of general
experimental psychology.* Worcester, Mass.:
Clark University Press, 1934, pp. 354–381.

———. (Ed.), *Comparative psychology.* (3rd ed.)
Englewood Cliffs, N.J.: Prentice-Hall, 1951.
(1934)

———. Effects of cortical destruction on reproductive behavior and maze learning in albino
rats. *J. comp. Psychol.,* 1938, *26,* 217–236.

———, & Barker, R. G. The attitudes and interests of premenarcheal and postmenarcheal girls.
J. genet. Psychol., 1939, *54,* 27–71.

————. Counteracting the retarding effects of inanition on the awakening of copulatory ability in male rats by testosterone propionate. *J. comp. Psychol.*, 1942, *33*, 97–105.

————. Multiply, vary, let the strongest live and the weakest die.—Charles Darwin. *Psychol. Bull.*, 1943, *40*, 1–24.

GUSTAV STORRING
1860-1946
German Psychologist (15)

Störring, G. *Vorlesungen über Psychopathologie in ihrer Bedeutung für die normale Psychologie mit Einschluss der psychologischen Grundlagen der Erkenntnistheorie.* Leipzig: Engelmann, 1900.

————. *Mental pathology in its relation to normal psychology.* Trans. by T. Loveday. New York: Macmillan, 1907. (1900)

————. *Die Erkenntnistheorie von Tetens.* Leipzig: Engelmann, 1901.

————. *Zur Lehre von den Allgemeinbegriffen. Phil. Stud.*, 1902, *20*, 323–335.

————. *Moralphilosophische Streitfragen.* Vol. 1. *Die Entstehung des sittlichen Bewusstseins.* Leipzig: Engelmann, 1903.

————. Experimentelle Beiträge zur Lehre vom Gefühl. *Arch. ges. Psychol.*, 1906, *6*, 316–356.

————. Experimentelle Untersuchungen über einfache Schlussprozesse. *Arch. ges. Psychol.*, 1908, *11*, 1–127.

————. Experimentelle und psychopathologische Untersuchungen über das Bewusstsein der Gültigkeit. *Arch. ges. Psychol.*, 1909, *14*, 1–42.

————. *Die Hebel der sittlichen Entwicklung der Jugend.* (2nd ed.) Leipzig: Engelmann, 1919. (1911)

————. Experimentelle Beiträge zur Lehre von den Bewegungs- und Kraftempfindungen. *Arch. ges. Psychol.*, 1912, *25*, 177–188.

————. Zur kritischen Würdigung der Freudschen Theorie. *Z. Pathopsychol.*, 1913, *2*, 144–149.

————. *Psychologie des menschlichen Gefühlslebens.* (2nd ed.) Bonn: Cohen, 1922. (1916)

————. Zur Psychologie der Erinnerungsgewissheit. *Arch. ges. Psychol.*, 1922, *43*, 24–31.

————. *Psychologie.* Leipzig: Engelmann, 1923.

————. Allgemeine Bestimmungen über Denkprozesse und kausale Behandlung einfacher experimentell gewonnener Schlussprozesse. *Arch. ges. Psychol.*, 1925, *52*, 1–60.

————. Psychologie der disjunktiven und hypothetischen Urteile und Schlüsse. *Arch. ges. Psychol.*, 1926, *54*, 23–84.

————. Psychologie der zweiten und dritten Schlussfigur und allgemeine Gesetzmässigkeiten der Schlussprozesse. *Arch. ges. Psychol.*, 1926, *55*, 47–110.

————. *Das urteilende und schliessende Denken in kausaler Behandlung.* Leipzig: Akademie Verlagsgesellschaft, 1926.

————. Zur Frage der geisteswissenschaftlichen und verstehenden Psychologie. *Arch. ges. Psychol.*, 1927, *58*, 389–448; 1928, *61*, 273–354. (Also Leipzig: Akademie Verlagsgesellschaft, 1928)

————. Methoden der Psychologie des fähreren Gefühlslebens. In E. Abderhalden (Ed.), *Handbuch der biologischen Arbeitsmethoden.* Vol. 6. *Methoden der experimentellen Psychologie.* Part B/2. Vienna: Urban & Schwarzenberg, 1931, pp. 1125–1646.

Störring, G. E., & ————. Experimentelle Untersuchungen zur allgemeinen Gefühlslehre. *Arch. ges. Psychol.*, 1931, *78*, 273–379.

————. *Zur Psychopathologie und Klinik der Angstzustände.* Berlin: Karger, 1934.

————. *Die moderne ethische Wertphilosophie.* Leipzig: Engelmann, 1935.

————. *Methoden der Psychologie des höheren Gefühlslebens auf Grund psychopathologischer, experimenteller und völkerpsychologischer Untersuchungen.* Berlin: Urban & Schwarzenberg, 1938.

SAMUEL ANDREW STOUFFER
1900-1960
American Sociologist (13)

Stouffer, S. A. *Social research to test ideas: Selected writings.* Intro. by P. F. Lazarsfeld. New York: Free Press, 1962.   **C**

Wooddy, C. H., & ———. Local option and public opinion. *Amer. J. Sociol.*, 1930–1931, *36*, 175–205.

Pearson, K., ———, & David, F. N. Further applications in statistics of the T*m*(x) Bessel function. *Biometrika*, 1932, *24*, 293–350.

———, & Tibbitts, C. Tests of significance in applying Westergard's method of expected cases to sociological data. *J. Amer. Stat. Ass.*, 1933, *28*, 293–307.

———. A technique for analyzing sociological data classified in non-quantitative groups. *Amer. J. Sociol.*, 1933–1934, *39*, 180–193.

———. A coefficient of "combined partial correlation" with an example from sociological data, *J. Amer. Stat. Ass.*, 1934, *29*, 70–71.

Tibbitts, C., & ———. Testing the significance of comparisons in sociological data. *Amer. J. Sociol.* 1934–1935, *40*, 357–363.

———. Statistical induction in rural social research. *Social Forces*, 1935, *13*, 505–515.

———. Reliability coefficients in a correlation matrix. *Psychometrika*, 1936, *1*, 17–20.

———. Evaluating the effect of inadequately measured variables in partial correlation analysis. *J. Amer. Stat. Ass.*, 1936, *31*, 348–360.

———, et al. Research memorandum on the family in the depression. *Soc. Sci. Res. Counc. Bull.*, 1937, No. 29.

———. Intervening opportunities: A theory relating mobility and distance. *Amer. sociol. Rev.*, 1940, *5*, 845–867.

———, et al. Memorandum on prediction and natural defense. *Soc. Sci. Res. Counc. Bull.*, 1941, No. 48, 157–178.

———. Notes on the case-study and unique case. *Sociometry*, 1941, *4*, 349–357.

———. Studying the attitudes of soldiers. *Proc. Amer. phil. Soc.*, 1948, *92*, 336–340.

McNall, *Sociological Perspectives;* Ross, *Social Order*

GEORGE FREDERICK STOUT
1860-1944
English Psychologist (26)

Stout, G. F. *Studies in philosophy and psychology.* New York: Macmillan, 1930.   **C**

———. The Herbartian psychology. *Mind*, 1888, *13*, 321–338, 473–498. Reprinted in *Studies in philosophy and psychology, op. cit.*, pp. 1–50.

———. Is mind synonymous with consciousness? *Proc. Arist. Soc.*, 1888, *1*(1), 11–12.

———. The scope and method of psychology. *Proc. Arist. Soc.*, 1888, *1*(1), 33–54.

———. Herbart compared with English psychologists and with Beneke. *Mind*, 1889, *14*, 1–26.

———. The psychological work of Herbart's disciples. *Mind*, 1889, *14*, 353–368.

———. The genesis of the cognition of physical reality. *Mind*, 1890, *15*, 22–45.

———. Is the distinction of feeling, cognition and conation valid as an ultimate distinction of the mental functions? (Symposium.) *Proc. Arist. Soc.*, 1890, *1*(3), 142–150.

———. Apperception and the movement of attention. *Mind*, 1891, *16*, 23–53.

———. Thought and language. *Mind*, 1891, *16*, 181–205.

———. Belief. *Mind*, 1891, *16*, 449–469.

———. Voluntary action. *Mind*. 1896, *5*(N.S.), 354–366.

———. *Analytic psychology.* (2 vols.) New York: Macmillan, 1896.

———. Prof. Angell's criticism of "analytic psychology." *Phil. Rev.*, 1898, *7*, 72–76.

———, & Mace, C. A. *A manual of psychology.* (5th ed.) London: University Tutorial Press, 1938. (1899) (Reprinted 1970)   **Bl**

———. The perception of change and duration. *Mind,* 1900, *9*(N.S.), 1–7. Reprinted in *Studies in philosophy and psychology, op. cit.,* pp. 67–73.

———. *The groundwork of psychology.* (2nd ed.) Rev. by R. H. Thouless. London: University of London Press, 1927. (1903)

———. Primary and secondary qualities. *Proc. Arist. Soc.,* 1904, *4,* 141–160.

———. Things and sensations. *Proc. Brit. Acad.,* 1905–1906, *2,* 169–181.

———. The nature of conation and mental activity. *Brit. J. Psychol.,* 1906–1908, *2,* 1–15.

———. Are presentations mental or physical? *Proc. Arist. Soc.,* 1909, *9,* 226–247.

———. IV. Instinct and intelligence. *Brit. J. Psychol.,* 1909–1910, *3,* 237–249.

———, Barker, H., & Hoernlé, R. F. A. Can there be anything obscure or implicit in a mental state? *Proc. Arist. Soc.,* 1913, *13,* 257–312.

Shand, A. F., McDougall, W., & ———. Instinct and emotion. *Proc. Arist. Soc.,* 1915, *15,* 22–99.

———. *The nature of universals and propositions.* London: Oxford University Press, 1921.

———. Ward as a psychologist. *Monist,* 1926, *36,* 20–55. Reprinted in *Studies in philosophy and psychology, op. cit.,* pp. 92–122.

———. *Mind and matter.* Vol. 1. New York: Macmillan, 1931.

———. *God and nature.* (Based on lectures 1919–1921.) Ed. by A. K. Stout. Cambridge: Cambridge University Press, 1952.   **B Bl**

Park & Burgess, *Sociology*

GEORGE MALCOLM STRATTON
1865-1957
American Psychologist (22)

Stratton, G. M. Ueber die Wahrnehmung von Druckänderungen bei verschiedenen Geschwindigkeiten. *Phil. Stud.,* 1896, *12,* 525–586.

———. The relation between psychology and logic. *Psychol. Rev.,* 1896, *3,* 313–320.

———. Some preliminary experiments on vision without inversion of the retinal image. *Psychol. Rev.,* 1896, *3,* 611–617.

———. Upright vision and the retinal image. *Psychol. Rev.,* 1897, *4,* 182–187.

———. Vision without inversion of the retinal image. *Psychol. Rev.* 1897, *4,* 341–360, 463–481.

———. A mirror pseudoscope and the limit of visible depth. *Psychol. Rev.,* 1898, *5,* 632–638.

———. The spatial harmony of touch and sight. *Mind,* 1899, *8*(N.S.), 492–505.

———. A new determination of the Minimum Visible and its bearings on localization and binocular depths. *Psychol. Rev.,* 1900, *7,* 429–435.

———. Visible motion and the space threshold. *Psychol. Rev.,* 1902, *9,* 433–443.

———. *Experimental psychology and its bearing upon culture.* New York: Macmillan, 1903. (Reprinted 1908, 1914)

———. Symmetry, linear illusions and the movements of the eye. *Psychol. Rev.,* 1906, *13,* 82–96.

———. Toward the correction of some rival methods in psychology. *Psychol. Rev.,* 1909, *16,* 67–84.

———. *Psychology of the religious life.* New York: Macmillan, 1911. (Reprinted 1970)

———. The psychology of change: How is the perception of movement related to that of succession? *Psychol. Rev.,* 1911, *18,* 262–293.

———. *Theophrastus and the Greek physiological psychology before Aristotle.* New York: Macmillan, 1917. (Reprinted 1964)

———. *Anger: Its religious and moral significance.* New York: Macmillan, 1923.

———. The color red and the anger of cattle. *Psychol. Rev.,* 1923, *30,* 321–325.

———. An experience during danger and the wider functions of emotion. In C. M. Campbell *et al.* (Eds.), *Problems of personality: Studies presented to Dr. Morton Prince, pioneer in American psychopathology.* New York: Harcourt, Brace, 1925, pp. 47–62.

——. Emotion and the incidence of disease. *J. abnorm. soc. Psychol.*, 1926–1927, *21*, 19–23.

——. The function of emotion as shown particularly in excitement. *Psychol. Rev.*, 1928, *35*, 351–366.

——. Excitement as an undifferentiated emotion. In M. L. Reymert (Ed.), *Feelings and emotions: The Wittenberg symposium.* Worcester, Mass.: Clark University Press, 1928, pp. 215–221.

——. *The social psychology of international conduct.* New York: Appleton, 1929.

——. The relation of emotion to sex, primogeniture and disease. *Amer. J. Psychol.*, 1934, *46*, 590–595.

Dember, *Perception ;* Herrnstein & Boring, *Source Book*

EDWARD KELLOGG STRONG
1884-1963
American Psychologist (20)

Strong, E. K. The relative merit of advertisements. *Arch. Psychol.*, N.Y., 1911, No. 17.

——. The effect of length of series upon recognition memory. *Psychol. Rev.*, 1912, *19*, 447–462.

——. Psychological methods as applied to advertising. *J. educ. Psychol.*, 1913, *4*, 393–404.

——. The effect of time-interval upon recognition memory. *Psychol. Rev.*, 1913, *20*, 339–372.

——. Work of the committee on classification of personnel in the Army. *J. appl. Psychol.*, 1918, *2*, 130–139.

——. *Psychology of selling and advertising.* New York: McGraw-Hill, 1925.

——. An interest test for personnel managers. *J. personnel Res.*, 1926–1927, *5*, 194–203.

——. Interest analysis of personnel managers. *J. personnel Res.*, 1926–1927, *5*, 235–242.

——. Differentiation of certified public accountants from other occupational groups. *J. educ. Psychol.*, 1927, *18*, 227–238.

——. Vocational Interest Test. *Educ. Rec.*, 1927, *8*, 107–121.

——. Vocational guidance of executives. *J. appl. Psychol.*, 1927, *11*, 331–347.

——. Vocational guidance of engineers. *Indust. Psychol.*, 1927, *2*, 291–298.

——. Diagnostic value of the Vocational Interest Test. *Educ. Rec.*, 1929, *10*, 59–68.

——. Interests of engineers: A basis for vocational guidance. *Personnel J.*, 1929, *7*, 441–454.

——. *Change of interests with age.* Stanford, Calif.: Stanford University Press, 1931.

——. Aptitudes versus attitudes in vocational guidance. *J. appl. Psychol.*, 1934, *18*, 501–515.

——. *The second-generation Japanese problem.* Stanford, Calif.: Stanford University Press, 1934. (Reprinted 1970)

——. Interests of men and women. *J. soc. Psychol.*, 1936, *7*, 49–67.

——. *Vocational interests of men and women.* Stanford, Calif.: Stanford University Press, 1943.

——. Personnel-psychologists at Stanford University. *Psychol. Bull.*, 1944, *41*, 474–489.

——. Vocational interests of accountants. *J. appl. Psychol.*, 1949, *33*, 474–481.

——. Norms for Strong's vocational interest tests. *J. appl. Psychol.*, 1951, *35*, 50–56.

——. Interest scores while in college of occupations engaged in 20 years later. *Educ. psychol. Measmt.*, 1951, *11*, 335–348.

——. Permanence of interest scores over 22 years. *J. appl. Psychol.*, 1951, *35*, 89–91.

——. Amount of change in occupational choice of college freshmen. *Educ. psychol. Measmt*, 1952, *12*, 677–691.

——, & Tucker, A. C. The use of vocational interest scales in planning a medical career. *Psychol. Monogr.*, 1952, *66*, No. 341.

——. Twenty-year follow-up of medical interests. In L. L. Thurstone (Ed.), *Application of psychology: Essays to honor Walter V. Bingham*. New York: Harper, 1952, pp. 111–131.

——. Nineteen-year follow-up of engineer interests. *J. appl. Psychol.*, 1952, *36*, 65–74.

——. Interests of Negroes and whites. *J. soc. Psychol.*, 1952, *35*, 139–150.

——. Validity of occupational choice. *Educ. psychol., Measmt*, 1953, *13*, 110–121.

——. *Vocational interests 18 years after college*. Minneapolis, Minn.: University of Minnesota Press, 1955.

——. Interests of fathers and sons. *J. appl. Psychol.*, 1957, *41*, 284–292.

——. Satisfactions and interests. *Amer. Psychologist*, 1958, *13*, 449–456. Reprinted in D. Wolfle (Ed.). *The discovery of talent*. Cambridge: Harvard University Press, 1969, pp. 89–106.

——, *et al.* Proposed scoring changes for the Strong Vocational Interest Blank. *J. appl. Psychol.*, 1964, *48*, 75–80.

Moore & Hartmann, *Industrial Psychology*

CARL STUMPF
1848-1936
German Psychologist (27)

Stumpf, C. *Philosophische Reden und Vorträge*. Leipzig: Barth, 1910.   **C**

——. *Erkenntnislehre*. (2 vols.) Ed. by F. Stumpf. Leipzig: Barth, 1939–1940.   **C**

——. *Ueber den psychologischen Ursprung der Raumvorstellung*. Leipzig: Hirzel, 1873. (Reprinted 1965)

——. Aus der vierten Dimension. *Phil. Monatsh.*, 1878, *14*, 13–20.

——. *Tonpsychologie*. (2 vols.) Leipzig: Hirzel, 1883–1890. (Reprinted 1965)

——. Lieder der Bellakula-Indianer. (1886) In A. J. Ellis *et al., Abhandlungen zur vergleichenden Musikwissenschaft*. Munich: Drei Masken, 1922, pp. 87–103.

——. *Leib und Seele und der Entwickelungsgedanke in der gegenwärtigen Philosophie.* (3rd ed.) Leipzig: Barth, 1909. (1890)

——. Ueber Vergleichungen von Tondistanzen. *Z. Psychol.*, 1890, *1*, 419–462.

——. *Psychologie und Erkenntnisstheorie*. Munich: Franz, 1891.

——. Wundts Antikritik. *Z. Psychol.*, 1891, *2*, 266–293.

——. Mein Schlusswort gegen Wundt. *Z. Psychol.*, 1891, *2*, 438–443.

——. Zum Begriff der Localzeichen. *Z. Psychol.*, 1893, *4*, 70–73.

——. Hermann von Helmholtz and the new psychology. *Psychol. Rev.*, 1895, *2*, 1–12.

——. *Tafeln zur Geschichte der Philosophie.* (2nd ed.) Berlin: Speyer & Peters, 1900. (1896)

——. *Ueber die Ermittlung von Obertönen*. Leipzig: Barth, 1896.

——. *Die pseudo-aristotelischen Probleme über Musik*. Berlin: Reiner, 1897.

——. *Geschichte der Konsonanzbegriffes*. Munich: Franz, 1897.

——. Neueres über Tonverschmelzung. *Z. Psychol.*, 1897, *15*, 280–303, 354.

——, & Meyer, M. F. Schwingungszahlbestimmungen bei sehr hohen Tönen. *Ann. Physik*, 1897, *61*, 760–779. (Also Leipzig: Barth, 1897)

——. Eröffnungsrede. *III. Inter. Cong. Psychol.* Munich, 1897, 3–16.

——, & Meyer, M. F. Massbestimmungen über die Reinheit consonanter Intervalle. *Z. Psychol.*, 1898, *18*, 321–404.

——. Die Unmusikalischen und die Tonverschmelzung. *Z. Psychol.*, 1898, *17*, 422–435.

——. Erwiderung. *Z. Psychol.*, 1898, *18*, 294–302.

——. Ueber den Begriff der Gemüthsbewegung. *Z. Psychol.*, 1899, *21*, 47–99.

——. Beobachtungen über subjective Töne und über Doppelthören. *Z. Psychol.*, 1899, *21*, 100–121.

———. *Der Entwicklungsgedanke in der gegenwärtigen Philosophie.* Leipzig: Barth, 1900.

———. Zur Methodik der Kinderpsychologie. *Z. pädag. Psychol.,* 1900, *2,* 1–21.

———. Ueber das Erkennen von Intervallen und Accorden bei sehr kurzer Dauer. *Z. Psychol.,* 1902, *27,* 148–186.

———. Erscheinungen und psychische Funktionen. *Abh. preuss. Akad. Wiss.,* phil.-hist. Kl., 1906, No. 4 (Also Berlin: Reimer, 1907).

———. Zur Einteilung der Wissenschaften. *Abh. preuss. Akad. Wiss.,* phil.-hist. Kl., 1906, No. 5.

———. *Die Wiedergeburt der Philosophie.* Leipzig: Barth, 1907.

———. *Erscheinungen und psychische Funktionen.* Berlin: Reimer, 1907.

———. Ueber Gefühlsempfindungen. *Z. Psychol.,* 1907, *44,* 1–49.

———. *Vom ethischen Skeptizismus.* Berlin: Schade, 1908.

———. Beobachtungen über Kombinationstöne. *Z. Psychol.,* 1910, *55,* 1–142.

———, & Hornbostel, E. M. v. Ueber die Bedeutung ethnologischer Untersuchungen für die Psychologie und Aesthetik der Tonkunst. *Ber. IV. Kong. exper. Psychol.,* Leipzig, 1911, pp. 256–269.

———. Konsonanz und Konkordanz. Nebst Bemerkungen über Wohlklang und Wohlgefälligkeit musikalischer Zusammenklänge. *Z. Psychol.,* 1911, *58,* 321–355.

———. Differenztöne und Konsonanz (Zweiter Artikel). *Z. Psychol.,* 1911, *59,* 161–175.

———. *Die Anfänge der Musik.* Leipzig: Barth, 1911.

———. Ueber neuere Untersuchungen zur Tonlehre. *Ber. VI. Kongr. exp. Psychol., Göttingen.* Leipzig, 1914, pp. 305–348.

———. Binaurale Tonmischung, Mehrheitsschwelle und Mitteltonbildung. *Z. Psychol.,* 1916, *75,* 330–350.

———. Die Attribute der Gesichtsempfindungen. *Abh. preuss. Akad. Wiss.,* phil.-hist. Kl., 1917, **No. 8.**

———. Die Struktur der Vokale. *Sitzber. preuss. Akad. Wiss.,* 1918, *17,* 333–358. (Also Berlin: Reimer, 1918)

———. Empfindung und Vorstellung. *Abh. preuss. Akad. Wiss.,* phil.-hist. Kl., 1918, No. 1.

———. Erinnerungen an Franz Brentano. In O. Kraus, *Franz Brentano: Zur Kenntnis seines Lebens und seiner Lehre.* Munich: Beck, 1919, pp. 87–149.　　　　　　　　　　　**B**

———. Zur Analyse der geflüsterten Vokale. *Beit. Anat. Ohres,* 1919, *12,* 234–254.

———. Zur Analyse der Konsonanten. *Beit. Anat. Ohres,* 1921, *17,* 151–181.

———. Veränderungen des Sprachverständnisses bei abwärts fortschreitender Vernichtung der Gehörsempfindung. *Beit. Anat. Ohres,* 1921, *17,* 182–190.

———. Carl Stumpf. In R. Schmidt (Ed.), *Die Philosophie der Gegenwart in Selbstdarstellungen.* Vol. 5. Leipzig: Meiner, 1924, pp. 105–265. Trans. without bibliog. in C. Murchison (Ed.), *A history of psychology in autobiography.* Vol. 1. Worcester, Mass.: Clark University Press, 1930, pp. 389–441.　　**B Bl**

———. *Die Sprachlaute: Experimentell-phonetische Untersuchungen nebst einem Anhang über Instrumental-Klänge.* Berlin: Springer Verlag, 1926.

———. *William James nach seinen Briefen.* Berlin: Pan-Verlag, 1928.

———. *Gefühl und Gefühlsempfindung.* Leipzig: Barth, 1928.

Rand, *Classical Psychologists;* Sahakian, *Psychology*

HARRY STACK SULLIVAN
1892-1949
American Psychiatrist (23)

Sullivan, H. S. *Clinical studies in psychiatry.* Ed. by Helen Swick Perry, Mary Ladd Gawel, & Martha Gibbon. New York: Norton, 1956. Reprinted in *Collected works,* Vol. 2, *vide infra.*　　　　　　　　　　　　　　　**C**

——. *Schizophrenia as a human process*. Intro. & commentary by Helen Swick Perry. New York: Norton, 1962. Reprinted in *Collected works*, Vol. 2, *vide infra*. **C**

——. *The fusion of psychiatry and social science*. Intro. & commentary by Helen Swick Perry. New York: Norton, 1964. Reprinted in *Collected works*, Vol. 2, *vide infra*. **C**

——. *The collected works of Harry Stack Sullivan*. Ed. by Helen Swick Perry *et al*. (2 vols.) New York: Norton, no date given (ca. 1965). **C**

——. Peculiarity of thought in schizophrenia. *Amer. J. Psychiat.*, 1925, *82*, 21–86. Reprinted in *Schizophrenia as a human process, op. cit.*, pp. 26–99.

——. The onset of schizophrenia. *Amer. J. Psychiat.*, 1927–1928, *84*, 105–134. Reprinted in *Schizophrenia as a human process, op. cit.*, pp. 104–136.

——. Research in schizophrenia. *Amer. J. Psychiat.*, 1929–1930, *86*, 553–568. Reprinted in *Schizophrenia as a human process, op. cit.*, pp. 186–202.

——. A note on the implications of psychiatry, the study of interpersonal relations, for investigations in the social sciences. *Amer. J. Sociol.*, 1936–1937, *42*, 848–861. Reprinted in *The fusion of psychiatry and social science, op. cit.*, pp. 15–29.

——. Introduction to the study of interpersonal relations. *Psychiatry*, 1938, *1*, 121–134. Reprinted in *The fusion of psychiatry and social science, op. cit.*, 1964, pp. 32–55.

——. Intuition, reason, and faith. *Science*, 1938, *88*, 601–609. Reprinted in *Psychiatry*, 1939, *2*, 129–132, & in *The fusion of psychiatry and social science, op. cit.*, 1964, pp. 60–65.

——. Conceptions of modern psychiatry. (2nd ed.) New York: Norton, 1953. (1940, 1945, 1947) Reprinted in *Collected works*, Vol. 1, *op. cit.*

——. The language of schizophrenia. In J. S. Kasanin (Ed.), *Language and thought in schizophrenia*. Berkeley, Calif.: University of California Press, 1944, pp. 4–15. (Reprinted 1964)

——. Remobilization for enduring peace and social progress. *Psychiatry*, 1947, *10*, 239–252. Reprinted in *The fusion of psychiatry and social science, op. cit.*, pp. 273–289.

——. The meaning of anxiety in psychiatry and in life. *Psychiatry*, 1948, *11*, 1–13. Reprinted in *The fusion of psychiatry and social science, op. cit.*, pp. 229–254.

——. The theory of anxiety and the nature of psychotherapy. *Psychiatry*, 1949, *12*, 3–12. Reprinted in H. Brand (Ed.), *The study of personality: A book of readings*. New York: Wiley, 1954, pp. 61–75.

——. Tensions interpersonal and international: A psychiatrist's view. In H. Cantril (Ed.), *Tensions that cause wars: Common statement and individual papers by a group of social scientists brought together by UNESCO*. Urbana, Ill.: University of Illinois Press, 1950, pp. 79–138. Reprinted in *The fusion of psychiatry and social science, op. cit.*, pp. 293–331.

——. *The interpersonal theory of psychiatry*. (1953) Ed. by Helen Swick Perry & Mary Ladd Gawel. New York: Norton, 1968. Reprinted in *Collected works*, Vol. 1, *op. cit.*

——. *The psychiatric interview*. Ed. by Helen Swick Perry & Mary Ladd Gawel. New York: Norton, 1954. Reprinted in *Collected works*, Vol. 1, *op. cit.*

——. *Personal psychopathology: Early formulations*. Intro. by Helen Swick Perry. New York: Norton, 1972.

Beck & Molish, *Reflexes;* Lindzey & Hall, *Personality;* Sahakian, *Personality*

JAMES SULLY
1842-1923
English Psychologist (22)

Sully, J. *Sensation and intuition: Studies in psychology and aesthetics*. (2nd ed.) London: King, 1880. (1874) **C**

——. Physiological psychology in Germany. *Mind*, 1876, *1*, 20–43.

——. The gratification derived from the infliction of pain. *Mind*, 1876, *1*, 285–286.

——. Art and psychology. *Mind,* 1876, *1,* 467–478.

——. The associationist theory of avarice. *Mind,* 1876, *1,* 567–568.

——. The laws of dream-fancy. *Cornhill Mag.,* 1876, *34,* 555–576 ; *Mind,* 1877, *2,* 111–112.

——. Pessimism: A history and a criticism. (2nd ed.) New York: Appleton, 1891. (1877)

——. The question of visual perception in Germany. *Mind,* 1878, *3,* 1–23, 167–195.

——. Harmony of colours. *Mind,* 1879, *4,* 172–191.

——. Les formes visuelles et le plaisir esthétique. *Rev. phil.,* 1880, *9,* 493–515.

——. Pleasure of visual form. *Mind,* 1880, *5,* 181–201.

——. Illusions: A psychological study. New York: Appleton, 1881.

——. On the definition of instinctive action. *Mind,* 1881, *6,* 114–116.

——. Versatility. *Mind,* 1882, *7,* 366–380.

——. *Outlines of psychology, with special references to the theory of education.* (2nd ed.) London: Longmans, Green, 1892. (1884)

——. Genius and insanity. *Nineteenth Cent.,* 1885, *17,* 948–969.

——. Comparison. *Mind,* 1885, *10,* 489–511.

——. *The teacher's handbook of psychology on the basis of "Outlines of psychology."* (5th ed.) New York: Appleton, 1910. (1886)

——. The psycho-physical process in attention. *Brain,* 1890, *13,* 145–164.

——. Mental elaboration. *Mind,* 1890, *15,* 469–488.

——. Psychology of conception. *Monist,* 1891–1892, *1,* 481–505.

——. *The human mind, a text-book of psychology.* (2 vols.) New York: Appleton, 1892. (1891)

——. *Studies of childhood.* (2nd ed.) New York: Appleton, 1910. (1895)

——. *Children's ways, being selections from the author's "Studies of childhood," with some additional matter.* New York: Appleton, 1897. (1895)

——. The new study of children. *Fortn. Rev.,* 1895, *58,* 723–737.

——. The child in recent English literature. *Fortn. Rev.,* 1897, *61,* 218–228.

——. Prolegomena to a theory of laughter. *Phil. Rev.,* 1900, *9,* 365–383.

——. *An essay on laughter, its forms, its causes, its development, and its value.* New York: Longmans, Green, 1902.

——. *My life & friends, a psychologist's memories.* London: Fisher, Unwin, 1918. **B**

EMANUEL SWEDENBORG
1688-1772
Swedish Theologian (11)

Swedenborg, E. *A compendium of the theological writings of Emanuel Swedenborg.* (3rd ed.) Ed. by S. M. Warren. New York: New-Church, 1888. (1853) **C**

——. *Miscellaneous theological works.* New York: Swedenborg Foundation, 1951. (1892) **C**

——. *Swedenborg's works.* (32 vols.) (Rotch edition) Boston: Houghton Mifflin, n.d. [ca. 1907] **C**

——. *Posthumous theological works.* (2 vols.) Ed. & trans. by J. Whitehead. New York: Swedenborg Foundation, 1928. **C**

——. *Three transactions on the cerebrum: A posthumous work.* (3 vols.) Trans. & ed. by A. Acton. Philadelphia: Swedenborg Scientific Association, 1938. **C**

——. *The principia or the first principles of natural things to which are added the minor principia and summary of the principia.* (2 vols.) Trans. by J. R. Rendell & I. Tansley. London: Swedenborg Society, 1912. (1734)

——. *The economy of the animal kingdom, considered anatomically, physically, and philosophically.* (2 vols.) Trans. by A. Clissold.

New York: The New Church Board of Publication, 1903. (1740–1741)

―――. *The animal kingdom considered anatomically, physically, and philosophically.* (2 vols.) Trans. by J. J. G. Wilkinson. Cincinnati, Ohio: Mendelholl, 1858. (1741)

―――. *Rational psychology.* Trans. by N. H. Rogers & A. Acton. Philadelphia: Swedenborg Scientific Association, 1950. (1742)

―――. *The five senses.* Ed. & trans. by E. S. Price. Philadelphia: Swedenborg Scientific Association, 1914. (1744)

―――. *Heaven and hell.* Trans. by F. Bayley. New York: Dutton, 1931. (1758)

―――. *Marital love: Its wise delights, after which follows scortatory love: Its insane pleasures.* Trans. by W. F. Wunsch. New York: Swedenborg Publishing Association, 1938. (1768)

―――. The intercourse between the soul and the body. (1769) In *Swedenborg's works,* Vol. 24, *op. cit.,* pp. 1–42.

―――. *Psychological transactions by Emanuel Swedenborg.* (2nd ed.) Ed. & trans. by A. Acton. Philadelphia: Swedenborg Scientific Association, 1955. (1846–1852)

―――. *The brain considered anatomically, physiologically and philosophically.* (2 vols.) Trans. & ed. by R. L. Tafel. London: Speirs, 1882–1887.

PERCIVAL MALLON SYMONDS
1893-1960
American Psychologist (11)

Symonds, P. M. On the loss of reliability in ratings due to coarseness of the scale. *J. exp. Psychol.,* 1924, 7, 456–461.

―――. The significance of intelligence tests in the University of Hawaii. *School & Soc.,* 1924, *20,* 601–606.

―――. Notes on rating. *J. appl. Psychol.,* 1925, *9,* 188–195.

―――. A social attitudes questionnaire. *J. educ. Psychol.,* 1925, *16,* 316–322.

―――. *Measurement in secondary education.* New York: Macmillan, 1927.

―――. *The nature of conduct.* New York: Macmillan, 1928.

―――, & Chase, Doris H. Practice vs. motivation. *J. educ. Psychol.,* 1929, *20,* 19–35.

―――. *Test and interest questionnaires in the guidance of high school boys.* New York: Teachers College Bureau of Publications, 1930.

―――. *Diagnosing personality and conduct.* New York: Appleton-Century, 1931.

―――, & Jackson, C. E. *Measurement of the personality adjustments of high school pupils.* New York: Columbia University Press, 1935.

―――. Securing rapport in interviewing. *Teach. Coll. Rec.,* 1938, *39,* 707–722.

―――. *Dynamics of human adjustment.* New York: Appleton-Century, 1946.

―――. *Adolescent fantasy.* New York: Columbia University Press, 1949.

―――. *The ego and the self.* New York: Appleton-Century-Crofts, 1951.

―――. *Dynamics of psychotherapy: The psychology of personality change.* Vol. 1. *Principles.* Vol. 2. *Process.* Vol. 3. *Procedures.* New York: Grune & Stratton, 1956–1958.

HIPPOLYTE ADOLPHE TAINE
1828-1893
French Philosopher (21)

Taine, H. *Essais de critique et d'histoire.* (6th ed.) Paris: Hachette, 1892. (1858)   C

―――. *Nouveaux essais de critique et d'histoire.* (8th ed.) Paris: Hachette, 1905. (1865)   C

―――. *Derniers essais de critique et d'histoire.* (6th ed.) Paris: Hachette, 1923. (1894)   C

―――. *Les philosophes classiques du XIXe siècle en France.* (11th ed.) Paris: Hachette, 1912. (1857)

―――. *History of English literature.* Trans. by H. Van Laun. New York: Holt, 1886. (1864)

———. *The philosophy of art.* Trans. by J. Durand. New York: Holt & Williams, 1873. (1865)

———. *Philosophie de l'art.* (Selections.) Ed. by J.-F. Revel. Paris: Hermann, 1964. (1865)

———. *On intelligence.* Trans. by T. D. Haye. New York: Holt & Williams, 1872. (1870)

———. Note sur l'acquisition de langage chez les enfants et dans l'espèce humaine. *Rev. phil.,* 1876, *1,* 3–23.

———. Les éléments et la formation de l'idée du moi. *Rev. phil.,* 1876, *1,* 289–294.

———. *Les origines de la France contemporaine: La révolution.* (28th ed.) (6 vols.) Paris: Hachette, 1920. (1878)

———. *Les origines de la France contemporaine: Le régime moderne.* (28th ed.) (3 vols.) Paris: Hachette, 1921. (1891)

———. De la volonté. *Rev. phil.,* 1900, *15,* 441–480.

Kessen, *Child.*

GABRIEL TARDE
1843-1904
French Sociologist (24)

Tarde, G. *Etudes pénales et sociales.* Lyon: Storck, 1892.   **C**

———. *Essais et mélanges sociologiques.* Paris: Maloine, 1895.   **C**

———. *Etudes de psychologie sociale.* Paris: Giard & Brière, 1898. (Reprinted 1971)   **C**

———. *Gabriel Tarde: Introduction et pages choisies par ses fils.* Pref. by H. Bergson. Paris: Michaud, 1909.   **Bl C**

———. *Gabriel Tarde on communication and social influence.* Ed. by T. N. Clark. Chicago: University of Chicago Press, 1969.   **Bl C**

———. La croyance et le désir. (1880) In *Essais et mélanges sociologiques, op. cit.,* pp. 237–308, & trans. in *On communication and social influence, op. cit.,* pp. 195–206.

———. La statistique criminelle du dernier demi-siècle. *Rev. phil.,* 1883, *15,* 49–82.

———. Darwinisme naturel et darwinisme social. *Rev. phil.,* 1884, *17,* 607–637.

———. Qu'est-ce qu'une société? *Rev. phil.,* 1884, *18,* 489–510.

———. *La criminalité comparée.* (5th ed.) Paris: Alcan, 1902. (1886)

———. La dialectique sociale. *Rev. phil.,* 1888, *26,* 20–41, 148–165.

———. *The laws of imitation.* (2nd ed.) Trans. by Elsie C. Parsons. New York: Holt, 1903. (1890) (Reprinted 1962)

———. *Penal philosophy.* Trans. by Rapelje Howell. Monclair, N.J.: Patterson Smith, 1968. (1890)

———. *Les transformations du droit.* (8th ed.) Paris: Alcan, 1922. (1893)

———. Questions sociales. (1893) In *Essais et mélanges sociologiques, op. cit.,* pp. 175–209.

———. Monadologie et sociologie. (1893). In *Essais et mélanges sociologiques, op. cit.,* pp. 309–389.

———. Les deux éléments de la sociologie (1894) Reprinted in *Etudes de psychologie sociale, op. cit.,* pp. 63–94, & trans. in *On communication and social influence, op. cit.,* pp. 112–135.

———. Human aggregation and crime. *Pop. Sci. Mon.,* 1894, *45,* 447–459.

———. *La logique sociale.* (2nd ed.) Paris: Alcan, 1898. (1895)

———. Sur l'idée de l'organisme social. *Rev. phil.,* 1896, *41,* 637–646.

———. *Underground man.* Trans. by C. Brereton. London: Duckworth, 1905.

———. L'idée d'opposition. *Rev. phil.,* 1897, *43,* 1–18, 160–175.

———. La graphologie. *Rev. phil.,* 1897, *44,* 337–363.

———. *L'opposition universelle.* Paris: Alcan, 1897. Excerpt trans. in *On communication and social influence, op. cit.,* pp. 222–241.

———. La sociologie. (1898) In *Etudes de psychologie sociale, op. cit.*, pp. 1–62. Excerpt trans. in *On communication and social influence, op. cit.*, pp. 73–105.

———. *Social laws: An outline of sociology.* Trans. by H. C. Warren. New York: Macmillan, 1899. (1898)

———. *Les transformations du pouvoir.* (2nd ed.) Paris: Alcan, 1909. (1899) Excerpt trans. in *On communication and social influence, op. cit.*, pp. 245–251.

———. *L'esprit de groupe. Arch. Anthrop. Crim.*, 1900, *15*, 5–28.

———. La realité sociale. *Rev. phil.*, 1901, *52*, 457–477.

———. *L'opinion et la foule.* Paris: Alcan, 1922. (1901)

———. Interpsychology: The interplay of human minds. (1901) Trans. by C. H. Page. *Int. Quart.*, 1902, *7*, 59–84.

———. *Psychologie économique.* (2 vols.) Paris: Alcan, 1902.

Sahakian, *Psychology*

LEWIS MADISON TERMAN
1877-1956
American Psychologist (27)

Terman, L. M. A preliminary study of the psychology and pedagogy of leadership. *J. genet. Psychol.*, 1904, *11*, 413–451.

———. Genius and stupidity: A study of some of the intellectual processes of seven "bright" and seven "stupid" boys. *J. genet. Psychol.*, 1906, *13*, 307–373.

———. The Binet-Simon scale for measuring intelligence: Impressions gained by its application upon four hundred nonselected children. *Psychol. Clin.*, 1911, *5*, 199–206, 239–244.

———, & Childs, H. G. A tentative revision and extension of the Binet-Simon measuring scale of intelligence. Part I. Introduction. Part II. Supplementary tests. 1. Generalization test: Interpretation of fables. The completion test. 3. Ball and field test of practical judgment. 4. Vocabulary test. Part III. Summary and criticisms. *J. educ. Psychol.*, 1912, *3*, 61–74, 133–143, 198–208, 277–289.

———. Suggestions for revising, extending, and supplementing the Binet intelligence tests. *J. Psycho.-Asthenics*, 1913, *18*, 20–33.

———, & Almack, J. C. *The hygiene of the school child.* Boston: Houghton Mifflin, 1929. (1914)

———, Lyman, Grace, Ordahl, G., Ordahl, Louise, Galbreath, Nena, & Tulbert, W. The Stanford revision of the Binet-Simon Scale, and some results from its application to one thousand nonselected children. *J. educ. Psychol.*, 1915, *6*, 551–562.

———. *The measurement of intelligence: An explanation of and a complete guide for the use of the Stanford revision and extension of the Binet-Simon intelligence scale.* Boston: Houghton Mifflin, 1916.

———, & Merrill, Maud. *The Stanford–Binet Scale: Manual for the third revision.* New York: Houghton Mifflin, 1960. (1916)

———. The vocabulary test as a measure of intelligence. *J. educ. Psychol.*, 1918, *9*, 452–466.

———. The use of intelligence tests in the Army. *Psychol. Bull.*, 1918, *15*, 177–187.

———. *The intelligence of school children.* Boston: Houghton Mifflin, 1919.

———, & Chase, J. M. The psychology, biology and pedagogy of genius. *Psychol. Bull.*, 1920, *17*, 397–409.

———. Intelligence and its measurement: A symposium. *J. educ. Psychol.*, 1921, *12*, 127–133.

———, & Whitmore, E. D. Age and grade norms for the national intelligence tests, scales A and B. *J. educ. Res.*, 1921, *3*, 124–132.

———. A new approach to the study of genius. *Psychol. Rev.*, 1922, *29*, 310–318.

———. The mental test as a psychological method. *Psychol. Rev.*, 1924, *31*, 93–117.

————, et al. *Genetic studies of genius*. Vol. I. *Mental and physical traits of a thousand gifted children*. Stanford, Calif.: Stanford University Press, 1925.

Cox, Catherine M., assisted by Lela O. Gillian, Ruth H. Livesay, & ————. *Genetic studies of genius*. Vol. 2. *The early mental traits of three hundred geniuses*. Stanford, Calif.: Stanford University Press, 1926.

————. The influence of nature and nurture upon intelligence scores: An evaluation of the evidence in Part I of the 1928 Yearbook of the National Society for the Study of Education. *J. educ. Psychol.*, 1928, *19*, 362–373.

Miles, Catherine C., & ————. Sex difference in the association of ideas. *Amer. J. Psychol.*, 1929, *41*, 165–206.

Burks, Barbara S., ————, et al. *Genetic studies of genius*. Vol. 3. *The promise of youth: Follow-up studies of a thousand gifted children*. Stanford, Calif.: Stanford University Press, 1930.

————, & Burks, Barbara S. The gifted child. In C. Murchison (Ed.), *Handbook of child psychology*. (2nd rev. ed.) Worcester, Mass.: Clark University Press, 1933, pp. 773–801. (1931)

————. Trails to psychology. In C. Murchison (Ed.), *A history of psychology in autobiography*. Vol. 2. Worcester, Mass.: Clark University Press, 1932, pp. 297–332.   **B**

————, & Buttenwieser, P. Personality factors in marital compatibility. *J. soc. Psychol.*, 1935, *6*, 143-171, 267–289.

————, & Miles, Catherine C. *Sex and personality: Studies in masculinity and femininity*. New York: McGraw-Hill, 1936. (Reprinted 1968)

McNemar, Q., & ————. Sex differences in variational tendency. *Genet. Psychol. Monogr.*, 1936, *18*, No. 1, 1–66.

————, & Merrill, Maud A. *Measuring intelligence*. Boston: Houghton Mifflin, 1959. (1937)

————, et al. *Psychological factors in marital happiness*. New York: McGraw-Hill, 1938.

————. Psychological approaches to the biography of genius. *Science*, 1940, *92*, 293–301.

————, & Oden, Melita H. The significance of deviates. II. Status of the California gifted group at the end of sixteen years. III. Correlates of adult achievement in the California gifted group. *Yearb. Nat. Soc. Stud. Educ.*, 1940, *39*(1), 67–74, 74–89.

————, & Tyler, Leona E. Psychological sex differences. In L. Carmichael (Ed.), *Manual of child psychology*. (2nd ed.) New York: Wiley, 1954, pp. 1064–1114. (1946)

————, & Oden, Melita H. *Genetic studies of genius*. Vol. 4. *The gifted child grows up: Twenty-five years' follow-up of a superior group*. Stanford, Calif.: Stanford University Press, 1947.

————. The discovery and encouragement of exceptional talent. *Amer. Psychologist*, 1954, *9*, 221–230. Reprinted in D. Wolfle (Ed.), *The discovery of talent*. Cambridge: Harvard University Press, 1969, pp. 1–23.

————. Scientists and nonscientists in a group of 800 gifted men. *Psychol. Monogr.*, 1954, *68*, No. 378.

————, & Oden, Melita H. *Genetic studies of genius*. Vol. 5. *The gifted group at mid-life: Thirty-five years' follow-up of the superior child*. Stanford, Calif.: Stanford University Press, 1959.

Beck & Molish, *Reflexes;* Cubberley, *Public Educators;* Dennis, *Psychology;* Dennis, *Readings Developmental;* Gruber, *Creative Thinking;* Jenkins & Paterson, *Individual Differences;* Pressey, *Casebook;* Rosenblith & Allinsmith, *Causes Behavior;* Sahakian, *Psychology;* Wrenn, *Contributions*

JOHANN NICHOLAS TETENS
1736-1807
German Philosopher (11)

Tetens, J. N. *Neudrucke seltener philosophischer Werke*. (4 vols.) Ed. by Kantgesellschaft. Berlin: Reuther & Reichard, 1911–1913.   **C**

————. *Die philosophischen Werke*. (4 vols.) Ed. by G. Tonelli. Hildesheim: Olms, 1968.   **C**

————. *Gedanken über einige Ursachen, warum in der Metaphysik nur wenige ausgemachte Wahrheiten sind.* Butzow: Berger, 1760.

————. *Abhandlung von den vorzüglichsten Beweisen des Daseins Gottes.* Wismar: Bödner, 1761.

————. *Commentatio de principio minimi.* Wismar: Bödner, 1769.

————. Ueber die allgemeine spekulativische Philosophie. (1775) In *Neudrucke seltener philosophischer Werke.* Vol. 4. Ed. by Kantgesellschaft. Berlin: Reuther & Reichard, 1913.

————. *Philosophische Versuche über die menschliche Natur und ihre Entwicklung.* (2 vols.) Berlin: Reuther & Reichard, 1913. (1777)

(SIR) GODFREY (HILTON) THOMSON
1881-1955
English Psychologist (23)

Brown, W., & Thomson, G. H. *The essentials of mental measurement.* (4th ed.) New York: Macmillan, 1940. (1911)

————. A comparison of the psycho-physical methods. *Brit. J. Psychol.,* 1912–1913, *5*, 203–241.

————. An inquiry into the best form of the method of serial groups. *Brit. J. Psychol.,* 1912–1913, *5*, 398–416.

————. Note on the probable error of Urban's formula for the method of just perceptible differences. *Brit. J. Psychol.,* 1913–1914, *6*, 217–222.

————. The accuracy of the phi-gamma process. *Brit. J. Psychol.,* 1914–1915, *7*, 44–55.

————. A hierarchy without a general factor. *Brit. J. Psychol.,* 1916–1917, *8*, 271–281.

————. The proof or disproof of the existence of general ability. *Brit. J. Psychol.,* 1917–1919, *9*, 321–336.

————. The hierarchy of abilities. *Brit. J. Psychol.,* 1917–1919, *9*, 337–344.

Garnett, J. C. M., & ————. Joint note on "the hierarchy of abilities." *Brit. J. Psychol.,* 1917–1919, *9*, 367–368.

————. On the degree of perfection of hierarchical order among correlational coefficients. *Biometrika,* 1919, *12*, 355–366.

————. On the cause of hierarchical order among the correlation coefficients of a number of varieties taken in pairs. *Proc. Roy. Soc.,* London, 1919, *95*, 400–408.

————. A direct deduction of the constant process used in the method of right and wrong cases. *Psychol. Rev.,* 1919, *26*, 454–464.

————. The general factor fallacy in psychology. *Brit. J. Psychol.,* 1919–1920, *10*, 319–326.

————. General versus group factors in mental activities. *Psychol. Rev.,* 1920, *27*, 173–190.

————. A new point of view in the interpretation of threshold measurements in psychophysics. *Psychol. Rev.,* 1920, *27*, 300–307.

————. Is thinking merely the action of language mechanisms? II. *Brit. J. Psychol.,* 1920–1921, *11*, 63–70.

————. The Northumberland mental tests. *Brit. J. Psychol.,* 1921–1922, *12*, 201–222.

————. A formula to correct for the effect of errors of measurement on the correlation of initial values with gains. *J. exp. Psychol.,* 1924, *7*, 321–324.

————. *Instinct, intelligence and character.* London: Allen & Unwin, 1924.

————. The interpretation of Burt's regression equation. *J. educ. Psychol.,* 1926, *17*, 301–308.

————. The mental age concept and the standardization of group tests. *Psychol. Rev.,* 1928, *35*, 398–413.

————. Fitting of frequency functions to Urban's lifted-weight results. *Amer. J. Psychol.,* 1929, *41*, 70–82.

————. *A modern philosophy of education.* London: Allen & Unwin, 1929.

————. The standardization of group tests and the scatter of intelligence quotients. *Brit. J. educ. Psychol.,* 1932, *2*, 92–112, 125–138.

————. Hotelling's method modified to give Spearman's *g. J. educ. Psychol.,* 1934, *25*, 366–374.

————. The theory of two factors versus the sampling theory of mental ability. *Nature,* London, 1934, *133,* 913.

————. The factorial analysis of human abilities. A rejoinder. *Hum. Factor,* 1935, *9,* 180–185, 361–363.

————. On complete families of correlation coefficients, and their tendency to zero tetrad-differences: Including a statement of the sampling theory of abilities. *Brit. J. Psychol.,* 1935–1936, *26,* 63–92.

————. Some points of mathematical technique in the factorial analysis of ability. *J. educ. Psychol.,* 1936, *27,* 37–54.

————. Maximising the specific factors in the analysis of ability. *Brit. J. educ. Psychol.,* 1938, *8,* 255–264.

————. *The factorial analysis of human ability.* (5th ed.) Boston: Houghton Mifflin, 1951. (1939)

————. *An analysis of performance test scores of a representative group of Scottish children.* London: University of London Press, 1940.

————. Weighting for battery reliability and prediction. *Brit. J. Psychol.,* 1940, *30,* 357–366.

————. The use of the Latin square in designing educational experiments. *Brit. J. educ. Psychol.,* 1941, *11,* 135–137.

————. Following up individual items in a group intelligence test. *Brit. J. Psychol.,* 1941–1942, *32,* 310–317.

————. The applicability of Karl Pearson's selection formulae in follow-up experiments. *Brit. J. Psychol.,* 1944, *34,* 105.

————. The trend of national intelligence. *Eugen. Rev.,* Cambridge, 1946, *38,* 9–18.

————. The maximum correlation of two weighted batteries (Hotelling's "most predictable criterion"). *Brit. J Psychol.* (Statist. Sec.), 1947, *1,* 27–34.

————. On estimating oblique factors. *Brit. J. Psychol.* (Statist. Sec.), 1949, *2,* 1–2.

————. Godfrey Thomson. In E. G. Boring *et al.* (Eds.), *A history of psychology in autobiography.* Vol. 4. Worcester, Mass.: Clark University Press, 1952, pp. 279–294.   **B**

Wiseman, *Intelligence*

EDWARD LEE THORNDIKE
1874-1949
American Psychologist (27)

Thorndike, E. L. *Selected writings from a connectionist's psychology.* New York: Appleton-Century-Crofts, 1949.   **C**

————. *Psychology and the science of education: Selected writings of Edward L. Thorndike.* Ed. by Geraldine M. Joncich. New York: Teachers College, Columbia University, 1962.   **C**

————. *Animal intelligence: Experimental studies.* New York: Macmillan, 1911. (1898) (Reprinted 1965)

————. The instinctive reaction of young chicks. *Psychol. Rev.,* 1899, *6,* 282–291.

Woodworth, R. S., & ————. Judgments of magnitude by comparison with a mental standard. *Psychol. Rev.,* 1900, *7,* 344–355. Reprinted in R. S. Woodworth, *Psychological issues: Selected papers of Robert S. Woodworth.* New York: Columbia University Press, 1939, pp. 61–71.

————. Mental fatigue. *Psychol. Rev.,* 1900, *7,* 466–482, 547–579.

Woodworth, R. S., & ————. The influence of improvement in one mental function upon the efficiency of other functions. *Psychol. Rev.,* 1901, *8,* 247–261, 384–395, 553–564. Reprinted in *Psychological issues: Selected papers of Robert S. Woodworth.* New York: Columbia University Press, 1939, pp. 335–369.

————. *Notes on child study.* (2nd ed.) New York: Macmillan, 1903. (1901)

————. The mental life of the monkeys. *Psychol. Monogr.,* 1901, No. 15.

————. *Educational psychology.* New York: Teachers College, Columbia University, 1914–1930. (1903)

———. *An introduction to the theory of mental and social measurements*. (2nd ed.) New York: Science Press, 1913. (1904)

———. Measurement of twins. *J. Phil.*, 1905, *2*, 547–553.

———. *The elements of psychology*. (2nd ed.) New York: Seiler, 1907. (1905)

———. *Principles of teaching based on psychology*. New York: Seiler, 1906.

———. *Empirical studies in the theory of measurements*. New York: Science Press, 1907.

———. The effect of practice in the case of a purely intellectual function. *Amer. J. Psychol.*, 1908, *19*, 374–384.

———. Darwin's contribution to psychology. *University of California Chronicle*, 1909, *12*, 65–80.

———. Handwriting. *Teachers College Rec.*, 1910, *11*(2), 1–81.

———. *Individuality*. Boston: Houghton Mifflin, 1911.

———. *Education: A first book*. New York: Macmillan, 1912.

———. The curve of work. *Psychol. Rev.*, 1912, *19*, 165–194.

———. The measurement of educational products. *School Rev.*, 1912, *20*, 289–299.

———. *The psychology of learning*. New York: Teachers College, Columbia University Press, 1913.

———. Ideo-motor action. *Psychol. Rev.*, 1913, *20*, 91–106.

———. *Educational psychology*. Vol. 1. *The original nature of man*. Vol. 2. *The psychology of learning*. Vol. 3. *Mental work and fatigue, and individual differences and their causes*. New York: Teachers College, Columbia University Press, 1913–1914.

———. *Educational psychology: Briefer course*. New York: Teachers College, Columbia University Press, 1914.

———. *Human nature club*. (2nd ed.) New York: Longmans, Green, 1901. (1900)

———. Measurements of ability to solve arithmetical problems. *J. genet. Psychol.*, 1914, *21*, 495–503.

———. Watson's "Behavior." *J. anim. Behav.*, 1915, *5*, 462–470.

———, Ruger, M. A., & McCall, W. A. The effects of outside air and recirculated air upon the intellectual achievement and improvement of school pupils (a second experiment). *School & Soc.*, 1916, *3*, 679–684; *4*, 260–264.

———, McCall, W. A., & Chapman, J. C. *Ventilation in relation to mental work*. New York: Teachers College, Columbia University, 1916.

———. Individual differences in judgments of the beauty of simple forms. *Psychol. Rev.*, 1917, *24*, 147–153.

———, & Kruse, P. J. The effect of humidification of a schoolroom upon the intellectual progress of pupils. *School & Soc.*, 1917, *5*, 657–660.

———. A standardized group examination of intelligence independent of language. *J. appl. Psychol.*, 1919, *3*, 13–32.

———. Intelligence examinations for college entrance. *J. educ. Res.*, 1920, *1*, 329–337.

———. Intelligence and its measurement: A symposium. *J. educ. Psychol.*, 1921, *12*, 124–127.

———. On the organization of intellect. *Psychol. Rev.*, 1921, *28*, 141–151.

———. *The psychology of arithmetic*. New York: Macmillan, 1922.

———. Practice effects in intelligence tests. *J. exp. Psychol.*, 1922, *5*, 101–107.

———. Intelligence scores of colored pupils in high schools. *School & Soc.*, 1923, *18*, 569–570.

———, et al. *The psychology of algebra*. New York: Macmillan, 1923.

———. Mental discipline in high school studies. *J. educ. Psychol.*, 1924, *15*, 1–22, 83–98.

———, et al. *The measurement of intelligence*. New York: Columbia University Press, 1926.

———. The law of effect. *Amer. J. Psychol.*, 1927, *39*, 212–222.

————. The influence of primacy. *J. exp. Psychol.*, 1927, *10*, 18–29.

————, et al. *Adult learning.* New York: Macmillan, 1928.

————. The resemblance of siblings in intelligence. *Yearb. Nat. Soc. Stud. Educ.*, 1928, *27*(1), 41–53.

————. *Human learning.* New York: Century, 1931. (Reprinted 1966)

————, et al. *The fundamentals of learning.* New York: Columbia University Press, 1932. (Reprinted 1970)

————. *Intelligence of animals and men.* Chicago: University of Chicago Press, 1932.

————. Reward and punishment in animal learning. *Comp. Psychol. Monogr.*, 1932, *8*, No. 39.

————. *An experimental study of rewards.* New York: Teachers College, Columbia University Press, 1933.

————. A theory of the action of the after-effects of a connection upon it. *Psychol. Rev.*, 1933, *40*, 434–439.

————. A proof of the law of effect. *Science*, 1933, *77*, 173–175.

————. The "spread" or "scatter" of the influence from a reward, in relation to Gestalt doctrines. *Science*, 1933, *77*, 368.

————. Rebounds from the target: More about "The prediction of vocational success." *Occupations*, 1934–1935, *13*, 329–333.

————, & Rock, R. T., Jr. Learning without awareness of what is being learned or intent to learn it. *J. exp. Psychol.*, 1934, *17*, 1–19.

————, Bregman, Elsie O., Lorge, I., Metcalfe, Zarda F., Robinson, Ellanore E., & Woodyard, Ella. *Prediction of vocational success.* New York: Commonwealth Fund, 1934.

————. The interests of adults. I. The permanence of interests. II. The interrelations of adult interests. *J. educ. Psychol.*, 1935, *26*, 401–410, 497–507.

————. *The psychology of wants, interests, and attitudes.* New York: Appleton, 1935.

————. *Adult interests.* New York: Macmillan, 1935.

Lorge, I., & ————. The influence of delay in the after-effect of a connection. *J. exp. Psychol.*, 1935, *18*, 186–194.

————, & Lorge, I. The influence of relevance and belonging. *J. exp. Psychol.*, 1935, *18*, 574–584.

————. Edward Lee Thorndike. In C. Murchison (Ed.), *A history of psychology in autobiography.* Vol. 3. Worcester, Mass.: Clark University Press, 1936, pp. 263–270.   **B**

————. Studies in the psychology of language. *Arch. Psychol.*, N. Y., 1938, No. 231.

————. *Your city.* New York: Harcourt, Brace, 1939.

————. *Human nature and the social order.* New York: Macmillan, 1940.

————. *Human nature and the social order.* Abridged by Geraldine J. Clifford. Cambridge: MIT Press, 1969. (1940)

————. Mental abilities. *Proc. Amer. Phil. Soc.*, 1941, *84*, 503–513.

————, & Woodyard, Ella. Differences within and between communities in the intelligence of the children. *J. educ. Psychol.*, 1942, *33*, 641–656.

————. James' influence on the psychology of perception and thought. *Psychol. Rev.*, 1943, *50*, 87–94.

————. *Man and his works.* Cambridge: Harvard University Press, 1943.

————. The causation of fraternal resemblance. *J. genet. Psychol.*, 1944, *64*, 249–264.

————, & Lorge, I. *The teacher's word book of 30,000 words.* New York: Teachers College, Columbia University, 1952. (1944)

————. Interests and abilities. *J. appl. Psychol.*, 1944, *28*, 43–52.

Anastasi, *Individual Differences;* Boe & Church, *Punishment;* Cubberley, *Public Educators;* Dennis, *Psychology;* Dennis, *Readings Developmental;* Grinder, *Genetic Psychology;* Herrnstein & Boring, *Source Book;* Jenkins & Paterson,

Individual Differences; Moore & Hartmann, *Industrial Psychology;* Park & Burgess, *Sociology;* Parsons, *Society;* Pressey, *Casebook;* Riopelle, *Problem Solving;* Sahakian, *Psychology*

LOUIS LEON THURSTONE
1887-1955
American Psychologist (27)

Thurstone, L. L. *The measurement of values.* Chicago: University of Chicago Press, 1959.
                                                    C

————. Mental tests for prospective telegraphers: A study of the diagnostic value of mental tests for predicting ability to learn telegraphy. *J. appl. Psychol.,* 1919, *3,* 110–117.

————. The learning curve equation. *Psychol. Monogr.,* 1919, *26,* No. 114.

————. The anticipatory aspect of consciousness. *J. Phil.,* 1919, *16,* 561–568.

————. Intelligence and its measurement: A symposium. *J. educ. Psychol.,* 1921, *12,* 201–207.

————. The predictive value of mental tests. *Educ. Rev.,* 1922, *63,* 11–22.

————. The stimulus-response fallacy in psychology. *Psychol. Rev.,* 1923, *30,* 354–369.

————. Contributions of Freudism to psychology. I. Influence of Freudism on theoretical psychology. *Psychol. Rev.,* 1924, *31,* 175–183.

————. *The nature of intelligence.* New York: Harcourt, Brace, 1924. (Reprinted 1960)

————. *The fundamentals of statistics.* New York: Macmillan, 1925.

————. A method of scaling psychological and educational tests. *J. educ. Psychol.,* 1925, *16,* 433–451.

————. The method of paired comparisons for social values. *J. abnorm. soc. Psychol.,* 1926–1927, *21,* 384–400. Reprinted in *The measurement of values, op. cit.,* pp. 67–81.

————. The mental age concept. *Psychol. Rev.,* 1926, *33,* 268–278.

————. Three psychophysical laws. *Psychol. Rev.,* 1927, *34,* 424–432. Reprinted in *The measurement of values, op. cit.,* pp. 61–66.

————. A law of comparative judgment. *Psychol. Rev.,* 1927, *34,* 273–286. Reprinted in *The measurement of values, op. cit.,* pp. 39–49.

————. The unit of measurement in educational scales. *J. educ. Psychol.,* 1927, *18,* 505–524.

————. A mental unit of measurement. *Psychol. Rev.,* 1927, *34,* 415–423. Reprinted in *The measurement of values, op. cit.,* pp. 50–56.

————. Psychophysical analysis. *Amer. J. Psychol.,* 1927, *38,* 368–389.

————. Equally often noticed differences. *J. educ. Psychol.,* 1927, *18,* 289–293. Reprinted in *The measurement of values, op. cit.,* pp. 57–60.

————. Scale construction with weighted observations. *J. educ. Psychol.,* 1928, *19,* 441–453.

————. Attitudes can be measured. *Amer. J. Sociol.,* 1928, *33,* 529–554. Reprinted in *The measurement of values, op. cit.,* pp. 215–233.

————. The measurement of opinion. *J. abnorm. soc. Psychol.,* 1928, *22,* 415–430. Reprinted in *The measurement of values, op. cit.,* pp. 234–247.

————. The phi-gamma hypothesis. *J. exp. Psychol.,* 1928, *11,* 293–305. Reprinted in *The measurement of values, op. cit.,* pp. 82–91.

————. An experimental study of nationality preferences. *J. gen. Psychol.,* 1928, *1,* 405–425. Reprinted in *The measurement of values, op. cit.,* pp. 248–265.

————. The absolute zero in intelligence measurement. *Psychol. Rev.,* 1928, *35,* 175–197.

————. Theory of attitude measurement. *Psychol. Rev.,* 1929, *36,* 222–241. Reprinted in *The measurement of values, op. cit.,* pp. 266–281.

————. Fechner's law and the method of equal-appearing intervals. *J. exp. Psychol.,* 1929, *12,* 214–224. Reprinted in *The measurement of values, op. cit.,* pp. 92–99.

————, & Ackerson, L. The mental growth curve for the Binet tests. *J. educ. Psychol.,* 1929, *20,* 569–583.

————, & Chave, E. J. *The measurement of attitude: A psychophysical method and some experiments with a scale for measuring attitude toward the church.* Chicago: University of Chicago Press, 1937. (1929)

————. A scale for measuring attitude toward the movies. *J. educ. Res.*, 1930, *22*, 89–94. Reprinted in *The measurement of values, op. cit.*, pp. 282–286.

————. The learning function. *J. gen. Psychol.*, 1930, *3*, 469–493.

————, & Thurstone, Thelma G. A neurotic inventory. *J. soc. Psychol.*, 1930, *1*, 3–30.

————. The relation between learning time and length of task. *Psychol. Rev.*, 1930, *37*, 44–53.

————. Rank order as a psychophysical method. *J. exp. Psychol.*, 1931, *14*, 187–201. Reprinted in *The measurement of values, op. cit.*, pp. 100–111.

————. The indifference function. *J. soc. Psychol.*, 1931, *2*, 139–167. Reprinted in *The measurement of values, op. cit.*, pp. 123–144.

————. The measurement of change in social attitude. *J. soc. Psychol.*, 1931, *2*, 230–235. Reprinted in *The measurement of values, op. cit.*, pp. 304–309.

————. Influence of motion pictures on children's attitudes. *J. soc. Psychol.*, 1931, *2*, 291–305. Reprinted in *The measurement of values, op. cit.*, pp. 309–319.

————. A multiple-factor study of vocational interests. *Personnel J.*, 1931, *10*, 198–205.

————. The measurement of social attitudes. *J. abnorm. soc. Psychol.*, 1931, *26*, 249–269. Reprinted in *The measurement of values, op. cit.*, pp. 287–303.

————, & Jenkins, R. L. *Order of birth, parentage, and intelligence.* Chicago: University of Chicago Press, 1931.

————. Multiple factor analysis. *Psychol. Rev.* 1931, *38*, 406–427.

————. *The reliability and validity of tests.* Ann Arbor, Mich.: Edwards Brothers, 1931. (Reprinted 1970)

————. Stimulus dispersions in the method of constant stimuli. *J. exp. Psychol.*, 1932, *15*, 284–297.

————, Richardson, M. W., Russell, J. T., & Stalnaker, J. M. *Manual of examination methods.* Chicago: University of Chicago Bookstore, 1933.

————. The error function in maze learning. *J. gen. Psychol.*, 1933, *9*, 288–301.

————. Unitary abilities. *J. gen. Psychol.*, 1934, *11*, 126–132.

————. The vectors of mind. *Psychol. Rev.*, 1934, *41*, 1–32.

————. *The vectors of mind: Multiple factor analysis for the isolation of primary traits.* Chicago: University of Chicago Press, 1935.

————. A new conception of intelligence. *Educ. Rec.*, 1936, *17*, 441–450.

————. The factorial isolation of primary abilities. *Psychometrika*, 1936, *1*, 175–182.

————. Psychology as a quantitative rational science. *Science*, 1937, *85*, 228–232. Reprinted in *The measurement of values, op. cit.*, pp. 3–11.

————. Current misuse of the factorial methods. *Psychometrika*, 1937, *2*, 73–76.

————. The perceptual factor. *Psychometrika*, 1938, *3*, 1–17.

————. A new rotational method in factor analysis. *Psychometrika*, 1938, *3*, 199–218.

————. *Primary mental abilities.* Chicago: University of Chicago Press, 1938.

————. Shifty and mathematical components: A critique of Anastasi's monograph on the influence of specific experience upon mental organization. *Psychol. Bull.*, 1938, *35*, 223–236.

————. Current issues in factor analysis. *Psychol. Bull.*, 1940, *37*, 189–236.

————. Experimental study of simple structure. *Psychometrika*, 1940, *5*, 153–168.

————, & Thurstone, Thelma G. *Factorial studies of intelligence.* Chicago: University of Chicago Press, 1941. (Reprinted 1970)

——. *A factorial study of perception.* Chicago: University of Chicago Press, 1944. (Reprinted 1970)

——. Second-order factors. *Psychometrika,* 1944, *9,* 71–100.

——. A multiple group method of factoring the correlation matrix. *Psychometrika,* 1945, *10,* 73–78.

——. The effects of selection in factor analysis. *Psychometrika,* 1945, *10,* 165–198.

——. The prediction of choice. *Psychometrika,* 1945, *10,* 237–253. Reprinted in *The measurement of values, op. cit.,* pp. 145–160.

——. Factor analysis and body types. *Psychometrika,* 1946, *11,* 15–21.

——. A single plane method of rotation. *Psychometrika,* 1946, *11,* 71–79.

——. Theories of intelligence. *Sci. Mon.,* N.Y., 1946, *62,* 101–112.

——. *Multiple-factor analysis: A development and expansion of the vectors of mind.* Chicago: University of Chicago Press, 1947.

——. Factorial analysis of body measurements. *Amer. J. Phys. Anthrop.,* 1947, *5,* 15–28.

——. Psychological implication of factor analysis. *Amer. Psychologist,* 1948, *3,* 402–408. Reprinted in M. Marx (Ed.), *Psychological theory: Contemporary readings.* New York: Macmillan, 1959, pp. 276–284.

——. The Rorschach in psychological science. *J. abnorm. soc. Psychol.,* 1948, *43,* 471–475.

——. Psychophysical methods. In T. G. Andrews (Ed.), *Methods of psychology.* New York: Wiley, 1948, pp. 124–157.

——, & Pemberton, Carol. An analysis of mechanical aptitude. *Psychomet. Lab. Rep. Univer. Chicago,* 1951, No. 62.

——. Factor analysis as a scientific method. *Psychomet. Lab. Rep. Univer. Chicago,* 1951, No. 65.

——. Experimental tests of temperament. In G. Ekman *et al.* (Eds.), *Essays in psychology.* Upsala: Almquist & Wiksells, 1951, pp. 248–262.

——. The dimensions of temperament. *Psychometrika,* 1951, *16,* 11–20.

——. L. L. Thurstone. In E. G. Boring *et al.* (Eds.), *A history of psychology in autobiography.* Vol. 4. Worcester, Mass.: Clark University Press, 1952, pp. 295–321.   **B**

——. Creative talent. In L. L. Thurstone (Ed.), *Applications of psychology: Essays to honor Walter V. Bingham.* New York: Harper, 1952, pp. 18–37.

——. A method of factoring without communalities. In *Proceedings of the 1954 invitational conference on testing problems.* Princeton, N.J.: Educational Testing Service, 1955, pp. 59–62.

——. The measurement of values. *Psychol. Rev.,* 1954, *61,* 47–58. Reprinted in *The measurement of values, op. cit.,* pp. 182–194.

——. An analytical method for simple structure. *Psychometrika,* 1954, *19,* 173–182.

——. The criterion problem in personality research. *Educ. psychol. Measmt,* 1955, *15,* 353–361.

Jones, L. V., & ——. The psychophysics of semantics: An experimental investigation. *J. appl. Psychol.,* 1955, *39,* 31–36.

——, & Jones, L. V. The rational origin for measuring subjective values. *J. Amer. Stat. Ass.,* 1957, *52,* 458–471.

Anastasi, *Individual Differences;* Beck & Molish, *Reflexes;* Jenkins & Paterson, *Individual Differences;* Miller, *Mathematics;* Moore & Hartmann, *Industrial Psychology;* O'Brien & Schrag, *Sociology;* Rosenblith & Allinsmith, *Causes Behavior;* Sahakian, *Psychology;* Valentine, *Experimental*

DIETRICH TIEDEMANN
1748-1803
German Philosopher (11)

Tiedemann, D. *Geist der spekulativen Philosophie.* (6 vols.) Marburg: Neue Akademische Buchhandlung, 1791–1797.   **C**

——. *Versuch einer Erklärung des Ursprunges der Sprache.* Riga: Hartknoch, 1772.

———. *System der stoischen Philosophie.* (3 vols.) Leipzig: Weidmann, 1776.

———. *Untersuchungen über den Menschen.* (3 vols.) Leipzig: Weidmann, 1777–1778. (Reprinted 1969)

———. *Griechenlands erste Philosophen.* Leipzig: Weidmann & Reich, 1780.

———. *Dialogorum Platonis argumenta.* Biponti: Typographia societatis, 1786.

———. *Tiedemann's record of infant-life: An English version of the French translation and commentary by Bernard Perez.* Ed. by L. Soldan. Syracuse, N.Y.: Bardeen, 1890. (1787)

———. *Tiedemann's Beobachtungen über die Entwicklung der Seelenthätigkeit bei Kindern.* Ed. by W. Rein. Altenburg: Bonde, 1897. (1787)

———. *Disputatio de quaestione quae fuerit artium magicarum origo.* Marburg: Nova officina Libraria Academica, 1787.

———. Tiedemann's observations on the development of the mental faculties of children. (1787) Trans. by Suzanne Langer & C. Murchison. *J. genet. Psychol.,* 1927, *34,* 205–230.

———. *Theätet oder über das menschliche Wissen: Ein Beitrag zur Vernunft-Kritik.* Brussels: Culture et Civilisation, 1968. (1794)

———. *Handbuch der Psychologie.* Ed. by L. Wachler. Leipzig: Barth, 1804.

Dennis, *Readings Developmental*

EDWARD BRADFORD TITCHENER
1867-1927
American Psychologist (27)

Titchener, E. B. The Leipsic school of experimental psychology. *Mind,* 1892, *1*(N.S.), 206–234.

———. Anthropometry and experimental psychology. *Phil. Rev.,* 1893, *2,* 187–192.

———. Two recent criticisms of modern psychology. *Phil. Rev.,* 1893, *2,* 450–458.

———. Zur Chronometrie des Erkennungsactes. *Phil. Stud.,* 1893, *8,* 139–144.

———. The psychology of "relation." *Phil. Rev.,* 1894, *3,* 193–196.

———. Affective attention. *Phil. Rev.,* 1894, *3,* 429–433.

———. Simple reactions. *Mind,* 1895, *4*(N.S.), 74–81.

———. The type-theory of the simple reaction. *Mind,* 1895, *4*(N.S.), 506–514; 1896, *5*(N.S.), 236–241.

———. *An outline of psychology.* (New ed.) New York: Macmillan, 1902. (1896) (Reprinted 1970)

———. *The primer of psychology.* New York: Macmillan, 1898.

———. The postulates of a structural psychology. *Phil. Rev.,* 1898, *7,* 449–465.

———. Zur Kritik der Wundt'schen Gefühlslehre. *Z. Psychol.,* 1899, *19,* 321–326.

———. Structural and functional psychology. *Phil. Rev.,* 1899, *8,* 290–299.

———. *Experimental psychology: A manual of laboratory practice.* (2 vols. in 4) New York: Macmillan, 1901–1905. (Reprinted 1967)

———. Ein Versuch, die Methode der paarweisen Vergleichung auf die verschiedenen Gefühlsrichtungen anzuwenden. *Phil. Stud.,* 1902, *20,* 382–406.

———. Were the earliest organic movements conscious or unconscious? *Pop. Sci. Mon.,* 1902, *60,* 458–469.

Bentley, I. M., & ———. Ebbinghaus' explanation of beats. *Amer. J. Psychol.,* 1904, *15,* 62–71.

———. The problems of experimental psychology. *Science,* 1904, *20*(N.S.), 786–798.

———. The problems of experimental psychology. *Amer. J. Psychol.,* 1905, *16,* 220–224.

———, & Pyle, W. H. The effect of imperceptible shadows on the judgment of distance. *Proc. Amer. Phil. Soc.,* 1907, *46,* 94–109.

———. *Lectures on the elementary psychology of feeling and attention.* New York: Macmillan, 1908.

———. The tri-dimensional theory of feeling. *Amer. J. Psychol.,* 1908, *19,* 213–231.

———. *A textbook of psychology*. (Rev. ed.) New York: Macmillan, 1910. (1909)

———. *Lectures on the experimental psychology of thought processes*. New York: Macmillan, 1909.

———. The psychophysics of climate. *Amer. J. Psychol.*, 1909, *20*, 1–14.

———. The past decade of experimental psychology. *Amer. J. Psychol.*, 1910, *21*, 404–421.

———. A note on the consciousness of self. *Amer. J. Psychol.*, 1911, *22*, 540–552.

———. Description *versus* statement of meaning. *Amer. J. Psychol.*, 1912, *23*, 165–182.

———. Prolegomena to a study of introspection. *Amer. J. Psychol.*, 1912, *23*, 427–448.

———. The schema of introspection. *Amer. J. Psychol.*, 1912, *23*, 485–508.

———. The method of examination. *Amer. J. Psychol.*, 1913, *24*, 429–440.

———. Memory and imagination: A restatement. *Psychol. Rev.*, 1912, *19*, 158–163.

———. Psychology: Science or technology? *Pop. Sci. Mon.*, 1914, *84*, 39–51.

———. On "psychology as the behaviorist views it." *Proc. Amer. Phil. Soc.*, 1914, *53*, 1–17.

———. A note on sensation and sentiment. *Amer. J. Psychol.*, 1914, *25*, 301–307.

———. An historical note on the James-Lange theory of emotion. *Amer. J. Psychol.*, 1914, *25*, 427–447.

———. *A beginner's psychology*. New York: Macmillan, 1915.

———. Sensation and system. *Amer. J. Psychol.*, 1915, *26*, 258–267.

———. On ethnological tests of sensation and perception, with special reference to tests of color vision and tactile discrimination in the reports of the Cambridge Anthropological Expedition to Torres Straits. *Proc. Amer. Phil. Soc.*, 1916, *55*, 204–236.

———. A note on the compensation of odors. *Amer. J. Psychol.*, 1916, *27*, 435–436.

———. A note on the sensory character of black. *J. Phil.*, 1916, *13*, 113–121.

———. A further word on black. *J. Phil.*, 1916, *13*, 649–655.

———. Professor Stumpf's affective psychology. *Amer. J. Psychol.*, 1917, *28*, 263–277.

———. The psychological concept of clearness. *Psychol. Rev.*, 1917, *24*, 43–61.

———. Brentano and Wundt: Empirical and experimental psychology. *Amer. J. Psychol.*, 1921, *32*, 108–120.

———. Wilhelm Wundt. *Amer. J. Psychol.*, 1921, *32*, 161–178. **B**

———. Functional psychology and the psychology of act. I. II. *Amer. J. Psychol.*, 1921, *32*, 519–542; 1922, *33*, 43–83.

———. Mach's "Lectures on psychophysics." *Amer. J. Psychol.*, 1922, *33*, 213–222.

———. A note on Wundt's doctrine of creative synthesis. *Amer. J. Psychol.*, 1922, *33*, 351–360.

———. Visual intensity. *Amer. J. Psychol.*, 1923, *34*, 310–311.

———. Relearning after forty-six years. *Amer. J. Psychol.*, 1923, *34*, 468–469.

———. The term "attensity." *Amer. J. Psychol.*, 1924, *35*, 156.

———. Experimental psychology: A retrospect. *Amer. J. Psychol.*, 1925, *36*, 313–323.

———. Empirical and experimental psychology. *J. gen. Psychol.*, 1928, *1*, 176–177.

———. *Systematic psychology: Prolegomena.* New York: Macmillan, 1929.

Beck & Molish, *Reflexes*; Dennis, *Psychology*; Herrnstein & Boring, *Source Book*; Mandler & Mandler, *Thinking*; Miller, *Mathematics*; Russell, *Motivation*; Sahakian, *Psychology*; Shipley, *Classics*

EDWARD CHACE TOLMAN
1886-1959
American Psychologist (27)

Tolman, E. C. *Collected papers in psychology.* Berkeley, Calif.: University of California Press, 1951. (Reprinted 1958 as *Behavior and psychological man.*) **Bl C**

——. More concerning the temporal relations of meaning and imagery. *Psychol. Rev.,* 1917, *24,* 114–138.

——. Retroactive inhibition as affected by conditions of learning. *Psychol. Monogr.,* 1917, *25,* No. 107.

——. Nerve process and cognition. *Psychol. Rev.,* 1918, *25,* 423–442.

——. Instinct and purpose. *Psychol. Rev.,* 1920, *27,* 217–233.

——. Can instincts be given up in psychology? *J. abnorm. soc. Psychol.,* 1922, *17,* 139–152. Reprinted in *Collected papers, op. cit.,* pp. 9–22.

——. A new formula for behaviorism. *Psychol. Rev.,* 1922, *29,* 44–53. Reprinted in *Collected papers, op. cit.,* pp. 1–8.

——. The effects of underlearning upon short- and long-time retentions. *J. exp. Psychol.,* 1923, *6,* 466–474.

——. The nature of instinct. *Psychol. Bull.,* 1923, *20,* 200–216.

——. A behavioristic account of the emotions. *Psychol. Rev.,* 1923, *30,* 217–227. Reprinted in *Collected papers, op. cit.,* pp. 23–31.

——. The inheritance of maze-learning ability in rats. *J. comp. Psychol.,* 1924, *4,* 1–18.

——. Behaviorism and purpose. *J. Phil.,* 1925, *22,* 36–41. Reprinted in *Collected papers, op. cit.,* pp. 32–37.

——Purpose and cognition: The determiners of animal learning. *Psychol. Rev.,* 1925, *32,* 285–297. Reprinted in *Collected papers, op. cit.,* pp. 38–47.

——. The nature of the fundamental drives. *J. abnorm. soc. Psychol.,* 1925–1926, *20,* 349–358.

——. A behavioristic theory of ideas. *Psychol. Rev.,* 1926, *33,* 352–369. Reprinted in *Collected papers, op. cit.,* pp. 48–62.

——. Habit formation and higher mental processes in animals. *Psychol. Bull.,* 1927, *24,* 1–35; 1928, *25,* 24–53.

——, & Nyswander, Dorothy B. The reliability and validity of maze-measures for rats. *J. comp. Psychol.,* 1927, *7,* 425–460.

——. A behaviorist's definition of consciousness. *Psychol. Rev.,* 1927, *34,* 433–439. Reprinted in *Collected papers, op. cit.,* pp. 63–68.

——. Purposive behavior. *Psychol. Rev.,* 1928, *35,* 524–530.

——, & Honzik, C. H. "Insight" in rats. *Univer. Calif. Publ. Psychol.,* 1930, *4,* 215–232.

——. Honzik, C. H., & Robinson, E. W. The effect of degrees of hunger upon the order of elimination of long and short blinds. *Univer. Calif. Publ. Psychol.,* 1930, *4,* 189–202.

——, & Honzik, C. H. Degrees of hunger, reward and non-reward, and maze learning in rats. *Univer. Calif. Publ. Psychol.,* 1930, *4,* 241–257.

——. Maze performance a function of motivation and of reward as well as of knowledge of the maze paths. *J. gen. Psychol.,* 1930, *4,* 338–342.

——, & Honzik, C. H. Introduction and removal of reward, and maze performance in rats. *Univer. Calif. Publ. Psychol.,* 1930, *4,* 257–275.

——. *Purposive behavior in animals and men.* New York: Century, 1932. (Reprinted 1967)

——, Hall, C. S., & Brentnall, E. P. A disproof of the law of effect and a substitution of the laws of emphasis, motivation, and disruption. *J. exp. Psychol.,* 1932, *15,* 601–614.

——. Lewin's concept of vectors. *J. gen. Psychol.,* 1932, *7,* 3–15.

——. The law of effect: A reply to Dr. Goodenough. *J. exp. Psychol.,* 1933, *16,* 463–470.

————, & Horowitz J. A reply to Mr. Koffka. *Psychol. Bull.,* 1933, *30,* 459–465.

————, & Krechevsky, I. Means-end-readiness and hypothesis: A contribution to comparative psychology. *Psychol. Rev.,* 1933, *40,* 60–70.

————. Sign-Gestalt or conditioned reflex? *Psychol. Rev.,* 1933, *40,* 246–255. Reprinted in *Collected papers, op. cit.,* pp. 69–76.

————. Gestalt and sign-Gestalt. *Psychol. Rev.,* 1933, *40,* 391–411. Reprinted in *Collected papers, op. cit.,* pp. 77–93.

————. Theories of learning. In F. A. Moss (Ed.), *Comparative psychology.* New York: Prentice-Hall, 1934, pp. 367–408.

————. Backward elimination of errors in two successive discrimination habits. *Univer. Calif. Publ. Psychol.,* 1934, *6,* 145–152.

————. Psychology versus immediate experience. *Phil. Sci.,* 1935, *2,* 356–380. Reprinted in *Collected papers, op. cit.,* pp. 94–114.

————, & Brunswik, E. The organism and the causal texture of the environment. *Psychol. Rev.,* 1935, *42,* 43–77. Reprinted in K. R. Hammond (Ed.), *The psychology of Egon Brunswik.* New York: Holt, Rinehart & Winston, 1966, pp. 457–486.

————. Connectionism: Wants, interests, and attitudes. *J. Pers.,* 1936, *4,* 245–253.

Honzik, C. H., & ————. The perception of spatial relations by the rat: A type of response not easily explained by conditioning. *J. comp. Psychol.,* 1936, *22,* 287–318.

————. Operational behaviorism and current trends in psychology. *Proc. 25th Anniv. Celebr. Inaug. Grad. Stud. Univer. So. Calif.* Los Angeles: University of Southern California Press, 1936, pp. 89–103. Reprinted in *Collected papers, op. cit.,* pp. 115–129, and in M. H. Marx (Ed.), *Psychological theory: Contemporary readings.* New York: Macmillan, 1951, pp. 87–102.

————. An operational analysis of "demands." *Erkenntnis,* 1937, *6,* 383–392.

————. Demands and conflicts. *Psychol. Rev.,* 1937, *44,* 158–169.

————. The acquisition of string-pulling by rats—conditioned response or sign-Gestalt? *Psychol. Rev.,* 1937, *44,* 195–211. Reprinted in *Collected papers, op. cit.,* pp. 130–143.

Honzik, C. H., & ————. The action of punishment in accelerating learning. *J. comp. Psychol.,* 1938, *26,* 187–200.

————. The determiners of behavior at choice point. *Psychol. Rev.,* 1938, *45,* 1–41. Reprinted in *Collected papers, op. cit.,* pp. 144–178.

————. A reply to Professor Guthrie. *Psychol. Rev.,* 1938, *45,* 163–164.

————. The law of effect: A round table discussion. II. *Psychol. Rev.,* 1938, *45,* 200–203.

————. Physiology, psychology and sociology. *Psychol. Rev.,* 1938, *45,* 228–241. Reprinted in *Collected papers, op. cit.,* pp. 179–189.

————. Prediction of vicarious trial and error by means of the schematic sowbug. *Psychol. Rev.,* 1939, *46,* 318–336. Reprinted in *Collected papers, op. cit.,* pp. 190–206.

————. Spatial angle and vicarious trial and error. *J. comp. Psychol.,* 1940, *30,* 129–135.

————. Motivation, learning, and adjustment. *Proc. Amer. Phil. Soc.,* 1941, *84,* 543–563.

————, Grier, F. M., & Levin, M. Individual differences in emotionality, hypothesis formation, vicarious trial and error, and visual discrimination learning in rats. *Comp. Psychol. Monogr.,* 1941, *17,* No. 3.

————. Psychological man. *J. soc. Psychol.,* 1941, *13,* 205–218. Reprinted in *Collected papers, op. cit.,* pp. 207–218.

————. Discrimination vs. learning and the schematic sowbug. *Psychol. Rev.,* 1941, *48,* 367–382.

————, & Minium, E. VTE in rats: Overlearning and difficulty of discrimination. *J. comp. Psychol.,* 1942, *34,* 301–306.

————. *Drives toward war.* New York: Appleton, 1942.

————. A drive-conversion diagram. *Psychol. Rev.,* 1943, *50,* 503–513. Reprinted in *Collected papers, op. cit.,* pp. 219–227.

————, & Ritchie, B. F. Correlation between VTE's on a maze and on a visual discrimination apparatus. *J. comp. Psychol.*, 1943, *36*, 91–98.

Geier, F. M., & ————. Goal distance and restless activity. I. The goal gradient of restless activity. *J. comp. Psychol.*, 1943, *35*, 197–204.

————. A stimulus-expectancy need-cathexis psychology. *Science*, 1945, *101*, 160–166. Reprinted in *Collected papers, op. cit.*, pp. 228–240.

————, Ritchie, B. F., & Kalish, D. Studies in spatial learning. I. Orientation and the short cut. II. Place learning vs. response learning. IV. The transfer of place learning to other starting paths. V. Response learning vs. place learning by the non-correction method. *J. exp. Psychol.*, 1946, *36*, 13–25, 221–229 ; 1947, *37*, 39–47, 285–292.

————. Cognitive maps in rats and men. *Psychol. Rev.*, 1948, *55*, 189–208. Reprinted in *Collected papers, op. cit.*, pp. 241–264.

————, & Gleitman, H. Studies in spatial learning. VII. Place and response learning under different degrees of motivation. *J. exp. Psychol.*, 1949, *39*, 653–659.

————, & Gleitman, H. Studies in learning and motivation. I. Equal reinforcements in both end-boxes, followed by shock in one end-box. *J. exp. Psychol.*, 1949, *39*, 810–819.

————. Discussion: Interrelationships between perception and personality: A symposium. *J. Pers.*, 1949, *18*, 48–50.

————. The psychology of social learning. *J. soc. Issues*, 1949, *5*, Suppl. No. 3, 5–18.

————. There is more than one kind of learning. *Psychol. Rev.*, 1949, *56*, 144–155.

————. The nature and functioning of wants. *Psychol. Rev.*, 1949, *56*, 357–369.

————. A psychological model. In T. Parsons & E. A. Shils (Eds.), *Toward a general theory of action*. Cambridge: Harvard University Press, 1951, pp. 279–361.

————. Edward Chace Tolman. In E. G. Boring *et al.* (Eds.), *A history of psychology in auto-biography*. Vol. 4. Worcester, Mass.: Clark University Press, 1952, pp. 323–339.   **B**

————. A theoretical analysis of the relations between sociology and psychology. *J. abnorm. soc. Psychol.*, 1952, *47*, 291–298.

————. A cognition-motivation model. *Psychol. Rev.*, 1952, *59*, 389–400.

————, & Postman, L. Learning. *Annu. rev. Psychol.*, 1954, *5*, 27–56.

————. Principles of performance. *Psychol. Rev.*, 1955, *62*, 315–326.

Postman, L., & ————. Brunswik's probabilistic functionalism. In S. Koch (Ed.), *Psychology: A study of a science*. Study 1. *Conceptual and systematic*. Vol. 1. *Sensory, perceptual, and physiological formulations*. New York: McGraw-Hill, 1959, pp. 502–564.

————. Principles of purposive behavior. In S. Koch (Ed.), *Psychology: A study of a science*. Study 1. *Conceptual and systematic*. Vol. 2. *General systematic formulations, learning, and special processes*. New York: McGraw-Hill, 1959, pp. 92–157.

Bindra & Stewart, *Motivation ;* Parsons, *Society ;* Perez, *Readings ;* Russell, *Motivation ;* Sahakian, *Psychology ;* Zajonc, *Animal Social*

LEONARD THOMPSON TROLAND
1889-1932
American Psychologist (21)

Troland, L. T. A definite physico-chemical hypothesis to explain visual response. *Amer. J. Physiol.*, 1913, *32*, 8–40.

————. The Freudian psychology and psychical research. *J. abnorm. Psychol.*, 1913–1914, *8*, 405–428.

————. Adaptation and the chemical theory of sensory response. *Amer. J. Psychol.*, 1914, *25*, 500–527.

————. The theory of practice of the artificial pupil. *Psychol. Rev.*, 1915, *22*, 167–176.

————. The absence of the Purkinje phenomenon in the fovea. *J. Franklin Inst.*, 1916, *182*, 111–112.

————. Apparent brightness: Its conditions and properties. *Trans. Illum. Eng. Soc.*, 1916, *11*, 947–966.

————. Philosophy and the world's peace. *J. Phil.*, 1916, *13*, 421–437.

————. On the measurement of visual stimulation intensities. *J. exp. Psychol.*, 1917, *2*, 1–33.

————. The nature of the visual receptor process. *J. opt. Soc. Amer.*, 1917, *1*, 3–15.

————. Biological enigmas and the theory of enzyme action. *Amer. Naturalist*, 1917, *51*, 321–350.

————. Paraphysical monism. *Phil. Rev.*, 1918, *27*, 39–62.

————. The heterochromatic differential threshold for brightness: I. Experimental. II. Theoretical. *Psychol. Rev.*, 1918, *25*, 305–329, 359–377.

————. The psychology of color, in relation to illumination. *Trans. Illum. Eng. Soc.*, 1918, *13*, 21–37.

————. A system for explaining affective phenomena. *J. abnorm. Psychol.*, 1920, *14*, 376–387.

————. The enigma of color vision. *Amer. J. physiol. Opt.*, 1920, *1*, 317–377; 1921, *2*, 23–48.

————. The "all or none" law in visual response. *J. opt. Soc. Amer.*, 1920, *4*, 161–186.

————. A rejoinder to Drs. Ferree and Rand's note. *Psychol. Bull.*, 1920, *17*, 135–142.

————. The physical basis of nerve functions. *Psychol. Rev.*, 1920, *27*, 323–350.

————. Henri Piéron on the physiological principles underlying the study of light. *Trans. Illum. Eng. Soc.*, 1921, *16*, 44–50.

————. The colors produced by equilibrium photopic adaptation. *J. exp. Psychol.*, 1921, *4*, 344–390.

————. The present status of visual science. *Bull. Nat. Res. Council*, 1922, *5*(27), 1–120.

————. Brilliance and chroma in relation to zone theories of vision. *J. opt. Soc. Amer.*, 1922, *6*, 3–26.

————. Helmholtz's contribution to physiological optics. *J. opt. Soc. Amer.*, 1922, *6*, 327–335.

————. Report of committee on colorimetry for 1920–1921. *J. opt. Soc. Amer.*, 1922, *6*, 527–596.

————. Psychophysics, the key to physics and metaphysics. *J. Wash. Acad. Sci.*, 1922, *12*, 141–162.

————. The significance of psychical monism for psychological theory. *Psychol. Rev.*, 1922, *29*, 201–211.

————, & Campbell, N. The interrelations of modern physics and modern psychology. *J. Franklin Inst.*, 1924, *197*, 479–504, 817–826.

————. The optics of the nervous system. *J. opt. Soc. Amer.*, 1924, *8*, 389–410. Also in *Amer. J. Physiol. Opt.*, 1924, *5*, 127–153.

————. *The mystery of mind*. New York: Van Nostrand, 1926.

————. Psychology of natural color motion pictures. *Amer. J. Physiol. Opt.*, 1926, *7*, 375–382.

————. *The fundamentals of human motivation*. New York: Van Nostrand, 1928.

————. Vision. I. Visual phenomena and their stimulus correlations. In C. Murchison (Ed.), *The foundations of experimental psychology*. Worcester, Mass.: Clark University Press, 1929, pp. 169–215.

————. The psychophysiology of auditory qualities and attributes. *J. gen. Psychol.*, 1929, *2*, 28–58.

————. Optics as seen by a psychologist. *J. opt. Soc. Amer.*, 1929, *18*, 223–236.

————. *Psychophysiology: A survey of modern scientific psychology.* Vol. 1. *Problems of psychology and perception.* Vol. 2. *Sensation.* Vol. 3. *Cerebration and action.* New York: Van Nostrand, 1929–1932. (Reprinted 1969)

————. Motivation. In C. Murchison (Ed.), *Psychologies of 1930*. Worcester, Mass.: Clark University Press, 1930, pp. 460–480.

——. Psychophysiological considerations relating to the theory of hearing. *J. acoust. Soc. Amer.,* 1930, *1,* 301–310.

——. An analysis of the literature concerning the dependency of visual functions upon illumination intensity. *Trans. Illum. Eng. Soc.,* 1931, *26,* 107–196.

——. Vision. I. Visual phenomena and their stimulus correlations. In C. Murchison (Ed.), *A handbook of general experimental psychology.* Worcester, Mass.: Clark University Press, 1934, pp. 653–703.

——. *A technique for the experimental study of telepathy and other alleged clairvoyant processes. A report on the work done at the Harvard Psychological Laboratory, under the gift of Mrs. John Wallace Riddell and the Hodgson Fund.* Albany, N.Y.: Brandlow Printing. (n.d.)

Bindra & Stewart, *Motivation*

EDWIN BURKET TWITMYER
1873-1943
American Psychologist (14)

Twitmyer, E. B. *A study of the knee-jerk.* Philadelphia: Winston, 1902.

——. Knee jerks without stimulation of the patellar tendon. *Psychol. Bull.,* 1905, *2,* 43–44.

——. Clinical studies of retarded children. *Psychol. Clin.,* 1907, *1,* 97–103.

——. The psychologist's approach to the problem of mental deficiency. *Proc. Addr. Amer. Ass. Stud. Feeblemind.,* 1927, *32,* 31–40.

——. The correction of speech defects. In R. A. Brotemarkle (Ed.), *Clinical psychology: Studies in honor of Lightner Witmer.* Philadelphia, Pa.: University of Pennsylvania Press, 1931, pp. 83–90.

——, & Nathanson, Y. S. *Correction of defective speech.* Philadelphia: Blakiston, 1932.

——, & Nathanson, Y. S. The determination of laterality. *Psychol. Clin.,* 1933–1934, *22,* 141–148.

——, & Nathanson, Y. S. Auditory perceptibility: Acuity and dominance. *Psychol. Clin.,* 1933–1934, *22,* 220–231.

(SIR) EDWARD BURNETT TYLOR
1832-1917
English Anthropologist (13)

Tylor, E. B. *Anahuac, or, Mexico and the Mexicans, ancient and modern.* London: Green, Longmans, Roberts, 1861. (Reprinted 1970)

——. Wild men and beast-children. *Anthrop. Rev.,* London, 1863, *1,* 21–32.

——. *Researches into the early history of mankind and the development of civilization.* London: Murray, 1865.

——. *Researches into the early history of mankind and the development of civilization.* (Abridged) Ed. by P. Bohannan. Chicago: University of Chicago Press, 1964. (1865)

——. The religion of savages. *Fortn. Rev.,* 1866, *6,* 71–86.

——. On the survival of savage thought in modern civilization. *Proc. Roy. Inst. Great Britain,* 1866–1869, *5,* 522–535.

——. On phenomena of the higher civilization traceable to a rudimentary origin among savage tribes. *Anthrop. Rev.,* 1867, *5,* 303–314.

——. The philosophy of religion among the lower races of mankind. *J. ethnol. Soc. London,* 1870, *2,* 369–381.

——. *Primitive culture: Researches into the development of mythology, philosophy, religion, language, art, and custom.* (2 vols.) Gloucester, Mass.: Smith, 1958. (1871)

——. Mr. Spencer's "Principles of Sociology." *Mind,* 1877, *2,* 141–156.

——. *Anthropology.* (2 vols). London: Watts, 1937. (1881)

——. *Anthropology.* Abridged by L. A. White. Ann Arbor, Mich.: University of Michigan Press, 1965. (1881)

——. On a method of investigating the development of institutions; applied to laws of marriage and descent. *J. Roy. Anthrop. Inst. Great Britain*, 1889, *18*, 245–272. Reprinted in F. W. Moore (Ed.), *Readings in cross-cultural methodology*. New Haven: HRAF Press, 1961, pp. 1–43.

Coser & Rosenberg, *Sociological Theory*; Fried, *Anthropology*; Goldschmidt, *Mankind*; Kroeber, *Source Book*; Thomas, *Source Book*

(BARON) JAKOB JOHANN VON UEXKULL
1864-1944
German Biologist (19)

Uexküll, J. v. Physiologische Untersuchungen an Eledone moschata. *Z. Biol.*, 1891, *28*, 550–566; 1894, *30*, 179–186, 317–327; 1895, *31*, 584–609.

Beer, T., Bethe, A., & ———. Vorschläge zu einer objektivierenden Nomenklatur in der Physiologie des Nervensystems. *Biol. Zbl.*, 1899, *19*, 517–521. (Also *Centbl. Physiol.*, 1899, *13*, 137–141.) Reprinted in E. Dzendolet, Behaviorism and sensation in the paper by Beer, Bethe & von Uexküll. (1899) *J. hist. Behav. Sci.*, 1967, *3*, 256–261.

———. Ueber die Stellung der vergleichenden Physiologie zur Hypothese der Tierseele. *Biol. Zbl.*, 1900, *20*, 497–502.

———. Die Physiologie des Seeigelstachels. *Z. Biol.*, 1900, *39*, 72–112.

———. Biophysik und Psychophysik. *Ergeb. Physiol.*, Abt. 2, 1904, *3*, 521.

———. *Leitfaden in das Studium der experimentellen Biologie der Wassertiere.* Wiesbaden: Bergmann, 1905.

———. *Umwelt und Innenwelt der Tiere.* Berlin: Springer-Verlag, 1909.

———. *Bausteine zu einer biologischen Weltanschauung.* Munich: Bruckmann, 1913.

———. *Theoretical biology.* Trans. by D. L. Mackinnon. New York: Harcourt, Brace, 1926. (1920) (Reprinted 1970)

———. *Theoretische Biologie.* (2nd ed.) Berlin: Springer-Verlag, 1928. (1920)

———. Die Rolle des Subjekts in der Biologie. *Naturwissenschaften*, 1931, *19*, 385–391.

———, & Kriszat, G. *Streifzüge durch die Umwelten von Tieren und Menschen.* (2nd ed.) Berlin: Springer-Verlag, 1956. (1934)

———. A stroll through the worlds of animals and men: A picture book of invisible worlds. In C. H. Schiller (Trans & Ed.), *Instinctive behavior: The development of a modern concept.* New York: International Universities Press, 1957, pp. 5–80.

———. Tier und Umwelt. *Z. Tierpsychol.*, 1939, *2*, 101–114.

———. *Bedeutungslehre.* Leipzig: Barth, 1940.

———. *Der Sinn des Lebens.* Godesberg: Küpper, 1947.

———. *Niegeschaute Welten.* Munich: List, 1957 (1949)   **B**

FRANCIS M. URBAN
ca 1883-ca 1950
American Psychologist (14)

Urban, F. M. *The application of statistical methods to the problems of psychophysics.* Philadelphia, Pa.: Psychological Clinic Press, 1908.

———. Die psychophysischen Massmethoden als Grundlagen empirischer Messungen. *Arch. ges. Psychol.*, 1909, *15*, 261–355; *16*, 168–227.

———. Ueber die Methode der mehrfachen Fälle. *Arch. ges. Psychol.*, 1910, *17*, 367–411.

———. Ein Beitrag zur Kenntnis der psychometrischen Funktionen im Gebiete der Schallempfindungen. *Arch. ges. Psychol.*, 1910, *18*, 400–410.

———. The method of constant stimuli and its generalizations. *Psychol. Rev.*, 1910, *17*, 229–259.

———. Eine Bemerkung über die Methode der ebenmerklichen Unterschiede. *Arch. ges. Psychol.*, 1911, *20*, 45–51.

———. The psychophysical measurement methods. *Psychol. Bull.*, 1911, *8*, 198–202; 1912, *9*, 209–215; 1913, *10*, 180–185; 1914, *11*, 171–177.

———. Der Einfluss der Uebung bei Gewichtsversuchen. *Arch. ges. Psychol.*, 1913, *29*, 271–311.

———. Ueber einige Begriffe und Aufgaben der Psychophysik. *Arch. ges. Psychol.*, 1913, *30*, 113–152.

———. Die empirische Darstellung der psychometrischen Funktionen. *Arch. ges. Psychol.*, 1915, *34*, 121–155.

———. The psychometric constant delta. *Amer. J. Psychol.*, 1950, *63*, 100–107.

———. The equality judgments. *Amer. J. Psychol.*, 1950, *63*, 282–284.

HANS VAIHINGER
1852-1933
German Philosopher (11)

Vaihinger, H. *Hartmann, Dühring, und Lange.* Iserlohn: Baedeker, 1876.

———. *Kommentar zu Kants "Kritik der reinen Vernunft."* Ed. by R. Schmidt. (2 vols.) Stuttgart: Union Deutsche Verlagsgesellschaft, 1922. (1881–1892) (Reprinted 1969)

———. Zu Kants Widerlegung des Idealismus. In E. Zeller (Ed.), *Strassburger Abhandlungen zur Philosophie.* Freiburg: Mohr, 1884, pp. 85–147.

———. *Nietzsche als Philosoph.* (5th ed.) Langensalza: Beyer, 1930. (1902)

———. *The philosophy of "as if": A system of the theoretical, practical and religious fictions of mankind.* (6th ed.) Trans. by C. K. Ogden New York: Barnes & Noble, 1952. (1911)

———. Hans Vaihinger. In R. Schmidt (Ed.), *Die Philosophie der Gegenwart in Selbstdarstellungen.* Vol. 2. (2nd ed.) Leipzig: Meiner, 1923, pp. 183–212. **B Bl**

CHARLES WILFRID VALENTINE
1879-1964
English Psychologist (13)

Valentine, C. W. Psychological theories of the horizontal-vertical illusion. *Brit. J. Psychol.*, 1912–1913, *5*, 8–35.

———. The effect of astigmatism on the horizontal-vertical illusion, and a suggested theory of the illusion. *Brit. J. Psychol.*, 1912–1913, *5*, 308–330.

———. The aesthetic appreciation of musical intervals among school children and adults. *Brit. J. Psychol*, 1913–1914, *6*, 190–216.

———. The colour perception and colour preferences of an infant in its fourth and eighth months. *Brit. J. Psychol.*, 1913–1914, *6*, 363–386.

———. *An introduction to the experimental psychology of beauty.* New York: Dodge, 1914. (1913)

———. *An introduction to experimental psychology in relation to education.* (5th ed.) Baltimore, Md.: Warwick & York, 1953. (1914)

———. The method of comparison in experiments with musical intervals and the effect of practice on the appreciation of discords. *Brit. J. Psychol.*, 1914–1915, 7, 118–135.

———. Mind and medium in art. *Brit. J. Psychol.*, 1920–1921, *11*, 47–54.

———. *The new psychology of the unconscious.* (4th ed.) New York: Macmillan, 1929. (1921).

———. The function of images in the appreciation of poetry. *Brit. J. Psychol.*, 1923–1924, *14*, 164–191.

———. Reflexes in early childhood: Their development, variability, evanescence, inhibition, and relation to instincts. *Brit. J. Med. Psychol.*, 1927, 7, 1–35.

———. The relative reliability of men and women in intuitive judgments of character. *Brit. J. Psychol.*, 1928–1929, *19*, 213–238.

———. *Growing up.* London: Kegan Paul, 1929.

———. The innate bases of fear. *J. genet. Psychol.*, 1930, *37*, 394–420.

————. The psychology of imitation with special reference to early childhood. *Brit. J. Psychol.,* 1930–1931, *21,* 105–132.

————. *Education of children under seven.* London: Kegan Paul, 1932.

————. *The reliability of examinations.* London: University of London Press, 1932.

————. An enquiry as to reasons for the choice of the teaching profession by university students. *Brit. J. educ. Psychol.,* 1934, *4,* 237–259.

————. A study of the beginnings and significance of play in infancy. *Brit. J. educ. Psychol.,* 1938, *8,* 188–200, 285–306.

————. *The difficult child and the problem of discipline.* London: Methuen, 1940. (Reprinted 1965)

————. The specific nature of temperament traits and a suggested report form. *Brit. J. educ. Psychol.,* 1940, *10,* 25–48.

————. *The psychology of early childhood: A study of mental development in the first years of life.* (3rd ed.) London: Methuen, 1946. (1942)

————. *The human factor in the army: Some applications of psychology to training, selection, morale and discipline.* (Rev. ed.) Aldershot: Gale & Polden, 1954. (1943)

————. Adolescence and some problems of youth training. *Brit. J. educ. Psychol.,* 1943, *13,* 57–68.

————. Some present day trends, dangers, and possibilities in the field of psychology. *Brit. J. educ. Psychol.,* 1948, *18,* 134–147.

————. *Psychology and its bearing on education.* London: Methuen, 1960. (1950)

————. *Parents and children: A first book on the psychology of child development and training.* New York: Philosophical Library, 1955. (1953)

————. *The normal child and some of his abnormalities: A general introduction to the psychology of childhood.* Baltimore, Md.: Penguin Books, 1956.

————. *The experimental psychology of beauty.* London: Methuen, 1962. (Reprinted 1968)

WILLARD LEE VALENTINE
1904-1947
American Psychologist (13)

Valentine, W. L. Note on the "binaural beat." *J. comp. Psychol.,* 1927, *7,* 357–368.

————, & Gorsuch, Cecelia. The effect of suggestion upon the perception of the binaural shift. *J. comp. Psychol.,* 1928, *8,* 361–367.

————. A study of learning curves. I. The application of Meyer's arc-cotangent function & Thurstone's hyperbola to the maze performance of white rats. *J. comp. Psychol.,* 1930, *10,* 421–435.

————. A study of learning curves. II. The relationship between the hyperbola and the arc-cotangent function. *J. gen. Psychol.,* 1930, *4,* 359–362.

————. A study of learning curves. III. The relationship between a growth curve and the arc-cotangent function. *J. gen. Psychol.,* 1931, *5,* 251–254.

————, & Wagner, I. Relative arm motility in the newborn infant. *Ohio Univer. Stud.,* 1934, No. 12, 53–68.

————. Common misconceptions of college students. *J. appl. Psychol.,* 1936, *20,* 633–658.

————, & Dockeray, F. C. The experimental study of the newborn. 1926–36. *Educ. Res. Bull. Ohio St. Univer.,* 1936, *15,* 127–133.

————, & Wickens, D. D. *Experimental foundations of general psychology.* (3rd ed.) New York: Rinehart, 1949. (1938)

MAX VERWORN
1863-1921
German Physiologist (14)

Verworn, M. *Psychophysiologische Protisten-Studien.* Jena: Fischer, 1889.

————. Gleichgewicht und Otolithenorgan: Experimentelle Untersuchungen. *Arch. ges. Physiol.,* 1891, *50,* 423–472.

————. *Die Bewegung der lebendigen Substanz.* Jena: Fischer, 1892.

———. Modern physiology. *Monist,* 1893–1894, *4,* 355–374.

———. *General physiology: An outline of the science of life.* (2nd ed.) Ed. & trans. by F. S. Lee. New York: Macmillan, 1899. (1895)

———. *Allgemeine Physiologie: Ein Grundriss der Lehre von Leben.* (7th ed.) Jena: Fischer, 1922. (1895)

———. Tonische Reflexe. *Arch. ges. Physiol.,* 1897, *65,* 63–80.

———. *Beiträge zur Physiologie des Centralnervensystems.* Vol. I. *Die sogenannte Hypnose der Thiere.* Jena: Fischer, 1898.

———. *Das Neuron in Anatomie und Physiologie.* (4th ed.) Jena: Fischer, 1903. (1900)

———. Ermüdung und Erholung. *Berl. klin. Wochensch.,* 1901, *38,* 125–132.

———. *Die Biogenhypothese: Eine kritisch-experimentelle Studie über die Vorgänge in der lebendigen Substanz.* Jena: Fischer, 1903.

———. *Prinzipienfragen in der Naturwissenschaft.* (2nd ed.) Jena: Fischer, 1917. (1905)

———. *Die Mechanik des Geisteslebens.* (3rd ed.) Leipzig: Teubner, 1919. (1907)

———. *Die Anfänge der Kunst. ein Vortrag.* (2nd ed.) Jena: Fischer, 1920. (1909)

———. *Die Entwicklung des menschlichen Geistes. ein Vortrag.* (4th ed.) Jena: Fischer, 1920. (1910)

———. *Irritability: A physiological analysis of the general effect of stimuli in living substance.* New Haven: Yale University Press, 1913.

———. *Die biologischen Grundlagen der Kulturpolitik. eine Betrachtung zum Weltkriege.* (2nd ed.) Jena: Fischer, 1916. (1915)

———. *Erregung und Lähmung. Eine allgemeine Physiologie der Reizwirkungen.* Jena: Fischer, 1914.

———. *Zur Psychologie der primitiven Kunst.* Jena: Fischer, 1968.

KARL VON VIERORDT
1818-1884
German Physiologist (17)

Fechner, G. T., Preyer, W., & Vierordt, K. v. *Wissenschaftliche Briefe von Gustav Theodore Fechner und W. Preyer nebst einem Briefwechsel zwischen K. von Vierordt und Fechner.* Ed. by W. Preyer. Hamburg: Voss, 1890.
B C

———. *Grundriss der Physiologie des Menschen.* (5th ed.) Tübingen: Laupp, 1877. (1859)

———. *Ueber die Messung der Sehschärfe. Arch. Ophthalm,* 1963, *9*(1), 161–163.

———. *Der Zeitsinn nach Versuchen.* Tübingen: Laupp, 1868.

———. Ueber die Ursache der verschiedenen Entwicklung des Ortssinnes der Haut. *Arch. ges. Physiol.,* 1869, *2,* 297–306.

———. Die Abhängigkeit der Ausbildung des Raumsinnes der Haut von Beweglichkeit der Körperteile. *Z. Biol.,* 1870, *6,* 53–72.

———. *Die Anwendung des Spektralapparates zur Messung und Vergleichung der Stärke des farbigen Lichtes.* Tübingen: Laupp, 1871.

———. Die Bewegungsempfindung. *Z. Biol.,* 1876, *12,* 226–240.

———. *Physiologie des Kindesalters.* Tübingen: Laupp, 1877.

———. Psychophysische Bemerkungen. *Z. Biol.,* 1882, *18,* 397–405.

———. *Die Schall- und Tonstärke und das Schallleitungsvermögen der Körper.* Tübingen: Laupp, 1885.

Clendening, *Source Book*

ALFRED WILHELM VOLKMANN
1800-1877
German Physiologist (12)

Volkmann, A. W. *Neue Beiträge zur Psychologie des Gesichtssinnes.* Leipzig: Breitkopf & Härtel, 1836.

———. *Die Lehre von dem leiblichen Leben des Menschen—ein anatomisch-physiologisches Handbuch zum Selbstunterricht für Gebildete.* Leipzig: Breitkopf, 1837.

———. Ueber Reflexbewegungen. *Arch. Anat. Physiol.,* 1838, 15–43.

———. Nervenphysiologie. In R. Wagner (Ed.), *Handwörterbuch der Physiologie.* Vol. 2. Brunswick: Vieweg, 1844, pp. 476–627.

———. Beitrag zur nähern Kenntniss der motorischen Nervenwirkungen. *Arch. Anat. Physiol.,* 1845, 407–429.

———. Sehen. In R. Wagner (Ed.), *Handwörterbuch der Physiologie.* Vol. 3. Part 1. Brunswick: Vieweg, 1846, pp. 265–351.

———. *Streifzüge im Gebiete der exacten Physiologie. Eine Streitschrift gegen Herrn Professor G. Valentin.* Leipzig: Breitkopf & Härtel, 1847.

———. Ueber einige Gesichtsphänomene, welche mit dem Vorhandensein eines unempfindlichen Flecks im Auge zusammenhängen. *Ber. sächs. Ges. Wiss. Leipzig,* math.-phys. Kl., 1953, *5,* 27–50.

———. Ueber das Vermögen, Grössenverhältnisse zu schätzen. *Ber. sächs. Ges. Wiss. Leipzig,* math.-phys. Kl., 1858, *10,* 173–204.

———. Versuche und Betrachtungen über Muskelcontractilität. *Arch. Anat. Physiol.,* 1858, 215–288.

———. Ueber den Einfluss der Uebung auf das Erkennen räumlicher Distanzen. *Ber. sächs. Ges. Wiss. Leipzig,* math.-phys. Kl., 1858, *10,* 38–69.

———. *Physiologische Untersuchungen im Gebiete der Optik.* (2 vols.) Leipzig: Breitkopf & Härtel, 1863–1864.

———. Zur Entscheidung der Frage: Ob die Zapfen der Netzhaut als Raumelemente beim Sehen fungieren. *Arch. Anat. Physiol.,* 1865, 395–403; 1866, 649–656.

———. Zur Mechanik der Augenmuskeln. *Ber. sächs. Ges. Wiss. Leipzig,* math.-phys. Kl., 1869, *21,* 28–69.

VOLTAIRE
(assumed name of
FRANCOIS MARIE AROUET)
1694-1778
French Philosopher (19)

Voltaire. *Lettres philosophiques.* (3rd ed.) (2 vols.) Ed. by G. Lanson. Paris: Hachette, 1924. (1734) **C**

———. *Oeuvres complètes de Voltaire.* (52 vols.) Ed. by L. Moland. Paris: Garnier, 1877–1885. **C**

———. *The works of Voltaire, a contemporary version.* Ed. by J. Morley. New York: St. Hubert Guild, 1901. **C**

———. *The portable Voltaire.* Ed. by B. R. Redman. New York: Viking Press, 1949. **C**

———. *Correspondance.* Ed. by T. Besterman. (107 vols.) Geneva: Institut et Musée Voltaire, 1953–1965. **B C**

———. *Mélanges.* Annotated by J. v. d. Heuvel. Paris: Gallimard, 1965. (1961) **C**

———. *Select letters.* Trans. by T. Besterman. New York: Nelson, 1963. **B C**

D'Alembert, J. L., & ———. *Correspondance avec Voltaire.* (1752–1778) Reprinted in J. L. d'Alembert, *Oeuvres complètes.* Vol. 5. Geneva: Slatkine, 1967, pp. 46–247. **B C**

———. *The complete works.* (ult. ? vols.) Ed. by T. Besterman. Toronto: University of Toronto Press, 1968– .

———. *Traité de métaphysique.* (2nd ed.) Ed. by H. T. Patterson. Manchester: Manchester University Press, 1957. (1734)

———. *The elements of Sir Isaac Newton's philosophy.* Trans. by J. Hanna. London: Cass, 1967. (1738)

———. *Candide: Or optimism.* Trans. & ed. by R. M. Adams. New York: Norton, 1966. (1759)

———. *Philosophical dictionary.* (7th ed.) (2 vols.) Ed. by P. Gay. New York: Basic Books, 1962. (1764)

———. Le philosophe ignorant. (1766) In *Mélanges, op. cit.,* pp. 877–930.

———. Lettre de Voltaire à M. Hume. (1766) In *Mélanges, op. cit.,* pp. 859–876.

Brinton, *Age Reason ;* Slotkin, *Anthropology ;* Torrey, *Les Philosophes*

LEO SEMENOVICH VYGOTSKY
1896-1934
Russian Psychologist (20)

Vygotsky, L. S. (*Selected psychological investigations.*) Ed. by A. N. Leontiev & A. R. Luria. Moscow: Akademiya Pedag. Nauk, 1956.   **C**

———. (*Development of higher mental functions: From the unpublished works.*) Ed. by A. N. Leontiev, A. R. Luria, & B. M. Teplov. Moscow: Akademiya Pedag. Nauk, 1960.   **C**

———. (Consciousness as a problem of the psychology of behavior.) *Psikhol. marksizma,* 1924, *1,* 175–199.

———. (*Pedagogical psychology.*) Moscow: Rabotnik Prosveshcheniya, 1926.

———. (*Development of active attention in a preschool child.*) Moscow: Giz, 1929.

———. (*Psychology of school-age children.*) Moscow: Pedgiz, 1929.

———. The problem of the cultural development of the child. (1928) *J. genet. Psychol.,* 1929, *36,* 415–433.

———. (Principal statements of the plan of pedological investigation of difficult children. *Pedologiya,* 1929, *3,* 34–42.

———, & Luria, A. R. The function and fate of egocentric speech. *Proc. 9th Internat. Congr.,* New Haven. Princeton, N.J.: Psychological Review Co., 1930, pp. 464–465.

———. (Studies on vivid imagery.) In V. A. Fingert & M. L. Shirvindt (Eds.), (*The principal trends in contemporary psychology.*) Moscow: Giz, 1930, pp. 178–205.

———. (*Imagination and creativity in childhood.*) Moscow: Rabotnik Prosveshcheniya, 1930. (Reprinted 1967)

———. Gestalt psychology. In V. A. Fingert & M. L. Shirvindt (Eds.), (*The principal trends in contemporary psychology.*) Moscow: Giz, 1930, pp. 84–125.

———, & Luria, A. R. (*Essays on the history of behavior.*) Moscow: Giz, 1930.

———. (The development of the higher forms of behavior in childhood.) *Mater. I. Vsesojuz. sez. izuch. poved. chelov.,* 1930, 138–139.

———. (*Pedology of the adolescent.*) Moscow: Uchpedgiz, 1931.

———. (The problem of relationship between psychology and pedology.) *Psikhologiya,* 1931, *1,* 78–100.

———. (Psychotechnique and pedagogy.) *Psikhofiziol. Truda Psikhotekh,* 1931, (2/3), 173–184.

———. (The problem of psychology of schizophrenia.) *Sov. Neuropatol.,* 1932, *1,* 352–364.

———. Thought in schizophrenia. *Arch. Neurol. Psychiat.,* Chicago, 1934, *31,* 1063–1077.

———. *Thought and language.* Trans. by Eugenia Hanfmann & Gertrude Vakar. New York & Cambridge: Wiley & MIT Press, 1962. (1934)

———. Thought and speech. (1934) *Psychiatry,* 1939, *2,* 29–54. Reprinted in S. Saporta (Ed.), *Psycholinguistics: A book of readings.* New York: Holt, Rinehart & Winston, 1961, pp. 509–537.

———. (*Fascism in psychoneurology.*) Moscow: Biomedgiz, 1934.

———. (*Mental development of children in the process of learning.*) Moscow: Uchpedgiz, 1935.

———. (The problem of emotions.) *Vop. Psikhol.,* 1958, *4,* 125–134.

———. Development of the higher mental functions. (1960) In A. N. Leontiev, A. R. Luria, & A. Smirnov (Eds.), *Psychological research in the USSR.* Vol. 1. Moscow: Progress, 1966, pp. 11–46.

————. *The psychology of art.* Trans. by Scripta Technica, & intro. by A. N. Leontiev. Cambridge: MIT Press, 1971. (1965)

————. Play and its role in the mental development of the child. (1966) *Sov. Psychol.,* 1967, *5*(3), 6–18.

————. Spinoza's theory of the emotions in light of contemporary psychoneurology. (1970) *Sov. Stud. Phil.,* 1971–1972, *10,* 362–382.

ALFRED RUSSEL WALLACE
1823-1913
English Biologist (15)

Wallace, A. R. *Natural selection and tropical nature: Essays in descriptive and theoretical biology. (Contains contributions to the theory of natural selection and tropical nature and other essays.)* New York: Macmillan, 1891. (1870, 1878) (Reprinted 1969)   **C**

————. *Studies, scientific and social.* (2 vols.) London: Macmillan, 1900.   **C**

————. *Alfred Russel Wallace: Letters and reminiscences.* (2 vols.) Ed. by J. Marchant. New York: Harper, 1916.   **B Bl C**

————. *Wallace and Bates in the tropics: An introduction to the theory of natural selection.* Ed. by Barbara G. Beddall. New York: Macmillan, 1969.   **C**

————. *A narrative of travels on the Amazon and Rio Negro, with an account of the native tribes, and observations on the climate, geology, and natural history of the Amazon Valley.* (3rd ed.) New York: Lock. 1890. (1853)

Darwin, C., & ————. *Evolution by natural selection.* Ed. & intro. by G. De Beer. Cambridge: Cambridge University Press, 1958. (1858)

————. The origin of human races and the antiquity of man deduced from the theory of "Natural Selection." *Anthrop. Rev.,* London, 1864, *2,* clviii–clxx.

————. *The Malay archipelago.* (New ed.) (2 vols.) New York: Macmillan, 1902. (1869)

————. *On miracles and modern spiritualism.* (2nd ed.) London: Trübner, 1881. (1875)

————. *The geographical distribution of animals. With a study of the relations of living and extinct faunas as elucidating the past changes of the earth's surface.* (2 vols.) New York: Harper, 1876.

————, *et al. The psychophysiological sciences and their assailants.* Boston: Colly & Rich, 1878.

————. *Island life or, the phenomena and causes of insular faunas and floras including a revision and attempted solution of the problem of geological climates.* (3rd ed.) New York: Macmillan, 1911. (1880)

————, & Dyer, W. T. T. *The distribution of life.* New York: Fitzgerald, 1885.

————. *Darwinism, an exposition of the theory of natural selection with some of its applications.* (3rd ed.) New York: Macmillan, 1923. (1889)

————. Human selection. (1890) Reprinted in *Studies, scientific and social,* Vol. 1, *op. cit.,* pp. 509–526.

————. Are individually acquired characters inherited? *Fortn. Rev.,* 1893, *59,* 490–498, 655–668. Reprinted in *Studies, scientific and social,* Vol. 1, *op. cit.,* pp. 315–344.

————. The problem of instinct. *Nat. Sci.,* 1897, *10,* 161–168. Reprinted in *Studies, scientific and social,* Vol. 1, *op. cit.,* pp. 497–508.

————. *The wonderful century, its successes and its failures.* (2nd ed.) New York: Dodd, Mead, 1903. (1898) (Reprinted 1970)

————. *Man's place in the universe.* (3rd ed.) London: Chapman & Hall, 1912. (1903)

————. *My life: A record of events and opinions.* (2nd ed.) (2 vols.) New York: Dodd, 1908. (1905) (Reprinted 1969)   **B**

————. *The world of life.* London: Chapman & Hall, 1910.

———. *Social environment and moral progress.* New York: Cassell, 1913.

———. *The revolt of democracy.* New York: Cassell, 1913.

Bodenheimer, *Biology;* Gabriel & Fogel, *Biology*

GRAHAM WALLAS
1858-1932
English Sociologist (11)

Wallas, G. *Men and ideas.* Ed. by M. Wallas. London: Allen & Unwin, 1940. (1901) (Reprinted 1971) **C**

———. *Human nature in politics.* New York: Crofts, 1931. (1908)

———. The beginning of modern socialism. *Sociol. Rev.,* 1910, *3,* 44–50.

———. *The great society: A psychological analysis.* New York: Macmillan, 1914. (Reprinted 1967)

———. Instinct and the unconscious. IV. *Brit. J. Psychol.,* 1919–1920, *10,* 24–26.

———. *Our social heritage.* New Haven: Yale University Press, 1921.

———. Jeremy Bentham. *Pol. Sci. Quart.,* 1923, *38,* 45–56.

———. *The art of thought.* New York: Harcourt, Brace, 1926.

———. *Physical and social science.* London: Macmillan, 1930.

———. *Social judgment.* New York: Harcourt, Brace, 1935. (1934)

HENRI PAUL HYACINTHE WALLON
1879-1962
French Psychologist (12)

Wallon, H. Buts et méthodes de la psychologie. Psychologie de l'enfant. *Enfance,* 1963, No. 1–2, pp. 5–171. **C**

———. *Délire de persécution: Le délire chronique à base d'interprétation.* Paris: Baillière, 1909.

———. Les psychonévroses de guerre. *Année psychol.,* 1914–1919, *21,* 215–236.

———. Lésions nerveuses et troubles psychiques de guerre. *J. Psychol. norm. path.,* 1920, *17,* 69–96.

———. La conscience et la vie subconsciente. *J. Psychol. norm. path.,* 1920, *17,* 97–120.

———. Emotion et épilepsie. *J. Psychol. norm. path.,* 1920, *17,* 367–377.

———. Les réactions motrices dans les crises dues à l'émotion. *Année psychol.,* 1920–1921, *22,* 143–166.

———. La conscience et la conscience du moi. *J. Psychol. norm. path.,* 1921, *18,* 51–64.

———. Psychonévroses et troubles d'origine sympathique. *J. Psychol. norm. path.,* 1921, *18,* 419–425.

———. Le problème biologique de la conscience. *Rev. phil.,* 1921, *91,* 161–185.

———. Le problème de la conscience. In G. Dumas (Ed.), *Traité de psychologie.* Vol. 1. Paris: Alcan, 1923, pp. 202–229.

———. La conscience et la vie subconsciente. In G. Dumas (Ed.), *Traité de psychologie.* Vol. 2. Paris: Alcan, 1924, pp. 479–521.

———. L'interrogation chez l'enfant. *J. Psychol. norm. path.,* 1924, *21,* 170–182.

———. La mentalité épileptique. *J. Psychol. norm. path.,* 1925, *22,* 500–515.

———. *L'enfant turbulent. Etude sur les retards et les anomalies du développement moteur et mental.* Paris: Alcan, 1925.

———. *Psychologie pathologique.* Paris: Alcan, 1926.

———. La "science des rêves" de S. Freud. *J. Psychol. norm. path.,* 1927, *24,* 759–764.

———. La maladresse. *J. Psychol. norm. path.,* 1928, *25,* 61–78.

———. La mentalité primitive et celle de l'enfant. *Rev. phil.,* 1928, *106,* 82–105.

———. Sélection et orientation professionnelles. *J. Psychol. norm. path.,* 1929, *26,* 710–727.

————. Le problème biologique de la conscience. In G. Dumas (Ed.), *Nouveau traité de psychologie*. Vol. 1. Paris: Alcan, 1930, pp. 293–331.

————. *Principes de psychologie appliquée: L'évolution psychologique de l'enfant.* Paris: Colin, 1930.

————. La psychologie appliquée. *Rev. phil.,* 1930, *109,* 97–107.

————. Science de la nature et science de l'homme: La psychologie. *Rev. Synthèse,* 1931, *2,* 35–39.

————. *Les origines du caractère chez l'enfant.* (2nd ed.) Paris: Presses Universitaires de France, 1949. (1934)

————. Psychologie et technique. *J. Psychol. norm. path.,* 1935, *32,* 161–182.

————. Le réel et le mental (à propos d'un livre récent). *J. Psychol. norm. path.,* 1935, *32,* 455–489.

————. Milieu et enseignement decrolyen. *Arch. belg. Sci. Educ.,* 1937, *2,* 173–180.

————. *L'évolution psychologique de l'enfant.* Paris: Colin, 1968. (1941)

————. *De l'acte à la pensée.* Paris: Flammarion, 1942.

————. La conscience et la vie subconsciente. In G. Dumas (Ed.), *Nouveau traité de psychologie*. Vol. 7. Book 1, Fasc. 1. Paris: Alcan, 1942, pp. 1–38.

————. *Les origines de la pensée chez l'enfant.* (3rd ed.) Paris: Presses Universitaires de France, 1963. (1945)

————. *Les principes de l'orientation à l'école et dans la profession: Conférence.* Paris: Sauvard, 1945.

————. La psychologie de Descartes. *Pensée,* 1950, *32,* 11–20.

————. *Les mécanismes de la mémoire en rapport avec ses objets.* Paris: Presses Universitaires de France, 1951.

————. Les références de la pensée courante chez l'enfant. *Année psychol.,* 1951, *51,* 387–402.

————. L'associationnisme de Pavlov. *Bull. Gr. Etud. Psychol.,* Univer. Paris, 1952, 11–16.

————. *L'oeuvre du Dr. O. Decroly.* Pantin (Seine): Secrétariat du C.F.E.P., 1954.

————. Psychologie et éducation de l'enfance. *Enfance,* 1959, No. 3–4, 195–450.

————, & Lurcat, Liliane. Espace postural et espace environnant (le schéma corporel). *Enfance,* 1962, No. 1, 1–33.

Hameline, *Anthologie*

JAMES WARD
1843-1925
English Psychologist (24)

Ward, J. *Essays in philosophy.* Cambridge: Cambridge University Press, 1927. (Reprinted 1968)   **C**

————. An attempt to interpret Fechner's law. *Mind,* 1876, *1,* 452–466.

————. Some notes on the physiology of the nervous system of the fresh-water crayfish (Astarus fluviatelis). *J. Physiol.,* 1879, *2,* 214–227.

————. Ueber die Auslösung von Reflexbewegungen durch eine Summe schwacher Reize. *Arch. Physiol.,* 1880, 72–91.

————. A general analysis of mind. *J. specul. Phil.,* 1882, *16,* 366–385.

————. Psychological principles. I. The standpoint of psychology. II. Fundamental facts and conceptions. III. Attention and the field of consciousness. *Mind,* 1883, *8,* 153–169, 465–486 ; 1887, *12,* 45–67.

————. Psychology. In *The Encyclopaedia Britannica.* (9th ed.) Vol. 20. Edinburgh: Black, 1886, pp. 37–85.

————. J. S. Mill's science of ethology. *Int. J. Ethics,* 1891, *1,* 441–459.

————. "Modern" psychology: A reflexion. *Mind,* 1893, *2*(N.S.), 54–82.

————. Assimilation and association. *Mind,* 1893, *2*(N.S.), 347–362 ; 1894, *3*(N.S.), 509–532.

——. *Naturalism and agnosticism.* (4th ed.) New York: Macmillan, 1915. (1899) (Reprinted 1971)

——. Reply to Herbert Spencer's psychology. *Fortn. Rev.,* 1900, *73,* 464–476.

——. On the definition of psychology. *Brit. J. Psychol.,* 1904–1905, *1,* 3–25.

——. Is "black" a sensation? *Brit. J. Psychol.,* 1904–1905, *1,* 407–427.

——. *Realm of ends or pluralism and theism.* (2nd ed.) Cambridge: Cambridge University Press, 1912. (1911)

——. *Heredity and memory.* Cambridge: Cambridge University Press, 1913.

——. A further note on the sensory character of black. *Brit. J. Psychol.,* 1915–1917, *8,* 212–221.

——. *Psychological principles.* (2nd ed.) Cambridge: Cambridge University Press, 1920. (1918) (Reprinted 1933)

——. Sense knowledge. I. II. III. *Mind,* 1919, *28,* 257–274, 447–462; 1920, *29,* 129–144.

——. *A study of Kant.* Cambridge: Cambridge University Press, 1922.

——. A theistic monadism. In J. H. Muirhead (Ed.), *Contemporary British philosophy: Personal statements.* (2nd series) New York: Macmillan, 1925, pp. 25–54.

——. *Psychology applied to education.* Cambridge: Cambridge University Press, 1926.

Herrnstein & Boring, *Source Book*

CARL JOHN WARDEN
1890-1961
American Psychologist (19)

Warden, C. J. (Ed.), *Animal motivation: Experimental studies on the albino rat.* New York: Columbia University Press, 1931.   **C**

——. Some factors determining the order of elimination of culs-de-sac in the maze. *J. exp. Psychol.,* 1923, *6,* 192–210.

——. The distribution of practice in animal learning. *Comp. Psychol. Monogr.,* 1923, *1,* No. 3.

——. Primacy and recency as factors in cul-de-sac elimination in a stylus maze. *J. exp. Psychol.,* 1924, *7,* 98–116.

——. The relative economy of various modes of attack in the mastery of a stylus maze. *J. exp. Psychol.,* 1924, *7,* 243–275.

——. The value of the preliminary period of feeding in the problem box. *J. comp. Psychol.,* 1925, *5,* 365–372.

Jenkins, T. N., Warner, L. H., & ——. Standard apparatus for the study of animal motivation. *J. comp. Psychol.,* 1926, *6,* 361–382. Reprinted in C. J. Warden (Ed.), *Animal motivation, op. cit.,* pp. 17–33.

——. A comparison of different norms of mastery in animal maze learning. *J. comp. Psychol.,* 1926, *6,* 159–179.

——, & Haas, E. L. The effect of short intervals of delay in feeding upon speed of maze learning. *J. comp. Psychol.,* 1927, *7,* 107–116. Reprinted in C. J. Warden (Ed.), *Animal motivation, op. cit.,* pp. 446–454.

——, & Warner, L. H. The development of a standardized animal maze. *Arch. Psychol.,* N.Y., 1927, No. 93.

——, & Aylesworth, Mercy. The relative value of reward and punishment in the formation of a visual discrimination habit in the white rat. *J. comp. Psychol.,* 1927, *7,* 117–127.

——, & Warner, L. H. The development of animal psychology in the United States during the past three decades. *Psychol. Rev.,* 1927, *34,* 196–205.

——. The historical development of comparative psychology. *Psychol. Rev.,* 1927, *34,* 57–85, 135–168.

——, & Warner, L. H. The sensory capacities and intelligence of dogs. *Quart. Rev. Biol.,* 1928, *3,* 1–28.

——, & Nissen, H. W. An experimental analysis of the obstruction method of measuring animal drives. *J. comp. Psychol.,* 1928, *8,* 325–

342. Reprinted in C. J. Warden (Ed.), *Animal motivation, op. cit.,* pp. 34–49.

———. The development of modern comparative psychology. *Quart. Rev. Biol.,* 1928, *3,* 486–522.

———, & Rowley, Jean B. The discrimination of absolute versus relative brightness in the ring dove (Turtor risorius). *J. comp. Psychol.,* 1929, *9,* 317–338.

Schneck, M. R., & ———. A comprehensive survey of the experimental literature on animal retention. *J. genet. Psychol.,* 1929, *36,* 1–28.

———, & Hamilton, E. L. The effect of variations in length of maze pattern upon rate of fixation in the white rat. *J. genet. Psychol.,* 1929, *36,* 229–239.

———, & Cummings, S. B. Primacy and recency factors in animal motor learning. *J. genet. Psychol.,* 1929, *36,* 240–254.

———. A note on the early history of experimental methods in comparative psychology. *J. genet Psychol.,* 1930, *38,* 466–471.

———. *The evolution of human behavior.* New York: Macmillan, 1932.

———. Motivation and maze learning: A reply to Professor Tolman. *J. gen. Psychol.,* 1932, *6,* 214–216.

———. The relative strength of the primary drives in the white rat. *J. genet. Psychol.,* 1932, *41,* 16–35.

———. Jenkins, T. N., & Warner, L. H. *Introduction to comparative psychology.* New York: Ronald Press, 1934.

———, Jenkins, T. N., & Warner, L. H. *Comparative psychology.* (3 vols.) New York: Ronald Press, 1935.

———, & Jackson, T. A. Imitative behavior in the rhesus monkey. *J. genet. Psychol.,* 1935, *46,* 103–125.

———. *The emergence of human culture.* New York: Macmillan, 1936.

———, Field, H. A., & Koch, A. M. Imitative behavior in cebus and rhesus monkeys. *J. gen.*

Psychol., 1940, *56,* 311–322. Reprinted in R. B. Zajonc (Ed.), *Animal social psychology: A reader of experimental studies.* New York: Wiley, 1969, pp. 65–83.

———, & Brown, H. C. A preliminary investigation of torm and motion acuity at low levels of illumination. *J. exp. Psychol.,* 1944, *34,* 437–449.

Boe & Church, *Punishment ;* Russell, *Motivation ;* Valentine, *Experimental ;* Zajonc, *Animal Social*

LUCIEN HYNES WARNER
1900-1963
American Psychologist (11)

Jenkins, T. N., ———, & Warden, C. J. Standard apparatus for the study of animal motivation. *J. comp. Psychol.,* 1926, *6,* 361–382. Reprinted in C. J. Warden (Ed.), *Animal motivation: Experimental studies on the albino rat.* New York: Columbia University Press, 1931, pp. 17–33.

Warden, C. J., & ———. The development of animal psychology in the United States during the past three decades. *Psychol. Rev.,* 1927, *34,* 196–205.

———. A study of sex behavior in the white rat by means of the obstruction method. *Comp. Psychol. Monogr.,* 1927, *4,* No. 22. Reprinted in C. J. Warden (Ed.), *Animal motivation, op. cit.,* pp. 119–178.

———. A study of hunger behavior in the white rat by means of the obstruction method. *J. comp. Psychol.,* 1928, *8,* 273–299. Reprinted in C. J. Warden (Ed.), *Animal motivation, op. cit.,* pp. 56–80.

———. A study of thirst behavior in the white rat by means of the obstruction method. *J. genet. Psychol.,* 1928, *35,* 178–192. Reprinted in C. J. Warden (Ed.), *Animal motivation, op. cit.,* pp. 100–114.

Warden, C. J., & ———. The sensory capacities and intelligence of dogs. *Quart. Rev. Biol.,* 1928, *3,* 1–28.

——. The association span of the white rat. *J. genet. Psychol.*, 1932, *41*, 57–90.

——. An experimental search for the "conditioned response." *J. genet. Psychol.*, 1932, *41*, 91–115.

Warden, C. J., Jenkins, T. N., & ——. *Introduction to comparative psychology.* New York: Ronald Press, 1934.

Warden, C. J., Jenkins, T. N., & ——. *Comparative psychology.* (3 vols.) New York: Ronald Press, 1935.

Valentine, *Experimental*

HOWARD CROSBY WARREN
1867-1934
American Psychologist (23)

Warren, H. C., & Shaw, W. J. Further experiments of memory for square size. *Psychol. Rev.*, 1895, *2*, 239–244.

——. The fundamental functions of consciousness. *Psychol. Bull.*, 1906, *3*, 217–227. (Also in *Princeton Contrib. Psychol.*, 1906, *4*, 97–107.)

——. The mental and the physical. *Psychol. Rev.*, 1914, *21*, 79–100.

——. A study of purpose. *J. Phil.*, 1916, *13*, 5–26, 29–49, 57–72.

——. Mental association from Plato to Hume. *Psychol. Rev.*, 1916, *23*, 208–230.

——. Mechanism vs. vitalism in the domain of psychology. *Phil. Rev.*, 1918, *27*, 597–615.

——. *Human psychology.* Boston: Houghton Mifflin, 1919.

——. A classification of reflexes, instincts, and emotional phenomena. *Psychol. Rev.*, 1919, *26*, 197–203.

——. *A history of the association psychology.* New York: Scribner's, 1921. (Reprinted 1967)

——. Psychology and the central nervous system. *Psychol. Rev.*, 1921, *28*, 249–269.

——. *Elements of human psychology.* Boston: Houghton Mifflin, 1922.

——. Awareness and behaviorism. *Phil. Rev.*, 1922, *31*, 601–605.

——. The significance of neural adjustment. *Psychol. Rev.*, 1922, *29*, 481–489.

——. Mechanism and teleology in psychology. *Psychol. Rev.*, 1925, *32*, 266–284.

——. Outline of a psychological standpoint. *Amer. J. Psychol.*, 1927, *39*, 23–41.

——. Howard C. Warren. In C. Murchison (Ed.), *A history of psychology in autobiography.* Vol. 1. Worcester, Mass.: Clark University Press, 1930, pp. 443–469.   **B**

——. In defense of some discarded concepts. *Psychol. Rev.*, 1931, *38*, 392–405.

——. Social nudism and the body taboo. *Psychol. Rev.*, 1933, *40*, 161–183.   **B**

——. *Dictionary of psychology.* New York: Houghton Mifflin, 1934.

MARGARET FLOY WASHBURN
1871-1939
American Psychologist (23)

Washburn, Margaret F. The perception of distance in the inverted landscape. *Mind*, 1894, *3*(N.S.), 438–440.

——. Ueber den Einfluss der Gesichtsassociationen auf die Raumwahrnehmungen der Haut. *Phil. Stud.*, 1895, *11*, 190–225.

——. The process of recognition. *Phil. Rev.*, 1897, *6*, 267–274.

——. Subjective colours and the after-image: Their significance for the theory of attention. *Mind*, 1899, *8*(N.S.), 25–34.

——. After-images. *Psychol. Rev.*, 1899, *6*, 653.

——. The color changes of the white light after-image, central and peripheral. *Psychol. Rev.*, 1900, *7*, 39–46.

——. Some examples of the use of psychological analysis in system-making. *Phil. Rev.*, 1902, *11*, 445–462.

————. *The animal mind: A textbook of comparative psychology.* (4th ed.) New York: Macmillan, 1936. (1908)

————. *Movement and mental imagery: Outlines of a motor theory of the complexer mental processes.* Boston: Houghton Mifflin, 1916.

————. Some thoughts on the last quarter century in psychology. *Phil. Rev.,* 1917, *26,* 46–55.

————. Dualism in animal psychology. *J. Phil.,* 1919, *16,* 41–44.

————, & Grose, Sarah L. Voluntary control of likes and dislikes: The effect of an attempt voluntarily to change the affective value of colors. *Amer. J. Psychol.,* 1921, *32,* 284–289.

————. Introspection as an objective method. *Psychol. Rev.,* 1922, *29,* 89–112.

————. Rowley, J., & Winter, G. A further study of revived emotions as related to emotional and calm temperaments. *Amer. J. Psychol.,* 1926, *37,* 280–283.

————. Gestalt psychology and motor psychology. *Amer. J. Psychol.,* 1926, *37,* 516–520.

————. Emotion and thought: A motor theory of their relations. In M. L. Reymert (Ed.), *Feelings and emotions: The Wittenberg symposium.* Worcester, Mass.: Clark University Press, 1928, pp. 104–115.

————, Keeler, K., New, K. B., & Parshall, F. M. Experiments on the relation of reaction-time, cube fluctuations, and mirror drawing to temperamental differences. *Amer. J. Psychol.,* 1929, *41,* 112–117.

————. A system of motor psychology. In C. Murchison (Ed.), *Psychologies of 1930.* Worcester, Mass.: Clark University Press, 1930, pp. 81–94.

————. Margaret Floy Washburn: Some recollections. In C. Murchison (Ed.), *A history of psychology in autobiography.* Vol. 2. Worcester, Mass.: Clark University Press, 1932, pp. 333–358.   **B**

JOHN BROADUS WATSON
1878-1958
American Psychologist (27)

Watson, J. B. *Animal education: The psychical development of the white rat.* Chicago: University of Chicago Press, 1903.

————. Kinesthetic and organic sensations: Their rôle in the reactions of the white rat to the maze. *Psychol. Monogr.,* 1907, *8,* No. 33.

————. Imitation in monkeys. *Psychol. Bull.,* 1908, *5,* 169–178.

Carr, H. A., & ————. Orientation in the white rat. *J. comp. Neurol.,* 1908, *18,* 27–44.

————. The behavior of noddy and sooty terns. *Carnegie Inst. Publ.,* 1908, No. 103.

Yerkes, R. M., & ————. Methods of studying vision in animals. *Behav. Monogr.,* 1911, *1,* No. 2.

————. Image and affection in behavior. *J. Phil.,* 1913, *10,* 421–428.

————, & Watson, Mary I. A study of the responses of rodents to monochromatic light. *J. anim. Behav.,* 1913, *3,* 1–14.

————. Psychology as the behaviorist views it. *Psychol. Rev.,* 1913, *20,* 158–177.

————. *Behavior: An introduction to comparative psychology.* New York: Holt, 1914.

Lashley, K. S., & ————. An historical and experimental study of homing. *Carnegie Inst. Publ.,* 1915, No. 211, pp. 7–60.

————. Behavior and the concept of mental disease. *J. Phil.,* 1916, *13,* 589–597.

————. The place of the conditioned-reflex in psychology. *Psychol. Rev.,* 1916, *23,* 89–116.

————. An attempted formulation of the scope of behavior psychology. *Psychol. Rev.,* 1917, *24,* 329–352.

————. The effect of delayed feeding upon reaction. *Psychobiology,* 1917, *1,* 51–60.

————, & Morgan, J. J. B. Emotional reactions and psychological experimentation. *Amer. J. Psychol.,* 1917, *28,* 163–174.

———. A schematic outline of the emotions. *Psychol. Rev.,* 1919, *26,* 165–196.

———. *Psychology from the standpoint of a behaviorist.* (3rd ed.) Philadelphia: Lippincott, 1929. (1919)

———, & Rayner, Rosalie. Conditioned emotional reactions. *J. exp. Psychol.,* 1920, *3,* 1–14.

———. Is thinking merely the action of language mechanism? V. *Brit. J. Psychol.,* 1920–1921, *11,* 87–104.

———, & Watson, Rosalie R. Studies in infant psychology. *Sci. Mon.,* N.Y., 1921, *13,* 493–515.

———. The unverbalized in human behavior. *Psychol. Rev.,* 1924, *31,* 273–280.

———. The place of kinaesthetic, visceral, and laryngeal organization in thinking. *Psychol. Rev.,* 1924, *31,* 339–347.

———. *Behaviorism.* (Rev. ed.) New York: Norton, 1930. (1924, 1925) (Reprinted 1970)

———. Behaviorism: A psychology based on reflex action. *J. phil. Stud.,* 1926, *1,* 454–466.

———. Behaviorism: A psychology based on reflexes. *Arch. Neurol. Psychiat.,* Chicago, 1926, *15,* 185–204.

———. What the nursery has to say about instincts. In C. Murchison (Ed.), *Psychologies of 1925.* (3rd ed.) Worcester, Mass.: Clark University Press, 1928, pp. 1–35. (1926)

———. Experimental studies on the growth of the emotions. In C. Murchison (Ed.), *Psychologies of 1925.* (3rd ed.) Worcester, Mass.: Clark University Press, 1928, pp. 37–57. (1926)

———. Recent experiments on how we lose and change our emotional equipment. In C. Murchison (Ed.), *Psychologies of 1925.* (3rd ed.) Worcester, Mass.: Clark University Press, 1928, pp. 59–81. (1926)

———. The origin and growth of behaviorism. *Arch. ges. Phil.,* 1927, *30,* 247–262.

———. The myth of the unconscious. *Harper's,* 1927, *155,* 502–508.

———. *The ways of behaviorism.* New York: Harper, 1928.

——— (with Rosalie R. Watson). *Psychological care of the infant and child.* New York: Norton, 1928.

———, & McDougall, W. *The battle of behaviorism.* New York: Norton, 1928.

———. John Broadus Watson. In C. Murchison (Ed.), *A history of psychology in autobiography.* Vol. 3. Worcester, Mass.: Clark University Press, 1936, pp. 271–281. **B**

Beck & Molish, *Reflexes;* Dennis, *Psychology;* Drever, *Sourcebook;* Grob & Beck, *American Ideas;* Herrnstein & Boring, *Source Book;* Kessen, *Child;* Park & Burgess, *Sociology;* Parsons, *Society;* Perez, *Readings;* Sahakian, *Psychology;* Shipley, *Classics*

HENRY JACKSON WATT
1879-1925
English Psychologist (19)

Watt, H. J. Experimentelle Beiträge zu einer Theorie des Denkens. *Arch. ges. Psychol.,* 1905, *4,* 289–436. (Also Leipzig: Engelmann, 1904)

———. Experimental contribution to a theory of thinking. *J. Anat. Physiol.,* 1906, *40,* 257–266.

———. *The economy and training of memory.* New York: Longmans, Green, 1909.

———. Some problems of sensory integration. *Brit. J. Psychol.,* 1909–1910, *3,* 323–347.

———. The elements of experience and their integration: Or modalism. *Brit. J. Psychol.,* 1911, *4,* 127–204.

———. The psychology of visual motion. *Brit. J. Psychol.,* 1913–1914, *6,* 26–43.

———. Are the intensity differences of sensation quantitative? III. *Brit. J. Psychol.,* 1913–1914, *6,* 175–183.

———. The main principles of sensory integration. *Brit. J. Psychol.,* 1913–1914, *6,* 239–260.

————. Psychological analysis and theory of hearing. *Brit. J. Psychol.*, 1914–1915, *7*, 1–43.

————. Stereoscopy as a purely visual, bisystemic, integrative process. *Brit. J. Psychol.*, 1915–1917, *8*, 131–169.

————. The typical form of the cochlea and its variation. *Proc. Roy. Soc.*, London, 1917, *89B*, 410–421.

————. *The psychology of sound.* London: Cambridge University Press, 1917.

————. *The foundations of music.* Cambridge: Cambridge University Press. 1919.

————. A theory of binaural hearing. *Brit. J. Psychol.*, 1920–1921, *11*, 163–171.

————. *Sensory basis and structure of knowledge.* London: Methuen, 1925.

————. *The common sense of dreams.* Worcester, Mass.: Clark University Press, 1929.
B Bl

Mandler & Mandler, *Thinking ;* Russell, *Motivation*

ERNST HEINRICH WEBER
1795-1878
German Physiologist (27)

Weber, E. H. *De pulsu, resorptione, auditu et tactu: Annotationes anatomicae et physiologiae.* Leipzig: Köhler, 1834. **C**

————. *Annotationes anatomicae et physiologicae: Programmata collecta.* Leipzig: Köhler, 1851. **C**

————. *De aure et auditu hominis et animalium.* Leipzig: Fleischer, 1820.

————, & Weber, W. E. *Wellenlehre auf Experimente gegründet.* Leipzig: Fleischer, 1825.

————. Ueber den Tastsinn. *Arch. Anat. Physiol. Berlin*, 1835, 152–159.

————. Muskelbewegung. In R. Wagner (Ed.), *Handwörterbuch der Physiologie.* Vol. 3, Part 2. Brunswick: Vieweg, 1846, pp. 1–122.

————. Der Tastsinn und Gemeingefühl. Ed. by E. Hering. Leipzig: Engelmann, 1905. (1846) Also in R. Wagner (Ed.), *Handwörterbuch der Physiologie.* Vol. 3, Part 2. Brunswick: Vieweg, 1846, pp. 481–588.

————. Ueber den Einfluss der Erwärmung und Erkältung der Nerven auf ihr Leitungsvermögen. *Arch. Anat. Physiol. Berlin*, 1847, 342–356.

————. Ueber die Umstände durch welche man geleitet wird, manche Empfindungen auf äussere Objecte zu beziehen. *Ber. sächs. Ges. Wiss. Leipzig*, math.-phys. Kl., 1848, *2*, 226–237.

————. Ueber die Tastorgane als die allein fähigen, uns die Empfindungen von Wärme, Kälte und Druck zu verschaffen. *Arch. Anat. Physiol. Berlin*, 1849, 273–282.

————. Ueber den Raumsinn und die Empfindungskreise in der Haut und im Auge. *Ber. sächs. Ges. Wiss. Leipzig*, math.-phys. Kl., 1852, *4*, 85–154.

————. Ueber den Raumsinn im Allgemeinen und einige Verhältnisse des Tastsinnes insbesondere. *Cbl. Naturwiss. Anthrop.*, 1853, *1*, 585–598.

Clarke & O'Malley, *Brain ;* Dennis, *Psychology ;* Fulton & Wilson, *Physiology ;* Herrnstein & Boring, *Source Book ;* Murphy, *Western ;* Rand, *Classical Psychologists*

MAX WEBER
1864-1920
German Sociologist (19)

Weber, M. *Gesammelte Aufsätze zur Religionssoziologie.* (2nd ed.) (3 vols.) Tübingen: Mohr, 1922–1923. (1921) **C**

————. *Gesammelte Aufsätze zur Wissenschaftslehre.* (2nd ed.) Tübingen: Mohr, 1951. (1922) **C**

————. *Gesammelte Aufsätze zur Soziologie und Sozialpolitik.* Tübingen: Mohr, 1924. **C**

————. *Gesammelte Aufsätze zur Sozial- und Wirtschaftsgeschichte.* Tübingen: Mohr, 1924. **C**

———. *From Max Weber: Essays in sociology.* Trans. & ed. by H. H. Gerth & C. W. Mills. New York: Oxford University Press, 1946. (Reprinted 1958)   **C**

———. *Schriften zur theoretischen Soziologie, zur Soziologie der Politik und Verfassung.* Ed. by M. Solms. Frankfurt: Schauer, 1947. **Bl C**

———. *Max Weber on the methodology of the lsocial sciences.* Trans. & ed. by E. Shils & H. A. Finch. Glencoe, Ill.: Free Press, 1949.   **C**

———. *Max Weber on law in economy and society.* Ed. by M. Rheinstein, & trans. by M. Rheinstein & E. Shils. Cambridge: Harvard University Press, 1954.   **C**

———. *Max Weber: Selections from his work.* Intro. by S. M. Miller. New York: Crowell, 1963.   **C**

———. *Max Weber on charisma and institution building: Selected writings.* Ed. & intro. by S. N. Eisenstadt. Chicago: University of Chicago Press, 1968.   **C**

———. *Zur Geschichte der Handelsgesellschaften im Mittelalter. Nach südeuropäischer Quellen.* Amsterdam: Bonset, 1970. (1889)

———. The social causes of the decay of ancient civilization. (1896) *J. gen. Educ.,* 1950, *5,* 75–88.

———. *The Protestant ethic and the spirit of capitalism.* Trans. by T. Parsons. New York: Scribner's, 1958. (1904–1905)

———. *The religion of China: Confucianism and Taoism.* Trans. by H. H. Gerth & D. Martindale. Glencoe, Ill.: Free Press, 1951. (1915)

———. *The religion of India: The sociology of Hinduism and Buddhism.* Trans. & ed. by H. H. Gerth & D. Martindale. Glencoe, Ill.: Free Press, 1958. (1916–1917)

———. *Ancient Judaism.* Ed. & trans. by H. Gerth. Glencoe, Ill.: Free Press, 1952. (1917–1919)

———. *The rational and social foundations of music.* Trans. & ed. by D. Martindale, J. Riedel, & Gertrude Neuwirth. Carbondale, Ill.: Southern Illinois University Press, 1958. (1921)

———. The three types of legitimate rule. (1922) In A. Etzione (Ed.), *Complex organizations: A sociological reader.* Trans. by H. Gerth. New York: Holt, 1961, pp. 4–14.

———. *The city.* Trans. by D. Martindale & Gertrude Neuwirth. Glencoe, Ill.: Free Press, 1958. (1922)

———. *The sociology of religion.* (4th ed.) Trans. by E. Fischoff. Boston: Beacon Press, 1963. (1922)

———. *Economy and society: An outline of interpretive sociology.* Ed. by G. Roth & C. Wittich, & trans. by E. Fischoff *et al.* New York: Bedminster Press, 1968. (1922)

———. *The theory of social and economic organization.* Trans. & ed. by A. M. Henderson & T. Parsons. Glencoe, Ill.: Free Press, 1964. (1922)

———. *General economic history.* Trans. by F. H. Knight. Glencoe, Ill.: Free Press, 1950. (1923)

———. Basic concepts in sociology. Trans. by H. P. Secher. New York: Philosophical Library, 1962. (1925) (Reprinted 1969)

———. Max Weber on race and society. (1924) Intro. by B. Nelson. *Soc. Res.,* 1971, *38,* 30–41.

Borgatta, *Present-day Sociology;* Coser, *Sociological Thought;* Coser & Rosenberg, *Sociological Theory;* Curtis, *Knowledge;* Goldschmidt, *Mankind;* McNall, *Sociological Perspective;* Parsons, *Society;* Ross, *Social Order*

ALBERT PAUL WEISS
1879-1931
American Psychologist (22)

Weiss, A. P. The Ebbinghaus method of conjectural examination. *J. exp. Ped.,* 1912, *4,* 320–334.

———. Apparatus and experiments on sound intensity. *Psychol. Monogr.,* 1916, *22,* No. 95.

———. Preliminary report on the relative intensity of successive, simultaneous, ascending, and descending tones. *Psychol. Rev.*, 1917, *24*, 154–158.

———. Relation between structural and behavior psychology. *Psychol. Rev.*, 1917, *24*, 301–317.

———. Relation between functional and behavior psychology. *Psychol. Rev.*, 1917, *24*, 353–368.

———. Conscious behavior. *J. Phil.*, 1918, *15*, 631–641.

———. The tone intensity reaction. *Psychol. Rev.*, 1918, *25*, 50–80.

———. The mind and the man-within. *Psychol. Rev.*, 1919, *26*, 327–334.

———. The relation between physiological psychology and behavior psychology. *J. Phil.*, 1919, *16*, 626–634.

———. The vowel character of fork tones. *Amer. J. Psychol.*, 1920, *31*, 166–193.

———. The stimulus error. *J. exp. Psychol.*, 1922, *5*, 223–226.

———. Behavior and the central nervous system. *Psychol. Rev.*, 1922, *29*, 329–343.

———. The aims of social evolution. *Ohio. J. Sci.*, 1923, *23*, 115–134.

———. Behaviorism and behavior. I. II. *Psychol. Rev.*, 1924, *31*, 32–50, 118–149.

———. *A theoretical basis of human behavior.* (2nd ed.) Columbus, Ohio: Adams, 1929. (1925)

———. One set of postulates for a behavioristic psychology. *Psychol. Rev.*, 1925, *32*, 83–87. Reprinted in *A theoretical basis of human behavior, op. cit.*, pp. 387–403.

———. Purposive striving as a fundamental category of psychology: Discussion. *Psychol. Rev.*, 1925, *32*, 171–177.

———. Linguistics and psychology. *Language*, *1*, 1925, 52–57.

———. Dr. Davies on "Mechanism, meaning and teleology in behavior." *Amer. J. Psychol.*, 1926, *37*, 450–459.

———. Behaviorism and ethics. *J. abnorm. soc. Psychol.*, 1927–1928, *22*, 388–397.

———. Feeling and emotion as forms of behavior. In M. L. Reymert (Ed.), *Feelings and emotions: The Wittenberg symposium.* Worcester, Mass.: Clark University Press, 1928, pp. 170–192.

———. The measurement of infant behavior. *Psychol. Rev.*, 1929, *36*, 453–471.

———. Bridgeman's new vision of science. *Sci. Mon.*, N.Y., 1929, *29*, 506–514.

———. The biosocial standpoint in psychology. In C. Murchison (Ed.), *Psychologies of 1930.* Worcester, Mass.: Clark University Press, 1930, pp. 301–306.

———. Solipsism in psychology. *Psychol. Rev.*, 1931, *38*, 474–486.

———. Value as an objective problem for psychology. *J. abnorm. soc. Psychol.*, 1932–1933, *27*, 111–129.

FREDERIC LYMAN WELLS
1884-1964
American Psychologist (11)

Wells, F. L. *Linguistic lapses, with especial reference to the perception of linguistic sounds.* New York: Science Press, 1906.

———. A statistical study of literary merit. *Arch. Psychol.*, N.Y., 1907, No. 7.

———. Normal performance in the tapping test before and during practice, with special reference to fatigue phenomena. *Amer. J. Psychol.*, 1908, *19*, 437–483.

———. Studies in retardation as given in the fatigue phenomena of the tapping test. *Amer. J. Psychol.*, 1909, *20*, 38–59.

———. Sex differences in the tapping test: An interpretation. *Amer. J. Psychol.*, 1909, *20*, 353–363.

———. Practice effects in free association. *Amer. J. Psychol.*, 1911, *22*, 1–13.

———, & Forbes, A. On certain electrical processes in the human body and their relation to emotional reactions. *Arch. Psychol.*, N.Y., 1911, No. 18.

——, & Woodworth, R. S. Association tests. *Psychol. Monogr.*, 1911, *13*, No. 57.

——. Some properties of the free association time. *Psychol. Rev.*, 1911, *18*, 1–23.

——. A preliminary note on the categories of association reactions. *Psychol. Rev.*, 1911, *18*, 229–233.

——. The question of association types. *Psychol. Rev.*, 1912, *19*, 253–270.

——. The personal factor in association reaction. *Amer. J. Insan.*, 1913, *69*, 897–906.

——. *Mental adjustments*. New York: Appleton, 1917.

——. Psychotic performance in cancellation and direction tests. *Psychol. Rev.*, 1919, *26*, 366–371.

——. Association types and personality. *Psychol. Rev.*, 1919, *26*, 371–376.

——. Autistic mechanisms in association reaction. *Psychol. Rev.*, 1919, *26*, 376–381.

——, & Kelly, C. M. Intelligence and psychosis. *Amer. J. Insan.*, 1920, *77*, 17–45.

——. The status of "clinical" psychology. *Ment. Hyg.*, N.Y., 1922, *6*, 11–22.

——. *Pleasure and behavior*. New York: Appleton, 1924.

——. Notes on "false" reactions. *Psychol. Rev.*, 1924, *31*, 311–320.

——. Reactions to visual stimuli in affective settings. *J. exp. Psychol.*, 1925, *8*, 64–76.

——. *Mental tests in clinical practice*. Yonkerson-Hudson, N.Y.: World Book, 1927.

——. Rorschach and the free association test. *J. gen. Psychol.*, 1935, *13*, 413–433.

——. Social maladjustments: Adaptive regression. In C. Murchison (Ed.), *A handbook of social psychology*. Worcester, Mass.: Clark University Press, 1935, pp. 845–915.

——. Intelligence and socialization. *Amer. J. Psychiat.*, 1937, *93*, 1265–1291.

——. Clinical aspects of functional transfer.

(Psychometric practice in adults of superior intelligence. IV.) *Amer. J. Orthopsychiat.*, 1939, *9*, 1–22.

——. Mental measurement and college objective. *Psychol. Rev.*, 1940, *47*, 425–450.

——, & Ruesch J. (Eds.), *Mental examiners handbook*. (2nd ed.) New York: Psychological Corporation, 1945. (1942)

——. A research focused upon the normal personality: A note. *J. Pers.*, 1944, *12*, 299–301.

——. Clinical psychology in retrospect and prospect. *J. Psychol.*, 1949, *27*, 125–142.

——. Psychometric patterns in adjustment problems at upper extremes of test "intelligence": cases 29–56, Department of Hygiene referrals. *J. genet. Psychol.*, 1950, *76*, 3–37.

——. Should this student be at Harvard? In L. L. Thurstone (Ed.), *Applications of psychology: Essays to honor Walter V. Bingham*. New York: Harper, 1952, pp. 88–110.

Beck & Molish, *Reflexes ;* Valentine, *Experimental*

HEINZ WERNER
1890-1964
German-American Psychologist (24)

Werner, H. Untersuchungen über den "blinden Fleck." *Arch. ges. Physiol.*, 1913, *153*, 475–490.

——. Ein Phänomen optischer Verschmelzung. *Z. Psychol.*, 1913, *66*, 263–270.

——. Die melodische Erfindung im frühen Kindesalter. *Sitzber. kais. Akad. Wiss. Wien*, 1917, *182*, No. 4.

——. Ueber optische Rhythmik. *Arch. ges. Psychol.*, 1918, *38*, 115–163.

——. *Die Ursprünge der Metapher*. Leipzig: Barth, 1919.

——. Grundfragen der Intensitätspsychologie. *Z. Psychol.*, 1922, Suppl. 10. (Also Leipzig: Barth, 1922)

——. *Die Ursprünge der Lyrik*. Munich: Reinhardt, 1924.

———. Studien über Strukturgesetze. I. Ueber Strukturgesetze und deren Auswirkung in den sogenannten geometrisch-optischen Täuschungen. II: Ueber das Problem der motorischen Gestaltung. *Z. Psychol.*, 1924, *94*, 248–264, 265–272.

———, & Lagercrantz, E. Studien über Strukturgesetze. III. Experimentell psychologische Studien über die Struktur des Wortes. *Z. Psychol.*, 1924, *96*, 316–363.

———. Studien über die Strukturgesetze. IV. Ueber Mikromelodik und Mikroharmonik. *Z. Psychol.*, 1925, *98*, 74–89.

———. *Einführung in die Entwicklungspsychologie.* (4th ed.) Leipzig: Barth, 1959. (1926)

———. Studien über Strukturgesetze. V. Ueber die Ausprägung von Tongestalten. *Z. Psychol.*, 1926, *101*, 159–181.

———, & Creuzer, H. Studien über Strukturgesetze. VI. Ueber einen Fall von Schichtspaltung beim Bewegungssehen. *Z. Psychol.*, 1927, *102*, 333–337.

Zietz, K., & ———. Studien über Strukturgesetze. VIII. Ueber die dynamische Struktur der Bewegung. *Z. Psychol.*, 1927, *105*, 226–249.

———. Ueber magische Verhaltungsweisen beim Kinde und Jugendlichen. *Z. pädag. Psychol.*, 1928, *29*, 465–476.

———. Ueber die Sprachphysiognomik als einer neue Methode der vergleichenden Sprachbetrachtung. *Z. Psychol.*, 1929, *109*, 337–363.

———. Untersuchungen über Empfindung und Empfinden. I. Das Problem des Empfindens und die Methode seiner experimentellen Prüfung. II. Die Rolle der Sprachempfindung im Prozess der Gestaltung ausdrucksmässig erlebter Worte. *Z. Psychol.*, 1930, *114*, 152–166, *117*, 230–254.

———. *Grundfragen der Sprachphysiognomik.* Leipzig: Barth, 1932.

———. Sprache als Ausdruck. *Ber. 12. Kongress exp. Psychol.*, 1932, 201–210.

———. L'unité des sens. *J. Psychol. norm. path.*, 1934, *31*, 190–205.

———. Studies on contour. I. Qualitative analyses. *Amer. J. Psychol.*, 1935, *47*, 40–64.

———. Process and achievement: A basic problem of education and developmental psychology. *Harvard educ. Rev.*, 1937, *7*, 353–368.

———. Dynamics in binocular depth perception. *Psychol. Monogr.*, 1937, *49*, No. 218.

———. Binocular depth contrast and the conditions of the binocular field. *Amer. J. Psychol.*, 1938, *51*, 489–497.

———. *Comparative psychology of mental development.* (3rd ed.) New York: International Universities Press, 1957. (1940) (Reprinted 1961)

Strauss, A. A., & ———. Qualitative analysis of the Binet test. *Amer. J. ment. Def.*, 1940, *45*, 50–55.

———, & Strauss, A. A. Causal factors in low performance. *Amer. J. ment. Def.*, 1940, *45*, 213–218.

———. Studies on contour: Strobostereoscopic phenomena. *Amer. J. Psychol.*, 1940, *53*, 418–422.

———. Perception of spatial relationship in mentally deficient children. *J. genet. Psychol.*, 1940, *57*, 93–100.

———, & Bowers, M. Auditory-motor organization in two clinical types of mentally deficient children. *J. genet. Psychol.*, 1941, *59*, 85–99.

———, & Strauss, A. A. The mental organization of the brain-injured mentally defective child. *Amer. J. Psychiat.*, 1941, *97*, 1195–1203.

———, & Thuma, B. D. Critical flicker-frequency in children with brain injury. *Amer. J. Psychol.*, 1942, *55*, 394–399.

Strauss, A. A., & ———. Disorders of conceptual thinking in the brain-injured child. *J. nerv. ment. Dis.*, 1942, *96*, 153–172.

———, & Carrison, Doris. Measurement and development of the finger schema in mentally retarded children; relation of arithmetic achievement to performance on the Finger Schema Test. *J. educ. Psychol.*, 1942, *33*, 252–264.

————, & Carrison, Doris. Animistic thinking in brain-injured mentally retarded children. *J. abnorm. soc. Psychol.*, 1944, *39,* 43–62.

————. Development of visuo-motor performance on the marble-board test in mentally retarded children. *J. genet. Psychol.*, 1944, *64,* 269–279.

Bijon, S. W., & ————. Language analysis in brain-injured and non-brain-injured mentally deficient children. *J. genet. Psychol.*, 1945, *66,* 239–254.

————. Perceptual behavior of brain-injured, mentally defective children: An experimental study by means of the Rorschach technique. *Genet. Psychol. Monogr.*, 1945, *31,* 51–110.

————. Motion and motion perception: A study on vicarious functioning. *J. Psychol.*, 1945, *19,* 317–327.

————. Abnormal and subnormal rigidity. *J. abnorm. soc. Psychol.*, 1946, *41,* 15–24.

————. The concept of rigidity: A critical evaluation. *Psychol. Rev.*, 1946, *53,* 43–52.

————. The effect of boundary strength on interference and retention. *Amer. J. Psychol.*, 1947, *60,* 598–607.

————. Thought disturbance with reference to figure-background impairment in brain-injured children. *Confina Neurol.*, 1949, *9,* 255–263.

Klapper, Zelda, & ————. Developmental deviations in brain-injured (cerebral-palsied) members of pairs of identical twins. *Quart. J. Child Behav.*, 1950, *2,* 288–313.

————, & Wapner, S. Sensory-tonic field theory of perception. *J. Pers.*, 1949, *18,* 88–107. Reprinted in J. S. Bruner & D. Krech (Eds.), *Perception and personality: A symposium.* Durham, N.C.: Duke University Press, 1950, pp. 88–107.

Wapner, S. ————, & Chandler, K. A. Experiments on sensory-tonic field theory of perception. I. Effect of extraneous stimulation on the visual perception of verticality. *J. exp. Psychol.*, 1951, *42,* 341–345.

————, Wapner, S., & Chandler, K. A. Experiments on sensory-tonic field theory of percep

tion. II. Effect of supported and unsupported tilt of the body on the visual perception of verticality. *J. exp. Psychol.*, 1951, *42,* 346–350.

Wapner, S., ————, & Morant, R. B. Experiments on sensory-tonic field theory of perception. III. Effect of body rotation on the visual perception of verticality. *J. exp. Psychol.*, 1951, *42,* 351–357.

————, & Kaplan, E. The acquisition of word meanings: A developmental study. *Monogr. Soc. Res. Child Developmt.*, 1952, *15,* No. 1.

Solomon, P., & ————. Studies on contour. III. Studies in negative after-images. *Amer. J. Psychol.*, 1952, *65,* 67–74.

————, & Wapner, S. Experiments on sensory-tonic field theory of perception. IV. Effect of initial position of a rod on apparent verticality. *J. exp. Psychol.*, 1952, *43,* 68–74.

————, & Wapner, S. Toward a general theory of perception. *Psychol. Rev.*, 1952, *59,* 324–338.

————, *et al.* Experiments on sensory-tonic field theory of perception. VI. Effect of position of head, eyes, and of object on position of the apparent median plane. *J. exp. Psychol.*, 1953, *46,* 293–299.

Wapner, S., ————, Bruell, J. H., & Goldstein, A. G. Experiments on sensory-tonic field theory of perception. VII. Effect of asymmetrical extent and starting positions of figures on the visual apparent median plane. *J. exp. Psychol.*, 1953, *46,* 300–307.

————. Change of meaning: A study of semantic processes through the experimental method. *J. genet. Psychol.*, 1954, *50,* 181–208.

————, & Wapner, S. Studies in physiognomic perception. I. Effect of configurational dynamics and meaning-induced sets on the position of the apparent median plane. *J. Psychol.*, 1954, *38,* 51–65.

————, & Wapner, S. Changes in psychological distance under conditions of danger. *J. Pers.*, 1955–1956, *24,* 153–167.

Wapner, S., ————, & Comalli, P. E., Jr. Space localization under conditions of danger. *J. Psychol.*, 1956, *41,* 335–346.

————, & Kaplan, B. The developmental approach to cognition: Its relevance to the psychological interpretation of anthropological and ethnolinguistic data. *Amer. Anthrop.*, 1956, *58*, 866–880.

————, & Kaplan, B. Symbolic mediation and organization of thought: An experimental approach by means of the line schematization technique. *J. Psychol.*, 1957, *43*, 3–25.

————, & Wapner S. Perceptual development. *Clark Univer. Monogr. Psychol.*, 1957, No. 2.

————. The concept of development from a comparative and organismic point of view. In D. B. Harris (Ed.), *The concept of development: An issue in the study of human behavior.* Minneapolis, Minn.: University of Minnesota Press, 1957, pp. 125–148.

Wapner, S., ————, & Comalli, P. E., Jr. Effect of enhancement of head boundary on head size and shape. *Percept. mot. Skills*, 1958, *8*, 319–325.

————, & Kaplan, B. *Symbol formation: An organismic-developmental approach to language and the expression of thought.* New York: Wiley, 1963.

Rand, G., Wapner, S., ————, & McFarland, J. H. Age differences in performances on the Stroop Color-Word Test. *J. Pers.*, 1963, *31*, 534–558.

Bauermeister, M., ————, & Wapner, S. The effect of body tilt on tactual-kinesthetic perception of verticality. *Amer. J. Psychol.*, 1964, *77*, 451–456.

Wapner, S., & ————. An experimental approach to body perception from the organismic-developmental point of view. In S. Wapner & H. Werner (Eds.), *The body percept.* New York: Random House, 1965, pp. 9–25.

Beardslee, *Perception*

MAX WERTHEIMER
1880-1943
German-American Psychologist (27)

Wertheimer, M. *Drei Abhandlungen zur Gestalttheorie.* Erlangen: Philosophische Akademie, 1925. **C**

————, & Klein, J. Psychologische Tatbestandsdiagnostik. *Arch. Kriminalanthrop. Kriminalistik*, 1904, *15*, 72–113.

————. Experimentelle Untersuchungen zur Tatbestandsdiagnostik. *Arch. ges. Psychol.*, 1905, *6*, 59–131.

————. Ueber die Assoziationsmethoden. *Arch. Kriminalanthrop. Kriminalistik*, 1906, *22*, 293–319.

Lipmann, O., & ————. Tatbestandsdiagnostische Kombinationsversuche. *Z. angew. Psychol.*, 1907, *1*, 119–128.

————. Musik der Wedda. *Sammelbände int. Musikges.*, 1910, *11*, 300–309.

————. Ueber das Denken der Naturvölker. I. Zahlen und Zahlgebilde. *Z. Psychol.*, 1912, *60*, 321–378. Abridged & trans. in W. D. Ellis (Ed.), *A source book of Gestalt psychology.* London: Routledge & Kegan Paul, 1967, pp. 265–273.

————. Experimentelle Studien über das Sehen von Bewegung. *Z. Psychol.*, 1912, *61*, 161–265. Reprinted in *Drei Abhandlungen zur Gestalttheorie, op. cit.*, & abridged trans. in T. Shipley (Ed.), *Classics in psychology.* New York: Philosophical Library, 1961, pp. 1032–1089.

Hornbostel, E. M. v., & ————. Ueber die Wahrnehmung der Schallrichtung. *Sitzber. preuss. Akad. Wiss.*, 1920, *20*, 388–396.

————. Untersuchungen zur Lehre von der Gestalt: I. Prinzipielle Bemerkungen. *Psychol. Forsch.*, 1922, *1*, 47–58. Abridged & trans. in W. D. Ellis (Ed.), *A source book of Gestalt psychology.* New York: Harcourt, Brace, 1938, pp. 12–16.

————. Bemerkungen zu Hillebrands Theorie der stroboskopischen Bewegungen. *Psychol. Forsch.*, 1923, *3*, 106–123.

————. Untersuchungen zur Lehre von der Gestalt. II. *Psychol. Forsch.*, 1923, *4*, 301–350. Abstracted & trans. in W. D. Ellis (Ed.), *A source book of Gestalt psychology.* London: Routledge & Kegan Paul, 1938, pp. 71–88 ; & in D. C. Beardsall & M. Wertheimer (Eds.), *Readings in perception.* Princeton, N.J.: Van Nostrand, 1958, pp. 115–135.

———. Ueber Gestalttheorie. *Symposion: Phil. Z. Forsch. Ausspr.*, 1925, *1*, 39–60. Abridged & trans. in W. D. Ellis (Ed.), *A source book of Gestalt psychology*. New York: Harcourt, Brace, 1938, pp. 1–11 ; & trans. in *Soc. Res.*, 1944, *11*, 78–99.

———. *Ueber Schlussprozesse im produktiven Denken*. Berlin: De Gruyter, 1920. Abstracted & trans. in W. D. Ellis (Ed.), *A source book of Gestalt psychology*. London: Routledge & Kegan Paul, 1967, pp. 274–282.

———. Zu dem Problem der Unterscheidung von Einzelinhalt und Teil. *Z. Psychol.*, 1933, *129*, 353–357. Reprinted & trans. in *Productive thinking*, vide infra, pp. 260–265.

———. On truth. *Social Res.*, 1934, *1*, 135–146. Reprinted in Mary Henle (Ed.), *Documents of Gestalt psychology*. Berkeley, Calif.: University of California Press, 1961, pp. 19–28.

———. Some problems in the theory of ethics. *Social. Res.*, 1935, *2*, 353–367. Reprinted in Mary Henle (Ed.), *Documents of Gestalt psychology*. Berkeley, Calif.: University of California Press, 1961, pp. 29–41.

———. On the concept of democracy. In M. Ascoli & F. Lehmann (Eds.), *Political and economic democracy*. New York: Norton, 1937, pp. 271–283. Reprinted in Mary Henle (Ed.), *Documents of Gestalt psychology*. Berkeley, Calif.: University of California Press, 1961, pp. 42–51.

———. A story of three days. In Ruth N. Anshen (Ed.), *Freedom: Its meaning*. New York: Harcourt, Brace, 1940, pp. 555–569. Reprinted in Mary Henle (Ed.), *Documents of Gestalt psychology*. Berkeley, Calif.: University of California Press, 1961, pp. 52–64.

———. *Productive thinking*. (Enlarged ed.) Ed. by M(ichael) Wertheimer. New York: Harper, 1959. (1945) **Bl**

———. On discrimination experiments I. Two logical structures. Ed. by Lise Wertheimer. *Psychol. Rev.*, 1959, *66*, 252–266.

Beardslee, *Perception ;* Gruber, *Creative Thinking ;* Herrnstein & Boring, *Source Book ;* Mandler & Mandler, *Thinking ;* Sahakian, *Psychology ;* Shipley, *Classics*

CHARLES WHEATSTONE
1802-1875
English Physicist (14)

Wheatstone, C. *Scientific papers*. London: Taylor & Francis, 1879. **C**

———. Remarks on Purkinje's experiments. *Brit. Ass. Rep.*, 1835, 551–553. Reprinted in *Scientific papers, op. cit.*, pp. 221–222.

———. Contributions to the physiology of vision. Part I. On some remarkable and hitherto unobserved phenomena of binocular vision. *Phil. Trans.*, 1838, *128*, 371–394. Reprinted in *Scientific papers, op. cit.*, pp. 225–259.

———. On a singular effect of the juxtaposition of certain colours under particular circumstances. *Brit. Ass. Rep.*, 1844, Pt. 2, 10. Reprinted in *Scientific papers, op. cit.*, p. 284.

———. Contributions to the physiology of vision. Part II. On some remarkable and hitherto unobserved phenomena of binocular vision. *Phil. Trans.*, 1852, 1–18. Reprinted in *Scientific papers, op. cit.*, pp. 260–283.

———. On the binocular microscope and on stereoscopic pictures of microscopic objects. *Trans. Microscop. Soc.*, 1853, *1*, 99–102.

Dember, *Perception ;* Herrnstein & Boring, *Source Book ;* Sahakian, *Psychology*

RAYMOND HOLDER WHEELER
1892-1961
American Psychologist (19)

Wheeler, R. H. Theories of the will and kinaesthetic sensations. *Psychol. Rev.*, 1920, *27*, 351–360.

———. The development of meaning. *Amer. J. Psychol.*, 1922, *33*, 223–233.

———, & Cutsforth, T. D. Synaesthesia, a form of perception. *Psychol. Rev.*, 1922, *29*, 212–220.

———. Analyzed versus unanalyzed experience. *Psychol. Rev.*, 1922, *29*, 425–446.

———. Some problems of meaning. *Amer. J. Psychol.*, 1923, *34*, 185–202.

——. Introspection and behavior. *Psychol. Rev.* 1923, *30*, 103–115.

——. Outline of a system of psychology. *Psychol. Rev.*, 1923, *30*, 151–163.

——. A psychological description of intelligence. *Psychol. Rev.*, 1924, *31*, 161–174.

——. Persistent problems in systematic psychology. I. A philosophical heritage. II. The psychological datum. III. Stimulus-error and complete introspection. V. Attention and association. *Psychol. Rev.*, 1925, *32*, 179–191, 251–265, 443–456; 1928, *35*, 1–18.

——. Persistent problems in systematic psychology. IV: Structural versus functional analysis. *J. gen. Psychol.*, 1928, *1*, 91–107.

——. The action consciousness. *Brit. J. Psychol.*, 1928–1929, *19*, 253–267.

——. *The science of psychology: An introductory study.* New York: Crowell, 1940. (1929)

Newman, E. B., Perkins, F. T., & ——. Cannon's theory of emotion: A critique. *Psychol. Rev.*, 1930, *37*, 305–326.

——. *The laws of human nature. A general view of Gestalt psychology.* New York: Appleton, 1932.

——, & Perkins, F. T. *Principles of mental development: A textbook in educational psychology.* New York: Crowell, 1932.

——, Perkins, F. T., & Bartley, S. H. Errors in the critiques of Gestalt psychology. II. Confused interpretations of the historical approach. *Psychol. Rev.*, 1933, *40*, 221–245.

——, Perkins, F. T., & Bartley, S. H. Errors in the critiques of Gestalt psychology. III. Inconsistencies in Thorndike's system. *Psychol. Rev.*, 1933, *40*, 303–323.

——, Perkins, F. T., & Bartley, S. H. Errors in the critiques of Gestalt psychology. IV. Inconsistencies in Woodworth, Spearman, and McDougall. *Psychol. Rev.*, 1933, *40*, 412–433.

——. Organismic vs. mechanistic logic. *Psychol. Rev.*, 1935, *42*, 335–353.

——. Organismic logic in the history of science. *Phil. Sci.*, 1936, *3*, 26–61.

Jenkins & Paterson, *Individual Differences*, Park & Burgess, *Sociology*

WILLIAM MORTON WHEELER
1865-1937
American Biologist (11)

Wheeler, W. M. *Essays in philosophical biology.* Ed. by G. H. Parker. Cambridge: Harvard University Press, 1939. (Reprinted 1967)   **C**

——. A neglected factor in evolution. *Science,* 1902, *15* (N.S.), 766–774.

——. On the founding of colonies of queen ants. *Bull. Amer. Mus. Nat. Hist.,* 1906, *22*, 33–105.

——. The queen ant as a psychological study. *Pop. Sci. Mon.,* 1906, *68*, 291–299.

——. The origin of slavery among ants. *Pop. Sci. Mon.,* 1907, *71*, 550–559.

——. Vestigial instincts in insects and other animals. *Amer. J. Psychol.,* 1908, *19*, 1–13.

——. *Ants: Their structure, development and behavior.* New York: Columbia University Press, 1910. (Reprinted 1960)

——. The ant-colony as an organism. *J. Morphol.,* 1911, *22*, 307–325. Reprinted in *Essays in philosophical biology, op. cit.,* pp. 3–27.

——. A study of some ant larvae, with a consideration of the origin and meaning of the social habit among insects. *Proc. Amer. Phil. Soc.,* 1918, *57*, 293–343.

——. The parasitic aculeata: A study in evolution. *Proc. Amer. Phil. Soc.,* 1919, *58*, 1–40.

——. The Termitodoxa; Or biology and society, *Sci. Mon., N.Y.,* 1920, *10*, 113–124. Reprinted in *Essays in philosophical biology, op. cit.,* pp. 71–88.

——. On instincts. *J. abnorm. Psychol.,* 1921, *15*, 295–318. Reprinted in *Essays in philosophical biology, op. cit.,* pp. 37–70.

———. *Social life among the insects.* New York: Harcourt, Brace, 1923.

———. A new word for an old thing. *Quart. Rev. Biol.,* 1926, *1,* 439–443.

———. Emergent evolution and the social. *Science,* 1926, *64,* 433–440. Reprinted in *Essays in philosophical biology, op. cit.,* pp. 143–169.

———. The physiognomy of insects. *Quart. Rev. Biol.,* 1927, *2,* 1–36.

———. *Emergent evolution and the development of societies.* New York: Norton, 1928.

———. *The social insects, their origin and evolution.* New York: Harcourt, Brace, 1928.

———. *Foibles of insects and men.* New York: Knopf, 1928.

———. Present tendencies in biological theory. *Sci. Mon., N.Y.,* 1929, *28,* 97–109. Reprinted in *Essays in philosophical biology, op. cit.,* pp. 185–210.

———. *Demons of the dust: A study in insect behavior.* New York: Norton, 1930.

———. Societal evolution. In E. V. Cowdry (Ed.), *Human biology and racial welfare.* New York: Hoeber, 1930, pp. 139–155.

———. Some attractions of the field study of ants. *Sci. Mon., N.Y.,* 1932, *34,* 397–402.

———. *Colony-founding among ants with an account of some primitive Australian species.* Cambridge: Harvard University Press, 1933.

———. Animal societies. *Sci. Mon., N.Y.,* 1934, *39,* 289–301. Reprinted in *Essays in philosophical biology, op. cit.,* pp. 232–261.

———. *Mosaics and other anomalies among ants.* Cambridge: Harvard University Press, 1937.

GUY MONTROSE WHIPPLE
1876-1941
American Psychologist (20)

Whipple, G. M. The influence of forced respiration on psychical and physical activity. *Amer. J. Psychol.,* 1898, *9,* 560–571.

———. An analytical study of the memory image and the process of judgment in the discrimination of clangs and tones. *Amer. J. Psychol.,* 1901, *12,* 409–457; 1902, *13,* 219–268.

———. Studies in pitch discrimination. *Amer. J. Psychol.,* 1903, *14,* 553–573.

———. Reaction-times as a test of mental ability. *Amer. J. Psychol.,* 1904, *15,* 489–498.

———. A range of information test. *Psychol. Rev.,* 1909, *16,* 347–351.

———. The vocabulary of a three-year-old boy, with some interpretative comments. *J. genet. Psychol.,* 1909, *16,* 1–22.

———. The effect of practice upon the range of visual attention and of visual apprehension. *J. educ. Psychol.,* 1910, *1,* 249–262.

———. *Manual of mental and physical tests.* Part 1. *Simpler processes.* Part 2. *Complex processes.* (3rd ed.) Baltimore, Md.: Warwick & York, 1924, 1921. (1910)

———. The use of mental tests in the school. *Yearb. Nat. Soc. Stud. Educ.,* 1916, *15*(1), 149–160.

———. *Classes for gifted children: An experimental study of method of selection and introduction.* Bloomington, Ill.: Public School Publishing, 1919.

———. Some features of the education of gifted children. *School & Soc.,* 1920, *12,* 175–179.

———. The national intelligence tests. *J. educ. Res.,* 1921, *4,* 16–31.

———. Endowment, maturity, and training as factors in intelligence scores. *Sci. Mon., N.Y.,* 1924, *18,* 496–507.

———. The education of gifted children: Historical and introductory. *Yearb. Nat. Soc. Stud. Educ.,* 1924, *23*(1), 1–24.

———. The transfer of training. *Yearb. Nat. Soc. Stud. Educ.,* 1928, *27*(2), 179–209.

———. Experiments in teaching students how to study. *J. educ. Res.,* 1929, *19,* 1–12.

——. Causes of retardation in reading and methods of eliminating them. *Peabody J. Educ.*, 1938, *16*, 191–200.

——. The contributions of this society (N.S.S.E.) to the scientific movement in education with special reference to the trends in problems and methods of inquiry. *Yearb. Nat. Soc. Stud. Educ.*, 1938, *37*(2), 257–272.

WILLIAM ALANSON WHITE
1870-1937
American Psychiatrist (14)

White, W A. *Outlines of psychiatry.* (14th ed.) Washington, D.C.: Nervous & Mental Disease Publishing, 1935. (1907)

——. The theory of the "Complex." *Interstate Med. J.*, 1909, *16*, 243–258.

——, & Franz, S. I. The use of association tests in determining mental contents. *Govt. Hosp. Insane Bull.*, 1909, *1*, 55–71.

——. The theory, methods, and psychotherapeutic value of psychoanalysis. *Interstate Med. J.*, 1910, *17*, 643–655.

——. Some recent psychological tendencies in psychiatry. *N. Y. Med. J.*, 1910, *91*, 1205–1209.

——. The diagnostics of dementia praecox. *J. nerv. ment. Dis.*, 1910, *37*, 139–144.

——. *Mental mechanisms.* New York: Nervous & Mental Disease Publishing, 1911.

——. Moon myth in medicine: The moon as libido symbol. *Psychoanal. Rev.*, 1914, *1*, 241–256.

——, & Jelliffe, S. E. *Diseases of the nervous system: A textbook of neurology and psychiatry.* (5th ed.) Philadelphia: Lea & Febiger, 1929. (1915)

——. Psychoanalytic parallels. *Psychoanal. Rev.*, 1915, *2*, 177–190.

——. *Mechanisms of character formation: An introduction to psychoanalysis.* New York: Macmillan, 1916.

——. Symbolism. *Psychoanal. Rev.*, 1916, *3*, 1–25.

——. *The principles of mental hygiene.* New York: Macmillan, 1917.

——. Psychoanalytic tendencies. *Amer. J. Insan.* 1917, *73*, 599–607.

——. Individuality and introversion. *Psychoanal. Rev.*, 1917, *4*, 1–11.

——. The mechanism of transference. *Psychoanal. Rev.*, 1917, *4*, 373–381.

——. *Thoughts of a psychiatrist on the war and after.* New York: Hoeber, 1919.

——. *The mental hygiene of childhood.* Boston: Little, Brown, 1919.

——. *Foundations of psychiatry.* Washington, D.C.: Nervous & Mental Disease Publishing, 1921.

——. The behavioristic attitude. *Ment. Hyg.*, N.Y., 1921, *5*, 1–18.

——. *Insanity and the criminal law.* New York: Macmillan, 1923.

——. *An introduction to the study of the mind.* Washington, D.C.: Nervous & Mental Disease Publishing, 1924.

——. *Essays in psychopathology.* Washington, D.C.: Nervous & Mental Disease Publishing, 1925.

——. Presidential address. (Delivered at 81st annual meeting of the American Psychiatric Association, Richmond, Va., May 12–15, 1925.) *Amer. J. Psychiat.*, 1925, *82*, 1–20.

——. The comparative method in psychiatry. *J. nerv. ment. Dis.*, 1925, *61*, 1–17.

——. *The meaning of disease: An inquiry in the field of medical philosophy.* Baltimore, Md.: William & Wilkins, 1926.

——. The language of schizophrenia. *Arch. Neurol. Psychiat.*, Chicago, 1926, *16*, 359–413.

——. The narrowing of the gap between the functional and organic. *Amer. J. Psychiat.*, 1927, *94*, 221–229.

——. *Lectures in psychiatry.* New York: Nervous & Mental Disease Publishing, 1928.

——. Psychiatry and the social sciences. (Read at a meeting of the Social Science Research

Council, Hanover, N.H., Aug. 26, 1927.) *Amer. J. Psychiat.*, 1928, *94*, 729–747.

———. *Medical psychology: The mental factor in disease.* New York: Nervous & Mental Disease Publishing, 1931.

———. *Forty years of psychiatry.* New York: Nervous & Mental Disease Publishing, 1933. **B**

———. *Crimes and criminals.* New York: Farrar & Rinehart, 1933.

———. *Twentieth century psychiatry.* New York: Norton, 1936.

———. *The autobiography of a purpose.* New York: Doubleday, Doran, 1938. **B Bl**

———. Medical philosophy: From the viewpoint of a psychiatrist. *Psychiatry*, 1947, *10*, 77–98, 191–210.

Park & Burgess, *Sociology*

ALFRED NORTH WHITEHEAD
1861-1947
English-American Philosopher (14)

Whitehead, A. N. *The aims of education, and other essays.* New York: Macmillan, 1967. (1909) **C**

———. *Essays in science and philosophy.* New York: Philosophical Library, 1947. **B C**

———. *Alfred North Whitehead: An anthology.* Ed. by F. S. C. Northop & M. W. Gross. New York: Macmillan, 1953. **C**

———. *Whitehead's American essays in social philosophy.* Ed. by A. H. Johnson. New York: Harper, 1959. **C**

———. *Alfred North Whitehead: His reflections on man and nature.* Ed. by Ruth N. Anshen. New York: Harper, 1961. **C**

———. *The interpretation of science: Selected essays.* Ed. by A. H. Johnson. Indianapolis, Ind.: Bobbs-Merrill, 1961. **C**

———. *A treatise on universal algebra, with applications.* Vol. 1. Cambridge: Cambridge University Press, 1898.

———, & Russell, B. *Principia mathematica.* (2nd ed.) (3 vols.) Cambridge: Cambridge University Press, 1957. (1910–1913)

———. *An introduction to mathematics.* New York: Holt, 1911.

———. *An enquiry concerning the principles of natural knowledge.* (2nd ed.) Cambridge: Cambridge University Press, 1955. (1919)

———. *The concept of nature.* Ann Arbor, Mich.: University of Michigan Press, 1959. (1920)

———. *The principle of relativity, with applications to physical science.* Cambridge: Cambridge University Press, 1922.

———. *Science and the modern world: Lowell lectures. 1925.* New York: Macmillan, 1925. (Reprinted 1948)

———. *Religion in the making: Lowell lectures, 1926.* New York: Macmillan, 1957. (1926)

———. *Symbolism: Its meaning and effect.* New York: Macmillan, 1958. (1927)

———. *The function of reason.* Princeton, N.J.: Princeton University Press, 1929.

———. *Process and reality: An essay in cosmology.* New York: Macmillan, 1929. (Reprinted 1960)

———. *Adventures of ideas.* New York: Macmillan, 1933. (Reprinted 1955)

———. *Nature and life.* Chicago: University of Chicago Press, 1934.

———. *Modes of thought: Six lectures delivered in Wellesley College, Massachusetts, and two lectures in the University of Chicago.* New York: Macmillan, 1938. (Reprinted 1958)

———. Autobiographical notes. (1941) In P. A. Schillp (Ed.), *The philosophy of A. N. Whitehead.* (2nd ed.) New York: Tudor, 1951, pp. 1–14. **B**

———. *Dialogues of Alfred North Whitehead.* Recorded by L. Price. Boston: Little, Brown, 1954. **B**

Gruber, *Creative Thinking ;* Madden, *Scientific Thought ;* Mueller, *American Philosophy ;* Strain, *Philosophies Education*

ROBERT WHYTT
1714-1766
Scottish Physiologist (15)

Whytt, R. *The works of Robert Whytt, M.D.* Edinburgh: Balfour, Auld, & Smellie, 1768. **C**

——. *An essay on the vital and other involuntary motions of animals.* (2nd ed.) Edinburgh: Hamilton Balfour & Neill, 1763. (1751) Reprinted in *Works, op. cit.,* pp. 1–208.

——. *Physiological essays.* (3rd ed.) Edinburgh: Balfour, 1766. (1755)

——. *Observations on the sensibility and irritability of the parts of men and other animals occasioned by the celebrated M. de Haller's late Treatise on those subjects.* Edinburgh: Balfour, 1755. Reprinted in *Works, op. cit.,* pp. 254–306.

——. *Observations on the nature, causes and cure of those disorders which are commonly called nervous, hypochondriac, or hysteric, to which are prefixed some remarks on the sympathy of nerves.* (3rd ed.) Edinburgh: Balfour, 1767. (1764) Reprinted in *Works, op. cit.,* pp. 487–713.

> Clarke & O'Malley, *Brain;* Fulton & Wilson, *Physiology;* Hall, *Source Book;* Herrnstein & Boring, *Source Book;* Hunter & Macalpine, *Psychiatry*

NORBERT WIENER
1894-1964
American Mathematician (18)

Wiener, N. The relation of space and geometry to experience. *Monist,* 1922, *32,* 12–60, 200–247, 364–394.

——. On the nature of mathematical thinking. *Austral. J. Psychol. Phil.,* 1923, *1,* 268–272.

Rosenblueth, A., ——, & Bigelow, J. Behavior, purpose and teleology. *Phil. Sci.,* 1943, *10,* 18–24. Reprinted in W. Buckley, (Ed.), *Modern systems research for the behavioral scientist: A sourcebook.* Chicago: Aldine, 1968, pp. 221–225.

——, & Rosenblueth, A. The role of models in science. *Phil. Sci.,* 1945, *12,* 316–321.

——. Time, communication, and the nervous system. *Ann. N.Y. Acad. Sci.,* 1948, *50,* 197–219.

——. *Cybernetics: Or control and communication in the animal and the machine.* (2nd ed.) Cambridge: MIT Press, 1961. (1948)

——. *The human use of human beings: Cybernetics and society.* (2nd ed.) Boston: Houghton Mifflin, 1954. (1950)

——. Some maxims for biologists and psychologists. *Dialectica,* 1950, *4,* 186–191.

Rosenblueth, A, & ——. Purposeful and non-purposeful behavior. *Phil. Sci.,* 1950, *17,* 318–326. Reprinted in W. Buckley (Ed.), *Modern systems research for the behavioral scientist: A sourcebook.* Chicago: Aldine, 1968, pp. 232–237.

——. Speech, language, and learning. *J. acoust. Soc. Amer.,* 1950, *22,* 690–697.

——. *Ex-prodigy: My childhood and youth.* Cambridge, Mass.: MIT Press, 1968. (1953) **B**

——. Optics and the theory of stochastic process. *J. Opt. Soc. Amer.,* 1953, *43,* 225–228.

——. *I am a mathematician: The later life of a prodigy.* Cambridge: MIT Press, 1968. (1956) **B**

——. Rhythms in psychology with particular reference to encephalography. *Proc. Rudolf Virchow Med. Soc. City New York,* 1957, *16,* 109–124.

——. My connection with cybernetics: Its origin and future. *Cybernetics,* 1958, Namur, Belgium, 1–14.

——. *God and Golem, Inc.* Cambridge: MIT Press, 1964.

——. Perspectives in neurocybernetics. In *Cybernetics of the nervous system.* Ed. by N. Wiener & J. P. Schadé. New York: Elsevier, 1965, pp. 399–415.

——. Cybernetics. *Sci. Amer.,* 1948, *179,* 14–19. Reprinted in D. M. Messick (Ed.), *Mathematical thinking in behavioral science.* San Francisco: Freeman, 1968, pp. 40–51.

ENNO DIRK WIERSMA
1858-1940
Dutch Psychiatrist (12)

Wiersma, E. D. Untersuchungen über sogenannten Aufmerksamkeitsschwankungen. *Z. Psychol.*, 1901, *26*, 168–200 ; 1902, *28*, 179–198 ; 1903, *31*, 110–126.

———. Die Ebbinghaus'sche Combinations–methode. *Z. Psychol.*, 1902, *30*, 196–222.

Heymans, G., & ———. Beiträge zur speziellen Psychologie auf Grund einer Massenunter-suchung. *Z. Psychol.*, 1906, *42*, 81–127, 258–301 ; 1906, *43*, 321–373 ; 1907, *45*, 1–42 ; 1908, *46*, 321–333 ; 1908, *49*, 414–439 ; 1909, *51*, 1–72 ; 1912, *62*, 1–59 ; 1918, *80*, 76–89. Reprinted in G. Heymans, *Gesammelte Schriften*. Vol. 3. The Hague : Nijhoff, 1927, pp. 41–414.

———. Intelligenzprüfungen nach Binet und Simon und ein Versuch zur Auffindung neuer Tests. *Z. angew. Psychol.*, 1914, *8*, 267–275.

———. On the value of the simultaneous registration of the plethysmogram and the psychologalvanic reactions. *Proc. Roy. Acad. Sci.*, Holland, 1915, *17*, 1154–1158.

———. The psychology of conditions of confusion. *Proc. Roy. Acad. Sci.*, Holland, 1918, *20*, 312–326.

———. Psychical inhibition. *Proc. Roy. Acad. Sci.*, Holland, 1921, *23*, 33–46.

———. Concordance of the laws of some psychological and physiological phenomena. *Proc. Roy. Acad. Sci.*, Holland, 1922, *24*, 1–11.

———. The psychology of epilepsy. *J. ment. Sci.*, 1923, *69*, 482–497.

———. Die Bedeutung der statistichen Untersuchungsmethode in der speziellen Psychologie. *Z. angew. Psychol.*, 1927, *28*, 333–346.

———. Psychology of dementia. I, II. *J. ment. Sci.*, 1930, *76*, 1–42.

———. *Lectures on psychiatry*. London : Lewis, 1932.

WILHELM WIRTH
1876-1952
German Psychologist (14)

Wirth, W. Vorstellungs- und Gefühlskontrast. *Z. Psychol.*, 1898, *18*, 49–90.

———. Der Fechner-Helmholtz'sche Satz über negative Nachbilder und seine Analogien. *Phil. Stud.*, 1900, *16*, 465–567 ; 1901, *17*, 311–430 ; 1903, *18*, 563–714.

———. Zur Theorie des Bewusstseinsumfanges und seiner Messug. *Phil. Stud.*, 1902, *20*, 487–669.

———. Die Klarheitsgrade der Regionen des Sehfeldes bei verschiedenen Verteilungen der Aufmerksamkeit. *Psychol. Stud.*, 1906, *2*, 30–88.

———. *Die experimentelle Analyse der Bewusst-seinsphänomene*. Brunswick : Vieweg, 1908.

———. Erwiderung gegen K. Marbe. *Z. Psychol.*, 1908, *46*, 429–438.

———. Zur Messung der Klarheitsgrade der Bewusstseinshalte. *Psychol. Stud.*, 1909, *5*, 48–72.

———. Die Probleme der psychologischen Studien von Theodor Lipps. *Arch. ges. Psychol.*, 1909, *14*, 217–278.

———. Die mathematischen Grundlagen der sogenannten unmittelbaren Behandlung psychophysischer Resultate. *Psychol. Stud.*, 1910, *6*, 141–156, 252–315, 430–454.

———. Zur erkenntnistheoretischen und mathematischen Begründung der Massmethoden für die Unterschiedsschwelle. (Kritische Betrachtungen über F. M. Urbans Behandlung der Methode der ebenmerklichen Unterschiede und G. F. Lipps' Verwertung der Gleichheitsfälle.) *Arch. ges. Psychol.*, 1911, *20*, 52–100 ; 1912, *24*, 276–312.

———. Ein einheitliches Präzisionsmass der Urteilsleistung bei der Methode der 3 Hauptfälle und seine Beziehungen zum mittleren Schätzungswert. *Arch. ges. Psychol.*, 1912, *24*, 141–171.

———. *Psychophysik. Darstellung der Methoden der experimentellen Psychologie.* Leipzig: Hirzel, 1912.

———. Ueber den Anstieg der inneren Tastempfindung. Nach Versuchen von J. Hermann bearbeitet (gemeinsam mit O. Klemm). *Psychol. Stud.*, 1913, *8*, 485–496.

———. Eine Bemerkung von G. F. Lipps zu den mathematischen Grundlagen der sog. unmittelbaren Behandlung psychophysischer Resultate. Kritisch erörtert. *Arch. ges. Psychol.*, 1913, *27*, 431–475.

———. *Zur Orientierung der Philosophie am Bewusstseinsbegriff.* Munich: Beck, 1919.

———. *Spezielle psychophysische Massmethoden.* Berlin: Urban & Schwarzenberg, 1920.

———. Zur Kritik einer verstehenden Psychologie der Weltanschauungen. *Arch. ges. Psychol.*, 1922, *43*, 72–109.

———. K. Pearsons angepasste Gerade (best fitting straight line) und die mittlere Regression. *Arch. ges. Psychol.*, 1923, *44*, 183–185.

———. Bedeutung und Gültigkeit des Fechner-Helmholtzschen Satzes über negative Nachbilder. *Arch. ges. Psychol.*, 1924, *46*, 125–187.

———. Grundfragen der Aesthetik. *Arch. ges. Psychol.*, 1925, *53*, 185–336. (Reprinted Leipzig: Akademische Verlagsgesellschaft, 1928)

———. Die psychotechnische Brauchbarkeit der Spearmanschen Rangkorrelationskoeffizienten, zumal für Augenmassprüfung. *Ind. Psychotechn.*, 1925, *2*, 22–31.

———. *Die Zeitwahrnehmung.* Leipzig: Pfeiffer, 1926.

———. Die Reaktionszeiten. In A. Bethe (Ed.), *Handbuch der normalen und pathologischen Physiologie.* Vol. 10. Berlin: Springer-Verlag, 1927, pp. 524–599.

———. Zur Widerlegung der Behauptungen von Krisen in der modernen Psychologie. In R. W. Schulte (Ed.), *Psycholog-Medizin.* Vol. 2. Stuttgart: Enke, 1927, pp. 100–131.

———. Das Wesen der psychophysischen Gesetzmässigkeit. *Arch. ges. Psychol.*, 1927, *60*, 205–234.

———. Zur Messung einer bestimmten Phase der lokalen Erregbarkeitsdifferenz im Sehorgan. *Arch. ges. Psychol.*, 1928, *65*, 163–190.

———. Die Neuen Psychologischen Studien: Kritisches Referat. *Arch. ges. Psychol.*, 1929, *70*, 417–462.

———. Die Konstanz des üblichen Masses für den simultanen Helligkeitskontrast. *Neue Psychol. Stud.*, 1930, *6*(3), 169–282.

———. Eine statistiche Gesetzmässigkeit der Verteilung psychophysischer Energie im Sehfeld. *Arch. ges. Psychol.*, 1930, *77*, 693–714.

———. Wie ich zur Philosophie und Psychologie kam. *Arch. ges. Psychol.*, 1931, *80*, 452–510. **B**

———. Die Bedeutung Wilhelm Wundts in der sogenannten Krise der Modernen Psychologie. *Wiss. Beiträge Leipzig Lehreztg.*, 1932, No. 4, 25–32.

———. Zur Berücksichtigung der Bewusstheitsgrade in der Gestalttheorie. *13. Kongr. Dtsch. Ges. Psychol.*, Leipzig, 1933, 185–186.

———. Zu den Bewusstseinsphänomenen der Gestaltauffassung. *Arch. ges. Psychol.*, 1934, *91*, 507–538.

———. Ein massmethodischer Beitrag zur Ganzheitspsychologie. *Neue psychol. Stud.*, 1934, *12*(2), 113–134.

———. Psychophysische Beiträge zur Lehre vom Zielen und Schiessen. *Arch. ges. Psychol.*, 1935, *94*, 1–32.

———. Wilhelm Wirth. In C. Murchison (Ed.), *A history of psychology in autobiography.* Vol. 3. Worcester, Mass.: Clark University Press, 1936, pp. 283–327. **B**

———. Die Zeitverhältnisse bei schnellem rechtshändigen Taktieren mit und ohne Nebenaufgabe der Rhythmisierung. *Arch. ges. Psychol.*, 1937, *98*, 245–278.

———. Die unmittelbare Teilung einer gegebenen Zeitstrecke. *Amer. J. Psychol.*, 1937, *50*, 79–96.

———. Schwankungen und Rhythmus in der Arbeitskurve. *Z. Arbeitspsychol.*, 1938, *2*, 122–127.

———. Die ersten Versuche der praktischen Anwendung eines psychophysischen Apparates zur Kontrolle des Abkommens beim Leerschuss in der Schiessausbildung. *Industr. Psychotechnik*, 1938, *15*, 19–33.

―――. Die Bedingungen der Genauigkeit psychophysischer Leistungen. *Nova Acta Leopolodina N.F.*, 1938, *6*, 41–80 ; 1939, *7*, 542–543.

―――. Psychologische Analysen des musikalischen Gehöres und seiner Typen (Zur Kritik einer Komponentenzerlegung der Tonhöhe und ihrer typologischen Auswirkungen). *Arch. ges. Psychol.*, 1941, *109*, 129–296.

―――. Erwiderung auf Welleks Verteidigung gegen meine Kritik seiner Musiktypologie des deutschen Volkes. *Arch. ges. Psychol.*, 1942–1943, *111*, 165–215.

CLARK WISSLER
1870-1947
American Anthropologist (14)

Wissler, C., & Richardson, W. W. Diffusion of the motor impulse. *Psychol. Rev.*, 1900, *7*, 29–38.

―――. The correlation of mental and physical tests. *Psychol. Monogr.*, 1901, *3*, No. 16.

―――. A review of progress in science tests. *J. Pedag.*, 1902, *14*, 203–213.

Boas, F., & ―――. Statistics of growth. *Rep. U.S. Commissioner Educ.*, *1904*, 1905, 25–132.

―――. The Spearman correlation formula. *Science*, 1905, *22*, 309–311.

―――. *North American Indians of the plain.* (3rd ed.) (Handbook Series, No. 1) New York: American Museum of Natural History, 1948. (1912)

―――. Influence of the horse in the development of plains culture. *Amer. Anthrop.*, 1914, *16*, 1–25.

―――. Material cultures of the North American Indians. *Amer. Anthrop.*, 1914, *16*, 447–505.

―――. Psychological and historical interpretations for culture. *Science*, 1916, *43*, 193–201.

―――. *The American Indian: An introduction to the anthropology of the New World.* (3rd ed.) Gloucester, Mass.: Smith, 1957. (1917)

―――. Opportunities for coordination in anthropological and psychological research. *Amer. Anthrop.*, 1920, *22*, 1–12.

―――. *Man and culture.* New York: Crowell, 1923. (Reprinted 1965)

―――. *The relation of nature to man in aboriginal America.* New York: Oxford University Press, 1926. (Reprinted 1970)

―――. The culture-area concept in social anthropology. *Amer. J. Sociol.*, 1927, *32*, 881–891.

―――. Recent developments in anthropology. In E. C. Hayes (Ed.), *Recent developments in the social sciences.* Philadelphia: Lippincott, 1927, pp. 50–96.

―――. *An introduction to social anthropology.* New York: Holt, 1929.

―――. *Growth of children in Hawaii: Based on observations by Louis R. Sullivan.* Bernice P. Bishop Memoirs, 1930, Vol. 11, No. 2. Honolulu, Hawaii: The Museum, 1930.

―――. Social history of the red man. In C. Murchison (Ed.), *A handbook of social psychology.* Worcester, Mass.: Clark University Press, 1935, pp. 268–308.

―――. Material culture. In C. Murchison (Ed.), *A handbook of social psychology.* Worcester, Mass.: Clark University Press, 1935, pp. 520–564.

―――. *Indian cavalcade: Or, life on the old-time Indian reservations.* New York: Sheridan House, 1938.

―――. *Indians of the United States: Four centuries of their history and culture.* (Rev. ed.) Ed. by Lucy W. Kluckhohn. Garden City, N.Y.: Doubleday, 1966. (1940)

―――. The American Indian and the American Philosophical Society. *Proc. Amer. Phil. Soc.*, 1943, *86*, 189–204.

Fried, *Anthropology* ; Herrnstein & Boring, *Source Book* ; Hoebel & Jennings, *Anthropology* ; Jenkins & Paterson, *Individual Differences* ; Kroeber, *Source Book*

STEPHAN WITASEK
1870-1915
German Psychologist (19)

Witasek, S. Versuche über das Vergleichen von Winkelverschiedenheiten. *Z. Psychol.,* 1896, *11,* 321–332.

——. Ueber willkürliche Vorstellungsverbindung. *Z. Psychol.,* 1896, *12,* 185–225.

——. Beiträge zur speciellen Dispositionspsychologie. *Arch. syst. Phil.,* 1897, *3,* 273–293.

——. Beiträge zur Psychologie der Komplexionen. *Z. Psychol.,* 1897, *14,* 401–435.

Meinong, A., & ——. Zur experimentellen Bestimmung der Tonverschmelzungsgrade. *Z. Psychol.,* 1897, *15,* 189–205.

——. Ueber die Natur der geometrisch-optischen Täuschungen. *Z. Psychol.,* 1899, *19,* 81–174.

——, & Höfler, A. *Psychologische Schulversuche mit Angabe der Apparate.* Leipzig: Barth, 1900.

——. Zur psychologischen Analyse der ästhetischen Einfühlung. *Z. Psychol.,* 1901, *25,* 1–49.

——. Wert und Schönheit. *Arch. syst. Phil.,* 1902, *8,* 164–193.

——. *Grundzüge der allgemeinen Aesthetik.* Leipzig: Barth, 1904.

——. *Psychologisches zur ethischen Erziehung.* Langensalza: Beyer, 1907.

——. Ueber Lesen und Rezitieren in ihrer Beziehungen zum Gedächtnis. *Z. Psychol.,* 1907, *44,* 161–185, 246–278.

——. *Grundlinien der Psychologie.* Leipzig: Meiner, 1908.

——. Zur Lehre von der Lokalisation im Sehraum. *Z. Psychol.,* 1909, *50,* 161–218.

——. Lokalisationsdifferenz und latente Gleichgewichtsstörung. *Z. Psychol.,* 1909, *53,* 61–96.

——. In Sachen der Lokalisationsdifferenz. (Zur Klärung und Abwehr.) *Z. Psychol.,* 1910, *56,* 85–103.

——. *Psychologie der Raumwahrnehmung des Auges.* Heidelberg: Winter, 1910.

——. Ueber ästhetische Objektivität. *Z. Phil., phil. Krit,* 1915, *157,* 87–113, 179–199.

——. Assoziation und Gestalteinprägung. *Z. Psychol.,* 1918, *79,* 161–210.

LIGHTNER WITMER
1867-1956
American Psychologist (19)

Witmer, L. The psychological analysis and physical basis of pleasure and pain. *J. nerv. ment. Dis.,* 1894, *21,* 209–228.

——. Zur experimentellen Aesthetik einfacher räumlicher Formverhältnisse. *Phil. Stud.,* 1894, *9,* 96–144, 209–263.

——. Practical work in psychology. *Pediatrics,* 1896, *2,* 462–471.

——. *Analytical psychology.* Boston: Ginn, 1902.

——. Clinical psychology. *Psychol. Clin.,* 1907, *1,* 1–9. Reprinted in R. A. Brotemarkle (Ed.), *Clinical psychology: Studies in honor of Lightner Witmer to commemorate the thirty-fifth anniversary of the founding of the first psychological clinic.* Philadelphia: University of Pennsylvania Press, 1931, pp. 341–352. **B**

——. University courses in psychology. *Psychol. Clin.,* 1907, *1,* 25–35.

——. A case of chronic bad spelling—Amnesia Visualis Verbalis, due to arrest of post-natal development. *Psychol. Clin.,* 1907, *1,* 53–64.

——. The hospital school. *Psychol. Clin.,* 1907, *1,* 138–146.

——. Retardation through neglect in children of the rich. *Psychol. Clin.,* 1907, *1,* 157–174.

——. Retrospect and prospect: An editorial. *Psychol. Clin.,* 1908–1909, *2,* 1–4.

——. The treatment and cure of a case of mental and moral deficiency. *Psychol. Clin.,* 1908–1909, *2,* 153–179.

——. The restoration of children of the slums. *Psychol. Clin.*, 1910, *3*, 266–280.

——. Courses in psychology at the Summer School of the University of Pennsylvania. *Psychol. Clin.*, 1911, *4*, 245–273.

——. *The special class for backward children.* Philadelphia: Psychological Clinic Press, 1911.

——. The Montessori method. *Psychol. Clin.*, 1914, *8*, 1–5.

——. On the relation of intelligence to efficiency. *Psychol. Clin.*, 1915, *9*, 61–86. Reprinted in R. A. Brotemarkle (Ed.), *Clinical psychology, op. cit.*, pp. 353–387.

——. Clinical records. *Psychol. Clin.*, 1915, *9*, 1–17.

——. Diagnostic education—an education for the fortunate few. *Psychol. Clin.*, 1917, *11*, 69–78.

——. Performance and success: An outline of psychology for diagnostic testing and teaching. *Psychol. Clin.*, 1919, *12*, 145–170.

——. The problem of educability. *Psychol. Clin.*, 1919, *12*, 174–178.

——. Efficiency and other factors of success. *Psychol. Clin.*, 1919, *12*, 241–247.

——. The training of very bright children. *Psychol. Clin.*, 1919–1920, *13*, 88–96.

——. Orthogenic cases. XIV. Don: A curable case of arrested development due to a fear psychosis, the result of shock in a three-year-old infant. *Psychol. Clin.*, 1919–1920, *13*, 97–111.

——. Intelligence—a definition. *Psychol. Clin.*, 1922, *14*, 65–67.

——. The analytical diagnosis. *Psychol. Clin.*, 1922, *14*, 129–135.

——. What is intelligence and who has it? *Sci. Mon.*, N.Y., 1922, *15*, 57–67.

——. Psychological diagnosis and the psychonomic orientation of analytic science. *Psychol. Clin.*, 1925, *16*, 1–18. Reprinted in R. A. Brotemarkle (Ed.), *Clinical psychology, op. cit.*, pp. 388–409.

Beck & Molish, *Reflexes*

(BARON) CHRISTIAN VON WOLFF (or WOLF) 1679-1754 German Philosopher (25)

Wolff, C. v. *Eigene Lebensbeschreibung.* Ed. by H. Wuttke. Leipzig: Weidmann, 1841.   **B C**

Leibniz, G. W., & ——. *Briefwechsel zwischen Leibniz und Christian Wolff.* Ed. by C. v. Gerhardt. Hildesheim: Olms, 1963. (1860)
B C

——. *Gesammelte Werke.* (Ult. 51 vols.) Ed. by J. Ecole *et al.* Hildesheim: Olms, 1962– .
B C Cl

——. *Logic, or rational thoughts on the powers of the human understanding: With their use and application in the knowledge and search of truth.* (9th ed.) London: Hawes *et al.*, 1770. (1713) Reprinted in German in *Gesammelte Werke*, Part 1, Vol. 1, *op. cit.*, 1965.

——. Elementa matheseos universae. (1713) Reprinted in *Gesammelte Werke*. Part 2, Vols. 29–32, *op. cit.*, 1968.

——. Mathematisches Lexikon. (1716) Reprinted in *Gesammelte Werke*, Part 1, Vol. 11, *op. cit.*, 1965.

——. *Vernünftige Gedanken von Gott, der Welt und der Seele, der Menschen auch allen Dingen überhaupt.* (New ed.) Halle: Renger, 1747. (1719)

——. *Vernünftige Gedanken von der Menschen Thun und Lassen zu Beförderung ihrer Glückseligkeit.* (New ed.) Halle: Renger, 1754. (1720)

——. *Vernünftige Gedanken von dem gesellschaftlichen Leben der Menschen.* (New ed.) Halle: Madgeburg, 1756. (1721)

——. *Vernünftige Gedanken von den Würkungen der Natur.* (5th ed.) Halle: Renger, 1746. (1723)

——. *Preliminary discourse on philosophy in general.* Trans. by R. J. Blackwell. Indianapolis, Ind.: Bobbs-Merrill, 1963. (1728)

——. *Philosophia rationalis, sive logica methodo scientifica pertractata et ad usum scientiarum atque vitae aptata.* (3rd ed.) Frankfurt: Renger, 1740. (1728)

——. Philosophia prima sive ontologia. (1730) Reprinted in *Gesammelte Werke,* Part 2, Vol. 3, *op. cit.,* 1962.

——. Cosmologia generalis methodo scientifica pertractata, qua ad solidam, imprimis Dei atque naturae, cognitionem via sternitur. (1731) Reprinted in *Gesammelte Werke,* Part 2, Vol. 4, *op. cit.,* 1964.

——. Psychologia empirica. (1732) Reprinted in *Gesammelte Werke,* Part 2, Vol. 5, *op. cit.,* 1968.

——. *Psychologia rationalis.* Frankfurt: Renger, 1734.

——. Jus naturae. (1740–1748) Reprinted in *Gesammelte Werke,* Part 2, Vols. 17–24, *op. cit.,* 1968.

——. *Jus gentium methodo scientifica pertractatum.* Eng. trans. of 1764 ed. by J. H. Drake. Oxford: Clarendon Press, 1934. (1749)

——. Institutiones juris naturae et gentium. (1750) Reprinted in *Gesammelte Werke,* Part 2, Vol. 29, *op. cit.,* 1969.

——. *Philosophia moralis sive ethica.* (5 vols.) Halle: Magdeburg, 1750–1753.

Rand, *Classical Psychologists*

ROBERT SESSIONS WOODWORTH
1869-1962
American Psychologist (27)

Woodworth, R. S. *Psychological issues: Selected papers of Robert S. Woodworth.* New York: Columbia University Press, 1939. (Reprinted 1970) **B Bl C**

Ladd, G. T., & ——. *Elements of physiological psychology.* (Rev. ed.) New York: Scribner's, 1911. (1887)

——. The accuracy of voluntary movement. *Psychol. Monogr.,* 1899, *3,* No. 13.

——, & Thorndike, E. L. Judgments of magnitude by comparison with a mental standard. *Psychol. Rev.,* 1900, *7,* 344–355. Reprinted in *Psychological issues, op. cit.,* pp. 61–71.

Thorndike, E. L., & ——. The influence of improvement in one mental function upon the efficiency of other functions. *Psychol. Rev.,* 1901, *8,* 247–261, 384–395, 553–564. Reprinted in *Psychological issues, op. cit.,* pp. 335–369.

——. On the voluntary control of the force of movement. *Psychol. Rev.,* 1901, *8,* 350–359. Reprinted in *Psychological issues, op. cit.,* pp. 287–295.

——. Maximal contraction, "staircase" contraction, refractory period, and compensatory pause of the heart. *Amer. J. Physiol.,* 1902, *8,* 213–248. Reprinted in *Psychological issues, op. cit.,* pp. 296–332.

——. *Le mouvement.* Paris: Doin, 1903.

——, & Sherrington, C. S. A pseudaffective reflex and its spinal path. *J. Physiol.,* 1904, *31,* 234–243.

——. The cause of a voluntary movement. In J. H. Tufts *et al.* (Eds.), *Studies in philosophy and psychology by former students of Charles Edward Garman.* Boston: Houghton, Mifflin, 1906, pp. 351–392. Reprinted in *Psychological issues, op. cit.,* pp. 29–60.

——. Psychiatry and experimental psychology. *Amer. J. Insan.,* 1906, *63,* 27–38. Reprinted in *Psychological issues, op. cit.,* pp. 166–176.

——. Imageless thought. *J. Phil.,* 1906, *3,* 701–708. Reprinted in *Psychological issues, op. cit.,* pp. 72–79.

——. Non-sensory components of sense perception. *J. Phil.,* 1907, *4,* 169–176. Reprinted in *Psychological issues, op. cit.,* pp. 80–88.

——. The consciousness of relation. *Essays, philosophical and psychological, in honor of William James.* New York: Longmans, Green, 1908, pp. 483–507. Reprinted in *Psychological issues, op. cit.,* pp. 89–102.

——. How the psychological mechanism works. *Psychotherapy,* 1909, *4,* 68–84. Reprinted in *Psychological issues, op. cit.,* pp. 177–191.

——. Racial differences in mental traits. *Science,* 1910, *31,* 171–186. Reprinted in *Psychological issues, op. cit.,* pp. 215–237.

———. The puzzle of color vocabularies. *Psychol. Bull.*, 1910, 7, 325–334. Reprinted in *Psychological issues, op. cit.*, pp. 238–248.

———, & Wells, F. L. Association tests. *Psychol. Monogr.*, 1911, *13*, No. 57.

———. On factors contributing to a low scientific productivity in America. *Science*, 1911, *33*, 374–379. Reprinted in *Psychological issues, op. cit.*, pp. 247–256.

———. Combining the results of several tests: A study in statistical method. *Psychol. Rev.*, 1912, *19*, 97–123. Reprinted in *Psychological issues, op. cit.*, pp. 257–283.

———. Professor Cattell's psychophysical contributions. *Arch. Psychol.*, N.Y., 1914, *30*, 60–74.

———. A revision of imageless thought. *Psychol. Rev.*, 1915, *22*, 1–27. Reprinted in *Psychological issues, op. cit.*, pp. 103–127.

———. Some criticisms of the Freudian psychology. *J. abnorm. Psychol.*, 1917, *12*, 174–194. Reprinted in *Psychological issues, op. cit.*, pp. 192–211.

———. *Dynamic psychology.* New York: Columbia University Press, 1918.

———, & Marquis, D. G. *Psychology.* (5th ed.) New York: Holt, 1947. (1921)

———. Four varieties of behaviorism. *Psychol. Rev.*, 1924, *31*, 257–264. Reprinted in *Psychological issues, op. cit.*, pp. 128–135.

———. Dynamic psychology. In C. Murchison (Ed.), *Psychologies of 1925.* (3rd ed.) Worcester, Mass.: Clark University Press, 1928, pp. 111–126. (1926)

———. Gestalt psychology and the concept of reaction stages. *Amer. J. Psychol.*, 1927, *39*, 62–69. Reprinted in *Psychological issues, op. cit.*, pp. 141–148.

———. A justification of the concept of instinct. *J. abnorm. soc. Psychol.*, 1927, *22*, 3–7. Reprinted in *Psychological issues, op. cit.*, pp.136–140.

———. How emotions are identified and classified. In M. L. Reymert (Ed.), *Feelings and emotions: The Wittenberg symposium.* Worcester, Mass.: Clark University Press, 1928, pp. 222–227.

———. Dynamic psychology. In C. Murchison (Ed.), *Psychologies of 1930.* Worcester, Mass.: Clark University Press, 1930, pp. 327–336.

———, & Sheehan, Mary R. *Contemporary schools of psychology.* (3rd ed.) New York: Ronald Press, 1964. (1931)   **Bl**

———. Robert S. Woodworth. In C. Murchison (Ed.), *A history of psychology in autobiography.* Vol. 2. Worcester, Mass.: Clark University Press, 1932, pp. 359–380. Reprinted in *Psychological issues, op. cit.*, pp. 3–25.   **B**

———. *Adjustment and mastery: Problems in psychology.* Baltimore, Md.: Williams & Wilkins, 1933.

———, & Sells, S. B. An atmosphere effect in formal syllogistic reasoning. *J. exp. Psychol.*, 1935, *18*, 451–460.

———. Situation-and-goal set. *Amer. J. Psychol.*, 1937, *50*, 130–140. Reprinted in *Psychological issues, op. cit.*, pp. 149–160.

———. The future of clinical psychology. *J. consult. Psychol.*, 1937, *1*, 4–5.

———. *Experimental psychology.* New York: Holt, 1938.

———, & Schlosberg, H. *Experimental psychology.* (Rev. ed.) New York: Holt, 1960. (1938)

———. Individual and group behavior. *Amer. J. Sociol.*, 1939, *44*, 823–828.

———. Heredity and environment. (A critical survey of recently published materials on twins and foster children.) *Soc. Sci. Res. Counc. Bull.*, 1941, No. 47.

———. *The Columbia University Psychological Laboratory: A fifty-year retrospect.* New York: Author, 1942.   **B**

———. The adolescence of American psychology. *Psychol. Rev.*, 1943, *50*, 10–32.

———. Reinforcement of perception. *Amer. J. Psychol.*, 1947, *60*, 119–124.

——. *Dynamics of behavior.* New York: Holt, Rinehart, & Winston, 1958.

Beck & Molish, *Reflexes;* Bindra & Stewart, *Motivation;* Herrnstein & Boring, *Source Book;* Jenkins & Paterson, *Individual Differences;* Kroeber, *Source Book;* Russell, *Motivation;* Sahakian, *Psychology*

WILHELM (MAX or MAXIMILIAN) WUNDT
1832-1920
German Psychologist (27)

Wundt, W. *Essays.* Leipzig: Engelmann, 1906. (1885) **C**

——. *Kleine Schriften.* (2 vols.) Leipzig: Engelmann, 1911. **C**

——. *Die Lehre von der Muskelbewegung. Nach eigenen Untersuchungen bearbeitet.* Brunswick: Vieweg, 1858.

——. *Beiträge zur Theorie der Sinneswahrnehmung.* (3rd ed.) Leipzig: Winter, 1897. (1862)

——. *Vorlesungen über die Menschen- und Thierseele.* (7th, 8th eds.) (2 vols.) Hamburg: Voss, 1922. (1863–1864)

——. *Lectures on human and animal psychology.* (2nd ed.) Trans. by J. E. Creighton & E. B. Titchener. New York: Macmillan, 1901. (1863–1864)

——. *Lehrbuch der Physiologie des Menschen.* (4th ed.) Stuttgart: Enke, 1878. (1864)

——. *Die physikalischen Axiome und ihre Beziehung zum Causalprincip.* Erlangen: Enke, 1866.

——. Ueber einige Zeitverhältnisse des Wechsels der Sinnesvorstellungen. *Deutsch. Klin.,* 1866, *18,* No. 9.

——. Die Entstehung räumlicher Gesichtswahrnehmungen. *Phil. Monatsh.,* 1869, *3,* 225–247.

——. *Untersuchungen zur Mechanik der Nerven und Nervencentren.* (2 vols. in 1.) Erlangen: Enke, 1871.

——. *Grundzüge der physiologischen Psychologie.* (6th ed.) (3 vols.) Leipzig: Engelmann, 1908–1911. (1873, 1874)

——. *Principles of physiological psychology.* Intro. & Part 1 of 5th German ed. Trans. by E. B. Titchener. New York: Macmillan, 1904. (1873, 1874)

——. *Ueber den Einfluss der Philosophie auf die Erfahrungswissenschaften.* Leipzig: Engelmann, 1876.

——. Central innervation and consciousness. *Mind,* 1876, *1,* 161–178.

——. Sur la théorie des signes locaux. *Rev. phil.,* 1878, *6,* 217–231.

——. Ueber den gegenwärtigen Zustand der Thierpsychologie. *Vtljsch. wiss. Phil.,* 1878, *2,* 137–149.

——. Ueber das Verhältniss der Gefühle zu den Vorstellungen. *Vtljsch. wiss. Phil.,* 1879, *3,* 129–151.

——. *Logik: Eine Untersuchung der Principien der Erkenntnis und der Methoden wissenschaftlicher Forschung.* (4th ed.) (3 vols.) Stuttgart: Enke, 1919–1921. (1880–1883)

——. Ueber die mathematische Induktion. *Phil. Stud.,* 1881–1883, *1,* 90–147.

——. Ueber psychologische Methoden. *Phil. Stud.,* 1881–1883, *1,* 1–38.

——. Ueber die Messung psychischer Vorgäme. *Phil. Stud.,* 1881–1883, *1,* 251–260.

——. Zur Lehre vom Willen. *Phil. Stud.,* 1881–1883 *1,* 337–378.

——. Weitere Bemerkungen über psychische Me ung. *Phil. Stud.,* 1881–1883, *1,* 463–472.

——. Schlusswort zum ersten Bande. *Phil. Stud.,* 1881–1883, *1,* 615–617.

——. Ueber das Weber'sche Gesetz. *Phil. Stud.,* 1883–1885, *2,* 1–36.

——. Erfundene Empfindungen. *Phil. Stud.,* 1883–1885, *2,* 298–305.

——. Zur Kritik des Seelenbegriffs. *Phil. Stud.,* 1883–1885, *2,* 483–494.

———. Kant's kosmologische Antinomien und das Problem der Unendlichkeit. *Phil. Stud.*, 1883–1885, *2*, 495–538.

———. *Ethics: An investigation of the facts and laws of the moral life.* (3 vols.) Trans. by E. B. Titchener. New York: Macmillan, 1879–1901. (1886)

———. Ueber Ziele und Wege der Völkerpsychologie. *Phil. Stud.*, 1887–1888, *4*, 1–27.

———. Selbstbeobachtung und innere Wahrnehmung. *Phil. Stud.*, 1887–1888, *4*, 292–309.

———. Die Empfindung des Lichts und der Farben. *Phil. Stud.*, 1887–1888, *4*, 311–389.

———. Zur Erinnerung an Gustav Theodor Fechner. Worte gesprochen an seinem Sarge 21. Nov., 1887. *Phil. Stud.*, 1887–1888, *4*, 471–478.

———. Ueber die Eintheilung der Wissenschaften. *Phil. Stud.*, 1888–1889, *5*, 1–55.

———. Biologische Probleme. *Phil. Stud.*, 1888–1889, *5*, 327–380.

———. *System der Philosophie.* (4th ed.) (3 vols.) Leipzig: Engelmann, 1919. (1889)

———. Zur Frage der Localisation der Grosshirnfunctionen. *Phil. Stud.*, 1890–1891, *6*, 1–25.

———. Ueber die Methoden der Messung des Bewusstseinsumfanges. *Phil. Stud.*, 1890–1891, *6*, 250–260.

———. Zur Lehre von den Gemüthsbewegungen. *Phil. Stud.*, 1890–1891, *6*, 335–393.

———. Ueber Vergleichungen von Tondistanzen. *Phil. Stud.*, 1890–1891, *6*, 605–640.

———. Zur Frage des Bewusstseinsumfanges. *Phil. Stud.*, 1892, *7*, 222–231.

———. Eine Replik C. Stumpfs. *Phil. Stud.*, 1891–1892, *7*, 298–327.

———. Bemerkungen zur Associationslehre. *Phil. Stud.*, 1891–1892, *7*, 329–361.

———. Auch ein Schlusswort. *Phil. Stud.*, 1891–1892, *7*, 633–636.

———. *Beiträge zur Theorie der Sinneswahrnehmung.* Leipzig: Winter, 1892.

———. Hypnotismus und Suggestion. *Phil. Stud.*, 1893, *8*, 1–85. (Also Leipzig: Engelmann, 1892)

———. Ist der Hörnerv direct durch Tonschwingungen erregbar? *Phil. Stud.*, 1893, *8*, 641–652.

———. Akustische Versuche an einer labyrinthlosen Taube. *Phil. Stud.*, 1894, *9*, 496–509

———. Ueber psychische Kausalität und das Princip des psychophysischen Parallelismus. *Phil. Stud.*, 1894, *10*, 1–124.

———. Zur Beurtheilung der zusammengesetzten Reactionen. *Phil. Stud.*, 1894, *10*, 485–498.

———. Ueber die Definition der Psychologie. *Phil. Stud.*, 1896, *12*, 1–66.

———. Ueber naiven und kritischen Realismus. *Phil. Stud.*, 1895–1896, *12*, 307–408; 1897–1898, *13*, 1–105, 323–433.

———. *Outlines of psychology.* (7th ed.) Trans. by C. H. Judd. Leipzig: Engelmann, 1907. (1896)

———. *Grundriss der Psychologie.* (10th ed.) Leipzig: Engelmann, 1911. (1896)

———. *Die geometrisch-optischen Täuschungen.* Leipzig: Teubner, 1898.

———. Zur Theorie der räumlichen Gesichtswahrnehmungen. *Phil. Stud.*, 1898, *14*, 1–118.

———. Bemerkungen zur Theorie der Gefühle. *Phil. Stud.*, 1899–1900, *15*, 149–182.

———. Zur Kritik tachistoskopischer Versuche. *Phil. Stud.*, 1899–1900, *15*, 287–317; 1900, *16*, 61–70.

———. Zur Technik des Complicationspendels. *Phil. Stud.*, 1899–1900, *15*, 579–582.

———. *Völkerpsychologie.* (10 vols.) Leipzig: Engelmann, 1900–1920. (Reprinted 1965–1969)

———. *Einleitung in die Philosophie.* (9th ed.) Leipzig: Kröner, 1922. (1901)

———. *Gustav Theodor Fechner: Rede zur Feier seines 100-jährigen Geburtstages.* Leipzig: Engelmann, 1901.

———. *Naturwissenschaft und Psychologie.* Leipzig: Engelmann, 1911. (1903)

———. Ueber Ausfrageexperimente und über die Methoden zur Psychologie des Denkens. *Psychol. Stud.,* 1907, *3,* 301–360.

———. Kritische Nachlese zur Ausfragemethode. *Arch. ges. Psychol.,* 1908, *11,* 445–459.

———. Das Institut für experimentelle Psychologie. *Festschrift zur Feier des 500-jährigen Bestehens der Universität.* Leipzig: Engelmann, 1909, *4, Pt. 1,* pp. 118–133.

———. Ueber rein und angewandte Psychologie. *Psychol. Stud.,* 1909, *5,* 1–47.

———. *Zur Psychologie und Ethik.* Leipzig: Reclam, 1911.

———. *Probleme der Völkerpsychologie.* Leipzig: Wiegandt, 1911.

———. *An introduction to psychology.* (2nd ed.) Trans. by R. Pintner. New York: Macmillan, 1912. (1911)

———. *Elements of folk psychology: Outlines of a psychological history of the development of mankind.* London: Allen, 1916. (1912)

———. *Ueber den wahrhaften Krieg.* Leipzig: Kröner, 1914.

———. *Erlebtes und Erkanntes.* Stuttgart: Kröner, 1920.   **B**

Dember, *Perception ;* Dennis, *Psychology ;* Herrnstein & Boring, *Source Book ;* Rand, *Classical Psychologists ;* Reeves, *Body Mind ;* Shipley, *Classics*

ROBERT MEARNS YERKES
1876-1956
American Psychologist (27)

Yerkes, R. M. Reaction of *Entromostraca* to stimulation by light. *Amer. J. Physiol.,* 1899, *3,* 157–182.

———. The formation of habits in the turtle. *Pop. Sci. Mon.,* 1901, *58,* 519–525.

———. The instincts, habits and reactions of the frog. *Psychol. Monogr.,* 1903, *4,* No. 17, 579–638.

———. Bahnung und Hemmung der Reactionen auf tactile Reize durch akustische Reize beim Frosche. *Arch. ges. Physiol.,* 1905, *107,* 207–237.

———. Animal psychology and criteria of the psychic. *J. Phil.,* 1905, *2,* 141–149.

———. Concerning the genetic relations of types of action. *J. comp. Neurol.,* 1905, *15,* 132–137.

———, & Urban, F. M. Time-estimation in its relation to sex, age, and physiological rhythms. *Havard psychol. Stud.,* 1906, *2,* 405–430.

———. The mutual relations of stimuli in the frog *Rana Clamata daudin. Harvard psychol. Stud.,* 1906, *2,* 545–574.

———. *The dancing mouse: A study in animal behavior.* New York: Macmillan, 1907.

———, & Dodson, J. D. The relation of strength of stimulus to rapidity of habit formation. *J. comp. Neurol.,* 1908, *18,* 459–482.

———, & Morgulis, S. The method of Pavlov in animal psychology. *Psychol. Bull.,* 1909, *6,* 257–273.

———. Psychology in its relation to biology. *J. Phil.,* 1910, *7,* 113–124.

———, & Bloomfield, D. Do kittens instinctively kill mice? *Psychol. Bull.,* 1910, *7,* 253–263.

———. *Introduction to psychology.* New York: Holt, 1911.

———, & Watson, J. B. Methods of studying vision in animals. *Behav. Monogr.,* 1911, *1,* No. 2.

———. The discrimination method. *J. anim. Behav.,* 1912, *2,* 142–144.

———. The intelligence of earthworms. *J. anim. Behav.,* 1912, *2,* 332–352.

———, & La Rue, D. W. *Outline of a study of the self.* Cambridge: Harvard University Press, 1913.

———. The heredity of savageness and wildness in rats. *J. anim. Behav.,* 1913, *3,* 286–296.

———. The study of human behavior. *Science,* 1914, *39,* 625–633.

————, Bridges, W., & Hardwick, Rose S. *A point scale for measuring mental ability*. Baltimore, Md.: Warwick & York, 1915.

————. The mental life of monkeys and apes. *Behav. Monogr.*, 1916, *3*, No. 12. (Also Boston: Holt, 1916)

————. Methods of exhibiting reactive tendencies characteristic of ontogenetic and phylogenetic stages. *J. anim. Behav.*, 1917, *7*, 11–28.

————. Behaviorism and genetic psychology. *J. Phil.*, 1917, *14*, 154–160.

————. Psychology in relation to the war. *Psychol. Rev.*, 1918, *25*, 85–115.

————. Report of the psychology committee of the National Research Council. *Psychol. Rev.*, 1919, *26*, 83–149.

Yoakum, C. S., & ————. *Army mental tests*. New York: Holt, 1920.

———— (Ed.), Psychological examining in the United States Army. *Mem. Nat. Acad. Sci.*, 1921, No. 15.

————. A new method of studying the ideational behavior of mentally defective and deranged as compared with normal individuals. *J. comp. Psychol.*, 1921, *1*, 369–394.

————. *Almost human.* New York: Century, 1925.

————, & Learned, Blanche W. *Chimpanzee intelligence and its vocal expressions*. Baltimore, Md.: Williams & Wilkins, 1925.

————. The mind of a gorilla. Parts 1 & 2. *Genet. Psychol. Monogr.*, 1927, *2*, 1–193, 375–551.

————. The mind of a gorilla. Part 3. Memory. *Comp. Psychol. Monogr.*, 1928, *5*, No. 2, 1–94.

————, & Yerkes, Ada W. *The great apes: A study of anthropoid life*. New Haven: Yale University Press, 1945. (1929)

————. Robert Mearns Yerkes: Psychobiologist. In C. Murchison (Ed.), *A history of psychology in autobiography*. Vol. 2. Worcester, Mass.: Clark University Press, 1932, pp. 381–407. **B**

————. Concerning the anthropocentrism of psychology. *Psychol. Rev.*, 1933, *40*, 209–212.

————. Modes of behavioral adaptation in chimpanzee to multiple-choice problems. *Comp. Psychol. Monogr.*, 1934, *10*, No. 47.

————, & Tomilin, M. I. Chimpanzee twins: Behavioral relations and development. *J. genet. Psychol.*, 1935, *46*, 239–263.

————, & Tomilin, M. I. Mother-infant relations in chimpanzee. *J. comp. Psychol.*, 1935, *20*, 321–359.

————, & Yerkes, Ada W. Social behavior in infrahuman primates. In C. Murchison (Ed.), *A handbook of social psychology*. Worcester, Mass.: Clark University Press, 1935, pp. 973–1033.

————. Primate coöperation and intelligence. *Amer. J. Psychol.*, 1937, *50*, 254–270.

Spence, K. W., & ————. Weight, growth and age in chimpanzees. *Amer. J. phys. Anthrop.*, 1937, *22*, 229–246.

————, & Nissen, H. W. Prelinguistic sign behavior in chimpanzee. *Science*, 1939, *89*, 585–587.

————. Social behavior of chimpanzees: Dominance between mates, in relation to sexual status. *J. comp. Psychol.*, 1940, *30*, 147–186.

————. *Chimpanzees: A laboratory colony*. New Haven: Yale University Press, 1943.

————. Psychology in world reconstruction. *J. consult. Psychol.*, 1946, *10*, 1–7.

Boe & Church, *Punishment;* Dennis, *Psychology;* Herrnstein & Boring, *Source Book;* Sahakian, *Psychology;* Valentine, *Experimental*

THOMAS YOUNG
1773-1829
English Physicist (23)

Young, T. *Miscellaneous works of the late Thomas Young*. (3 vols.) Vols. 1 & 2 ed. by G. Peacock; Vol. 3 ed. by J. Leitch. London: Murray, 1855. (Reprinted 1971) **C**

————. Observations on vision. *Phil. Trans.*, 1793, *83*, 169–181. Reprinted in *Miscellaneous works*, Vol. 1, *op. cit.*, pp. 1–11.

——. Outlines of experiments and inquiries respecting sound and light. *Phil. Trans.*, 1800, *90*, 106–150. Reprinted in *Miscellaneous works*, Vol. 1, *op. cit.*, pp. 64–98.

——. On the mechanism of the eye. *Phil. Trans.*, 1801, *91*, 23–88. Reprinted in *Miscellaneous works*, Vol. 1, *op. cit.*, pp. 12–63.

——. On the theory of light and colours. *Phil. Trans.*, 1802, *92*, 12–48. Reprinted in *Miscellaneous works*, Vol. 1, *op. cit.*, pp. 140–169, & in part in H. Crew (Ed.), *The wave theory of light*. New York: American Book, 1900, pp. 47–61.

——. An account of some cases of the production of colours not hitherto described. *Phil. Trans.*, 1802, *92*, 387–397. Reprinted in *Miscellaneous works*, Vol. 1, *op. cit.*, pp. 170–178, & in part in H. Crew (Ed.), *The wave theory of light*. New York: American Book, 1900, pp. 62–67.

——. *A course of lectures on natural philosophy and the mechanical arts.* (New ed.) (2 vols.) Ed. by P. Kelland. London: Taylor & Walton, 1845. (1807) (Reprinted 1972)

——. *An introduction to medical literature, including a system of practical nosology. Intended as a guide to students and an assistant to practitioners.* London: Howlett, 1813.

——. Remarks on the probabilities of error in physical observations, and on the density of the earth, considered, especially with regard to the reduction of experiments on the pendulum, in a letter to Capt. Henry Kater, F.R.S. *Phil. Trans.*, 1819, *109*, 70–95. Reprinted in *Miscellaneous works*, Vol. 2, *op. cit.*, pp. 8–28.

Dember, *Perception ;* Dennis, *Psychology ;* Herrnstein & Boring, *Source Book ;* MacAdam, *Color Science ;* Murphy, *Western ;* Teevan, *Vision*

GEORGE UDNY YULE
1871-1951
English Statistician (20)

Yule, G. U. *Statistical papers of George Udny Yule.* Ed. by A. Stuart & M. G. Kendall. London: Griffin, 1971. **B C**

——. On the significance of Bravais' formulae for regression, etc., in the case of skew correlation. *Proc. Roy. Soc.*, London, 1897, *60A*, 477–489.

——. Note on the teaching of the theory of statistics at the University College. *J. Roy. Stat. Soc.*, 1897, *60A*, 456–458.

——. On the theory of correlation. *J. Roy. Stat. Soc.*, 1897, *60A*, 812–854.

——. On the association of attributes in statistics: With illustrations from the material of the childhood, society etc. *Phil. Trans.*, 1900, *194A*, 257–319.

——. On the theory of consistence of logical class-frequencies, and its geometrical representation. *Phil. Trans.*, 1901, *197A*, 91–133.

——. Notes on the theory of association of attributes in statistics. *Biometrika*, 1902–1903, *2*, 121–134.

——. Mendel's laws and their probable relation to intra-racial heredity. *New Phytologist*, 1902, *1*, 193–207, 223–238.

——. The introduction of the words "statistics," "statistical" into the English language. *J. Roy. Stat. Soc.*, 1905, *68*, 391–396.

——, & Hooker, R. H. Note on estimating the relative influence of two variables upon a third. *J. Roy. Stat. Soc.*, 1906, *69*, 197–200.

——. On the theory of correlation for any number of variables, treated by a new system of notation. *Proc. Roy. Soc.*, London, 1907, *79A*, 182–193.

——. The applications of the method of correlation to social and economic statistics. *J. Roy. Stat. Soc.*, 1909, *72*, 721–730.

——. On the interpretation of correlations between indices or ratios. *J. Roy. Stat. Soc.*, 1910, *73*, 644–647.

——, & Kendall, M. G. *An introduction to the theory of statistics.* (14th ed.) London: Griffin, 1958. (1911)

——. On the methods of measuring association between two attributes. *J. Roy. Stat. Soc.*, 1912, *75*, 579–652.

Greenwood, M., & ———. The statistics of anti-typhoid and anti-cholera inoculation and the interpretation of such statistics in general. *Roy. Soc. Med.,* Sect. epidem. stat. med., 1915, *8,* part 2, 113–194.

Greenwood, M., & ———. An enquiry into the nature of frequency distributions representative of multiple happenings with particular reference to the occurrence of multiple attacks of disease or of repeated accident. *J. Roy. Stat. Soc.,* 1920, *83,* 255–279.

———. On the application of the χ^2 method to association and contingency tables, with experimental illustrations. *J. Roy. Stat. Soc.,* 1922, *85,* 95–104.

———. A mathematical theory of evolution, based on the conclusions of Dr. J. C. Willis, F.R.S. *Phil. Trans.,* 1925, *213B,* 21–87.

———. The growth of population and the factors which control it. *J. Roy. Stat. Soc.,* 1925, *88,* 1–58.

———. Why do we sometimes get nonsense correlations between time-series? A study in sampling and the nature of time-series. *J. Roy. Stat. Soc.,* 1926, *89,* 1–64.

———. On a method of investigating periodicities in disturbed series, with special reference to Wolfer's sunspot numbers. *Phil. Trans.,* 1927, *226A,* 267–298.

———. On some points relating to vital statistics, more especially statistics of occupational mortality. *J. Roy. Stat. Soc.,* 1934, *97,* 1–72.

———. On a parallelism between differential coefficients and regression coefficients. *J. Roy. Stat. Soc.,* 1936, *99,* 770–776.

———. *The statistical study of literary vocabulary.* Cambridge: Cambridge University Press, 1944. (Reprinted 1968)

———. On a method of studying time series based on their internal correlations. *J. Roy. Stat. Soc.,* 1945, *108,* 208–225.

———. Cumulative sampling: A speculation as to what happens in copying manuscripts. *J. Roy. Stat. Soc.,* 1946, *109,* 44–52.

———. Puyol's Classes A and B of tests of the "De Imitatione Christi." *Recherches de théologie ancienne et médiévale,* 1947, *14,* 65–88.

KARL EDWARD ZENER
1903-1964
American Psychologist (15)

Zener, K. E. The significance of behavior accompanying conditioned salivary secretion for theories of the conditioned response. *Amer. J. Psychol.,* 1937, *50,* 384–403.

———, & McCurdy, H. G. Analysis of motivational factors in conditioned behavior. I. The differential effect of changes in hunger upon conditioned, unconditioned, and spontaneous salivary secretion. *J. Psychol.,* 1939, *8,* 321–350.

Bevan, W., Jr., & ———. Some influences of past experience upon the perceptual thresholds of visual form. *Amer. J. Psychol.,* 1952, *65,* 434–442.

———. The significance of experience of the individual for the science of psychology. In H. Feigl, M. Scriven, & G. Maxwell (Eds.), *Minnesota studies in the philosophy of science.* Vol. 2. *Concepts, theories, and the mind-body problem.* Minneapolis, Minn.: University of Minnesota Press, 1958, pp. 354–369.

Crovitz, H. F., Datson, P. G., & ———. Laterality and a phenomenon of localization. *Percept. mot. skills,* 1959, *9,* 282.

———, & Gaffron, Mercedes. Perceptual experience: An analysis of its relations to the external world through internal processing. In S. Koch (Ed.), *Psychology: A study of a science.* Study 2. *Empirical substructures and relations with other sciences.* Vol. 4. *Biologically oriented fields: Their place in psychology and in biological science.* New York: McGraw-Hill, 1962, pp. 515–618.

Crovitz, H. F., & ———. A group-test for assessing hand-and-eye dominance. *Amer. J. Psychol.,* 1962, *75,* 271–276.

THEODOR ZIEHEN
1862-1950
German Psychiatrist (18)

Ziehen, T. *Leitfaden der physiologischen Psychologie in 16 Vorlesungen.* (15th ed.) Jena: Fischer, 1924. (1891)

———. *Introduction to physiological psychology.* (4th ed.) Trans. by C. C. v. Liew & O. W. Beyer. New York: Macmillan, 1909. (1891)

———. *Psychiatrie.* (4th ed.) Leipzig: Hirzel, 1911. (1894)

———. *Die Erkennung und Behandlung der Melancholie in der Praxis.* (2nd ed.) Halle: Marhold, 1907. (1896)

———. *Psychophysiologische Erkenntnistheorie.* (2nd ed.) Jena: Fischer, 1907. (1898)

———. Psychotherapie. In A. Eulenburg & S. Samuel (Eds.), *Lehrbuch der allgemeinen Therapie und der therapeutischen Methodik.* Vol. 2. Vienna: Urban & Schwarzenberg, 1898, pp. 637–696.

———. *Die Ideenassoziation des Kindes.* (2 vols.) Berlin: Reuther & Reichard, 1898, 1900.

———. *Handbuch der Anatomie des Zentralnervensystems des Menschen.* (2 vols.) Jena: Fischer, 1899, 1920.

———. *Das Verhältnis der Herbartschen Psychologie zur physiologisch-experimentellen Psychologie.* (2nd ed.) Berlin: Reuther & Reichard, 1911. (1900)

———. *Ueber die allgemeinen Beziehungen zwischen Gehirn und Seelenleben.* (3rd ed.) Leipzig: Barth, 1912. (1903)

———. Erkenntnisstheoretische Auseinandersetzungen. *Z. Psychol.,* 1902, 27, 305–343.

———. Einige Bemerkungen zur Anwendung der Methode der richtigen und falschen Fälle bei psychologischen Untersuchungen. *Monatssch. Psychiat. Neurol.,* 1904, 15, 64–66.

———. *Die Prinzipien und Methoden der Begabungs- insbesondere der Intelligenzprüfung.* (5th ed.) Berlin: Karger, 1923. (1908)

———. Zur Lehre der Aufmerksamkeit. *Monatssch. Psychiat. Neurol.,* 1908, 24, 173–178.

———. *Die Erkennung der psychopathischen Konstitutionen und die öffentliche Fürsorge für psychopathisch veranlagte Kinder.* Berlin: Karger, 1912.

———. *Zum gegenwärtigen Standpunkt der Erkenntnistheorie (zugleich Versuch einer Einteilung der Erkenntnistheorien).* Wiesbaden: Bergmann, 1914.

———. Ueber den gegenwärtigen Stand der experimentellen Aesthetik. *Z. Aesth.,* 1914, 9, 16–46.

———. *Die Grundlagen der Psychologie.* (2 vols.) Leipzig: Teubner, 1938. (1915)

———. *Die Geisteskrankheiten des Kindesalters einschliesslich des Schwachsinns und der psychopathischen Konstitutionen im Kindesalter.* Halle: Marhold, 1926. (2 vols.) (1915–1917)

———. Beitrag zur Lehre vom absoluten Eindruck. *Z. Psychol.,* 1915, 71, 177–287.

———. *Die Psychologie grosser Heerführer. Der Krieg und die Gedanken der Philosophen und Dichter vom ewigen Frieden.* Leipzig: Barth, 1916.

———. *Ueber das Wesen der Beanlagung und ihre methodische Erforschung.* (4th ed.) Langensalza: Beyer, 1929. (1918)

———. *Die Beziehungen der Lebenserscheinungen zum Bewusstsein.* Berlin: Bornträger, 1921.

Haecker, V., & ———. *Zur Vererbung und Entwicklung der musikalischen Begabung.* Leipzig: Barth, 1922.

———. *Grundlagen der Naturphilosophie.* Leipzig: Quelle & Meyer, 1922.

———. In R. Schmidt (Ed.), *Die Philosophie der Gegenwart in Selbstdarstellungen.* Vol. 4. Leipzig: Meiner, 1923, pp. 219–235.   **B Bl**

———. *Das Seelenleben der Jugendlichen.* (4th ed.) Langensalza: Beyer, 1931. (1923)

———. Charakterologische Studien an Verbrechern. *Jb. Charakterol.,* 1927, 4, 196–209.

———. *Die Grundlagen der Religionsphilosophie.* Leipzig: Meiner, 1928.

——. *Die Grundlagen der Charakterologie.* Langensalza: Beyer, 1930.

——. Theodor Ziehen. In C. Murchison (Ed.), *A history of psychology in autobiography.* Vol. 1. Worcester, Mass.: Clark University Press, 1930, pp. 471–489.   **B Bl**

GREGORY ZILBOORG
1890-1959
American Psychoanalyst (17)

Zilboorg, G. *Psychoanalysis and religion.* Ed. by Margaret S. Zilboorg. New York: Farrar, Strauss & Cudahy, 1962.

——. The dynamics of schizophrenic reactions related to pregnancy and childbirth. *Amer. J. Psychiat.,* 1929, *8,* 733–766.

——. Sidelights on parent-child antagonism. *Amer. J. Orthopsychiat.,* 1932, *2,* 35–43.

——. Anxiety without affect. *Psychoanal. Quart.,* 1933, *2,* 48–67.

——. The problem of constitution in psychopathology. *Psychoanal. Quart.,* 1934, *3,* 339–362.

——. *The medical man and the witch during the Renaissance.* Baltimore, Md.: Johns Hopkins Press, 1935.

——. Some sidelights on the psychology of murder. *J. nerv. ment. Dis.,* 1935, *81,* 442–444.

——. Differential diagnostic types of suicide. *Arch. Neurol. Psychiat.,* Chicago, 1936, *35,* 270–291.

——. Suicide among civilized and primitive races. *Amer. J. Psychiat.,* 1936, *92,* 1347–1396.

——. Considerations on suicide, with particular reference to that of the young. *Amer. J. Orthopsychiat.,* 1937, *7,* 15–31.

——. *I won't apologize: Two letters by Dr. Gregory Zilboorg.* Stamford, Conn.: Overbook Press, 1938.   **B**

——. Loneliness: Its relation to narcissism. *Atlantic Mon.,* 1938, *161,* 45–54.

——. Some observations on the transformation of instincts. *Psychoanal. Quart.,* 1938, *7,* 1–24.

——. Overestimation of psychopathology. *Amer. J. Orthopsychiat.,* 1939, *9,* 86–94.

——. Ambulatory schizophrenias. *Psychiatry,* 1941, *4,* 149–155.

——, & Henry, G. W. *A history of medical psychology.* New York: Norton, 1941.

——. Psychology and culture. *Psychoanal. Quart.,* 1942, *11,* 1–16.

——. Russian psychiatry—its historical and ideological background. *Bull. N.Y. Acad. Med.,* 1943, *19,* 713–728.

——. *Mind, medicine and man.* New York: Harcourt, Brace, 1943.

——. Fear of death. *Psychoanal. Quart.,* 1943, *12,* 465–475.

——. Psychopathology of social prejudice. *Psychoanal. Quart.,* 1947, *16,* 303–324.

——. The struggle for and against the individual in psychotherapy. *Amer. J. Psychiat.,* 1948, *104,* 524–527.

——. *Sigmund Freud: His exploration of the mind of man.* New York: Scribner's, 1951.

——. Some sidelights on free associations. *Int. J. Psycho-Anal.,* 1952, *33,* 489–495.

——. *The psychology of the criminal act and punishment.* New York: Harcourt, Brace, 1954.

——. *Freud and religion. A restatement of an old controversy.* Westminster, Md.: Newman Press, 1958.

HENDRIK ZWAARDEMAKER
1857-1930
Dutch Physiologist (23)

Zwaardemaker, H. Compensation von Gerüchen mittelst des Doppelriechmessers. *Fortschr. Med.,* 1889, *7,* 721–731.

——. Sur la norme de l'acuité olfactive. *Arch. néerl. sci. exact.,* 1892, *35,* 131–148.

Zwaardemaker — 468 —

———. Der Einfluss der Schallintensität auf die Lage der oberen Tongrenze. *Z. Ohrenh.*, 1893, *24*, 303–313.

———. *Die Physiologie des Geruchs.* Trans. by A. J. v. Landegg. Leipzig: Engelmann, 1895.

———. Ein verbesserter Riechmesser, *Arch. Laryngol. Rhinol.*, 1895, *3*, 367–371.

———. Les sensations olfactives, leurs combinaisons et leurs compensations. *Année psychol.*, 1898, *5*, 202–225.

———, & Lans, L. J. Ueber ein Studium relativer Unerregbarkeit als Ursache des intermittirenden Charakters des Lidschlagreflexes. (1899) *Zbl. Physiol.*, 1900, *13*, 325–329.

———, & Reuter, C. *Qualitative Geruchsmessung.* Utrecht: Reeks, 1900.

———. Präzisions-Olfactometrie. *Arch. Laryngol. Rhinol.*, 1904, *15*, 171–177.

———, & Quix, F. H. Akustische Funktionsstörungen bei Labyrinthaffektionen. *Z. Ohrenh.*, 1905, *50*, 29–57.

———. *Leerboek der physiologie.* (3rd ed.) (2 vols.) Haarlem: Bohn, 1921. (1910)

———. Odeur et chimisme. *Arch. néerl. Physiol.*, 1921–1922, *6*, 336–354.

———. *L'odorat.* Paris: Doin, 1925.

———. H. Zwaardemaker: An intellectual history of a physiologist with psychological aspirations. In C. Murchison (Ed.), *A history of psychology in autobiography.* Vol. 1. Worcester, Mass.: Clark University Press, 1930, pp. 491–516.   **B**

———. Geruch. In R. Dittler & G. Joos (Eds.), *Handwörterbuch der Naturwissenschaften.* (2nd ed.) Vol. 4. Jena: Fischer, 1935, pp. 1129–1136.

———. Geschmack. In R. Dittler & G. Joos (Eds.), *Handwörterbuch der Naturwissenschaften.* (2nd ed.) Vol. 4. Jena: Fischer, 1935, pp. 1195–1201.

ADDENDA

Beers, C. W. An intimate account of the origin and growth of the mental hygiene movement. *Ment. Hyg.,* N.Y., 1931, *15,* 673–684. **B**

Bentham, J. *The collected works of Jeremy Bentham: Of laws in general.* Ed. by H. L. A. Hart. London: Athlone Press, 1970. (1945)

Calkins, Mary W. The philosophical credo of an absolutistic personalist. In G. P. Adams & W. P. Montague (Eds.), *Contemporary American philosophy: Personal statements.* Vol. 1. New York: Macmillan, 1930, pp. 199–218.

Claparède, E. *Psychologie de l'enfant et pédagogie expérimentale.* (2 vols.) Neuchâtel: Delachaux & Niestlé, 1946–1947. **C**

Dilthey, W. Zur Weltanschauungslehre. (1903) Reprinted in *Gesammelte Schriften, op. cit.,* Vol. 8, pp. 220–226. Trans. in part as The dream in W. Kluback, *Wilhelm Dilthey's philosophy of history.* New York: Columbia University Press, 1956, pp. 103–109. Reprinted in H. Meyerhoff, *The philosophy of history in our time.* Garden City, N.Y.: Doubleday, 1954, pp. 40–43.

———. II. Das Verstehen anderer Personen und ihrer Lebensäusserungen. (1910) In *Gesammelte Schriften, op cit.,* Vol. 7, pp. 205–230. Trans. as The understanding of other persons and their life-expressions. Trans J. J. Kuehl. In P. Gardiner (Ed.), *Theories of history.* New York: Free Press, 1959, pp. 213–225.

Dix, Dorothea L. *On behalf of the insane poor: Selected reports. 1843–1952.* New York: Arno Presss, 1971. **C**

Donders, F. C. (Autobiography.) In H. J. M. v. Weve & G. ten Doesschate (Eds.). *Het jubileum van Professor F. C. Donders gevierd te Utrecht op 27 en 28 Mei 1888. Gedenkboek uitgegeven door de Commissie.* Utrecht: Van de Weijer, 1889, pp. 115–232. **B**

Graefe, A. V., & ———. *Die Briefe Albrecht von Gräfes an F. C. Donders (1852-1870).* Ed. by H. J. M. v. Weve & G. ten Doesschate. Stuttgart: Enke, 1935. **B**

———. *De harmonie van het dierlijke leven.* Intro. by P. H. Kylstra. Utrecht: Oosthoek, 1972. (1848)

Freud, S., & Jung, C. G. *The Freud-Jung letters.* Ed. by W. McGuire. Princeton, N.J.: Princeton University Press, 1974. **B C**

Helmholtz, V. v. *Hermann von Helmholtz über sich selbst.* Ed. by D. Goetz. Leipzig: Teubner, 1966. **B C**

Klages, L. *Die Problem der Graphologie.* Leipzig: Barth, 1910. Reprinted in E. Frauchiger *et al.* (Eds.), *Ludwig Klages Sämtliche Werke.* Vol. 7. Bonn: Bouvier, 1971, pp. 1–284.

Kraepelin, E. *Manic depressive insanity and paranoia.* Trans. by R. M. Barclay. Edinburgh: Livingstone, 1921. (1913, 1915)

Landis, C. Statistical evaluation of psychotherapeutic methods. In S. E. Hinsie (Ed.), *Concepts and problems of psychotherapy.* New York: Columbia University Press, 1937, pp. 155–169.

Merleau-Ponty, M. *L'union de l'âme et au corps chez Malebranche, Maine de Biran et Bergson.* Ed. by J. Deprun. Paris: Vrin, 1968.

Mira y Lopez, E. Estado atual da psicologia do pensamento. Resumo critico do trabalho da Escola Wurzburg. *Arg. Brasil. Psicotec.,* 1963, *15* (2), 33–43.

Nietzsche, F. W. *Nietzsche: A self-portrait from his letters.* Ed. & trans. by P. Fuss & H. Shapiro. Cambridge: Havard University Press, 1971. **B C**

———. *Nietzsches Werke. Kritische Gesamtausgabe.* (Ult. 30+ vols.) Ed. by G. Colli & M. Montinari. Berlin: De Gruyter, 1967–. **C**

Ramon y Cajal, S. Pensamientos de tendencia educativa, y ideal de la ciencia. Intro. & trans.

by G. V. Russell. *Texas Rep. Biol. Med.,* 1972. 30 (1). 1–8.

Rubinstein, S. (*Problems of general psychology.*) Ed. by E. V. Soroxova. Moscow: Akademiya Pedag. Nauk, 1973.   **C**

Rush, B. *Two Essays on the mind.* Intro. by E. T. Carlson. New York: Brunner/Mazel. 1972. **C**

Simon, T. *Inédits d'Alfred Binet.* Cahors: Couselant, 1960.   **C**

Weber, M. *Max Weber: The interpretation of social reality.* Ed. & intro. essay by J. E. T. Eldridge. London: Joseph, 1971.   **C**

Wiersma, E. D. Ein Versuch zur Erklärung der retrograden Amnesien. *Z. ges. Neurol. Psychiat.,* 1914, *22,* 519–527.

————. Psychische Nachwirkungen. *Z. ges. Neurol. Psychiat.,* 1917, *35,* 191–203.

————. On pathological lying. *J. Pers.,* 1933, *2,* 48–61.

————. Children of the happily and unhappily married. *Proc. Roy. Acad. Sci.,* Holland, 1934, *37,* 1–15.

————. The mental condition of the happily and unhappily married. *Proc. Roy. Acad. Sci.,* Holland, 1939, *39,* 1–39.

Yerkes, R. M. Early days of comparative psychology. *Psychol. Rev.,* 1943, *50,* 74–76.